IMPROVE YOUR GRADE!

STUDENTS START HERE ▶

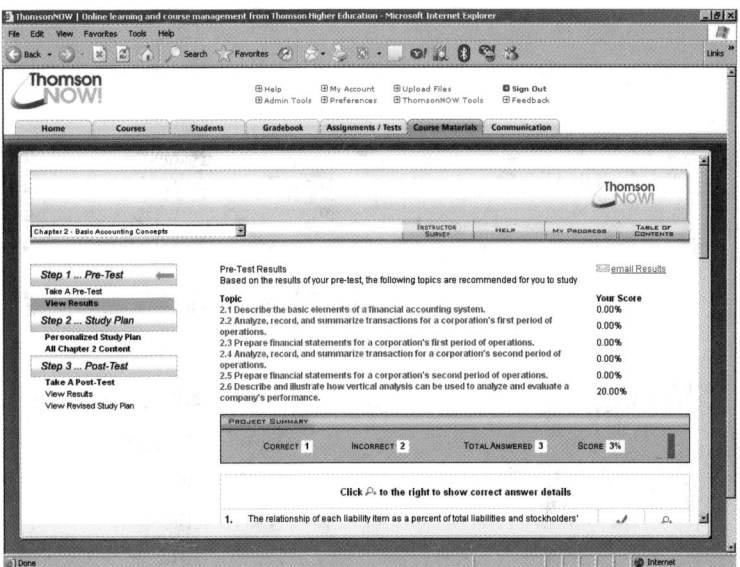

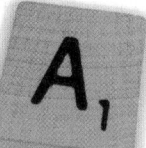

PERSONALIZED STUDY PLANS STRENGTHEN STUDENT COMPREHENSION

Diagnostic pre- and post-assessment quizzes identify gaps in knowledge and help you develop a Personalized Study Plan. The plan provides practice with links to videos, eBook content, and other multimedia tools.

SUCCESSFULLY COMPLETE HOMEWORK ONLINE

All end-of-chapter problems and exercises are available online with hints and links to tools. These additional review opportunities help you effectively complete assignments. You can easily view assignments completed, due dates, and current grades from one convenient screen.

GAMES REINFORCE CONCEPTS

Interactive accounting games reinforce key concepts and provide you with immediate feedback.

eBOOK BRINGS CONTENT TO LIFE

ThomsonNOW features a full-color eBook, allowing you to reference pages from homework assignments and end-of-chapter activities. This immediate and convenient access to the text is ideal for study and review.

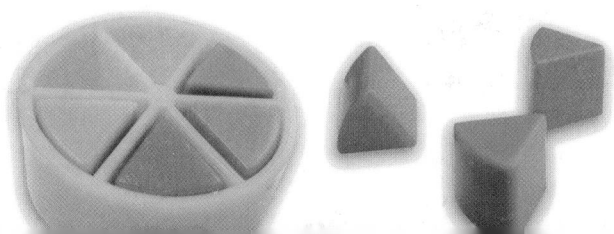

TENTH EDITION

ACCOUNTING
Concepts and Applications

W. STEVE ALBRECHT
PhD, CPA, CIA, CFE
Brigham Young University

•

EARL K. STICE
PhD
Brigham Young University

•

JAMES D. STICE
PhD
Brigham Young University

•

MONTE R. SWAIN
PhD, CPA, CMA
Brigham Young University

THOMSON
™
SOUTH-WESTERN

Australia · Brazil · Canada · Mexico · Singapore · Spain · United Kingdom · United States

THOMSON

SOUTH-WESTERN

Accounting: Concepts & Applications, 10e
W. Steve Albrecht, Earl K. Stice, James D. Stice, and Monte R. Swain

VP/Editorial Director:
Jack W. Calhoun

Publisher:
Rob Dewey

Executive Editor:
Sharon Oblinger

Developmental Editor:
Aaron Arnsparger

Marketing Manager:
Kristen Hurd

Content Project Manager:
Starratt E. Alexander

Manager of Technology, Editorial:
John Barans

Technology Project Editor:
Scott Hamilton

Manufacturing Coordinator:
Doug Wilke

Production House/Composition:
LEAP Publishing Services and
GGS Information Services

Printer:
R R Donnelley
Willard Manufacturing Division

Art Director:
Bethany Casey

Internal Designer:
C Miller Design

Cover Designer:
Bethany Casey

Cover Illustrations:
© Larry Moore, Scott Hull Associates

Photography Manager:
Deanna Ettinger

Photo Researcher:
Robin Samper

Library of Congress Control Number:
2006940161

For more information about our
products, contact us at:

Thomson Learning Academic
Resource Center

1-800-423-0563

Thomson Higher Education
5191 Natorp Boulevard
Mason, OH 45040
USA

STREAMLINED SOLUTIONS
ADD UP TO SUCCESS

FINANCIAL CHAPTERS LEAVE NOTHING TO CHANCE

- Based on your feedback, **the financial statement analysis chapter appears as the last chapter** (Ch. 14) in the financial section. This now serves as a capstone chapter, getting students into analysis.

- The **unique chapter on financial statement integrity** (now Ch. 5) provides a strong ethical foundation for students to better understand the impact of the Sarbanes-Oxley Act and today's increased focus on earnings management.

MANAGERIAL CHAPTER REVISIONS ON THE ROLL

Completely reorganized, streamlined managerial chapters now center around a new conceptual model that covers topics in a logical progression that's ideal for the introductory level.

- Chapters now begin with traditional product costing methods and discussion of cost flows before moving to control topics, such as budgeting and variances.

- Managerial chapters now conclude with decision-making subjects, such as CVP and investments.

Streamlined chapter on activity-based costing (Ch. 17) provides an intriguing presentation that's careful not to overwhelm students. The **use of a continuing example** – Lily Ice Cream Company – is featured to allow students to see ongoing applications of accounting concepts in decision-making.

MODIFIED TABLE OF CONTENTS

Based on your feedback, the table of contents has been modified to introduce topics similar to the order they are presented on the balance sheet.

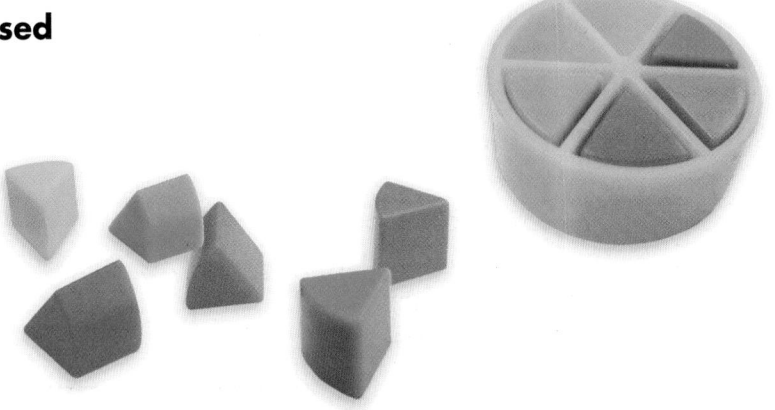

GAME ON! UNRAVEL THE PUZZLE

LEARNING FEATURES STUDENTS REALLY USE

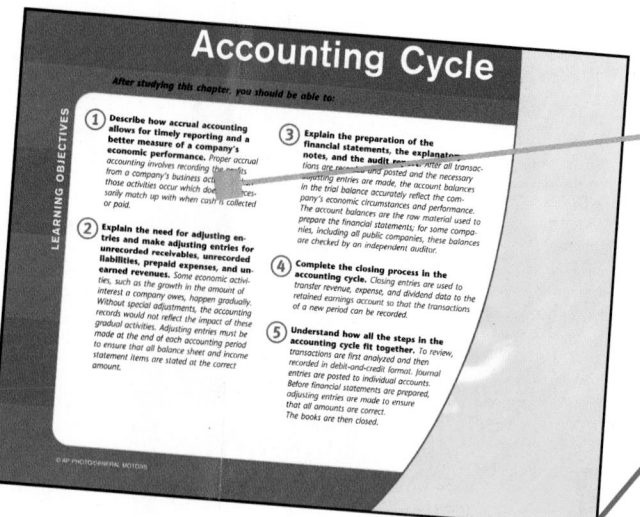

NEW! **Brief Explanations that accompany Learning Objectives** at the beginning of every chapter direct students' attention while reading. They are an ideal resource to refresh student understanding before lectures and tests.

NEW! **Revised *Remember This... Summaries*** at the end of each topical section of the chapter highlight the most important material within that section. Bulleted lists assist with retention, while tables visually demonstrate important relationships or connections.

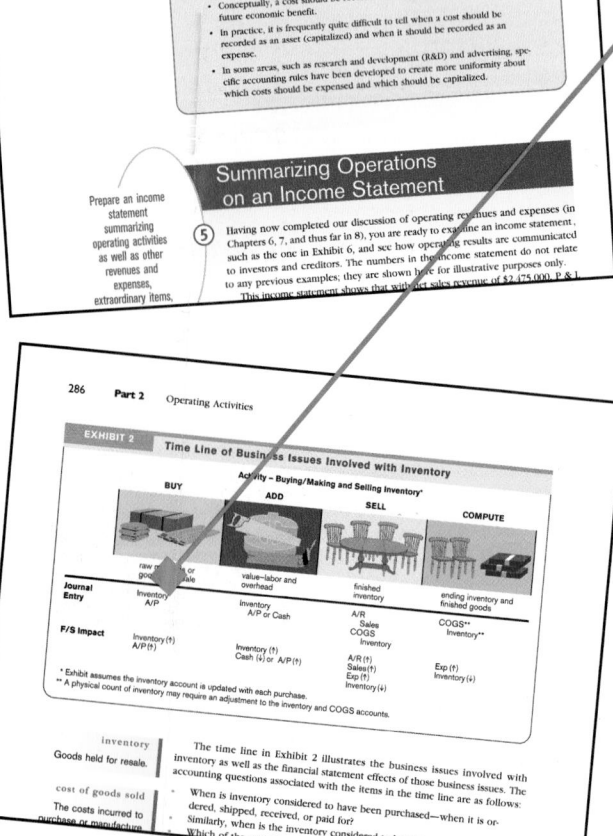

NEW! **Improved Chapter-Opening Exhibits** place events in context, while showing both the timeline of events for a particular business activity and the impact of these events on the financial statements. These enhanced exhibits provide a clear visual aid as students begin to conceptualize the relationships between various activities of a business and the proper accounting procedures that accompany them.

FYI boxes draw examples from real business events or situations to show students the immediate relevance of the information they are learning.

Stop and Think features highlight thought-provoking issues or concepts that reinforce the importance of developing critical-thinking skills for success in today's competitive business world.

Caution boxes remind students of the important points to consider when resolving more difficult situations or learning more complex concepts.

TAKE A LOOK AT THE BEST GAME IN TOWN

ACCOUNTING: CONCEPTS AND APPLICATIONS, 10E
WHERE FUTURE BUSINESS CHAMPIONS BEGIN

Staying on top of the game in today's competitive world means consistently looking for ways to improve, building upon existing strengths, and maximizing every opportunity. **Accounting: Concepts and Applications, 10e** *does just that to give you and your students a competitive edge in accounting today. See for yourself how proven accounting leaders Albrecht, Stice, Stice, and Swain have improved this edition to help you and your students achieve your personal best — in today's classroom and the business world beyond.*

A STRATEGY FOR SUCCESS

Accounting, 10e continues to build upon a winning strategy designed to help you meet the diverse needs of both accounting majors and non-majors in your course. The text's solid presentation of procedures blends with a balanced emphasis on decision-making. Students learn how to effectively use and prepare accounting information.

With an emphasis on the activities of a business, **Accounting, 10e** demonstrates accounting in action using a wealth of actual examples from numerous leading companies throughout the world. Student-focused learning features place concepts within a business context. No matter what your students' career choices, this edition has the coverage to make them winners in the game of life.

THE WINNING SOLUTION – STRONGER WITH EVERY ROUND

Building on the strengths that make this a market-leading text, this edition takes the accounting experience to a new level. The flexibility of expanded coverage, new applications in every chapter, reorganized and streamlined content, and the innovative online ThomsonNOW™ course management system are everything you need to put your students ahead of the game!

Now It's Your Turn.
Take a look for yourself!

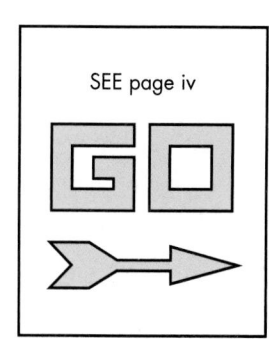

SEE page iv

GO

YOU WIN WITH FLEXIBILITY TAILORED TO YOUR COURSE NEEDS

Always a hallmark of this text, **expanded coverage within each chapter,** in addition to solid **basic coverage** of essential accounting concepts, allows you to choose how much depth you wish for exploring advanced topics. The result is maximum flexibility for your class.

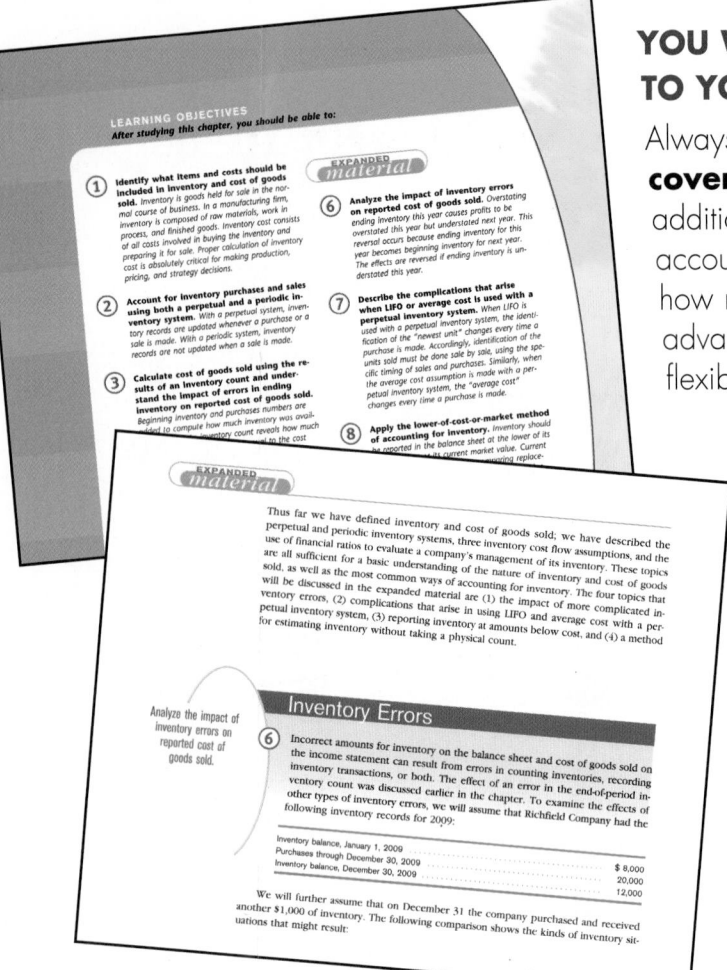

ORGANIZATION PLAYS TO TODAY'S BUSINESS STRENGTHS

The text's unique approach, emphasizing business activities, provides a solid framework for understanding how an organization performs its primary business activities. This realistic approach makes it easier for students to understand accounting's role.

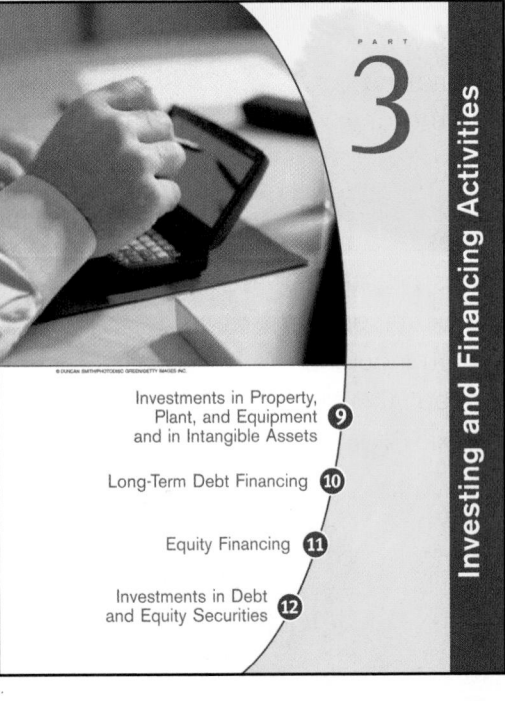

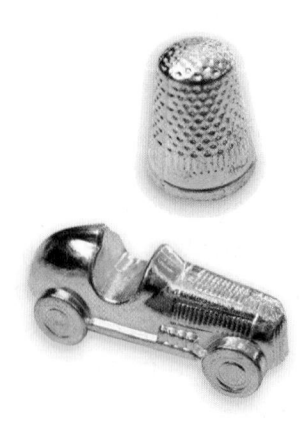

VARIETY IS THE NAME OF THE GAME!
EXCEPTIONAL END-OF-CHAPTER RESOURCES

FROM NOVICE TO PROFESSIONAL

A **variety of homework and assignment opportunities** at the end of each chapter provides a wealth of hands-on, focused practice.

■ **Practice Exercises** offer quick-hit concept checks ideal for in-class practice.

■ **Exercises and Problems** delve deeper into concepts, testing students' retention of critical topics and procedures.

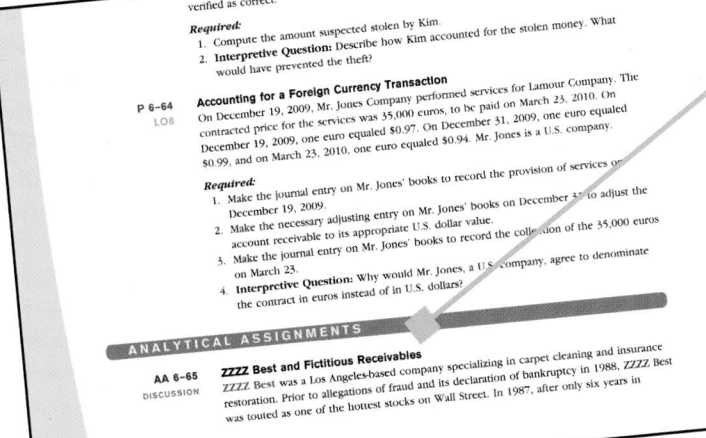

NEW!

Margin References to Learning Objectives have been added to all exercise and problem materials for quick reference and focused practice.

NEW!

Analytical Assignments, following the problems in each chapter, provide dynamic new discussion and critical-thinking activities. From discussion cases and judgment calls, to assignments that require the analysis of real company financial statements, this new section is a source for assignments that take learning a step beyond the typical.

End-of-chapter practice exercises and problems are now available online through the innovative **ThomsonNOW™ for Accounting, 10e** with instant grading and homework management capabilities!

JUST WHAT YOU NEED TO
KNOW AND DO **NOW**

IT'S YOUR TURN TO SAVE TIME AND ENSURE INTERACTIVE LEARNING

■ **Assign Online Homework** – All end-of-chapter problems and exercises are available online with hints and links to the eBook. This helps students to effectively complete assignments.

■ **Check Course Credibility and Compliance** – ThomsonNOW identifies assignment and test bank questions as they relate to AACSB, AICPA, and IMA standards with customizable reports that allow you to track progress as well as course content.

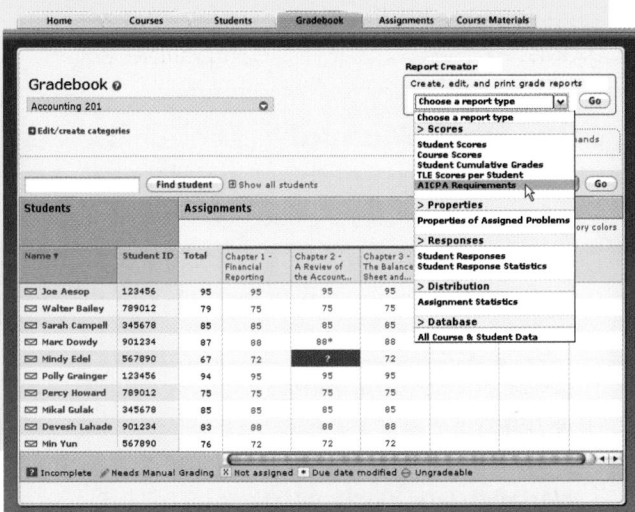

■ **Manage Your Gradebook with Ease** – ThomsonNOW automatically grades homework and tests and provides students with immediate results. Students take responsibility for their own assignments as they can easily view assignments completed, due dates, and current grades from one convenient screen. You can even weight grades to best fit your overall course plan.

■ **Integrated eBook Brings Content to Life** – Students can read the latest edition sequentially or follow links from specific assignments and end-of-chapter activities for remedial review.

■ **Interactive Learning Games and Assignments Reinforce Key Concepts** – Multimedia games provide a fun way to learn accounting concepts. Both creative and challenging, these games reinforce core content and provide immediate feedback to help students improve knowledge and skills.

■ **Personalized Study Plans Reinforce Student Comprehension** – Diagnostic pre- and post-assessment quizzes identify gaps in knowledge and help students develop Personalized Study Plans that provide practice with links to tutorials, demonstration exercises, videos, eBook content, accounting games and other multimedia tools.

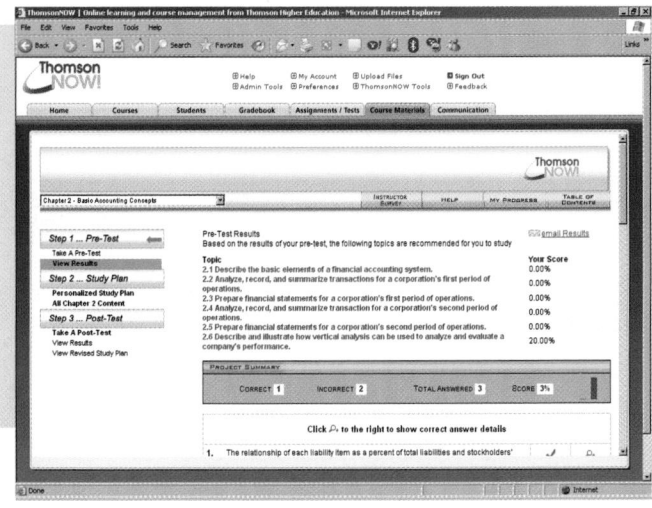

QUALITY RESOURCES HELP SOLVE
THE ACCOUNTING PUZZLE!

FULL SUITE OF INSTRUCTOR SUPPORT GIVES YOU THE WINNING HAND

A complete selection of reliable supplements, including PowerPoint® slides and a revised Test Bank edited personally by the authors, ensures consistency throughout your course and full continuity with the text! In addition to the innovative new technology offered with ThomsonNOW™, **Accounting, 10e** delivers a wealth of choices for your teaching convenience. Here are just a few highlights from the complete package:

- **Experience Accounting Videos** highlight managerial accounting concepts in **Accounting, 10e.** These 14 video clips cover many industry segments by spanning manufacturing, retail, and service industries. Students watch managerial accounting concepts come to life as they view brief videos that feature familiar organizations such as Hard Rock Café and BP. The videos are ideal for launching a dynamic, interactive lecture in the classroom. These videos are available in ThomsonNOW or as a standalone item.

- **Improved Test Bank** now tags questions to **AACSB** standards as well as **AICPA** (in the Financial portion) and **IMA** standards (in the Managerial portion) so you can efficiently monitor student progress. This is particularly valuable during the accreditation process or when your school wants to standardize assessment. Test bank questions are also identified as **easy, moderate,** and **difficult** to help you create exams best suited for your individual students.

- **ExamView® Electronic Testing Software** allows you to easily generate and customize tests from the reliable test bank questions for traditional or online quizzes or exams.

- **Instructor's Manual** includes an overview of chapter Learning Objectives, detailed lecture outlines, descriptions of key illustrations and boxed items with page references, and a topical overview grid of end-of-chapter assignments with assignments classified by level of difficulty and estimated time of completion.

Companion Web Site

www.thomsonedu.com/accounting/albrecht

Find all of the resources you and your students need on the text's companion Web site. Online, password-protected access allows you to easily download numerous valuable resources and teaching tools, including Solutions Manual, Instructor's Manual, PowerPoint® slides, and Spreadsheet Solutions.

Students can easily access Student Spreadsheet Templates. They can test their understanding with interactive online quizzes and other interactive learning tools.

ACKNOWLEDGMENTS

The tenth edition of *Accounting: Concepts and Applications* reflects many comments from colleagues and students, all of which are deeply appreciated. In particular we would like to thank the following:

Laurie Hays
Western Michigan University

Samuel Tiras
University of Buffalo

Bob Hartman
University of Iowa

Cathy Lumbattis
Southern Illinois University-Carbondale

Hubert Glover
Howard University

Diane Tanner
University of North Florida

Kem Edwards
Bryant College

James Bannister
University of Hartford

Linda Chase
Baldwin Wallace College

K.D. Hatheway-Dial
University of Idaho

Doug Asbury
University of Findlay

Louann Cummings
University of Findlay

Josie Mathias
Mercer County Community College

Ibrahim Badawi
St. John's University

Christie Comunale
Long Island University-C.W. Post

Keren Deal
Auburn University

Rafik Elias
California State University-Los Angeles

Marian Boscia
Kings College

Mary MacAusland
Reading Area Community College

Bonnie Slager
Santiago Canyon College

Joey Styron
Augusta State University

Robert Holtfreter
Central Washington University

Donald Raux
Siena College

William Braberry
Bluefield State College

William Goodman
Bluefield State College

Anne Rich
Quinnipac University

Paul Holt
Texas A&M University-Kingsville

Ralph Lindeman
Kent State University

Susan Minke
Indiana University-Purdue University at Fort Wayne

Lynne Shoaf
Belmont Abbey College

In addition, we would like to thank the following content providers and verifiers for their professional services and consideration in providing a more concise, higher-quality product.

Content Providers:

Cameron Pratt
Brigham Young University

Jason Bond
Brigham Young University

John Morley
Brigham Young University

Michael and Becky Blue
Bloomsburg University

David O'Dell
McPherson College

Dave Cottrell
Brigham Young University

Verifiers:

James Emig
Villanova University

Beth Woods
Howell, MI

W. Steve Albrecht
James D. Stice
Earl K. Stice
Monte R. Swain

W. Steve Albrecht

W. Steve Albrecht is the Associate Dean of the Marriott School of Management and Andersen Professor at Brigham Young University. Dr. Albrecht, a certified public accountant, certified internal auditor, and certified fraud examiner, came to BYU in 1977 after teaching at Stanford and at the University of Illinois. Earlier, he worked as a staff accountant for Deloitte & Touche. Prior to becoming associate dean of the Marriott School, Dr. Albrecht served for nine years as the director of the School of Accountancy and Information Systems at BYU.

Dr. Albrecht received a bachelor's degree in accounting from Brigham Young University and his MBA and PhD degrees from the University of Wisconsin at Madison. He is past President of the American Accounting Association and the Association of Certified Fraud Examiners. He was a former member of the Board of Regents of the Institute of Internal Auditors and the Board of Directors of the Utah Association of CPAs. He was also president of the Accounting Program Leadership Group (chairs of accounting departments and programs) and served on the task force of the American Institute of CPAs that wrote a fraud auditing standard. He was a member of the Committee of Sponsoring Organizations (COSO) from 1997–2000 and is past president of Beta Alpha Psi, the national accounting honors fraternity. He was a member of the AICPA Council and chaired their Pre-Certification Executive Education Committee.

Dr. Albrecht has done extensive research on business fraud. His research has resulted in the publication of over one hundred articles in academic and professional journals. He is the author or co-author of over 20 books or monographs, several of which are on fraud. His financial and principles of accounting textbooks are in their 10th editions. In 2000, he completed a major study (Accounting Education: Charting the Course through a Perilous Future) on the future of accounting education in the United States. His fraud textbook is currently in its second edition. He is a frequent speaker on the topics of fraud examination, accounting education, and personal financial planning.

Dr. Albrecht has received numerous awards and honors, including BYU's highest faculty honor, the Karl G. Maeser Distinguished Faculty Lecturer Award for superior scholarship and teaching. He has also received the BYU School of Management's Outstanding Faculty Award and the BYU Outstanding Researcher Award. He has been recognized by Beta Alpha Psi, the Federation of Schools of Accountancy, the Auditing Section of the American Association and the AICPA as Educator of the Year. He has also received awards for outstanding teaching at Stanford University, the University of Illinois, and the University of Wisconsin. In 1997, 2001, 2002, and 2003 he was chosen as one of the 100 most influential accounting professionals in the United States by *Accounting Today* magazine. In 1998, he received the Cressey Award from the Association of Certified Fraud Examiners, the highest award given for a lifetime of achievement in fraud detection and deterrence. (Past winners were Jane Bryant Quinn of *Newsweek* magazine and Rudolph Giuliani, past United States Attorney for the Southern District of New York and past mayor of New York City.) In 2002, in honor of his contribution in fighting fraud, the Association of Certified Fraud Examiners named one of the buildings at their headquarters after Dr. Albrecht. And in 2001, in recognition of his contributions to BYU and to academia, an anonymous donor endowed the W. Steve Albrecht Professorship in Accounting.

Dr. Albrecht has consulted with numerous organizations, including a variety of Fortune 500 companies, major financial institutions, the United Nations, FBI, and other organizations, and he has been an expert witness in some of the largest fraud cases in America. He currently serves on the audit committees and boards of directors of four public and three private companies. Dr. Albrecht is married to the former LeAnn Christiansen, and they have six children and ten grandchildren.

Earl K. Stice

Earl K. Stice is the PricewaterhouseCoopers Professor of Accounting in the School of Accountancy and Information Systems at Brigham Young University where he has been on the faculty since 1998. He holds bachelor's and master's degrees from Brigham Young University and a PhD from Cornell University. Dr. Stice has taught at Rice University, the University of Arizona, Cornell University, and the Hong Kong University of Science and Technology (HKUST). He won the Phi Beta Kappa teaching award at Rice University and was twice selected at HKUST as one of the ten best lecturers on campus. Dr. Stice has also taught in a variety of executive education and corporate training programs in the United States, Hong Kong, China, and South Africa, and he is currently on the executive MBA faculty of the China Europe International Business School in Shanghai. He has published papers in the *Journal of Financial and Quantitative Analysis, The Accounting Review, Review of Accounting Studies, Issues in Accounting Education*, and the *Journal of Accounting Education*, and his research on stock splits has been cited in *Business Week, Money*, and *Forbes*. Dr. Stice has presented his research results at seminars in the United States, Finland, Taiwan, Australia, and Hong Kong. He is co-author of *Intermediate Accounting, 16th edition* and *Financial Accounting: Reporting and Analysis, 7th Edition*. Dr. Stice and his wife, Ramona, are the parents of seven children: Derrald, Han, Ryan Marie, Lorien, Lily, Taraz, and Kamila.

James D. Stice

James D. Stice is the Distinguished Teaching Professor in the Marriott School of Management at Brigham Young University. He is currently the Director of the Marriott School's MBA Program. He holds bachelor's and master's degrees from BYU and a PhD from the University of Washington, all in accounting. Professor Stice has been on the faculty at BYU since 1988. During that time, he has been selected by graduating accounting students as "Teacher of the Year" on numerous occasions, he was selected by his peers in the Marriott School at BYU to receive the "Outstanding Teaching Award" in 1995, and in 1999 he was selected by the University to receive its highest teaching award, the Maeser Excellence in Teaching Award. Professor Stice has taught at INSEAD in France and at the China Europe International Business School in Shanghai. Professor Stice has published articles in *The Journal of Accounting Research, The Accounting Review, Decision Sciences, Issues in Accounting Education, The CPA Journal*, and other academic and professional journals. In addition to this textbook, he has published two other textbooks: *Financial Accounting: Reporting and Analysis*, and *Intermediate Accounting*. In addition to his teaching and research, Dr. Stice has been involved in executive education for such companies as IBM, Bank of America, Ernst & Young, RSM McGladrey and currently serves on the board of directors of Nutraceutical Corporation. Dr. Stice and his wife, Kaye, have seven children: Crystal, J.D., Ashley, Whitney, Kara, Skyler, and Cierra and two grandchildren.

Monte R. Swain

Monte R. Swain is the Deloitte Professor of Accounting in the School of Accountancy at Brigham Young University. He received his PhD in managerial accounting and information systems from Michigan State University and joined the BYU faculty in 1991. His dissertation, which examined the impact of information load on capital budgeting decision processes, was awarded an Institute of Management Accountants Dissertation Grant. At BYU, Dr. Swain has received the Teaching Excellence Award for Management Skills in 1994, 1995, and 1997; the Marriott School of Management Outstanding Teacher in 1999. In addition to his research work involving human decision processes, Dr. Swain studies and writes on activity-based costing, the Balanced Scorecard, and the Theory of Constraints in management information systems. He has published papers in leading academic and practitioner journals such as *Behavioral Research in Accounting, Decision Sciences, Strategic Finance*, and *The Internal Auditor*. In addition, Dr. Swain is deeply committed to the scholarship of teaching and has published a number of papers and cases on education in *Issues in Accounting Education, Journal of Accounting Education, The Journal of Accounting Case Research, Journal of Education for Business*, and the *Case Research Journal*. Dr. Swain sits on the editorial board for *Issues in Accounting Education*. Dr. Swain has spent significant time working with or researching organizations such as IBM, Clorox, and Deere and Company. He is a Certified Public Accountant and a Certified Management Accountant. Dr. Swain took an academic leave from BYU from July 1999 to July 2000 to serve as the Chief Financial Officer for Authorize.Net (payment-processing service for e-commerce). As a result of that experience, he has published papers and cases on the impact of eCommerce on financial and managerial accounting. Dr. Swain is active in the American Accounting Association where he serves in various capacities helping to promote the objectives of that organization. He and his wife, Shannon, have seven children.

SUPPLEMENTS

For the Instructor.......

ThomsonNOW™ for *Accounting: Concepts and Applications, 10e*

Description:
Save time and ensure all of your students—regardless of their major—have the understanding they need of accounting procedures and concepts with the integrated, online innovation of ThomsonNOW™. This integrated online course management and learning system combines the best of current technology to save you time in planning your course and managing student assignments. You can teach with the latest built-in technology support, reinforce comprehension with customized student learning paths, and efficiently test and automatically grade assignments with reports that correspond to AACSB, AICPA, and IMA standards. ThomsonNOW™ is effective for the standard lecture-based course or can serve as a strong foundation for full distance-learning programs. For your convenience, ThomsonNOW™ is even compatible with WebCT® and Blackboard®.

For more information, visit **www.thomsonedu. com/thomsonnow**.

Experience Accounting Videos

Description:
The ideal tool for launching a dynamic, interactive lecture in your course, these new Experience Accounting Videos highlight managerial accounting concepts in action from Accounting, 10e. Each brief video clip, which is approximately five minutes, features recognizable companies, such as Hard Rock Café and BP, that are using managerial accounting to strengthen their business performance. These videos are available in ThomsonNOW™ or standalone via the Web.

Instructor's Manual

Description:
Simplify class preparation with these detailed lecture outlines, overview of Learning Objectives, descriptions of key illustrations and boxed items with page references, and topical overview grid of end-of-chapter assignments with assignments classified by level of difficulty and estimated time of completion. Available online or on the Instructor's Resource CD-ROM.

Instructor's Resource CD-ROM
ISBN: **0324645783**

Description:
Place all of the key teaching resources you need for a winning course at your fingertips with this all-in-one source. Find everything you need to plan, teach, grade, and assess student understanding and progress. This CD includes the Solutions Manual, Instructor's Manual, Test Bank in Word and ExamView®, PowerPoint® slides, spreadsheet solutions, and solutions to the Cumulative Spreadsheet Analysis assignments from the textbook.

PowerPoint® Presentation Slides

Description:
Bring your lectures to life and clarify difficult concepts with these slides for this edition to capture and keep your students' attention. Ideal as guides for student note-taking and study, you can print the slides or simply use with an overhead projector. Available online or on the Instructor's Resource CD-Rom.

Solutions Manual
ISBN: **0324648308 and 0324648316**

Description:
Carefully verified to ensure accuracy, these solutions and answers to all end-of-chapter materials from the textbook help you easily plan, assign, and efficiently grade assignments.

Solutions Transparencies
ISBN: **0324645848 and 032464583X**

Description:
Clarify learning for students with these acetate masters that detail solutions for the exercises and problems from the text. These are specifically created for instructors who wish to use overheads in class.

Test Bank
ISBN: **0324645775 and 0324645767**

Description:
This revised test bank helps you efficiently assess your students' understanding with problems and questions that are now tagged to AACSB and AICPA standards. This is particularly valuable during the accreditation process or when your school wants to standardize assessment. Test bank questions are also identified by easy, medium, or challenging level of difficulty for easy selection.

ExamView® 5.0 Computerized Test Bank

Description:
This easy-to-use test-creation program for Microsoft® Windows or Macintosh contains all questions from the printed Test Bank with AACSB, AICPA, and IMA standards and level of difficulty indicated for each question. It's simple to customize tests to your specific class needs as you edit or create questions and

store customized exams. This is an ideal tool for online testing. Available on the IRCD.

WebTutor™ Toolbox for Blackboard® and WebCT
ISBN: **0534272401 (Blackboard) or 053427241x (WebCT)**

Description:

Leverage the power of the Internet and bring your course to life with this course management program. You or your students can use this wealth of interactive resources with those on the text's companion Web site to supplement the classroom experience and ensure positive outcomes. Use this effective resource as an integrated solution for your distance learning or web-enhanced course. Visit **http://webtutor. swlearning.com.**

Working Papers t/a Financial Accounting (Chapters 1–14)
ISBN: **0324648227**

Description:

Verified by the text authors to ensure accuracy and quality consistent with the text, the working papers for problems from the financial accounting chapters in the textbook are provided together in one convenient resource.

Albrecht/Stice/Stice/Swain's *Accounting: Concepts and Applications, 10e* **Companion Web Site**
URL: **http://www.thomsonedu.com/accounting/albrecht**

Description:

Now you and your students can reach the top of your game in accounting with immediate access to a rich array of teaching and learning resources at *Accounting: Concepts and Applications, 10e*'s interactive companion Web site. This resource features chapter-by-chapter online tutorial quizzes, a final exam, chapter outlines and review, online learning games, flashcards, expanded coverage of certain topics not found in the textbook, and more! Easily download the instructor resources you need from the password-protected, instructor-only section of the site.

For Students....

Companion Web Site

Description:

Now you can stay on top of your game, master the procedures and concepts of accounting and earn the grade you want in your accounting course with the rich array of learning resources at the *Accounting: Concepts and Applications, 10e* interactive companion Web site. Designed specifically for your accounting needs, this Web site features chapter-by-chapter online quizzes and solutions, learning games, flashcards, expanded coverage of topics not covered in the text, and more!

Working Papers t/a Financial Accounting (Chapters 1–14)
ISBN: **0324648227**

Description:

The working papers for problems from the textbook are provided together in one resource for your convenience. Verified by the text authors to ensure accuracy and consistent quality, you'll find the tools you need to enhance your learning experience.

BRIEF CONTENTS

CONTENTS

▶ PART TWO

OPERATING ACTIVITIES 223

▶ PART THREE

INVESTING AND FINANCING ACTIVITIES 387

EXPANDED
material

EXPANDED
material

▶ PART FOUR

OTHER DIMENSIONS OF FINANCIAL REPORTING 611

▶ PART FIVE

FOUNDATIONS OF MANAGEMENT ACCOUNTING 725

EXPANDED *material*

▶ PART SEVEN

MAKING DECISIONS USING MANAGEMENT ACCOUNTING 1007

20 COST BEHAVIOR AND DECISIONS USING C-V-P ANALYSIS . . . 1009

EXPANDED *material*

21 RELEVANT INFORMATION AND DECISIONS 1075

EXPANDED
material

▶ PART EIGHT

CONTINUOUS IMPROVEMENT IN MANAGEMENT ACCOUNTING 1175

APPENDICES

INDEXES

© DUNCAN SMITH/PHOTODISC GREEN/GETTY IMAGES INC.

Accounting Information: Users and Uses

After studying this chapter, you should be able to:

LEARNING OBJECTIVES

① **Describe the purpose of accounting and explain its role in business and society.** *Accounting is the recording of the day-to-day financial activities of a company and the organization of that information into summary reports used by people inside and outside the company to make decisions.*

② **Identify the primary users of accounting information.** *Among the users of accounting information are lenders, investors, company management, suppliers, customers, employees, competitors, government agencies, politicians, and the press.*

③ **Describe the environment of accounting, including the effects of generally accepted accounting principles, international business, ethical considerations, and technology.** *The practice of accounting involves adherence to the established national and (increasingly) international accounting rules as well as the use of judgment. Because accounting data are typically captured and summarized by computer systems, the practice of accounting requires familiarity with information technology.*

④ **Analyze the reasons for studying accounting.** *Every job requires you to prepare, use, respond to, or be evaluated using accounting data. Those people who better understand accounting are better able to function in any organization.*

In 1913, a young CPA named Arthur Andersen partnered with a gentleman named Clarence DeLany to form the public accounting firm of **Andersen, DeLany & Co**. At the time, there were only about 2,200 CPAs in the United States, and at the age of 23, Mr. Andersen was one of the youngest. Mr. DeLany later left the firm, and in 1918 it was renamed **Arthur Andersen**. From that beginning, the company grew to the point where in 2001, Andersen had operations in 84 countries and over 85,000 employees. Revenues for 2002 were $9.3 billion. Some of the companies whose financial statements were audited by Andersen included **Colgate-Palmolive**, **Delta Air Lines**, **FedEx Corp.**, **Hershey Foods**, **Hilton Hotels**, and **Merck**.

On August 31, 2002, Arthur Andersen closed its doors and ceased to be an auditor of the financial statements of companies whose stock was traded on public stock exchanges. How did this dramatic "about face" occur? In a word—Enron. Arthur Andersen was the external auditor for a Texas-based energy company named **Enron**.[1] To make its financial statements appear as though the company was performing better than it actually was, Enron officials created several companies, established partnerships with those companies, and then used those partnerships to hide hundreds of millions of dollars in debt. Andersen officials knew about these companies and approved the accounting for the transactions. While the details of the accounting for these transactions are far beyond the scope of this accounting class, suffice it to say that it was complicated.

When the SEC began investigating the Enron scandal, Arthur Andersen undertook a series of events that led to its eventual demise. Company officials ordered that documents relating to the Enron audit be shredded, and Andersen attorneys asked that certain internal correspondence with Enron officers that had not yet been made public be changed to hide the firm's knowledge of certain transactions. Investigation by the SEC into charges of obstruction of justice by Andersen officials led to the firm closing its doors in August of 2002.

I
n this textbook, you will begin your study of accounting. You will learn to speak and understand accounting, "the language of business." Without an understanding of accounting, business investments, taxes, and money management will be like a foreign language to you. In brief, an understanding of accounting facilitates the interpretation of financial information, which allows for better economic decisions.

interpret and use financial information prepared using accounting techniques and procedures. With the knowledge you obtain from this exposure to accounting, you will be able to "read" the financial statements of companies, understand the information that is being conveyed, and use accounting information to make good business decisions. Also, through discussion of the business environment in which accounting is used, you will increase your understanding of general business concepts such as corporations, leases, annuities, leverage, investments, and so forth.

You will become convinced that accounting is not "bean counting." Time after time you will see that accountants must exercise judgment about how to best summarize and report the results of business transactions. This judgment was at the heart of the Enron, WorldCom, and other scandals. As a result, you will gain a respect for the complexity of accounting and develop a healthy skepticism about the precision of any financial reports you see.

CAUTION

Don't be too concerned with all the new and unfamiliar terms you see in the first chapter of the book. Learning a "new language" takes time. Be patient. Before too long, you will be speaking the "language of business" (accounting) quite fluently.

The major objectives of this text are to provide you with a basic understanding of the language of accounting and with the ability to

---

[1] In addition to Enron, several other Andersen clients including WorldCom, Qwest, Sunbeam, and Waste Management also had major financial statement frauds. These near-term failures also contributed to Andersen's demise.

Finally, you will see the power of accounting. Financial statements are not just paper reports that get filed away and forgotten. As an example, the misleading financial statement numbers associated with Enron, WorldCom, and Tyco (another financial statement fraud) resulted in tens of thousands of employees being laid off and investors losing billions of dollars. You will see that financial statement numbers, and, indirectly, the accountants who prepare them, determine who receives loans and who doesn't, which companies attract investors and which don't, which managers receive salary bonuses and which don't, and which companies are praised in the financial press and which aren't.

So, let's get started.

What's the Purpose of Accounting?

Describe the purpose of accounting and explain its role in business and society.

(1) Imagine a long distance telephone company with no system in place to document who calls whom and how long they talk. Or a manager of a 300-unit apartment complex who has forgotten to write down which tenants have and have not paid this month's rent. Or an accounting professor who, the day before final grades are due, loses the only copy of the disk containing the spreadsheet of all the homework, quiz, and exam scores. Each of these scenarios illustrates a problem with bookkeeping, the least glamorous aspect of accounting. **Bookkeeping** is the preservation of a systematic, quantitative record of an activity. Bookkeeping systems can be very primitive—cutting notches in a stick to tally how many sheep you have or moving beads on a string to track the score in a billiards game. But the importance of routine bookkeeping cannot be overstated; without bookkeeping, business is impossible.

bookkeeping

The preservation of a systematic, quantitative record of an activity.

Rudimentary bookkeeping is ancient, probably predating both language and money. The modern system of double-entry bookkeeping still in use today (described in Chapter 3) was developed in the 1300s–1400s in Italy by the merchants in the trading and banking centers of Florence, Venice, and Genoa. The key development in accounting in the last 500 years has been the use of the bookkeeping data, not just to keep track of things, but to evaluate the performance and health of a business.

This use of bookkeeping data as an evaluation tool may seem obvious to you, but it is a step that is often not taken. Let's consider a bookkeeping system with which most of us are familiar—a checking account. Your checking account involves (or should involve) careful recording of the dates and amounts of all checks written and all deposits made, the maintenance of a running account total, and reconciliations with the monthly bank statement. Now, assume that you have a perfect checking account bookkeeping system. Will the system answer the following questions?

- Are you spending more for groceries this year than you did last year?
- What proportion of your monthly expenditures are fixed, meaning that you can't change them except through a drastic change in lifestyle?
- You plan to study abroad next year; will you be able to save enough between now and then to pay for it?

accounting system

The procedures and processes used by a business to analyze transactions, handle routine bookkeeping tasks, and structure information so it can be used to evaluate the performance and health of the business.

In order to answer these kinds of evaluation questions, each check must be analyzed to determine the type of expenditure, your checks must then be coded by type of expenditure, the data must be boiled down into summary reports, and past data must be used to forecast future patterns. How many of us use our checking account data like this? Not many. We do the bookkeeping (usually), but we don't structure the information to be used for evaluation.

In summary, an **accounting system** is used by a business to (1) analyze transactions, (2) handle routine bookkeeping tasks, and (3) structure information so it can be used to evaluate the performance and health of the business. Exhibit 1 illustrates the three functions of the accounting system.

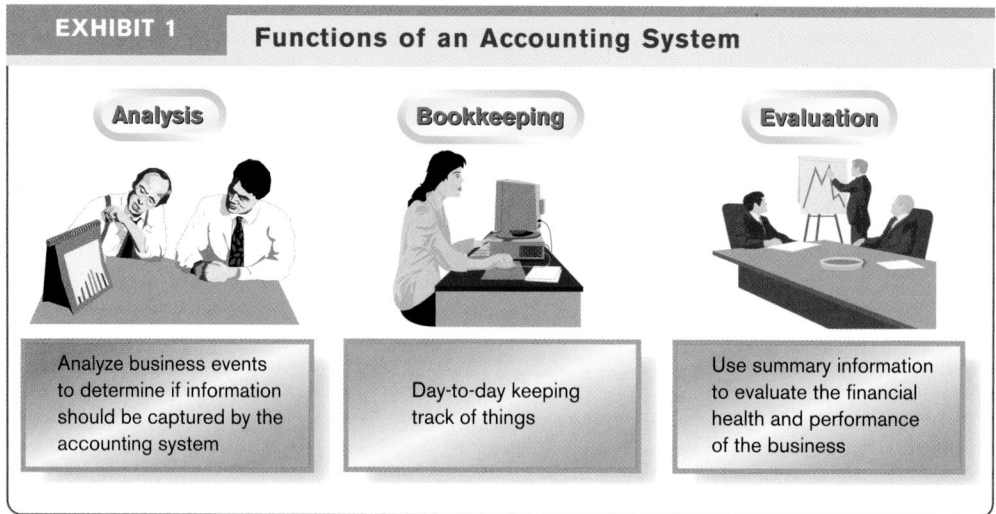

EXHIBIT 1   Functions of an Accounting System

Analysis — Analyze business events to determine if information should be captured by the accounting system

Bookkeeping — Day-to-day keeping track of things

Evaluation — Use summary information to evaluate the financial health and performance of the business

accounting

A system for providing quantitative, financial information about economic entities that is useful for making sound economic decisions. Accounting is often called the "language of business" because it provides the means of recording and communicating business activities and the results of those activities.

Accounting is formally defined as a system for providing "quantitative information, primarily financial in nature, about economic entities that is intended to be useful in making economic decisions."[2] The key components of this definition are:

- *Quantitative.* Accounting relates to numbers. This is a strength because numbers can be easily tabulated and summarized. It is a weakness because some important business events, such as a toxic waste spill and the associated lawsuits and countersuits, cannot be easily described by one or two numbers.
- *Financial.* The health and performance of a business are affected by and reflected in many dimensions—financial, personal relationships, community and environmental impact, and public image. Accounting focuses on just the financial dimension.
- *Useful.* The practice of accounting is supported by a long tradition of theory. U.S. accounting rules have a theoretical conceptual framework. Some people actually make a living as accounting theorists. However, in spite of its theoretical beauty, accounting exists only because it is useful.
- *Decisions.* Although accounting is the structured reporting of what has already occurred, this past information can only be useful if it impacts decisions about the future.

Making good decisions is critical for success in any business enterprise. When an important decision must be made, it is essential to use a rational decision-making process. The process is basically the same no matter how complex the issue. First, the issue or question must be clearly identified. Next, the facts surrounding the situation must be gathered and analyzed. Then, several alternative courses of action should be identified and considered before a decision is finally reached. This decision-making process is summarized in Exhibit 2.

---

[2] Statement of the Accounting Principles Board No. 4, "Basic Concepts and Accounting Principles Underlying Financial Statements of Business Enterprises," New York: American Institute of Certified Public Accountants, 1970, par. 40.

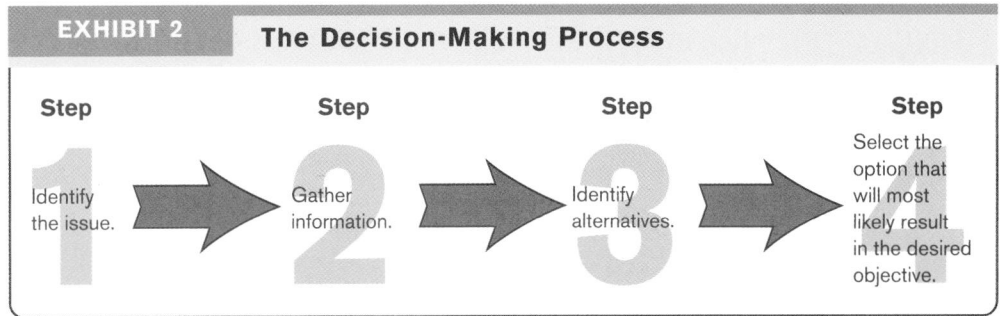

EXHIBIT 2   **The Decision-Making Process**

Step 1 Identify the issue.

Step 2 Gather information.

Step 3 Identify alternatives.

Step Select the option that will most likely result in the desired objective.

One must be careful to make a distinction between a good decision and a good outcome. Often, many factors outside the control of the decision maker affect the outcome of a decision. The decision-making process does not guarantee a certain result; it only ensures that a good decision is made. The outcome always has an element of chance. Part of business is learning how to protect yourself against bad outcomes. The first step in achieving a favorable outcome begins with making a good decision.

business

An organization operated with the objective of making a profit from the sale of goods or services.

nonprofit organization

An entity without a profit objective, oriented toward providing services efficiently and effectively.

Accounting plays a vital role in the decision-making process. An accounting system provides information in a form that can be used to make knowledgeable financial decisions. The information supplied by accounting is in the form of quantitative data, primarily financial in nature, and relates to specific economic entities. An economic entity may be an individual, a business enterprise, or a nonprofit organization. A **business**, such as a grocery store or a car dealership, is operated with the objective of making a profit for its owners. The goal of a **nonprofit organization**, such as a city government or a university, is to provide services in an effective and efficient manner. Every entity, regardless of its size or purpose, must have a way to keep track of its economic activities and measure how well it is accomplishing its goals. Accounting provides the means for tracking activities and measuring results.

The Relationship of Accounting to Business

Business is the general term applied to the activities involved in the production and distribution of goods and services. Accounting is used to record and report the financial effects of business activities. Thus, as mentioned earlier, accounting is often called the "language of business." It provides the means of recording and communicating the successes and failures of business organizations. Without accounting information, many important financial decisions would be made blindly. Investors, for example, would have no way to distinguish between a profitable company and one that is on the verge of failure; bankers could not evaluate the riskiness of potential loans; corporate managers would have no basis for controlling costs, setting prices, or investing the company's resources; and governments would have no basis for taxing income.

All business enterprises have some activities in common. As shown in Exhibit 3, one common activity is the acquisition of monetary resources. These resources, often referred to as "capital," come from three sources: (1) investors (owners), (2) creditors (lenders), and (3) the business itself in the form of earnings that have been retained. Once resources are obtained, they are used to buy land, buildings, and equipment; to purchase materials and supplies; to pay employees; and to meet any other operating expenses involved in the production and marketing of goods or services. When the product or service is sold, additional monetary resources (revenues) are generated. These resources can be used to pay loans, to pay taxes, and to buy new materials, equipment,

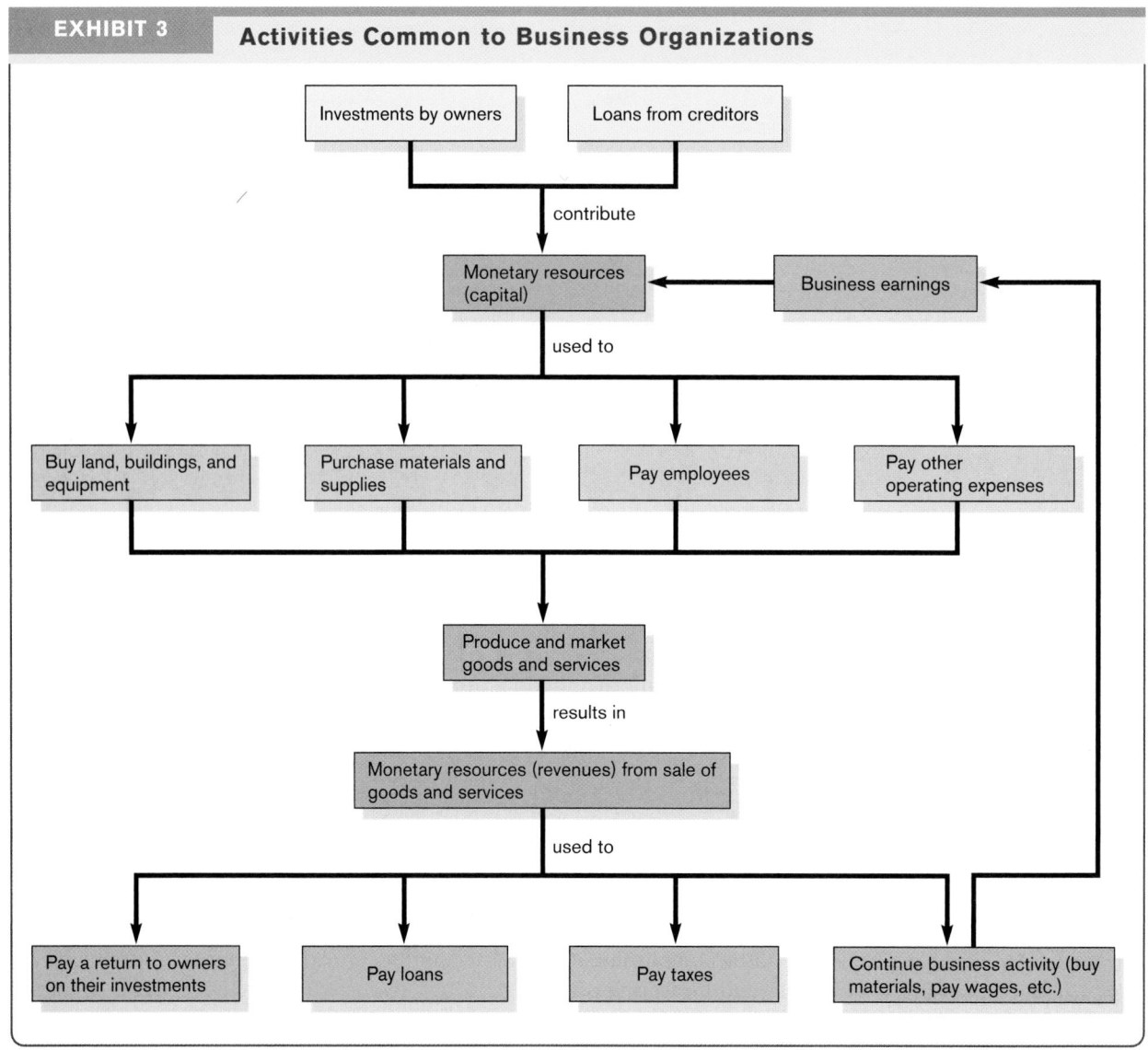

EXHIBIT 3   **Activities Common to Business Organizations**

and other items needed to continue the operations of the business. In addition, some of the resources may be distributed to owners as a return on their investment. **Wal-Mart**, for example, uses the earnings from its operations to open new stores and purchase inventory for those new stores. Once the new stores are opened, they produce more funds that can then be used to open more stores. Wal-Mart also distributes many of its resources back to its owners. Owners also receive a return on their investment through increases in the value of the stock.

Accountants play two roles with regard to these activities. First, they measure and communicate (report) the results of these activities—in other words, accountants keep score. In order to measure these results as accurately as possible, accountants follow a fairly standard set of procedures, usually referred to as the **accounting cycle**. The cycle includes several steps, which involve analyzing, recording, classifying, summarizing, and reporting the transactions of a business. These steps are explained in detail in Chapters 3 and 4. Second, accountants advise managers on how to structure these activities so as to achieve the goals of the business—be those goals to generate a profit, to minimize costs, to provide efficient services, etc.

accounting cycle

The procedure for analyzing, recording, classifying, summarizing, and reporting the transactions of a business.

Who Uses Accounting Information?

Identify the primary users of accounting information.

(2) The accounting system generates output in the form of financial reports. As shown in Exhibit 4, there are two major categories of reports: internal and external. Internal reports are used by those who direct the day-to-day operations of a business enterprise. These individuals are collectively referred to as "management," and the related area of accounting is called **management accounting** (see page 10 for definition). Management accounting focuses on the information needed for planning, implementing plans, and controlling costs. Managers and executives who work inside a company have access to specialized management accounting information that is not available to outsiders. For example, the management of **McDonald's Corporation** has detailed management accounting data on exactly how much it costs to produce each food and drink item on the menu. Further, if **Burger King** or **Wendy's** starts a local burger price war in, say, Missouri, McDonald's managers can request daily sales summaries for each store in the area to measure the impact.

EXHIBIT 4	Output of the Accounting Cycle

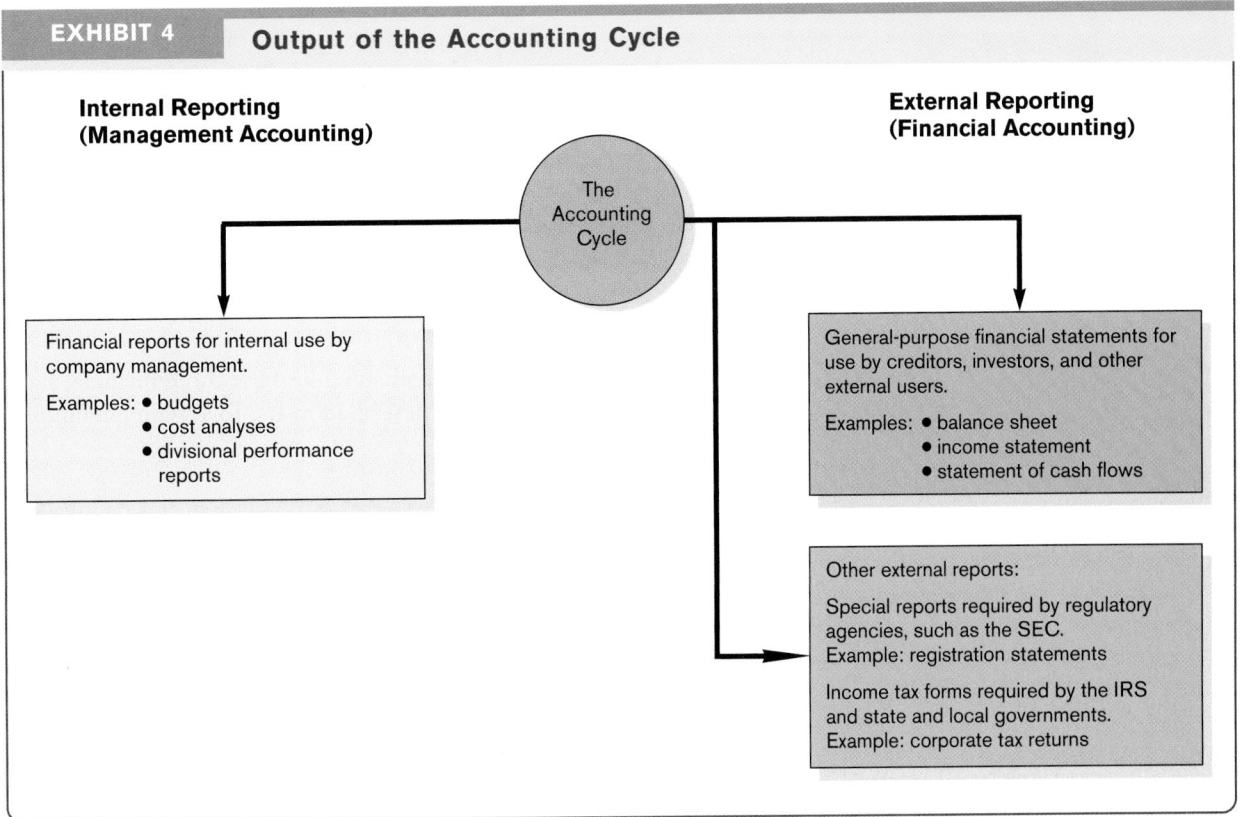

management accounting

The area of accounting concerned with providing internal financial reports to assist management in making decisions.

annual report

A document that summarizes the results of operations and financial status of a company for the past year and outlines plans for the future.

financial statements

Reports such as the balance sheet, income statement, and statement of cash flows, which summarize the financial status and results of operations of a business entity.

financial accounting

The area of accounting concerned with reporting financial information to interested external parties.

Other examples of decisions made using management accounting information are whether to produce a product internally or purchase it from an outside supplier, what prices to charge, and which costs seem excessive. Consider those companies that produce computers. Most computers are shipped with an operating system already installed. More than 90% of computers have **Microsoft's** Windows pre-installed. The computer makers must decide whether to develop their own operating system or pay Microsoft a licensing fee to use Windows. Most computer manufacturers have determined it is cost effective to license from Microsoft. Companies such as **Sears** and **Radio Shack** often use products produced by outside suppliers rather than manufacture the products themselves. The products are then labeled with the "Kenmore" or "Realistic" brand names and sold to customers. These are just two examples of decisions that must be made by management given available financial information.

External financial reports, included in the firm's **annual report**, are used by individuals and organizations that have an economic interest in the business but are not part of its management. Information is provided to these "external users" in the form of general-purpose **financial statements** and special reports required by government agencies. The general-purpose information provided by **financial accounting** is summarized in the three primary financial statements: balance sheet, income statement, and statement of cash flows (more formally introduced in Chapter 2), and explanatory notes and discussion that supports these statements.

- The *balance sheet*—reports the resources of a company (the assets), the company's obligations (the liabilities), and the owners' equity, which represents the difference between what is owned (assets) and what is owed (liabilities).
- The *income statement*—reports the amount of net income earned by a company during a period, with annual and quarterly income statements being the most common. Net income is the excess of a company's revenues over its expenses; if the expenses are more than the revenues, then the company has suffered a loss for the period. The income statement represents the accountant's best effort at measuring the economic performance of a company.
- The *statement of cash flows*—reports the amount of cash collected and paid out by a company in the following three types of activities: operating, investing, and financing. The statement of cash flows is the most objective of the financial statements because, as you will see in subsequent chapters, it involves fewer accounting estimates and judgments.

Examples of external users of the information contained in these three financial statements, along with other available information, are described in the following paragraphs.

Lenders

Lenders (creditors) are interested in one thing—being repaid, with interest. If you were to approach a bank for a large loan, the bank would ask you for the following types of information in order to evaluate whether you would be able to repay the loan:

- A listing of your assets and liabilities
- Payroll stubs, tax returns, and other evidence of your income
- Details about any monthly payments (car, rent, credit cards, etc.) you are obligated to make
- Copies of recent bank statements to document the flow of cash into and out of your account

In essence, the bank would be asking you for a balance sheet, an income statement, and a statement of cash flows. Similarly, banks use companies' financial statements in making decisions about commercial loans. The financial statements are useful because they help the lender predict the future ability of the borrower to repay the loan.

In the case of Wal-Mart, a review of its balance sheet indicates that the company has several formal lenders. In addition, Wal-Mart reports a balance in its "accounts payable" account. This amount represents amounts owed to vendors from whom Wal-Mart has purchased on credit. Considering Wal-Mart's reputation, this "lending" is very low risk.

Investors

Investors want information to help them estimate how much cash they can expect to receive in the future if they invest in a business now. Financial statements, coupled with a knowledge of business plans, market forecasts, and the character of management, can aid investors in assessing these future cash flows. Many companies have broad ownership with a few individuals owning a large portion of the company's stock. At Wal-Mart, the Walton Family (the founders of Wal-Mart) own 1,701,604,926 shares (40.8% of total shares outstanding).

Obviously, millions of Americans invest in McDonald's, Wal-Mart, **Cisco Systems**, **General Electric**, and other public companies without ever seeing the financial statements of these companies. Investors can feel justifiably safe in doing this because large companies are followed by armies of financial analysts who would quickly blow the whistle if they found information suggesting that investors in these companies were at serious risk. But what about investing in a smaller company, one that the financial press doesn't follow, or in a local family business that is seeking outside investors for the first time? In cases such as these, investing without looking at the financial statements is like jumping off the high dive without looking first to see if there is any water in the pool.

F Y I

One of the concerns with online "day trading" in stocks is that investors make significant investment decisions without ever seeing, or even thinking about, a company's reported financial position.

Management

In addition to using management accounting information available only to those within the firm, managers of a company can use the general financial accounting information that is also made available to outsiders. Company goals are often stated in terms of financial accounting numbers, such as a target of sales growth in excess of 5%. Also, reported "net income" is frequently used in calculating management bonuses. Finally, managers of a company can analyze the general-purpose financial statements (using the techniques introduced in Chapter 6 and discussed in detail in Chapter 14) in order to pinpoint areas of weakness about which more detailed management accounting information can be sought.

Other Users of Financial Information

There are many other external users of financial information, including suppliers, customers, employees, competitors, government agencies, and the press. These are described below.

Suppliers and Customers
In some settings, suppliers and customers are interested in the long-run staying power of a company. On the supplier side, if **Boeing** receives an order from an airline for 30 new 747s over the next 10 years, Boeing wants to know whether the airline will be around in the future to take delivery of and pay for the planes. On the customer side, a homeowner who has foundation repair work done wants to know whether the company making the repairs will be around long enough to honor its 50-year guarantee. Financial statements provide information that suppliers and customers can use to assess the long-run prospects of a company.

Employees   Employees are interested in financial accounting information for a variety of reasons. As mentioned earlier, financial statement data are used in determining employee bonuses. In addition, financial accounting information can help an employee evaluate the likelihood that the employer will be able to fulfill its long-run promises, such as pensions and retiree health-care benefits. Financial statements are also important in contract negotiations between labor unions and management.

Competitors   If you were a manager at **PepsiCo**, would you be interested in knowing the relative profitability of **Coca-Cola**'s operations in the United States, Brazil, Japan, and France? Of course you would, because that information could help you identify strategic opportunities for marketing efforts where potential profits are high or where your competitor is weak. Wal-Mart can use the information in financial statements to track its competitors and identify new opportunities to grow and use its market share in retail to increase its revenues in other ventures.

Government Agencies   Federal and state government agencies make frequent use of financial accounting information. For example, to make sure that investors have sufficient information to make informed investment decisions, the Securities and Exchange Commission monitors the financial accounting disclosures of companies (both U.S. and foreign) whose stocks trade on U.S. stock exchanges. The International Trade Commission uses financial accounting information to determine whether the importation of Ecuadorian roses or Chinese textiles is harming U.S. companies through unfair trade practices. The Justice Department uses financial statement data to evaluate whether companies (such as Microsoft) are earning excessive monopolistic profits. In Microsoft's case, from 2003 to 2005, it reported profits of $0.26 on every dollar of sales. During that same period, General Electric, one of America's most admired companies, generated profits of $0.12 on every dollar of sales.

The Press   Financial statements are a great place for a reporter to find background information to flesh out a story about a company. For example, a story about Wal-Mart can be enhanced by using the sales data shown in its annual report. In addition, a surprising accounting announcement, such as a large drop in reported profits, is a trigger for an investigative reporter to write about what is going on in a company.

In summary, who uses financial accounting information? Everyone does, or at least everyone should. External financial reports come within the area of accounting referred to as financial accounting. Most of the data needed to prepare both internal and external reports are provided by the same accounting system. A major difference between management and financial accounting is the types of financial reports prepared. Internal reports are tailored to meet the needs of management and may vary considerably among businesses. General-purpose financial statements and other external reports, however, follow certain standards or guidelines and are thus more uniform among companies. The first fourteen chapters of *Accounting: Concepts and Applications* focus on financial accounting, specifically on the primary financial statements (discussed and illustrated in Chapter 2). The remaining chapters, 15 through 23, focus on management accounting.

> ## REMEMBER THIS...
>
> - Management accounting focuses on providing reports for INTERNAL use by management to assist in making operating decisions and in planning and controlling a company's activities.
> - Financial accounting provides information to meet the needs of EXTERNAL users.
> - The three general-purpose financial statements are the balance sheet, the income statement, and the statement of cash flows.
> - The financial statements are used by interested external parties such as investors, creditors, suppliers, customers, employees, competitors, the government, and the press.

Within What Kind of Environment Does Accounting Operate?

Describe the environment of accounting, including the effects of generally accepted accounting principles, international business, ethical considerations, and technology.

(3) Accounting functions in a dynamic environment. Changes in technology as well as economic and political factors can significantly influence accounting practice. For example, the downfall of Enron and WorldCom and the resulting demise of Arthur Andersen have significantly changed the way accounting is done. As a result of these scandals, the U.S. government has taken a more active role in the development of accounting rules and oversight of the accounting industry. Four particularly important factors that influence the environment in which accounting operates are the development of "generally accepted accounting principles" (GAAP), international business, ethical considerations, and technology.

The Significance and Development of Accounting Standards

Imagine a company that compensates a key employee in the following ways:

- Paying a cash salary of $80,000.
- Offering the option to become, a year from now, a 10% owner of the company in exchange for an investment of $200,000.

If the company does well in the coming year, the company will increase in value, the $200,000 price tag for 10% ownership will look like a great deal, and the employee will exercise the option. If the company does poorly, it will decline in value, the $200,000 price will be too high, and the employee will throw the option away and forget the whole thing. Assume the company then sells the ownership option to interested outside investors for $25,000.

The accounting question is how to summarize in one number the company's compensation cost associated with this employee. We would probably all agree to include the $80,000 cash salary as compensation. What about the option? Both of the following arguments could be put forward:

1. If the employee were to buy the option from the company, just like any other outside investor, the employee would have to pay $25,000. Therefore, giving the option to the employee is just like paying him or her $25,000 cash. The $25,000 value of the option should be added to compensation cost.
2. The option doesn't cost the company a thing. In fact, the option merely increases the probability that the employee will invest $200,000 in the company in the future. The option doesn't add a penny to compensation cost.

So, which argument is right? Should each company decide for itself whether to include the $25,000 option value as part of compensation cost, or should there be an overall accounting standard followed by all companies? And if there is a standard, who sets it?[3]

There are many situations in business, such as the option compensation case just described, in which reasonable people can disagree about how certain items should be handled for accounting purposes. And, since financial accounting information is designed to be used by people outside a company, it is important that outsiders understand the rules and assumptions used by the company in constructing its financial statements. This would be extremely difficult and costly for outsiders to find out if every company formulated its own set of accounting rules. Accordingly, in most countries in the world, there exists a committee or board that establishes the accounting rules for that country.

---

[3] The answer to this surprisingly controversial question of the accounting for option compensation is given in Chapter 8. Just to show how influential accounting can be, this exact issue was debated on the floor of the U.S. Senate.

The Financial Accounting Standards Board

Financial Accounting Standards Board (FASB)

The private organization responsible for establishing the standards for financial accounting and reporting in the United States.

In the United States, accounting standards for publicly listed companies are set by the **Financial Accounting Standards Board (FASB)**. The FASB is based in Norwalk, Connecticut, and its seven full-time members are selected from a variety of backgrounds—professional accounting, business, government, and academia. An important thing to note about the FASB is that it is not a government agency; the FASB is a private body established and supported by fees received from companies that are audited by public accounting firms. Because the FASB is not a government agency, it has no legal power to enforce the accounting standards it sets. The FASB gets its authority to establish rules from the Securities and Exchange Commission (discussed later).

The FASB maintains its influence as the accounting standard setter for the United States (and the most influential accounting body in the world) by carefully protecting its prestige and reputation for setting good standards. In doing so, the FASB must walk a fine line between constant improvement of accounting practices to provide more full and fair information for external users and practical constraints on financial disclosure to appease businesses that are reluctant to disclose too much information to outsiders. To balance these opposing forces, the FASB seeks consensus by requesting written comments and sponsoring public hearings on all its proposed standards. The end result of this public process is a set of accounting rules that are described as being **generally accepted accounting principles (GAAP)**.

generally accepted accounting principles (GAAP)

Authoritative guidelines that define accounting practice at a particular time.

As you study this text, you will be intrigued by the interesting conceptual issues the FASB must wrestle with in setting accounting standards. The FASB has deliberated over the correct way to compute motion picture profits, the appropriate treatment of the cost of dismantling a nuclear power plant, the best approach for reflecting the impact of changes in foreign currency exchange rates, and the proper accounting for complex financial instruments such as commodity futures and interest rate swaps. And since U.S. companies are always suspicious that any change in the accounting rules will make them look worse on paper, almost all FASB decisions are made in the midst of controversy.

STOP & THINK

Why is it important for the FASB to remain completely independent?

Other Organizations

In addition to the FASB, several other organizations affect accounting standards and are important in other ways to the practice of accounting. Some of these organizations are discussed below.

Securities and Exchange Commission In response to the Stock Market Crash of 1929, Congress created the **Securities and Exchange Commission (SEC)** to regulate U.S. stock exchanges. Part of the job of the SEC is to make sure that investors are provided with full and fair information about publicly-traded companies. The SEC is not charged with protecting investors from losing money; instead, the SEC seeks to create a fair information environment in which investors can buy and sell stocks without fear that companies are hiding or manipulating financial data.

Securities and Exchange Commission (SEC)

The government body responsible for regulating the financial reporting practices of most publicly-owned corporations in connection with the buying and selling of stocks and bonds.

As part of its regulatory role, the SEC has received from Congress specific legal authority to establish accounting standards for companies soliciting investment funds from the American public. Generally, the SEC refrains from exercising this authority and allows the FASB to set U.S. accounting standards. However, as a result of the accounting scandals of the early 2000s, the SEC was given more responsibility and authority to monitor financial reporting. Congress provided this

certified public accountant (CPA)

A special designation given to an accountant who has passed a national uniform examination and has met other certifying requirements.

American Institute of Certified Public Accountants (AICPA)

The national organization of CPAs in the United States.

additional authority with the Sarbanes-Oxley Act. This Act created, among other things, a Public Company Accounting Oversight Board. The Act also required the SEC to implement many changes in the way corporations are governed.

While the FASB is charged with creating the rules that dictate financial reporting practices, the SEC is always looming in the background, legally authorized to take over the setting of U.S. accounting standards should the FASB lose its credibility with the public.

American Institute of Certified Public Accountants The label "CPA" has two different uses—there are individuals who are CPAs and there are CPA firms. A **certified public accountant (CPA)** is someone who has taken a minimum number of college-level accounting classes, has passed the CPA exam administered by the **American Institute of Certified Public Accountants (AICPA)**, and has met other requirements set by his or her state. In essence, the CPA label guarantees that the person has received substantial accounting training.

The second use of the label "CPA" is in association with a CPA firm. A CPA firm is a company that performs accounting services, just as a law firm performs legal services. Obviously, a CPA firm employs a large number of accountants, not all of whom have received the training necessary to be certified public accountants. CPA firms help companies establish accounting systems, formulate business plans, redesign their operating procedures, and just about anything else you can think of. A good way to think of a CPA firm is as a freelance business-advising firm with a particular strength in accounting issues.

CPA firms are also hired to perform independent audits of the financial statements of a company. The important role of the independent audit in ensuring the reliability of the financial statements is discussed in Chapter 5.

(?) FYI

Other tasks accountants perform are planning for acquisitions and mergers, measuring efficiency improvements from new technology, managing quality, and developing accounting software.

(?) FYI

Besides CPAs, other accounting-related certifications also exist. Examples include the Certified Management Accountant (CMA), Certified Internal Auditor (CIA), and the Certified Fraud Examiner (CFE).

Internal Revenue Service Financial accounting reports are designed to provide information about the economic performance and health of a company. Income tax rules are designed to tax income when the tax can be paid and to provide concrete rules to minimize inefficient arguing between taxpayers and the **Internal Revenue Service (IRS)**. Financial accounting and tax accounting involve different sets of rules because they are designed for different purposes. The implication of these two different sets of rules is that companies must maintain two sets of books—one set from which the financial statements can be prepared and the other set to comply with income tax regulations. There is nothing shady or underhanded about this. Individuals studying accounting often confuse financial accounting standards and income tax regulations. Keep in mind that what is done for accounting purposes is not necessarily accounted for in the same way for tax purposes.

International Business

One of the significant environmental changes in recent years has been the expansion of business activity on a worldwide basis. As consumers, we are familiar with the wide array of products from other countries, such as electronics from Japan

Internal Revenue Service (IRS)

A government agency that prescribes the rules and regulations that govern the collection of tax revenues in the United States.

© GETTY IMAGES INC.

Because of the expansion of international business, consumers are familiar with products from other countries, such as Hong Kong.

and clothing made in China. On the other hand, many U.S. companies have operating divisions in foreign countries. Other American companies are located totally within the United States but have extensive transactions with foreign companies. The economic environment of today's business is truly based on a global economy. As an example, in 2005 almost 62% of **IBM**'s sales were to individuals and companies located outside the United States.

International Accounting Standards Board (IASB)

The committee formed in 1973 to develop worldwide accounting standards.

Accounting practices among countries vary widely. Attempts are being made to make those practices more consistent among countries. In an attempt to harmonize conflicting national standards, the **International Accounting Standards Board (IASB)** was formed in 1973 to develop worldwide accounting standards. The IASB includes representatives from the eight major accounting standard-setting boards around the world including the United States. Like the FASB, the IASB develops proposals, circulates them among interested organizations, receives feedback, and then issues a final pronouncement.

The accounting standards produced by the IASB are referred to as International Financial Reporting Standards (IFRS's). IFRS's are envisioned to be a set of standards that can be used by all companies regardless of where they are based. In the extreme, IFRS's could supplement or even replace standards set by national standard setters such as the FASB. IASB standards are gaining increasing acceptance throughout the world. Thus far, however, the SEC has not recognized IASB standards and has barred foreign companies from listing their shares on U.S. stock exchanges unless those companies agree to provide financial statements in accordance with U.S. accounting rules (or at least provide a reconciliation between IASB GAAP and U.S. GAAP). Disclosure requirements in the United States are the strictest in the world, and foreign companies are reluctant to submit to the SEC requirement. This conflict between IASB GAAP and U.S. GAAP will be interesting to watch in the coming years: Will the SEC maintain a hard line and ultimately force U.S. accounting rules on the rest of the world? Or will the IASB standards gain increasing acceptance and become the worldwide standard? We'll see.

 F Y I

Since international accounting standards often differ from GAAP, foreign companies may be required to adjust their books to be listed on the New York Stock Exchange. For example, when Germany's **Daimler-Benz** (makers of Mercedes Benz) became a NYSE-listed company in 1994, its GAAP-adjusted books showed a loss of $748 million, whereas its German standard books reported earnings of $636 million. Note: Daimler-Benz subsequently merged with **Chrysler** to become **DaimlerChrysler**.

F Y I

In 2001, the IASB restructured itself as an independent body with closer links to national standard-setting bodies. At that time, the IASB adopted its current name and dropped its original name of the International Accounting Standards Committee (IASC).

At numerous points throughout this text, we will point out certain international applications of accounting as well as some differences that might exist in accounting rules between the United States and other countries. In addition, each chapter includes a case in the end-of-chapter material dealing with an international accounting issue.

Ethics in Accounting

Another environmental factor affecting accounting, and business in general, is the growing concern over ethics. This concern has been a focus of the accounting scandals of the early 2000s. Enron, WorldCom, and Tyco (to name a few) each resulted from upper management's falsifying financial reports (with the help of the company's internal accountants) and external auditors not detecting those falsifications. Accounting rules and the resulting information are designed to capture and reflect the underlying performance of a company. When management is tempted to use accounting numbers to misrepresent a company's performance, accountants (both inside and outside the company) are perceived by the public as being responsible for ensuring that the misrepresentation does not occur. The public's confidence in the accounting profession was weakened when these scandals came to light with the common denominator being that accounting information was used to mislead the public.

As mentioned previously, the SEC has taken action to see that public confidence in the accounting profession is restored. In addition, other organizations (like the Auditing Standards Board and the major stock exchanges) have taken measures to increase the public's confidence in the role of accountants and auditors and to restore the image of the accounting professional as being ethical and competent.

This concern over ethics and the accounting profession was highlighted in an almost prophetic speech given by then chairman of the SEC, Arthur Levitt, in September 1998 and was reinforced in 2001 with the business failures of Enron and WorldCom. In his speech, entitled "The Number's Game," Chairman Levitt identified several major accounting techniques that he believed were being used to undermine the integrity of financial reporting. As you will find, accounting involves significant judgment. Chairman Levitt expressed concern that this accounting judgment was giving way to pressure to "meet the numbers." In other words, Wall Street's expectations about a company, rather than the company's actual business performance, were driving the reported accounting numbers.

The ethical dilemmas facing businesses and their accountants often revolve around pressures placed on companies by investors, creditors, and potential investors and creditors. As Chairman Levitt mentioned, these pressures can sometimes cause company officials to become involved in "accounting hocus-pocus." Because accounting involves judgment, the reported accounting numbers can differ significantly depending on the assumptions made by those preparing the financial statements. As a simple example of how this can occur, consider again the case of Microsoft. When a customer buys a Microsoft product, part of the purchase price relates to promised customer service and future product upgrades. So the question is this: How much of the sales price should Microsoft report as a "sale" on the date of the sale, and how much relates to future services to be provided? As you can imagine, that is a difficult question to answer, and any answer will involve an estimate.

To quote again from Chairman Levitt's speech, accounting principles "allow for flexibility to adapt to changing circumstances." It is this flexibility that creates many of the ethical dilemmas faced by accountants. As businesses come under pressure to report favorable performance, accountants may also come under pressure to "flex" the rules just a little too far.

Don't let yourself naively think that ethical dilemmas in business are rare. Such issues occur quite frequently. To help prepare you to enter the business world and to recognize and deal with ethical issues, we have included at least one accounting-related ethics case at the end of each chapter. Ethics is an important topic that should be considered carefully, with the ultimate goal of improving individual and collective behavior in society.

Technology

Few developments have changed the way business is conducted as much as computers have. Computer technology allows businesses to do things that 20 years ago were unimaginable. Consider being able to use your desktop computer to track the status of a package shipped from Los Angeles to New York. Companies such as **UPS** and **FedEx** incorporate this type of technology as an integral part of their business. Financial institutions use computer technology to wire billions of dollars each day to locations around the world.

So how have computers changed the way accounting is done? That question can be addressed on several levels. First, computer technology allows companies to easily gather vast amounts of information about individual transactions. For example, information relating to the customer, the salesperson, the product being sold, and the method of payment can be easily gathered for each transaction using computer technology.

Second, computer technology allows large amounts of data to be compiled quickly and accurately, thereby significantly reducing the likelihood of errors. As you will soon discover, a large part of the mechanics of accounting involves moving numbers to and from various accounting records as well as adding and subtracting a lot of figures. Computers have made this process virtually invisible. What once occupied a large part of an accountant's time can now be done in an instant.

Third, in the precomputer world of limited analytical capacity, it was essential for lenders and investors to receive condensed summaries of a company's financial activities. Now, lenders and investors have the ability to receive and process gigabytes of information, so why should the report of Wal-Mart's financial performance be restricted to three short financial statements? Why can't Wal-Mart provide access to much more detailed information online? In fact, why can't Wal-Mart allow investors to directly tap into its own internal accounting database? Information technology has made this type of information acquisition and analysis possible; the question accountants face now is how much information companies should be required to make available to outsiders. Ten years ago, the only way you could get a copy of Wal-Mart's financial statements was to call or write to receive paper copies in the mail. Now you can download those summary financial statements from Wal-Mart's Web site. How will you get financial information 10 years from now? No one knows, but the rapid advances in information technology guarantee that it will be different from anything we are familiar with now.

Finally, and most importantly, although technology has changed the way certain aspects of accounting are carried out, on a fundamental level the mechanics of accounting

THE SECRETS TO DOING WELL
in an Accounting Class

Step one in succeeding in an accounting class is to stay current with your studies and with your assignments. Many of the concepts in accounting are new, and some time is required between the introduction of a new concept and the mastery of that concept. Some students try to "cram" all their accounting study into a short period of time right before an exam, and they almost always find, through sad experience, that the cramming strategy doesn't work in accounting. Some of you may be skeptical of this advice because you have successfully used the cramming strategy in other courses. For you, we suggest the following experiment: pair up with a classmate, with one of you

studying your accounting on a regular basis and the other waiting until two days before the first exam to start studying. We guarantee that the "crammer" will have a humbling experience on that first exam whereas the regular studier will have reasonable success. We also strongly suggest that if you try this experiment, you take the role of the regular studier and let your friend be the crammer.

Second, realize that many of the concepts in accounting build on one another. As a result, missing class or skipping a couple of homework assignments can be catastrophic. An initial concept must be understood before a subsequent concept can be attempted.

are still the same as they were 500 years ago. People are still required to analyze complex business transactions and input the results of that analysis into the computer. Technology has not replaced judgment.

So if you are asking "Why do I need to understand accounting—can't computers just do it?"—the answer is a resounding "No!" You need to know what the computer is doing if you are to understand and interpret the information resulting from the accounting process. You need to understand that since judgment was required when the various pieces of information were put into the accounting systems, judgment will be required to appropriately use that information. We have included numerous end-of-chapter opportunities for you to experience how technology helps in the accounting process. These opportunities will illustrate the important role that technology can play in the accounting process as well as emphasize the critical role that the accountant plays as well.

REMEMBER THIS...

- The rules governing financial accounting are called generally accepted accounting principles (GAAP).
- In the United States, GAAP is set by a private, nongovernmental group called the Financial Accounting Standards Board (FASB).
- Worldwide GAAP is set by the International Accounting Standards Board (IASB) based in London.
- Other U.S. organizations that are important to the practice of accounting are the SEC, the AICPA, and the IRS.
- Because the practice of accounting requires professional judgment, accountants are frequently faced with ethical dilemmas.
- Technology has changed the way accounting information is collected, analyzed, and used. However, computers have not replaced the accountant nor eliminated the need for qualified decision makers.

For example, imagine trying to learn to do algebra after having skipped the lessons on addition and subtraction. Similarly, jumping into Chapter 6 in this book is a difficult feat if you don't understand the material covered in Chapter 3.

The third step in having a good experience in your accounting class is to make sure you understand the big picture. We have included learning objectives to cover each major point in the chapter. The introductions associated with each learning objective should help you understand WHY you are studying the issue in addition to HOW to do accounting. In most cases, when you understand the "why" of something, you find it much easier to grasp the "how."

Finally, if you need help, don't delay in finding it. Your instructor is a valuable resource and you should take advantage of his or her office hours. (Note: Instructors love students who come in with written lists of specific questions. On the other hand, instructors get frustrated with students who view office hours as a time for the instructor to repeat, for an audience of one, a lecture that the student missed.) In addition, many students find that accounting study groups are beneficial. A well-organized study group is an example of the classic economic concept of specialization and trade; group members can rotate in taking the lead in studying difficult concepts and then explaining them to the rest of the group.

Good luck, and enjoy the ride!

So, Why Should I Study Accounting?

④ You may still be asking, "But why do I need to study accounting?" Even if you have no desire to be an accountant, at some point in your life you will need financial information to make certain decisions, such as whether to buy or lease an automobile, how to budget your monthly income, where to invest your savings, or how to finance your (or your child's) college education. You can make each of these decisions without using financial information and then hope everything turns out okay, but that would be bad decision making. As noted in the discussion of Exhibit 3, a good decision does not guarantee a good outcome, but a bad decision guarantees one of two things—a bad outcome or a lucky outcome. And you cannot count on lucky outcomes time after time. On a personal level, each of us needs to understand how to collect and use accounting information.

Odds are that each of you will have the responsibility of providing some form of income for yourself and your family. Would you prefer to work for a company that is doing well and has a promising future or one that is on the brink of bankruptcy? Of course we all want to work for companies that are doing well. But how would you know? Accounting information will allow you to evaluate your employer's short- and long-term potential.

When you graduate and secure employment, it is almost certain that accounting information will play some role in your job. Whether your responsibilities include sales (where you will need information about product availability and costs), production (where you will need information regarding the costs of materials, labor, and overhead), quality control (where you will need information relating to variances between expected and actual production), or human resources (where you will need information relating to the costs of employees), you will use accounting information. The more you know about where accounting information comes from, how it is accumulated, and how it is best used, the better you will be able to perform your job.

Everyone is affected by accounting information. Saying you don't need to know accounting doesn't change the fact that you are affected by accounting information. Ignoring the value of that information simply puts you at a disadvantage. Those who recognize the value of accounting information and learn how to use it to make better decisions will have a competitive advantage over those who don't. It's as simple as that.

 F Y I

The AICPA provides a Web site that introduces students to career opportunities in accounting. The Web site is **http://www.startheregoplaces.com**.

> **REMEMBER THIS...**
>
> - Everyone is affected by accounting.
> - Each individual needs some accounting skills in order to organize his or her personal finances.
> - Each person in a business, charity, or other organization can use accounting information to make better decisions.

REVIEW OF LEARNING OBJECTIVES

(1) Describe the purpose of accounting and explain its role in business and society.

- Accounting is a service activity designed to accumulate, measure, and communicate financial information about businesses and other organizations to provide information for making informed decisions about how to best use available resources.
- Accounting is often called the "language of business."

(2) Identify the primary users of accounting information.

	Managerial Accounting	**Financial Accounting**
Focus	Internal reporting	External reporting
Reports	Budgets	Balance sheet
	Cost analyses	Income statement
	Performance reports	Statement of cash flows
Users	Company management	Investors
		Creditors
		Suppliers
		Customers
		Employees
		Competitors
		The government
		The press

(3) Describe the environment of accounting, including the effects of generally accepted accounting principles, international business, ethical considerations, and technology.

- Generally accepted accounting principles (GAAP)
  - Set by the FASB in the United States.
  - Set by the IASB worldwide.
- Other U.S. organizations that are important to the practice of accounting:
  - SEC—regulates U.S. stock exchanges and requires financial disclosures by companies listed on those exchanges.
  - AICPA—national association of professional accountants in the United States.
  - IRS—government agency responsible for tax accounting rules.
- Do accountants need ethics? Yes, because they are called on to make accounting judgments and estimates which impact the reported performance of a company.
- Do accountants use computers? Yes, computers have changed the way accounting information is collected, analyzed, and used. However, computers have not replaced the accountant nor eliminated the need for qualified decision makers.

(4) Analyze the reasons for studying accounting.

- Everyone is affected by accounting.
- Each individual needs some accounting skills in order to organize his or her personal finances.
- Each person in a business, charity, or other organization can use accounting information to make better decisions.

KEY TERMS & CONCEPTS

accounting, 6
accounting cycle, 8
accounting system, 5
American Institute
of Certified Public
Accountants
(AICPA), 15
annual report, 10

bookkeeping, 5
business, 7
certified public
accountant (CPA), 15
financial accounting, 10
Financial Accounting
Standards Board
(FASB), 14

financial statements, 10
generally accepted
accounting principles
(GAAP), 14
Internal Revenue Service
(IRS), 15
International
Accounting

Standards Board
(IASB), 16
management
accounting, 10
nonprofit organization, 7
Securities and
Exchange Commission
(SEC), 14

DISCUSSION QUESTIONS

1. What are the three functions of an accounting system?
2. What are the essential elements in decision making, and how does accounting fit into the process?
3. What types of personal decisions have required you to use accounting information?
4. What does the term *business* mean to you?
5. Why is accounting often referred to as the "language of business"?
6. In what ways are the needs of internal and external users of accounting information the same? In what ways are they different?
7. What are generally accepted accounting principles (GAAP)? Who currently develops and issues GAAP? What is the purpose of GAAP?
8. Why is it important for financial statements and other external reports to be based on generally accepted accounting principles?

9. What are the respective roles of the Securities and Exchange Commission (SEC) and the Internal Revenue Service (IRS) in the setting of accounting standards?
10. For you as a potential investor, what is the problem with different countries having different accounting standards? For you as the president of a multinational company, what is the problem with different countries having different accounting standards?
11. Ethical considerations affect all society. Why are ethical considerations especially important for accountants?
12. Given significant technological advances, can we expect to see less demand for accountants and accounting-type services?
13. Other than that it is a requirement for your major or that your mom or dad is making you, why should you study accounting?

EXERCISES

E 1-1   **The Role and Importance of Accounting**
LO1   Assume that you are applying for a part-time job as an accounting clerk in a retail clothing establishment. During the interview, the store manager asks how you expect to contribute to the business. How would you respond?

E 1-2   **Bookkeeping Is Everywhere**
LO1   Describe how bookkeeping is applied in each of the following settings:
   a. Your college English class.
   b. The National Basketball Association.
   c. A hospital emergency room.
   d. Jury selection for a major murder trial.
   e. Four college roommates on a weekend skiing trip.

E 1-3   **Accounting Information and Decision Making**
LO1   You are the owner of Automated Systems, Inc., which sells **Apple** computers and related data processing equipment. You are currently trying to decide whether to continue selling the Apple computer line or to distribute the Windows-based computers instead. What information do you need to consider in order to determine how successful your business is or will be? What information would help you decide whether to sell the Apple or the

(continued)

Windows-based personal computer line? Use your imagination and general knowledge of business activity.

E 1-4 **Allocation of Limited Resources**

LO1 Assume you are a small business owner trying to increase your company's profits. How can accounting information help you efficiently allocate your limited resources to maximize your business profit?

E 1-5 **Users of Financial Information**

LO2 Why might each of the following individuals or groups be interested in a firm's financial statements? (a) The current stockholders of the firm; (b) the creditors of the firm; (c) the management of the firm; (d) the prospective stockholders of the firm; (e) the Internal Revenue Service (IRS); (f) the SEC; (g) the firm's major labor union.

E 1-6 **Structuring Information for Use in Evaluation**

LO2 You work in a small convenience store. The store is very low-tech; you ring up the sales on an old-style cash register that merely records the amount of the sale. The store owner uses this cash register tape at the end of each day to verify that the correct amount of cash is in the cash register drawer.

In addition to verifying the cash amount, how else could the information on the cash register tape be used to evaluate the store's operation? What additional bookkeeping procedures would be necessary to make these additional uses possible?

E 1-7 **Investing in the Stock Market**

LO2 Assume your grandparents have just given you $20,000 on the condition that you invest the money in the stock market. As you contemplate making your investment choices, what accounting information do you want to help identify companies that will have high future rates of return?

E 1-8 **Management versus Financial Accounting**

LO2 This chapter discusses two areas of accounting: management and financial accounting. Contrast management and financial accounting with respect to the following:

- Overall purpose
- Type of financial reports used (i.e., external, internal, or both)
- Users of the information

Also, in what ways are these two fields of accounting similar?

E 1-9 **The Role of the SEC**

LO2 It is not often that the federal government has allowed the private sector to govern itself, but that is exactly what has happened with the field of accounting. The SEC has delegated the responsibility of rule making to the FASB, a group of seven individuals who are hired full-time to discuss issues, research areas of interest, and determine what GAAP is and will be. What are the advantages of allowing the private sector to determine accounting standards? Identify any advantages that the SEC might gain if it established the rules that govern the practice of accounting.

E 1-10 **Why Two Sets of Books?**

LO2 This past year you were married. This coming April you will be faced with preparing your first tax return since mom and dad said "you are now on your own." As you review the IRS regulations, you notice several differences from what you learned in your accounting class. It appears that businesses must keep two sets of books: one for the IRS and one in accordance with GAAP. Why aren't GAAP and IRS rules the same?

E 1-11 **Career Opportunities in Accounting**

LO2 You are scheduled to graduate from college with a degree in accounting, and your mother would like to know what you plan to do with the rest of your life. She assumes

(continued)

that your only option is to be a bookkeeper like Bob Cratchit in the story *A Christmas Carol*. What can you tell Mom regarding the options available to you with your degree in accounting?

E 1-12
LO3
Differences in Accounting across Borders

In the United States, accounting for inventory is a difficult issue. Inventory is comprised of those items either purchased or manufactured to be resold at a profit. Numerous methods are available to account for inventory for financial reporting purposes. A very commonly used method—called LIFO (last-in, first-out)—minimizes a company's tax obligation. In the United Kingdom, however, LIFO is not permitted for tax purposes and thus is not used very often for financial reporting. In Turkey, the use of LIFO is severely restricted, and in Russia, LIFO is a foreign term. Only in Germany, where the tax laws have been modified to allow the use of LIFO, is LIFO being adopted. Different accounting methods are available for numerous other issues in accounting. Identify some major problems associated with comparing the financial statements of companies from different countries.

E 1-13
LO3
Ethics in Accounting

The text has pointed out that ethics is an important topic, especially for CPAs. Derek Bok, former law professor and president of Harvard University, has suggested that colleges and universities have a special opportunity and obligation to train students to be more thoughtful and perceptive about moral and ethical issues. Other individuals have concluded that it is not possible to "teach" ethics. What do you think? Can ethics be taught? If you agree that colleges and universities can teach ethics, how might the ethical dimensions of accounting be presented to students?

E 1-14
LO3
Challenges to the Accounting Profession

As the business world continues to change the way in which business is conducted, accountants are faced with the challenge of accounting for these changes. Who, for example, could have anticipated the risks associated with asbestos? Or the decline of communism? Or the increasingly litigious environment in the United States? Each of these events, and many more, has influenced business—which has, in turn, influenced accounting. From your general understanding of accounting and the current business environment, what are some of the challenges you see facing the accounting profession?

E 1-15
LO4
Why Do I Need to Know Accounting?

One of your college friends recently graduated from school with a major in music (specifically piano). He has told you that he is going to start his own piano instructional business. He plans to operate the business from home. You ask him how he is going to account for his business, and his reply is, "I graduated in music, not accounting. I am going to teach music, not number crunching. I didn't need accounting in college and I don't need it now!" Is your friend right? What financial information might he find useful in operating his business?

ANALYTICAL ASSIGNMENTS

AA 1-16
DISCUSSION
To Lend or Not To Lend–That Is the Question

Sam Love is vice president and chief lending officer of the Meeker First National Bank. Recently, Bill McCarthy, a new farmer, moved to town. Sam has not dealt with Bill previously and knows little about the Mountain Meadow Ranch that Bill operates. Bill would like to borrow $100,000 to purchase some equipment and yearling steers for his ranch. What information does Sam need to help make the lending decision? What type of information should Bill collect and analyze before even requesting the loan?

AA 1-17
DISCUSSION
Information Needs to Remain Competitive

In 2005, **Intel** owned the microprocessor industry with a market share of over 80%. Its nearest competition was **Advanced Micro Devices (AMD)** with a market share of 17.6%.

(continued)

What type of information, accounting or otherwise, do you think the management of AMD may want and need as they try to compete with Intel and other companies?

AA 1-18
DISCUSSION

International Happenings

July 1, 1997, marked a historic date as Hong Kong reverted to political and economic control by mainland China. The Stock Exchange of Hong Kong offers the opportunity to invest in both local Hong Kong companies and in "red-chip offerings," which are stocks of companies that are listed in Hong Kong but controlled by mainland China interests. As an international investor, what accounting information might be helpful as you consider investing in the Hong Kong stock market? For which variables in this situation is accounting information unlikely to be very helpful?

AA 1-19
DISCUSSION

Is Better Accounting the Solution to All of Life's Problems?

Your friend has just completed an introductory accounting course. She has heard that you are now taking accounting, and she has come to give you the benefit of her experience. You discover that your friend is enamored with the field of accounting, and she now believes that most business problems can be easily solved through better accounting. In fact, your friend believes that most government, social, and spiritual problems can also be solved by a better application of good accounting principles. Given what you have read in Chapter 1, do you agree with your friend? Explain.

AA 1-20
DISCUSSION

We Don't Have Time for Good Accounting!

Your sister and her business partner have just launched their own software company. They have developed software that compresses and packages email text and voice messages, allowing email and phone messages to be safely transmitted over a wireless network even while flying in a commercial airliner. Orders for the software have been pouring in, and your sister and her business partner estimate that they will make at least $10 million within the next three months. You suggest to your sister that she hire an accountant and begin to set up an accounting system within her new company. Your sister replies that accounting systems are for old-fashioned companies such as **General Motors** and **Procter & Gamble**; she wants to focus her time on hiring new software developers and on working on ideas for her company's next generation of software products. Is your sister correct? Explain.

AA 1-21
DISCUSSION

Is the Proposed Electricity Rate Increase Fair?

The governor of your state has just appointed you to the state's public utility rate commission. Your job is to set fair prices for the electricity and natural gas sold to residents of the state by a select number of public utilities. The state's primary electric utility has just proposed a 5.3% rate increase. How should you use accounting information to evaluate this proposed rate hike?

AA 1-22
JUDGMENT CALL

You Decide: How much education is necessary for an accountant?

You are at your family reunion when some relatives start asking you about your studies and plans after school. Upon learning your intentions to be an accountant, everyone was alarmed that it took five to six years to get a master's degree in accounting. Your uncle says, "All you have to do is go to a computer store and pick up a copy of QuickBooks. Computers do everything these days. The computer will do all the work and you can collect a paycheck!" Is five to six years too much time and effort to prepare to be an accountant, or is it necessary?

AA 1-23
JUDGMENT CALL

You Decide: Should the Emerging Issues Task Force (a group organized to assist the FASB in developing accounting positions) be allowed to have members of large corporations sit on their committee and vote on accounting issues that are facing today's companies, or should it be left to the accounting firms?

That is what happened with **J.P. Morgan** at a June 2002 meeting of the EITF (Emerging Issues Task Force), an extension of the FASB. J.P. Morgan blocked a vote that would have barred companies from recognizing immediate profits or losses upon entering an energy-trading contract, a move that is critical to the financial statements of J.P. Morgan and others in its industry.

Wal-Mart

In Appendix A at the back of this text is **Wal-Mart's** Form 10-K for the year ended January 31, 2006. Review the Form 10-K and identify its major areas. How many pages of the Form 10-K are devoted to a narrative of the prior three years' performance? How many pages focus on explaining technical accounting and business-related issues and procedures? In your opinion, given your limited knowledge of accounting, what is the most interesting part of the Form 10-K? What is the least interesting?

General Motors

Below is a condensed listing of the assets and liabilities of **General Motors** as of December 31, 2005. All amounts are in millions of U.S. dollars.

Assets		Liabilities	
Cash	$ 50,452	Payables	$315,663
Loans receivable	218,236	Pensions	11,304
Inventories	14,354	Other retiree benefits	33,997
Property & equipment	82,740	Other liabilities	99,478
Other assets	110,296		
Total assets	$476,078	Total liabilities	$460,442

1. Among its assets, General Motors lists more than $218 billion in loans receivable. This represents loans that General Motors has made and expects to collect in the future. This is exactly the kind of asset reported among the assets of banks. Given what you know about General Motors' business, how do you think the company acquired these loans receivable?
2. The difference between the reported amount of General Motors' assets and liabilities is $15.636 billion ($476.078 – $460.442). What does this difference represent?

Should the SEC Choose the FASB or the IASB?

The SEC has received from Congress the legal authority to set accounting standards in the United States. Historically, the SEC has allowed the FASB to set those standards. In addition, the SEC has refused to allow foreign companies to seek investment funds in the United States unless they agree to provide U.S. investors with financial statements prepared using FASB rules.

The number of foreign companies seeking to list their shares on U.S. stock exchanges is increasing. Even more would likely sell stock to the American public if the SEC were to agree to accept financial statements prepared according to usually less stringent IASB standards.

Why do you think the SEC has so far insisted on financial statements prepared using FASB rules? Do you agree with its policy? Explain.

Disagreement with the Boss

You recently graduated with your degree in accounting and have accepted an entry-level accounting position with BigTec, Inc. One of your first responsibilities is to review expense reports submitted by various executives. The expense reports include such items as receipts for taking clients to dinner and hotel receipts for business travel. In conducting this review, you note that your boss has submitted for reimbursement several items that are clearly outside the established guidelines of the corporation. In questioning your boss about the items, he told you to process the items and not worry about them. What would you do?

The Language of Business

Accounting is known as the "language of business." Prepare a one- to two-page paper explaining why all business students should have some accounting education. Also include a discussion of how accounting applies to at least five different types of businesses, such as a grocery store, a university, or a movie theater.

AA 1-29
WRITING

Visiting an Accounting Professional

Select a field of accounting you are interested in. Visit a professional who works in that area and discuss the career opportunities available in that specific accounting field. After the visit, prepare a one- to two-page paper summarizing what you learned from your discussion with the accounting professional.

© AP PHOTO/BEN MARGOT

Financial Statements:
An Overview

(1) Understand the basic elements, uses, and limitations of the balance sheet. *The balance sheet reports a company's financial position at a point in time and lists the company's resources (assets), obligations (liabilities), and net ownership interest (owners' equity).*

(2) Understand the basic elements and uses of the income statement. *The income statement describes a company's financial performance for a period of time. A company's expenses are subtracted from its revenues in computing net income.*

(3) Understand the categories and uses of the statement of cash flows and see how the primary financial statements tie together. *The statement of cash flows details how a company obtained and spent cash during a period of time. All of a company's cash transactions are categorized as either operating, investing, or financing activities.*

(4) Recognize the need for financial statement notes and identify the types of information included in the notes. *The notes to the financial statements provide information on the accounting assumptions used in preparing the statements and also provide supplemental information not included in the statements themselves.*

(5) Describe the purpose of an audit report and the incentives the auditor has to perform a good audit. *An audit performed by accountants from outside the company increases the reliance that users can place on the information in the company's financial statements. The audit firm does a thorough and fair audit in order to protect its reputation and to reduce the risk of a costly lawsuit.*

(6) Explain the fundamental concepts and assumptions that underlie financial accounting. *The financial statements are prepared for the business itself, excluding items related strictly to the personal affairs of the owner or owners. The dollar amounts recorded in the financial statements come from market transactions and are assumed to be a fair reflection of the underlying value of the items exchanged.*

In addition to founding the brokerage firm of **Merrill Lynch**, in 1926 Charles Merrill was instrumental in the consolidation of several grocery store chains in the western United States to form one big holding company called **Safeway**. In 1955, control of Safeway passed to Robert Magowan, Merrill's son-in-law. Under Magowan's leadership, Safeway expanded to become, in 1971, the largest supermarket chain in the United States.

During the 1970s, Safeway became too cautious and conservative (in the view of many). In 1980, Robert Magowan's 37-year-old son, Peter (who had started out in Safeway as a teenager bagging groceries), became chairman of the board of directors. As he assumed leadership of Safeway, Magowan faced a host of problems: an overall decrease in the size of the grocery market due to an increased tendency by Americans to eat at fast-food restaurants; union contracts that resulted in higher labor costs for Safeway than many of its competitors; high corporate overhead; and stores that were too small and too close together.

Under Peter Magowan's leadership, Safeway eliminated 2,000 office and warehouse jobs and embarked upon an impressive program of new construction and remodeling. During much of the early 1980s, Safeway spent more on capital expenditures than any other U.S. company, averaging nearly $600 million per year. In November 1986, Safeway was acquired by **Kohlberg, Kravis, Roberts & Co. (KKR)** for $5.3 billion in what was then the second-largest debt-financed buyout of all time.

So, how is Safeway doing today? In the 2005 Fortune 500 survey, Safeway, with 2004 sales of $35.8 billion, ranks as the fourth-largest food and drug chain in the United States, behind **Kroger** ($56.4 billion in sales), **Albertson's** ($40.1 billion in sales)[1], and **Walgreen** ($37.5 billion in sales). Sales volume isn't the only financial measure that can be used to evaluate a company. For example, Safeway reported net income in 2004 of ($560) million, compared to the net loss reported by Kroger ($128 million) and net income reported by Albertson's ($444 million) and Walgreen ($1,360 million). Also, Safeway's cash income ("cash from operations") was $2,226 million.

To adequately answer the question of how Safeway is doing today, one must have a working knowledge of financial statements. In this chapter, you will learn that the financial statements are summary reports that show how a business is doing and what its successes and failures are. The financial statements covered in this chapter are the same as those used every day by millions of business owners, investors, and creditors to evaluate how well or poorly organizations are doing.

Hopefully, you will come away from this chapter convinced that the purpose of accounting is not to fill out dull reports that are then filed away in dusty cabinets, but rather to prepare summary financial performance measures to be used as the basis for thousands of economic decisions every day.

The Financial Statements

The job of a mortgage loan officer is to evaluate each mortgage applicant to determine the likelihood that he or she will repay the mortgage loan. A key piece of evidence in each applicant's file is the financial information included as part of the loan application. A loan officer can use this information to evaluate whether an applicant will generate enough income to make the monthly mortgage payments and continue to make the required payments on other obligations. In fact, it is difficult to imagine how a mortgage loan officer could make an informed decision without this financial information.

Gaining access to an applicant's financial information clearly helps the mortgage lender make a better loan decision, but the applicant also benefits from making these

---

[1] In 1999, Albertson's merged with **American Stores** to form what was, at the time, the largest supermarket chain in the United States. Coincidentally, American Stores traces its roots back to the Skaggs family, whose stores also formed the backbone of the original Safeway chain organized by Charles Merrill in 1926.

**primary financial
statements**

The balance sheet, income statement, and statement of cash flows, used by external groups to assess a company's economic standing.

**balance sheet
(statement of financial
position)**

The financial statement that reports a company's assets, liabilities, and owners' equity at a particular date.

**income statement
(statement of
earnings)**

The financial statement that reports the amount of net income earned by a company during a period.

**statement of cash
flows**

The financial statement that reports the amount of cash collected and paid out by a company during a period of time.

financial disclosures. If no financial disclosures were provided, lenders would be forced to make loan decisions in the absence of reliable financial information about applicants. With greater uncertainty about applicants' ability to repay loans, a lender's risk would increase, causing the lender to raise the interest rate charged on loans. Thus, disclosure of financial information allows a lender to make better lending decisions and also allows an applicant to reduce the lender's uncertainty, leading to a lower interest rate on the loan.

The financial statements prepared by companies yield the same benefits as do the financial disclosures provided by mortgage applicants. Financial statement information provides potential lenders and investors with a reliable basis for evaluating the past performance and future prospects of a company. Because financial statements are used by so many different groups (investors, creditors, managers, etc.), they are sometimes called *general-purpose financial statements*. The three **primary financial statements** are the balance sheet, the income statement, and the statement of cash flows. These statements provide answers to the following questions:

1. What is the company's current financial status?
2. What were the company's operating results for the period?
3. How did the company obtain and use cash during the period?

> The **balance sheet** (or **statement of financial position**) reports the resources of a company (assets), the company's obligations (liabilities), and the difference between what is owned (assets) and what is owed (liabilities), called owners' equity.
>
> The **income statement** (or **statement of earnings**) reports the amount of net income earned by a company during a period, with annual and quarterly income statements being the most common. (Net income is discussed later in the chapter.) The income statement represents the accountant's best effort at measuring the economic performance of a company.
>
> The **statement of cash flows** reports the amount of cash collected and paid out by a company in the following three types of activities: operating, investing, and financing.

For illustrative purposes, we will reference **Wal-Mart**'s financial statements in this chapter and throughout the rest of the book. Those financial statements can be found in the back of the text in Appendix A.

The Balance Sheet

① Understand the basic elements, uses, and limitations of the balance sheet.

In the movie *The Princess Bride*, the hero, Wesley, was "mostly dead all day" until being revived by a miracle pill. Wesley was immediately challenged to come up with a plan to stop the imminent marriage of his true love, Buttercup, to the evil Prince Humperdinck. In formulating his plan, Wesley's first question to his conspirators was "What are our liabilities?" followed by "What are our assets?" In essence, the recently revived hero was saying, "Let me see a balance sheet." Similarly, the first questions asked about any business by potential investors and creditors are "What are the resources of the business?" and "What are its existing obligations?" The balance sheet answers these questions.

The three categories of the balance sheet—assets, liabilities, and owners' equity—are each explained on the following page.

assets

Economic resources that
are owned or controlled
by a company.

Assets   Assets are economic resources that are owned or controlled[2] by a company. Exhibit 1 contains a list of common assets along with a brief explanation of each asset. To be summarized and aggregated on a balance sheet, each asset must be assigned a dollar amount. A balance sheet wouldn't be very useful with the following asset listing: one bank account, two warehouses full of goods, three trucks, and four customers who owe us money. As emphasized throughout this text, the monetary measurement and valuation of assets is an area in which accountants must exercise considerable professional judgment.

 F Y I

The insurmountable difficulties in valuing some assets can cause important economic assets to be excluded from a company's balance sheet. For example, how does one put a monetary value on the worldwide reputation of Coca-Cola or on the genius and leadership of Bill Gates? These assets, though incredibly valuable, are not listed in the balance sheets of **The Coca-Cola Company** or of **Microsoft**.

Liabilities   Liabilities are obligations to pay cash, transfer other assets, or provide services to someone else. Your personal liabilities might include unpaid phone bills, the remaining balance on an automobile loan, or an obligation to complete work for which you have already been paid. Exhibit 2 includes a listing of some of the more common liabilities. Like assets, liabilities must be measured in dollars or whatever the currency being used is (monetary amounts.) And, as with assets, quantifying the amount of a liability can require extensive judgment. As one example, consider the difficulties faced by a company to quantify its obligation to clean up a particular toxic waste site when the cleanup will take years to complete; the exact extent of the environmental damage at the site is still in dispute; and legal responsibility for the toxic mess is still being debated in the courts. Properly valuing a company's liabilities is one of the biggest (if not *the* biggest) challenges that an accountant faces.

liabilities

Obligations to pay cash,
transfer other assets, or
provide services to
someone else.

Owners' Equity   The remaining claim against the assets of a business, after the liabilities have been deducted, is **owners' equity**. Thus, owners' equity is a

owners' equity

The ownership interest in
the net assets of an entity; equals total assets
minus total liabilities.

EXHIBIT 1	Common Assets	
	Common Assets	
Asset	**Definition**	**Example**
Cash	Coins, currency, checks.	The amount in a company's checking account.
Accounts Receivable	Amounts owed to a company that sold goods or services to a customer on credit.	If you have a balance on your credit card, the credit card company classifies the amount you owe them as an account receivable.
Inventory	Items that are purchased or manufactured by a company and are resold.	The items you see on the shelves in **Wal-Mart** are considered by Wal-Mart as inventory.
Buildings	Structures used in the operations of a business.	To continue the previous example, the store itself is classified by Wal-Mart as a building.

---

[2] An example of an asset that a company technically does not own, but does economically control, is a building that the company uses under a long-term, noncancelable lease agreement.

EXHIBIT 2	Common Liabilities	

Common Liabilities

Liability	Definition	Example
Accounts Payable	Amount owed as a result of the purchase of goods and services on credit.	The amount owed by a company for inventory that was purchased on credit and has not been paid for yet.
Taxes Payable	Amount owed to federal and state governments resulting from the application of tax laws.	Corporate income tax owed but not yet paid; employment taxes owed but not yet paid.
Mortgage Payable	Amount owed relating to the purchase of property.	The loan associated with the purchase of a home or building would be called a Mortgage Payable.
Unearned Revenue	When customers pay for service or product in advance, the company owes service or product (not money) to the customer.	If you pay for a 12-month magazine subscription, the publishing company owes you magazines.

net assets

The owners' equity of a business; equal to total assets minus total liabilities.

residual amount; it represents the **net assets** (total assets minus total liabilities) available after all obligations have been satisfied. Exhibit 3 contains a listing of common sources of owners' equity. Obviously, if there are no liabilities (an unlikely situation, except at the start of a business), then the total assets are exactly equal to the owners' claims against those assets—the owners' equity.

In order to get a business started, investors transfer resources, usually cash, to the business in return for part ownership. Ownership of a company can be restricted to one person (a sole proprietorship), to a small group (a partnership), or to a diverse group of owners who often don't even know one another (a corporation). When owners initially invest money in a corporation, they receive evidence of their ownership in the form of shares of stock, represented by stock certificates. These shares of stock may then be privately traded among existing owners of the corporation, privately sold to new owners, or traded publicly on an organized stock exchange such as the New York Stock Exchange (NYSE) (where **Safeway's** shares are traded) or the NASDAQ exchange (where Microsoft's shares are traded). The owners of a corporation are called **stockholders** or **shareholders**, and the

stockholders (shareholders)

The owners of a corporation.

EXHIBIT 3	Sources of Owners' Equity	

Sources of Owners' Equity

Owners' Equity	Definition	Example
Capital Stock	The amount given by shareholders to obtain shares of stock from a company.	A company sells shares of stock to the public. The amount the company receives is Capital Stock. Capital Stock is usually divided into two accounts: Common Stock and Additional Capital Stock that will be explained later.
Retained Earnings	Earnings that are retained in the business.	If a company reports net income for the year of $100,000 and reinvests the entire amount in the business (doesn't distribute dividends to its owners), retained earnings is $100,000.

stockholders' equity

The owners' equity section of a corporate balance sheet.

owners' equity section of a corporate balance sheet is sometimes referred to as **stockholders' equity**.

Owners' equity is increased when owners make additional investments in a business or when the business generates profits that are retained in the business. Owners' equity is decreased when the owners take back part of their investment. If the business is a corporation, distributions to the owners (stockholders) are called **dividends**. Owners' equity can also be decreased if operations generate a loss instead of a profit. In the extreme, very poor performance can result in the loss of all the assets originally invested by the owners. For a corporation, the amount of accumulated earnings of the business that have not been distributed to owners is called **retained earnings**. The portion of owners' equity contributed by owners in exchange for shares of stock is called **capital stock**. The amount of retained earnings plus the amount of capital stock equals the corporation's total owners' equity.

Although the emphasis in this book is on corporations, most of the same principles also apply to proprietorships and partnerships. Differences in accounting for proprietorships and partnerships are explained in detail in this text's website at **http://www.thomsonedu.com/accounting/albrecht.**

dividends

Distributions to the owners (stockholders) of a corporation.

retained earnings

The amount of accumulated earnings of the business that have not been distributed to owners.

Accounting Equation   The balance sheet presents information based on the basic **accounting equation**:

Assets = Liablities + Owners' Equity

In fact, the name *balance sheet* comes from the fact that a proper balance sheet must always balance—total assets must equal the total of liabilities and owners' equity. The accounting equation is not some miraculous coincidence; it is true by definition. Liabilities and owners' equity are just the methods used to finance the purchase of assets; that is, they are the claims (creditors' claims and owners' claims) against the assets. They can also be thought of as the sources of the funds that were used to purchase the assets. So, another way to view the accounting equation is that the total amount of the assets is equal to the total amount of financing needed to buy the assets. The total resources, therefore, equal the claims against those resources. This is illustrated in Exhibit 4.

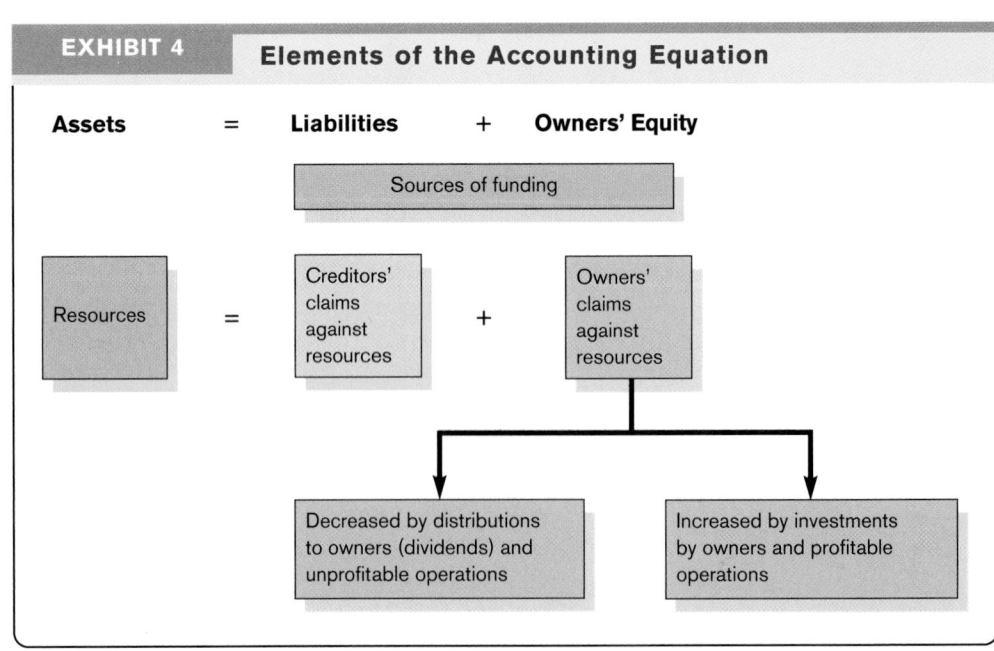

The accounting equation is presented here merely to give you a glimpse of **double-entry accounting**. Chapter 3 gives an in-depth discussion of the equation elements and the mechanics of double-entry accounting.

The Format of a Balance Sheet

A balance sheet, adapted from Safeway's 2005 balance sheet is shown in Exhibit 5. Note that a balance sheet is presented for a particular date because it reports a company's financial position at a point in time.

As illustrated, the balance sheet is divided into the major sections we have described: assets, liabilities, and owners' equity. The asset section identifies the types of assets owned by Safeway (cash, for example) and the monetary amounts associated with those assets. The liability section defines the extent and nature of Safeway's debts (income taxes not yet paid, for example).

Owners' equity completes the balance sheet. This section identifies the portion of Safeway's resources that were contributed by owners, either in exchange for shares of stock or as undistributed earnings since Safeway's inception. Together with liabilities, owners' equity indicates how a company is financed (whether by borrowing or by owner contributions and operating profits). You can see that Safeway has been financed primarily through liabilities. Because total liabilities are over 70% of Safeway's total assets, we can say that most of Safeway's assets are financed using some form of liabilities.

Classified and Comparative Balance Sheets

Imagine that two people each owe you $10,000. You ask to see the balance sheets of each. Borrower A has assets of $10,000 in the form of cash. Borrower B has assets of $10,000 in the form of undeveloped land. If you need to collect the loan in the next two weeks, which of the two borrowers is more likely to be able to pay you back? Borrower A is more likely to be able to repay you quickly because the assets of A are more *liquid*, meaning that they are in the form of cash or can be easily converted into cash. Assets such as undeveloped land are said to be *illiquid* in that it takes time and effort to convert them into cash. This illustration shows that not all assets are the same. For some purposes, it is very important to distinguish between current assets, which are generally more liquid, and long-term assets. A balance sheet that distinguishes between current and long-term assets is called a **classified balance sheet**.

Note that in the balance sheet in Exhibit 5, Safeway's assets are classified as current, or short-term, and long-term. **Current assets** include cash and other assets that are expected to be converted to cash within a year. Current assets generally are listed in decreasing order of **liquidity** (see page 36 for definition); cash is listed first, followed by the other current assets, such as accounts receivable. **Long-term assets**, such as land, buildings, and equipment, are those that a company needs in order to operate its business over an extended period of time (see page 37 for definition).

Like assets, liabilities usually are classified as either **current liabilities** (obligations expected to be paid within a year) or **long-term liabilities** (see page 37 for definitions). Accounts payable, for example, usually would be paid within 30 to 60 days, whereas a mortgage may remain on the books for 20 to 30 years before it is fully paid.

Safeway's balance sheet in Exhibit 5 includes financial information for both the current year and the preceding year. Most companies prepare such **comparative financial statements** so that readers can identify any significant changes in particular items (see page 37 for definition). For example, notice that Safeway's

---

capital stock

The portion of stockholders' equity that represents investment by owners in exchange for shares of stock. Also referred to as paid-in capital.

accounting equation

An algebraic equation that expresses the relationship between assets (resources), liabilities (obligations), and owners' equity (net assets, or the residual interest in a business after all liabilities have been met): Assets = Liabilities + Owners' Equity.

double-entry accounting

A system of recording transactions in a way that maintains the equality of the accounting equation.

> ⓘ **CAUTION**
>
> Don't worry about fully understanding all the items in Safeway's classified balance sheet, such as the "Obligations under capital leases" and the "Accumulated other comprehensive income." If there was nothing else to learn, this book would be much shorter and this accounting class would last only two weeks.

classified balance sheet

A balance sheet in which assets and liabilities are subdivided into current and long-term categories.

current assets

Cash and other assets that can be easily converted to cash within a year.

EXHIBIT 5	Classified Balance Sheets for Safeway

Safeway, Inc.
Comparative Balance Sheet
Year-End 2005 and 2004
(amounts in millions)

	2005	2004
ASSETS		
Current assets:		
Cash and equivalents	$ 373.3	$ 266.8
Receivables	350.6	339.0
Merchandise inventories, net of LIFO reserve of $48.4 and $48.6	2,766.0	2,740.7
Prepaid expenses and other current assets	212.5	251.2
Total current assets	$ 3,702.4	$ 3,597.7
Property, plant & equipment:		
Land	$ 1,413.9	$ 1,396.0
Plant and equipment	14,714.9	13,646.7
	$16,128.8	$15,042.7
Less accumulated depreciation and amortization	(7,031.7)	(6,353.3)
Total property, net	$ 9,097.1	$ 8,689.4
Goodwill	2,402.4	2,406.6
Other assets	555.0	683.7
Total assets	$15,756.9	$15,377.4
LIABILITIES AND STOCKHOLDERS' EQUITY		
Current liabilities:		
Current portion of long-term debt	$ 753.3	$ 639.7
Accounts payable	2,151.5	1,759.4
Accrued salaries and wages	526.1	426.4
Income taxes	124.2	270.3
Other accrued liabilities	708.8	696.3
Total current liabilities	$ 4,263.9	$ 3,792.1
Long-term debt:		
Notes and debentures	$ 4,961.2	$ 5,469.7
Obligations under capital leases	644.1	654.0
Total long-term debt	$ 5,605.3	$ 6,123.7
Deferred income taxes	223.1	463.6
Accrued claims and other liabilities	744.9	691.1
Total liabilities	$10,837.2	$11,070.5
Stockholders' equity:		
Common stock: par value $0.01 per share; 1,500 shares authorized; 580.1		
and 578.5 shares outstanding	$ 5.8	$ 5.8
Additional capital stock and other	3,445.1	3,357.9
Treasury stock at cost; 130.7 and 130.8 shares	(3,875.7)	(3,879.7)
Accumulated other comprehensive income	172.8	144.9
Retained earnings	5,171.7	4,678.0
Total stockholders' equity	$ 4,919.7	$ 4,306.9
Total liabilities and stockholders' equity	$15,756.9	$15,377.4

liquidity

The ability of a company to pay its debts in the short run.

total assets increased by $379.5 million ($15,756.9 − $15,377.4) from 2004 to 2005. In addition, notice that Safeway's total liabilities decreased by $233.3 million. An increase in total assets coupled with a decrease in total liabilities often indicates a company is doing well. The fact that the company reported net income of $561.1 million confirms that the company is having success.

Limitations of a Balance Sheet   Although the balance sheet is useful in showing the financial status of a company, it does have some limitations. The primary limitation of

long-term assets

Assets that a company needs in order to operate its business over an extended period of time.

current liabilities

Liabilities expected to be satisfied within a year or the current operating cycle, whichever is longer.

long-term liabilities

Liabilities that are not expected to be satisfied within a year.

comparative financial statements

Financial statements in which data for two or more years are shown together.

market value

The value of a company as measured by the number of shares of stock outstanding multiplied by the current market price of the stock; the current value of a business.

book value

The value of a company as measured by the amount of owners' equity; that is, assets less liabilities.

the balance sheet is that it does not reflect the current value or worth of a company. Refer to the balance sheet numbers for Wal-Mart in the appendix. If the balance sheet were perfect, meaning that it included all economic assets reported at their current market values, then the amount of owners' equity would be equal to the market value of the company. In the case of Wal-Mart, the value of the company would be $70.8 billion, which is the amount of assets that would remain after all the liabilities were repaid. The actual market value of Wal-Mart on May 9, 2006, however, was $200 billion. How could the balance sheet be so wrong?

The discrepancy between recorded balance sheet value and actual market value is the result of the following two factors:

1. Accountants record many assets at their purchase cost, not at their current market value. **Market value** is the price that would have to be paid to buy the same asset today. For example, if land was obtained ten years ago, it would still be reported on the balance sheet at its original cost, even though its market value may have increased dramatically.
2. Not all economic assets are included in the balance sheet. For example, some of the most important economic assets of Wal-Mart are its distribution channels, its name recognition, and its reputation for low prices. These intangible factors are all very valuable economic assets. In fact, they are by far the most valuable assets Wal-Mart has. Nevertheless, these important economic assets are outside the normal accounting process.

Because the balance sheet can underreport the value of some long-term assets, and not report other important economic assets, the accounting **book value** of a company (measured by the amount of owners' equity) is usually less than the company's market value, measured by the market price per share times the number of shares of stock. This is illustrated in Exhibit 6 using data for the ten largest companies (in terms of market value) in the United States.

Despite its deficiencies, the balance sheet is a useful source of information regarding the financial position of a business. A lender would never loan a company money without knowing what assets the company has and what other loans the company is already obligated to repay. An investor shouldn't pay money in exchange for ownership in a company without knowing something about the company's existing resources and obligations. When a balance sheet is classified, and when comparative data are provided, the balance sheet provides an informative picture of a company's financial position.

REMEMBER THIS...

- Balance sheet—a summary of the financial position of a company at a particular date
- Asset—economic resource owned or controlled by a company
- Liability—economic obligation to deliver assets or provide a service
- Equity—equal to total assets minus total liabilities and representing the book value of the assets that belongs to the owners after the liability obligations have been satisfied; stems from direct owner investment and past profits retained in the business
- Accounting equation—Assets = Liabilities + Owners' Equity
- Format—in the balance sheet, assets and liabilities are typically separated into current and long-term items with data for both the current and the preceding year reported for comparison
- Limitations—the balance sheet reflects assets acquired at their historical cost, thus frequently ignoring changes in value and gradual development of intangible assets

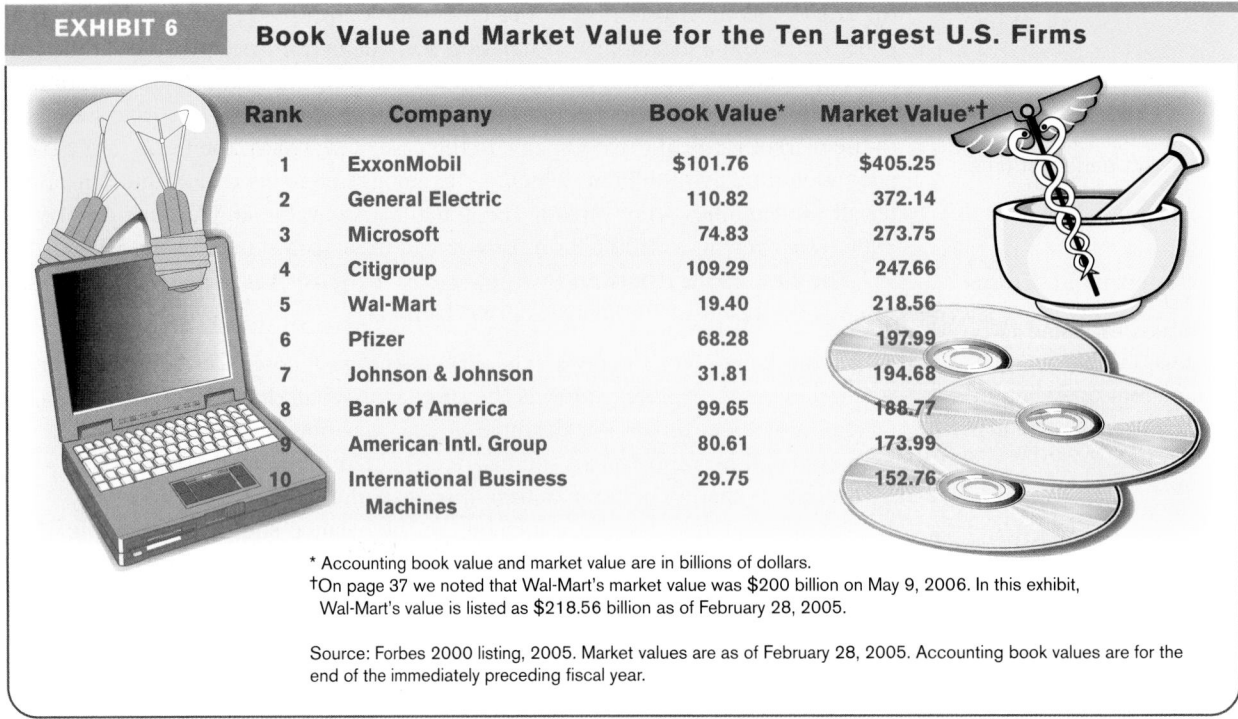

Rank	Company	Book Value*	Market Value*†
1	ExxonMobil	$101.76	$405.25
2	General Electric	110.82	372.14
3	Microsoft	74.83	273.75
4	Citigroup	109.29	247.66
5	Wal-Mart	19.40	218.56
6	Pfizer	68.28	197.99
7	Johnson & Johnson	31.81	194.68
8	Bank of America	99.65	188.77
9	American Intl. Group	80.61	173.99
10	International Business Machines	29.75	152.76

EXHIBIT 6   Book Value and Market Value for the Ten Largest U.S. Firms

* Accounting book value and market value are in billions of dollars.

†On page 37 we noted that Wal-Mart's market value was $200 billion on May 9, 2006. In this exhibit, Wal-Mart's value is listed as $218.56 billion as of February 28, 2005.

Source: Forbes 2000 listing, 2005. Market values are as of February 28, 2005. Accounting book values are for the end of the immediately preceding fiscal year.

The Income Statement

2 Understand the basic elements and uses of the income statement.

Almost every day, *The Wall Street Journal* includes articles detailing the income forecasts of many publicly-traded companies. The stock prices of companies go up or down depending on whether information disclosed about a company has a positive or negative impact on the firm's expected earnings. For example, on March 31, 2006, the following events occurred:

- **Google**'s stock price fell $6.54 per share on news that the Internet search giant would sell 5.3 million new shares. Additional stock raises concerns about dilution for current shareholders, so the market reacted negatively.
- **Ruby Tuesday**'s stock price rose by $1.58 per share. The casual-dining chain's fiscal third-quarter earnings were better than expected. In addition, the restraurant-level profit margins exceeded predictions. This announcement means investors earned more return on their investment than expected and will continue to do so since profit margins are higher than expected. Because of this announcement, the market reacted positively.

As companies provide additional information about revenue and income numbers, it is apparent that investors find these accounting numbers useful in evaluating the health and performance of a business.

Net income is reported in the income statement. The income statement shows the results of a company's operations for a period of time (a month, a quarter, or a year). The income statement summarizes the revenues generated and the costs incurred (expenses) to generate those revenues. The "bottom line" of an income statement is net income (or net loss), the difference between revenues and expenses. To help you understand an income statement, we must first define its elements—revenues, expenses, and net income (or net loss).

revenue

Increase in a company's resources from the sale of goods or services.

Revenues   Revenue is the amount of assets created through business operations. Think of revenue as another way for a company to acquire assets. In the same way that assets can be acquired by borrowing or by owners' investment, assets can also be acquired by providing a product or service for which customers are willing to pay. Manufacturing and merchandising companies receive revenues from the sale of merchandise. For example, Safeway's revenue is the cash that customers pay in exchange for groceries. A service enterprise generates revenues from the fees it charges for the services it performs. Companies might also earn revenues from other activities, such as charging interest or collecting rent. When goods are sold or services performed, the resulting revenue is in the form of cash or accounts receivable (a promise from the buyer to pay for the goods or services by a specified date in the future). Revenues thus generally represent an increase in total assets. These new assets are not tied to any liability obligation; therefore, the assets belong to the owners and thus represent an increase in owners' equity.

expenses
Costs incurred in the normal course of business to generate revenues.

Expenses Expenses are the amount of assets consumed through business operations. Expenses are the costs incurred in normal business operations to generate revenues. Employee salaries and utilities used during a period are two common examples of expenses. For Safeway, the primary expense is the wholesale cost of the groceries that it sells to its customers at retail. Just as revenues represent an increase in assets and equity, expenses generally represent a decrease in assets and in equity.

> In considering revenues and expenses, remember that not all inflows of assets are revenues; nor are all outflows of assets considered to be expenses. For example, cash may be received by borrowing from a bank, which is an increase in a liability, not a revenue. Similarly, cash may be paid for supplies, which is an exchange of one asset for another asset, not an expense. The details of properly identifying revenues and expenses will be discussed further in Chapter 3.

net income (net loss)
An overall measure of the performance of a company; equal to revenues minus expenses for the period.

Net Income (or Net Loss) Net income, sometimes called earnings or profit, is an overall measure of the performance of a company. Net income reflects the company's accomplishments (revenues) in relation to its efforts (expenses) during a particular period of time. If revenues exceed expenses, the result is called net income (revenues − expenses = net income). If expenses exceed revenues, the difference is called **net loss**. Because net income results in an increase in resources from operations, owners' equity is also increased; a net loss decreases owners' equity. Exhibit 7 lists the ten U.S. companies with the highest net incomes in 2004.

It is important to note the difference between revenues and net income. Both concepts represent an increase in the net assets (assets − liabilities) of a firm. However, revenues represent total resource increases; expenses are subtracted from revenues to derive net income or net loss. Thus, whereas revenue is a "gross" concept, income (or loss) is a "net" concept.

It is also important to note the difference between revenues and assets. Revenues are one activity of a company that generates assets. For example, selling a product (which is revenue) results in an asset (either cash or an accounts receivable). Assets can also be generated by other activities. For example, borrowing money from a bank would not be considered a revenue-generating activity, but it would result in an asset—cash. To summarize, activities involving revenue result in assets, but assets can result from many different activities.

The Format of an Income Statement Comparative income statements for Safeway are presented in Exhibit 8. In contrast to the balance sheet, which is "as of" a particular date, the income statement refers to the "year ended." Remember, the income statement covers a period of time; the balance sheet is a report at a point in time. The multi-step format illustrated here highlights several profit measurements including gross profit, operating income, and net income.

EXHIBIT 7   **Top Ten U.S. Companies, Ranked by Net Income**

Company Name	Net Income*
ExxonMobil	$25,330
Citigroup	17,046
General Electric	16,593
Bank of America Corp.	14,143
ChevronTexaco	13,328
Pfizer	11,361
American Intl. Group	11,050
Wal-Mart Stores	10,267
Altria Group	9,416
Johnson & Johnson	8,509

*Net income is in millions of dollars.

Source: Fortune 500 listing, 2005.

EXHIBIT 8   **Adapted Comparative Income Statements for Safeway**

Safeway, Inc.

Comparative Income Statement

For Years Ended 2005 and 2004

(amounts in millions)

	2005	2004
Sales	$ 38,416.0	$ 35,822.9
Cost of goods sold	(27,303.1)	(25,227.6)
Gross profit	$ 11,112.9	$ 10,595.3
Operating and administrative expense	(9,898.2)	(9,422.5)
Operating profit	$ 1,214.7	$ 1,172.8
Interest expense	(402.6)	(411.2)
Other income, net	36.9	32.3
Income from continuing operations before income taxes	$ 849.0	$ 793.9
Income taxes	(287.9)	(233.7)
Net income (loss)	$ 561.1	$ 560.2
BASIC (LOSS) EARNINGS PER SHARE:	$1.25	$1.26

The income statement usually shows two main categories, revenues and expenses, although several subcategories may also be presented (as illustrated). Revenues are listed first. Typical operating expenses for most businesses are employee salaries, utilities, and advertising. For Safeway, as with any retail firm, the largest expense is for cost of goods sold. The difference between sales and cost of goods sold represents the difference between the retail price Safeway receives from a grocery sale and the wholesale cost of the groceries that are sold. This difference (sales − cost of goods sold) is called **gross profit** or **gross margin**.

Expenses are sometimes divided into operating and nonoperating categories. The primary nonoperating expenses are interest and income taxes. These expenses are called nonoperating because they have no connection with the specific nature of the operation of the business. For example, Safeway and Wal-Mart

gross profit (gross margin)

The excess of net sales revenue over the cost of goods sold.

deal with interest and income taxes in a similar way, even though the two companies operate using different strategies.

gains (losses)

Money made or lost on activities outside the normal operation of a company.

Two other items that frequently appear in the income statement are **gains** and **losses**. Gains and losses refer to money made or lost on activities outside the normal business of a company. For example, when Safeway receives cash for selling groceries, it is called revenue. But when Safeway makes money by selling an old delivery truck, the amount is called a gain, not revenue, because Safeway is not in the business of selling trucks.

earnings (loss) per share (EPS)

The amount of net income (earnings) related to each share of stock; computed by dividing net income by the number of shares of stock outstanding during the period.

One final bit of information required on the income statements of corporations is **earnings (loss) per share (EPS)**. This EPS amount is computed by dividing the net income (earnings or loss) for the current period by the number of shares of stock outstanding during the period. Earnings per share information tells the owner of a single share of stock how much of the net income for the year belongs to him or her. Often two EPS figures are disclosed—basic and diluted. Basic EPS is based on historical transactions and involves dividing net income by actual average shares outstanding during the period. Diluted EPS is a bit more complicated and involves estimating what EPS would be if certain stock transactions (that will be discussed later) had occurred.

F Y I

Recently, companies have been providing an additional measure of income—comprehensive income. The wealth of a company is affected in a variety of ways that have nothing to do with the business operations of the company. **Comprehensive income** is the number used to reflect an overall measure of the change in a company's wealth during the period. The most common examples of items included in comprehensive income include changes in foreign currency exchange rates, changes in the value of certain investment securities, and changes in the value of certain derivative financial instruments. Each of these items is affected by market conditions, affects a company's reported assets and liabilities yet cannot be influenced in any large degree by the company. Therefore, they are reported as part of a firm's comprehensive income.

Like the balance sheet, the income statement usually shows the comparative results for two or more periods, allowing investors and creditors to evaluate how profitable an enterprise has been during the current period as compared with earlier periods. For example, examination of Safeway's comparative income statements in Exhibit 8 shows that net income in 2005 was over $0.9 million higher ($561.1 − $560.2) than in 2004. Further analysis of the income statement is reinforced throughout the text.

The Statement of Retained Earnings

In addition to an income statement, corporations sometimes prepare a **statement of retained earnings** (see page 42 for definition). This statement identifies changes in retained earnings from one accounting period to the next. Exhibit 9 illustrates the statement of retained earnings for Safeway. The statement shows a beginning retained earnings balance, the net income for the period, a deduction for any dividends paid (which were $67.4 million for Safeway), and an ending retained earnings balance.

comprehensive income

A measure of the overall change in a company's wealth during a period; consists of net income plus changes in wealth resulting from changes in investment values and exchange rates.

Note how the accounting equation is affected by the elements reported in the statement of retained earnings. Net income results in an increase in net assets and a corresponding increase in Retained Earnings, which increases Owners' Equity.

$$(\uparrow)\text{Assets} = \text{Liabilities} + \text{Owners' Equity} (\uparrow)$$

Capital Stock   Retained Earnings ($\uparrow$)

Dividends reduce net assets (e.g., cash) and similarly reduce Retained Earnings, which reduces Owners' Equity.

$$(\downarrow)\text{Assets} = \text{Liabilities} + \text{Owners' Equity} (\downarrow)$$

Capital Stock   Retained Earnings ($\downarrow$)

EXHIBIT 9	Illustrated Statement of Retained Earnings for Safeway

Safeway, Inc.
Illustrated Statement of Retained Earnings
For the Year Ended December 31, 2005
(in millions)

Retained earnings, January 1, 2005	$4,678.0
Plus net income for the year	561.1
	$5,239.1
Less dividends	(67.4)
Retained earnings, December 31, 2005	$5,171.7

statement of retained earnings

A report that shows the changes in retained earnings during a period of time.

It is worth taking a moment to review just what exactly Retained Earnings is and what Retained Earnings isn't. Retained Earnings is the amount of earnings of a business that have been retained in the business (hence, the name Retained Earnings). The earnings that have not been retained in the business have been distributed to owners in the form of a dividend. The earnings that have been retained have been reinvested back into the business to become inventory and equipment and to pay down debt. To see where a company has reinvested the earnings it has retained would require you to examine the assets on the firm's balance sheet. Odds are that many of those assets will have been provided by the earnings that have been reinvested in the business.

Now, what isn't Retained Earnings? Retained Earnings is not cash. Some of the earnings that have been retained in a business may be retained in the form of cash, but it is more likely that the cash has been used to purchase other assets or to pay off liabilities. Students often make the mistake of assuming that if a company has Retained Earnings, the company has cash. That is not true. To determine how much cash a company has, you would examine the balance in the company's cash account—not the balance in the company's retained earnings account.

Corporations sometimes present a *statement of stockholders' equity* instead of a statement of retained earnings. The statement of stockholders' equity is more detailed and includes changes in capital stock as well as changes in retained earnings.

REMEMBER THIS...

- Income statement—a report of a company's performance for a particular period of time
- Revenue—an INCREASE in a company's resources through a normal business transaction
- Expense—a DECREASE in a company's resources through a normal business transaction
- Net income—equal to revenues minus expenses and represents the net amount of assets created through business operations during a particular period of time
- Format—usually several years of income statement data are reported side by side for comparison
- Computation of retained earnings—retained earnings is equal to the total earnings that have been retained in the company; this amount accumulates each year and is computed as beginning retained earnings plus net income minus dividends

The Statement of Cash Flows

③ Net income is the single best measure of a company's economic performance. However, anyone who has paid rent or college tuition knows that bills must be paid with cash, not with "economic performance." Accordingly, in addition to net income, investors and creditors also desire to know how much actual cash a company's operations generate during a period and how that cash is used. The statement of cash flows shows the cash inflows (receipts) and cash outflows (payments) of an entity during a period of time. As shown in Exhibit 10, companies receive cash primarily by selling goods or providing services, by selling other assets, by borrowing, and by receiving cash from investments by owners. Companies use cash to pay current operating expenses such as wages, utilities, and taxes; to purchase additional buildings, land, and otherwise expand operations; to repay loans; and to pay their owners a return on the investments that have been made.

In the statement of cash flows, individual cash flow items are classified according to three main activities: operating, investing, and financing.

Understand the categories and uses of the statement of cash flows and see how the primary financial statements tie together.

operating activities

Activities that are part of the day-to-day business of a company.

investing activities

Activities associated with buying and selling long-term assets.

financing activities

Activities whereby cash is obtained from or repaid to owners and creditors.

> **Operating Activities**   Operating activities are those activities that are part of the day-to-day business of a company. Cash receipts from selling goods or from providing services are the major operating cash inflow. Major operating cash outflows include payments to purchase inventory and to pay wages, taxes, interest, utilities, rent, and similar expenses.
>
> **Investing Activities**   The primary investing activities are the purchase and sale of land, buildings, and equipment. You can think of investing activities as those activities associated with buying and selling long-term assets.
>
> **Financing Activities** Financing activities are those activities whereby cash is obtained from or repaid to owners and creditors. For example, cash received from owners' investments, cash proceeds from a loan, or cash payments to repay loans would all be classified under financing activities.

Conceptually, the statement of cash flows is the easiest to prepare of the three primary financial statements. Imagine examining every check and deposit slip you have written in the past year and sorting them into three piles—operating, investing, and financing. You would have to exercise some judgment in deciding which pile some items go into (for example, is the payment of interest an operating or a financing activity?). But overall, the three-way categorization of cash flows is not that difficult. In essence, this is all that is involved in the preparation of a statement of cash flows. As you will see in Chapter 13, however, actual preparation of a statement of cash flows can sometimes be challenging.

Exhibit 11 contains the statement of cash flows for Safeway for 2005 and 2004. As with balance sheets and income statements, companies usually provide comparative statements of cash flows.

How can Safeway report such a small amount of income on the income statement and yet be generating almost $2 billion in cash flow from operating activities? The simple answer is that Safeway reported a large number of noncash expenses on its 2005 income statement. This issue gets at the heart of accrual accounting which is introduced in Chapter 4. The details relating to the statement of cash flows will be explored in Chapter 13.

EXHIBIT 10 **Cash Flows**

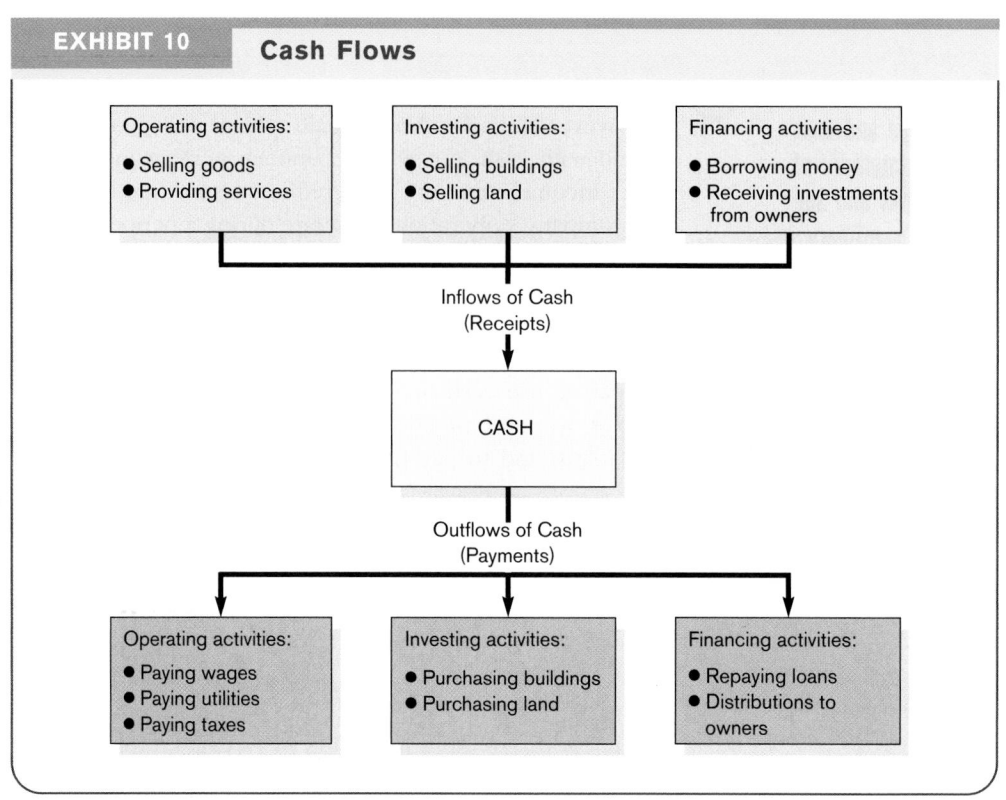

EXHIBIT 11 **Statement of Cash Flows for Safeway, Inc.**

Safeway Inc. and Subsidiaries
Consolidated Statements of Cash Flows
For Year Ended December 2005 and 2004*

	2005	2004
CASH FLOWS FROM OPERATING ACTIVITIES		
Cash collected from customers	$ 38,404.4	$ 35,867.1
Cash paid for		
Inventory	(26,936.3)	(25,076.3)
Operating and administrative expenses	(8,550.6)	(8,085.8)
Interest	(412.1)	(434.8)
Taxes	(624.4)	(43.8)
NET CASH FLOWS FROM OPERATING ACTIVITIES	1,881.0	2,226.4
CASH FLOWS FROM INVESTING ACTIVITIES		
Cash paid for property additions	(1,383.5)	(1,212.5)
Proceeds from sale of property	105.1	194.7
Other	(35.1)	(52.5)
NET CASH FLOWS USED BY INVESTING ACTIVITIES	(1,313.5)	(1,070.3)
CASH FLOWS FROM FINANCING ACTIVITIES		
Additions to short-term borrowings	13.0	11.2
Payments on short-term borrowings	(23.8)	(1.5)
Additions to long-term borrowings	754.5	1,173.5
Payments on long-term borrowing	(1,188.6)	(2,278.6)
Purchase of treasury stock	(1.5)	(0.4)
Dividends paid	(44.9)	–
Other	30.3	31.7
NET CASH FLOWS USED BY FINANCING ACTIVITIES	(461.0)	(1,064.1)
INCREASE IN CASH FOR THE PERIOD	$ 106.5	$ 92.0

*Adapted.

EXHIBIT 12   **How the Financial Statements Tie Together**

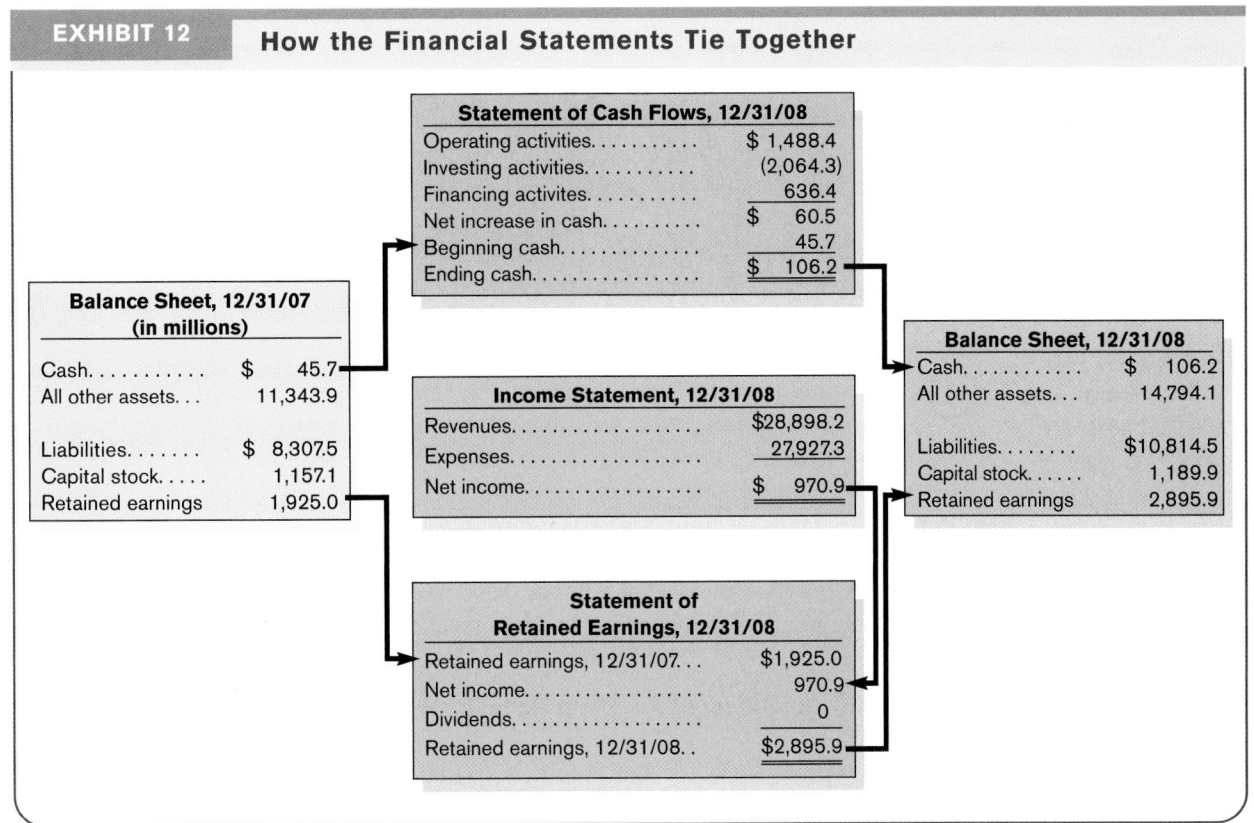

How the Financial Statements Tie Together

Although we have introduced the primary financial statements as if they were independent of one another, they are interrelated and tie together. In accounting language, they "articulate." **Articulation** refers to the relationship between an operating statement (the income statement or the statement of cash flows) and comparative balance sheets, whereby an item on the operating statement helps explain the change in an item on the balance sheet from one period to the next.

articulation

The interrelationships among the financial statements.

Exhibit 12 shows how the financial statements tie together. Note that the beginning amount of cash from the 2004 balance sheet is added to the net increase

REMEMBER THIS...

- Statement of cash flows—a report of a company's cash inflows and outflows categorized into operating, investing, and financing activities
- Operating activities—activities that are part of a company's day-to-day business; examples include collecting cash from customers, paying employees, and purchasing inventory
- Investing activities—activities involving the purchase and sale of long-term assets such as buildings, trucks, and equipment
- Financing activities—activities surrounding acquiring the capital needed to purchase the company's assets; examples include getting cash from loans, repaying loans, receiving invested cash from owners, and paying dividends
- Format—usually several years of cash flow data are reported side by side for comparison
- Articulation—the three primary financial statements tie together as follows:
  - the income statement explains the change in the retained earnings balance in the balance sheet
  - the statement of cash flows explains the change in the cash balance in the balance sheet

or decrease in cash (from the statement of cash flows) to derive the cash balance as reported on the 2005 balance sheet. Similarly, the retained earnings balance as reported on the 2005 balance sheet comes from the beginning retained earnings balance (2004 balance sheet) plus net income for the period (from the income statement) less dividends paid. As you study financial statements, these relationships will become clearer and you will understand the concept of articulation better.

Notes to the Financial Statements

Recognize the need for financial statement notes and identify the types of information included in the notes.

(4) The three primary financial statements contain a lot of information. Still, three summary reports cannot possibly tell financial statement users everything they want to know about a company. Additional information is given in the **notes to the financial statements**. In fact, in a typical annual report, the notes go on for 15 pages or more, whereas the primary financial statements fill only 3 pages. The notes tell about the assumptions and methods used in preparing the financial statements and also give more detail about specific items.

The financial statement notes are of the following four general types:

1. Summary of significant accounting policies.
2. Additional information about the summary totals found in the financial statements.
3. Disclosure of important information that is not recognized in the financial statements.
4. Supplementary information required by the Financial Accounting Standards Board (FASB) or the Securities and Exchange Commission (SEC).

notes to the financial statements

Explanatory information considered an integral part of the financial statements.

Summary of Significant Accounting Policies

As mentioned earlier, accounting involves making assumptions, estimates, and judgments. In addition, in some settings, there is more than one acceptable method of accounting for certain items. For example, there are a variety of acceptable ways of estimating how much a building depreciates (wears out) in a year. In order for financial statement users to be able to properly interpret the three primary financial statements, they must know what procedures were used in preparing those statements. This information about accounting policies and practices is given in the financial statement notes.

 F Y I

In its 1920 annual report, **IBM** included zero pages of notes (and the dollar amounts were carried out to the penny). In 1966, there were four pages of notes (and dollar amounts were rounded to the nearest dollar). In 2005, IBM's annual report included 46 pages of notes (and dollar amounts were rounded to the nearest million).

Additional Information about Summary Totals

For a large company, such as **Wal-Mart** or **Safeway**, one summary number in the financial statements represents literally thousands of individual items. For example, the $4.961 billion in long-term notes and debentures included in Safeway's 2005 balance sheet (see Exhibit 5) represents loans comprised of mortgages, senior secured debentures, senior subordinated debentures, commercial paper, short-term unsecured bank borrowings, an unsecured bank credit agreement, and more. The balance sheet includes only one number, with the details in the notes.

Disclosure of Information Not Recognized

One way to report financial information is to include the estimates and judgments in the financial statements. This is called *recognition*. The key assumptions and estimates are then described in a note to the financial statements. Another approach is to not include

EXHIBIT 13 **Safeway's Note Disclosure**

NOTE L: COMMITMENTS AND CONTINGENCIES

LEGAL MATTERS In July 1988, there was a major fire at the Company's dry grocery warehouse in Richmond, California. Through March 1, 2006, in excess of 126,000 claims for personal injury and property damage arising from the fire have been settled for an aggregate amount of approximately $125 million. The Company's loss as a result of the fire damage to its property and settlement of the above claims was substantially covered by insurance.

As of March 1, 2006, there were still pending approximately 175 claims against the Company for personal injury (including punitive damages), arising from the smoke, ash and embers generated by the fire. A substantial percentage of these claims have been asserted in lawsuits against the Company filed in the Superior Court for Alameda County, California. There can be no assurance that the pending claims will be settled or otherwise disposed of for amounts and on terms comparable to those settled to date. Safeway continues to believe that coverage under its insurance policy will be sufficient and available for resolution of all remaining personal injury and property damage claims arising out of the fire.

estimates and judgments in the financial statements but instead to explain them in the notes to the financial statements. This is called *disclosure*. Disclosure is the accepted way to convey information to users when the information is too uncertain to be recognized. For example, in July 1988, Safeway suffered a fire in one of its warehouses in Richmond, California. As of March 1, 2006, there were still 175 unsettled personal injury lawsuits against Safeway stemming from the fire. It is impossible to summarize the complexity of the potential outcome of these lawsuits in a number that can be reported on the financial statements; so, Safeway describes the situation, in some detail, in the notes to the financial statements. The related note from Safeway's annual report is included in Exhibit 13.

Supplementary Information

The FASB and SEC both require supplementary information that must be reported in the financial statement notes. For example, the FASB requires the disclosure of quarterly financial information and of business segment information. A sample of this type of disclosure can be seen in Wal-Mart's Form 10-K in Appendix A. In the notes to its financial statements, Wal-Mart reports that almost 20% of its 2006 revenue was generated outside of the United States.

REMEMBER THIS...

The notes to the financial statements contain additional information not included in the financial statements themselves. The notes:

- explain the company's accounting assumptions and practices,
- provide details of financial statement summary numbers and additional disclosure about complex events, and
- report supplementary information required by the SEC or the FASB.

The External Audit

Describe the purpose of an audit report and the incentives the auditor has to perform a good audit.

⑤ Refer back to the opening scenario for this chapter. Following the November 1986 buyout by **Kohlberg, Kravis, Roberts & Co. (KKR), Safeway** decided to again issue shares to the public. In April 1990, Safeway issued shares at a price of $11.25 per share. The $11.25 price implied that the market value of KKR's initial investment had risen from $130 million to $731 million. The $11.25 price was determined by investment bankers and potential investors after examining the financial statements of Safeway. Now, consider the following questions:

- Who controlled the preparation of the Safeway financial statements used by investors in arriving at the $11.25 price? The owners and managers of Safeway, led by KKR.
- Did KKR have any incentive to bias the reported financial statement numbers? Absolutely. The better the numbers, the higher the stock offering price and the more money raised by KKR.
- Since KKR had control of the preparation of the financial statements and stood to benefit substantially if those statements looked overly favorable, how could the financial statements be trusted? Good question.

This situation illustrates a general truth: the owners and managers of a company have an incentive to report the most favorable results possible. Poor reported financial performance can make it harder to get loans, can lower the amount that managers receive as salary bonuses, and can lower the stock price when shares are issued to the public. With these incentives to stretch the truth, the financial statements would not be reliable unless they were reviewed by an external party.

audit report

A report issued by an independent CPA that expresses an opinion about whether the financial statements fairly present a company's financial position, operating results, and cash flows in accordance with generally accepted accounting principles.

To provide this external review, a company's financial statements are often audited by an independent certified public accountant (CPA). A CPA firm issues an **audit report** that expresses an opinion about whether the statements fairly present a company's financial position, operating results, and cash flows in accordance with generally accepted accounting principles. Note that the financial statements are the responsibility of a company's management and not of the CPA. Although not all company records have to be audited, audits are needed for many purposes. For example, a banker may not make a loan without first receiving audited financial statements from a prospective borrower. As another example, most securities cannot be sold to the general public until they are registered with the SEC. Audited financial statements are required for this registration process.

? FYI

Notice that **Wal-Mart**'s audit report is dated March 25, 2006. This means that it took less than two months (from the end of the fiscal year on January 31) for the completion of the audit. Obviously, much audit work was conducted during the year to make this happen.

Though an audit report does not guarantee accuracy, it does provide added assurance that the financial statements are not misleading since they have been examined by an independent professional. However, the CPA cannot examine every transaction upon which the summary figures in the financial statements are based. The accuracy of the statements must remain the responsibility of the company's management. An example of a typical audit report is found in Wal-Mart's 2006 financial statements included in the appendix. Wal-Mart's financial statements were audited by **Ernst & Young LLP**, one of the large international audit firms.

One final question: Who hires and pays Ernst & Young to do the audit of Wal-Mart's financial statements? Wal-Mart does. At first glance, this situation appears to be similar to allowing students in an accounting class to choose and pay the graders of the examinations. However, two economic factors combine to allow us to trust the quality of the audit, even though the auditor was hired by the company being audited:

- *Reputation*. Ernst & Young, as one of the large accounting firms, has a reputation for doing high-quality audits (as do almost all independent auditors in the United States). It would be very reluctant to risk this reputation by signing off on a questionable set of financial statements.
- *Lawsuits*. Auditors are sued all the time, even when they conduct a good audit. Investors who lose money claim that they lost the money by relying on bogus financial statements that were certified by an external auditor. If even honest auditors

get sued, then an auditor who intentionally approves a false set of financial statements is at great risk of losing a big lawsuit.

The business scandals of the early 2000s have reinforced the important role that auditors play in ensuring the integrity of financial statements. We will discuss the role of auditing and auditors in much greater detail in Chapter 5.

> **REMEMBER THIS...**
>
> - An audit report is issued by an independent CPA firm and verifies that a set of financial statements has been prepared in accordance with generally accepted accounting principles.
> - CPA firms have an economic incentive to perform good audits in order to preserve their reputations and avoid lawsuits.

Fundamental Concepts and Assumptions

Explain the fundamental concepts and assumptions that underlie financial accounting.

⑥ Certain fundamental concepts and assumptions underlie financial accounting practice and the resulting financial statements. These ideas are so fundamental to any economic activity that they usually are taken for granted in conducting business. Nevertheless, it is important to be aware of them because these assumptions, together with certain basic concepts and procedures, determine the rules and set the boundaries of accounting practice. They indicate which events will be accounted for and in what manner. In total, they provide the essential characteristics of the traditional **accounting model**.

This section will describe the **separate entity concept**, the assumption of arm's-length transactions, the cost principle, the monetary measurement concept, and the going concern assumption. The concept of double-entry accounting was already introduced on page 35 as the basis for the accounting equation. Remember that accounting is the language of business, and it takes time to learn a new language. The terms and concepts we introduce here will become much more familiar as your study continues.

accounting model

The basic accounting assumptions, concepts, principles, and procedures that determine the manner of recording, measuring, and reporting a company's transactions.

The Separate Entity Concept

Because business involves the exchange of goods or services between entities, it follows that accounting records should be kept for those entities. For accounting purposes, an **entity** is defined as the organizational unit for which accounting records are maintained—for example, **IBM Corporation**. It is a focal point for identifying, measuring, and communicating accounting data. Furthermore, the entity is considered to be separate from its individual owners.

separate entity concept

The idea that the activities of an entity are to be separated from those of the individual owners.

The Assumption of Arm's-Length Transactions

Accounting is based on the recording of economic transactions. Viewed broadly, **transactions** include not only exchanges of economic resources between separate entities, but also events that have an economic impact on a business independently (see page 50 for definition). The borrowing and lending of money and the sale and purchase of goods or services are examples of the former. The loss in value of equipment due to obsolescence or fire is an example of the latter. Collectively, transactions provide the data that are included in accounting records and reports.

entity

An organizational unit (a person, partnership, or corporation) for which accounting records are kept and about which accounting reports are prepared.

© PHOTOLINK/GETTY IMAGES INC.

The balance sheets of major league sports teams are based on historical costs. The market value of the teams is often much higher than is reflected on the books.

Accounting for economic transactions enables us to measure the success of an entity. However, the data for a transaction will not accurately represent that transaction if any bias is involved. Therefore, unless there is evidence to the contrary, accountants assume **arm's-length transactions**. That is, they make the assumption that both parties—for example, a buyer and a seller— are rational and free to act independently; each trying to make the best deal possible in establishing the terms of the transaction.

> **⚠ CAUTION**
>
> When reading accounting reports, remember that many reported values are historical costs, reflecting exchange prices at various transaction dates.

The Cost Principle

To further ensure objective measurements, accountants record transactions at **historical cost**, the amount originally paid or received for goods and services in arm's-length transactions. The historical cost is assumed to represent the fair market value of the item at the date of the transaction because it reflects the actual use of resources by independent parties. In accounting, this convention of recording transactions at cost is often referred to as the **cost principle**.

The historical cost figure may be modified in the future to reflect new information. While historical cost is a reliable number in that it results from an arm's-length transaction, it may not always provide information that is as relevant as financial statement users would like.

transactions

Exchange of goods or services between entities (whether individuals, businesses, or other organizations), as well as other events having an economic impact on a business.

The Monetary Measurement Concept

Accountants do not record all the activities of economic entities. They record only those that can be measured in monetary terms. Thus, the concept of **monetary measurement** becomes another important characteristic of the accounting model. For example, employee morale cannot be measured directly in monetary terms and is not reported in the accounting records. Wages paid or owed, however, are quantifiable in terms of money and are reported. In accounting, all transactions are recorded in monetary amounts, whether or not cash is involved. In the United States, the dollar is the unit of exchange and is thus the measuring unit for accounting purposes.

arm's-length transactions

Business dealings between independent and rational parties who are looking out for their own interests.

historical cost

The dollar amount originally exchanged in an arm's-length transaction; an amount assumed to reflect the fair market value of an item at the transaction date.

The Going Concern Assumption

The **Safeway** balance sheet in Exhibit 5 was prepared under the assumption that Safeway would continue in business for the foreseeable future. This is called the **going concern assumption**. Without this assumption, preparation of the balance sheet would be much more difficult. For example, the $2.8 billion inventory for Safeway in 2005 is reported at the cost originally paid to purchase the inventory. This is a reasonable figure because, in the normal course of business, Safeway can expect to sell the inventory for this amount, plus some profit. But if it were assumed that Safeway

cost principle

The idea that transactions are recorded at their historical costs or exchange prices at the transaction date.

monetary measurement

The idea that money, as the common medium of exchange, is the accounting unit of measurement, and that only economic activities measurable in monetary terms are included in the accounting model.

going concern assumption

The idea that an accounting entity will have a continuing existence for the foreseeable future.

would go out of business tomorrow, the inventory would suddenly be worth a lot less. The going concern assumption allows the accountant to record assets at what they are worth to a company in normal use, rather than what they would sell for in a liquidation sale.

REMEMBER THIS...

- Entity concept—Financial statements are prepared for a specific economic entity; the private affairs of the owners are not to be mixed in with the business transactions.
- Arm's-length transaction—A market price accurately reflects underlying value when the transaction occurs between two unrelated parties, each bargaining for his or her own interests.
- Cost principle—In general, financial statement items are measured at their cost on the original transaction date.
- Monetary measurement concept—In order to be included in the financial statements, the value of an item must be measurable in terms of dollars.
- Going concern assumption—When preparing the financial statements, the accountant assumes that the business will survive for the foreseeable future. Without this assumption, balance sheet items would be recorded at emergency liquidation amounts.

REVIEW OF LEARNING OBJECTIVES

① **Understand the basic elements, uses, and limitations of the balance sheet.**

Assets   =   Liabilities   +   Owners' Equity

Sources of funding

Resources = Creditors' claims against resources + Owners' claims against resources

- In the balance sheet, assets and liabilities are typically separated into current and long-term items with data for both the current and the preceding year reported for comparison.
- The balance sheet reflects assets acquired at their historical cost, thus frequently ignoring changes in value and gradual development of intangible assets.

② **Understand the basic elements and uses of the income statement.**

INCOME STATEMENT

REVENUE	an INCREASE in a company's resources through a normal business transaction
− EXPENSE	a DECREASE in a company's resources through a normal business transaction
= NET INCOME	equal to revenues minus expenses and representing the net amount of assets created through business operations during a particular period of time

- Format—usually several years of income statement data are reported side by side for comparison

STATEMENT OF RETAINED EARNINGS	
RETAINED EARNINGS, BEGINNING	cumulative retained earnings from all prior years
+ NET INCOME	the net amount of assets created through business operations during the year; these assets belong to the owners
– DIVIDENDS	amount of business profits (usually in the form of cash) paid out to the owners during the year
= RETAINED EARNINGS, ENDING	as of the end of the year, the amount of the company's assets that have come through owners' reinvestment of their profits into the business

(3) Understand the categories and uses of the statement of cash flows and see how the primary financial statements tie together.

STATEMENT OF CASH FLOWS	
+ Operating Activities	activities that are part of a company's day-to-day business; examples include collecting cash from customers, paying employees, and purchasing inventory
+ Investing Activities	activities involving the purchase and sale of long-term assets such as buildings, trucks, and equipment
+ Financing Activities	activities surrounding acquiring the capital needed to purchase the company's assets; examples include getting cash from loans, repaying loans, receiving invested cash from owners, and paying dividends
= Net Change in Cash	change in the cash balance from the beginning of the period to the end of the period

- Format—usually several years of cash flow data are reported side by side for comparison
- Articulation—the three primary financial statements tie together as follows:
  - the income statement explains the change in the retained earnings balance in the balance sheet
  - the statement of cash flows explains the change in the cash balance in the balance sheet

(4) Recognize the need for financial statement notes and identify the types of information included in the notes.
- The notes to the financial statements contain additional information not included in the financial statements themselves.
- The notes explain the company's accounting assumptions and practices, provide details of financial statement summary numbers and additional disclosure about complex events, and report supplementary information required by the SEC or the FASB.

(5) Describe the purpose of an audit report and the incentives the auditor has to perform a good audit.
- An audit report is issued by an independent CPA firm and verifies that a set of financial statements has been prepared in accordance with generally accepted accounting principles.
- CPA firms have an economic incentive to perform good audits in order to preserve their reputations and avoid lawsuits.

Explain the fundamental concepts and assumptions that underlie financial accounting.

FUNDAMENTAL CONCEPT OR ASSUMPTION	DESCRIPTION
Entity concept	Financial statements are prepared for a specific economic entity; the private affairs of the owners are not to be mixed in with the business transactions.
Arm's-length transaction	A market price accurately reflects underlying value when the transaction occurs between two unrelated parties, each bargaining for his or her own interests.
Cost principle	In general, financial statement items are measured at their cost on the original transaction date.
Monetary measurement concept	In order to be included in the financial statements, the value of an item must be measurable in terms of dollars.
Going concern assumption	When preparing the financial statements, the accountant assumes that the business will survive for the foreseeable future. Without this assumption, balance sheet items would be recorded at emergency liquidation amounts.

KEY TERMS & CONCEPTS

accounting
equation, 35
accounting model, 49
arm's-length
transactions, 50
articulation, 45
assets, 32
audit report, 48
balance sheet
(statement
of financial
position), 31
book value, 37
capital stock, 35
classified balance
sheet, 35
comparative financial
statements, 37

comprehensive
income, 41
cost principle, 51
current assets, 35
current
liabilities, 37
dividends, 34
double-entry
accounting, 35
earnings (loss) per
share (EPS), 41
entity, 49
expenses, 39
financing
activities, 43
gains (losses), 41
going concern
assumption, 51

gross profit (gross
margin), 40
historical cost, 50
income statement
(statement of
earnings), 31
investing activities, 43
liabilities, 32
liquidity, 36
long-term assets, 37
long-term liabilities, 37
market value, 37
monetary
measurement, 51
net assets, 33
net income (net loss), 39
notes to the financial
statements, 46

operating activities, 43
owners' equity, 32
primary financial
statements, 31
retained earnings, 34
revenue, 38
separate entity
concept, 49
statement of cash
flows, 31
statement of retained
earnings, 42
stockholders
(shareholders), 33
stockholders'
equity, 34
transactions, 50

REVIEW PROBLEM

The Income Statement and the Balance Sheet

Shirley Baum manages The Copy Shop. She has come to you for help in preparing an income statement and a balance sheet for the year ended December 31, 2009. Several amounts, determined as of December 31, 2009, are presented below. No dividends were paid this year.

(continued)

Capital stock (10,000		Mortgage payable	$72,000
shares outstanding)	$ 40,000	Accounts payable	6,000
Retained earnings (12/31/08)	12,400	Land	24,000
Advertising expense	2,000	Supplies	2,000
Cash	17,000	Salary expense	20,000
Rent expense	2,400	Revenues	42,000
Building (net)	100,000	Other expenses	1,300
Interest expense	700	Accounts receivable	3,000

Required:

1. Prepare an income statement for the year ended December 31, 2009, including EPS.
2. Determine the amount of retained earnings at December 31, 2009.
3. Prepare a classified balance sheet as of December 31, 2009.

Solution

1. Income Statement

The first step in solving this problem is to separate the balance sheet items from the income statement items. Asset, liability, and owners' equity items reflect the company's financial position and appear on the balance sheet; revenues and expenses are reported on the income statement.

Balance Sheet Items

Capital stock
Retained earnings
Cash
Building (net)
Mortgage payable
Accounts payable
Land
Supplies
Accounts receivable

Income Statement Items

Advertising expense
Rent expense
Interest expense
Salary expense
Revenues
Other expenses

After the items have been separated, the income statement and the balance sheet may be prepared using a proper format.

The Copy Shop
Income Statement
For the Year Ended December 31, 2009

Revenues		$42,000
Expenses:		
Advertising expense	$ 2,000	
Rent expense	2,400	
Interest expense	700	
Salary expense	20,000	
Other expenses	1,300	26,400
Net income		$15,600
EPS = $15,600 ÷ 10,000 shares = $1.56		

(continued)

2. Retained Earnings

The amount of Retained Earnings at December 31, 2009, may be calculated as follows:

Retained earnings (12/31/08)	$12,400
Add: Net income for year	15,600
Subtract: Dividends for year	0
Retained earnings (12/31/09)	$28,000

Since no dividends were paid during 2009, the ending balance in Retained Earnings is simply the beginning balance plus net income for the year.

3. Balance Sheet

The Copy Shop
Balance Sheet
December 31, 2009

Assets			Liabilities and Owners' Equity		
Current assets:			**Current liabilities:**		
Cash	$ 17,000		Accounts payable	$ 6,000	
Accounts receivable	3,000				
Supplies	2,000	$ 22,000	**Long-term liabilities:**		
			Mortgage payable	72,000	
Long-term assets:			Total liabilities		$ 78,000
Land	$ 24,000				
Building (net)	100,000	124,000	**Owners' equity:**		
			Capital stock	$ 40,000	
			Retained earnings	28,000*	68,000
Total assets		$146,000	Total liabilities and owners' equity		$146,000

*See item 2 for calculation.

DISCUSSION QUESTIONS

1. As an external user of financial statements, perhaps an investor or creditor, what type of accounting information do you need?
2. What is the major purpose of:
   a. A balance sheet?
   b. An income statement?
   c. A statement of cash flows?
3. Assume you want to invest in the stock market, and your friends tell you about a company's stock that is "guaranteed" to have an annual growth rate of 150%. Should you trust your friends and invest immediately, or should you research the company's financial statements before investing? Explain.
4. Why are classified and comparative financial statements generally presented in annual reports to shareholders?
5. Why are owners' equity and liabilities considered the "sources" of assets?
6. Owners' equity is not cash; it is not a liability; and it generally is not equal to the current worth of a business. What is the nature of owners' equity?
7. What are the limitations of the balance sheet? Why is it important to be aware of them when evaluating a company's growth potential?
8. Some people feel that the income statement is more important than the balance sheet. Do you agree? Why or why not?
9. How might an investor be misled by looking only at the "bottom line" (the net income or EPS number) on an income statement?
10. Why is it important to classify cash flows according to operating, investing, and financing activities?
11. You are thinking of investing in one of two companies. In one annual report, the auditor's opinion states that the financial statements were prepared in accordance with generally accepted accounting principles. The other makes no such claim. How important is that to you? Explain.

12. Some people think that auditors are responsible for ensuring the accuracy of financial statements. Are they correct? Why or why not?
13. What are the four general types of financial statement notes typically included in annual reports to stockholders?

14. Explain why each of the following is important in accounting:
    a. The separate entity concept
    b. The assumption of arm's-length transactions
    c. The cost principle
    d. The monetary measurement concept
    e. The going concern assumption

PRACTICE EXERCISES

PE 2-1   **Total Assets**

LO1   Using the following information, compute total assets.

Equipment	$10,000
Accounts payable	900
Capital stock	1,500
Cash	800
Loan payable	9,000
Wages payable	500
Accounts receivable	1,000
Retained earnings	3,400
Inventory	3,500

PE 2-2   **Total Liabilities**

LO1   Refer to the data in PE 2-1. Compute total liabilities.

PE 2-3   **Total Owners' Equity**

LO1   Refer to the data in PE 2-1. Compute total owners' equity.

PE 2-4   **The Accounting Equation**

LO1   For the following four cases, use the accounting equation to compute the missing quantity.

	Assets	Liabilities	Owners' Equity
Case A	$10,000	$ 4,000	A
Case B	8,000	B	$3,500
Case C	C	5,500	7,000
Case D	13,000	15,000	D

PE 2-5   **Balance Sheet**

LO1   Using the data in PE 2-1, prepare a balance sheet.

PE 2-6   **Current Assets**

LO1   Using the following information, compute total current assets.

Land	$7,000
Machinery	1,300
Accounts payable	1,600
Cash	625
Buildings	7,500
Accounts receivable	800
Retained earnings	2,200
Inventory	2,100

PE 2-7 **Current Liabilities**

LO1 Using the following information, compute total current liabilities.

Inventory	$ 9,000
Loan payable (due in 14 months)	1,100
Capital stock	1,750
Cash	400
Mortgage payable (due in 30 years)	10,000
Loan payable (due in 6 months)	250
Accounts payable	700
Retained earnings	5,000

PE 2-8 **Book Value and Market Value of Equity**

LO1 For the following four cases, compute (1) the book value of equity and (2) the market value of equity.

	Assets	Liabilities	Number of Shares of Stock Outstanding	Market Price per Share
Case A	$ 10,000	$ 4,000	1,000	$15
Case B	8,000	7,000	500	10
Case C	13,500	5,500	300	20
Case D	100,000	150,000	1,000	7

PE 2-9 **Total Revenues**

LO2 Using the following information, compute total revenues. Caution: Not all of the items listed should be included in the computation of total revenues.

Cost of goods sold	$10,200	Wages payable	$ 475
Interest revenue	900	Accounts receivable	950
Advertising expense	2,150	Retained earnings	6,400
Cash	700	Consulting revenue	2,700
Sales	13,600		

PE 2-10 **Total Expenses**

LO2 Using the data in PE 2-9, compute total expenses. Caution: Not all of the items listed should be included in the computation of total expenses.

PE 2-11 **Computation of Net Income**

LO2 For the following four cases, compute net income (or net loss). Caution: Not all of the items listed should be included in the computation of net income.

	Case A	Case B	Case C	Case D
Cost of goods sold	$ 60,000	$ 30,000	$60,000	$110,000
Interest expense	18,000	47,000	25,000	31,000
Cash	3,000	4,500	2,100	6,000
Retained earnings	50,000	15,000	31,000	70,000
Sales	100,000	150,000	70,000	200,000
Accounts payable	12,000	20,000	5,000	38,000
Rent revenue	5,000	1,000	12,000	10,000
Machinery	175,000	60,000	50,000	185,000

PE 2-12 **Income Statement**

LO2 Using the following information, prepare an income statement.

(continued)

Cost of goods sold	$ 7,300
Interest expense	1,200
Wage expense	900
Cash	600
Sales	12,000
Accounts payable	400
Accounts receivable	750
Retained earnings	3,300
Income tax expense	800

PE 2-13

LO2

Computation of Ending Retained Earnings

For the following four cases, compute the ending amount of retained earnings. Caution: Not all of the items listed should be included in the computation of ending retained earnings.

	Case A	Case B	Case C	Case D
Capital stock	$ 60,000	$ 30,000	$60,000	$110,000
Long-term loan payable	18,000	47,000	25,000	31,000
Dividends	3,000	4,500	2,100	6,000
Retained earnings (beginning)	50,000	15,000	31,000	70,000
Inventory	100,000	150,000	70,000	200,000
Cash	12,000	20,000	5,000	38,000
Net income (loss)	5,000	1,000	12,000	(10,000)
Machinery	175,000	60,000	50,000	185,000

PE 2-14

LO2

Expanded Accounting Equation

For the following four cases, use the expanded accounting equation to compute the missing quantity.

	Assets	Liabilities	Capital Stock	Retained Earnings
Case A	$23,000	$11,000	A	$ 4,500
Case B	17,500	B	$ 4,500	3,600
Case C	C	14,000	11,000	27,000
Case D	45,000	29,000	18,000	D

PE 2-15

LO3

Computing Cash from Operating Activities

Using the following data, compute cash flow from operating activities.

		Cash Inflow (Outflow)
a.	Cash received from sale of a building	$ 5,600
b.	Cash paid for interest	(450)
c.	Cash paid to repay a loan	(1,000)
d.	Cash collected from customers	10,000
e.	Cash paid for dividends	(780)
f.	Cash paid for income taxes	(1,320)
g.	Cash received upon the issuance of new shares of stock	3,000
h.	Cash received from tenants renting part of a building	600
i.	Cash paid to purchase land	(12,000)

PE 2-16

LO3

Computing Cash from Investing Activities

Refer to the information in PE 2-15. Use that information to compute cash flow from investing activities.

PE 2-17

LO3

Computing Cash from Financing Activities

Refer to the information in PE 2-15. Use that information to compute cash flow from financing activities.

PE 2-18   **Preparing a Statement of Cash Flows**

LO3   Refer to the information in PE 2-15. Use that information to prepare a complete statement of cash flows. The beginning cash balance for the year was $2,000.

PE 2-19   **Financial Statement Articulation**

LO3   For the following four cases, use the principle of financial statement articulation to compute the missing amounts.

	Case A	Case B	Case C	Case D
Dividends	$ 6,500	$ 7,300	$ 800	G
Cash, beginning	13,000	C	4,200	$ 22,000
Retained earnings, ending	A	16,000	15,500	35,000
Net increase (decrease) in cash	8,200	5,300	E	(6,300)
Net income (loss)	18,000	25,000	F	(11,000)
Retained earnings, beginning	41,000	D	22,000	51,000
Cash, ending	B	21,000	1,600	H

EXERCISES

E 2-20   **Classification of Financial Statement Elements**

LO1   Indicate for each of the following items whether it would appear on a balance sheet (BS) or an income statement (IS). If a balance sheet item, is it an asset (A), a liability (L), or an owners' equity item (OE)?

1. Accounts Payable
2. Sales Revenue
3. Accounts Receivable
4. Advertising Expense
5. Cash
6. Supplies
7. Consulting Revenue
8. Land
9. Capital Stock
10. Rent Expense
11. Equipment
12. Interest Receivable
13. Mortgage Payable
14. Notes Payable
15. Buildings
16. Salaries & Wages Expense
17. Retained Earnings
18. Utilities Expense

E 2-21   **Accounting Equation**

LO1   Compute the missing amounts for companies A, B, and C.

	A	B	C
Cash	$31,000	$ 8,400	$13,000
Accounts receivable	14,000	13,000	16,500
Land and buildings	95,000	?	67,000
Accounts payable	?	16,000	23,000
Mortgage payable	80,000	31,000	41,500
Owners' equity	45,000	17,000	?

E 2-22   **Comprehensive Accounting Equation**

LO1, LO2   Assuming no additional investments by or distributions to owners, compute the missing amounts for companies X, Y, and Z.

	X	Y	Z
Assets: January 1, 2009	$360	$?	$230
Liabilities: January 1, 2009	280	460	?
Owners' equity: January 1, 2009	?	620	150
Assets: December 31, 2009	380	?	310
Liabilities: December 31, 2009	?	520	90
Owners' equity: December 31, 2009	?	720	?
Revenues in 2009	80	?	400
Expenses in 2009	100	116	?

E 2-23 **Computing Elements of Owners' Equity**

LO1, LO2 From the information provided, determine:

1. The amount of retained earnings at December 31.
2. The amount of revenues for the period.

Totals	January 1	December 31
Current assets	$ 10,000	$ 15,000
All other assets	190,000	180,000
Liabilities	65,000	45,000
Capital stock	60,000	?
Retained earnings	75,000	?

Additional data:

Expenses for the period were $75,000.

Dividends paid were $11,500.

Capital stock increased by $10,000 during the period.

E 2-24 **Balance Sheet Relationships**

LO1, LO2 Correct the following balance sheet.

Canfield Corporation
Balance Sheet
December 31, 2009

Assets		Liabilities and Owners' Equity	
Cash	$ 55,000	Buildings	$325,000
Accounts payable	65,000	Accounts receivable	75,000
Interest receivable	20,000	Mortgage payable	150,000
Capital stock	200,000	Sales revenue	350,000
Rent expense	60,000	Equipment	85,000
Retained earnings	145,000	Utilities expense	5,000
		Total liabilities	
Total assets	$545,000	and owners' equity	$990,000

E 2-25 **Balance Sheet Preparation**

LO1, LO2 From the following data, prepare a classified balance sheet for Taylorsville Construction Company at December 31, 2009.

Accounts payable	$ 74,300
Accounts receivable	113,500
Buildings	512,000
Owners' equity, 1/1/09	314,300
Cash	153,600
Distributions to owners during 2009	48,100
Supplies	4,250
Land	90,000
Mortgage payable	423,400
Net income for 2009	109,450
Owners' equity, 12/31/09	?

E 2-26 **Income Statement Computations**

LO2 Following are the operating data for an advertising firm for the year ended December 31, 2009.

(continued)

Revenues	$175,000
Supplies expense	45,000
Salaries expense	70,000
Rent expense	1,500
Administrative expense	6,000
Income taxes (30% of income before taxes)	?

For 2009, determine:

1. Income before taxes.
2. Income taxes.
3. Net income.
4. Earnings per share (EPS), assuming there are 15,000 shares of stock outstanding.

E 2-27 **Income Statement Preparation**

LO2 The following selected information is taken from the records of Pickard and Associates.

Accounts payable	$ 143,000
Accounts receivable	95,000
Advertising expense	14,500
Cash	63,000
Supplies expense	31,500
Rent expense	12,000
Utilities expense	2,500
Income taxes (30% of income before taxes)	?
Miscellaneous expense	5,100
Owners' equity	215,000
Salaries expense	78,000
Fees (revenues)	476,000

1. Prepare an income statement for the year ended December 31, 2009. (Assume that 11,000 shares of stock are outstanding.)
2. Explain what the EPS ratio tells the reader about Pickard and Associates.

E 2-28 **Income and Retained Earnings Relationships**

LO2 Assume that retained earnings increased by $375,000 from December 31, 2008, to December 31, 2009, for Jarvie Distribution Corporation. During the year, a cash dividend of $135,000 was paid.

1. Compute the net income for the year.
2. Assume that the revenues for the year were $830,000. Compute the expenses incurred for the year.

E 2-29 **Retained Earnings Computations**

LO2 During 2009, Edgemont Corporation had revenues of $230,000 and expenses, including income taxes, of $190,000. On December 31, 2008, Edgemont had assets of $350,000, liabilities of $80,000, and capital stock of $210,000. Edgemont paid a cash dividend of $25,000 in 2009. No additional stock was issued. Compute the retained earnings on December 31, 2008, and 2009.

E 2-30 **Preparation of Income Statement and Retained Earnings Statement**

LO2 Prepare an income statement and a statement of retained earnings for Big Sky Corporation for the year ended June 30, 2009, based on the following information:

(continued)

Capital stock (1,500 shares @ $100)		$150,000
Retained earnings, July 1, 2008		76,800
Dividends		6,500
Ski rental revenue		77,900
Expenses:		
Rent expense	$ 6,000	
Salaries expense	38,600	
Utilities expense	2,400	
Advertising expense	7,500	
Miscellaneous expense	7,700	
Income taxes	2,100	64,300

E 2-31

LO2

Articulation: Relationships between a Balance Sheet and an Income Statement

The total assets and liabilities of Omni Company at January 1 and December 31, 2009, are presented below.

	January 1	December 31
Assets	$103,000	$167,000
Liabilities	72,000	88,000

Determine the amount of net income or loss for 2009, applying each of the following assumptions concerning the additional issuance of stock and dividends paid by the firm. Each case is independent of the others.

1. Dividends of $12,100 were paid and no additional stock was issued during the year.
2. Additional stock of $18,000 was issued and no dividends were paid during the year.
3. Additional stock of $72,000 was issued and dividends of $12,400 were paid during the year.

E 2-32

LO3

Cash Flow Computations

From the following selected data, compute:

1. Net cash flow provided (used) by operating activities.
2. Net cash flow provided (used) by investing activities.
3. Net cash flow provided (used) by financing activities.
4. Net increase (decrease) in cash during the year.
5. The cash balance at the end of the year.

Cash receipts from:	
Customers	$270,000
Investments by owners	54,000
Sale of building	90,000
Proceeds from bank loan	60,000
Cash payments for:	
Wages	$ 82,000
Utilities	3,000
Advertising	4,000
Rent	36,000
Taxes	67,000
Dividends	20,000
Repayment of principal on loan	40,000
Purchase of land	106,000
Cash balance at beginning of year	$386,000

E 2-33

LO3

Cash Flow Classifications

For each of the following items, indicate whether it would be classified and reported under the operating activities (OA), investing activities (IA), or financing activities (FA) section of a statement of cash flows:

a. Cash receipts from selling merchandise

b. Cash payments for wages and salaries

(continued)

    c. Cash proceeds from sale of stock

    d. Cash purchase of equipment

    e. Cash dividends paid

    f. Cash received from bank loan

    g. Cash payments for inventory

    h. Cash receipts from services rendered

    i. Cash payments for taxes

    j. Cash proceeds from sale of property no longer needed as expansion site

E 2-34
LO4

Notes to Financial Statements

Refer to **Wal-Mart's** Form 10-K in Appendix A at the end of the book. How important are the notes to financial statements? What are the major types of notes that Wal-Mart includes in its Form 10-K?

E 2-35
LO6

The Cost Principle

On January 1, 2009, Save-More Construction Company paid $150,000 in cash for a parcel of land to be used as the site of a new office building. During March, the company petitioned the city council to rezone the area for professional office buildings. The city council refused, preferring to maintain the area as a residential zone. After nine months of negotiation, Save-More Construction convinced the council to rezone the property for commercial use, thus raising its value to $200,000.

    For accounting purposes, what value should be used to record the transaction on January 1, 2009? At what value would the property be reported at year-end, after the city council rezoning? Explain why accountants use historical costs to record transactions.

E 2-36
LO6

The Monetary Measurement Concept

Many successful companies, such as **Ford Motor Company**, **ExxonMobil**, and **Marriott Corporation**, readily acknowledge the importance and value of their employees. In fact, the employees of a company are often viewed as the most valued asset of the company. Yet in the asset section of the balance sheets of these companies there is no mention of the asset Employees. What is the reason for this oversight and apparent inconsistency?

E 2-37
LO6

The Going Concern Assumption

Assume that you open an auto repair business. You purchase a building and buy new equipment. What difference does the going concern assumption make with regard to how you would account for these assets?

PROBLEMS

P 2-38
LO1

Balance Sheet Classifications and Relationships

Stoker and Co. has the following balance sheet elements as of December 31, 2009.

Land	$136,000	Mortgage payable	$253,000
Cash	?	Capital stock	200,000
Building	225,000	Retained earnings	186,000
Accounts payable	101,000	Inventory	72,000
Notes payable (short-term)	98,000	Accounts receivable	119,000
Equipment	215,000		

Required:

Compute the total amount of:

    1. Current assets.

    2. Long-term assets.

    3. Current liabilities.

    4. Long-term liabilities.

    5. Stockholders' equity.

P 2-39   **Preparation of a Classified Balance Sheet**

LO1, LO2   Following are the December 31, 2009, account balances for Siraco Company.

Cash	$ 1,950
Accounts receivable	2,500
Supplies	1,800
Equipment	11,275
Accounts payable	3,450
Wages payable	250
Dividends paid	1,500
Capital stock	775
Retained earnings, January 1, 2009 ...	12,000
Revenues	10,000
Miscellaneous expense	1,550
Supplies expense	3,700
Wages expense	2,200

Required:

1. Prepare a classified balance sheet as of December 31, 2009.
2. **Interpretive Question:** On the basis of its 2009 earnings, was this company's decision to pay dividends of $1,500 a sound one?

P 2-40   **Balance Sheet Preparation with a Missing Element**

LO1   The following data are available for Schubert Products Inc., as of December 31, 2009.

Cash	$ 7,500
Accounts payable	24,000
Capital stock	42,000
Accounts receivable	20,000
Building	49,500
Supplies	2,000
Retained earnings	?
Land	20,000

Required:

1. Prepare a balance sheet for Schubert Products Inc.
2. Determine the amount of retained earnings at December 31, 2009.
3. **Interpretive Question:** In what way is a balance sheet a depiction of the basic accounting equation?

P 2-41   **Income Statement Preparation**

LO2   Listed below are the results of Rulon Candies' operations for 2008 and 2009. (Assume 4,000 shares of outstanding stock for both years.)

	2009	**2008**
Sales	$300,000	$350,000
Utilities expenses	15,000	8,500
Employee salaries	115,000	110,000
Advertising expenses	10,000	20,000
Income tax expense	9,000	36,500
Interest expense	25,000	15,000
Cost of goods sold	115,000	85,000
Interest revenue	10,000	10,000

Required:

1. Prepare a comparative income statement for Rulon Candies, Inc., for the years ended December 31, 2009, and 2008. Be sure to include figures for gross margin, operating income, income before taxes, net income, and earnings per share.

(continued)

2. **Interpretive Question:** What advice would you give Rulon Candies, Inc., to improve its profitability for the year 2010?

P 2-42

LO2

Income Statement Preparation

The following information is taken from the records of Wadley's Car Wash for the year ended December 31, 2009.

Income taxes	$ 45,000
Service revenues	210,000
Rent expense	6,000
Salaries expense	41,000
Miscellaneous expense	970
Utilities expense	4,300
Supplies expense	10,300

Required:

Prepare an income statement for Wadley's Car Wash for the year ended December 31, 2009. (Assume that 3,000 shares of stock are outstanding.)

P 2-43

LO1, LO2

Expanded Accounting Equation

At the end of 2009, Spencer Systems, Inc., had a fire that destroyed the majority of its accounting records. Spencer Systems, Inc., was able to gather the following financial information for 2009.

a. Retained earnings was changed only as a result of net income and a $25,000 dividend payment to Spencer's investors.

b. All other account changes for the year are listed below. The amount of change for each account is shown as a net increase or decrease.

	Increase or (Decrease)
Cash	$ 12,500
Interest receivable	(7,500)
Inventory	50,000
Accounts receivable	(11,750)
Building	157,500
Accounts payable	22,500
Mortgage payable	137,500
Wages payable	(35,250)
Capital stock	26,250

Required:

Using the accounting equation, compute Spencer's net income for 2009.

P 2-44

LO2

Income Statement Preparation

Precision Corporation has been a leading supplier of magnetic storage disks for three years. Following are the results of Precision's operations for 2009.

Sales revenue	$68,000
Advertising expense	1,530
Income taxes	4,360
Delivery expense	480
Packaging expense	355
Salaries expense	18,350
Supplies expense	8,410
EPS	3.45

Required:

1. Prepare an income statement for the year ended December 31, 2009.
2. How many shares of stock were outstanding?

P 2-45   **Net Income**

LO2   A summary of the operations of Streuling Company for the year ended May 31, 2009, is shown below.

Advertising expense	$ 2,760
Supplies expense	37,820
Rent expense	1,500
Salaries expense	18,150
Miscellaneous expense	4,170
Dividends	12,400
Retained earnings (6/1/08)	156,540
Income taxes	21,180
Consulting fees (revenues)	115,100
Administrative expense	7,250

Required:

1. Determine the net income for the year by preparing an income statement. (Assume that 3,000 shares of stock are outstanding.)
2. **Interpretive Question:** Assuming an operating loss for the year, is it a good idea for Streuling to still pay its shareholders dividends?

P 2-46   **Net Income and Statement of Retained Earnings**

LO2   A summary of the operations of Quincy Company for the year ended May 31, 2009, is shown below.

Advertising expense	$ 4,650
Supplies expense	38,410
Rent expense	2,400
Salaries expense	25,340
Miscellaneous expense	10,200
Dividends	19,500
Retained earnings (6/1/08)	175,670
Income taxes	20,760
Consulting fees (revenues)	176,400
Administrative expense	13,900

Required:

1. Determine the net income for the year by preparing an income statement. (There are 8,000 shares of stock outstanding.)
2. Prepare a statement of retained earnings for the year ended May 31, 2009.
3. Prepare a statement of retained earnings assuming that Quincy had a net loss for the year of $38,000.
4. **Interpretive Question:** Assuming a loss as in (3), is it a good idea for Quincy to still pay its shareholders dividends?

P 2-47   **Comprehensive Financial Statement Preparation**

LO1, LO2   The following information was obtained from the records of Wilcox, Inc., as of December 31, 2009.

Land	$ 42,500
Buildings	197,550
Salaries expense	125,350
Utilities expense	5,250
Accounts payable	38,050
Revenues	389,950
Supplies	72,500
Retained earnings (1/1/09)	311,000

(continued)

Capital stock (2,000 shares outstanding)	$ 65,000
Accounts receivable	90,000
Supplies expense	110,600
Cash	?
Notes payable (long-term)	63,800
Rent expense	21,200
Dividends in 2009	95,500
Other expenses	11,250
Income taxes	35,000

Required:
1. Prepare an income statement for the year ended December 31, 2009.
2. Prepare a classified balance sheet as of December 31, 2009.
3. **Interpretive Question:** Why is the balance in Retained Earnings so large as compared with the balance in Capital Stock?

P 2-48

LO1, LO2

Elements of Comparative Financial Statements

The following report is supplied by Maxwell Sons Company.

Maxwell Sons Company					
Comparative Balance Sheets					
As of December 31, 2009 and 2008					
Assets	**2009**	**2008**	**Liabilities and Owners' Equity**	**2009**	**2008**
Cash	$ 28,000	$19,000	Accounts payable	$ 9,000	$ 8,000
Accounts receivable	21,000	14,000	Salaries and commissions		
Notes receivable	10,000	12,000	payable	11,000	12,000
Land	43,000	43,000	Notes payable	32,000	35,000
			Capital stock	15,000	15,000
			Retained earnings	35,000	18,000
			Total liabilities and		
Total assets	$102,000	$88,000	owners' equity	$102,000	$88,000

Operating expenses for the year included utilities of $5,700, salaries and commissions of $38,700, and miscellaneous expenses of $2,200. Income taxes for the year were $4,500, and the company paid dividends of $8,000.

Required:
1. Compute the total expenses, including taxes, incurred in 2009.
2. Compute the net income or net loss for 2009.
3. Compute the total revenue for 2009.
4. **Interpretive Question:** Why are comparative financial statements generally of more value to users than statements for a single period?

P 2-49

LO3

Statement of Cash Flows

Pratt & Jordan Development, Inc., constructs homes and offices and sells them to customers. The financial information shown below was gathered from its accounting records for 2009. Assume any increase or decrease in the balances from 1/1/09 to 12/31/09 resulted from either receiving or paying cash in the transaction. For example, during 2009 the balance on loans for land holdings increased $75,000 because the company received $75,000 in cash by taking out an additional loan on the land.

(continued)

Items	Balance as of 1/1/09	Balance as of 12/31/09
Cash	$130,000	$175,000
Cash receipts from customers	–	750,000
Loans on land holdings	225,000	300,000
Cash distributions to owners	–	60,000
Loan on building	130,000	80,000
Investments in securities	600,000	845,000
Cash payments for other expenses	–	32,000
Cash payments for taxes	–	43,000
Cash payments for operating expenses	–	215,000
Cash payments for wages and salaries	–	135,000

Required:

1. Prepare a statement of cash flows for Pratt & Jordan Development, Inc., for the year ended December 31, 2009.
2. **Interpretive Question:** Does Pratt & Jordan Development, Inc., appear to be in good shape from a cash flow standpoint? What other information would help you analyze the situation?

P 2-50
LO3

Statement of Cash Flows

The cash account for Esplin Enterprises shows the following for the year ended December 31, 2009.

Beginning cash balance	$?
Cash receipts during year from:	
Services	2,214,000
Investments by owners	93,000
Sale of land	194,000
Cash payments during year for:	
Operating expenses	1,735,000
Taxes	207,000
Purchase of building	352,000
Distributions to owners	68,000
Ending cash balance	815,000

Required:

Prepare a statement of cash flows for Esplin Enterprises for the year ended December 31, 2009.

ANALYTICAL ASSIGNMENTS

AA 2-51
DISCUSSION

Creditor and Investor Information Needs

Ink Spot is a small company that has been in business for two years. Wilford Smith, the president of the company, has decided that it is time to expand. He needs $10,000 to purchase additional equipment and to pay for increased operating expenses. Wilford can either apply for a loan at First City Bank, or he can issue more stock (1,000 shares are outstanding) to new investors. Assuming that you are the loan officer at First City Bank, what information would you request from Ink Spot before deciding whether to make the loan? As a potential investor in Ink Spot, what information would you need to make a good investment decision?

AA 2-52
DISCUSSION

Analyzing Trends and Key Financial Relationships

An investor may choose from several investment opportunities: the stocks of different companies; rental property or other real estate; or savings accounts, money market certificates, and similar financial instruments. When considering an investment in the stock of a particular

(continued)

company, comparative financial data presented in the annual report to stockholders help an investor identify key relationships and trends. As an illustration, comparative operating results for Prime Properties, Inc., from its 2009 annual report are provided. (Dollars are presented in thousands except for earnings per share.)

	Year Ended December 31		
	2009	**2008**	**2007**
Revenues:			
Property management fees	$ 58,742	$ 63,902	$ 66,204
Appraisal fees	55,641	60,945	62,320
Total revenues	$114,383	$124,847	$128,524
Expenses:			
Selling and advertising	$ 64,371	$ 75,403	$ 80,478
Administrative expenses	30,671	31,115	31,618
Other expenses	9,265	9,540	9,446
Interest expense	2,047	1,468	26
Total expenses	$106,354	$117,526	$121,568
Income before taxes	$ 8,029	$ 7,321	$ 6,956
Income taxes	2,409	2,196	2,087
Net income	$ 5,620	$ 5,125	$ 4,869
Earnings per share*	$2.25	$2.05	$1.95

*2.5 million shares outstanding

What trends are indicated by the comparative income statement data for Prime Properties, Inc.? Which of these trends would be of concern to a potential investor? What additional information would an investor need in order to make a decision about whether to invest in this company?

AA 2-53

DISCUSSION

How Many Accounting Equations Are There?

You have recently completed Chapter 2 in your introductory accounting course and have been enthusiastically explaining the accounting equation to all of your friends. One of your friends reports that he took accounting last year and that actually there isn't just one accounting equation. For example, he says that in addition to the equation Assets = Liabilities + Owners' Equity, there are also the equations Revenues = Assets, Net Income = Cash from Operating Activities, and Retained Earnings = Cash. Comment on these three additional accounting "equations" listed by your friend.

AA 2-54

DISCUSSION

Can Financial Statement Information Be Used to Successfully Pick Stocks?

For most companies, the only reliable source of information about the company's performance is found in the company's financial statements. However, for the 15,000 publicly-traded companies in the United States (those whose ownership shares can be bought and sold on a stock exchange), there is much information generated by business reporters and financial analysts to supplement the financial statements. In addition, ownership shares of these publicly-traded companies are bought and sold by investors, large and small, every day. For these publicly-traded companies, can the financial statements be used to pick winning and losing stocks, that is, those stocks that will go up in value and those that will decline in value in the future? Explain.

AA 2-55

DISCUSSION

Who Audits American Companies?

Your sister is a biochemist, but she prides herself on keeping a close eye on the business news. It is her opinion that the U.S. federal government should increase the amount that it pays to the auditors of the financial statements of U.S. companies. She is convinced that tax-payers would support this increase, even if it means increased income taxes. She thinks that

(continued)

increased government audit fees will attract more qualified auditors and will result in a dramatic rise in the reliability of the financial statements released by U.S. companies. This increased reliability will help U.S. companies compete in the global marketplace. Comment on your sister's opinion.

AA 2-56
DISCUSSION

Accounting for the Proper Entity

You have been hired to prepare the financial reports for White River Building Supply, a proprietorship owned by Bill Masters. Upon encountering several payments made from the company bank account to a nearby university, you contact Bill Masters to find out how to classify these payments. Masters explains that those checks were written to pay his daughter's tuition and to purchase her textbooks and miscellaneous supplies. He then tells you to include the payments with other expenses of the business. "This way," he explains, "I can deduct the payments on my tax return. Why not, since it all comes out of the same pocket?" How would you respond to Masters?

AA 2-57
JUDGMENT CALL

You Decide: What is the most important number in the financial statements—net income or EPS?

You were talking with some of your friends, who are finance majors, and they said that the most important number in the financial statements is the earnings per share figure on the income statement. One friend said, "EPS is the only number Wall Street cares about!" Some of your fellow students in accounting believe, however, that net income and the income statement are much more important than a single EPS figure.

AA 2-58
JUDGMENT CALL

You Decide: Is the cash flow statement necessary?

You were at dinner with some family and friends when one of them started talking about the long hours he has been putting in at work—a local waste management company. He said that cash flows have been bad and he has been staying up late trying to figure out the problem. When asked about the condition of his statement of cash flows, he said, "We don't have one of those statements to assess cash flows, we just use EBITDA (earnings before interest, taxes, depreciation, and amortization). Besides, everything I need to know is in either the balance sheet or income statement." Is a statement of cash flows necessary, or is the information it contains redundant of the balance sheet and income statement?

AA 2-59
JUDGMENT CALL

You Decide: Should Wall Street place so much importance on the EPS figure or not?

Recently, your mom came to you with questions about some of her investments. A year ago, she made an investment in 10 companies that are traded on the S&P 500. She tried to pick enough different companies to "diversify" her portfolio. Last week, one of her companies came out with "lower than expected EPS." In the two days following the news, the stock price dropped almost 30%! She wanted to know why so many people cared about one number. How do you respond?

AA 2-60
JUDGMENT CALL

You Decide: Are the notes to the financial statements necessary?

Do the notes to the financial statements add value to investors, or have they evolved from tradition? You were listening to talk radio on your way home from work a couple weeks ago when you heard someone say, "Everything you need to know about a company should be either in the balance sheet, income statement, or statement of cash flows. If you can't find it in there, it is not worth knowing! Besides that, the notes are too complex to understand!" Do you agree with this assumption?

AA 2-61
REAL COMPANY
ANALYSIS

Wal-Mart

The 2006 Form 10-K for **Wal-Mart** can be found in Appendix A. Answer the following questions:

1. Locate Wal-Mart's 2006 balance sheet. What percentage of its total assets consists of cash and cash equivalents? How much long-term debt does Wal-Mart have?

(continued)

2. Find Wal-Mart's 2006 income statement. Have revenues increased or decreased over the last three years? Is the rate of increase rising?

3. Find Wal-Mart's statement of stockholders' equity. Did Wal-Mart pay a dividend in 2006? Did Wal-Mart buy or sell any stock in 2006?

4. Review Wal-Mart's statement of cash flows. What activity generates most of Wal-Mart's cash? What is Wal-Mart doing with all its money—buying back its own stock, investing in other companies, or something else?

AA 2-62

REAL COMPANY ANALYSIS

Safeway

At the start of this chapter you learned a little about **Safeway** and its history. Now let's take a look at the company's financial performance in recent years. Refer back to Safeway's income statement (on page 40), the balance sheet (on page 36), and the statement of cash flows (on page 44).

Based on information contained in these financial statements, answer the following questions:

1. As a percentage of total assets, did current assets increase or decrease from 2004 to 2005? What was the primary reason for the change?

2. Divide gross profit by sales for 2004 and 2005. For which year is the gross profit percentage higher? What does that change represent?

3. In 2005, did Safeway generate enough cash from operations to fund all of its investing activities? Looking at the financing activities section of the statement of cash flows, would you predict that long-term debt on the balance sheet went up or down in 2005?

AA 2-63

INTERNATIONAL

Diageo

Diageo is a United Kingdom (UK) consumer products firm, best known in the United States for the following brand names: Smirnoff, Johnnie Walker, J&B, Gordon's, Guinness, Pillsbury, and Häagen-Dazs. Diageo's 2005 balance sheet is shown on the next page.

(continued)

Diageo
Consolidated Balance Sheet
30 June 2005
(in millions of pounds)

Fixed assets		
Intangible assets	4,252	
Tangible assets	2,097	
Investment in associates	1,334	
Other investments	719	
		8,402
Current assets		
Stocks	2,335	
Debtors–due within one year	1,664	
Debtors–due after one year	68	
Cash at bank and liquid resources	817	
	4,884	
Creditors–due within one year		
Borrowings	(869)	
Other creditors	(3,183)	
	(4,052)	
Net current (liabilities)/assets		832
Total assets less current liabilities		9,234
Creditors–due after one year		
Borrowings	(3,677)	
Other creditors	(98)	
		(3,775)
Provisions for liabilities and charges		(723)
Post employment charges		(902)
Net Assets		3,834
Capital and reserves		
Called-up share capital		883
Share premium account	1,337	
Revaluation reserve	111	
Capital redemption reserve	3,060	
Profit and loss account	(1,750)	
Reserves attributable to equity shareholders		2,758
Shareholders' funds		3,641
Minority interests		193
		3,834

1. Can you identify any major differences between Wal-Mart's and Diageo's balance sheets in terms of the order in which major categories are displayed?
2. What is Diageo's total assets? Is it as easy to determine as Wal-Mart's total assets?
3. Take a look at the following list of accounts and identify, given your knowledge of assets, liabilities, and owners' equity, what the American equivalent of those accounts might be (you might want to reference Wal-Mart's balance sheet for comparison):
   - Stocks
   - Debtors
   - Called-up share capital
   - Profit and loss account

AA 2-64

ETHICS

Violating a Covenant

Often banks will require a company that borrows money to agree to certain restrictions on its activities in order to protect the lending institution. These restrictions are called "debt covenants." An example of a common debt covenant is requiring a company to maintain its current ratio (which is current assets ÷ current liabilities) at a certain level, say, 2.0.

(continued)

Your boss has just come to you and asked, "How can you make our current ratio higher?" You know that the company has a line of credit with a local bank that requires the company to maintain its current ratio at 1.5. You also know that the company was dangerously close to violating this covenant during the previous quarter. The end of the fiscal period is next week, and some action must be taken to increase the current ratio. If the covenant is violated, the lending agreement allows the bank to significantly modify the terms of the debt (in the bank's favor) and also gives the bank a seat on the company's board of directors. Management would prefer not to have the bank involved in the day-to-day affairs of the business, nor do they want to alter the terms of the lending agreement.

Identify ways in which the current ratio can be increased. Would any of the alternatives you identify be good for the business, e.g., selling equipment might raise the current ratio but would that be good for the business? Should a company engage in these types of transactions?

AA 2-65

WRITING

The Most Important Financial Statement

As you have discovered, there are three primary financial statements—balance sheet, income statement, and statement of cash flows. In no more than two pages, answer the following question: If you could have access to only one of the primary financial statements, which would it be and why? As you provide support for the financial statement of your choice, also provide reasons as to why you would not pick the other two statements.

AA 2-66

CUMULATIVE
SPREADSHEET
PROJECT

Creating a Balance Sheet and Income Statement

Starting with this chapter, each chapter in this text will include a spreadsheet assignment based on the financial information of a fictitious company named Handyman. The first assignments are simple—in this chapter you are asked to do little more than set up financial statement formats and input some numbers. In succeeding chapters, the spreadsheets will get more complex so that by the end of the course you will have constructed a spreadsheet that allows you to forecast operating cash flow for five years in the future and adjust your forecast depending on the operating parameters that you think are most reasonable.

So, let's get started with the first spreadsheet assignment.

1. The following numbers are for Handyman Company for 2009:

Short-Term Loans Payable	$ 10	Long-Term Debt	$207
Interest Expense	9	Income Tax Expense	4
Capital Stock	50	Retained Earnings (as of 1/1/06)	31
Cash	10	Receivables	27
Dividends	0	Sales	700
Accumulated Depreciation	9	Accounts Payable	74
Inventory	153	Property, Plant, & Equipment	199
Cost of Goods Sold	519	Other Operating Expenses	160

Your assignment is to create a spreadsheet containing a balance sheet and an income statement for Handyman Company.

2. Handyman is wondering what its balance sheet and income statement would have looked like if the following numbers were changed as indicated:

	Change	
	From	**To**
Sales	700	730
Cost of Goods Sold	519	550
Other Operating Expenses	160	165

Create a second spreadsheet with the numbers changed as indicated. *Note:* After making these changes, your balance sheet may no longer balance. Assume that any discrepancy is eliminated by increasing or decreasing Short-Term Loans Payable as much as necessary.

The Mechanics of Accounting

After studying this chapter, you should be able to:

(1) Understand the process of transforming transaction data into useful accounting information. *Transforming raw transaction data into useful accounting information involves analyzing, recording, and summarizing a large amount of transaction data so that financial reports can be prepared.*

(2) Analyze transactions and determine how those transactions affect the accounting equation (step one of the accounting cycle). *Accountants analyze transactions using debits and credits. Whether a debit or credit represents an increase or decrease depends on the type of account being considered. The accounting equation (Assets = Liabilities + Owners' Equity) represents the fact that the amount of a company's assets is always equal to the amount of financing (from investors and creditors) used to acquire those assets.*

(3) Record the effects of transactions using journal entries (step two of the accounting cycle). *Journal entries are the accountant's way of recording the debit and credit effects of both simple and complex business transactions. Journal*

entries are recorded in the journal which is a chronological listing of transactions coded in debit and credit language.

(4) Summarize the resulting journal entries through posting and prepare a trial balance (step three of the accounting cycle). *Once journal entries are made, their effects must be sorted and copied, or posted, to the individual accounts. All of the individual accounts are collected in the ledger. A trial balance lists all of the accounts in the ledger, along with their balances.*

(5) Describe how technology has affected the first three steps of the accounting cycle. *Computers now take care of the routine aspects of bookkeeping, such as posting, trial balance preparation, and analysis of common transactions. Knowledge of the process helps one understand the flow of information within a company.*

Ray Kroc, a 51-year-old milkshake machine distributor, first visited the McDonald brothers' drive-in (in San Bernardino, California) in July of 1954 because he wanted to know why a single "hamburger stand" needed 10 milkshake machines. That first day, Kroc spent the lunch rush hour watching the incredible volume of business the small drive-in was able to handle. By the time he left town, Kroc had received a personal briefing on the "McDonald's Speedee System" from Dick and Mac McDonald and had secured the rights to duplicate the system throughout the United States.

Ray Kroc opened his first outlet in Chicago in 1955, and 50 years later the number of McDonald's locations had expanded to over 31,500. The essence of **McDonald's** business seems fairly simple: revenues come from selling Big Macs, Happy Meals, Chicken McNuggets, etc.; operating costs include the costs of the raw materials to produce the food items, labor costs, building rentals, income taxes, and so forth. But the magnitude of McDonald's operations in terms of volume (sales average over $100 million per day) as

accounting cycle

The procedure for analyzing, recording, summarizing, and reporting the transactions of a business.

well as geography (McDonald's has locations in 121 countries throughout the world) makes compiling this information a challenge. In order to prepare its year-end financial reports, McDonald's must accumulate financial information from its various locations throughout the world, summarize that information according to U.S. accounting standards, and make the report available to the public within a short time (45 days beginning in 2007) after the end of the year. In fact, McDonald's annual report for the period ended December 31, 2005, was finished on February 20, 2006.

With the number of transactions that occur on a daily basis, the accounting for McDonald's would be impossible were it not for a systematic method for analyzing these transactions and collecting and recording transaction related information. What is the process by which McDonald's and other entities transform raw transaction data into useful information? Certainly, shareholders and others would not understand how McDonald's has performed if the company merely published volumes of raw transaction data. How are millions of transactions summarized and eventually reported in the primary financial statements? This transformation process is referred to as the **accounting cycle**, or the bookkeeping part of accounting.

n the first two chapters, we provided an overview of accounting. We discussed the environment of accounting and its objectives, some basic concepts and assumptions of accounting, and the primary financial statements. Now we begin our study of the "accounting cycle."

This simply means that we will examine the procedures for analyzing, recording, summarizing, and reporting the transactions of a business. In this chapter, we describe the first three steps in the cycle. The remaining step (preparing reports for external users) is explained in Chapter 4.

How Can We Collect All This Information?

Understand the process of transforming transaction data into useful accounting information.

1 Suppose you were asked, "What was the total cost, to the nearest dollar, of your college education last year?" To answer this question would require that you (1) gather information (in the form of receipts, credit card statements, and canceled checks) for all your expenditures, (2) analyze that information to determine which outflows relate to your college education, and (3) summarize those outflows into one number—the cost of your college education. Once you have answered that question, answer this one, "How much did you spend on food last year?" Again you would have to go through the same process of

© GHISLAIN & MARIE DAVID DELOSSY/GETTY IMAGES INC.

Businesses, such as a college bookstore, have many exchange transactions in which they trade one thing for another—like textbooks for cash.

collecting data, analyzing the information to identify those expenditures relating to food, and then summarizing those expenditures into one number. From these two examples you can see that, without a method for gathering and organizing day-to-day financial data, answers to seemingly routine questions can get quite complex.

Now you may be thinking, "Doesn't my checkbook allow me to easily answer these questions?" Your checkbook (also known as your check register) would certainly help, but it is limited in that it tracks only the transactions that go through your checking account. It does not track the cash in your pocket, in your savings accounts, or in other investment accounts. It also is not yet summarized.

Now consider the dilemma for businesses. They typically have far more transactions than you, and the kinds of transactions are more varied. Businesses buy and sell goods or services; borrow and invest money; pay wages to employees; purchase land, buildings, and equipment; distribute earnings to owners; and pay taxes to the government. These activities are referred to as "exchange transactions" because the entity is actually trading (exchanging) one thing for another. A college bookstore, for example, exchanges textbooks for cash. **Business documents**, such as a sales invoice, a purchase order, or a check stub, are often used (1) to confirm that a transaction has occurred, (2) to establish the amounts to be recorded, and (3) to facilitate the analysis of business events.

business documents

Records of transactions used as the basis for recording accounting entries; include invoices, check stubs, receipts, and similar business papers.

To determine how well an entity is managing its resources, the results of transactions must be analyzed. The accounting cycle makes the analysis possible by recording and summarizing an entity's transactions and preparing reports that present the summary results. Exhibit 1 shows the sequence of the accounting cycle. Later, we will discuss these general categories and the specific steps of the cycle.

Keeping track of a company's transactions requires a system of accounting that is tailor-made to the needs of that particular enterprise. Obviously, the accounting system of a large multinational corporation with millions of business transactions each day will be much more complex than the system needed by a small Internet start-up company. The more complex and detailed the accounting system, the more likely it is to be automated. Even small companies generally use some type of inexpensive accounting software. Such software helps reduce the number of routine clerical functions and improves the accuracy and timeliness of the accounting records.

Although a computer-based system is faster and requires less labor than a manual system, the steps in the process are basically the same for both: transactions are first recorded on source documents; they are then analyzed, journalized, and posted to the accounts; and the resulting information is summarized, reported, and used for evaluation purposes. The difference lies in who (or what) does the work. With a computer-based system, the software transforms the recorded data, summarizes the data into categories, and prepares the financial statements and other reports. Nevertheless,

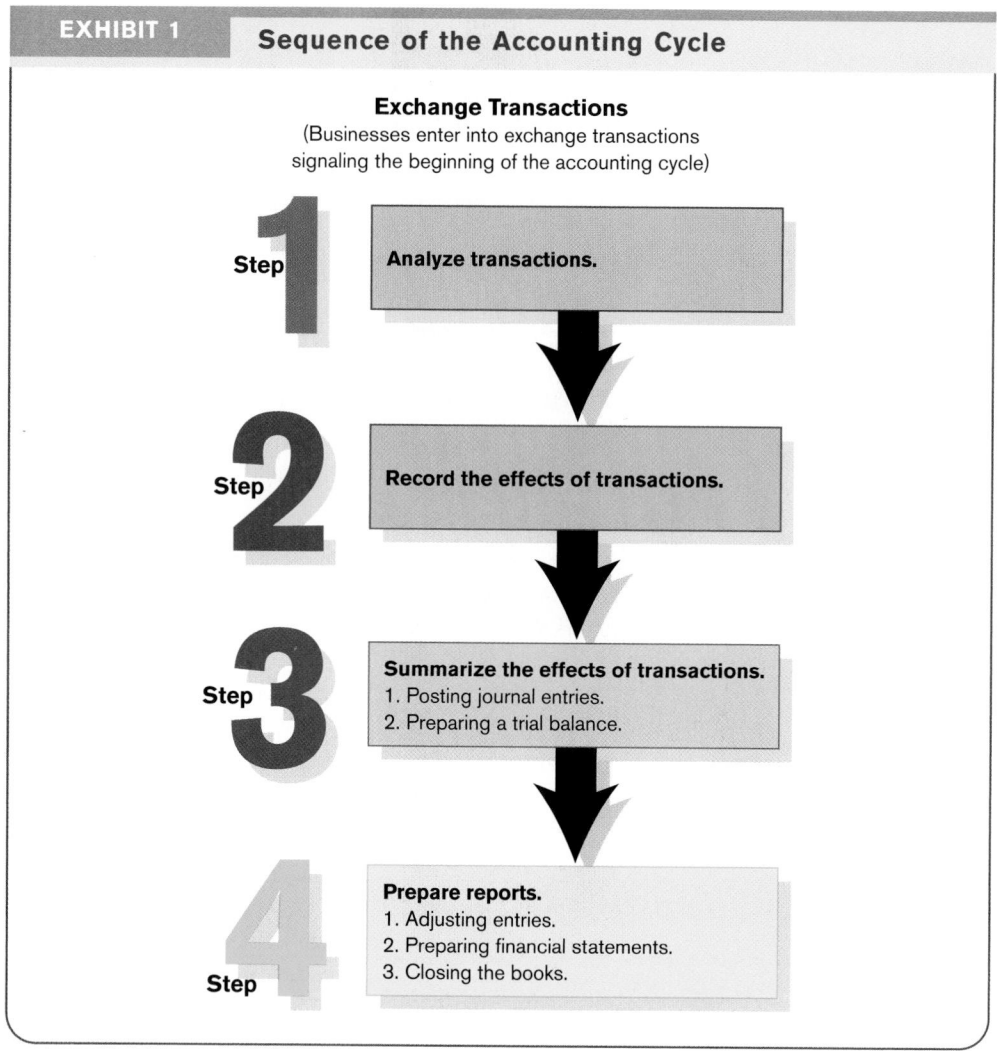

EXHIBIT 1   **Sequence of the Accounting Cycle**

Exchange Transactions
(Businesses enter into exchange transactions
signaling the beginning of the accounting cycle)

Step 1   Analyze transactions.

Step 2   Record the effects of transactions.

Step 3   Summarize the effects of transactions.
1. Posting journal entries.
2. Preparing a trial balance.

Step 4   Prepare reports.
1. Adjusting entries.
2. Preparing financial statements.
3. Closing the books.

human judgment is still essential in analyzing and recording transactions, especially those of a non-routine nature.

Because a manual accounting system is easier to understand, we will use a manual system for the examples in this text. As you begin studying the steps in the accounting cycle, it is important that you understand the accounting equation and double-entry accounting more fully. This concept was briefly introduced in Chapter 2. You will recall that the accounting model is built on this basic equation. You now need to learn how to use the equation in accounting for the transactions of a business.

REMEMBER THIS...

Accounting is designed to accumulate and report in summary form the results of a company's transactions, thereby transforming the financial data into useful information for decision making. The four steps in the accounting cycle are as follows.

1. Analyze transactions.
2. Record the effects of transactions.
3. Summarize the effects of transactions.
4. Prepare reports.

How Do Transactions Affect the Accounting Equation?

Analyze transactions and determine how those transactions affect the accounting equation (step one of the accounting cycle).

② Often, the most difficult aspect of accounting is determining which events are to be reflected in the accounting records and which are not. Suppose, for example, that **Burger King** introduced a Big Mac clone at half the Big Mac price. The proliferation of Big Mac clones could have a serious impact on the future of **McDonald's**. However, as discussed in Chapter 2, events that cannot be measured in monetary terms will not be reflected in the financial statements. It would be virtually impossible to reliably quantify the impact that Big Mac clones could have on the future profitability of McDonald's, and thus, that information would not be reflected in the financial statements.

Now you may be saying to yourself, "We have an obligation to inform financial statement users about this attack on the Big Mac." We would all agree that this information should be shared, but the financial statements are not the place to do it. As you review a company's annual report to shareholders, you will notice that the financial statements are only one part of the information provided to users. Information relating to the competitive environment, product development, and marketing and sales efforts is included in the annual report, but not as part of the accounting information.

After determining the amount of a transaction, the event must be analyzed to determine if an arm's-length transaction has occurred. Accounting is concerned primarily with reflecting the effects of transactions between two independent entities. So **Delta Air Lines** signing a contract with **Boeing** to purchase airplanes in the future would not be reflected in the financial statements until the airplanes are manufactured and Delta has contracted to pay for the planes.

Transactions between independent parties must be analyzed to determine their effect on the accounting equation. This analysis is often what separates an accountant from a bookkeeper. While many transactions are routine, some business events are quite complex and require a comprehensive analysis to determine how the event should be reflected in the financial statements. Consider the following example:

• A company buys a building. In addition to paying $20,000 cash, the company agrees to pay $10,000 per year for the next 10 years. The company will also pay a $2,000 property tax bill associated with the building from last year. As part of the purchase, the company gave the former owners of the building 500 shares of stock. Finally, the building will require $23,000 worth of repairs and renovations before it can be used. How much should be recorded as the cost of the building?

As this example illustrates, transactions can become quite complex. The good news is that the transaction analysis framework introduced in this chapter allows you to break complex transactions into manageable pieces and also provides a self-checking mechanism to ensure that you haven't forgotten anything. Once a transaction is properly analyzed and the affected accounts identified (along with the direction of those effects), the remainder of the accounting cycle can proceed without much difficulty.

The Accounting Equation

So let's begin our analysis of transactions by first reviewing some of the basics. Recall that the fundamental accounting equation is:

Assets	=	**Liabilities**	+	**Owners' Equity**
[Resources]		[A method of financing resources that requires repayment]*		[A method of financing resources that does not require repayment and represents ownership interests in the business]

---

*Not all liabilities represent a method of financing assets. In some cases, liabilities arise during the course of business that are not associated with the financing of assets. For example, an obligation to clean up a toxic waste spill is not associated with an asset but still represents a liability. Still, the majority of liabilities are incurred to finance assets.

The accounting equation must always remain in balance. To see how this balance is maintained when accounting for business transactions, consider the following activities:

Business Activity (Transaction)	Effect in Terms of the Accounting Equation
1. Investment of $50,000 by owners	Increase asset (Cash), increase owners' equity (Capital Stock): A ↑ $50,000 = OE ↑ $50,000
2. Borrowed $25,000 from bank	Increase asset (Cash), increase liability (Notes Payable): A ↑ $25,000 = L ↑ $25,000
3. Purchased $14,000 worth of inventory on credit (will pay later). The inventory is to be resold at a later date.	Increase asset (Inventory), increase liability (Accounts Payable): A ↑ $14,000 = L ↑ $14,000
4. Purchased equipment costing $15,000 for cash	Decrease asset (Cash), increase asset (Equipment): A ↓ $15,000 = A ↑ $15,000

For each of the transactions, the terms in parentheses are the specific accounts affected by the transactions, as will be explained in the next section.

In each case, the equation remains in balance because an identical amount is added to both sides, subtracted from both sides, or added to and subtracted from the same side of the equation. Following each transaction, we can ensure that the accounting equation balances. Note how the following spreadsheet keeps track of the equality of the accounting equation for these four transactions:

TRANSACTION #	ASSETS		LIABILITIES		OWNERS' EQUITY
Beginning Balance	$ 0	=	$ 0	+	$ 0
1	+50,000				+50,000
Subtotal	$50,000	=	$ 0	+	$50,000
2	+25,000		+25,000		
Subtotal	$75,000	=	$25,000	+	$50,000
3	+14,000		+14,000		
Subtotal	$89,000	=	$39,000	+	$50,000
4	+15,000				
	−15,000				
Total	$89,000	=	$39,000	+	$50,000

Using Accounts to Categorize Transactions

In Chapter 2, the balance sheet and the income statement were introduced as two of the three primary financial statements, the third being the statement of cash flows. We learned that the elements of the balance sheet are assets, liabilities, and owners' equity; the elements of the income statement are revenues and expenses. Now we must learn how each of these elements is comprised of many different accounts.

account

An accounting record in which the results of transactions are accumulated; shows increases, decreases, and a balance.

An **account** is a specific accounting record that provides an efficient way to categorize similar transactions. Thus, we may designate asset accounts, liability accounts, and owners' equity accounts. Examples of asset accounts are Cash, Inventory, and Equipment. Liability accounts include Accounts Payable and Notes Payable. The equity accounts for a corporation are Capital Stock and Retained

Earnings. You can think of an individual account as a summary of every transaction affecting a certain item (such as cash); the summary may be recorded on one page of a book or in one column of a spreadsheet (seen as follows).

| Transaction # | ASSETS | | | | LIABILITIES | | | OWNER'S EQUITY |
	Cash	Inventory	Equipment		Accounts Payable	Notes Payable		Capital Stock
Beginning Balance	$ 0	$ 0	$ 0	=	$ 0	$ 0	+	$ 0
1	+50,000							+50,000
Subtotal	$50,000	$ 0	$ 0	=	$ 0	$ 0	+	$50,000
2	+25,000					+25,000		
Subtotal	$75,000	$ 0	$ 0	=	$ 0	$25,000	+	$50,000
3		+14,000			+14,000			
Subtotal	$75,000	$14,000	$ 0	=	$14,000	$25,000	+	$50,000
4	−15,000		+15,000					
Total	$60,000	$14,000	$15,000	=	$14,000	$25,000	+	$50,000

Using the previous transactions, we can easily see how the accounting equation can be expanded to include specific accounts under the headings of assets, liabilities, and owners' equity. We can also see that after each transaction, the equality of the accounting equation can be determined simply by adding up the balances of all the asset accounts and comparing the total to the sum of all the liability and owners' equity accounts.

Now suppose that a company has 200 accounts and 10,000 transactions each month. Obviously, this spreadsheet would quickly get very big. Today, computers help in compiling this massive amount of data. Five hundred years ago, when double-entry accounting was formalized, all the adding and subtracting was done by hand. You can imagine the difficulties of tracking multiple accounts, involving hundreds of transactions, using the spreadsheet method described above while doing all the computations by hand. Mixing "+" and "−" in one column would provide ample opportunity to make mistakes.

T-account

A simplified depiction of an account in the form of a letter T.

This problem was solved by separating the "+" and the "−" for each account into separate columns, totaling each column, and then computing the difference between the columns to arrive at an ending balance. The simplest, most fundamental format is the configuration of the letter T. This is called a **T-account**. Note that a T-account is an abbreviated representation of an actual account (illustrated later) and is used as a teaching and learning tool. The following are examples of T-accounts, representing the transactions described previously.

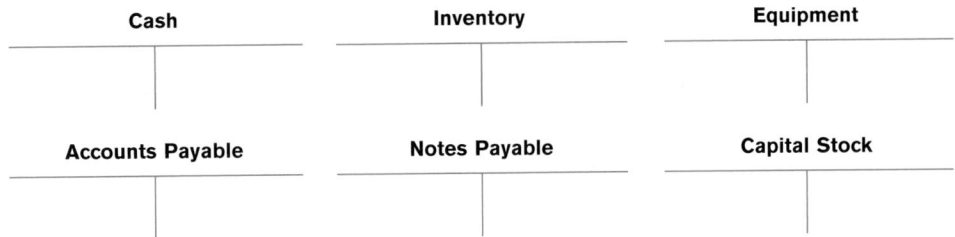

The account title (Cash, for example) appears at the top of the T-account. Transaction amounts may be recorded on both the left side and the right side of the T-account. Instead of using the terms left and right to indicate which side of a T-account is affected, terms unique to accounting were developed. **Debit (abbreviated Dr)** is used to indicate the left side of a T-account, and

debit

An entry on the left side of a T-account.

credit

An entry on the right side of a T-account.

credit (abbreviated **Cr**) is used to indicate the right side of a T-account. Debit means left, credit means right—nothing more, nothing less.

Besides representing the left and right sides of an account, the terms *debit* and *credit* take on additional meaning when coupled with a specific account. By convention, for asset accounts, debits refer to increases and credits to decreases. For example, to increase the cash account, we debit it; to decrease the cash account, we credit it. Since we expect the total increases in the cash account to be greater than the decreases, the cash account will usually have a debit balance after accounting for all transactions. Thus, we can make this generalization—asset accounts will usually have debit balances. The opposite relationship is true of liability and owners' equity accounts; they are decreased by *debits* and increased by *credits*. As a result, liability and owners' equity accounts will typically have credit balances. The effect of this system is shown here, with an increase indicated by (+) and a decrease by (−).

Assets		=	Liabilities		+	Owners' Equity	
DR	CR		DR	CR		DR	CR
(+)	(−)		(−)	(+)		(−)	(+)

F Y I

Where does the "DR" come from when the term debit doesn't have an "r" in it? Recall that accounting, as we know it today, was formalized in the 1500s in Italy. The Italian and Latin (a common language back then) verb forms of debit are *addebitare* and *debere,* respectively. Thus, the "DR" represents an Italian or Latin abbreviation of debit.

CAUTION

Just a reminder that asset accounts will typically have debit balances, whereas liabilities and owners' equity accounts will typically have credit balances.

In addition to assets equaling liabilities and owners' equity, debits should always also equal credits. If you fully grasp the meaning of these two equalities, you are well on your way to mastering the mechanics of accounting or learning the language of accounting. Debits and credits allow us to take a shortcut to ensure that the accounting equation balances. **If, for every transaction, debits equal credits, then the accounting equation will balance.**

To understand why this happens, keep in mind three basic facts regarding double-entry accounting:

1. Debits are always entered on the left side of an account and credits on the right side.
2. For every transaction, there must be at least one debit and one credit.
3. Debits must always equal credits for each transaction.

Now notice what this means for one of the business transactions shown earlier (page 80): investment by owners. An asset account (Cash) is debited; it is increased. An owners' equity account (Capital Stock) is credited; it is also increased. There is both a debit and a credit for the transaction, and we have increased accounts on both sides of the equation by an equal amount, thus keeping the accounting equation in balance.

Be careful not to let the general, non-accounting meanings of the words *credit* and *debit* confuse you. In general conversation, credit has an association with plus and debit with minus. But on the asset side of the accounting equation, where debit means increase and credit means decrease, this association can lead you astray. In accounting, debit simply means left and credit simply means right. To make sure you understand the relationship between debits and credits, the various accounts, and the accounting equation, let us examine further the transactions listed on page 80.

Business Activity (Transaction)	Effect in Terms of the Accounting Equation						
	Assets		=	Liabilities	+	Owners' Equity	
1. Investment by owners	Cash DR (+)					Capital Stock CR (+)	
2. Borrowed money from bank	Cash DR (+)			Notes Payable CR (+)			
3. Purchased inventory on credit	Inventory DR (+)			Accounts Payable CR (+)			
4. Purchased equipment for cash	Equipment DR (+)	Cash CR (−)					

Note that every time an account is debited, other accounts have to be credited for the same amount. This is the major characteristic of the double-entry accounting system: *the debits must always equal the credits.* This important characteristic creates a practical advantage: the opportunity for "self-checking." If debits do not equal credits, an error has been made in analyzing and recording the entity's activities.

Before proceeding any further, let's stop for a moment and review the relationship between the various types of accounts and debits and credits. It is in your best interest not to go on until you understand these very important relationships.

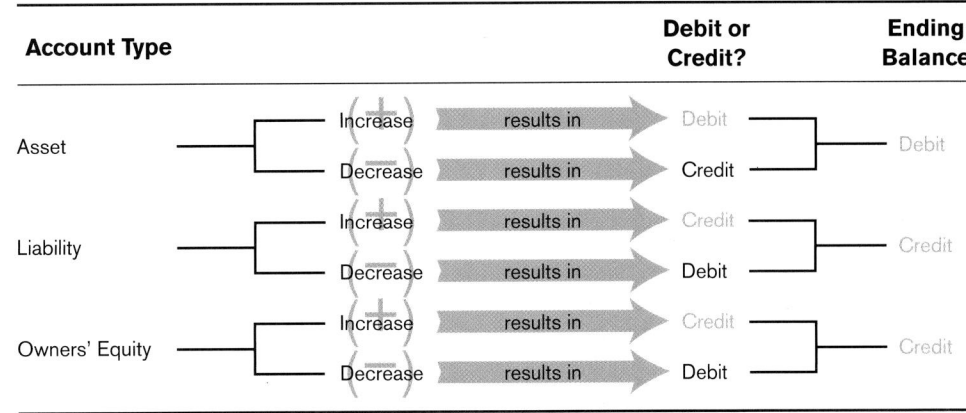

Account Type		Debit or Credit?	Ending Balance
Asset	Increase → results in	Debit	Debit
	Decrease → results in	Credit	
Liability	Increase → results in	Credit	Credit
	Decrease → results in	Debit	
Owners' Equity	Increase → results in	Credit	Credit
	Decrease → results in	Debit	

Expanding the Accounting Equation to Include Revenues, Expenses, and Dividends

At this point, we must bring revenues and expenses into the picture. Obviously, they are part of every ongoing business. Revenues provide resource inflows; they are increases in resources from the sale of goods or services. Expenses represent resource outflows; they are costs incurred in generating revenues. Note that revenues are not synonymous with cash or other assets, but are a way of describing where the assets came from. For example, cash received from the sale of a product would be considered revenue. Cash received by borrowing from the bank would not be revenue, but an increase in a liability. By the same token, expenses are a way of describing how an asset has been used. Thus, cash paid for interest on a loan is an expense, but cash paid to buy a building represents the exchange of one asset for another.

 CAUTION

We stated previously that owners' equity accounts will have credit balances. However, expenses, a component of Retained Earnings, will almost always have debit balances. Since revenues will usually exceed expenses, the net effect on Retained Earnings will result in a credit balance.

How do revenues and expenses fit into the accounting equation? Remember that revenues minus expenses equals net income; and net income is a major source of change in owners' equity from one accounting period to the next. Revenues and expenses, then, may be thought of as *temporary* subdivisions of owners' equity. Revenues increase owners' equity and so, like all owners' equity accounts, are increased by credits. Expenses reduce owners' equity and are therefore increased by debits. As will be explained in Chapter 4, all revenue and expense accounts are "closed" into the retained earnings account at the end of the accounting cycle.

dividends

Distributions to the owners (stockholders) of a corporation.

One other temporary account affects owners' equity. It is the account that shows distributions of earnings to owners. For a corporation, this account is called **Dividends**. Since dividends reflect payments to the owners, thereby reducing owners' equity, the dividends account is increased by a debit and decreased by a credit. The dividends account, like revenues and expenses, is also "closed" into the retained earnings account.

Just a warning here: students who have trouble grasping debits and credits usually get hung up on the revenue and expense accounts. Remember that revenues and expenses are subcategories of Retained Earnings. When you credit a revenue account, you are essentially increasing Retained Earnings. When you debit an expense account, you are increasing the amount of expense, which in turn reduces Retained Earnings.

Using the corporate form of business as an example, the accounting equation may be expanded to include revenues, expenses, and dividends, as shown in Exhibit 2.

Why Should I Understand the Mechanics of Accounting?

If computers now take care of all the routine accounting functions, why does a businessperson need to know anything about debits, credits, journals, posting, T-accounts, and trial balances? Good question. First of all, even though computers now do most of

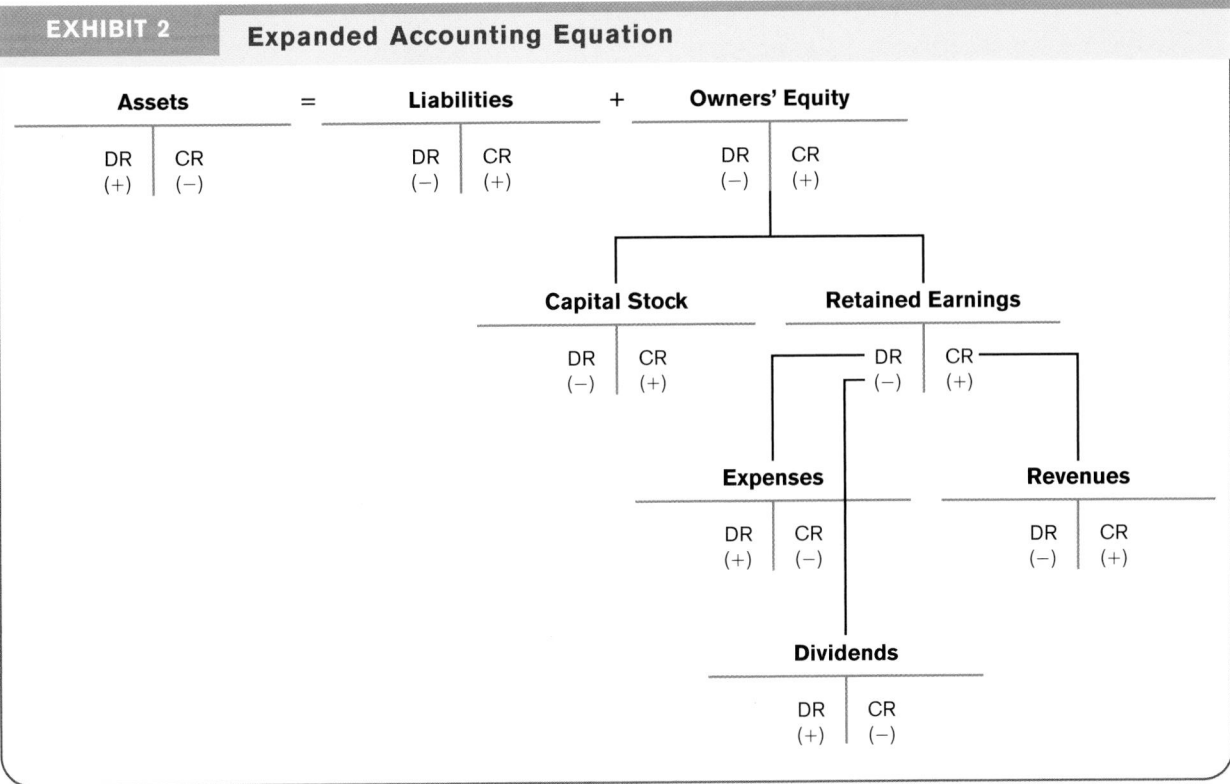

EXHIBIT 2   **Expanded Accounting Equation**

the dirty work, the essence of double-entry accounting is unchanged from the days of quill pens and handwritten ledgers. Thus, understanding the process explained in this chapter is still relevant to a computer-based accounting system. In addition, with or without computers, the use of debits, credits, and T-accounts still provides an efficient and widely used shorthand method of analyzing transactions. At a minimum, all businesspeople should be familiar enough with the language of accounting to understand, for example, why a credit balance in Cash or a debit balance in Retained Earnings is something unusual enough to merit investigation. Finally, an understanding of the accounting cycle—analyzing, recording, summarizing, and preparing—gives one insight into how information flows within an organization. And great advantages accrue to those who understand information flow.

REMEMBER THIS...

	Debit	Credit
Asset	↑	↓
Liability	↓	↑
Owners' Equity	↓	↑
Revenue	↓	↑
Expense	↑	↓
Dividend	↑	↓

- Revenues increase owners' equity.
- Expenses decrease owners' equity.
- Dividends decrease owners' equity.
- If debits = credits, then Assets = Liabilities + Owners' Equity

How Do We Record the Effects of Transactions?

(3) With our knowledge of the different types of accounts (assets, liabilities, and owners' equity) and the use of the terms *debit* and *credit* (debit means left and credit means right), we are now ready to actually record the effects of transactions.

The second step in the accounting cycle is to record the results of transactions in a **journal**. Journals provide a chronological record of all transactions of a business. They show the dates of the transactions, the amounts involved, and the particular accounts affected by the transactions. Sometimes a detailed description of the transaction is also included.

journal

An accounting record in which transactions are first entered; provides a chronological record of all business activities.

This chronological recording of transactions in a journal (sometimes called a book of original entry) provides a company with a complete record of its activities. If amounts were recorded directly in the accounts, it would be difficult, if not impossible, for a company to trace a transaction that occurred, say, six months previously.

Smaller companies, such as a locally owned pizza restaurant, may use only one journal, called a "general journal," to record all transactions. Larger companies having thousands of transactions each year may use special journals (for example, a cash receipts journal) as well as a general journal.

journalizing

Recording transactions in a journal.

A specific format is used in **journalizing** (recording) transactions in a general journal. The debit entry is listed first; the credit entry is listed second and is indented to the right. Normally, the date and a brief explanation of the transaction are considered essential parts of the **journal entry**. (In the text, we often ignore dates and explanations to simplify the examples.) Dollar signs usually are omitted. Unless otherwise noted, this format will be used whenever a journal entry is presented.

journal entry

A recording of a transaction where debits equal credits; usually includes a date and an explanation of the transaction.

General Journal Entry Format

Date	Debit Entry	xx	
	Credit Entry		xx
	Explanation.		

Exhibit 3 is a partial page from a general journal, showing typical journal entries. Study this exhibit carefully because the entire accounting cycle is based on journal entries. If journal entries are incorrect, the resulting financial information will be inaccurate.

To give you additional exposure to analyzing transactions and recording journal entries, we are going to start our own business. Rather than spend the summer flipping burgers at the local hamburger house, you decide that you want to have an outdoor job—one that allows you to enjoy the summer sun, engage in rigorous physical activity, and sharpen your skills as an entrepreneur. You are going to start your own landscaping business. This business will involve mowing lawns, pulling weeds, trimming and planting shrubs, and so forth. We will use your new business to illustrate the journal entries used to record some common transactions of a business enterprise.[1] These transactions fit into the following four general categories: acquiring cash, acquiring other assets, selling goods or providing services, and collecting cash and paying obligations. Obviously, we cannot present all possible transactions in this chapter. In studying the illustrations, strive to understand the conceptual basis of transaction analysis rather than memorizing specific journal entries. Pay particular attention to the dual effect of each transaction on the company in terms of the basic accounting equation (that is, its impact on assets and on liabilities and owners' equity). Remember that business activity involves revenues, expenses, and distributions to owners as well, and that these accounts eventually increase or decrease the retained earnings account in owners' equity.

---

[1] Normally, a small business like this one would be started as a sole proprietorship or as a partnership. We assume a corporation here to show a complete set of transactions.

EXHIBIT 3	General Journal

	JOURNAL			Page 1
Date	**Description**	**Post. Ref.**	**Debits**	**Credits**
2009 July 1	Cash		2,000	
	Capital Stock			2,000
	Issued 200 shares of capital stock at $10 per share.			
5	Truck		800	
	Cash			800 ·
	Purchased a used truck.			
5	Equipment		250	
	Accounts Payable			250
	Purchased a lawnmower on account.			
5	Supplies		180	
	Cash			180
	Purchased supplies for cash.			

Acquiring Cash, Either from Owners or by Borrowing

Your first task in starting this business is to acquire cash, either through owners' investments or by borrowing. Your parents indicate that they will match any funds that you are going to put into your business. You have $1,000 in savings, and coupled with your parents' matching funds, you decide to issue 200 shares of stock.

Example 1   The following transaction illustrates investments by owners:

assets (+)	Cash 2,000
owners' equity (+)	Capital Stock 2,000
	Issued 200 shares of capital stock at $10 per share.

This transaction increases cash as a result of capital stock being issued to investors, or stockholders. The cash account is debited, and the capital stock account is credited. The economic impact of this situation may be summarized as follows:

	ASSETS					=	**LIABILITIES**		+	**OWNERS' EQUITY**
Transaction	**Cash**	**Inventory**	**Equipment**	**Supplies**	**Truck**		**Accounts Payable**	**Notes Payable**		**Capital Stock**
Beginning Balance	$ 0	$0	$0	$0	$0	=	$0	$0	+	$ 0
Invested money in the business	2,000	—	—	—	—		—	—		2,000
Subtotal	$2,000	$0	$0	$0	$0	=	$0	$0	+	$2,000

Example 2   Suppose that in addition to coming up with the money yourself or from your parents, you went to a bank and convinced the loan officer to lend you the money. The journal entry for such a transaction would be:

assets (+)   Cash 2,000
liabilities (+)   Notes Payable   2,000
                    Borrowed $2,000 from First National Bank, signing a
                    12-month note at 12% interest.

Here, the cash account is debited, and the notes payable account is credited. The accounting equation captures the economic impact of borrowing the money as follows:

	ASSETS					=	LIABILITIES		+	OWNERS' EQUITY
Transaction	Cash	Inventory	Equipment	Supplies	Truck		Accounts Payable	Notes Payable		Capital Stock
Beginning Balance	$ 0	$0	$0	$0	$0	=	$0	$ 0	+	$ 0
Invested money in the business	2,000	—	—	—	—		—	—		2,000
Borrowed money from a bank	2,000	—	—	—	—		—	2,000		—
Subtotal	$4,000	$0	$0	$0	$0	=	$0	$2,000	+	$2,000

Acquiring Other Assets

Now that you have obtained the funds necessary to start your business, either from owner investment or by borrowing, you can use that money to acquire other assets needed to operate the business. Such assets include supplies (such as fertilizer), inventory (perhaps shrubs that you will plant), and equipment (for example, a lawnmower and a truck for hauling). These assets may be purchased with cash or on credit. Credit purchases require payment after a period of time, for example, 30 days. Normally, interest expense is incurred when assets are bought on a time-payment plan that extends beyond two or three months. (To keep our examples simple here, we will not include interest expense. We will show how to account for interest on page 94, where we discuss the payment of obligations.) Examples of transactions involving the acquisition of noncash assets follow.

Example 1   The first thing you need is a lawnmower and some form of transportation. You find an old 1988 pickup truck for sale for $800, and you buy it paying cash.

assets (+)   Truck 800
assets (−)   Cash   800
                    Purchased a used truck.

The accounting equation shows:

Transaction	ASSETS					=	LIABILITIES		+	OWNERS' EQUITY
	Cash	Inventory	Equipment	Supplies	Truck		Accounts Payable	Notes Payable		Capital Stock
Beginning Balance	$ 0	$0	$0	$0	$ 0	=	$0	$ 0	+	$ 0
Invested money in the business	2,000	—	—	—	—		—	—		2,000
Borrowed money from a bank	2,000	—	—	—	—		—	2,000		—
Purchased a truck paying cash	−800	—	—	—	800		—	—		—
Subtotal	$3,200	$0	$0	$0	$800	=	$0	$2,000	+	$2,000

Next, you drive to the local Sears store and purchase a Craftsman lawnmower and gas can for $250. Instead of paying for the mower with cash, you open a charge account, which will allow you to pay for the mower in 30 days with no interest charge. (If you wait and pay beyond this 30-day grace period, an interest charge will apply.) The journal entry to record this purchase is:

assets (+)	Equipment 250	
liabilities (+)	Accounts Payable	250
	Purchased a lawnmower and gas can on account.	

The accounting equation is shown below. When you pay for the mower, cash will be reduced, and the liability, Accounts Payable, will also be reduced, thus keeping the equation in balance.

Transaction	ASSETS					=	LIABILITIES		+	OWNERS' EQUITY
	Cash	Inventory	Equipment	Supplies	Truck		Accounts Payable	Notes Payable		Capital Stock
Beginning Balance	$ 0	$0	$ 0	$0	$ 0	=	$ 0	$ 0	+	$ 0
Invested money in the business	2,000	—	—	—	—		—	—		2,000
Borrowed money from a bank	2,000	—	—	—	—		—	2,000		—
Purchased a truck paying cash	−800	—	—	—	800		—	—		—
Purchased a mower on account	—	—	250	—	—		250	—		—
Subtotal	$3,200	$0	$250	$0	$800	=	$250	$2,000	+	$2,000

Example 2   Off you go to the neighborhood Home Depot store to purchase fertilizer, gloves, a rake, a shovel, and other assorted supplies. The total cost is $180, which you pay in cash; an increase in one asset (supplies) results in a decrease in another asset (cash).

assets (+)	Supplies	180
assets (−)	Cash	180
	Purchased supplies for cash.	

The accounting equation shows:

		ASSETS				=	LIABILITIES		+	OWNERS' EQUITY
Transaction	**Cash**	**Inventory**	**Equipment**	**Supplies**	**Truck**		**Accounts Payable**	**Notes Payable**		**Capital Stock**
Beginning Balance	$ 0	$0	$ 0	$ 0	$ 0	=	$ 0	$ 0	+	$ 0
Invested money in the business	2,000	−	−	−	−		−	−		2,000
Borrowed money from a bank	2,000	−	−	−	−		−	2,000		−
Purchased a truck paying cash	−800	−	−	−	800		−	−		−
Purchased a mower on account	−	−	250	−	−		250	−		−
Purchased supplies for cash	−180	−	−	180	−		−	−		−
Subtotal	$3,020	$0	$250	$180	$800	=	$250	$2,000	+	$2,000

Example 3   On your way home from the hardware store, you drive past a greenhouse and notice a big sign advertising a "50% off" sale on shrubs. Since you anticipate that planting shrubs will be part of your business, you stop and purchase for cash $150 worth of shrubs as inventory. You plan to make money in two ways with the shrubs: (1) revenue from the labor associated with planting them and (2) a profit on selling the shrubs for more than you paid. (This is fair; after all, you are saving your client the time and trouble of having to go to the greenhouse.)

assets (+)	Inventory	150
assets (−)	Cash	150
	Purchased inventory for cash.	

The accounting equation is shown at the top of the following page.

	ASSETS					=	LIABILITIES		+	OWNERS' EQUITY
Transaction	**Cash**	**Inventory**	**Equipment**	**Supplies**	**Truck**		**Accounts Payable**	**Notes Payable**		**Capital Stock**
Beginning Balance	$ 0	$ 0	$ 0	$ 0	$ 0	=	$ 0	$ 0	+	$ 0
Invested money in the business	2,000	–	–	–	–		–	–		2,000
Borrowed money from a bank	2,000	–	–	–	–		–	2,000		–
Purchased a truck paying cash	–800	–	–	–	800		–	–		–
Purchased a mower on account	–	–	250	–	–		250	–		–
Purchased supplies for cash	–180	–	–	180	–		–	–		–
Purchased inventory for cash	–150	150	–	–	–		–	–		–
Subtotal	$2,870	$150	$250	$180	$800	=	$250	$2,000	+	$2,000

Selling Goods or Providing Services

Now that you have your lawnmower, your transportation, your supplies, and your inventory, it is time to go to work. The next category of common transactions involves the sale of services or merchandise. Revenues are generated and expenses incurred during this process. Sometimes services and merchandise are sold for cash; at other times, they are sold on credit (on account to be collected later), and a receivable is established for collection at a later date. Therefore, revenues indicate the source not only of cash but of other assets as well, all of which are received in exchange for the merchandise or services provided. Similarly, expenses may be incurred and paid for immediately by cash, or they may be incurred on credit—that is, they may be "charged," with a cash payment to be made at a later date. Illustrative transactions follow. Note the effect of revenues and expenses on owners' equity is indicated in brackets for each transaction.

Example 1   As soon as people find out that you are in the lawn care and landscaping business, your phone begins ringing off the hook. Although most of your clients pay you immediately when you perform the service, some prefer to pay you once a month. As a result, a portion of your revenues is received immediately in cash, while the balance becomes receivables. The journal entry to record your first week's revenue for lawn care services is:

assets (+)	Cash	270	
assets (+)	Accounts Receivable	80	
revenues (+) [equity (+)]	Lawn Care Revenue		350
	To record revenue for lawn care services.		

compound journal entry

A journal entry that involves more than one debit or more than one credit or both.

As the journal entry illustrates, more than two accounts can be involved in recording a transaction. This type of entry is called a **compound journal entry**. Because revenues increase owners' equity, the accounting equation shows:

Assets   =   Liabilities   +   Owners' Equity (Revenues)
(increase $350)   (no change)   (increase $350)

The detailed effect of this transaction and of each of the following transactions is summarized in Exhibit 4 on page 96.

Example 2   One of your customers asks if you will plant some shrubs in her backyard. You mention that you have some shrubs and describe them to her; she is thrilled that you have just the shrubs she wants, thereby saving her a trip to the greenhouse. You use one-half of your inventory of shrubs in this customer's yard, and it takes you three hours to complete the job. She pays you in cash. In this instance, we are dealing with two different types of revenue—profit from the sale of the shrubs and revenue from your labor. Let's deal with each type of revenue separately.

Sale of Shrubs.   Sales, whether made on account or for cash, require entries that reflect not only the sale, but also the cost of the inventory sold. The "cost of goods sold" is an expense and, as such, is offset with the sales revenue to determine the profitability of sales transactions. The special procedures for handling inventory are described in Chapter 7. It is sufficient here to show an example of the impact of the transaction on the accounting equation.

In this example, you charged your customer $90 for one-half of the shrubs you purchased earlier.

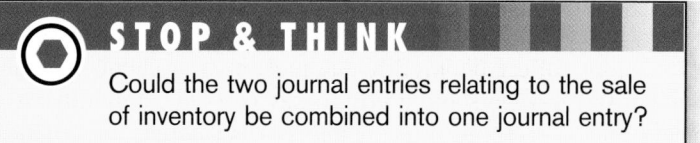

assets (+)   Cash   90
revenues (+) [equity (+)]   Sales Revenue   90

expenses (+) [equity (−)]   Cost of Goods Sold   75
assets (−)   Inventory   75
                              To record the cost of inventory sold and to reduce inventory for its cost.

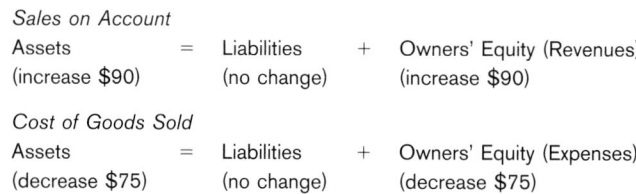

STOP & THINK

Could the two journal entries relating to the sale of inventory be combined into one journal entry?

In this example, inventory costing you $75 is being sold for $90. The effect on the accounting equation for each transaction is:

Sales on Account
Assets   =   Liabilities   +   Owners' Equity (Revenues)
(increase $90)   (no change)   (increase $90)

Cost of Goods Sold
Assets   =   Liabilities   +   Owners' Equity (Expenses)
(decrease $75)   (no change)   (decrease $75)

Labor for Planting.   In addition to making a profit on the sale of the shrubs, you also generated revenue planting them. The journal entry to record this revenue is:

assets (+)
revenues (+) [equity (+)]

Cash	45	
Landscaping Revenue		45
To record revenue for landscaping services.		

The effect of the transaction on the accounting equation is:

Assets	=	Liabilities	+	Owners' Equity (Revenues)
(increase $45)		(no change)		(increase $45)

Example 3   In addition to expenses relating to the sale of inventory, other expenses are also incurred in operating a business. Examples include gas for your lawnmower and your truck and the wages you agreed to pay your little brother for working for you (Mom said you had to let him help). The following journal entries illustrate how these expenses would be accounted for:

expenses (+) [equity (−)]
assets (−)

Gasoline Expense	50	
Cash		50
Paid cash for gas for the truck and the mower.		

expenses (+) [equity (−)]
assets (−)

Wages Expense	60	
Cash		60
Paid wages expense.		

The effect on the accounting equation of the gasoline expense is:

Assets	=	Liabilities	+	Owners' Equity
(decrease $50)		(no change)		(decrease $50)

The entry for Wages Expense affects the equation in the same manner, the only difference being the amount, $60.

Collecting Cash and Paying Obligations

Obviously, once merchandise or services are sold on account, the receivables must be collected. The cash received is generally used to meet daily operating expenses and to pay other obligations. Excess cash can be reinvested in the business or distributed to the owners as a return on their investment.

Example 1   The collection of accounts receivable is an important aspect of most businesses. Receivables are created when you allow certain customers to pay for your services at a later date. When receivables are collected, that asset is reduced and cash is increased, as shown here.

assets (+)
assets (−)

Cash	80	
Accounts Receivable		80
Collected $80 of receivables.		

The effect of collecting the receivables on the accounting equation is:

Assets	=	Liabilities	+	Owners' Equity
(increase $80; decrease $80)		(no change)		(no change)

Note that no revenue is involved here. Revenue is recorded when the original sales transaction creates the accounts receivable. The cash collection on account merely involves exchanging one asset for another.

Example 2   Remember that lawnmower and gas can you purchased on account? Well, now you have to pay for them. The entry to record the payment of obligations with cash is:

liabilities (−)	Accounts Payable	250	
assets (−)	Cash		250
	Paid $250 for the lawnmower and gas can previously purchased.		

After payment of accounts payable, the accounting equation shows:

Assets	=	Liabilities	+	Owners' Equity
(decrease $250)		(decrease $250)		(no change)

Remember that two parties are always involved in exchange transactions. What one buys, the other sells. When sales are on credit, the seller will record a receivable and the buyer will record a payable. The two accounts are inversely related. The seller of merchandise records a receivable and a sale, and simultaneously records an expense for the cost of goods sold and a reduction of inventory (as in Example 2 on page 92). The buyer records the receipt of the merchandise and, at the same time, records an obligation to pay the seller at some future time. When payment is made, the buyer reduces Accounts Payable and Cash (as in this example), whereas the seller increases Cash and reduces Accounts Receivable (as in Example 1 on page 93).

Example 3   On page 88, we showed the entry required when cash was borrowed from the bank. In that entry, you borrowed $2,000 to be paid over 12 months. Suppose you are required to make monthly loan payments of $178 with a portion of each payment being attributed to interest and a portion to reducing the liability—just like a mortgage on a house. As the following compound journal entry shows, a note payable or similar obligation requires an entry for payment, as well as for the interest due. Note that "interest" is the amount charged for using money, as will be more fully explained in later chapters.

liabilities (−)	Notes Payable.	158	
expenses (+) [equity (−)]	Interest Expense	20	
assets (−)	Cash		178
	Paid first monthly payment on note with interest ($2,000 × 0.12 × 1/12).		

Analysis of this transaction reveals that assets have decreased for two reasons. First, a portion of a liability has been paid with cash. Second, interest expense at 12% for one month on the note payable has been paid. This relationship will generally be present in most long-term and some short-term liability transactions. Since the interest charge is an expense and decreases owners' equity, the impact of the entry on the accounting equation is:

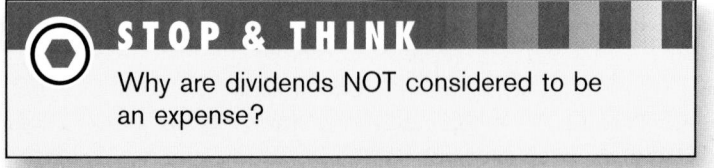

STOP & THINK

Why are dividends NOT considered to be an expense?

Assets	=	Liabilities	+	Owners' Equity (Expenses)
(decrease $178)		(decrease $158)		(decrease $20)

Example 4 Recall that you obtained financing in two ways to start your business—investors (you, Mom, and Dad) and the bank. In the previous journal entry, we illustrated how the bank receives a return on its investment. Well, Mom and Dad would like a return as well. Corporations that are profitable generally pay dividends to their stockholders. "Dividends" represent a distribution to the stockholders of part of the earnings of a company. The following entry illustrates the payment of a cash dividend:

dividends (+) [equity (−)]	Dividends	50
assets (−)	Cash	50
	Paid a $50 cash dividend.	

As noted earlier, dividends, like revenues and expenses, affect owners' equity. Unlike revenues and expenses, dividends are a distribution of profits and, therefore, are not considered in determining net income. Because dividends reduce the retained earnings accumulated by a corporation, they decrease owners' equity. The payment of a $50 dividend affects the accounting equation as follows:

Assets	=	Liabilities	+	Owners' Equity (Dividends)
(decrease $50)		(no change)		(decrease $50)

See Exhibit 4 on the next page for a summary of the transactions shown in this chapter and their effect on the accounting equation.

FYI

Many students have a little trouble getting used to debits, credits, and journal entries. So you are not alone if you are feeling a little overwhelmed. But remember, riding a bike wasn't easy the first time either. Like riding a bike, you will soon find that debits, credits, and journal entries aren't that difficult.

A Note on Journal Entries

When preparing a journal entry, a systematic method may be used in analyzing every transaction. A journal entry involves a three-step process:

1. Identify which accounts are involved.
2. For each account, determine if it is increased or decreased.
3. For each account, determine by how much it has changed.

The answer to step 1 tells you if the accounts involved are asset, liability, or owners' equity accounts. The answer to step 2, when considered in light of your answer to step 1, tells you if the accounts involved are to be debited or credited. Consider the instance where $25,000 is borrowed from a bank. The two accounts involved are Cash and Notes Payable. Cash increased, and since Cash is an asset and assets increase with debits, then Cash must be debited. Notes Payable increased (we owe more money), and since Notes Payable is a liability and liabilities increase with credits, then Notes Payable must be credited. The answer to step 3 completes the journal entry. Cash is debited for $25,000, and Notes Payable is credited for $25,000.

EXHIBIT 4   **Summary of Transactions**

		ASSETS					=	LIABILITIES	
	Cash	**Accounts Receivable**	**Inventory**	**Equipment**	**Supplies**	**Truck**		**Accounts Payable**	**Notes Payable**
Balance (from page 91)	$2,870	–	$150	$250	$180	$800	=	$ 250	$2,000
Revenue from lawn care	270	80	–	–	–	–		–	–
Sold inventory for cash	90	–	–75	–	–	–		–	–
Revenue from landscaping	45	–	–	–	–	–		–	–
Paid for gasoline	–50	–	–	–	–	–		–	–
Paid wages	–60	–	–	–	–	–		–	–
Collected receivables	80	–80	–	–	–	–		–	–
Paid accounts payable	–250	–	–	–	–	–		–250	–
Paid loan payment	–178	–	–	–	–	–		–	–158
Paid dividend	–50	–	–	–	–	–		–	–
Total	$2,767	$ 0	$ 75	$250	$180	$800	=	$ 0	$1,842

This three-step process will always work, even for complex transactions. Consider the case where inventory costing $60,000 is sold on account for $75,000. Using the three-step process results in the following:

1. *Step 1:* What accounts are involved?
   - Accounts Receivable (an asset), Inventory (an asset), Cost of Goods Sold (an expense—part of owners' equity), and Sales Revenue (a revenue account—part of owners' equity).
2. *Step 2:* Did the accounts increase or decrease?
   - Accounts Receivable increased (customers owe us more money). Since Accounts Receivable is an asset, it is increased with a debit.
   - Inventory decreased (we don't have it anymore). Since Inventory is an asset, it is decreased with a credit.
   - Cost of Goods Sold increased (an expense causing owners' equity to decrease). Since owners' equity decreases with a debit, Cost of Goods Sold must be debited.
   - Sales Revenue increased (a revenue causing owners' equity to increase). Since owners' equity increases with a credit, Sales Revenue must be credited.
3. *Step 3:* By how much did each account change?
   - The answer to step 3 results in the following journal entries:

Accounts Receivable	75,000	
Sales Revenue		75,000
Cost of Goods Sold.	60,000	
Inventory.		60,000

+					OWNERS' EQUITY					
					Retained Earnings					
	Capital Stock	Lawn Care Revenue	Sales Revenue	Landscaping Revenue	Cost of Goods Sold*	Gasoline Expense*	Wages Expense*	Interest Expense*	Dividends*
+	$2,000	–	–	–	–	–	–	–	–
	–	350	–	–	–	–	–	–	–
	–	–	90	–	–75	–	–	–	–
	–	–	–	45	–	–	–	–	–
	–	–	–	–	–	–50	–	–	–
	–	–	–	–	–	–	–60	–	–
	–	–	–	–	–	–	–	–	–
	–	–	–	–	–	–	–	–	–
	–	–	–	–	–	–	–	–20	–
	–	–	–	–	–	–	–	–	–50
+	$2,000	$350	$90	$45	–$75	–$50	–$60	–$20	–$50

*Recall that an increase in these accounts actually decreases owners' equity, hence the – (minus sign).

REMEMBER THIS...

Making a journal entry involves the following three steps:

1. Identify which accounts are involved.
2. For each account, determine if it is increased or decreased.
3. For each account, determine by how much it has changed.

Posting Journal Entries and Preparing a Trial Balance

Summarize the resulting journal entries through posting and prepare a trial balance (step three of the accounting cycle).

(4) Once transactions have been analyzed and recorded in a journal, it is necessary to classify and group all similar items. This is accomplished by the bookkeeping procedure of **posting** all the journal entries to appropriate accounts (see page 98 for definition). As indicated earlier, accounts are records of like items. They show transaction dates, increases and decreases, and balances. For example, all increases and decreases in cash arising from transactions recorded in the journal are accumulated in one account called Cash. Similarly, all sales transactions are grouped together in the sales revenue account.

Posting is no more than sorting all journal entry amounts by account and copying those amounts to the appropriate account. No analysis is needed; all the necessary analysis is performed when the transaction is first recorded in the journal.

posting

The process of transferring amounts from the journal to the ledger.

ledger

A book of accounts in which data from transactions recorded in journals are posted and thereby summarized.

chart of accounts

A systematic listing of all accounts used by a company.

All accounts are maintained in an accounting record called a "ledger." A **ledger** (the main ledger is called a general ledger) is a "book of accounts." Exhibit 5 shows how the three cash transactions in the general journal would be posted to the cash account in the general ledger, with arrows depicting the posting procedures. Observe that a number has been inserted in the "posting reference" column in both books. This number serves as a cross-reference between the general journal and the accounts in the general ledger. In the journal, it identifies the account to which the journal entry has been posted. In the ledger, it identifies the page on which the entry appears in the general journal. For example, the GJ1 notation in the cash account for the July 1 entry means that the $2,000 has been posted from page 1 of the general journal. As you will discover, these posting references are useful in tracking down mistakes. With a computer system, the software automatically generates these posting references.

A particular company will have as many (or as few) accounts as it needs to provide a reasonable classification of its transactions. The list of accounts used by a company is known as its **chart of accounts**. The normal order of a chart of accounts is assets (current and long-term), then liabilities (current and long-term), followed by owners' equity, sales, and expenses. Exhibit 6 on page 100 shows some accounts that might appear in a typical company's chart of accounts.

! CAUTION

Common mistakes when manually posting include posting a debit to the credit side of an account, transposing numbers (e.g., a 45 magically becomes a 54), and posting to the wrong account (e.g., Supplies instead of Inventory). The lesson—be very careful or mistakes will creep into your work. Thankfully, posting is a task done almost exclusively by computers these days.

Determining Account Balances

At the end of an accounting period, the accounts in the general ledger are reviewed to determine each account's balance. Asset, expense, and dividend accounts normally have debit balances; liability, owners' equity, and revenue accounts normally have credit balances. In other words, the balance is normally on the side that increases the account.

To illustrate how to determine an account balance, consider the following T-account depicting all the cash transactions from our landscaping business (with dates being added). The beginning cash account balance plus all Cash debit entries, less total credits to Cash, equals the ending balance in the cash account.

Cash

Beg. Bal.	0		
7/1	2,000		
7/1	2,000	7/5	800
7/9	270	7/5	180
7/14	90	7/7	150
7/14	45	7/18	50
7/30	80	7/23	60
		7/31	250
		7/31	178
		7/31	50
	4,485		(1,718)
	(1,718)		
End. Bal.	2,767		

EXHIBIT 5	Posting to the General Ledger

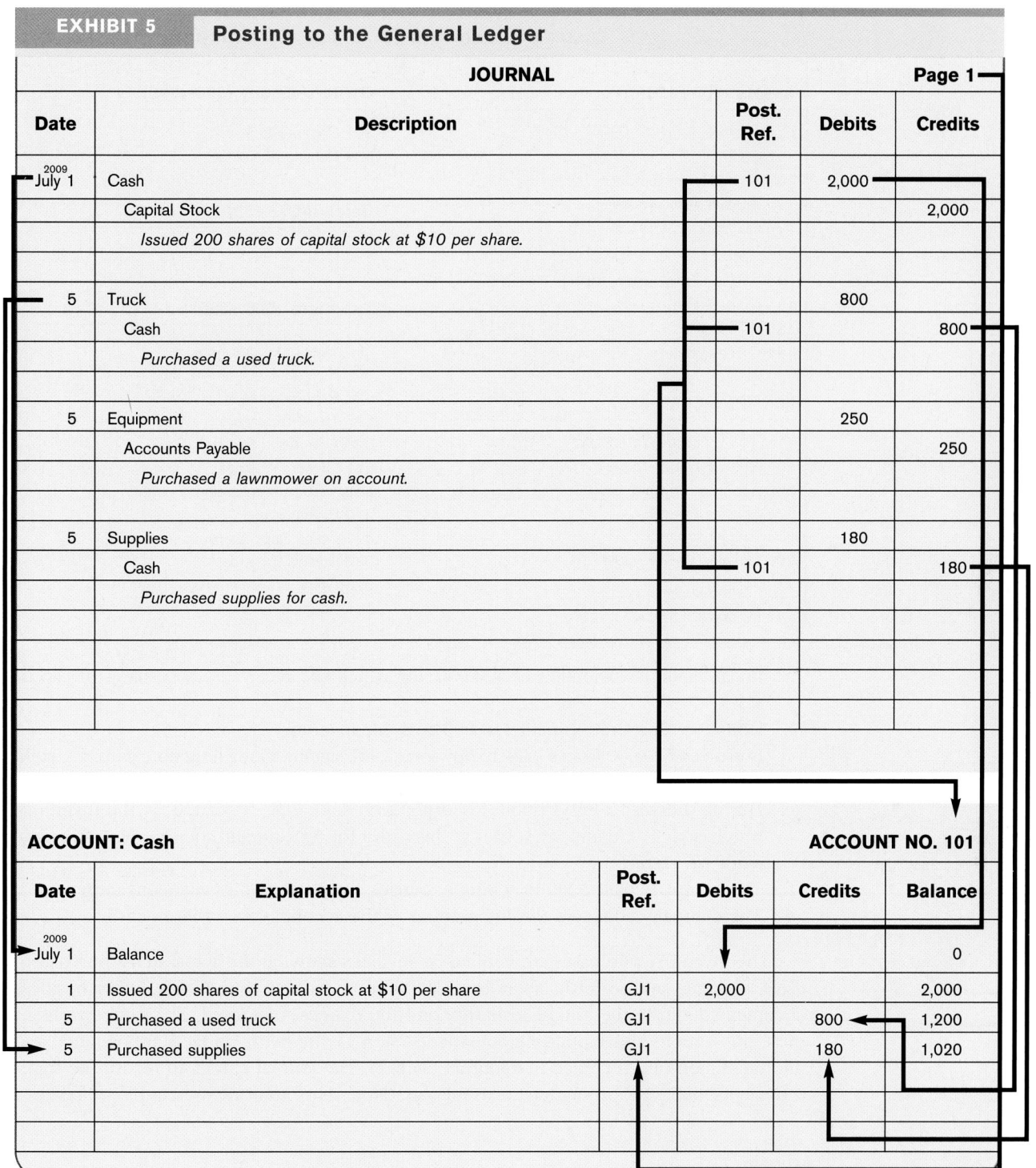

JOURNAL   Page 1

Date	Description	Post. Ref.	Debits	Credits
2009 July 1	Cash	101	2,000	
	Capital Stock			2,000
	Issued 200 shares of capital stock at $10 per share.			
5	Truck		800	
	Cash	101		800
	Purchased a used truck.			
5	Equipment		250	
	Accounts Payable			250
	Purchased a lawnmower on account.			
5	Supplies		180	
	Cash	101		180
	Purchased supplies for cash.			

ACCOUNT: Cash   **ACCOUNT NO. 101**

Date	Explanation	Post. Ref.	Debits	Credits	Balance
2009 July 1	Balance				0
1	Issued 200 shares of capital stock at $10 per share	GJ1	2,000		2,000
5	Purchased a used truck	GJ1		800	1,200
5	Purchased supplies	GJ1		180	1,020

Illustration of the First Three Steps in the Accounting Cycle

We have introduced the first three steps in the accounting cycle. A simple illustration will help reinforce what you have learned about the relationship of assets, liabilities, and owners' equity, as well as revenues, expenses, and dividends, and the mechanics of double-entry accounting. Katherine Kohler established the Double K Corporation in 2009. The following transactions occurred.

EXHIBIT 6	**Chart of Accounts for a Typical Company**

Assets (100–199)

Current Assets (100–150):
101 Cash
103 Notes Receivable
105 Accounts Receivable
107 Inventory
108 Supplies

Long-Term Assets (151–199):
151 Land
152 Buildings
154 Office Furniture or Equipment

Liabilities (200–299)

Current Liabilities (200–219):
201 Notes Payable
202 Accounts Payable
203 Salaries Payable
204 Interest Payable
206 Income Taxes Payable

Long-Term Liabilities (220–239):
222 Mortgage Payable

Owners' Equity (300–399)

301 Capital Stock
330 Retained Earnings

Sales (400–499)

400 Sales Revenue

Expenses (500–599)

500 Cost of Goods Sold
501 Sales Salaries and Commissions
523 Rent Expense
525 Travel Expense
528 Advertising Expense
551 Officers' Salaries
553 Administrative Salaries
570 Payroll Taxes
571 Office Supplies Expense
573 Utilities Expense
578 Office Equipment Rent Expense
579 Accounting and Legal Fees

a. Initial capital contribution of $20,000, for which she received 1,000 shares of capital stock.
b. Double K Corporation paid $10,000 cash for inventory.
c. Borrowed $20,000 from a bank to buy some land, signing a long-term note with the bank.
d. Land was purchased for $25,000 cash.
e. During the year 2009, Double K Corporation sold 20%, or $2,000, of the inventory purchased. The company sold that inventory for $3,200, and the sale was originally made on credit.
f. The company paid $200 in selling expenses and $100 in miscellaneous expenses.
g. The company collected the full amount of the account receivable in cash.

The inventory purchases are verified by invoices showing the actual items purchased, dates, amounts, and so forth. There is a $20,000 note payable to the bank. Other business documents indicate the sale of inventory and the expenses incurred. Through analysis of these transactions and supporting documents (step 1), the pertinent facts are obtained and the transactions are recorded in a journal (step 2). The journal entries to record the transactions of Double K Corporation are as follows. (Note that letters are used in place of dates.)

Business Transaction	Account Category and Direction	Journal Entries	Debits	Credits
Issued stock	assets (+)	(a) Cash	20,000	
	owners' equity (+)	(a) Capital Stock		20,000
		Issued 1,000 shares of capital stock for $20,000.		
Purchased	assets (+)	(b) Inventory	10,000	
inventory	assets (−)	(b) Cash		10,000
		Purchased $10,000 of inventory for cash.		

(continued)

Business Transaction	Account Category and Direction	Journal Entries	Debits	Credits
Borrowed	assets (+)	(c) Cash	20,000	
money	liabilities (+)	(c) Notes Payable		20,000
		Borrowed $20,000 from a bank.		
Purchased	assets (+)	(d) Land	25,000	
land	assets (−)	(d) Cash		25,000
		Purchased land for cash.		
Sold inventory	assets (+)	(e) Accounts Receivable	3,200	
	revenues (+)	(e) Sales Revenue		3,200
		Sold inventory for $3,200 on account.		
	expenses (+)	(e) Cost of Goods Sold	2,000	
	assets (−)	(e) Inventory		2,000
		To record the cost of goods or inventory sold.		
Paid expenses	expenses (+)	(f) Selling Expenses	200	
	expenses (+)	(f) Miscellaneous Expenses	100	
	assets (−)	(f) Cash		300
		Paid selling and miscellaneous expenses.		
Collected cash	assets (+)	(g) Cash	3,200	
	assets (−)	(g) Accounts Receivable		3,200
		Collected accounts receivable.		

Next, the transactions are posted to the ledger accounts (step 3, part 1). T-accounts are used to illustrate this process, with the letters (a) through (g) showing the cross-references to the journal entries. A balance is shown for the end of the period. (Where only one transaction is involved, the amount of the transaction is also the account balance.)

	Cash				**Accounts Receivable**				**Inventory**				**Land**	
(a)	20,000	(b)	10,000	(e)	3,200	(g)	3,200	(b)	10,000	(e)	2,000	(d)	25,000	
(c)	20,000	(d)	25,000											
(g)	3,200	(f)	300	Bal.	0			Bal.	8,000					
Bal.	7,900													

	Notes Payable			**Capital Stock**			**Sales Revenue**	
		(c)	20,000		(a)	20,000		(e)	3,200

	Cost of Goods Sold			**Selling Expenses**			**Miscellaneous Expenses**	
(e)	2,000		(f)	200		(f)	100	

The effect of these transactions can also be visualized using a spreadsheet format as shown in Exhibit 7.

EXHIBIT 7	Effects of Business Transactions on the Accounting Equation

Transaction	ASSETS				=	LIABILITIES	+		OWNERS' EQUITY				
	Cash	Inventory	Land	Accounts Receivable		Notes Payable		Capital Stock	Retained Earnings				
Beginning Balance	$ 0	$ 0	$ 0	$ 0	=	$ 0	+	$ 0	Sales Revenue	Cost of Goods Sold*	Selling Expenses*	Misc. Expenses*
A	20,000	–	–	–		–		20,000	–	–	–	–
B	–10,000	10,000	–	–		–		0	–	–	–	–
C	20,000	–	–	–		20,000		–	–	–	–	–
D	–25,000	–	25,000	–		–		–	–	–	–	–
E	–	–2,000	–	3,200		–		–	3,200	–2,000	–	–
F	–300	–	–	–		–		–	–	–	–200	–100
G	3,200	–	–	–3,200		–		–	–	–	–	–
Total	$ 7,900	$ 8,000	$25,000	$ 0	=	$20,000	+	$20,000	$3,200	–$2,000	–$200	–$100

*Recall that an increase in these accounts actually decreases owners' equity, hence the – (minus sign).

trial balance

A listing of all account balances; provides a means of testing whether total debits equal total credits for all accounts.

After the account balances have been determined, a trial balance is usually prepared (step 3, part 2). A **trial balance** lists each account with its debit or credit balance, as shown in Exhibit 8. By adding all the debit balances and all the credit balances, the accountant can see whether total debits equal total credits. Even if the trial balance does show total debits equal to total credits, there may be errors. A transaction may have been omitted completely, or it may have been recorded incorrectly or posted to the wrong account. These types of errors will not be discovered by preparing a trial balance; additional analysis would be required. In this case, total debits equal total credits.

EXHIBIT 8	Trial Balance

Double K Corporation
Trial Balance
December 31, 2009

	Debits	Credits
Cash	$ 7,900	
Accounts Receivable	0	
Inventory	8,000	
Land	25,000	
Notes Payable		$20,000
Capital Stock		20,000
Sales Revenue		3,200
Cost of Goods Sold	2,000	
Selling Expenses	200	
Miscellaneous Expenses	100	
Totals	$43,200	$43,200

Thus, the accounting equation is in balance. The balances are taken from each ledger account.

Students frequently mistake a trial balance and the balance sheet for one another. In fact, they are very different reports. A trial balance is strictly an internal document used to summarize all of the account balances (assets, liabilities, owners' equity, revenues, expenses, and dividends) in a company's accounting system. Few people outside a company's accounting department ever see the trial balance; most businesspeople never see a real trial balance during their entire business career. The balance sheet, on the other hand, is a more formal summary document that is frequently provided to interested parties both inside and outside a company.

From the data in the trial balance, an income statement and a balance sheet can be prepared. Exhibit 9 shows these two financial statements for Double K Corporation. Notice that there is no retained earnings account in the trial balance but there is one on the balance sheet. The reason for this is that all the income statement accounts such as Revenue, Cost of Goods Sold, and expenses are eventually accumulated into Retained Earnings. That is, earnings are reflected on the income statement. The business then decides the amount of those earnings to be retained. Those earnings that are to be retained are then disclosed on the balance sheet.

Also, the statement of cash flows can be prepared by categorizing the items in the cash account as operating, investing, or financing, as shown in Exhibit 10.

Three final notes: First, the preparation of financial statements is rarely so simple. In reality, the procedure also involves the adjustment of some ledger accounts, which need to be brought current before they can be included in the balance sheet or the income statement. In Chapter 4, we will explain how accounts are adjusted (step 4, part 1) so that the financial statements will accurately reflect the current financial position and operating results of an enterprise.

EXHIBIT 9	**Income Statement and Balance Sheet**

Double K Corporation
Income Statement
For the Year Ended December 31, 2009

Sales revenue		$3,200
Expenses:		
Cost of goods sold	$2,000	
Selling expenses	200	
Miscellaneous expenses	100	2,300
Net income		$ 900
EPS ($900 ÷ 1,000 shares)		$ 0.90

Double K Corporation
Balance Sheet
December 31, 2009

Assets		**Liabilities and Owners' Equity**	
Cash	$ 7,900	Notes payable	$20,000
Inventory	8,000	Capital stock (1,000 shares)	20,000
Land	25,000	Retained earnings	900*
Total assets	$40,900	Total liabilities and	
		owners' equity	$40,900

*Beginning retained earnings plus net income minus dividends.

EXHIBIT 10   **Statement of Cash Flows**

Double K Corporation
Statement of Cash Flows
For the Year Ended December 31, 2009

Operating activities:		
Collections from customers.	$ 3,200	
Purchase of inventory	(10,000)	
Paid expenses.	(300)	$ (7,100)
Investing activities:		
Purchased land.		(25,000)
Financing activities:		
Issued stock	$20,000	
Borrowed from bank.	20,000	40,000
Net increase in cash.		$ 7,900
Beginning cash balance		0
Ending cash balance		$ 7,900

Second, net income does not usually equal the ending retained earnings balance. Only in the first year of a company's operations would this be the case. Double K Corporation began operations in 2009 and paid no dividends during the year; so, its $900 net income on the income statement equals the retained earnings figure on the balance sheet. In future years, the figures would be different, since retained earnings is an accumulation of earnings from past years adjusted for dividends and other special items.

REMEMBER THIS...

- Posting involves sorting and copying the journal entry items to individual accounts.
- Account balances are computed by summing the debit and credit entries in each account.
- A trial balance is prepared by listing each account along with its balance.
- An income statement and a balance sheet can be prepared from this trial balance.
- A statement of cash flows is prepared by analyzing the inflows and outflows of cash as detailed in the cash account.

Where Do Computers Fit In All This?

Describe how technology has affected the first three steps of the accounting cycle.

5 Students often ask, "Do I really need to know the difference between a debit and a credit? Haven't computers taken care of that?" Computers have greatly facilitated a business's ability to quickly process huge amounts of information without making mathematical errors. Most computers can make millions of calculations per second and produce more documents in 10 minutes than a person could in an entire week. The time spent posting journal entries and summarizing accounts into a trial balance has been greatly reduced as a result of computers.

But computers still can't think. That's your job. Walk up to a computer terminal and show it a sales invoice and the computer will just sit there and wait.

Wait for what? For the answers to three questions: (1) What accounts are involved? (2) Did those accounts increase or decrease? (3) By how much did each account change?

Let's consider how the best-selling money management software package, Quicken®, has changed the accounting process. Quicken works a lot like a check register. For each check, you indicate the date, the check number, the payee, and the amount. Quicken then prompts you to indicate the nature of the expenditure by selecting from a list of accounts. For example, if the expenditure relates to your purchase of groceries, you would select the account "Food." Thus, all your transactions relating to "Food" will be grouped together, allowing you to quickly determine all food expenditures.

Now let's review what Quicken has done. First of all, since you indicated the transaction involved a check, Quicken knows that cash decreased. Quicken is programmed to know that when cash decreases, it involves a credit to the cash account. Quicken also has been programmed to know that debits have to equal credits, and since Cash was credited, the program knows that something was debited. Since you indicated "Food" (an expense) was the other account, Quicken debits that account, causing your expense account to increase (we now know that expenses increase with debits). Instead of telling Quicken which accounts to debit and credit, you are required to identify the accounts (question 1) and indicate if they increased or decreased (question 2). Quicken is able to determine, based on the answer to these two questions, which accounts were debited and which accounts were credited.

So has Quicken fundamentally changed the accounting process? No. It has increased the accuracy and speed with which the posting process is done, as well as the speed with which a variety of reports can be prepared. Quicken has also eliminated the need for the user to specify debit or credit. Because computers are so fast, the two-step process of identifying accounts and the direction of their change can be done as quickly as you can say "credit Cash." So why don't accountants get rid of these 500-year-old terms, debit and credit? The reason is that all accountants are familiar with and comfortable using these terms. When someone says "credit Cash," accountants everywhere know exactly what that means. Thus, debit and credit provide a useful shorthand method of communication.

The computer has also enhanced step 3 of the accounting cycle—summarizing. In fact, only in the smallest of businesses will you find the posting of journal entries and the preparation of a trial balance being done by hand. But in every business, from the largest to the smallest, you will find accountants still actively involved in analyzing transactions and turning those transactions into journal entries and eventually into useful accounting reports.

REMEMBER THIS...

- Computers have made posting and the preparation of reports and statements much easier.
- Computers have *not* replaced the need for accountants to analyze transactions and determine their effect on the accounting equation.

REVIEW OF
LEARNING OBJECTIVES

(1) **Understand the process of transforming transaction data into useful accounting information.** The objective of the accounting process is to gather and transform transaction data into useful information that measures and communicates the results of business activity. The four steps in the accounting cycle are as follows:

Step 1. Analyze transactions.
Step 2. Record the effects of transactions.
Step 3. Summarize the effects of transactions.
Step 4. Prepare reports.

(2) **Analyze transactions and determine how those transactions affect the accounting equation (step one of the accounting cycle).**

Assets	=	Liabilities	+	Owners' Equity
DR CR		DR CR		DR CR
(+) (−)		(−) (+)		(−) (+)

The following types of accounts are sub-categories of Retained Earnings which is an Owners' Equity account.

Expenses	Dividends	Revenues
DR CR	DR CR	DR CR
(+) (−)	(+) (−)	(−) (+)

- More expense, a debit, means less owners' equity.
- More dividends, a debit, means less owners' equity.
- More revenue, a credit, means more owners' equity.

(3) **Record the effects of transactions using journal entries (step two of the accounting cycle).** Making a journal entry involves the following three steps:

1. Identify which accounts are involved.
2. For each account, determine if it is increased or decreased.
3. For each account, determine by how much it has changed.

(4) **Summarize the resulting journal entries through posting and prepare a trial balance (step three of the accounting cycle).**
- Posting involves sorting and copying the journal entry items to individual accounts.
- Account balances are computed by summing the debit and credit entries in each account.
- A trial balance is prepared by listing each account along with its balance.
- An income statement and a balance sheet can be prepared from this trial balance.
- A statement of cash flows is prepared by analyzing the inflows and outflows of cash as detailed in the cash account.

(5) **Describe how technology has affected the first three steps of the accounting cycle.**
- Computers have made posting and the preparation of reports and statements much easier.
- Computers have **not** replaced the need for accountants to analyze transactions and determine their effect on the accounting equation.

KEY TERMS & CONCEPTS

account, 80

accounting cycle, 76

business documents, 77

chart of accounts, 98

compound journal entry, 92

credit, 82

debit, 81

dividends, 84

journal, 86

journal entry, 86

journalizing, 86

ledger, 98

posting, 98

T-account, 81

trial balance, 102

REVIEW PROBLEM

The First Three Steps in the Accounting Cycle

Journal entries are given below for January 2009, the first month of operation for the Svendsen Service Company.

Jan.	2	Cash	40,000	
		Capital Stock		40,000
		Issued capital stock for cash.		
	2	Insurance Expense	500	
		Cash		500
		Purchased a one-month insurance policy.		
	2	Rent Expense	750	
		Cash		750
		Paid rent for the month of January.		
	3	Shop Equipment	8,000	
		Cash		8,000
		Purchased shop equipment for cash.		
	4	Supplies	3,000	
		Accounts Payable		3,000
		Purchased shop supplies on account.		
	5	Automotive Equipment	11,500	
		Cash		3,500
		Notes Payable		8,000
		Purchased a truck. Paid $3,500 cash and issued a 30-day note for the balance.		
	8	Cash	1,750	
		Service and Repair Revenue		1,750
		Received cash for repairs.		
	9	Advertising Expense	300	
		Cash		300
		Paid cash for radio spot announcements.		
	12	Automotive Expense	200	
		Cash		200
		Paid gas, oil, and service costs on the truck.		
	14	Accounts Payable	3,000	
		Cash		3,000
		Paid $3,000 on account.		
	16	Accounts Receivable	1,200	
		Service and Repair Revenue		1,200
		Repaired truck for Acme Drilling Company on account.		
	18	Telephone Expense	75	
		Cash		75
		Paid for installation and telephone service for one month.		
	19	Automotive Expense	180	
		Cash		180
		Paid for minor repairs on the truck.		
	20	Cash	1,000	
		Notes Receivable	1,450	
		Service and Repair Revenue		2,450
		Collected $1,000 cash from Jones for truck repairs; accepted a 60-day note for the balance.		

(continued)

Jan. 24	Repairs and Maintenance Expense	150	
	Cash		150
	Paid cleaning and painting expenses on the building.		
25	Cash	1,500	
	Service and Repair Revenue		1,500
	Received cash for repairs and services from Hamilton, Inc.		
27	Supplies	2,500	
	Cash		2,500
	Purchased shop supplies.		
29	Office Equipment	1,250	
	Cash		1,250
	Purchased a computer.		
30	Cash	1,200	
	Accounts Receivable		1,200
	Collected receivables from Acme Drilling Company.		
31	Utilities Expense	900	
	Cash		900
	Paid the monthly utility bill.		
31	Automotive Expense	350	
	Cash		350
	Paid for gas, oil, and servicing of the truck.		

Required:

Set up T-accounts, post all journal entries to the accounts, balance the accounts, and prepare a trial balance.

Solution

The first step in solving this problem is to set up T-accounts for each item; then post all journal entries to the appropriate ledger accounts, as shown. Once the amounts are properly posted, account balances can be determined.

Cash

1/2	40,000	1/2	500
1/8	1,750	1/2	750
1/20	1,000	1/3	8,000
1/25	1,500	1/5	3,500
1/30	1,200	1/9	300
		1/12	200
		1/14	3,000
		1/18	75
		1/19	180
		1/24	150
		1/27	2,500
		1/29	1,250
		1/31	900
		1/31	350
Bal.	23,795		

Notes Receivable

1/20	1,450		

Accounts Receivable

1/16	1,200	1/30	1,200
Bal.	0		

Supplies

1/4	3,000		
1/27	2,500		
Bal.	5,500		

Shop Equipment

1/3	8,000		

Automotive Equipment

1/5	11,500		

Office Equipment

1/29	1,250		

Notes Payable

		1/5	8,000

Accounts Payable

1/14	3,000	1/4	3,000
		Bal.	0

Capital Stock

		1/2	40,000

Service and Repair Revenue

		1/8	1,750
		1/16	1,200
		1/20	2,450
		1/25	1,500
		Bal.	6,900

Insurance Expense

1/2	500		

Rent Expense

1/2	750		

Advertising Expense

1/9	300		

Automotive Expense

1/12	200		
1/19	180		
1/31	350		
Bal.	730		

(continued)

Telephone Expense		Repairs and Maintenance Expense		Utilities Expense	
1/18 75		1/24 150		1/31 900	

The final step is to prepare a trial balance to see whether total debits equal total credits for all accounts. List all the accounts with balances; then enter the balance in each account.

Svendsen Service Company
Trial Balance
January 31, 2009

	Debits	Credits
Cash	$23,795	
Accounts Receivable	0	
Notes Receivable	1,450	
Supplies	5,500	
Shop Equipment	8,000	
Automotive Equipment	11,500	
Office Equipment	1,250	
Accounts Payable		$ 0
Notes Payable		8,000
Capital Stock		40,000
Service and Repair Revenue		6,900
Insurance Expense	500	
Rent Expense	750	
Advertising Expense	300	
Automotive Expense	730	
Telephone Expense	75	
Repairs and Maintenance Expense	150	
Utilities Expense	900	
Totals	$54,900	$54,900

DISCUSSION QUESTIONS

1. What is the basic objective of the accounting cycle?
2. Explain the first three steps in the accounting cycle.
3. What are the advantages of a computer-based accounting system? Does such a system eliminate the need for human judgment? Explain.
4. In a double-entry system of accounting, why must total debits always equal total credits?
5. Explain the increase/decrease, debit/credit relationship of asset, liability, and owners' equity accounts.
6. How are revenues, expenses, and dividends related to the basic accounting equation?
7. In what ways are dividend and expense accounts similar, and in what ways are they different?
8. How does understanding the mechanics of accounting help a businessperson who has no intention of practicing accounting?
9. Distinguish between a journal and a ledger.
10. Assume that Company A buys $1,500 of merchandise from Company B for cash. The merchandise originally cost Company B $1,000. What entries should the buyer and seller make, and what is the relationship of the accounts for this transaction?
11. Indicate how each of the following transactions affects the accounting equation.
    a. Purchase of supplies on account.
    b. Payment of wages.
    c. Cash sales of goods for more than their cost.
    d. Payment of monthly utility bills.
    e. Purchase of a building with a down payment of cash plus a mortgage.
    f. Cash investment by a stockholder.
    g. Payment of a cash dividend.
    h. Sale of goods on account for more than their cost.
    i. Sale of land at less than its cost.
12. What is a chart of accounts? What is its purpose?
13. If a trial balance appears to be correct (debits equal credits), does that guarantee complete accuracy in the accounting records? Explain.

14. What is the difference between a trial balance and a balance sheet?

15. Have computers eliminated the need to analyze transactions? Explain.

PRACTICE EXERCISES

For PE 3-1 through 3-5, do the following for each transaction:
a. List the accounts impacted by the transaction.
b. For each account, indicate whether the transaction increased or decreased the account.
c. For each account, indicate how much the transaction increased or decreased the account.
d. Compute the impact of the transaction on total assets, total liabilities, and total owners' equity.

PE 3-1   **Impact of a Transaction**
LO2   The company borrowed $85,000 in cash from Eastern Bank.

PE 3-2   **Impact of a Transaction**
LO2   The company used $45,000 in cash to purchase land on the west side of Hatu Lake.

PE 3-3   **Impact of a Transaction**
LO2   The company used $30,000 in cash to repay a portion of its bank loan (see PE 3-1). For simplicity, assume that there is no interest on the loan.

PE 3-4   **Impact of a Transaction**
LO2   The company received $75,000 in cash as an additional investment by the stockholders (owners) of the company.

PE 3-5   **Impact of a Transaction**
LO2   The company purchased a building for $130,000. The company paid $50,000 of the purchase price in cash and signed a mortgage contract obligating it to pay the remaining $80,000 over the next 10 years.

PE 3-6   **Computing Ending Account Balances**
LO2   Refer to PE 3-1 through 3-5. Construct a spreadsheet similar to the one shown on page 91. Enter each transaction into the spreadsheet and compute the ending balance in each account.

PE 3-7   **Understanding Debits**
LO2   Below is a list of accounts. For each account, indicate whether a *debit* increases or decreases the account balance.

	Account	Debit
0.	Cash	Increases
1.	Accounts Payable	
2.	Capital Stock	
3.	Land	
4.	Inventory	
5.	Loan Payable	
6.	Mortgage Payable	
7.	Building	

PE 3-8   **Understanding Credits**

LO2   Below is a list of accounts. For each account, indicate whether a credit increases or decreases the account balance.

	Account	Credit
0.	Cash	Decreases
1.	Accounts Receivable	
2.	Capital Stock	
3.	Equipment	
4.	Inventory	
5.	Accounts Payable	
6.	Building	
7.	Notes Payable	

PE 3-9   **Understanding Debits, Credits, and Retained Earnings**

LO2   Below is a list of accounts and whether the account is being debited or credited. For each item, indicate whether the account balance will be increased or decreased.

	Account	Debit or Credit	Account Balance
0.	Salary Expense	Debit	Increased
1.	Sales Revenue	Credit	
2.	Retained Earnings	Debit	
3.	Insurance Expense	Credit	
4.	Dividends	Credit	
5.	Interest Revenue	Debit	
6.	Advertising Expense	Debit	
7.	Rent Revenue	Credit	

PE 3-10   **Understanding Retained Earnings**

LO2   Below is a list of accounts with corresponding balances. Using these accounts, along with the fact that the beginning balance in Retained Earnings is $9,000, compute the ending balance in Retained Earnings. *Note:* Not all of the listed account balances enter into the calculation of Retained Earnings.

	Account	Account Balance
a.	Insurance Expense	$1,600
b.	Cash	1,200
c.	Sales Revenue	7,500
d.	Advertising Expense	1,800
e.	Accounts Payable	2,100
f.	Dividends	600
g.	Interest Revenue	350

PE 3-11   **Journal Entries**

LO3   Refer to PE 3-1. Make the journal entry necessary to record the transaction.

PE 3-12   **Journal Entries**

LO3   Refer to PE 3-2. Make the journal entry necessary to record the transaction.

PE 3-13   **Journal Entries**

LO3   Refer to PE 3-3. Make the journal entry necessary to record the transaction.

PE 3-14   **Journal Entries**

LO3   Refer to PE 3-4. Make the journal entry necessary to record the transaction.

PE 3-15

LO3

Journal Entries

Refer to PE 3-5. Make the journal entry necessary to record the transaction.

PE 3-16

LO3

Journal Entries with Revenues, Expenses, and Dividends

Make the journal entries necessary to record the following eight transactions.

a. Purchased inventory on account for $130,000.

b. Sold goods for $100,000 cash. The goods originally cost $65,000.

c. Paid $27,000 cash for employee wages.

d. Paid $12,500 cash for advertising.

e. Sold goods for $25,000 cash and $60,000 on account (a total of $85,000). The goods originally cost $57,000.

f. Collected cash of $47,000 from the $60,000 receivable on account; the remaining $13,000 is expected to be collected later.

g. Paid cash of $55,000 on the $130,000 payable on account; the remaining $75,000 is expected to be paid later.

h. Paid cash dividends of $8,500.

PE 3-17

LO4

Posting

Refer to the journal entries made in PE 3-11 through PE 3-15. Construct a T-account representing each account impacted by those five transactions. Post all of the journal entries to these T-accounts. Compute the ending balance in each account. Assume that the beginning balance in each T-account is zero.

PE 3-18

LO4

Posting with Revenues, Expenses, and Dividends

Refer to the journal entries made in PE 3-16. Construct a T-account representing each account impacted by those eight transactions. Post all of the journal entries to these T-accounts. Compute the ending balance in each account. Assume that the beginning balance in each T-account is zero.

PE 3-19

LO4

Preparing a Trial Balance

Refer to the T-accounts constructed in PE 3-17 and PE 3-18. Using the ending balances in those T-accounts, construct a trial balance. *Note:* The only account that is common to these two sets of T-accounts is the cash account; add the two cash account balances together to get the total balance.

PE 3-20

LO4

Using a Trial Balance to Prepare an Income Statement

Using the trial balance given below, prepare an income statement.

	Debit	Credit
Cash	$ 68,000	
Accounts Receivable	126,000	
Inventory	216,000	
Land	90,000	
Building	200,000	
Accounts Payable		$ 150,000
Loan Payable		270,000
Capital Stock		250,000
Dividends	17,000	
Sales Revenue		370,000
Cost of Goods Sold	244,000	
Utilities Expense	54,000	
Rental Expense	25,000	
Totals	$1,040,000	$1,040,000

PE 3-21   **Using a Trial Balance to Prepare a Balance Sheet**

LO4   Using the trial balance given in PE 3-20, prepare a balance sheet. *Note:* The ending retained earnings balance is equal to the beginning balance (which is assumed to be $0) plus the amount of net income less the amount of dividends.

PE 3-22   **Preparing a Statement of Cash Flows**

LO4   Refer to the transactions described in PE 3-1 through PE 3-5 as well as to the eight transactions in PE 3-16. Using all of these transactions, prepare a statement of cash flows. *Note:* For the building purchase described in PE 3-5, the portion of the purchase financed with the mortgage ($80,000) is considered to be a noncash transaction; accordingly, the only portion of the transaction that impacts the statement of cash flows is the $50,000 cash down payment.

EXERCISES

E 3-23   **Basic Accounting Equation**

LO2   The fundamental accounting equation can be applied to your personal finances. For each of the following transactions, show how the accounting equation would be kept in balance. Example: Paid for semester's tuition (decrease assets: cash account; decrease owners' equity: expense account increases).

     1. Took out a school loan for college.
     2. Paid this month's rent.
     3. Sold your old computer for cash at what it cost to buy it.
     4. Received week's paycheck from part-time job.
     5. Received interest on savings account.
     6. Paid monthly payment on car loan (part of the payment is principal; the remainder is interest).

E 3-24   **Accounting Elements: Increase/Decrease, Debit/Credit Relationships**

LO2   The text describes the following accounting elements: assets, liabilities, owners' equity, capital stock, retained earnings, revenues, expenses, and dividends. Which of these elements are increased by a debit entry, and which are increased by a credit entry? Give a transaction for each item that would result in a net increase in its balance.

E 3-25   **Expanded Accounting Equation**

LO2   Payless Department Store had the following transactions during the year:

     1. Purchased inventory on account.
     2. Sold merchandise for cash, assuming a profit on the sale.
     3. Borrowed money from a bank.
     4. Purchased land, making cash down payment and issuing a note for the balance.
     5. Issued stock for cash.
     6. Paid salaries for the year.
     7. Paid a vendor for inventory purchased on account.
     8. Sold a building for cash and notes receivable at no gain or loss.
     9. Paid cash dividends to stockholders.
    10. Paid utilities.

Using the following column headings, identify the accounts involved and indicate the net effect of each transaction on the accounting equation (+ increase; − decrease; 0 no effect). Transaction 1 has been completed as an example.

Transaction	Assets	=	Liabilities	+	Owners' Equity
1	+		+		0
	(Inventory)		(Accounts Payable)		

E 3-26
LO2
Classification of Accounts

For each of the accounts listed, indicate whether it is an asset (A), a liability (L), or an owners' equity (OE) account. If it is an account that affects owners' equity, indicate whether it is a revenue (R) or expense (E) account.

1. Cash
2. Sales
3. Accounts Receivable
4. Cost of Goods Sold
5. Insurance Expense
6. Capital Stock
7. Mortgage Payable
8. Salaries and Wages Expense
9. Retained Earnings
10. Salaries Payable
11. Accounts Payable
12. Interest Revenue
13. Inventory
14. Interest Receivable
15. Notes Payable
16. Equipment
17. Office Supplies
18. Utilities Expense
19. Interest Payable
20. Rent Expense

E 3-27
LO2
Normal Account Balances

For each account listed in E 3-26, indicate whether it would normally have a debit (DR) balance or a credit (CR) balance.

E 3-28
LO2
Relationships of the Expanded Accounting Equation

Skibbe, Inc., had the following information reported. From these data, determine the amount of:

1. Capital stock at December 31, 2008.
2. Retained earnings at December 31, 2009.
3. Revenues for the year 2009.

	December 31, 2008	December 31, 2009
Total assets	$125,000	$150,000
Total liabilities	30,000	35,000
Capital stock	?	25,000
Retained earnings	75,000	?
Revenues for 2009		?
Expenses for 2009		102,500
Dividends paid during 2009		2,500

E 3-29
LO3
Journalizing Transactions

Record each of the following transactions in Raintree's general journal. (Omit explanations.)

1. Issued capital stock for $90,000 cash.
2. Borrowed $45,000 from a bank. Signed a note to secure the debt.
3. Paid salaries and rent of $53,000 and $4,100, respectively.
4. Purchased inventory from a supplier on credit for $6,300.
5. Paid the supplier for the inventory purchased in (4) above.
6. Sold inventory that cost $1,350 for $2,400 on credit.
7. Collected $2,400 from customers on transaction (6) above.

E 3-30
LO3
Journalizing Transactions

Silva Company had the following transactions:

1. Purchased a new building, paying $20,000 cash and issuing a note for $50,000.
2. Purchased $15,000 of inventory on account.
3. Sold inventory costing $5,000 for $6,000 on account.
4. Paid for inventory purchased on account (item 2).
5. Issued capital stock for $25,000.

(continued)

6. Collected $4,500 of accounts receivable.
7. Paid utility bills totaling $360.
8. Sold old building for $27,000, receiving $10,000 cash and a $17,000 note (no gain or loss on the sale).
9. Paid $2,000 cash dividends to stockholders.

Record the above transactions in general journal format. (Omit explanations.)

E 3-31

LO3

Journal Entries

During July 2009, Krogue, Inc., completed the following transactions. Prepare the journal entry for each transaction.

July	2	Received $320,000 for 80,000 shares of capital stock.
	4	Purchased $90,000 of equipment, with 75% down and 25% on a note payable.
	5	Paid utilities of $2,300 in cash.
	9	Sold equipment for $15,000 cash (no gain or loss).
	13	Purchased $250,000 of inventory, paying 40% down and 60% on credit.
	14	Paid $6,000 cash insurance premium for July.
	18	Sold inventory costing $62,000 for $81,000 to customers on account to be paid at a later date.
	20	Collected $7,500 from accounts receivable.
	24	Sold inventory costing $32,000 for $43,000 to customers for cash.
	27	Paid property taxes of $1,200.
	30	Paid $150,000 of accounts payable for inventory purchased on July 13.

E 3-32

LO3

Challenging Journal Entries

The accountant for Han Company is considering how to journalize the following transactions:

a. The employees of Han Company earned $105,000. The employees received $90,000 in cash and were promised that they will receive the remaining $15,000 as a pension payment on the date that they retire.
b. On August 1, 2009, Han Company paid $1,800 cash for one year of rent on a building it is using. This one year of rent is scheduled to be in effect for the 12 months starting on August 1, 2009.

1. What journal entry should be made on the books of Han Company to record the employee compensation information in (a)?
2. Describe any assumptions necessary in making the employee compensation journal entry in (1).
3. Make the necessary journal entry on Han Company's books on August 1 to record the payment for the building rent described in (b).
4. Consider the journal entry made in (3). Is any adjustment to Han's books necessary as of December 31, 2009, as a consequence of the rent journal entry made on August 1?

E 3-33

LO3

Journal Entries

The following transactions are for the Pickard Construction Company:

a. The firm bought equipment for $64,000 on credit.
b. The firm purchased land for $450,000, $160,000 of which was paid in cash and a note payable signed for the balance.

(continued)

c.   The firm paid $41,000 it owed to its suppliers.

d.   The firm arranged for a $225,000 line of credit (the right to borrow funds as needed) from the bank. No funds have yet been borrowed.

e.   The firm sold some of its products for $34,000—$18,000 for cash, the remainder on account.

f.   Cost of sales in (e) are $22,000.

g.   The firm borrowed $84,000 on its line of credit.

h.   The firm paid a $10,000 cash dividend to its stockholders.

i.   An investor invested an additional $60,000 in the company in exchange for additional capital stock.

j.   One of the primary investors borrowed $90,000 from a bank. The loan is a personal loan.

k.   The firm repaid $16,000 of its line of credit.

l.   The firm received a $1,000 deposit from a customer for a product to be sold and delivered to that customer next month.

Analyze and record the transactions as journal entries. (Omit explanations.)

E 3-34   **Analysis of Journal Entries**

LO3   The following journal entries are from the books of Kara Elizabeth Company:

a.	Buildings	90,000	
	Cash		35,000
	Mortgage Payable		55,000
b.	Cash	25,000	
	Capital Stock		25,000
c.	Cash	40,000	
	Loan Payable		40,000
d.	Salary Expense	12,000	
	Cash		12,000
e.	Inventory	12,500	
	Accounts Payable		12,500
f.	Accounts Receivable	84,000	
	Sales		84,000
	Cost of Goods Sold	51,000	
	Inventory		51,000
g.	Cash	62,000	
	Accounts Receivable		62,000
h.	Accounts Payable	38,000	
	Cash		38,000

For each of the journal entries, prepare an explanation of the business event that is being represented.

E 3-35   **Journal Entry to Correct an Error**

LO3   Legolas Company paid $5,000 cash for executive salaries. When the journal entry to record this $5,000 payment was made, the payment was mistakenly added to the cost of land purchased by Legolas. The $5,000 should have been recorded as salary expense. Make the journal entry necessary to correct this error.

E 3-36

Journalizing and Posting Transactions

LO3, LO4

Given the following T-accounts, describe the transaction that took place on each specified date during July:

Cash			
7/5	9,500	7/1	3,420
7/28	8,000	7/23	2,000
		7/25	5,000
		7/30	5,500
Bal.	1,580		

Accounts Receivable			
7/14	18,000	7/5	9,500
		7/28	8,000
Bal.	500		

Inventory			
7/10	20,000	7/14	15,000
Bal.	5,000		

Equipment			
7/30	1,500		

Land			
7/30	4,000		

Accounts Payable			
7/25	5,000	7/10	20,000
		Bal.	15,000

Sales Revenue		
	7/14	18,000

Cost of Goods Sold		
7/14	15,000	

Rent Expense		
7/23	2,000	

Advertising Expense		
7/1	3,420	

E 3-37

Posting Journal Entries

LO4

Post the journal entries prepared in E 3-31 to T-accounts, and determine the final balance for each account. (Assume all beginning account balances are zero.)

E 3-38

Trial Balance

LO4

The account balances from the ledger of Arigato, Inc., as of July 31, 2009, are listed here in alphabetical order. The balance for Retained Earnings has been omitted. Prepare a trial balance, and insert the missing amount for Retained Earnings.

Accounts Payable	$ 10,300	Land	$31,000
Accounts Receivable	8,100	Miscellaneous Expenses	1,300
Buildings	44,000	Mortgage Payable (due 2012)	32,000
Capital Stock	21,000	Rent Expense	4,300
Cash	19,600	Retained Earnings	?
Equipment	22,000	Salary Expense	11,000
Fees Earned	44,500	Supplies	550
Insurance Expense	5,100	Utilities Expense	1,150

E 3-39

Trial Balance

LO4

Assume you work in the accounting department at Marshall, Inc. Your boss has asked you to prepare a trial balance as of November 30, 2009, using the following account balances from the company's ledger. Prepare the trial balance and insert the missing amount for Cost of Goods Sold.

(continued)

Accounts Payable	$ 55,000	Notes Payable	$250,000
Accounts Receivable	25,000	Notes Receivable	20,000
Advertising Expense	5,000	Other Expenses	1,000
Buildings	150,000	Property Tax Expense	1,500
Capital Stock	173,000	Rent Expense	7,500
Cash	35,000	Retained Earnings	40,000
Cost of Goods Sold	?	Salaries Expense	155,000
Equipment	55,000	Salaries Payable	2,000
Inventory	200,000	Sales Revenue	375,000
Land	125,000	Short-Term Investments	15,000
Mortgage Payable	95,000	Utilities Expense	7,000

PROBLEMS

P 3-40
LO2, LO3

Transaction Analysis and Journal Entries

Browne Motors, Inc., entered into the following transactions during the month of June:

a. Purchased a total of eight new cars and trucks from Jerry's Motors, Inc., for a total of $105,600, one-half of which was paid in cash. The balance is due within 45 days. The total cost of the vehicles to Jerry's Motors was $91,000.

b. Purchased $3,300 of supplies on account from White Supply Company. The cost of the supplies to White Supply Company was $2,400.

c. Paid $720 to Mountain Electric for the monthly utility bill.

d. Sold a truck to Dave's Delivery, Inc. A $2,800 down payment was received with the balance of $14,500 due within 30 days. The cost of the delivery truck to Browne Motors was $13,200.

e. Paid $4,950 to Steve's Automotive for repair work on cars for the current month.

f. Sold one of the new cars purchased from Jerry's Motors to the town mayor, Rachel Mecham. The sales price was $16,250, and was paid by Mecham upon delivery of the car. The cost of the particular car sold to Mecham was $11,800.

g. Borrowed $25,000 from a local bank to be repaid in one year with 12% interest.

Required:

1. For each of the transactions, make the proper journal entry on the books of Browne Motors. (Omit explanations.)

2. For each of the transactions, make the proper journal entry on the books of the other party to the transaction, for example, (a) Jerry's Motors, Inc., (b) White Supply Company. (Omit explanations.)

3. **Interpretive Question:** Why do some of the journal entries for Browne Motors and other companies involved appear to be "mirror images" of each other?

P 3-41
LO3, LO4

Journal Entries and Trial Balance

As of January 1, 2009, Gammon Corporation had the following balances in its general ledger:

	Debits	Credits
Cash	$ 63,000	
Accounts Receivable	47,000	
Inventory	184,000	
Office Building	416,000	
Accounts Payable		$ 33,000
Mortgage Payable		360,000
Notes Payable		137,000
Capital Stock		115,000
Retained Earnings		65,000
Totals	$710,000	$710,000

(continued)

Gammon had the following transactions during 2009. All expenses were paid in cash, unless otherwise stated.

a. Collected $42,000 of receivables.

b. Accounts Payable as of January 1, 2009, were paid off.

c. Purchased inventory for $70,000 cash.

d. Paid utilities of $12,600.

e. Sold $370,000 of merchandise, 90% for cash and 10% for credit. The Cost of Goods Sold was $197,000.

f. Paid $50,000 mortgage payment, of which $30,000 represents interest expense.

g. Paid salaries expense of $120,000.

h. Paid installment of $10,000 on note.

Required:

1. Prepare journal entries to record each listed transaction. (Omit explanations.)

2. Set up T-accounts with the proper account balances at January 1, 2009, post the journal entries to the T-accounts, and prepare a trial balance for Gammon Corporation at December 31, 2009.

3. **Interpretive Question:** If the debit and credit columns of the trial balance are in balance, does this mean that no errors have been made in journalizing the transactions? Explain.

P 3-42

LO3, LO4

Journalizing and Posting

Assume you are interviewing for a part-time accounting job at Spilker & Associates, Inc., and the interviewer gives you the following list of company transactions in September 2009.

Sept. 1	Received $150,000 for capital stock issued.
2	Paid $20,000 cash to employees for wages earned in September 2009.
4	Purchased $75,000 of running shoes and clothing on account for resale.
5	Paid utilities of $1,800 for September 2009.
9	Paid $1,500 cash for September's insurance premium.
11	Sold inventory of running shoes and clothing costing $35,000 for $70,000, with $20,000 received in cash and the remaining balance on credit.
15	Purchased $2,500 of supplies on account.
21	Received $25,000 from customers as payments on their accounts.
25	Paid $75,000 of accounts payable.

Using this list, you have been asked to do the following in the interview:

Required:

1. Journalize each of the transactions for September. (Omit explanations.)

2. Set up T-accounts, and post each of the journal entries made in (1).

3. **Interpretive Question:** If the business owners wanted to know at any given time how much cash the company had, where would you tell the owners to look? Why?

P 3-43

LO3, LO4

Journal Entries from Ledger Analysis

T-accounts for JCB Industries, Inc., are shown below.

	Cash				Accounts Receivable				Inventory		
(a)	140,000	(b)	70,000	(e)	35,000	(i)	22,000	(d)	43,000	(e)	25,000
(c)	60,000	(d)	8,000								
(e)	35,000	(f)	18,000								
(i)	22,000	(g)	63,000								
		(h)	35,000								

(continued)

Building	
(b) 210,000	

Accounts Payable	
(h) 35,000	(d) 35,000

Mortgage Payable	
	(b) 140,000

Notes Payable	
(g) 60,000	(c) 60,000

Capital Stock	
	(a) 140,000

Sales Revenue	
	(e) 70,000

Cost of Goods Sold	
(e) 25,000	

Interest Expense	
(g) 3,000	

Wages Expense	
(f) 18,000	

Required:
1. Analyze these accounts and detail the appropriate journal entries that must have been made by JCB Industries, Inc. (Omit explanations.)
2. Determine the amount of net income/loss from the account information.

P 3-44
LO3, LO4

Journalizing and Posting Transactions

Anna Regina, owner of Anna's Beauty Supply, completed the following business transactions during March 2009.

Mar. 1	Purchased $26,500 of inventory on credit.
4	Collected $2,500 from customers as payments on their accounts.
5	Purchased equipment for $1,500 cash.
6	Sold inventory that cost $15,000 to customers on account for $20,000.
10	Paid rent for March, $525.
15	Paid utilities for March, $50.
17	Paid a $150 monthly salary to the part-time helper.
20	Collected $16,500 from customers as payments on their accounts.
25	Paid property taxes for March of $600.
26	Sold inventory that cost $10,000 to customers for $15,000 cash.
28	Paid $26,500 cash on account payable. (See March 1 entry.)

Required:
1. For each transaction, give the entry to record it in the company's general journal. (Omit explanations.)
2. Set up T-accounts, and post the journal entries to their appropriate accounts.

P 3-45
LO3, LO4

Unifying Concepts: Compound Journal Entries, Posting, Trial Balance

Shaw Mercantile Company had the following transactions during 2009.

a. Jon Shaw began business by investing the following assets, receiving capital stock in exchange:

Cash	$ 30,000
Inventory	34,000
Land	20,000
Building	165,000
Equipment	13,500*
Totals	$262,500

*A note of $6,000 on the equipment was assumed by the company.

(continued)

b. Sold merchandise that cost $32,000 for $52,000; $20,000 cash was received immediately, and the other $32,000 will be collected in 30 days.

c. Paid off the note of $6,000 plus $500 interest.

d. Purchased merchandise costing $14,000, paying $6,000 cash and issuing a note for $8,000.

e. Exchanged $6,000 cash and $6,000 in capital stock for office equipment costing $12,000.

f. Purchased a truck for $25,000 with $5,000 down and a one-year note for the balance.

Required:

1. Journalize the transactions. (Omit explanations.)
2. Post the journal entries using T-accounts for each account.
3. Prepare a trial balance at December 31, 2009.

P 3-46

LO3, LO4

Unifying Concepts: Journal Entries, T-Accounts, Trial Balance

Jethro Company, a retailer, had the following account balances as of April 30, 2009:

Cash	$ 5,050	
Accounts Receivable	2,450	
Inventory	8,000	
Land	13,000	
Building	12,000	
Furniture	2,000	
Notes Payable		$12,500
Accounts Payable		6,000
Capital Stock		15,000
Retained Earnings		9,000
Totals	$42,500	$42,500

During May, the company completed the following transactions.

May 3 Paid one-half of 4/30/09 accounts payable.

4 Purchased inventory on account, $5,000.

6 Collected all of 4/30/09 accounts receivable.

7 Sold inventory costing $3,850 for $3,000 cash and $2,000 on account.

8 Sold one-half of the land for $6,500, receiving $4,000 cash plus a note for $2,500.

15 Paid installment of $2,500 on notes payable (entire amount reduces the liability account).

21 Issued additional capital stock for $1,000 cash.

23 Sold inventory costing $2,000 for $3,750 cash.

25 Paid salaries of $1,000.

26 Paid rent of $250.

29 Purchased desk for $250 cash.

Required:

1. Prepare the journal entry for each transaction.
2. Set up T-accounts with the proper account balances at April 30, 2009, and post the entries to the T-accounts.
3. Prepare a trial balance as of May 31, 2009.

P 3-47

LO3, LO4

Unifying Concepts: First Steps in the Accounting Cycle

The following balances were taken from the general ledger of Holland Company on January 1, 2009:

(continued)

	Debits	Credits
Cash	$14,500	
Short-Term Investments	9,000	
Accounts Receivable	17,500	
Inventory	22,000	
Land	30,000	
Buildings	70,000	
Equipment	15,000	
Notes Payable		$15,500
Accounts Payable		19,500
Salaries and Wages Payable		7,500
Mortgage Payable		32,500
Capital Stock (7,000 shares outstanding)		70,000
Retained Earnings		33,000

During 2009, the company completed the following transactions:

a. Purchased inventory for $95,000 on credit.

b. Issued an additional $40,000 of capital stock (4,000 shares) for cash.

c. Paid property taxes of $5,200 for the year 2009.

d. Paid advertising and other selling expenses of $6,500.

e. Paid utilities expense of $4,800 for 2009.

f. Paid the salaries and wages owed for 2008. Paid additional salaries and wages of $23,000 during 2009.

g. Sold merchandise costing $111,000 for $167,000. Of total sales, $38,000 were cash sales and $129,000 were credit sales.

h. Paid off notes of $15,500 plus interest of $1,200.

i. On November 1, 2009, received a loan of $15,000 from the bank.

j. On December 30, 2009, made annual mortgage payment of $3,300 and paid interest of $700.

k. Collected receivables for the year of $132,000.

l. Paid off accounts payable of $110,500.

m. Received dividends and interest of $1,100 on short-term investments during 2009. (Record as Miscellaneous Revenue.)

n. Purchased additional short-term investments of $12,000 during 2009. (*Note:* Short-term investments are current assets.)

o. Paid 2009 corporate income taxes of $6,300.

p. Paid cash dividends of $6,100.

Required:

1. Journalize the 2009 transactions. (Omit explanations.)

2. Set up T-accounts with the proper account balances at January 1, 2009, and post the journal entries to the T-accounts.

3. Determine the account balances, and prepare a trial balance at December 31, 2009.

4. Prepare an income statement and a balance sheet. (Remember that the dividends account and all revenue and expense accounts are temporary retained earnings accounts.)

5. **Interpretive Question**: Why are revenue and expense accounts used at all?

P 3-48   **Unifying Concepts: T-Accounts, Trial Balance, and Income Statement**

LO2, LO4   The following list is a selection of transactions from Trafalga, Inc.'s business activities during 2009, the first year of operations.

a. Received $50,000 cash for capital stock.

b. Paid $5,000 cash for equipment.

(continued)

c. Purchased inventory costing $18,000 on account.

d. Sold $25,000 of merchandise to customers on account. Cost of goods sold was $15,000.

e. Signed a note with a bank for a $10,000 loan.

f. Collected $9,500 cash from customers who had purchased merchandise on account.

g. Purchased land, $10,000, and a building, $60,000, for $15,000 cash and a 30-year mortgage of $55,000.

h. Made a first payment of $2,750 on the mortgage principal plus $2,750 in interest.

i. Paid $12,000 of accounts payable.

j. Purchased $1,500 of supplies on account.

k. Paid $2,500 of accounts payable.

l. Paid $7,500 in wages earned during the year.

m. Received $10,000 cash and $3,000 of notes in settlement of customers' accounts.

n. Received $3,250 in payment of a note receivable of $3,000 plus interest of $250.

o. Paid $600 cash for a utility bill.

p. Sold excess land for its cost of $3,000.

q. Received $1,500 in rent for an unused part of a building.

r. Paid off $10,000 note, plus interest of $1,200.

Required:

1. Set up T-accounts, and appropriately record the debits and credits for each transaction directly in the T-accounts. Leave room for a number of entries in the cash account.

2. Prepare a trial balance.

3. Prepare an income statement for the period. (Ignore income taxes and the EPS computation.)

P 3-49
LO4

Correcting a Trial Balance

The following trial balance was prepared by a new employee.

Trial Balance
Jeppson Company, Inc.
For the Year Ended November 30, 2009

	Credits	Debits
Cash	$ 19,000	
Mortgage Payable		$ 75,200
Advertising Expense	9,600	
Capital Stock	110,000	
Equipment		36,900
Notes Payable		197,350
Inventory		142,000
Wages Expense	87,900	
Notes Receivable		12,000
Accounts Payable		23,450
Accounts Receivable	5,300	
Rent Expense		8,750
Wages Payable	12,000	
Furniture		18,000
Other Expenses	1,950	
Sales Revenue	225,600	
Buildings	110,700	
Cost of Goods Sold		113,650
Property Tax Expense		1,300
Land		95,850
Retained Earnings		21,400
Utilities Expense	2,100	
Totals	$584,150	$745,850

(continued)

Required:

Prepare the corrected company trial balance. (Assume all accounts have "normal" balances and the recorded amounts are correct.)

ANALYTICAL ASSIGNMENTS

AA 3-50
DISCUSSION

How Does Wal-Mart (and Other Companies) Do It?

Wal-Mart's revenues exceeded $312 billion in 2005. These revenues were generated by millions of transactions all over the world: in the United States, Canada, Europe, South America, and Asia. What is the process used by Wal-Mart to transform this tremendous amount of transaction data into summarized information reported to the general public in the form of financial statements?

AA 3-51
DISCUSSION

Advantages and Disadvantages of a Computerized Accounting System

Your soon-to-be father-in-law owns a small retail store. He has manually kept his business accounting records for over 20 years, but he is currently thinking about switching to a computerized accounting system. What advice would you give him about the advantages and the disadvantages of using a computerized accounting system?

AA 3-52
DISCUSSION

When Is a Debit a Debit?

Your new roommate, Susan, is confused. She has just received a notice from her bank indicating that her account has been debited for the cost of new checks. This has reduced her cash account. Susan just learned in her introductory accounting class that debiting Cash increases the account. She wonders why the bank has reduced her account by debiting it. How can you help Susan understand this situation?

AA 3-53
DISCUSSION

Understanding the Mechanics of Accounting

As the CFO (chief financial officer) of Rollins Engineering Company, you are looking for someone to fill the position of office manager. Part of the job description is to maintain the company's accounting records. This means that the office manager must be able to journalize transactions, post them to the ledger accounts, and prepare monthly trial balances. You have just interviewed the first applicant, Jay McMahon, who claims that he has studied accounting. As an initial check on his understanding of the basic mechanics of accounting, you give Jay a list of accounts randomly ordered and with assumed balances and ask him to prepare a trial balance. Jay prepares the following.

Trial Balance		
	Debits	**Credits**
Accounts Payable		$ 4,500
Salaries Expense		175,000
Consulting Revenues	$269,000	
Cash	82,100	
Utilities Expense	12,000	
Accounts Receivable		44,000
Supplies	11,000	
Rent Expense	30,000	
Capital Stock		77,000
Supplies Expense	33,000	
Office Equipment	15,000	
Retained Earnings		24,000
Other Expenses	6,400	
Salaries Payable	34,000	
Totals	$492,500	$324,500

(continued)

Based solely on your assessment of Jay McMahon's understanding of accounting, would you hire him as office manager? Explain. Prepare a corrected trial balance that you can use as a basis for your discussion with Jay and future applicants. Explain how the basic accounting equation and the system of double-entry accounting provide a check on the accounting records.

AA 3-54
DISCUSSION

Exercising Accounting Judgment

You have recently started business as an accounting consultant. Companies come to you when they face difficult decisions about how to make certain journal entries. You are currently working on the following two problems, which are independent of one another.

a. Baggins Company sells hamburgers for $1.00 each. The cost of the materials used to make each hamburger is 30 cents. Baggins has a compensation plan in which its employees are paid in the form of cash and hamburgers. During 2009, Baggins paid cash salaries of $500,000 and also issued certificates to employees entitling them to 200,000 free hamburgers. The certificates are not redeemable until 2010. What journal entry or entries should Baggins make in 2009 to record this employee compensation information?

b. Radagast Company purchased a building for $100,000 cash on January 1, 2009. Because of poor business decisions, as of December 31, 2009, the building is worthless. Make all journal entries necessary in 2009 in connection with this building.

AA 3-55
JUDGMENT CALL

You Decide: **Is understanding the accounting cycle essential to being a good accountant, or is it a waste of time?**

John, a family friend who didn't go to college, was talking to you about his job, as bookkeeper, at a local bookstore. "It is no longer necessary to learn the accounting cycle to be a good accountant," he said. "Computers do most of the work anyway. Unless you work in a small family-owned business, it doesn't make any sense to learn the correct method for posting debits and credits. If you just understand the financial statements, you will be ok!" Do you agree or disagree? Explain.

AA 3-56
JUDGMENT CALL

You Decide: **If you major in accounting, will you enjoy a rewarding career, or will the field be extinct in 20 years?**

I thought an accounting degree would give me the solid, fundamental understanding of business I was looking for but some of my friends seem to think that accountants won't have jobs a few years from now. They argue that as computers become smarter and more powerful, they will develop enough capacities to make good business decisions. They say I am making a mistake by majoring in a field that will not be around in 20 years. What do you think?

AA 3-57
REAL COMPANY
ANALYSIS

Wal-Mart

The 2006 Form 10-K for **Wal-Mart** is included in Appendix A. Locate that Form 10-K and consider the following questions:

1. Find Wal-Mart's 2006 income statement. Assume that operating, selling, general, and administrative expenses were paid in cash. What journal entry did Wal-Mart make in 2006 to record these expenses?

2. Find Wal-Mart's 2006 cash flow statement. What journal entry did Wal-Mart make in 2006 to record the issuance of long-term debt?

3. Again, looking at the cash flow statement, what journal entry did Wal-Mart make in 2006 to record the purchase of property and equipment?

AA 3-58
REAL COMPANY
ANALYSIS

McDonald's

A brief history of the origin of the **McDonald's Corporation** is given at the start of this chapter. The following questions are adapted from information appearing in McDonald's 2005 annual report.

1. In 2005, total sales at all McDonald's stores worldwide were $54.3 billion. There were 31,886 McDonald's stores operating in 2005. Estimate how many customers per day visit an average McDonald's store.

2. For the stores owned by the McDonald's Corporation (as opposed to those owned by franchisees), total sales in 2005 were $15.4 billion, and total cost of food and packaging

(continued)

was $5.207 billion. What journal entries would McDonald's make to record a $10 sale and to record the cost of food and packaging associated with the $10 sale?

3. McDonald's reported payment of cash dividends of $842.0 million in 2005. What journal entry was required?

4. McDonald's reported that the total income tax it owed for 2005 was $1,137.7 million. However, only $795.1 million in cash was paid for taxes during the year. What compound journal entry did McDonald's make to record its income tax expense for the year?

AA 3-59
INTERNATIONAL

Shanghai Petrochemical Company Limited

In July 1993, **Shanghai Petrochemical Company Limited** became the first company organized under the laws of the People's Republic of China to publicly issue its shares on the worldwide market. Shanghai Petrochemical's shares now trade on the stock exchanges in Shanghai, Hong Kong, and New York. The following questions are adapted from information appearing in Shanghai Petrochemical's 1995 annual report.

1. In 1995, Shanghai Petrochemical reported sales of 11.835 billion renminbi (US$ 1 = 8.33 RMB) and cost of sales of RMB 9.016 billion. Make the necessary journal entries, using renminbi as the currency.

2. In 1995, Shanghai Petrochemical declared cash dividends of RMB 851.5 million. However, cash paid for dividends during the year was only RMB 818.8 million. Make the necessary compound journal entry to record the declaration and payment of cash dividends for the year.

3. In China, a 17% value added tax (VAT) is added to the invoiced value of all sales. This VAT is collected by the seller from the buyer and then held to be forwarded to the government. What journal entry would Shanghai Petrochemical make to record the sale, on account, of crude oil with an invoice sales value of $100 and a cost of $70?

AA 3-60
ETHICS

Should You Go the Extra Mile?

You work in a small convenience store. The store is very low-tech; you ring up the sales on an old-style cash register that merely records the amount of the sale. The store owner uses this cash register tape at the end of each day to verify that the correct amount of cash is in the cash register drawer. On a day-to-day basis, no other financial information is collected about store operations.

Since you started studying accounting, you have become a bit uneasy about your job because you see many ways that store operations could be improved through the gathering and use of financial information. Even though you are not an expert, you are quite certain that you could help the store owner set up an improved information system. However, you also know that this will take extra effort on your part, with no real possibility of receiving an increase in pay.

Should you say anything to the store owner, or should you just keep quiet and save yourself the trouble?

AA 3-61
WRITING

Accounting Is Everywhere!

Financial accounting information is frequently used in newspaper and magazine articles to provide background data on companies. Prepare a one-page report on the use of financial accounting data by the press. Proceed as follows:

1. Scan the articles in a recent copy of one of the popular business periodicals (such as *The Wall Street Journal*, *Forbes*, *Fortune*, or *Business Week*) for examples of the use of financial accounting data.

2. Identify and describe three interesting examples:
   - Detail the nature of the accounting data used.
   - Outline the point that the writer is trying to make by using the particular accounting data.

AA 3-62
CUMULATIVE
SPREADSHEET
PROJECT

Analyzing Transactions

This spreadsheet assignment is a continuation of the spreadsheet assignment given in Chapter 2. If you completed that spreadsheet, you have a head start on this one.

   Determine the impact of each of the following transactions on total assets, total liabilities, and total owners' equity. Treat each transaction independently, meaning that before determining the impact of each new transaction, you should reset the financial statement values to their original amounts. Each of the hypothetical transactions is assumed to occur on the last day of the year.

a. Collected $20 cash from customer receivables.

b. Purchased $30 in inventory on account.

c. Purchased $100 in property, plant, and equipment. The entire amount of the purchase was financed with a mortgage. Principal repayment for the mortgage is due in 10 years.

d. Purchased $100 in property, plant, and equipment. The entire amount of the purchase was financed with new stockholder investment.

e. Borrowed $20 with a short-term loan payable. The $20 was paid out as a dividend to stockholders.

f. Received $20 as an investment from stockholders. The $20 was paid out as a dividend to stockholders.

Completing the Accounting Cycle

After studying this chapter, you should be able to:

LEARNING OBJECTIVES

(1) **Describe how accrual accounting allows for timely reporting and a better measure of a company's economic performance.** *Proper accrual accounting involves recording the profits from a company's business activities when those activities occur which does not necessarily match up with when cash is collected or paid.*

(2) **Explain the need for adjusting entries and make adjusting entries for unrecorded receivables, unrecorded liabilities, prepaid expenses, and unearned revenues.** *Some economic activities, such as the growth in the amount of interest a company owes, happen gradually. Without special adjustments, the accounting records would not reflect the impact of these gradual activities. Adjusting entries must be made at the end of each accounting period to ensure that all balance sheet and income statement items are stated at the correct amount.*

(3) **Explain the preparation of the financial statements, the explanatory notes, and the audit report.** *After all transactions are recorded and posted and the necessary adjusting entries are made, the account balances in the trial balance accurately reflect the company's economic circumstances and performance. The account balances are the raw material used to prepare the financial statements; for some companies, including all public companies, these balances are checked by an independent auditor.*

(4) **Complete the closing process in the accounting cycle.** *Closing entries are used to transfer revenue, expense, and dividend data to the retained earnings account so that the transactions of a new period can be recorded.*

(5) **Understand how all the steps in the accounting cycle fit together.** *To review, transactions are first analyzed and then recorded in debit-and-credit format. Journal entries are posted to individual accounts. Before financial statements are prepared, adjusting entries are made to ensure that all amounts are correct. The books are then closed.*

General Motors, the brainchild of William Durant, was formed through the acquisition of a number of preexisting car makers. **Buick** and **Oldsmobile** were acquired in 1908; **Cadillac** and **Pontiac** (originally called **Oakland**) were added in 1909. With so many acquisitions in those early years, General Motors' financing was quickly depleted, and Durant lost control of his company. With Durant fighting to regain the reins of General Motors, the company was in such turmoil that, at one point, **Chevrolet Motor Company** (another Durant creation) owned a majority of GM stock. After many deals, Durant found himself back in charge in 1916, and Chevrolet became a subsidiary of GM in 1918.

Following the end of World War I, an economic slowdown stretched Durant's financial resources past the breaking point, and in 1920 he lost control of General Motors for good. Under the direction of Alfred P. Sloan, General Motors eventually became the dominant car maker in the world, a position it still holds.

Although General Motors' global market share has declined with stiff competition from Japanese (**Toyota, Honda,** etc.), European (including **DaimlerChrysler**), and domestic (**Ford**) competitors, General Motors still sells more cars and trucks than any other company in the world. In 2005, GM sold 65 million vehicles, nearly 14% of the worldwide total. GM also remains one of the largest private employers in the United States with 325,000 employees at the end of 2005.

But recent stiff competition has resulted in General Motors falling on hard times. In 2005, the company reported a net loss of over $10.5 billion. During the same period it was reporting this huge loss on its income statement, GM reported an even larger negative cash flow from operations on its cash flow statement. In fact, in 2005, GM's negative cash flow from operations was $16.9 billion. In 2004, GM reported net income of $2.8 billion and cash flow from operations of $9.4 billion.

How can a company incur such a large loss on the income statement and an even larger negative cash flow and still stay in business? Why the large discrepancy in 2004 and 2005 between net income (loss) and cash flow from operations? The differences came from business expenses that General Motors incurred but which required no cash or had either paid for in earlier years or would pay for in subsequent years. As an example, consider post-retirement benefits. These benefits are recorded as expenses (a cost of doing business) to the company now as employees work, but General Motors won't actually have to make the cash payments related to these benefits until the employees retire in the future. Proper accounting requires recording now all business expenses—both those that are paid in cash and those that involve promises of payment in the future.

As the General Motors scenario illustrates, adjustments or true-ups (to the original transaction data recorded in the accounts) usually are needed so that the financial statements will accurately reflect a company's economic performance during the period and its economic condition as of the end of the period. This is a part of completing the accounting cycle. In addition to the true-up adjustments, certain accounts must be "closed" (brought to a zero balance) at the end of an accounting period to prepare the records for a new accounting cycle. The nature of year-end adjustments and the remaining steps in the accounting cycle are discussed in this chapter.

Accrual Accounting

Describe how accrual accounting allows for timely reporting and a better measure of a company's economic performance.

1 In 2008, two brothers sign a contract for a consulting project. The total contract price is $20,000. The brothers do most of the consulting work in 2008 and finish the job in 2009. They receive a $2,000 cash payment from the contract in 2008 and receive the remaining $18,000 cash in 2009. On December 31, 2008, the brothers prepare a 2008 income statement to use in applying for a bank loan. What amount of revenue should the brothers report for 2008?

This simple example illustrates why accounting is much more than merely tabulating cash receipts and cash payments. A proper measure of the brothers' economic performance in 2008 requires estimating the amount of the work completed in 2008; to report 2008 revenue as only the $2,000 cash received grossly understates the actual economic output produced during the year. In addition, the need for the year-end income statement means that the brothers can't wait until after the final contract payment is received before preparing a summary of their activities; the bank wants the income statement now.

Accrual accounting is the process of recording expenses and revenues when incurred and earned, regardless of when cash is received and of adjusting original transaction data into refined measures of a firm's past economic performance and current economic condition. As the following sections explain, this accrual process is necessary because a business requires periodic, timely financial reports and accrual information better measures a firm's performance than do cash flow data.

The difficulty in using accrual accounting to generate a performance measure is represented in Exhibit 1. Each horizontal bar in the exhibit represents a business deal such as the production and sale of a car, the delivery of legal services for a specific lawsuit, or the development, delivery, and support of a piece of software. Some deals last less than a day from start to finish, such as when a barber provides a haircut in exchange for cash. The obligations and responsibilities associated with other deals can stretch on for years. For example, when you buy a **General Motors** car, the deal is not done from your standpoint until four or five years later after you have received all of the GM warranty services promised to you. And, from GM's standpoint, the deal is not done until 40 or 50 years later after GM has paid the assembly-line workers all of the pension benefits they earned through the labor hours spent assembling your car. Even though the economic loose ends of some business deals extend for years, financial statement users still require periodic reports about a company's operating performance. As you can see in Exhibit 1, the beginning and the end of a year are arbitrary breaks in the life of an ongoing business. The job of accountants is to consider all business deals that were at least partially completed during a year and to measure the revenues, expenses, and profit associated with those deals. This profit is then reported as net income for the year. As you can see, accrual accounting is much more than mere "bean counting."

Periodic Reporting

All businesses, large or small, periodically issue their financial statements so that users can make sound economic decisions. Current owners, prospective investors, bankers, and others need up-to-date reports in order to compare and judge a company's financial position and operating results on a continuing, timely basis. They need to know the financial position of a company (from the balance sheet), the relative success or failure of

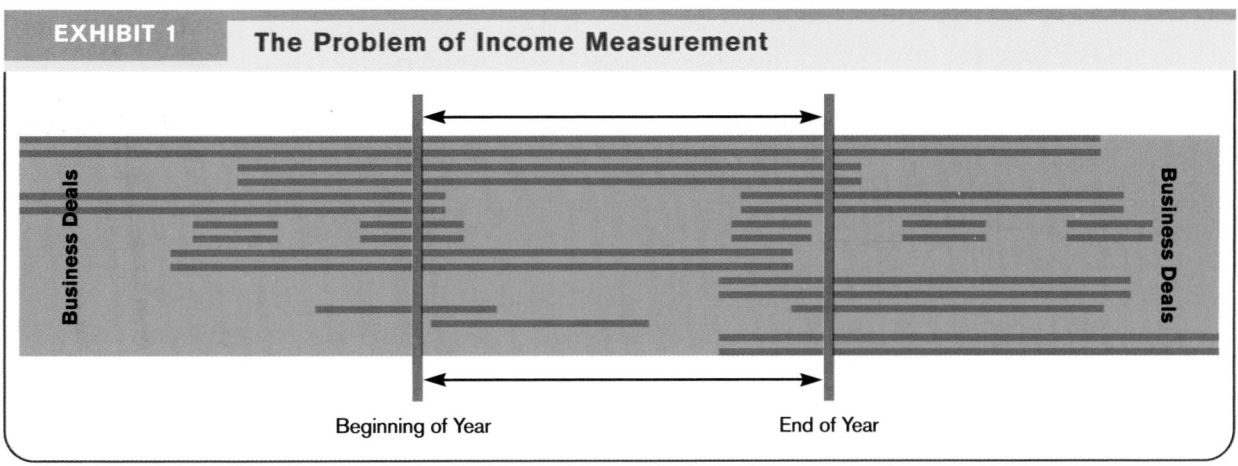

EXHIBIT 1   **The Problem of Income Measurement**

Business Deals

Business Deals

Beginning of Year

End of Year

time-period concept

The idea that the life of a business is divided into distinct and relatively short time periods so that accounting information can be timely.

fiscal year

An entity's reporting year, covering a 12-month accounting period.

calendar year

An entity's reporting year, covering 12 months and ending on December 31.

current operations (from the income statement), and the nature and extent of cash flows (from the statement of cash flows).

The financial picture of a company—its success or failure in meeting its economic objectives—cannot really be complete until the "life" of a business is over. However, managers, owners, and creditors cannot wait 10, 20, or 100 years to receive an exact accounting of a business. In order to provide timely accounting information, the time-period concept divides the life of an enterprise into distinct and relatively short (generally 12 months or less) accounting periods. The 12-month accounting period is referred to as the fiscal year. When an entity closes its books on December 31, its reports are based on a calendar year.

Most large corporations, and even many small companies, issue a report to stockholders as of a fiscal year-end. Also, most corporations prepare reports on a quarterly basis as well. As noted in Chapters 1 and 2, this annual report includes the primary financial statements (balance sheet, income statement, and statement of cash flows) and other financial data, such as a management discussion and analysis of operations.

Although periodic reporting is vital to a firm's success, the frequency of reporting forces accountants to use some data that are based on judgments and estimates. Ideally, accounting judgments are made carefully and estimates are based on reliable evidence, but the limitations of accounting reports should be understood and kept in mind.

> **? F Y I**
>
> About two-thirds of large U.S. companies choose December 31 as the end of their fiscal year.

Accrual- versus Cash-Basis Accounting

Closely related to the time-period concept is the concept of accrual-basis accounting. This important characteristic of the traditional accounting model simply means that—

accrual-basis accounting

A system of accounting in which revenues and expenses are recorded as they are earned and incurred, not necessarily when cash is received or paid.

> revenues are recognized (recorded) when earned without regard for when cash is received; expenses are recorded as incurred without regard for when they are paid. Accrual accounting requires that revenues and expenses be assigned to their proper accounting periods, which do not necessarily coincide with the periods in which cash is received or paid.

> **STOP & THINK**
>
> Since almost all companies have their financial records on computer, what stops them from preparing financial statements every day?

Revenue Recognition   How do we assign revenues to particular periods? First, we must determine when revenues have actually been earned. The revenue recognition principle states that revenues are recorded when two main criteria have been met.

1. The earnings process is substantially complete; generally, a sale has been made or services have been performed.
2. Cash has been collected or collectibility is reasonably assured.

These two criteria ensure that both parties to the transaction have fulfilled their commitment or are formally obligated to do so. In simple terms, satisfying the first criterion demonstrates that the seller has done something; satisfying the second criterion demonstrates that the buyer has done something. The seller generally records sales revenue when goods are shipped or when services are performed. When this occurs, the seller has

revenue recognition principle

The idea that revenues should be recorded when (1) the earnings process has been substantially completed and (2) cash has either been collected or collectibility is reasonably assured.

completed his or her part of the transaction. The seller assumes, when shipment is made or services performed, that the buyer has given a valid promise to pay (if this promise is not implied, then the seller probably will not ship). The promise to pay, or the actual payment, would complete the buyer's part of the transaction. If, for example, General Motors sold and shipped $800 million of cars in 2009, but will not receive the cash proceeds until 2010, the $800 million would still be recognized as revenue in 2009, when it is earned and a promise of payment is received. Both of the revenue recognition principle criteria have been met. On the other hand, if General Motors is paid in 2009 for cars to be shipped in 2010, it would not record those payments as revenues until the cars are actually shipped. Referring back to the example that began this section, the two brothers would recognize as consulting revenue the amount associated with the proportion of the job that was completed in 2008. For example, if an objective estimate indicated that 80% of the consulting project was completed in 2008, then it would be appropriate for the brothers to recognize $16,000 ($20,000 × 0.8) as revenue in 2008—assuming that they felt they had received a valid promise that they would be paid for the consulting work.

F Y I

Determining when to recognize revenues is usually the most difficult accounting decision most companies have to make. And, there have been more financial statement frauds involving improper revenue recognition than any other type of financial statement misstatement.

The Matching Principle Once a company determines which revenues should be recognized during a period, how does it iden-

matching principle

The concept that all costs and expenses incurred in generating revenues must be recognized in the same reporting period as the related revenues.

tify the expenses that have been incurred? The matching principle requires that all costs and expenses incurred to generate revenues must be recognized in the same accounting period as the related revenues. The cost of the merchandise sold, for example, should be matched to the revenue derived from the sale of that merchandise during the period. Expenses that cannot be matched with revenues are assigned to the accounting period in which they are incurred. For example, the exact amount of electricity used to make an automobile generally cannot be determined, but since the amount used for a month or a year is known, that amount can be matched to the revenues earned during the same period.

As shown in Exhibit 2, this process of matching expenses with recognized revenues determines the amount of net income reported on the income statement. Net income is the most widely used indicator of how well a company has performed during a period. The subject of income determination, including revenue recognition and expense matching, is discussed more completely in Chapters 6, 7, and 8.

To illustrate the difference between cash- and accrual-basis accounting, and to demonstrate why accrual-basis accounting provides a more meaningful measure of income, assume that during 2009, Karas Brothers billed clients $50,500 for consulting

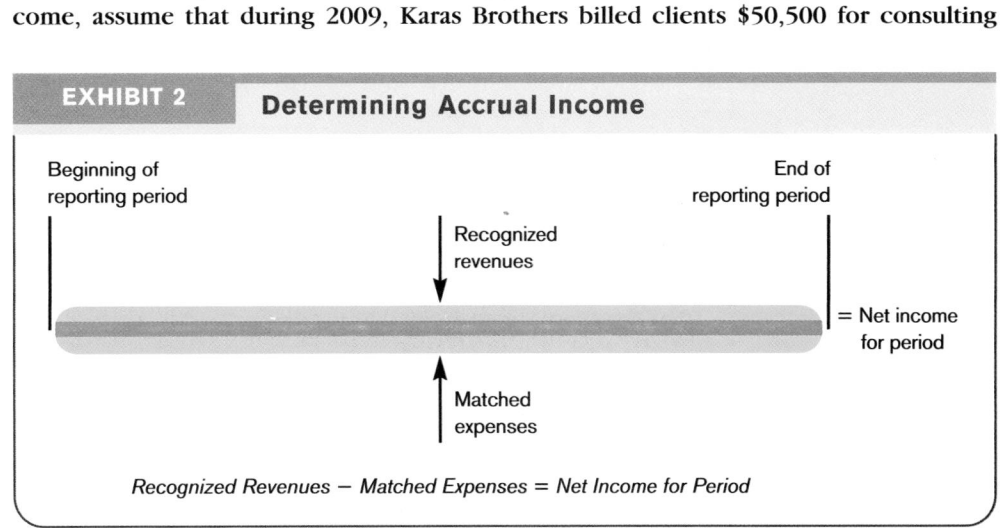

EXHIBIT 2 **Determining Accrual Income**

Beginning of reporting period

End of reporting period

Recognized revenues

= Net income for period

Matched expenses

Recognized Revenues − Matched Expenses = Net Income for Period

services performed in 2009. By December 31, Karas had received $22,000 in cash from customers, with the $28,500 balance expected in 2010. During 2009, Karas paid $21,900 for various expenses that had been incurred. At December 31, 2009, Karas still owed $11,200 for additional expenses incurred. These expenses will be paid during January 2010. How much income should Karas Brothers report for 2009? The answer depends on whether cash-basis or accrual-basis accounting is used. As shown below, with cash-basis accounting, reported income would be $100. With accrual-basis accounting, reported income would be $17,400.

Karas Brothers
Reported Income for 2009

Cash-Basis Accounting		Accrual-Basis Accounting	
Cash receipts	$22,000	Revenues earned	$50,500
Cash disbursements	21,900	Expenses incurred	33,100
Income	$ 100	Income	$17,400

cash-basis accounting

A system of accounting in which transactions are recorded and revenues and expenses are recognized only when cash is received or paid.

How do we explain this $17,300 difference? Under **cash-basis accounting**, Karas Brothers would report only $22,000 in revenue, the total amount of cash received during 2009. Similarly, the company would report only $21,900 of expenses (the amount actually paid) during 2009. The additional $11,200 of expenses incurred but not yet paid would not be reported. Using accrual-basis accounting, however, Karas earned $50,500 in revenues, which is the total increase in resources for the period (an increase of $22,000 in cash plus $28,500 in receivables). Similarly, Karas incurred a total of $33,100 in expenses, which should be matched with revenues earned to produce a realistic income measurement. The combined result of increasing revenues by $28,500 while increasing expenses by only $11,200 creates the $17,300 difference in net income ($28,500 − $11,200 = $17,300).

 CAUTION

Although accrual-basis net income is the measure of Karas Brothers' economic performance for the year, the cash flow information is useful in evaluating the need to obtain short-term loans, the ability to repay existing loans, and the like. The statement of cash flows is an essential companion to the accrual-basis income statement.

As this example shows, accrual-basis accounting provides a more accurate picture of a company's profitability. It matches earned revenues with the expenses incurred to generate those revenues. This helps investors, creditors, and others to better assess the operating results of a company and make more informed judgments concerning its profitability and earnings potential. Accrual-basis accounting is required by generally accepted accounting principles (GAAP).

REMEMBER THIS...

- Accrual accounting is the process of recording expenses and revenues when incurred and earned, regardless of when cash is received. Accrual accounting is required by GAAP because it provides a better measure of performance than does cash-basis accounting.
- The revenue recognition principle states that revenue is reported when the work is done which is often not the same time period as when the cash is collected.
- The matching principle states that expenses are reported when the corresponding asset or service is used which is often not the same time period as when cash is paid.

Adjusting Entries

Explain the need for adjusting entries and make adjusting entries for unrecorded receivables, unrecorded liabilities, prepaid expenses, and unearned revenues.

② As discussed in Chapter 3, transactions generally are recorded in a journal in chronological order and then posted to the ledger accounts. The entries are based on the best information available at the time. Although the majority of accounts are up-to-date at the end of an accounting period and their balances can be included in the financial statements, some accounts require adjustment to reflect current circumstances. In general, these accounts are not updated throughout the period because it is impractical or inconvenient to make such entries on a daily or weekly basis. At the end of each accounting period, in order to report all asset, liability, and owners' equity amounts properly and to recognize all revenues and expenses for the period on an accrual basis, accountants are required to make any necessary adjustments prior to preparing the financial statements. The entries that reflect these adjustments are called **adjusting entries**. It is important to note that adjusting entries are not made based on transactions; rather, they are the entries needed after careful analysis of revenues earned and expenses incurred.

adjusting entries

Entries required at the end of each accounting period to recognize, on an accrual basis, revenues and expenses for the period and to report proper amounts for asset, liability, and owners' equity accounts.

One difficulty with adjusting entries is that the need for an adjustment is not signaled by a specific event such as the receipt of a bill or the receipt of cash from a customer. Rather, adjusting entries are recorded on the basis of an analysis of the circumstances at the close of each accounting period.

This analysis involves just two steps:

1. Determine whether the amounts recorded for all assets and liabilities are correct. If not, debit or credit the appropriate asset or liability account. In short, fix the balance sheet.
2. Determine what revenue or expense adjustments are required as a result of the changes in recorded amounts of assets and liabilities indicated in step 1. Debit or credit the appropriate revenue or expense account. In short, fix the income statement.

It should be noted that these two steps are interrelated and may be reversed. That is, revenue and expense adjustments may be considered first to fix the income statement, indicating which asset and liability accounts need adjustment to fix the balance sheet. As you will see, *each adjusting entry involves at least one income statement account and one balance sheet account*. T-accounts are helpful in analyzing adjusting entries and will be used in the illustrations that follow.

The areas most commonly requiring analysis to see whether adjusting entries are needed are:

1. Unrecorded receivables
2. Unrecorded liabilities
3. Prepaid expenses
4. Unearned revenues

As we illustrate and discuss adjusting entries, remember that the basic purpose of adjustments is to make account balances current in order to report all asset, liability, and owners' equity amounts properly and to recognize all revenues and expenses for the period on an accrual basis. This is done so that the income statement and the balance sheet will reflect the proper operating results and financial position, respectively, at the end of the accounting period.

Unrecorded Receivables

In accordance with the revenue recognition principle of accrual accounting, revenues should be recorded when earned, regardless of when the cash is received. If revenue is earned but not yet collected in cash, a receivable exists. To ensure that all receivables are properly reported on the balance sheet in the correct amounts, an analysis should be made at the end of each accounting period to see whether there are any revenues that have been earned but have not yet been collected or recorded. These **unrecorded receivables** are earned and represent amounts that are receivable in the future; therefore, they should be recognized as assets.

unrecorded receivables

Revenues earned during a period that have not been recorded by the end of that period.

To illustrate, we will pick up with the landscaping business we started in Chapter 3. Recall that we mow lawns, pull weeds, plant shrubs, and perform other related services. We are able to provide these services year round because we live in a region with a very mild climate. Our company reports on a calendar-year basis and has determined the following on December 31, 2009:

> On November 1, we entered into a year-long contract with an apartment complex to provide general landscaping services each week and bill the customer every three months. The terms of the contract state that we will earn $400 per month. As of December 31, Lawn Care Revenue of $800 ($400 for November and $400 for December) has not been recorded and will not be billed or received until the end of January 2010. No entry has been made since the end of October with respect to this contract.

As of year-end, no asset has been recorded, but an $800 receivable exists ($400 × 2), because two months' worth of revenue has been earned. To record this receivable, we must debit (increase) the asset Accounts Receivable for $800. With the debit, we have accomplished step 1 by fixing the balance sheet with regard to this transaction. Step 2 requires that we use the other half of the adjusting entry, the credit of $800, to fix the income statement. We know that the credit must be to either a revenue or an expense account, and the nature of the transaction suggests that we should credit Lawn Care Revenue for $800. The adjusting entry is:

Dec. 31	Accounts Receivable....................................	800	
	Lawn Care Revenue...................................		800
	To record two months of earned revenue not yet received.		

Adjusting entries are recorded in the general journal and are posted to the accounts in the general ledger in the same manner as other journal entries. Again note that each adjusting entry must involve at least one balance sheet account and at least one income statement account.

After this adjusting entry has been journalized and posted, the receivable will appear as an asset on the balance sheet, and the lawn care revenue is reported on the income statement. Through the adjusting entry, the asset (receivable) accounts are properly stated and revenues are appropriately reported.

Unrecorded Liabilities

Just as assets are created from revenues being earned before they are collected or recorded, liabilities can be created by expenses being incurred prior to being paid or recorded. These expenses, along with their corresponding liabilities, should be recorded when incurred, no matter when they are paid. Thus, adjusting entries are required at the end of an accounting period to recognize any **unrecorded liabilities** in the proper period and to record the corresponding expenses. As the expense is recorded (increased by a debit), the offsetting liability is also recorded (increased by a credit), showing the entity's obligation to pay for the expense.

unrecorded liabilities

Expenses incurred during a period that have not been recorded by the end of that period.

If such adjustments are not made, the net income measurement for the period will not reflect all appropriate expenses and the corresponding liabilities will be understated on the balance sheet.

To illustrate, we will assume that on December 31, 2009, our landscaping company has determined the following:

1. Your brother has worked for the company since its inception. He is paid every two weeks. The next payday is on Friday, January 5, 2010. On that day, your brother will be paid $700, the amount he earns every two weeks. Since December 31 falls halfway through the pay period, one-half of his wages should be allocated to 2009.

2. Recall from Chapter 3 that one of our options for financing our company was to borrow money from a bank. We borrowed $2,000 with the promise that on the first of every month we would make a $178 payment—a portion of that payment being attributed to interest[1] and a portion to principal. Our next payment is due on January 1, 2010, but the interest expense associated with that payment should be attributed to the period in which the money was actually used—December 2009. Assume that interest of $20 must be recognized on December 31, 2009.

To represent its current financial position and earnings, our landscaping company must record the impact of these events in the accounts, even though cash transactions have not yet occurred. The wages will not be paid until 2010. Under accrual-basis accounting, however, these costs are expenses of 2009 and should be recognized on this year's income statement, with the corresponding liability shown on the balance sheet as of the end of the year. To fix the balance sheet, Wages Payable must be credited (increased) for $350; recognition of this liability ensures that the balance sheet properly reports this liability, which was created during 2009 and exists as of the end of the year. The debit of this adjusting entry is to Wages Expense, resulting in the proper inclusion of this expense in the 2009 income statement. The adjusting journal entry is as follows:

Dec. 31	Wages Expense	350	
	Wages Payable		350
	To record obligation for wages.		

The liability for the interest for the month of December is recorded by a credit (increase) to Interest Payable; this fixes the balance sheet. The debit of the adjusting entry is to Interest Expense, which properly includes this expense on the 2009 income statement. The adjusting entry is:

Dec. 31	Interest Expense	20	
	Interest Payable		20
	To record interest incurred.		

The wages expense and interest expense would be reported on the income statement for the year ended December 31, and the liabilities (wages payable and interest payable) would be reported on the balance sheet as of December 31. Because of the adjusting entries, both the income statement

CAUTION

A liability is not recorded for the total amount of interest that will have to be paid over the entire life of the loan. If we repay the loan on December 31, the future interest will not have to be paid, but the interest for the month of December that has passed will still be due.

---

[1] As noted in Chapter 3, interest is the cost of using money. The amount borrowed or lent is the principal. The interest rate is an annual rate stated as a percentage. The period of time involved may be stated in terms of a year. For example, if interest is to be paid for 3 months, time is 3/12, or 1/4 of a year. If interest is to be paid for 90 days, time is 90/365 of a year. Thus, the formula for computing interest is Interest = Principal × Interest Rate × Time (fraction of a year).

and the balance sheet will more accurately reflect the financial situation of our landscaping company.

Prepaid Expenses

Payments that a company makes in advance for items normally charged to expense are known as **prepaid expenses**. An example would be the payment of an insurance premium for the next 18 months. Theoretically, every resource acquisition is an asset, at least temporarily. Thus, the entry to record an advance payment should be a debit to an asset account (Prepaid Expenses) and a credit to Cash, showing the exchange of cash for another asset.[2]

An expense is the using up of an asset. For example, when supplies are purchased, they are recorded as assets; when they are used, their cost is transferred to an expense account. The purpose of making adjusting entries for prepaid expenses is to show the complete or partial consumption of an asset. If the original entry is to an asset account, the adjusting entry reduces the asset to an amount that reflects its remaining future benefit and at the same time recognizes the actual expense incurred for the period.

> **! CAUTION**
>
> Prepaid Expenses is a tricky name for an asset. Assets are reported in the balance sheet. Don't make the mistake of including Prepaid Expenses with the expenses on the income statement.

For the unrecorded assets and liabilities discussed earlier, there was no original entry; the adjusting entry was the first time these items were recorded in the accounting records. For prepaid expenses, this is not the case. Because cash has already been paid (in the case of prepaid expenses), an original entry has been made to record the cash transaction. Therefore, the amount of the adjusting entry is the difference between what the updated balance should be and the amount of the original entry already recorded.

To illustrate adjustments for Prepaid Expenses, we will assume the following about our landscaping company:

1. On November 1, 2009, we purchased a six-month insurance policy on our old truck, paying a $600 premium.
2. On December 15, 2009, we purchased several months' of supplies (fertilizer, weed killer, etc.) at a total cost of $350. At year-end, $225 worth of supplies were still on hand.

For the prepaid insurance, we record the payment of $600 on November 1 as follows:

Nov. 1	Prepaid Insurance	600	
	Cash		600
	Paid a six-month insurance premium in advance.		

This entry shows that one asset (Cash) has been exchanged for another asset (Prepaid Insurance). Over the next six months we will use the auto insurance and the asset, Prepaid Insurance, will slowly be used up. As the asset is used, its cost is recorded as an expense.

At year-end, only those assets that still offer future benefits to the company should be reported on the balance sheet. Thus, an adjustment is required to reduce the prepaid

---

[2] It is also possible that the initial expenditure could be recorded with a debit to an expense account. This would require a different adjusting entry. This possibility is discussed in the web material associated with the text at **http://www.thomsonedu.com/accounting/albrecht**.

insurance account to reflect the fact that only four months of prepaid insurance remain. See the following time line.

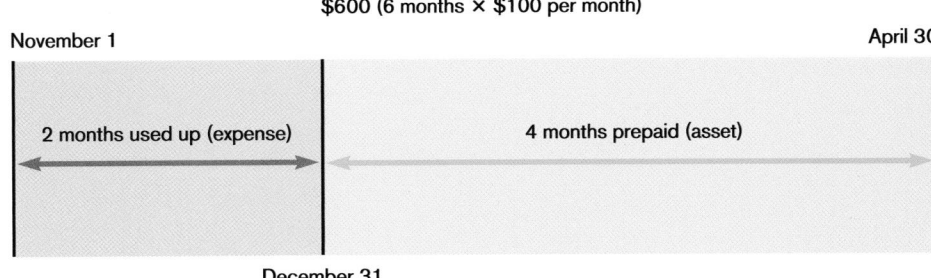

$600 (6 months × $100 per month)

November 1   April 30

2 months used up (expense)   4 months prepaid (asset)

December 31

The adjusting journal entry to bring the original amounts to their updated balances at year-end is:

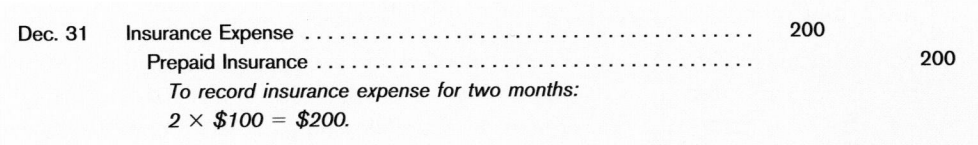

Dec. 31	Insurance Expense	200
	Prepaid Insurance	200
	To record insurance expense for two months:	
	2 × $100 = $200.	

When the adjusting entry is journalized and posted, the proper amount of insurance expense ($200) will be shown as an expense on the income statement and the proper amount of prepaid insurance ($400) will be carried forward to the next period as an asset on the balance sheet. This is illustrated in the following T-accounts:

	Prepaid Insurance		**Cash**		**Insurance Expense**	
Original entry (11/1/09)	600		600			
Adjusting entry (12/31/09)		200			200	
Updated balances (12/31/09)	400				200	
	To balance sheet				To income statement	

CAUTION

The terms *supplies* and *inventory* are often confused. Supplies include such items as paper, pencils, and soap that might be used in an office or a warehouse. Inventory includes only those items held for resale to customers or for direct use in the manufacture of products.

When supplies are consumed in the normal course of business, the asset account (Supplies on Hand) must be adjusted and the used up portion charged as an operating expense (Supplies Expense) on the income statement. Thus, the adjustment for supplies is handled the same way as for any other prepaid asset.

We initially recorded $350 of supplies as an asset:

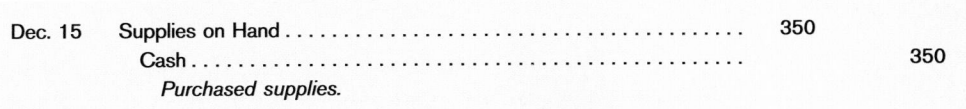

Dec. 15	Supplies on Hand	350
	Cash	350
	Purchased supplies.	

At year-end, an adjustment must be made to recognize that only $225 of supplies remains. This also implies that $125 ($350 − $225) of the supplies have been used and should be charged to expense. The entries are summarized in the following T-accounts:

	Supplies on Hand			Cash			Supplies Expense	
Original entry (12/15/09)	350			350				
Adjusting entry (12/31/09)		125					125	
Updated balances (12/31/09)	225						125	
	To balance sheet						To income statement	

The adjusting entry is:

Dec. 31	Supplies Expense	125	
	Supplies on Hand		125
	To record the use of supplies.		

unearned revenues

Cash amounts received before they have been earned.

Unearned Revenues

Amounts received before the actual earning of revenues are known as **unearned revenues**. They arise when customers pay in advance of the receipt of goods or services. Because the company has received cash but has not yet given the customer the purchased goods or services, the unearned revenues are in fact liabilities. That is, the company must provide something in return for the amounts received. For example, a building contractor may require a deposit before proceeding on construction of a house. Upon receipt of the deposit, the contractor has unearned revenue, a liability. The contractor must construct the house to earn the revenue. If the house is not built, the contractor will be obligated to repay the deposit.

 CAUTION

Unearned Revenue is a tricky name for a liability. Liabilities are reported in the balance sheet. Don't make the mistake of including Unearned Revenue with the revenues on the income statement.

To illustrate the adjustments for unearned revenues, we will assume the following about our landscaping company:

> On December 1, a client pays you $225 for three months of landscaping services to be provided for the period beginning December 1, 2009, and ending February 28, 2010. This client is going to Hawaii for an extended vacation and would like you to take care of the grounds in her absence.

Typically, the original entry to record unearned revenue involves a debit to Cash and a credit to a liability account.[3] In our example of landscaping revenue received three months in advance, the liability account would be Unearned Revenue, as shown below.

Dec. 1	Cash...	225	
	Unearned Revenue		225
	Received three months' revenue in advance:		
	$75 × 3 = $225.		

The credit to the liability account, Unearned Revenue, is logically correct; until we provide the landscaping service, the revenue received in advance is unearned and is thus an obligation (liability).

---

[3] It is also possible that the initial expenditure could be recorded with a credit to a revenue account. This would require a different adjusting entry. This possibility is discussed in the web material associated with the text at **http://www.thomsonedu.com/accounting/albrecht**.

Preparing Financial Statements

Explain the preparation of the financial statements, the explanatory notes, and the audit report.

③ Once all transactions have been analyzed, journalized, and posted and all adjusting entries have been made, the accounts can be summarized and presented in the form of financial statements. Financial statements can be prepared directly from the data in the adjusted ledger accounts. The data must be organized into appropriate sections and categories so as to present them as simply and clearly as possible. The following process describes how the financial statements are prepared from the information taken from the trial balance:

1. Identify all revenues and expenses—these account balances are used to prepare the income statement.
2. Compute net income—subtract expenses from revenues.
3. Compute the ending retained earnings balance—this process was described in Chapter 2 and is illustrated here. Retained Earnings from the previous period is the starting point. Net income (computed in step 2) is added to the beginning retained earnings balance, and dividends for the period are subtracted.
4. Prepare a balance sheet using the balance sheet accounts from the trial balance and the modified retained earnings balance computed from step 3.

Note: No account on the trial balance shows up on both the income statement and the balance sheet.

CAUTION

Students often make the mistake of using the beginning retained earnings balance on the end-of-year balance sheet. As we shall see in the next section, the ending retained earnings balance is arrived at when the books are closed for the year.

Once the financial statements are prepared, explanatory notes are written. These notes clarify the methods and assumptions used in preparing the statements. In addition, the auditor must review the financial statements to make sure they are accurate, reasonable, and in accordance with generally accepted accounting principles. Finally, the financial statements are distributed to external users who analyze them in order to learn more about the financial condition of the company.

Financial Statement Preparation

To illustrate the preparation of financial statements from adjusted ledger accounts, a simplified adjusted trial balance for **General Motors** as of December 31, 2005, is provided in Exhibit 3.

From these data, an income statement and a balance sheet may be prepared for General Motors, as shown in Exhibits 4 and 5.

The ending retained earnings balance for General Motors for 2005 ($2,361), as reported on the balance sheet, is computed as follows:

Beginning retained earnings balance	$14,062
(from the adjusted trial balance)	
Add: Net income (loss) for the period	(10,567)
(from the income statement)	
Subtract: Dividends for the period	(1,134)
(from the adjusted trial balance)	
Ending retained earnings balance	$ 2,361

This follows the computation of retained earnings discussed in Chapter 2.

EXHIBIT 3	Simplified Adjusted Trial Balance

General Motors Corporation
Simplified Adjusted Trial Balance
December 31, 2005
(in millions)

	Debits	Credits
Cash	$ 30,726	
Investments	23,017	
Receivables	218,236	
Inventories	14,354	
Property and Equipment	78,401	
Intangible Assets	4,339	
Deferred Taxes	29,889	
Other Assets	77,116	
Accounts Payable		$ 29,913
Notes and Loans Payable		285,750
Pensions and Other Retirement Benefits		45,301
Accrued Expenses and Other Liabilities		99,478
Capital Stock and Other		17,267
Accumulated Other Comprehensive Loss	3,992	
Retained Earnings		14,062
Dividends	1,134	
Net Sales and Revenues		192,604
Cost of Sales and Other Expenses	170,547	
Selling, General and Administrative Expenses	22,734	
Interest Expense	15,768	
Income Tax (Benefit) Expense		5,878
Totals	$690,253	$690,253

EXHIBIT 4	Income Statement

General Motors Corporation
Statement of Income
For the Year Ended December 31, 2005
(in millions)

Net sales and revenues		$192,604
Cost of sales and other expenses	$170,547	
Selling, general and administrative expenses	22,734	
Total operating expenses		193,281
Operating income		$ (677)
Interest expense	$ 15,768	
Income tax (benefit) expense	(5,878)	
Total other expenses		9,890
Net loss		$ (10,567)

A statement of cash flows is not shown here. To prepare a statement of cash flows, we need more detailed information about the nature of the cash receipts and cash disbursements during the year. The preparation of a statement of cash flows will be illustrated in Chapter 13.

EXHIBIT 5	Balance Sheet

General Motors Corporation
Balance Sheet
December 31, 2005
(in millions)

Assets		
Cash	$ 30,726	
Investments	23,017	
Receivables	218,236	
Inventories	14,354	
Total current assets		$286,333
Property and equipment	$ 78,401	
Intangible assets	4,339	
Deferred taxes	29,889	
Other assets	77,116	
Total long-term assets		189,745
Total assets		$476,078
Liabilities and Owners' Equity		
Accounts payable	$ 29,913	
Accrued expenses and other liabilities	99,478	
Total current liabilities		$129,391
Notes and loans payable		285,750
Pensions and other retirement benefits		45,301
Total liabilities		$460,442
Owners' equity		
Capital stock and other	$ 17,267	
Accumulated other comprehensive loss	(3,992)	
Retained earnings	2,361	
Total owners' equity		15,636
Total liabilities and owners' equity		$476,078

Note: This balance sheet is not an exact replica of General Motors' actual balance sheet due to simplifying modifications for this exhibit.

The Notes

As discussed in Chapter 2, the notes to the financial statements tell about the assumptions and methods used in preparing the financial statements and also give more detail about specific items. A sample of the kind of information that appears in the notes for General Motors' financial statements is illustrated in Exhibit 6. The first note on revenue recognition illustrates how financial statement notes can summarize the accounting policies and assumptions that underlie the financial statements. The second note, on the debt associated with GM's financing subsidiary (GMAC), provides detailed information about a summary number that was reported in the financial statements. The third note, on GM's labor force, provides information that is deemed to be important to financial statement users, such as future labor costs, but that does not directly affect any of the reported historical financial statement numbers.

The financial statement notes serve to augment the summarized, numerical information contained in the financial statements. To highlight the importance of the notes, many financial statements have the following message printed at the bottom: "The notes are an integral part of these financial statements."

EXHIBIT 6	General Motors: Notes to the Financial Statements

General Motors Corporation
Notes to the Financial Statements (partial list)
For the Year Ended December 31, 2005

Revenue Recognition: Sales generally are recorded when products are shipped . . . to independent dealers or other third parties.

Debt: For Automotive and Other Operations, long-term debt and loans payable were as follows (dollars in millions):

	Weighted-Average Interest Rate		December 31,	
	2005	2004	2005	2004
Long-term debt and loans payable				
Payable within one year:				
Current portion of long-term debt	5.8%	5.7%	$ 564	$ 584
All other	7.4%	3.0%	955	1,478
Total loans payable			$ 1,519	$ 2,062
Payable beyond one year	6.9%	6.8%	31,084	30,425
Unamortized discount			(97)	(103)
Mark to market adjustment			27	138
Total long-term debt			31,014	30,460
Total long-term debt and loans payable			$32,533	$32,522

Labor Force: GM, on a worldwide basis, has a concentration of its labor supply in employees working under union collective bargaining agreements, of which certain contracts expired in 2003.

The Audit

As mentioned in Chapter 2, an independent audit, by CPAs from outside the company, is often conducted to ensure that the financial statements have been prepared in conformity with generally accepted accounting principles. With respect to the financial statements of General Motors, the audit procedures conducted by the external auditor, **Deloitte & Touche**, would probably include the following checks.

Review of Adjustments As you learned in the first part of this chapter, adjusting entries usually require more analysis, and more judgment, than do the regular journal entries recorded throughout the year. As part of the audit, the auditor will review these adjusting entries.

When conducting the audit of the financial statements, auditors are concerned that accounts are properly adjusted. Auditors are able to focus their efforts as illustrated in Exhibit 7. Companies usually are more concerned about and make sure that assets

EXHIBIT 7	How Auditors Spend Their Time

	Too much recorded	Too little recorded
Assets	Auditors must critically scrutinize each recorded amount to ensure it does not overstate the asset's value.	Little worry for the auditor—companies themselves will work hard to make sure that assets are not understated.
Liabilities	Little worry for the auditor—companies themselves will work hard to make sure that liabilities are not overstated.	Auditors must search for unrecorded liabilities as a company might not work as hard in an effort to increase its own liabilities.

are not UNDERstated and that liabilities are not OVERstated. Auditors will make special effort to ensure that assets are not OVERstated and that liabilities are not UNDERstated.

Sample of Selected Accounts

For a number of accounts, the auditor undertakes a sampling process to see whether the items reported in the balance sheet actually exist. For example, General Motors reports an ending cash and equivalents balance of $30,726,000,000. The auditor will ask to see bank statements and will probably call the bank(s) to verify the existence of the cash. For inventory, the auditor will ask to physically see the inventory and will conduct a spot check to see whether the company inventory records match what is actually in the warehouse.

Review of Accounting Systems

The auditor will also evaluate General Motors' accounting systems. If a company has a good accounting system, with all transactions being recorded in an efficient, orderly way, then the auditor has greater reason to be confident that the financial statements are reliable. On the other hand, if the company's accounting system is haphazard, with many missing documents and unexplained discrepancies, then the auditor must do more detailed work to verify the financial statements.

If the auditor finds that the financial statements have been prepared in conformance with generally accepted accounting principles, then the auditor provides a report to that effect. This report is attached and distributed as part of the financial statements. The audit report is discussed in more detail in Chapter 5.

work sheet

A tool used by accountants to facilitate the preparation of financial statements.

Using a Work Sheet

A work sheet is a tool used by accountants to facilitate the preparation of financial statements. Unlike the financial statements, work sheets are for internal use only; they are not distributed to "outsiders." Although the use of work sheets is optional, most accountants find them helpful for organizing large quantities of data. Many work sheets are now prepared on electronic spreadsheets, using a software package such as Lotus 1-2-3, Excel, or Quattro Pro. Using a work sheet to assist in the preparation of financial statements is explained in detail on the text Web site at **http://www.thomsonedu.com/accounting/albrecht**.

Financial Statement Analysis

Financial statements are prepared so that they can be used. Once the balance sheet, income statement, and statement of cash flows of a company are completed, the whole package is distributed to bankers, suppliers, and investors to be used in evaluating the company's financial health.

Financial statement analysis involves the examination of both relationships among financial statements numbers and the trends in those numbers over time. One purpose of financial statement analysis is to use the past performance of a company to predict how well it will do in the future. Another purpose of financial statement analysis is to evaluate the performance of a company with an eye toward identifying problem areas. Financial statement analysis is both diagnosis, identifying where a firm has problems, and prognosis, predicting how a firm will perform in the future.

Relationships between financial statement amounts are called financial ratios. For example, net income divided by sales is a financial ratio called "return on sales." Return on sales tells you how many pennies of profit a company makes on each dollar of sales. There are hundreds of different financial ratios, each shedding light on a different aspect of the health of a company.

In subsequent chapters, we will introduce a variety of ratios that help financial statement users evaluate a company's financial health. In Chapter 14, we will provide a comprehensive overview of financial statement analysis.

REMEMBER THIS...

- The adjusted trial balance provides the raw material for the preparation of the balance sheet and the income statement. Accounts in the adjusted trial balance are reported in either the balance sheet or the income statement, but not both.
- The notes to the financial statements provide further information about the methods and assumptions used in preparing the financial statements as well as further detail about certain financial statement items.
- The audit is conducted by a CPA from outside the company who reviews the adjusting entries, performs tests to check the balances of selected accounts, and reviews the condition of the accounting systems.
- Financial statement analysis involves examining the relationship of financial statement numbers across time for the same company and across companies at the same point in time.

Closing the Books

Complete the closing process in the accounting cycle.

④ We have almost reached the end of the accounting cycle for a period. Thus far, the accounting cycle has included analyzing documents, journalizing transactions, posting to the ledger accounts, determining account balances, preparing a trial balance, making adjusting entries, and preparing the financial statements. Just two additional steps are needed: (1) journalizing and posting closing entries and (2) preparing a post-closing trial balance.

Real and Nominal Accounts

real accounts

Accounts that are not closed to a zero balance at the end of each accounting period; permanent accounts appearing on the balance sheet.

To explain the closing process, we must first define two new terms. Certain accounts are referred to as real accounts. These accounts report the cumulative increases and decreases in certain account balances from the date the company was organized. Real accounts (assets, liabilities, and owners' equity) appear on the balance sheet and are permanent; they are not closed to a zero balance at the end of each accounting period. Balances existing in real accounts at the end of a period are carried forward to the next period.

nominal accounts

Accounts that are closed to a zero balance at the end of each accounting period; temporary accounts generally appearing on the income statement.

Other accounts are known as nominal accounts. These accounts (revenues, expenses, and dividends) are temporary; they are really just subcategories of Retained Earnings and are reduced to a zero balance through the closing process at the end of each accounting period. Thus, nominal accounts begin with a zero balance at the start of each accounting cycle. Transactions throughout the period (generally a year) are journalized and posted to the nominal accounts. These are used to accumulate and classify all revenue and expense items, and also dividends, for that period. At the end of the accounting period, adjustments are made, the income statement is prepared, and the balances in the temporary accounts are then closed to Retained Earnings, a permanent account.

Closing entries bring the income statement accounts back to a zero balance, which makes the accounts ready for a new accounting period. In addition, the closing entries transfer the net income or loss for the accounting period to Retained Earnings and reduce Retained Earnings for any dividends. Without closing entries, revenue and expense balances would extend from period to period, making it difficult to isolate the operating results of each accounting period.

Closing Entries

Unlike adjusting entries, the actual mechanics of the closing process are not complicated. Revenue accounts normally have credit balances and are closed by being debited; expense accounts generally have debit balances and are closed by being credited. The difference between total revenues and total expenses represents the net income (or net loss) of the entity. For a corporation, net income is credited to Retained Earnings because income increases owners' equity. A net loss would be debited to Retained Earnings because a loss decreases owners' equity.

To illustrate the closing process, we will again refer to **General Motors'** financial information as discussed earlier on pages 143–146. The closing journal entry is:

Dec. 31	Net Sales and Revenues	192,604	
	Cost of Sales and Other Expenses		170,547
	Selling, General and Administrative Expenses		22,734
	Interest Expense		15,768
	Income Tax Expense	5,878	
	Retained Earnings	10,567	
	To close revenues and expenses to Retained Earnings.		

closing entries

Entries that reduce all nominal, or temporary, accounts to a zero balance at the end of each accounting period, transferring their preclosing balances to a permanent balance sheet account.

Closing entries must be posted to the appropriate ledger accounts. Once posted, all nominal accounts will have a zero balance; that is, they will be "closed."

The dividends account is also a nominal (temporary) account that must be closed at the end of the accounting period. However, dividends are not expenses and will not be reported on an income statement; they are distributions to stockholders of part of a corporation's earnings. Thus, dividends reduce retained earnings. When dividends are declared by the board of directors of a corporation, the amount that will be paid is debited to Dividends and credited to a liability account, Dividends Payable, or to Cash if paid immediately. Because Dividends is a temporary account, it must be closed to Retained Earnings at the end of the accounting period. The dividends account is closed by crediting it and by debiting Retained Earnings, thereby reducing owners' equity, as illustrated below for General Motors.

Dec. 31	Retained Earnings	1,134	
	Dividends		1,134
	To close Dividends to Retained Earnings.		

The books are now ready for a new accounting cycle. The closing process for the revenues, expenses, and dividends of a corporation is shown schematically in Exhibit 8.

Preparing a Post-Closing Trial Balance

An optional last step in the accounting cycle is to balance the accounts and to prepare a **post-closing trial balance** (see page 150 for definition). The accounts are to be

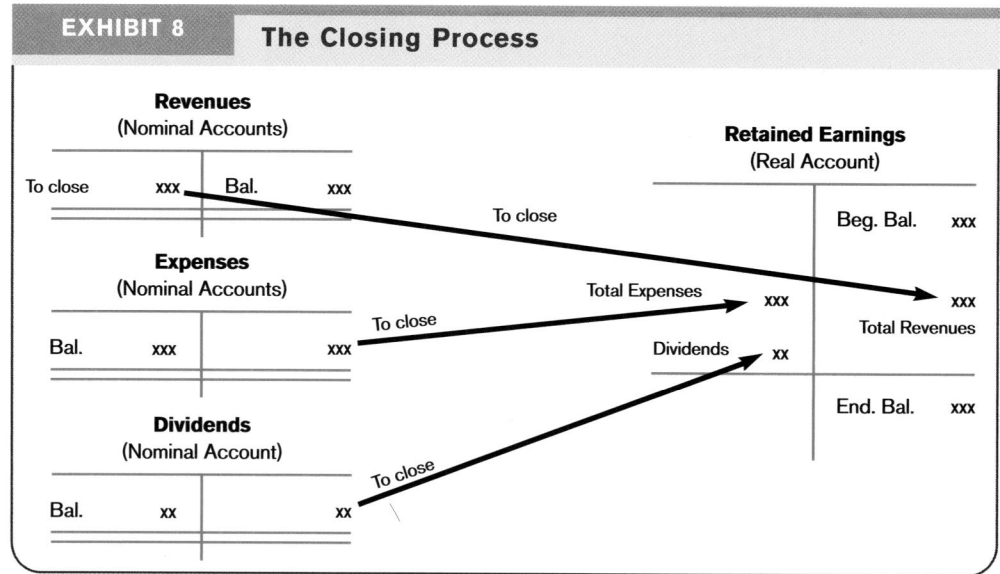

EXHIBIT 8 The Closing Process

post-closing trial balance

A listing of all real account balances after the closing process has been completed; provides a means of testing whether total debits equal total credits for all real accounts prior to beginning a new accounting cycle.

balanced—debits and credits added and a balance determined—only after the closing entries have been recorded and posted in the general ledger. The information for the post-closing trial balance is then taken from the ledger. The nominal accounts will not be shown since they have been closed and thus have zero balances. Only the real accounts will have current balances. This step is for internal purposes only and is designed to provide some assurance that the previous steps in the cycle have been performed properly, prior to the start of a new accounting period. Exhibit 9 illustrates a post-closing trial balance for General Motors Corporation.

EXHIBIT 9 Post-Closing Trial Balance

General Motors Corporation
Post-Closing Trial Balance
December 31, 2005
(in millions)

	Debits	Credits
Cash	$ 30,726	
Investments	23,017	
Receivables	218,236	
Inventories	14,354	
Property and Equipment	78,401	
Intangible Assets	4,339	
Deferred Taxes	29,889	
Other Assets	77,116	
Accounts Payable		$ 29,913
Notes and Loans Payable		285,750
Pensions and Other Retirement Benefits		45,301
Accrued Expenses and Other Liabilities		99,478
Capital Stock and Other		17,267
Accumulated Other Comprehensive Loss	3,992	
Retained Earnings		2,361
Totals	$480,070	$480,070

REMEMBER THIS...

- Nominal (temporary) accounts = revenues, expenses, and dividends
- Real (permanent) accounts = assets, liabilities, and owners' equity
- Two objectives of closing entries:
  - Close all revenue, expense, and dividend accounts to zero in preparation for the start of a new period.
  - Transfer all revenue, expense, and dividend balances to Retained Earnings.

A Summary of the Accounting Cycle

Understand how all the steps in the accounting cycle fit together.

(5) We have now completed our discussion of the steps that are performed each period in the accounting cycle. By way of review, Exhibit 10 lists the sequence of the accounting cycle (presented earlier in Chapter 3). Many of the steps, such as analyzing transactions, occur continuously. Other steps, such as preparing the financial statements, generally occur only once during the cycle.

The financial statements that result from the accounting cycle provide useful information to investors, creditors, and other external users. These statements are included in the annual reports provided to stockholders. As illustrated earlier

EXHIBIT 10	**Sequence of the Accounting Cycle**

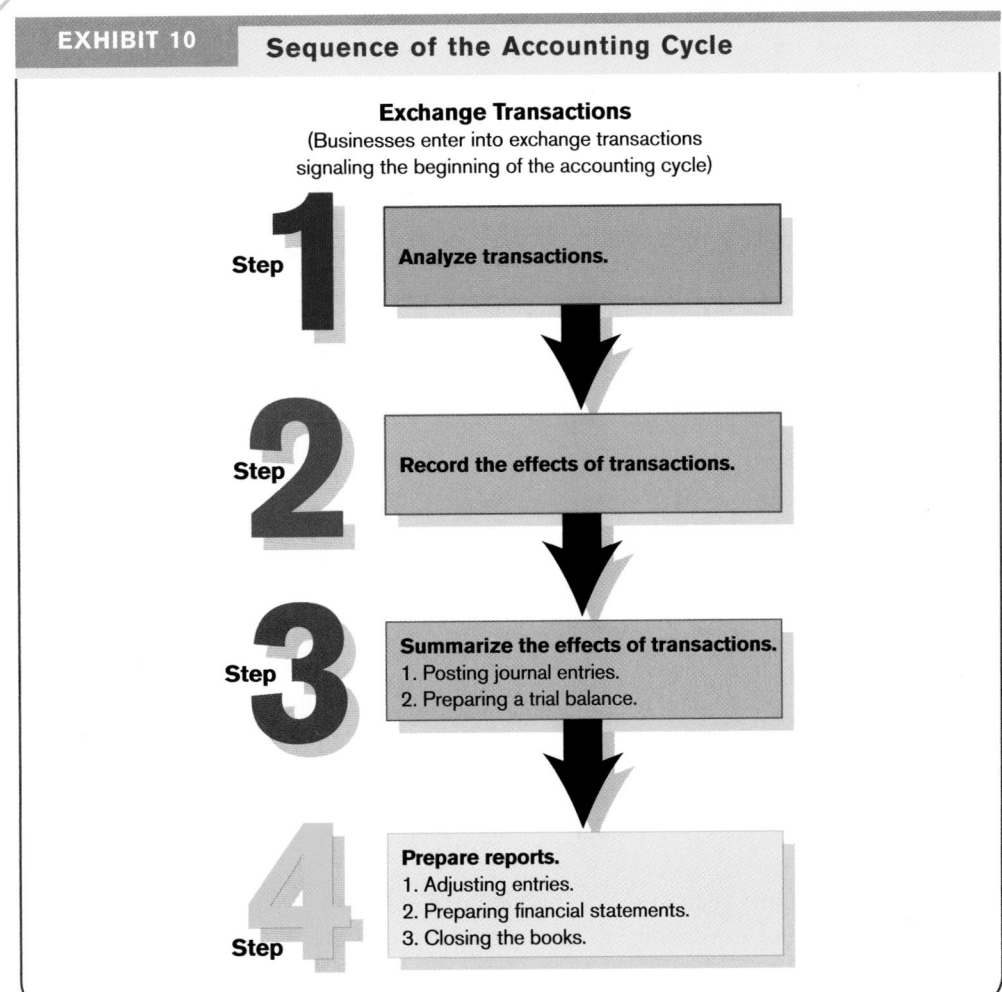

Exchange Transactions
(Businesses enter into exchange transactions signaling the beginning of the accounting cycle)

Step 1 Analyze transactions.

Step 2 Record the effects of transactions.

Step 3 Summarize the effects of transactions.
1. Posting journal entries.
2. Preparing a trial balance.

Step 4 Prepare reports.
1. Adjusting entries.
2. Preparing financial statements.
3. Closing the books.

in the chapter, once the financial statements are made available to users, they can then be analyzed and compared to the financial statements of similar firms to detect strengths and weaknesses.

REMEMBER THIS...

The four steps in the accounting cycle are as follows:

1. Analyze transactions.
2. Record the effects of transactions.
3. Summarize the effects of transactions.
4. Prepare reports, with the following detailed steps as covered in this chapter.
   - Adjusting entries
   - Financial statements
   - Closing entries

REVIEW OF LEARNING OBJECTIVES

(1) Describe how accrual accounting allows for timely reporting and a better measure of a company's economic performance. Accrual-basis accounting means that:

- revenues are recognized as they are earned, not necessarily when cash is received;
- expenses are recognized as they are incurred, not necessarily when cash is paid.

Accrual-basis accounting provides a more accurate picture of a company's financial position and operating results than does cash-basis accounting.

(2) Explain the need for adjusting entries and make adjusting entries for unrecorded receivables, unrecorded liabilities, prepaid expenses, and unearned revenues.

Adjusting entry for	Debit	Credit
Unrecorded receivable	Asset	Revenue
Unrecorded liability	Expense	Liability
Prepaid expense	Expense	Asset
Unearned revenue	Liability	Revenue

(3) Explain the preparation of the financial statements, the explanatory notes, and the audit report.

- The adjusted trial balance provides the raw material for the preparation of the balance sheet and the income statement. Accounts in the adjusted trial balance are reported in either the balance sheet or the income statement, but not both.
- The notes to the financial statements provide further information about the methods and assumptions used in preparing the financial statements as well as further detail about certain financial statement items.
- The audit is conducted by a CPA from outside the company who:
  - reviews the adjusting entries,
  - performs tests to check the balances of selected accounts, and
  - reviews the condition of the accounting systems.

Financial statements are prepared to be used. Financial statement analysis exams relationships between financial numbers across companies at the same point in time and across time for the same company.

(4) Complete the closing process in the accounting cycle.

Closing entry for	Debit	Credit
Revenue	Revenue	Retained Earnings
Expense	Retained Earnings	Expense
Dividends	Retained Earnings	Dividends

(5) Understand how all the steps in the accounting cycle fit together. The accounting cycle consists of specific steps to analyze, record, classify, summarize, and report the transactions of a business. The three detailed steps of "reporting" covered in this chapter are:

- making adjusting entries,
- preparing financial statements, and
- making closing entries.

KEY TERMS & CONCEPTS

accrual-basis
   accounting, 132
adjusting entries, 135
calendar year, 132
cash-basis
   accounting, 134

closing entries, 149
fiscal year, 132
matching principle, 133
nominal accounts, 148
post-closing trial
   balance, 150

prepaid expenses, 138
real accounts, 148
revenue recognition
   principle, 133
time-period
   concept, 132

unearned revenues, 140
unrecorded
   liabilities, 136
unrecorded
   receivables, 136
work sheet, 147

REVIEW PROBLEM

The Accounting Cycle

This review problem provides a useful summary of the entire accounting cycle. The following post-closing trial balance is for Sports Haven Company as of December 31, 2008.

Sports Haven Company
Post-Closing Trial Balance
December 31, 2008

	Debits	Credits
Cash	$17,500	
Accounts Receivable	17,000	
Inventory	28,800	
Supplies on Hand	1,200	
Prepaid Building Rental	24,000	
Accounts Payable		$18,000
Capital Stock (3,600 shares outstanding)		54,000
Retained Earnings		16,500
Totals	$88,500	$88,500

(continued)

Following is a summary of the company's transactions for 2009.
a. At the beginning of 2009, the company issued 1,500 new shares of stock at $20 per share.
b. Total inventory purchases were $49,500; all purchases were made on credit and are recorded in the inventory account.
c. Total sales were $125,000; $102,900 were on credit, the rest were for cash. The cost of goods sold was $47,500; the inventory account is reduced at the time of each sale.
d. In December, a customer paid $3,500 cash in advance for merchandise that was temporarily out of stock. The advance payments received from customers are initially recorded as liabilities. The $3,500 is not included in the sales figures in (c) above.
e. The company paid $66,500 on accounts payable during the year.
f. The company collected $102,000 of accounts receivable during the year.
g. The company purchased $600 of supplies for cash during 2009, debiting Supplies on Hand.
h. The company paid $850 for advertising during the year, debiting Prepaid Advertising.
i. Total salaries paid during the year were $45,000.
j. The company paid $650 during the year for utilities.
k. Dividends of $7,500 were paid to stockholders in December.

On December 31, 2009, the company's accountant gathers the following information to adjust the accounts:

l. As of December 31, salaries of $750 had been earned by employees but will not be paid until January 3, 2010.
m. A count at December 31 shows $800 of supplies still on hand.
n. The prepaid advertising paid during 2009 includes $400 paid on December 1, 2009, for a series of radio advertisements to be broadcast throughout December 2009 and January 2010. The balance in the account, $450, represents advertisements that were broadcast during 2009.
o. On December 31, 2008, the company rented an office building for two years and paid $24,000 in cash (the full rental fee for 2009 and 2010). The payment was recorded with a debit to Prepaid Building Rental. No entries have been made for building rent in 2009.

p. On December 20, 2009, a bill for $150 was received for utilities. No entry was made to record the receipt of the bill, which is to be paid on January 4, 2010.
q. As of December 31, 2009, the merchandise paid for in advance [transaction (d)] was still out of stock. The company expects to receive the merchandise and fill the order by January 15, 2010.
r. The company's income is taxed at a rate of 15%.

Required:
1. Make entries in the general journal to record each of the transactions [items (a) through (k)].
2. Using T-accounts to represent the general ledger accounts, post the transactions recorded in the general journal. Enter the beginning balances in the accounts that appear in the December 31, 2008, post-closing trial balance before posting 2009 transactions. When all transactions have been posted to the T-accounts, determine the balance for each account.
3. Prepare a trial balance as of December 31, 2009.
4. Record adjusting entries [items (l) through (r)] in the general journal; post these entries to the general ledger (T-accounts).
5. Prepare an income statement and balance sheet for 2009.
6. Record closing entries [label (s) and (t)] in the general journal; post these entries to the general ledger (T-accounts).
7. Prepare a post-closing trial balance.

(continued)

Solution

1. Following are the journal entries to record the transactions for the year. Several of these are summary entries representing numerous individual transactions.

(a) Cash   30,000
      Capital Stock   30,000

    The company issued additional shares of stock, so Capital Stock must be credited to reflect the increase in owners' equity. Since the company received cash of $30,000 (1,500 shares at $20 per share), Cash is also increased.

(b) Inventory   49,500
      Accounts Payable   49,500

    The company purchased $49,500 of goods on credit. Inventory is increased (debited) for this amount. Accounts Payable is credited to show the increase in liabilities.

(c) Accounts Receivable   102,900
     Cash   22,100
      Sales Revenue   125,000

    Total sales were $125,000, so Sales Revenue must be increased (credited) by that amount. Of this amount, $102,900 were on credit, and $22,100 were cash sales. We increase the asset accounts, Accounts Receivable and Cash, by debiting them.

(c) Cost of Goods Sold   47,500
      Inventory   47,500

    The cost of the merchandise sold during the year was $47,500. Cost of Goods Sold (expense) must be increased (debited) by this amount. Since the goods were sold, Inventory (asset) must be reduced by a credit of $47,500.

(d) Cash   3,500
      Unearned Sales Revenue   3,500

    Cash is debited (increased) by the amount received from the customer. The company recorded the advance payments for merchandise by crediting a liability account, Unearned Sales Revenue.

(e) Accounts Payable   66,500
      Cash   66,500

    The company's payments on its accounts reduce the amount of its obligation to creditors, so Accounts Payable (liability) is debited to decrease it by the amount paid. Cash must also be decreased (credited).

(f) Cash   102,000
      Accounts Receivable   102,000

    Since the company has collected some of its receivables from customers, Accounts Receivable is credited to show a decrease. Cash is increased (debited).

(g) Supplies on Hand   600
      Cash   600

    The company purchased $600 of supplies. By debiting Supplies on Hand, an increase is shown in that asset account. Cash must be credited to show a decrease.

(h) Prepaid Advertising   850
      Cash   850

    The company purchased $850 of advertising and chose to initially debit an asset account, Prepaid Advertising. Since cash was paid, it must be reduced by a credit.

(i) Salaries Expense   45,000
      Cash   45,000

(continued)

| (j) | Utilities Expense | 650 | |
| | Cash | | 650 |

For transactions (i) and (j), an expense account must be debited to show that expenses have been incurred. Cash must be credited (reduced).

| (k) | Dividends | 7,500 | |
| | Cash | | 7,500 |

Dividends must be debited to show a decrease in owners' equity resulting from a distribution of earnings. Cash must be reduced by a credit.

2. T-accounts with the beginning balances and journal entries posted are shown here. (Note that accounts with more than one entry must be "balanced" by drawing a rule and entering the debit or credit balance below it.)

Cash

Beg.		(e)	66,500
bal.	17,500	(g)	600
(a)	30,000	(h)	850
(c)	22,100	(i)	45,000
(d)	3,500	(j)	650
(f)	102,000	(k)	7,500
Updated			
bal.	54,000		

Accounts Receivable

Beg.		(f)	102,000
bal.	17,000		
(c)	102,900		
Updated			
bal.	17,900		

Inventory

Beg.		(c)	47,500
bal.	28,800		
(b)	49,500		
Updated			
bal.	30,800		

Supplies on Hand

Beg.		
bal.	1,200	
(g)	600	
Updated		
bal.	1,800	

Prepaid Building Rental

Beg.		
bal.	24,000	

Prepaid Advertising

(h)	850	

Accounts Payable

(e)	66,500	Beg.	
		bal.	18,000
		(b)	49,500
		Updated	
		bal.	1,000

Unearned Sales Revenue

		(d)	3,500

Capital Stock

		Beg.	
		bal.	54,000
		(a)	30,000
		Updated	
		bal.	84,000

Retained Earnings

		Beg.	
		bal.	16,500

Dividends

(k)	7,500	

Sales Revenue

		(c)	125,000

Cost of Goods Sold

(c)	47,500	

Salaries Expense

(i)	45,000	

Utilities Expense

(j)	650	

3. The balance of each account is entered in a trial balance. Each column in the trial balance is totaled to determine that total debits equal total credits.

(continued)

Sports Haven Company
Trial Balance
December 31, 2009

	Debits	Credits
Cash	$ 54,000	
Accounts Receivable	17,900	
Inventory	30,800	
Supplies on Hand	1,800	
Prepaid Building Rental	24,000	
Prepaid Advertising	850	
Accounts Payable		$ 1,000
Unearned Sales Revenue		3,500
Capital Stock		84,000
Retained Earnings		16,500
Dividends	7,500	
Sales Revenue		125,000
Cost of Goods Sold	47,500	
Salaries Expense	45,000	
Utilities Expense	650	
Totals	$230,000	$230,000

4. The adjusting entries for Sports Haven Company are presented in journal form and explained. Updated T-accounts are provided showing the posting of the adjusting entries.

(l) Salaries Expense 750
    Salaries Payable 750

As of December 31, there is an unrecorded liability and expense of $750 for salaries owed to employees. Because the salaries were earned in 2009, the liability and related expense must be recorded in 2009.

(m) Supplies Expense 1,000
    Supplies on Hand 1,000

Supplies on Hand (asset) has a debit balance before adjustment of $1,800 [beginning balance of $1,200 plus $600 of supplies purchased during the year, transaction (g)]. Since $800 of supplies are on hand at the end of the year, Supplies on Hand should be reduced (credited) by $1,000. Supplies Expense must be debited to show that $1,000 of supplies were used during the period.

(n) Advertising Expense 650
    Prepaid Advertising 650

Prepaid Advertising has a debit balance before adjustment of $850, the total amount paid for advertising during the year [transaction (h)]. This amount includes $400 that was paid for radio advertising throughout December 2009 and January 2010. Only that portion that applies to 2010 should be shown as Prepaid Advertising, $200 ($400 ÷ 2 months), since it is not an expense of the current year. The remainder, $650, is advertising expense for the period. Thus, the asset account, Prepaid Advertising, must be credited for $650, and Advertising Expense must be increased by a debit of $650.

(o) Building Rent Expense 12,000
    Prepaid Building Rental 12,000

The original entry at the end of 2008 was a debit to the asset account, Prepaid Building Rental, and a credit to Cash. An adjusting entry is needed to record rent expense of $12,000 for 2009 ($24,000 ÷ 2 years). The expense account must be debited and the asset account must be reduced by a credit. The remaining $12,000 in Prepaid Building Rental reflects the portion of the total payment for building rent expense in 2010.

(p) Utilities Expense 150
    Utilities Payable 150

(continued)

As of December 31, 2009, there is an unrecorded liability and expense of $150 for utilities. Because the expense was incurred in 2009, an adjusting entry is needed to record the liability and related expense.

(q)   No entry required.

The original entry to record the advance payment from a customer was made by crediting a liability [transaction (d)]. As of December 31, no revenue has been earned. The company still has an obligation to deliver goods or refund the advanced payment. Therefore, no adjustment is required, since the liability is already properly recorded.

(r)	Income Tax Expense	2,595	
	Income Taxes Payable		2,595

The remaining adjustment is for income taxes. The difference between total revenues and total expenses is the amount of income before taxes, $17,300. This amount is multiplied by the applicable tax rate of 15% to determine income taxes for the period. The expense account is debited to show the income taxes incurred for the year and the liability account is credited to show the obligation to the government.

Cash

Beg.		(e)	66,500
bal.	17,500	(g)	600
(a)	30,000	(h)	850
(c)	22,100	(i)	45,000
(d)	3,500	(j)	650
(f)	102,000	(k)	7,500
Updated			
bal.	54,000		

Accounts Receivable

Beg.		(f)	102,000
bal.	17,000		
(c)	102,900		
Updated			
bal.	17,900		

Inventory

Beg.		(c)	47,500
bal.	28,800		
(b)	49,500		
Updated			
bal.	30,800		

Supplies on Hand

Beg.		(m)	1,000
bal.	1,200		
(g)	600		
Updated			
bal.	800		

Prepaid Building Rental

Beg.		(o)	12,000
bal.	24,000		
Updated			
bal.	12,000		

Prepaid Advertising

(h)	850	(n)	650
Updated			
bal.	200		

Accounts Payable

(e)	66,500	Beg.	
		bal.	18,000
		(b)	49,500
		Updated	
		bal.	1,000

Salaries Payable

(l)	750

Utilities Payable

(p)	150

Income Taxes Payable

(r)	2,595

Unearned Sales Revenue

(d)	3,500

Capital Stock

		Beg.	
		bal.	54,000
		(a)	30,000
		Updated	
		bal.	84,000

(continued)

Retained Earnings				Dividends				Sales Revenue	
	Beg.		(k)	7,500				(c)	125,000
	bal.	16,500							

Cost of Goods Sold			Salaries Expense			Utilities Expense	
(c)	47,500	(i)	45,000		(j)	650	
		(l)	750		(p)	150	
		Updated			Updated		
		bal.	45,750		bal.	800	

Advertising Expense			Supplies Expense			Building Rent Expense	
(n)	650		(m)	1,000		(o)	12,000

Income Tax Expense	
(r)	2,595

5. Data for the financial statements may be taken from the adjusted ledger accounts and reported as follows:

Sports Haven Company
Income Statement
For the Year Ended December 31, 2009

Sales revenue	$125,000	
Less cost of goods sold	47,500	
Gross profit		$77,500
Less operating expenses:		
Salaries expense	$ 45,750	
Utilities expense	800	
Advertising expense	650	
Supplies expense	1,000	
Building rent expense	12,000	60,200
Income before income taxes		$17,300
Income tax expense		2,595
Net income		$14,705
Earnings per share:		
$14,705 ÷ 5,100 shares = $2.88 (rounded)		

(continued)

Sports Haven Company
Balance Sheet
December 31, 2009

Assets

Cash	$54,000	
Accounts receivable	17,900	
Inventory	30,800	
Supplies on hand	800	
Prepaid building rental	12,000	
Prepaid advertising	200	
Total assets		$115,700

Liabilities and Owners' Equity

Liabilities:

Accounts payable	$ 1,000	
Salaries payable	750	
Utilities payable	150	
Income taxes payable	2,595	
Unearned sales revenue	3,500	
Total liabilities		$ 7,995
Owners' equity:		
Capital stock (5,100 shares outstanding)	$84,000	
Retained earnings	23,705*	
Total owners' equity		107,705
Total liabilities and owners' equity		$115,700

*Note that in preparing the balance sheet, net income must be added to the beginning balance in Retained Earnings and dividends must be subtracted ($16,500 + $14,705 − $7,500 = $23,705).

---

6. The next step is to record the closing entries in the general journal and then post those entries to the general ledger (T-accounts). T-accounts are shown with all previous entries and the closing entries [items (s) and (t)] posted.

   The first entry is to close the revenue account and each of the expense accounts. Sales Revenue has a credit balance; it is debited to reduce the balance to zero. The expense accounts are closed by crediting them. The difference in total revenues and total expenses is $14,705 (net income for the period). Net income represents an increase in retained earnings. All of this is captured in the single, compound closing entry(s), as follows:

(s)	Sales Revenue	125,000	
	Cost of Goods Sold		47,500
	Salaries Expense		45,750
	Utilities Expense		800
	Advertising Expense		650
	Supplies Expense		1,000
	Building Rent Expense		12,000
	Income Tax Expense		2,595
	Retained Earnings		14,705

Second, Dividends, a nominal account, must also be closed to Retained Earnings.

(t)	Retained Earnings	7,500	
	Dividends		7,500

(continued)

Cash

Beg.			(e)	66,500
bal.	17,500		(g)	600
(a)	30,000		(h)	850
(c)	22,100		(i)	45,000
(d)	3,500		(j)	650
(f)	102,000		(k)	7,500
Updated				
Bal.	54,000			

Accounts Receivable

Beg.			(f)	102,000
bal.	17,000			
(c)	102,900			
Updated				
bal.	17,900			

Inventory

Beg.			(c)	47,500
bal.	28,800			
(b)	49,500			
Updated				
bal.	30,800			

Supplies on Hand

Beg.			(m)	1,000
bal.	1,200			
(g)	600			
Updated				
bal.	800			

Prepaid Building Rental

Beg.			(o)	12,000
bal.	24,000			
Updated				
bal.	12,000			

Prepaid Advertising

(h)	850		(n)	650
Updated				
bal.	200			

Accounts Payable

(e)	66,500		Beg.	
			bal.	18,000
			(b)	49,500
			Updated	
			bal.	1,000

Salaries Payable

			(l)	750

Utilities Payable

			(p)	150

Income Taxes Payable

			(r)	2,595

Unearned Sales Revenue

			(d)	3,500

Capital Stock

			Beg.	
			bal.	54,000
			(a)	30,000
			Updated	
			bal.	84,000

Retained Earnings

(t)	7,500		Beg.	
			bal.	16,500
			(s)	14,705
			Updated	
			bal.	23,705

Dividends

(k)	7,500		(t)	7,500

Sales Revenue

(s)	125,000		(c)	125,000

Cost of Goods Sold

(c)	47,500		(s)	47,500

Salaries Expense

(i)	45,000		(s)	45,750
(l)	750			

Utilities Expense

(j)	650		(s)	800
(p)	150			

Advertising Expense

(n)	650		(s)	650

Supplies Expense

(m)	1,000		(s)	1,000

Building Rent Expense

(o)	12,000		(s)	12,000

Income Tax Expense

(r)	2,595		(s)	2,595

(continued)

7. The final (optional) step in the accounting cycle is to prepare a post-closing trial balance. This procedure is a check on the accuracy of the closing process. It is a listing of all ledger account balances at year-end. Note that only real accounts appear because all nominal accounts have been closed to a zero balance in preparation for the next accounting cycle.

Sports Haven Company
Post-Closing Trial Balance
December 31, 2009

	Debits	Credits
Cash	$ 54,000	
Accounts Receivable	17,900	
Inventory	30,800	
Supplies on Hand	800	
Prepaid Building Rental	12,000	
Prepaid Advertising	200	
Accounts Payable		$ 1,000
Salaries Payable		750
Utilities Payable		150
Income Taxes Payable		2,595
Unearned Sales Revenue		3,500
Capital Stock		84,000
Retained Earnings		23,705
Totals	$115,700	$115,700

DISCUSSION QUESTIONS

1. Why are financial reports prepared on a periodic basis?
2. Distinguish between reporting on a calendar-year and on a fiscal-year basis.
3. When are revenues generally recognized (recorded)?
4. What is the matching principle?
5. Explain why accrual-basis accounting is more appropriate than cash-basis accounting for most businesses.
6. Why are accrual-based financial statements considered somewhat tentative?
7. Why are adjusting entries necessary?
8. Since there are usually no source documents for adjusting entries, how does the accountant know when to make adjusting entries and for what amounts?
9. The analysis process for preparing adjusting entries involves two basic steps. Identify the two steps and explain why both are necessary.

10. Why are supplies not considered inventory? What type of account is Supplies on Hand?
11. Cash is not one of the accounts increased or decreased in an adjusting entry. Why?
12. Which are prepared first: the year-end financial statements or the general journal adjusting entries? Explain.
13. Of what value are the notes to the financial statements and the audit report, both of which are usually included in the annual report to shareholders?
14. Distinguish between real and nominal accounts.
15. What is the purpose of closing entries?
16. What is the purpose of the post-closing trial balance? Explain where the information for the post-closing trial balance comes from.

PRACTICE EXERCISES

PE 4-1   **Periodic Reporting**

LO1   Which one of the following statements is true with respect to periodic reporting?

a. All companies in the United States are required to have a fiscal year that ends on December 31.

b. The issuance of frequent periodic financial reports reduces the need for accountants to make estimates and judgments.

c. In the United States, only large businesses (those with total assets in excess of $650 million) prepare periodic financial statements.

d. Some financial reports may be prepared on a daily basis.

e. The Securities and Exchange Commission (SEC) requires all publicly-traded companies in the United States to file monthly financial statements.

PE 4-2   **Revenue Recognition**

LO1   In which one of the following situations should revenue be recognized?

a. The earnings process has begun and cash collectibility is reasonably assured.

b. The earnings process has begun and cash has been collected.

c. The earnings process is substantially complete and cash collectibility is not yet reasonably assured.

d. The earnings process will soon begin and cash has been collected.

e. The earnings process is substantially complete and cash collectibility is reasonably assured.

PE 4-3   **Matching**

LO1   Select the one phrase below that best completes the following statement: According to the matching principle, . . .

a. The amount of cash collected should be matched and recognized in the same period as the related revenue.

b. Expenses should be matched and recognized in the same period as the related revenue.

c. The amount of cash collected should be matched and recognized in the same period as the related expense.

d. Revenue should be matched and recognized in the same period as the related cash collection.

e. Expenses should be matched and recognized in the same period as the related shareholder investment.

PE 4-4   **Cash-Basis Accounting**

LO1   A lawn care company started business on January 1, 2009. The company billed clients $85,000 for lawn care services completed in 2009. By December 31, the company had received $61,000 cash from the customers, with the $24,000 balance expected to be collected in 2010. During 2009, the company paid $58,000 cash for various expenses. At December 31, the company still owed $29,000 for additional expenses incurred which have not yet been paid in cash. These expenses will be paid during January 2010. How much income should the company report for 2009? Note: The company computes income using cash-basis accounting.

PE 4-5   **Accrual-Basis Accounting**

LO1   Refer to PE 4-4. Compute income for 2009 assuming that the company uses accrual-basis accounting.

PE 4-6   **Unrecorded Receivable: Original Entry**

LO2   Greg operates a sizeable newspaper delivery service. On the last day of each month, Greg receives a statement from the newspaper publisher detailing how much money Greg earned

(continued)

that month from delivering papers. On the 10th day of the following month, Greg receives the cash for the preceding month's deliveries. On December 10, Greg received $12,300 cash for deliveries made in November. Make the journal entry necessary on Greg's books on December 10 to record the receipt of this cash, assuming that Greg did not make any adjusting entry as of the end of November.

PE 4-7
LO2
Unrecorded Receivable: Adjusting Entry

Refer to PE 4-6. On December 31, Greg received a statement from the newspaper publisher notifying him that he had earned $13,700 for his December deliveries. Because December 31 is the end of Greg's fiscal year, he makes adjusting entries at that time. (1) Make the adjusting journal entry necessary on Greg's books on December 31 to record the $13,700 in delivery revenue earned during December and (2) make the journal entry necessary on Greg's books on January 10 to record the receipt of the $13,700 in cash. Note: When making the January 10 entry, don't forget the adjusting entry that was made on December 31.

PE 4-8
LO2
Unrecorded Liability: Original Entry

On May 1, the company borrowed $75,000 from Bank of Salt Lake. The loan is for five years and bears an annual interest rate of 9%. Interest on the loan is to be paid in cash each year on April 30; the $75,000 loan amount is to be repaid in full after five years. Make the journal entry necessary on the company's books to record the receipt of this loan on May 1.

PE 4-9
LO2
Unrecorded Liability: Adjusting Entry

Refer to PE 4-8. (1) Make the adjusting entry necessary on the company's books with respect to this loan on December 31. (2) Make the journal entry necessary on the company's books on the following April 30 to record payment of interest for the first year of the loan. Note: When making this April 30 entry, don't forget the adjusting entry that was made on December 31.

PE 4-10
LO2
Prepaid Expense: Original Entry

On August 1, the company paid $72,000 cash for a four-year insurance policy. The policy went into effect on August 1. Make the journal entry necessary on the company's books to record the payment for the insurance on August 1.

PE 4-11
LO2
Prepaid Expense: Adjusting Entry

Refer to PE 4-10. (1) Make the adjusting entry necessary on the company's books on December 31 with respect to this insurance policy and (2) compute the ending balance in the prepaid insurance account; assume that the balance as of the beginning of the year was $0.

PE 4-12
LO2
Unearned Revenue: Original Entry

The company provides security services to its clients. On April 1, the company received $270,000 cash for a three-year security contract. The contract went into effect on April 1. Make the journal entry necessary on the company's books to record the receipt of the payment for the contract on April 1.

PE 4-13
LO2
Unearned Revenue: Adjusting Entry

Refer to PE 4-12. (1) Make the adjusting entry necessary on the company's books on December 31 with respect to this security contract and (2) compute the ending balance in the unearned security revenue account; assume that the balance as of the beginning of the year was $0.

PE 4-14
LO2
Wages Payable: Adjusting Entry and Subsequent Payment

The company pays its employees at the end of the day Friday for work done during that five-day work week. Total wages for a week are $24,000. In the current year, December 31 occurred on a Tuesday. (1) Make the adjusting entry necessary on the company's books on December 31 with respect to unpaid employee wages and (2) make the journal entry necessary on Friday, January 3, of the following year to record the cash payment of wages for the

(continued)

week. Ignore the new year's holiday season and assume that employees worked each of the five days. Note: When making the January 3 entry, don't forget the adjusting entry that was made on December 31.

PE 4-15
LO2
Supplies: Original Purchase and Adjusting Entry

On January 1, the company had office supplies costing $4,600. On March 23, the company bought additional office supplies costing $8,200; the company paid cash. On December 31, a physical count of office supplies revealed that supplies costing $2,900 remained. (1) Make the journal entry necessary on the company's books on March 23 to record the purchase of office supplies and (2) make the adjusting entry necessary on December 31 with respect to office supplies.

PE 4-16
LO3
Preparing an Adjusted Trial Balance

Before any adjusting entries were made, the company prepared the following trial balance as of December 31:

	Debit	Credit
Cash	$ 68,000	
Notes Receivable	126,000	
Prepaid Rent	216,000	
Building	290,000	
Accounts Payable		$ 150,000
Unearned Fee Revenue		270,000
Capital Stock		150,000
Retained Earnings		100,000
Dividends	17,000	
Fee Revenue		370,000
Wages Expense	244,000	
Utilities Expense	79,000	
Totals	$1,040,000	$1,040,000

In order to make the adjusting entries, the following information has been assembled:
a. The notes receivable were issued on June 1. The annual interest rate on the notes is 12%. Interest is to be received each year on May 31; accordingly, no interest has been received.
b. The unearned fee revenue represents cash received in advance on February 1. This $270,000 relates to a three-year contract which began on February 1. It is expected that the fees will be earned evenly over the three-year contract period. As of December 31, no revenue had yet been recognized on this contract.
c. The prepaid rent represents cash paid in advance on October 1. This $216,000 relates to a five-year rental agreement that began on October 1. As of December 31, no expense had yet been recognized in association with this rental agreement.
d. As of December 31, unpaid (and unrecorded) wages totaled $22,000.

(1) Prepare the necessary adjusting journal entries and (2) prepare an adjusted trial balance.

PE 4-17
LO3
Using an Adjusted Trial Balance to Prepare an Income Statement

Refer to PE 4-16. Using the adjusted trial balance prepared in part (2), prepare an income statement for the year.

PE 4-18
LO3
Using an Adjusted Trial Balance to Prepare a Balance Sheet

Refer to PE 4-16. Using the adjusted trial balance prepared in part (2), prepare a balance sheet as of the end of the year. Note: The ending retained earnings balance is equal to the beginning balance plus the amount of net income less the amount of dividends.

PE 4-19

LO3

Adjusting Entries and the Audit

Consider the auditor's review of a company's adjusting entries. For which one of the following would a concerned auditor be required to make a search of items not included in the accounting records?

a. Overstated assets
b. Overstated liabilities
c. Understated assets
d. Understated liabilities

PE 4-20

LO4

Closing Entries: Revenues

Below is a list of accounts with corresponding ending balances.

	Account	Account Balance
a.	Prepaid Insurance	$3,200
b.	Cash	1,650
c.	Sales Revenue	5,500
d.	Retained Earnings	4,100
e.	Accounts Payable	2,300
f.	Capital Stock	1,000
g.	Interest Revenue	100

Prepare one summary entry to close those accounts that should be closed at the end of the year.

PE 4-21

LO4

Closing Entries: Expenses

Below is a list of accounts with corresponding ending balances.

	Account	Account Balance
a.	Insurance Expense	$1,300
b.	Cash	750
c.	Accounts Receivable	4,000
d.	Cost of Goods Sold	2,300
e.	Interest Payable	1,500
f.	Building	450
g.	Interest Receivable	200

Prepare one summary entry to close those accounts that should be closed at the end of the year.

PE 4-22

LO4

Closing Entries: Everything

Below is a list of accounts with corresponding ending balances.

	Account	Account Balance
a.	Inventory	$1,800
b.	Dividends	900
c.	Sales Revenue	7,900
d.	Wages Expense	5,100
e.	Cash	1,900
f.	Cost of Goods Sold	3,200
g.	Rent Revenue	800
h.	Retained Earnings (beginning)	1,300

(1) Prepare all entries necessary to close those accounts that should be closed at the end of the year and (2) compute the ending balance in the retained earnings account.

PE 4-23

LO4

Post-Closing Trial Balance

Refer to PE 4-16. Prepare a post-closing trial balance. For this exercise, ignore the adjustments described in PE 4-16; just use the reported trial balance.

EXERCISES

E 4-24
LO1

Reporting Income: Cash versus Accrual Accounting

On December 31, 2009, Matt Morgan completed the first year of operations for his new computer retail store. The following data were obtained from the company's accounting records:

Sales to customers	$197,000
Collections from customers	145,000
Interest earned and received on savings accounts	2,500
Cost of goods sold	98,500
Amounts paid to suppliers for inventory	103,000
Wages owed to employees at year-end	3,500
Wages paid to employees	40,000
Utility bill owed: to be paid next month	1,100
Interest due at 12/31 on loan to be paid in March of next year	1,200
Amount paid for one and one-half years' rent, beginning Jan. 1, 2009	17,500
Income taxes owed at year-end	4,000

1. How much net income (loss) should Matt report for the year ended December 31, 2009, according to (a) cash-basis accounting and (b) accrual-basis accounting?
2. Which basis of accounting provides the better measure of operating results for Matt?

E 4-25
LO1

Reporting Income: Cash versus Accrual Accounting

On December 31, Daniel McGrath completed the first year of operations for his new business. The following data are available from the company's accounting records:

Sales to customers	$265,000
Collections from customers	185,000
Interest earned and received on savings accounts	1,100
Amount paid on January 1 for one and one-half years' rent	18,000
Utility bill owed: to be paid next month	1,350
Cost of goods sold	123,000
Amount paid to suppliers for materials	104,500
Wages paid to employees	71,000
Wages owed to employees at year-end	3,500
Interest due at 12/31 on a loan to be paid the middle of next year	950

1. How much net income (loss) should Daniel report for the year ended December 31 according to (a) cash-basis accounting and (b) accrual-basis accounting?
2. Which basis of accounting provides the better measure of operating results for Daniel?

E 4-26
LO2

Classifications of Accounts Requiring Adjusting Entries

For each type of adjustment listed, indicate whether it is an unrecorded receivable, an unrecorded liability, an unearned revenue, or a prepaid expense at December 31, 2009.
1. Property taxes that are for the year 2009, but are not to be paid until 2010.
2. Rent revenue earned during 2009, but not collected until 2010.
3. Salaries earned by employees in December 2009, but not to be paid until January 5, 2010.
4. A payment received from a customer in December 2009 for services that will not be performed until February 2010.
5. An insurance premium paid on December 29, 2009, for the period January 1, 2010, to December 31, 2010.
6. Gasoline charged on a credit card during December 2009. The bill will not be received until January 15, 2010.
7. Interest on a certificate of deposit held during 2009. The interest will not be received until January 7, 2010.
8. A deposit received on December 15, 2009, for rental of storage space. The rental period is from January 1, 2010, to December 31, 2010.

E 4-27

LO2

Adjusting Entries: Prepaid Expenses and Unearned Revenues

Kearl Associates is a professional corporation providing management consulting services. The company initially debits assets in recording prepaid expenses and credits liabilities in recording unearned revenues. Give the entry that Kearl would use to record each of the following transactions on the date it occurred. Prepare the adjusting entries needed on December 31, 2009.

1. On July 1, 2009, the company paid a three-year premium of $5,400 on an insurance policy that is effective July 1, 2009, and expires June 30, 2012.
2. On February 1, 2009, Kearl paid its property taxes for the year February 1, 2009, to January 31, 2010. The tax bill was $2,400.
3. On May 1, 2009, the company paid $360 for a three-year subscription to an advertising journal. The subscription starts May 1, 2009, and expires April 30, 2012.
4. Kearl received $3,600 on September 15, 2009, in return for which the company agreed to provide consulting services for 18 months beginning immediately.
5. Kearl rented part of its office space to Davis Realty. Davis paid $900 on November 1, 2009, for the next six months' rent.
6. Kearl loaned $80,000 to a client. On November 1, the client paid $14,400, which represents two years' interest in advance (November 1, 2009, through October 31, 2011).

E 4-28

LO2

Adjusting Entries: Prepaid Expenses and Unearned Revenues

Erickson Group provides computer network consulting services. The company initially debits assets in recording prepaid expenses and credits liabilities in recording unearned revenues. Give the appropriate entry that Erickson would use to record each of the following transactions on the date it occurred. Prepare the adjusting entries needed on December 31, 2009. (Round all numbers to the nearest dollar.)

1. On March 15, 2009, Erickson received $35,000 for a contract to provide consulting services for 18 months beginning immediately.
2. On April 1, 2009, the company paid $350 for a two-year subscription to a computer networking journal. The subscription starts April 1, 2009, and expires March 31, 2011.
3. On May 1, 2009, Erickson paid $4,500 in property taxes for the year May 1, 2009, to April 30, 2010.
4. Erickson rented part of its office building to Boss Graphics, LLC. Boss paid $1,900 on August 1, 2009, for the next six months' rent.
5. On September 1, 2009, the company paid a two-year premium of $20,000 on an insurance policy that is effective September 1, 2009, and expires August 31, 2011.
6. Erickson loaned $250,000 to a client. On October 1, 2009, the client paid $21,000 for interest in advance (October 1, 2009, to September 30, 2010).

E 4-29

LO2

Adjusting Entries

Shop Rite Services is ready to prepare its financial statements for the year ended December 31, 2009. The following information can be determined by analyzing the accounts:

1. On August 1, 2009, Shop Rite received a $4,800 payment in advance for rental of office space. The rental period is for one year beginning on the date payment was received. Shop Rite recorded the receipt as unearned rent.
2. On March 1, 2009, Shop Rite paid its insurance agent $3,000 for the premium due on a 24-month corporate policy. Shop Rite recorded the payment as prepaid insurance.
3. Shop Rite pays its employee wages the middle of each month. The monthly payroll (ignoring payroll taxes) is $22,000.
4. Shop Rite received a note from a customer on June 1, 2009, as payment for services. The amount of the note is $1,000 with interest at 12%. The note and interest will be paid on June 1, 2011.
5. On December 20, 2009, Shop Rite received a $2,500 check for services. The transaction was recorded as unearned revenue. By year-end, Shop Rite had completed three-fourths

(continued)

of the contracted services. The rest of the services won't be completed until at least the middle of January 2010.

6. On September 1, Shop Rite purchased $500 worth of supplies. At December 31, 2009, one-fourth of the supplies had been used. Shop Rite initially recorded the purchase of supplies as an asset.

Where appropriate, prepare adjusting journal entries at December 31, 2009, for each of these items.

E 4-30

LO2

Adjusting Entries

Consider the following two independent situations:

1. On June 1, Hatch Company received $3,600 cash for a two-year subscription to its monthly magazine. The term of the subscription begins on June 1. Make the entry to record the receipt of the subscription on June 1. Also make the necessary adjusting entry at December 31. The company uses an account called Unearned Subscription Revenue.

2. Clark Company pays its employees every Friday for a five-day workweek. Salaries of $150,000 are earned equally throughout the week. December 31 of the current year is a Tuesday.
   a. Make the adjusting entry at December 31.
   b. Make the entry to pay the week's salaries on Friday, January 3, of the next year. Assume that all employees are paid for New Year's Day.

E 4-31

LO2

Adjusting Entries

Consider the following items for Williams Company:

1. On July 1 of the current year, Williams Company borrowed $300,000 at 9% interest. As of December 31, no interest expense has been recognized.

2. On September 1 of the current year, Williams Company rented to another company some excess space in one of its buildings. Williams Company received $24,000 cash on September 1. The rental period extends for six months, starting on September 1. Williams Company credited the account Unearned Rent Revenue upon receipt of the rent paid in advance.

3. At the beginning of the year, Williams Company had $750 of supplies on hand. During the year, another $3,900 of supplies were purchased for cash and recorded in the asset account Office Supplies. At the end of the year, Williams Company determined that $980 of supplies remained on hand.

4. On February 1 of the current year, Williams Company loaned Botts Company $125,000 at 8% interest. The loan amount, plus accrued interest, will be repaid in one year.

For each of the items, make the appropriate adjusting journal entry, if any, necessary in Williams Company's books as of December 31.

E 4-32

LO2

Adjusting Entries

Davis Company opened a Web page design business on January 1 of the current year. The following information relates to Davis Company's operations during the current year:

1. On February 1, Davis Company rented a new office. Before moving in, it prepaid a year's rent of $24,000 cash.

2. On March 31, Davis Company borrowed $50,000 from a local bank at 15%. The loan is to be repaid, with interest, after one year. As of December 31, no interest payments had yet been made.

3. Davis Company bills some of its customers in advance for its design services. During the year, Davis received $60,000 cash in advance from its customers. As of December 31, Davis's accountant determined that 40% of that amount had not yet been earned.

(continued)

4. On June 15, Davis Company purchased $1,400 of supplies for cash. On September 14, Davis made another cash purchase of $1,100. As of December 31, Davis's accountant determined that $1,700 of supplies had been used during the year.

5. Before closing its books, Davis Company found a bill for $800 from a free-lance programmer who had done work for the company in November. Davis had not yet recorded anything in its books with respect to this bill. Davis plans to pay the bill in January of next year.

For each of the items, make the initial entry, where appropriate, to record the transaction and, if necessary, the adjusting entry at December 31.

E 4-33
LO2

Adjusting Entries

Wallin Enterprises disclosed the following information on December 31, 2009 (before any adjusting entries were made):

1. In June, Wallin purchased an insurance premium for $54,000 for the 18 months beginning July 1, 2009.
2. On November 1, Wallin received $12,000 from Judy Phan for six months of rent beginning on November 1.
3. On February 1, Wallin borrowed $50,000 at 10% interest. Wallin has not recognized any interest expense this year.
4. On October 1, Wallin loaned Chris Spiker $15,000 at 12% interest. No interest revenue has been collected or recorded.

For each item listed, prepare the necessary adjusting entries to be made on December 31, 2009.

E 4-34
LO2

Adjusting Entries

Consider the following information related to the Timmy Thompson Company:

1. At the beginning of the year, the company had $460 in supplies on hand. During the year, the company purchased $5,300 in supplies. At the end of the year, the company had $1,320 in supplies on hand.
2. The company pays its employees on the 15th of each month. The monthly payroll (ignoring payroll taxes) is $19,000.
3. On November 1, the company received a $10,000 check for services. The transaction was recorded as unearned revenue. By year-end, the Timmy Thompson Company had completed one-fourth of the required work related to this service. Timmy expects to complete the rest of the work within the first two months of the next year.
4. On December 15, Timmy paid $4,800 for factory rental related to January of the next year.

For each item listed, prepare the necessary adjusting entries to be made on December 31.

E 4-35
LO2

Adjusting Entries

Consider the following information related to Pendleton Consulting:

1. On October 1, 2009, Pendleton Consulting entered into an agreement to provide consulting services for six months to Soelberg Company. Soelberg agreed to pay Pendleton $750 for each month of service. Payment will be made at the end of the contract (March 31, 2010).
2. On April 30, Pendleton borrowed $40,000 from a local bank at 12%. The loan is to be repaid, with interest, after one year. As of December 31, no interest expense had been recognized.
3. On February 25, Pendleton paid $36,000 for 12 months of rent beginning on March 1. On February 25, Pendleton made a journal entry debiting Prepaid Rent Expense.

(continued)

4. At the beginning of 2009, Pendleton had $825 in supplies on hand. During 2009, Pendleton purchased $7,290 in supplies. On December 31, 2009, Pendleton had $1,035 in supplies on hand.

For each item listed, prepare the necessary adjusting entries to be made on December 31, 2009.

E 4-36
LO2
Analysis of Accounts

Answer the following questions:

1. If office supplies on hand amounted to $3,500 at the beginning of the period and total purchases of office supplies during the period amounted to $18,000, determine the ending balance of office supplies on hand if office supplies expense for the period amounted to $19,500.
2. If beginning and ending accounts receivable were $22,000 and $26,000, respectively, and total sales made on account for the period amounted to $73,000, determine the amount of cash collections from customers on account for the period.
3. Assume all rent revenues are received in advance and accounted for as unearned rent, and beginning and ending balances of unearned rent are $4,000 and $4,500, respectively. If total rent revenue for the period amounts to $18,000, determine the amount of rent collections in advance for the period.

E 4-37
LO3
Classifying Account Balances

For each of the following accounts, indicate whether it would be found in the income statement or in the balance sheet.

1. Cash	10. Interest Receivable	19. Sales Revenue
2. Inventory	11. Capital Stock	20. Insurance Expense
3. Salaries Expense	12. Accounts Payable	21. Machinery
4. Prepaid Salaries	13. Buildings	22. Land
5. Retained Earnings	14. Mortgage Payable	23. Salaries Payable
6. Office Supplies Expense	15. Interest Expense	24. Prepaid Insurance
7. Accounts Receivable	16. Accounts Payable	25. Notes Payable
8. Cost of Goods Sold	17. Notes Receivable	26. Dividends
9. Maintenance Expense	18. Office Supplies	

E 4-38
LO4
Real and Nominal Accounts

Classify each of the following accounts as either a real account (R) or a nominal account (N):

1. Cash	14. Prepaid Salaries
2. Sales Revenue	15. Utilities Expense
3. Accounts Receivable	16. Notes Payable
4. Cost of Goods Sold	17. Inventory
5. Prepaid Insurance	18. Property Tax Expense
6. Capital Stock	19. Rent Expense
7. Retained Earnings	20. Interest Payable
8. Insurance Expense	21. Income Taxes Payable
9. Salaries Payable	22. Dividends
10. Interest Expense	23. Buildings
11. Insurance Premiums Payable	24. Office Supplies
12. Salaries Expense	25. Income Tax Expense
13. Accounts Payable	

E 4-39   **Closing Entry**

LO4   The income statement for Roberts Enterprises for the year ended June 30, 2009, is provided.

Roberts Enterprises	
Income Statement	
For the Year Ended June 30, 2009	
Sales revenue	$ 263,000
Cost of goods sold	(148,000)
Selling and general expenses	(21,300)
Income before income taxes	$ 93,700
Income tax expense	(33,000)
Net income	$ 60,700

1. Prepare a journal entry to close the accounts to Retained Earnings.
2. What problem may arise in closing the accounts if the information from the income statement is used?

E 4-40   **Closing Entry**

LO4   Revenue and expense accounts of Reschke Training Services for November 30, 2009, are given as follows. Prepare a compound journal entry that will close the revenue and expense accounts to the retained earnings account.

	Debit	Credit
Sales Revenue		$372,000
Cost of Goods Sold	$189,500	
Salaries Expense	42,000	
Interest Expense	2,500	
Rent Expense	12,600	
Insurance Expense	2,800	
Property Tax Expense	900	
Supplies Expense	1,600	
Advertising Expense	13,000	

E 4-41   **Closing Entries**

LO4   Johstoneaux, Inc. reports the following numbers for 2009:

Johstoneaux, Inc.	
Income Statement	
For the Year Ended December 31, 2009	
Sales	$ 420,300
Cost of goods sold	(230,000)
Insurance expense	(3,000)
Selling and administrative expenses	(90,000)
Income before taxes	$ 97,300
Income tax expense	(30,100)
Net income	$ 67,200

Prepare journal entries to close the revenue and expense accounts to the retained earnings account.

E 4-42   **Closing Entries**

LO4   The following information relates to the Wycherly Company:

Wycherly Company

Income Statement

For the Year Ended December 31, 2009

Sales revenue	$ 906,000
Interest revenue	23,000
Net revenue	$ 929,000
Cost of goods sold	(450,000)
Selling and administrative expenses	(140,000)
Income before taxes	$ 339,000
Income tax expense	(135,600)
Net income	$ 203,400

Prepare journal entries to close the revenue and expense accounts to the retained earnings account.

E 4-43   **Closing Dividends and Preparing a Post-Closing Trial Balance**

LO4   A listing of account balances taken from the adjusted ledger account balances of The Miners' Guild shows the following:

Cash	$ 45,160	Salaries Payable	$ 18,000
Accounts Receivable	112,960	Taxes Payable	48,800
Inventory	156,720	Unearned Rent	30,400
Prepaid Insurance	13,040	Mortgage Payable	180,000
Land	272,000	Capital Stock	88,000
Accounts Payable	57,280	Dividends	40,000
Notes Payable	80,000	Retained Earnings	137,400

All revenue and expense accounts have been closed to Retained Earnings. Dividends has not yet been closed.

Prepare (1) the closing entry for Dividends and (2) a post-closing trial balance for December 31, 2009.

E 4-44   **Closing Dividends and Preparing a Post-Closing Trial Balance**

LO4   Below is a listing of account balances taken from the adjusted ledger account balances of Jolley Manufacturing Corporation.

Cash	$ 16,400	Income Taxes Payable	$ 7,000
Accounts Receivable	23,500	Mortgage Payable	82,500
Inventory	71,000	Notes Payable	23,000
Prepaid Advertising	4,000	Unearned Rent	4,200
Building	110,000	Capital Stock	80,000
Land	45,000	Dividends	14,800
Accounts Payable	24,000	Retained Earnings	56,000
Wages Payable	8,000		

All revenues and expense accounts have been closed to Retained Earnings. Dividends has not yet been closed.

Prepare (1) the closing entry for Dividends and (2) a post-closing trial balance for December 31, 2009.

PROBLEMS

P 4-45   **Cash- and Accrual-Basis Accounting**

LO1   In the course of your examination of the books and records of Karen Company, you find the following data:

Salaries earned by employees in 2009	$ 61,000
Salaries paid in 2009	53,000
Total sales revenue in 2009	927,000
Cash collected from sales in 2009	952,000
Utilities expense incurred in 2009	7,500
Utility bills paid in 2009	6,300
Cost of goods sold in 2009	602,000
Cash paid on purchases in 2009	613,000
Inventory at December 31, 2009	416,000
Tax assessment for 2009	6,210
Taxes paid in 2009	5,930
Rent expense for 2009	36,000
Rent paid in 2009	41,000

Required:

1. Compute Karen's net income for 2009 using cash-basis accounting.
2. Compute Karen's net income for 2009 using accrual-basis accounting.
3. **Interpretive Question:** Why is accrual-basis accounting normally used? Can you see any opportunities for improperly reporting income under cash-basis accounting? Explain.

P 4-46   **Adjusting Entries**

LO2   The information presented below is for MedQuest Pharmacy, Inc.

a. Salaries for the period December 26, 2009, through December 31, 2009, amounted to $17,840 and have not been recorded or paid. (Ignore payroll taxes.)

b. Interest of $5,225 is payable for three months on an 11%, $190,000 loan and has not been recorded.

c. Rent of $36,000 was paid for six months in advance on December 1 and debited to Prepaid Rent.

d. Rent of $76,000 was credited to an unearned revenue account when received. Of this amount, $42,100 is still unearned at year-end.

e. The expired portion of an insurance policy is $2,400. Prepaid Insurance was originally debited.

f. Interest revenue of $400 from a $4,000 note has been earned but not collected or recorded.

Required:

Prepare the adjusting entries that should be made on December 31, 2009. (Omit explanations.)

P 4-47   **Adjusting Entries**

LO2   The information presented below is for Susan's Sweet Shop.

a. Interest of $9,600 is payable for September 2009 through December 2009 on a 9%, $320,000 loan and has not been recorded.

b. Rent of $93,500 was credited to an unearned revenue account when received. Of this amount, $42,250 is still unearned at year-end.

c. Interest revenue of $9,450 from a $105,000 note has been earned but not collected or recorded.

d. The expired portion of an insurance policy is $4,960. Prepaid Insurance was originally debited.

e. Rent of $30,000 was paid for six months in advance on November 15, 2009, and debited to Prepaid Rent.

(continued)

f. Salaries for the period December 26, 2009, to December 31, 2009, amounted to $15,300 and have not been recorded or paid. (Ignore payroll taxes.)

Required:

Prepare the adjusting entries that should be made on December 31, 2009. (Omit explanations.)

P 4-48
LO2

Year-End Analysis of Accounts

An analysis of cash records and account balances of Wells, Inc., for 2009 is as follows:

	Account Balances Jan. 1, 2009	Account Balances Dec. 31, 2009	Cash Received or Paid in 2009
Wages Payable	$2,600	$3,000	
Unearned Rent	4,500	5,000	
Prepaid Insurance	100	120	
Paid for wages			$29,600
Received for rent			12,000
Paid for insurance			720

Required:

Determine the amounts that should be included on the 2009 income statement for (1) wages expense, (2) rent revenue, and (3) insurance expense.

P 4-49
LO2

Year-End Analysis of Accounts

An analysis of cash records and account balances of Apartment Renters, Inc., for 2009 is as follows:

	Account Balances Jan. 1, 2009	Account Balances Dec. 31, 2009	Cash Received or Paid in 2009
Salaries Payable	$15,600	$18,400	
Unearned Rent	10,350	14,100	
Prepaid Insurance	3,300	2,000	
Paid for salaries			$134,000
Received for rent			48,500
Paid for insurance			13,800

Required:

Determine the amounts that should be included on the 2009 income statement for (1) salaries expense, (2) rent revenue, and (3) insurance expense.

P 4-50
LO4

Account Classifications and Debit-Credit Relationships

Using the format provided, for each account identify (1) whether the account is a balance sheet (B/S) or an income statement (I/S) account; (2) whether it is an asset (A), a liability (L), an owners' equity (OE), a revenue (R), or an expense (E) account; (3) whether the account is a real or a nominal account; (4) whether the account will be "closed" or left "open" at year-end; and (5) whether the account normally has a debit or a credit balance. The following example is provided:

Account Title	(1) B/S or I/S	(2) A, L, OE, R, E	(3) Real or Nominal	(4) Closed or Open	(5) Debit/ Credit
Cash	B/S	A	Real	Open	Debit

(continued)

1. Accounts Receivable	13. Supplies on Hand
2. Accounts Payable	14. Utilities Expense
3. Prepaid Insurance	15. Income Taxes Payable
4. Mortgage Payable	16. Interest Revenue
5. Rent Expense	17. Notes Payable
6. Sales Revenue	18. Income Tax Expense
7. Cost of Goods Sold	19. Wages Payable
8. Dividends	20. Unearned Rent Revenue
9. Capital Stock	21. Land
10. Inventory	22. Unearned Consulting Fees
11. Retained Earnings	23. Interest Receivable
12. Prepaid Rent	24. Consulting Fees

P 4-51

LO4

Closing Entries

The income statement for Joe's Asphalt, Inc., for the year ended December 31, 2009, is as follows:

Joe's Asphalt, Inc.
Income Statement
For the Year Ended December 31, 2009

Sales revenue		$904,000
Less expenses:		
Cost of goods sold	$726,000	
Salaries expense	144,000	
Interest expense	10,500	
Office supplies expense	7,640	
Insurance expense	9,860	
Property tax expense	22,400	
Total expenses		920,400
Net loss		$ (16,400)

Required:

Dividends of $36,000 were paid on December 30, 2009.

1. Give the entry required on December 31, 2009, to properly close the income statement accounts.
2. Give the entry required to close the dividends account at December 31, 2009.

P 4-52

LO4

Closing Entries

The income statement for Squared Carpentry, Inc., for the year ended December 31, 2009, is as follows:

Squared Carpentry, Inc.
Income Statement
For the Year Ended December 31, 2009

Sales revenue		$843,200
Less expenses:		
Cost of goods sold	$567,100	
Wages expense	102,750	
Utilities expense	4,890	
Insurance expense	6,930	
Property tax expense	10,510	
Rent expense	49,000	
Advertising expense	15,640	
Interest expense	9,800	
Total expenses		766,620
Net income		$ 76,580

(continued)

Dividends of $18,600 were paid on December 30, 2009.

Required:

1. Give the entry required on December 31, 2009, to properly close the income statement accounts.
2. Give the entry required to close the dividends account at December 31, 2009.

P 4-53

LO2, LO4

Unifying Concepts: Adjusting and Closing Entries

The unadjusted and adjusted trial balances of White Company as of December 31, 2009, are presented below.

| | White Company Trial Balance December 31, 2009 | | | |
| | Unadjusted | | Adjusted | |
	Debits	Credits	Debits	Credits
Cash	$ 21,250		$ 21,250	
Accounts Receivable	11,250		11,250	
Supplies on Hand	5,195		3,895	
Prepaid Rent	17,545		7,545	
Prepaid Insurance	1,985		1,100	
Buildings (net)	95,000		95,000	
Land	45,720		45,720	
Accounts Payable		$ 9,350		$ 9,350
Wages Payable				5,700
Income Taxes Payable				580
Interest Payable		450		1,050
Notes Payable		65,000		65,000
Capital Stock		84,320		84,320
Consulting Fees Earned		142,380		142,380
Wages Expense	92,335		98,035	
Rent Expense			10,000	
Interest Expense	3,500		4,100	
Insurance Expense	585		1,470	
Supplies Expenses	4,365		5,665	
Income Tax Expense	2,770		3,350	
Totals	$301,500	$301,500	$308,380	$308,380

Required:

1. Prepare the journal entries that are required to adjust the accounts at December 31, 2009.
2. Prepare the journal entry that is required to close the accounts at December 31, 2009.

P 4-54

LO3, LO4

Unifying Concepts: Analysis of Accounts

The bookkeeper for Davey James Company accidentally pressed the wrong computer key and erased the amount of Retained Earnings. You have been asked to analyze the following data and provide some key numbers for the board of directors meeting, which is to take place in 30 minutes. With the exception of Retained Earnings, the following account balances are available at December 31, 2009.

(continued)

Cash	$ 61,000	Accounts Receivable	$ 49,000
Furniture (net)	40,000	Inventory	160,000
Accounts Payable	120,000	Notes Payable	250,000
Land	260,000	Supplies on Hand	10,000
Buildings (net)	240,000	Capital Stock	300,000
Sales Revenue	415,000	Dividends	20,000
Salaries Expense	50,000	Retained Earnings	?
Cost of Goods Sold	220,000		

Required:

1. Compute the amount of total assets at December 31, 2009.
2. Compute the amount of net income for the year ended December 31, 2009.
3. After all closing entries are made, what is the amount of Retained Earnings at December 31, 2009?
4. What was the beginning Retained Earnings balance at January 1, 2009?

P 4-55
LO5

Unifying Concepts: Analysis and Correction of Errors

At the end of November 2009, the general ledger of Peacock Clothing Company showed the following amounts:

Assets	$103,070
Liabilities	53,300
Owners' Equity	76,300

The company's bookkeeper is new on the job and does not have much accounting experience. Because the bookkeeper has made numerous errors, total assets do not equal liabilities plus owners' equity. The following is a list of errors made.

a. Inventory that cost $64,000 was sold, but the entry to record cost of goods sold was not made.
b. Credit sales of $23,400 were posted to the general ledger as $32,400. The accounts receivable were posted correctly.
c. Inventory of $14,800 was purchased on account and received before the end of November, but no entry to record the purchase was made until December.
d. November salaries payable of $4,000 were not recorded until paid in December.
e. Common stock was issued for $25,000 and credited to Accounts Payable.
f. Inventory purchased for $42,030 was incorrectly posted to the asset account as $24,500. No error was made in the liability account.

Required:

Determine the correct balances of assets, liabilities, and owners' equity at the end of November.

P 4-56
LO5

Unifying Concepts: The Accounting Cycle

The post-closing trial balance of Anderson Company at December 31, 2008, is shown here.

(continued)

Anderson Company Post-Closing Trial Balance December 31, 2008	Debits	Credits
Cash	$ 15,000	
Accounts Receivable	20,000	
Inventory	30,000	
Land	150,000	
Accounts Payable		$ 25,000
Notes Payable		35,000
Capital Stock		125,000
Retained Earnings		30,000
Totals	$215,000	$215,000

During 2009, Anderson Company had the following transactions:

a. Inventory purchases were $80,000, all on credit (debit Inventory).

b. An additional $10,000 of capital stock was issued for cash.

c. Merchandise that cost $100,000 was sold for $180,000; $100,000 were credit sales and the balance were cash sales. (Debit Cost of Goods Sold and credit Inventory for sale of merchandise.)

d. The notes were paid, including $7,000 interest.

e. $105,000 was collected from customers.

f. $95,000 was paid to reduce accounts payable.

g. Salaries expense was $30,000, all paid in cash.

h. A $10,000 cash dividend was declared and paid.

Required:

1. Prepare journal entries to record each of the 2009 transactions.

2. Set up T-accounts with the proper balances at January 1, 2009, and post the journal entries to the T-accounts.

3. Prepare an income statement for the year ended December 31, 2009, and a balance sheet as of that date. Also prepare a statement of retained earnings.

4. Prepare the entries necessary to close the nominal accounts, including Dividends.

5. Post the closing entries to the ledger accounts [label (i) and (j)] and prepare a post-closing trial balance at December 31, 2009.

ANALYTICAL ASSIGNMENTS

AA 4-57

DISCUSSION

Using Financial Statements for Investment Decisions

Several doctors are considering the purchase of a small real estate business as an investment. Because you have some training in the mechanics of the accounting cycle, they have hired you to review the real estate company's accounting records and to prepare a balance sheet and an income statement for their use. In analyzing various business documents, you verify the following data.

The account balances at the beginning of the current year were as follows:

Cash in Bank	$ 7,800
Notes Receivable (from Current Owner)	10,000
Supplies on Hand	750
Prepaid Office Rent	4,500
Accounts Payable	450
Owners' Equity	22,600

(continued)

During the current year, the following summarized transactions took place:

a. The owner paid $1,200 to the business to cover the interest on the note receivable ($10,000 × 0.12 × 1 year). Nothing was paid on the principal.

b. Real estate commissions earned during the year totaled $45,500. Of this amount, $1,000 has not been received by year-end.

c. The company purchased $500 of supplies during the year. A count at year-end shows $300 worth still on hand.

d. The $4,500 paid for office rental was for 18 months, beginning in January of this year.

e. Utilities paid during the year amounted to $1,500.

f. During the year, $400 of accounts payable were paid; the balance in Accounts Payable at year-end is $300, with the adjustment being debited to Miscellaneous Office Expense.

g. The owner paid himself $1,500 a month as a salary and paid a part-time secretary $2,400 for the year. (Ignore payroll taxes.)

On the basis of the above data, prepare a balance sheet and an income statement for the real estate business. Does the business appear profitable? Does the balance sheet raise any questions or concerns? What other information might the doctors want to consider in making this investment decision?

AA 4-58
DISCUSSION

Accounting and Ethical Issues Involving the Closing Process

Silva and Wanita Rodriques are the owners of Year-Round Landscape, Inc., a small landscape and yard service business in southern California. The business is three years old and has grown significantly, especially during the past year. To sustain this growth, Year-Round Landscape must expand operations.

In the past, the Rodriques have been able to secure funds for the business from personal resources. Now those resources are exhausted, and the Rodriques are seeking a loan from a local bank.

To satisfy bank requirements, Year-Round Landscape, Inc., must provide a set of financial statements, including comparative income statements showing the growth in earnings over the past three years. In analyzing the records, Silva notices that the nominal accounts have not yet been closed for this year. Furthermore, Silva is aware of a major contract that is to be signed on January 3, only three days after the December 31 year-end for the business. Silva suggests that the closing process be delayed one week so that this major contract can be included in this year's operating results. Silva estimates that this contract will increase current year earnings by 20%.

What accounting issues are involved in this case? What are the ethical issues?

AA 4-59
DISCUSSION

Wrestling with Your Conscience and GAAP

You are the controller for South Valley Industries. Your assistant has just completed the financial statements for the current year and has given them to you for review. A copy of the statements also has been given to the president of the company. The income statement reports net income for the year of $50,000 and earnings per share of $2.50.

In reviewing the statements, you realize the assistant neglected to record adjusting entries. After making the necessary adjustments, the company shows a net loss of $10,000. The difference is due to an unusually large amount of unrecorded expenses at year-end. You realize that these expenses are not likely to be found by the independent auditors.

You wonder if it would be better to delay the recording of the expenses until the first part of the subsequent year in order to avoid reporting a net loss on the income statement for the current year. A significant increase in revenues is expected in the coming year, and the expenses in question could be "absorbed" by the higher revenues.

What issues are involved in this case? What course of action would you take?

AA 4-60
JUDGMENT CALL

You Decide: Should deferred compensation packages be disclosed in the notes to the financial statements, or should they be recorded as liabilities?

Recently, corporate accounting scandals have brought about an increased scrutiny of executive compensation. Companies are being criticized for their role in accounting for stock

(continued)

options, inflated salaries, and personal loans to executives. However, there is one hidden treasure that should not be overlooked: deferred compensation packages for executives. These are retirement packages that will allow executives to set aside, pretax, up to 100% of their cash compensation, earning as much as a 10% return. For many companies, these deferred compensation packages represent corporate liabilities that are not in the financial statements or even disclosed in the notes. How should they be reported and/or disclosed, if at all?

AA 4-61
JUDGMENT CALL

You Decide: **Should intellectual properties be recorded as assets on the balance sheet or disclosed in the notes to the financial statements?**

Intellectual property refers to creations of the mind. Examples include inventions, symbols, names, images, logos, and designs used in commerce. For example, the annual reports for a mutual fund company will often list all fund managers with their associated professional credentials, academic history, and honors they have received. This provides useful information to the investors and helps individuals realize the value of good fund managers. Is there a way to "quantify" this type of information so that it can appear in the balance sheet as an asset to the firm?

AA 4-62
JUDGMENT CALL

You Decide: **Can wages payable be deferred to make the financial statements look better?**

It is early December and you have just been hired as an accountant for a local computer hardware store. Business is expanding due to the increased number of sales reps your boss just hired. Your boss is excited about expanding the business into other nearby communities, but will need a loan from the bank to do so. He has hired you to clean up the books and get the company's financial information ready so he can present it to the bank's loan officer after the first of the year. On December 30, your boss asks you not to record the sales force's wages for the month of December because he won't be able to pay them until mid-January. He wants the financial statements to be in good shape when he visits the loan officer. What should you do?

AA 4-63
REAL COMPANY
ANALYSIS

Wal-Mart

Using **Wal-Mart's** 2006 Form 10-K contained in Appendix A, answer the following questions:

1. Find note #1 in Wal-Mart's annual report. Specifically locate the "Revenue Recognition" heading. In the case of Wal-Mart and SAM'S CLUB shopping cards, does the company recognize revenue when the card is purchased?
2. SAM'S CLUB sells 12-month membership cards. Are the revenues associated with the sale of those cards recognized when the card is sold, at the end of the 12 months, or at some other point?

AA 4-64
REAL COMPANY
ANALYSIS

Home Depot

Selected financial statement information for **Home Depot** is given in the table below. Using this information, answer the following questions:

(all numbers in millions)
Retained Earnings balance—02/02/2003 $15,971 million

	Net Income	Dividends
For year ended February 1, 2004	$4,304	$595
For year ended January 30, 2005	5,001	719
For year ended January 29, 2006	5,838	857

1. Compute Home Depot's Retained Earnings balance at the end of each year.
2. Divide dividends into net income for each year. The result is termed the "dividend payout ratio." Did Home Depot's dividend payout ratio increase or decrease over time?

AA 4-65
REAL COMPANY
ANALYSIS

Campbell Soup

Information from the 2005 income statement for **Campbell Soup Company** is shown below.

(in millions, except per-share amounts)	2005	2004	2003
Net Sales	$7,548	$7,109	$6,678
Costs and expenses			
Cost of products sold	4,491	4,187	3,805
Marketing and selling expenses	1,185	1,153	1,145
Administrative expenses	571	542	507
Research and development expenses	95	93	88
Other expenses	(4)	(13)	59
Restructuring charge	–	32	–
Total costs and expenses	6,338	5,994	5,604
Earnings Before Interest and Taxes	$1,210	$1,115	$1,074
Interest expense	184	174	186
Interest income	4	6	5
Earnings before taxes	1,030	947	893
Taxes on earnings	323	300	298
Net Earnings	$ 707	$ 647	$ 595

Using the information from the income statement, perform the following:
1. Prepare the entries made by Campbell to close the 2005 revenue and expense accounts to Retained Earnings.
2. Campbell Soup paid dividends of $280 million in 2005. Provide the entry made to close the dividends account to Retained Earnings.
3. If the beginning balance in Campbell's Retained Earnings was $5,642 million, what would the ending balance be after the above closing entries have been posted?

AA 4-66
INTERNATIONAL

Exchange Rate Adjustments

Given the international economy in which many firms operate, it is not unusual for companies to have transactions with companies in foreign countries. Relatedly, it is becoming common for some of those transactions to be denominated in a foreign currency. That is, if a company in the United States makes a purchase from a company in Japan, it is possible that the U.S. company will have to pay Japanese yen when the invoice comes due.

For example, suppose American, Inc., purchased inventory from Japan, Inc., on December 15, 2008. Japan, Inc., expects to receive 1,000,000 Japanese yen in 30 days. To record a journal entry for this purchase, you would need to know what 1,000,000 yen are worth today. Suppose that on December 15, 2008, one yen is worth $0.07 (this is called an exchange rate). What journal entry would be made on American, Inc.'s books?

Since exchange rates change every day, the amount of U.S. dollars to be paid on January 15, 2009, will likely be different than the originally recorded $70,000. In addition, to correctly state the liability on December 31, 2008, an adjustment will be required. Suppose that at year-end, one Japanese yen is worth $0.08. What adjusting entry would be made to reflect this change in exchange rates as of December 31, 2008? (Hint: The accounts being adjusted with this journal entry will be the accounts payable account and an exchange gain or loss.)

When the invoice is paid on January 15, 2009, it is likely that the number of U.S. dollars required to purchase 1,000,000 Japanese yen will again have changed. Suppose exchange rates have increased to $0.09. Provide the journal entry to pay the invoice.

AA 4-67
ETHICS

Do Two Wrongs Make a Right?

Jex Varner, chief financial officer of Wyndam, Inc., is involved in a meeting with the firm's newly hired external auditors, Ernst & Price. The external auditors have noted several

(continued)

adjusting entries that they believe should be reflected in the current period's financial statements. Specifically, there are questions regarding $400,000 of cash that has been received (and recorded as revenue) but not yet earned. The auditors feel that this amount should be recognized as a liability.

Jex counters that the firm's policy has always been to recognize revenue when the cash is received. He states that $350,000 of cash was received in December of last year, earned in January, and no adjustment was made. To be consistent, he continues, he doesn't believe any adjustments should be made this year.

As a member of the external auditing team, do you agree with Jex's reasoning? If you think that an adjustment needs to be made, what journal entry would you propose? What should be done about the $350,000 that has been earned this year even though the cash was received last year?

AA 4-68
WRITING

Are Adjusting Entries More Trouble Than They Are Worth?

You are taking an introductory accounting class. You think that making regular journal entries is not too difficult, but making adjusting entries is still a bit of a mystery. You have found that your answers to homework questions on adjusting entries are incorrect at least half the time. You mentioned your difficulties to the other members of your study group, and they all agreed—adjusting entries are brutal. As you and your study colleagues shared your frustration with adjusting entries, the following consensus formed: adjusting entries are more trouble than they are worth. You were selected by your study group to pass this sentiment along to your accounting instructor. She agreed that adjusting entries can be difficult, but she insisted that they are worth the effort. She has now given you the following writing assignment: write a one-page paper describing the value of adjusting entries.

AA 4-69
CUMULATIVE
SPREADSHEET
PROJECT

Preparing Forecasts

This spreadsheet assignment is a continuation of the spreadsheet assignments given in earlier chapters. If you completed those spreadsheets, you have a head start on this one.

1. Refer back to the balance sheet and income statement created using the financial statement numbers for Handyman Company for 2009 [given in part (1) of the Cumulative Spreadsheet Project assignment in Chapter 2]. With these historical numbers for 2009 as a starting point, Handyman wishes to prepare a forecasted balance sheet and a forecasted income statement for 2010. In preparing the forecasted financial statements for 2010, consider the following additional information:

   a. Sales in 2010 are expected to increase by 40% over 2009 sales of $700.

   b. In the forecasted balance sheet for 2010, cash, receivables, inventory, and accounts payable will all increase at the same rate as sales (40%) relative to 2009. These increases occur because, with the planned 40% increase in the volume of business and no plans to significantly change its methods of operation, Handyman will probably also experience a 40% increase in the levels of its current operating assets and liabilities.

   c. In 2010, Handyman expects to acquire new property, plant, and equipment costing $80.

   d. Accumulated depreciation is the cumulative amount of depreciation expense that Handyman has reported over its years in business. Thus, the forecasted amount of accumulated depreciation for 2010 can be computed as accumulated depreciation as of the end of 2009 plus the forecasted depreciation expense for 2010.

   e. New short-term loans payable will be acquired in an amount sufficient to make Handyman's current ratio (current assets divided by current liabilities) in 2010 exactly equal to 2.0.

   f. No new long-term debt will be acquired in 2010.

   g. No cash dividends will be paid in 2010. Remember that the amount of retained earnings at the end of any year is the beginning retained earnings amount plus net income minus dividends.

(continued)

h. In this exercise, the forecasted amount of paid-in capital is the "plug" figure. In other words, the forecasted balance in paid-in capital at the end of 2010 is the amount necessary to make the forecasted balance sheet balance such that forecasted total assets equal forecasted total liabilities. A key reason for preparing forecasted financial statements is to identify in advance whether any additional financing will be required.

i. The $160 in operating expenses reported in 2009 breaks down as follows: $5 depreciation expense, $155 other operating expenses.

j. In the forecasted income statement for 2010, cost of goods sold and other operating expenses will both increase at the same rate as sales (40%) relative to 2009. This is another way of saying that the amount of these expenses, relative to the amount of sales, will probably stay about the same year to year unless Handyman plans to significantly change the way it does business.

k. The amount of Handyman's depreciation expense is determined by how much property, plant, and equipment the company has. In 2009, Handyman had $5 of depreciation expense on $199 of property, plant, and equipment, meaning that depreciation was equal to 2.5% ($5/$199) of the amount of property, plant, and equipment. It is expected that the same relationship will hold in 2010.

l. Interest expense depends on how much interest-bearing debt a company has. In 2009, Handyman reported interest expense of $9 on long-term debt of $207. (Note: To simplify this exercise, we will ignore interest expense on the short-term loan payable.) Because Handyman is expected to have the same amount of long-term debt in 2010, our best guess is that interest expense will remain the same.

m. Income tax expense is determined by how much pretax income a company has. And, the most reasonable assumption to make is that a company's tax rate, equal to income tax expense divided by pretax income, will stay constant from year to year. Handyman's income tax rate in 2009 was 33% ($4/$12).

2. Repeat (1) assuming that forecasted sales growth in 2010 is 20% instead of 40%. Clearly state any assumptions that you make.

Ensuring the Integrity of Financial Information

After studying this chapter, you should be able to:

(1) Identify the types of problems that can appear in financial statements. *Mechanical errors in the recording or posting process and mistakes in accounting estimates can result in incorrect financial statement numbers. Financial statements can also be intentionally misstated by managers seeking to fraudulently deceive investors and creditors.*

(2) Describe the safeguards employed to ensure that financial statements are free from problems. *Ethical and careful managers are much more likely to establish conditions and procedures that result in fair financial statements. Such managers insist on a carefully designed accounting system that captures all company transactions. These managers also ensure that internal checks and balances prevent accidental loss and intentional theft and fraud.*

(3) Understand the concept of earnings management and why it occurs. *Managers of companies sometimes are motivated to manage reported earnings in order to meet internal targets and to look good to outsiders. When a manager decides to manage earnings, he or she can fall into a downward spiral of deception which can result in a massive loss of reputation for the manager and the company.*

(4) Understand the major parts of the Sarbanes-Oxley Act and how it impacts financial reporting. *The Sarbanes-Oxley Act was passed by Congress in 2002 in response to the public uproar over a rash of large corporate accounting scandals. The Act places a personal responsibility on corporate managers to produce reliable financial reports. The Act also raises the standards for external auditors.*

(5) Describe the role of auditors and how their presence affects the integrity of financial statements. *Auditors increase the reliance that users can place on financial reports. Internal auditors monitor accounting processes in a company on an ongoing basis. External auditors certify that the financial statements released to the public are a fair representation of the company's financial position and performance.*

(6) Explain the role of the Securities and Exchange Commission in adding credibility to financial statements. *The SEC has legal authority to set financial accounting standards in the United States; in practice, the SEC allows the FASB to set these standards. The SEC also oversees the certification of external auditors. The SEC requires publicly-traded companies to provide quarterly financial statements to the public.*

Until 2002, **WorldCom**, a telecom giant, appeared to be one of the greatest corporate success stories ever. In 1983, a group of partners led by former basketball coach Bernard Ebbers sketched out their idea for a long distance telephone company on a napkin in a coffee shop in Hattiesburg, Mississippi. Soon after, their company **LDDS** (Long Distance Discount Service) began providing service as a long distance reseller. For 15 years, it grew quickly through acquisitions and mergers. Bernard Ebbers was named CEO in 1985, and the company sold shares of stock to the public in August 1989. Its $40 billion merger with **MCI** in 1998 was the largest corporate merger in history at the time. The company was also a favorite with investors and Wall Street analysts. The stock reached a peak of $64.51 per share in June 1999.

Not long after, however, the success of the company's finances began to unravel with the accumulation of debt and expenses, the fall of the stock market, and drops in long distance rates and revenue. While it would take nearly two years for the extent of these problems to become public, in the end, WorldCom disclosed massive financial statement fraud and filed for Chapter 11 bankruptcy, the largest in U.S. history. In 2002, WorldCom became a horror story that involved the largest accounting fraud ever reported, SEC investigations, the resignation of CEO Bernard Ebbers, a $101.9 billion dollar bankruptcy, and a stock that was worth less than a pay phone call.[1]

While there were several different types of financial statement frauds committed by WorldCom, by far the largest was the manipulation of expenses and assets. In a court filing in New York in November 2002, the Securities and Exchange Commission (SEC) said that WorldCom admitted that it concealed over $9 billion in expenses, all of which was converted into false profits.

As you learned in earlier chapters, expenditures should be classified as assets and listed on the balance sheet if they have future value, such as expenditures for buildings or equipment. If expenditures are for current operating costs such as salaries or rent, however, you learned that they should be expensed as incurred and reported as expenses on the income statement.

In simple terms, instead of expensing costs that had been incurred, the company was listing these costs as assets and putting them on the balance sheet. These expenditures should have been subtracted from revenues on the income statement and reported as expenses when incurred. The result was that reported expenses were lower than they should have been on the income statement and reported assets and owners' equity were higher than they should have been on the balance sheet.

The simple WorldCom fraud was discovered when some obscure tips provided to the company's internal auditors were pursued by Cynthia Cooper, Gene Morse, and Glyn Smith, all internal auditors working for the company. The subsequent investigation resulted in testimony from David Myers, an accountant with WorldCom, who stated: "I was instructed on a quarterly basis by Scott Sullivan, chief financial officer, to ensure that entries were made to falsify WorldCom's books to reduce WorldCom's reported actual costs and therefore to increase WorldCom's reported earnings." He said that Scott Sullivan and he would "... work backward, picking the earnings numbers that they knew Wall Street analysts expected to see, and then force WorldCom's financials to match those numbers." While these shenanigans worked for a time, in the end, WorldCom's total market value (number of shares of stock times stock price) went from a high of about $120 billion to almost nothing and several individuals were indicted for fraud.

(?) **F Y I**

On April 14, 2002, WorldCom announced that it was changing its name to MCI—the company it purchased in 1998. In 2005, it was sold to **Verizon** for $6.7 billion or about $20.75 per share of stock.

---

[1] CEO Bernie Ebbers was sentenced in July 2005 to 25 years in prison for his role in orchestrating the WorldCom financial statement fraud. His sentence is the longest ever for a CEO found guilty of committing corporate crimes while running a Fortune 500 company.

In Chapters 1 and 2, you were introduced to financial accounting and shown the outputs (financial statements) of the financial reporting process. You learned that the balance sheet, income statement, and statement of cash flows are reports used by organizations to summarize their financial results for various users. In Chapters 3 and 4, the accounting cycle, the method of entering and processing financial transaction information in the accounting records, was described. You learned that transaction data are captured by journal entries, journal entry data are summarized in accounts and ledgers, ledger information is summarized on trial balances, and trial balance information provides the basis for the balance sheet, income statement, and statement of cash flows.

In Chapters 1 through 4, the assumption was made that the financial reporting process always works the way it should and that the resulting financial statements are accurate. In reality, however, because of unintentional errors, as well as intentional deception or fraud (such as in the WorldCom case), the resulting financial statements sometimes contain errors or omissions that can mislead investors, creditors, and other users.

In this chapter, we show how financial statements might be manipulated, and we discuss the safeguards built into the financial reporting system to prevent these abuses. We also examine the role that auditors play in ensuring that the financial statements fairly represent the financial performance of the firm.

The Types of Problems That Can Occur

Identify the types of problems that can appear in financial statements.

1 Obviously, most businesses do not engage in massive frauds like those that occurred at **WorldCom**. Financial deception does not come about mainly for two reasons: (1) the vast majority of business managers are honest, possess integrity, and would not be associated with fraudulent activity, and (2) safeguards have been built into the accounting system to prevent and detect activities that are inconsistent with the objectives of a business. These safeguards attempt to eliminate problems from being introduced into the financial statements. However, during the past few years, there have been numerous financial statement frauds disclosed at companies such as **Enron**, **WorldCom**, **Adelphia**, **Global Crossing**, **Xerox**, **Quest**, **Waste Management**, **Cendant**, **AniCom**, **Homestore**, **Sunbeam**, **Tyco**, and others.

Before proceeding further, we need to make an important distinction regarding these problems. Problems in the financial statements can result for several different reasons.

1. *Errors*—result when unintentional mistakes are made in recording transactions, posting transactions, summarizing accounts, and so forth. Errors are *not intentional* and when detected are immediately corrected. Errors can result from sloppy accounting, bad assumptions, misinformation, miscalculations, and other factors.
2. *Disagreements*—result when different people arrive at different conclusions based on the same set of facts. Because accounting involves judgment and estimates, opportunities for honest disagreements in judgment abound. These disagreements often come about because of the different incentives that motivate those involved with producing the financial statements. An example of a disagreement might be differing views about what percentage of reported receivables will be collected or how long equipment and other assets will last.
3. *Frauds*—result from intentional errors. Fraudulent financial reporting occurs when management chooses to intentionally manipulate the financial statements to serve their own purposes, such as meeting Wall Street's earnings forecasts as was the case with WorldCom.

An accounting system should be designed to significantly reduce the possibility that problems, in whatever form, will make their way into financial statements. When it is discovered that the financial statements of public companies are wrong, for whatever reason, they must be restated (reissued with correct amounts). In recent years, the number of restatements has increased, as shown below.

Year	Number of U.S. Restatements
2000	233
2001	270
2002	330
2003	323
2004	619
2005	1295[2]

Types of Errors in the Reporting Process

Errors, and other problems, can occur in most stages of the accounting cycle. We will first describe the kinds of errors that can occur and then identify controls to minimize these errors.

Errors in Transactions and Journal Entries   Transactions, such as selling products or services, paying salaries, buying inventory, and paying taxes, are entered into the accounting records through journal entries. For example, if $5,000 is paid to an attorney for legal services, the following journal entry is made:

Legal Expense...	5,000	
Cash		5,000
Paid an attorney $5,000 for legal services.		

An invoice from the law firm should support this entry. Errors could be introduced into the financial reporting process if (1) the invoice from the law firm was lost and the legal expense was not entered into the accounting records, (2) the amount entered into the accounting records was incorrect, or (3) the accounts involved were incorrectly identified.

Errors in Accounts and Ledgers   Even when journal entries properly summarize legitimate transactions, errors and misstatements can be introduced into the financial records because journal entry data are not summarized appropriately or accurately in the ledgers. Using the previous example of paying an attorney $5,000, errors could occur at the posting stage of the accounting cycle if the legal expense is entered in the wrong account in the ledger or if an incorrect amount is posted to the correct account. Posting the correct amount to the wrong expense account would result in the correct total for all expenses, but individual expense account balances would be incorrect.

A more severe error occurs at the ledger stage if amounts that should be included in asset or liability accounts are improperly included in expense or revenue accounts, or vice versa. Examples include (1) recording insurance expense as prepaid insurance (an asset), (2) recording purchases of goods for resale as inventory (an asset) when they should be reported as cost of goods sold (an expense), (3) recording money received from customers as revenue when it should be recorded as unearned revenue (a liability), or (4) not reporting supplies used as an expense.

---

[2] 1,195 of these were by U.S. companies and 100 were by foreign private issues with U.S.-listed stocks. This information comes from a 2006 Glass Lewis Report and includes restatements of both quarterly and annual financial statements.

Disagreements in Judgment

Many people think that accounting involves exactness and precision and that accountants simply record the facts, total the numbers, and present unbiased results. Nothing could be further from the truth. Accountants are constantly making judgments and estimates regarding the past and the future. Let's return to the landscaping business that we introduced in Chapters 3 and 4 to illustrate some of the judgments involved in the accounting process.

As your lawn care and landscaping business has become more and more successful, you have been able to obtain bigger and better jobs. Recently, you signed a contract to provide all the landscaping for a new condominium complex currently under construction. The terms of the contract call for payment of one-half of the contract amount up front and the remaining one-half upon completion. You begin working on the condominium landscaping in early December, but it looks as though you will not finish until well into January. To prepare financial statements at the end of December, how much of the condominium contract should you report as revenue? The answer depends on how close to completion the job is. If you are 25% complete, it makes sense to report 25% of the contract amount as revenue. If you are 75% complete, report 75% of the contract amount as revenue. The hard part is determining how much of the job has been completed.

Suppose you contact two landscapers (friendly competitors) and ask them to provide you with an estimate of how complete the landscaping job is at year-end. Would it be possible for these two people to arrive at different conclusions regarding the percentage of completion? Which one would be right? Different people can look at the same set of facts and arrive at different conclusions. They're not wrong, just different. In this case, the different estimates would result in different financial statement numbers. These different numbers could make the difference between your company showing a profit or reporting a loss.

Consider another example. Most of your customers pay promptly, but some take a little longer to pay. A few customers discontinue their lawn care service and never pay for some of the services they received. Your problem is that when you provide a service for a customer, you do not know if that customer will be a "prompt payer," a "slow payer," or a "no payer." Recognizing that a certain percentage of your customers will be "no payers," should you record a receivable (and a revenue) for the full amount of every sale? As you will learn in Chapter 6, most businesses recognize that a certain percentage of receivables will be uncollectible. How should you arrive at the amount of your receivables that won't be collected? Is it possible that your estimate will be slightly off? Could different people legitimately arrive at different estimates? Of course. These different estimates will then affect the results reported in the financial statements. There are many more estimates like these required when preparing financial statements for most companies.

Fraudulent Financial Reporting

As mentioned previously, fraudulent financial reporting is intentional. To illustrate, consider the journal entry made previously related to legal expense. Assume that a company's accountant embezzles $5,000 and prepares the following journal entry to conceal the fraud:

Legal Expense	5,000	
Cash		5,000
Paid an attorney $5,000 for legal services.		

The accountant could prepare the journal entry without supporting documentation (e.g., an invoice) or create a fictitious invoice from a phantom law firm.

Unless someone is watching closely, the theft may go undetected. Because the accountant made a fictitious entry to Legal Expense, the accounting records appear to be correct, and the accounting equation still balances. Cash, an asset, is stolen, and the recognition of an expense results in owners' equity being reduced by the same amount.

Assets	=	Liablities	+	Owners' Equity
(decreased by $5,000)				(decreased by $5,000)

While this illustration is small and the dishonest act was committed by an employee against the company, it is intentional and results in financial statements that are incorrect. More serious financial statement fraud occurs when top management intentionally manipulates the financial statements in much larger amounts.

There are many different ways for management to commit financial statement fraud. Examples are listing sales that don't exist (as was the case with **Waste Management**, the trash disposal company, which was making false entries to record revenues and receivables that overstated income by as much as 35% in 1996 and a total of $1.7 billion from 1992–1997); not recording sales returns or uncollectible receivables (as was the case with the vacuum maker, **Regina**, which did not record the return of over 40,000 vacuums); and not recording various expenses, understating liabilities, and overstating assets such as inventory or receivables (as was the case with **Phar-Mor**, which overstated its assets by shipping products back and forth between stores when inventory was counted).

STOP & THINK

Before reading about the safeguards designed to minimize the types of problems we have just discussed, can you think of things that could be done to ensure that errors, disagreements in judgment, and fraudulent financial reporting do not occur?

REMEMBER THIS...

The financial reports for most companies are accurate.
Inaccurate financial reports can result from any one of the following:

- Unintentional errors
- Disagreements in judgment
- Fraud

Safeguards Designed to Minimize Problems

Describe the safeguards employed to ensure that financial statements are free from problems.

Accounting is a language just as is English. In the same way that a falsehood can be written in English, a misleading story can be expressed by financial statements. By far, the vast majority of financial statements are as accurate as possible, and the preparers are honest. **Federal Express**, the shipping company, as do all public companies, requires that its executives annually sign off on a code of ethics that gives assurances in writing that they have no conflicts of interest or know of no improprieties. The company's policy requires that any employee involved in any kind of dishonesty be immediately terminated and prosecuted. According to FedEx's policy, ". . . magnitude is not the issue. It doesn't matter if the impropriety involves a thousand or a million dollars, our company will not tolerate anything that is done unethically or inappropriately." Almost all organizations prepare accounting records and financial reports with integrity, and in most cases, preparers are even conservative when judgments and estimates are required. To help ensure that financial reports are accurate and to prevent problems such as those that occurred at **WorldCom**, several safeguards have been built into the financial reporting system and structure of most organizations in the United States. As a future user of accounting information, you should be aware of these safeguards and the reasons for their existence.

internal control structure

Safeguards in the form of policies and procedures established to provide management with reasonable assurance that the objectives of an entity will be achieved.

Most organizations build controls into their organization and financial reporting processes so that abuses are difficult. These safeguards, called the **internal control structure**, are internal to the organization preparing the financial statements. The American Institute of Certified Public Accountants (AICPA) has defined *internal control* as "the policies and procedures established to provide reasonable assurance that specific entity objectives will be achieved."[3] These internal controls protect investors and creditors and even help management in their efforts to run their organizations as effectively and efficiently as possible. If you encounter an organization or financial statements that do not have these controls and safeguards, you should exercise extreme care.

Most companies have the following five concerns in mind when they are designing internal controls:

1. To provide accurate accounting records and financial statements containing reliable data for business decisions.
2. To safeguard assets and records. Most companies think of their assets as including their financial assets (such as cash or property), their employees, their confidential information, and their reputation and image.
3. To effectively and efficiently run their operations, without duplication of effort or waste.
4. To follow management policies.
5. To comply with the Foreign Corrupt Practices and Sarbanes-Oxley Acts, which require companies to maintain proper record-keeping systems and controls.

Foreign Corrupt Practices Act (FCPA)

Legislation requiring any company that has publicly-traded stock to have an adequate system of internal accounting controls.

Sarbanes-Oxley Act

A law passed by Congress in 2002 that gives the SEC significant oversight responsibility and control over companies issuing financial statements and their external auditors.

The responsibility for establishing and maintaining the internal control structure belongs to a company's management. Until several years ago, this responsibility was only implied; there was no formal legal requirement. However, in the wake of illegal political campaign contributions, business frauds, and numerous illegal payments to foreign officials in exchange for business favors, in 1977, Congress passed the **Foreign Corrupt Practices Act (FCPA)**. As a result of this legislation, all companies whose stock is publicly traded are required by law to keep records that represent the firm's transactions accurately and fairly. In addition, they must maintain adequate systems of internal accounting control. Following the rash of reported financial statement frauds in 2001 and 2002, Congress passed the **Sarbanes-Oxley Act** (known as the corporate responsibility act) in 2002. This far-sweeping corporate reform act requires, among other things, that every company's annual report contain an "internal control report," which must (1) state the responsibility of management for establishing and maintaining an adequate internal control structure and procedures for financial reporting, (2) contain an assessment of the effectiveness of the internal control structure by management, (3) contain an independent auditor's assessment of the concurrence with the way management assessed the reliability of its internal controls, and (4) contain an independent assessment of the reliability of internal controls by the independent auditor.

---

[3] AU Section 319, par. 06, Codification of Statements on Auditing Standards, CCH Inc., 1994, p. 98.

(This act, by the way, requires that the CEO and CFO of every public company prepare and sign a statement to accompany their financial statements that certifies the "appropriateness of the financial statements and disclosures contained in the report.")

A company's internal control structure can be divided into five basic categories:[4] (1) the control environment, (2) risk assessment, (3) control activities, (4) information and communication, and (5) monitoring. In this chapter, we will only briefly cover the control environment and control activities (sometimes called control procedures), as well as the need for monitoring (the areas of risk assessment and information and communication are left to courses covering the details of auditing).

The Control Environment

control environment

The actions, policies, and procedures that reflect the overall attitudes of top management about control and its importance to the entity.

The **control environment** consists of the actions, policies, and procedures that reflect the overall attitudes of top management, the directors, and the owners about control and its importance to the company. In a strong control environment, management believes control is important and makes sure that everyone responds conscientiously to the control policies and procedures. In addition, a company with a good control environment generally develops an organizational structure that identifies clear lines of authority and responsibility. A complex **organizational structure** can make it easier to conceal dishonest transactions.

organizational structure

Lines of authority and responsibility.

Another element of a good control environment relates to independent oversight of significant management decisions. This oversight is generally exhibited through a board of directors which consists of individuals both internal and external to the firm.

audit committee

Members of a company's board of directors who are responsible for dealing with the external and internal auditors.

Every major company has a board of directors. A good control environment would suggest that a subset of these directors should form an **audit committee**. The audit committee should be comprised of independent, outside directors (members of the board who are not officers of the company). The internal and external auditors would then be accountable to this audit committee. Under the Sarbanes-Oxley Act, members of the audit committee must be financially literate. The audit committee must be directly responsible for the appointment, compensation, and oversight of the work of the external auditor and must have the authority to engage independent legal counsel or other advisors if it suspects any wrongdoing. External auditors who suspect wrongdoing in financial reporting should forward those concerns to the audit committee.

Control Activities (Procedures)

control activities (procedures)

Policies and procedures used by management to meet their objectives.

Control activities or **control procedures** are those policies and procedures, in addition to the control environment and accounting system, that management has adopted to provide reasonable assurance that the company's established objectives will be met and that financial reports are accurate. Generally, control activities fall into five categories: adequate segregation of duties, proper procedures for authorization, physical control over assets and records, adequate documents and records, and independent checks on performance. The first three are referred to as **preventative controls** because they "prevent" problems from occurring. The last two are referred to as **detective controls** because they help catch problems that are occurring before the problems become large.

preventative controls

Internal control activities that are designed to prevent the occurrence of errors and fraud.

detective controls

Internal control activities that are designed to detect the occurrence of errors and fraud.

---

[4] These five categories were outlined in a document created by the Committee of Sponsoring Organizations (COSO). Most companies use the COSO framework to assess the reliability of their internal controls.

Adequate Segregation of Duties

segregation of duties

A strategy to provide an internal check on performance through separation of authorization of transactions from custody of related assets, separation of operational responsibilities from record-keeping responsibilities, and separation of custody of assets from accounting personnel.

Adequate Segregation of Duties   A good internal control system should provide for the appropriate segregation of duties. This means that no one department or individual should be responsible for handling all or conflicting phases of a transaction. In some small businesses, this segregation is not possible because the limited number of employees prevents division of all the conflicting functions. Nevertheless, there are three functions that should be performed by separate departments or by different people whenever possible.

1. *Authorization.* Authorizing and approving the execution of transactions; for example, approving the sale of a building or land.
2. *Record keeping.* Recording the transactions in the accounting records.
3. *Custody of assets.* Having physical possession of or control over the assets involved in transactions, including operational responsibility; for example, having the key to the safe in which cash or investment securities are kept or, more generally, having control over the production function.

By separating the responsibilities for these duties, a company realizes the efficiency derived from specialization and also reduces the errors, both intentional and unintentional, that might otherwise occur.

Proper Procedures for Authorization   A strong system of internal control requires proper authorization for every transaction. In the typical corporate organization, this authorization originates with the stockholders who elect a board of directors. It is then delegated from the board of directors to upper-level management and eventually throughout the organization. While the board of directors and upper-level management possess a fairly general power of authorization, a clerk usually has limited authority. Thus, the board would authorize dividends, a general change in policies, or a merger; a clerk would be restricted to authorizing credit or a specific cash transaction. Only certain people should be authorized to enter data into accounting records and prepare accounting reports.

As an example of journal entries and misstated financial statements that were not authorized, consider the following example:

> In one of the large financial statement frauds that became public in 2002, the CFO instructed the chief accountant to increase earnings by $105 million. The chief accountant was skeptical about the purpose of these instructions, but he did not challenge them. The mechanics were left to the chief accountant to carry out. The chief accountant created a spreadsheet containing seven pages of improper journal entries that he determined were necessary to carry out the CFO's instructions. These types of fictitious and unauthorized journal entries were made over a five-year period.

physical safeguards

Physical precautions used to protect assets and records, such as locks on doors, fireproof vaults, password verification, and security guards.

Physical Control Over Assets and Records   Some of the most crucial policies and procedures involve the use of adequate physical safeguards to protect resources. For example, a bank would not allow significant amounts of money to be transported in an ordinary car. Similarly, a company should not leave its valuable assets or records unprotected. Examples of physical safeguards are fireproof vaults for the storage of classified information, currency, and marketable securities; and guards, fences, and remote control cameras for the protection of equipment, materials, and merchandise. Re-creating lost or destroyed records can be costly and time-consuming, so companies make backup copies of records.

Adequate Documents and Records   A key to good controls is an adequate system of documentation and records. As explained in Chapter 3, documents are the physical,

© ROYALTY-FREE/CORBIS

Many companies use physical safeguards, such as surveillance cameras, to protect their resources.

objective evidence of accounting transactions. Their existence allows management to review any transaction for appropriate authorization. Documents are also the means by which information is communicated throughout an organization. In short, adequate documentation provides evidence that the recording and summarizing functions that lead to financial reports are being performed properly. A well-designed document has several characteristics: (1) it is easily interpreted and understood, (2) it has been designed with all possible uses in mind, (3) it has been pre-numbered for easy identification and tracking, and (4) it is formatted so that it can be handled quickly and efficiently. Documents can be actual pieces of paper or information in a computer database.

Independent Checks on Performance
Having **independent checks** on performance is a valuable control technique. Independent checks incorporate reviews of functions, as well as the internal checks created from a proper segregation of duties.

There are many ways to independently check performance. Using independent reviewers, such as auditors, is one of the most common. In addition, mandatory vacations, where another employee performs the vacationing person's duties, periodic rotations or transfers, or merely having someone independent of the accounting records reconcile the bank statement are all types of independent checks.

As stated previously, all public companies are required to include in their annual report a statement signed by management that describes and accepts responsibility for the internal controls of the company. The statement shown in Exhibit 1 was included in the 2005 annual report of **IBM Corporation**.

independent checks

Procedures for continual internal verification of other controls.

REMEMBER THIS...

Most organizations have an internal control system that, among other things, helps ensure integrity in financial reports. The various elements of control that relate to financial reporting are summarized as follows.

Control Environment	**Control Activities (Procedures)**
1. Management philosophy and operating style.	1. Segregation of duties (preventative control).
2. Organizational structure.	2. Proper procedures for authorization (preventative control).
3. Audit committee.	3. Physical control over assets and records (preventative control).
	4. Adequate documents and records (detective control).
	5. Independent checks on performance (detective control).

| EXHIBIT 1 | **IBM Corporation's 2005 Management Letter** |

Report of Management

Management's Report on Internal Control Over Financial Reporting

Management is responsible for establishing and maintaining adequate internal control over financial reporting of the company. Internal control over financial reporting is a process designed to provide reasonable assurance regarding the reliability of financial reporting and the preparation of financial statements for external purposes in accordance with accounting principles generally accepted in the United States of America.

The company's internal control over financial reporting includes those policies and procedures that (1) pertain to the maintenance of records that, in reasonable detail, accurately and fairly reflect the transactions and dispositions of the assets of the company; (2) provide reasonable assurance that transactions are recorded as necessary to permit preparation of financial statements in accordance with accounting principles generally accepted in the United States of America, and that receipts and expenditures of the company are being made only in accordance with authorizations of management and directors of the company; and (3) provide reasonable assurance regarding prevention or timely detection of unauthorized acquisition, use, or disposition of the company's assets that could have a material effect on the financial statements.

Because of its inherent limitations, internal control over financial reporting may not prevent or detect misstatements. Also, projections of any evaluation of effectiveness to future periods are subject to the risk that controls may become inadequate because of changes in conditions, or that the degree of compliance with the policies or procedures may deteriorate.

Management conducted an evaluation of the effectiveness of internal control over financial reporting based on the framework in Internal Control-Integrated Framework issued by the Committee of Sponsoring Organizations of the Treadway Commission (COSO). Based on this evaluation, management concluded that the company's internal control over financial reporting was effective as of December 31, 2005. Management's assessment of the effectiveness of the company's internal control over financial reporting as of December 31, 2005 has been audited by PricewaterhouseCoopers LLP, an independent registered public accounting firm, as stated in their report which is included herein.

Samuel J. Palmisano
Chairman of the Board,
President and Chief Executive Officer
February 28, 2006

Mark Loughridge
Senior Vice President,
Chief Financial Officer
February 28, 2006

Reasons for Earnings Management

Understand the concept of earnings management and why it occurs.

③ Accountants, using the concepts of accrual accounting and the accounting standards that have been issued, add information value by using estimates and assumptions to convert the raw cash flow data into accrual data. However, the same flexibility that allows accountants to use professional judgment to produce financial statements that accurately portray a company's financial condition also allows desperate managers to "manage" the reported numbers.[5]

This section describes four reasons for managing reported earnings. These aren't necessarily good reasons. However, they do reflect the forces that are often spoken of as pushing managers to manipulate reported earnings. These four reasons are as follows:

- Meet internal targets.
- Meet external expectations.
- Income smoothing.
- Window dressing for an IPO or a loan.

---

[5] As we will learn in the subsequent discussion, extreme "earnings management" may result from fraudulent activities. But it is important to note that not all earnings management activities are fraudulent.

Meet Internal Targets

internal earnings targets

Financial goals established within a company.

Internal earnings targets are an important tool in motivating managers to increase sales efforts, control costs, and use resources more efficiently. But as with any performance measurement tool, it is a fact of life that the person being evaluated will have a tendency to forget the economic factors underlying the measurement and instead focus on the measured number itself.

Meet External Expectations

A wide variety of external stakeholders have an interest in the financial performance of a company. For example, employees and customers want a company to do well so that it can survive for the long run and make good on its long-term pension and warranty obligations. Suppliers want assurance that they will receive payment and, more importantly, that the purchasing company will be a reliable purchaser for many years into the future. For these stakeholders, signs of financial weakness, such as the reporting of negative earnings, are very bad news indeed. Accordingly, we shouldn't be surprised that in some companies when the initial computations reveal that a company will report a net loss, the company's accountants are asked to go back to the accrual judgments and estimates to see if just a few more dollars of earnings can be squeezed in order to get earnings to be positive.

Income Smoothing

Examine the time series of earnings for Company A and Company B shown in Exhibit 2. For Company A, the amount of earnings increases steadily for each year from Year 1 through Year 10. For Company B, the earnings series is like a roller coaster ride. Companies A and B have the same earnings in Year 1 and the same earnings in Year 10, and they also have the same total earnings over the 10-year period included in the graph. At the end of Year 10, if you were asked which company you would prefer to loan money to or to invest in, you would almost certainly choose Company A. The earnings stream of Company A gives you a sense of stability, reliability, and reduced risk.

Now, imagine yourself as the chief executive officer of Company B. You know that through aggressive accounting assumptions, you can strategically defer or accelerate the

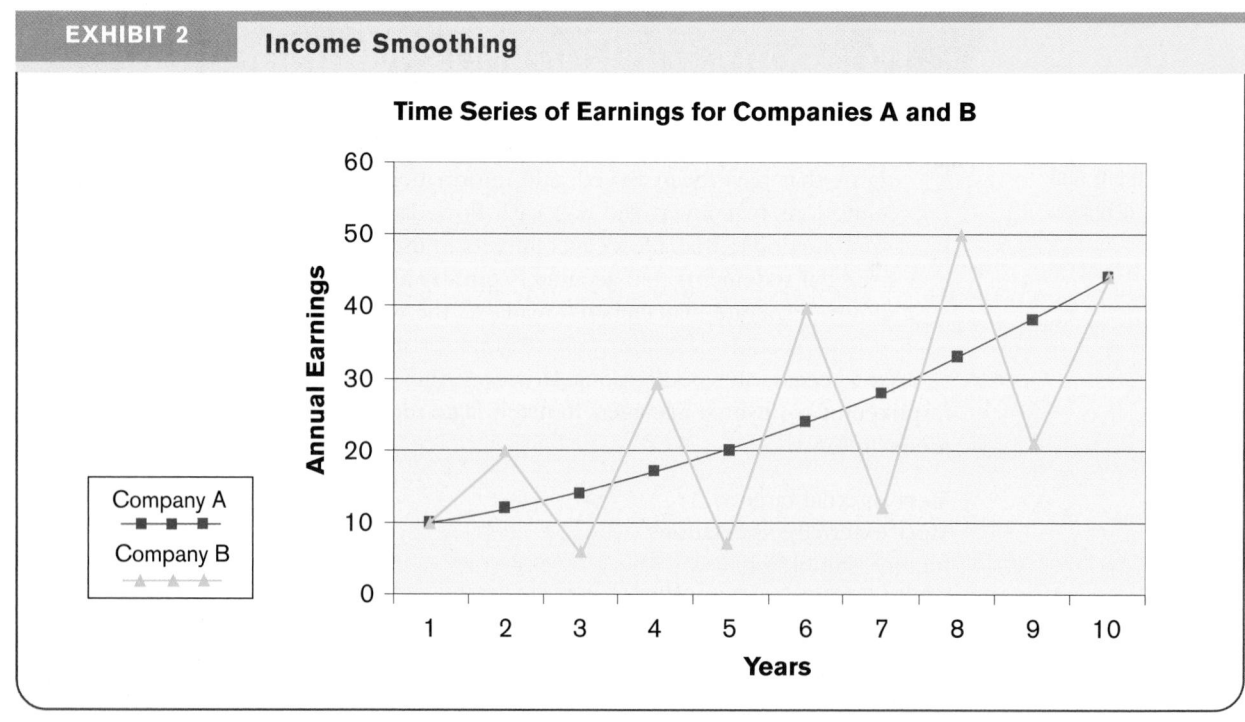

EXHIBIT 2   **Income Smoothing**

Time Series of Earnings for Companies A and B

income smoothing

The practice of carefully timing the recognition of revenues and expenses to even out the amount of reported earnings from one year to the next.

recognition of some revenues and expenses and smooth your reported earnings stream to be exactly like that shown for Company A. Would you be tempted to do so? The practice of carefully timing the recognition of revenues and expenses to even out the amount of reported earnings from one year to the next is called **income smoothing**. By making a company appear to be less volatile, income smoothing can make it easier for a company to obtain a loan on favorable terms and to attract investors.

Window Dressing for an IPO or a Loan

For companies entering phases where it is critical that reported earnings look good, accounting assumptions can be stretched—sometimes to the breaking point. Such phases include just before making a large loan application or just before the initial public offering (IPO) of stock. Many studies have demonstrated the tendency of managers in U.S. companies to boost their reported earnings using accounting assumptions in the period before an IPO.

With all of the incentives to manage earnings, it isn't surprising that managers occasionally do use the flexibility inherent in accrual accounting to actually manage earnings. And the more accounting training one has, the easier it is to see ways in which accounting judgments and estimates can be used to "enhance" the reported numbers. In fact, there have been nationwide seminars on exactly how to effectively manage earnings. One popular seminar sponsored by the National Center for Continuing Education in 2001 was titled, "How to Manage Earnings in Conformance with GAAP." The target audience for the two-day seminar was described as CFOs, CPAs, controllers, auditors, bankers, analysts, and securities attorneys.

 F Y I

In the wake of the accounting scandals that occurred in 2001 and 2002, the National Center for Continuing Education decided to change the title of the earnings management seminar to "How to Detect Manipulative Accounting Practices." However, the course outline was exactly the same as the original "How to Manage Earnings" seminar.

The Earnings Management Continuum

Not all earnings management schemes are created equal. The continuum in Exhibit 3 illustrates that earnings management can range from savvy timing of transactions to outright fraud. The discussion in this section discusses each activity on the earnings management continuum. Keep in mind that in most companies, earnings management, if it is practiced at all, does not extend beyond the savvy transaction timing found at the left end of the continuum in Exhibit 3. However, because of the importance, and economic significance, of the catastrophic reporting failures that are sometimes associated with companies that engage in more elaborate earnings management, the entire continuum is discussed here.

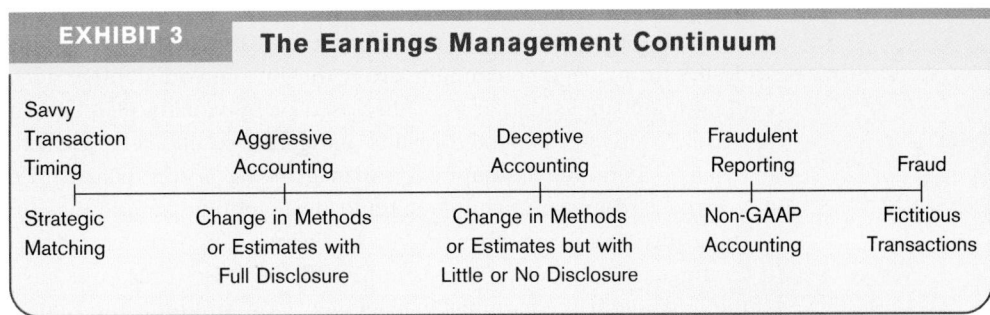

EXHIBIT 3	**The Earnings Management Continuum**			
Savvy Transaction Timing	Aggressive Accounting	Deceptive Accounting	Fraudulent Reporting	Fraud
Strategic Matching	Change in Methods or Estimates with Full Disclosure	Change in Methods or Estimates but with Little or No Disclosure	Non-GAAP Accounting	Fictitious Transactions

Strategic Matching   As mentioned in the earlier discussion of income smoothing, through awareness of the benefits of consistently meeting earnings targets or of reporting a stable income stream, a company can make extra efforts to ensure that certain key transactions are completed quickly, or delayed, in order for them to be recognized in the most advantageous quarter.

Change in Methods or Estimates with Full Disclosure   Companies frequently change accounting estimates regarding bad debts, return on pension funds, depreciation lives, and so forth. Although such changes are a routine part of adjusting accounting estimates to reflect the most current information available, they can be used to manage the amount of reported earnings. Because the impact of such changes is fully disclosed, any earnings management motivation could be detected by financial statement users willing to do a little detective work.

Change in Methods or Estimates with Little or No Disclosure   In contrast to the accounting changes referred to in the preceding paragraph, other accounting changes are sometimes made without full disclosure. For example, in 1999 **Xerox** reported that the company changed the estimated interest rate used in recording sales-type leases without describing the change in the notes to the financial statements. While one might debate whether the new estimated interest rate was more appropriate, what is certain is that failing to disclose the impact of the change resulted in financial statement users being misled. These users evaluated the reported earnings of Xerox under the incorrect assumption that the results were compiled using a consistent set of accounting methods and estimates and could therefore be meaningfully compared to prior-year results. As indicated by the label in Exhibit 3, this constitutes deceptive accounting.

Non-GAAP Accounting   Toward the right end of the earnings management continuum lies the earnings management tool that can be politely called "non-GAAP accounting." A more descriptive label in many cases is "fraudulent reporting," although non-GAAP accounting can also be the result of inadvertent errors. For example, a brief description of some of **Enron's** accounting practices was given in Chapter 1. It is clear that some (though certainly not all) of these accounting practices were established for the express purpose of hiding information from financial statement users. In so doing, Enron violated the spirit of the accounting standards. In some cases, Enron also violated the letter of the standards by using some accounting practices that were not allowed under GAAP.

Fictitious Transactions   As mentioned previously in this chapter, **Regina** did not record the return of over 40,000 vacuums. In fact, the company rented secret warehouses in which to store returned merchandise in order to avoid recording the returns. This is an example of outright fraud, which is the deceptive concealment of transactions (like the sales returns) or the creation of fictitious transactions.

The five items displayed in Exhibit 3 also mirror the progression in earnings management strategies followed by individual companies. These activities start small and legitimate and really reflect nothing more than the strategic timing of transactions to smooth reported results. In the face of operating results that fall short of targets, a company might make some cosmetic changes in accounting estimates in order to meet earnings expectations, but would fully disclose these changes to avoid deceiving serious financial statement users. If operating results are far short of expectations, an increasingly desperate management might cross the line into deceptive accounting by making accounting changes that are not disclosed or by violating GAAP completely. Finally, when the gap between expected results and actual results is so great that it cannot be closed by any accounting assumption, a manager who is still fixated on making the target number must resort to out-and-out fraud by inventing transactions and customers. The key thing to remember is that the forces encouraging managers and accountants to manage earnings are real, and if one is not aware of those forces it is easy to gradually slip from the left side of the earnings management continuum to the right side.

Is Earnings Management Ethical?

Refer back to Exhibit 3. Everyone agrees that the creation of fictitious transactions, at the far right side of the earnings management continuum, is unethical. But there the universal agreement ends with respect to what is and is not ethical. For example, managers and their auditors frequently disagree about what constitutes fraudulent, non-GAAP reporting. In the **WorldCom** example mentioned earlier, the company's CFO vigorously defended the capitalization, rather than the expensing, of the disputed $3.8 billion in local phone access charges. The CFO reiterated this defense, based on his understanding of the appropriate accounting standards, in a multi-day series of meetings with the external auditor and the audit committee. In the view of the CFO, this "fraudulent reporting" was both ethical and in conformity with GAAP. And as one moves even further to the left on the earnings management continuum, disagreement about whether a certain act is or is not ethical increases. For example, when a company makes an accounting change, how can a bright line be drawn between sufficient and deceptive disclosure? And who is to judge whether the strategic timing of gains and losses by a company is unethical or just prudent business practice?

Exhibit 4 contains a figure called the **GAAP oval**. This oval represents the flexibility a manager has, within GAAP, to report one earnings number from among many possibilities based on different methods and assumptions. Clearly, reporting a number corresponding with points D or E, which are both outside the GAAP oval, is unethical. The difficult ethical question is whether the manager has a responsibility to try to report an earnings number exactly in the middle of the possible range, such as point B in Exhibit 4. Or does the manager have a responsibility to report the most conservative, worst-case number, like point A in the exhibit? Is it wrong for the manager to try to use accounting flexibility to report an earnings number corresponding with point C, which is the highest possible earnings number that is still in conformity with GAAP? And what cost is there, in terms of credibility, for a manager who makes a conservative

GAAP oval

A diagram that represents the flexibility a manager has, within GAAP, to report one earnings number from among many possibilities based on different methods and assumptions.

? F Y I

Nonaccountants are under the impression that there is no GAAP oval. Instead, they believe that there is only a GAAP point, a single quantity that represents the one, true earnings number. Managers must be aware that because of this attitude the public can be very unforgiving of companies that are found to have "innocently" managed earnings.

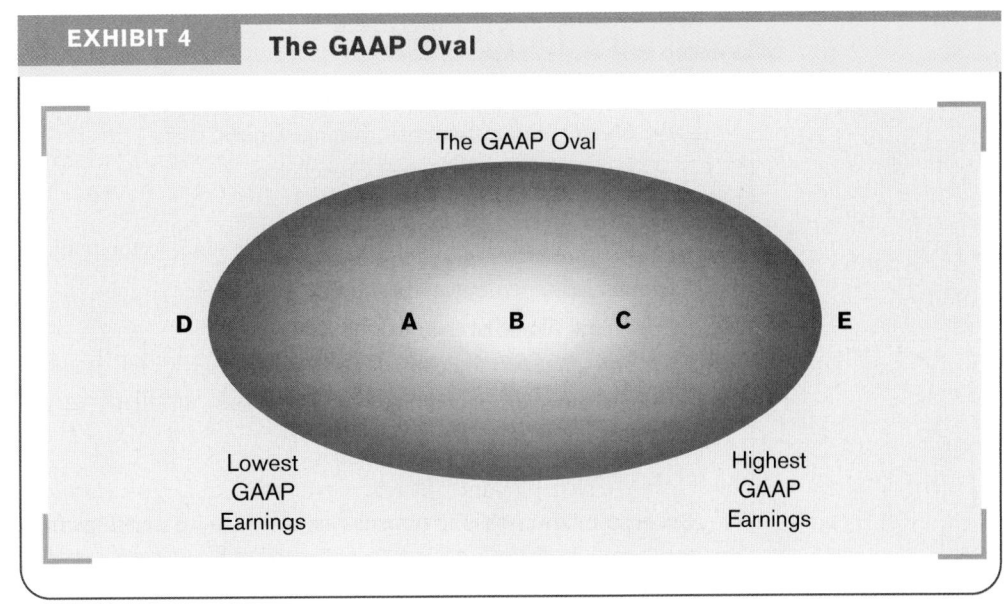

EXHIBIT 4   **The GAAP Oval**

The GAAP Oval

D   A   B   C   E

Lowest GAAP Earnings   Highest GAAP Earnings

set of accounting assumptions one year, perhaps when overall operating performance is good, and an aggressive set of assumptions the next year, perhaps to try to hide lackluster operating performance? Finally, note also that the boundary of the oval is fuzzy, so it sometimes is not clear whether a certain set of computations is or is not in conformity with GAAP.

Of course, whether a manager actually does manage earnings, and whether he or she crosses the line and violates GAAP to do so, is partially a function of the fear (and costs) of getting caught and of the general ethical culture of the company. But it is also a function of the personal ethics of the manager, and the manager's ability to recognize that fraudulent and deceptive financial reporting is part of a continuum that starts with innocent window dressing but can end with full-scale fraud. There is no neon sign giving a final warning saying, "Beware, don't cross this line!" Thus, each individual must be constantly aware of where he or she is with respect to the earnings management continuum in Exhibit 3 and the GAAP oval in Exhibit 4. Boards of directors and financial statement preparers should also be aware that, as a group, managers are notoriously overoptimistic about the future business prospects of their companies. Therefore, a company policy of having a consistently conservative approach to accounting is a good counterbalance to managers who might try to justify optimistic accounting assumptions on the basis of a business turnaround that is "just around the corner."

Personal Ethics

Personal ethics is not a topic one typically expects to study in a financial accounting course. However, the large number of accounting scandals in 2001 and 2002 demonstrated that personal ethics and financial reporting are inextricably connected. The GAAP oval in Exhibit 4 illustrates that there is a range of earnings numbers a company can report for a year and still be in strict conformity with GAAP. Thus, earnings management can and does occur without any violation of the accounting rules. If one takes a strictly legalistic view of the world, then it is clear that managers should manage earnings, when they have concluded that the potential costs in terms of lost credibility are outweighed by the financial reporting benefits, because earnings can be managed without violating any rules.

A contrasting view is that the practice of financial accounting is not a matter of simply applying a list of rules to a set of objective facts. Management intent often enters into the decision of how to report a particular item. For example, land is reported as a long-term

---

REMEMBER THIS...

The reasons that management might manage earnings include:
- pressure to meet internal earnings targets,
- pressure to meet external expectations,
- smoothing income, and
- preparing to apply for a loan or to offer stock to the public.

Earnings management can take the form of:
- careful timing of transactions,
- changing accounting methods or estimates with full disclosure,
- changing accounting methods or estimates WITHOUT adequate disclosure,
- non-GAAP accounting, and
- fictitious transactions.

Because of the possible abuses associated with earnings management, it is important that accountants be persons of high personal integrity.

asset in the balance sheet unless management intends to sell the land within one year of the balance sheet date. In the context of earnings management, an important consideration is whether savvy transaction timing or changes in accounting methods or estimates are done to better communicate the economic performance of the business to financial statement users or whether the earnings management techniques are used with the intent to deceive. And if earnings management is done to deceive, who is management trying to deceive? If management is trying to deceive potential investors, lenders, regulatory authorities, employees, or other company stakeholders, then managing earnings poses a real risk of lost credibility in the future. And there is one final important item to consider— most of us believe that intentionally trying to deceive others is wrong, no matter what the economic consequences.

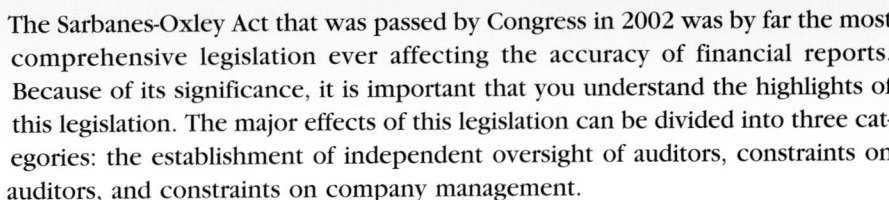

The Sarbanes-Oxley Act

(4) Understand the major parts of the Sarbanes-Oxley Act and how it impacts financial reporting.

The Sarbanes-Oxley Act that was passed by Congress in 2002 was by far the most comprehensive legislation ever affecting the accuracy of financial reports. Because of its significance, it is important that you understand the highlights of this legislation. The major effects of this legislation can be divided into three categories: the establishment of independent oversight of auditors, constraints on auditors, and constraints on company management.

Public Company Accounting Oversight Board

Public Company Accounting Oversight Board (PCAOB)

Board of five full-time members established by the Sarbanes-Oxley Act to oversee the accounting and auditing profession.

Sarbanes-Oxley required the establishment of a **Public Company Accounting Oversight Board (PCAOB)**, with five full-time members, to oversee the accounting and auditing profession. This board is required to:

- Register all public accounting firms that provide audits for public companies.
- Establish standards relating to the preparation of audit reports for public companies.
- Conduct inspections (reviews) of accounting firms.
- Conduct investigations and disciplinary proceedings and impose appropriate sanctions on pubic accounting firms whose performance is inadequate.
- Enforce compliance with the Sarbanes-Oxley Act.

 FYI

Who are Sarbanes and Oxley? Paul Sarbanes is a Democratic senator from Maryland, and Michael Oxley is a Republican member of the House of Representatives from Ohio. These two gentlemen co-sponsored this sweeping reform.

Constraints on Auditors

To ensure that external auditors remain independent, Sarbanes-Oxley requires the following:

- Accounting firms that audit public companies are prohibited from providing several non-audit services to their clients, including: (1) bookkeeping or other services related to the accounting records or financial statements, (2) financial information systems design and implementation, (3) appraisal or valuation services, (4) actuarial services, (5) internal audit outsourcing services, (6) management functions or human resources, (7) broker or dealer, investment adviser or investment banking services, (8) legal services and expert services unrelated to the audit, and (9) any other service that the Board determines is impermissible.

- Requires that audit partners on engagements be rotated off the audit every five years.
- Requires that auditors report to and be retained by the audit committee rather than the CFO or other members of the company's management.

Constraints on Management

Restoring public confidence in the financial reporting process will require that management ensure financial statement users of the steps taken to provide quality financial information. To that end, Sarbanes-Oxley requires management to do the following:

- The CEO and CFO of each public company are required to prepare a statement to accompany the audit report to certify to the appropriateness of the financial statements and disclosures. As discussed earlier, management is still required to provide an assessment of internal controls in each annual report.
- All public companies are required to develop and enforce an officer code of ethics.
- Loans to executive officers and directors are prohibited.
- Support a much stronger board and audit committee in each public company. The audit committee is a subset of the board of directors and consists only of individuals who are not part of the management team of the company.

Only time will tell how effective this law is in preventing and deterring financial statement misstatements. One thing is for sure, however, and that is that because of this legislation, public companies are taking their financial reporting responsibilities much more seriously than ever before.

REMEMBER THIS...

The Sarbanes-Oxley Act has the following major provisions.

- Public Company Accounting Oversight Board—established to oversee the certification of auditors
- Constraints on auditors—stricter rules to ensure that external auditors maintain their independence
- Constraints on management—provisions to make corporate CEOs and CFOs personally responsible for reliable financial statements

---

The Role of Auditors in the Accounting Process

Describe the role of auditors and how their presence affects the integrity of financial statements.

(5) Someone needs to check and make sure that the accounting system is running as designed and that the resulting financial statements fairly present the financial performance of the company. Auditors are that "someone." Auditors provide management (and stockholders) with some assurance that the internal control system is functioning properly and that the financial statements fairly represent the financial performance of the firm. Two types of auditors are typically employed by management—internal and external auditors.

Internal Auditors

Most large organizations have a staff of **internal auditors**, an independent group of experts in controls, accounting, and operations. This group's major purpose is to monitor

internal auditors

An independent group of experts (in controls, accounting, and operations) who monitor operating results and financial records, evaluate internal controls, assist with increasing the efficiency and effectiveness of operations, and detect fraud.

operating results and financial records, evaluate internal controls, assist with increasing the efficiency and effectiveness of operations, and even detect fraud. The internal audit staffs in some large organizations include over 100 individuals. The audit manager reports directly to the president (or other high-level executive officer) and to the audit committee of the board of directors. By performing independent evaluations of an organization's internal controls, the internal auditors are helping preserve integrity in the reporting process. Employees who know that internal auditors are reviewing operations and reports are less likely to manipulate records. Even if they do, their actions may be discovered by the work of the internal auditors.

Internal auditors' responsibilities vary considerably, depending upon the organization. Some internal audit staffs consist of only one or two employees who spend most of their time performing reviews of financial records or internal controls. Other organizations may have a large number of auditors who search for and investigate fraud, work to improve operational efficiency and effectiveness, and make sure their organization is complying with various laws and regulations.

Organizations that have a competent group of internal auditors generally have fewer financial reporting problems than do organizations that don't have internal auditors.

External Auditors

external auditors

Independent CPAs who are retained by organizations to perform audits of financial statements.

generally accepted auditing standards (GAAS)

Auditing standards developed by the PCAOB for public companies and AICPA for private companies.

Probably the greatest safeguard in the financial reporting system in the United States is the requirement that firms have external audits of their financial statements and internal controls. **External auditors** examine an organization's financial statements to determine if they are prepared and presented in accordance with generally accepted accounting principles and are free from material (significant) misstatement. They also issue opinions about management's assessment of the reliability of an organization's internal controls and their own assessment of the reliability of internal controls. External audits are performed by certified public accounting (CPA) firms. CPA audits are required by the Securities and Exchange Commission and the major stock exchanges for all companies whose stock is publicly traded. Even companies that are not public, however, often employ CPAs to perform audits of their financial statements. Banks and other lenders usually require audits, and audits can instill confidence in users of financial reports. In conducting audits, CPAs are required by **generally accepted auditing standards (GAAS)** to provide reasonable assurance that significant fraud or misstatement is not present in financial statements. Because CPAs cannot audit every transaction of an organization, and because detecting collusive management deception is sometimes impossible, it is not possible for auditors to guarantee that financial statements are "correct." Instead, they can only provide reasonable assurance that financial statements are "presented fairly." Even with audits, there are still a few occasions when major financial statement fraud is not detected. As we have already discussed in this chapter, the Sarbanes-Oxley Act of 2002 made major reforms in the way CPAs must conduct their audits, who they report to, and what their penalties are for not conducting proper audits.

CPA audits of financial statements have become very important in the United States because of the enormous size of many

⊘ FYI

As of 2006, four international public accounting firms—the "Big 4": **Ernst & Young, PricewaterhouseCoopers, Deloitte & Touche,** and **KPMG**—were responsible for auditing the majority of the Fortune 500 companies, as well as most other large, publicly-traded companies in the United States. Until 2001, there were five large firms but as you learned in Chapter 1, **Arthur Andersen's** involvement in **Waste Management, Enron,** and **WorldCom** dealt a one-two-three knockout punch that put Arthur Andersen out of business.

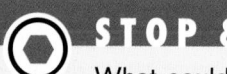

STOP & THINK

What could auditors do to ensure that the financial reporting system in a company is working properly? Be specific.

corporations. Because the stockholders, who own corporations, are usually different individuals from a company's management, audits provide comfort to these owners/investors that management is carrying out its stewardship function appropriately.

What Do Auditors Do?

While management has the primary responsibility to prepare the financial statements and ensure that the internal control system is functioning properly, internal auditors provide an independent assessment of how well the controls are working. External auditors usually study the internal control system to see if they can rely on it as they perform their audits, provide an opinion on management's assessment of the reliability of internal controls, and issue their own independent opinion about the adequacy of the internal controls. If the internal control system is functioning correctly, it increases the likelihood that the resulting financial information is reliable.

CAUTION

External auditors are responsible for evaluating the assumptions and estimates of management as well as testing the internal control system. The external auditors do not make the assumptions and estimates, nor are they responsible for designing the internal control system.

Auditors gain confidence in the quality of the reporting process using several different processes: interviews, observation, sampling, confirmation, and analytical procedures. Several of these processes are used by both internal and external auditors, while some are used primarily by external auditors. Exhibit 5 provides a summary of these procedures and indicates who uses them most often. A brief discussion of each process then follows.

Interviews Auditors *interview* employees to ensure that procedures are understood, proper documentation is being made, and proper authorization is being obtained. Through interviews, auditors identify potential weaknesses in the control system that will be examined using testing procedures.

Observation *Observation* is done to verify compliance with procedures and to ensure that accounting records agree with physical records. For example, auditors in a bank will count the cash in a vault to ensure that recorded amounts agree with the actual cash on hand. Auditors will also verify the existence of inventory by doing a physical count of product. In addition to using observation to verify the existence of assets, auditors will also use observation to ensure that employees are complying with proper procedures.

Sampling As mentioned previously, auditors cannot examine every transaction. Typically, they will select a *sample of transactions* for analysis. Based on the results of

EXHIBIT 5	Audit Processes Used by Auditors	
	Internal Auditors	**External Auditors**
Interviews	X	X
Observation	X	X
Sampling	X	X
Confirmation	–	X
Analytical procedures	–	X

their analysis of the sample, they may conclude that the internal control procedures are being complied with, resulting in reliable financial information. Auditors may also conclude from the results that the internal control system is not reliable, resulting in further testing being required.

Confirmation   Used primarily by external auditors, *confirmations* are used to verify the balances in accounts that result from transactions with outsiders. For example, customers are often contacted and asked to verify account balances. Banks are contacted to verify loan amounts, lines of credit, and other account balances. This procedure ensures that the balances listed on the financial statements do, in fact, exist.

Analytical Procedures   *Analytical procedures* are used to provide guidance to external auditors as they attempt to identify areas that may deserve attention. Analytical procedures involve the use of such techniques as comparative ratio analysis. By comparing the results of ratio analysis from one period to the next, auditors may be able to identify areas where additional investigation may be appropriate.

At the completion of an audit, the auditors issue a report that accompanies the financial statements and describes to readers, in very general terms, what was done by the audit firm and whether accounting rules were followed; the report also indicates an opinion as to whether the financial statements and the accompanying notes fairly represent the financial condition of the firm.

As an example of an auditors' report, **Wal-Mart's** 2006 independent auditors' report, taken from the company's 2006 financial statements, is included in Exhibit 6.

EXHIBIT 6	**Wal-Mart's 2006 Independent Auditors' Report**

Report of Independent Registered Accounting Firm

The Board of Directors and Shareholders of Wal-Mart Stores, Inc.

We have audited the accompanying consolidated balance sheets of Wal-Mart Stores, Inc. as of January 31, 2006 and 2005, and the related consolidated statements of income, shareholders' equity and cash flows for each of the three years in the period ended January 31, 2006. These financial statements are the responsibility of the Company's management. Our responsibility is to express an opinion on these financial statements based on our audits.

We conducted our audits in accordance with the standards of the Public Company Accounting Oversight Board (United States). Those standards require that we plan and perform the audit to obtain reasonable assurance about whether the financial statements are free of material misstatement. An audit includes examining, on a test basis, evidence supporting the amounts and disclosures in the financial statements. An audit also includes assessing the accounting principles used and significant estimates made by management, as well as evaluating the overall financial statement presentation. We believe that our audits provide a reasonable basis for our opinion.

In our opinion, the financial statements referred to above present fairly, in all material respects, the consolidated financial position of Wal-Mart Stores, Inc. at January 31, 2006 and 2005, and the consolidated results of its operations and its cash flows for each of the three years in the period ended January 31, 2006, in conformity with accounting principles generally accepted in the United States of America.

We have also audited, in accordance with the standards of the Public Company Accounting Oversight Board (United States), the effectiveness of the Wal-Mart Stores, Inc.'s internal control over financial reporting as of January 31, 2006 based on the criteria established in *Internal Control–Integrated Framework* issued by the Committee of Sponsoring Organizations of the Treadway Commission, and our report dated March 27, 2006, expressed an unqualified opinion thereon.

ERNST & YOUNG LLP
Ernst & Young LLP
Rogers, Arkansas

March 27, 2006

Are Outside (Independent) Auditors Independent?

Independent auditors are hired by the audit committee of the board of directors to make sure that the financial statements prepared by *management* fairly represent the financial performance of the company. Since the company being audited is paying the auditors, is there a danger that the auditors may not be independent? Is there a possibility that auditors will go along with whatever management says because management is paying them? That possibility exists, but there are a number of factors that work as a counterbalance.

First, recall from our discussion of the internal control structure that the Foreign Corrupt Practices and Sarbanes-Oxley acts require companies to maintain an adequate system of internal controls. If management knowingly violate this law, they can go to jail (a number of top managers have) and would be subject to personal fines. In addition, the company is subject to corporate fines. Thus, management would be taking a big risk if they interfere with the auditors.

Second, external auditors have a responsibility to financial statement users to ensure that financial statements are fairly presented. The legal system in the United States provides auditors with financial incentives to remain independent. As an example, the auditors in the **Phar-Mor** financial statement fraud case were sued by plaintiffs for over $1 billion. A jury held the audit firm liable, and that firm settled with the plaintiffs for a lesser, though undisclosed (but not insignificant), amount. Thus, external auditors are taking a big risk if they allow their independence and integrity to be compromised.

Third, auditors have a reputation to protect. The reason auditors are hired at all is because the investing public believes they provide an independent check on the reliability and integrity of the financial information. If an audit firm were no longer perceived in this manner, companies would cease to employ it. CPA firms obtain audit clients based on the quality of their reputation. Would they sell that reputation to the highest bidder? That would be very shortsighted indeed.

FYI

This give and take between the auditors and management typically results in financial statements that fairly reflect the financial performance of a business. For example, in 2004, of 6,319 audits conducted for firms listed on the New York, American, and NASDAQ stock exchanges, only 3 involved significant issues on which auditors and management could not reach agreement on disclosure.

Knowing the incentives that influence auditors to provide fair and reliable financial information, we can now begin to see how the issues relating to disagreements in judgment can work themselves out. On the one hand, we have a management team that has an incentive to provide financial statement information that portrays the company in the most favorable position possible. On the other hand, we have auditors who are responsible to ensure that the information being provided is unbiased and fair. If auditors don't live up to their charge, they can end up paying to litigants much more than they ever received in audit fees.

The Securities and Exchange Commission (SEC) and the new Public Company Accounting Oversight Board are working with public accounting firms to ensure that independence remains a keystone of the auditing profession.

If management is allowed to paint an overly optimistic picture of the firm's performance by using estimates that bias the financial reports, the audit firm will pay (via litigation) if those estimates prove to be materially wrong in the future. To protect itself, the audit firm would actually prefer that management use conservative estimates, but management will not always go along with the auditors in this regard. It is this tension, resulting from differing incentives, that provides financial statement users with information that, taken as a whole, fairly represents the financial performance of a business.

REMEMBER THIS...

- Auditors provide a check and balance to ensure that the financial statements fairly reflect the financial performance of a business.
- Internal auditors ensure integrity in the financial records and evaluate and encourage adherence to the organization's internal controls.
- External certified public accountants ensure the integrity in the financial reporting process with independent audits of financial statements.
- Independent financial statement audits are required for all public companies, and often by creditors and other users.

The Securities and Exchange Commission

Explain the role of the Securities and Exchange Commission in adding credibility to financial statements.

(6)

In addition to the role of independent internal and external auditors, the U.S. government plays a role in ensuring the integrity of financial information. The **Securities and Exchange Commission (SEC)** is responsible for ensuring that investors, creditors, and other financial statement users are provided with reliable information upon which to make investment decisions.

The SEC is an agency of the federal government. The SEC was organized in the 1930s because of financial reporting and stock market abuses. One such abuse was price manipulation. It was not uncommon in the 1920s for stockbrokers or dealers to indulge in "wash sales" or "matched orders," in which successive buy and sell orders created a false impression of stock activity and forced prices up. This maneuver allowed those involved to reap huge profits before the price fell back to its true market level. Outright deceit by issuing false and misleading financial statements was another improper practice. The objective of these manipulative procedures was to make profits at the expense of unwary investors.

The Securities Act of 1933 requires most companies planning to issue new debt or stock securities to the public to submit a registration statement to the SEC for approval. The SEC examines these statements for completeness and adequacy before permitting companies to sell securities through securities exchanges. The Securities Exchange Act of 1934 requires all public companies to file detailed periodic reports with the SEC.

Securities and Exchange Commission (SEC)

The government body responsible for regulating the financial reporting practices of most publicly-owned corporations in connection with the buying and selling of stocks and bonds.

The SEC requires a considerable amount of information to be included in these filings. Among other things, a company must submit financial statements that have been audited by CPAs and that contain an opinion issued by those CPAs.

Of the many reports required by the SEC, the following have the most direct impact on financial reporting:

FYI

The first chairman of the SEC was Joseph P. Kennedy, father of the late President John F. Kennedy.

- *Registration statements.* These include various forms that must be filed and approved before a company can sell securities through the securities exchanges.
- *Form 10-K.* This report must be filed annually for all publicly held companies. The report contains extensive financial information, including audited financial

statements by independent CPAs. The 10-K also requires additional disclosure beyond that typically provided in the audited financial statements. Examples of additional information include the executive compensation of top management and the details of property, plant, and equipment transactions.

- *Form 10-Q.* This report must be filed quarterly for all publicly held companies. It contains certain financial information and requires a CPA's involvement.

Because the SEC has statutory power to mandate any reporting requirement it feels is needed, it has considerable influence in setting generally accepted accounting principles and disclosure requirements for financial statements. Generally, the SEC accepts the accounting pronouncements of the Financial Accounting Standards Board and other bodies such as the AICPA. In addition, the SEC has the power to establish rules for any CPA associated with audited financial statements submitted to the commission.

The SEC is given broad enforcement powers under the 1934 Act. If the rules of operation for stock exchanges prove to be ineffectual in implementing the requirements of the SEC, the SEC can alter or supplement them. The SEC can suspend trading of a company's stock for not more than 10 days (a series of orders has enabled the SEC to suspend trading for extended periods, however) and can suspend all trading on any exchange for up to 90 days. If substantive hearings show that the issuer failed to comply with the requirements of the securities laws, the SEC can "de-list" any security. Brokers and dealers can be prevented, either temporarily or permanently, from working in the securities market, and investigations can be initiated, if deemed necessary, to determine violations of any of the Acts or rules administered by the SEC.

The Effect of the 1934 Act on Independent Accountants

Accountants are involved in the preparation and review of a major portion of the reports and statements required by the 1934 Act. Accountants also can be censured, and their work is subject to approval by the SEC. The financial statements in the annual report to stockholders and in the 10-K report must be audited. In addition, accountants consult and assist in the preparation of the quarterly 10-Q reports and the other periodic reports.

More recently, the Sarbanes-Oxley Act has strengthened the authority of the SEC to monitor financial reporting. Under the Act, the SEC is given more resources and authority, has oversight for the new Public Company Accounting Oversight Board, has more control over auditors and reporting companies, and, in general, has a greater responsibility to protect investors and creditors who rely on financial reports.

REMEMBER THIS...

- The Securities and Exchange Commission (SEC) is an agency of the federal government.
- The purpose of the SEC is to assist investors in public companies by regulating stock and bond markets and by requiring certain disclosures.
- The SEC has statutory authority to establish accounting principles, but it basically accepts pronouncements of the FASB and AICPA as authoritative.
- Common reports required by the SEC are registration statements and Forms 10-K and 10-Q.
- The SEC can suspend trading and even de-list securities.

REVIEW OF LEARNING OBJECTIVES

① Identify the types of problems that can appear in financial statements. Three types of problems can affect financial statements.

Errors	Unintentional mistakes that can enter the accounting system at the transaction and journal entry stage or when journal entries are posted to accounts
Disagreements in judgment	Differences in opinion about what numbers should be reported in the financial statements based on different estimates
Fraud	Intentional misrepresentations in the financial statements

② Describe the safeguards employed to ensure that financial statements are free from problems. Internal controls are safeguards built into an organization that help to protect assets and increase reliability of the accounting records.
The three basic internal control structure categories are:

(1) the control environment,
(2) the accounting systems, and
(3) the control procedures.

The five types of control procedures are:

(1) segregation of duties,
(2) procedures for authorizations,
(3) documents and records,
(4) physical safeguards, and
(5) independent checks.

③ Understand the concept of earnings management and why it occurs.

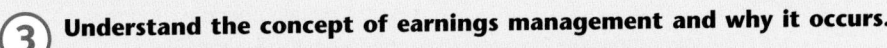

Reasons for earnings management	• pressure to meet internal earnings targets • pressure to meet external expectations • smoothing income • preparing to apply for a loan or to offer stock to the public
Techniques of earnings management	• careful timing of transactions • changing accounting methods or estimates with full disclosure • changing accounting methods or estimates withOUT adequate disclosure • non-GAAP accounting • fictitious transactions

④ Understand the major parts of the Sarbanes-Oxley Act and how it impacts financial reporting.

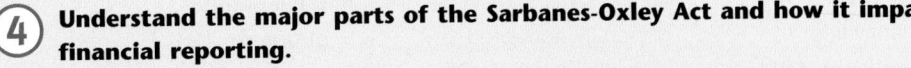

Public Company Accounting Oversight Board (PCAOB)	• register all public accounting firms • establish auditing standards • inspect public accounting firms
Constraints on auditors	• auditors are prohibited from providing non-audit services to audit clients • audit partners must rotate every five years • auditors must report to the audit committee of the board of directors

Constraints on management	• the CEO and the CFO must personally certify the reliability of the financial statements • companies must have a code of ethics • loans to company executives are prohibited • audit committees must be strengthened

(5) Describe the role of auditors and how their presence affects the integrity of financial statements.

Internal auditors	• evaluate internal controls • monitor operating results • ensure compliance with laws and company policy • detect fraud
External auditors	Gather evidence to be able to certify the fairness of the financial statements through: • interviews • observation • sampling • confirmation • analytical procedures

• External audits are required of most public companies by the Securities and Exchange Commission.
• External audits must be performed by CPAs who are licensed by the individual states in which they practice.

(6) Explain the role of the Securities and Exchange Commission in adding credibility to financial statements.

• The SEC is the agency of the federal government charged with the responsibility of assisting investors by making sure they are provided with reliable information upon which to make investment decisions.
• The SEC was organized in the 1930s and requires certain periodic reports such as the Forms 10-Q and 10-K of companies that sell stock publicly in the United States.
• The SEC adds credibility to financial statements by:
  • requiring independent audits,
  • reviewing financial statements itself, and
  • sanctioning firms that violate its standards.

KEY TERMS & CONCEPTS

audit committee, 192
control activities (procedures), 192
control environment, 192
detective controls, 192
external auditors, 203
Foreign Corrupt Practices Act (FCPA), 191

GAAP oval, 199
generally accepted auditing standards (GAAS), 203
income smoothing, 197
independent checks, 194
internal auditors, 203

internal control structure, 191
internal earnings target, 196
organizational structure, 192
physical safeguards, 193
preventative controls, 192

Public Company Accounting Oversight Board (PCAOB), 201
Sarbanes-Oxley Act, 191
Securities and Exchange Commission (SEC), 207
segregation of duties, 193

DISCUSSION QUESTIONS

1. How can a person tell whether an entry to an expense account is payment for a legitimate expenditure or a means of concealing a theft of cash?

2. How would it be possible to overstate revenues? What effect would an overstatement of revenues have on total assets?

3. What is the Foreign Corrupt Practices Act, and how is it important to financial reporting?

4. What are the major elements of a system of internal controls?

5. Identify five different types of control procedures.

6. What are the four factors that might motivate a manager to attempt to manage earnings?

7. (a) What is the purpose of internal earnings targets?
   (b) What is the risk associated with internal earnings targets?

8. What is meant by the term *income smoothing*?

9. What are the five labels in the earnings management continuum (see Exhibit 3), and what general types of actions are associated with each of the labels?

10. Is there anything wrong with using a different accounting estimate this year compared to last year, as long as both estimates fall within a generally accepted range for your industry?

11. Refer to the GAAP oval in Exhibit 4. (a) In what important way is point E different from point C?

(b) In what important way is point A different from point C?

12. The Sarbanes-Oxley Act established the Public Company Accounting Oversight Board. Identify the duties of that board.

13. What constraints were placed on auditors as a result of the Sarbanes-Oxley Act?

14. As a result of the Sarbanes-Oxley Act, public companies are required to make changes in the way they do business. What practice does Sarbanes-Oxley forbid?

15. How do internal auditors add to the credibility of financial statements?

16. What is the purpose of a financial statement audit by CPAs?

17. Do you believe that outside auditors (CPAs) who examine the financial statements of a company, while being paid by that company, can be truly independent?

18. The SEC requires companies to register with it when they sell stocks or bonds and also requires periodic reporting thereafter. Which of these reports, the initial registration statements or the subsequent periodic reports, do you believe would be scrutinized more closely by the SEC?

19. What do you suspect is the relationship between the FASB and the SEC?

EXERCISES

E 5-1 Accounting Errors–Transaction Errors

LO1 How would the following errors affect the account balances and the basic accounting equation, *Assets = Liabilities + Owners' Equity*? How do the misstatements affect income?

a. The purchase of a truck is recorded as an expense instead of an asset.

b. A cash payment on accounts receivable is received but not recorded.

c. Fictitious sales on account are recorded.

d. A clerk misreads a handwritten invoice for repairs and records it as $1,500 instead of $1,800.

e. Payment is received on December 31 for the next three months' rent and is recorded as revenue.

E 5-2 Errors in Financial Statements

LO1 The following financial statements are available for Sherwood Real Estate Company:

(continued)

Balance Sheet

Assets		Liabilities		
Cash	$ 1,300	Accounts payable	$ 100,000	
Receivable from sale		Mortgage payable	6,000,000	
of real estate	5,000,000	Total liabilities		$ 6,100,000
Interest receivable*	180,000			
Real estate properties . . .	6,000,000	**Stockholders' Equity**		
		Capital stock	$ 10,000	
		Retained earnings	5,071,300	
		Total stockholders' equity . . .		5,081,300
		Total liabilities and		
Total assets	$11,181,300	stockholders' equity		$11,181,300

*Interest Receivable applies to Receivable from sale of real estate.

Income Statement

Gain on sale of real estate	$3,200,000
Interest income*	180,000
Total revenues	$3,380,000
Expenses	1,200,000
Net income	$2,180,000

*Interest Income applies to Receivable from sale of real estate.

Sherwood Company is using these financial statements to entice investors to buy stock in the company. However, a recent FBI investigation revealed that the sale of real estate was a fabricated transaction with a fictitious company that was recorded to make the financial statements look better. The sales price was $5,000,000 with a zero cash down payment and a $5,000,000 receivable. Prepare financial statements for Sherwood Company showing what its total assets, liabilities, stockholders' equity, and income really are with the sale of real estate removed.

E 5-3

LO1, LO3

Appropriateness of Accounting Rules

In the early 1990s, the top executive of a large oil refining company (based in New York) was convicted of financial statement fraud. One of the issues in the case involved the way the company accounted for its oil inventories. In particular, the company would purchase crude oil from exploration companies and then process the oil into finished oil products, such as jet fuel, diesel fuel, and so forth. Because there was a ready market for these finished products, as soon as the company purchased the crude oil, it would value its oil inventory at the selling prices of the finished products less the cost to refine the oil. Although the case involved fraud, the type of accounting used was also questioned because it allowed the company to recognize profit before the actual sale (and even refining) of the oil. Nevertheless, one of the large CPA firms attested to the use of this method. If you were the judge in this case, would you be critical of this accounting practice?

E 5-4

LO2

Internal Control Procedures

As an auditor, you have discovered the following problems with the accounting system control procedures of Jim's Supply Store. For each of the following occurrences, tell which of the five internal control procedures was lacking. Also, recommend how the company should change its procedures to avoid the problem in the future.

a. Jim's Supply's losses due to bad debts have increased dramatically over the past year. In an effort to increase sales, the managers of certain stores have allowed large credit sales to occur without review or approval.

(continued)

b. An accountant hid his theft of $200 from the company's bank account by changing the monthly reconciliation. He knew the manipulation would not be discovered.

c. Mark Peterson works in the storeroom. He maintains the inventory records, counts the inventory, and has unlimited access to the storeroom. He occasionally steals items of inventory and hides the theft by including the value of the stolen goods in his inventory count.

d. Receiving reports are sometimes filled out days after shipments have arrived.

E 5-5   Internal Auditing–Staffing Internal Audits

LO5   A manufacturing corporation recently reassigned one of its accounting managers to the internal audit department. He had successfully directed the western-area accounting office, and the corporation thought his skills would be valuable to the internal audit department. The director of the internal audit division knew of this individual's experience in the western-area accounting office and assigned him to audit that same office.

Should the internal auditor be assigned to audit the same office in which he recently worked? What problems could arise in this situation?

E 5-6   Internal Auditing

LO5   Which of the following is not applicable to the internal audit function?

a. Deter or catch employee fraud.

b. Issue an opinion for investors regarding the reliability of the financial statements.

c. Be guided by its own set of professional standards.

d. Help to ensure that the accounting function is performed correctly and that the financial statements are prepared accurately.

E 5-7   Internal Auditing–External Auditor's Reliance on Internal Auditors

LO5   Pierson, CPA, is planning an audit of the financial statements of Generic Company. In determining the nature, timing, and extent of the auditing procedures, Pierson is considering Generic's internal audit function, which is staffed by Shawn Goff.

1. In what ways may Goff's work be relevant to Pierson?

2. What factors should Pierson consider, and what inquiries should Pierson make in deciding whether to rely on Goff's work?

E 5-8   Ensuring the Integrity of Financial Reporting

LO5, LO6   Three college seniors with majors in accounting are discussing alternative career plans. All three want to enter careers that will help to ensure the integrity of financial reporting. The first wants to become an internal auditor. She believes that by ensuring appropriate internal controls within a company, the financial statements will be reliable. The second wants to go to work in public accounting and perform external audits of companies. He believes that external auditors are independent and can make sure that financial statements are correct. The third student believes that neither choice will be adding much value to the integrity of financial statements because, in both cases, the auditors will be receiving their pay (either directly or indirectly) from the companies they audit. He believes the only way to make a real difference is to work for the Securities and Exchange Commission, using the "arm of government regulation" to force companies to issue appropriate financial statements and then punishing them (through jail sentences and large fines) when their financial statements are misleading. In your opinion, which of these three students will make the largest contribution toward ensuring integrity in the financial statements?

E 5-9   External Auditors–Purpose of an Audit

LO5   What is the purpose of external auditors providing an opinion on a company's financial statements?

E 5-10   **Auditing Financial Statements**

LO5   The Utah Lakers professional basketball team has recently decided to sell stock and become a public company. In determining what it must do to file a registration statement with the SEC, the company realizes that it needs to have an audit opinion to accompany its financial statements. The company has recently approached two accounting students at a major university and asked them to "audit" its financial statements to be submitted to the SEC. Should the two accounting students accept the work and perform the audit?

E 5-11   **Auditing Negligence**

LO5   A few years ago, the officers of **Phar-Mor**, a discount retail chain, were convicted of issuing fraudulent financial statements. It was learned at the trial that the company overstated its inventory by moving inventory from store to store and counting the same inventory several times. For example, a case of Coca-Cola would be counted at one store and then moved to another store and counted again. In a separate civil trial, Phar-Mor's auditors were accused of performing negligent audits because they didn't catch these inventory movements. Do you believe that the external auditors were negligent in this case?

E 5-12   **Securities and Exchange Commission–Authority to Set Accounting**

LO6   **Standards**

Which organization—the Securities and Exchange Commission, the American Institute of Certified Public Accountants, or the Financial Accounting Standards Board—has federal government authority to set accounting standards and reporting requirements? Some people have argued that all accounting rule making should be done by the federal government. Do you agree? Why or why not?

E 5-13   **Securities and Exchange Commission–Role of the SEC**

LO6   Describe the role of the Securities and Exchange Commission and its influence on the practice of auditing.

E 5-14   **Securities and Exchange Commission–Information Needed for Investing**

LO6   As an investor you are considering buying stock in a relatively new company. Medical Horizons, Inc., has been in existence for 10 years and is now about to go public. The first stock offering will be listed on the New York Stock Exchange next week.

1. What kind of information would you like to know before investing in the company? Where can you find this information?
2. How does the SEC protect the securities market from companies that are fraudulent or in poor financial condition?
3. Besides stock market investors, what other parties might be interested in knowing financial data about companies?

E 5-15   **Securities and Exchange Commission**

LO6   Many people have argued that the purpose of the SEC is to protect investors. Some believe that the best way to do this is by preventing weak companies from issuing stock. Others say that the SEC should require full disclosure and then let the buyer beware. Which do you think is more appropriate: a preventive role or a disclosure role?

ANALYTICAL ASSIGNMENTS

AA 5-16
DISCUSSION

Auditing a Company

Jerry Stillwell, the owner of a small company, asked Jones, a CPA, to conduct an audit of the company's financial statements. Stillwell told Jones that the audit needed to be completed in time to submit audited financial statements to a bank as part of a loan application. Jones immediately accepted the assignment and agreed to provide an auditor's report within two weeks.

Because Jones was busy, he hired two accounting students to perform the audit. After two hours of instruction, he sent them off to conduct the audit. Jones told the students not to spend time reviewing the internal controls, but instead to concentrate on proving the mathematical accuracy of the ledgers and other financial records.

The students followed Jones's instructions, and after 10 days, they provided the financial statements, which did not include notes. Jones reviewed the statements and prepared an auditor's report. The report did not refer to generally accepted accounting principles and contained no mention of any qualifications or disclosures. Briefly describe the problems with this audit.

AA 5-17
DISCUSSION

Auditing Practice

A few years ago, the owners of an electronics wholesale company committed massive fraud by overstating revenues on the financial statements. They recorded three large fictitious sales near the end of the year to the retailers **Silo**, **Circuit City**, and **Wal-Mart**. The three transactions overstated revenues, receivables, and income by nearly $20 million. As part of the audit procedures, the external auditors sent requests for confirmation to the three stores to ensure that they did, in fact, owe the electronics company $20 million. In the meantime, the owners of the electronics company rented mailboxes in the cities where the three "customers" were headquartered, using names very similar to those of the three "customers." The requests for confirmation were sent to the mailboxes. The owners completed the confirmations and sent them back to the auditors, confirming the $20 million in receivables. With respect to the fraud, answer the following two questions:

1. What journal entries would the fraud perpetrators have entered into the financial records to overstate revenues?
2. Should the external auditors be held liable for not catching the fraud?

AA 5-18
DISCUSSION

Income Smoothing and an IPO

You are an analyst for an investment fund that invests in initial public offerings (IPOs). You are looking at the financial statements of two companies, Clark Company and Durfee Company, that plan to go public soon. Net income for the past three years for the two companies has been as follows (in thousands):

Year	Clark Net Income	Durfee Net Income
2008	$10,000	$17,000
2009	14,000	1,000
2010	20,000	26,000

If both companies issue the same number of shares and if the initial share prices are the same, which of the two companies appears to be a more attractive investment? Explain your reasoning. Also, what alternate sources of data would you look at to find out if the reported earnings amounts accurately portray the business performance of these two companies over the past three years?

AA 5-19
DISCUSSION

If It Isn't Fraud, Then It's Ethical

Cruella DeVil is the chief financial officer (CFO) of a local publicly-traded company. Cruella was recently invited to speak to accounting students at the local university. One of the students asked Cruella whether she thought earnings management was ethical. Cruella laughed and responded that her view was that anything that was not explicitly prohibited by the accounting standards or by government regulations was ethical. What do you think of Cruella's opinion?

AA 5-20
DISCUSSION

GAAP Is a Point, Not an Oval!

You are the chief financial officer (CFO) of Lorien Company, which is publicly traded. At the annual shareholders' meeting, you have been asked to discuss the company's recent reported results. As part of your presentation, you illustrated the minimum and maximum values for net income that could have been reported by Lorien using a range of accounting assumptions used by other companies in your industry. Your statement prompted a cry of outrage from one of the shareholders present at the meeting. This shareholder accused you of being an unprincipled liar. This shareholder stated that any suggestion that there is a range of possible net income values for a given company in a given year indicates an overly liberal approach to financial reporting. This shareholder has moved that your employment contract be immediately terminated because of an apparent lack of moral character. The shareholder's arguments have been persuasive to a large number of people present at the meeting. What can you say to defend yourself?

AA 5-21
JUDGMENT CALL

You Decide: Which is more important–having a good system of internal controls or hiring honest employees?

Is an internal control structure really necessary? Your uncle doesn't seem to think so. He works for a regional employment staffing service and recently commented, "As long as a company hires hard-working, honest people, fraud and abusive financial reporting cases will be almost nonexistent. People with integrity will always make the right choice. In the last six months, we haven't placed anyone for employment who has been fired or let go for fraudulent activity!" A friend argues, however, that anyone presented with the right pressures can commit fraud and that opportunities must be eliminated through an effective internal control structure. Who do you agree with?

AA 5-22
JUDGMENT CALL

You Decide: Can auditors rely on client personnel to assist them with their audit?

Should external auditors do all audit procedures themselves, or should the relationship between the auditor and the client be more friendly? You have just graduated from college and are now working as an auditor for a public accounting firm. Your first client is a major shipping company on the west coast that specializes in sending goods to China. As part of your first assignment, you are asked to count the number of metal containers in the storage warehouse and also verify their contents. As you begin, the warehouse manager (and long-time friend of the firm) comes to you and says, "Don't worry about looking inside the containers. Our guys did that last week and we are running low on time." What should you do?

AA 5-23
REAL COMPANY ANALYSIS

Wal-Mart

The 2006 Form 10-K for **Wal-Mart** is included in Appendix A. Locate that Form 10-K and consider the following questions:

1. With respect to the report of the external auditors to "the Board of Directors and Shareholders of Wal-Mart Stores, Inc.":
   a. Who is Wal-Mart's external auditor?
   b. How long after the end of Wal-Mart's fiscal year did the external auditor complete the audit?

(continued)

2. With respect to the report of management concerning the financial statements:
    a. Who is responsible for the financial statements?
    b. After reading the paragraph on internal control, indicate whether you agree or disagree with the following statement: "The purpose of an internal control system is to ensure that all transactions are always recorded and that all assets are always completely safeguarded."
    c. After looking at the description of the members of the audit committee (in the second paragraph), do you think that any members of the Walton family are members of that committee?

AA 5-24

REAL COMPANY
ANALYSIS

Circle K

At one time, **Circle K** was the second-largest convenience store chain in the United States (behind **7-Eleven**). At its peak, Circle K, based in Phoenix, Arizona, operated 4,685 stores in 32 states. Circle K's rapid expansion was financed through long-term borrowing. Interest on this large debt, combined with increased price competition from convenience stores operated by oil companies, squeezed the profits of Circle K. For the fiscal year ended April 30, 1990, Circle K reported a loss of $773 million. In May 1990, Circle K filed for Chapter 11 bankruptcy protection. Subsequently, Circle K was taken over by **Tosco**, a large independent oil company.

1. In the fiscal year ended April 30, 1989, Circle K experienced significant financial difficulty. Reported profits were down 74.5% from the year before. In the president's letter to the shareholders, Circle K explained that 1989 was a "disappointing" year and that management was seeking some outside company to come in and buy out the Circle K shareholders. How do you think all this bad news was reflected in the auditor's report accompanying the financial statements dated April 30, 1989?

2. As mentioned, Circle K reported a loss of $773 million for the year ended April 30, 1990. Just a week after the end of the fiscal year, the CEO was fired. One week after that, Circle K declared bankruptcy. The audit report was completed approximately two months later. How do you think the news of the bankruptcy was reflected in the auditor's report accompanying the financial statements dated April 30, 1990?

AA 5-25

INTERNATIONAL

Do the Financial Statements Give a True and Fair View?

Swire Pacific, Ltd., based in Hong Kong, is one of the largest companies in the world. The primary operations of the company are in the region of Hong Kong, China, and Taiwan where it has operated for over 125 years. Swire operates **Cathay Pacific Airways** and has extensive real estate holdings in Hong Kong. The 2005 auditor's report (prepared by **Pricewaterhouse-Coopers**) for Swire Pacific, dated March 9, 2006, read as follows (in part):

> An audit includes examination, on a test basis, of evidence relevant to the amounts and disclosures in the accounts. It also includes an assessment of the significant estimates and judgments made by the Directors in the preparation of the accounts, and of whether the accounting policies are appropriate to the circumstances of the Company and the group consistently applied and adequately disclosed....
>
>   In our opinion the accounts give a true and fair view of the state of affairs of the company and of the group as at 31st December 2005....

Although the concept of a "true and fair view" is not part of the auditor's terminology in the United States, it is used by auditors all over the world and is also discussed as part of International Accounting Standards (IAS). The "true and fair view" concept states that an auditor must make sure that the financial statements give an honest representation of the economic status of the company, even if the company violates generally accepted accounting principles in order to do so.

(continued)

1. Review the opinion language in the auditor's report for **Wal-Mart** (see Appendix A). Does the audit report state unconditionally that Wal-Mart's financial statements are a fair representation of the economic status of the company?

2. Auditors in the United States concentrate on performing audits to ensure that financial statements are prepared in accordance with generally accepted accounting principles. What economic and legal realities in the United States would make it difficult for U.S. auditors to apply the "true and fair view" concept?

AA 5-26

ETHICS

Blowing the Whistle on Former Partners

On St. Patrick's Day in 1992, **Chambers Development Company**, one of the largest landfill and waste management firms in the United States, announced that it had been engaging in improper accounting for years. Wall Street fear (over what this announcement implied about the company's track record of steady earnings growth) sent Chambers' stock price plunging by 62% in one day.

The improper accounting by Chambers had been discovered in the course of the external audit. The auditors found that $362 million in expenses had not been reported since Chambers first became a public company in 1985. If this amount of additional expense had been reported, it would have completely wiped out all the profit reported by Chambers since it first went public. The difficult part of this situation was that a large number of the financial staff working for Chambers were former partners in the audit firm performing the audit. These accountants had first worked as independent external auditors at Chambers, then were hired by Chambers, and subsequently were audited by their old partners.

What ethical and economic issues did the auditors of Chambers Development Company face as they considered whether to blow the whistle on their former partners?

AA 5-27

WRITING

External Auditors

Visit or call a local CPA firm (or the local office of a multi-office CPA firm). Ask about career opportunities, the size of the firm's staff, who some of its major clients are, and other facts about the firm. Then, write a one-page summary of your visit.

AA 5-28

CUMULATIVE
SPREADSHEET
PROJECT

Analyzing the Impact of Errors

This spreadsheet assignment is a continuation of the spreadsheet assignment given in Chapter 2. If you completed that spreadsheet, you have a head start on this one.

1. Refer back to the financial statement numbers for Handyman Company for 2009 [given in part (1) of the Cumulative Spreadsheet Project assignment in Chapter 2]. Using the balance sheet and income statement created with those numbers, create spreadsheet cell formulas to compute and display values for the following ratios:
   a. Current assets divided by current liabilities (often called the current ratio)
   b. Total liabilities divided by total assets (often called the debt ratio)
   c. Sales divided by total assets (often called asset turnover)
   d. Net income divided by total stockholders' equity (often called return on equity)

   The details of these ratios will be discussed in detail in subsequent chapters.

2. To observe the impact that errors and fraudulent transactions can have on the financial statements, determine what the ratios computed in (1) would have been if (1) each of the following transactions was recorded as described and (2) the transaction was recorded correctly. Treat each transaction independently, meaning that before determining the impact of each new transaction you should reset the financial statement values to their original amounts. Each of the hypothetical transactions is assumed to occur on the last day of the year.

(continued)

a. Created receivables by creating fictitious sales of $140 all on account.
b. Purchased $80 of inventory on account but incorrectly increased the property, plant, and equipment account instead of increasing Inventory.
c. Borrowed $60 with a short-term payable. The liability was incorrectly recorded as Long-Term Debt.
d. An inventory purchase on account in the amount of $90 was not recorded until the next year.

As a recently hired accountant for a small business, Bearing, Inc., you are provided with last year's balance sheet, income statement, and post-closing trial balance to familiarize yourself with the business.

Bearing, Inc.
Balance Sheet
December 31, 2009

Assets

Cash	$22,100	
Accounts receivable	27,000	
Inventory	13,500	
Supplies	600	
Total assets		$63,200

Liabilities and Stockholders' Equity

Liabilities:		
Accounts payable	$17,000	
Salaries payable	3,500	
Income taxes payable	3,200	
Total liabilities		$23,700
Stockholders' equity:		
Capital stock (10,000 shares outstanding)	$20,000	
Retained earnings	19,500	
Total stockholders' equity		39,500
Total liabilities and stockholders' equity		$63,200

Bearing, Inc.
Income Statement
For the Year Ended December 31, 2009

Sales revenue	$143,000	
Rent revenue	4,000	
Total revenues		$147,000
Less cost of goods sold		85,000
Gross margin		$ 62,000
Less operating expenses:		
Supplies expense	$ 1,200	
Salaries expense	31,000	
Miscellaneous expense	6,400	38,600
Income before taxes		$ 23,400
Less income taxes		8,190
Net income		$ 15,210
Earnings per share ($15,210 ÷ 10,000 shares)		$ 1.52

Bearing, Inc.
Post-Closing Trial Balance
December 31, 2009

	Debits	Credits
Cash	$22,100	
Accounts Receivable	27,000	
Inventory	13,500	
Supplies	600	
Accounts Payable		$17,000
Salaries Payable		3,500
Income Taxes Payable		3,200
Capital Stock		20,000
Retained Earnings		19,500
Totals	$63,200	$63,200

You are also given the following information that summarizes the business activity for the current year, 2010.

a. Issued 6,000 additional shares of capital stock for $30,000 cash.
b. Borrowed $10,000 on January 2, 2010, from Metropolis Bank as a long-term loan. Interest for the year is $700, payable on January 2, 2011.
c. Paid $5,100 cash on September 1 to lease a truck for one year.
d. Received $1,800 on November 1 from a tenant for six months' rent.
e. Paid $900 on December 1 for a one-year insurance policy.
f. Purchased $250 of supplies for cash.
g. Purchased inventory for $80,000 on account.
h. Sold inventory for $105,000 on account; cost of the merchandise sold was $60,000.
i. Collected $95,000 cash from customers' accounts receivable.
j. Paid $65,000 cash for inventories purchased during the year.
k. Paid $34,000 for sales reps' salaries, including $3,500 owed at the beginning of 2010.
l. No dividends were paid during the year.
m. The income taxes payable for 2009 were paid.
n. For adjusting entries, all prepaid expenses are initially recorded as assets, and all unearned revenues are initially recorded as liabilities.
o. At year-end, $400 worth of supplies are on hand.
p. At year-end, an additional $4,000 of sales salaries are owed, but have not yet been paid.
q. Income tax expense is based on a 35% corporate tax rate.

You are asked to do the following:

1. Journalize the transactions for the current year, 2010, using the accounts listed on the financial statements and other appropriate accounts (you may omit explanations).
2. Set up T-accounts and enter the beginning balances from the December 31, 2009, post-closing trial balance for Bearing. Post all current year journal entries to the T-accounts.
3. Journalize and post any necessary adjusting entries at the end of 2010. (*Hint:* Items b, c, d, e, m, o, and p require adjustment.)
4. After the adjusting entries are posted, prepare a trial balance, a balance sheet, and an income statement for 2010. (*Hint:* Income before income taxes should equal $8,175.)
5. Journalize and post closing entries for 2010 and prepare a post-closing trial balance.

© DUNCAN SMITH/PHOTODISC RED/GETTY IMAGES INC.

PART

2

Operating Activities

Selling a Product or a Service

(1) Understand the three basic types of business activities: operating, investing, and financing. *Operating activities are the day-to-day activities of a business such as selling products, purchasing inventory, and paying for wages. Investing activities primarily relate to the purchase of property, plant, and equipment and the sale of those assets after they have been used. Financing activities are the borrowing of money, and its repayment, and the receipt of funds from investors and payment of dividends back to those investors.*

(2) Use the two revenue recognition criteria to decide when the revenue from a sale or service should be recorded in the accounting records. *Companies should recognize revenue only after they provide a good or service and after they receive a valid promise of payment. Deciding when to recognize revenue is a critical issue in accounting judgment because companies almost always want to recognize revenue sooner rather than later.*

(3) Properly account for the collection of cash and describe the business controls necessary to safeguard cash. *Companies frequently sell on credit, collecting the cash after the sales revenue has already been recorded. Sales discounts are used to encourage early payment of accounts. Cash is a tempting target for theft or fraud, so adequate safeguards must be established within a business to protect the cash.*

(4) Record the losses resulting from credit customers who do not pay their bills. *In order to match bad debt expense with revenue in the appropriate year, the amount of the accounts that will ultimately be uncollectible must be forecasted before individual bad debts are specifically identified. Two ways to perform this estimate are the percentage of sales and aging.*

(5) Evaluate a company's management of its receivables by computing and analyzing appropriate financial ratios. *A company's credit policy can be evaluated by computing how quickly the company collects its receivables.*

(6) Match revenues and expenses by estimating and recording future warranty and service costs associated with a sale. *When warranty promises are made, the total cost to be associated with those promises is estimated and recorded as an expense at the time of the sale.*

EXPANDED *material*

(7) Reconcile a checking account. *A bank reconciliation is a detailed explanation of why the amount of cash a company or individual has in the bank differs from the amount recorded in the company or individual's own records. Most of the differences are caused by timing. For example, a company subtracts a payment amount as soon as it mails the check; the bank doesn't reduce the account balance until the check is presented for payment.*

(8) Account for the impact of changing exchange rates on the value of accounts receivable denominated in foreign currencies. *Making sales denominated in a foreign currency exposes a company to risk because the U.S. dollar value of that currency can fluctuate between the time of the sale and the actual collection. These fluctuations create foreign currency gains and losses.*

Jerry Yang and David Filo met while graduate students at Stanford. Jerry and David's friendship was strengthened when they both went on a six-month academic exchange program to Japan in 1992. In 1993, Jerry and David were supposed to be working on their Ph.D. theses in computer-aided design at Stanford. Instead, they found themselves spending more and more research time surfing through the incredible amount of information available on the newly created "World Wide Web." Jerry and David quickly learned that the key to surfing the vast quantities of information on the Web was to be able to organize the information. They compiled a list of their favorite Web sites, which they e-mailed to friends and posted on the Web. The Web site eventually became known as "**Yahoo!**"

By 1994, thousands were using Yahoo! to access information on the Web. In fact, the demand was so great that Jerry and David were spending 20-plus hours a day on their "hobby." In addition, the resources of the Stanford computer network were being taxed by Yahoo! users, and university officials asked Jerry and David to find another computer to host their service.

F Y I

Jonathan Swift coined the word *yahoo* in his book *Gulliver's Travels*. The "yahoos" were savage humans who lived in a land where horses were the dominant species. Swift, a noted satirist, used the term yahoo to illustrate how easy it is to justify committing atrocities against people once they are categorized with an unfavorable label.

In March 1995, Jerry and David were finally convinced that their Web search hobby could actually be turned into a business. They accepted a $4 million investment from a **venture capital firm**. Realizing that they lacked business expertise, they chose Tim Koogle, another Stanford graduate who was running a $400 million high-tech equipment company, to join them in running their company. This team has turned Yahoo! into one of the most

venture capital firm

A company that provides needed cash to companies in return for an ownership interest.

recognized names among Internet companies. In January of 2000, the company was worth over $100 billion. Then the "Internet bubble" burst. The year 2000 saw many Internet companies fall by the wayside and those that remained had market value a fraction of what they once were. For example, Yahoo!'s value in May of 2006 was approximately $45.5 billion.

So what happened to Internet companies? Investors were afraid of missing out on the next "Microsoft." As a result, the value of many high-tech companies was based on rumors, beta versions, and vaporware. Once investors realized the outlandish prices being paid for these tech companies, they began focusing on the basics of a business—revenues and profits. Many Internet companies never posted a profit—Yahoo! did not report its first profitable year until 1999. Once investors began expecting companies to post profits and generate cash, many Internet companies went out of business—the "bubble" burst.

So, how does Yahoo! make money? Throughout its history, Yahoo! has generated almost all of its revenue through the sale of advertising space on its Web pages. For example, in 2005, 87% of Yahoo!'s $5.3 billion in revenue was generated through marketing services. Yahoo! has various methods of marketing and advertising and is very specific in its annual report as to how revenue is recognized for each of its revenue sources. For example, "The Company recognizes revenue related to the display of advertisements on the Yahoo! Properties as 'impressions' are delivered. An 'impression' is delivered when an advertisement appears in pages viewed by users." Another source of advertising revenue is text-link advertisements, and revenues from that source are recognized when "'click-throughs' occur. A 'click-through' occurs when a user clicks on an advertiser's listing." As you can see, companies are very careful when it comes to the recognition of revenue—and for good reason. The recent accounting scandals coupled with the bursting of the Internet bubble have placed a renewed emphasis on "when should revenue be recognized?"

For Internet companies such as Yahoo!, investors are extremely interested in the amount of revenue reported in the income statement. In fact, in the gold rush of e-commerce, investors were more concerned about how much e-business a company was doing than about whether the company was able to generate immediate profits. The amount of revenue reported by an Internet company is a key indicator of how large the company is in the Internet economy. For example, until 2003, Amazon.com had never reported a profit (revenue minus expenses) in its history; the company lost $149 million in 2002 alone. Yet, because of the $3.9 billion in revenue it reported in 2002, Amazon.com was viewed as a major player in the Internet economy. As a result, Amazon.com had a market value of $12 billion in May 2003.

Exhibit 1 illustrates how the stock of both Yahoo! and Amazon.com has performed since 1998. The Internet boom peaked in January of 2000 and in one year both companies had lost significant market value. The bright side is that both of these companies are still in existence. Many Internet companies are gone.

The amount of revenue reported by traditional companies, such as General Motors, Wal-Mart, and General Electric, is also of interest to investors because increased revenues almost always lead to increased profits. Consequently, there is sometimes great pressure on companies to report as much revenue as possible. To balance this pressure, accounting rules have been established to govern exactly when it is appropriate for a company to report the revenue from a transaction in the income statement. These accounting rules are not just conceptual toys for accountants; investor concern about whether Microstrategy, a software company, was correctly applying the accounting rules associated with revenue caused the company's stock price to drop from $333 per share on March 10, 2000, to $22.25 per share just 10 weeks later.

In this chapter, you will study the accounting rules governing the proper recognition of revenue. You will also learn how to account for cash collections and how to handle customer accounts that are uncollectible. Selling goods and services, collecting the cash, and handling customer accounts are fundamental to the operation of any business. Accordingly, properly recording these activities is fundamental to the practice of accounting.

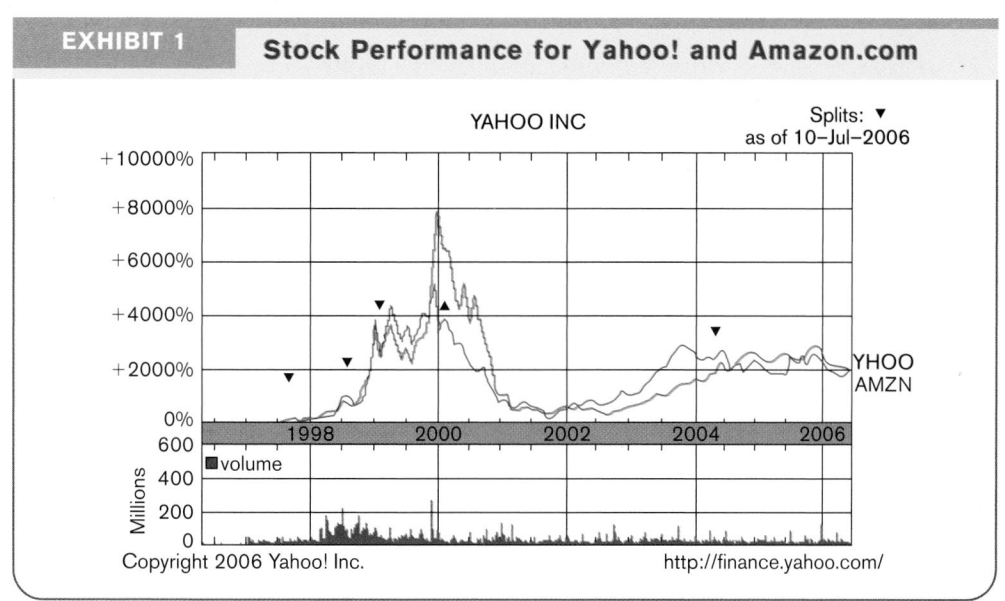

EXHIBIT 1   **Stock Performance for Yahoo! and Amazon.com**

YAHOO INC

Splits: ▼ as of 10–Jul–2006

YHOO
AMZN

Copyright 2006 Yahoo! Inc.   http://finance.yahoo.com/

SETTING THE STAGE

Major Activities of a Business

1 In the first five chapters, you were introduced to the accounting environment, the basic financial statements, and the accounting cycle (the way business transactions are entered into the accounting records). That material was necessary for you to understand some basic terminology and procedures used in accounting. Accounting has often been called the language of business. By studying the first five chapters, you should now be somewhat familiar with this new business language.

Understand the three basic types of business activities: operating, investing, and financing.

With the basics behind us, it is now time to use accounting to understand how businesses work, how the various activities of business are accounted for, and how businesses report their operating results to investors. The activities of most businesses can be divided into three groups:

- Operating activities
- Investing activities
- Financing activities

operating activities

Transactions and events that involve selling products or services and incurring the necessary expenses associated with the primary activities of the business.

Operating activities involve selling products or services, buying inventory for resale, and incurring and paying for necessary expenses associated with the primary activities of the business. The operating activities of a motel, for example, would include renting rooms (the selling activity); buying soap, shampoo, and other supplies to operate the motel; and incurring and paying for electricity, heat, water, cleaning, television and telephone service; and salaries and taxes of workers. The operating activities of a grocery store would include buying produce, meats, canned goods, and other items for resale; selling products to customers; and incurring and paying for expenses associated with the store's operations such as utilities, salaries, and taxes. The operating activities of **Yahoo!** include selling advertising space on the company's Web pages, paying employees to maintain the Yahoo! system and to develop new software, and paying to advertise the Yahoo! brand name on TV and in magazines. It is easy to identify operating activities because they are always associated with the primary purpose of a business.

In this chapter we cover the operating activities for selling products and services, the recognition of revenues from those sales, accounting for cash, and problems associated with collecting receivables arising from sales. In Chapter 7 we examine the purchase of inventory for resale to customers and the necessary accounting procedures. In Chapter 8 we conclude our discussion of operating activities by considering other operating expenses and how revenues and expenses are combined to compute the net income of a business. Incurring and paying for operating expenses such as employee compensation, insurance, advertising, research and development, and income taxes are also covered in Chapter 8.

investing activities

Transactions and events that involve the purchase and sale of property, plant, equipment, and other assets not generally held for resale.

Investing activities involve the purchase of assets for use in the business. The assets purchased as part of investing activities include property, plant, and equipment, as well as financial assets such as investments in stocks and bonds of other companies. Investing activities are distinguishable from operating activities because they occur less frequently and the amounts involved in each transaction are usually quite large. For example, while most businesses buy and sell inventory or services to customers on a daily basis (operating activities), only rarely do they buy and sell buildings, equipment, and stocks and bonds of other companies. It is important to note that buying inventory for resale is an operating activity, not an investing activity. Investing activities are covered in Chapters 9 and 12.

financing activities

Transactions and events whereby resources are obtained from, or repaid to, owners (equity financing) and creditors (debt financing).

Financing activities involve raising money to finance a business by means other than operations. In addition to earning money through profitable operations, there are two other ways to fund a business: (1) money can be borrowed from creditors (debt financing), or (2) money can be raised by selling stock or

A motel deals with operating activities on a daily basis when renting rooms, buying supplies, and paying utility expenses.

ownership interests in the business to investors (equity financing). Debt financing is the subject of Chapter 10, while equity financing will be discussed in Chapter 11.

Once you have studied Chapters 6 through 12, you will have a good understanding of how businesses operate, invest, and are financed. That knowledge should be helpful in the future if you own your own business, invest in companies as a stockholder, work for a financial institution (or other lender of funds), or work in any position where a knowledge of business is essential.

After studying the operating, investing, and financing activities of a business, you will be ready to combine your knowledge of how businesses operate with the basic accounting knowledge you gained from Chapters 1 through 5. To do this, we will study in detail the statement of cash flows, which is structured around the three activities of a business (Chapter 13). You will discover that preparation of a statement of cash flows requires a sound understanding of the balance sheet and the income statement, as well as a good grasp of how the activities of a business tie together. Throughout Chapters 6 through 12 we will be discussing how financial statement numbers are used to make decisions. In Chapter 14, we will bring together in one chapter all of the financial ratios that have been discussed as well as provide a framework for the various financial statement ratios and how they are used. Exhibit 2 provides a graphical road map of the business and reporting activities that will be discussed in the subsequent eight chapters.

Although Chapters 6 through 12 are organized around business activities, it is important to understand how these activities relate to the basic financial statements. To help you understand these relationships, at the beginning of each of the next seven chapters where possible, we present an exhibit that identifies the time line of transactions that will

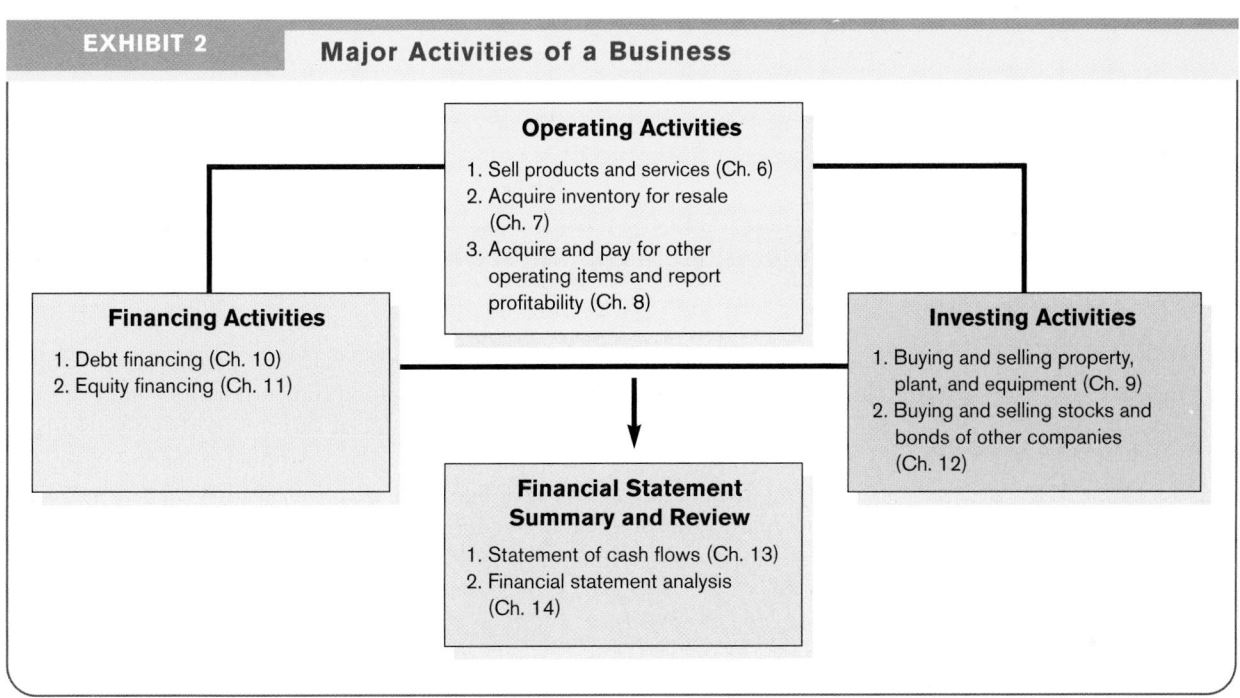

EXHIBIT 2   Major Activities of a Business

Operating Activities
1. Sell products and services (Ch. 6)
2. Acquire inventory for resale (Ch. 7)
3. Acquire and pay for other operating items and report profitability (Ch. 8)

Financing Activities
1. Debt financing (Ch. 10)
2. Equity financing (Ch. 11)

Investing Activities
1. Buying and selling property, plant, and equipment (Ch. 9)
2. Buying and selling stocks and bonds of other companies (Ch. 12)

Financial Statement Summary and Review
1. Statement of cash flows (Ch. 13)
2. Financial statement analysis (Ch. 14)

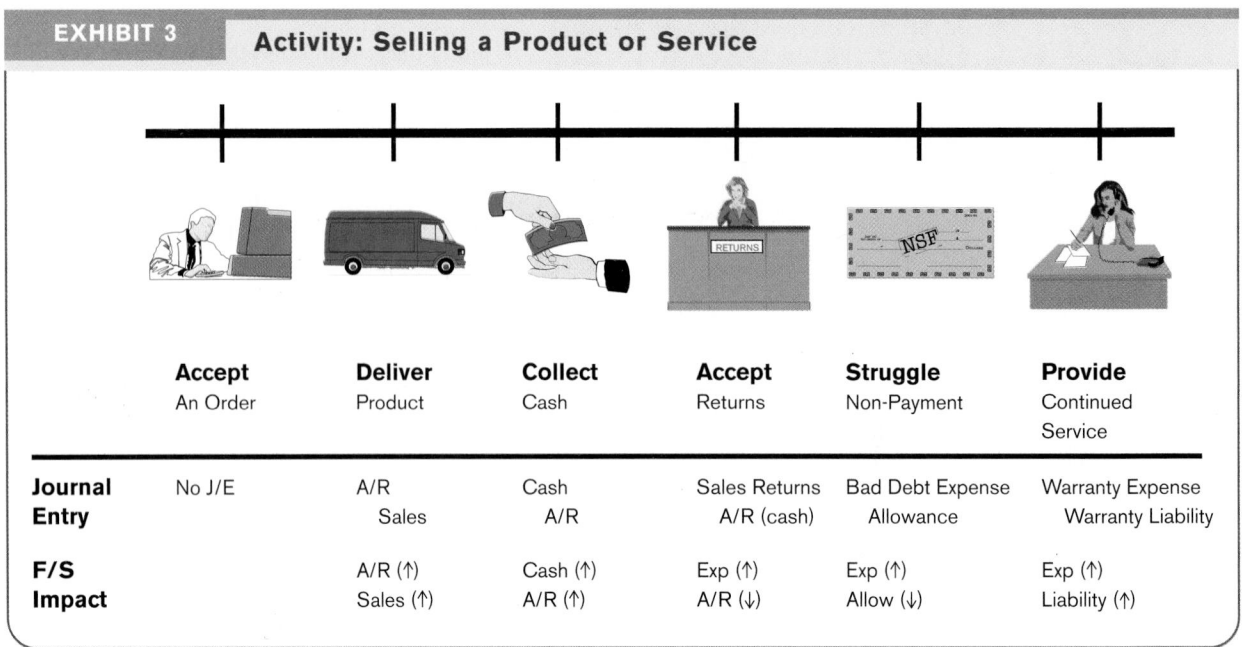

	Accept An Order	**Deliver** Product	**Collect** Cash	**Accept** Returns	**Struggle** Non-Payment	**Provide** Continued Service

**Journal
Entry**
	No J/E	A/R
		   Sales
			Cash
			   A/R
				Sales Returns
				   A/R (cash)
					Bad Debt Expense
					   Allowance
						Warranty Expense
						   Warranty Liability

F/S Impact		A/R (↑) Sales (↑)	Cash (↑) A/R (↑)	Exp (↑) A/R (↓)	Exp (↑) Allow (↓)	Exp (↑) Liability (↑)

be covered in that chapter, the specific accounts associated with those transactions, summary journal entries relating to those accounts, and how the financial statements are ultimately affected because of those transactions. As you can see in Exhibit 3, Cash, Accounts Receivable, and Warranty Liability on the balance sheet; Sales, Bad Debt Expense, and Warranty Expense on the income statement; and Receipts from Customers on the statement of cash flows are covered in Chapter 6.

> **REMEMBER THIS...**
>
> - Operating activities involve selling products or services, buying inventory for resale, and incurring and paying for necessary expenses associated with the primary activities of a business.
> - Investing activities include purchasing assets for use in the business and making investments in such items as stocks and bonds.
> - Financing activities include raising money to finance a business by means other than operations.

Recognizing Revenue

Use the two revenue recognition criteria to decide when the revenue from a sale or service should be recorded in the accounting records.

(2) The operations of a business revolve around the sale of a product or a service. **Mcdonald's** sells fast food; **Wal-Mart** sells food and other household goods; **Bank of America** loans money and sells financial services; **Yahoo!** sells advertising space on its Web pages. Just as the sale of a product or service is at the heart of any business, proper recording of the revenue from sales and services is fundamental to the practice of accounting.

Consideration of this time line raises a number of very interesting accounting questions:

- When should revenue be recognized—when the initial order is placed, when the good or service is provided, when the cash is collected, or later, when there is no longer any chance that the customer will return the product or demand a refund because of faulty service?

- What accounting procedures are used to manage and safeguard cash as it is collected?
- How do you account for bad debts, that is, customers who don't pay their bills?
- How do you account for the possibility that sales this year may obligate you to make warranty repairs and provide continuing customer service for many years to come?

The following sections will address these accounting issues, beginning with the important question of when to recognize revenue.

When Should Revenue Be Recognized?

revenue recognition

The process of recording revenue in the accounting records; occurs after (1) the work has been substantially completed and (2) cash collection is reasonably assured.

Revenue recognition is the phrase that accountants use to refer to the recording of a sale through a journal entry in the formal accounting records. Revenue is usually recognized when two important criteria have been met:

1. The work has been substantially completed (the company has done something), and
2. Cash, or a valid promise of future payment, has been received (the company has received something in return).

As a practical matter, most companies record sales when goods are shipped to customers. Credit sales are recognized as revenues before cash is collected, and revenue from services is usually recognized when the service is performed, not necessarily when cash is received.

To illustrate, we will assume that on a typical business day Farm Land Products sells 30 sacks of fertilizer for cash and 20 sacks on credit, all at $10 per sack. Given these data, the $500 of revenue is recorded as follows:

Cash	300	
Accounts Receivable	200	
Sales Revenue		500

Sold 30 sacks of fertilizer for cash and 20 sacks on credit.

 FYI

In the majority of companies, the most frequent types of journal entries are those to record sales, cash collections, purchases, and payments to suppliers. Because such transactions are so frequent, most firms maintain four separate special journals: (1) the sales journal, (2) the purchases journal, (3) the cash receipts journal, and (4) the cash disbursements journal. These journals are discussed in detail in this text's Interactive Study Center at **http://www.thomsonedu.com/accounting/ albrecht**.

Although the debit entries are made to different accounts, the credit entry for the full amount is to a revenue account. Thus, accrual-basis accounting requires the recognition of $500 in revenue instead of the $300 that would be recognized if the focus were merely on cash collection.

This example is a simple illustration of how sales are recorded and revenue is recognized. In reality, sales transactions are usually more complex, involving such things as uncertainty about exactly when the transaction is actually completed and whether a valid promise of payment has actually been received from the customer. These difficulties are compounded by the fact that companies often have an understandable desire to report revenue as soon as possible in order to enhance their reported performance and make it easier to get loans or attract investors. The discussion below will further examine the two revenue recognition criteria (work done and cash collectible) to see how accountants apply these rules to ensure that reported revenue fairly reflects the economic performance of a business.

Application of the Revenue Recognition Criteria

The Farm Land example was used to illustrate a straightforward case of revenue recognition at the time a sale is made. The Farm Land customers bought $500 worth of fertilizer, paying $300 cash and promising to pay $200 later; the $500 of revenue was recognized immediately. But what if the terms of the sale had also required Farm Land to deliver the fertilizer to the customers at no extra charge? In this case, proper application of the "work done" revenue recognition criterion would require that the revenue not be recorded until actual delivery had taken place. Alternatively, assume that the fertilizer sale was accompanied by a guarantee that, within 30 days, customers could return the unused portion of fertilizer for a full refund. If very few customers ever seek a refund, revenue should still be recognized at the time of sale. But, for example, if over 70% of fertilizer customers later seek refunds, the "cash collectible" revenue recognition criterion suggests that no revenue should be recognized until the completion of the 30-day return period; Farm Land then becomes reasonably assured of the amount of cash it will collect from the $500 in sales. This situation illustrates the need for accountants to exercise professional judgment and account for the economic reality of a transaction instead of blindly relying on technical legal rules about whether a sale has taken place. Other examples of the application of the revenue recognition criteria are given below.

Yahoo! As mentioned in the opening scenario of this chapter, **Yahoo!** derives most of its revenue from the sale of banner advertising space on its Web pages. As mentioned, Yahoo! recognizes advertising revenue as the impressions occur. This revenue recognition practice makes sense if Yahoo! is reasonably certain of collecting payment for these impressions because Yahoo! has completed its work of providing the impressions. Yahoo! often guarantees an advertiser a minimum number of impressions. To the extent that the minimum guaranteed impressions are not met as of the date the financial statements are prepared, Yahoo! delays recognizing the advertising revenue until the guaranteed number of impressions is reached.

 STOP & THINK

As you might expect, not all software companies support this revenue recognition practice; they would prefer to recognize all of the revenue from a software sale immediately at the time of the sale. Microsoft, on the other hand, has been very supportive of the rule. Why do you think Microsoft supports the accounting rule that many other software firms oppose?

Microsoft The nature of the computer software industry presents several sticky revenue recognition issues. The installation of software and the promise of software upgrades require software companies to consider when the earnings process is substantially complete. Are the revenue recognition criteria satisfied at the point of sale, when the software is installed, or after promised upgrades are delivered? **Microsoft** recognizes a portion (about 80% for the Office 2003 software) of the software price as revenue immediately upon delivery of the software to you. The rest of the software price is recognized as revenue gradually over time as the technical support service is provided.

Boeing   **Boeing** recognizes revenue from commercial aircraft sales at the time the aircraft is delivered to the airline. For example, in 2005 Boeing recognized revenue from the delivery of 290 commercial aircraft, including 212 737s. In contrast, many of Boeing's government contracts require years of work before any product is delivered. If Boeing did not recognize any revenue during this extended production period, its economic activity for that period would be understated. Thus, the accounting rules allow Boeing to recognize revenue piecemeal as it reaches "scheduled performance milestones." This type of "proportional performance" technique is commonly used to recognize revenue from transactions that extend over a long time period, such as for highway construction projects or season tickets for a professional sports team.

Rent-A-Center   **Rent-A-Center** operates 2,753 rent-to-own stores in the United States under both its own name and the names, "Get It Now" and "ColorTyme." Customers rent furniture, VCRs, and other consumer goods under an agreement giving them ownership of the item if they continue to make their payments for the entire rental period. Rent-to-own stores attract customers who cannot afford the outright purchase of consumer goods and who anticipate difficulty in receiving credit through normal channels. Thus, a big concern for Rent-A-Center is collecting the full amount of cash due under a rental contract. In fact, Rent-A-Center states that only about 25% of its customers complete the full term of their agreement. With such a high likelihood of customers stopping payments on their rental agreements, Rent-A-Center recognizes revenue from a specific contract only gradually as the cash is actually collected.

F Y I

According to generally accepted auditing standards, auditors are often required to confirm Accounts Receivable balances directly with the company that supposedly owes the money. This can provide an independent check on the existence of the receivables.

As mentioned initially, the accounting for most sales transactions is straightforward—the revenue is recognized when the sale is made. However, as illustrated by the examples in this section, when the "work" associated with a sale extends over a significant period of time, or when cash collectibility is in doubt, the accountant must use professional judgment in applying the revenue recognition criteria to determine the proper time to record the sale.

Properly recognizing revenue is made more difficult by the fact that companies often have an understandable desire to report revenue as soon as possible. For example, for a company that is applying for a large loan or making an initial public offering of stock, it is critical that reported revenue, and thus reported net income, be as high as possible. In addition, company managers are often scrambling to make revenue or profit targets. In many cases, the managers' bonuses depend on whether these targets are met.

STOP & THINK

Many colleges and universities prepare financial statements that are released to the public. When do you think a college or university should recognize revenue from student tuition?

Accordingly, managers often have great interest in making sure that revenue is recognized this year rather than waiting until next year. Receivables and revenue continue to be ripe areas for abuse or outright fraud because the associated accounting journal entry is so temptingly easy to make: debit Accounts Receivable and credit Revenue.

> **REMEMBER THIS...**
>
> - Revenue is recognized after:
>   - the work is done **and**
>   - cash collectibility is reasonably assured.
> - The entry to record revenue from the sale of merchandise or from the performance of a service is:
>
> | | | |
> |---|---:|---:|
> | Cash (and/or Accounts Receivable) .... | XXX | |
> | Sales Revenue (or Service Revenue)......................... | | XXX |

Cash Collection

3 — *Properly account for the collection of cash and describe the business controls necessary to safeguard cash.*

Recall the Farm Land Products example in which fertilizer was sold, partially for cash and partially on credit. Farm Land recorded the sales as follows:

Cash	300	
Accounts Receivable	200	
Sales Revenue		500
Sold 30 sacks of fertilizer for cash and 20 sacks on credit.		

Subsequent collection of the $200 accounts receivable is recorded as follows:

Cash	200	
Accounts Receivable		200
Collected cash for $200 credit sale.		

Note that Sales Revenue is not credited again when the cash is collected; the revenue was already recognized when the sale was made.

The following T-accounts show that the net result of these two transactions is an increase in Cash and Sales Revenue of $500.

	Cash		Accounts Receivable		Sales Revenue	
Original sale	300		200			500
Collection of account	200			200		
Final balances	500		0			500
	To balance sheet					To income statement

These two entries illustrate simple sales and collection transactions. Many companies, however, offer sales discounts and must deal with merchandise returns. The accounting for discounts and returns is explained next.

Sales Discounts

sales discount

A reduction in the selling price that is allowed if payment is received within a specified period.

In many sales transactions, the buyer is given a discount if the bill is paid promptly. Such incentives to pay quickly are called **sales discounts**, or cash discounts, and the discount terms are typically expressed in abbreviated form. For example, 2/10, n/30 means that a buyer will receive a 2% discount from the selling price if payment is made within 10 days of the date of purchase, but that the full amount must be paid within 30 days or it will be considered past due. (Other common terms are 1/10, n/30 and 2/10, EOM. The latter means that a 2% discount is granted if payment is made within 10 days after the date of sale; otherwise the balance is due at the end of the month.) A 2% discount is a strong incentive for a customer to pay within 10 days because it is equivalent to paying an annual interest rate of about 36% to wait and pay after the discount period. In fact, if the amount owed is substantial, most firms will borrow money, if necessary, to take advantage of a sales discount. The interest rate they will have to pay a lending institution to borrow the money is considerably less than the effective interest rate of missing the sales discount.

If an account receivable is paid within a specified discount period, the entry to record the receipt of cash is different from the cash receipt entry shown earlier. Thus, if the $200 in Farm Land credit sales were made with discount terms of 2/10, n/30, and if the customers paid within the discount period, the entry to record the receipt of cash is:

Cash	196	
Sales Discounts ($200 × 0.02)	4	
Accounts Receivable		200
Collected cash within the discount period for $200 credit sale.		

contra account

An account that is offset or deducted from another account.

Sales Discounts is a **contra account** (specifically, a contra-revenue account), which means that it is deducted from sales revenue on the income statement. This account is included with other revenue accounts in the general ledger, but unlike other revenue accounts, it has a debit balance rather than a credit balance.

Sales Returns and Allowances

Customers often return merchandise, either because the item is defective or for a variety of other reasons. Most companies generally accept merchandise returns in order to maintain good customer relations. When merchandise is returned, the company must make an entry to reduce revenues and to reduce either Cash (a cash refund) or Accounts Receivable (an adjustment to the customer's account). A similar entry is required when the sales price is reduced because the merchandise was defective or damaged during shipment to the customer.

To illustrate the type of entry needed, we will assume that before any payments on account are made, Farm Land customers return goods costing $150; $100 in returns were made by cash customers, and $50 in returns were made by credit customers. The entry to record the return of merchandise is:

Sales Returns and Allowances	150	
Cash		100
Accounts Receivable		50
Received $150 of returned merchandise; $100 from cash customers and $50 from credit customers.		

sales returns and allowances

A contra-revenue account in which the return of, or allowance for reduction in the price of, merchandise previously sold is recorded.

The credit customers will be sent a credit memorandum for the return, stating that credit has been granted and that the balance of their accounts (in total) is now $150 ($200 original credit purchase − $50 returns). Like Sales Discounts, **Sales Returns and Allowances** is a contra account that is deducted from sales revenue on the income statement. The income statement presentation for the revenue accounts, assuming payment within the discount period on the $150 balance in Accounts Receivable, is shown on the following page.

Income Statement

Sales revenue	$ 500
Less: Sales discounts*	(3)
Less: Sales returns and allowances	(150)
Net sales revenue	$347

*($200 − $50) × 0.02 = $3

Note that when merchandise is returned, sales discounts for the subsequent payment are granted only on the selling price of the merchandise not returned.

It might seem that the use of contra accounts (Sales Discounts and Sales Returns and Allowances) involves extra steps that would not be necessary if discounts and returns of merchandise were deducted directly from Sales Revenue. Although such direct deductions would have the same final effect on net income, the contra accounts separate initial sales from all returns, allowances, and discounts. This permits a company's management to analyze the extent to which customers are returning merchandise, receiving allowances, and taking advantage of discounts. If management find that excessive amounts of merchandise are being returned, they may decide that the company's sales returns policy is too liberal or that the quality of its merchandise needs improvement.

gross sales

Total recorded sales before deducting any sales discounts or sales returns and allowances.

A company's total recorded sales, before any discounts or returns and allowances, are referred to as **gross sales**. When sales discounts or sales returns and allowances are deducted from gross sales, the resulting amount is referred to as **net sales**.

net sales

Gross sales less sales discounts and sales returns and allowances.

Control of Cash

cash

Coins, currency, money orders, checks, and funds on deposit with financial institutions; the most liquid of assets.

Cash includes coins, currency, money orders and checks (made payable or endorsed to the company), and money on deposit with banks or savings institutions that are available for use to satisfy the company's obligations. All the various transactions involving these forms of cash are usually summarized and reported under a single balance sheet account, Cash.

Because it is the easiest asset to spend if it is stolen, cash is a tempting target and must be carefully safeguarded. Several control procedures have been developed to help management monitor and protect cash. Because cash is particularly vulnerable to loss or misuse we will discuss three important controls that are an integral part of accounting for cash.

One of the most important controls is that the handling of cash be separated from the recording of cash. The purpose of this separation of duties is that it becomes more difficult for theft or errors to occur when two or more people are involved. If the cash records are maintained by an employee who also has access to the cash itself, cash can be stolen or "borrowed," and the employee can cover up the shortage by falsifying the accounting records.

In its balance sheet (see Appendix A), **Wal-Mart** follows the common practice of combining cash and short-term investments (bonds and U.S. Treasury securities) for the total Cash amount.

A second cash control practice is to require that all cash receipts be deposited daily in bank accounts. This disciplined, rigid process ensures that personal responsibility for the handling of cash is focused on the individual assigned to make the regular deposit. In addition, this process prevents the accumulation of a large amount of cash—even the most trusted employee can be tempted by a large cash hoard.

A third cash control practice is to require that all cash expenditures (except those paid out of a miscellaneous petty cash fund) be made with prenumbered checks. As we all know from managing our personal finances, payments made with pocket cash are quickly forgotten and easily concealed. In contrast, payments made by check are well documented, both in our personal check registers and by our bank.

In addition to safeguarding cash, a business must ensure that cash is wisely managed. In fact, many businesses establish elaborate control and budgeting procedures for monitoring cash balances and estimating future cash needs. Companies also try to keep only minimum balances in no-interest or low-interest checking accounts; other cash is kept in more high-yielding investments such as certificates of deposit.

REMEMBER THIS...

- Net sales can be calculated as follows:

    Gross Sales
    − Sales Discounts
    − Sales Returns and Allowances
    = Net Sales

- Common cash controls include:

    - separation of duties in handling and accounting for cash,
    - daily deposits of all cash receipts, and
    - payment of all expenditures by prenumbered checks.

Accounting for Credit Customers Who Don't Pay

Record the losses resulting from credit customers who do not pay their bills.

(4) The term **receivables** refers to a company's claims for money, goods, or services. Receivables are created through various types of transactions, the two most common being the sale of merchandise or services on credit and the lending of money. On a personal level, we are all familiar with credit. Because credit is so readily available, we can buy such items as cars, refrigerators, and big-screen TVs, even when we cannot afford to pay cash for them. Major retail companies such as **Sears**, oil companies such as **Shell**, and credit card companies such as **Visa, Mastercard**, and **American Express** have made credit available to almost every person in the United States. We live in a credit world—not only on the individual level, but also at the wholesale and manufacturing business levels.

receivables

Claims for money, goods, or services.

In business, credit sales give rise to the most common type of receivables: accounts receivable. **Accounts receivable** are the amounts owed to a business by its credit customers and are usually collected in cash within 10 to 60 days (see page 238 for definition). Accounts receivable result from agreements between a company and its credit customers; a more formal contract, including interest on the unpaid balance, is called a note receivable. Receivables that are to be converted to cash within a year (or the normal operating cycle) are classified as current assets and listed on the balance sheet below Cash. In

? F Y I

Credit card sales can be viewed as a way for a business to reap the benefit of increased credit sales without having to set up a bookkeeping and collection service for accounts receivable. The credit card company screens customers based on their creditworthiness, sends out the bills, collects the cash, and bears the cost of any uncollectible accounts. A business that accepts credit card sales pays a fee ranging from 1 to 5% of credit card sales.

accounts receivable

A current asset representing money due for services performed or merchandise sold on credit.

bad debt

An uncollectible account receivable.

this section of the chapter, we discuss the accounting issues associated with credit customers who don't pay.

When companies sell goods and services on credit (as most do), there are usually some customers who do not pay for the merchandise they purchase; these are referred to as **bad debts**. In fact, most businesses expect a small percentage of their receivables to be uncollectible. If a firm tries too hard to eliminate the possibility of losses from nonpaying customers, it usually makes its credit policy so restrictive that valuable sales are lost. On the other hand, if a firm extends credit too easily, the total cost of maintaining the accounts receivable system may exceed the benefit gained from attracting customers by allowing them to buy on credit (due to the number of accounts to track and uncollectible receivables to try to collect). Because of this dilemma, most firms carefully monitor their credit sales and accounts receivable to ensure that their policies are neither too restrictive nor too liberal.

When an account receivable becomes uncollectible, a firm incurs a bad debt loss. This loss is recognized as a cost of doing business, so it is classified as a selling expense. There are two ways to account for losses from uncollectible accounts: the direct write-off method and the allowance method.

Sometimes companies need cash prior to the due dates of their receivables. Often, in these circumstances, such companies will sell or "factor" their accounts receivables to financing or factoring companies. To learn more about how companies account for the "factoring" of receivables, visit this text's Interactive Study Center at **http://www.thomsonedu.com/ accounting/albrecht**.

direct write-off method

The recording of actual losses from uncollectible accounts as expenses during the period in which accounts receivable are determined to be uncollectible.

Direct Write-Off Method

With the **direct write-off method**, an uncollectible account is recognized as an expense at the time it is determined to be uncollectible. For example, assume that during the year 2009, Farm Land Products had total credit sales of $300,000. Of this amount, $250,000 was subsequently collected in cash during the year, leaving a year-end balance in Accounts Receivable of $50,000 ($300,000 − $250,000). The summary journal entries to record this information are:

Accounts Receivable	300,000	
Sales Revenue		300,000
To record total credit sales for the year.		
Cash	250,000	
Accounts Receivable		250,000
To record total cash collections for the year.		

Assume that one credit customer, Jake Palmer, has an account balance of $1,500 that remains unpaid for several months in 2010. If, after receiving several past-due notices, Palmer still does not pay, Farm Land will probably turn the account over to an attorney or a collection agency. Then, if collection attempts fail, the company may decide that the Palmer account will not be collected and write it off as a loss. The entry to record the expense under the direct write-off method is:

Bad Debt Expense	1,500	
Accounts Receivable		1,500
To write off the uncollectible account of Jake Palmer.		

bad debt expense

An account that represents the portion of the current period's credit sales that are estimated to be uncollectible.

Bad Debt Expense is usually considered a selling expense on the income statement. Although the direct write-off method is objective (the account is written off at the time it proves to be uncollectible), it most likely would violate the matching principle, which requires that all costs and expenses incurred in generating revenues be identified with those revenues period by period. With the direct write-off method, sales made near the end of one accounting period may not be recognized as uncollectible until the next period. In this example, the revenue from the sale to Jake Palmer is recognized in 2009, but the expense from the bad debt is not recognized until 2010. As a result, expenses are understated in 2009 and overstated in 2010. This makes the direct write-off method unacceptable from a theoretical point of view. The direct write-off method is allowable only if bad debts involve small, insignificant amounts.

The Allowance Method

allowance method

The recording of estimated losses due to uncollectible accounts as expenses during the period in which the sales occurred.

The **allowance method** satisfies the matching principle because it accounts for uncollectibles during the same period in which the sales occurred. With this method, a firm uses its experience (or industry averages) to estimate the amount of receivables arising from this year's credit sales that will ultimately become uncollectible. That estimate is recorded as bad debt expense in the period of sale. Although the use of estimates may result in a somewhat imprecise expense figure, this is generally thought to be a less serious problem than the direct write-off method's failure to match bad debt expenses with the sales that caused them. In addition, with experience, these estimates tend to be quite accurate.

To illustrate the allowance method, assume that Farm Land Products estimates that the bad debts created by its $300,000 in credit sales in 2009 will ultimately total $4,500. Note that this is a statistical estimate—on average, bad debts will be $4,500, but Farm Land does not yet know exactly which customers will be the ones who will fail to pay. The entry to record this estimated bad debt expense for 2009 is:

Bad Debt Expense	4,500	
Allowance for Bad Debts		4,500
To record the estimated bad debt expense for the current year.		

allowance for bad debts

A contra account, deducted from Accounts Receivable, that shows the estimated losses from uncollectible accounts.

Bad Debt Expense is a selling expense on the income statement, and **Allowance for Bad Debts** is a contra account to Accounts Receivable on the balance sheet. An allowance account is used because the company does not yet know which receivables will not be collected. Later on, for example, in 2010, as actual losses are recognized, the balance in Allowance for Bad Debts is reduced. For example, if in 2010 Jake Palmer's receivable for $1,500 is specifically identified as being uncollectible, the entry is:

Allowance for Bad Debts	1,500	
Accounts Receivable		1,500
To write off the uncollectible account of Jake Palmer.		

Note that the write-off entry in 2010 does not affect net income in 2010. Instead, the net income in 2009, when the credit sale to Jake Palmer was originally made, already reflects the estimated bad debt expense. Think of this entry as follows: The $1,500 Jake Palmer account has been shown to be bad, so it is "thrown away" via a credit to Accounts Receivable. In addition, Allowance for Bad Debts, which is a general estimate of the amount of bad accounts, is reduced by $1,500 because the bad Palmer account has been specifically identified and eliminated. In one entry, the amounts in Accounts Receivable and Allowance for Bad Debts have been reduced. Assume that the balance in Accounts Receivable was $50,000 and the balance in Allowance for Bad Debts was $4,500 before the Palmer account was written off. The net amount in Accounts Receivable after the $1,500 write-off is exactly the same as it was before the entry, as shown here.

Before Write-Off Entry		After Write-Off Entry	
Accounts receivable	$50,000	Accounts receivable ($50,000 − $1,500)	$48,500
Less allowance for bad debts	4,500	Less allowance for bad debts ($4,500 − $1,500)	3,000
Net balance	$45,500	Net balance	$45,500

net realizable value of accounts receivable

The net amount that would be received if all receivables considered collectible were collected; equal to total accounts receivable less the allowance for bad debts.

The net balance of $45,500 reflects the estimated **net realizable value of accounts receivable**, that is, the amount of receivables the company actually expects to collect.

The following T-account shows the kinds of entries that are made to Allowance for Bad Debts:

Allowance for Bad Debts

Actual write-offs of uncollectible accounts	Estimates of uncollectible accounts

Occasionally, a customer whose account has been written off as uncollectible later pays the outstanding balance. When this happens, the company reverses the entry that was used to write off the account and then recognizes the payment. For example, if Jake Palmer pays the $1,500 after his account has already been written off, the entries to correct the accounting records are:

Accounts Receivable	1,500	
Allowance for Bad Debts		1,500
To reinstate the balance previously written off as uncollectible.		
Cash	1,500	
Accounts Receivable		1,500
Received payment in full of previously written-off accounts receivable.		

Because customers sometimes pay their balances after their accounts are written off, it is important for a company to have good control over both the cash collection procedures and the accounting for accounts receivable. Otherwise, such payments as the previously written-off $1,500 could be pocketed by the employee who receives the cash, and it would never be missed. This is one reason that most companies separate the handling of cash from the recording of cash transactions in the accounts.

Because the amount recorded in Bad Debt Expense affects both the reported net realizable value of the receivables and net income, companies must be careful to use good estimation procedures. These estimates can focus on an examination of either the total number of credit sales during the period or the outstanding receivables at year-end to determine their collectibility.

Estimating Uncollectible Accounts Receivable as a Percentage of Credit Sales

One method of estimating bad debt expense is to estimate uncollectible receivables as a percentage of credit sales for the period. If a company uses this method, the amount of uncollectibles will be a straight percentage of the current year's credit sales. That percentage will be a projection based on experience in prior years, modified for any changes expected for the current period. For example, in the Farm Land example, credit sales for the year of $300,000 are expected to generate bad debts of $4,500, indicating that 1.5% of all credit sales are expected to be uncollectible ($4,500/$300,000 = 1.5%). Farm Land would evaluate the percentage each year, in light of its continued experience, to see whether the same percentage still seems reasonable. In addition, if economic conditions have changed for Farm Land's customers (such as the onset of a recession making it more likely that debts will remain uncollected), the percentage would be adjusted.

When this percentage of sales method is used, the existing balance (if there is one) in Allowance for Bad Debts does not affect the amount computed and is not included in the adjusting entry to record bad debt expense. The 1.5% of the current year's sales that is estimated to be uncollectible is calculated and entered separately, and then added to the existing balance. For example, if the existing credit balance is $2,000, the $4,500 will be added, making the new credit balance $6,500. The rationale for not considering the existing $2,000 balance in Allowance for Bad Debts is that it relates to previous periods' sales and reflects the company's estimate (as of the beginning of the year) of prior years' accounts receivable that are expected to be uncollectible.

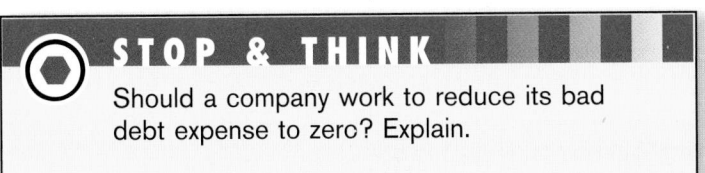

STOP & THINK

Should a company work to reduce its bad debt expense to zero? Explain.

In determining the percentage of credit sales that will be uncollectible, a company must estimate the total amount of loss on the basis of experience or industry averages. Obviously, a company that has been in business for several years should be able to make more accurate estimates than a new company. Many established companies use a three- or five-year average as the basis for estimating losses from uncollectible accounts.

Estimating Uncollectible Accounts Receivable as a Percentage of Total Receivables

Another way to estimate uncollectible receivables is to use a percentage of total receivables. Using this method, the amount of uncollectibles is a percentage of the total receivables balance at the end of the period. Assume that Farm Land decides to use this method and determines that 12% of the $50,000 in the year-end Accounts Receivable will ultimately be uncollectible. Accordingly, the credit balance in Allowance for Bad Debts should be $6,000 ($50,000 × 0.12). If there is no existing balance in Allowance for Bad Debts representing the estimate of bad accounts left over from prior years, then an entry for $6,000 is made. If the account has an existing balance, however, only the net amount needed to bring the credit balance to $6,000 is added. For example, an existing credit balance of $2,000 in Allowance for Bad Debts results in the following adjusting entry:

Bad Debt Expense	4,000	
Allowance for Bad Debts		4,000
To adjust the allowance account to the desired balance		
($6,000 − $2,000 = $4,000).		

In all cases, the ending balance in Allowance for Bad Debts should be the amount of total receivables estimated to be uncollectible.

In estimating bad debt expense, the percentage of sales method focuses on an estimation based directly on the level of the current year's credit sales. With the percentage of total receivables method, the focus is on estimating total bad debts existing at the end of the period; this number is compared to the leftover bad debts from prior years, and the difference is bad debt expense, the new bad debts created in the current period. These two techniques are merely alternative estimation approaches. In practice, as a check, a company would probably use both procedures to ensure that they yield roughly consistent results.

Aging Accounts Receivable.   In the example just given, the correct amount of the ending Allowance for Bad Debts balance was computed by applying the estimated uncollectible percentage (12%) to the entire Accounts Receivable balance ($50,000). In a more refined method of estimating the appropriate ending balance in Allowance for Bad Debts, a company bases its calculations on how long its receivables have been outstanding. With this procedure, called **aging accounts receivable**, each receivable is categorized according to age, such as current, 1–30 days past due, 31–60 days past due, 61–90 days past due, 91–120 days past due, and over 120 days past due. Once the receivables in each age classification are totaled, each total is multiplied by an appropriate uncollectible percentage (as determined by experience), recognizing that the older the receivable, the less likely the company is to collect. Exhibit 4 shows how Farm Land could use an aging accounts receivable analysis to estimate the amount of its $50,000 ending balance in Accounts Receivable that will ultimately be uncollectible.

> **aging accounts receivable**
>
> The process of categorizing each account receivable by the number of days it has been outstanding.

EXHIBIT 4	Aging Accounts Receivable							

Customer	Balance	Current	1–30	31–60	61–90	91–120	Over 120
A. Adams	$10,000	$10,000					
R. Bartholomew	6,500			$ 5,000			$1,500
F. Christiansen	6,250	5,000	$1,250				
G. Dover	7,260			7,260			
M. Ellis	4,000	4,000					
G. Erkland	2,250				$2,250		
R. Fisher	1,500		500			$1,000	
J. Palmer	1,500		1,500				
E. Zeigler	10,740	4,000	6,740				
Totals	$50,000	$23,000	$9,990	$12,260	$2,250	$1,000	$1,500

Estimate of Losses from Uncollectible Accounts

Age	Balance	Percentage Estimated to Be Uncollectible	Amount
Current	$23,000	1.5	$ 345
1–30 days past due	9,990	4.0	400
31–60 days past due	12,260	20.0	2,452
61–90 days past due	2,250	40.0	900
91–120 days past due	1,000	60.0	600
Over 120 days past due	1,500	80.0	1,200
Totals	$50,000		$5,897*

*Receivables that are likely to be uncollectible.

The allowance for bad debts estimate obtained using the aging method is $5,897. If the existing credit balance in Allowance for Bad Debts is $2,000, the required adjusting entry is:

Bad Debt Expense	3,897	
Allowance for Bad Debts		3,897

*To adjust the allowance account to the desired ending
balance ($5,897 − $2,000 = $3,897).*

CAUTION

The aging method is merely a more refined technique for estimating the desired balance in Allowance for Bad Debts.

The aging of accounts receivable is probably the most accurate method of estimating uncollectible accounts. It also enables a company to identify its problem customers. Companies that base their estimates of uncollectible accounts on credit sales or total outstanding receivables also often age their receivables as a way of monitoring the individual accounts receivable balances.

Real-World Illustration of Accounting for Bad Debts

The application of bad debt accounting is illustrated using the financial statements of **Yahoo!** for 2003–2005. As shown in Exhibit 5, Yahoo! reported accounts receivable at the end of 2005 of $763.6 million and a bad debt allowance for bad debts of $41.9 million. In other words, credit customers owed Yahoo! $763.6 million as of the end of 2005; however, Yahoo!'s best estimate was that $41.9 million of this amount would never be collected. This bad debt allowance amounted to 5.5% of the Accounts Receivable balance, down from 6.7% in 2004 and 10.2% in 2003. For a company operating in a stable economic environment with little change in the nature of its credit customers, this percentage would be expected to be about the same from year to year. In the case of Yahoo!, operating in the volatile Internet economy, it appears that there has been some variation in the collectibility of accounts receivable from one year to the next.

EXHIBIT 5	Bad Debt Expense for Yahoo!		
Year of	**Ending Accounts Receivable**	**Ending Bad Debt Allowance**	**Bad Debt Allowance as a Percentage of Accounts Receivable**
2003	$314,376*	$31,961	10.2%
2004	514,208	34,215	6.7%
2005	763,580	41,857	5.5%

*Dollar amounts are in thousands.

REMEMBER THIS...

Two ways of accounting for losses from uncollectible receivables include:

- allowance method (generally accepted)
- direct write-off method (NOT generally accepted)

Two ways of estimating losses from uncollectible receivables include:

- percentage of credit sales (existing balance is ignored)
- fraction of total outstanding receivables (often determined by aging the accounts receivable) (existing balance is considered)

Assessing How Well Companies Manage Their Receivables

(5) As introduced in Chapter 4, information from the financial statements can be used to evaluate a company's performance. An important element of overall company performance is the efficient use of assets. With regard to accounts receivable, inefficient use means that too much cash is tied up in the form of receivables. A company that collects its receivables on a timely basis has cash to pay its bills. Companies that do not do a good job of collecting receivables are often cash poor, paying interest on short-term loans to cover their cash shortage or losing interest that could be earned by investing cash.

There are several methods of evaluating how well an organization is managing its accounts receivable. The most common method involves computing two ratios, accounts receivable turnover and average collection period. The **accounts receivable turnover** ratio is an attempt to determine how many times during the year a company is "turning over" or collecting its receivables. It is a measure of how many times old receivables are collected and replaced by new receivables. Accounts receivable turnover is calculated as follows:

accounts receivable turnover

A measure used to indicate how fast a company collects its receivables; computed by dividing sales by average accounts receivable.

$$\text{Accounts Receivable Turnover} = \frac{\text{Sales Revenue}}{\text{Average Accounts Receivable}}$$

Notice that the numerator of this ratio is sales revenue, not credit sales. Conceptually, one might consider comparing the level of accounts receivable to the amount of credit sales instead of total sales. However, companies rarely, if ever, disclose how much of their sales are credit sales. For this ratio, you can think of cash sales as credit sales with a very short collection time (0 days). Also note that the denominator uses average accounts receivable instead of the ending balance. This recognizes that sales are generated throughout the year; the average Accounts Receivable balance is an approximation of the amount that prevailed during the year. If the Accounts Receivable balance is relatively unchanged during the year, then using the ending balance is acceptable and common. The following are the accounts receivable turnover ratios for two well-known companies for 2005:

$$\text{Wal-Mart} \quad \frac{\$312.47 \text{ billion}}{\$2.189 \text{ billion}} = 142.7 \text{ times}$$

$$\text{Boeing} \quad \frac{\$54.845 \text{ billion}}{\$4.950 \text{ billion}} = 11.1 \text{ times}$$

From this analysis, you can see that **Wal-Mart** turns its receivables over much more often than does **Boeing**. This is not surprising given the different nature of the two businesses. Wal-Mart sells primarily to retail customers for cash. Remember, from Wal-Mart's standpoint, a credit card sale is the same as a cash sale since Wal-Mart receives its money instantly; it is the credit card company that must worry about collecting the receivable. Boeing, on the other hand, sells to airlines and governments that have established business credit relationships with Boeing. Thus, the nature of its business dictates that Boeing has a much larger fraction of its sales tied up in the form of accounts receivable than does Wal-Mart.

Accounts receivable turnover can then be converted into the number of days it takes to collect receivables by computing a ratio called **average collection period**. This ratio is computed by dividing 365 (or the number of days in a year) by the accounts receivable turnover as follows:

average collection period

A measure of the average number of days it takes to collect a credit sale; computed by dividing 365 days by the accounts receivable turnover.

$$\text{Average Collection Period} = \frac{365}{\text{Accounts Receivable Turnover}}$$

Computing this ratio for both Wal-Mart and Boeing shows that it takes Wal-Mart only 2.6 days (365 ÷ 142.7) on average to collect its receivables, while Boeing takes an average of 32.9 days (365 ÷ 11.1).

Consider what might happen to Boeing's average collection period during an economic recession. During a recession, purchasers are often strapped for cash and try to delay paying on their accounts for as long as possible. Boeing might be faced with airlines that still want to buy airplanes but wish to stretch out the payment period. The result would be a rise in Boeing's average collection period; more of Boeing's resources would be tied up in the form of accounts receivable. In turn, Boeing would have to increase its borrowing in order to pay its own bills since it would be collecting less cash from its slow-paying customers. Proper receivables management involves balancing the desire to extend credit in order to increase sales with the need to collect the cash quickly in order to pay off your own bills.

REMEMBER THIS...

Careful management of accounts receivable is a balance between:

- extending credit to increase your sales and
- collecting cash quickly to reduce your need to borrow.

Two ratios commonly used in monitoring the level of receivables are:

- accounts receivable turnover (Sales Revenue ÷ Average Accounts Receivable) and
- average collection period (365 ÷ Accounts Receivable Turnover).

Recording Warranty and Service Costs Associated with a Sale

Match revenues and expenses by estimating and recording future warranty and service costs associated with a sale.

(6) Let's return to the Farm Land example in which 50 sacks of fertilizer were sold for $500. Assume that as part of each sale, Farm Land offers to send a customer service representative to the home or place of business of any purchaser who wants more detailed instructions on how to apply the fertilizer. Historical experience suggests that the buyer of one fertilizer sack in 10 will request a visit from a Farm Land representative, and the material and labor cost of each visit averages $35. So, with 50 sacks of fertilizer sold, Farm Land has obligated itself to provide, on average, $175 in future customer service [(50 ÷ 10) × $35]. Proper matching requires that this $175 expense be estimated and recognized in the same period in which the associated sale is recognized. Otherwise, if the company waited to record customer service expense until the actual visits are requested, this period's sales revenue would be reported in the same income statement with customer service expense arising from last period's sales. The accountant is giving up some precision because the service expense must be estimated in advance. This sacrifice in precision is worth the benefit of being able to better match revenues and expenses.

The entry to recognize Farm Land's estimated service expense from the sale of 50 sacks of fertilizer is as follows:

Customer Service Expense	175	
Estimated Liability for Service		175
Estimated customer service costs on sales [(50 ÷ 10) × $35].		

The credit entry, Estimated Liability for Service, is a liability. When actual expenses are incurred in providing the customer service, the liability is eliminated with the following type of entry:

Estimated Liability for Service	145	
Wages Payable (to service employees)		100
Supplies		45
Actual customer service costs incurred.		

This entry shows that supplies and labor were required to honor the service agreements. This procedure results in the service expense being recognized at the time of sale, not necessarily when the actual service occurs.

After these two journal entries are made, the remaining balance in Estimated Liability for Service will be $30, shown as follows:

Estimated Liability for Service

Estimate at time of sale		175
Actual service costs incurred	145	
Remaining balance		30

The $30 balance represents the estimated amount of service that still must be provided in the future resulting from the sale of the 50 sacks of fertilizer. If actual experience suggests that the estimated service cost is too high, a lower estimate would be made in connection with subsequent fertilizer sales. If estimated liability for service is too low, a higher estimate is made for subsequent sales. The important point is that the accountant would not try to go back and "fix" an estimate that later proves to be inexact; the accountant merely monitors the relationship between the estimated and actual service costs in order to adjust future estimates accordingly.

The accounting just shown for estimated service costs is the same procedure used for estimated warranty costs. For example, **General Motors** promises automobile buyers that it will fix, at no charge to the buyer, certain mechanical problems for a certain period of time. GM estimates and records this warranty expense at the time the automobile sales are made. At the end of 2005, GM reported an existing liability for warranty costs of $9.1 billion. This amount is what GM estimates it will have to spend on warranty repairs in 2006 (and later years) on cars sold in 2005 (and earlier).

REMEMBER THIS...

If a company makes promises about future warranty repairs or continued customer service as part of the sale, the value of these promises should be estimated and recorded as an expense at the time of the sale. The entry has the following general format:

Expense	XXX	
Warranty Liability		XXX

EXPANDED material

Thus far the chapter has covered the main topics associated with selling goods or services, collecting the proceeds from those sales, and estimating and recording bad debt expense and service expense. The expanded material will cover two additional topics. First, an important tool of cash control, the bank reconciliation, will be explained. Second, the financial statement implications of making sales denominated in foreign currencies will be illustrated.

Reconciling the Bank Account

Reconcile a checking account.

⑦

With the exception of small amounts of petty cash kept for miscellaneous purposes, most cash is kept in various bank accounts. Generally, only a few employees are authorized to sign checks, and they must have their signatures on file with the bank.

Each month the business receives a bank statement that shows the cash balance at the beginning of the period, the deposits, the amounts of the checks processed, and the cash balance at the end of the period. With the statement, the bank includes all of that month's canceled checks (or at least a listing of the checks), as well as debit and credit memos [for example, an explanation of charges for **NSF (not sufficient funds) checks** and service fees]. From a bank's perspective, customers' deposits are liabilities; hence, debit memos reduce the company's cash balance, and credit memos increase the balance.

NSF (not sufficient funds) check

A check that is not honored by a bank because of insufficient cash in the check writer's account.

The July bank statement for one of Hunt Company's accounts is presented in Exhibit 6. This statement shows all activity in the cash account as recorded by the bank and includes four bank adjustments to Hunt's balance—a bank service charge of $7 (the bank's monthly fee), $60 of interest paid by First Security Bank on Hunt's average balance, a $425 transfer into another account, and a $3,200 direct deposit made by a customer who regularly deposits payments directly to Hunt's bank account. Other adjustments that are commonly made by a bank to a company's account include:

1. *NSF (not sufficient funds).* This is the cancellation of a prior deposit that could not be collected because of insufficient funds in the check writer's (payer's) account. When a check is received and deposited in the payee's account, the check is assumed to represent funds that will be collected from the payer's bank. When a bank refuses to honor a check because of insufficient funds in the account on which it was written, the check is returned to the payee's bank and is marked "NSF." The amount of the check, which was originally recorded as a deposit (addition) to the payee's account, is deducted from the account when the check is returned unpaid.
2. *MS (miscellaneous).* Other adjustments made by a bank.
3. *ATM (automated teller machine) transactions.* These are deposits and withdrawals made by the depositor at automated teller machines.
4. *Withdrawals for credit card transactions paid directly from accounts.* These types of cards, called debit cards, are like using plastic checks. Instead of the card holder getting a bill or statement, the amount charged is deducted from the card holder's bank balance.

It is unusual for the ending balance on the bank statement to equal the amount of cash recorded in a company's cash account. The most common reasons for differences are:

1. *Time period differences.* The time period of the bank statement does not coincide with the timing of the company's postings to the cash account.
2. *Deposits in transit.* These are deposits that have not been processed by the bank as of the bank statement date, usually because they were made at or near the end of the month.
3. *Outstanding checks.* These are checks that have been written and deducted from a company's cash account but have not cleared or been deducted by the bank as of the bank statement date.
4. *Bank debits.* These are deductions made by the bank that have not yet been recorded by the company. The most common are monthly service charges, NSF checks, and bank transfers out of the account.
5. *Bank credits.* These are additions made by the bank to a company's account before they are recorded by the company. The most common source is interest paid by the bank on the account balance.

| EXHIBIT 6 | July Bank Statement for Hunt Company |

First Security Bank
Helena, Montana 59601

Statement of Account

```
HUNT COMPANY                        Account Number 325-78126
1900 S. PARK LANE
HELENA, MT 59601                    Date of Statement JULY 31, 2009
```

Check Number	Checks and Withdrawals	Deposits and Additions	Date	Balance
			6/30	13,000
620	140		7/01	12,860
621	250	1,500	7/03	14,110
622	860		7/05	13,250
623	210		7/08	13,040
		2,140	7/09	15,180
624	205		7/10	14,975
626	310		7/14	14,665
	425 T		7/15	14,240
		3,200 D	7/18	17,440
628	765		7/19	16,675
629	4,825		7/22	11,850
630	420		7/24	11,430
632	326	1,600	7/25	12,704
		2,100	7/26	14,804
633	210		7/29	14,594
635	225		7/31	14,369
	7 SC	60 I	7/31	14,422
	9,178 TOTAL CHECKS AND WITHDRAWALS	10,600 TOTAL DEPOSITS AND ADDITIONS		14,422 BALANCE

NSF = Not Sufficient Funds   D = Direct Deposit   I = Interest   T = Transfer Out of Account
SC = Service Charge   MS = Miscellaneous   ATM = Automated Teller Machine Transaction

6. *Accounting errors.* These are numerical errors made by either the company or the bank. The most common is transposition of numbers.

bank reconciliation

The process of systematically comparing the cash balance as reported by the bank with the cash balance on the company's books and explaining any differences.

The process of determining the reasons for the differences between the bank balance and the company's cash account balance is called a **bank reconciliation**. This usually results in adjusting both the bank statement and the book (cash account) balances. If the balances were not reconciled (if the cash balance were left as is), the figure used on the financial statements would probably be incorrect, and external users would not have accurate information for decision making. More importantly, the bank reconciliation can serve as an independent check to ensure that the cash is being accounted for correctly within the company.

We will use Hunt Company's bank account to illustrate a bank reconciliation. The statement shown in Exhibit 6 indicates an ending balance of $14,422 for the month of July. After arranging the month's canceled checks in numerical order and examining the bank statement, Hunt's accountant notes the following:

1. A deposit of $3,100 on July 31 was not shown on the bank statement. (It was in transit at the end of the month.)

EXHIBIT 7	**July Bank Reconciliation for Hunt Company**

Hunt Company
Bank Reconciliation
July 31, 2009

Balance per bank statement		$14,422	Balance per books		$13,937
Additions to bank balance:			*Additions to book balance:*		
Deposit in transit		3,100	Direct deposit	$3,200	
Total		$17,522	Interest	60	3,260
			Total		$17,197
Deductions from bank balance:			*Deductions from book balance:*		
Outstanding checks: 625	$326		Service charge	$ 7	
631	426		Bank transfer	425	
634	185	(937)	Error in recording check No. 630		
			(for Jones's wages)	180	(612)
Adjusted bank balance		**$16,585**	**Adjusted book balance**		**$16,585**

2. Checks No. 625 for $326, No. 631 for $426, and No. 634 for $185 are outstanding. Check No. 627 was voided at the time it was written.
3. The bank's service charge for the month is $7.
4. A direct deposit of $3,200 was made by Joy Company, a regular customer.
5. A transfer of $425 was made out of Hunt's account into the account of Martin Custodial Service for payment owed.
6. The bank paid interest of $60 on Hunt's average balance.
7. Check No. 630 for Thelma Jones's wages was recorded in the accounting records as $240 instead of the correct amount, $420.
8. The cash account in the general ledger shows a balance on July 31 of $13,937.

The bank reconciliation is shown in Exhibit 7. Since the bank and book balances now agree, the $16,585 adjusted cash balance is the amount that will be reported on the financial statements. If the adjusted book and bank balances had not agreed, the accountant would have had to search for errors in bookkeeping or in the bank's figures. When the balances finally agree, any necessary adjustments are made to the cash account to bring it to the correct balance. The entries to correct the balance include debits to Cash for all reconciling additions to the book balance and credits to Cash for all reconciling deductions from the book balance. Additions and deductions from the bank balance do not require adjustments to the company's books; the deposits in transit and the outstanding checks have already been recorded by the company, and, of course, bank errors are corrected by notifying the bank and having the bank make corrections. The adjustments required to correct Hunt's cash account are:

Cash	3,260	
Accounts Receivable		3,200
Interest Revenue		60
To record the additions due to the July bank reconciliation		
(a $3,200 deposit made by Joy Company and $60 interest).		
Custodial Expense	425	
Miscellaneous Expense	7	
Wages Expense	180	
Cash		612
To record the deductions due to the July bank reconciliation		
(service charge, $7; a $180 recording error, check No. 630;		
bank transfer of $425 to Martin Custodial Service).		

- A bank reconciliation has the following general format:

  Balance per bank
  +   Deposits in transit
  −   Outstanding checks
  +/− Bank errors or other adjustments for things that the bank doesn't yet know about
  =   Adjusted balance per bank

  Balance per books
  +   Interest received, automatic deposits, and other additions revealed in the bank statement
  −   Service fees and other subtractions revealed in the bank statement
  +/− Book errors or other adjustments for things heretofore unreflected in the books
  =   Adjusted balance per books

- The reconciliation is not done until the adjusted balance per books is equal to the adjusted balance per bank.

Foreign Currency Transactions

Account for the impact of changing exchange rates on the value of accounts receivable denominated in foreign currencies.

⑧ All of the sales illustrated to this point in the text have been denominated in U.S. dollars. However, many U.S. companies do a large portion of their business in foreign countries. For example, **Wal-Mart** reports that sales in 2005 were denominated in currencies other than the U.S. dollar, including the euro, Japanese yen, British pound, and Canadian dollar. So, what would Wal-Mart have to do to record a software sale denominated in Japanese yen or British pounds? This section answers that question.

When a U.S. company sells a good or provides a service to a party in a foreign country, the transaction amount is frequently denominated in U.S. dollars. The U.S. dollar is a relatively stable currency, and buyers from Azerbaijan to Zimbabwe are often eager to avoid the uncertainty associated with payments denominated in their local currencies. For example, no matter where they are located, buyers and sellers of crude oil almost always write the contract price in terms of U.S. dollars. A U.S. company accounts for a sales contract with a foreign buyer with the sales price denominated in U.S. dollars in the way illustrated previously in this chapter; no new accounting issues are raised. However, if a U.S. company enters into a transaction in which the price is denominated in a foreign currency, the U.S. company must use special accounting procedures to recognize the change in the value of the transaction as foreign currency exchange rates fluctuate. For example, if Wal-Mart makes a credit sale with a price of 100,000 Indonesian rupiah, Wal-Mart knows that it will eventually collect 100,000 rupiah, but Wal-Mart does not know what those rupiah will be worth, in U.S. dollar terms, until the actual rupiah payment is received. Such a transaction is called a **foreign currency transaction**; the accounting for these transactions is demonstrated in the following section.

foreign currency transaction

A sale in which the price is denominated in a currency other than the currency of the seller's home country.

Foreign Currency Transaction Example

To illustrate the accounting for a sale denominated in a foreign currency, assume that American Company sold goods with a price of 20,000,000 Korean won on March 23 to one of its Korean customers. Payment in Korean won is due July 12. American Company prepares quarterly financial statements on June 30. The following exchange rates apply:

	U.S. Dollar Value of One Korean Won	Event
April 23	$0.0010	Sale
June 30	0.0007	Financial statements prepared
July 12	0.0008	Payment received on account

On April 23, each Korean won is worth one-tenth of one U.S. cent. In other words, it takes 1,000 Korean won (1/0.0010) to buy one U.S. dollar. At this exchange rate, the 20,000,000-Korean-won contract is worth $20,000 (20,000,000 × $0.0010).

On April 23, American Company records the sale and the account receivable in its books as follows:

Accounts Receivable (fc)	20,000	
Sales Revenue		20,000

Note that this journal entry is exactly the same as those illustrated earlier in the chapter. The (fc) indicates that the Accounts Receivable asset is denominated in a foreign currency and, thus, subject to exchange rate fluctuations. Because the financial statements of American Company are reported in U.S. dollars, all transaction amounts must be converted into their U.S. dollar equivalents when they are entered into the formal accounting system.

On June 30, American Company prepares its quarterly financial statements. Because the 20,000,000-Korean-won contract price has not yet been collected in cash, American Company still has a receivable denominated in Korean won and must reflect the effect of the change in the exchange rate on the U.S. dollar value of that receivable. In this case the Korean won has decreased in value and is worth only $0.0007 on June 30. If American Company had to settle the contract on June 30, it would receive only $14,000 (20,000,000 × $0.0007). Thus, American Company must recognize an exchange loss of $6,000, or 20,000,000 × ($0.0010 − $0.0007). On July 12, American Company receives payment from its Korean customer. In the interim the value of the Korean won has increased slightly to $0.0008. When the receivable is collected, the 20,000,000 Korean won are worth $16,000 (20,000,000 × $0.0008), so now American Company has experienced a gain relative to its position on June 30. The effects of the fluctuation in the value of the Korean won can be summarized as follows:

 F Y I

The wide fluctuations in exchange rates in this illustration are unusual, but not unprecedented. For example, as part of the Asian financial crisis of 1997, the number of Korean won needed to purchase one U.S. dollar increased from 917.77 on October 23, 1997, to 1,952.68 on December 23, 1997.

	U.S. Dollar Value of the Receivable	Gain or Loss
April 23	$20,000	Not applicable
June 30	14,000	$6,000 loss
July 12	16,000	$2,000 gain

This information would be reported in American Company's three primary financial statements in the second quarter (ending June 30) and the third quarter (beginning July 1) as follows:

Second Quarter:

Income Statement		Balance Sheet		Statement of Cash Flows	
Sales revenue	$20,000	Accounts receivable	$14,000	Cash collected from customers	$ 0
Foreign exchange loss	(6,000)				

Third Quarter:

Income Statement		Balance Sheet		Statement of Cash Flows	
Sales revenue	$ 0	Cash	$16,000	Cash collected from customers	$16,000
Foreign exchange gain	2,000	Accounts receivable	0		

The net result of the sale in the second quarter, the collection of cash in the third quarter, and the changing exchange rates in between is to record a sale of $20,000, the collection of cash of $16,000, and a net exchange loss of $4,000 (a $6,000 loss in the second quarter and a $2,000 gain in the third quarter). The important point to note is that the sale is measured at the exchange rate on the date of sale and that any fluctuations between the sale date and the settlement date are recognized as exchange gains or losses.

What could American Company have done in the previous example to reduce its exposure to the risk associated with changing exchange rates? The easiest thing would have been to denominate the transaction in U.S. dollars. Then the risk of exchange rate changes would have fallen on the Korean company. Secondly, American Company could have locked in the price of Korean won by entering into a forward contract with a foreign currency broker. A forward contract is an example of a derivative contract. Derivatives are becoming more and more commonplace in today's business environment.

REMEMBER THIS...

- When a U.S. company makes a sale that is denominated in a foreign currency, the sale is called a foreign currency transaction.
  - Sale: measured at the exchange rate on the date of sale
  - Cash collection: measured at the exchange rate on the date of collection
- Any fluctuations between the sale date and the cash collection date are recognized as exchange gains or losses.

REVIEW OF
LEARNING OBJECTIVES

(1) Understand the three basic types of business activities: operating, investing, and financing.

Operating Activities	• selling products or services
	• buying inventory for resale
	• incurring and paying for necessary expenses associated with the primary activities of a business
Investing Activities	• purchasing assets for use in the business
	• making investments in such items as stocks and bonds
Financing Activities	• borrowing money and repaying loans
	• issuing new shares of stock
	• paying cash dividends

(2) Use the two revenue recognition criteria to decide when the revenue from a sale or service should be recorded in the accounting records. Revenue is recognized after:

• the work is done **and**
• cash collectibility is reasonably assured.

Revenue for long-term contracts is recognized in proportion to the amount of the contract completed.

(3) Properly account for the collection of cash and describe the business controls necessary to safeguard cash.

• Net sales can be calculated as follows:

    Gross Sales
   − Sales Discounts
   − Sales Returns and Allowances
   = Net Sales

• Common cash controls include:
  • separation of duties in handling and accounting for cash,
  • daily deposits of all cash receipts, and
  • payment of all expenditures by prenumbered checks.

(4) Record the losses resulting from credit customers who do not pay their bills. Two ways of accounting for losses from uncollectible receivables:

• allowance method (generally accepted)
• direct write-off method (NOT generally accepted)

Two ways of estimating losses from uncollectible receivables:

• percentage of credit sales
• fraction of total outstanding receivables (often determined by aging the accounts receivable)

(5) Evaluate a company's management of its receivables by computing and analyzing appropriate financial ratios. Careful management of accounts receivable is a balance between:

• extending credit to increase your sales and
• collecting cash quickly to reduce your need to borrow.

Two ratios commonly used in monitoring the level of receivables are:

• accounts receivable turnover (Sales Revenue ÷ Average Accounts Receivable) and
• average collection period (365 ÷ Accounts Receivable Turnover).

(6) **Match revenues and expenses by estimating and recording future warranty and service costs associated with a sale.** If a company makes promises about future warranty repairs or continued customer service as part of the sale, the value of these promises should be estimated and recorded as an expense (and liability) at the time of the sale.

(7) **Reconcile a checking account.**

Balance per bank
+ Deposits in transit
− Outstanding checks
+/− Bank errors or other adjustments for things that the bank doesn't yet know about
= Adjusted balance per bank

Balance per books
+ Interest received, automatic deposits, and other additions revealed in the bank statement
− Service fees and other subtractions revealed in the bank statement
+/− Book errors or other adjustments for things heretofore unreflected in the books
= Adjusted balance per books

(8) **Account for the impact of changing exchange rates on the value of accounts receivable denominated in foreign currencies.** When a U.S. company makes a sale that is denominated in a foreign currency, the sale is called a foreign currency transaction.
• Sale: measured at the exchange rate on the date of sale
• Cash collection: measured at the exchange rate on the date of collection

Any fluctuations between the sale date and the cash collection date are recognized as exchange gains or losses.

KEY TERMS & CONCEPTS

accounts receivable, 238
accounts receivable
  turnover, 244
aging accounts
  receivable, 242
allowance for bad
  debts, 239
allowance method, 239
average collection
  period, 244

bad debt, 238
bad debt expense, 239
cash, 236
contra account, 235
direct write-off
  method, 238
financing activities, 228
gross sales, 236
investing
  activities, 228

net realizable value
  of accounts
  receivable, 240
net sales, 236
operating activities, 228
receivables, 237
revenue recognition, 231
sales discounts, 234
sales returns and
  allowances, 235

venture capital firm, 226

EXPANDED *material*

bank reconciliation, 248
foreign currency
  transaction, 250
NSF (not sufficient
  funds) checks, 247

REVIEW PROBLEM

Accounting for Receivables and Warranty Obligations

Douglas Company sells furniture. Approximately 10% of its sales are cash; the remainder are on credit. During the year ended December 31, 2009, the company had net credit sales of $2,200,000. As of December 31, 2009, total accounts receivable were $800,000, and Allowance for Bad Debts had a debit balance of $1,100 prior to adjustment. In the past, approximately 1% of credit sales have proved to be uncollectible. An aging analysis of the individual accounts receivable revealed that $32,000 of the Accounts Receivable balance appeared to be uncollectible.

(continued)

The largest credit sale during the year occurred on December 4, 2009, for $72,000 to Aaron Company. Terms of the sale were 2/10, n/30. On December 13, Aaron Company paid $60,000 of the receivable balance and took advantage of the 2% discount. The remaining $12,000 was still outstanding on March 31, 2010, when Douglas Company learned that Aaron Company had declared bankruptcy. Douglas wrote the receivable off as uncollectible.

On December 31, 2009, Douglas Company estimated that it would cost $11,000 in labor and various expenditures to service the furniture it had sold (under 90-day warranty agreements) during the last three months of 2009. During January 2010, the company spent $430 in labor and $600 for supplies to perform service on defective furniture that was sold during the year 2009.

Required:
Prepare the following journal entries:

1. The sale of $72,000 of furniture on December 4, 2009, to Aaron Company on credit.
2. The collection of $58,800 from Aaron Company on December 13, 2009, assuming the company allows the discount on partial payment.
3. Record Bad Debt Expense on December 31, 2009, using the percentage of credit sales method.
4. Record Bad Debt Expense on December 31, 2009, using the aging of receivables method.
5. Record estimated warranty expense on December 31, 2009.
6. Record actual expenditures to service defective furniture under the warranty agreements on January 31, 2010.
7. Write off the balance of the Aaron Company receivable as uncollectible, March 31, 2010.

Solution
The journal entries would be recorded as follows:

1.	Dec. 4, 2009	Accounts Receivable	72,000	
		Sales Revenue		72,000
		Sold $72,000 of furniture to Aaron Company on credit.		
2.	Dec. 13, 2009	Cash	58,800	
		Sales Discounts	1,200	
		Accounts Receivable		60,000
		Collected $58,800 from Aaron Company on December 4 sale and recognized the 2% discount taken (0.02 × $60,000 = $1,200).		
3.	Dec. 31, 2009	Bad Debt Expense	22,000	
		Allowance for Bad Debts		22,000
		Recorded bad debt expense as 1% of credit sales of $2,200,000 ($2,200,000 × 0.01 = $22,000).		

Note: When using the percentage of credit sales method to estimate bad debt expense, the existing balance in the allowance for bad debts account is ignored.

4.	Dec. 31, 2009	Bad Debt Expense	33,100	
		Allowance for Bad Debts		33,100
		Recorded bad debt expense using the aging of accounts receivable method ($32,000 + $1,100 debit balance).		

Note: When using the percentage of total receivables method (e.g., by aging receivables) to estimate bad debt expense, the existing balance in Allowance for Bad Debts must be taken into consideration so that the new balance is the amount of receivables not expected to be collected.

5.	Dec. 31, 2009	Customer Service Expense	11,000	
		Estimated Liability for Service		11,000
		Estimated customer service (warranty) costs on furniture sold during the last three months of 2009. (The warranty period is 90 days.)		

(continued)

6.	Jan. 31, 2010	Estimated Liability for Service	1,030	
		Wages Payable (to service employees)		430
		Supplies		600
		Actual customer service costs incurred.		
7.	Mar. 31, 2010	Allowance for Bad Debts	12,000	
		Accounts Receivable		12,000
		Wrote off the balance in the Aaron Company		
		account as uncollectible.		

DISCUSSION QUESTIONS

1. What are the three types of basic business activities?
2. Why is the purchase of inventory for resale to customers classified as an operating activity rather than an investing activity?
3. When should revenues be recognized and reported?
4. Why do you think misstatement of revenues (e.g., recognizing revenues before they are earned) is one of the most common ways to manipulate financial statements?
5. Why is it important to have separate sales returns and allowances and sales discounts accounts? Wouldn't it be much easier to directly reduce the sales revenue account for these adjustments?
6. Why do companies usually have more controls for cash than for other assets?
7. What are three generally practiced controls for cash, and what is the purpose of each control?
8. Why do most companies tolerate having a small percentage of uncollectible accounts receivable?
9. Why does the accounting profession require the use of the allowance method of accounting for losses due to bad debts rather than the direct write-off method?
10. With the allowance method, why is the net balance, or net realizable value, of Accounts

Receivable the same after the write-off of a receivable as it was prior to the write-off of the uncollectible account?
11. Why is the "aging" of accounts receivable usually more accurate than basing the estimate on total receivables?
12. Why is it important to monitor operating ratios such as accounts receivable turnover?
13. Why must the customer service expense (warranty) sometimes be recorded in the period prior to when the actual customer services will be performed?

EXPANDED *material*

14. What are the major reasons that the balance of a bank statement is usually different from the cash book balance (Cash per the general ledger)?
15. Why don't the additions and deductions from the bank balance on a bank reconciliation require adjustment by the company?
16. Do all transactions by U.S. companies with foreign parties require special accounting procedures by the U.S. companies? Explain.

PRACTICE EXERCISES

PE 6-1   **Classifying Major Business Activities**

LO1   Classify each of the following business activities as an operating, investing, or financing activity.

a. Acquiring inventory for resale.
b. Buying and selling stocks and bonds of other companies.
c. Selling shares of stock to investors for cash.
d. Selling products or services.
e. Buying property, plant, or equipment.
f. Acquiring and paying for other operating items.
g. Selling property, plant, or equipment.
h. Borrowing cash from creditors.

PE 6-2   **Revenue Recognition**

LO2   In which one of the following situations should revenue be recognized?
a. The earnings process has begun and cash collectibility is reasonably assured.
b. The earnings process has begun and cash has been collected.
c. The earnings process is substantially complete and cash collectibility is not yet reasonably assured.
d. The earnings process will soon begin and cash has been collected.
e. The earnings process is substantially complete and cash collectibility is reasonably assured.

PE 6-3   **Revenue Recognition**

LO2   Make the journal entry necessary to record the sale of 120 books at $32 per book. Sixty-five of the books were sold for cash, and 55 were sold on credit.

PE 6-4   **Cash Collection**

LO3   Refer to the data in PE 6-3. Make the journal entry necessary when the company receives payment for the 55 books sold on credit.

PE 6-5   **Sales Discounts**

LO3   Refer to the data in PE 6-3. Assume that all of the books were sold to a single customer and that the terms of the credit sale were 2/10, n/30. Make the journal entry necessary to record the receipt of the cash payment assuming that (1) the customer paid the balance on the account five days after the purchase and (2) the customer paid the balance on the account 20 days after the purchase.

PE 6-6   **Sales Returns and Allowances**

LO3   Refer to the data in PE 6-3. Assume a customer found that 20 of the books were misprinted and returned the 20 books for a refund. Prepare the journal entry necessary in the records of the selling company to record the receipt of the returned books assuming that (1) the books were returned by a cash customer and (2) the books were returned by a credit customer.

PE 6-7   **Computing Net Sales**

LO3   Using the following data, compute net sales.

Sales discounts	$ 50,000
Accounts receivable, ending	125,000
Gross sales	2,500,000
Inventory, ending	200,000
Sales returns and allowances	75,000

PE 6-8   **Control of Cash**

LO3   Which one of the following is *not* an important control associated with cash?
a. All cash expenditures must be made with prenumbered checks.
b. The cash balance must never fall below the sum of inventory and accounts receivable.
c. All cash receipts must be deposited daily.
d. The handling of cash must be separated from the recording of cash.

PE 6-9   **The Direct Write-Off Method**

LO4   The company has an accounts receivable balance of $3,000,000 at the end of the year. The company decides that $90,000 of those accounts receivable are uncollectible because the customers associated with those accounts had filed for bankruptcy protection during the year. Using the direct write-off method of accounting for bad debt expense, make the journal entry necessary to record bad debt expense for the year.

PE 6-10 **The Allowance Method**

LO4 The company had credit sales of $2,500,000 during the year, its first year of business. The company has estimated that $50,000 of these sales on account will ultimately be uncollectible. In addition, a year-end review of accounts identified that of the $200,000 in accounts outstanding as of the end of the year, $43,000 were worthless because the business customers associated with those accounts had gone bankrupt. Using the allowance method of accounting for bad debt expense, make the journal entries necessary to record (1) bad debt expense for the year and (2) the write-off of uncollectible accounts at the end of the year.

PE 6-11 **Computing Net Accounts Receivable**

LO4 Refer to the data in PE 6-10. Taking into account the allowance for bad debts established at the end of the year, compute the net realizable value of accounts receivable (1) before the write-off of uncollectible accounts and (2) after the write-off of uncollectible accounts.

PE 6-12 **Collecting an Account Previously Written Off**

LO4 Refer to the data in PE 6-10. Assume that one customer, whose account had previously been written off, returned from exile in the Bahamas and paid his account of $7,000. Make the journal entry or entries necessary to record the receipt of this payment.

PE 6-13 **Estimating Uncollectible Accounts Receivable as a Percentage of Credit Sales**

LO4 The company had an Accounts Receivable balance of $85,000 and an Allowance for Bad Debts balance of $3,400 (credit) at the end of the year (before any adjusting entry). Credit sales for the year totaled $860,000. The accountant determined that 1% of this year's credit sales will ultimately be uncollectible. Make the journal entry necessary to record bad debt expense for the year.

PE 6-14 **Estimating Uncollectible Accounts Receivable as a Percentage**

LO4 **of Total Receivables**

The company had an Accounts Receivable balance of $85,000 and an Allowance for Bad Debts balance of $3,400 (credit) at the end of the year (before any adjusting entry). Credit sales for the year totaled $860,000. The accountant determined that 10% of the ending accounts receivable will ultimately be uncollectible. Make the journal entry necessary to record bad debt expense for the year.

PE 6-15 **Estimating Uncollectible Accounts Receivable Using Aging Accounts Receivable**

LO4 The company reports the following aging accounts receivable data:

| Customer | Balance | Current | Days Past Due | | | | |
			1–30	31–60	61–90	91–120	Over 120
T. Gardner	$ 3,750	$ 2,250	$1,500				
J. Gammon	4,000	1,000		$2,500		$ 500	
M. Orser	2,000		2,000				
K. Saxton	1,000			750	$250		
K. Welch	4,000						$4,000
R. Beckstrom	10,900	8,000	2,900				
B. Roberts	3,900			3,900			
L. Wilcox	5,850	5,200			650		
J. Gagon	1,500					1,500	
A. Wycherly	1,750		1,750				
Totals	$38,650	$16,450	$8,150	$7,150	$900	$2,000	$4,000

(continued)

In addition, the company provides the following estimates for accounts that will ultimately be uncollectible:

Age	Percentage Estimated to Be Uncollectible
Current	1.75%
1–30 days past due	6
31–60 days past due	15
61–90 days past due	35
91–120 days past due	65
Over 120 days past due	90

Using this information, make the journal entry necessary to record bad debt expense. Assume that: (1) the balance in the allowance for bad debts account (before adjustment) is $2,000 (credit) and (2) the balance in the allowance for bad debts account (before adjustment) is $3,600 (debit).

PE 6-16
LO4

Evaluating Quality of Accounts Receivable

The company reports the following data for the past three years:

Year	Ending Accounts Receivable	Ending Allowance for Bad Debts
Year 3	$60,450	$10,360
Year 2	50,250	7,690
Year 1	43,200	4,400

Compute the allowance for bad debts as a percentage of accounts receivable and evaluate the quality of accounts receivable over the three-year period.

PE 6-17
LO5

Accounts Receivable Turnover

Using the following data, calculate the company's accounts receivable turnover.

Accounts receivable balance, December 31	$ 54,000
Inventory balance, December 31	59,000
Sales revenue	520,000
Cost of goods sold	310,000
Accounts receivable balance, January 1	46,000

PE 6-18
LO5

Average Collection Period

Refer to the data in PE 6-17. Calculate the company's average collection period.

PE 6-19
LO6

Warranty Expense

The company has determined, based on past experience, that 15% of all tires sold will need repairs within the warranty period. When customers request a tire repair under the warranty agreement, each visit costs an average of $20 in parts and labor. The company sold 600 tires during the year. Make the journal entry necessary to record warranty expense for the year.

PE 6-20
LO6

Repairs under Warranty

Refer to the data in PE 6-19. Assume that during the following year, 20 customers bring in 80 tires for warranty repairs. The labor and supplies associated with these repairs were $900 and $350, respectively. Make the journal entry necessary to record the performance of these warranty services.

PE 6-21   Bank Reconciliation
LO7

The company received a bank statement at the end of the month. The statement contained the following:

Ending balance	$33,000
Bank service charge for the month	250
Interest earned and added by the bank to the account balance	110

In comparing the bank statement to its own cash records, the company found the following:

Deposits made but not yet recorded by the bank	$11,200
Checks written and mailed but not yet recorded by the bank	21,300

Before making any adjustments suggested by the bank statement, the cash balance according to the books is $23,040. What is the correct cash balance as of the end of the month? Verify this amount by reconciling the bank statement with the cash balance on the books.

PE 6-22   Journal Entries from a Bank Reconciliation
LO7

Refer to PE 6-21. Make all journal entries necessary on the company's books to adjust the reported cash balance in response to the receipt of the bank statement.

PE 6-23   Journal Entry to Record a Foreign Currency Transaction
LO8

On November 6 of Year 1, the company provided services (on account) to a client located in Thailand. The contract price is 100,000 Thai baht. On November 6, the exchange rate was 50 baht for one U.S. dollar. On December 31, the exchange rate was 40 baht for one U.S. dollar. The company received payment on the account on March 23 of Year 2. On that date, the exchange rate was 100 baht for one U.S. dollar. Make the journal entry necessary on November 6 to record the performance of the service.

PE 6-24   Computation of Foreign Exchange Gains and Losses
LO8

Refer to PE 6-23. Compute the foreign exchange gain or loss that should be reported in (1) Year 1 and (2) Year 2.

EXERCISES

E 6-25   Recognizing Revenue
LO2

Supposedly, there is an over 200-year wait to buy **Green Bay Packers** season football tickets. The fiscal year-end (when they close their books) for the Green Bay Packers is March 30 of each year. If the Packers sell their season football tickets in February for the coming football season, when should the revenue from those ticket sales be recognized?

E 6-26   Recognizing Revenue
LO2

James Dee Company cleans the outside walls of buildings. The average job generates revenue of $800,000 and takes about two weeks to complete. Customers are required to pay for a job within 30 days after its completion. James Dee Company guarantees its work for five years—if the building walls get dirty within five years, James Dee will clean them again at no charge. James Dee is considering recognizing revenue using one of the following methods:

a. Recognize revenue when James Dee signs the contract to do the job.

b. Recognize revenue when James Dee begins the work.

c. Recognize revenue immediately after the completion of the job.

(continued)

d. Recognize revenue 30 days after the completion of the job when the cash is collected.

e. Wait until the five-year guarantee period is over before recognizing any revenue.

Which revenue recognition option would you recommend to James Dee? Explain your answer.

E 6-27

LO2

Recognizing Revenue–Long-Term Construction Projects

In the year 2002, Salt Lake City, Utah, hosted the Winter Olympics. To get ready for the Olympics, most of the major roads and highways in and around Salt Lake City were renovated. It took over three years to complete the highway projects, and **Wasatch Constructors**, the construction company performing the work, didn't want to wait until the work was completed to recognize revenue. How should the revenue on these highway construction projects have been recognized?

E 6-28

LO2

Revenue Recognition

Yummy, Inc., is a franchiser that offers for sale an exclusive franchise agreement for $30,000. Under the terms of the agreement, the purchaser of a franchise receives a variety of services associated with the construction of a Yummy Submarine and Yogurt Shop, access to various product supply services, and continuing management advice and assistance once the retail unit is up and running. The contract calls for the franchise purchaser to make cash payments of $10,000 per year for three years to Yummy, Inc.

How should Yummy, Inc., account for the sale of a franchise contract? Specifically, when should the revenue and receivable be recognized?

E 6-29

LO3

Control of Cash

Molly Maloney is an employee of Marshall Company, a small manufacturing concern. Her responsibilities include opening the daily mail, depositing the cash and checks received into the bank, and making the accounting entries to record the receipt of cash and the reduction of receivables. Explain how Maloney might be able to misuse some of Marshall's cash receipts. As a consultant, what control procedures would you recommend?

E 6-30

LO3

Recording Sales Transactions

On June 24, 2009, Sudweeks Company sold merchandise to Brooke Bowman for $70,000 with terms 2/10, n/30. On June 30, Bowman paid $39,200 on her account and was allowed a discount for the timely payment. On July 20, Bowman paid $21,000 on her account and returned $9,000 of merchandise, claiming that it did not meet contract terms.

Record the necessary journal entries for Sudweeks Company on June 24, June 30, and July 20.

E 6-31

LO3

Recording Sales Transactions

Lee Company sold merchandise on account to Peart Company for $16,000 on June 3, 2009, with terms 2/10, n/30. On June 7, 2009, Lee Company received $650 of returned merchandise from Peart Company and issued a credit memorandum for the appropriate amount. Lee Company received payment for the balance of the bill on June 21, 2009.

Record the necessary journal entries for Lee Company on June 3, June 7, and June 21.

E 6-32

LO4

Estimating Bad Debts

The trial balance of Sparkling Jewelry Company at the end of its 2009 fiscal year included the following account balances:

Account	
Accounts receivable	$66,400
Allowance for bad debts	1,300 (debit balance)

The company has *not yet* recorded any bad debt expense for 2009.

(continued)

Determine the amount of bad debt expense to be recognized by Sparkling Jewelry Company for 2009, assuming the following independent situations:

1. An aging accounts receivable analysis indicates that probable uncollectible accounts receivable at year-end amount to $3,900.
2. Company policy is to maintain a provision for uncollectible accounts receivable equal to 4% of outstanding accounts receivable.
3. Company policy is to estimate uncollectible accounts receivable as equal to 1% of the previous year's annual sales, which were $350,000.

E 6-33

LO4

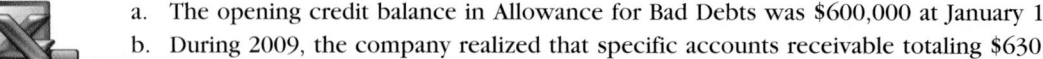

Accounting for Bad Debts

The following data were associated with the accounts receivable and uncollectible accounts of Julia Jay, Inc., during 2009:

a. The opening credit balance in Allowance for Bad Debts was $600,000 at January 1, 2009.
b. During 2009, the company realized that specific accounts receivable totaling $630,000 had gone bad and had been written off.
c. An account receivable of $35,000 was collected during 2009. This account had previously been written off as a bad debt in 2008.
d. The company decided that Allowance for Bad Debts would be $650,000 at the end of 2009.

1. Prepare journal entries to show how these events would be recognized in the accounting system using:
   a. The direct write-off method.
   b. The allowance method.
2. Discuss the advantages and disadvantages of each method with respect to the matching principle.

E 6-34

LO4

Accounting for Uncollectible Accounts Receivable

Dodge Company had the following information relating to its accounts receivable at December 31, 2008, and for the year ended December 31, 2009:

Accounts receivable balance at 12/31/08	$ 900,000
Allowance for bad debts at 12/31/08 (credit balance)	50,000
Gross sales during 2009 (all credit)	5,000,000
Collections from customers during 2009	4,500,000
Accounts written off as uncollectible during 2009	60,000
Estimated uncollectible receivables at 12/31/09	110,000

Dodge Company uses the percentage of receivables method to estimate bad debt expense.

1. At December 31, 2009, what is the balance of Dodge Company's Allowance for Bad Debts? What is the bad debt expense for 2009?
2. At December 31, 2009, what is the balance of Dodge Company's gross accounts receivable?

E 6-35

LO4

Aging of Accounts Receivable

Smoot Company's accounts receivable reveal the following balances:

Age of Accounts	Receivable Balance
Current	$720,000
1–30 days past due	395,000
31–60 days past due	105,000
61–90 days past due	52,000
91–120 days past due	13,000

(continued)

The credit balance in Allowance for Bad Debts is now $42,000. After a thorough analysis of its collection history, the company estimates that the following percentages of receivables will eventually prove uncollectible:

Current	0.5%
1–30 days past due	3.0
31–60 days past due	16.0
61–90 days past due	52.5
91–120 days past due	92.0

Prepare an aging schedule for the accounts receivable, and give the journal entry for recording the necessary change in the allowance for bad debts account.

E 6-36

LO4

Aging of Accounts Receivable

The following aging of accounts receivable is for Harry Company at the end of its first year of business:

Aging of Accounts Receivable **December 31, 2009**					
	Overall	**Less Than 30 Days**	**31 to 60 Days**	**61 to 90 Days**	**Over 90 Days**
Ken Nelson	$ 10,000	$ 8,000		$1,000	$1,000
Elaine Anderson	40,000	31,000	$ 4,000		5,000
Bryan Crist	12,000	3,000	4,000	2,000	3,000
Renee Warner	60,000	50,000	10,000		
Nelson Hsia	16,000	10,000	6,000		
Stella Valerio	25,000	20,000		5,000	
Totals	$163,000	$122,000	$24,000	$8,000	$9,000

Harry Company has collected the following bad debt information from a consultant familiar with Harry's industry:

Age of Account	**Percentage Ultimately Uncollectible**
Less than 30 days	2%
31–60 days	10
61–90 days	30
Over 90 days	75

1. Compute the appropriate Allowance for Bad Debts as of December 31, 2009.
2. Make the journal entry required to record this allowance. Remember that, since this is Harry's first year of operations, the allowance account at the beginning of the year was $0.
3. What is Harry's net accounts receivable balance as of December 31, 2009?

E 6-37

LO4

Direct Write-Off versus Allowance Method

The vice president for Tres Corporation provides you with the following list of accounts receivable written off in the current year. (These accounts were recognized as bad debt

(continued)

expense at the time they were written off; i.e., the company was using the direct write-off method.)

Date	Customer	Amount
March 30	Rasmussen Company	$12,000
July 31	Dodge Company	7,500
September 30	Larsen Company	10,000
December 31	Peterson Company	12,000

Tres Corporation's sales are all on a n/30 credit basis. Sales for the current year total $3,600,000, and analysis has indicated that uncollectible receivable losses historically approximate 1.5% of sales.

1. Do you agree or disagree with Tres Corporation's policy concerning recognition of bad debt expense? Why or why not?
2. If Tres were to use the percentage of sales method for recording bad debt expense, by how much would income before income taxes change for the current year?

E 6-38

LO4

Accounting for Uncollectible Receivables–Percentage of Sales Method

The trial balance of Beecher's Sporting Warehouse, Inc., shows a $110,000 outstanding balance in Accounts Receivable at the end of 2008. During 2009, 90% of the total credit sales of $4,400,000 was collected, and no receivables were written off as uncollectible. The company estimated that 1.5% of the credit sales would be uncollectible. During 2010, the account of Damon Shilling, who owed $7,300, was judged to be uncollectible and was written off. At the end of 2010, the amount previously written off was collected in full from Mr. Shilling.

Prepare the necessary journal entries for recording all the preceding transactions relating to uncollectibles on the books of Beecher's Sporting Warehouse, Inc.

E 6-39

LO4

Comparing the Percentage of Sales and the Percentage of Receivables Methods

Keefer Company uses the percentage of sales method for computing bad debt expense. As of January 1, 2009, the balance of Allowance for Bad Debts was $200,000. Write-offs of uncollectible accounts during 2009 totaled $240,000. Reported bad debt expense for 2009 was $320,000, computed using the percentage of sales method.

Keith & Harding, the auditors of Keefer's financial statements, compiled an aging accounts receivable analysis of Keefer's accounts at the end of 2009. This analysis has led Keith & Harding to estimate that, of the accounts receivable Keefer has as of the end of 2009, $700,000 will ultimately prove to be uncollectible.

Given their analysis, Keith & Harding, the auditors, think that Keefer should make an adjustment to its 2009 financial statements. What adjusting journal entry should Keith & Harding suggest?

E 6-40

LO5

Ratio Analysis

The following are summary financial data for Parker Enterprises, Inc., and Boulder, Inc., for three recent years:

	Year 3	Year 2	Year 1
Net sales (in millions):			
Parker Enterprises, Inc.	$ 3,700	$ 3,875	$ 3,882
Boulder, Inc.	17,825	16,549	15,242
Net accounts receivable (in millions):			
Parker Enterprises, Inc.	1,400	1,800	1,725
Boulder, Inc.	5,525	5,800	6,205

1. Using the above data, compute the accounts receivable turnover and average collection period for each company for years 2 and 3.
2. Which company appears to have the better credit management policy?

E 6-41

LO5

Assessing How Well Companies Manage Their Receivables

Assume that Hickory Company has the following data related to its accounts receivable:

	2008	2009
Net sales	$1,425,000	$1,650,000
Net receivables:		
Beginning of year	375,000	333,500
End of year	420,000	375,000

Use these data to compute accounts receivable turnover ratios and average collection periods for 2008 and 2009. Based on your analysis, is Hickory Company managing its receivables better or worse in 2009 than it did in 2008?

E 6-42

LO5

Measuring Accounts Receivable Quality

The following accounts receivable information is for Kayley Company:

	2009	2008	2007
Accounts receivable	$670,000	$580,000	$500,000
Allowance for bad debts	47,000	44,000	41,000

Did the creditworthiness of Kayley's customers increase or decrease between 2007 and 2009? Explain.

E 6-43

LO6

Accounting for Warranties

Rick Procter, president of Sharp Television Stores, has been concerned recently about declining sales due to increased competition in the area. Rick has noticed that many of the national stores selling television sets and appliances have been placing heavy emphasis on warranties in their marketing programs. In an effort to revitalize sales, Rick has decided to offer free service and repairs for one year as a warranty on his television sets. Based on experience, Rick believes that first-year service and repair costs on the television sets will be approximately 5% of sales. The first month of operations following the initiation of Rick's new marketing plan showed significant increases in sales of TV sets. Total sales of TV sets for the first three months under the warranty plan were $10,000, $8,000, and $12,000, respectively.

1. Assuming that Rick prepares adjusting entries and financial statements for his own use at the end of each month, prepare the appropriate entry to recognize customer service (warranty) expense for each of these first three months.
2. Prepare the appropriate entry to record services provided to repair sets under warranty in the second month, assuming that the following costs were incurred: labor (paid in cash), $550; supplies, $330.

E 6-44

LO6

Accounting for Warranties

Ainge Auto sells used cars and trucks. During 2009, it sold 53 cars and trucks for a total of $1,400,000. Ainge provides a 24-month, 30,000-mile warranty on the used cars and trucks sold. Ainge estimates that it will cost $25,000 in labor and $20,000 in parts to service (during the following year) the cars and trucks sold in 2009.

In January 2010, Joleen Glassett brought her truck in for warranty repairs. Ainge Auto fixed the truck under its warranty agreement. It cost Ainge $450 in labor and $310 in parts to fix Joleen Glassett's truck. Prepare the journal entries to record (1) Ainge Auto's estimated customer service liability as of December 31, 2009, and (2) the costs incurred in repairing the truck in January 2010.

E 6-45
LO7

Preparing a Bank Reconciliation

Prepare a bank reconciliation for Eugene Company at January 31, 2009, using the information shown.

1. Cash per the accounting records at January 31 amounted to $145,604; the bank statement on this same date showed a balance of $129,004.
2. The canceled checks returned by the bank included a check written by the LeRoy Company for $3,528 that had been deducted from Eugene's account in error.
3. Deposits in transit as of January 31, 2009, amounted to $21,856.
4. The following amounts were adjustments to Eugene Company's account on the bank statement:
   a. Service charges of $52.
   b. An NSF check of $2,800.
   c. Interest earned on the account, $80.
5. Checks written by Eugene Company that have not yet cleared the bank include four checks totaling $11,556.

E 6-46
LO7

Preparing a Bank Reconciliation

The records of Denna Corporation show the following bank statement information for December:

a. Bank balance, December 31, 2009, $87,450
b. Service charges for December, $50
c. Rent collected by bank, $1,000
d. Note receivable collected by bank (including $300 interest), $2,300
e. December check returned marked NSF (check was a payment of an account receivable), $200
f. Bank erroneously reduced Denna's account for a check written by Dunna Company, $1,000
g. Cash account balance, December 31, 2009, $81,200
h. Outstanding checks, $9,200
i. Deposits in transit, $5,000

1. Prepare a bank reconciliation for December.
2. Prepare the entry to correct the cash account as of December 31, 2009.

E 6-47
LO7

Reconciling Book and Bank Balances

Jensen Company has just received the September 30, 2009, bank statement summarized in the following schedule:

	Charges	Deposits	Balance
Balance, September 1			$ 5,100
Deposits recorded during September		$27,000	32,100
Checks cleared during September	$27,300		4,800
NSF check, J. J. Jones	50		4,750
Bank service charges	10		4,740
Balance, September 30			4,740

Cash on hand (recorded on Jensen's books but not deposited) on September 1 and September 30 amounted to $200. There were no deposits in transit or checks outstanding at September 1, 2009. The cash account for September reflected the following:

Cash

Sept. 1 Balance	5,300	Sept. Checks	28,000
Sept. Deposits	29,500		

(continued)

Answer the following questions. (*Hint:* It may be helpful to prepare a complete bank reconciliation.)

1. What is the ending balance per the cash account before adjustments?
2. What adjustments should be added to the depositor's books?
3. What is the total amount of the deductions from the depositor's books?
4. What is the total amount to be added to the bank's balance?
5. What is the total amount to be deducted from the bank's balance?

E 6-48

LO8

Foreign Currency Transaction

Apple Core, a U.S. company, sold 125,000 cases of tropical fruit to Minh Market, a Vietnamese firm, for 3.2 billion Vietnamese dong. The sale was made on November 17, 2009, when one U.S. dollar equaled 16,000 dong. Payment of 3.2 billion Vietnamese dong was due to Apple Core on January 16, 2010. At December 31, 2009, one U.S. dollar equaled 18,000 dong, and on January 16, 2010, one U.S. dollar equaled 18,400 dong.

1. What will be the value of the accounts receivable on December 31, 2009, in Vietnamese dong?
2. What will be the value of the accounts receivable on December 31, 2009, in U.S. dollars?
3. Will Apple Core recognize an exchange gain or loss at December 31, 2009? Explain.
4. Will Apple Core recognize an exchange gain or loss on January 16, 2010? Explain.
5. In connection with this sale, what amount will Apple Core report as Sales Revenue in its income statement for 2009?
6. In connection with this sale, what amount will Apple Core report as Cash Collected from Customers in its statement of cash flows for 2010?

E 6-49

LO8

Foreign Currency Transaction

American, Inc., sells one widget to Japanese Company at an agreed-upon price of 1,000,000 yen. On the day of the sale, one yen is equal to $0.01. American, Inc., maintains its accounting records in U.S. dollars. Therefore, the amount in yen must be converted to U.S. dollars.

1. Provide the journal entry that would be made by American, Inc., on the day of the sale, assuming Japanese Company pays for the widget on the day of the sale.
2. Most sales are on account, meaning that payment will not be received for 30 days or even longer. What issues will arise for American, Inc., if the sale is made with payment due in 30 days? (*Hint:* What might happen to the value of the yen in relation to the dollar during the 30-day period?)
3. Suppose that 30 days from the date of the sale the value of one yen is equal to $0.008. What journal entry would be made when the 1,000,000 yen are received by American, Inc.?

PROBLEMS

P 6-50

LO2

Recognizing Revenue

Brad Company sells ships. Each ship sells for over $25 million. Brad never starts building a ship until it receives a specific order from a customer. Brad usually takes about four years to build a ship. After construction is completed and during the first three years the customer uses the ship, Brad agrees to repair anything on the ship free of charge. The customers pay for the ships over a period of 10 years after the date of delivery.

Brad Company is considering the following alternatives for recognizing revenue from its sale of ships:

a. Recognize revenue when Brad receives the order to do the job.
b. Recognize revenue when Brad begins the work.
c. Recognize revenue proportionately during the four-year construction period.
d. Recognize revenue immediately after the customer takes possession of the ship.
e. Wait until the three-year guarantee period is over before recognizing any revenue.
f. Wait until the 10-year payment period is over before recognizing any revenue.

(continued)

Required:

1. Which of the methods, (a) through (f), should Brad use to recognize revenue? Support your answer.

2. **Interpretive Question:** A member of Congress has introduced a bill that would require the SEC to crack down on lenient revenue recognition practices by shipbuilding companies. This bill would require Brad Company to use method (f) above. The "logic" behind the congressperson's bill is that no revenue should ever be recognized until the complete amount of cash is in hand. You have been hired as a lobbyist by Brad Company to speak against this bill. What arguments would you use on Capitol Hill to sway representatives to vote against this bill?

P 6-51
LO2

Recognizing Revenue

The Ho Man Tin Tennis Club sells lifetime memberships for $20,000 each. A lifetime membership entitles a person to unlimited access to the club's tennis courts, weight room, exercise equipment, and swimming pool. Once a lifetime membership fee is paid, it is not refundable for any reason.

Judy Chan and her partners are the owners of Ho Man Tin Tennis Club. In order to overcome a cash shortage, they intend to seek investment funds from new partners. Judy and her partners are meeting with their accountant to provide information for preparation of financial statements. They are considering when they should recognize revenue from the sale of lifetime memberships.

Required:

Answer the following questions:

1. When should the lifetime membership fees be recognized as revenue? Remember, they are nonrefundable.

2. **Interpretive Question:** What incentives would Judy and her partners have for recognizing the entire amount of the lifetime membership fee as revenue at the time it is collected? Since the entire amount will ultimately be recognized anyway, what difference does the timing make?

P 6-52
LO3

Sales Transactions

Money Company and Profit Company entered into the following transactions:

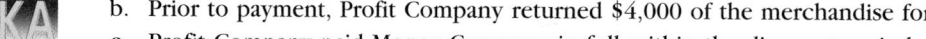

a. Money Company sold merchandise to Profit Company for $60,000, terms 2/10, n/30.
b. Prior to payment, Profit Company returned $4,000 of the merchandise for credit.
c. Profit Company paid Money Company in full within the discount period.
d. Profit Company paid Money Company in full after the discount period. [Assume that transaction (c) did not occur.]

Required:

Prepare journal entries to record the transactions for Money Company (the seller).

P 6-53
LO3

Cash Fraud

Mac Faber was the controller of the Lewiston National Bank. In his position of controller, he was in charge of all accounting functions. He wrote cashier's checks for the bank and reconciled the bank statement. He alone could approve exceptions to credit limits for bank customers, and even the internal auditors reported to him. Unknown to the bank, Mac had recently divorced and was supporting two households. In addition, many of his personal investments had soured, including a major farm implement dealership that had lost $40,000 in the last year. Several months after Mac had left the bank for another job, it was discovered that a vendor had paid twice and that the second payment had been deposited in Mac's personal account. Because Mac was not there to cover his tracks (as he had been on previous occasions), an investigation ensued. It was determined that Mac had used his position in the bank to steal $117,000 over a period of two years. Mac was prosecuted and sentenced to 30 months in a federal penitentiary.

(continued)

Required:

1. What internal control weaknesses allowed Mac to perpetrate the fraud?
2. What motivated Mac to perpetrate the fraud?

P 6-54

LO4

Analysis of Allowance for Bad Debts

Boulder View Corporation accounts for uncollectible accounts receivable using the allowance method.

As of December 31, 2008, the credit balance in Allowance for Bad Debts was $130,000. During 2009, credit sales totaled $10,000,000, $90,000 of accounts receivable were written off as uncollectible, and recoveries of accounts previously written off amounted to $15,000. An aging of accounts receivable at December 31, 2009, showed the following:

Classification of Receivable	Accounts Receivable Balance as of December 31, 2009	Percentage Estimated Uncollectible
Current	$1,140,000	2%
1–30 days past due	600,000	10
31–60 days past due	400,000	23
Over 60 days past due	120,000	75
	$2,260,000	

Required:

1. Prepare the journal entry to record bad debt expense for 2009, assuming bad debts are estimated using the aging of receivables method.
2. Record journal entries to account for the actual write-off of $90,000 uncollectible accounts receivable and the collection of $15,000 in receivables that had previously been written off.

P 6-55

LO4

Accounting for Accounts Receivable

Assume that Dominum Company had the following balances in its receivable accounts on December 31, 2008:

Accounts receivable	$ 640,000
Allowance for bad debts	20,600 (credit balance)

Transactions during 2009 were as follows:

Gross credit sales	$2,100,000
Collections of accounts receivable ($1,840,000 less cash discounts of $32,000)	1,808,000
Sales returns and allowances (from credit sales)	24,000
Accounts receivable written off as uncollectible	9,400
Balance in Allowance for Bad Debts on December 31, 2009 (based on percent of total accounts receivable)	21,800

Required:

1. Prepare entries for the 2009 transactions.
2. What amount will Dominum Company report for:
   a. Net sales in its 2009 income statement?
   b. Total accounts receivable on its balance sheet of December 31, 2009?

P 6-56

LO4

Analysis of Receivables

Juniper Company was formed in 1999. Sales have increased on the average of 5% per year during its first 10 years of existence, with total sales for 2008 amounting to $400,000. Since incorporation, Juniper Company has used the allowance method to account for uncollectible accounts receivable.

(continued)

On January 1, 2009, the company's Allowance for Bad Debts had a credit balance of $5,000. During 2009, accounts totaling $3,500 were written off as uncollectible.

Required:

1. What does the January 1, 2009, credit balance of $5,000 in Allowance for Bad Debts represent?
2. Since Juniper Company wrote off $3,500 in uncollectible accounts receivable during 2009, was the prior year's estimate of uncollectible accounts receivable overstated?
3. Prepare journal entries to record:
    a. The $3,500 write-off of receivables during 2009.
    b. Juniper Company's 2009 bad debt expense, assuming an aging of the December 31, 2009, accounts receivable indicates that potential uncollectible accounts at year-end total $9,000.

P 6-57

LO4

Computing and Recording Bad Debt Expense

During 2009, Wishbone Corporation had a total of $5,000,000 in sales, of which 80% were on credit. At year-end, the Accounts Receivable balance showed a total of $2,300,000, which had been aged as follows:

Age	Amount
Current	$1,900,000
1–30 days past due	200,000
31–60 days past due	100,000
61–90 days past due	70,000
Over 90 days past due	30,000
	$2,300,000

Prepare the journal entry required at year-end to record the bad debt expense under each of the following independent conditions. Assume, where applicable, that Allowance for Bad Debts had a credit balance of $5,500 immediately before these adjustments.

Required:

1. Use the direct write-off method. (Assume that $60,000 of accounts are determined to be uncollectible and are written off in a single year-end entry.)
2. Based on experience, uncollectible accounts existing at year-end are estimated to be 3% of total accounts receivable.
3. Based on experience, uncollectible accounts are estimated to be the sum of:

    1% of current accounts receivable
    6% of accounts 1–30 days past due
    10% of accounts 31–60 days past due
    20% of accounts 61–90 days past due
    30% of accounts over 90 days past due

P 6-58

LO4

Unifying Concepts: Aging of Accounts Receivable and Uncollectible Accounts

Capital Edge Company has found that, historically, 0.5% of its current accounts receivable, 3% of accounts 1 to 30 days past due, 4.5% of accounts 31 to 60 days past due, 8% of accounts 61 to 90 days past due, and 10% of accounts over 90 days past due are uncollectible. The following schedule shows an aging of the accounts receivable as of December 31, 2009:

		Days Past Due			
	Current	**1–30**	**31–60**	**61–90**	**Over 90**
Balance	$105,600	$31,400	$14,200	$3,600	$900

(continued)

The balances at December 31, 2009, in selected accounts are as follows. (Assume that the allowance method is used.)

Sales revenue	$560,100
Sales returns	10,300
Allowance for bad debts	1,100 (credit balance)

Required:

1. Given these data, make the necessary adjusting entry (or entries) for uncollectible accounts receivable on December 31, 2009, on Capital Edge's books.
2. On February 14, 2010, Shannon Johnson, a customer, informed Capital Edge Company that she was going bankrupt and would not be able to pay her account of $89. Make the appropriate entry (or entries).
3. On June 29, 2010, Shannon Johnson was able to pay the amount she owed in full. Make the appropriate entry (or entries).
4. Assume that Allowance for Bad Debts at December 31, 2009, had a debit balance of $1,100 instead of a credit balance of $1,100. Make the necessary adjusting journal entry that would be needed on December 31, 2009.

P 6-59
LO4

Estimating Uncollectible Accounts

Ulysis Corporation makes and sells clothing to fashion stores throughout the country. On December 31, 2009, before adjusting entries were made, it had the following account balances on its books:

Accounts receivable	$ 2,320,000
Sales revenue, 2009 (60% were credit sales)	16,000,000
Allowance for bad debts (credit balance)	4,000

Required:

1. Make the appropriate adjusting entry on December 31, 2009, to record the allowance for bad debts if uncollectible accounts receivable are estimated to be 3% of accounts receivable.
2. Make the appropriate adjusting entry on December 31, 2009, to record the allowance for bad debts if uncollectible accounts receivable are estimated on the basis of an aging of accounts receivable; the aging schedule reveals the following:

	Balance of Accounts Receivable	Percent Estimated to Become Uncollectible
Current	$1,200,000	0.5%
1–30 days past due	800,000	1
31–60 days past due	200,000	4
61–90 days past due	80,000	20
Over 90 days past due	40,000	30

3. Now assume that on March 3, 2010, it was determined that a $64,000 account receivable from Petite Corners is uncollectible. Record the bad debt, assuming:
   a. The direct write-off method is used.
   b. The allowance method is used.
4. Further assume that on June 4, 2010, Petite Corners paid this previously written-off debt of $64,000. Record the payment, assuming:
   a. The direct write-off method had been used on March 3 to record the bad debt.
   b. The allowance method had been used on March 3 to record the bad debt.
5. **Interpretive Question:** Which method of accounting for bad debts, direct write-off or allowance, is generally used? Why?

P 6-60

LO4

The Aging Method

The following aging of accounts receivable is for Coby Company at the end of 2009:

| | | **Aging of Accounts Receivable** **December 31, 2009** | | | |
	Overall	**Less Than 30 Days**	**31 to 60 Days**	**61 to 90 Days**	**Over 90 Days**
Travis Campbell	$ 50,000	$ 40,000	$ 5,000	$ 2,000	$ 3,000
Linda Reed	35,000	31,000	4,000		
Jack Riding	110,000	100,000	10,000		
Joy Riddle	20,000	3,000	10,000	4,000	3,000
Afzal Shah	90,000	60,000	21,000	4,000	5,000
Edna Ramos	80,000	60,000	16,000		4,000
Totals	$385,000	$294,000	$66,000	$10,000	$15,000

Coby Company had a credit balance of $20,000 in its allowance for bad debts account at the beginning of 2009. Write-offs for the year totaled $16,500. Coby Company makes only one adjusting entry to record bad debt expense at the end of the year. Historically, Coby Company has experienced the following with respect to the collection of its accounts receivable:

Age of Account	Percentage Ultimately Uncollectible
Less than 30 days	1%
31–60 days	5
61–90 days	30
Over 90 days	90

Required:

1. Compute the appropriate balance of allowance for bad debts as of December 31, 2009.
2. Make the journal entry required to record this allowance for bad debts balance. Remember that the allowance account already has an existing balance.
3. What is Coby's net accounts receivable balance as of December 31, 2009?

P 6-61

LO5

Analysis of Accounts Receivable Quantity and Quality

The following accounts receivable information is for Rouge Company:

	2009	**2008**	**2007**
Accounts receivable	$ 98,000	$ 50,000	$ 70,000
Allowance for bad debts	5,000	2,800	4,000
Sales revenue	190,000	175,000	165,000

Required:

1. With the big increase in Allowance for Bad Debts in 2009, Rouge Company is concerned that the creditworthiness of its customers declined from 2008 to 2009. Is there any support for this view in the accounts receivable data? Explain.
2. **Interpretive Question:** Is there any cause for alarm in the accounts receivable data for 2009? Explain.

EXPANDED
material

P 6-62

LO7

Preparing a Bank Reconciliation

Milton Company has just received the following monthly bank statement for June 2009.

Date	Checks	Deposits	Balance
June 01			$25,000
June 02	$ 150		24,850
June 03		$ 6,000	30,850
June 04	750		30,100
June 05	1,500		28,600
June 07	8,050		20,550
June 09		8,000	28,550
June 10	3,660		24,890
June 11	2,690		22,200
June 12		9,000	31,200
June 13	550		30,650
June 17	7,500		23,150
June 20		5,500	28,650
June 21	650		28,000
June 22	700		27,300
June 23		4,140†	31,440
June 25	1,000		30,440
June 30	50*		30,390
Totals	$27,250	$32,640	

*Bank service charge.

†Note collected, including $140 interest.

Data from the cash account of Milton Company for June are as follows:

June 1 balance $20,440

Checks written:

June 1	$ 1,500
4	8,500
6	2,690
8	550
9	7,500
12	650
19	700
22	1,000
26	1,300
27	1,360
	$25,750

Deposits:

June 2	$ 6,000
5	8,000
10	9,000
18	5,500
30	6,000
	$34,500

At the end of May, Milton had three checks outstanding for a total of $4,560. All three checks were processed by the bank during June. There were no deposits outstanding at the end of May. It was discovered during the reconciliation process that a check for $8,050, written on June 4 for supplies, was improperly recorded on the books as $8,500.

Required:

1. Determine the amount of deposits in transit at the end of June.
2. Determine the amount of outstanding checks at the end of June.
3. Prepare a June bank reconciliation.
4. Prepare the journal entries to correct the cash account.
5. **Interpretive Question:** Why is it important that the cash account be reconciled on a timely basis?

P 6-63

LO7

Determining Where the Cash Went

Kim Lee, the bookkeeper for Briton Company, had never missed a day's work for the past 10 years until last week. Since that time, he has not been located. You now suspect that Kim may have embezzled money from the company. The following bank reconciliation, prepared by Kim last month, is available to help you determine if a theft occurred:

Briton Company		
Bank Reconciliation for August 2009		
Prepared by Kim Lee		

Balance per bank statement	$192,056		Balance per books	$169,598
Additions to bank balance:			Additions to book balance:	
Deposits in transit	8,000		Note collected by bank	250
			Interest earned	600
Deductions from bank balance:			Deductions from book balance:	
Outstanding checks:			NSF check	(1,800)
#201	(19,200)		Bank service charges	(48)
#204	(5,000)			
#205	(4,058)			
#295	(195)			
#565	(1,920)			
#567	(615)			
#568	(468)			
Adjusted bank balance	$168,600		**Adjusted book balance**	$168,600

In examining the bank reconciliation, you decide to review canceled checks returned by the bank. You find that check stubs for check nos. 201, 204, 205, and 295 indicate that these checks were supposedly voided when written. All other bank reconciliation data have been verified as correct.

Required:

1. Compute the amount suspected stolen by Kim.
2. **Interpretive Question:** Describe how Kim accounted for the stolen money. What would have prevented the theft?

P 6-64

LO8

Accounting for a Foreign Currency Transaction

On December 19, 2009, Mr. Jones Company performed services for Lamour Company. The contracted price for the services was 35,000 euros, to be paid on March 23, 2010. On December 19, 2009, one euro equaled $0.97. On December 31, 2009, one euro equaled $0.99, and on March 23, 2010, one euro equaled $0.94. Mr. Jones is a U.S. company.

Required:

1. Make the journal entry on Mr. Jones' books to record the provision of services on December 19, 2009.
2. Make the necessary adjusting entry on Mr. Jones' books on December 31 to adjust the account receivable to its appropriate U.S. dollar value.
3. Make the journal entry on Mr. Jones' books to record the collection of the 35,000 euros on March 23.
4. **Interpretive Question:** Why would Mr. Jones, a U.S. company, agree to denominate the contract in euros instead of in U.S. dollars?

ANALYTICAL ASSIGNMENTS

AA 6-65

DISCUSSION

ZZZZ Best and Fictitious Receivables

ZZZZ Best was a Los Angeles-based company specializing in carpet cleaning and insurance restoration. Prior to allegations of fraud and its declaration of bankruptcy in 1988, ZZZZ Best was touted as one of the hottest stocks on Wall Street. In 1987, after only six years in

(continued)

business, the company had a market valuation exceeding $211 million, giving its "genius" president a paper fortune of $109 million. Lawsuits, however, alleged that the company was nothing more than a massive fraud scheme that fooled major banks, two CPA firms, an investment banker, and a prestigious law firm.

ZZZZ Best was started as a carpet-cleaning business by Barry Minkow, a 15-year-old high school student, in 1981. Although ZZZZ Best had impressive growth as a carpet-cleaning business, the growth was not nearly fast enough for the impatient Minkow. In 1985, ZZZZ Best announced that it was expanding into the insurance restoration business, restoring buildings that had been damaged by fire, floods, and other disasters. During 1985 and 1986, ZZZZ Best reported undertaking several large insurance restoration projects. The company reported high profits from these restoration jobs. A public stock offering in 1986 stated that 86% of ZZZZ Best Corporation's business was in the insurance restoration area.

Based on the company's high growth and reported income in 1987, a spokesperson for a large brokerage house was quoted in *Business Week* as saying that "Barry Minkow is a great manager and ZZZZ Best is a great company." He recommended that his clients buy ZZZZ Best stock. That same year, the Association of Collegiate Entrepreneurs and the Young Entrepreneurs' Organization placed Minkow on their list of the top 100 young entrepreneurs in America; and the mayor of Los Angeles honored Minkow with a commendation that said that he had "set a fine entrepreneurial example of obtaining the status of a millionaire at the age of 18."

Unfortunately, ZZZZ Best's insurance business, its impressive growth, and its high reported income were totally fictitious. In fact, the company never once made a legitimate profit. Barry Minkow himself later said that he was a "fraudster" who convincingly deceived almost everyone involved with the company. Through the use of widespread collusion among company officials, Minkow was even able to hide the fraud from ZZZZ Best's external auditor. For example, when ZZZZ Best reported an $8.2 million contract to restore a building in San Diego, the external auditor demanded to see the building; this was difficult since neither the building nor the job existed. However, officials of ZZZZ Best gained access to a construction site and led the auditor through a tour of an unfinished building in San Diego to show that the "restoration" work was ongoing. The situation became very complicated for ZZZZ Best when the auditor later asked to see the finished job. ZZZZ Best had to spend $1 million to lease the building and hire contractors to finish six of the eight floors in 10 days. The auditor was led on another tour and wrote a memo saying, "Job looks very good." The auditor was subsequently faulted for looking only at what ZZZZ Best officials chose to show, without making independent inquiries.

Minkow's house of cards finally came crashing down as it became apparent to banks, suppliers, investors, and the auditors that the increasing difficulty ZZZZ Best was having with paying its bills was entirely inconsistent with a company reporting so much revenue and profit. In January 1988, a federal grand jury in Los Angeles returned a 57-count indictment, charging 11 individuals—including ZZZZ Best founder and president, Barry Minkow—with engaging in a massive fraud scheme. Minkow was later convicted and sentenced to 25 years in a federal penitentiary in Colorado.

ZZZZ Best grossly inflated its operating results by reporting bogus revenue and receivables. What factors prevent a company from continuing to report fraudulent results indefinitely? What could the auditor have done to uncover the ZZZZ Best fraud?

Source: This description is based on articles in *The Wall Street Journal*, *Forbes*, and investigative proceedings of the U.S. House of Representatives, Subcommittee on Energy and Commerce hearings: *The Wall Street Journal*, July 7, 1987, p. 1; July 9, 1987, p. 1; August 23, 1988, p. 1; U.S. House of Representatives, Subcommittee on Oversight and Investigation of the Committee on Energy and Commerce, January 27, 1988; U.S. House of Representatives, Subcommittee on Oversight and Investigation of the Committee on Energy and Commerce, February 1, 1988; Daniel Akst, "How Barry Minkow Fooled the Auditors," *Forbes*, October 2, 1989, p. 126.

AA 6-66

DISCUSSION

Recognizing Revenue

HealthCare, Inc.,* operates a number of medical testing facilities around the United States. Drug manufacturers, such as **Merck** and **Bristol-Myers Squibb**, contract with HealthCare

---

*The name of the actual company has been changed.

(continued)

for testing of their newly developed drugs and other medical treatments. HealthCare advertises, gets patients, and then administers the drugs or other experimental treatments, under a doctor's care, to determine their effectiveness. The Food and Drug Administration requires such human testing before allowing drugs to be prescribed by doctors and sold by pharmacists. A typical contract might read as follows:

> HealthCare, Inc., will administer the new drug, "Lexitol," to 50 patients, once a week for 10 weeks, to determine its effectiveness in treating male baldness. Merck will pay HealthCare, Inc., $100 per patient visit, to be billed at the conclusion of the test period. The total amount of the contract is $50,000 (50 patients $\times$ 10 visits $\times$ $100 per visit).

Given these kinds of contracts, when should HealthCare recognize revenue—when contracts are signed, when patient visits take place, when drug manufacturers are billed, or when cash is collected?

AA 6-67
DISCUSSION

Credit Policy Review

The president, vice president, and sales manager of Moorer Corporation were discussing the company's present credit policy. The sales manager suggested that potential sales were being lost to competitors because of Moorer Corporation's tight restrictions on granting credit to consumers. He stated that if credit policies were loosened, the current year's estimated credit sales of $3,000,000 could be increased by at least 20% next year with an increase in uncollectible accounts receivable of only $10,000 over this year's amount of $37,500. He argued that because the company's cost of sales is only 25% of revenues, the company would certainly come out ahead.

The vice president, however, suggested that a better alternative to easier credit terms would be to accept consumer credit cards such as **Visa** or **Mastercard**. She argued that this alternative could increase sales by 40%. The credit card finance charges to Moorer Corporation would be 4% of the additional sales.

At this point, the president interrupted by saying that he wasn't at all sure that increasing credit sales of any kind was a good thing. In fact, he suggested that the $37,500 of uncollectible accounts receivable was altogether too high. He wondered whether the company should discontinue offering sales on account.

With the information given, determine whether Moorer Corporation would be better off under the sales manager's proposal or the vice president's proposal. Also, address the president's suggestion that credit sales of all types be abolished.

AA 6-68
JUDGMENT CALL

You Decide: **Which method is better–the direct write-off method or the allowance method?**

Your father-in-law has asked you to help him with some basic accounting duties dealing with a local irrigation company of which he is president. The company has issued shares of stock allowing shareholders the right to use a specified amount of water every week from a water canal that passes through town. Your main duties would consist of billing and collecting yearly dues from the shareholders and maintaining the books with a canned software system. There are less than 60 shareholders in the company. Should you write off receivables from customers when it is determined they will not pay, or should you estimate the percentage of receivables that will be uncollectible and establish an allowance? Your father-in-law does not want an allowance because he believes all customers will pay. What should you do?

AA 6-69
JUDGMENT CALL

You Decide: **Can pre-billing customers increase revenues?**

For the past year, you have been working as an accountant for a local Internet Service Provider. Business is growing steadily with the holiday season just around the corner. The

(continued)

company hopes to reach more customers next year through additional advertising. In order to do so, it will need a loan from the bank. You overheard your boss say that if revenues increase 5% by year-end, the company will be in good enough shape to receive the loan. Your boss asks you to send out invoices to a handful of customers charging them for a service that won't be provided until the next year and to recognize the billings as revenue. He says they will eventually receive the service but it is more important to recognize the sale now. What should you do?

AA 6-70
JUDGMENT CALL

You Decide: **Can a company overestimate bad debts in good years and then use lower estimates when times are bad?**

The company you work for has been highly profitable this year. Your boss tells you to overestimate the allowance for doubtful accounts. He says the income statement can handle the charge this year and the excess reserve can be used to increase earnings in future years. Is his proposal acceptable?

AA 6-71
REAL COMPANY ANALYSIS

Wal-Mart

The 2006 Form 10-K for **Wal-Mart** is included in Appendix A. Locate that Form 10-K and consider the following questions:

1. Provide the summary journal entry that Wal-Mart would have made to record its revenue for the fiscal year ended January 31, 2006 (assume all sales were on account).
2. Given Wal-Mart's beginning and ending balances in accounts receivable, along with your journal entry from part (1), estimate the amount of cash collected from customers during the year.
3. Locate Wal-Mart's note on revenue recognition. What is Wal-Mart's revenue recognition policy?

AA 6-72
REAL COMPANY ANALYSIS

Bank of America

Bank of America is one of the oldest banks in America, as well as one of the largest. Founded in the late 1800s, Bank of America has grown from a strictly California-based bank to one with operations in 29 states. Information from Bank of America's annual report follows. (Amounts are in millions.)

	2005	2004
Bad debt expense	$4,021	$2,868
Write-off of uncollectible accounts	5,834	4,147
Allowance for bad debts (year-end)	8,045	8,626

Using this information, answer the following questions:

1. Provide the journal entry made by Bank of America to record bad debt expense for 2005.
2. Provide the journal entry made by Bank of America to record the write-off of actual bad debts during 2005.
3. Estimate the amount of bad debts previously written off that Bank of America recovered in 2005.

AA 6-73
REAL COMPANY ANALYSIS

Microsoft and IBM

Information from comparative income statements and balance sheets for **Microsoft** and **IBM** is given below. (Amounts are in millions.)

	Microsoft		IBM	
	2005	2004	2005	2004
Sales	$39,788	$36,835	$91,134	$96,293
Accounts receivable	7,180	5,890	9,540	10,522

(continued)

Use this information to answer the following questions:

1. Without doing any computations, which company do you think has the lowest average collection period?
2. Compute Microsoft's average collection period for 2005.
3. Compute IBM's average collection period for 2005.

AA 6-74

INTERNATIONAL

Samsung

The economic downturn in South Korea in late 1997 focused world attention on what had heretofore been viewed as one of the world's economic powerhouses. Symptomatic of the economic collapse was the freefall in Korea's currency, the won, which declined in value from 845 won per U.S. dollar on December 31, 1996, to 1,695 won per dollar on December 31, 1997.

When Korea's economy soured, many sought to blame the economy's unusual structure, which concentrates a large fraction of the economic activity in the hands of just a few companies, called chaebol. Chaebol are large Korean conglomerates (groups of loosely connected firms with central ownership) that are usually centered around a family-owned parent company. The growth of the chaebol in the years since the Korean War has been aided by government nurturing—it is said that the chaebol have received government assistance in getting loans and obtaining trading licenses, for example.

In Korea there are now four super-chaebol—**Hyundai, Samsung, Daewoo,** and **Lucky Goldstar.** Collectively, these four conglomerates account for between 40 and 45% of South Korea's gross national product.

Samsung, one of the four super-chaebol, was founded in 1938 in Taegu, Korea. The company had humble beginnings; its original products included fruit, dried seafood, flour, and noodles, and its original exports were squid and apples. Now, Samsung has a worldwide presence in electronics, machinery, automobiles, chemicals, and financial services. To illustrate the size of Samsung's operations, it is estimated that one out of every five televisions or monitors in the world was made by Samsung.

The following information is from Samsung's 1997 annual report. All numbers are in trillions of Korean won.

	1997	1996
Net sales	91.519	74.641
Accounts receivable	10.064	6.233

1. Did Samsung's sales increase in 1997, relative to 1996, in terms of U.S. dollars? Explain. What exchange rate information would allow you to make a more accurate calculation?
2. Compute Samsung's average collection period for both 1996 and 1997. Instead of using the average accounts receivable balance, use the end-of-year balance.
3. Comment on the change in the average collection period from 1996 to 1997, especially in light of the economic conditions in Korea in 1997.
4. What do you think happened to Samsung's accounts payable balance in 1997, relative to 1996? Explain.

AA 6-75

ETHICS

Changing Our Estimates in Order to Meet Analysts' Expectations

John Verner is the controller for BioMedic, Inc., a biotechnology company. John is finishing his preparation of the preliminary financial statements for a meeting of the board of directors scheduled for later in the day. At the board's prior meeting, members discussed the need to report earnings of at least $1.32 per share. It was not mentioned specifically at the meeting, but everyone on the board knows that financial analysts have forecast that BioMedic will report earnings per share (EPS) of $1.32; failure to meet analysts' expectations could hurt BioMedic's chances of going forward with its planned initial public offering (IPO) later this year.

(continued)

Unfortunately for John and the company, the preliminary EPS figure is coming up short. John knows that the board will take a serious look at the estimates and assumptions made in preparing the income statement. In anticipation of the board's review, John has identified the following two issues:

1. In the past, bad debt expense has been computed using the percentage of sales method. The percentage used has varied between 3 and 3.5%. This year, John assumed a rate of 3%. If he were to modify his estimate of bad debt expense to 2.5% of sales, income would increase by $700,000.

2. BioMedic, Inc., offers a warranty on many of the products it sells. Like bad debt expense, warranty expense is computed as a percentage of sales. John is considering modifying his estimate of warranty expense from 1.4% of sales down to 1.1%. This modification would result in a $420,000 increase in net income.

These two changes, considered together, would result in BioMedic being able to report EPS of $1.33 per share, thereby allowing the company to publicly announce that it had exceeded analysts' expectations. Without these changes, BioMedic will report EPS of $1.21 per share.

What issues should John consider before he makes the changes to the income statement? Would John be doing something wrong by making these changes? Would John be breaking the law?

AA 6-76
WRITING

Revenue Recognition for Health Clubs

The health fitness business has become increasingly popular as the sedentary lifestyle of most Americans has caused a large percentage of the population to feel, and be, out of shape. Health clubs have popped up all over, and with these clubs come some interesting accounting issues. Members typically sign up for one year and pay an up-front fee, followed by a monthly payment. The up-front fee covers, among other things, a health assessment by a club expert as well as a customized training program. For the monthly fee, members get the use of the facilities. The big accounting question is: How should the up-front fee be accounted for? Can the entire amount of the up-front fee be recognized at the beginning of the contract, or should it be recognized over the course of the year? Prepare a one-page paper explaining your point of view.

AA 6-77
CUMULATIVE
SPREADSHEET
PROJECT

Creating a Forecasted Balance Sheet and Income Statement

This spreadsheet assignment is a continuation of the spreadsheet assignments given in earlier chapters. If you completed those spreadsheets, you have a head start on this one. If needed, review the spreadsheet assignment for Chapter 4 to refresh your memory on how to construct forecasted financial statements.

1. Handyman wishes to prepare a forecasted balance sheet and income statement for 2010. Use the original financial statement numbers for 2009 [given in part (1) of the Cumulative Spreadsheet Project assignment in Chapter 2] as the basis for the forecast, along with the following additional information:

   a. Sales in 2010 are expected to increase by 40% over 2009 sales of $700.

   b. In 2010, Handyman expects to acquire new property, plant, and equipment costing $80.

   c. The $160 in other operating expenses reported in 2009 includes $5 of depreciation expense.

   d. No new long-term debt will be acquired in 2010.

   e. No cash dividends will be paid in 2010.

   f. New short-term loans payable will be acquired in an amount sufficient to make Handyman's current ratio in 2010 exactly equal to 2.0.

Note: These statements were constructed as part of the spreadsheet assignment in Chapter 4; you can use that spreadsheet as a starting point if you have completed that assignment.

(continued)

For this exercise, the current assets are expected to behave as follows:

   i. Cash and inventory will increase at the same rate as sales.

   ii. The forecasted amount of accounts receivable in 2010 is determined using the forecasted value for the average collection period. For simplicity, do the computations using the end-of-period accounts receivable balance instead of the average balance. The average collection period for 2010 is expected to be 14.08 days.

Clearly state any additional assumptions that you make.

2. Repeat (1), with the following change in assumptions:

   a. Average collection period is expected to be 9.06 days.

   b. Average collection period is expected to be 20.00 days.

3. Comment on the differences in the forecasted values of accounts receivable in 2010 under each of the following assumptions about the average collection period: 14.08 days, 9.06 days, and 20.00 days. Under which assumption will Handyman's forecasted cash flow from operating activities be higher? Explain.

Inventory

(1) **Identify what items and costs should be included in inventory and cost of goods sold.** *Inventory is goods held for sale in the normal course of business. In a manufacturing firm, inventory is composed of raw materials, work in process, and finished goods. Inventory cost consists of all costs involved in buying the inventory and preparing it for sale. Proper calculation of inventory cost is absolutely critical for making financial reporting, production, pricing, and strategy decisions.*

(2) **Account for inventory purchases and sales using both a perpetual and a periodic inventory system.** *With a perpetual system, inventory records are updated whenever a purchase or a sale is made. With a periodic system, inventory records are not updated when a sale is made.*

(3) **Calculate cost of goods sold using the results of an inventory count and understand the impact of errors in ending inventory on reported cost of goods sold.** *Beginning inventory and purchases numbers are added to compute how much inventory was available for sale. An inventory count reveals how much was not sold; the difference is equal to the cost of goods sold. Overstating the amount of ending inventory causes profits to be overstated as well.*

(4) **Apply the four inventory cost flow alternatives: specific identification, FIFO, LIFO, and average cost.** *In order to calculate cost of goods sold and ending inventory, the accountant must make an assumption about which units are sold first. With FIFO, the oldest units are assumed to be sold first. With LIFO, the newest units are assumed to be sold first. With the average cost assumption, all units are assigned the same average cost, independent of their specific actual cost.*

(5) **Use financial ratios to evaluate a company's inventory level.** *The length of the operating cycle is the time from the purchase of inventory to the collection of cash from the sale of that inventory; this interval is equal to the number of days' sales in inventory plus the average collection period. The length of this interval should be compared to the average time taken to pay for inventory purchases.*

EXPANDED *material*

(6) **Analyze the impact of inventory errors on reported cost of goods sold.** *Overstating ending inventory this year causes profits to be overstated this year but understated next year. This reversal occurs because ending inventory for this year becomes beginning inventory for next year. The effects are reversed if ending inventory is understated this year.*

(7) **Describe the complications that arise when LIFO or average cost is used with a perpetual inventory system.** *When LIFO is used with a perpetual inventory system, the identification of the "newest unit" changes every time a purchase is made. Accordingly, identification of the units sold must be done sale by sale, using the specific timing of sales and purchases. Similarly, when the average cost assumption is made with a perpetual inventory system, the "average cost" changes every time a purchase is made.*

(8) **Apply the lower-of-cost-or-market method of accounting for inventory.** *Inventory should be reported in the balance sheet at the lower of its historical cost or its current market value. Current market value is computed by comparing replacement cost to the inventory's net realizable value (selling price less selling cost).*

(9) **Explain the gross margin method of estimating inventories.** *Knowledge of a company's historical gross profit percentage can be used to estimate a company's cost of goods sold. This estimate, combined with sales and purchases data, can be used to estimate the amount of inventory a company has.*

Sears, Roebuck & Company began as the result of an inventory mistake. In 1886, a shipment of gold watches was mistakenly sent to a jeweler in Redwood Falls, Minnesota. When the jeweler refused to accept delivery of the unwanted watches, they were purchased by an enterprising railroad agent who saw an opportunity to make some money. Richard Sears sold all of those watches, ordered more, and started the **R. W. Sears Watch Company**. The next year, Sears moved his operation to Chicago, where he found a partner in watchmaker Alvah Roebuck, and in 1893 they incorporated under the name "Sears, Roebuck & Co."

The company's initial growth was fueled by mail-order sales to farmers. Sears bought goods in volume from manufacturers. Then, taking advantage of cheap parcel post and rural free delivery (RFD) rates, Sears shipped the goods directly to the customers, thereby bypassing the profit markups of the chain of middlemen usually standing between manufacturers and farmers. Sales growth was partially driven by the persuasive advertising copy written by Richard Sears for the famous Sears catalog. In fact, his product descriptions have been politely called "fanciful." But the company compensated by backing its products with an unconditional money-back guarantee for dissatisfied customers.

Sears began as a retailer buying inventory in bulk and selling it to the masses. In the 1980s Sears diversified its operations and began selling auto insurance (through **Allstate**), financial services (through **Dean Witter**), and real estate (through **Coldwell Banker**). In the early 1990s, the diversified Sears empire began to show increasing weakness, culminating in a reported loss of almost $2.3 billion in 1992. The company's management responded by going back to the basics of retail marketing. The financial services operations and the real estate operations (along with the famous Sears Tower in Chicago) were sold. Sears focused on clothing sales in its mall-base stores and appliance and automotive product sales in its off-the-mall stores.

Sears is continuing to leverage one of its biggest assets—its in-house brand names such as Kenmore and Craftsman. In fact, sales of Sears appliances and tools make up two-thirds of the company's annual revenue. Currently, Sears is the leader in appliance sales and outsells the next 12 competitors combined. In an attempt to overhaul its clothing lines, Sears bought the well-known catalog and Internet retailer, **Land's End**, in June 2002 and in March 2005, Sears and **Kmart** merged forming a retailing powerhouse to compete with **Wal-Mart**.

Like Sears, every business has products or services that it sells. Some companies, usually referred to as diversified companies or conglomerates, sell many unrelated products and services, just as Sears did in the 1980s. Other companies focus on a core set of products or services, as Sears did in the 1990s.

In Chapter 6, the focus was on revenues and receivables arising from the sale of products and services. In this chapter, the focus is on accounting for the products and services that are sold.

Traditionally, companies have been divided into two groups: service companies and product companies. Companies such as hotels, cable TV networks, banks, carpet cleaners, and lawyers, accountants, and engineers all sell services. In contrast, supermarkets, steel mills, and book stores sell products. Because the practice of accounting evolved in a business environment dominated by manufacturing and merchandising firms, the accounting for service companies is significantly less developed than the accounting for companies that sell products. In this chapter we discuss traditional accounting for product companies, emphasizing cost of goods sold and inventory. In Chapter 8 we will discuss operating expenses that are common to both service and product firms. Further discussion of the developing area of accounting for service companies is included in Chapter 16 in the management accounting section of *Accounting: Concepts and Applications*.

Inventory accounting is considerably more complex for manufacturing firms than for merchandising firms. In a retail or wholesale business, the cost of goods sold is simply the costs incurred in purchasing the merchandise sold during the period; inventory is simply the cost of products purchased and not yet sold. Manufacturing firms, however, produce the goods they sell, so inventory and cost of goods sold must include all manufacturing costs of the products produced and sold. Because it is much

EXHIBIT 1   **How Much Inventory Do Companies Have?**

Inventory Levels for the 50 Largest Companies, 1979–2005

Source: Standard and Poor's COMPUSTAT.

easier to understand the concept of inventory and cost of goods sold in the context of retail and wholesale firms, manufacturing firms will not be considered in detail in this chapter. The details of inventory accounting for manufacturing firms will be covered in Chapter 16 in the management accounting section of *Accounting: Concepts and Applications.*

Fifty years ago, inventory was arguably the most important asset on the balance sheet. However, changes in the economy have led to a decrease in the relative importance of inventory. For example, as illustrated in Exhibit 1, inventory for the 50 largest companies in the United States declined steadily from over 15% of total assets in 1979 to 6.8% of total assets in 2005. This trend is a result of two factors: more efficient management of inventory because of improved information technology and a decrease in the prominence of old-style, smokestack industries that carried large inventories. Companies in the growth industries of services, technology, and information often have little or no inventory.

> ## STOP & THINK
>
> The clear separation between product and service companies is disappearing. For example, does **Microsoft** sell a product or a service? What about **McDonald's**—product or service?

Inventory and Cost of Goods Sold

Identify what items and costs should be included in inventory and cost of goods sold.

(1)   **Inventory** is the name given to goods that are either manufactured or purchased for resale in the normal course of business (see page 286 for definition). A car dealer's inventory is comprised of automobiles; a grocery store's inventory consists of vegetables, meats, dairy products, canned goods, and bakery items; **Sears'** inventory is composed of shirts, Kenmore appliances, DieHard® batteries, and more. Like other items of value, such as cash or equipment, inventory is classified as an asset and reported on the balance sheet. When products are sold, they are no longer assets. The costs to purchase or manufacture the products must be removed from the asset classification (inventory) on the balance sheet and reported on the income statement as an expense—**cost of goods sold** (see page 286 for definition).

EXHIBIT 2 **Time Line of Business Issues Involved with Inventory**

Activity – Buying/Making and Selling Inventory*

	BUY	ADD	SELL	COMPUTE
	raw materials or goods for resale	value–labor and overhead	finished inventory	ending inventory and finished goods
Journal Entry	Inventory A/P	Inventory A/P or Cash	A/R Sales COGS Inventory	COGS** Inventory**
F/S Impact	Inventory ($\uparrow$) A/P ($\uparrow$)	Inventory ($\uparrow$) Cash ($\downarrow$) or A/P ($\uparrow$)	A/R ($\uparrow$) Sales ($\uparrow$) Exp ($\uparrow$) Inventory ($\downarrow$)	Exp ($\uparrow$) Inventory ($\downarrow$)

* Exhibit assumes the inventory account is updated with each purchase.
** A physical count of inventory may require an adjustment to the inventory and COGS accounts.

---

inventory

Goods held for resale.

cost of goods sold

The costs incurred to purchase or manufacture the merchandise sold during a period.

The time line in Exhibit 2 illustrates the business issues involved with inventory as well as the financial statement effects of those business issues. The accounting questions associated with the items in the time line are as follows:

- When is inventory considered to have been purchased—when it is ordered, shipped, received, or paid for?
- Similarly, when is the inventory considered to have been sold?
- Which of the costs associated with the "value added" process are considered to be part of the cost of inventory, and which are simply business expenses for that period?
- How should total inventory cost be divided between the inventory that was sold (cost of goods sold) and the inventory that remains (ending inventory)?

These questions are addressed in the following sections of the chapter.

What is Inventory?

raw materials

Materials purchased for use in manufacturing products.

work in process

Partially completed units in production.

finished goods

Manufactured products ready for sale.

In a merchandising firm, either wholesale or retail, inventory is composed of the items that have been purchased in order to be resold. In a supermarket, milk is inventory, a shopping cart is not. In a manufacturing company, there are three different types of inventory: raw materials, work in process, and finished goods.

Raw Materials **Raw materials** are goods acquired in a relatively undeveloped state that will eventually compose a major part of the finished product. If you are making bicycles, one of the raw materials is tubular steel. For a computer assembler, raw materials inventory is composed of plastic, wires, and **Intel** Pentium® chips.

Work in Process **Work in process** consists of partially finished products. When you take a tour of a manufacturing plant, you are seeing work-in-process inventory.

Finished Goods **Finished goods** are the completed products waiting for sale. A completed car rolling off the automobile assembly line is part of finished goods inventory.

What Costs Are Included in Inventory Cost?

Inventory cost consists of all costs involved in buying the inventory and preparing it for sale. In the case of raw materials or goods acquired for resale by a merchandising firm, cost includes the purchase price, freight, and receiving and storage costs.

manufacturing overhead

The indirect manufacturing costs associated with producing inventory.

The cost of work-in-process inventory is the sum of the costs of the raw materials, the production labor, and some share of the **manufacturing overhead** required to keep the factory running. The cost of an item in finished goods inventory is the total of the materials, labor, and overhead costs used in the production process for that item. As you can imagine, accumulating these costs and calculating a cost per unit is quite a difficult task. The cost of a finished automobile includes the cost of the steel and rubber; the salaries and wages of assembly workers, inspectors, and testers; the factory insurance; the workers' pension benefits; and much more. This costing process is a key part of management accounting and is covered in Chapter 16 in the management accounting section of *Accounting: Concepts and Applications*.

The costs just described are all costs expended in order to get inventory produced and ready to sell. These costs are appropriately included in inventory costs. Those costs incurred in the sales effort itself are *not* inventory costs, but instead should be reported as operating expenses in the period in which they are incurred. For example, the costs of maintaining the finished goods warehouse or the retail showroom are period expenses. Salespersons' salaries are period expenses, as is the cost of advertising (a more detailed discussion of advertising is included in Chapter 8). In addition, general non-factory administrative costs are also period expenses. Examples are the costs of the corporate headquarters and the company president's salary.

FOB (free-on-board) destination

A business term meaning that the seller of merchandise bears the shipping costs and maintains ownership until the merchandise is delivered to the buyer.

Who Owns the Inventory?

As a general rule, goods should be included in the inventory of the business holding legal title. So, a merchandising firm is considered to have purchased inventory once it has legal title to the inventory. Similarly, the inventory is considered to be sold when legal title passes to the customer. In most cases, this "legal title" rule is easy to apply—if you go into a business and look around, it is probably safe to assume that the inventory you see belongs to that business. In the case of goods in transit and goods on consignment, however, this "legal title" rule can be rather difficult to apply.

FOB (free-on-board) shipping point

A business term meaning that the buyer of merchandise bears the shipping costs and acquires ownership at the point of shipment.

Goods in Transit When goods are being shipped from the seller to the buyer, who owns the inventory that is on a truck or railroad car—the seller or the buyer? If the seller pays for the shipping costs, the arrangement is known as **FOB (free-on-board) destination**, and the seller owns the merchandise from the time it is shipped until it is delivered to the buyer. If the buyer pays the shipping costs, the arrangement is known as **FOB (free-on-board) shipping point**, and the buyer owns the merchandise during transit. Thus, in determining which items should be counted and included in the inventory balance for a period, a company must note the amount of merchandise in transit and the terms under which it is being shipped. In all cases, merchandise should be included in the inventory of the party who owns it; for goods in transit, this is generally the party who is paying the shipping costs. The impact of shipping terms on the ownership of goods in transit is summarized in Exhibit 3.

consignment

An arrangement whereby merchandise owned by one party, the consignor, is sold by another party, the consignee, usually on a commission basis.

Goods on Consignment Sometimes the inventory a firm stocks in its warehouse has not actually been purchased from suppliers. With a **consignment** arrangement, suppliers (the consignors) provide inventory for resale while

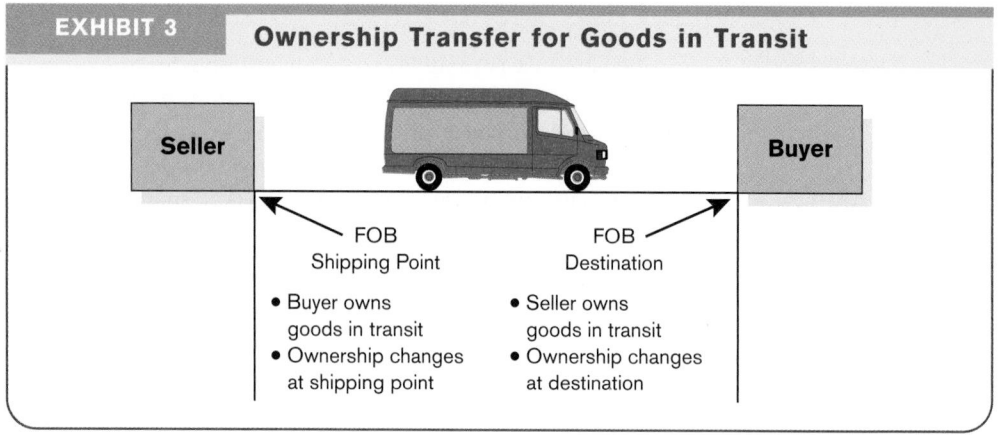

EXHIBIT 3   **Ownership Transfer for Goods in Transit**

Seller

Buyer

FOB
Shipping Point
• Buyer owns
  goods in transit
• Ownership changes
  at shipping point

FOB
Destination
• Seller owns
  goods in transit
• Ownership changes
  at destination

retaining ownership of the inventory until it is sold. (This is referred to in the business world as a "sale-through" arrangement as opposed to a "sell-in" arrangement where sales to distributors are recorded as revenue.) The firm selling the merchandise (the consignee) merely stocks and sells the merchandise for the supplier/owner and receives a commission on any sales as payment for services rendered. Through a consignment arrangement, the manufacturer enables dealers to acquire a broad sample of inventory without incurring the purchase and finance charges required to actually buy the inventory. It is extremely important that goods being held on consignment not be included in the inventory of the firm holding the goods for sale even though they are physically on that firm's premises. It is equally important that the supplier/owner properly include all such goods in its records even though the inventory is not on its premises.

An example of a company that successfully uses consignment sales as part of its business strategy is **International Airline Support Group, Inc.** This company is a leading distributor of aircraft spare parts for large jet airplanes. The company uses consignments because, as stated in its annual report, this arrangement allows it "to obtain parts inventory on a favorable basis without committing its capital to purchasing inventory."

Ending Inventory and Cost of Goods Sold

cost of goods available for sale

The cost of all merchandise available for sale during the period; equal to the sum of beginning inventory and net purchases.

Inventory purchased or manufactured during a period is added to beginning inventory, and the total cost of this inventory is called the **cost of goods available for sale**. At the end of an accounting period, total cost of goods available for sale must be allocated between inventory still remaining (to be reported in the balance sheet as an asset) and inventory sold during the period (to be reported in the income statement as an expense, Cost of Goods Sold).

This cost allocation process is extremely important because the more cost that is said to remain in ending inventory, the less cost is reported as cost of goods sold in the income statement. This is why accurately determining who owns the inventory is such a big issue. Making a mistake with inventory ownership will result in misstating both the income statement and the balance sheet. For this reason, accountants must be careful of inventory errors because they directly affect reported net income. The impact of inventory errors is illustrated later in the chapter.

The cost allocation process also involves a significant amount of accounting judgment. Identical inventory items are usually purchased at varying prices throughout the year, so to calculate the amount of ending inventory and cost of goods sold, the accountant must determine which items (the low cost or high cost) remain and which were sold. Again, this decision can directly affect the amount of reported cost of goods sold and net income. The use of inventory cost flow assumptions is discussed later in the chapter.

REMEMBER THIS...

- Inventory is composed of goods held for sale in the normal course of business.
- For a manufacturing firm, the three types of inventory are raw materials, work in process, and finished goods.
- All costs incurred in producing and getting inventory ready to sell should be added to inventory cost.
- Inventory should be recorded on the books of the company holding legal title.
- At the end of an accounting period, the total cost of goods available for sale during the period must be allocated between ending inventory and cost of goods sold.

Accounting for Inventory Purchases and Sales

Account for inventory purchases and sales using both a perpetual and a periodic inventory system.

(2) To begin a more detailed study of inventory accounting, we must first establish a solid understanding of the journal entries used to record inventory transactions. The accounting procedures for recording purchases and sales using both a periodic and a perpetual inventory system are detailed in this section.

Overview of Perpetual and Periodic Systems

Some businesses track changes in inventory levels on a continuous basis, recording inventory increases and decreases with each individual purchase and sale to maintain a running total of the inventory balance. This is called a perpetual inventory system. Other businesses rely on quarterly or yearly inventory counts to reveal which inventory items have been sold. This is called a periodic inventory system.

Perpetual   You own a discount appliance superstore. Your biggest-selling items are washers, dryers, refrigerators, microwaves, and dishwashers. You advertise your weekly sale items on local TV stations, and your sales volume is quite heavy. You have 50 sales-people who work independently of one another. You have found that customers get very upset if they come to buy an advertised item and you have run out. In this business environment, would it make sense to keep a running total of the quantity remaining of each inventory item and update it each time a sale is made? Yes, the benefit of having current information on each inventory item would make it worthwhile to spend a little extra time to update the inventory records when a sale is made.

perpetual inventory system

A system of accounting for inventory in which detailed records of the number of units and the cost of each purchase and sales transaction are prepared throughout the accounting period.

This appliance store would probably use a **perpetual inventory system**. With a perpetual system, inventory records are updated whenever a purchase or a sale is made. In this way, the inventory records at any given time reflect how many of each inventory item should be in the warehouse or out on the store shelves. A perpetual system is most often used when each individual inventory item has a relatively high value or when there are large costs to running out of or overstocking specific items.

Periodic   You operate a newsstand in a busy metropolitan subway station. Almost all of your sales occur during the morning and the evening rush hours. You sell a diverse array of items—newspapers, magazines, pens, snacks, and other odds and ends. During rush hour, your business is a fast-paced pressure cooker; the longer you take with one customer, the more chance that the busy commuters waiting in line for service will tire of waiting and you will lose sales. In this business environment,

A newsstand will wait until the end of the day to count inventory by comparing what items it started with to what is left. This is an example of a periodic inventory system.

would it make sense to make each customer wait while you meticulously check off on an inventory sheet exactly which items were sold? No, the delay caused by this detailed bookkeeping would cause you to lose customers. It makes more sense to wait until the end of the day, count up what inventory you still have left, compare that to what you started with, and use those numbers to deduce how many of each inventory item you sold during the day.

This subway newsstand scenario is an example of a situation where a **periodic inventory system** is appropriate. With a periodic system, inventory records are not updated when a sale is made; only the dollar amount of the sale is recorded. Periodic systems are most often used when inventory is composed of a large number of diverse items, each with a relatively low value.

periodic inventory system

A system of accounting for inventory in which cost of goods sold is determined and inventory is adjusted at the end of the accounting period, not when merchandise is purchased or sold.

Impact of Information Technology   Over the past 25 years, advances in information technology have lowered the cost of maintaining a perpetual inventory system. As a result, more businesses have adopted perpetual systems so that they can more closely track inventory levels. A visible manifestation of this trend is in supermarkets. Twenty years ago, the checkout clerk rang up the price of each item on a cash register. After the customers walked out of the store with their groceries, the store knew the total amount of the sale but did not know which individual items had been sold. This was a periodic inventory system. Now, with laser scanning equipment tied into the supermarket's computer system, most supermarkets operate under a perpetual system. The store manager knows exactly what you bought and exactly how many of each item should still be left on the store shelves.

Perpetual and Periodic Journal Entries

The following transactions for Grantsville Clothing Store will be used to illustrate the differences in bookkeeping procedures between a business using a perpetual inventory system and one using a periodic inventory system:

a.   Purchased on account: 1,000 shirts at a cost of $10 each for a total of $10,000.
b.   Purchased on account: 300 pairs of pants at a cost of $18 each for a total of $5,400.
c.   Paid cash for separate shipping costs on the shirts purchased in (a), $970. The supplier of the pants purchased in (b) included the shipping costs in the $18 purchase price.
d.   Returned 30 of the shirts (costing $300) to the supplier because they were stained.
e.   Paid for the shirt purchase. A 2% discount was given on the $9,700 bill [(1,000 purchased − 30 returned) × $10] because of payment within the 10-day discount period (payment terms were 2/10, n/30).

(Continued)

f.   Paid $5,400 for the pants purchase. No discount was allowed because payment was made after the discount period.

g.   Sold on account: 600 shirts at a price of $25 each for a total of $15,000.

h.   Sold on account: 200 pairs of pants at a price of $40 each for a total of $8,000.

i.   Accepted return of 50 shirts by dissatisfied customers.

STOP & THINK

If you buy your groceries with a credit card or a bank debit card, what kind of information can the supermarket accumulate about you?

The journal entries for the perpetual inventory system should seem familiar to you—a perpetual system has been assumed in all earlier chapters of the text. A perpetual system was assumed because it is logical and is the system all companies would choose if there were no cost to updating the inventory records each time a sale or purchase is made. As mentioned, a periodic inventory system is sometimes a practical necessity.

Purchases   With a perpetual system, all purchases are added (debited) directly to Inventory. With a periodic system, the inventory balance is only updated using an inventory count at the end of the period; inventory purchases during the period are recorded in a temporary holding account called Purchases. As will be illustrated later, at the end of the period, the balance in Purchases is closed to Inventory in connection with the computation of cost of goods sold.

Entries (a) and (b) to record the shirt and pants purchases are given below.

	Perpetual			**Periodic**		
a.	Inventory	10,000		Purchases	10,000	
	Accounts Payable		10,000	Accounts Payable		10,000
b.	Inventory	5,400		Purchases	5,400	
	Accounts Payable		5,400	Accounts Payable		5,400

Transportation Costs   The cost of transporting the inventory is an additional inventory cost. Sometimes, as with the pants in the Grantsville Clothing example, the shipping cost is already included in the purchase price, so a separate entry to record the transportation costs is not needed. When a separate payment is made for transportation costs, it is recorded as follows:

	Perpetual			**Periodic**		
c.	Inventory	970		Freight In	970	
	Cash		970	Cash		970

With a perpetual inventory system, transportation costs are added directly to the inventory balance. With a periodic inventory system, another temporary holding account, Freight In, is created, and transportation costs are accumulated in this account during the period. Like the purchases account, Freight In is closed to Inventory at the end of the period in connection with the computation of cost of goods sold.

Purchase Returns   With a perpetual system, the return of unsatisfactory merchandise to the supplier results in a decrease in Inventory. In addition, since no payment will have to be made for the returned merchandise, Accounts Payable is reduced by the same amount. With a periodic system, the amount of the returned merchandise is recorded in yet another temporary holding account called Purchase Returns. Purchase Returns is a contra account to Purchases and is also closed to Inventory as part of the computation of cost of goods sold.

	Perpetual				**Periodic**		
d.	Accounts Payable	300			Accounts Payable	300	
	Inventory		300		Purchase Returns		300

If the returned merchandise had already been paid for, the supplier would most likely return the purchase price. In this case, the debit would be to Cash instead of to Accounts Payable.

Purchase Discounts As discussed in Chapter 6, sellers sometimes offer inducements for credit customers to pay quickly. In this example, Grantsville Clothing takes advantage of purchase discounts to save money on the payment for the shirts. The amount of the purchase discount is $194 ($9,700 × 0.02), so the total payment for the shirts is $9,506 ($9,700 − $194). The amount recorded for inventory should reflect the actual amount paid to purchase the inventory. With a perpetual inventory system, this is shown by subtracting the purchase discount amount from the inventory account. With a periodic inventory system, another holding account is created to accumulate purchase discounts taken during the period.

	Perpetual				**Periodic**		
e.	Accounts Payable	9,700			Accounts Payable	9,700	
	Inventory		194		Purchase Discounts		194
	Cash		9,506		Cash		9,506
f.	Accounts Payable	5,400			Accounts Payable	5,400	
	Cash		5,400		Cash		5,400

Note that the payment for the pants is made after the discount period, so the full amount must be paid. Since this transaction had no impact on Inventory, the entry is the same for both the perpetual and the periodic system.

In terms of journal entries, you should recognize that the difference between a perpetual and a periodic inventory system is that all adjustments to inventory under a perpetual system are entered directly in the inventory account; with a periodic system, all inventory adjustments are accumulated in an array of temporary holding accounts: Purchases, Freight In, Purchase Returns, and Purchase Discounts.

Sales The sales of shirts and pants would be recorded as follows:

	Perpetual				**Periodic**		
g.	Accounts Receivable	15,000			Accounts Receivable	15,000	
	Sales (600 × $25)		15,000		Sales		15,000
	Cost of Goods Sold	6,000					
	Inventory (600 × $10)		6,000				
h.	Accounts Receivable	8,000			Accounts Receivable	8,000	
	Sales (200 × $40)		8,000		Sales		8,000
	Cost of Goods Sold	3,600					
	Inventory (200 × $18)		3,600				

These entries reflect the primary difference between a perpetual and a periodic inventory system—with a periodic system, no attempt is made to recognize cost of goods sold on a transaction-by-transaction basis. In fact, with a periodic system, Grantsville Clothing would not even know how many shirts and how many pairs of pants had been sold. Instead, only total sales of $23,000 ($15,000 + $8,000) would be known.

For simplicity, we have recorded the cost of goods sold for the shirts as $10 each. The actual cost per shirt, after adjusting for freight in and purchase discounts, is $10.80, computed as follows:

Total purchase price (1,000 shirts)	$10,000
Plus: Freight in	970
Less: Purchase returns (30 shirts)	(300)
Less: Purchase discounts	(194)
Total cost of shirts (970 shirts)	$10,476
Total cost $10,476 ÷ 970 shirts = $10.80 per shirt	

In practice, it is unlikely that a firm using a perpetual inventory system would bother to adjust unit costs for the effects of freight cost and purchase discounts on an ongoing basis. The cost of doing these calculations could easily outweigh any resulting improvement in the quality of cost information.

Sales Returns   As discussed in Chapter 6, dissatisfied customers sometimes return their purchases. The journal entries to record the return of 50 shirts are as follows:

	Perpetual			**Periodic**	
i.	Sales Returns (50 × $25) 1,250		Sales Returns	1,250	
	Accounts Receivable	1,250	Accounts Receivable		1,250
	Inventory (50 × $10) 500				
	Cost of Goods Sold	500			

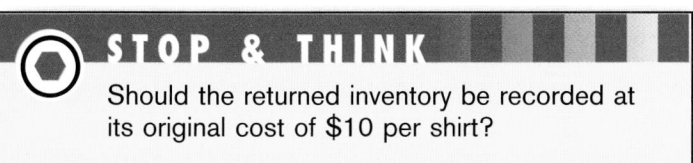

STOP & THINK

Should the returned inventory be recorded at its original cost of $10 per shirt?

Under the perpetual system, not only are the sales for the returned items canceled, but the cost of the returned inventory is also removed from Cost of Goods Sold and restored to the inventory account.

Closing Entries   After all of the journal entries are posted to the ledger, the T-accounts for Inventory and Cost of Goods Sold, under a perpetual system, would appear as follows:

Inventory				**Cost of Goods Sold**			
(a)	10,000	(d)	300	(g)	6,000	(i)	500
(b)	5,400	(e)	194	(h)	3,600		
(c)	970	(g)	6,000				
(i)	500	(h)	3,600				
Bal.	6,776			Bal.	9,100		

These numbers, after being verified by a physical count of the inventory (as described in the next section), would be reported in the financial statements—the $6,776 of Inventory in the balance sheet and the $9,100 of Cost of Goods Sold in the income statement.

Review the journal entries (a) through (i) under the periodic inventory system and notice that none of the amounts have been entered in either Inventory or Cost of Goods Sold. As a result, both of these accounts will have zero balances at year-end. Actually, the inventory account would have the same balance it had at the beginning of the period, which, in this example, we will assume to be zero.

With a periodic inventory system, the correct balances are recorded in Inventory and Cost of Goods Sold through a series of closing entries. Two entries are made:

1. Transfer all the temporary holding accounts to the inventory account balance. At this point, the inventory account balance is equal to the cost of goods available for sale (beginning inventory plus the net cost of purchases for the period).

2. Reduce Inventory by the amount of Cost of Goods Sold. At this point, the inventory account balance is equal to the ending inventory amount, and the appropriate cost of goods sold amount is also recognized.

To illustrate, the information for Grantsville Clothing will be used. The entry to transfer all the temporary holding accounts to the inventory account is as follows:

Inventory	15,876	
Purchase Returns	300	
Purchase Discounts	194	
Freight In		970
Purchases		15,400

Closing of temporary inventory accounts for periodic system.

net purchases

The net cost of inventory purchased during a period, after adding the cost of freight in and subtracting returns and discounts.

The inventory debit of $15,876 is the amount of **net purchases** for the period. Notice that, after this entry has been posted, the balances in all the temporary holding accounts will have been reduced to zero. As mentioned, after the addition of net purchases, the inventory account balance represents cost of goods available for sale (the sum of beginning inventory and net purchases). Remember that, in this example, beginning inventory is assumed to be zero.

The second closing entry involves the adjustment of Inventory to its appropriate ending balance and the creation of the cost of goods sold account. This cost of goods sold account would be closed when other nominal accounts (e.g., Sales Salaries, Interest Expense, etc.) are closed. If the year-end physical count indicates that the ending inventory balance should be $6,776, the appropriate entry is as follows:

Cost of Goods Sold	9,100	
Inventory ($15,876 − $6,776)		9,100

Adjustment of inventory account to appropriate ending balance.

In this example, the values for both ending inventory ($6,776) and cost of goods sold ($9,100) are the same with either a perpetual or a periodic inventory system. So, what is the practical difference between the two systems? One difference is that a perpetual system can tell you the inventory balance and the cumulative cost of goods sold at any time during the period. With a periodic system, on the other hand, you must wait until the inventory is counted at the end of the period to compute the amount of inventory or cost of goods sold. Another difference is that, with a perpetual system, you can compare the inventory records to the amount of inventory actually on hand and thus determine whether any inventory has been lost or stolen. As described in the next section, this comparison is not possible with a periodic system.

> **REMEMBER THIS...**
>
> - With a perpetual inventory system, the amount of inventory and cost of goods sold for the period are tracked on an ongoing basis.
> - With a periodic inventory system, inventory and cost of goods sold are computed using an end-of-period inventory count.
> - With a periodic system, inventory-related items are recorded in temporary holding accounts that are transferred to the inventory account at the end of the period.

Counting Inventory and Calculating Cost of Goods Sold

Calculate cost of goods sold using the results of an inventory count and understand the impact of errors in ending inventory on reported cost of goods sold.

(3) Regular physical counts of the existing inventory are essential to maintaining reliable inventory accounting records. With a perpetual system, the physical count can be compared to the recorded inventory balance to see whether any inventory has been lost or stolen. With a periodic system, a physical count is the only way to get the information necessary to compute cost of goods sold.

Taking a Physical Count of Inventory

No matter which inventory system a company is using, periodic physical counts are a necessary and important part of accounting for inventory. With a perpetual inventory system, the physical count either confirms that the amount entered in the accounting records is accurate or highlights shortages and clerical errors. If, for example, employees have been stealing inventory, the theft will show up as a difference between the balance in the inventory account and the amount physically counted.

A physical count of inventory involves two steps:

1. *Quantity count.* In most companies, physically counting all inventory is a time-consuming activity. Because sales transactions and merchandise deliveries can complicate matters, inventory is usually counted on holidays or after the close of business on the inventory day. Special care must be taken to ensure that all inventory owned, wherever its location, is counted and that inventory on hand but not owned (consignment inventory) is not counted.
2. *Inventory costing.* When the physical count has been completed, each type of merchandise is assigned a unit cost. The quantity of each type of merchandise is multiplied by its unit cost to determine the dollar value of the inventory. These amounts are then added to obtain the total ending inventory for the business. This is the amount reported as Inventory on the balance sheet. The ending balance in the inventory account may have to be adjusted for any shortages discovered.

To illustrate the impact of a physical inventory count on the accounting records for both a periodic and a perpetual system, we will refer back to the Grantsville Clothing Store example used earlier. Assume that a physical count, combined with inventory costing analysis, suggests that the correct amount for ending inventory is $5,950. This information can be combined with previous information from the accounting system as follows:

	Periodic System	Perpetual System
Beginning inventory	$ 0	$ 0
Plus: Net purchases	15,876	15,876
Cost of goods available for sale	$15,876	$15,876
Less: Ending inventory	5,950	6,776 (from inventory system)
Cost of goods sold	$ 9,926	$ 9,100 (from inventory system)
Goods lost or stolen	unknown	826 ($6,776 − $5,950)
Total cost of goods sold, lost, or stolen	$ 9,926	$ 9,926

Recall that, in this example, the beginning inventory is assumed to be zero. The amount of net purchases is a combination of the items affecting the amount paid for inventory purchases during the period: purchase price, freight in, purchase returns, and purchase discounts. The $15,876 amount for net purchases was computed earlier in connection with the closing entry for the periodic system.

This cost of goods sold computation highlights the key difference between a periodic and a perpetual inventory system. With a periodic system, the company does not know what ending inventory *should be* when the inventory count is performed. The best the company can do is count the inventory and assume that the difference between the cost of goods available for sale and the cost of goods still remaining (ending inventory) must represent the cost of goods that were sold. Actually, a business using a periodic system has no way of knowing whether these goods were sold, lost, stolen, or spoiled—all it knows for sure is that the goods are gone.

inventory shrinkage

The amount of inventory that is lost, stolen, or spoiled during a period; determined by comparing perpetual inventory records to the physical count of inventory.

With a perpetual system, the accounting records themselves yield the cost of goods sold during the period, as well as the amount of inventory that should be found when the physical count is made. In the Grantsville Clothing example, the predicted ending inventory is $6,776 (from the T-account shown earlier); the actual ending inventory, according to the physical count, is only $5,950. The difference of $826 ($6,776 − $5,950) represents inventory lost, stolen, or ruined during the period. This amount is called inventory shrinkage. The adjusting entry needed to record this **inventory shrinkage** is as follows:

Inventory Shrinkage	826	
Inventory ($6,776 − $5,950)		826
Adjustment of perpetual inventory balance to reflect inventory		
shrinkage.		

 F Y I

CVS is a leader in the retail drugstore industry in the United States with net sales of $24.2 billion in fiscal 2002. Inventory shrinkage for CVS for 2002 was $288 million, or almost 1.2% of sales. The company has since ceased to report actual inventory shrinkage numbers and instead reported in 2005 that inventory shrinkage had improved.

For internal management purposes, the amount of inventory shrinkage would be tracked from one period to the next to detect whether the amount of "shrinkage" for any given period is unusually high. For external reporting purposes, the shrinkage amount would probably be combined with normal cost of goods sold, and the title "Cost of Goods Sold" would be given to the total. Notice that if this practice is followed, reported cost of goods sold would be the same under both a perpetual and a periodic inventory system. The difference is that, with a perpetual system, company management knows how much of the goods was actually sold and how much represents inventory shrinkage.

With a periodic inventory system, no journal entry for inventory shrinkage is made because the amount of shrinkage is unknown. Instead, the ending inventory amount derived from the physical count is used to make the second periodic inventory closing entry (refer back to the previous section). Using the $5,950 ending inventory amount, the appropriate periodic inventory closing entry is:

Cost of Goods Sold	9,926	
Inventory ($15,876 − $5,950)		9,926
Adjustment of inventory account to appropriate ending balance.		

The Income Effect of an Error in Ending Inventory

As shown in the previous section, the results of the physical inventory count directly affect the computation of cost of goods sold with a periodic system and inventory shrinkage with a perpetual system. Errors in the inventory count will cause the amount of cost of goods sold or inventory shrinkage to be misstated. To illustrate, assume that the correct inventory count for Grantsville Clothing is $5,950 but that the ending inventory value is mistakenly computed to be $6,450. The impact of this $500 ($6,450 − $5,950) inventory overstatement is as follows:

	Periodic System	Perpetual System
Beginning inventory	$ 0	$ 0
Plus: Net purchases	15,876	15,876
Cost of goods available for sale	$15,876	$15,876
Less: Ending inventory	6,450	6,776 (from inventory system)
Cost of goods sold	$ 9,426	$ 9,100 (from inventory system)
Goods lost or stolen	unknown	326 ($6,776 − $6,450)
Total cost of goods sold, lost, or stolen	$ 9,426	$ 9,426

The $500 inventory overstatement reduces the reported cost of goods sold, lost, or stolen by $500, from $9,926 (computed earlier) to $9,426. This is because if we mistakenly think that we have more inventory remaining, then we will also mistakenly think that we must have sold less. Conversely, if the physical count understates ending inventory, total cost of goods sold will be overstated.

Since an inventory overstatement decreases reported cost of goods sold, it will also increase reported gross margin and net income. For this reason, the managers of a firm that is having difficulty meeting profit targets are sometimes tempted to "mistakenly" overstate ending inventory. Because of this temptation, auditors must take care to review a company's inventory counting process and also to physically observe a sample of the actual inventory. Many new accounting graduates who are hired by public accounting firms spend a portion of their first year on the job checking the inventory counts done by clients. The benefits of this exposure are twofold: (1) these new auditors get an opportunity to see what a business actually does, and (2) the inventory count provides assurance that the inventory amount stated on the financial statements is accurate.

REMEMBER THIS...

- A physical inventory count is necessary to ensure that inventory records match the actual existing inventory.
- If a perpetual system is used, an inventory count can be used to compute the amount of inventory shrinkage during the period.
- An error in the reported ending inventory amount can have a significant effect on reported cost of goods sold, gross margin, and net income. For example, overstatement of ending inventory results in understatement of cost of goods sold and overstatement of net income.

Inventory Cost Flow Assumptions

Apply the four inventory cost flow alternatives: specific identification, FIFO, LIFO, and average cost.

Consider the following transactions for the Ramona Rice Company for the year 2009.

Mar. 23	Purchased 10 kilos of rice, $4 per kilo.
Nov. 17	Purchased 10 kilos of rice, $9 per kilo.
Dec. 31	Sold 10 kilos of rice, $10 per kilo.

The surprisingly difficult question to answer with this simple example is "How much income did Ramona make in 2009?" As you can see, it depends on which rice was sold on December 31. There are three possibilities:

	Case #1 Sold Old Rice	Case #2 Sold New Rice	Case #3 Sold Mixed Rice
Sales ($10 × 10 kilos)	$100	$100	$100
Cost of goods sold (10 kilos)	40	90	65
Gross margin	$ 60	$ 10	$ 35

FIFO (first in, first out)

An inventory cost flow assumption whereby the first goods purchased are assumed to be the first goods sold so that the ending inventory consists of the most recently purchased goods.

LIFO (last in, first out)

An inventory cost flow assumption whereby the last goods purchased are assumed to be the first goods sold so that the ending inventory consists of the first goods purchased.

average cost

An inventory cost flow assumption whereby cost of goods sold and the cost of ending inventory are determined by using an average cost of all merchandise available for sale during the period.

specific identification

A method of valuing inventory and determining cost of goods sold whereby the actual costs of specific inventory items are assigned to them.

In Case #1, it is assumed that the 10 kilos of rice sold on December 31 were the old ones, purchased on March 23 for $4 per kilo. Accountants call this a **FIFO (first in, first out)** assumption. In Case #2, it is assumed that the company sold the new rice, purchased on November 17 for $9 per kilo. Accountants call this a **LIFO (last in, first out)** assumption. In Case #3, it is assumed that all the rice is mixed together, so the cost per kilo is the average cost of all the rice available for sale, or $6.50 per kilo [($40 + $90) ÷ 20 kilos]. Accountants call this an **average cost** assumption.

The point of the Ramona Rice example is this: in most cases, there is no feasible way to track exactly which units were sold. Accordingly, in order to compute cost of goods sold, the accountant must make an assumption. Note that this is not a case of tricky accountants trying to manipulate the reported numbers; instead, this is a case in which income simply cannot be computed unless the accountant uses his or her judgment and makes an assumption.

All three of the assumptions described in the example—FIFO, LIFO, and average cost—are acceptable under U.S. accounting rules. An interesting question is whether a company would randomly choose one of the three acceptable methods, or whether the choice would be made more strategically. For example, if Ramona Rice were preparing financial statements to be used to support a bank loan application, which assumption would you suggest that the company make? On the other hand, if Ramona were completing its income tax return, which assumption would be best? This topic of strategic accounting choice will be discussed later in this chapter.

In the following sections, we will examine in more detail the different cost flow assumptions used by companies to determine inventories and cost of goods sold.

Specific Identification Inventory Cost Flow

An alternative to the assumptions just described is to specifically identify the cost of each particular unit that is sold. This approach, called **specific identification**, is often used by automobile dealers and other businesses that sell a limited number of units at a high price. To illustrate the specific identification inventory costing method, we will consider the September 2009 records of Nephi Company, which sells one type of bicycle.

Sept.   1   Beginning inventory consisted of 10 bicycles costing $200 each.
        3   Purchased 8 bicycles costing $250 each.
       18   Purchased 16 bicycles costing $300 each.
       20   Purchased 10 bicycles costing $320 each.
       25   Sold 28 bicycles, $400 each.

These inventory records show that during September the company had 44 bicycles (10 from beginning inventory and 34 that were purchased during the month) that it could have sold. However, only 28 bicycles were sold, leaving 16 on hand at the end of

September. Using the specific identification method of inventory costing requires that the individual costs of the actual units sold be charged against revenue as cost of goods sold. To compute cost of goods sold and ending inventory amounts with this alternative, a company must know which units were actually sold and what the unit cost of each was.

Suppose that of the 28 bicycles sold by Nephi on September 25, 8 came from the beginning inventory, 4 came from the September 3 purchase, and 16 came from the September 18 purchase. With this information, cost of goods sold and ending inventory are computed as follows:

	Bicycles	Costs
Beginning inventory	10	$ 2,000
Net purchases	34	10,000
Goods available for sale	44	$12,000
Ending inventory	16	4,600
Cost of goods sold	28	$ 7,400

The cost of ending inventory is the total of the individual costs of the bicycles still on hand at the end of the month, or:

2 bicycles from beginning inventory, $200 each	$ 400
4 bicycles purchased on September 3, $250 each	1,000
0 bicycles purchased on September 18, $300 each	0
10 bicycles purchased on September 20, $320 each	3,200
Total ending inventory (16 units)	$4,600

Similarly, the cost of goods sold is the total of the costs of the specific bicycles sold, or:

8 bicycles from beginning inventory, $200 each	$1,600
4 bicycles purchased on September 3, $250 each	1,000
16 bicycles purchased on September 18, $300 each	4,800
0 bicycles purchased on September 20, $320 each	0
Total cost of goods sold (28 units)	$7,400

For many companies, it is impractical, if not impossible, to keep track of specific units. In that case, an assumption must be made as to which units were sold during the period and which are still in inventory, as illustrated earlier in the Ramona Rice example.

It is very important to remember that the accounting rules do not require that the assumed flow of goods for costing purposes match the actual physical movement of goods purchased and sold. In some cases, the assumed cost flow may be similar to the physical flow, but firms are not required to match the assumed accounting cost flow to the physical flow. A grocery store, for example, usually tries to sell the oldest units first to minimize spoilage. Thus, the physical flow of goods would reflect a FIFO pattern, but the grocery store could use a FIFO, LIFO, or average cost assumption in determining the ending inventory and cost of goods sold numbers to be reported in the financial statements. On the other hand, a company that stockpiles coal must first sell the coal purchased last since it is on top of the pile. That company might use the LIFO cost assumption, which reflects physical flow, or it might use one of the other alternatives.

In the next few sections, we will illustrate the FIFO, LIFO, and average inventory costing methods. The bicycle inventory data for Nephi Company will again be used in illustrating the different inventory cost flows.

FIFO Cost Flow Assumption

With FIFO, it is assumed that the oldest units are sold and the newest units remain in inventory. Using the FIFO inventory cost flow assumption, the ending inventory and cost of goods sold for Nephi Company are:

	Bicycles	Costs
Beginning inventory	10	$ 2,000
Net purchases	34	10,000
Goods available for sale	44	$12,000
Ending inventory	16	5,000
Cost of goods sold	28	$ 7,000

The $7,000 cost of goods sold and $5,000 cost of ending inventory are determined as follows:

FIFO cost of goods sold (oldest 28 units):	
10 bicycles from beginning inventory, $200 each	$2,000
8 bicycles purchased on September 3, $250 each	2,000
10 bicycles purchased on September 18, $300 each	3,000
Total FIFO cost of goods sold	$7,000

FIFO ending inventory (newest 16 units):	
6 bicycles purchased on September 18, $300 each	$1,800
10 bicycles purchased on September 20, $320 each	3,200
Total FIFO ending inventory	$5,000

LIFO Cost Flow Assumption

LIFO is the opposite of FIFO. With LIFO, the cost of the most recent units purchased is transferred to cost of goods sold. When prices are rising, as they are in the Nephi Company example, LIFO provides higher cost of goods sold, and hence lower net income, than FIFO. This is because the newest (high-priced) goods are assumed to have been sold. Using the LIFO inventory cost flow assumption, the ending inventory and cost of goods sold for Nephi Company are:

	Bicycles	Costs
Beginning inventory	10	$ 2,000
Net purchases	34	10,000
Goods available for sale	44	$12,000
Ending inventory	16	3,500
Cost of goods sold	28	$ 8,500

The $8,500 cost of goods sold and $3,500 cost of ending inventory are determined as follows:

LIFO cost of goods sold (newest 28 units):	
10 bicycles purchased on September 20, $320 each	$3,200
16 bicycles purchased on September 18, $300 each	4,800
2 bicycles purchased on September 3, $250 each	500
Total LIFO cost of goods sold	$8,500

LIFO ending inventory (oldest 16 units):	
10 bicycles from beginning inventory, $200 each	$2,000
6 bicycles purchased on September 3, $250 each	1,500
Total LIFO ending inventory	$3,500

Average Cost Flow Assumption

With average costing, an average cost must be computed for all the inventory available for sale during the period. The average unit cost for Nephi Company during September is computed as follows:

	Bicycles	Costs
Beginning inventory	10	$ 2,000
Net purchases	34	10,000
Goods available for sale	44	$12,000
$12,000 ÷ 44 units = $272.73 per unit		

With the average cost assumption, cost of goods sold is computed by multiplying the number of units sold by the average cost per unit. Similarly, the cost of ending inventory is computed by multiplying the number of units in ending inventory by the average cost per unit. These calculations are as follows:

Average Cost of Goods Sold: 28 Units × $272.73 per Unit = $7,636 (rounded)
Average Ending Inventory: 16 Units × $272.73 per Unit = $4,364 (rounded)

This information can be shown as follows:

	Bicycles	Costs
Beginning inventory	10	$ 2,000
Net purchases	34	10,000
Goods available for sale	44	$12,000
Ending inventory	16	4,364
Cost of goods sold	28	$ 7,636

A Comparison of All Inventory Costing Methods

The cost of goods sold and ending inventory amounts we have calculated using the three cost flow assumptions are summarized along with the resultant gross margins as follows:

	FIFO	LIFO	Average
Sales revenue (28 × $400)	$11,200	$11,200	$11,200
Cost of goods sold	7,000	8,500	7,636
Gross margin	$ 4,200	$ 2,700	$ 3,564
Ending inventory	$ 5,000	$ 3,500	$ 4,364

Note that the net result of each of the inventory cost flow assumptions is to allocate the total cost of goods available for sale of $12,000 between cost of goods sold and ending inventory.

Conceptual Comparison From a conceptual standpoint, LIFO gives a better reflection of cost of goods sold in the income statement than does FIFO because the most recent goods ("last in"), with the most recent costs, are assumed to have been sold. Thus, LIFO cost of goods sold matches current revenues with current costs. Average cost is somewhere between LIFO and FIFO. On the balance sheet, however, FIFO gives a better measure of inventory value because, with the FIFO assumption, the "first in" units are sold and the remaining units are the newest ones with the most recent costs. In summary, LIFO gives a conceptually better measure of income, but FIFO gives a conceptually better measure of inventory value on the balance sheet.

Financial Statement Impact Comparison   As illustrated in the Nephi Company example, in times of rising inventory prices (the most common situation in the majority of industries today), cost of goods sold is highest with LIFO and lowest with FIFO. As a result, gross margin, net income, and ending inventory are lowest with LIFO and highest with FIFO. With the impact on the reported financial statement numbers being so uniformly bad, you may be wondering why any company would ever voluntarily choose to use LIFO (during times of inflation). It might further surprise you to learn that, since 1974, hundreds of U.S. companies have voluntarily switched from FIFO to LIFO and that over half of the large companies in the United States currently use LIFO in accounting for at least some of their inventories.

The attractiveness of LIFO can be explained with one word—TAXES. If a company uses LIFO in a time of rising prices, reported cost of goods sold is higher, reported taxable income is lower, and cash paid for income taxes is lower. In fact, LIFO was invented in the 1930s in the United States for the sole purpose of allowing companies to lower their income tax payments. In most instances where accounting alternatives exist, firms are allowed to use one accounting method for tax purposes and another for financial reporting. In 1939, however, when the Internal Revenue Service (IRS) approved the use of LIFO, it ruled that firms may use LIFO for tax purposes only if they also use LIFO for financial reporting purposes. Therefore, companies must choose between reporting higher profits and paying higher taxes with FIFO or reporting lower profits and paying lower taxes with LIFO.

STOP & THINK

Over the entire life of a company—from its beginning with zero inventory until its final closeout when the last inventory item is sold—is aggregate cost of goods sold more, less, or the same as aggregate purchases? How is this relationship affected by the inventory cost flow assumption used?

REMEMBER THIS...

- In most cases, an accountant must make an inventory cost flow assumption in order to compute cost of goods sold and ending inventory.
- With FIFO (first in, first out), it is assumed that the oldest inventory units are sold first.
- With LIFO (last in, first out), it is assumed that the newest units are sold first.
- With the average cost assumption, the total goods available for sale are used to compute an average cost per unit for the period; this average cost is then used in calculating cost of goods sold and ending inventory.
- LIFO produces a better matching of current revenues and current expenses in the income statement; FIFO yields a balance sheet inventory value that is closer to the current value of the inventory.
- The primary practical attraction of LIFO is that it lowers income tax payments during times of inflation.

Assessing How Well Companies Manage Their Inventories

Use financial ratios to evaluate a company's inventory level.

(5)   Money tied up in the form of inventories cannot be used for other purposes. Therefore, companies try hard to minimize the necessary investment in inventories while at the same time assuring that they have enough inventory on hand to meet customer demand. In recent years a method of inventory management called just-in-time (JIT) inventory has become popular. JIT, which will be described in Chapter 23 of *Accounting: Concepts and Applications*, is an inventory management method that attempts to have exactly enough inventory arrive just in time for sale. Its purpose is to minimize the amount of money needed to purchase and hold inventory.

Evaluating the Level of Inventory

inventory turnover

A measure of the efficiency with which inventory is managed; computed by dividing cost of goods sold by average inventory for a period.

Two widely used measurements of how effectively a company is managing its inventory are the inventory turnover ratio and number of days' sales in inventory. **Inventory turnover** provides a measure of how many times a company turns over, or replenishes, its inventory during a year. The calculation is similar to the accounts receivable turnover discussed in Chapter 6. It is calculated by dividing cost of goods sold by average inventory as follows:

$$\text{Inventory Turnover} = \frac{\text{Cost of Goods Sold}}{\text{Average Inventory}}$$

The average inventory amount is the average of the beginning and ending inventory balances. The inventory turnover ratios for **Sears**, **Safeway**, and **Caterpillar** for 2005 are as follows (dollar amounts are in billions):

	Sears	Safeway	Caterpillar
Cost of goods sold	$35.505	$27.303	$26.558
Beginning inventory	3.281	2.741	4.675
Ending inventory	9.068	2.766	5.224
Average inventory	6.175	2.754	4.950
Inventory turnover	5.75	9.91	5.37

number of days' sales in inventory

An alternative measure of how well inventory is being managed; computed by dividing 365 days by the inventory turnover ratio.

From this analysis, you can see that Safeway, the supermarket, turns its inventory over more frequently than Sears, the department store, and Caterpillar, the equipment dealer. This result is what we would have predicted given that the companies are in different businesses and have different types of inventory.

Inventory turnover can also be converted into the **number of days' sales in inventory**. This ratio is computed by dividing 365, or the number of days in a year, by the inventory turnover, as follows:

$$\frac{\text{Number of Days'}}{\text{Sales in Inventory}} = \frac{365}{\text{Inventory Turnover}}$$

Computing this ratio for Sears, Safeway, and Caterpillar yields the following:

	Number of Days' Sales in Inventory
Sears	63.5 days
Safeway	36.8 days
Caterpillar	68.0 days

CAUTION

Sometimes these two inventory ratios are computed using ending inventory rather than average inventory. This is appropriate if the inventory balance does not change much from the beginning to the end of the year.

Individuals analyzing how effective a company's inventory management is would compare these ratios with those of other firms in the same industry and with comparable ratios for the same firm in previous years.

Impact of the Inventory Cost Flow Assumption

As mentioned previously, in times of rising prices, the use of LIFO results in higher cost of goods sold and lower inventory values. All three of the companies in the ratio illustration above use LIFO. Each company includes supplemental disclosures in the financial statement notes that allow users to compute what reported inventory and cost of goods sold would have been if the company had used FIFO. To illustrate the impact that the choice of inventory cost flow assumption can have on the reported numbers, consider the following comparison for Caterpillar for 2005:

	Reported LIFO Numbers	Numbers if Using FIFO
Cost of goods sold	$26.558	$26.337
Average inventory	4.950	6.013
Inventory turnover	5.37	4.38
Number of days' sales in inventory	68.0 days	83.3 days

The difference in cost of goods sold for 2005 is not great because inflation was relatively low in that year. However, the difference in the reported average inventory balance reflects the cumulative effect of inflation for the many years since Caterpillar first started using LIFO. The impact on the ratio values is dramatic. Of course, the difference between LIFO and FIFO is not as great for most companies as shown here for Caterpillar, but the general point is that the choice of inventory cost flow assumption can affect the conclusions drawn about the financial statements—if the financial statement user is not careful.

Number of Days' Purchases in Accounts Payable

In Chapter 6, we introduced the average collection period ratio. In this chapter we have discussed the computation of the number of days' sales in inventory. Taken together, these two ratios indicate the length of a firm's operating cycle. The two ratios measure the amount of time it takes, on average, from the point when inventory is purchased to the point when cash is collected from the customer who purchased the inventory. For example, Sears' 131-day operating cycle for 2005 is depicted below.

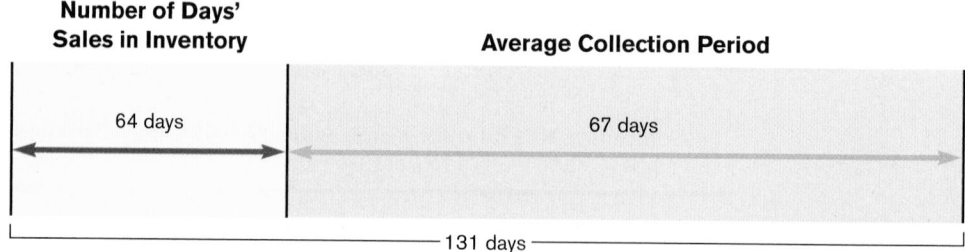

Is Sears' operating cycle too long, too short, or just right? That is difficult to tell without information from prior years and from competitors. But by including one additional ratio in the analysis, we can learn more about how Sears is managing its operating cash flow.

**number of days'
purchases in accounts
payable**

A measure of how well
operating cash flow is
being managed;
computed by dividing
total inventory purchases
by average accounts
payable and then dividing
365 days by the result.

The number of days' purchases in accounts payable reveals the average length of time that elapses between the purchase of inventory on account and the cash payment for that inventory. The **number of days' purchases in accounts payable** is computed by dividing total inventory purchases by average accounts payable and then dividing the result into 365 days:

$$\frac{\text{Number of Days' Purchases}}{\text{in Accounts Payable}} = \frac{365\ \text{Days}}{\text{Purchases/Average Accounts Payable}}$$

The amount of inventory purchased during a year is computed by combining cost of goods sold with the change in the inventory balance for the year. If inventory increased during the year, then inventory purchases are equal to cost of goods sold plus the increase in the inventory balance. Similarly, if inventory decreased during the year, inventory purchases are equal to cost of goods sold minus the decrease in the inventory balance.

The number of days' purchases in accounts payable indicates how long a company takes to pay its suppliers. For example, Sears' number of days' purchases in accounts payable for 2005 is computed as follows (dollar figures are in millions):

Cost of goods sold for 2005	$35,505
Add increase in inventory during 2005	5,787
Inventory purchases during 2005	$41,292
Average accounts payable during 2005	$ 2,193

$$\frac{\text{Number of Days' Purchases}}{\text{in Accounts Payable}} = \frac{365\ \text{Days}}{\$41,292/\$2,193}$$

$$= 19\ \text{days}$$

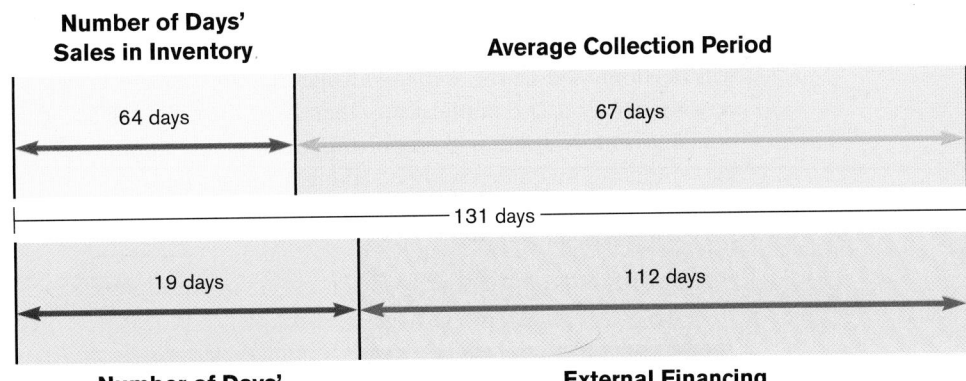

Number of Days' Sales in Inventory — 64 days | Average Collection Period — 67 days | 131 days | 19 days | 112 days | Number of Days' Purchases in Accounts Payable | External Financing Needed

CAUTION

This computation of the number of days' purchases in accounts payable assumes that only inventory purchases on account are included in accounts payable. It is likely that the accounts payable balance also includes such items as supplies purchased on account. Nevertheless, the purchase of inventory is typically the most significant element of accounts payable.

Sears must pay its suppliers in 19 days but must wait for 131 days before receiving the cash from its customers. Sears must finance the remaining 112 days (131 days − 19 days) of its operating cycle with bank loans or additional stockholder investment or by charging interest to those using its credit card debt. Sears is famous for using the last option—charging customers for the use of credit. In 2005 alone, Sears reported revenue from its credit card activities of over $213 million.

These calculations illustrate that proper management of the sales/collection cycle, coupled with prudent financing of inventory purchases on account, can reduce a company's reliance on external financing.

REMEMBER THIS...

- Proper inventory management seeks a balance between keeping a lower inventory level to avoid tying up excess resources and maintaining a sufficient inventory balance to ensure smooth business operation.

- Companies assess how well their inventory is being managed by using two ratios: (1) inventory turnover and (2) number of days' sales in inventory.

- A company's choice of inventory cost flow assumption can significantly affect the values of these inventory ratios; intelligent ratio analysis requires considering possible accounting differences among companies.

- Comparison of the average collection period, number of days' sales in inventory, and number of days' purchases in accounts payable reveals how much of a company's operating cycle it must finance through external financing.

Thus far we have defined inventory and cost of goods sold; we have described the perpetual and periodic inventory systems, three inventory cost flow assumptions, and the use of financial ratios to evaluate a company's management of its inventory. These topics are all sufficient for a basic understanding of the nature of inventory and cost of goods sold, as well as the most common ways of accounting for inventory. The four topics that will be discussed in the expanded material are (1) the impact of more complicated inventory errors, (2) complications that arise in using LIFO and average cost with a perpetual inventory system, (3) reporting inventory at amounts below cost, and (4) a method for estimating inventory without taking a physical count.

Inventory Errors

Analyze the impact of inventory errors on reported cost of goods sold.

6 Incorrect amounts for inventory on the balance sheet and cost of goods sold on the income statement can result from errors in counting inventories, recording inventory transactions, or both. The effect of an error in the end-of-period inventory count was discussed earlier in the chapter. To examine the effects of other types of inventory errors, we will assume that Richfield Company had the following inventory records for 2009:

Inventory balance, January 1, 2009	$ 8,000
Purchases through December 30, 2009	20,000
Inventory balance, December 30, 2009	12,000

We will further assume that on December 31 the company purchased and received another $1,000 of inventory. The following comparison shows the kinds of inventory situations that might result:

The $1,000 of merchandise purchased on December 31 was	**Incorrect*** not recorded as a purchase and not counted as inventory	**Incorrect** recorded as a purchase but not counted as inventory	**Incorrect** not recorded as a purchase but counted as inventory	**Correct** recorded as a purchase and counted as inventory
Beginning inventory	$ 8,000 (OK)**	$ 8,000 (OK)	$ 8,000 (OK)	$ 8,000 (OK)
Net purchases	20,000 (↓)	21,000 (OK)	20,000 (↓)	21,000 (OK)
Cost of goods available for sale	$28,000 (↓)	$29,000 (OK)	$28,000 (↓)	$29,000 (OK)
Ending inventory	12,000 (↓)	12,000 (↓)	13,000 (OK)	13,000 (OK)
Cost of goods sold	$16,000 (OK)	$17,000 (↑)	$15,000 (↓)	$16,000 (OK)

*This calculation produces the correct cost of goods sold but by an incorrect route–the errors in purchases and ending inventory offset each other.
**For the amount, ↓ indicates it is too low, ↑ means it is too high, and OK means it is correct.

In these calculations, the beginning inventory plus purchases equals the cost of goods that were "available for sale." In other words, everything that "could be sold" must have either been on hand at the beginning of the period (beginning inventory) or purchased during the period (net purchases). Then, ending inventory (what wasn't sold) was subtracted from the cost of goods available for sale. The result is the cost of goods that were sold. Everything on hand (available) had to be either sold or left in ending inventory. From this example, you can see how inventory and cost of goods sold can be misstated by the improper recording of inventory purchases or counting of inventory.

Similar errors can occur when inventory is sold. If a sale is recorded but the merchandise remains in the warehouse and is counted in the ending inventory, cost of goods sold will be understated, whereas gross margin and net income will be overstated. If a sale is not recorded but inventory is shipped and not counted in the ending inventory, gross margin and net income will be understated, and cost of goods sold will be overstated.

To illustrate these potential inventory errors, we will again consider the data of Richfield Company. Note that sales figures have been added and the ending inventory and the 2009 purchases now correctly include the $1,000 purchase of merchandise made on December 31, 2009.

Sales revenue through December 30, 2009 (200% of cost)	$32,000
Inventory balance, January 1, 2009	8,000
Net purchases during 2009	21,000
Inventory balance, December 31, 2009	13,000

In addition, assume that on December 31, inventory that cost $1,000 was sold for $2,000. The merchandise was delivered to the buyer on December 31. The following analysis shows the kinds of situations that might result:

The $2,000 sale on December 31 was	**Incorrect** not recorded and the merchandise was counted as inventory	**Incorrect** recorded and the merchandise was counted as inventory	**Incorrect** not recorded and the merchandise was excluded from inventory	**Correct** recorded and the merchandise was excluded from inventory
Sales revenue	$32,000 (↓)*	$34,000 (OK)	$32,000 (↓)	$34,000 (OK)
Cost of goods sold:				
Beginning inventory	$ 8,000 (OK)	$ 8,000 (OK)	$ 8,000 (OK)	$ 8,000 (OK)
Net purchases	21,000 (OK)	21,000 (OK)	21,000 (OK)	21,000 (OK)
Cost of goods available for sale	$29,000 (OK)	$29,000 (OK)	$29,000 (OK)	$29,000 (OK)
Ending inventory	13,000 (↑)	13,000 (↑)	12,000 (OK)	12,000 (OK)
Cost of goods sold	$16,000 (↓)	$16,000 (↓)	$17,000 (OK)	$17,000 (OK)
Gross margin	$16,000 (↓)	$18,000 (↑)	$15,000 (↓)	$17,000 (OK)

*For the amount, ↓ indicates it is too low, ↑ means it is too high, and OK means it is correct.

To reduce the possibility of these types of inventory cutoff errors, most businesses close their warehouses at year-end while they count inventory. If they are retailers, they will probably count inventory after hours. During the inventory counting period, businesses do not accept or ship merchandise, nor do they enter purchase or sales transactions in their accounting records.

As explained, an error in inventory results in cost of goods sold being overstated or understated. This error has the opposite effect on gross margin and, hence, on net income. For example, if at the end of the accounting period $2,000 of inventory is not counted, cost of goods sold will be $2,000 higher than it should be, and gross margin and net income will be understated by $2,000. Such inventory errors affect gross margin and net income not only in the current year but in the following year as well. A recording delay resulting in an understatement of purchases in one year, for example, results in an overstatement in the next year.

To illustrate how inventory errors affect gross margin and net income, let us first assume the following correct data for Salina Corporation:

		2008		2009
Sales revenue			$50,000	$40,000
Cost of goods sold:				
Beginning inventory	$10,000		$ 5,000	
Net purchases	20,000		25,000	
Cost of goods available for sale	$30,000		$30,000	
Ending inventory	5,000		10,000	
Cost of goods sold		25,000		20,000
Gross margin		$25,000		$20,000
Operating expenses		10,000		10,000
Net income		$15,000		$10,000

Now suppose that ending inventory in 2008 was overstated; that is, instead of the correct amount of $5,000, the count erroneously showed $7,000 of inventory on hand. The following analysis shows the effect of the error on net income in both 2008 and 2009:

		2008		2009
Sales revenue			$50,000	$40,000
Cost of goods sold:				
Beginning inventory	$10,000		$ 7,000 (↑)	
Net purchases	20,000		25,000	
Cost of goods available for sale	$30,000		$32,000 (↑)	
Ending inventory	7,000 (↑)*		10,000	
Cost of goods sold		23,000 (↓)		22,000 (↑)
Gross margin		$27,000 (↑)		$18,000 (↓)
Operating expenses		10,000		10,000
Net income		$17,000 (↑)		$ 8,000 (↓)

*For the amount, ↑ means it is too high, ↓ means it is too low.

When the amount of ending inventory is overstated (as it was in 2008), both gross margin and net income are overstated by the same amount ($2,000 in 2008). If the ending inventory amount had been understated, net income and gross margin would also have been understated, again by the same amount.

Since the ending inventory in 2008 becomes the beginning inventory in 2009, the net income and gross margin for 2009 are also misstated. In 2009, however, beginning inventory is overstated, so gross margin and net income are understated, again by $2,000.

Thus, the errors in the two years offset or counterbalance each other, and if the count taken at the end of 2009 is correct, income in subsequent years will not be affected by this error.

> **REMEMBER THIS...**
>
> - A misstatement of an ending inventory balance affects net income, both in the current year and in the next year.
> - Errors in beginning and ending inventory have the opposite effect on cost of goods sold, gross margin, and net income.
> - Errors in inventory correct themselves after two years if the physical count at the end of the second year shows the correct amount of ending inventory for that period.

Complications of the Perpetual Method with LIFO and Average Cost

Describe the complications that arise when LIFO or average cost is used with a perpetual inventory system.

(7) In the Nephi Company bicycle example used earlier in the chapter, the simplifying assumption was made that all 28 bicycles were sold at the end of the month. In essence, this is the assumption made when a periodic inventory system is used—goods are assumed to be sold at the end of the period because the exact time when particular goods are sold is not recorded. Computation of average cost and LIFO under a perpetual system is complicated because the average cost of units available for sale changes every time a purchase is made, and the identification of the "last in" units also changes with every purchase.

These perpetual system complications are illustrated below using the same Nephi Company example used earlier, but now assuming that sales occurred at different times during the month.

Sept. 1   Beginning inventory consisted of 10 bicycles costing $200 each.
     3   Purchased 8 bicycles costing $250 each.
     5   Sold 12 bicycles, $400 each.
   18   Purchased 16 bicycles costing $300 each.
   20   Purchased 10 bicycles costing $320 each.
   25   Sold 16 bicycles, $400 each.

When a perpetual system is used and sales occur during the period, the identification of the "last in" units must be evaluated at the time of each individual sale, as follows:

September 5 sale of 12 bicycles, identification of "last in" units:		
8 bicycles purchased on September 3, $250 each	$2,000	
4 bicycles in beginning inventory, $200 each	800	$2,800
September 25 sale of 16 bicycles, identification of "last in" units:		
10 bicycles purchased on September 20, $320 each	$3,200	
6 bicycles purchased on September 18, $300 each	1,800	5,000
Total perpetual LIFO cost of goods sold		$7,800

This $7,800 amount for LIFO cost of goods sold under a perpetual inventory system compares to the $8,500 LIFO cost of goods sold computed earlier in the chapter assuming a periodic inventory system. Again, the difference arises because the "last in" units are identified at the end of the period with a periodic system; with a perpetual system, the "last in" units are identified at the time of each individual sale.

A similar difference arises with the average cost method because, with a perpetual system, a new average cost per unit must be determined at the time each individual sale is made. This process is illustrated as follows:

September 5 sale of 12 bicycles, determination of average cost:

10 bicycles in beginning inventory, $200 each	$2,000	
8 bicycles purchased on September 3, $250 each	2,000	
Total cost of goods available for sale on September 5		$4,000

Average cost on September 5: $4,000 ÷ 18 bicycles = $222.22 per bicycle
September 5 cost of goods sold:
   12 bicycles × $222.22 per bicycle = $2,667 (rounded)

September 25 sale of 16 bicycles, determination of average cost:

6 (18 − 12) bicycles; remaining cost ($4,000 − $2,667)	$1,333	
16 bicycles purchased on September 18, $300 each	4,800	
10 bicycles purchased on September 20, $320 each	3,200	
Total cost of goods available for sale on September 25		$9,333

Average cost on September 25: $9,333 ÷ 32 bicycles = $291.66 per bicycle
September 25 cost of goods sold:
   16 bicycles × $291.66 per bicycle = $4,667 (rounded)

Total cost of goods sold: $2,667 + $4,667 = $7,334

This $7,334 cost of goods sold under the perpetual average method compares with $7,636 cost of goods sold under the periodic average method. Again, the difference is that one overall average cost for all goods available for sale during the period is used with a periodic system; with a perpetual system, a new average cost is computed at the time of each sale.

By the way, no complications arise in using FIFO with a perpetual system. This is because, no matter when sales occur, the "first in" units are always the same ones. So, FIFO periodic and FIFO perpetual yield the same numbers for cost of goods sold and ending inventory.

Because of the complications associated with computing perpetual LIFO and perpetual average cost, many businesses that use average cost or LIFO for financial reporting purposes use a simple FIFO assumption in maintaining their day-to-day perpetual inventory records. The perpetual FIFO records are then converted to periodic average cost or LIFO for the financial reports.

REMEMBER THIS...

- Using the average cost and LIFO inventory cost flow assumptions with a perpetual inventory system leads to some complications.
- These complications arise because the identity of the "last in" units changes with each new inventory purchase, as does the average cost of units purchased up to that point.

Reporting Inventory at Amounts below Cost

(8) All the inventory costing alternatives we have discussed in this chapter have one thing in common: they report inventory at cost. Occasionally, however, it becomes necessary to report inventory at an amount that is less than cost. This happens when the future value of the inventory is in doubt—when it is damaged, used, or obsolete, or when it can be replaced new at a price that is less than its original cost.

Inventory Valued at Net Realizable Value

net realizable value

The selling price of an item less reasonable selling costs.

When inventory is damaged, used, or obsolete, it should be reported at no more than its **net realizable value**. This is the amount the inventory can be sold for, minus any selling costs. Suppose, for example, that an automobile dealer has a demonstrator car that originally cost $18,000 and now can be sold for only $16,000. The car should be reported at its net realizable value. If a commission of $500 must be paid to sell the car, the net realizable value is $15,500, or $2,500 less than cost. This loss is calculated as follows:

Cost		$18,000
Estimated selling price	$16,000	
Less selling commission	500	15,500
Loss		$ 2,500

To achieve a proper matching of revenues and expenses, a company must recognize this estimated loss as soon as it is determined that an economic loss has occurred (even before the car is sold). The journal entry required to recognize the loss and reduce the inventory amount of the car is:

Loss on Write-Down of Inventory (Expense)	2,500	
Inventory		2,500
To write down inventory to its net realizable value.		

By writing down inventory to its net realizable value, a company recognizes a loss when it happens and shows no profit or loss when the inventory is finally sold. Using net realizable values means that assets are not being reported at amounts that exceed their future economic benefits.

lower-of-cost-or-market (LCM) rule

A basis for valuing inventory at the lower of original cost or current market value.

ceiling

The maximum market amount at which inventory can be carried on the books; equal to net realizable value.

Inventory Valued at Lower of Cost or Market

Inventory must also be written down to an amount below cost if it can be replaced new at a price that is less than its original cost. In the electronics industry, for instance, the costs of computers and compact disc players have fallen dramatically in recent years. When goods remaining in ending inventory can be replaced with identical goods at a lower cost, the lower unit cost must be used in valuing the inventory (provided that the replacement cost is not higher than net realizable value or lower than net realizable value minus a normal profit). This is known as the **lower-of-cost-or-market (LCM) rule**. (In a sense, a more precise name would be the lower-of-actual-or-replacement-cost rule.)

The **ceiling**, or maximum market amount at which inventory can be carried on the books, is equivalent to net realizable value, which is the selling price less

floor

The minimum market amount at which inventory can be carried on the books; equal to net realizable value minus a normal profit.

estimated selling costs. The ceiling is imposed because it makes no sense to value an inventory item above the amount that can be realized upon sale. For example, assume that a company purchased an inventory item for $10 and expected to sell it for $14. If the selling costs of the item amounted to $3, the ceiling or net realizable value would be $11 ($14 − $3).

The **floor** is defined as the net realizable value minus a normal profit. Thus, if the inventory item costing $10 had a normal profit margin of 20%, or $2, the floor would be $9 (net realizable value of $11 less normal profit of $2). This is the lowest amount at which inventory should be carried in order to prevent showing losses in one period and large profits in subsequent periods.

In applying this LCM rule, you can follow certain basic guidelines:

1. Define market value as:
    a. replacement cost, if it falls between the ceiling and the floor.
    b. the floor, if the replacement cost is less than the floor.
    c. the ceiling, if the replacement cost is higher than the ceiling.
        (As a practical matter, when replacement cost, ceiling, and floor are compared, market is always the middle value.)
2. Compare the defined market value with the original cost and choose the lower amount.

The following chart gives four separate examples of the application of the LCM rule; the resulting LCM amount is highlighted in each case.

				Market	
Item	Number of Items in Inventory	Original Cost (LIFO FIFO, etc.)	Replacement Cost	Net Realizable Value (Ceiling)	Net Realizable Value Minus Normal Profit (Floor)
A	10	$17	$16	$15	$10
B	8	21	18	23	16
C	30	26	21	31	22
D	20	19	16	34	25

The LCM rule can be applied in one of three ways: (1) by computing cost and market figures for each item in inventory and using the lower of the two amounts in each case, (2) by computing cost and market figures for the total inventory and then applying the LCM rule to that total, or (3) by applying the LCM rule to categories of inventory. For a clothing store, categories of inventory might be all shirts, all pants, all suits, or all dresses.

To illustrate, we will use the above data to show how the LCM rule would be applied to each inventory item separately and to total inventory. (The third method is similar to the second, except that it may involve several totals, one for each category of inventory.)

Item	Number of Items in Inventory	Original Cost	Market Value	LCM for Individual Items
A	10	$17 × 10 units = $ 170	$15 × 10 units = $ 150	$ 150
B	8	$21 × 8 units = 168	$18 × 8 units = 144	144
C	30	$26 × 30 units = 780	$22 × 30 units = 660	660
D	20	$19 × 20 units = 380	$25 × 20 units = 500	380
		$1,498	$1,454	$1,334

$44
$164

Using the first method, applying the LCM rule to individual items, inventory is valued at $1,334, a write-down of $164 from the original cost. With the second method, using total inventory, the lower of total cost ($1,498) or total market value ($1,454) is used for a write-down of $44. The write-down is smaller when total inventory is used because the increase in market value of $120 in item D offsets decreases in items A, B, and C. In practice, each of the three methods is acceptable, but once a method has been selected, it should be followed consistently.

The journal entry to write down the inventory to the lower of cost or market applying the LCM rule to individual items is:

Loss on Write-Down of Inventory (Expense)	164	
Inventory		164
To write down inventory to lower of cost or market.		

The amount of this entry would have been $44 if the LCM rule had been applied to total inventory.

The LCM rule has gained wide acceptance because it reports inventory on the balance sheet at amounts that are consistent with future economic benefits. With this method, losses are recognized when they occur, not necessarily when a sale is made.

REMEMBER THIS...

- The recorded amount of inventory should be written down (1) when it is damaged, used, or obsolete and (2) when it can be replaced (purchased new) at an amount that is less than its original cost.
- In the first case, inventory is reported at its net realizable value, an amount that allows a company to break even when the inventory is sold.
- In the second case, inventory is written down to the lower of cost or market.
- When using the lower-of-cost-or-market rule, market is defined as falling between the ceiling and floor.
- Ceiling is defined as the net realizable value; floor is net realizable value minus a normal profit margin.
- In no case should inventory be reported at an amount that exceeds the ceiling or is less than the floor.
- These reporting alternatives are attempts to show assets at amounts that reflect realistic future economic benefits.

Method of Estimating Inventories

Explain the gross margin method of estimating inventories.

(9) We have assumed that the number of inventory units on hand is known by a physical count that takes place at the end of each accounting period. For the periodic inventory method, this physical count is the only way to determine how much inventory is on hand at the end of a period. For the perpetual inventory method, the physical count verifies the quantity on hand or indicates the amount of inventory shrinkage or theft. There are times, however, when a company needs to know the dollar amount of ending inventory, but a physical count is either impossible or impractical. For example, many firms prepare quarterly, or even monthly, financial statements, but it is too expensive and time-consuming to count the inventory at the end of each period. In such cases, if the perpetual inventory method is being used, the balance in the inventory account is usually assumed to be

gross margin method

A procedure for estimating the amount of ending inventory; the historical relationship of cost of goods sold to sales revenue is used in computing ending inventory.

correct. With the periodic inventory method, however, some estimate of the inventory balance must be made. A common method of estimating the dollar amount of ending inventory is the gross margin method.

The Gross Margin Method

With the **gross margin method**, a firm uses available information about the dollar amounts of beginning inventory and purchases, and the historical gross margin percentage to estimate the dollar amounts of cost of goods sold and ending inventory.

To illustrate, we will assume the following data for Payson Brick Company:

Net sales revenue, January 1 to March 31	$100,000
Inventory balance, January 1	15,000
Net purchases, January 1 to March 31	65,000
Gross margin percentage (historically determined percentage of net sales)	40%

With this information, the dollar amount of inventory on hand on March 31 is estimated as follows:

		Dollars	**Percentage of Sales**
Net sales revenue		$100,000	100%
Cost of goods sold:			
Beginning inventory	$15,000		
Net purchases	65,000		
Total cost of goods available for sale	$80,000		
Ending inventory ($80,000 − $60,000)	20,000 (3)*		
Cost of goods sold ($100,000 − $40,000)		60,000 (2)*	60%
Gross margin ($100,000 × 0.40)		$ 40,000 (1)*	40%

*The numbers indicate the order of calculation.

In this example, gross margin is first determined by calculating 40% of sales (step 1). Next, cost of goods sold is found by subtracting gross margin from sales (step 2). Finally, the dollar amount of ending inventory is obtained by subtracting cost of goods sold from total cost of goods available for sale (step 3). Obviously, the gross margin method of estimating cost of goods sold and ending inventory assumes that the historical gross margin percentage is appropriate for the current period. This assumption is a realistic one in many fields of business. In cases where the gross margin percentage has changed, this method should be used with caution.

The gross margin method of estimating ending inventories is also useful when a fire or other calamity destroys a company's inventory. In these cases, the dollar amount of inventory lost must be determined before insurance claims can be made. The dollar amounts of sales, purchases, and beginning inventory can be obtained from prior years' financial statements and from customers, suppliers, and other sources. Then the gross margin method can be used to estimate the dollar amount of inventory lost.

REMEMBER THIS...

- The gross margin method is a common technique for estimating the dollar amount of inventory.
- The historical gross margin percentage is used in conjunction with sales to estimate cost of goods sold.
- This estimated cost of goods sold amount is subtracted from cost of goods available for sale to yield an estimate of ending inventory.

REVIEW OF LEARNING OBJECTIVES

(1) Identify what items and costs should be included in inventory and cost of goods sold.

- Inventory:
  - is composed of goods held for sale in the normal course of business,
  - includes all costs incurred in producing and getting it ready to sell,
  - includes raw materials, work in process, and finished goods in a manufacturing company, and
  - should be recorded on the books of the company holding legal title.

(2) Account for inventory purchases and sales using both a perpetual and a periodic inventory system.

- With a perpetual inventory system, the amount of inventory and cost of goods sold for the period are tracked on an ongoing basis.
- With a periodic inventory system, inventory and cost of goods sold are computed using an end-of-period inventory count.

(3) Calculate cost of goods sold using the results of an inventory count and understand the impact of errors in ending inventory on reported cost of goods sold.

- If a perpetual system is used, an inventory count can be used to compute the amount of inventory shrinkage during the period.
- An error in the reported ending inventory amount can have a significant effect on reported cost of goods sold, gross margin, and net income. For example, overstatement of ending inventory results in understatement of cost of goods sold and overstatement of net income.

(4) Apply the four inventory cost flow alternatives: specific identification, FIFO, LIFO, and average cost.

Specific Identification	No assumptions made; costs of specific units included in ending inventory and in cost of goods sold.
FIFO	Assume that the oldest inventory units are sold and that the newest remain in ending inventory.
LIFO	Assume that the newest inventory units are sold and that the oldest remain in ending inventory.
Average Cost	Assign a common average cost per unit to all units, both in cost of goods sold and in ending inventory.

(5) Use financial ratios to evaluate a company's inventory level.

- Proper inventory management seeks a balance between keeping a lower inventory level to avoid tying up excess resources and maintaining a sufficient inventory balance to ensure smooth business operation.
- Companies assess how well their inventory is being managed by using two ratios: (1) inventory turnover and (2) number of days' sales in inventory.
- Comparison of the average collection period, number of days' sales in inventory, and number of days' purchases in accounts payable reveals how much of a company's operating cycle it must finance through external financing.

(6) Analyze the impact of inventory errors on reported cost of goods sold.

- A misstatement of an ending inventory balance affects net income, both in the current year and in the next year.
- Errors in beginning and ending inventory have the opposite effect on cost of goods sold, gross margin, and net income.
- Errors in inventory correct themselves after two years if the physical count at the end of the second year shows the correct amount of ending inventory for that period.

(7) Describe the complications that arise when LIFO or average cost is used with a perpetual inventory system.

- When LIFO is used with a perpetual inventory system, the identification of the "newest unit" changes every time a purchase is made. Accordingly, identification of the units sold must be done sale by sale, using the specific timing of sales and purchases.
- When the average cost assumption is made with a perpetual inventory system, the "average cost" changes every time a purchase is made.

(8) Apply the lower-of-cost-or-market method of accounting for inventory.

- When using the lower-of-cost-or-market rule, market is defined as falling between the ceiling and floor.
- Ceiling is defined as the net realizable value; floor is net realizable value minus a normal profit margin.
- In no case should inventory be reported at an amount that exceeds the ceiling or is less than the floor.

(9) Explain the gross margin method of estimating inventories.

- The historical gross margin percentage can be used in conjunction with sales to estimate cost of goods sold.
- This estimated cost of goods sold amount is subtracted from cost of goods available for sale to yield an estimate of ending inventory.

KEY TERMS & CONCEPTS

average cost, 298
consignment, 287
cost of goods available
  for sale, 288
cost of goods sold, 286
FIFO (first in, first out), 298
finished goods, 286
FOB (free-on-board)
  destination, 287
FOB (free-on-board)
  shipping point, 287

inventory, 286
inventory shrinkage, 296
inventory turnover, 303
LIFO (last in, first
  out), 298
manufacturing
  overhead, 287
net purchases, 294
number of days'
  purchases in accounts
  payable, 305

number of days'
  sales in
  inventory, 303
periodic inventory
  system, 290
perpetual inventory
  system, 289
raw materials, 286
specific
  identification, 298
work in process, 286

EXPANDED *material*

ceiling, 311
floor, 312
gross margin
  method, 314
lower-of-cost-or-market
  (LCM) rule, 311
net realizable value, 311

REVIEW PROBLEMS

Inventory Cost Flow Alternatives

Lehi Wholesale Distributors buys printers from manufacturers and sells them to office supply stores. During January 2009, its periodic inventory records showed the following:

Jan. 1   Beginning inventory consisted of 26 printers at $200 each.
   10   Purchased 10 printers at $220 each.
   15   Purchased 20 printers at $250 each.
   28   Purchased 9 printers at $270 each.
   31   Sold 37 printers.

Required:

Calculate ending inventory and cost of goods sold, using:

1. FIFO inventory.
2. LIFO inventory.
3. Average cost.

Solution

When computing ending inventory and cost of goods sold, it is usually easiest to get an overview first. The following calculations are helpful:

Beginning inventory, 26 units at $200 each	$ 5,200
Purchases: 10 units at $220	$ 2,200
20 units at $250	5,000
9 units at $270	2,430
Total purchases (39 units)	$ 9,630
Cost of goods available for sale (65 units)	$14,830
Less ending inventory (28 units)	?
Cost of goods sold (37 units)	?

Given a beginning inventory, only ending inventory and cost of goods sold will vary with the different inventory costing alternatives. Because ending inventory and cost of goods sold are complementary numbers whose sum must equal total goods available for sale, you can calculate only one of the two missing numbers in each case and then compute the other by subtracting the first number from goods available for sale. Thus, in the calculations that follow, we will always calculate ending inventory first.

1. FIFO Inventory

Since we know that 28 units are left in ending inventory, we look for the last 28 units purchased because the first units purchased would all be sold. The last 28 units purchased were:

9 units at $270 each on January 28 =	$2,430
19 units at $250 each on January 15 =	4,750
Ending inventory	$7,180

Ending inventory is $7,180, and cost of goods sold is $7,650 ($14,830 - $7,180).

(continued)

2. LIFO Inventory

The first 28 units available would be considered the ending inventory (since the last ones purchased are the first ones sold). The first 28 units available were:

```
Beginning inventory: 26 units at $200 = $5,200
January 10 purchase: 2 units at $220 =    440
    Ending inventory ............    $5,640
```

Thus,

```
Cost of goods available for sale .....   $14,830
Ending inventory ...............           5,640
Cost of goods sold ............         $ 9,190
```

3. Average Cost

The total cost of goods available for sale is divided by total units available for sale to get a weighted average cost:

$$\frac{\text{Cost of Goods Available for Sale}}{\text{Units Available for Sale}} = \frac{\$14,830}{65} = \$228.15 \text{ per Unit}$$

```
Cost of goods available for sale ..............................   $14,830
Less ending inventory (28 units at $228.15) .....................     6,388
Cost of goods sold (37 units at $228.15) ......................   $ 8,442
```

Note: With the average cost alternative, the computed amounts may vary slightly due to rounding.

EXPANDED *material*

Perpetual Inventory Cost Flow Alternatives

Using the above example, we assume Lehi Wholesale Distributors buys printers from manufacturers and sells them to office supply stores. During January 2009, its inventory records showed the following:

Jan.   1   Beginning inventory consisted of 26 printers at $200 each.
   10   Purchased 10 printers at $220 each.
   12   Sold 15 printers.
   15   Purchased 20 printers at $250 each.
   17   Sold 14 printers.
   19   Sold 8 printers.
   28   Purchased 9 printers at $270 each.

Required:

Calculate ending inventory and cost of goods sold, using:
1. Perpetual FIFO inventory.
2. Perpetual LIFO inventory.
3. Perpetual average cost.

(continued)

Solution

When computing ending inventory and cost of goods sold, it is usually easiest to get an overview first. The following calculations are helpful:

Beginning inventory, 26 units at $200 each	$ 5,200
Purchases: 10 units at $220	$ 2,200
20 units at $250	5,000
9 units at $270	2,430
Total purchases (39 units)	$ 9,630
Cost of goods available for sale (65 units)	$14,830
Less ending inventory (28 units)	?
Cost of goods sold (37 units)	?

Given a beginning inventory, only ending inventory and cost of goods sold will vary with the different inventory costing alternatives. Because ending inventory and cost of goods sold are complementary numbers whose sum must equal total goods available for sale, you can calculate only one of the two missing numbers in each case, and then compute the other by subtracting the first number from goods available for sale. Thus, in the calculations that follow, we will always calculate ending inventory first.

1. Perpetual FIFO Inventory

With this alternative, records must be maintained throughout the period, as shown. The final calculation is:

Cost of goods available for sale	$14,830
Ending inventory [(19 × $250) + (9 × $270)]	7,180
Cost of goods sold	$ 7,650

PERPETUAL FIFO CALCULATIONS

Date	Purchased Number of Units	Unit Cost	Total Cost	Sold Number of Units	Unit Cost	Total Cost	Remaining Number of Units	Unit Cost	Total Cost
Beginning inventory							26	$200	$5,200
January 10	10	$220	$2,200				36	26 at $200 10 at $220	$7,400
12				15	15 at $200	$3,000	21	11 at $200 10 at $220	$4,400
15	20	$250	5,000				41	11 at $200 10 at $220 20 at $250	$9,400
17				14	11 at $200 3 at $220	2,860	27	7 at $220 20 at $250	$6,540
19				8	7 at $220 1 at $250	1,790	19	19 at $250	$4,750
28	9	$270	2,430	—		——	28	19 at $250 9 at $270	$7,180
Totals	39		$9,630	37		$7,650			

(continued)

2. Perpetual LIFO Inventory

With this alternative, as shown below, the calculation is:

Cost of goods available for sale	$14,830
Ending inventory	6,230
Cost of goods sold	$ 8,600

PERPETUAL LIFO CALCULATIONS

Date	Purchased Number of Units	Unit Cost	Total Cost	Sold Number of Units	Unit Cost	Total Cost	Remaining Number of Units	Unit Cost	Total Cost
Beginning inventory							26	$200	$5,200
January 10	10	$220	$2,200				36	26 at $200 10 at $220	$7,400
12				15	10 at $220 5 at $200	$3,200	21	21 at $200	$4,200
15	20	$250	5,000				41	21 at $200 20 at $250	$9,200
17				14	14 at $250	3,500	27	21 at $200 6 at $250	$5,700
19				8	6 at $250 2 at $200	1,900	19	19 at $200	$3,800
28	9	$270	2,430	—		—	28	19 at $200 9 at $270	$6,230
Totals	39		$9,630	37		$8,600			

3. Perpetual Average Cost

With this alternative, a new average cost of inventory items must be calculated each time a purchase is made, as shown in the following table:

Cost of goods available for sale	$14,830
Ending inventory	6,748
Cost of goods sold	$ 8,082

PERPETUAL AVERAGE COST CALCULATIONS

	Purchased	Sold	Remaining	Computations
Beginning inventory			26 units at $200.00 = $5,200	
January 10	10 units at $220 = $2,200		36 units at $205.56 = $7,400	$5,200 + $2,200 = $7,400; $7,400 ÷ 36 = $205.56
12		15 units at $205.56 = $3,083	21 units at $205.56 = $4,317	
15	20 units at $250 = $5,000		41 units at $227.24 = $9,317	$4,317 + $5,000 = $9,317; $9,317 ÷ 41 = $227.24
17		14 units at $227.24 = $3,181	27 units at $227.24 = $6,135	
19		8 units at $227.24 = $1,818	19 units at $227.24 = $4,318	
28	9 units at $270 = $2,430		28 units at $241.00 = $6,748	$4,318 + $2,430 = $6,748; $6,748 ÷ 28 = $241.00

DISCUSSION QUESTIONS

1. In wholesale and retail companies, inventory is composed of the items that have been purchased for resale. What types of inventory does a manufacturing firm have?
2. What comprises the cost of inventory?
3. Why is it more difficult to account for the inventory of a manufacturing firm than for that of a merchandising firm?
4. Who owns merchandise during shipment under the terms FOB shipping point?
5. When is the cost of inventory transferred from an asset to an expense?
6. Which inventory method (perpetual or periodic) provides better control over a firm's inventory?
7. Is the accounting for purchase discounts and purchase returns the same with the perpetual and the periodic inventory methods? If not, what are the differences?
8. Are the costs of transporting inventory into and out of a firm treated the same way? If not, what are the differences?
9. Why is it usually important to take advantage of purchase discounts?
10. Why are the closing entries for inventory under a periodic system more complicated than those for a perpetual system?
11. Why is it necessary to physically count inventory when the perpetual inventory method is being used?
12. What adjusting entries to Inventory are required when the perpetual inventory method is used?
13. What is the effect on net income when goods held on consignment are included in the ending inventory balance?

14. Explain the difference between cost flow and the movement of goods.
15. Which inventory cost flow alternative results in paying the least amount of taxes when prices are rising?
16. Would a firm ever be prohibited from using one inventory costing alternative for tax purposes and another for financial reporting purposes?
17. Why is it necessary to know which inventory cost flow alternative is being used before the financial performances of different firms can be compared?
18. What can the inventory turnover ratio tell us?

19. Is net income under- or overstated when purchased merchandise is counted and included in the inventory balance but not recorded as a purchase?
20. Is net income under- or overstated if inventory is sold and shipped but not recorded as a sale?
21. Why do the LIFO and average cost inventory cost flow assumptions result in different inventory numbers for the perpetual and periodic inventory methods?
22. When should inventory be valued at its net realizable value?
23. When should inventory be valued at the lower of cost or market?
24. When firms cannot count their inventory, how do they determine how much inventory is on hand for the financial statements?

PRACTICE EXERCISES

PE 7-1 **Inventory Identification**
LO1 Which one of the following is *not* an example of inventory?
   a. Cranes at a construction site
   b. Books on the shelves of a bookstore
   c. Apples in a supermarket
   d. Screws to be used in assembling tables at a carpentry shop
   e. Computer software for sale at a computer store

PE 7-2 **Costs Included in Inventory**
LO1 Which one of the following costs is *not* included in inventory?
   a. Salaries paid to assembly workers
   b. Direct materials used in assembly
   c. Salary paid to the company president
   d. Rent paid for use of the company factory
   e. Salary paid to the factory supervisor

PE 7-3   **Goods in Transit**

LO1   Collin Wholesale sold $2,500 inventory to Jennifer Company on December 27, year 1, with shipping terms of FOB destination. The inventory arrived on January 2, year 2. Which company owns the inventory at year-end (December 31, year 1)?

PE 7-4   **Computing Cost of Goods Sold**

LO1   Using the following data, compute cost of goods sold.

Inventory, December 31	$ 51,000
Inventory, January 1	63,000
Cash, December 31	19,000
Purchases during the year	287,000
Sales during the year	505,000

PE 7-5   **Perpetual and Periodic Inventory Systems**

LO2   For each of the following businesses, indicate whether the business would be more likely to use a perpetual or a periodic inventory system.

a. Automobile dealer
b. Summer snow-cone stand
c. Supermarket

d. Large appliance retailer
e. Newsstand
f. Discount clothing retailer

PE 7-6   **Inventory Purchases**

LO2   The company purchased (on account) 180 tables to be resold to customers. The cost of each table was $200. Make the journal entry to record this transaction under (1) a perpetual inventory system and (2) a periodic inventory system.

PE 7-7   **Transportation Costs**

LO2   The company incurred $830 in shipping costs related to the inventory purchases in PE 7-6. The company paid for the shipping costs in cash. Make the journal entry necessary to record this transaction under (1) a perpetual inventory system and (2) a periodic inventory system.

PE 7-8   **Purchase Returns**

LO2   The company returned 15 of the tables purchased in PE 7-6 because of defects in assembly. Make the journal entry necessary to record this return under (1) a perpetual inventory system and (2) a periodic inventory system.

PE 7-9   **Purchase Discounts**

LO2   The company paid for the tables purchased in PE 7-6 (less the tables returned in PE 7-8). Because the company paid within 10 days, it received a 2% discount on the purchase. Make the journal entry necessary to record this transaction under (1) a perpetual inventory system and (2) a periodic inventory system.

PE 7-10   **Sales**

LO2   The company sold 70 tables on account for $240 each. Make the journal entry or entries necessary to record this transaction under (1) a perpetual inventory system and (2) a periodic inventory system. Don't forget the impact of the 2% discount described in PE 7-9 and the transportation costs mentioned in PE 7-7.

PE 7-11   **Sales Returns**

LO2   A dissatisfied customer returned six of the tables that were sold in PE 7-10. Make the journal entry or entries necessary to record this transaction under (1) a perpetual inventory system and (2) a periodic inventory system.

PE 7-12   **Closing Inventory Entries for a Periodic System**

LO3   Refer to the data in PE 7-6 through PE 7-11. Assume the beginning balance in the inventory account was $0 for the periodic inventory system. A physical count of the inventory at the

(continued)

end of the period shows the ending balance of inventory is $19,970. Prepare the necessary entries for a periodic inventory system (1) to close the temporary accounts to the inventory account and (2) to adjust the inventory account to the appropriate ending balance.

PE 7-13
LO3

Inventory Shrinkage

The company's perpetual inventory records show that the ending inventory balance should be $182,000. However, a physical count of the inventory reveals the true ending balance of inventory to be $178,500. Prepare the journal entry necessary to record inventory shrinkage for the period.

PE 7-14
LO3

Computing Cost of Goods Sold with a Periodic System

The company uses a periodic inventory system. Beginning inventory was $6,000. Net purchases (including freight in, purchase returns, and purchase discounts) were $23,000. The physical count of inventory at the end of the year revealed ending inventory to be $7,500. Compute cost of goods sold.

PE 7-15
LO3

Errors in Ending Inventory

The company uses a periodic inventory system and overstated its ending inventory by $20,000. How will this inventory error affect reported net income for the company?

PE 7-16
LO4

Specific Identification Inventory Cost Flow

The company reports the following activity during October related to its inventory of cameras:

Oct. 1   Beginning inventory consisted of 8 cameras costing $100 each.
      3   Purchased 12 cameras costing $110 each.
     14   Purchased 7 cameras costing $115 each.
     20   Purchased 15 cameras costing $125 each.
     29   Sold 26 cameras for $150 each.

The 26 cameras sold on October 29 consisted of the following: 4 cameras from the beginning inventory, 5 cameras purchased on October 3, 3 cameras purchased on October 14, and 14 cameras purchased on October 20. Determine (1) the cost of goods sold for the month and (2) the ending inventory balance for October 31 using the specific identification cost flow assumption.

PE 7-17
LO4

FIFO Cost Flow Assumption

Refer to the data in PE 7-16. Determine (1) the cost of goods sold for the month and (2) the ending inventory balance for October 31 using the FIFO cost flow assumption.

PE 7-18
LO4

LIFO Cost Flow Assumption

Refer to the data in PE 7-16. Determine (1) the cost of goods sold for the month and (2) the ending inventory balance for October 31 using the LIFO cost flow assumption.

PE 7-19
LO4

Average Cost Flow Assumption

Refer to the data in PE 7-16. Determine (1) the cost of goods sold for the month and (2) the ending inventory balance for October 31 using the average cost flow assumption. Round unit costs to the nearest tenth of a cent.

PE 7-20
LO5

Inventory Turnover

Using the following data, compute inventory turnover.

Inventory, December 31, year 1	$ 82,000
Cost of goods sold	342,000
Sales	694,000
Inventory, January 1, year 1	74,000

PE 7-21   **Number of Days' Sales in Inventory**

LO5   Refer to the data in PE 7-20. Compute number of days' sales in inventory.

PE 7-22   **Number of Days' Purchases in Accounts Payable**

LO5   Using the following data, compute number of days' purchases in accounts payable.

Accounts payable, December 31, year 1	$ 52,000
Cost of goods sold	358,000
Accounts payable, January 1, year 1	46,000
Purchases	364,000

EXPANDED
material

PE 7-23   **Inventory Errors–Multiple Years**

LO6   At the beginning of year 1, the company's inventory level was stated correctly. At the end of year 1, inventory was *understated* by $2,000. At the end of year 2, inventory was *overstated* by $450. Reported net income was $3,000 in year 1 and $3,000 in year 2. Compute the correct amount of net income in year 1.

PE 7-24   **Inventory Errors–Multiple Years**

LO6   Refer to PE 7-23. Compute the correct amount of net income in year 2.

PE 7-25   **LIFO and a Perpetual Inventory System**

LO7   The company reported the following inventory data for the year:

	Units	Cost per Unit
Beginning inventory	300	$17.50
Purchases:		
July 15	900	18.00
October 11	1,200	18.25
Units remaining at year-end: 300		

Sales occurred as follows:

	Units Sold
January 16	200
July 23	600
November 1	1,300
Total	2,100

Compute (1) cost of goods sold and (2) ending inventory making a LIFO cost flow assumption. The company uses a *perpetual* inventory system.

PE 7-26   **Average Cost and a Perpetual Inventory System**

LO7   Refer to PE 7-25. Compute (1) cost of goods sold and (2) ending inventory making an average cost assumption. The company uses a perpetual inventory system.

PE 7-27   **Lower of Cost or Market**

LO8   The following information pertains to the company's ending inventory:

	Original Cost	Net Realizable Value	Replacement Cost	Normal Profit
Item A	$ 720	$ 740	$ 710	$ 80
Item B	390	400	310	70
Item C	1,250	1,300	1,230	250

Apply lower-of-cost-or-market accounting to each inventory item individually. What total amount should be reported as inventory in the balance sheet?

PE 7-28   **Recording an Inventory Write-Down**

LO9   The company started business at the beginning of year 1. The company applies the lower-of-cost-or-market (LCM) rule to its inventory as a whole. Inventory cost and market value as of the end of year 1 were as follows:

	Cost	Market Value
Year 1	$1,200	$900

The market value number already includes consideration of the replacement cost, the ceiling, and the floor. Make the journal entry necessary to record the LCM adjustment at the end of year 1.

PE 7-29   **Estimating Inventory**

LO9   On August 17, the company's inventory was destroyed in a hurricane-related flood. For insurance purposes, the company must reliably estimate the amount of inventory on hand on August 17. The company uses a periodic inventory system. The following data have been assembled:

Inventory, January 1	$1,650,000
Purchases, January 1–August 17	4,130,000
Sales, January 1–August 17	6,500,000
Historical gross profit percentages:	
Last year	60%
Two years ago	65%

Estimate the company's inventory as of August 17 using (1) last year's gross profit percentage and (2) the gross profit percentage from two years ago.

EXERCISES

E 7-30   **Goods on Consignment**

LO1   Company A has consignment arrangements with Supplier B and with Customer C. In particular, Supplier B ships some of its goods to Company A on consignment, and Company A ships some of its goods to Customer C on consignment. At the end of 2009, Company A's accounting records showed:

Goods on consignment from Supplier B	$ 8,000
Goods on consignment with Customer C	10,000

(continued)

1. If a physical count of inventory reveals that $30,000 of goods are on hand, what amount of ending inventory should be reported?
2. If the amount of the beginning inventory for the year was $27,000 and purchases during the year were $59,000, then what is the cost of goods sold for the year? (Assume the ending inventory from question 1.)
3. If, instead of these facts, Company A had only $4,000 of goods on consignment with Customer C, but had $10,000 of consigned goods from Supplier B, and physical goods on hand totaled $36,000, what would the correct amount of the ending inventory be?
4. With respect to question 3, if beginning inventory totaled $24,000 and the cost of goods sold was $47,500, what were the purchases?

E 7-31

LO2

Recording Sales Transactions–Perpetual Inventory Method

On June 24, 2009, Reed Company sold merchandise to Emily Clark for $95,000 with terms 2/10, n/30. On June 30, Clark paid $44,100, receiving the cash discount on her payment, and returned $15,000 of merchandise, claiming that it did not meet contract terms.

Assuming that Reed uses the perpetual inventory method, record the necessary journal entries on June 24 and June 30. The cost of merchandise to Reed Company is 60% of its selling price.

E 7-32

LO2

Perpetual Inventory Method

Orser Furniture purchases and sells dining room furniture. Its management uses the perpetual method of inventory accounting. Journalize the following transactions that occurred during October 2009:

Oct. 2 Purchased on account $27,000 of inventory with payment terms 2/10, n/30, and paid $650 in cash to have it shipped from the vendor's warehouse to the Orser showroom.
       5 Sold inventory costing $4,900 for $8,250 on account.
      10 Paid $13,950 of accounts payable (from October 2 purchase) and received the cash discount.
      14 Returned two damaged tables purchased on October 2 (costing $550 each) to the vendor.
      19 Received payment of $4,560 from customers.
      20 Paid the balance of the account from October 2 purchase.
      22 Sold inventory costing $3,800 for $5,200 on account.
      24 A customer returned a dining room set that she decided didn't match her home. She paid $3,250 for it, and its cost to Orser was $1,800.

Assuming the balance in the inventory account is $12,000 on October 1, and no other transactions relating to inventory occurred during the month, what is the inventory balance at the end of October?

E 7-33

LO2

Recording Sales Transactions–Periodic Inventory Method

On June 24, 2009, Mowen Company sold merchandise to Jack Simpson for $80,000 with terms 2/10, n/30. On June 30, Simpson paid $39,200, receiving the cash discount on his payment, and returned $16,000 of merchandise, claiming that it did not meet contract terms.

Assuming that Mowen Company uses the periodic inventory method, record the necessary journal entries on June 24 and June 30.

E 7-34

LO2

Cost of Goods Sold Calculations

Complete the Cost of Goods Sold section for the income statements of the following five companies:

	Able Company	Baker Company	Carter Company	Delmont Company	Eureka Company
Beginning inventory	$16,000	$24,800			$19,200
Purchases	26,500		$43,000	$89,500	
Purchase returns		1,000	1,800	200	2,200
Cost of goods available for sale	42,100		58,300		81,500
Ending inventory		22,200	15,200	28,800	
Cost of goods sold	33,400	67,200		93,400	68,400

E 7-35

LO2

Journalizing Inventory Transactions

Shannon Parts uses the periodic method of inventory accounting.

1. Journalize the following transactions relating to the company's purchases in 2009:

Jan. 24 Purchased $18,000 of inventory on credit, terms 2/10, n/30.

30 Paid $17,640 to pay off the debt from the January 24 purchase.

Mar. 14 Purchased $140,000 of inventory on credit, terms 2/10, n/30. Paid $1,150 in cash for transportation.

Apr. 1 Returned defective machinery worth $25,000 from the March 14 purchase to manufacturer.

13 Paid $115,000 to pay off the debt from the March 14 purchase.

2. Assuming these were the only purchases in 2009, compute the cost of goods sold. Beginning inventory was $23,400 and ending inventory was $26,250.

E 7-36

LO3

Adjusting Inventory (Perpetual Method)

Deer Company's perpetual inventory records show an inventory balance of $120,000. Deer Company's records also show cost of goods sold totaling $240,000. A physical count of inventory on December 31, 2009, showed $92,000 of ending inventory.

Adjust the inventory records assuming that the perpetual inventory method is used.

E 7-37

LO3

Adjusting Inventory and Closing Entries (Periodic Method)

As of December 31, 2009, Whitney Company had the following account balances:

Inventory (beginning)	$140,000
Purchases	230,000
Purchase returns	6,000

A physical count of inventory on December 31, 2009, showed $104,000 of ending inventory. Prepare the closing entries that are needed to adjust the inventory records and close the related purchases accounts, assuming that the periodic inventory method is used.

E 7-38

LO3

Cost of Goods Sold Calculation

The accounts of Berrett Company have the following balances for 2009:

Purchases	$520,000
Inventory, January 1, 2009	80,000
Purchase returns	15,280
Purchase discounts	1,760
Freight in	24,800
Freight out (selling expense)	4,800
Cash	8,000

The inventory count on December 31, 2009, is $96,000. Using the information given, compute the cost of goods sold for Berrett Company for 2009.

E 7-39   **Adjusting Inventory Records for Physical Counts**

LO3   Cleopatra, Inc., which uses the perpetual inventory method, recently had an agency count its inventory of frozen burritos. The agency left the following inventory sheet:

Type of Merchandise	Date Purchased	Quantity on Hand	Unit Cost	Inventory Amount
Chicken Burrito	2/12/09	50	$2.50	(a)
Beef Burrito	2/18/09	19	(b)	$60.80
Bean Burrito	2/08/09	(c)	$2.10	$65.10
Veggie Burrito	2/15/09	43	(d)	$81.70

Complete the inventory calculations for Cleopatra (items a–d) and provide the journal entry necessary to adjust ending inventory, if necessary. The balance in Inventory before the physical count was $321.10.

E 7-40   **Specific Identification Method**

LO4   E's Diamond Shop is computing its inventory and cost of goods sold for November 2009. At the beginning of the month, these items were in stock:

	Quantity	Cost	Total
Ring A	8	$600	$ 4,800
Ring A	10	650	6,500
Ring B	5	300	1,500
Ring B	6	350	2,100
Ring B	3	450	1,350
Ring C	7	200	1,400
Ring C	8	250	2,000
			$19,650

During the month, the shop purchased four type A rings at $600, two type B rings at $450, and five type C rings at $300 and made the following sales:

Ring Type	Quantity Sold	Price	Cost
A	2	$1,000	$600
A	3	1,050	600
A	1	1,200	650
B	2	850	450
B	2	800	350
C	4	450	200
C	3	500	250
C	1	550	250

Because of the high cost per item, E's uses specific identification inventory costing.

1. Calculate the cost of goods sold and ending inventory balances for November.
2. Calculate the gross margin for the month.

E 7-41   **Inventory Costing Methods**

LO4   For each of the descriptions listed below, identify the inventory costing method to which it applies. The costing methods are: average cost, LIFO, and FIFO.

1. The value of ending inventory does not include the cost of the most recently acquired goods.
2. In a period of rising prices, cost of goods sold is highest.
3. In a period of rising prices, ending inventory is highest.
4. Ending inventory is between the levels of the other two methods.
5. The balance of the inventory account may be unrealistic because inventory on hand is valued at old prices.

E 7-42   **FIFO and LIFO Inventory Costing**

LO4   Jefferson's Jewelry Store is computing its inventory and cost of goods sold for November 2009. At the beginning of the month, the following jewelry items were in stock (rings were purchased in the order listed):

	Quantity	Cost	Total
Ring A	8	$600	$ 4,800
Ring A	10	650	6,500
Ring B	5	300	1,500
Ring B	6	350	2,100
Ring B	3	450	1,350
Ring C	7	200	1,400
Ring C	8	250	2,000
			$19,650

During the month, the following rings were purchased: four type A rings at $600, two type B rings at $450, and five type C rings at $300. Also during the month, these sales were made:

Ring Type	Quantity Sold	Price
A	2	$1,000
A	3	1,050
A	1	1,200
B	2	850
B	2	800
C	4	450
C	3	500
C	1	550

Jefferson's uses the periodic inventory method. Calculate the cost of goods sold and ending inventory balances for November using FIFO and LIFO.

E 7-43   **FIFO, LIFO, and Average Cost Calculations (Periodic Inventory Method)**

LO4   The following transactions took place with respect to Model B computers in Jackson's Computer Store during November 2009:

Nov.	1	Beginning inventory	60 computers at $1,350
	5	Purchase of Model B computers	14 computers at $1,400
	11	Purchase of Model B computers	12 computers at $1,500
	24	Purchase of Model B computers	18 computers at $1,750
	30	Sale of Model B computers	40 computers at $2,700

Assuming the periodic inventory method, compute cost of goods sold and ending inventory using the following inventory costing alternatives: (a) FIFO, (b) LIFO, and (c) average cost.

E 7-44   **Inventory Ratios**

LO5   The following data are available for 2009, regarding the inventory of two companies:

	Atkins Computers	Burbank Electronics
Beginning inventory	$ 40,000	$ 80,000
Ending inventory	48,000	95,000
Cost of goods sold	690,000	910,000

Compute inventory turnover and number of days' sales in inventory for both companies. Which company is handling its inventory more efficiently?

E 7-45

LO5

Analysis of the Operating Cycle

The following information was taken from the records of Dallen Company for the year 2010:

Sales	$600,000
Beginning inventory	$114,000
Ending inventory	$87,000
Beginning accounts receivable	$68,000
Average collection period	44 days
Beginning accounts payable	$36,000
Ending accounts payable	$42,000
Gross profit percentage	37%

1. Compute the number of days' sales in inventory.
2. Compute the ending balance in Accounts Receivable.
3. Compute the number of days' purchases in accounts payable.
4. How many days elapse, on average, between the time Dallen must pay its suppliers for inventory purchases and the time Dallen collects cash from its customers for the sale of that same purchased inventory?
5. Repeat the computations in (1), (2), (3), and (4) using the end-of-year balance sheet balances rather than the average balances.

E 7-46

LO6

Inventory Errors

As the accountant for Synergy Solutions, you are in the process of preparing the income statement for the year ended December 31, 2009. In doing so, you have noticed that merchandise costing $3,500 was sold for $5,000 on December 31.

Before the effects of the $5,000 sale were taken into account, the relevant income statement figures were:

Sales revenue	$95,000
Beginning inventory	21,000
Purchases	38,000
Ending inventory	19,000

1. Prepare a partial income statement through gross margin under each of the following three assumptions:
   a. The sale is recorded in the 2009 accounting record; the inventory is included in the ending physical inventory count.
   b. The sale is recorded in 2009; the inventory is not included in ending inventory.
   c. The sale is not recorded in the 2009 accounting records; the merchandise is not included in the ending inventory count.
2. Under the given circumstances, which of the three assumptions is correct?
3. Which assumption overstates gross margin (and therefore net income)?

E 7-47

LO7

FIFO, LIFO, and Average Cost Calculations (Perpetual Inventory Method)

The July 2009 inventory records of Mario's Bookstore showed the following:

July	1	Beginning inventory	28,000 at $2.00 = $56,000
	5	Sold	4,000
	13	Purchased	6,000 at $2.25 = 13,500
	17	Sold	3,000
	25	Purchased	8,000 at $2.50 = 20,000
	27	Sold	5,000
			$89,500

(continued)

1. Using the perpetual inventory method, compute the ending inventory and cost of goods sold balances with (a) FIFO, (b) LIFO, and (c) average cost. Compute unit costs to the nearest cent.
2. Which of the three alternatives is best? Why?

E 7-48

LO8

Lower of Cost or Market

Prepare the necessary journal entries to account for the purchases and year-end adjustments of the inventory of Payson Manufacturing Company. All purchases are made on account. Payson uses the periodic inventory method.

1. Purchased 50 standard widgets for $8 each to sell at $14 per unit.
2. Purchased 15 deluxe widgets at $20 each to sell for $30 per unit.
3. At the end of the year, the standard widgets could be purchased for $9 and are selling for $15.
4. At the end of the year, the deluxe widgets could be purchased for $10 and are selling for $16 per unit. Selling costs are $4 per unit, and normal profit is $6 per unit. Inventory is 15 units.
5. At the end of the second year, standard widgets could be purchased for $6 and are selling for $8. Selling costs are $1 per widget, and normal profit is $2 per widget. Inventory is 50 units.
6. At the end of the second year, the deluxe widgets could be purchased for $9 and are selling for $20. Selling costs and normal profit remain as in (4). Inventory is 15 units.

E 7-49

LO8

Lower of Cost or Market

Duncan Company sells lumber. Inventory cost data per 1,000 board feet of lumber for Duncan Company are as follows:

Item	Plywood	Maple	Pine	Redwood
Quantity on hand	21	23	38	16
Original cost	$450	$1,900	$700	$1,600
Current replacement cost	400	1,700	550	1,650
Net realizable value	350	1,850	650	1,700
Net realizable value minus normal profit	250	1,600	600	1,500

1. By what amount, if any, should each item (considered separately) be written down?
2. Make the appropriate journal entry (or entries):
   a. Assuming that each inventory item is considered separately.
   b. Assuming that LCM is applied to total inventory.

E 7-50

LO9

Gross Margin Method of Estimating Inventory

Jason Company needs to estimate the inventory balance for its quarterly financial statements. The periodic inventory method is used. Records show that quarterly sales totaled $400,000, beginning inventory was $80,000, and net purchases totaled $280,000; the historical gross margin percentage has averaged approximately 40%.

1. What is the approximate amount of ending inventory?
2. If a physical count shows only $100,000 in inventory, what could be the explanation for the difference?

E 7-51

LO9

Estimating Inventory Amounts

Erin's Boutique was recently destroyed by fire. For insurance purposes, she must determine the value of the destroyed inventory. She knows the following information about her 2009 operations before the fire occurred:

Beginning inventory	$ 5,750
Net purchases	58,000
Sales	91,300
Profit margin	35%

Estimate the cost of Erin's destroyed inventory.

E 7-52

LO9

Estimating Inventory

Ted Smyth manages an electronics store. He suspects that some employees are stealing items from inventory. Determine the cost of the missing inventory. The following information is available from the accounting records:

Beginning inventory	$ 300,000
Sales	2,000,000
Net purchases	1,600,000
Actual ending inventory	450,000
Historical profit margin	30%

PROBLEMS

P 7-53

LO1

What Should Be Included in Inventory?

Howard is trying to compute the inventory balance for the December 31, 2008, financial statements of his automotive parts shop. He has computed a tentative balance of $61,800 but suspects that several adjustments still need to be made. In particular, he believes that the following could affect his inventory balance:

a. A shipment of goods that cost $2,000 was received on December 28, 2008. It was properly recorded as a purchase in 2008 but not counted with the ending inventory.

b. Another shipment of goods (FOB destination) was received on January 2, 2009, and cost $1,200. It was properly recorded as a purchase in 2009 but was counted with 2008's ending inventory.

c. A $3,400 shipment of goods to a customer on January 3 was recorded as a sale in 2009 but was not included in the December 31, 2008, ending inventory balance. The goods cost $2,300.

d. The company had goods costing $8,000 on consignment with a customer, and $6,000 of merchandise was on consignment from a vendor. Neither amount was included in the $61,800 figure.

e. The following amounts represent merchandise that was in transit on December 31, 2008, and recorded as purchases and sales in 2008 but not included in the December 31 inventory.

   1. Ordered by Howard, $2,600, FOB destination.
   2. Ordered by Howard, $900, FOB shipping point.
   3. Sold by Howard, cost $3,400, FOB shipping point.
   4. Sold by Howard, cost $5,100, FOB destination.

Required:

1. Determine the correct amount of ending inventory at December 31, 2008.
2. Assuming net purchases (before any adjustment, if any) totaled $79,200 and beginning inventory (January 1, 2008) totaled $38,700, determine the cost of goods sold in 2008.

P 7-54

LO2

Perpetual and Periodic Journal Entries

The following transactions for Goodmonth Tire Company occurred during the month of March 2009:

a. Purchased 500 automobile tires on account at a cost of $40 each for a total of $20,000.

b. Purchased 300 truck tires on account at a cost of $80 each for a total of $24,000.

c. Returned 12 automobile tires to the supplier because they were defective.

d. Paid for the automobile tires.

e. Paid for half the truck tires.

(continued)

f. Paid the remaining balance owed on the truck tires.

g. Sold on account 400 automobile tires at a price of $90 each for a total of $36,000.

h. Sold on account 200 truck tires at a price of $150 each for a total of $30,000.

i. Accepted return of 7 automobile tires from dissatisfied customers.

Required:

1. Prepare journal entries to account for the above transactions assuming a periodic inventory system.

2. Prepare journal entries to account for the above transactions assuming a perpetual inventory system.

3. Assume that inventory levels at the beginning of March (before these transactions) were 100 automobile tires that cost $40 each and 70 truck tires that cost $80 each. Also, assume that a physical count of inventory at the end of March revealed that 184 automobile tires and 164 truck tires were on hand. Given these inventory amounts, prepare the closing entries to account for inventory and related accounts as of the end of March.

P 7-55

LO2

Income Statement Calculations

Stout Company has gross sales of 250% of cost of goods sold. It has also provided the following information for the calendar year 2009:

Inventory balance, January 1, 2009	$ 22,000
Total cost of goods available for sale	84,000
Sales returns	4,200
Purchase returns	2,000
Freight in	800
Sales (net of returns)	169,800
Operating expenses	7,500

Using the available information, compute the following. (Ignore income taxes.)

Required:

1. Gross sales for 2009.
2. Net purchases and gross purchases for 2009.
3. Cost of goods sold for 2009.
4. Inventory balance at December 31, 2009.
5. Gross margin for 2009.
6. Net income for 2009.

P 7-56

LO2

Income Statement Calculations

	Company A	Company B	Company C	Company D
Sales revenue	$2,000	(4) _____	$480	$1,310
Beginning inventory	200	76	0	600
Purchases	(1) _____	423	480	249
Purchase returns	(20)	(19)	(0)	(8) _____
Ending inventory	300	110	(6) _____	195
Cost of goods sold	1,200	370	(7) _____	(9) _____
Gross margin	(2) _____	(5) _____	155	(10) _____
Operating expenses	108	22	34	129
Net income	(3) _____	107	121	546

Required:

Complete the income statement calculations by filling in all missing numbers.

P 7-57   **Inventory Cost Flow Alternatives**

LO4   Stocks, Inc., sells weight-lifting equipment. The sales and inventory records of the company for January through March 2009 were as follows:

	Weight Sets	Unit Cost	Total Cost
Beginning inventory, Jan. 1	460	$30	$13,800
Purchase, Jan. 16	110	32	3,520
Sale, Jan. 25 ($45 per set)	216		
Purchase, Feb. 16	105	36	3,780
Sale, Feb. 27 ($40 per set)	307		
Purchase, March 10	150	28	4,200
Sale, March 30 ($50 per set)	190		

Required:

1. Determine the amounts for ending inventory, cost of goods sold, and gross margin under the following costing alternatives. Use the periodic inventory method, which means that all sales are assumed to occur at the end of the period no matter when they actually occurred. Round amounts to the nearest dollar.
   a. FIFO
   b. LIFO
   c. Average cost

2. **Interpretive Question:** Which alternative results in the highest gross margin? Why?

P 7-58   **Periodic Inventory Cost Flow Method**

LO4   Fresh Wholesale buys peaches from farmers and sells them to canneries. During May 2009, Fresh's inventory records showed the following:

			Cases	Price
May	1	Beginning inventory	5,100	$10.50
	4	Purchase	1,210	12.00
	9	Sale	1,020	19.65
	13	Purchase	1,050	12.50
	19	Sale	1,750	19.65
	26	Purchase	2,120	13.00
	30	Sale	2,340	19.65

Fresh Wholesale uses the periodic inventory method to account for its inventory, which means that all sales are assumed to occur at the end of the period no matter when they actually occurred.

Required:

Calculate the cost of goods sold and ending inventory using the following cost flow alternatives. (Calculate unit costs to the nearest cent.)

1. FIFO
2. LIFO
3. Average cost

P 7-59   **Calculating and Interpreting Inventory Ratios**

LO5   Captain Geech Boating Company sells fishing boats to fishermen. Its beginning and ending inventories for 2009 are $462 million and $653 million, respectively. It had cost of goods sold of $1,578 million for the year ended December 31, 2009. Merchant Marine Company also sells fishing boats. Its beginning and ending inventories for the year 2009 are $120 million and $90 million, respectively. It had cost of goods sold of $1,100 million for the year ended December 31, 2009.

(continued)

Required:

1. Calculate the inventory turnover and number of days' sales in inventory for the two companies.
2. **Interpretive Question:** Are the results of these ratios what you expected? Which company is managing its inventory more efficiently?

EXPANDED *material*

P 7-60

LO6

The Effect of Inventory Errors

The accountant for Steele Company reported the following accounting treatments for several purchase transactions (FOB shipping point) that took place near December 31, 2009, the company's year-end:

Date Inventory Was Shipped	Was the Purchase Recorded in the Books on or before December 31, 2009?	Amount	Was the Inventory Counted and Included in Inventory Balance on December 31, 2009?
2009:			
December 26	Yes	$1,100	Yes
December 29	Yes	800	No
December 31	No	1,800	Yes
2010:			
January 1	No	300	Yes
January 1	Yes	3,000	No
January 1	No	600	No

Required:

1. If Steele Company's records reported purchases and ending inventory balances of $80,800 and $29,800, respectively, for 2009, what would the proper amounts in these accounts have been?
2. What would be the correct amount of cost of goods sold for 2009, if the beginning inventory balance on January 1, 2009, was $20,200?
3. By how much would cost of goods sold be over- or understated if the corrections in question (1) were not made?

P 7-61

LO6

Correction of Inventory Errors

The annual reported income for Salazar Company for the years 2006–2009 is shown here. However, a review of the inventory records reveals inventory misstatements.

	2006	2007	2008	2009
Reported net income	$30,000	$40,000	$35,000	$45,000
Inventory overstatement, end of year		3,000		2,000
Inventory understatement, end of year	4,000		1,000	

Required:

Using the data provided, calculate the correct net income for each year.

P 7-62

LO6

The Effect of Inventory Errors

You have been hired as the accountant for Christman Company, which uses the periodic inventory method. In reviewing the firm's records, you have noted what you think are several accounting errors made during the current year, 2009. These potential mistakes are listed as follows:

a. A $51,000 purchase of merchandise was properly recorded in the purchases account, but the related accounts payable account was credited for only $4,000. *(continued)*

b. A $4,400 shipment of merchandise received just before the end of the year was properly recorded in the purchases account but was not physically counted in the inventory and, hence, was excluded from the ending inventory balance.

c. A $5,600 purchase of merchandise was erroneously recorded as a $6,500 purchase.

d. A $1,200 purchase of merchandise was not recorded either as a purchase or as an account payable.

e. During the year, $3,100 of defective merchandise was sent back to a supplier. The original purchase had been recorded, but the merchandise return entry was not recorded.

f. During the physical inventory count, inventory that cost $800 was counted twice.

Required:

1. If the previous accountant had tentatively computed the 2009 gross margin to be $25,000, what would be the correct gross margin for the year?

2. If these mistakes are not corrected, by how much will the 2010 net income be in error?

P 7-63

LO7

Unifying Concepts: Inventory Cost Flow Alternatives

Stan's Wholesale buys canned tomatoes from canneries and sells them to retail markets. During August 2009, Stan's inventory records showed the following:

			Cases	Price
Aug.	1	Beginning inventory	4,100	$10.50
	4	Purchase	1,500	11.00
	9	Sale	950	19.95
	13	Purchase	1,000	11.00
	19	Sale	1,450	19.95
	26	Purchase	1,700	11.50
	30	Sale	1,900	19.95

Even though it requires more computational effort, Stan's uses the perpetual inventory method because management feels that the advantage of always having current knowledge of inventory levels justifies the extra cost.

Required:

Calculate the cost of goods sold and ending inventory using the following cost flow alternatives. (Calculate unit costs to the nearest cent.)

1. FIFO
2. LIFO
3. Average cost

P 7-64

LO7

Perpetual Inventory Cost Flow Alternatives

Pump-It, Inc., sells weight-lifting equipment. The sales and inventory records of the company for January through March 2009 were as follows:

	Weight Sets	Unit Cost	Total Cost
Beginning inventory, Jan. 1	460	$30	$13,800
Purchase, Jan. 16	110	32	3,520
Sale, Jan. 25 ($45 per set)	216		
Purchase, Feb. 16	105	36	3,780
Sale, Feb. 27 ($40 per set)	307		
Purchase, March 10	150	28	4,200
Sale, March 30 ($50 per set)	190		

(continued)

Required:

1. Determine the amounts for ending inventory, cost of goods sold, and gross margin under the following costing alternatives. Use the perpetual inventory method. Round amounts to the nearest dollar.

   a. FIFO

   b. LIFO

   c. Average cost (calculate unit costs to the nearest cent)

2. **Interpretive Question:** Which alternative results in the highest gross margin? Why?

P 7-65

LO9

Unifying Concepts: Inventory Estimation Method

McCarlie Clothing Store has the following information available:

	Cost	Selling Price	Other
Purchases during March 2009	$215,000	$400,000	
Inventory balance, March 1, 2009	60,000	95,000	
Sales during March		510,000	
Average gross margin rate for the last three years			52%

Required:

1. On the basis of this information, estimate the cost of inventory on hand at March 31, 2009, using the gross margin method. Round to the nearest whole percent.

2. How accurate do you think this method is?

ANALYTICAL ASSIGNMENTS

AA 7-66

DISCUSSION

Why Use a Perpetual System?

You are a consultant for the ABC Consulting Company. You have been hired by Eddie's Electronics, a company that owns 25 electronics stores selling radios, televisions, compact disc players, stereos, and other electronic equipment. Since the company began business 10 years ago, it has been using a periodic inventory system. However, Mark Eddie just returned from a seminar where some of his competitors told him he should be using the perpetual inventory method. Mr. Eddie is not sure he should believe his competitors. He wants you to advise him about his inventory choices and make a recommendation about the inventory method he should use.

AA 7-67

DISCUSSION

Should We Reduce Inventory?

It has now been two years since you advised Mr. Eddie to switch to the perpetual inventory method. He is very happy with the additional information he has about inventory levels and theft. He has hired you for advice once again. This time, Mr. Eddie has been to an inventory management seminar where he heard that most companies have too much money tied up in inventory. He wonders if his company could be much more profitable if it reduced its inventory levels. What would you tell him?

AA 7-68

JUDGMENT CALL

You Decide: Should inventory be recorded at cost or fair market value?

You recently ran into Bill Autograph, a friend from high school who has been really busy getting his sports collectible/memorabilia business off the ground. When he heard you were an accountant, he became very interested and wanted you to clarify something. One concept he seemed particularly confused about was the fact that when inventory is purchased, it is recorded on the books at cost but the books are not adjusted for subsequent increases in the value of the inventory. This concept is of particular importance to Bill because he often buys collectibles that will increase in value depending on how successful a particular player or team becomes. Can he record increases in the value of his sports memorabilia inventory?

Wal-Mart

Using **Wal-Mart**'s 2006 Form 10-K in Appendix A, answer the following questions:
1. What type of items compose Wal-Mart's inventory?
2. Review Wal-Mart's balance sheet to determine the amount of inventory on hand on January 31, 2006.
3. What inventory method does Wal-Mart use?

General Electric

Selected financial statement information relating to inventories for **General Electric (GE)** is given below.

December 31 (in millions)	2005	2004
Cost of goods sold	$46,169	$42,645
Inventory–FIFO valuation	11,171	10,439
Inventory–LIFO valuation	10,474	9,778

1. Compute GE's number of days' sales in inventory for 2005 using (a) the FIFO valuation for inventory and (b) the LIFO valuation for inventory. Are the differences significant enough to concern you?
2. Suppose that GE purchases its inventory with the terms "net 30 days." That is, GE's creditors expect payment in 30 days. Is GE going to have a cash flow problem?

La-Z-Boy and McDonald's

The following information is taken from the 2005 financial statements of **La-Z-Boy, Inc.**, maker of recliners and other home furnishings, and the 2005 financial statements of **McDonald's**, maker of the Big Mac® and other fast foods.

	La-Z-Boy	McDonald's
Cost of goods sold	$1,583.14*	$14,136.00*
Beginning inventory	250.57	147.50
Ending inventory	260.56	147.00

*Amounts in millions.

1. Before you do any computations, forecast which of the two companies will have a lower number of days' sales in inventory.
2. Compute each company's number of days' sales in inventory. Was your forecast in (1) correct?
3. How can these two very successful companies have number of days' sales in inventory that are so different?

Why No LIFO?

The LIFO method of accounting for inventory is primarily a U.S. invention. Many countries around the world will not allow LIFO to be used, and other countries discourage its use. For example, the International Accounting Standards Board calls LIFO an undesirable but "allowable" method. In the United Kingdom, LIFO is allowable under corporate law but is unacceptable under professional accounting standards.

Why do you think other countries have such an unfavorable opinion of LIFO? Think about these issues: In periods of rising prices, does the amount shown on the balance sheet relating to inventory reflect current cost? If a company's inventory on the balance sheet reflected costs from years past, what would happen to the income statement if those inventory costs were suddenly moved to Cost of Goods Sold? Would the result reflect a firm's actual performance?

AA 7-73

ETHICS

Shipping Bricks

In 1989 the U.S. Department of Justice Criminal Division discovered a massive inventory fraud that was being conducted by managers at **Miniscribe Corporation.** MiniScribe manufactured and sold computer disk drives. The fraud included placing bricks in disk drive boxes, shipping those boxes to customers, and recording a sale when the box was shipped. MiniScribe managers also knowingly shipped defective drives and recorded sales even though they knew those drives would be returned.

What would be the effect on the income statement and the balance sheet of shipping bricks and recording those shipments as sales? (*Hint:* Think about the journal entry that would have been made by MiniScribe accountants when a box of bricks was shipped to customers who were expecting disk drives.) Would company officials be able to fool financial statement users for a long time using this type of deception? What could financial statement users have looked for to detect this type of fraud?

AA 7-74

WRITING

Estimating Inventory

Jon Johnson, an accountant with a local CPA firm, has just completed an inventory count for Mom & Pop's Groceries. Mom and Pop provide audited financial statements to their bank annually, and part of that audit requires an inventory count. Don Squire, a partner with the CPA firm, has also conducted an analysis to estimate this period's ending inventory. Don used the gross margin method, a method whereby the prior period's gross margin percentage is used to infer this period's percentage, to estimate ending inventory. In addition, the store is equipped with cash registers that scan each product as it is sold and, as a result, provide a perpetual inventory record.

These three inventory analysis methods have resulted in three very different answers, which are summarized in the following table:

Method	Inventory Value
Inventory count	$ 98,500
Gross margin analysis	119,750
Point-of-sale scanners	111,500

In evaluating the results, Jon and Don are curious as to why the three methods result in such large differences. Since the inventory count reports actual inventory on hand, they begin to wonder if Mom and Pop have an inventory theft problem. Write a short memo explaining why the other two methods, gross margin analysis and point-of-sale scanners, can result in significantly different answers without there being a theft problem.

AA 7-75

CUMULATIVE
SPREADSHEET
PROJECT

Preparing New Forecasts

This spreadsheet assignment is a continuation of the spreadsheet assignments given in earlier chapters. If you completed those spreadsheets, you have a head start on this one. If needed, review the spreadsheet assignment for Chapter 4 to refresh your memory on how to construct forecasted financial statements.

1. Handyman wishes to prepare a forecasted balance sheet and income statement for 2010. Use the original financial statement numbers for 2009 [given in part (1) of the Cumulative Spreadsheet Project assignment in Chapter 2] as the basis for the forecast, along with the following additional information:

    a. Sales in 2010 are expected to increase by 40% over 2009 sales of $700.

    b. Cash will increase at the same rate as sales.

    c. The forecasted amount of accounts receivable in 2010 is determined using the forecasted value for the average collection period. For simplicity, do the computations using the end-of-period accounts receivable balance instead of the average balance. The average collection period for 2010 is expected to be 14.08 days.

    d. In 2010, Handyman expects to acquire new property, plant, and equipment costing $80.

(continued)

e. The $160 in operating expenses reported in 2009 breaks down as follows: $5 depreciation expense, $155 other operating expenses.
f. No new long-term debt will be acquired in 2010.
g. No cash dividends will be paid in 2010.
h. New short-term loans payable will be acquired in an amount sufficient to make Handyman's current ratio in 2010 exactly equal to 2.0.

Note: These statements were constructed as part of the spreadsheet assignment in Chapter 6; you can use that spreadsheet as a starting point if you have completed that assignment. *Clearly state any additional assumptions that you make.*

For this exercise, add the following additional assumptions:

i. The forecasted amount of inventory in 2010 is determined using the forecasted value for the number of days' sales in inventory (computed using the end-of-period inventory balance). The number of days' sales in inventory for 2010 is expected to be 107.6 days.
ii. The forecasted amount of accounts payable in 2010 is determined using the forecasted value for the number of days' purchases in accounts payable (computed using the end-of-period accounts payable balance). The number of days' purchases in accounts payable for 2010 is expected to be 48.34 days.

2. Repeat (1), with the following changes in assumptions:
   a. Number of days' sales in inventory is expected to be 66.2 days.
   b. Number of days' sales in inventory is expected to be 150.0 days.
3. Comment on the differences in the forecasted values of cash from operating activities in 2010 under each of the following assumptions about the number of days' sales in inventory: 107.6 days, 66.2 days, and 150.0 days.
4. Is there any impact on the forecasted level of accounts payable when the number of days' sales in inventory is changed? Why or why not?
5. What happens to the forecasted level of short-term loans payable when the number of days' sales in inventory is reduced to 66.2 days? Explain.

Completing the Operating Cycle

After studying this chapter, you should be able to:

(1) Account for the various components of employee compensation expense. *In addition to wages and salaries, companies also compensate their employees through bonuses, stock options, pensions, and other benefits. Computing total compensation expense involves a significant element of estimation and assumption.*

(2) Compute income tax expense, including appropriate consideration of deferred tax items. *Reported income tax expense reflects all of the tax implications of transactions and events occurring during the year. Because financial accounting rules and income tax rules are not the same, income tax expense this year sometimes reflects items that will not actually impact the legal computation of income taxes until future years.*

(3) Distinguish between contingent items that should be recognized in the financial statements and those that should be merely disclosed in the financial statement notes. *A contingent item is an uncertain circumstance involving a potential gain or loss that will not be resolved until some future event occurs. Contingent losses are recognized when they* are probable and estimable; they are not recognized but are only disclosed when they are just possible.

(4) Understand when an expenditure should be recorded as an asset and when it should be recorded as an expense. *Conceptually, a cost should be recorded as an asset whenever it has a probable future economic benefit. In practice, it is frequently quite difficult to tell when a cost should be recorded as an asset (capitalized) and when it should be recorded as an expense.*

(5) Prepare an income statement summarizing operating activities as well as other revenues and expenses, extraordinary items, and earnings per share. *Because the items in the income statement are carefully arranged and sequenced, emphasis is placed on the portion of income that is generated by the ongoing core operations of the business.*

Before 1850, the primary use for petroleum was as a medicine. Known variously as Seneca oil, American oil, and rock oil, a mixture of water and petroleum was reportedly good for rheumatism, chronic cough, ague, toothache, corns, neuralgia, urinary disorders, indigestion, and liver ailments.

Gradually, additional properties of oil were discovered. It was found that oil could serve as a lubricant for the machinery that was becoming more common as the Industrial Revolution progressed. In addition, distilled oil was found to burn well in the household lamps that had traditionally burned vegetable oil or sperm whale oil. As the demand for petroleum increased, the search for oil began in earnest. In late August 1859, oil was struck in northwestern Pennsylvania at a depth of 69½ feet, creating an oil well that yielded 25 barrels per day. This discovery touched off an oil rush in western Pennsylvania, and the opportunities to get rich were soon fanned by the increased demand for lubricating oil associated with the North's war production during the Civil War.

The oil boom did not hit Texas until 1901 when a well on Spindletop Hill, south of Beaumont, Texas, began to gush 100,000 barrels of oil a day.

In those early days, Cleveland, Ohio, was the center of oil refining, and one of the earliest players in the refining business was John D. Rockefeller. Rockefeller had started his business career in Cleveland as a bookkeeper(!) in 1855. By saving his earnings, he acquired some investment capital, and, with a partner, he put up $4,000 to begin a refinery in Cleveland in 1862. Rockefeller subsequently created an empire of oil companies located in various states. These companies were eventually consolidated into a holding company called the **Standard Oil Company of New Jersey**.

John D. Rockefeller used some of his Standard Oil profits to found the University of Chicago in 1891.

In the early 1890s, the spirit of reform spread over the United States. Many people felt that Big Business was too powerful and must be reined in by the federal government. In 1911, the U.S. Supreme Court mandated the breakup of the Standard Oil Company into 34 smaller companies. Many of those companies are still very well known, as evidenced by the partial list contained in Exhibit 1.

The largest piece of the dismembered Standard Oil Trust was the Standard Oil Company of New Jersey, which changed its named to **Exxon** in 1972. Exxon now

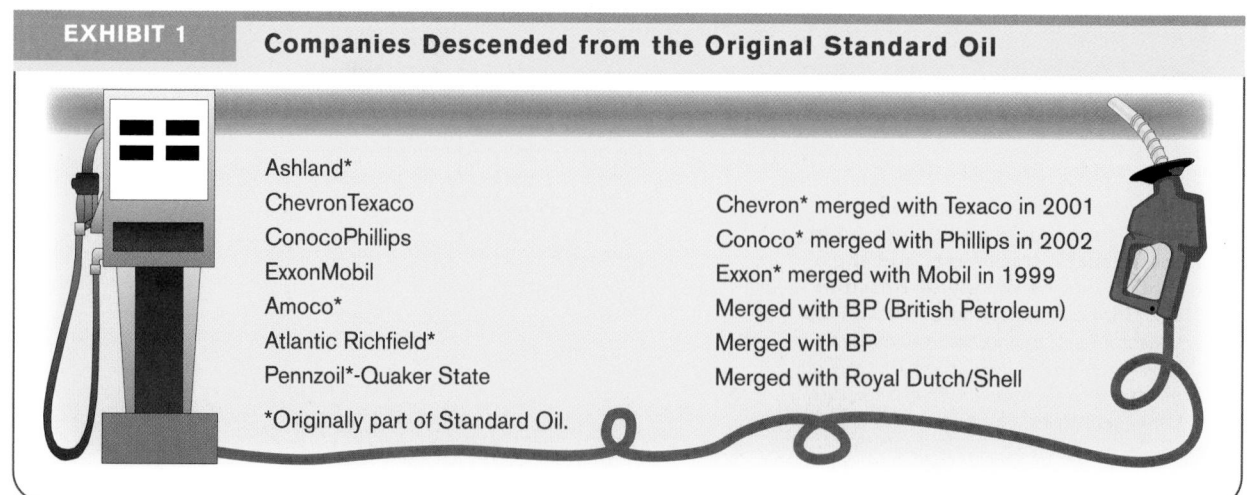

EXHIBIT 1	**Companies Descended from the Original Standard Oil**
Ashland*	
ChevronTexaco	Chevron* merged with Texaco in 2001
ConocoPhillips	Conoco* merged with Phillips in 2002
ExxonMobil	Exxon* merged with Mobil in 1999
Amoco*	Merged with BP (British Petroleum)
Atlantic Richfield*	Merged with BP
Pennzoil*-Quaker State	Merged with Royal Dutch/Shell
*Originally part of Standard Oil.	

F Y I

The federal antitrust case against **Microsoft** was compared to the Standard Oil case of 1911, with Bill Gates playing the role of a modern-day Rockefeller.

operates in over 100 countries, exploring for oil, producing petrochemical products, and transporting oil and natural gas. In many places, the company is known as **Esso**, representing the initials "SO" for Standard Oil. On December 1, 1998, Exxon (the former Standard Oil Company of New Jersey) announced an agreement to merge with **Mobil** (the former **Standard Oil Company of New York**), thus reuniting these two pieces of the vast empire built by John D. Rockefeller. The formal joining of the two companies was completed on November 30, 1999, creating **ExxonMobil**.[1] To illustrate the size of ExxonMobil's operations, the company had worldwide proven oil reserves of 11.2 billion barrels and proven natural gas reserves of 66.9 trillion cubic feet as of December 31, 2005.

I n Chapters 6 and 7, we discussed the accounting for sales and the cost of inventory sold. For firms that sell a product, the cost of the inventory sold typically represents the largest expense. For example, cost of goods sold was the largest expense category for ExxonMobil in 2005, totaling 57% of sales. For Wal-Mart, cost of goods sold was 77% of sales in 2005. Although cost of goods sold represents a significant expense for those companies such as ExxonMobil and Wal-Mart that manufacture and/or sell a product, it is certainly not the only expense. And for those companies that sell a service, other expenses such as employee compensation or advertising can be far more significant than cost of goods sold.

In this chapter, we discuss a number of these other significant operating issues. We will begin with a discussion of two significant operating expenses that are incurred by almost every firm: employee compensation and income taxes. We also discuss the accounting for the costs associated with contingencies, which are items that are not fully resolved at the time the financial statements are prepared. Two common examples of contingencies are lawsuits and environmental cleanup obligations. Also in this chapter we discuss how one determines whether a cost should be recorded as an asset (capitalized) or recorded as an expense. The expense versus capitalize issue has arisen many times over the years as accountants have wrestled with how to account for advertising costs, research costs, and others.

The financial statement items covered in this chapter are illustrated in Exhibit 2. Various operating items affecting the income statement are covered in the chapter. The two most significant are employee compensation and income taxes. The balance sheet items discussed are pension liabilities, deferred income tax liabilities, and contingent liabilities. The accounting aspects of these balance sheet items are intriguing in that both the pension and deferred tax items are sometimes reported as assets rather than liabilities. In addition, contingent liabilities are frequently not reported on the balance sheet at all. The details of all these topics, and more, are discussed in this chapter.

---

[1] Information for this description was obtained from Daniel J. Boorstin, *The Americans: The Democratic Experience* (New York: Random House, 1973) and Ida M. Tarbell, *The History of the Standard Oil Company* (New York: MacMillan Company, 1904).

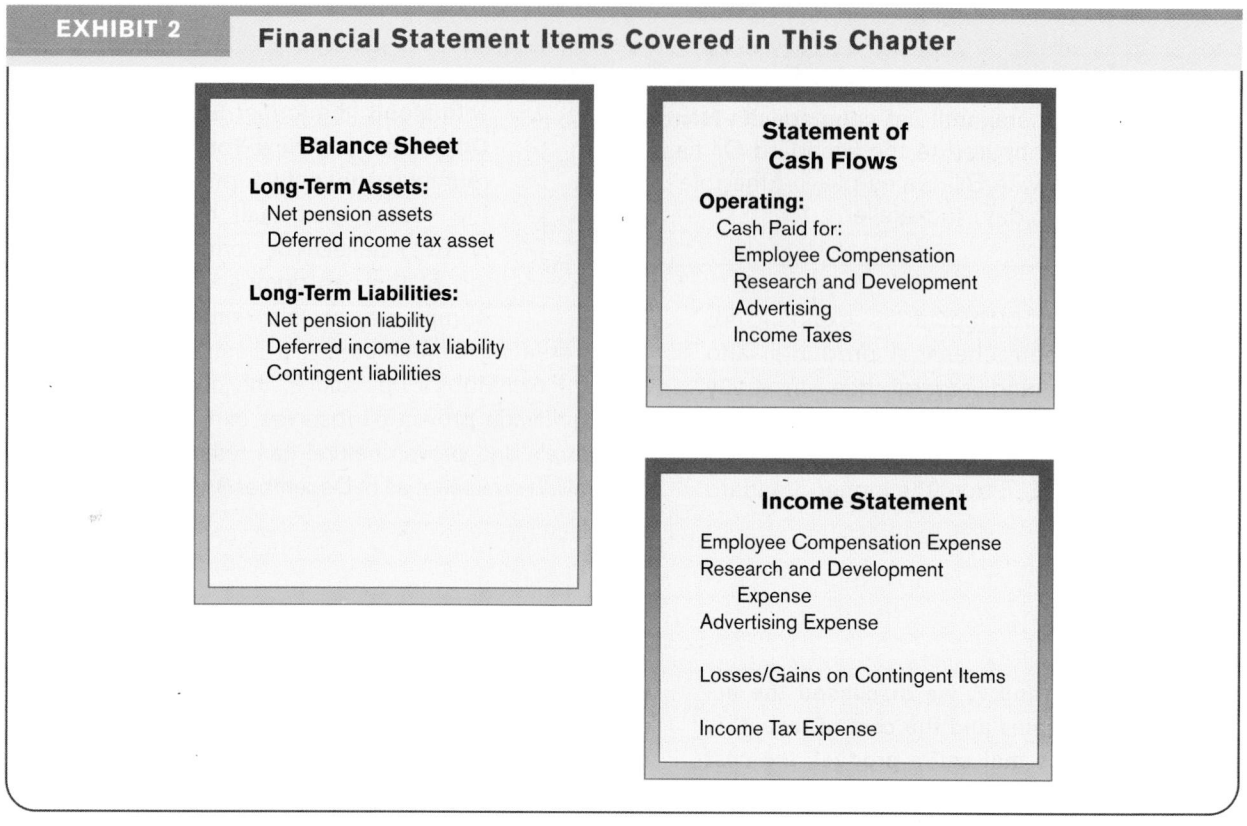

EXHIBIT 2   **Financial Statement Items Covered in This Chapter**

Balance Sheet

Long-Term Assets:
  Net pension assets
  Deferred income tax asset

Long-Term Liabilities:
  Net pension liability
  Deferred income tax liability
  Contingent liabilities

Statement of Cash Flows

Operating:
  Cash Paid for:
    Employee Compensation
    Research and Development
    Advertising
    Income Taxes

Income Statement

  Employee Compensation Expense
  Research and Development
        Expense
  Advertising Expense

  Losses/Gains on Contingent Items

  Income Tax Expense

Employee Compensation

Account for the various components of employee compensation expense.

① Often, one of the largest operating expenses of a business is the salaries and wages of its employees. But the cost of employees is not simply the expense associated with the current period's wages. As the following time line illustrates, issues associated with employee compensation can extend long after the employee has retired.

Payroll relates to the salaries and wages earned by employees for work done in the current period. Wages are paid anywhere from weekly to monthly, depending on the company. Compensated absences exist when an employer agrees to pay workers for sick days or vacation days. These obligations must be estimated and accrued in the period that the employee earns those days off. Many employees are paid bonuses based on some measure of performance (such as income or sales

Employee Compensation Event Line

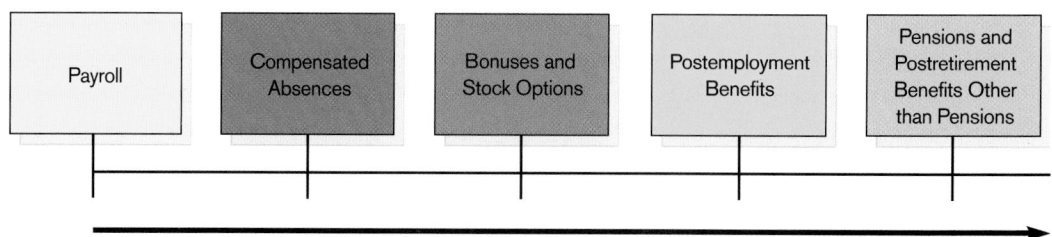

| Payroll | Compensated Absences | Bonuses and Stock Options | Postemployment Benefits | Pensions and Postretirement Benefits Other than Pensions |

Time

volume). Those bonuses are often paid quarterly or annually. One way to provide bonuses to employees is through the granting of stock options. In some cases, employees may earn what are termed "postemployment benefits," which kick in if an employee is laid off or terminated. Finally, firms offer benefits to their employees upon retirement. We will discuss each of these items in further detail in the sections that follow.

Payroll

In its simplest form, accounting for payroll involves debiting Salaries Expense and crediting Salaries Payable when employees work and then debiting Salaries Payable and crediting Cash when wages are paid. However, accounting for salaries and related payroll taxes is never quite that simple and can, in fact, be quite complex. This is primarily because every business is legally required to withhold certain taxes from employees' salaries and wages.

Social Security (FICA) taxes

Federal Insurance Contributions Act taxes imposed on the employee and the employer; used mainly to provide retirement benefits.

Very few people receive their full salary as take-home pay. For example, an employee who earns $30,000 a year probably takes home between $20,000 and $25,000. The remainder is withheld by the employer to pay the employee's federal and state income taxes, **Social Security (FICA) taxes**,[2] and any voluntary or contractual withholdings that the employee has authorized (such as union dues, medical insurance premiums, and charitable contributions). Thus, the accounting entry to record the expense for an employee's monthly salary (computed as 1/12 of $30,000) might be:

Salaries Expense	2,500	
FICA Taxes Payable, Employees		191
Federal Withholding Taxes Payable		400
State Withholding Taxes Payable		200
Salaries Payable		1,709
To record Mary Perrico's salary for July.		

All the credit amounts (which are arbitrary in this example) are liabilities that must be paid by the employer to the federal and state governments and to the employee. It should be noted that these withholdings do not represent an additional expense to the employer because the employee actually pays them. The employer merely serves as an agent for the governments for collecting and paying these withheld amounts.

In addition to remitting employees' income and FICA taxes, companies must also pay certain payroll-related taxes, such as the employer's portion of the FICA tax (an amount equal to the employee's portion) and state and federal unemployment taxes. The payroll-related taxes paid by employers are expenses to the company and are included in operating expenses on the income statement. An entry to record the company's share of payroll taxes relating to Mary Perrico's employment (again using arbitrary amounts) would be:

Payroll Tax Expense	279	
FICA Taxes Payable, Employer		191
Federal Unemployment Taxes Payable		18
State Unemployment Taxes Payable		70
To record employer payroll tax liabilities associated with Mary Perrico's salary for July.		

---

[2] Congress has split FICA taxes into two parts—Social Security and Medicare. For the purposes of this chapter, we will combine the two.

The different liabilities recorded in the preceding two entries for payroll would be eliminated as payments are made. The entries to account for the payments are:

FICA Taxes Payable	382	
Federal Withholding Taxes Payable	400	
Federal Unemployment Taxes Payable	18	
Cash		800
Paid July withholdings and payroll taxes to federal government.		
State Withholding Taxes Payable	200	
State Unemployment Taxes Payable	70	
Cash		270
Paid July withholdings and payroll taxes to state government.		
Salaries Payable	1,709	
Cash		1,709
Paid July salary to Mary Perrico.		

As these entries show, three checks are written for payroll-related expenses: one to the federal government, one to the state, and one to the employee.

One further point about salaries and wages needs to be made. The period of time covered by the payroll may not coincide with the last day of the year for financial reporting. Thus, if the reporting year ends on Wednesday, December 31, and the salaries and wages for that week will be paid Monday, January 5 of the following year, then the company must show the salaries and wages earned from Monday through Wednesday (December 29, 30, and 31) as a liability on the December 31 balance sheet. To accomplish this, the company would record an end-of-year adjusting entry to record the salaries and wages earned for those three days.

Compensated Absences

Suppose that you work for a business that provides each employee one day of sick leave for each full month of employment. When should that sick day (or compensated absence) be accounted for? When it is taken by the employee? When it is earned by the employee? And how much of an accrual should be associated with the compensated absences?

The matching principle requires that the expense associated with the compensated absence be accounted for in the period in which it is earned by the employee. Some of the conceptual issues associated with accounting for compensated absences are similar to those addressed in accounting for bad debts. In the case of bad debts, if we waited until we were sure a customer wasn't going to pay, then we could be certain about our bad debt expense. But we may not find out that we are not going to be paid until several periods later, and as a result, the bad debt expense would be reflected in the wrong accounting period. So instead of waiting until accounts are dishonored, we estimate the expense for each period. The same is true with compensated absences. Although we could wait until those sick days are taken and then know exactly what they will cost, it may be years before we know. Rather than wait, we estimate instead. For example, if you earn both $100 a day and one sick day per month, then it makes sense for your employer to recognize an expense (and accrue a liability) of $100 per month related to your sick pay. This would be done with the following journal entry:

Salaries Expense	100	
Sick Days Payable		100
To recognize accrued sick pay.		

When you take that sick day (and let's not forget that the government will take its share of your sick pay also), the journal entry would be:

Sick Days Payable	100	
Various Taxes Payable		20
Cash		80
To record payment of sick day net of FICA, federal, and state taxes.		

Now suppose that you don't take your sick day until next year. Assume also that you received a $10 raise per day. This makes our estimate of $100 incorrect, so we will fix that estimate in the period in which you take the sick day. The journal entry in this instance would be:

Sick Days Payable	100	
Salaries Expense	10	
Various Taxes Payable		22
Cash		88
To record payment of sick day net of FICA, federal, and state taxes.		

The same procedures would apply when accounting for accrued vacation pay or other types of compensated absences.

Bonuses

bonus

Additional compensation, beyond the regular compensation, that is paid to employees if certain objectives are achieved.

Many companies offer employee **bonus** plans that allow employees to receive additional compensation should certain objectives be achieved. These bonus plans sometimes apply to all employees although more often they are restricted to members of top management. In many instances, the terms of the bonus plan are defined using financial statement numbers. For example, in its 2005 proxy statement filed with the Securities and Exchange Commission (SEC), **ExxonMobil** disclosed that it paid $9.15 million in bonuses to its top six executives. ExxonMobil's chief executive officer (CEO), Lee R. Raymond, received the lion's share of that bonus amount at $4.9 million (this on top of his regular annual compensation of $4.0 million).

The purpose of an earnings-based bonus plan is to encourage managers to work harder and smarter to improve the performance of the company. However, such a plan also increases the incentive of managers to manipulate reported earnings. In fact, one of the factors looked at by auditors in evaluating the risk of financial statement fraud in a company is whether the company has an earnings-based management bonus plan.

Stock Options

employee stock options

Rights given to employees to purchase shares of stock of a company at a predetermined price.

Employee stock options have become an increasingly popular way to compensate top executives. Under a stock option plan, managers are given the option of purchasing shares of the company's stock in the future at a price that is specified today. For example, in 2002, Lee Raymond, CEO of ExxonMobil, was granted 1,050,000 options, each allowing him to buy one share of ExxonMobil stock in the future for $37.12, which was the market value of ExxonMobil shares on the date the options were granted. Raymond will make money from these options if he is able to improve the performance of ExxonMobil and increase its stock price. In August of 2006, a share of ExxonMobil stock was worth $68 making those options worth $32,424,000 [1,050,000 × ($68.00 − $37.12)]. Stock options are an attractive way to compensate top management because the options pay off only if the managers are able to increase the value of the company, which is exactly what the owners of the company (the stockholders) desire.

There has been significant debate in the United States about how to compute the compensation expense associated with employee stock options. The debate centered around the issue of what the value of an option is. The FASB has determined the proper way to value options is the fair value method. This method is described below.

Fair Value Method The "fair value" of an option stems from the possibility that the employee may want to exercise the option in the future if the company's stock price goes up. For example, even if an option exercise price of $50 is equal to the stock price on the date the option is granted to an employee, there is a chance that the stock price may increase during the life of the option. This means that an option with no "intrinsic value" can still have substantial economic value because the employee holding the option may be able to buy the stock at less than its market value some time in the future. Exact computation of the fair value of options involves complex formulas derived using stochastic calculus, but commercially available software packages make option valuation no more difficult than using a spreadsheet.

Postemployment Benefits

postemployment benefits

Benefits paid to employees who have been laid off or terminated.

Postemployment benefits are perhaps the least common of the topics covered in this section on employee compensation. **Postemployment benefits** are those benefits that are incurred after an employee has ceased to work for an employer but before that employee retires. A common example is a company-provided severance package for employees who have been laid off. This severance package might include salary for a certain time period, retraining costs, education costs, and the like. Accounting standards require that the amount of the postemployment cost be estimated and accrued in the period in which the employee is actually terminated. For example, suppose a company decides to close a segment of its operations, thereby laying off a certain percentage of its labor force. The company must estimate the costs associated with the benefits offered to those laid-off employees and would record the following journal entry when the employees are actually terminated:

Salaries Expense	xxx	
Benefits Payable		xxx
To record postemployment benefits for laid-off employees.		

pension

An agreement between an employer and employees that provides for benefits upon retirement.

When the benefits are paid, a journal entry would be made to reduce the payable and to record the cash outflow.

Pensions

A **pension** is cash compensation received by an employee after that employee has retired. Two primary types of pension plans exist. A **defined contribution plan** requires the company to place a certain amount of money into a pension fund each year on behalf of the employees. Then, after the employees retire, they receive the money contributed to the pension fund plus the earnings on those contributions. With a **defined benefit plan**, on the other hand, the company promises the employees a certain monthly cash amount after they retire, based on factors such as number of years worked by the employee, employee's highest salary, and so forth.

defined contribution plan

A pension plan under which the employer contributes a defined amount to the pension fund; after retirement, the employees receive the amount contributed plus whatever it has earned.

The accounting for a defined contribution plan is quite simple—a company merely reports pension expense equal to the amount of cash it is required to contribute to its employees' pension fund during the year. Normally, no balance sheet liability is reported in connection with a defined contribution plan because, once the company has made the required contribution to the pension fund, it has no remaining obligation to the employees.

defined benefit plan

A pension plan under which the employer defines the amount that retiring employees will receive and contributes enough to the pension fund to pay that amount.

The accounting issues associated with defined benefit plans are much more complex because the ultimate amount that a company will have to pay into its employees' pension fund depends on how long the employees work before retiring, what their highest salaries are, how long the employees live after they retire, and how well the investments in the pension fund perform. The accounting concept underlying this complexity, however, is still the same basic idea of matching: the income statement this year should contain all expenses related to generating revenue this year, whether those expenses are paid in cash this year (like cash wages) or are not expected to be paid for many years (like pension benefits).

STOP & THINK

Who bears the risks associated with a defined contribution plan—the employer or the employee? Which party bears the risks associated with a defined benefit plan?

Pension-Related Items in the Financial Statements Each of the major balance sheet and income statement items related to pension accounting is briefly introduced below.

- *Pension fund.* When a company has a defined benefit pension plan, it is required by U.S. federal law to establish a separate pension fund to ensure that employees receive the defined benefits promised under the plan. The pension fund is basically a large investment fund of stocks and bonds. The company still owns these pension fund assets, but it cannot use them for any purpose except to pay pension benefits to employees.

- *Pension obligation.* The promise to make defined benefit pension payments to employees represents a liability to the company making the promise. The amount of this liability is quite difficult to estimate because it depends on future salary increases, employee turnover, employee life span, and so forth. The estimation of the liability is done by professionals called actuaries. These are the same individuals who provide the computations that life insurance companies use in setting premiums.

- *Net pension asset or liability.* One possible way to present the pension information on a balance sheet is to list the pension plan assets among the long-term assets and the pension liability as a long-term liability. However, the accounting standards stipulate that these two items be offset against one another and a single net amount be shown as either a net pension asset or a net pension liability.

- *Pension-related interest cost.* The estimated pension obligation represents an amount owed by a company to its employees. Accordingly, a pension-related interest cost is recognized each year; the amount of this interest cost is the increase in the pension obligation resulting from interest on the unpaid pension obligation.

- *Service cost.* The amount of a company's pension obligation increases each year as employees work and earn more pension benefits. This increase in the pension obligation is an expense associated with work done during the year and is called the pension service cost.

- *Return on pension fund assets.* The cost of a company's pension plan is partially offset by the return that the company earns on the assets in its pension fund.

- *Pension expense.* Just as pension liabilities and assets are offset against one another to arrive at a single net liability or asset to be reported on the balance sheet, the three components of pension expense (interest cost, service cost, and return on pension fund assets) are netted against one another to yield a single number that is reported on the income statement.

Illustration from ExxonMobil's Financial Statements In the notes to its 2005 financial statements, ExxonMobil discloses the following about its pension benefit obligation and its pension fund. All numbers are in millions of dollars.

	U.S. Plans	Non-U.S. Plans	Total
Pension benefit obligation	$11,181	$19,310	$30,491
Pension fund assets	7,250	12,063	19,313
Net pension liability	$ 3,931	$ 7,247	$11,178

Note that ExxonMobil has separated its pension plans into those covering employees in the United States and those covering employees located outside the United States. This is a useful separation because the laws governing the maintenance of pension plans vary from country to country; U.S. laws are generally viewed as giving more protection to the rights of the employees covered by pension plans than foreign laws do. Also note that ExxonMobil's pension plans are "underfunded," meaning that the market value of the assets in the pension funds is less than the estimated pension liability. ExxonMobil also provides the following information about its pension expense in 2005. Again, all of the numbers are in millions.

	U.S. Plans	Non-U.S. Plans	Total
Service cost	$ 330	$ 382	$ 712
Interest cost	611	834	1,445
Less: Expected return on fund assets	(629)	(789)	(1,418)
Other miscellaneous items	397	434	831
Net pension expense	$ 709	$ 861	$1,570

Note the significant reduction in reported pension expense caused by the expected return on pension fund assets; without the return on the pension fund, ExxonMobil's pension expense would be more than twice as high.

CAUTION

The expected, not the actual, return on the pension fund assets is subtracted in computing pension expense. The accounting for the difference between expected and actual return involves deferring gains and losses, corridor amounts, and other complexities best left for an intermediate accounting course.

Postretirement Benefits Other Than Pensions

In addition to pension benefits, employers often offer employees other benefits after their retirement. For example, ExxonMobil promises its employees that it will continue to cover them with health-care and life insurance plans after retirement. These types of plans are typically less formal than pension plans and often are not backed by assets accumulated in a separate fund. For example, ExxonMobil has only a $456 million separate fund set up to cover its estimated $5.4 billion obligation to cover the post-retirement health-care needs of employees.

The accounting rules require companies to currently recognize the expense and long-term liability associated with the postretirement benefits that are earned in the current year, in keeping with the normal practice of matching expenses to the period in which they are initially incurred. The actual accounting is complex but similar to that required for pensions. The potential liabilities for these future payments can be quite significant for many firms. **General Motors** has the largest postretirement benefit plan in the United States, with a nonpension postretirement obligation totaling $84.941 billion as of December 31, 2005.

As illustrated in this section, compensation expense includes much more than just wages and salaries. Companies presumably have calculated that the value of the services provided by employees justifies the additional compensation cost beyond salaries and wages. The fact that employees earn benefits in one year that they do not receive until later, sometimes many years later, necessitates careful accounting to ensure that compensation expense is reported in the year in which it is earned.

REMEMBER THIS...

- Employee compensation is not limited to just the current period's payroll. The cost of employees also includes compensated absences, bonuses, stock options, postemployment benefits, pensions, and other postretirement benefits.
- Companies account for employee stock options using the fair value method.
- A pension obligation is reported on the balance sheet as the difference between the obligation and the amount in an associated pension fund.
- Pension expense is the sum of interest cost and service cost, less the expected return on the pension fund assets.

Taxes

Compute income tax expense, including appropriate consideration of deferred tax items.

(2) In addition to the payroll taxes described in the previous section, companies are responsible for paying several other taxes to federal, state, and/or local governments, including sales taxes, property taxes, and income taxes. The accounting for these taxes is described next.

Sales Taxes

Most states and some cities charge a sales tax on retail transactions. These taxes are paid by customers to the seller, who in turn forwards them to the state or city. Sales taxes collected from customers represent a current liability until remitted to the appropriate governmental agency. For example, assume that a sporting goods store in Denver prices a pair of skis at $200 and that the combination of state and city sales tax is 6.5%. When the store sells the skis, it collects $213 and records the transaction as follows:

Cash	213	
Sales Revenue		200
Sales Tax Payable		13

Sold a pair of skis for $200. Collected $213, including 6.5% sales tax.

sales tax payable

Money collected from customers for sales taxes that must be remitted to local governments and other taxing authorities.

The sales revenue is properly recorded at $200, and the $13 is recorded as **Sales Tax Payable**, a liability. Then, on a regular basis, a sales tax return is completed and filed with the state or city tax commission, and sales taxes collected are paid to those agencies. Note that the collection of the sales tax from customers creates a liability to the state but does not result in the recognition of revenue when collected or an expense when paid to the state. The company acts as an agent of the state in collecting the sales tax and recognizes a liability only until the collected amount is remitted to the state.

Property Taxes

Property taxes are usually assessed by county or city governments on land, buildings, and other company assets. The period covered by the assessment of property taxes is often from July 1 of one year to June 30 of the next year. If a property taxpayer is on a calendar-year financial reporting basis (or on a fiscal-year basis ending on a day other than June 30), the property tax assessment year and the company's financial reporting year will not coincide. Therefore, when the company prepares its financial statements at calendar-year end, it must report a prepaid tax asset (if taxes are paid at the beginning of the tax year) or a property tax liability (if taxes are paid at the end of the tax year) for the taxes associated with the first portion of the assessment year. To illustrate, assume that Yokum Company pays its property taxes of $3,600 on June 30, 2008, for the period July 1, 2008, to June 30, 2009. If the company is on a calendar-year basis and records the prepayment as an asset, then the adjusting entry at December 31, 2008, would be:

Property Tax Expense	1,800	
Prepaid Property Taxes		1,800
To record property tax expense for six months.		

The prepaid property taxes account balance of $1,800 would be shown on Yokum's balance sheet at December 31, 2008, as a current asset. On June 30, 2009, property tax expense would be recognized for the period January 1, 2009, through June 30, 2009, with the following entry:

Property Tax Expense	1,800	
Prepaid Property Taxes		1,800
To record property tax expense for the property assessment		
period January 1–June 30, 2009.		

Income Taxes

Corporations pay income taxes just as individuals do. This corporate income tax is usually reported as the final expense on the income statement. For example, in 2005, three lines from **ExxonMobil**'s income statement relating to taxes were as follows, with all numbers in millions:

	2005	2004	2003
Income before income taxes	$59,432	$41,241	$31,966
Income taxes	23,302	15,911	11,006
Income from continuing operations	$36,130	$25,330	$20,960

The $23.302 billion in income tax expense reported by ExxonMobil in 2005 is not necessarily equal to the amount of cash paid for income taxes during the year. In fact, ExxonMobil paid $22.535 billion for income taxes in 2005. Reported income tax expense may differ from the actual amount of cash paid for taxes for two reasons. First, like many other expenses, income taxes are not necessarily paid in cash in the year in which they are incurred. The important point to remember is that reported income tax expense reflects the amount of income taxes attributable to income earned during the year, whether the tax was actually paid in cash during the year or not.

The second reason reported income tax expense may differ from the actual amount of cash paid for taxes is that income tax expense is based on reported financial accounting income, whereas the amount of cash paid for income taxes is dictated by the applicable government tax law. The $23.302 billion income tax expense reported by ExxonMobil in 2005 reflects the total estimated amount of income tax the company expects will eventually be paid based on the income reported in the current year's income statement. However, because the income computed using the tax rules is almost always different from the income computed using financial accounting standards, some of this tax may not have to be paid for several years. In addition, tax rules may require income tax to be paid on income before the financial accounting standards consider that income to be "earned." These differences in tax law income and financial accounting income give rise to deferred income tax items, which are discussed in this section.

Corporations in the United States compute two different income numbers—financial income for reporting to stockholders and taxable income for reporting to the Internal Revenue Service (IRS). The existence of these two "sets of books" seems unethical to some, illegal to others. However, the difference between the stockholders' need for information and the government's need for efficient revenue collection makes the computation of the two different income numbers essential. The different purposes of these reporting systems were summarized by the U.S. Supreme Court in the *Thor Power Tool case* (1979):

> The primary goal of financial accounting is to provide useful information to management, shareholders, creditors, and others properly interested; the major responsibility of the accountant is to protect these parties from being misled. The primary goal of the income tax system, in contrast, is the equitable collection of revenue.

In summary, U.S. corporations compute income in two different ways, and rightly so. Nevertheless, the existence of these two different numbers that can each be called "income before taxes" makes it surprisingly difficult to define what is meant by "income tax expense."

Deferred Tax Example

Assume that you invest $1,000 by buying shares in a mutual fund on January 1. Also assume that the income tax rate is 40%. According to the tax law, any economic gain you experience through an increase in the value of your mutual fund shares is not taxed until you actually sell your shares. The rationale behind this tax rule is that until you sell your shares, you don't have the cash to pay any tax. Now, assume further that the economy does well and that the value of your mutual fund shares increases to $1,600 by December 31. You decide to prepare partial financial statements to summarize your holdings and the performance of your shares during the year. These financial statements are as follows:

Balance Sheet		Income Statement	
Assets:		Revenues:	
Mutual Fund Shares	$1,600	Gain on Mutual Fund Investment	$600

A moment's consideration reveals that this balance sheet and income statement are misleading. Yes, it is true that your shares are now worth $1,600, but if and when you liquidate the shares, you will have to pay income tax of $240 [($1,600 − $1,000) × 0.40]. Thus, you are overstating your economic position by only reporting the $1,600 in mutual fund shares; you should also report that a liability of $240 exists in relation to these shares. Similarly, it is misleading to report the $600 gain on your income statement without also reporting that, at some future time, you will have to pay $240 in income tax on that gain. A more accurate set of financial statements would appear as follows:

Balance Sheet		Income Statement	
Assets:		Revenues:	
Mutual Fund Shares	$1,600	Gain on Mutual Fund Investment	$600
Liabilities:		Expenses:	
Deferred Income Tax Liability	$ 240	Income Tax Expense	$240

The appropriate journal entry to recognize income tax expense in this case is as follows:

Income Tax Expense	240	
Deferred Income Tax Liability		240

Note that the deferred income tax liability is not a legal liability because, as far as the IRS is concerned, you do not currently owe any tax on the increase in the value of your mutual fund. Nevertheless, the deferred tax liability is an economic liability that should be reported now because it reflects an obligation that will have to be paid in the future as a result of an event (the increase in the value of the mutual fund shares) that occurred this year.

Now, what if the mutual fund shares had decreased in value from $1,000 to $400? Consider whether the following set of financial statements would accurately reflect your economic position and performance:

Balance Sheet		**Income Statement**	
Assets:		Revenues:	
Mutual Fund Shares	$400	Loss on Mutual Fund Investment	$600

Again, these financial statements are somewhat misleading because they ignore the future tax implications of the change in the value of the mutual fund shares. In this case, when the shares are sold, you will realize a taxable loss of $600. If you have other investment income, that loss can be used to reduce your total taxable income by $600, which will save you $240 ($600 × 0.40) in income taxes. Thus, in a real sense, this loss on the mutual funds is not all bad because it will provide you with a $240 reduction in income taxes in the year in which you sell the shares. This reduction in taxes is an asset, a deferred income tax asset, because it represents a probable future economic benefit that has arisen from an event (the drop in the value of the mutual fund shares) that occurred this year. Similarly, the income statement effect of this future savings in taxes is to soften the blow of the reported $600 loss. The loss that occurred this year will result in an income tax benefit in the future, so the benefit is reported on this year's income statement, as follows:

Balance Sheet		**Income Statement**	
Assets:		Expenses:	
Mutual Fund Shares	$400	Loss on Mutual Fund Investment	$ 600
		Less: Income Tax Benefit	(240)
Deferred Income Tax Asset	$240		
		Net Loss	$ 360

The journal entry to recognize the income tax "expense" is as follows:

Deferred Income Tax Asset	240	
Income Tax Expense		240

Notice that Income Tax Expense is credited, or reduced, in this entry. If there are other income taxes for the year, this credit will result in a reduction in reported income tax expense. If there are no other income taxes, then the credit amount will be reported on the income statement as an addition to income under the title "income tax benefit."

The value of the deferred tax asset depends on your having other investment income in the future against which the loss on the mutual fund shares can be offset. Thus, accounting for deferred tax assets is complicated by the fact that one must make an assumption about the likelihood that a company will have enough taxable income in the future to be able to take advantage of the deferred tax benefit.

As this simple mutual fund example illustrates, the amount of income tax expense reported on a company's income statement is not necessarily the same as the amount of income tax the company must pay on taxable income generated during the year. There are literally hundreds of accounting areas in which income is taxed by the taxing authorities in a different year than the year in which the income is reported to the financial statement users in the income statement. The details of deferred income tax accounting are among the most complicated issues covered in intermediate accounting courses.

REMEMBER THIS...

- The amount of sales tax collected is reported as a liability until the funds are forwarded to the appropriate government agency.

- When property taxes are paid in advance, the amount is reported as a prepaid asset until the time period covered by the property tax has expired.

- Reported income tax expense is not merely the amount of income tax that a company legally owes for a given year.

- Because of differences between financial accounting rules and income tax rules, revenues and expenses can enter into the computation of income in different years for financial accounting purposes and for income tax purposes.

- Proper accounting for deferred income taxes ensures that reported income tax expense for a year represents all of the income tax consequences arising from transactions undertaken during the year.

Contingencies

Distinguish between contingent items that should be recognized in the financial statements and those that should be merely disclosed in the financial statement notes.

(3) By its very nature, business is full of uncertainty. As discussed in relation to employee compensation and taxes, proper recording of an expense in the current period frequently requires making estimates about what will occur in future periods. Sometimes the very existence of an asset or liability depends on the occurrence, or nonoccurrence, of a future event. For example, whether a company will have to make a payment as a result of a lawsuit arising from events occurring this year depends on a judge or jury ruling that may not be known for several years. In accounting terms, a **contingency** is an uncertain circumstance involving a potential gain or loss that will not be resolved until some future event occurs. In this section, we discuss the conceptual issues associated with contingencies and the accounting for events for which the outcome is uncertain.

contingency

Circumstances involving potential losses or gains that will not be resolved until some future event occurs.

If you were a financial statement user, would you want to be informed of events known to management that might have an adverse effect on the company's future? Consider as an example a lawsuit filed against a company. Because litigation can take years, how should that company account for the possibility of a loss? Would you want the company to wait until the lawsuit is resolved before informing financial statement users of the litigation? Of course not. You would want to know about the lawsuit if the outcome could potentially materially affect the operations of the company. But would you want to know about every lawsuit filed against the company? Probably not.

Accounting standard-setters have addressed this issue and determined that the proper disclosure for a contingency depends upon the assessed outcome. The first thing to note is that accounting standard-setters determined that accounting for contingent gains is, in most cases, inappropriate. Contingent gains are typically not accounted for until the future event relating to the contingent gain resolves itself. Contingent liabilities are to be accounted for differently depending on an assessment of the likely outcome of the contingency. Exhibit 3 contains the relevant terms, definitions, and proper accounting for contingent liabilities.

If you think about it, this probability spectrum makes a great deal of sense. For example, if it is likely that your company will lose a lawsuit in which it is the defendant, then it would be appropriate to account for that outcome now by recognizing a loss and establishing a payable. If the likelihood of your company losing the case is slight, then it makes sense to do nothing. And if you are unsure of the outcome, then disclosure in the notes seems appropriate.

The problem in implementing these terms relates to assessing the likelihood of an outcome. Who is to say if your company will lose a lawsuit? The company must obtain objective assessments as to the possible outcome of future events. In the case of litigation, the company would ask its attorneys about the possible outcome. The firm auditing the company might use its own attorneys to assess the possible outcome. In any case, companies are required to make objective assessments as to the likely outcome of contingent events and then account for those events based on that assessment.

Wal-Mart's 2006 Form 10-K (see Appendix A) contains the company's disclosure relating to contingencies. At the time, the company was involved in several lawsuits regarding labor laws. Contrast Wal-Mart's disclosure with the 2005 disclosure provided by **Altria Group**, the parent of tobacco company **Philip Morris**, relating to its involvement in ongoing tobacco litigation. The company provides over eight pages of disclosure relating to its potential tobacco-related liability.

STOP & THINK

Why might a company hesitate to assess the likelihood of losing an ongoing lawsuit as being probable? If you were the attorney for the plaintiff, how could you use the resulting information from the financial statements?

environmental liabilities

Obligations incurred because of damage done to the environment.

Environmental Liabilities

Environmental liabilities have gained increasing attention of late because of their potential magnitude. **Environmental liabilities** are obligations incurred because of damage done by companies to the environment. Common environmental liabilities include cleanup costs associated with oil spills, toxic waste dumps,

EXHIBIT 3	Accounting for Contingent Liabilities	
Term	**Definition**	**Accounting**
Probable	The future event is likely to occur.	Estimate the amount of the contingency and make the appropriate journal entry; provide detailed disclosure in the notes.
Reasonably possible	The chance of the future event occurring is more than remote but less than likely.	Provide detailed disclosure of the possible liability in the notes.
Remote	The chance of the future event occurring is slight.	No disclosure required.

or air pollution. These liabilities are usually brought to the company's attention as a result of fines or penalties imposed by the federal government or when damage that is caused by the company is recognized. Although the accounting and disclosures associated with environmental liabilities fall under the guidelines for contingencies discussed in the previous section, environmental liabilities present a unique problem.

In the case of a lawsuit, one can typically make a reasonable estimate as to the upper bound of the potential settlement. For example, if your company is being sued for $4 million, it is unlikely that any potential settlement will be higher than that amount. In the case of environmental liabilities, it is often very difficult to estimate the cost of environmental cleanup. Thus, while the company may deem it probable that a liability exists, estimating that liability can be difficult. Recall that the contingency standard requires a liability to be recorded on the company's books if it is probable and estimable. If a potential liability is possible and estimable, the standards require note disclosure.

What about the situation where a potential liability is probable but cannot be estimated with much accuracy, as is often the case with environmental liabilities? Obviously, if a company cannot estimate a probable obligation, it makes sense to provide extensive note disclosure. Most companies will estimate at least a minimum amount and provide note disclosure as to the possibility of additional costs. As an illustration, **ExxonMobil** disclosed the information in Exhibit 4 in its 1991 and 2005 annual reports in connection

---

EXHIBIT 4	**ExxonMobil–1991 and 2005 Disclosures Concerning *Exxon Valdez* Oil Spill**

Disclosure in 1991

On March 24, 1989, the Exxon Valdez, a tanker owned by Exxon Shipping Company, a subsidiary of Exxon Corporation, ran aground on Bligh Reef in Prince William Sound off the port of Valdez, Alaska, and released approximately 260,000 barrels of crude oil. More than 315 lawsuits, including class actions, have been brought in various courts against Exxon Corporation and certain of its subsidiaries.

On October 8, 1991, the United States District Court for the District of Alaska approved a civil agreement and consent decree. . . . These agreements provided for guilty pleas to certain misdemeanors, the dismissal of all felony charges and the remaining misdemeanor charges by the United States, and the release of all civil claims against Exxon . . . by the United States and the state of Alaska. The agreements also released all claims related to or arising from the oil spill by Exxon. . . .

Payments under the plea agreement totaled $125 million–$25 million in fines and $100 million in payments to the United States and Alaska for restoration projects in Alaska. Payments under the civil agreement and consent decree will total $900 million over a ten-year period. The civil agreement also provides for the possible payment, between September 1, 2002, and September 1, 2006, of up to $100 million for substantial loss or decline in populations, habitats, or species in areas affected by the oil spill which could not have been reasonably anticipated on September 25, 1991.

The remaining cost to the corporation from the Valdez accident is difficult to predict and cannot be determined at this time. It is believed the final outcome, net of reserves already provided, will not have a materially adverse effect upon the corporation's operations or financial condition.

Disclosure in 2005

A number of lawsuits, including class actions, were brought in various courts against Exxon Mobil Corporation and certain of its subsidiaries relating to the accidental release of crude oil from the tanker Exxon Valdez in 1989. The vast majority of the compensatory claims have been resolved and paid. All of the punitive damage claims were consolidated in the civil trial that began in 1994. The first judgment from the United States District Court for the District of Alaska in the amount of $5 billion was vacated by the United States Court of Appeals for the Ninth Circuit as being excessive under the Constitution. The second judgment in the amount of $4 billion was vacated by the Ninth Circuit panel without argument and sent back for the District Court to reconsider in the light of the recent U.S. Supreme Court decision in *Campbell v. State Farm*. The most recent District Court judgment for punitive damages was for $4.5 billion plus interest and was entered in January 2004. ExxonMobil and the plaintiffs have appealed this decision to the Ninth Circuit. The Corporation has posted a $5.4 billion letter for credit. Oral arguments were held before the Ninth Circuit on January 27, 2006. Management believes that the likelihood of the judgment being upheld is remote. While it is reasonably possible that a liability may have been incurred from the Exxon Valdez grounding, it is not possible to predict the ultimate outcome or to reasonably estimate any such potential liability.

with lawsuits filed as a result of the *Exxon Valdez* oil spill. Note that in 1991, the company sounds quite optimistic that it has settled the bulk of the claims related to the oil spill and that any further claims "will not have a materially adverse effect" upon the company. This optimistic disclosure is particularly interesting in light of the $4.5 billion adverse judgment discussed in the 2005 disclosure.

REMEMBER THIS...

- Contingent liabilities depend on some future event to determine if a liability actually exists.
- Companies are required to assess the likelihood of certain future events occurring and then, based on that assessment, provide appropriate disclosure.
- If the company deems the future event to be likely, the journal entries are made and the liability is accrued.
- If the future event is deemed reasonably possible, note disclosure is required.
- For those events considered remote, no disclosure is required.
- Environmental liabilities represent a case where a liability exists but measurement is difficult. A minimum liability is typically established along with extensive note disclosure.

Capitalize versus Expense

Understand when an expenditure should be recorded as an asset and when it should be recorded as an expense.

(4) To this point in the text, we have assumed that the decision of expensing a cost to the income statement or capitalizing an expenditure and placing it on the balance sheet as an asset is an easy one. In reality, that decision is often difficult and one that makes accounting judgment critical. For example, should a building that cost $1 million and is expected to benefit 20 future periods be capitalized and placed on the balance sheet? The answer is pretty clear—of course. What about office supplies that are used this period? Will they benefit future periods? No, and as a result, the costs of those supplies should be expensed. What about research and development costs? Should they be capitalized as an asset or expensed to the income statement? Now you see the problem. Sometimes it is difficult to determine whether an expenditure will benefit the future. Exhibit 5 provides an expense/asset continuum that demonstrates the difficulty of the decision to capitalize or expense a cost.

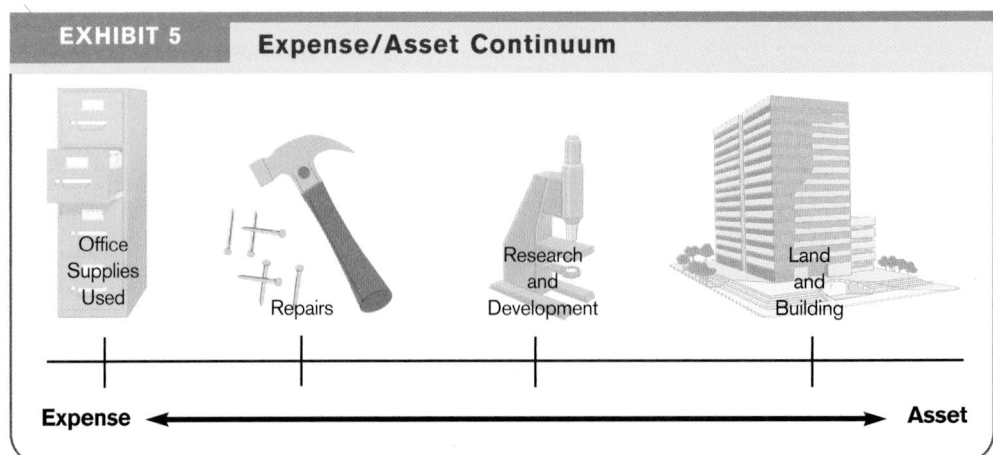

EXHIBIT 5   Expense/Asset Continuum

Office Supplies Used

Repairs

Research and Development

Land and Building

Expense ← → Asset

The endpoints of the continuum are easy. The decision starts to get fuzzy, though, once you leave the endpoints. Do repairs and maintenance benefit future periods (and therefore need to be capitalized), or are they necessary expenditures just to keep a machine running (and should be expensed)? To illustrate the issues involved in deciding whether an expenditure should be capitalized or expensed, two specific areas will be discussed—research and development (R&D) and advertising.

Research and Development

Research is an activity undertaken to discover new knowledge that will be useful in developing new products, services, or processes. Development involves the application of research findings to develop a plan or design for new or improved products and processes. **ExxonMobil** reports that, from 2003 through 2005, it spent an average of $660 million per year on R&D activities.

Because of the uncertainty surrounding the future economic benefit of R&D activities, the FASB decided in 1974 that research and development expenditures should be expensed in the period incurred. Among the arguments for expensing R&D costs is the frequent inability to find a definite causal relationship between the expenditures and future revenues. Sometimes very large expenditures do not generate any future revenue, while relatively small expenditures lead to significant discoveries that generate large revenues. The FASB found it difficult to establish criteria that would distinguish between those R&D expenditures that would most likely benefit future periods and those that would not.

In summary, the FASB concluded that R&D expenditures are undertaken to benefit future periods, but that it is impractical to identify which R&D expenditures actually do provide future economic benefit. Accordingly, all R&D costs are to be recorded as expenses in the year they are incurred. This rule leads to a systematic overstatement of R&D expenses and a systematic understatement of R&D assets.

STOP & THINK

Would you expect that a rule requiring all firms to expense R&D outlays would cause R&D expenditures to decrease? Why or why not?

FYI

The International Accounting Standards Board (IASB) has established an R&D accounting rule that many think is superior to the FASB rule. The IASB rule requires research costs to be expensed and development costs to be capitalized. Research costs are defined as those R&D costs incurred before technological feasibility has been established.

Advertising

Every year in the two weeks of hype preceding the Super Bowl, we hear about the incredible number of media people covering the event and about how much money advertisers are paying for a 30-second spot during the broadcast. We also hear a little bit about the football teams. With advertising costs running in excess of $2 million for 30 seconds, one has to believe that the advertisers expect some future economic benefit from the advertising. So, should advertising costs be capitalized or expensed?

For accounting purposes, the general presumption is that advertising costs should be expensed because of the uncertainty of the future benefits. However, in selected cases in which the future benefits are more certain, advertising costs should be capitalized. This type of advertising involves targeted advertising to customers who have purchased products in the past. Such advertising is also characterized by the ability to estimate how many customers will respond favorably.

As these discussions of R&D and advertising illustrate, capitalize-or-expense decisions can be quite difficult from a conceptual standpoint. The general rule of thumb is that, when there is significant uncertainty about whether an expenditure should be capitalized or expensed, expense it. This approach is in line with the traditional conservatism of accounting, but be aware that it can result in a significant understatement of the economic assets of a company.

REMEMBER THIS...

- Conceptually, a cost should be recorded as an asset whenever it has a probable future economic benefit.
- In practice, it is frequently quite difficult to tell when a cost should be recorded as an asset (capitalized) and when it should be recorded as an expense.
- In some areas, such as research and development (R&D) and advertising, specific accounting rules have been developed to create more uniformity about which costs should be expensed and which should be capitalized.

Summarizing Operations on an Income Statement

Prepare an income statement summarizing operating activities as well as other revenues and expenses, extraordinary items, and earnings per share.

(5) Having now completed our discussion of operating revenues and expenses (in Chapters 6, 7, and thus far in 8), you are ready to examine an income statement, such as the one in Exhibit 6, and see how operating results are communicated to investors and creditors. The numbers in the income statement do not relate to any previous examples; they are shown here for illustrative purposes only.

This income statement shows that with net sales revenue of $2,475,000, P & L Company had net income of $385,000. The income statement classifies and accounts for the other $2,090,000 ($2,475,000 − $385,000). Sales revenue, cost of goods sold, and operating expenses (which are separated into selling expenses and general and administrative expenses on the income statement) have already been explained. It is important to note that operating income of $726,000 shows how much P & L Company earned from carrying on its major operations. These items constitute the major ongoing components of the income statement. Items shown at the bottom of the income statement are not part of the main operations of the business or are unusual and nonrecurring in nature.

other revenues and expenses

Items incurred or earned from activities that are outside of, or peripheral to, the normal operations of a firm.

Other Revenues and Expenses

Other revenues and expenses are those items incurred or earned from activities outside of, or peripheral to, the normal operations of a firm. For example, a manufacturing company that receives dividends from its investments in the stock of another firm would show those dividend revenues as "Other Revenues and Expenses." This way, investors can see how much of a firm's income is from its major operating activity and how much is from peripheral activities, such as investing in other companies. The most common items reported in this section are interest and investment revenues and expenses. The other revenues and expenses category also includes gains and losses from the sale of assets other than inventory, such as land and buildings.

extraordinary items

Nonoperating gains and losses that are unusual in nature, infrequent in occurrence, and material in amount.

Extraordinary Items

The **extraordinary items** section of an income statement is reserved for reporting special nonoperating gains and losses. This category is restrictive and

EXHIBIT 6   **Sample Income Statement**

P & L Company
Income Statement
For the Year Ended December 31, 2009

Revenues:			
Gross sales revenue		$2,500,000	
Less: Sales returns		(12,000)	
Less: Sales discounts		(13,000)	
Net sales revenue			$2,475,000
Cost of goods sold			1,086,000
Gross margin			$1,389,000
Operating expenses:			
Selling expenses:			
Sales salaries expense	$200,000		
Sales commissions expense	60,000		
Advertising expense	45,000		
Delivery expense	14,000		
Total selling expenses		$ 319,000	
General and administrative expenses:			
Administrative salaries expense	$278,000		
Rent expense, office equipment	36,000		
Property tax expense	22,000		
Miscellaneous expenses	8,000		
Total general and administrative expenses		344,000	
Total operating expenses			663,000
Operating income			$ 726,000
Other revenues and expenses:			
Dividend revenue		$ 5,000	
Gain on sale of land		4,000	
Interest expense		(85,000)	
Net other revenues and expenses			(76,000)
Income from operations before income taxes			$ 650,000
Income taxes on operations (30%)			195,000
Income before extraordinary item			$ 455,000
Extraordinary item:			
Flood loss		$ (100,000)	
Income tax effect (30%)		30,000	(70,000)
Net income			$ 385,000
Earnings per share (100,000 shares outstanding):			
Income before extraordinary item			$4.55
Extraordinary loss			(0.70)
Net income			$3.85

Another item that is reported in a separate section of the income statement relates to discontinued operations. When a company decides to cease the operations of a segment or a division, it must provide careful disclosure as to the past profitability of the segment and the expected costs associated with closing the segment.

includes only those items that are (1) unusual in nature, (2) infrequent in occurrence, and (3) material in amount. They are separated from other revenues and expenses so that readers can identify them as onetime, or nonrecurring, events. Extraordinary items are rare but can include losses or gains from floods, fires, earthquakes, and so on. For example, in 1980 when Mount St. Helens erupted in Washington, mudslides and flooding adversely affected much of the **Weyerhaeuser Company**'s timberlands.

The 1980 eruption of Mount St. Helens caused **Weyerhaeuser Company** to report an extraordinary loss of $66.7 million. However, it's not likely Weyerhaeuser will have to worry about that extraordinary event happening again anytime soon!

Weyerhaeuser reported an extraordinary loss of $66.7 million in 1980 to cover standing timber, buildings, equipment, and other damaged items. Interestingly enough, the attack on the World Trade Center in September of 2001 was not accounted for as an extraordinary item. Accounting standard-setters determined that the economic effects of the World Trade Center attack were so pervasive as to make it impossible to separate the direct costs stemming from the attack from the economic costs (including lost revenue) created by the transformation of the economic landscape created by the attack.

If a firm has an extraordinary loss, its taxes are lower than they would be on the basis of ordinary operations. P & L Company, for example, actually paid only $165,000 ($195,000 based on operations less a $30,000 tax benefit from the extraordinary loss) in taxes. On the other hand, if a firm has an extraordinary gain, its taxes are increased. Therefore, to ensure that the full effect of the gain or loss is presented, extraordinary items are always shown together with their tax effects so that a net-of-tax amount can be seen. Thus, income tax expense may appear in two places on the income statement: below operating income before income taxes and in the extraordinary items section.

Earnings per Share

earnings per share (EPS)

The amount of net income (earnings) related to each share of stock; computed by dividing net income by the number of shares of stock outstanding during the period.

As noted in Chapter 2, a company is required to show **earnings per share (EPS)** on the income statement. If extraordinary items are included on the income statement, a firm will report EPS figures on income before extraordinary items, on extraordinary items, and on net income. Earnings per share is calculated by dividing a firm's net income by the number of shares of stock outstanding during the period. Exhibit 6 assumes that 100,000 shares of stock are outstanding. Earnings-per-share amounts are important because they allow potential investors to compare the profitability of all firms, whether large or small. Thus, the performance of a company earning $200 million and having 200,000 shares of stock outstanding can be compared with a company earning $60,000 and with 30,000 shares outstanding.

Income statements will often report two EPS figures—basic and diluted. The basic earnings per share figure is based on historical information. The diluted earnings per share number considers stock transactions that might occur in the future, the most common example being the exercise of stock options. Consider the following simplified example.

Burt Company reported net income for the year 2009 of $300,000. As of January 1, Burt had 100,000 shares of stock outstanding; those shares of stock were outstanding throughout the year. In addition, as of January 1, Burt had stock options outstanding that allowed certain executives to receive 50,000 shares of stock *for free* at a time of their choosing. As of December 31, the executives had not yet exercised the options.

basic earnings per share

An earnings per share figure that divides net income by the number of shares of stock outstanding.

diluted earnings per share

An earnings per share figure that considers the effect on net income and shares outstanding of events that will likely occur in the future, such as the exercising of favorable stock options.

Burt Company will compute two EPS numbers for 2009. The **basic earnings per share** is a straightforward computation based on Burt's reported net income and number of shares outstanding during the year. In this case, basic EPS is $3.00 per share ($300,000 net income/100,000 shares outstanding). Burt also computes **diluted earnings per share**. The diluted EPS number can be thought of as the earnings per share that would have been earned by each owner of one share *if* the holders of favorable contracts, such as the stock options in the case of Burt Company, had decided to exercise their rights at the beginning of the year. The diluted EPS number is really a future-oriented number; it gives the shareholders an indication of what their earnings per share next year might be if existing contracts, such as the options in this case, are exercised and new shares are issued. In this case, the diluted EPS is $2.00 per share [$300,000/(100,000 shares + 50,000 potential shares)]. Options are just one example of contracts that can "dilute" the earnings per share of existing shareholders; another example is bonds (basically corporate IOUs) that can be converted into shares of stock. Bonds are discussed in Chapter 10.

Differing Income Statement Formats

The income statement featured in Exhibit 6 demonstrates detailed disclosure of a company's operations. Most companies do not provide that level of detail. The information contained in income statements varies from company to company. For example, **Wal-Mart** (see Appendix A) summarizes the results of its operations in 19 lines. **IBM**, on the other hand, provides detailed revenue and cost figures on the face of its income statements for each of its five operating segments (hardware, global services, software, global financing, and enterprise investments). **Ford Motor Company** provides detail in its income statements as to the operations of its two very different lines of business—automotive and financial services. Keep in mind that the format of the income statement will vary across companies but the information contained in the income statement is the same—revenues and expenses.

> **REMEMBER THIS...**
>
> - The results of operating activities are summarized and reported on an income statement.
> - On an income statement, cost of goods sold is subtracted from net sales to arrive at gross margin, or the amount a company marks up its inventory.
> - Operating expenses are then subtracted from gross margin to arrive at operating income.
> - Nonoperating items, such as other revenues and expenses, extraordinary items, and earnings per share, are reported on the income statement below operating income.

REVIEW OF LEARNING OBJECTIVES

(1) **Account for the various components of employee compensation expense.**
Total employee compensation can involve some or all of the following:

- Payroll
- Compensated absences
- Bonuses
- Stock options
- Postemployment benefits
- Pensions
- Postretirement benefits other than pensions

(2) **Compute income tax expense, including appropriate consideration of deferred tax items.**

- Sales tax–Reported as a liability until the funds are forwarded to the appropriate government agency.
- Property tax–When paid in advance, the amount is reported as a prepaid asset until the time period covered by the property tax has expired.
- Income tax–Deferred income taxes reported to ensure that reported income tax expense for a year represents all of the income tax consequences arising from transactions undertaken during the year.

(3) **Distinguish between contingent items that should be recognized in the financial statements and those that should be merely disclosed in the financial statement notes.**

- **Probable**–expense and liability recognized
- **Possible**–note disclosure required
- **Remote**–no disclosure required

(4) **Understand when an expenditure should be recorded as an asset and when it should be recorded as an expense.**

- Conceptually, a cost should be recorded as an asset whenever it has a probable future economic benefit.
- In practice, it is frequently quite difficult to tell when a cost should be recorded as an asset (capitalized) and when it should be recorded as an expense.
- In some areas, such as research and development (R&D) and advertising, specific accounting rules have been developed to create more uniformity about which costs should be expensed and which should be capitalized.

(5) **Prepare an income statement summarizing operating activities as well as other revenues and expenses, extraordinary items, and earnings per share.**

- On an income statement, cost of goods sold is subtracted from net sales to arrive at gross margin, or the amount a company marks up its inventory.
- Operating expenses are then subtracted from gross margin to arrive at operating income.
- Nonoperating items, such as other revenues and expenses, extraordinary items, and earnings per share, are reported on the income statement below operating income.

KEY TERMS & CONCEPTS

basic earnings per
   share, 363
bonus, 347
contingency, 355
defined benefit plan, 349
defined contribution
   plan, 348

diluted earnings per
   share, 363
earnings per share
   (EPS), 362
employee stock
   options, 347

environmental
   liabilities, 356
extraordinary
   items, 360
other revenues and
   expenses, 360

pension, 348
postemployment
   benefits, 348
sales tax payable, 351
Social Security (FICA)
   taxes, 345

REVIEW PROBLEM

The Income Statement

From the following information, prepare an income statement for Southern Corporation for the year ended December 31, 2009. Assume that there are 200,000 shares of stock outstanding.

Sales Returns	$ 50,000
Sales Discounts	70,000
Gross Sales Revenue	9,000,000
Flood Loss	80,000
Income Taxes on Operations	500,000
Administrative Salaries Expense	360,000
Sales Salaries Expense	800,000
Rent Expense (General and Administrative)	32,000
Utilities Expense (General and Administrative)	4,000
Supplies Expense (General and Administrative)	16,000
Delivery Expense (Selling)	6,300
Payroll Tax Expense (Selling)	6,000
Automobile Expense (General and Administrative)	3,800
Insurance Expense (General and Administrative)	34,000
Advertising Expense (Selling)	398,000
Interest Revenue	6,000
Interest Expense	92,000
Insurance Expense (Selling)	7,000
Entertainment Expense (Selling)	7,200
Miscellaneous Selling Expenses	15,000
Miscellaneous General and Administrative Expenses	10,800
Cost of Goods Sold	5,950,000
Tax rate applicable to flood loss	30%

Solution

The first step in preparing an income statement is classifying items, as follows:

Revenue Accounts	
Sales Returns	$ 50,000
Sales Discounts	70,000
Gross Sales Revenue	9,000,000

(continued)

Cost of Goods Sold Accounts	
Cost of Goods Sold	$5,950,000

Selling Expense Accounts	
Sales Salaries Expense	$800,000
Delivery Expense	6,300
Payroll Tax Expense	6,000
Advertising Expense	398,000
Insurance Expense	7,000
Entertainment Expense	7,200
Miscellaneous Selling Expenses	15,000

General and Administrative Expense Accounts	
Administrative Salaries Expense	$360,000
Rent Expense	32,000
Utilities Expense	4,000
Supplies Expense	16,000
Automobile Expense	3,800
Insurance Expense	34,000
Miscellaneous General and Administrative Expenses	10,800

Other Revenue and Expense Accounts	
Interest Revenue	$ 6,000
Interest Expense	92,000

Miscellaneous Accounts	
Income Taxes on Operations	$500,000

Extraordinary Item Accounts	
Flood Loss	$80,000
Tax rate	30%

Once the accounts are classified, the income statement is prepared by including the accounts in the following format:

	Net Sales Revenue (Gross Sales Revenue − Sales Returns − Sales Discounts)
−	Cost of Goods Sold
=	Gross Margin
−	Selling Expenses
−	General and Administrative Expenses
=	Operating Income
+/−	Other Revenues and Expenses (add Net Revenues, subtract Net Expenses)
=	Income before Income Taxes

(continued)

- Income Taxes on Operations
= Income before Extraordinary Items
+/− Extraordinary Items (add Extraordinary Gains, subtract Extraordinary Losses, net of applicable taxes)
= Net Income

After net income has been computed, earnings per share is calculated and added to the bottom of the statement. It is important that the proper heading be included.

Southern Corporation
Income Statement
For the Year Ended December 31, 2009

Revenues:			
Gross sales revenue		$9,000,000	
Less: Sales returns		(50,000)	
Less: Sales discounts		(70,000)	
Net sales revenue			$8,880,000
Cost of goods sold			5,950,000
Gross margin			$2,930,000
Operating expenses:			
Selling expenses:			
Sales salaries expense	$800,000		
Delivery expense	6,300		
Payroll tax expense	6,000		
Advertising expense	398,000		
Insurance expense	7,000		
Entertainment expense	7,200		
Miscellaneous expenses	15,000		
Total selling expenses		$1,239,500	
General and administrative expenses:			
Administrative salaries expense	$360,000		
Rent expense	32,000		
Utilities expense	4,000		
Supplies expense	16,000		
Automobile expense	3,800		
Insurance expense	34,000		
Miscellaneous expenses	10,800		
Total general and administrative expenses		460,600	
Total operating expenses			1,700,100
Operating income			$1,229,900
Other revenues and expenses:			
Interest revenue		$ 6,000	
Interest expense		(92,000)	
Net other revenues and expenses			(86,000)
Income from operations before income taxes			$1,143,900
Income taxes on operations			500,000
Income before extraordinary item			$ 643,900
Extraordinary item:			
Flood loss		$ (80,000)	
Income tax effect (30%)		24,000	(56,000)
Net income			$ 587,900
Earnings per share:			
Before extraordinary items		$ 3.22	($643,900 ÷ 200,000 shares)
Extraordinary loss		(0.28)	($ 56,000 ÷ 200,000 shares)
Net income		$ 2.94	($587,900 ÷ 200,000 shares)

DISCUSSION QUESTIONS

1. Why is the accounting for payroll-related liabilities more complicated than the accounting for other current liabilities?
2. If the period of time covered by a company's payroll does not coincide with the last day of the year for financial reporting, how is accounting for the payroll affected by this situation?
3. What is a compensated absence?
4. What danger is there in basing a manager's bonus on reported net income?
5. Why might a company offer stock options to an employee instead of simply paying the employee cash? Why might the employee accept stock options instead of asking to be paid in cash?
6. For a stock option to be valuable at some future point in time, what must happen to the company's stock price?
7. Severance benefits resulting from a company restructuring are reported as an expense in the period that the restructuring decision is made rather than when the benefits are actually paid. Why?
8. What is the difference between a defined contribution pension plan and a defined benefit pension plan?
9. How is a company's pension obligation reported in its balance sheet?
10. List and briefly discuss the three components of pension expense discussed in the chapter.
11. In what ways do postretirement health-care and life insurance benefit plans differ from postretirement pension plans?

12. Why is an end-of-year adjusting entry for property taxes often necessary?
13. In your opinion, what is the primary objective of determining pretax financial accounting income? How does this objective differ from the objectives of determining taxable income as defined by the IRS?
14. When and how does a company record the amount owed to the government for income taxes for a given year?
15. What causes deferred income taxes?
16. What is the difference between a "contingent liability" and a "liability"?
17. Escalating environmental liabilities are a major concern of companies today. How does a company know when to record such liabilities?
18. Currently **Microsoft** spends a tremendous amount of money on research and development costs to continuously develop new products. How are such R&D costs accounted for?
19. XYZ Corporation pays for advertising costs all the time. Sometimes the company records these payments as assets, and sometimes it records them as expenses. Why would XYZ use different accounting treatments?
20. What types of items would be included on an income statement as "other revenues and expenses"?
21. More than ever before, tremendous attention is being paid to a company's earnings-per-share number. Why do you think investors and creditors pay so much attention to earnings per share?

PRACTICE EXERCISES

PE 8-1   Salaries Expense Calculation
LO1   Using the following data, compute salaries expense.

State Withholding Taxes Payable	$ 6,100
FICA Taxes Payable, Employer	6,503
Salaries Payable	59,647
Federal Unemployment Taxes Payable	720
Federal Withholding Taxes Payable	12,750
State Unemployment Taxes Payable	2,380
FICA Taxes Payable, Employees	6,503

PE 8-2   Salaries Expense Journal Entry
LO1   Refer to the data in PE 8-1. Make the journal entry necessary to record salaries expense for the period.

PE 8-3   Payroll Tax Expense Calculation
LO1   Refer to the data in PE 8-1. Compute payroll tax expense.

PE 8-4 **Payroll Tax Expense Journal Entry**

LO1 Refer to the data in PE 8-1. Make the journal entry necessary to record payroll tax expense for the period.

PE 8-5 **Salaries and Payroll Tax Payments**

LO1 Refer to the data in PE 8-1. Make the journal entries necessary to record the payment of the payable accounts related to salaries expense and payroll tax expense to (1) the federal government, (2) the state government, and (3) the employees.

PE 8-6 **Accruing Compensated Absences**

LO1 Assume an employee earns $150 per day and accrues one sick day each month. Make the journal entry necessary at the end of the quarter to record the accrual of the sick days during the quarter.

PE 8-7 **Using Compensated Absences**

LO1 The employee mentioned in PE 8-6 used one sick day. For simplicity, combine the various taxes into one account called "Various Taxes Payable." The effective tax rate for all of the various taxes is 20%. Make the journal entry necessary to record the use of the sick day.

PE 8-8 **Accounting for Employee Stock Options**

LO1 An employee receives stock options as part of her compensation package. Those options allow the employee to purchase 1,000 shares of stock for $40 per share. If after one year the stock price has increased to $58 per share and the employee elects to exercise all of her stock options, how much will the employee net from the options?

PE 8-9 **Postemployment Benefits**

LO1 Because of a drop in demand for its products, the company found it necessary to lay off 350 employees. The employment contract grants termination benefits worth an estimated $10,000 to each employee. Make the journal entry necessary to record the termination of the employees.

PE 8-10 **Pension Terminology**

LO1 Identify which one of the following terms correctly matches the following definition: The amount a company's pension obligation increases as a result of employees working and earning more benefits.
a. Pension fund
b. Pension-related interest cost
c. Service cost
d. Pension expense
e. Return on pension fund

PE 8-11 **Net Pension Asset/Liability**

LO1 Companies A, B, and C report the following information:

	A	B	C
Pension benefit obligation	$ 3,920	$ 9,230	$1,302
Service cost	235	500	150
Pension fund assets	2,004	11,023	1,350
Expected return on pension fund assets	200	1,000	120

For each of the companies, determine the amount of the net pension asset/liability. Be sure to specify whether the amount is an asset or a liability.

PE 8-12   **Pension Expense**

LO1   Using the following numbers, compute pension expense.

Expected return on fund assets	$ 445
Pension benefit obligation	3,200
Service cost	265
Interest cost	320
Pension fund assets	4,100

PE 8-13   **Sales Tax**

LO2   The company sold merchandise for $448; this price does *not* include sales tax. The state sales tax rate is 6.25%. Make the journal entry necessary to record this transaction.

PE 8-14   **Property Taxes**

LO2   The company paid $10,800 in advance for one year of property taxes on September 24. The property taxes are for the one-year period beginning October 1. Make the journal entries necessary to record (1) the payment of the property taxes and (2) the year-end adjusting entry on December 31.

PE 8-15   **Income Tax Expense**

LO2   Which one of the following statements correctly describes income tax expense?
a. The amount of cash paid for income taxes during the year.
b. The amount of income tax owed as of the end of the year.
c. The amount of cash that will be paid for income taxes next year.
d. The amount of income taxes attributable to the income earned during the year.
e. The amount of income taxes payable as reported in a company's income tax return.

PE 8-16   **Deferred Tax Liability**

LO2   The company invested $2,500 in a mutual fund on April 1. By December 31, the value of the mutual fund had increased to $3,100, and the company did *not* sell any portion of the mutual fund during the year. The company's income tax rate is 35%. Prepare the journal entry necessary to record the deferred income tax liability.

PE 8-17   **Deferred Tax Assets**

LO2   The company invested $5,600 in a mutual fund on August 1. By December 31, the value of the mutual fund had declined to $3,900, and the company did not sell any portion of the mutual fund during the year. The company's income tax rate is 25%. Prepare the journal entry necessary to record the deferred income tax asset.

PE 8-18   **Contingent Liabilities**

LO3   Which one of the following correctly describes the circumstances in which a contingent liability should be recognized as a liability in the financial statements?
a. The chance of the future event occurring is remote.
b. The chance of the future event occurring is possible.
c. The chance of the future event occurring is probable.
d. The chance of the future event occurring is slight.
e. The chance of the future event occurring is more likely than not.

PE 8-19   **Capitalize versus Expense**

LO4   Which one of the following statements is correct?
a. When there is significant uncertainty about whether an expenditure should be capitalized or expensed, capitalize it.
b. When there is significant uncertainty about whether an expenditure should be capitalized or expensed, expense it.

(continued)

c. Generally, advertising costs are capitalized because it is easy for firms to trace advertising dollars spent to revenue generated from such advertisements.

d. Expenditures made for equipment and buildings should be expensed in the period of the purchase.

e. Research and development expenditures are typically capitalized in the period in which they are incurred.

PE 8-20   **Income Statement Classification**

LO5   Using the following data, prepare a classified income statement. The income tax rate on all items is 25%. (*Hint:* Net income is $52,050.)

Advertising expense	$ 4,000
Sales returns	5,000
Cost of goods sold	80,000
Dividend revenue	2,000
Gain on sale of equipment	1,000
Interest expense	5,000
Rent expense	3,600
Sales discounts	10,000
Salaries expense	11,000
Gross sales	215,000
Tornado loss	30,000

PE 8-21   **Earnings per Share**

LO5   The company had 300,000 shares of stock outstanding throughout the year. In addition, as of January 1 the company had issued stock options that allowed employees to receive 50,000 shares of stock for free at a time of their choosing in the future. As of the end of the year, none of the options had been exercised. Net income for the year was $510,000. Compute (1) basic earnings per share and (2) diluted earnings per share.

EXERCISES

E 8-22   **Payroll Accounting**

LO1   Stockbridge Stores, Inc., has three employees, Frank Wall, Mary Jones, and Susan Wright. Summaries of their 2009 salaries and withholdings are as follows:

Employee	Gross Salaries	Federal Income Taxes Withheld	State Income Taxes Withheld	FICA Taxes Withheld
Frank Wall	$54,000	$6,500	$2,500	$4,131
Mary Jones	39,000	4,800	1,900	2,984
Susan Wright	34,000	4,250	1,500	2,601

1. Prepare the summary entry for salaries paid to the employees for the year 2009.

2. Assume that, in addition to FICA taxes, the employer has incurred $192 for federal unemployment taxes and $720 for state unemployment taxes. Prepare the summary journal entry to record the payroll tax liability for 2009, assuming no taxes have yet been paid.

3. **Interpretive Question:** What other types of items are frequently withheld from employees' paychecks in addition to income taxes and FICA taxes?

E 8-23   **Bonus Computation and Journal Entry**

LO1

Chris Anger is the president of Anger Company, and his brother, George Anger, is the vice president. Their compensation package includes bonuses of 5% for Chris Anger and 4% for George Anger of net income that exceeds $325,000. Net income for the year 2009 has just been computed to be $745,000.

1. Compute the amount of bonuses to be paid to Chris and George Anger.
2. Prepare the journal entries to record the accrual and payment of the bonuses. Summarize all withholding taxes related to the bonuses in an account called Various Taxes Payable. Taxes payable on the bonuses total $8,400 for Chris and $6,720 for George.

E 8-24   **Stock Options: Fair Value Method**

LO1

On January 1, 2009, the Magily Company established a stock option plan for its senior employees. A total of 60,000 options were granted that permit employees to purchase 60,000 shares of stock at $48 per share. Each option had a fair value of $11 on the date the options were granted. The market price for Magily stock on January 1, 2009, was $50. The employees are required to remain with Magily Company for the entire year of 2009 in order to be able to exercise these options.

Compute the total amount of compensation expense to be associated with these options under the fair value method.

E 8-25   **Stock Options: Fair Value Method**

LO1

Refer to the information in E 8-24. If those holding stock options can purchase a share of stock for $48 and the market value of a share of stock on 1/1/09 is $50, how can the option to purchase the share be worth $11. What factors would cause the option to be worth more than $2 ($50 − $48)? Remember, the options cannot be exercised until the end of the year.

E 8-26   **Pensions on the Balance Sheet**

LO1

Pension plan information for Brassfield Company is as follows:

December 31, 2009	
Pension obligation liability	$4,300,000
December 31, 2009	
Pension fund assets	4,640,000
During 2009	
Total pension expense	250,000

How will this information be reported on Brassfield's balance sheet as of December 31, 2009?

E 8-27   **Computing Pension Expense**

LO1

Chanelle Company reports the following pension information for 2009:

Pension-related interest cost for the year	$ 65,000
Pension fund assets, end of year	895,000
Pension obligation liability, end of year	930,000
Pension service cost for the year	90,000
Return on pension fund assets for the year	115,000

1. What pension amount would Chanelle report on its balance sheet as of the end of the year?
2. Compute the amount to be reported on the income statement as pension expense for the year.

E 8-28 **Pension Computations**

LO1 The following pension information is for three different companies. For each company, compute the missing amount or amounts.

	Company 1	Company 2	Company 3
Pension fund assets	$100,000	$75,000	$ (e)
Pension obligation liability	(a)	80,000	100,000
Net pension asset (liability)	20,000	(c)	(25,000)
Pension-related interest cost	$ 10,000	$ (d)	$ 20,000
Service cost	8,000	6,000	23,000
Return on pension plan assets	5,000	8,000	(f)
Pension expense	(b)	10,000	35,000

E 8-29 **Accounting for Property Taxes**

LO2 In June 2008, Hans Company received a bill from the county government for property taxes on its land and buildings for the period July 1, 2008, through June 30, 2009. The amount of the tax bill is $17,400, and payment is due August 1, 2008. Hans Company uses the calendar year for financial reporting purposes.

1. Prepare the journal entries to record payment of the property taxes on August 1, 2008.
2. Prepare the adjusting entry for property taxes on December 31, 2008.

E 8-30 **Deferred Income Taxes**

LO2 Yosef Company began operating on January 1, 2009. At the end of the first year of operations, Yosef reported $750,000 income before income taxes on its income statement but only $660,000 taxable income on its tax return. This difference arose because $90,000 in income earned during 2009 was not yet taxable according to the income tax regulations. The tax rate is 35%.

1. Compute the amount of income tax that Yosef legally owes for taxable income generated during 2009.
2. Compute the amount of income tax expense to be reported on Yosef's income statement for 2009.
3. State whether Yosef has a deferred income tax asset or a deferred income tax liability as of the end of 2009. What is the amount of the asset or liability?

E 8-31 **Deferred Income Taxes**

LO2 Oranjestad Company began operating on January 1, 2009. At the end of the first year of operations, Oranjestad reported $650,000 income before income taxes on its income statement but taxable income of $720,000 on its tax return. This difference arose because $70,000 in expenses incurred during 2009 were not yet deductible for income tax purposes according to the income tax regulations. The tax rate is 35%.

1. Compute the amount of income tax that Oranjestad legally owes for taxable income generated during 2009.
2. Compute the amount of income tax expense to be reported on Oranjestad's income statement for 2009.
3. State whether Oranjestad has a deferred income tax asset or a deferred income tax liability as of the end of 2009. What is the amount of the asset or liability?

E 8-32 **Contingent Liabilities**

LO3 Rayn Company is involved in the following legal matters:

a. A customer is suing Rayn for allegedly selling a faulty and dangerous product. Rayn's attorneys believe that there is a 40% chance of Rayn's losing the suit.
b. A federal agency has accused Rayn of violating numerous employee safety laws. The company faces significant fines if found guilty. Rayn's attorneys feel that the company

(continued)

has complied with all applicable laws, and they therefore place the probability of incurring the fines at less than 10%.

c. Rayn has been named in a gender discrimination lawsuit. In the past, Rayn has systematically promoted its male employees at a faster rate than it has promoted its female employees. Rayn's attorneys judge the probability that Rayn will lose this lawsuit at more than 90%.

For each item, determine the appropriate accounting treatment.

E 8-33   **Classifying Expenditures as Assets or Expenses**

LO4   Determining whether an expenditure should be expensed or capitalized is often difficult. Consider each of the following independent situations and indicate whether you would recommend that the cost be expensed or capitalized as an asset. Explain your answer.

1. Splash.com has spent $1.5 million for a 30-second advertisement to be aired during the Super Bowl. The ad introduces the company's new Web-based product, and the company expects the ad to increase sales for at least 18 months.
2. Chromosome.com has spent $8 million on research related to genetic diseases. The company expects this research to lead to substantial revenues, beginning in the next year.
3. Catalog.com is an online catalog sales company. Catalog.com has just spent $5 million designing a targeted advertising campaign that will encourage regular customers of the company's online catalog service to buy new products.
4. Food.com is an online seller of groceries. The company just spent $4 million building a new warehouse. The warehouse is expected to be useful for the next 15 years.

E 8-34   **Preparing an Income Statement**

LO5   Bateman Company is preparing financial statements for the calendar year 2009. The following totals for each account have been verified as correct:

Office Supplies on Hand	$ 730
Insurance Expense	420
Gross Sales Revenue	18,000
Cost of Goods Sold	8,700
Sales Returns	800
Interest Expense	150
Accounts Payable	490
Accounts Receivable	610
Extraordinary Loss	1,980
Selling Expenses	860
Office Supplies Used	240
Cash	750
Revenue from Investments	430
Number of shares of capital stock	200

Prepare an income statement. Assume a 35% income tax rate on both income from operations and extraordinary items. Include EPS numbers.

E 8-35   **Unifying Concepts: The Income Statement**

LO5   Use the following information to prepare an income statement for Fairchild Corporation for the year ended December 31, 2009. You should show separate classifications for revenues, cost of goods sold, gross margin, selling expenses, general and administrative expenses, operating income, other revenues and expenses, income before income taxes, income taxes, and net income. (*Hint:* Net income is $27,276.)

(continued)

Sales Returns	$ 4,280
Income Taxes	26,000
Interest Revenue	2,400
Office Supplies Expense (General and Administrative)	400
Utilities Expense (General and Administrative)	3,980
Office Salaries Expense (General and Administrative)	12,064
Miscellaneous Selling Expenses	460
Insurance Expense (Selling)	1,160
Advertising Expense	6,922
Sales Salaries Expense	40,088
Sales Discounts	3,644
Interest Expense	1,170
Miscellaneous General and Administrative Expenses	620
Insurance Expense (General and Administrative)	600
Payroll Tax Expense (General and Administrative)	3,600
Store Supplies Expense (Selling)	800
Delivery Expense (Selling)	2,198
Inventory, January 1, 2009	79,400
Sales Revenue	395,472
Cost of Goods Sold	262,610
Purchases	230,560
Purchases Discounts	3,050
Inventory, December 31, 2009	44,300
Average number of shares of stock outstanding	10,000

PROBLEMS

P 8-36

LO1

Payroll Accounting

Orange County Bank has three employees, Albert Myers, Juan Moreno, and Michi Endo. During January 2009, these three employees earned $6,000, $4,200, and $4,000, respectively. The following table summarizes the required withholding rates on each individual's income for the month of January:

Employee	Federal Income Tax Withholdings	State Income Tax Withholdings	FICA Tax
Albert Myers	33%	3%	7.65%
Juan Moreno	28	4	7.65
Michi Endo	28	5	7.65

You are also informed that the bank is subject to the following unemployment tax rates on the salaries earned by the employees during January 2009:

Federal unemployment tax	0.8%
State unemployment tax	3.0%

Required:
1. Prepare the journal entry to record salaries payable for the month of January.
2. Prepare the journal entry to record payment of the January salaries to employees.
3. Prepare the journal entry to record the bank's payroll taxes for the month of January.

P 8-37

LO1

Determining Payroll Costs

Parley Pharmaceuticals pays its salespeople a base salary of $2,000 per month plus a commission. Each salesperson starts with a commission of 1.5% of total gross sales for the month. The commission is increased thereafter according to seniority and productivity, up to a maximum of 5%. Parley has five salespeople with gross sales for the month of July and commission rates as follows:

	Commission Rate	Gross Sales
Jordan	3.0%	$140,000
Alisa	4.5	200,000
Kasey	1.5	110,000
Trevor	5.0	180,000
Chad	2.5	90,000

The FICA tax rate is 7.65%. In addition, state and federal income taxes of 20% are withheld from each employee.

Required:

1. Compute Parley's total payroll expense (base salary plus commissions) for the month.
2. Compute the total amount of cash paid to employees for compensation for the month.
3. **Interpretive Question:** Briefly outline the advantages and disadvantages of having no income taxes withheld, but instead relying on individual taxpayers to pay the entire amount of their income tax at the end of the year when they file their tax return.

P 8-38

LO1

Stock Options

On January 1, 2009, Tiger Man Company established a stock option plan for its senior employees. A total of 400,000 options were granted that permit employees to purchase 400,000 shares of stock at $20 per share. Each option had a fair value of $5 on the grant date. The market price for Tiger Man stock on January 1, 2009, was $20. The employees are required to remain with Tiger Man for three years (2009, 2010, and 2011) in order to be able to exercise these options. Tiger Man's net income for 2009, before including any consideration of compensation expense, is $675,000.

Required:

1. Compute the compensation expense associated with these options for 2009 under the fair value method. Note that the period of time that the employees must work to be able to exercise the options is three years.
2. **Interpretive Question:** You are a Tiger Man stockholder. What objections might you have to Tiger Man's employee stock option plan?

P 8-39

LO1

Accounting for Pensions

The following information is available from John Gammon Company relating to its defined benefit pension plan:

Balances as of January 1, 2009:	
Pension obligation liability	$4,300
Pension fund assets	3,800
Activity for 2009:	
Service cost	$ 550
Contributions to pension fund	240
Benefit payments to retirees	200
Return on plan assets	340
Pension-related interest cost	344

(continued)

Required:

1. Compute the amount of pension expense to be reported on the income statement for 2009.
2. Determine the net pension amount to be reported on the balance sheet at the end of the year. *Note:* The benefit payments to retirees are made out of the pension fund assets. These payments reduce both the amount in the pension fund and the amount of the remaining pension obligation.
3. **Interpretive Question:** You are an employee of John Gammon Company and have just received the above information as part of the company's annual report to the employees on the status of the pension plan. Does anything in this information cause you concern? Explain.

P 8-40
LO1

Accounting for Pensions

Marseille Company reported the following information relating to its pension plan for the years 2007 through 2010:

	Year-End Obligation	Year-End Plan Assets	Interest Cost	Service Cost	Return on Assets
2007	$792,300	$598,700	–	–	–
2008	846,807	616,044	$71,307	$74,200	$71,844
2009	917,455	643,669	76,213	79,435	73,925
2010	995,026	695,009	82,571	76,300	77,240

Required:

1. Compute the amount of pension expense to be reported on the income statement for each of the years 2008 through 2010.
2. Determine the net pension amount to be reported on the balance sheet at the end of each year 2007 through 2010. Clearly indicate whether the amount is an asset or a liability.
3. Each year, the amount of the pension obligation is increased by the interest cost and the service cost. The pension obligation is reduced by the amount of pension benefits paid. Compute the amount of pension benefits paid in each of the years 2008 through 2010.
4. Each year, the amount in the pension fund is increased by contributions to the fund and by the return earned on the fund assets. The pension fund amount is reduced by the amount of pension benefits paid. Compute the amount of contributions to the pension fund in each of the years 2008 through 2010.

P 8-41
LO2

Life Cycle of a Deferred Tax Item

Black Kitty Company recorded certain revenues of $10,000 and $20,000 on its books in 2007 and 2008, respectively. However, these revenues were not subject to income taxation until 2009. Company records reveal pretax financial accounting income and taxable income for the three-year period as follows:

	Financial Income	Taxable Income
2007	$44,000	$34,000
2008	38,000	18,000
2009	21,000	51,000

Assume Black Kitty's tax rate is 40% for all periods.

Required:

1. Determine the amount of income tax that will be paid each year from 2007 through 2009.
2. Determine the amount of income tax expense that will be reported on the income statement each year from 2007 through 2009.

(continued)

3. Compute the amount of deferred tax liability that would be reported on the balance sheet at the end of each year.

4. **Interpretive Question:** Why would the IRS allow Black Kitty to defer payment of taxes on some of the revenue earned in 2007 and 2008?

P 8-42

LO5

Unifying Concepts: The Income Statement

From the following information, prepare an income statement for Moriancumer, Inc., for the year ended December 31, 2009. (*Hint:* Net income is $98,500.) Assume that there are 15,000 shares of capital stock outstanding.

Gross Sales Revenue	$4,230,000
Income Taxes	99,000
Cost of Goods Sold	3,116,000
Sales Salaries Expense	350,000
Rent Expense (Selling)	16,000
Payroll Tax Expense (Selling)	4,900
Entertainment Expense (Selling)	1,500
Miscellaneous Selling Expenses	6,300
Miscellaneous General and Administrative Expenses	5,400
Automobile Expense (Selling)	3,500
Insurance Expense (General and Administrative)	700
Interest Expense	39,000
Interest Revenue	2,000
Sales Returns	8,000
Advertising and Promotion Expense	204,000
Insurance Expense (Selling)	17,000
Delivery Expense (Selling)	3,100
Office Supplies Expense (General and Administrative)	8,000
Utilities Expense (General and Administrative)	1,100
Administrative Salaries Expense	200,000
Fire Loss (net of tax)	50,000

P 8-43

LO5

Income Statement Analysis

The following table represents portions of the income statements of Brinkerhoff Company for the years 2007–2009:

	2009	2008	2007
Gross sales revenue	$56,000	$ (9)	$47,600
Sales discounts	0	300	200
Sales returns	0	100	400
Net sales revenue	56,000	(10)	(1)
Beginning inventory	(15)	8,700	(2)
Purchases	33,400	(11)	25,000
Purchases discounts	700	400	800
Freight-in	(16)	0	700
Cost of goods available for sale	40,500	37,800	(3)
Ending inventory	6,900	(12)	(4)
Cost of goods sold	(17)	(13)	(5)
Gross margin	(18)	20,400	(6)
Selling expenses	4,500	(14)	(7)
General and administrative expenses	(19)	3,100	2,800
Income before income taxes	14,300	14,000	11,900
Income taxes	4,250	4,200	(8)
Net income	(20)	9,800	8,400

Required:

Fill in the missing numbers. Assume that gross margin is 40% of net sales revenue.

ANALYTICAL ASSIGNMENTS

AA 8-44
DISCUSSION

Recording Liabilities and the Effect on Bonuses

John Flowers, president of Marquette Company, is paid a salary plus a bonus equal to 10% of pretax income. The company has just computed its pretax income to be $3.4 million. Based on this income, Flowers expects to receive a bonus of $340,000. However, the company has just been told by outside experts that it may have an environmental liability of $2.1 million and that, based on new actuarial estimates, the recorded amount of postretirement benefits is too low by $1.2 million. The experts recommend that both of these liabilities be recorded, which would reduce income to $100,000 and Flowers' bonus to $10,000. Flowers believes he does not need to record the adjustments for the following reasons: the environmental liability is not certain, the amount of the potential liability can't be accurately estimated, and "actuarial estimates" are always changing. Is Flowers violating GAAP if he refuses to allow the company to adjust pretax income, or is the decision to not record the adjustments acceptable because of the uncertainty of the liabilities and the amounts?

AA 8-45
DISCUSSION

Questioning the Accounting for Pensions, Research, and Income Taxes

Tatia Wilks, the president of Lewbacca Company, is concerned about the low earnings that Lewbacca is scheduled to report this year. She called the company's accounting staff into her office to question them about the accounting treatment of several items. She raised the following points:

a. Why do we have to report an expense this year associated with our pension plan? Our company is new, and none of our employees is within even 15 years of retirement. Accordingly, the pension plan won't cost us anything for at least 15 years.

b. Research to find new products and improve our old products is one of our key competitive advantages. However, you tell me that all of the money we spend on research is reported as an expense this year. This is silly because the results of our research comprise our biggest economic asset.

c. We have an excellent staff of tax planners who work hard to legally minimize the amount of income taxes we pay each year. However, I see in the notes to the financial statements that you are requiring our company to report a "deferred income tax expense" for taxes that we don't even owe yet! Why?

How would you respond to each of these points?

AA 8-46
JUDGMENT CALL

You Decide: Are stock options and bonus plans an appropriate incentive or a cause for corruption?

Do employee bonus plans provide incentives to work harder and achieve personal and corporate goals, or are they a catalyst for corporate corruption? For example, assume you work for a Fortune 500 company. You are the chief financial officer of the company and are in charge of the company's accounting. The company is doing well; in fact, you have just been informed that members of top management will each receive 10,000 stock options to purchase company stock if earnings meet forecasts. Your associate tells you that the options will create pressure to meet the forecasts. Is he right?

AA 8-47
JUDGMENT CALL

You Decide: Should start-up costs be capitalized or expensed?

Your spouse is setting up a home-based Web design business. Her purpose for setting up the business is to earn some extra income now and, in two to three years, sell the business. Your spouse is wondering whether she can capitalize the start-up costs or whether they must be expensed. She has heard from other business owners that in order to minimize taxes, it is a lot better to expense as much as you can. With this end goal in mind, what should your spouse do?

Wal-Mart

The 2006 Form 10-K for **Wal-Mart** is included in Appendix A. Locate that Form 10-K and consider the following questions:

1. Find Wal-Mart's financial statement note on "Income taxes."
   a. Using the current tax information and the information given on income before income taxes, compute Wal-Mart's 2005 effective tax rate for both U.S. and international income. The effective tax rate is computed by dividing current taxes by income before income taxes.
   b. As of January 31, 2006, Wal-Mart had $4,097 million in deferred income tax liabilities. What was the source of most of this deferred tax liability?
2. Find Wal-Mart's financial statement note concerning "share-based compensation plans."
   c. Briefly describe Wal-Mart's employee stock option plan.
   d. Wal-Mart's employee stock option plan allows employees to buy Wal-Mart stock at a fixed price in the future. If Wal-Mart's stock price continues to rise, these options could be very valuable. Wal-Mart is required to estimate the value of these options and expense the value of these options as employee compensation. How much stock compensation expense did Wal-Mart recognize in the year ended January 31, 2006?

General Motors

General Motors has the largest set of private pension plans in the world. The company has many different pension plans covering different groups of employees. The following information was extracted from the notes to GM's 2005 financial statements. All numbers are in millions of U.S. dollars. As you can see, for reporting purposes these plans are separated into U.S. plans and non-U.S. plans.

	U.S. Plans Pension Benefits		Non-U.S. Plans Pension Benefits	
	2005	2004	2005	2004
Fair value of plan assets at end of year	$95,250	$90,886	$ 9,925	$ 9,023
Projected benefit obligation at end of year	89,133	90,760	20,641	18,056
Funded status	$ 6,117	$ 126	$(10,716)	$(9,033)

1. The projected benefit obligation is the measure of the value of the pension benefits earned by GM's employees that has not yet been paid. What is GM's total projected benefit obligation?
2. To ensure that employees will be able to collect their pension benefits, GM is required by law to set aside funds in a pension plan. What is the total value of assets in all of these pension funds?
3. Why do you think GM is required to separate its disclosure of pension plans into U.S. and non-U.S. plans?

IBM

Note P to **IBM**'s 2005 financial statements describes how taxes affect IBM's operations. Among the information given is the following (all amounts are in millions of U.S. dollars):

For the year ended December 31:	2005	2004	2003
Income from continuing operations before income taxes:			
U.S. operations	$ 7,450	$ 4,400	$3,662
Non-U.S. operations	4,776	6,269	5,755
Total income from continuing operations before income taxes	$12,226	$10,669	$9,417

(continued)

The continuing operations provision for income taxes by geographic operations is as follows:

For the year ended December 31:	2005	2004	2003
U.S. operations	$2,988	$1,492	$ 937
Non-U.S. operations	1,244	1,680	1,892
Total continuing operations provision for income taxes	$4,232	$3,172	$2,829
Provision for social security, real estate, personal property, and other taxes	$3,501	$3,449	$3,372

1. a. Compute the effective tax rate (income taxes/earnings before income taxes) for both U.S. and non-U.S. operations for 2003, 2004, and 2005.
   b. For each year 2003–2005, compute the percentage of the total tax burden that was made up of income taxes.
2. A deferred tax asset is a tax deduction that has already occurred and has been reported as a financial accounting expense but cannot be used to reduce income taxes until a future year. As of December 31, 2005, IBM reports that it has a deferred tax asset of $3.039 billion related to retirement-related benefits. How would such a deferred tax asset arise?

AA 8-51

INTERNATIONAL

Hutchison Whampoa

In Hong Kong, Li Ka-shing is known as "Superman." Li's personal wealth is estimated to be in excess of $1 billion, and there is a saying in Hong Kong that for every dollar spent, five cents goes into Li's pocket. Li and his family fled from China in 1940 in order to escape the advancing Japanese army. Li dropped out of school at age 13 to support his family by selling plastic trinkets on the streets of Hong Kong. Later, he scraped together enough money to buy a company that produced plastic flowers. His big success came when he bought the real estate surrounding his factory and watched the land skyrocket in value. Today, Li continues his simple lifestyle even though the companies he controls comprise over 10% of the value of the Hong Kong stock market. When asked why his sons have much nicer houses and cars than he does, Li responded, "My sons have a rich father; I did not."

Li is chairman of **Hutchison Whampoa Limited**. Hutchison has five major business segments: property development, container port operations, retailing, telecommunications, and energy. In 2005, Hutchison Whampoa reported net income of HK$13.554 billion (equivalent to approximately US$1.738 billion).

1. Assume that one of Hutchison Whampoa's overseas subsidiaries earns income of $1,000. The income tax rate in Hong Kong is 15%. When this income of $1,000 is transferred to the parent company in Hong Kong, it will be taxed, but no income tax is owed until then. What journal entry should Hutchison Whampoa make to record the income tax consequences of this $1,000 in income?
2. In 2005, Hutchison Whampoa reported earnings per share of HK$3.36. How many shares were outstanding during the year? (*Note:* See the net income information given above.)
3. Hutchison Whampoa reports that it records as assets the costs it incurs to sign up new subscribers to its cellular phone service network. These signup costs are then systematically transferred to expense over the following three years. What is the theoretical justification for this accounting practice?

AA 8-52

ETHICS

Twisting the Contingency Rules to Save the Environment

You are a member of an environmental group that is working to clean up Valley River, which runs through your town. Right now, the group is focusing on forcing Allied Industrial, a manufacturer with a large plant located on the river, to conduct its operations in a more environmentally friendly way.

The leader of your group, Frank Bowers, is a political science major at the local university. Frank discovers that Allied Industrial is involved in ongoing litigation with respect to

(continued)

toxic waste cleanup at 13 factory sites in other states. Frank is shocked to learn that Allied itself estimates that the total cost to clean up the toxic waste at these 13 sites could be as much as $140 million yet has not reported any liability on its balance sheet. Frank found this information buried in the notes to Allied Industrial's financial statements.

Frank is convinced that he has found a public relations tool that can be used to force Allied Industrial to clean up Valley River. He has called a press conference and plans to accuse Allied of covering up its $140 million obligation to clean up the toxic waste at the 13 sites. His primary piece of evidence is the fact that the $140 million obligation is not mentioned anywhere in Allied's primary financial statements.

You have taken a class in accounting and are somewhat troubled by Frank's interpretation of Allied's financial statement disclosures. You look at Allied's annual report and see that it does give complete disclosure about the possible obligation although it does not report the $140 million as a liability. The report also states that, in the opinion of its legal counsel, it is possible but not probable that Allied will be found liable for the $140 million toxic waste cleanup cost.

The press conference is scheduled for 3 P.M. What should you do?

AA 8-53
WRITING

Computing the Total Compensation for a Professor

Eunice Burns is a new assistant professor of phrenology at the University of Winnemucca. Her academic year salary is $30,000. In addition, she receives a summer salary equal to two-ninths (approximately 22%) of her academic year salary. The university agrees to contribute an amount equal to 7% of Eunice's academic year salary to a pension fund. Eunice acquires legal title to these pension contributions only if she stays at the university for five years or more. Historically, approximately 60% of new assistant professors have remained with the university at least five years. The university withholds $840 per year from Eunice's salary as her contribution to medical coverage. It costs the university $3,000 per year per employee for medical coverage. Eunice has a term-life insurance policy through the university because of the favorable group rate she can get. The $300 annual cost is withheld from her salary. If she were to get the same insurance on her own, it would cost $450. The FICA tax rate is 7.65%. This amount is withheld from Eunice's pay, and in addition, the university must match this amount and pay it to the federal government. Federal income taxes totaling 15% of income are withheld from Eunice's pay. Both the FICA tax and the federal income tax withholding are applied only to Eunice's academic year salary; no amounts are withheld from her summer salary.

You have just been hired as an assistant to the chief financial officer of the university. You have been asked to compute the total cost to the university of having Eunice Burns on the faculty. Write a one-page memo to the chief financial officer of the university outlining your calculations. Be sure to explain any assumptions that you make.

AA 8-54
CUMULATIVE
SPREADSHEET
PROJECT

Computing Changes in Debt Ratio and Return on Equity

This spreadsheet assignment is a continuation of the spreadsheet assignments given in earlier chapters. If you completed those spreadsheets, you have a head start on this one.

This assignment is based on the spreadsheet prepared in part (1) of the spreadsheet assignment for Chapter 7. Review that assignment for a summary of the assumptions made in preparing a forecasted balance sheet and income statement for 2010 for Handyman Company. Using those financial statements, complete the following two independent sensitivity exercises.

1. Handyman is involved in a class-action lawsuit in which a number of customers allege that they injured their thumbs while using hammers purchased at Handyman. These customers are seeking $50 million in compensatory and punitive damages. (*Note:* All of the numbers in Handyman's financial statements are in millions.) In making the financial statement projections for Handyman for 2010, it has been assumed that losing this lawsuit is possible, but not probable. Compute how each of the following quantities would be affected if a loss in this lawsuit becomes probable during 2010:
    a. Debt ratio (total liabilities/total assets) as of the end of 2010.
    b. Return on equity (net income/ending stockholders' equity) for 2010.

(continued)

2. Ignore the lawsuit described in (1). It is expected that Handyman's total "other operating expenses" will be $217 million in 2010. Of this amount, $20 million is for expected development costs that would be capitalized if Handyman were allowed to use International Accounting Standards. Compute how the capitalization of these development costs in 2010 would affect the following quantities. (*Note:* This is a hypothetical exercise because, as a U.S. company, Handyman is not currently allowed to use International Accounting Standards in preparing its financial statements.)

   a. Debt ratio (total liabilities/total assets) as of the end of 2010.

   b. Return on equity (net income/ending stockholders' equity) for 2010.

Fray Enterprises is a small business that purchases electronic personal information managers (PIM) from manufacturers and sells them to consumers. These PIMs keep track of appointments, phone numbers, to-do lists, and the like. Fray conducts business via the Internet and, at this point, carries only one model of PIM, the ZL-420. Fray provides the following trial balance as of January 1, 2009.

Fray Enterprises
Trial Balance
January 1, 2009

	Debits	Credits
Cash	$ 9,200	
Accounts Receivable	26,800	
Allowance for Bad Debts		$ 804
Inventory	31,650	
Prepaid Rent	1,100	
Office Supplies	900	
Accounts Payable		19,100
Wages Payable		2,800
Taxes Payable		3,400
Common Stock (10,000 shares)		30,000
Retained Earnings		13,546
Total	$69,650	$69,650

Fray uses the periodic FIFO inventory method in accounting for its inventory. The inventory of ZL-420 consists of the following inventory layers:

Layer	Units	Price per Unit	Total Price
1 (oldest purchase)	50	$120	$ 6,000
2	80	130	10,400
3	70	135	9,450
4 (most recent purchase)	40	145	5,800
Total	240		$31,650

Fray provides the following additional relevant information:

- The company uses the percentage of receivables method in estimating bad debts; 2% of the ending receivables balance is deemed to be uncollectible.
- Fray conducts an actual physical count of its inventory and office supplies at the end of each month.
- Fray rents its warehouse, office facilities, and computer equipment. Rent on the computer equipment is paid at the beginning of each month. Rent on the warehouse and office space is paid on the 15th of each month.
- Payroll is paid on the 5th and the 20th (pay periods end on the 15th and the last day of the month).
- Taxes Payable represents payroll taxes that are due by the 5th of the following month.
- All sales and all inventory purchases are on account.

The following transactions occurred for Fray during January of 2009:

Jan. 1   Paid rent on the computer equipment, $1,400.

5   Recorded sales for the week, 130 units at $210 per unit. (The company uses a periodic inventory system.)

5   Paid wages payable and taxes payable from the prior period.

5   Collected $19,000 from customers on account during the week.

8   Purchased office supplies for cash, $300.

10   Received 70 ZL-420s from the manufacturer at a cost of $145 per unit.

11   Paid accounts payable, $16,900.

12   Collected $22,000 from customers on account during the week.

12   Recorded sales for the week, 120 units at $210 per unit.

15   Paid monthly rent for the office and warehouse, $2,200.

15   Received 130 ZL-420s from the manufacturer at a cost of $150 per unit.

18   A customer returned a ZL-420 and requested a refund. A check was immediately mailed to the customer in the amount of $210.

19   Collected $30,000 from customers on account during the week.

19   Recorded sales for the week, 140 units at $210 per unit.

20   Paid the semimonthly payroll for the pay period ending on January 15. Salaries and wages total $4,800 and payroll taxes were as follows: FICA taxes payable, employee, $367; FICA taxes payable, employer, $367; state withholding taxes payable, $310; federal withholding taxes payable, $780; federal unemployment taxes payable, $60; state unemployment taxes payable, $180.

22   Received notice that a customer owing Fray $630 had filed bankruptcy and would be unable to pay.

23   Paid the taxes payable from the payroll on January 20.

24   Received 180 ZL-420s from the manufacturer at a cost of $150 per unit.

25   Purchased office supplies for cash, $480.

25   Paid accounts payable, $43,000.

26   Collected $30,500 from customers on account during the week.

26   Recorded sales for the week, 135 units at $220 per unit.

29   Customers returned 7 ZL-420s and requested refunds. Checks were immediately mailed to each customer in the amount of $210 each.

30   Received 140 ZL-420s from the manufacturer at a cost of $145 per unit.

31   Collected $29,900 from customers on account.

31   Recorded sales for the partial week, 70 units at $220 per unit.

31   Accrued the semimonthly payroll for the pay period ending on January 31. Salaries and wages total $5,000 and payroll taxes were as follows: FICA taxes payable, employee, $382; FICA taxes payable, employer, $382; state withholding taxes payable, $230; federal withholding taxes payable, $810; federal unemployment taxes payable, $65; state unemployment taxes payable, $190.

Required:

1. Provide the required journal entries to record each of the above events.
2. Make the adjusting entries necessary (1) to record bad debt expense for the period and (2) to adjust inventory and office supplies. A count of inventory and office supplies revealed 165 ZL-420s on hand and supplies valued at $1,000.
3. Prepare a trial balance as of January 31, 2009.
4. Prepare an income statement and a balance sheet for Fray Enterprises.
5. Compute Fray's number of days' sales in inventory, number of days' sales in accounts receivable, and number of days' purchases in accounts payable ratios. What can you conclude about the company's liquidity position based on this analysis?

© DUNCAN SMITH/PHOTODISC GREEN/GETTY IMAGES INC.

PART

3

Investing and Financing Activities

© AP PHOTO/SARA D. DAVIS

Investments in Property, Plant, and Equipment and in Intangible Assets

LEARNING OBJECTIVES

After studying this chapter, you should be able to:

(1) **Identify the two major categories of long-term operating assets: property, plant, and equipment and intangible assets.** *A company needs an infrastructure of long-term operating assets in order to produce and distribute its products and services. In addition to property, plant, and equipment, long-term operating assets also include intangible items such as patents and licenses.*

(2) **Understand the factors important in deciding whether to acquire a long-term operating asset.** *A company should purchase a long-term operating asset if the future cash flows expected to be generated by the asset are "large" in comparison to the cost to purchase the asset.*

(3) **Record the acquisition of property, plant, and equipment through a simple purchase as well as through a lease, by self-construction, and as part of the purchase of several assets at once.** *The recorded cost of property, plant, or equipment includes all costs needed to purchase the asset and prepare it for its intended use. Assets can be acquired through purchase, leasing, exchange, self-construction, or through the purchase of an entire company.*

(4) **Compute straight-line and units-of-production depreciation expense for plant and equipment.** *Depreciation is the process of systematically allocating the cost of a long-term asset over the service life of that asset. If that service life is measured in years, then a reasonable way to allocate the cost is equally over the years; this is called straight-line depreciation.*

(5) **Account for repairs and improvements of property, plant, and equipment.** *Postacquisition costs that increase an asset's capacity or extend its life are called improvements and are capitalized meaning that they are added to the cost of the asset. Routine maintenance costs are called repairs and are expensed.*

(6) **Identify whether a long-term operating asset has suffered a decline in value and record the decline.** *When a long-term operating asset suffers a significant decline in value (as indicated by a decline in the cash flows expected to be generated by the asset), it is said to be impaired. When an asset is impaired, its recorded value is reduced and an impairment loss is recognized. Increases in asset values are not recognized in the financial statements.*

(7) **Record the discarding and selling of property, plant, and equipment.** *Upon the disposal of a long-term operating asset, a gain or loss is recognized if the disposal proceeds are more or less, respectively, than the remaining book value of the asset.*

(8) **Account for the acquisition and amortization of intangible assets and understand the special difficulties associated with accounting for intangibles.** *Because the traditional accounting model is designed for manufacturing and retail companies, many intangible assets go unrecorded. Intangible assets are recorded only when they are purchased, either individually or as part of a set of assets. Goodwill is the excess of the purchase price over the fair value of the net identifiable assets in a business acquisition.*

(9) **Use the fixed asset turnover ratio as a measure of how efficiently a company is using its property, plant, and equipment.** *The fixed asset turnover ratio is computed as sales divided by the amount of property, plant, and equipment (fixed assets). This ratio can be used as a general measure of how efficiently a company is using its property, plant, and equipment.*

EXPANDED *material*

(10) **Compute declining-balance and sum-of-the-years'-digits depreciation expense for plant and equipment.** *Many long-term operating assets wear out proportionately more in the early years of their lives. For these assets, more depreciation is recorded in the early years; this is called accelerated depreciation. Two mathematical techniques used to generate this accelerated pattern are declining-balance depreciation and sum-of-the-years'-digits depreciation.*

(11) **Account for changes in depreciation estimates and methods.** *Depreciation expense involves making estimates relating to pattern of use, estimated useful life, and salvage value. Changes in estimated salvage value or useful life and changes in depreciation method are reflected in the computation of depreciation expense for the current and future periods. The undepreciated book value is allocated over the remaining life based on the revised estimates or method.*

Thomas Edison received $300,000 in investment funds in 1878 in order to start his **Edison Electric Light Company**. Today, **General Electric** is the direct descendant of Edison's company and, with a market value of $354 billion (as of May 2006), is the second most valuable company in the world (behind **ExxonMobil**). General Electric has been a fixture in corporate America since the late 1800s and is the only one of the 12 companies in the original Dow Jones Industrial Average that is still included among the 30 companies making up the Dow today.[1]

The stated purpose of the creation of the Edison Electric Light Company was the development of an economically practical electric light bulb. After a year of experimentation, Thomas Edison discovered that carbonized bamboo would provide a long-lasting light filament that was also easy to produce. Edison quickly found that delivering electric light to people's homes required more than a light bulb, however. So, he developed an entire electricity generation and distribution system, inventing new pieces of equipment when he couldn't find what he needed. The first public electric light system was built in London, followed soon after by the Pearl Street Station system in New York City in 1882. In 1892, Edison's company merged with the **Thomson-Houston Electric Company** [developer of alternating-current

(AC) equipment that could transmit over longer distances than Edison's direct-current (DC) system], and the General Electric Company (GE) was born.

From the beginning, General Electric's strength has been research. In addition to improving the design of the light bulb (including the development in the early 1900s of gas-filled, tungsten-filament bulbs that are the model for bulbs still used today), GE was also instrumental in developing almost every familiar household appliance—the iron, washing machine, refrigerator, range, air conditioner, dishwasher, and more. In addition, GE research scientists helped create FM radio, aircraft jet engines, and nuclear-power reactors.

Today, General Electric operates in a diverse array of businesses, ranging from train locomotives to medical CT scanners to consumer financing to the NBC television network. To support its broad array of businesses, General Electric maintains a vast quantity of long-term assets that cost almost $112 billion to acquire. In 2005 alone, GE spent an additional $14.4 billion in acquiring long-term operating assets and received $6.0 billion for disposing of old assets. Its long-term assets include $3.3 billion in rail cars, $32.9 billion in aircraft, $15.6 billion in buildings, $25.8 billion in machinery, and $81.7 billion in "intangible" assets.

I n Chapters 6 through 8, operating activities of a business and the assets and liabilities arising from those operations were discussed. In this and the next three chapters, investing and financing activities are covered. In this chapter, investments in long-term assets that are used in the business, such as buildings, property, land, and equipment, are discussed.

long-term operating assets

Assets expected to be held and used over the course of several years to facilitate operating activities.

In Chapter 10, long-term debt financing is covered. In Chapter 11, equity financing is discussed. Once you understand debt and equity securities, as discussed in Chapters 10 and 11, you will understand how these

same securities can be purchased as investments. Therefore, in Chapter 12, investments in stocks and bonds (securities) of other companies are discussed. Exhibit 1 illustrates the time line of important business issues associated with long-term operating assets and shows the financial statement impact of the items that will be covered in this chapter.

The two primary categories of long-term assets discussed in this chapter are (1) property, plant, and equipment and (2) intangible assets. Because property, plant, and equipment and intangible assets are essential to a business in carrying out its operating activities, they are sometimes called long-term operating assets. Unlike inventories, these long-term operating assets are

---

[1] This description is based on General Electric Company History at **http://ge.com/en/company/companyinfo/ at_a_glance/hist_leader.htm**; General Electric Company, *International Directory of Company Histories*, vol. 12 (Detroit: St. James Press, 1996), pp. 193–197; 1999 Annual Report of the General Electric Company.

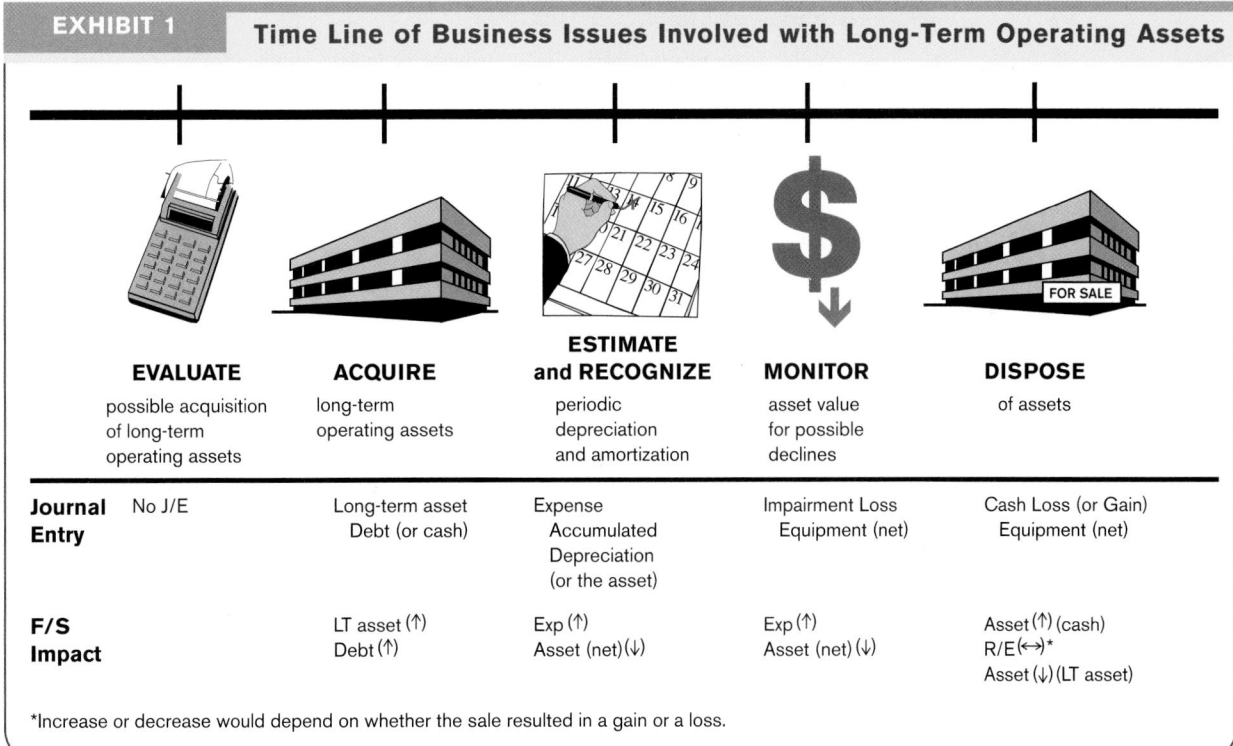

EXHIBIT 1   Time Line of Business Issues Involved with Long-Term Operating Assets

	EVALUATE	ACQUIRE	ESTIMATE and RECOGNIZE	MONITOR	DISPOSE
	possible acquisition of long-term operating assets	long-term operating assets	periodic depreciation and amortization	asset value for possible declines	of assets
Journal Entry	No J/E	Long-term asset Debt (or cash)	Expense Accumulated Depreciation (or the asset)	Impairment Loss Equipment (net)	Cash Loss (or Gain) Equipment (net)
F/S Impact		LT asset (↑) Debt (↑)	Exp (↑) Asset (net)(↓)	Exp (↑) Asset (net) (↓)	Asset (↑) (cash) R/E(↔)* Asset (↓)(LT asset)

*Increase or decrease would depend on whether the sale resulted in a gain or a loss.

SETTING THE STAGE

not acquired for resale to customers but are held and used by a business to generate revenues. As illustrated by the numbers given for General Electric at the beginning of the chapter, long-term operating assets often comprise a significant portion of the total assets of a company.

Nature of Long-Term Operating Assets

Identify the two major categories of long-term operating assets: property, plant, and equipment and intangible assets.

(1)   Businesses make money by selling products and services. A company needs an infrastructure of long-term operating assets in order to profitably produce and distribute these products and services. For example, **General Electric** needs factories in which to manufacture the locomotives and light bulbs that it sells. GE also needs patents on its unique technology to protect its competitive edge in the marketplace. A factory is an example of a long-term operating asset that is classified as property, plant, and equipment. A patent is an example of an intangible asset. **Property, plant, and equipment** refers to tangible, long-lived assets acquired for use in business operations. This category includes land, buildings, machinery, equipment, and furniture. **Intangible assets** are long-lived assets that are used in the operation of a business but do not have physical substance (see page 392 for definition). In most cases, they provide their owners with competitive advantages over other firms. Typical intangible assets are patents, licenses, franchises, and goodwill.

The following section outlines the process used in deciding whether to acquire a long-term operating asset. The subsequent sections discuss the accounting issues that arise when a long-term operating asset is acquired: accounting for the acquisition of the asset, recording periodic depreciation, accounting for new costs and changes in asset value, and properly removing the asset from the books upon disposition.

property, plant, and equipment

Tangible, long-lived assets acquired for use in business operations; include land, buildings, machinery, equipment, and furniture.

REMEMBER THIS...

intangible assets

Long-lived assets without physical substance that are used in business, such as licenses, patents, franchises, and goodwill.

- Long-term operating assets provide an infrastructure in which to conduct operating activities.
- The category of property, plant, and equipment refers to tangible, long-lived assets such as land and equipment.
- Examples of intangible assets are patents and licenses.

Understand the factors important in deciding whether to acquire a long-term operating asset.

Deciding Whether to Acquire a Long-Term Operating Asset

(2) As mentioned in the previous section, long-term operating assets are acquired to be used over the course of several years. The decision to acquire a long-term asset depends on whether the future cash flows generated by the asset are expected to be large enough to justify the asset cost. The process of evaluating a long-term project is called **capital budgeting**. This process is briefly introduced here and is covered in more detail in Chapter 22 in the management accounting section of *Accounting: Concepts and Applications*.

capital budgeting

Systematic planning for long-term investments in operating assets.

Assume that Yosef Manufacturing makes joysticks and other computer game accessories. Yosef is considering expanding its operations by buying an additional production facility. The cost of the new factory is $100 million. Yosef expects to be able to sell the joysticks and other items made in the factory for $80 million per year. At that level of production, the annual cost of operating the factory (wages, insurance, materials, maintenance, etc.) is expected to total $65 million. The factory is expected to remain in operation for 20 years. Should Yosef buy the new factory for $100 million?

To summarize the information in the preceding paragraph, Yosef must decide whether to pay $100 million for a factory that will generate a net profit of $15 million ($80 million − $65 million) per year for 20 years. At first glance, you might think that the decision is obvious because the factory costs only $100 million but will generate $300 million in profit ($15 million × 20 years) during its 20-year life. But this analysis ignores the important fact that dollars received in the future are not worth as much as dollars received right now. For example, if you can invest your money and earn 10%, receiving $1 today is the same as receiving $6.73 20 years from now because the $1 received today could be invested and would grow to $6.73 in 20 years. This important concept is called the **time value of money** and is essential to properly evaluating whether to acquire any long-term asset.

time value of money

The concept that a dollar received now is worth more than a dollar received in the future.

Using the time value of money calculations that will be explained in detail in Chapter 10, it can be shown that receiving the future cash flows from the factory of $15 million per year for 20 years is the same as receiving $128 million in one lump sum right now, if the prevailing interest rate is 10%. Thus, the decision to acquire the factory boils down to the following comparison: Should we pay $100 million to buy a factory now if the factory will generate future cash flows that are worth the equivalent of $128 million now? The decision is yes, because the $128 million value of the expected cash inflows is greater than the $100 million cost of the factory. On the other hand, if the factory were expected to generate only $10 million per year, then, using the computations that will be explained in Chapter 10, it can be calculated that the value of the cash flows would be only $85 million, and the factory should not be purchased for $100 million.

The important concept to remember here is that long-term operating assets have value because they are expected to help a company generate cash flows in the future. If events occur that change the expectation concerning those future cash flows, then the value of the asset changes. For example, if consumer demand for computer joysticks dries up, the value of a factory built to produce joysticks can plunge overnight even though the factory itself is still as productive as it ever was. Accounting for this type of decline in the value of a long-term operating asset is discussed later in the chapter.

REMEMBER THIS...

- Long-term operating assets have value because they help companies generate future cash flows.
- The decision to acquire a long-term operating asset involves comparing the cost of the asset to the value of the expected cash inflows, after adjusting for the time value of money.
- An asset's value can decline or disappear if events cause a decrease in the expected future cash flows generated by the asset.

Record the acquisition of property, plant, and equipment through a simple purchase as well as through a lease, by self-construction, and as part of the purchase of several assets at once.

Accounting for Acquisition of Property, Plant, and Equipment

(3) Like all other assets, property, plant, and equipment are initially recorded at cost. The cost of an asset includes not only the purchase price but also any other costs incurred in acquiring the asset and getting it ready for its intended use. Examples of these other costs include shipping, installation, and sales taxes. The items that should be included in the acquisition cost of various types of property, plant, and equipment are outlined in Exhibit 2.

Property, plant, and equipment are usually acquired by purchase. In some cases, assets are acquired by leasing but are accounted for as assets in much the same way as purchased assets. Plant and equipment can also be constructed by a business for its own use. Also, a company can in one transaction purchase several different assets or even another entire company. The accounting for each of these types of acquisition is explained below and on the following pages.

EXHIBIT 2	**Items Included in the Acquisition Cost of Property, Plant, and Equipment**
Land	Purchase price, commissions, legal fees, escrow fees, surveying fees, clearing and grading costs.
Land improvements (e.g., landscaping, paving, fencing)	Cost of improvements, including expenditures for materials, labor, and overhead.
Buildings	Purchase price, commissions, reconditioning costs.
Equipment	Purchase price, taxes, freight, insurance, installation, and any expenditures incurred in preparing the asset for its intended use, e.g., reconditioning and testing costs.

Assets Acquired by Purchase

A company can purchase an asset by paying cash, incurring a liability, exchanging another asset, or by a combination of these methods. If a single asset is purchased for cash, the accounting is relatively simple. To illustrate, we assume that Wheeler Resorts, Inc., purchases a new delivery truck for $15,096 (purchase price, $15,000, less 2% discount for paying cash, plus sales tax of $396). The entry to record this purchase is:

Delivery Truck	15,096	
Cash		15,096
Purchased a delivery truck for $15,096		
($15,000 − $300 cash discount + $396 sales tax).		

In this instance, cash was paid for a single asset, the truck. An alternative would be to borrow part of the purchase price. If the company had borrowed $12,000 of the $15,096 from a bank, the entry would have been:

Delivery Truck	15,096	
Cash		3,096
Notes Payable		12,000
Purchased a delivery truck for $15,096; paid $3,096 cash		
and issued a note for $12,000 to Chemical Bank.		

lease

A contract that specifies the terms under which the owner of an asset (the lessor) agrees to transfer the right to use the asset to another party (the lessee).

The $12,000 represents the principal of the note; it does not include any interest charged by the lending institution. (The interest is recognized later as interest expense.)

When one long-term operating asset is acquired in exchange for another, the cost of the new asset is usually set equal to the market value of the asset given up in exchange.

Assets Acquired by Leasing

lessee

The party that is granted the right to use property under the terms of a lease.

lessor

The owner of property that is leased (rented) to another party.

operating lease

A simple rental agreement.

Leases are often short-term rental agreements in which one party, the **lessee**, is granted the right to use property owned by another party, the **lessor**. For example, as a student, you may decide to lease (rent) an apartment to live in while you are attending college. The owner of the apartment (lessor) will probably require you to sign a lease specifying the terms of the arrangement. The lease states the period of time in which you will live in the apartment, the amount of rent you will pay, and when each rent payment is due. When the lease expires, you will either sign a new lease or move out of the apartment, which would then be rented to someone else.

Companies enter into similar types of lease arrangements. For example, Wheeler Resorts might decide to lease a building because it needs additional office space. Assume Wheeler signs a two-year lease requiring monthly rental payments of $1,000. When the lease expires, Wheeler will either move out of the building or negotiate a new lease with the owner. Accounting for this type of rental agreement, called an **operating lease**, is straightforward. When rent is paid each month, Wheeler records the following journal entry:

Rent (or Lease) Expense	1,000	
Cash		1,000
To record monthly rent of office building.		

Some lease agreements, however, are not so simple. Suppose Wheeler has decided to expand its operations and wants to acquire a hotel in the Phoenix, Arizona, area.

A college student (lessee) often rents an apartment while attending college. The apartment owner (lessor) will require the student to sign a lease stating the terms of the arrangement.

Wheeler's alternatives are to buy land and build a new hotel, purchase an existing hotel, or lease a hotel. Assume Wheeler locates a desirable piece of land, and the owner of the land agrees to build a hotel and lease the property to Wheeler. The lease agreement is noncancelable and requires Wheeler to make annual lease payments of $100,000 for 20 years. At the end of 20 years, Wheeler will become the owner of the property. Clearly, this is not a simple rental agreement, even though the transaction is called a lease by the parties involved. In reality, this transaction is a purchase of the property with the payments being spread over 20 years. The result is the same as if Wheeler had borrowed money on a 20-year mortgage and purchased the property.

Generally accepted accounting principles require that the recording of a transaction reflect its true economic nature, not its form. Instead of recognizing the individual lease payments as an expense as was done with the operating lease, Wheeler records the property as an asset and also records a liability reflecting the obligation to the lessor. The amount to be recorded is the cash amount that Wheeler would have to pay right now in order to completely pay off the obligation to make the future lease payments. This amount is called the present value of the lease payments (in the Wheeler example, the present value of 20 annual payments of $100,000) and takes into account the time value of money. As mentioned earlier, the time value concept will be explained in more detail in Chapter 10.

Continuing the example, assume that, at the beginning of the lease term, the present value of the future lease payments is $851,360. Wheeler makes the following journal entry to record the lease:

Leased Property	851,360	
Lease Liability		851,360
To record hotel acquired under a 20-year noncancelable lease.		

capital lease

A leasing transaction that is recorded as a purchase by the lessee.

This type of lease is called a **capital lease** because the lessee records (capitalizes) the leased asset the same as if the asset had been acquired in an outright purchase. The asset is reported with Property, Plant, and Equipment on the lessee's balance sheet. The lessee (Wheeler Resorts) also shows the lease liability on the balance sheet as a long-term liability.

When annual lease payments are made, Wheeler will not record the payment as rent expense. Instead, the payment will be recorded as a reduction in the lease liability, with part of each payment being interest on the outstanding obligation. The difference between the total lease payments (20 years × $100,000, or $2 million) and the "cost" or present value of the property is the amount of interest that will be paid over the term of the lease. To illustrate, assume that the first payment is made one year after the lease term begins and includes interest of $85,136 and a $14,864 reduction in the liability. The payment is recorded as follows:

Lease Liability	14,864	
Interest Expense	85,136	
Cash		100,000

To record annual lease payment under capital lease.

Accounting for payments on capital leases is discussed in more detail in Chapter 10.

Classifying Leases As illustrated, an operating lease is accounted for as a simple rental, whereas a capital lease is accounted for as a purchase of the leased asset. Because the accounting treatment of a lease can have a major impact on the financial statements, the accounting profession has established criteria for determining whether a lease should be classified as an operating or a capital lease. If a lease is noncancelable and meets any one of the following four criteria, it is recorded as a capital lease:

1. The lease transfers ownership of the leased asset to the lessee by the end of the lease term (as in the Wheeler Resorts example).
2. The lease contains an option allowing the lessee to purchase the asset at the end of the lease term at a bargain price, essentially guaranteeing that ownership will eventually transfer to the lessee.
3. The lease term is equal to 75% or more of the estimated economic life of the asset, meaning that the lessee will use the asset for most of its economic life.
4. The present value of the lease payments at the beginning of the lease is 90% or more of the fair market value of the leased asset. Meeting this criterion means that, in agreeing to make the lease payments, the lessee is agreeing to pay almost as much as the cash price to purchase the asset outright.

If just one of the above criteria is met, then the lease agreement is classified as a capital lease and is accounted for by the lessee as a debt-financed purchase. A lease that does not meet any of the capital lease criteria is considered an operating lease. Keep in mind that these two types of leases are not alternatives for the same transaction. If the terms of the lease agreement meet any one of the capital lease criteria, the lease must be accounted for as a capital lease.

The accounting for leases has been a thorn in the side of accounting standard-setters for at least 50 years. From the beginning, the crucial issue has been how to require companies to report leased assets and lease liabilities in the balance sheet when a lease constitutes an effective transfer of ownership. The four lease criteria outlined above were issued by the FASB in 1976, with the thought that the rigidity and strictness of the criteria would result in most leases being reported on lessee companies' balance sheets as capital leases. In practice, U.S. companies have taken these four criteria as a challenge and have carefully crafted their lease agreements so that none of the criteria is satisfied, allowing the leases to continue to be accounted for as operating leases.

One of the largest leasing companies in the United States is a subsidiary of **General Electric** called **GE Capital Services**. GE Capital Services leases industrial equipment, aircraft, factory buildings, rail cars, shipping containers, computers, medical equipment, and more. In 2005, the total original cost of assets leased by GE Capital Services to other companies was $72.4 billion.

FYI

One of the most interesting accounting manipulations involving the four lease criteria relates to the 90% threshold for the present value of the minimum lease payments. By hiring an insurance company to guarantee a portion of the lease payments, a lessee is able to exclude these payments from the present value computations, lowering the present value below the 90% threshold.

Assets Acquired by Self-Construction

Sometimes buildings or equipment are constructed by a company for its own use. This may be done to save on construction costs, to utilize idle facilities or idle workers, or to meet a special set of technical specifications. Self-constructed assets, like purchased assets, are recorded at cost, including all expenditures incurred to build the asset and make it ready for its intended use. These costs include the materials used to build the asset, the construction labor, and some reasonable share of the general company overhead (electricity, insurance, supervisors' salaries, etc.) during the time of construction.

capitalized interest

Interest that is recorded as part of the cost of a self-constructed asset.

Another cost that is included in the cost of a self-constructed asset is the interest cost associated with money borrowed to finance the construction project. Just as the cost to rent a crane to be used to construct a building would be included in the cost of the building, the cost to "rent" money to finance the construction project should also be included in the building cost. Interest that is recorded as part of the cost of a self-constructed asset is called **capitalized interest**. The amount of interest that should be capitalized is that amount that could have been saved if the money used on the construction project had instead been used to repay loans.

The following illustration demonstrates the computation of the cost of a self-constructed asset. Wheeler Resorts decided to construct a new hotel using its own workers. The construction project lasted from January 1 to December 31, 2009. Building materials costs for the project were $4,500,000. Total labor costs attributable to the project were $2,500,000. Total company overhead (costs other than materials and labor) for the year was $10,000,000; of this amount, it is determined that 15% can be reasonably assigned as part of the cost of the construction project. A construction loan was negotiated with Wheeler's bank; during the year, Wheeler was able to borrow from the bank to pay for materials, labor, etc. The total amount of interest paid on this construction loan during the year was $500,000. The total cost of the self-constructed hotel is computed as follows:

Materials	$4,500,000
Labor	2,500,000
Overhead allocation ($10,000,000 × 0.15)	1,500,000
Capitalized interest	500,000
Total hotel cost	$9,000,000

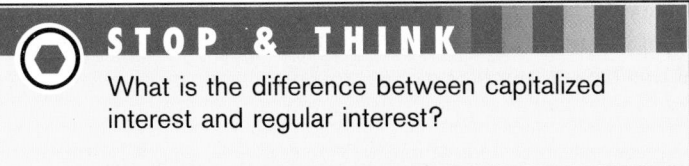

STOP & THINK

What is the difference between capitalized interest and regular interest?

The new hotel would be reported in Wheeler's balance sheet at a total cost of $9,000,000. As with other long-term operating assets, self-constructed assets are reported at the total cost necessary to get them ready for their intended use.

The amount of capitalized interest reported by several large U.S. companies, relative to their total interest expense, is displayed in Exhibit 3. As you can see, General Electric capitalized only an insignificant amount of its $15.187 billion in interest during 2005. On the other hand, **ExxonMobil** capitalized almost one-half of its interest during 2005.

Acquisition of Several Assets at Once

basket purchase

The purchase of two or more assets acquired together at a single price.

A **basket purchase** occurs when two or more assets are acquired together at a single price. A typical basket purchase is the purchase of a building along with the land on which the building sits. Because there are differences in the accounting for land and buildings, the purchase price must be allocated between the two assets on some reasonable basis. The relative fair market values of the

| EXHIBIT 3 | **Magnitude of Capitalized Interest for Several Large U.S. Companies** |

Company	Capitalized Interest	Interest Expense**	Capitalized, as a Percentage of Total Interest
General Electric*	$ 0	$15,187	0.0%
General Motors	45	15,768	0.3
ExxonMobil	434	496	46.7
McDonald's	5	356	1.4
Disney	77	597	11.4

Note: Numbers are for 2005 and are in millions of dollars.
*Once again, GE reports it capitalized only an "insignificant" amount.
**These amounts come from the income statement, and are net of capitalized interest, which explains the high percentage for ExxonMobil.

assets are usually used to determine the respective costs to be assigned to the land and the building.

To illustrate, we will assume that Wheeler Resorts purchases a 40,000-square-foot building on 2.6 acres of land for $3,600,000. How much of the total cost should be assigned to the land and how much to the building? If an appraisal indicates that the fair market values of the land and the building are $1,000,000 and $3,000,000, respectively, the resulting allocated costs would be $900,000 and $2,700,000, calculated as follows:

Asset	Fair Market Value	Percentage of Total Value	Apportionment of Lump-Sum Cost
Land	$1,000,000	25%	0.25 × $3,600,000 = $ 900,000
Building	3,000,000	75	0.75 × $3,600,000 = 2,700,000
Total	$4,000,000	100%	$3,600,000

In this case, the fair market value of the land is $1,000,000, or 25% of the total market value of the land and building. Therefore, 25% of the actual cost, or $900,000, is allocated to the land, and 75% of the actual cost, or $2,700,000, is allocated to the building. The journal entry to record this basket purchase is:

Land	900,000	
Building	2,700,000	
Cash		3,600,000

Purchased 2.6 acres of land and a 40,000-square-foot building.

If part of the purchase price is financed by a bank, an additional credit to Notes Payable or Mortgage Payable would be included in the entry.

Sometimes one company will buy all the assets of another company. For example, in its 2006 annual report, **Wal-Mart** discloses that, in December 2005, it purchased **Sonae Distribuicao Brasil S.A.** (a retail operation in Southern Brazil) for $720 million in cash. The purchase of an entire company raises a number of accounting issues. The first, already discussed above, is how to allocate the purchase price to the various assets acquired. In general, all acquired assets are recorded on the books of the acquiring company at their fair values as of the acquisition date.

goodwill

An intangible asset that exists when a business is valued at more than the fair market value of its net assets, usually due to strategic location, reputation, good customer relations, or similar factors; equal to the excess of the purchase price over the fair market value of the net assets purchased.

The second major accounting issue associated with the purchase of an entire company is the recording of goodwill. **Goodwill** represents all the special competitive advantages enjoyed by a company, such as a trained staff, good credit rating, reputation for superior products and services, and an established network of suppliers and customers. These factors allow an established business to earn more profits than would a new business, even though the new business might have the same type of building, the same equipment, and the same type of production processes.

When one company purchases another established business, the excess of the purchase price over the value of the identifiable net assets is assumed to represent the purchase of goodwill. The accounting for goodwill is illustrated later in the chapter.

REMEMBER THIS...

- Property, plant, and equipment cost = All costs to purchase and get ready for use.
- Leases:
    - Operating lease—accounted for as a rental; nothing on the balance sheet.
    - Capital lease—accounted for as a purchase; asset and liability on the balance sheet.
- Self-construction cost = Materials, labor, reasonable overhead, and interest.
- When two or more assets are acquired for a single price in a basket purchase, the relative fair market values are used to determine the respective costs.

Calculating and Recording Depreciation Expense

Compute straight-line and units-of-production depreciation expense for plant and equipment.

(4) The second element in accounting for plant and equipment is the allocation of an asset's cost over its useful life. The matching principle requires that this cost be assigned to expense in the periods benefited from the use of the asset. The allocation procedure is called **depreciation**, and the allocated amount, recorded in a period-ending adjusting entry, is an expense that is deducted from revenues in order to determine income. It should be noted that the asset "plant" normally refers to buildings only; land is recorded as a separate asset and is not depreciated because it is usually assumed to have an unlimited useful life.

depreciation

The process of cost allocation that assigns the original cost of plant and equipment to the periods benefited.

Accounting for depreciation is often confusing because students tend to think that depreciation expense reflects the decline in an asset's value. The concept of depreciation is nothing more than a systematic write-off of the original cost of an asset. The undepreciated cost is referred to as **book value**, which represents that portion of the original cost not yet assigned to the income statement as an expense. A company never claims that an asset's recorded book value is equal to its market value. In fact, market values of assets could increase at the same time that depreciation expense is being recorded.

book value

For a long-term operating asset, the asset's original cost less any accumulated depreciation.

To calculate depreciation expense for an asset, you need to know (1) its original cost, (2) its estimated useful life, and (3) its estimated salvage, or residual, value. **Salvage value** is the amount expected to be received when the asset is sold at the end of its useful life (see page 400 for definition). When an asset is purchased, its actual life and salvage value are obviously unknown. They must be

salvage value

The amount expected to be received when an asset is sold at the end of its useful life.

straight-line depreciation method

The depreciation method in which the cost of an asset is allocated equally over the periods of an asset's estimated useful life.

units-of-production method

The depreciation method in which the cost of an asset is allocated to each period on the basis of the productive output or use of the asset during the period.

estimated as realistically as is feasible, usually on the basis of experience with similar assets. In some cases, an asset will have little or no salvage value. If the salvage value is not significant, it is usually ignored in computing depreciation.

Several methods can be used for depreciating the costs of assets for financial reporting. In the main part of this chapter, we describe two: straight-line and units-of-production. In the expanded material section of this chapter, we describe two more depreciation methods: sum-of-the-years'-digits and declining-balance.

The **straight-line depreciation method** assumes that an asset will benefit all periods equally and that the cost of the asset should be assigned on a uniform basis for all accounting periods. If an asset's benefits are thought to be related to its productive output (miles driven in an automobile, for example), the **units-of-production method** is usually appropriate.

To illustrate straight-line and units-of-production depreciation methods, we assume that Wheeler Resorts purchased a van on January 1 for transporting hotel guests to and from the airport. The following facts apply:

Acquisition cost	$24,000
Estimated salvage value	$2,000
Estimated life:	
In years	4 years
In miles driven	60,000 miles

Straight-Line Method of Depreciation

The straight-line depreciation method is the simplest depreciation method. It assumes that an asset's cost should be assigned equally to all periods benefited. The formula for calculating annual straight-line depreciation is:

$$\frac{\text{Cost} - \text{Salvage value}}{\text{Estimated useful life (years)}} = \text{Annual depreciation expense}$$

With this formula, the annual depreciation expense for the van is calculated as:

$$\frac{\$24,000 - \$2,000}{4 \text{ years}} = \$5,500 \text{ depreciation expense per year}$$

When the depreciation expense for an asset has been calculated, a schedule showing the annual depreciation expense, the total accumulated depreciation, and the asset's book value (undepreciated cost) for each year can be prepared. The depreciation schedule for the van (using straight-line depreciation) is shown in Exhibit 4.

EXHIBIT 4	Depreciation Schedule with Straight-Line Depreciation		
	Annual Depreciation Expense	**Accumulated Depreciation**	**Book Value**
Acquisition date	–	–	$24,000
End of year 1	$ 5,500	$ 5,500	18,500
End of year 2	5,500	11,000	13,000
End of year 3	5,500	16,500	7,500
End of year 4	5,500	22,000	2,000
	$22,000		

The entry to record straight-line depreciation each year is:

Depreciation Expense	5,500	
Accumulated Depreciation, Hotel Van		5,500
To record annual depreciation for the hotel van.		

F Y I

A comparison of the amounts of cost and accumulated depreciation reveals how old the plant and equipment is relative to its total expected life.

Depreciation Expense is reported on the income statement. Accumulated Depreciation is a contra-asset account that is offset against the cost of the asset on the balance sheet. Book value is equal to the asset account balance, which retains the original cost of the asset as a debit balance, minus the credit balance in the accumulated depreciation account.

At the end of the first year, the acquisition cost, accumulated depreciation, and book value of the van are presented on the balance sheet as follows:

Property, Plant, and Equipment:	
Hotel van	$24,000
Less: Accumulated depreciation	5,500
Book value	$18,500

Similar information is provided in the annual reports of all companies with property, plant, and equipment. For example, **General Electric** reported the following in the notes to its 2005 financial statements:

	Original Cost (in millions)	
(December 31)	**2005**	**2004**
GE		
Land and improvements	$ 1,366	$ 1,562
Buildings, structures, and related equipment	10,044	9,617
Machinery and equipment	25,811	25,811
Leasehold costs and manufacturing plant under construction	2,157	2,157
	$ 39,378	$ 39,147
GE Capital Services		
Buildings and equipment	$ 5,547	$ 5,684
Equipment leased to others		
Aircraft	32,941	26,837
Vehicles	23,208	23,056
Railroad rolling stock	3,327	3,390
Mobile and modular space	2,889	2,965
Construction and manufacturing	1,609	1,772
All other	2,834	3,021
	$ 72,355	$ 66,725
	$111,733	$105,872

	Accumulated Depreciation and Amortization	
GE	$22,874	$22,391
GE Capital Services		
Buildings and equipment	2,431	2,389
Equipment leased to others	18,900	17,989
	$44,205	$42,769

Using this information, one can calculate that the property, plant, and equipment used by General Electric had been used for 58% ($22,874/$39,378) of its useful life as of the end of 2005. Similarly, the buildings and equipment used by **GE Capital Services** had been used for 44% ($2,431/$5,547) of its life, and the equipment leased by GE Capital Services to others had been used for 28% ($18,900/$66,808) of its useful life.

Units-of-Production Method of Depreciation

The units-of-production depreciation method allocates an asset's cost on the basis of use rather than time. This method is used primarily when a company expects that asset usage will vary significantly from year to year. If the asset's usage pattern is uniform from year to year, the units-of-production method will produce the same depreciation pattern as the straight-line method. Assets with varying usage patterns for which this method of depreciation may be appropriate include automobiles and other vehicles whose life is estimated in terms of number of miles driven. It is also used for certain machines whose life is estimated in terms of number of units produced or number of hours of operating life. The formula for calculating the units-of-production depreciation for the year is:

$$\frac{\text{Cost} - \text{Salvage value}}{\substack{\text{Total estimated life in} \\ \text{units, hours, or miles}}} \times \substack{\text{Number of units produced,} \\ \text{hours used, or miles driven} \\ \text{during the year}} = \text{Current year's depreciation expense}$$

To illustrate, we again consider Wheeler Resorts' van, which has an expected life of 60,000 miles. With the units-of-production method, if the van is driven 12,000 miles during the first year, the depreciation expense for that year is calculated as follows:

$$\frac{\$24,000 - \$2,000}{60,000 \text{ miles}} \times 12,000 \text{ miles} = \$4,400 \text{ depreciation expense}$$

The entry to record units-of-production depreciation at the end of the first year of the van's life is:

Depreciation Expense	4,400	
Accumulated Depreciation, Hotel Van		4,400
To record depreciation for the first year of the hotel van's life.		

The depreciation schedule for the four years is shown in Exhibit 5. This exhibit assumes that 18,000 miles were driven the second year, 21,000 the third year, and 9,000 the fourth year.

Note that part of the formulas for straight-line and units-of-production depreciation is the same. In both cases, cost − salvage value is divided by the asset's useful life. With straight-line, life is measured in years; with units-of-production, life is in miles or hours.

EXHIBIT 5	**Depreciation Schedule with Units-of-Production Depreciation**			
	Miles Driven	**Depreciation Expense**	**Accumulated Depreciation**	**Book Value**
Acquisition date	–	–	–	$24,000
End of year 1	12,000	$ 4,400	$ 4,400	19,600
End of year 2	18,000	6,600	11,000	13,000
End of year 3	21,000	7,700	18,700	5,300
End of year 4	9,000	3,300	22,000	2,000
		$22,000		

With units-of-production, the depreciation per mile or hour must then be multiplied by the usage for the year to determine depreciation expense.

What if the van lasts longer than four years or is driven for more than 60,000 miles? Once the $22,000 difference between cost and salvage value has been recorded as depreciation expense, there is no further expense to record. Thus, any additional years or miles are "free" in the sense that no depreciation expense will be recognized in connection with them. However, as other vans are purchased in the future, the initial estimates of their useful lives will be adjusted to reflect the experience with previous vans.

What if the van lasts less than four years or is driven fewer than 60,000 miles? This topic is covered later in the chapter in connection with the accounting for the disposal of property, plant, and equipment.

A Comparison of Depreciation Methods

The amount of depreciation expense will vary according to the depreciation method used by a company. Exhibit 6 compares the annual depreciation expense for Wheeler Resorts' van under the straight-line and units-of-production depreciation methods. As this schedule makes clear, the total amount of depreciation is the same regardless of which method is used.

Straight-line is by far the most commonly used depreciation method because it is the simplest to apply and makes intuitive sense. For example, in the notes to its 2006 financial statements (see Appendix A), **Wal-Mart** discloses that it depreciates its property, plant, and equipment using the straight-line method over useful lives ranging from 3 to 50 years.

Partial-Year Depreciation Calculations

Thus far, depreciation expense has been calculated on the basis of a full year. Businesses purchase assets at all times during the year, however, so partial-year depreciation calculations are often required. To compute depreciation expense for less than a full year, first calculate the depreciation expense for the year and then distribute it evenly over the number of months the asset is held during the year.

To illustrate, assume that Wheeler Resorts purchased its $24,000 van on July 1 instead of January 1. The depreciation calculations for the first one and one-half years, using straight-line depreciation, are shown in Exhibit 7. The units-of-production method has been omitted from the exhibit; midyear purchases do not complicate the calculations with this method because it involves number of miles driven, hours flown, and so on, rather than time periods.

In practice, many companies simplify their depreciation computations by taking a full year of depreciation in the year an asset is purchased and none in the year the asset is

EXHIBIT 6	**Comparison of Depreciation Expense Using Different Depreciation Methods**	
	Straight-Line Depreciation	**Units-of-Production Depreciation**
End of year 1	$ 5,500	$ 4,400
End of year 2	5,500	6,600
End of year 3	5,500	7,700
End of year 4	5,500	3,300
Totals	$22,000	$22,000

| | | EXHIBIT 7 | Partial-Year Depreciation | | |

Method	Full-Year Depreciation	Depreciation 1st Year (6 months)	Depreciation 2nd Year (12 months)
Straight-line	$5,500	$2,750 ($5,500 × ½)	$5,500

natural resources

Assets that are physically consumed or waste away, such as oil, minerals, gravel, and timber.

depletion

The process of cost allocation that assigns the original cost of a natural resource to the periods benefited.

sold. This is allowed because depreciation is based on estimates, and in the long run, the difference in the amounts is usually immaterial.

Units-of-Production Method with Natural Resources

Another common use for the units-of-production method is with natural resources. **Natural resources** include such assets as oil wells, timber tracts, coal mines, and gravel deposits. Like all other assets, newly purchased or developed natural resources are recorded at cost. This cost must be written off as the assets are extracted or otherwise depleted. This process of writing off the cost of natural resources is called **depletion** and involves the calculation of a depletion rate for each unit of the natural resource. Conceptually, depletion is exactly the same as depreciation; with plant and equipment, the accounting process is called depreciation, whereas with natural resources it is called depletion.

To illustrate, assume that Power-T Company purchases a coal mine for $1,200,000 cash. The entry to record the purchase is:

Coal Mine	1,200,000	
Cash		1,200,000
Purchased a coal mine for $1,200,000.		

If the mine contains an estimated 200,000 tons of coal deposits (based on a geologist's estimate), the depletion expense for each ton of coal extracted and sold will be $6 ($1,200,000/200,000 tons). Here, the unit of production is the extraction of one ton of coal. If 12,000 tons of coal are mined and sold in the current year, the depletion entry is:

Depletion Expense	72,000	
Accumulated Depletion, Coal Mine		72,000
To record depletion for the year: 12,000 tons at $6 per ton.		

After the first year's depletion expense has been recorded, the coal mine is shown on the balance sheet as follows:

Coal mine	$1,200,000
Less: Accumulated depletion	72,000
Book value	$1,128,000

But how do you determine the number of tons of coal in a mine? Because most natural resources cannot be counted, the amount of the resource owned is an estimate. The depletion calculation is therefore likely to be revised as new information becomes available. When an estimate is changed, a new depletion rate per unit is calculated and used to compute depletion during the remaining life of the natural resource or until another new estimate is made. Coverage of accounting for changes in estimates is included in the expanded material section of this chapter.

REMEMBER THIS...

- Depreciation is the process whereby the cost of an asset is allocated over its useful life.
- The straight-line and units-of-production methods allocate cost proportionately over an asset's life on the bases of time and use, respectively.
- Straight-line depreciation expense = (Cost − Salvage value) ÷ Estimated useful life
- Units-of-production depreciation expense =
  [(Cost − Salvage value) ÷ Estimated life in units] × Units produced
- Depreciation for natural resources is called depletion and is similar to units-of-production depreciation.

Account for repairs and improvements of property, plant, and equipment.

Repairing and Improving Property, Plant, and Equipment

(5) Sometime during its useful life, an asset will probably need to be repaired or improved. The accounting issue associated with these postacquisition expenditures is whether they should be immediately recognized as an expense or be added to the cost of the asset (capitalized). Remember from the discussion in Chapter 8 that an expenditure should be capitalized if it is expected to have an identifiable benefit in future periods.

Two types of expenditures can be made on existing assets. The first is ordinary expenditures for repairs, maintenance, and minor improvements. For example, a truck requires oil changes and periodic maintenance. Because these types of expenditures typically benefit only the period in which they are made, they are expenses of the current period.

The second type is an expenditure that lengthens an asset's useful life, increases its capacity, or changes its use. These expenditures are capitalized; that is, they are added to the asset's cost instead of being expensed in the current period. For example, overhauling the engine of a delivery truck involves a major expenditure to extend the useful life of the truck. To qualify for capitalization, an expenditure should meet three criteria: (1) it must be significant in amount; (2) it should benefit the company over several periods, not just during the current one; and (3) it should increase the productive life or capacity of the asset.

To illustrate the differences in accounting for capital and ordinary expenditures, assume that Wheeler Resorts also purchases a delivery truck for $42,000. This truck has an estimated useful life of eight years and a salvage value of $2,000. The straight-line depreciation is $5,000 per year [($42,000 − $2,000)/8 years]. If the company spends $1,500 each year for normal maintenance, its annual recording of these expenditures is:

Repairs and Maintenance Expense	1,500	
Cash		1,500
Spent $1,500 for maintenance of delivery truck.		

This entry has no effect on either the recorded cost or the depreciation expense of the truck. Now suppose that at the end of the sixth year of the truck's useful life, Wheeler spends $8,000 to overhaul the engine. This expenditure will increase the truck's remaining life from two to four years, but will not change its estimated salvage value. The depreciation for the last four years will be $4,500 per year, calculated as shown below.

	Depreciation before Overhaul		Depreciation after Overhaul
Original cost	$42,000	Original cost	$42,000
Less salvage value	2,000	Accumulated depreciation	
Cost to be allocated (depreciable amount)	$40,000	(prior to overhaul)	30,000
Original life of asset	8 years	Remaining book value	$12,000
Original depreciation per year ($40,000/8)	$5,000	Capital expenditure (overhaul)	8,000
Usage before overhaul	× 6 years	New book value	$20,000
Accumulated depreciation prior to overhaul	$30,000	Less salvage value	2,000
		New depreciable amount	$18,000
		Remaining life	4 years
		New annual depreciation ($18,000/4)	$ 4,500

The journal entry to record the $8,000 capitalized expenditure is:

Delivery Truck	8,000	
Cash		8,000
Spent $8,000 to overhaul the engine of the $42,000 truck.		

Another example of a capital expenditure is the cost of land improvements. Certain improvements are considered permanent, such as moving earth to change the land contour. Such an expenditure would be capitalized as part of the land account. Other expenditures may have a limited life, such as those incurred in building a road, a sidewalk, or a fence. These expenditures would be capitalized in a separate land improvements account and be depreciated over their useful lives.

It is often difficult to determine whether a given expenditure should be capitalized or expensed. The two procedures produce a different net income, however, so it is extremely important that such expenditures be properly classified. When in doubt, accepted practice is to record an expenditure as an expense to ensure that the asset is not reported at an amount that exceeds its future benefit.

REMEMBER THIS...

- When an expenditure is capitalized, it is recorded as an addition to the cost of an asset.
- To be capitalized, an expenditure must:
  1. be significant in amount,
  2. provide benefits for more than one period, and
  3. increase the productive life or capacity of an asset.
- Ordinary expenditures, such as repairs, merely maintain an asset's productive capacity at the level originally projected and are expenses of the current period.

Recording Impairments of Asset Value

Identify whether a long-term operating asset has suffered a decline in value and record the decline.

(6) As mentioned earlier, the value of a long-term asset depends on the future cash flows expected to be generated by that asset. Occasionally, events occur after the purchase of an asset that significantly reduce its value. For example, a decline in the consumer demand for high-priced athletic shoes can cause the value of a shoe-manufacturing plant to plummet. Accountants call this **impairment**. When an asset is impaired, the event should be recognized in the financial statements, both as a reduction in the reported value of the asset in the balance sheet and as a loss in the income statement. Of course, the value of long-term assets can also increase after the purchase date. In the United States, these increases are not recorded, as explained more fully later in this section.

impairment

A decline in the value of a long-term operating asset.

Recording Decreases in the Value of Property, Plant, and Equipment

According to U.S. accounting rules, the value of an asset is impaired when the sum of estimated future cash flows from that asset is less than the book value of the asset. This computation ignores the time value of money. As illustrated in the example below, this is a strange impairment threshold—a more reasonable test would be to compare the book value to the fair value of the asset.

Once it has been determined that an asset is impaired, the amount of the impairment is measured as the difference between the book value of the asset and the fair value. To summarize, the existence of an impairment loss is determined using the sum of the estimated future cash flows from the asset, ignoring the time value of money. The amount of the impairment loss is measured using the fair value of the asset, which does incorporate the time value of money. The practical result of this two-step process is that an impairment loss is not recorded unless it is quite certain that the asset has suffered a permanent decline in value.

To illustrate, assume that Wheeler Resorts purchased a fitness center building five years ago for $600,000. The building has been depreciated using the straight-line method with a 20-year useful life and no residual value. Wheeler estimates that the building has a remaining useful life of 15 years, that net cash inflow from the building will be $25,000 per year, and that the fair value of the building is $230,000.

Annual depreciation for the building has been $30,000 ($600,000 ÷ 20 years). The current book value of the building is computed as follows:

Original cost	$600,000
Accumulated depreciation ($30,000 × 5 years)	150,000
Book value	$450,000

The book value of $450,000 is compared with the $375,000 ($25,000 × 15 years) sum of future cash flows (ignoring the time value of money) to determine whether the building is impaired. The sum of future cash flows is only $375,000, which is less than the $450,000 book value, so an impairment loss should be recognized. The loss is equal to the $220,000 ($450,000 – $230,000) difference between the book value of the building and its fair value. The impairment loss would be recorded as follows:

Accumulated Depreciation, Building	150,000	
Loss on Impairment of Building	220,000	
Building ($600,000 – $230,000)		370,000
Recognized $220,000 impairment loss on building.		

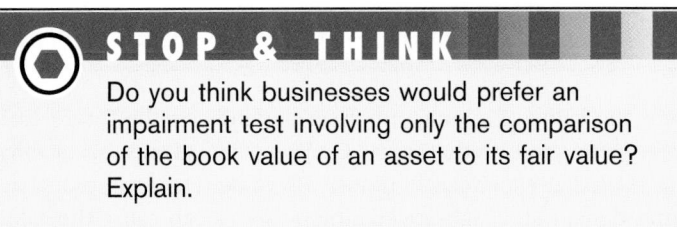

STOP & THINK

Do you think businesses would prefer an impairment test involving only the comparison of the book value of an asset to its fair value? Explain.

This journal entry basically records the asset as if it were being acquired brand new at its fair value of $230,000. The existing accumulated depreciation balance is wiped clean, and the new recorded value of the asset is its fair value of $230,000 ($600,000 − $370,000). After an impairment loss is recognized, no restoration of the loss is allowed even if the fair value of the asset later recovers.

The odd nature of the impairment test can be seen if the facts in the Wheeler example are changed slightly. Assume that net cash inflow from the building will be $35,000 per year and that the fair value of the building is $330,000. With these numbers, no impairment loss is recognized, even though the fair value of $330,000 is less than the book value of $450,000, because the sum of future cash flows of $525,000 ($35,000 × 15 years) exceeds the book value. Thus, in this case the asset would still be recorded at its book value of $450,000, even though its fair value is actually less. As mentioned above, the practical impact of the two-step impairment test is that no impairment losses are recorded unless the future cash flow calculations offer very strong evidence of a permanent decline in asset value. The impairment test is summarized in Exhibit 8.

AOL Time Warner set a world record when it recorded an impairment loss in 2002 of $99.737 billion. Over half of that amount related to a write-off of goodwill associated with the 2000 merger of **AOL** and **Time Warner**. This record write-off resulted in AOL Time Warner reporting a net loss for the year of $98.7 billion.

Recording Increases in the Value of Property, Plant, and Equipment

Under U.S. accounting standards, increases in the value of property, plant, and equipment are not recognized. Gains from increases in asset value are recorded only if and when the asset is sold. Thus, in the Wheeler example discussed above, if the fair value of the building rises to $800,000, the building would still be reported in the financial statements at its depreciated book value of $450,000. This is an example of the conservative bias that often exists in the accounting rules: losses are recognized when they occur, but the recognition of gains is deferred until the asset is sold.

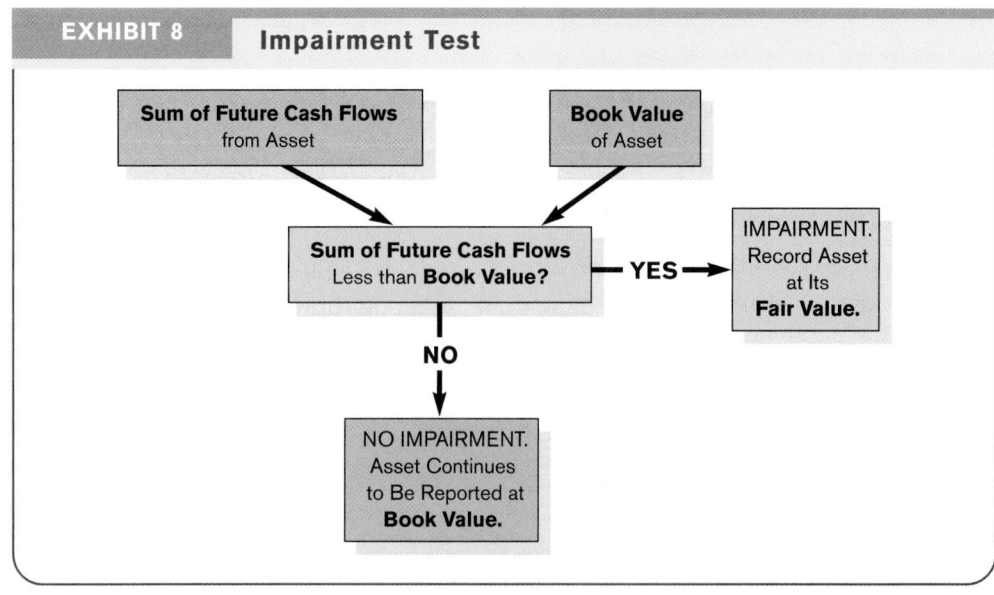

EXHIBIT 8 **Impairment Test**

Although increases in the value of property, plant, and equipment are not recognized in the United States, accounting rules in other countries do allow for their recognition. For example, companies in Great Britain often report their long-term operating assets at their fair values. Because this upward revaluation of property, plant, and equipment is allowable under international accounting standards, it will be interesting to watch over the next decade or so to see whether sentiment grows to allow this practice in the United States as well.

> **REMEMBER THIS...**
>
> - When an asset's value declines after it is purchased, it is said to be impaired.
> - Recording an impairment loss is a two-step process.
>   1. Compare the recorded book value of the asset to the sum of future cash flows expected to be generated by the asset.
>   2. If the book value is higher, recognize a loss in an amount equal to the difference between the book value of the asset and its FAIR value.
> - According to U.S. accounting rules, increases in the value of property, plant, and equipment are not recognized.

Disposal of Property, Plant, and Equipment

Record the discarding and selling of property, plant, and equipment.

 Plant and equipment eventually become worthless or are sold. When a company removes one of these assets from service, it has to eliminate the asset's cost and accumulated depreciation from the accounting records. There are basically three ways to dispose of an asset: (1) discard or scrap it, (2) sell it, or (3) exchange it for another asset.

Discarding Property, Plant, and Equipment

When an asset becomes worthless and must be scrapped, its cost and its accumulated depreciation balance should be removed from the accounting records. If the asset's total cost has been depreciated, there is no loss on the disposal. If, on the other hand, the cost is not completely depreciated, the undepreciated cost represents a loss on disposal.

To illustrate, we assume that Wheeler Resorts, Inc., purchases a computer for $15,000. The computer has a five-year life and no estimated salvage value and is depreciated on a straight-line basis. If the computer is scrapped after five full years, the entry to record the disposal is as follows:

Accumulated Depreciation, Computer	15,000	
Computer		15,000
Scrapped $15,000 computer.		

If Wheeler must pay $300 to have the computer dismantled and removed, the entry to record the disposal is:

Accumulated Depreciation, Computer	15,000	
Loss on Disposal of Computer	300	
Computer		15,000
Cash		300
Scrapped $15,000 computer and paid disposal costs of $300.		

If the computer had been scrapped after only four years of service (and after $12,000 of the original cost has been depreciated), there would have been a loss on disposal of $3,300 (including the disposal cost), and the entry would have been:

Accumulated Depreciation, Computer	12,000	
Loss on Disposal of Computer	3,300	
Computer		15,000
Cash		300
Scrapped $15,000 computer and paid disposal costs of $300.		

Don't think of the losses recognized above as "bad" or gains as "good." A loss on disposal simply means that, given the information we now have, it appears that we didn't record enough depreciation expense in previous years. As a result, the book value of the asset is higher than the amount we can get on disposal. Similarly, a gain means that too much depreciation expense was recognized in prior years, making the book value of the asset lower than its actual disposal value.

Selling Property, Plant, and Equipment

A second way of disposing of property, plant, and equipment is to sell it. If the sales price of the asset exceeds its book value (the original cost less accumulated depreciation), there is a gain on the sale. Conversely, if the sales price is less than the book value, there is a loss.

To illustrate, we refer again to Wheeler's $15,000 computer. If the computer is sold for $600 after five full years of service, assuming no disposal costs, the entry to record the sale is:

Cash	600	
Accumulated Depreciation, Computer	15,000	
Computer		15,000
Gain on Sale of Computer		600
Sold $15,000 computer at a gain of $600.		

Because the asset was fully depreciated, its book value was zero and the $600 cash received represents a gain. If the computer had been sold for $600 after only four years of service, there would have been a loss of $2,400 on the sale, and the entry to record the sale would have been:

Cash	600	
Accumulated Depreciation, Computer	12,000	
Loss on Sale of Computer	2,400	
Computer		15,000
Sold $15,000 computer at a loss of $2,400.		

The $2,400 loss is the difference between the sales price of $600 and the book value of $3,000 ($15,000 – $12,000). The amount of a gain or loss is thus a function of two factors: (1) the amount of cash received from the sale, and (2) the book value of the asset at the date of sale. The book value can vary from the market price of the asset for two reasons: (1) the accounting for the asset is not intended to show market value in the financial statements, and (2) it is difficult to estimate salvage value and useful life at the outset of an asset's life.

Exchanging Property, Plant, and Equipment

A third way of disposing of property, plant, and equipment is to exchange it for another asset. Such exchanges occur regularly with cars, trucks, machines, and other types of large equipment. When dissimilar assets are exchanged, such as a truck for a computer, the transaction is accounted for exactly as outlined previously: the acquired asset is recorded in the books at its fair market value, and a gain or loss may be recognized depending on the difference between this market value and the book value of the asset that was disposed of. Accounting for exchanges of similar assets can be more complicated and therefore is not discussed in this text. For a full treatment of the accounting for the exchange of similar assets, see an intermediate accounting text.

REMEMBER THIS...

- There are three ways of disposing of assets:
    1. discarding (scrapping),
    2. selling, and
    3. exchanging.
- If a scrapped asset has not been fully depreciated, a loss equal to the undepreciated cost or book value is recognized.
- When an asset is sold, there is a gain if the sales price exceeds the book value and a loss if the sales price is less than the book value.

Accounting for Intangible Assets

⑧ Account for the acquisition and amortization of intangible assets and understand the special difficulties associated with accounting for intangibles.

Intangible assets are rights and privileges that are long-lived, are not held for resale, have no physical substance, and usually provide their owner with competitive advantages over other firms. Familiar examples are **patents**, franchises, licenses, and goodwill.

The importance of intangible assets can be illustrated by considering **General Electric**. As mentioned in Chapter 2, if the balance sheet were perfect, the amount of owners' equity would be equal to the market value of the company. On December 31, 2005, GE's reported equity was equal to $109.354 billion. The actual market value of GE on December 31, 2005, was $367 billion. The reason for the large difference between the recorded value and the actual value is that a traditional balance sheet excludes many important intangible economic assets. Examples of GE's important intangible economic assets are its track record of successful products and its entrenched market position in the many industries in which it operates. These intangible factors are by far the most valuable assets owned by GE, but they fall outside the traditional accounting process.

patent

An exclusive right granted for 20 years by the federal government to manufacture and sell an invention.

As with many accounting issues, accounting for intangibles involves a trade-off between relevance and reliability. Information concerning intangible assets is relevant, but to meet the standard for recognition in the financial statements, the recorded amount for the intangible must also be reliable. The most important distinction in intangible assets for accounting purposes is between those intangible assets that are internally generated and those that are externally purchased. This distinction is important because the transfer of externally-purchased intangible assets in an arm's-length market transaction provides reliable evidence that the intangibles have probable future economic benefit. Such reliable evidence does not exist for most internally-generated intangibles. Accordingly, as discussed in Chapter 8, most costs associated with generating and maintaining internally-generated intangibles are expensed as incurred.

Keep in mind, however, that an intangible asset that is internally generated (and therefore not recorded as an asset on a company's books) is still valued by the stock market. As an illustration, consider Exhibit 9, which lists the 10 most valuable brands in the

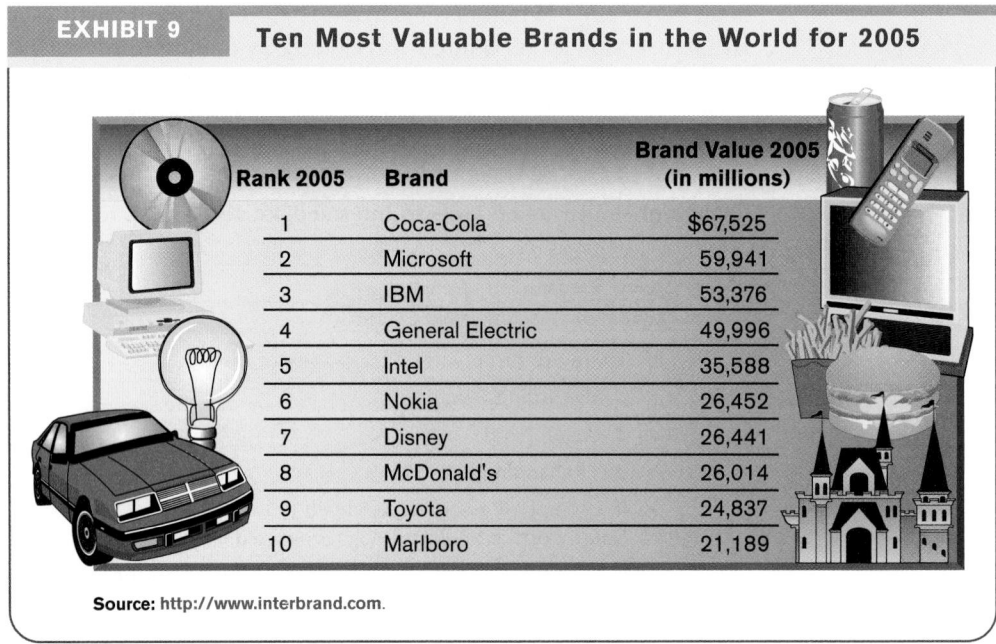

EXHIBIT 9   Ten Most Valuable Brands in the World for 2005

Rank 2005	Brand	Brand Value 2005 (in millions)
1	Coca-Cola	$67,525
2	Microsoft	59,941
3	IBM	53,376
4	General Electric	49,996
5	Intel	35,588
6	Nokia	26,452
7	Disney	26,441
8	McDonald's	26,014
9	Toyota	24,837
10	Marlboro	21,189

Source: http://www.interbrand.com.

world in 2005. Each of these brands represents a valuable economic asset that has been internally generated. For example, the $67.5 billion Coca-Cola brand name has been created over the years by **The Coca-Cola Company** through successful business operations and relentless marketing. But because the valuation of this asset is not deemed sufficiently reliable to meet the standard for financial statement recognition, it is not included in The Coca-Cola Company's balance sheet. However, as explained below, if another company were to buy The Coca-Cola Company, an important part of recording the transaction would be allocating the total purchase price to the various economic assets acquired, including previously unrecorded intangible assets.

In the future, financial reporting will move toward providing more information about internally-generated intangibles. Whether this will involve actual valuation and recognition of these intangibles in the financial statements, or simply more extensive note disclosure, remains to be seen.

A short description of some of the common types of intangible assets is given below.

Trademark   A trademark is a distinctive name, symbol, or slogan that distinguishes a product or service from similar products or services. Well-known examples include Coke, Windows, Yahoo!, and the Nike Swoosh. As shown in Exhibit 9 above, it was estimated in 2005 that the value of the Coca-Cola trademark was in excess of $67 billion. Because the Coca-Cola trademark is an internally-generated intangible asset, it is not reported in The Coca-Cola Company's balance sheet. However, the company has purchased other trademarks (such as Minute Maid), with a total cost of $2.3 billion; these are reported in The Coca-Cola Company's balance sheet.

Franchises   Franchise operations have become so common in everyday life that we often don't realize we are dealing with them. In fact, these days it is difficult to find a non-franchise business in a typical shopping mall. When a business obtains a **franchise**, the

franchise

An entity that has been licensed to sell the product of a manufacturer or to offer a particular service in a given area.

recorded cost of the franchise includes any sum paid specifically for the franchise right as well as legal fees and other costs incurred in obtaining it. Although the value of a franchise at the time of its acquisition may be substantially in excess of its cost, the amount recorded should be limited to actual outlays. For example, approximately 60% of **McDonald's** locations are operated under franchise agreements. A McDonald's franchisee must contribute an initial cash amount of $200,000, which is used to buy some of the equipment and signs and also to pay the initial franchise fee. The value of a McDonald's franchise alone is much more

The original Coca-Cola bottling franchise sold for $1.

than $200,000, but the franchisee would only record a franchise asset in his or her financial statements equal to the cost (not value) of the franchise. However, if a franchise right is included when one company purchases another company, presumably the entire value is included in the purchase price, and the fair value attributable to the franchise right is recorded as an intangible asset in the acquirer's books.

Goodwill   Goodwill is the business contacts, reputation, functioning systems, staff camaraderie, and industry experience that make a business much more than just a collection of assets. As mentioned above, if these factors are the result of a contractual right or are associated with intangibles that can be bought and sold separately, then the value of the factor should be reported as a separate intangible asset. In essence, goodwill is a residual number, the value of all of the synergies of a functioning business that cannot be specifically identified with any other intangible factor. Goodwill is recognized only when it is purchased as part of the acquisition of another company. In other words, a company's own goodwill, its homegrown goodwill, is not recognized. Goodwill will be discussed more in depth later in the chapter. Exhibit 10 provides a summary of a number of intangible assets and how they are valued.

Estimating the Fair Value of an Intangible   The most difficult part of recording an amount for an intangible asset is not in identifying the asset but instead is in estimating a fair value of the asset. The objective in estimating the fair value is to duplicate the

---

EXHIBIT 10	**Acquisition Costs of Goodwill and Other Intangible Assets**	
Patent	An exclusive right granted by a national government that enables an inventor to control the manufacture, sale, or use of an invention. In the United States, legal life is 20 years from patent application date.	**COST:** Purchase price, filing and registry fees, cost of subsequent litigation to protect right. Does not include internal research and development costs.
Trademark	An exclusive right granted by a national government that permits the use of distinctive symbols, labels, and designs, e.g., McDonald's golden arches, Nike's Swoosh, Apple's computer name and logo. Legal life is virtually unlimited.	**COST:** Same as Patent.
Copyright	An exclusive right granted by a national government that permits an author to sell, license, or control his/her work. In the United States, copyrights expire 50 years after the death of the author.	**COST:** Same as Patent.
Franchise agreement	An exclusive right or privilege received by a business or individual to perform certain functions or sell certain products or services.	**COST:** Expenditures made to purchase the franchise. Legal fees and other costs incurred in obtaining the franchise.
Acquired customer list	A list or database containing customer information such as name, address, past purchases, and so forth. Companies that originally develop such a list often sell or lease it to other companies, unless prohibited by customer confidentiality agreements.	**COST:** Purchase price when acquired from another company. Costs to internally develop a customer list are expensed as incurred.
Goodwill	Miscellaneous intangible resources, factors, and conditions that allow a company to earn above-normal income with its identifiable net assets. Goodwill is recorded only when a business entity is acquired by a purchase.	**COST:** Portion of purchase price that exceeds the sum of the current market value for all identifiable net assets, both tangible and intangible.

Source: Some of these illustrations are taken from SFAS No. 141, "Business Combinations," Appendix A.

price at which the intangible asset would change hands in an arm's-length market transaction. If there is a market for similar intangibles assets, then the best estimate of fair value is made with reference to these observable market prices.

To illustrate the accounting for the purchase of an intangible patent, assume that Wheeler Resorts, Inc., acquires, for $200,000, a patent granted seven years earlier to another firm. The entry to record the purchase of the patent is:

Patent	200,000	
Cash		200,000
Purchased patent for $200,000.		

The one exception to valuing purchased intangibles at market value involves goodwill, which arises when an entire business is purchased. Goodwill is best thought of as a residual amount, the amount of the purchase price of a business that is left over after all other tangible and intangible assets have been identified. As such, goodwill is that intangible something that makes the whole company worth more than its individual parts. In general, goodwill represents all the special advantages, not otherwise separately identifiable, enjoyed by an enterprise, such as a high credit standing, reputation for superior products and services, experience with development and distribution processes, favorable government relations, and so forth. These factors allow a business to earn above-normal income with the identifiable assets, tangible and intangible, employed in the business.

To illustrate the accounting for goodwill, assume that, in order to cater to the medicinal needs of its guests, Wheeler Resorts purchases Valley Drug Store for $400,000. At the time of purchase, the recorded assets and liabilities of Valley Drug have the following fair market values:

Inventory	$220,000
Long-term operating assets	110,000
Other assets (prepaid expenses, etc.)	10,000
Liabilities	(20,000)
Total net assets	$320,000

Note that Wheeler Resorts records these items at their fair market values on the date purchased, just as it does when purchasing individual assets.

Because Wheeler was willing to pay $400,000 for Valley Drug, there must have been other favorable, intangible factors worth approximately $80,000. These factors are called goodwill, and the entry to record the purchase of the drug store is:

Inventory	220,000	
Long-term Operating Assets	110,000	
Other Assets	10,000	
Goodwill	80,000	
Liabilities		20,000
Cash		400,000
Purchased Valley Drug Store for $400,000.		

amortization

The process of cost allocation that assigns the original cost of an intangible asset to the periods benefited.

Amortization of Intangible Assets

Like tangible assets, intangible assets are recorded at their historical costs. Unlike tangible assets, the costs associated with intangible assets are not always allocated as expenses over time. The periodic allocation to expense of an intangible asset's cost is called **amortization**. Conceptually, depreciation (with plant and equipment), depletion (with natural resources), and amortization (with intangible assets) are exactly the same thing. Straight-line amortization is generally used for intangible assets.

In accounting for an intangible asset after its acquisition, a determination first must be made as to whether the intangible asset has a finite life. If no economic, legal, or contractual factors cause the intangible to have a finite life, then its life is said to be indefinite, and the asset is not to be amortized until its life is determined to be finite. An indefinite life is one that extends beyond the foreseeable horizon. An example of an intangible asset that has an indefinite life is a broadcast license which includes an extension option that can be renewed indefinitely. If an intangible asset is determined to have a finite life, then the asset is to be amortized over its estimated life; the useful life estimate should be reviewed periodically.

To illustrate the amortization of an intangible asset, let us continue with the patent example with Wheeler Resorts, Inc., used earlier. Recall that the patent, with a legal life of 20 years, was purchased from another company after seven years. Because seven years of its 20-year legal life have already elapsed, the patent now has a legal life of only 13 years, although it may have a shorter useful life. If its useful life is assumed to be eight years, one-eighth of the $200,000 cost should be amortized each year for the next eight years. The entry each year to record the patent amortization expense is:

Amortization Expense, Patent	25,000	
Patent		25,000
To amortize one-eighth of the cost of the patent.		

Notice that in the above entry, the patent account was credited. Alternatively, a contra-asset account, such as Accumulated Amortization, could have been credited. In practice, however, crediting the intangible asset account directly is more common. This is different from the normal practice of crediting Accumulated Depreciation for buildings or equipment.

Many intangible assets that used to be amortized are no longer amortized. For example, goodwill used to be amortized over a 40-year period. Goodwill is now no longer amortized.

Impairment of Intangible Assets

While many intangible assets are not amortized, all intangible assets must be evaluated every year to determine if (1) their estimated useful life has changed and (2) the intangible asset has become impaired. Previously in this chapter the issue of asset impairment was discussed with regard to tangible assets. While the specifics of the various impairment tests associated with the different kinds of intangible assets are beyond the scope of this textbook, suffice it to say that when evaluating whether or not an intangible asset has become impaired, the objective is to ensure that the intangible assets recorded on the books of a company are not overstated. If an intangible asset is determined to be impaired, an impairment loss is recorded on the income statement and the intangible asset is reduced on the books of the company.

REMEMBER THIS...

- Intangible assets are long-term rights and privileges that have no physical substance but provide competitive advantages to owners. Common intangible assets are patents, franchises, licenses, and goodwill.
- Intangible assets are only recognized in the financial statements if they have been purchased through an arm's-length transaction.
- The cost of recorded intangible assets is expensed as follows:
  - Certain intangible assets are amortized over the economic life of the asset.
  - Many intangible assets are not amortized because their economic lives are not limited.
  - All intangible assets, including goodwill, must be analyzed to determine if impairment has occurred. If it has, then an impairment loss is recognized.

Use the fixed asset turnover ratio as a measure of how efficiently a company is using its property, plant, and equipment.

Measuring Property, Plant, and Equipment Efficiency

In this section we discuss the fixed asset turnover ratio, which uses financial statement data to give a rough indication of how efficiently a company is utilizing its property, plant, and equipment to generate sales. We also illustrate that the fixed asset turnover ratio must be interpreted carefully because, as with most other financial ratios, acceptable values for this ratio differ significantly from one industry to the next.

Evaluating the Level of Property, Plant, and Equipment

fixed asset turnover

The number of dollars in sales generated by each dollar of fixed assets; computed as sales divided by property, plant, and equipment.

Fixed asset turnover can be used to evaluate the appropriateness of the level of a company's property, plant, and equipment. Fixed asset turnover is computed as sales divided by average property, plant, and equipment (fixed assets) and is interpreted as the number of dollars in sales generated by each dollar of fixed assets. This ratio is also often called PP&E turnover. The computation of the fixed asset turnover for **General Electric** is given below. All financial statement numbers are in millions.

	2005	2004
Sales	$148,019	$133,417
Property, plant, and equipment		
Beginning of year	$ 63,103	$ 53,388
End of year	67,528	63,103
Average fixed assets	$ 65,316	$ 58,246
Fixed asset turnover	2.27 times	2.29 times

The fixed asset turnover calculations suggest that GE used its fixed assets to generate sales a little less efficiently in 2005 than in 2004. In 2005, each dollar of fixed assets generated $2.27 in sales, down from $2.29 in 2004.

Industry Differences in Fixed Asset Turnover

As with all ratios, the fixed asset turnover ratio must be used carefully to ensure that erroneous conclusions are not made. For example, fixed asset turnover ratio values for two companies in different industries cannot be meaningfully compared. This point can be illustrated using the fact that General Electric is composed of two primary parts—General Electric, the manufacturing company, and GE Capital Services, the financial services firm. The fixed asset turnover ratio computed earlier was for both these parts combined. Because GE Capital Services does not use property, plant, and equipment for manufacturing but instead leases the assets to other companies in order to earn financial revenue, one would expect its fixed asset turnover ratio to be quite unlike that for a manufacturing firm. In fact, as shown below, the fixed asset turnover ratio for the manufacturing segments of General Electric was 5.44 in 2005, over double the ratio value for the company as a whole.

Fixed Asset Turnover Ratio
General Electric–Manufacturing Segments Only

	2005	2004
Sales	$90,430	$82,214
Property, plant, and equipment		
Beginning of year	$16,756	$14,566
End of year	16,504	16,756
Average fixed assets	$16,630	$15,661
Fixed asset turnover	5.44 times	5.25 times

REMEMBER THIS...

- The fixed asset turnover ratio can be used as a general measure of how efficiently a company is using its property, plant, and equipment.
- Fixed asset turnover is computed as sales divided by average property, plant, and equipment and is interpreted as the number of dollars in sales generated by each dollar of fixed assets.
- Standard values for this ratio differ significantly from industry to industry.

EXPANDED material

Two topics related to operational assets that are traditionally covered in introductory accounting classes were not covered in the main part of this chapter. These two topics relate to depreciation—accelerated depreciation methods and changes in depreciation estimates.

Accelerated Depreciation Methods

Compute declining-balance and sum-of-the-years'-digits depreciation expense for plant and equipment.

(10) Earlier in the chapter, straight-line and units-of-production depreciation methods were discussed. Both of these methods allocate the cost of an asset evenly over its life. With straight-line depreciation, each time period during the asset's useful life is assigned an equal amount of depreciation. With units-of-production depreciation, each mile driven, hour used, or other measurement of useful life is assigned an equal amount of depreciation. Sometimes, a depreciation method that does not assign costs equally over the life of the asset is preferred. For example, if most of an asset's benefits will be realized in the earlier periods of the asset's life, the method used should assign more depreciation to the earlier years and less to the later years. Examples of these "accelerated" depreciation methods are the declining-balance and the sum-of-the-years'-digits methods. These methods are merely ways of assigning more of an asset's depreciation to earlier periods and less to later periods.

To illustrate these depreciation methods, we will again use the Wheeler Resorts example from earlier in the chapter. Assume again that Wheeler Resorts purchased a van for transporting hotel guests to and from the airport. The following facts apply:

Acquisition cost	$24,000
Estimated salvage value	$2,000
Estimated life:	
In years	4 years
In miles driven	60,000 miles

Declining-Balance Method of Depreciation

declining-balance depreciation method

An accelerated depreciation method in which an asset's book value is multiplied by a constant depreciation rate (such as double the straight-line percentage, in the case of double-declining-balance).

The **declining-balance depreciation method** provides for higher depreciation charges in the earlier years of an asset's life than does the straight-line method. The declining-balance method involves multiplying a fixed rate, or percentage, by a decreasing book value. This rate is a multiple of the straight-line rate. Typically, it is twice the straight-line rate, but it also can be 175, 150, or 125% of the straight-line rate. Our depreciation of Wheeler's hotel van will illustrate the declining-balance method using a fixed rate equal to twice the straight-line rate. This method is often referred to as the double-declining-balance depreciation method.

Declining-balance depreciation differs from the other depreciation methods in two respects: (1) the initial computation ignores the asset's salvage value, and (2) a constant depreciation rate is multiplied by a decreasing book value. The salvage value is not ignored completely because the depreciation taken during the asset's life cannot reduce the asset's book value below the estimated salvage value.

The double-declining-balance (DDB) rate is twice the straight-line rate, computed as follows:

$$\frac{1}{\text{Estimated life (years)}} \times 2 = \text{DDB rate}$$

This rate is multiplied times the book value at the beginning of each year (cost − accumulated depreciation) to compute the annual depreciation expense for the year. If the 150% declining balance were being used instead, the 2 in the rate formula would be replaced by 1.5 and so on for any other percentages.

To illustrate, the depreciation calculation for the van using the 200% (or double) declining-balance method is:

Straight-line rate	4 years = 1/4 = 25%
Double the straight-line rate	25% × 2 = 50%
Annual depreciation	50% × undepreciated cost (book value)

Based on this information, the formula for double-declining-balance depreciation can be expressed as (straight-line rate × 2) × (cost − accumulated depreciation) = current year's depreciation expense. The double-declining-balance depreciation for the four years is shown in Exhibit 11. As you review this exhibit, note that the book value of the van at the end of year 4 is $2,000, its salvage value.

 CAUTION

With declining-balance depreciation, the asset is not depreciated below its salvage value, though this figure is ignored in the initial computations.

EXHIBIT 11	**Depreciation Schedule with Double-Declining-Balance Depreciation**			
	Computation	**Annual Depreciation Expense**	**Accumulated Depreciation**	**Book Value**
Acquisition date	—	—	—	$24,000
End of year 1	$24,000 × 0.50	$12,000	$12,000	12,000
End of year 2	12,000 × 0.50	6,000	18,000	6,000
End of year 3	6,000 × 0.50	3,000	21,000	3,000
End of year 4	*	1,000	22,000	2,000
		$22,000		

*In year 4, depreciation expense cannot exceed $1,000 because the book value cannot be reduced below salvage value.

If Wheeler had applied the declining-balance method to depreciate the hotel van on the basis of 150% of the straight-line rate, the fixed rate would have been 37.5%, computed as follows: 25% × 1.50 = 37.5%. Using the 37.5% fixed rate, the annual depreciation of the hotel van would have been as follows:

First year: $24,000 × 37.5% = $9,000
Second year: $24,000 − $9,000 = $15,000 × 37.5% = $5,625
Third year: $15,000 − $5,625 = $9,375 × 37.5% = $3,516
Fourth year: $9,375 − $3,516 = $5,859 − $2,000 salvage value = $3,859

Since a total book value of $5,859 remains at the end of year 3, the remaining book value less the estimated salvage value is expensed in year 4.

Depreciation for Income Tax Purposes   Net income reported on the financial statements prepared for stockholders, creditors, and other external users often differs from taxable income reported on income tax returns. The most common cause of differences between financial reporting and tax returns is the computation of depreciation. Depreciation for income tax purposes must be computed in accordance with federal income tax law, which specifies rules to be applied in computing tax depreciation for various categories of assets. Income tax rules are designed to achieve economic objectives, such as stimulating investment in productive assets.

The income tax depreciation system in the United States is called the Modified Accelerated Cost Recovery System (MACRS). MACRS is based on declining-balance depreciation and is designed to allow taxpayers to quickly deduct the cost of assets acquired. Allowing this accelerated depreciation deduction for income tax purposes gives companies tax benefits for investing in new productive assets. Presumably, this will spur investment, create jobs, and make voters more likely to reelect their representatives.

Sum-of-the-Years'-Digits Method of Depreciation

sum-of-the-years'-digits (SYD) depreciation method

The accelerated depreciation method in which a constant balance (cost minus salvage value) is multiplied by a declining depreciation rate.

Like the declining-balance method, the **sum-of-the-years'-digits (SYD) depreciation method** provides for a proportionately higher depreciation expense in the early years of an asset's life. It is therefore appropriate for assets that provide greater benefits in their earlier years (such as trucks, machinery, and equipment) as opposed to assets that benefit all years equally (as buildings do). The formula for calculating SYD is:

$$\frac{\text{Number of years of life remaining at beginning of year}}{\text{Sum-of-the-years'-digits}} \times (\text{Cost} - \text{Salvage value}) = \text{Depreciation expense}$$

The numerator is the number of years of estimated life remaining at the beginning of the current year. The van, with a four-year life, would have four years remaining at the beginning of the first year, three at the beginning of the second, and so on. The denominator is the sum of the years of the asset's life. The sum of the years' digits for the van is 10 (4 + 3 + 2 + 1). In other words, the numerator decreases by one year each year, whereas the denominator remains the same for each year's calculation of depreciation. Also note that the asset's cost is reduced by the salvage value in computing the annual depreciation expense as is done for the straight-line method but not for the declining-balance method.

The depreciation on the van for the first two years is:

First year: 4/10 × ($24,000 − $2,000) = $8,800
Second year: 3/10 × ($24,000 − $2,000) = $6,600

The depreciation schedule for four years is shown in Exhibit 12.

EXHIBIT 12	Depreciation Schedule with Sum-of-the-Years'-Digits Depreciation

	Annual Depreciation Expense	Accumulated Depreciation	Book Value
Acquisition date	–	–	$24,000
End of year 1	$ 8,800	$ 8,800	15,200
End of year 2	6,600	15,400	8,600
End of year 3	4,400	19,800	4,200
End of year 4	2,200	22,000	2,000
Total	$22,000		

The entry to record the sum-of-the-years'-digits depreciation for the first year is:

Depreciation Expense 8,800
    Accumulated Depreciation, Hotel Van 8,800
      To record the first year's depreciation for the hotel van.

Subsequent years' depreciation entries would show depreciation expense of $6,600, $4,400, and $2,200.

When an asset has a long life, the computation of the denominator (the sum-of-the-years'-digits) can become quite involved. There is, however, a simple formula for determining the denominator. It is:

$$\frac{n(n + 1)}{2} \quad \text{where n is the life (in years) of the asset}$$

Given that the van has a useful life of four years, the formula works as follows:

$$\frac{4(5)}{2} = 10$$

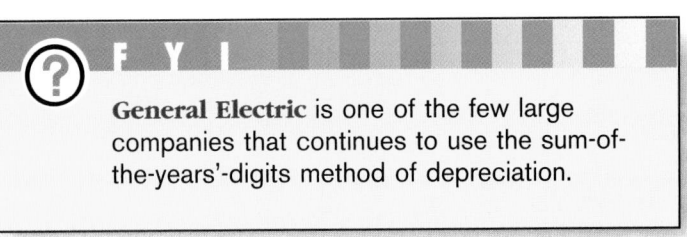

General Electric is one of the few large companies that continues to use the sum-of-the-years'-digits method of depreciation.

As you can see, the answer is the same as if you had added the years' digits (4 + 3 + 2 + 1). If an asset has a 10-year life, the sum of the years' digits is:

$$\frac{10(11)}{2} = 55$$

The depreciation fraction in year 1 would be 10/55, in year 2, 9/55, and so on.

A Comparison of Depreciation Methods

Now that you have been introduced to the four most common depreciation methods, we can compare them both graphically and by using the Wheeler Resorts van example. Exhibit 13 compares the straight-line, sum-of-the-years'-digits, and declining-balance depreciation methods with regard to the relative amount of depreciation expense incurred in each year for an asset that has a five-year life. The units-of-production method is not illustrated because there would not be a standard pattern of cost allocation. Exhibit 14 shows the results for the Wheeler Resorts' van for all four depreciation methods.

EXHIBIT 13	**Comparison of Depreciation Methods**

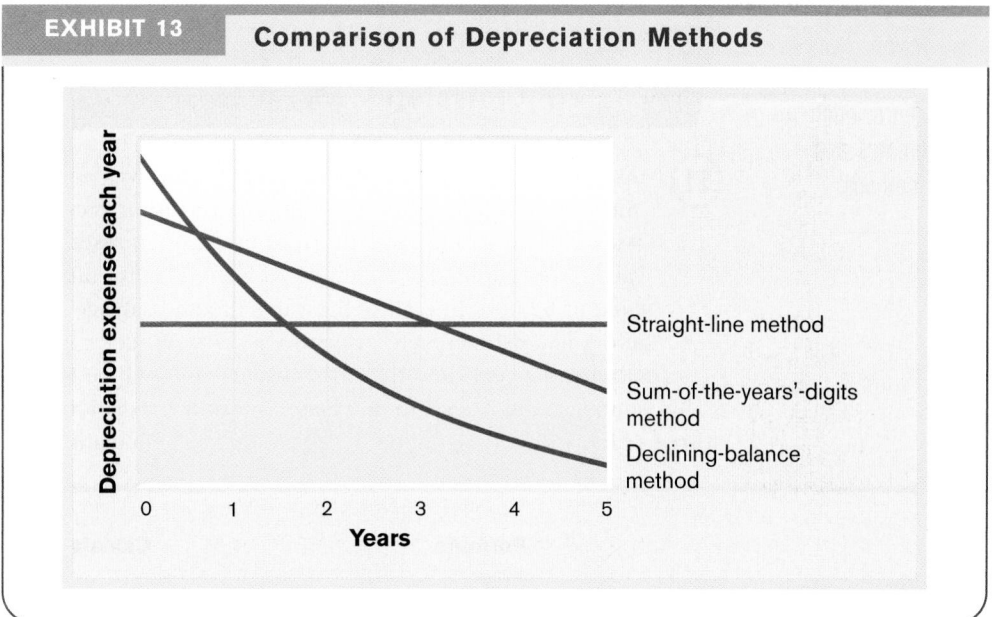

EXHIBIT 14	**Comparison of Depreciation Expense Using Different Depreciation Methods**

	Straight-Line Depreciation	Units-of-Production Depreciation	DDB Depreciation	SYD Depreciation
Year 1	$ 5,500	$ 4,400	$12,000	$ 8,800
Year 2	5,500	6,600	6,000	6,600
Year 3	5,500	7,700	3,000	4,400
Year 4	5,500	3,300	1,000	2,200
Totals	$22,000	$22,000	$22,000	$22,000

REMEMBER THIS...

- Two depreciation methods that allow for more depreciation expense in the early years of an asset's life are the declining-balance and the sum-of-the-years'-digits methods.

- The declining-balance method involves multiplying the asset's declining book value by a fixed rate that is a multiple of the straight-line rate.

- Sum-of-the-years'-digits depreciation is computed by multiplying (cost − salvage value) by a declining ratio based on the number of years in the asset's estimated life.

Changes in Depreciation Estimates and Methods

Account for changes in depreciation estimates and methods.

(11) As mentioned earlier in the chapter, useful lives and salvage values are only estimates. In addition, the various depreciation methods are simply alternative ways for estimating the pattern of usage of an asset over time. Wheeler Resorts' van, for example, was assumed to have a useful life of four years and a salvage value of $2,000. In reality, the van's life and salvage value may be different from the original estimates. If, after three years, Wheeler realizes that the van will last another three years and that the salvage value will be $3,000 instead of $2,000, the accountant would need to calculate a new depreciation expense for the remaining three years. Using straight-line depreciation, the calculations would be as follows:

	Formula	Calculation	Total Depreciation
Annual depreciation for the first three years	$\dfrac{\text{Cost} - \text{Salvage value}}{\text{Estimated useful life}} = \dfrac{\text{Depreciation}}{\text{expense}}$	$\dfrac{\$24,000 - \$2,000}{4 \text{ years}} = \$5,500$	$16,500
Book value after three years	$\dfrac{\text{Cost} - \text{Accumulated}}{\text{depreciation to date}} = \text{Book value}$	$24,000 - $16,500 = $7,500	
Annual depreciation for last three years (based on new total life of six years and new salvage value of $3,000	$\dfrac{\text{Book value} - \text{Salvage value}}{\text{Remaining useful life}} = \dfrac{\text{Depreciation}}{\text{expense}}$	$\dfrac{\$7,500 - \$3,000}{3 \text{ years}} = \$1,500$	4,500
Total depreciation			$21,000

 F Y I

To illustrate the uncertainty about depreciation life estimates, consider that **Boeing** 727 airplanes are lasting a lot longer than initially expected. The first Boeing 727 was delivered in 1963; the last was built in 1984. As of January 2001, almost 1,300 of the 1,831 727s delivered were still in service.

The example shows that a change in the estimate of useful life or salvage value does not require a modification of the depreciation expense already taken. New information affects depreciation only in future years. Exhibit 15 shows the revised depreciation expense. Similar calculations, although more complex, would apply if either the sum-of-the-years'-digits or the declining-balance depreciation method had been

EXHIBIT 15	Depreciation Schedule When There Is a Change in Estimate		
	Annual Depreciation Expense	Accumulated Depreciation	Book Value
Acquisition date	–	–	$24,000
Year 1	$ 5,500	$ 5,500	18,500
Year 2	5,500	11,000	13,000
Year 3	5,500	16,500	7,500
Change			
Year 4	1,500	18,000	6,000
Year 5	1,500	19,500	4,500
Year 6	1,500	21,000	3,000
Total	$21,000		

used. Had the company changed from the straight-line method to another method, the procedures used would be the same. The book value on the date the change is made would be used and the assumptions associated with the new depreciation method would be applied to this book value.

REMEMBER THIS...

- Because depreciation is only an estimate, changes in estimates of useful life, salvage value, or pattern of use may be required as new information becomes available.
- When there is a change in estimate, past periods' depreciation amounts remain the same.
- The change is reflected in future years' depreciation, as follows:
  - Change in life—The remaining book value (less old salvage value) is allocated over the new life.
  - Change in salvage value—The remaining book value, less the new salvage value, is allocated over the old life.
  - Change in method—The remaining book value, less the old salvage value, is allocated over the remaining life using the new method.

REVIEW OF LEARNING OBJECTIVES

(1) Identify the two major categories of long-term operating assets: property, plant, and equipment and intangible assets.

Categories of Long-Term Operating Assets	Examples
Property, Plant, and Equipment	Land, buildings, machines
Intangible Assets	Patents, licenses, goodwill

(2) Understand the factors important in deciding whether to acquire a long-term operating asset.

- Long-term operating assets have value because they help companies generate future cash flows. An asset's value can decline or disappear if events cause a decrease in the expected future cash flows generated by the asset.
- The decision to acquire a long-term operating asset (called capital budgeting) involves comparing the cost of the asset to the value of the expected cash inflows, after adjusting for the time value of money.

(3) Record the acquisition of property, plant, and equipment through a simple purchase as well as through a lease, by self-construction, and as part of the purchase of several assets at once.

Ways to Acquire Property, Plant, and Equipment	Things to Remember
Simple Purchase	Include all costs to purchase the asset and get it ready for its intended use.
Leasing	• Operating lease–accounted for as a rental; nothing on the balance sheet. • Capital lease–accounted for as a purchase; asset and liability on the balance sheet.
Self Construction	Include the cost of materials, labor, reasonable overhead, and interest.
Basket Purchase	Allocate the basket purchase price based on relative fair values.

(4) Compute straight-line and units-of-production depreciation expense for plant and equipment.

Straight-Line Depreciation	(Cost − Salvage value) ÷ Estimated useful life
Units-of-Production Depreciation	[(Cost − Salvage value) ÷ Estimated life in units] × Units produced
Depletion	Same as units-of-production depreciation

(5) Account for repairs and improvements of property, plant, and equipment.

Record an expenditure as an asset (that is, capitalize it) when–	The expenditure is: • significant in amount, • provides benefits for more than one period, and • increases the productive life or capacity of an asset.
Record an expenditure as an expense when–	The expenditure merely maintains an asset's productive capacity at the level originally projected.

(6) Identify whether a long-term operating asset has suffered a decline in value and record the decline.

- Recording an impairment loss is a two-step process.
  (1) Compare the recorded book value of the asset to the sum of future cash flows expected to be generated by the asset.
  (2) If the book value is higher, recognize a loss in an amount equal to the difference between the book value of the asset and its FAIR value.
- According to U.S. accounting rules, increases in the value of property, plant, and equipment are not recognized.

(7) Record the discarding and selling of property, plant, and equipment.

- If a scrapped asset has not been fully depreciated, a loss equal to the undepreciated cost or book value is recognized.
- When an asset is sold, there is a gain if the sales price exceeds the book value and a loss if the sales price is less than the book value.

(8) Account for the acquisition and amortization of intangible assets and understand the special difficulties associated with accounting for intangibles.

- Intangible assets are only recognized in the financial statements if they have been purchased through an arm's-length transaction.
- The cost of recorded intangible assets is expensed as follows:
  - Certain intangible assets are amortized over the economic life of the asset.
  - Many intangible assets are not amortized because their economic lives are not limited.
  - All intangible assets, including goodwill, must be analyzed to determine if impairment has occurred. If it has, then an impairment loss is recognized.

(9) Use the fixed asset turnover ratio as a measure of how efficiently a company is using its property, plant, and equipment.

- Fixed asset turnover is computed as sales divided by average property, plant, and equipment and is interpreted as the number of dollars in sales generated by each dollar of fixed assets.
- Standard values for this ratio differ significantly from industry to industry.

(10) **Compute declining-balance and sum-of-the years'-digits depreciation expense for plant and equipment.**

- The declining-balance method involves multiplying the asset's declining book value by a fixed rate that is a multiple of the straight-line rate.
- Sum-of-the-years'-digits depreciation is computed by multiplying (cost − salvage value) by a declining ratio based on the number of years in the asset's estimated life.

(11) **Account for changes in depreciation estimates and methods.**

- A change in depreciation estimate is reflected in future years' depreciation, as follows:
  - Change in life—The remaining book value (less old salvage value) is allocated over the new life.
  - Change in salvage value—The remaining book value, less the new salvage value, is allocated over the old life.
  - Change in method—The remaining book value, less the old salvage value, is allocated over the remaining life using the new method.

KEY TERMS & CONCEPTS

amortization, 414
basket purchase, 397
book value, 399
capital budgeting, 392
capital lease, 395
capitalized interest, 397
depletion, 404
depreciation, 399
fixed asset turnover, 416

franchise, 412
goodwill, 399
impairment, 407
intangible assets, 392
lease, 394
lessee, 394
lessor, 394
long-term operating
   assets, 390

natural resources, 404
operating lease, 394
patent, 411
property, plant, and
   equipment, 391
salvage value, 400
straight-line depreciation
   method, 400
time value of money, 392

units-of-production
   method, 400

declining-balance depre-
   ciation method, 418
sum-of-the-years'-digits
   (SYD) depreciation
   method, 419

REVIEW PROBLEMS

Property, Plant, and Equipment

Swift Motor Lines is a trucking company that hauls crude oil in the Rocky Mountain states. It currently has 20 trucks. The following information relates to a single truck:

a. Date truck was purchased, July 1, 2006.
b. Cost of truck:

Truck	$125,000
Paint job	3,000
Sales tax	7,000

c. Estimated useful life of truck, 120,000 miles.
d. Estimated salvage value of truck, $27,000.
e. 2008 expenditures on truck:
   (1) $6,000 on new tires and regular maintenance.
   (2) On January 1, spent $44,000 to completely rework the truck's engine; increased the total life to 200,000 miles but left expected salvage value unchanged.

(continued)

f. Miles driven:

2006	11,000
2007	24,000
2008 (after reworking of engine)	20,000
2009	14,000

Required:

Record journal entries to account for the following. (Use the units-of-production depreciation method.)

1. The purchase of the truck.
2. The expenditures on the truck during 2008.
3. Depreciation expense for:
    a. 2006
    b. 2007
    c. 2008
    d. 2009

Solution

1. Truck Purchase

The cost of the truck includes both the amount paid for it and all costs incurred to get it in working condition. In this case, the cost includes both the paint job and the sales tax. Thus, the entry to record the purchase is:

Truck	135,000	
Cash		135,000
Purchased truck for cash.		

2. Expenditures

The expenditure of $6,000 is an ordinary expenditure and is expensed in the current year. The engine overhaul is capitalized. The entries are:

Repairs and Maintenance Expense	6,000	
Cash		6,000
Recorded purchase of new tires and regular maintenance on truck.		
Truck	44,000	
Cash		44,000
Recorded major overhaul to truck's engine.		

3. Depreciation Expense

The formula for units-of-production depreciation on the truck is:

$$\frac{\text{Cost} - \text{Salvage value}}{\text{Total miles expected to be driven}} \times \frac{\text{Number of miles}}{\text{driven in any year}} = \text{Depreciation expense}$$

Journal entries and calculations are as follows:

a. 2006:

Depreciation Expense	9,900	
Accumulated Depreciation, Truck		9,900
Recorded depreciation expense for 2006.		

$$\frac{\$135,000 - \$27,000}{120,000 \text{ miles}} \times 11,000 \text{ miles} = \$9,900 \text{ or } \$0.90 \text{ per mile} \times 11,000 \text{ miles}$$

(continued)

b. 2007:

Depreciation Expense	21,600	
Accumulated Depreciation, Truck		21,600
Recorded depreciation expense for 2007.		

$$\$0.90 \times 24{,}000 \text{ miles} = \$21{,}600$$

c. 2008:

Depreciation Expense	14,600	
Accumulated Depreciation, Truck		14,600
Recorded depreciation expense for 2008.		

$$\frac{\begin{array}{c}\$135{,}000 - \$9{,}900 - \$21{,}600 \\ + \$44{,}000 - \$27{,}000\end{array}}{\underset{(200{,}000 - 11{,}000 - 24{,}000)}{165{,}000 \text{ miles}}} \times 20{,}000 \text{ miles} = \$14{,}600 \text{ or } \$0.73^* \text{ per mile} \times 20{,}000 \text{ miles}$$

*Rounded to the nearest cent.

d. 2009:

Depreciation Expense	10,220	
Accumulated Depreciation, Truck		10,220
Recorded depreciation expense for 2009.		

$$\$0.73 \times 14{,}000 \text{ miles} = \$10{,}220$$

EXPANDED *material*

Property, Plant, and Equipment

Swift Motor Lines is a trucking company that hauls crude oil in the Rocky Mountain states. It currently has 20 trucks. The following information relates to a single truck:

  a. Date truck was purchased, July 1, 2006.
  b. Cost of truck:

Truck	$125,000
Paint job	3,000
Sales tax	7,000

  c. Estimated useful life of truck, eight years.
  d. Estimated salvage value of truck, $27,000.
  e. 2008 expenditures on truck:
     (1) $6,000 on new tires and regular maintenance.
     (2) On January 1, spent $44,000 to completely rework the truck's engine. As a result of the engine work, the remaining life of the truck is increased to nine years, but the expected salvage value remains the same.

Required:

Record journal entries to account for the following. (Use the sum-of-the-years'-digits depreciation method.)
  1. The purchase of the truck.
  2. Depreciation expense for:
     a. 2006
     b. 2007
     c. 2008
  3. The expenditures on the truck during 2008.

(continued)

Solution

1. Truck Purchase

The cost of the truck includes both the amount paid for it and all costs incurred to get it in working condition. In this case, the cost includes both the paint job and the sales tax. Thus, the entry to record the purchase is:

Truck 135,000

    Cash 135,000

      Purchased truck for cash.

2. Depreciation Expense

The formula for sum-of-the-years'-digits depreciation on the truck is:

$$\frac{\text{Number of years of life remaining at beginning of year}}{\text{Sum-of-the-years'-digits}} \times (\text{Cost} - \text{Salvage value}) = \text{Depreciation expense}$$

Depreciation for the three years is calculated as follows:

2006: $\frac{8}{36} \times (\$135{,}000 - \$27{,}000) = \$24{,}000; \$24{,}000 \times 1/2 \text{ year} = \$12{,}000$

2007: $\frac{7.5}{36} \times (\$135{,}000 - \$27{,}000) = \$22{,}500$

2008: $\frac{9}{45} \times [(\$135{,}000 + \$44{,}000) - (\$12{,}000 + \$22{,}500) - \$27{,}000] = \$23{,}500$

The depreciation entries are:

a.   2006:

    Depreciation Expense 12,000

      Accumulated Depreciation, Truck 12,000

        Recorded depreciation expense for 2006.

b.   2007:

    Depreciation Expense 22,500

      Accumulated Depreciation, Truck 22,500

        Recorded depreciation expense for 2007.

c.   2008:

    Depreciation Expense 23,500

      Accumulated Depreciation, Truck 23,500

        Recorded depreciation expense for 2008.

3. Expenditures

The first expenditure of $6,000 is an ordinary expenditure and is expensed in the current year. The $44,000 expenditure is capitalized because it lengthens the truck's life. The entries are:

Repairs and Maintenance Expense 6,000

    Cash 6,000

      Recorded purchase of new tires and regular maintenance on truck.

Truck 44,000

    Cash 44,000

      Recorded major overhaul of truck engine.

DISCUSSION QUESTIONS

1. What are the major characteristics of property, plant, and equipment?
2. When buying a long-term asset such as a building or piece of equipment, the time value of money must be considered. With respect to time value, it is often said that the last payment (say, 20 years in the future) doesn't cost as much as the next payment today. Explain.
3. Why are expenditures other than the net purchase price included in the cost of an asset?
4. Why would a company include leased assets in the property, plant, and equipment section of its balance sheet when the assets are owned by another entity?
5. A company that borrows money to construct its own building generally should include the interest paid on the loan during the construction period in the cost of the building. Why?
6. Why are fair market values used to determine the cost of operating assets acquired in a basket purchase?
7. Companies usually depreciate assets such as buildings even though those assets may be increasing in value. Why?
8. How does the company accountant decide whether an expenditure should be capitalized or expensed?
9. If a firm is uncertain whether an expenditure will benefit one or more than one accounting period, or whether it will increase the capacity or useful life of an operational asset, most firms will expense rather than capitalize the expenditure. Why?
10. Sometimes long-term assets experience sudden dramatic decreases in value. For example, a waste dump might suddenly be constructed next to an office building. When such impairment of value occurs, should the decrease in value be recognized immediately, or should the same amount of depreciation expense be recognized as in past years?
11. Accountants in other countries sometimes write up the recorded amounts of long-term assets when their values increase. Why are U.S. accountants reluctant to increase the recorded value of property, plant, and equipment when their value increases?
12. Why is it common to have a gain or loss on the disposal of a long-term operating asset? Is it true that if the useful life and salvage value of an asset could be known with certainty and were realized, there would never be such a gain or loss?
13. When recording the disposal of a long-term operating asset, why is it necessary to debit the accumulated depreciation of the old asset?
14. Why are intangible assets considered assets although they have no physical substance?
15. Goodwill can be recorded only when a business is purchased. Does this result in similar businesses having incomparable financial statements?
16. How is fixed asset turnover calculated, and what does the resulting ratio value mean?

EXPANDED *material*

17. Which of the depreciation methods discussed in this chapter will usually result in the highest net income in the early years of an asset's life?
18. How does the declining-balance method of depreciation differ from other methods of depreciation?
19. Modified accelerated cost recovery system (MACRS) depreciation is allowed by the IRS but usually is not used in financial reporting. Why do you think this is the case?
20. When changing the estimate of the useful life of an asset, should depreciation expense for all the previous years be recalculated? If not, how do you account for a change in this estimate?
21. Why is it often necessary to recalculate the depletion rate for natural resources?

PRACTICE EXERCISES

PE 9-1   **Long-Term Operating Assets**

LO1   Which one of the following is not an example of a long-term operating asset?
     a. Buildings
     b. Land
     c. Goodwill
     d. Equipment
     e. Office Supplies

PE 9-2   **Decision of Long-Term Asset Acquisition**

LO2   Pekka Inc. has the option to purchase a new drilling machine for $50,000 today. The company expects a net cash flow of $13,000 per year from using the machine, and the machine

(continued)

will last five years. According to the time value of money, the value today of $13,000 per year for five years is $46,862. Should the company purchase the new drilling machine?

PE 9-3   **Asset Purchased with Cash**

LO3   The company used cash to purchase a stamping machine. The retail price on the machine is $35,000, but the company received a 2% discount. It also paid $2,150 in sales tax for the purchase. Make the necessary journal entry(ies) to record this transaction.

PE 9-4   **Asset Purchased Partially with Cash**

LO3   Refer to the data in PE 9-3. Assume the company borrowed $15,000 of the purchase price from a bank. Make the necessary journal entry(ies) to record this transaction.

PE 9-5   **Operating Lease**

LO3   On January 1, XYZ Company entered into a lease for equipment rental. The company agreed to pay $4,500 per year for ten years. The present value of all ten lease payments is $27,651. Assuming the company classified the lease as an operating lease, make the necessary journal entry(ies) to record the payment of the first year's rent expense for the equipment. The first lease payment is made at the end of the year.

PE 9-6   **Capital Lease Acquisition**

LO3   On January 1, XYZ Company entered into a lease for equipment rental. The company agreed to pay $4,500 per year for ten years. The present value of all ten lease payments is $27,651. Assuming the company classified the lease as a capital lease, make the necessary journal entry(ies) to record the acquisition of the equipment. The first lease payment is made at the end of the year.

PE 9-7   **Capital Lease Payments**

LO3   Refer to the data in PE 9-6. The interest included in the first lease payment is $2,765. Make the necessary journal entry(ies) to record the first $4,500 lease payment at the end of the first year.

PE 9-8   **Classifying Leases**

LO3   Which one of the following characteristics of a lease would not cause the lease to be classified as a capital lease?
  a. Lease ownership transfers to the lessee at the end of the lease.
  b. The present value of the lease payments at the beginning of the lease is 90% or more of the fair market value of the leased asset.
  c. The lease term is equal to 50% of the estimated economic life of the asset.
  d. The lease contains a bargain purchase option.

PE 9-9   **Assets Acquired by Self-Construction**

LO3   Using the following data, compute the total cost of a self-constructed office building.

Percentage of overhead attributable to construction of office building	30%
Direct materials	$1,450,000
Capitalized interest	140,000
Direct labor	860,000
Total overhead incurred during year	2,450,000

PE 9-10   **Acquisition of Several Assets at Once**

LO3   The company purchased a building and the accompanying land for $890,000 cash. Independent appraisers estimated the fair market value of the building and the land to be $720,000 and 240,000, respectively. Make the necessary journal entry(ies) to record this transaction.

PE 9-11   **Straight-Line Method of Depreciation**

LO4   Using the following data and the straight-line method of depreciation, compute depreciation expense, and make the necessary journal entry to record depreciation expense for the first year.

(continued)

Cost of machine	$1,000,000
Estimated useful life (years)	8 years
Salvage value	$40,000
Estimated useful life (units)	1,600,000
Units produced during the first year	180,000

PE 9-12

LO4

Units-of-Production Method of Depreciation

Refer to the data in PE 9-11. Using the units-of-production method of depreciation, compute depreciation expense, and make the necessary journal entry to record depreciation expense for the first year.

PE 9-13

LO4

Partial-Year Depreciation Calculations

On September 30, the company purchased a $25,000 delivery truck. The company estimates the truck will last five years and have a salvage value of $5,000 at the end of five years. Using the straight-line method of depreciation, compute the amount of depreciation in the first two years of the truck's service.

PE 9-14

LO4

Units-of-Production Method with Natural Resources

The company purchased an oil field for $4,200,000 cash. The oil field contains an estimated 600,000 barrels of oil. During the first year of operation, the company extracts and sells 70,000 barrels of oil. Compute the amount of depletion expense, and make the necessary journal entry(ies) to record depletion expense for the year.

PE 9-15

LO5

Repairing and Improving Property, Plant, and Equipment

The company has a molding machine with a historical cost of $150,000 and accumulated depreciation of $110,000. On January 1, the company performed a major motor overhaul costing $24,000. The company expects the machine will last seven more years and have a salvage value of $8,000. Compute depreciation expense for the current year using the straight-line method.

PE 9-16

LO6

Determining Asset Impairment

The company purchased a building 14 years ago for $720,000. The building has accumulated depreciation of $504,000 and a fair market value of $150,000. The company expects the building will generate a net cash inflow of $30,000 per year for the next six years. Determine whether, from an accounting point of view, the building is impaired.

PE 9-17

LO6

Recording Decreases in the Value of Property, Plant, and Equipment

Using the information in PE 9-16, determine the amount of impairment and record the impairment loss.

Original cost	$720,000
Accumulated depreciation	504,000
Book value	$216,000
Sum of future cash flows ($30,000 × 6 years)	$180,000

PE 9-18

LO7

Discarding Property, Plant, and Equipment

The company scrapped a truck with a historical cost of $60,000 and accumulated depreciation of $48,000. In addition, the company had to pay $500 to discard the truck. Make the necessary journal entry(ies) to record this transaction.

PE 9-19

LO7

Selling Property, Plant, and Equipment

The company sold a truck with a historical cost of $30,000 and accumulated depreciation of $24,000 for $7,000 cash. Make the necessary journal entry(ies) to record this transaction.

PE 9-20
LO8

Patents

On January 1, the company purchased a 13-year-old patent from another company for $210,000. The patent has a seven-year legal life remaining. Make the necessary journal entry(ies) to record amortization for the year the patent was acquired.

PE 9-21
LO8

Goodwill

Parent Company purchased Daughter Company for $200,000. At the time of purchase, the fair market value of Daughter Company's assets and liabilities was as follows:

Inventory	$ 25,000
Property, plant, and equipment	140,000
Other assets	64,000
Liabilities	59,000

Make the necessary journal entry(ies) (on Parent's books) to record the purchase of Daughter Company.

PE 9-22
LO9

Fixed Asset Turnover

Using the following data, compute the fixed asset turnover.

Current assets, end of year	$ 35,000
Fixed assets, end of year	180,000
Fixed assets, beginning of year	195,000
Sales during the year	595,000

EXPANDED material

PE 9-23
LO10

Declining-Balance Method of Depreciation

Using the following data and the declining-balance method of depreciation, compute depreciation expense for the first two years.

Cost of machine	$1,500,000
Estimated useful life (years)	10 years
Salvage value	$100,000

PE 9-24
LO10

Sum-of-the-Years'-Digits Method of Depreciation

Using the data in PE 9-23 and the sum-of-the-years'-digits method of depreciation, compute depreciation expense for the first two years.

PE 9-25
LO11

Changes in Depreciation Estimates

Using the information in PE 9-11, the company computed depreciation expense of $120,000 per year. After two years, the company determined that the machine would last 10 more years (for a total of 12 years). Compute depreciation expense for the third year.

EXERCISES

E 9-26
LO3

Acquisition Decision

Johnson Company is considering acquiring a new airplane. It has looked at two financing options. The first is to lease the airplane for 10 years with lease payments of $70,000 each year. The second is to purchase the airplane, making a down payment of $250,000 and

(continued)

annual payments of $40,000 for 10 years. If the present value of the two financing options is the same, what other factors must be considered in deciding whether to purchase or to lease?

E 9-27
LO3

Accounting for the Acquisition of a Long-Term Asset

Action Jackson Company acquired a new machine in order to expand its productive capacity. The costs associated with the machine purchase were as follows:

Purchase price	$25,000
Installation costs	750
Cost of initial testing	900
Sales tax	1,563

1. Make the journal entry to record the acquisition of the machine. Assume that all costs were paid in cash.
2. Make the journal entry to record the acquisition of the machine. Assume that Action Jackson Company signed a note payable for the $25,000 purchase price and paid the remaining costs in cash.

E 9-28
LO3, LO4

Computing Asset Cost and Depreciation Expense

Freddy's Restoration Company decided to purchase a new floor-polishing machine for its shop in New York City. After a long search, it found the appropriate polisher in Chicago. The machine costs $45,000 and has an estimated 15-year life and no salvage value. Freddy's Restoration Company made the following additional expenditures with respect to this purchase:

Sales tax	$2,000
Delivery costs (FOB shipping point)	1,000
Assembly cost	1,400
Painting of machine to match the décor	600

1. What is the cost of the machine to Freddy's Restoration Company?
2. What is the amount of the first full year's depreciation if Freddy's uses the straight-line method?

E 9-29
LO3, LO4

Acquisition and Depreciation of Assets

Vandre Oil Company, which prepares financial statements on a calendar-year basis, purchased new drilling equipment on July 1, 2009, using check numbers 1035 and 1036. The check totals are shown here, along with a breakdown of the charges.

1035 (Payee—Oil Equipment, Inc.):	
Cost of drilling equipment	$150,000
Cost of cement platform	50,000
Installation charges	26,000
Total	$226,000
1036 (Payee—Red Ball Freight):	
Freight costs for drilling equipment	$ 4,000

Assume that the estimated life of the drilling equipment is 10 years and its salvage value is $7,000.

1. Record the disbursements on July 1, 2009, assuming that no entry had been recorded for the drilling equipment.
2. Disregarding the information given about the two checks, assume that the drilling equipment was recorded at a total cost of $195,000. Calculate the depreciation expense for 2009 using the straight-line method.

E 9-30

LO3

Accounting for Leased Assets

On January 1, 2009, Hanks Company leased a copy machine with an integrated laser printer from Officeneeds, Inc. The five-year lease is noncancelable and requires monthly payments of $200 at the end of each month, with the first payment due on January 31, 2009. At the end of five years, Hanks will own the equipment. The present value of the lease payments at the beginning of the lease is determined to be $9,413.

1. Prepare journal entries to record:
    a. The lease agreement on January 1, 2009.
    b. The first lease payment on January 31, 2009, assuming that $78 of the $200 payment is interest.

2. Now assume that the lease expires after one year at which time a new lease can be negotiated or Hanks can return the equipment to Officeneeds. Prepare any journal entries relating to the lease that would be required on January 1 and January 31, 2009.

E 9-31

LO3

Interest Capitalization

Litton Company is constructing a new office building. Costs of the building are as follows:

Wages paid to construction workers	$185,000
Building materials purchased	456,000
Interest expense on construction loan	13,800
Interest expense on mortgage loan during the first year subsequent to the building's completion	22,000

Given the above costs, at what amount should the building be recorded in the accounting records?

E 9-32

LO3

Accounting for the Acquisition of Assets–Basket Purchase

Sealise Corporation purchased land, a building, and equipment for a total cost of $450,000. After the purchase, the property was appraised. Fair market values were determined to be $120,000 for the land, $280,000 for the building, and $80,000 for the equipment. Given these appraisals, record the purchase of the property by Sealise Corporation.

E 9-33

LO4

Depreciation Calculations

Garns Photography Company purchased a new car on July 1, 2008, for $26,000. The estimated life of the car was five years or 110,000 miles, and its salvage value was estimated to be $1,000. The car was driven 9,000 miles in 2008 and 24,000 miles in 2009.

1. Compute the amount of depreciation expense for 2008 and 2009 using the following methods:
    a. Straight-line.
    b. Units-of-production.

2. Which depreciation method more closely reflects the used-up service potential of the car? Explain.

E 9-34

LO4

Depreciation Calculations

Denver Hardware Company has a giant paint mixer that cost $31,500 plus $400 to install. The estimated salvage value of the paint mixer at the end of its useful life in 15 years is estimated to be $1,900. Denver estimates that the machine can mix 850,000 cans of paint during its lifetime. Compute the second full year's depreciation expense, using the following methods:

1. Straight-line.
2. Units-of-production, assuming that the machine mixes 51,000 cans of paint during the second year.

E 9-35

LO3, LO5

Acquisition and Improvement of Assets

Prepare entries in the books of Sanmara, Inc., to reflect the following. (Assume cash transactions.)

(continued)

1. Purchased a lathing machine to be used by the firm in its production process.

Invoice price	$45,000
Cash discount taken	900
Installation costs	1,200
Sales tax on machine	1,800

2. Performed normal periodic maintenance on the lathing machine at a cost of $200.
3. Added to the lathing machine a governor costing $400, which is expected to increase the machine's useful life.

E 9-36   **Asset Impairment**

LO6   Consider the following three independent scenarios:

	1	2	3
Original cost of asset	$1,400	$1,400	$1,400
Accumulated depreciation	400	400	400
Sum of future cash flows	1,500	1,500	900
Fair value of the asset	1,100	800	800

1. For each of the three scenarios, answer the following questions:
   a. Is the asset impaired?
   b. At what amount (net of accumulated depreciation) should the asset be reported?
2. Make the journal entry required in Scenario 3.

E 9-37   **Asset Impairment**

LO6   In 2004, Yorkshire Company purchased land and a building at a cost of $700,000, of which $150,000 was allocated to the land and $550,000 was allocated to the building. As of December 31, 2008, the accounting records related to these assets were as follows:

Land	$150,000
Building	550,000
Accumulated Depreciation, Building	150,000

On January 1, 2009, it is determined that there is toxic waste under the building and the future cash flows associated with the land and building are less than the recorded total book value for those two assets. The fair value of the land and building together is now only $120,000, of which $50,000 is land and $70,000 is the building. How should this impairment in value be recognized? Make the entry on January 1, 2009, to record the impairment of the land and building.

E 9-38   **Accounting for the Disposal of Assets**

LO7   Canlas Concrete Company has a truck that it wants to sell. The truck had an original cost of $80,000, was purchased four years ago, and was expected to have a useful life of eight years with no salvage value.

Using straight-line depreciation, and assuming that depreciation expense for four full years has been recorded, prepare journal entries to record the disposal of the truck under each of the following independent conditions:

1. Canlas Concrete Company sells the truck for $45,000 cash.
2. Canlas Concrete Company sells the truck for $38,000 cash.
3. The old truck is wrecked and Canlas Concrete Company hauls it to the junkyard.

E 9-39
LO7

Disposal of an Asset

Aeronautics Company purchased a machine for $115,000. The machine has an estimated useful life of eight years and a salvage value of $7,000. Journalize the disposal of the machine under each of the following conditions. (Assume straight-line depreciation.)

1. Sold the machine for $97,000 cash after two years.
2. Sold the machine for $36,000 cash after five years.

E 9-40
LO8

Accounting for Intangible Assets

Gaylord Research, Inc., has the following intangible assets:

Asset	Cost	Date Purchased	Expected Useful or Legal Life
Goodwill	$ 16,000	January 1, 2000	Unlimited
Patent	136,000	January 1, 2002	20 years

1. Record the amortization expense for both of these intangible assets for 2009 assuming neither of the assets is impaired.
2. Prepare the intangible assets section of the balance sheet for Gaylord Research, Inc., as of December 31, 2009.

E 9-41
LO8

Intangible Assets

On January 1, 2008, Landon Company purchased a patent for $250,000 to allow it to improve its product line. On July 1, 2008, Landon Company purchased another existing business in a nearby city for a total cost of $750,000. The market value of the land, building, equipment, and other tangible assets was $550,000. The excess $200,000 was recorded as goodwill.

Assuming Landon Company amortizes patents over a 20-year period, record the following:

1. The purchase of the patent on January 1, 2008.
2. The amortization of the patent at December 31, 2008.
3. Under what conditions would goodwill be amortized on the books of Landon?

E 9-42
LO8

Computing Goodwill

Stringtown Company purchased Stansbury Island Manufacturing for $1,800,000 cash. The book value and fair value of the assets of Stansbury Island as of the date of the acquisition are listed below:

	Book Value	Market Value
Cash	$ 30,000	$ 30,000
Accounts receivable	300,000	300,000
Inventory	350,000	600,000
Property, plant, and equipment	500,000	900,000
Totals	$1,180,000	$1,830,000

In addition, Stansbury Island had liabilities totaling $400,000 at the time of the acquisition.

1. At what amounts will the individual assets of Stansbury Island be recorded on the books of Stringtown, the acquiring company?
2. How will Stringtown account for the liabilities of Stansbury Island?
3. How much goodwill will be recorded as part of this acquisition?

E 9-43

LO9

Fixed Asset Turnover

The Store Next Door reported the following asset values in 2008 and 2009:

	2009	2008
Cash	$ 45,000	$ 27,000
Accounts receivable	500,000	430,000
Inventory	550,000	480,000
Land	300,000	280,000
Buildings	800,000	660,000
Equipment	150,000	110,000

In addition, The Store Next Door had sales of $3,200,000 in 2009. Cost of goods sold for the year was $1,900,000.

Compute The Store Next Door's fixed asset turnover ratio for 2009.

EXPANDED *material*

E 9-44

LO3, LO4, LO10

Acquisition and Depreciation of Assets

Brough Oil Company, which prepares financial statements on a calendar-year basis, purchased new drilling equipment on July 1, 2009. A breakdown of the cost follows:

Cost of drilling equipment	$125,000
Cost of cement platform	35,000
Installation charges	22,000
Freight costs for drilling equipment	3,000
Total	$185,000

Assuming that the estimated life of the drilling equipment is 20 years and its salvage value is $10,000:

1. Record the purchase on July 1, 2009.
2. Assume that the drilling equipment was recorded at a total cost of $140,000. Calculate the depreciation expense for 2009 using the following methods:
   a. Sum-of-the-years'-digits.
   b. Double-declining-balance.
   c. 150% declining-balance.
3. Prepare the journal entry to record the depreciation for 2009 in accordance with part (2)a.

E 9-45

LO3, LO4, LO10

Acquisition and Depreciation

At the beginning of 2009, Beef's Steak House constructed a new walk-in freezer that had a useful life of 10 years. At the end of 10 years, the motor could be salvaged for $3,500. In addition to construction costs that totaled $15,000, the following costs were incurred:

Sales taxes on components	$1,100
Delivery costs	700
Installation of motor	300
Painting of both interior and exterior of freezer	200

1. What is the cost of the walk-in freezer to Beef's Steak House?
2. Compute the amount of depreciation to be taken in the first year assuming Beef's Steak House uses the
   a. Double-declining-balance method.
   b. Sum-of-the-years'-digits method.

E 9-46   **Depreciation Computations**

LO10   Hsin-Yo Company purchases an $850,000 piece of equipment on January 2, 2007, for use in its manufacturing process. The equipment's estimated useful life is 10 years with no salvage value. Hsin-Yo uses 150% declining-balance depreciation for all its equipment.

1. Compute the depreciation expense for 2007, 2008, and 2009.
2. Compute the book value of the equipment on December 31, 2009.

E 9-47   **Depreciation Calculations**

LO10   Letha Enterprises purchased a new van on January 1, 2008, for $35,000. The estimated life of the van was four years or 76,000 miles, and its salvage value was estimated to be $3,000. Compute the amount of depreciation expense for 2008, 2009, and 2010 using the following methods:

1. Double-declining-balance.
2. 175% declining-balance.
3. Sum-of-the-years'-digits.

E 9-48   **Depreciation Calculations**

LO10   On January 1, 2008, MAC Corporation purchased a machine for $60,000. The machine cost $800 to deliver and $2,000 to install. At the end of 10 years, MAC expects to sell the machine for $2,000. Compute depreciation expense for 2008 and 2009 using the following methods:

1. Double-declining-balance.
2. 150% declining-balance.
3. Sum-of-the-years'-digits.

E 9-49   **Accounting for Natural Resources**

LO3, LO4, LO11   On January 1, 2008, Georgetown Holdings Corporation purchased a coal mine for cash, having taken into consideration the favorable tax consequences and the inevitable energy crunch in the future. Georgetown paid $960,000 for the mine. Shortly before the purchase, an engineer estimated that there were 120,000 tons of coal in the mine.

1. Record the purchase of the mine on January 1, 2008.
2. Record the depletion expense for 2008, assuming that 30,000 tons of coal were mined during the year.
3. Assume that on January 1, 2009, the company received a new estimate that the mine now contained 150,000 tons of coal. Record the entry (if any) to show the change in estimate.
4. Record the depletion expense for 2009, assuming that another 30,000 tons of coal were mined.

E 9-50   **Change in Estimated Useful Life**

LO4, LO11   On January 1, 2007, Landon Excavation Company purchased a new bulldozer for $120,000. The equipment had an estimated useful life of 10 years and an estimated residual value of $10,000. On January 1, 2009, Landon determined that the bulldozer would have a total useful life of only 8 years instead of 10 years with no change in residual value. Landon uses straight-line depreciation.

Compute depreciation expense on this bulldozer for 2007, 2008, and 2009.

PROBLEMS

P 9-51   **Acquisition, Depreciation, and Disposal of Assets**

LO3, LO4, LO7   On January 2, 2009, Dale Company purchased a building and land for $580,000. The most recent appraisal values for the building and the land are $420,000 and $180,000, respectively. The building has an estimated useful life of 25 years and a salvage value of $30,000.

(continued)

Required:

1. Assuming cash transactions and straight-line depreciation, prepare journal entries to record:
   a. Purchase of the building and land on January 2, 2009.
   b. Depreciation expense on December 31, 2009.
2. Assume that after three years the property (land and building) was sold for $470,000. Prepare the journal entry to record the sale.

P 9-52 **Purchasing Property, Plant, and Equipment**

LO3 Jordon Company is considering replacing its automated stamping machine. The machine is specialized and very expensive. Jordon is considering three acquisition alternatives. The first is to lease a machine for 10 years at $1 million per year, after which time Jordon can buy the machine for $1 million. The second alternative is to pay cash for the machine at a cost of $7 million. The third alternative is to make a down payment of $3 million, followed by 10 annual payments of $550,000. The company is trying to decide which alternative to select.

Required:

1. Assuming the present value of the lease payments is $7.2 million and the present value of the 10 loan payments of $550,000 is $4.1 million, determine which alternative Jordon should choose.
2. **Interpretive Question:** Your decision in part (1) was based only on financial factors. What other qualitative issues might influence your decision?

P 9-53 **Acquisition of an Asset**

LO3 Ray's Printing Company purchased a new printing press. The invoice price was $184,250. The company paid for the press within 10 days, so it was allowed a 2% discount. The freight cost for delivering the press was $3,000. A premium of $1,200 was paid for a special insurance policy to cover the transportation of the press. The company spent $3,400 to install the press and an additional $655 in start-up costs to get the press ready for regular production.

Required:

1. At what amount should the press be recorded as an asset?
2. What additional information must be known before the depreciation expense for the first year of operation of the new press can be computed?
3. **Interpretive Question:** What criterion is used to determine whether the start-up costs of $655 are included in the cost of the asset? Explain.

P 9-54 **Accounting for Leased Assets**

LO3 On January 2, 2009, Yardley Company contracted to lease a computer on a noncancelable basis for six years at an annual rental of $55,000, payable at the end of each year. The computer has an estimated economic life of seven years. There is no bargain purchase option, and the computer will be returned to the lessor at the end of the six-year term of the lease. At the beginning of the lease, the computer has a fair market value of $245,000, and the present value of the lease payments equals $239,539.

Required:

1. Is this a capital lease or an operating lease? Explain.
2. Assuming that the lease is an operating lease, prepare the journal entries for Yardley Company for 2009.
3. Assuming that the lease is a capital lease, prepare the journal entries for Yardley Company for 2009. Assume the lease payment at the end of 2009 includes interest of $23,954.

P 9-55 **Accounting for Leased Assets**

LO3 The board of directors of Swogen Company authorized the president to lease a corporate jet to facilitate her travels to domestic and international subsidiaries of the company. After

(continued)

extensive investigation of the alternatives, the company agreed to lease a jet for $300,548 each year for five years, payable at the end of each year. Title to the jet will pass to Swogen Company at the end of five years with no further payments required. The lease agreement starts on January 2, 2009. The jet has an economic life of eight years. The lease contract is noncancelable and contains an interest rate of 8%, resulting in a present value of the lease payments of $1,200,000 as of January 2, 2009.

Required:

1. Does this lease contract meet the requirements to be accounted for as a capital lease? Why or why not?
2. Assuming that the lease contract is to be accounted for as a capital lease, prepare the journal entries for Swogen Company for 2009. Interest included in the first payment is $96,000.

P 9-56   **Interest Capitalization**

LO3   Jennifer Cosmetics wants to construct a new building. It has two building options, as follows:

    a. Hire a contractor to do all the work. Jennifer has a bid of $850,000 from a reputable contractor to complete the project.

    b. Construct the building itself by taking out a construction loan of $800,000. Using this alternative, Jennifer believes materials and labor will cost $800,000, and interest on the construction loan will be calculated as follows:

$200,000 @ 12% for 9 months
$300,000 @ 12% for 6 months
$200,000 @ 12% for 3 months
$100,000 @ 12% for 1 month

Required:

1. What will be the recorded cost of the building under each alternative?
2. Assuming the building is depreciated over a 20-year period using straight-line depreciation with no salvage value, how much is the annual depreciation expense under each alternative?

P 9-57   **Depreciation Calculations**

LO4   On January 1, Clauser Company purchased a $79,000 machine. The estimated life of the machine was four years, and the estimated salvage value was $4,000. The machine had an estimated useful life in productive output of 90,000 units. Actual output for the first two years was: year 1, 25,000 units; year 2, 18,000 units.

Required:

1. Compute the amount of depreciation expense for the first year, using each of the following methods:
    a. Straight-line.
    b. Units-of-production.
2. What was the book value of the machine at the end of the first year, assuming that straight-line depreciation was used?
3. If the machine is sold at the end of the third year for $20,000, how much should the company report as a gain or loss (assuming straight-line depreciation)?

P 9-58   **Purchase of Multiple Assets for a Single Sum**

LO3, LO4   On April 1, 2009, Cajun Company paid $210,000 in cash to purchase land, a building, and equipment. The appraised fair market values of the assets were as follows: land, $70,000; building, $120,000; and equipment, $60,000. The company incurred legal fees of $8,000 to determine that it would have a clear title to the land. Before the facilities could be used, Cajun had to spend $4,000 to grade and landscape the land, $3,500 to put the equipment in working order, and $14,000 to renovate the building. The equipment was then estimated

(continued)

to have a useful life of seven years with no salvage value, and the building would have a useful life of 20 years with a net salvage value of $10,000. Both the equipment and the building are to be depreciated on a straight-line basis. The company is on a calendar-year reporting basis.

Required:
1. Allocate the single purchase price to the individual assets acquired.
2. Prepare the journal entry to acquire the land, building, and equipment.
3. Prepare the journal entry to record the title search, landscape, put the equipment in working order, and renovate the building.
4. Prepare the journal entries on December 31, 2009, to record the depreciation on the building and the equipment.

P 9-59

LO3, LO4

Basket Purchase and Partial-Year Depreciation

On April 1, 2009, Rosenberg Company purchased for $200,000 a tract of land on which was located a fully equipped factory. The following information was compiled regarding this purchase:

	Market Value	Seller's Book Value
Land	$ 75,000	$ 30,000
Building	100,000	75,000
Equipment	50,000	60,000
Totals	$225,000	$165,000

Required:
1. Prepare the journal entry to record the purchase of these assets.
2. Assume that the building is depreciated on a straight-line basis over a remaining life of 20 years and the equipment is depreciated on a straight-line basis over five years. Neither the building nor the equipment is expected to have any salvage value. Compute the depreciation expense for 2009 assuming the assets were placed in service immediately upon acquisition.

P 9-60

LO3, LO4, LO7

Acquisition, Depreciation, and Sale of an Asset

On January 2, 2007, Union Oil Company purchased a new airplane. The following costs are related to the purchase:

Airplane, base price	$112,000
Cash discount	3,000
Sales tax	4,000
Delivery charges	1,000

Required:
1. Prepare the journal entry to record the payment of these items on January 2, 2007.
2. Ignore your answer to part (1) and assume that the airplane cost $90,000 and has an expected useful life of five years or 1,500 hours. The estimated salvage value is $3,000. Using units-of-production depreciation and assuming that 300 hours are flown in 2008, calculate the amount of depreciation expense to be recorded for the second year.
3. Ignore the information in parts (1) and (2) and assume that the airplane costs $90,000, that its expected useful life is five years, and that its estimated salvage value is $5,000. The company now uses the straight-line depreciation method. On January 1, 2010, the following balances are in the related accounts:

(continued)

Airplane	$90,000
Accumulated Depreciation, Airplane	51,000

Prepare the necessary journal entries to record the sale of this airplane on July 1, 2010, for $40,000.

P 9-61
LO3, LO4, LO7

Acquisition, Depreciation, and Sale of an Asset

On July 1, 2009, Philip Ward bought a used pickup truck at a cost of $5,300 for use in his business. On the same day, Ward had the truck painted blue and white (his company's colors) at a cost of $800. Mr. Ward estimates the life of the truck to be three years or 40,000 miles. He further estimates that the truck will have a $450 scrap value at the end of its life, but that it will also cost him $50 to transfer the truck to the junkyard.

Required:
1. Record the following journal entries:
    a. July 1, 2009: Paid all bills pertaining to the truck. (No previous entries have been recorded concerning these bills.)
    b. December 31, 2009: The depreciation expense for the year, using the straight-line method.
    c. December 31, 2010: The depreciation expense for 2010, again using the straight-line method.
    d. January 2, 2011: Sold the truck for $2,600 cash.
2. What would the depreciation expense for 2009 have been if the truck had been driven 8,000 miles and the units-of-production method of depreciation had been used?
3. **Interpretive Question:** In part (1)d, there is a loss of $650. Why did this loss occur?

P 9-62
LO4

Accounting for Natural Resources

On May 31, 2007, Barren Oil Company purchased an oil well, with estimated reserves of 200,000 barrels of oil, for $2.0 million cash.

Required:
Prepare journal entries for the following:
1. Record the purchase of the oil well.
2. During 2007, 16,000 barrels of oil were extracted from the well. Record the depletion expense for 2007.
3. During 2008, 21,000 barrels of oil were extracted from the well. Record the depletion expense for 2008.

P 9-63
LO6

Asset Impairment

Delta Company owns plant and equipment on the island of Lagos. The cost and book value of the building are $2,800,000 and $2,400,000, respectively. Until this year, the market value of the factory was $7 million. However, a new dictator just came to power and declared martial law. As a result of the changed political status, the future cash inflows from the use of the factory are expected to be greatly reduced. Delta now believes that the output from the factory will generate cash inflows of $100,000 per year for the next 20 years. In addition, the market value of the factory building is now just $1,300,000. Delta is not sure how to account for the sudden impairment in value.

Required:
1. Explain how to decide whether an impairment loss is to be recognized.
2. Prepare the necessary journal entry, if any, to account for an impairment in the value of the factory.

P 9-64
LO8

Accounting for Intangible Assets (Goodwill)

On January 1, 2009, InterGalactic Company purchased the following assets and liabilities from Immensity Company for $325,000:

(continued)

	Book Value	Fair Market Value
Inventory	$ 60,000	$ 70,000
Building	100,000	130,000
Land	70,000	90,000
Accounts receivable	30,000	30,000
Accounts payable	(15,000)	(15,000)

Required:
Prepare a journal entry to record the purchase of Immensity by InterGalactic.

P 9-65
LO8

Accounting for Goodwill

On January 1, 2009, Fishing Creek Company purchased Skull Valley Technologies for $8,800,000 cash. The book value and fair value of Skull Valley's assets as of the date of the acquisition are listed below.

	Book Value	Market Value
Cash	$ 100,000	$ 100,000
Accounts receivable	500,000	500,000
Inventory	950,000	1,200,000
Property, plant, and equipment	1,500,000	1,900,000
Trademark	0	2,000,000
Totals	$3,050,000	$5,700,000

In addition, Skull Valley had liabilities totaling $4,000,000 at the time of the acquisition.

Required:
1. At what amount will Skull Valley's trademark be recorded on the books of Fishing Creek, the acquiring company?
2. How much goodwill will be recorded as part of this acquisition?
3. **Interpretive Question:** What was Skull Valley's recorded stockholders' equity immediately before the acquisition? Under what circumstances does stockholders' equity yield a poor measure of the fair value of a company?

P 9-66
LO9

Fixed Asset Turnover Ratio

Waystation Company reported the following asset values in 2008 and 2009:

	2009	2008
Cash	$ 40,000	$ 30,000
Accounts receivable	500,000	400,000
Inventory	700,000	500,000
Land	300,000	200,000
Buildings	800,000	600,000
Equipment	400,000	300,000

In addition, Waystation had sales of $4,000,000 in 2009. Cost of goods sold for the year was $2,500,000.

As of the end of 2008, the fair value of Waystation's total assets was $2,500,000. Of the excess of fair value over book value, $50,000 resulted because the fair value of Waystation's inventory was greater than its recorded book value. As of the end of 2009, the fair value of Waystation's total assets was $3,500,000. As of December 31, 2009, the fair

(continued)

value of Waystation's inventory was $100,000 greater than the inventory's recorded book value.

Required:
1. Compute Waystation's fixed asset turnover ratio for 2009.
2. Using the fair value of fixed assets instead of the book value of fixed assets, recompute Waystation's fixed asset turnover ratio for 2009. State any assumptions that you make.
3. **Interpretive Question:** Waystation's primary competitor is Handy Corner. Handy Corner's fixed asset turnover ratio for 2009, based on publicly available information, is 2.8 times. Is Waystation more or less efficient at using its fixed assets than is Handy Corner? Explain your answer.

P 9-67

LO10

Depreciation Calculations

Neilson's Hardware Company has a giant paint mixer that cost $51,300 plus $700 to install. The estimated salvage value of the paint mixer at the end of its useful life in eight years is estimated to be $4,000. Neilson's estimates that the machine can mix 720,000 cans of paint during its lifetime.

Required:
Compute the second full year's depreciation expense, using the following methods:
1. Double-declining-balance.
2. Sum-of-the-years'-digits.

P 9-68

LO3, LO10

Depreciation Calculations

On January 1, Top Flight Company purchased a $68,000 machine. The estimated life of the machine was five years, and the estimated salvage value was $5,000. The machine had an estimated useful life in productive output of 75,000 units. Actual output for the first two years was: year 1, 20,000 units; year 2, 15,000 units.

Required:
1. Compute the amount of depreciation expense for the first year, using each of the following methods:
   a. Straight-line.
   b. Units-of-production.
   c. Sum-of-the-years'-digits.
   d. Double-declining-balance.
2. What was the book value of the machine at the end of the first year, assuming that straight-line depreciation was used?
3. If the machine is sold at the end of the fourth year for $15,000, how much should the company report as a gain or loss (assuming straight-line depreciation)?

P 9-69

LO3, LO10

Financial Statement Effects of Depreciation Methods

On July 1, 2008, the consulting firm of Little, Smart, and Quick bought a new computer for $120,000 to help it service its clients more efficiently. The new computer was estimated to have a useful life of five years with an estimated salvage value of $20,000 at the end of five years. It was further estimated that the computer would be in operation about 1,500 hours in each of the five years with some variation of use from year to year. Janet Little, who manages the firm's internal operations, has asked you to help her decide which depreciation method should be selected for the new computer. The methods being considered are straight-line, double-declining-balance, and sum-of-the-years'-digits.

(continued)

Required:

1. Prepare a schedule showing depreciation for 2008, 2009, and 2010 for each of the three methods being considered.
2. For each of the three methods, compute the asset book value that would be reported on the balance sheet at December 31, 2010.
3. **Interpretive Question:** Which method would maximize income for the three years (2008–2010), and which would minimize income for the same period?

P 9-70

LO3, LO10

Depreciation Calculations

Gretchen, Inc., a firm that makes oversized boots, purchased a machine for its factory. The following data relate to the machine:

Price	$46,000
Delivery charges	$350
Installation charges	$650
Date purchased	May 1, 2008
Estimated useful life:	
In years	10 years
In hours of production	25,000 hours of operating time
Salvage value	$2,000

During 2008, the machine was used 1,800 hours. During 2009, the machine was used 2,900 hours.

Required:

Determine the depreciation expense and the year-end book values for the machine for the years 2008 and 2009, assuming that:

1. The straight-line method is used.
2. The double-declining-balance method is used.
3. The units-of-production method is used.
4. The sum-of-the-years'-digits method is used.
5. **Interpretive Question:** If you were Gretchen, which method would you use in order to report the highest profits in 2008 and 2009 combined?

P 9-71

LO5, LO11

Changes in Depreciation Estimates and Capitalization of Expenditures

Ironic Metal Products, Inc., acquired a machine on January 2, 2007, for $76,600. The useful life of the machine was estimated to be eight years with a salvage value of $4,600. Depreciation is recorded on December 31 of each year using the sum-of-the-years'-digits method.

At the beginning of 2009, the company estimated the remaining useful life of the machine to be four years and changed the estimated salvage value from $4,600 to $2,600. On January 2, 2010, major repairs on the machine cost the company $34,000. The repairs added two years to the machine's useful life and increased the salvage value to $3,000.

Required:

1. Prepare journal entries to record:
   a. The purchase of the machine.
   b. Annual depreciation expense for the years 2007 and 2008.
   c. Depreciation in 2009 under the revised estimates of useful life and salvage value.
   d. The expenditure for major repairs in 2010.
   e. Depreciation expense for 2010.
2. Compute the book value of the machine at the end of 2010.

P 9-72

LO3, LO4, LO11

Unifying Concepts: Accounting for Natural Resources

Forest Products, Inc., buys and develops natural resources for profit. Since 2006, it has had the following activities:

1/1/06   Purchased for $800,000 a tract of timber estimated to contain 1,600,000 board feet of lumber.

1/1/07   Purchased for $600,000 a silver mine estimated to contain 30,000 tons of silver ore.

7/1/07   Purchased for $60,000 a uranium mine estimated to contain 5,000 tons of uranium ore.

1/1/08   Purchased for $500,000 an oil well estimated to contain 100,000 barrels of oil.

Required:

1. Provide the necessary journal entries to account for the following:
   a. The purchase of these assets.
   b. The depletion expense for 2008 on all four assets, assuming that the following were extracted:
      (1) 200,000 board feet of lumber.
      (2) 5,000 tons of silver.
      (3) 1,000 tons of uranium.
      (4) 10,000 barrels of oil.
2. Assume that on January 1, 2009, after 20,000 tons of silver had been mined, engineers' estimates revealed that only 4,000 tons of silver remained. Record the depletion expense for 2009, assuming that 2,000 tons were mined.
3. Compute the book values of all four assets as of December 31, 2009, assuming that the total extracted to date is:
   a. Timber tract, 800,000 board feet.
   b. Silver mine, 22,000 tons [only 2,000 tons are left per part (2)].
   c. Uranium mine, 3,000 tons.
   d. Oil well, 80,000 barrels.

P 9-73

LO3, LO4, LO5

Unifying Concepts: Property, Plant, and Equipment

Logan Corporation owns and operates three sawmills that make lumber for building homes. The operations consist of cutting logs in the forest, hauling them to the various sawmills, sawing the lumber, and shipping it to building supply warehouses throughout the western part of the United States. To haul the logs, Logan has several trucks. Relevant data pertaining to one truck are:

a. Date of purchase, July 1, 2007.
b. Cost:

Truck	$40,000
Trailer	25,000
Paint job (to match company colors)	3,000
Sales tax	4,000

c. Estimated useful life of the truck, 120,000 miles.
d. Estimated salvage value, zero.
e. 2008 expenditures on truck:
   (1) Spent $4,500 on tires, oil changes, greasing, and other miscellaneous items.
   (2) Spent $18,000 to overhaul the engine and replace the transmission on January 1, 2008. This expenditure increased the life of the truck by 85,000 miles.

Required:

Record journal entries to account for:

1. The purchase of the truck.
2. The 2007 depreciation expense using units-of-production depreciation and assuming the truck was driven 35,000 miles.

(continued)

3. The expenditures relating to the truck during 2008.
4. The 2008 depreciation expense using the units-of-production method and assuming the truck was driven 50,000 miles.

ANALYTICAL ASSIGNMENTS

AA 9-74
DISCUSSION

Intangible Assets

Renford Company owns two restaurants. One, located in Tacoma, was purchased from a previous owner and the other, located in Seattle, was built by Renford Company. The restaurant was built nine years ago. The Tacoma restaurant was purchased last year and has goodwill of $550,000 on the books. As it turns out, the Seattle restaurant does twice as much business as the Tacoma restaurant and is much more profitable. The Seattle restaurant is in a prime location, and business keeps increasing each year. The Tacoma restaurant does about the same amount of business each year, and it doesn't look as if it will ever do any better. Does it make sense to you to have goodwill on the books of the less profitable restaurant? Should Renford record goodwill on the books of the Seattle restaurant, or should it write off the goodwill on the Tacoma restaurant's books?

AA 9-75
DISCUSSION

EXPANDED
material

Straight-Line versus Accelerated Depreciation

Dennis Company currently depreciates its assets using the straight-line method for both tax and financial accounting. Total depreciation expense for this year will be $250,000 using straight-line depreciation. A consultant has just advised the company that it should use accelerated depreciation methods for both tax and financial accounting because "paying lower taxes is better than recognizing higher income." Using accelerated depreciation methods, total depreciation expense this year would be $400,000. The company has an effective tax rate of 40%. Do you agree with the consultant? Why or why not?

AA 9-76
JUDGMENT CALL

You Decide: Should companies leasing equipment be required to record the equipment and leases as assets and liabilities on the balance sheet or as expenses on the income statement?

Current rules require that leases meeting any one of the following requirements should be classified as an asset and liability on the balance sheet:

- A transfer of ownership.
- A bargain purchase option.
- A lease term equal to 75% or more of the economic life of the asset.
- The present value of the payments are 90% or more of the fair market value of the asset at the beginning of the lease term.

However, what if a company leasing the asset decides to structure the lease so that the lease term is 73% of the economic life of the asset or the present value of the lease payments equals 88% of the fair market value of the asset? Should a company be able to use creative techniques in order to structure a lease so that it does not appear on the balance sheet?

AA 9-77
REAL COMPANY
ANALYSIS

Wal-Mart

Using **Wal-Mart**'s 2006 Form 10-K contained in Appendix A, answer the following questions:

1. As a percentage of total assets, is Wal-Mart's investment in property, plant, and equipment increasing or decreasing over time? Which of Wal-Mart's assets is increasing the

(continued)

fastest as a percentage of total assets? What does that indicate Wal-Mart is doing? *Hint:* Include property under capital lease as PP&E in calculating percentages.

2. Reference the notes to the financial statements. Which depreciation method does Wal-Mart use? Estimate the average useful life of Wal-Mart's depreciable assets (i.e., not including land) by dividing the ending balance in the depreciable asset accounts by the depreciation expense for the year. Does the resulting estimated useful life seem reasonable? *Hint:* Include property under capital lease as PP&E in your calculations.

3. Wal-Mart notes in its statement of cash flows that $14.563 billion of property, plant, and equipment was purchased in 2005. Using that information along with the detailed information from the balance sheet, compute (a) the original cost of the equipment disposed of during 2005 and (b) the accumulated depreciation associated with that equipment. (*Hint:* For property, plant, and equipment, beginning balance + purchases − disposals = ending balance; a similar calculation is used for accumulated depreciation.)

AA 9-78

REAL COMPANY ANALYSIS

FedEx

FedEx delivers packages around the world. To accomplish this task, FedEx has made huge investments in long-term assets.

1. Identify what you consider to be the major long-term assets of FedEx. Review the information shown below from FedEx's balance sheet (numbers are in millions) to see how well you did.

May 31	2005	2004
Property and Equipment, at Cost		
Aircraft and related equipment	$ 7,610	$ 7,001
Package handling and ground support equipment	3,366	3,395
Computer and electronic equipment	3,893	3,537
Vehicles	1,994	1,919
Facilities and other	5,154	4,459
	$22,017	$20,311
Less accumulated depreciation and amortization	12,374	11,274
Net property and equipment	$ 9,643	$ 9,037

2. FedEx uses the straight-line depreciation method in depreciating most of its assets. For each major category—aircraft and related equipment, package handling and ground support equipment, computer and electronic equipment, vehicles (mainly trucks and buildings), and facilities and other—provide an estimate (or a range) as to what you would deem a reasonable useful life for each category.

3. Using the information above, compute the accumulated depreciation associated with the property and equipment sold during 2005 given that depreciation for the year was $1.438 billion.

AA 9-79

REAL COMPANY ANALYSIS

U.S. Steel

1. **U.S. Steel** provides the following information in the notes to its financial statements relating to its use of the straight-line method of depreciation. Can you interpret the information contained in the note?

Property, plant and equipment—U.S. Steel records depreciation on a modified straight-line or straight-line method utilizing a composite or group asset approach based upon estimated lives of assets. The modified straight-line method is utilized for domestic steel producing assets and is based upon raw steel production levels. The modification factors applied to straight-line calculations range from a minimum of 85% at a production level below 81% of capability, to a maximum of 105% for a 100% production level. No modification is made at the 95% production level, considered the normal long-range level.

(continued)

2. U.S. Steel also provides information relating to the balances in its individual property, plant and equipment accounts, as shown below. In very general terms, how old is the company's property, plant, and equipment? Provide support for your answer.

(in millions)	December 31	
	2005	2004
Land and depletable property	$ 165	$ 175
Buildings	727	673
Machinery and equipment	10,235	9,827
Leased machinery and equipment	189	189
Total	$11,316	$10,864
Less accumulated depreciation, depletion and amortization	7,301	7,237
Net	$ 4,015	$ 3,627

AA 9-80

INTERNATIONAL

Swire Pacific

Swire Pacific, Ltd., based in Hong Kong, is one of the largest companies in the world. The primary operations of the company are in the regions of Hong Kong, China, and Taiwan where it has operated for over 125 years. Swire operates **Cathay Pacific Airways** and has extensive real estate holdings in Hong Kong.

Swire includes in its fixed assets those long-term assets held as investment properties. In 2002, the company noted that it revalued those assets each year for increases and decreases in fair value. During 2002, Swire reduced the value of those assets on their books by $5.161 billion in Hong Kong dollars.

1. Can you compose the journal entry made by Swire Pacific accountants to write the assets down in value? What would be the debit portion of the journal entry? (*Hint:* Although you may not know the exact answer, think about it and make an educated guess. Would the debit be to another asset account? Would it be to a liability account?)
2. Suppose that in the next year, the assets were again revalued and it was determined that a difference existed between market value and book value of only $3 billion Hong Kong dollars. How would this year's journal entry differ from the previous year's?

AA 9-81

ETHICS

Strategic Accounting Method Choices

You saw in Chapter 6 that a company's management selects the percentage to be used when computing bad debt expense. You noted in Chapter 7 that management is allowed to choose the method for valuing inventory. In this chapter you found that management gets to choose the method used for depreciating assets, the estimated salvage value, and the estimated useful life.

Suppose that you are involved in negotiations with the local labor union regarding wages for your company's employees. Labor leaders are asking that their members be given an average annual raise of 12%. The company president has asked you to prepare a set of financial statements that portrays the company's performance as being mediocre at best. The president also makes it clear that she does not want you to prepare fraudulent financial statements. All estimates must be within the bounds of reason.

So you come up with the following:

- Change the percentage used for estimating bad debts from 1.5% to 2%.
- Elect to use the LIFO method for valuing inventory because the prices associated with inventory have been rising.
- Change the average estimated salvage value of long-term assets from 15% to 10% of historical cost.
- Change the depreciation method from straight-line to an accelerated method.
- Change the average estimated useful life of long-term assets from 10 years to 7 years.

(continued)

As you know, each of these changes will result in net income being lower. Each of these changes is also still within the bounds of reason required by the company president.

1. Would it be appropriate to make the changes described above in order to obtain favorable terms from the labor union negotiators?
2. If the above changes are made, what sort of disclosure do you think should be required?

AA 9-82

WRITING

Gains Are Good, Losses Are Bad–Right?

When a long-term asset is sold for more than its book value, we record a gain. When a long-term asset is sold for less than its book value, we record a loss.

Your assignment is to write a two-page memo addressing the following questions:

1. What factors affect a long-term asset's book value?
2. What factors affect a long-term asset's fair value?
3. Should financial statement users expect an asset's book value to equal its fair value?
4. In the case of an asset sold for a loss, if we knew when we purchased the asset what we know at the point of sale, how would depreciation expense have differed if our objective was to ensure that book value equaled fair value when the asset was sold?
5. Is recognizing a loss on the sale of a long-term asset a bad thing? Is a gain good?

AA 9-83

CUMULATIVE SPREADSHEET PROJECT

Preparing New Forecasts

This spreadsheet project is a continuation of the spreadsheet projects in earlier chapters. If you completed those spreadsheets, you have a head start on this one.

1. Handyman wishes to prepare a forecasted balance sheet and income statement for 2010. Use the original financial statement numbers for 2009 [given in part (1) of the Cumulative Spreadsheet Project assignment in Chapter 2] as the basis for the forecast, along with the following additional information:
   a. Sales in 2010 are expected to increase by 40% over 2009 sales of $700.
   b. Cash will increase at the same rate as sales.
   c. The forecasted amount of accounts receivable in 2010 is determined using the forecasted value for the average collection period. For simplicity, do the computations using the end-of-period accounts receivable balance instead of the average balance. The average collection period for 2010 is expected to be 14.08 days.
   d. The forecasted amount of inventory in 2010 is determined using the forecasted value for the number of days' sales in inventory (computed using the end-of-period inventory balance). The number of days' sales in inventory for 2010 is expected to be 107.6 days.
   e. The forecasted amount of accounts payable in 2010 is determined using the forecasted value for the number of days' purchases in accounts payable (computed using the end-of-period accounts payable balance). The number of days' purchases in accounts payable for 2010 is expected to be 48.34 days.
   f. The $160 in operating expenses reported in 2009 breaks down as follows: $5 depreciation expense, $155 other operating expenses.
   g. No new long-term debt will be acquired in 2010.
   h. No cash dividends will be paid in 2010.
   i. New short-term loans payable will be acquired in an amount sufficient to make Handyman's current ratio in 2010 exactly equal to 2.0.

   Note: These statements were constructed as part of the spreadsheet assignment in Chapter 7; you can use that spreadsheet as a starting point if you have completed that assignment.

   Clearly state any additional assumptions that you make.

   For this exercise, add the following additional assumptions:

   j. The forecasted amount of property, plant, and equipment (PP&E) in 2010 is determined using the forecasted value for the fixed asset turnover ratio. For simplicity,

(continued)

compute the fixed asset turnover ratio using the end-of-period gross PP&E balance. The fixed asset turnover ratio for 2010 is expected to be 3.518 times.

k. In computing depreciation expense for 2010, use straight-line depreciation and assume a 30-year useful life with no residual value. Gross PP&E acquired during the year is only depreciated for half the year. In other words, depreciation expense for 2010 is the sum of two parts: (1) a full year of depreciation on the beginning balance in PP&E, assuming a 30-year life and no residual value, and (2) a half-year of depreciation on any new PP&E acquired during the year, based on the change in the gross PP&E balance.

Clearly state any additional assumptions that you make.

2. Repeat (1), with the following changes in assumptions:
   a. Fixed asset turnover ratio is expected to be 6.000 times.
   b. Fixed asset turnover ratio is expected to be 2.000 times.

3. Comment on the differences in the forecasted values of the following items in 2010 under each of the following assumptions about the fixed asset turnover ratio: 3.518 times, 6.000 times, and 2.000 times:
   a. Property, plant, and equipment.
   b. Depreciation expense.
   c. Income tax expense.
   d. Paid-in capital.

4. Return the fixed asset turnover ratio to 3.518 times. Now, repeat (1), with the following changes in assumptions:
   a. Estimated useful life is expected to be 15 years.
   b. Estimated useful life is expected to be 60 years.

5. Comment on the differences in the forecasted values of the following items in 2010 under each of the following assumptions about the estimated useful life of property, plant, and equipment: 30 years, 15 years, and 60 years.
   a. Depreciation expense.
   b. Income tax expense.

Long-Term Debt Financing

After studying this chapter, you should be able to:

LEARNING OBJECTIVES

① **Use present value concepts to measure long-term liabilities.** *The proper measure of the economic obligation associated with a long-term liability is the present value of the future cash flows instead of the simple sum of the future cash flows.*

② **Account for long-term liabilities, including notes payable and mortgages payable.** *Long-term notes payable are frequently repaid through regular interest payments with the entire balance of the note (the principal) being repaid at the end of the term of the note. With a mortgage, the liability is typically repaid through a series of equal payments, with some interest and some principal repayment included in each payment amount.*

③ **Account for capital lease obligations and understand the significance of operating leases being excluded from the balance sheet.** *For accounting purposes, leases are considered to be either rentals (called operating leases) or asset purchases with borrowed money (called capital leases). A company using a leased asset tries to have the lease classified as an operating lease in order to keep the lease obligation off the balance sheet.*

④ **Account for bonds, including the original issuance, the payment of interest, and the retirement of bonds.** *Bonds are a way to borrow funds from many difference sources rather than borrowing the entire amount from one source, such as a bank. Depending on the market interest rate at the time it is issued, a bond can be issued for more or less than its face value.*

⑤ **Use debt-related financial ratios to determine the degree of a company's financial leverage and its ability to repay loans.** *Debt-related financial ratios give an indication of the degree of a company's leverage and how much cushion operating profits give in terms of being able to make periodic interest payments.*

EXPANDED
material

⑥ **Amortize bond discounts and bond premiums using either the straight-line method or the effective-interest method.** *A bond discount arises when the coupon rate on the bonds is less than the market interest rate; a premium arises when the coupon rate is more than the market rate. Premium and discount balances are gradually reduced to zero over the life of the bond. A premium reduces bond interest expense; a discount increases bond interest expense.*

In 1923, two brothers, Walt and Roy Disney, founded the **Disney Brothers Studio** as a partnership to produce animated features for film. Five years later, the Disney Brothers Studio released its first animated film with sound effects and dialogue, *Steamboat Willie*, featuring a soon-to-become-famous mouse, Mickey. Pluto was introduced to American audiences in 1930, and Goofy was created just two years later. Donald Duck appeared on the scene in 1934, and in 1937 *Snow White and the Seven Dwarfs* was released, accompanied by the first comprehensive merchandising campaign.

But Walt Disney's vision encompassed more than animated films. In 1952, Disney began designing and creating Disneyland, which opened on July 17, 1955. Beginning in the late 1950s, the television shows *Disneyland* (which ran for 29 seasons under various names) and The *Mickey Mouse Club* were also successful Disney ventures. Though Walt Disney passed away in 1966, his influence is still felt around the world. We have Walt Disney World in Florida and Disneylands in Anaheim, California; Paris; Tokyo; and Hong Kong.

Disney's company has expanded far beyond what even he could have foreseen. **The Walt Disney Company** is now involved in television and radio stations; international film distribution; home video production; live theatrical entertainment; online computer programs; interactive computer games; telephone company partnerships; cruise lines; Disney Stores; newspaper, magazine, and book publishing; Internet marketing; and the convention business. In the past decade, The Walt Disney Company has grown over 300%. How has the company financed this growth? In part through very successful operations, but these have not been enough. The company has also borrowed to finance its expansion. As of October 1, 2005, The Walt Disney Company had long-term debt totaling over $10 billion. This long-term financing includes loans with U.S. banks as well as loans denominated (or made) in Hong Kong dollars and euros. The effective interest rates on Disney's loans range from 2.13 to 9.07%.[1]

F Y I

Not everything that Disney touches turns to gold. Disney opened an indoor theme park—DisneyQuest—in Chicago in June 1999 and closed the park in September 2001 citing a lack of long-range financial return potential.

In this chapter, we will introduce various types of long-term liabilities. We will explain a concept used in measuring the present value of an obligation due in the future. This concept—the time value of money—is useful for computing the value of bonds and notes, as in the Disney example, as well as for computing mortgage payments and pension obligations. In the main part of this chapter, we discuss the measurement of long-term liabilities and introduce numerous types of long-term liabilities—notes, mortgages, leases, and bonds. The basic accounting procedures associated with several of these liabilities are also discussed. In the expanded material, the complexities associated with the amortization of a bond issued at a premium or discount are discussed. Exhibit 1 highlights the financial statement accounts discussed in this chapter.

---

[1] The information for this scenario was obtained from Disney's Web site at **http://www.disney.com.**

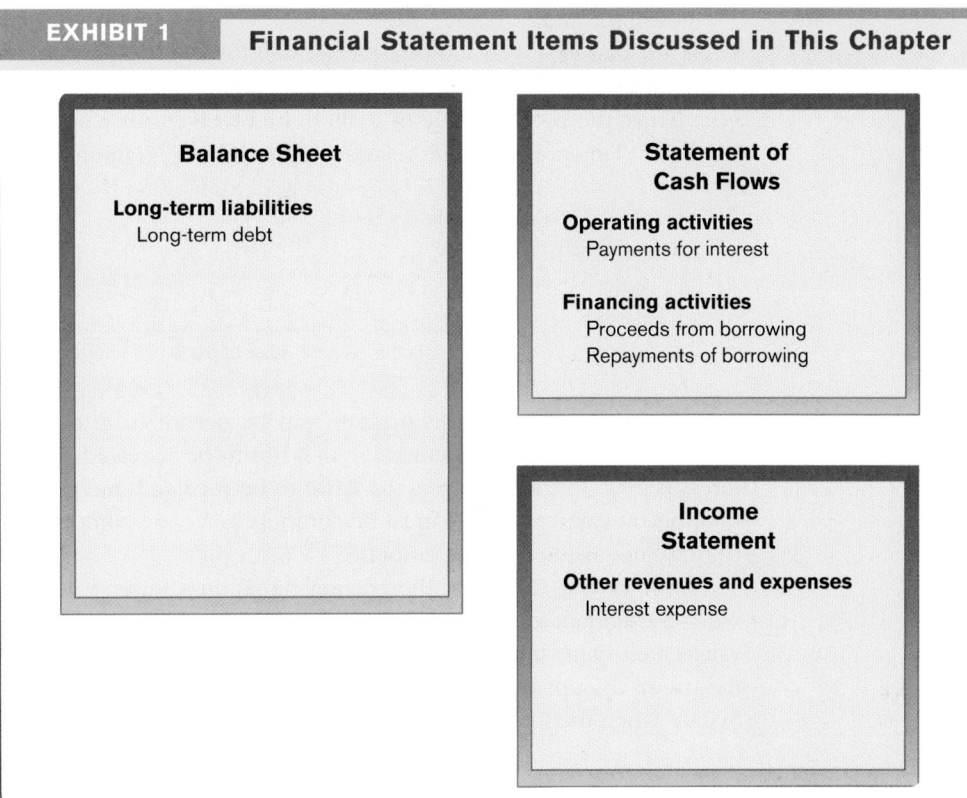

| EXHIBIT 1 | Financial Statement Items Discussed in This Chapter |

Balance Sheet

Long-term liabilities
Long-term debt

Statement of Cash Flows

Operating activities
Payments for interest

Financing activities
Proceeds from borrowing
Repayments of borrowing

Income Statement

Other revenues and expenses
Interest expense

SETTING THE STAGE

Measuring Long-Term Liabilities

Use present value concepts to measure long-term liabilities.

① Conceptually, the value of a liability is the cash that would be required to pay the liability in full today. Because money has a time value—usually referred to as interest, most people are willing to accept less money today than they would if a liability were paid in the future. Therefore, with the exception of short-term Accounts Payable, liabilities to be paid in the future usually involve interest.

Accounting for **long-term liabilities** is complex because usually payments of interest, or in some cases principal and interest, are made periodically over the period in which the liability is outstanding. Further, in some cases the amount of the liability in a noncash transaction may not be readily apparent. The time value of money concept is used in measuring and recording these liabilities.

Present Value and Future Value Concepts

long-term liabilities

Debts or other obligations that will not be paid within one year.

The concepts of present value and future value are used to measure the effect of time on the value of money. To illustrate, if you are to receive $100 one year from today, is it worth $100 today? Obviously not, because if you had the $100 today you could either spend it now or invest it and earn interest. If the $100 won't be received for one year, those options are not available. The **present value of $1** is the value today of $1 to be received or paid in the future, given a specified interest rate. To determine the value today of money to be received or paid in the future, we must "discount" the future amount (reduce the future amount to its present value) by an appropriate interest rate. For example, if money can earn 10% per year, $100 to be received one year from now is approximately equal to $90.91 received today.

present value of $1

The value today of $1 to be received or paid at some future date, given a specified interest rate.

Putting it another way, if $90.91 is invested today in an account that earns 10% interest for one year, the interest earned will be $9.09 ($90.91 × 10% × 1 year = $9.09). The sum of the $90.91 principal and the $9.09 interest will equal $100 at the end of one year. Thus, the present value of $100 to be received (or paid) in one year at 10% interest is $90.91. This present value relationship can be diagrammed as follows:

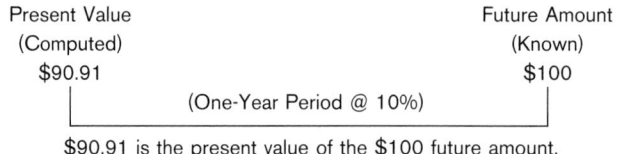

Present Value		Future Amount
(Computed)		(Known)
$90.91		$100
	(One-Year Period @ 10%)	

$90.91 is the present value of the $100 future amount.

The relationships in this diagram can be described in two ways. We have just seen that the $90.91 is the present value of $100 to be received one year from now when interest is 10%. In this example, the $100 to be received one year from now is known, and the present value of $90.91 must be computed. We are computing a present value amount from a known future value amount.

Another way to look at the relationship is on a future value basis. Future values apply when the amount today ($90.91) is known, and the future amount must be calculated. Future values are exactly the opposite of present values. Thinking in terms of future values, $100 is the future amount we can expect to receive in one year, given a present known amount of $90.91 when the interest rate is 10%. We can diagram this relationship as follows:

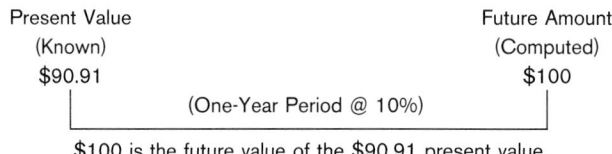

Present Value		Future Amount
(Known)		(Computed)
$90.91		$100
	(One-Year Period @ 10%)	

$100 is the future value of the $90.91 present value.

Present and future values can be calculated using formulas. If more than one period is involved, however, the formula is exponential, and the calculations become rather complicated. Therefore, it is more convenient to use either a present value table or a calculator that gives the present value of $1 for various numbers of periods and interest rates (see Table I, page 484) or a future value table that gives the future value of $1 for various numbers of periods and interest rates (see Table III, page 486). We will illustrate the use of both a present value table and a future value table as well as the keystrokes needed when using a standard business calculator.

Computing the Present Value of a Single Amount   To use a present value table, you simply locate the appropriate number of periods in the leftmost column and the interest rate in the row at the top of the table. The intersection of the row and column is the factor representing the present value of $1 for the number of periods and the relevant interest rate. To find the present value of an amount other than $1, multiply the factor in the table by that amount.

To illustrate the use of a present value table (Table I) to find the present value of a known future amount, assume that $10,000 is to be paid four years from today when the interest rate is 10%. What is the present value of the $10,000 payment?

Amount of payment	$ 10,000
Present value factor of $1 to be paid in 4 periods	
at 10% interest (from Table I)	× 0.6830
Present value of payment	$ 6,830

This present value amount, $6,830, is the amount that could be paid today to satisfy the obligation that is due four years from now if money earns 10% annually. As indicated, this procedure is sometimes referred to as "discounting." Thus, we say that $10,000 discounted for four years at 10% is $6,830. Stated another way, if $6,830 is invested today in an account that pays 10% interest, in four years the balance in that account will be $10,000.

Another way to compute this same amount is to use a business calculator. The keystrokes described below are for a Hewlett-Packard 10BII business calculator; similar keystrokes are used with other business calculators. To compute the present value of $10,000 to be received four years from today, with a prevailing interest rate of 10%, make the following keystrokes:

Hewlett-Packard Keystrokes:

a. Always **CLEAR ALL** before doing anything else. With a Hewlett-Packard 10BII, one does this by pressing the yellow key, then pressing "C." This has the effect of clearing out any information left over from a prior computation.

b. Always set **P/YR** (payments per year) to the correct number—"1" in this case. With a Hewlett-Packard 10BII, one does this by pressing "1," then pressing the yellow key, then pressing "PMT." This has the effect of telling the calculator that each year is being viewed as a separate period. As described later in this chapter, interest can be compounded over different periods, such as monthly, quarterly, daily, or even continuously. Setting **P/YR** equal to 1 means that the interest rate is compounded annually. Sometimes, the default for this amount is "12" because the calculator is set to compute monthly payments. Until you are comfortable using your calculator, your best strategy is to set this amount to "1" to avoid having the calculator doing too many mysterious things automatically.

1. 10,000   Press **FV**.
2. 4   Press **N**.
3. 10   Press **I/YR**.
4. Press **PV** for the answer of $6,830.13.

Computing the Future Value of a Single Amount   To find the future value of an amount that is known today, use a future value table. When using a future value table, simply locate the appropriate number of periods in the leftmost column and the interest rate in the row at the top of the table. The intersection of the row and column is the factor representing the future value of $1 for the number of periods and the relevant interest rate. To find the future value of an amount other than $1, multiply the factor in the table by that amount.

To illustrate the use of a future value table (Table III), we will use the same information as before, except that we will now assume that the present value of $6,830 is known, not the future amount of $10,000. Assume that we have a savings account with a current balance of $6,830 that earns interest of 10%. What will be the balance in that account in four years?

Present value in savings account	$ 6,830*
Future value factor of $1 in 4 periods at 10% interest (from Table III)	× 1.4641*
Future value	$ 10,000*

*Rounded; other calculations in chapter will also be rounded.

Hewlett-Packard Keystrokes:
a. **CLEAR ALL**.
b. Set **P/YR** to 1.

1. 6,830   Press **PV**.
2. 4   Press **N**.
3. 10   Press **I/YR**.
4. Press **FV** for the answer of $9,999.80. (You would round to $10,000.)

When computing future values, we often use the term *compounding* to mean the frequency with which interest is added to the principal. Thus, we say that interest of 10% has been compounded once a year (annually) to arrive at a future value at the end of four years of $10,000. If the interest is added more or less frequently than once a year, the future amount will be different.

compounding period

The period of time for which interest is computed.

The preceding example assumed annual **compounding periods** for interest. If the 10% interest had been compounded semiannually (twice a year) for four years, the calculation would have used a 5% (one-half of the 10%) rate for eight periods (4 years × 2 periods per year) instead of 10% for four periods. To illustrate, what is the present value of $10,000 to be paid in four years if interest of 10% is compounded semiannually?

Amount of payment	$ 10,000
Present value factor of $1 to be paid in 8 periods at 5% interest (from Table I)	× 0.6768
Present value of payment	$ 6,768

Thus, the present value of $10,000 to be paid in four years is $6,768 if interest is compounded semiannually. Likewise, if semiannual compounding is used to determine the future value of $6,768 in four years at 10% compounded semiannually, the result is as follows:

Present value in savings account	$ 6,768
Future value factor of $1 in 8 periods at 5% interest (from Table III)	× 1.4775
Future value	$ 10,000

Note that the present value ($6,768) is lower with semiannual compounding than with annual compounding ($6,830). The more frequently interest is compounded, the greater the total amount of interest deducted (in computing present values) or added (in computing future values).

For practice using semiannual compounding with a business calculator, try the following set of keystrokes:

Hewlett-Packard Keystrokes:
a. **CLEAR ALL**.
b. Set **P/YR** to 1. There is a simple way to tell the calculator to automatically compute the impact of semiannual compounding. Look in your calculator instruction book if you are interested in knowing how to do this. Alternatively, you can do some of the calculations yourself (divide the interest rate by two and double the number of periods) and use the keystrokes below.

1. 6,768   Press **PV**.
2. 8   Press **N**.
3. 5   Press **I/YR**.
4. Press **FV** for the answer of $9,999.42.

S T O P & T H I N K

Without referencing the present value
tables, answer these questions: As interest
rates increase, would you expect the
present value factors to increase or decrease?
Why?

Because interest may also be compounded quarterly, monthly, or for some other period, you should learn the relationship of interest to the compounding period. Semiannual interest means that you double the interest periods and halve the annual interest rate; with quarterly interest, you quadruple the periods and take one-fourth of the annual interest rate. The formula for interest rate is:

$$\frac{\text{Yearly interest rate}}{\text{Compounding periods per year}} = \frac{\text{Interest rate per}}{\text{compounding period}}$$

The number of interest periods is simply the number of periods per year times the number of years. That formula is:

$$\frac{\text{Compounding}}{\text{periods per year}} \times \frac{\text{Number of}}{\text{years}} = \frac{\text{Number of}}{\text{interest periods}}$$

Computing the Present Value of an Annuity

annuity

A series of equal amounts to be received or paid at the end of equal time intervals.

present value of an annuity

The value today of a series of equally spaced, equal-amount payments to be made or received in the future given a specified interest rate.

In discussing present values and future values, we have assumed only a single present value or future value with one of the amounts known and the other to be computed. With liabilities, we generally know the future amount that must be paid and would like to compute the present value of that future payment. Because this chapter focuses on liabilities, we will concentrate on present value calculations.

Many long-term liabilities involve a series of payments rather than one lump-sum payment. For example, a company might purchase equipment under an installment agreement requiring payments of $5,000 each year for five years. Determining the value today (present value) of a series of equally spaced, equal-amount payments (called an **annuity**) is more complicated than determining the present value of a single future payment. If you were to try to calculate the **present value of an annuity** by hand, you would have to discount the first payment for one period, the second payment for two periods, and so on, and then add all the present values together. Because such calculations are time-consuming, a table is generally used (see Table II, page 485). The factors in the table are the sums of the individual present values of all future payments. Based on the present value of an annuity of $1, the table provides factors for various interest rates and number of payments.

To illustrate the use of a present value of an annuity table (Table II), we will assume that $10,000 is to be paid at the end of each of the next 10 years. This series of payments is illustrated below.

 C A U T I O N

Use care when referencing the present value and future value tables. You can do all your computations correctly, but if you pull the factor from the wrong table, your answer will be wrong.

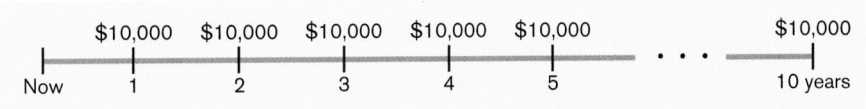

If the interest rate is 12% compounded annually, Table II shows a present value factor of 5.6502. This factor means that the present value of $1 paid each year for 10 years discounted at 12% is approximately $5.65. Applying this factor to payments of $10,000 results in the following:

Amount of the annual payment	$ 10,000
Present value factor of an annuity of $1	
discounted for 10 payments at 12%	× 5.6502
Present value	$ 56,502

This amount, $56,502, is the amount (present value) that could be paid today to satisfy the obligation to pay $10,000 per year for 10 years if the interest rate is 12%.

The present value of an annuity can also be computed with a business calculator as follows:

Hewlett-Packard Keystrokes:
a. **CLEAR ALL.**
b. Set **P/YR** to 1.

1. 10,000   Press **PMT**.
2. 10   Press **N**.
3. 12   Press **I/YR**.
4. Press **PV** for the answer of $56,502.23.

Computing Periodic Payments   With some modifications, the same calculations used to compute the present value of an annuity can be used to compute the proper amount of a periodic loan payment. For example, consider the task of computing the appropriate monthly payment on an automobile loan of $20,000 if the interest rate is 12% compounded monthly (i.e., 1% per month) and the loan period is 60 months. This problem can be viewed as follows:

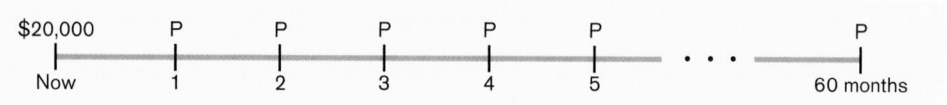

In this case, we know the present value of the annuity—it is $20,000, or the amount we would have to pay today to pay off the entire loan. What we want to know is what series of 60 payments (P in the diagram) has a present value exactly equal to the $20,000 that we owe. The calculation of the payment amount can be set up as follows:

Amount of the annual payment	Payment
Present value factor of an annuity of $1	
discounted for 60 payments at 1%	× 44.9550
Present value	$ 20,000

In equation format, this can be written as follows:

$$\$20,000 = \text{Payment} \times 44.9550$$
$$\text{Payment} = \$20,000/44.9550$$
$$\text{Payment} = \$444.89$$

In other words, paying $444.89 per month for 60 months is the same as paying $20,000 right now, if the interest rate on borrowed money is 12% compounded monthly (1% per month). (Note that the total paid would be $26,693.40 ($444.89 × 60) and that the total interest would be $6693.40.)

This payment amount can also be computed with a business calculator as follows:

Hewlett-Packard Keystrokes:
a. **CLEAR ALL**.
b. Set **P/YR** to 1.

1. 20,000   Press **PV**.
2. 60   Press **N**.
3. 1   Press **I/YR**.
4. Press **PMT** for the answer of $444.88895.

REMEMBER THIS...

- Long-term liabilities are debts or other obligations that will not be paid or satisfied within one year. Present value concepts, which equate the value of money received or paid in different periods, are used to measure long-term liabilities.

- An annuity is a series of equal payments to be made or received in the future. A lump sum is one payment to be made or received in the future.

- Future value computations are performed to calculate how much a lump-sum payment or an annuity will have grown, because of interest, at some point in the future.

- Present value computations are performed to calculate how much money right now is economically equivalent to a lump sum or annuity to occur in the future.

- Present and future value amounts can be computed using tables, a business calculator, or a spreadsheet.

- In calculating present and future values, you must consider the compounding period and the interest rate. For other than annual payments, the number of periods used is the number of periods per year times the number of years; the interest rate used is the annual rate divided by the number of periods per year.

- The same type of computations used to compute the present value of an annuity can also be used to compute the proper amount of a periodic payment, such as the monthly payment on a car loan.

Accounting for Long-Term Liabilities

Account for long-term liabilities, including notes payable and mortgages payable.

(2) Now that we have explained how present value concepts are applied in measuring long-term liabilities, we are ready to discuss the accounting for those liabilities. The time line in Exhibit 2 illustrates the business events associated with long-term liabilities.

A company's first decision is to determine the type of long-term financing to use. In this chapter, we will discuss four different types of financing: notes payable, mortgages payable, leasing, and bonds. There are advantages and disadvantages to each type of financing. For example, bonds (which are sold in $1,000 increments) allow a company to borrow a little bit of money from a lot of different people, whereas notes involve borrowing a lot of money from one lender (or perhaps a consortium of lenders). The benefit of a mortgage is typically a lower interest rate because the property being purchased is used as collateral on the loan, thereby providing the lender with less risk. Leases have the advantage of typically requiring a lower

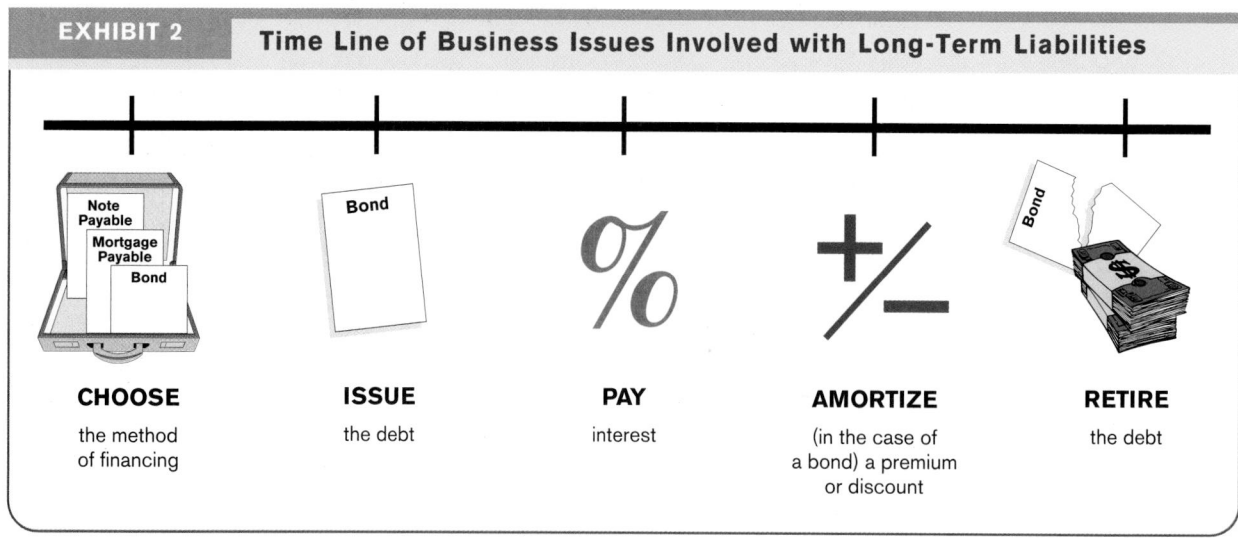

EXHIBIT 2   **Time Line of Business Issues Involved with Long-Term Liabilities**

CHOOSE	ISSUE	PAY	AMORTIZE	RETIRE
the method of financing	the debt	interest	(in the case of a bond) a premium or discount	the debt

down payment as there are no risks associated with product obsolescence. (At the end of many leases, the asset being leased is returned to the original owner.) Once the pros and cons of the various types of financing are analyzed, and the company selects an option, the accounting differs, depending upon the type of financing chosen. In this section, we will discuss the recording of long-term debt, including notes payable and mortgages payable.

Interest-Bearing Notes

To illustrate the accounting for a long-term interest-bearing note payable, assume that on January 1, 2009, Giraffe Company borrowed $10,000 from City Bank for three years at 10% interest. Assume also that interest is payable annually on December 31. The entries to account for the note are:

2009			
Jan. 1	Cash	10,000	
	Note Payable		10,000
	Borrowed $10,000 from City Bank for three years.		
Dec. 31	Interest Expense	1,000	
	Cash		1,000
	Made first annual interest payment on		
	City Bank note ($10,000 × 0.10).		
2010			
Dec. 31	Interest Expense	1,000	
	Cash		1,000
	Made second annual interest payment		
	on City Bank note ($10,000 × 0.10).		
2011			
Dec. 31	Interest Expense	1,000	
	Note Payable	10,000	
	Cash		11,000
	Made final interest payment ($10,000 × 0.10)		
	and repaid principal on City Bank note.		

A long-term note such as this three-year note should be recorded in the books at the present value of the future cash payments to be made in connection with the note. If the market interest rate is 10%, then the present value of the cash payments on the note is computed as follows:

Present value of interest payments:		
Amount of each interest payment	$ 1,000	
Table II factor for 3 payments at 10%	× 2.4869	
Present value of annuity		$ 2,487
Present value of principal payment:		
Amount of principal payment	$10,000	
Table I factor for 3 periods at 10%	× 0.7513	
Present value of single payment		7,513
Present value of interest and principal		$10,000

The total present value is the sum of the present values of the interest payments (an annuity) and the single principal payment due in three years. In this case, the present value of the cash payments on the note is exactly equal to the note's face amount of $10,000. This is because the annual interest payments of 10% are equal to the market rate of interest, or the rate of interest that lenders would insist on earning for lending money in exchange for the note.

In the notes to its 2005 financial statements, **The Walt Disney Company** reported the existence of a variety of notes payable, including notes for which the amounts to be repaid were stated in euros, Hong Kong dollars, and U.S. dollars. These notes included various types of debt instruments including "fixed or floating rate notes, U.S. dollar or foreign currency denominated notes, redeemable notes, index linked and dual currency notes."

Mortgages Payable

mortgage payable

A written promise to pay a stated amount of money at one or more specified future dates; a mortgage is secured by the pledging of certain assets, usually real estate, as collateral.

A **mortgage payable** is similar to a note payable in that it is a written promise to pay a stated sum of money at one or more specified future dates. It differs from a note in the way it is applied. Whereas money borrowed with a note can often be used for any business purpose, mortgage money is usually related to a specific asset, typically real estate. Assets purchased with a mortgage are usually pledged as security or collateral on the loan. Individuals commonly obtain home mortgages, and companies frequently use plant mortgages. In either case, a mortgage generally requires periodic (usually monthly) payments of principal plus interest.

To illustrate the accounting for a mortgage, we will assume that McGiven Automobile Company borrows $100,000 on January 1 to purchase a new showroom and signs a mortgage agreement pledging the showroom as collateral on the loan. If the mortgage is at 8% for 30 years, and the monthly payment is $733.76, payable on January 31 with subsequent payments due at the end of each month thereafter, the entries to record the acquisition of the mortgage and the first monthly payment are:

Jan. 1	Cash	100,000	
	Mortgage Payable		100,000
	Borrowed $100,000 to purchase the automobile		
	showroom.		
Jan. 31	Mortgage Payable	67.09	
	Interest Expense	666.67	
	Cash		733.76
	Made first month's mortgage payment.		

As this entry shows, only $67.09 of the $733.76 payment is applied to reduce the mortgage; the remainder is interest ($100,000 × 0.08 × ½). In each successive month, the amount applied to reduce the mortgage will increase slightly until, toward the end of

EXHIBIT 3	Mortgage Amortization Schedule – Year 1 ($100,000, 30-Year Mortgage at 8%)

Payment	Monthly Payment	Interest Portion	Principal Portion	Outstanding Mortgage Balance
				$100,000.00
1	$733.76	$666.67	$67.09	99,932.91
2	733.76	666.22	67.54	99,865.37
3	733.76	665.77	67.99	99,797.38
4	733.76	665.32	68.44	99,728.93
5	733.76	664.86	68.90	99,660.03
6	733.76	664.40	69.36	99,590.67
7	733.76	663.94	69.82	99,520.85
8	733.76	663.47	70.29	99,450.56
9	733.76	663.00	70.76	99,379.80
10	733.76	662.53	71.23	99,308.58
11	733.76	662.06	71.70	99,236.87
12	733.76	661.58	72.18	99,164.69

mortgage amortization schedule

A schedule that shows the breakdown between interest and principal for each payment over the life of a mortgage.

the 30-year mortgage, almost all of the payment will be reductions in the mortgage balance. A **mortgage amortization schedule** identifies how much of each mortgage payment is interest and how much is principal reduction, as shown in Exhibit 3 (for the first year of the mortgage). A similar table could be prepared for each year of the mortgage.

The following table shows how much the monthly payment and total amount paid and what the qualifying annual income (the monthly payment is recommended not to exceed 28% of a person's monthly gross income) would have to be on a $100,000, 25-year mortgage. You can see that as the interest rate increases, so does the monthly payment and total amount paid over the life of the loan.

$100,000, 25-Year Mortgage			
Interest Rate	Monthly Payment	Total Amount Paid	Qualifying Annual Income
7%	$ 707	$212,100	$30,300
8%	772	231,600	33,086
9%	839	251,700	35,957
10%	909	272,700	38,957
11%	980	294,000	42,000
12%	1,053	315,900	45,129
13%	1,128	338,400	48,343
14%	1,204	361,200	51,600

At the end of each year, a mortgage is reported on the balance sheet in two places: (1) the principal to be paid during the next year is shown as a current liability, and (2) the balance of the mortgage payable is shown as a long-term liability. Further, any accrued interest on the mortgage is reported as a current liability, and the interest expense for the year is included with other expenses on the income statement.

> **REMEMBER THIS...**
>
> - Long-term interest-bearing notes are obligations that will be repaid over several years.
> - Interest on the note is computed by multiplying the outstanding balance of the note by the rate of interest.
> - Mortgages payable are long-term liabilities that arise when companies borrow money to buy land, construct buildings, or purchase additional operating assets. Mortgages are tied to specific assets.
> - Mortgages are amortized over a period of time and involve periodic, usually monthly, payments that include both principal and interest.

Accounting for Lease Obligations

Account for capital lease obligations and understand the significance of operating leases being excluded from the balance sheet.

(3) As discussed in Chapter 9, a company may choose to lease rather than purchase an asset. If a lease is a simple, short-term rental agreement, called an operating lease, lease payments are recorded as Rent Expense by the lessee and as Rent Revenue by the lessor. However, if the terms of a lease agreement meet specific criteria (see Chapter 9, page 396), the transaction is classified as a capital lease and is accounted for as if the asset had been purchased with long-term debt. The lessee records the leased property as an asset and recognizes a liability to the lessor.

In Chapter 9, we focused on the recording of assets acquired under capital leases, using assumed amounts for the present value. Here we will explain how the present value of a capital lease is determined. To illustrate the measurement and recording of a capital lease, we will assume that Malone Corporation leases a mainframe computer from Macro Data, Inc., on December 31, 2008. The lease requires annual payments of $10,000 for 10 years, with the first payment due on December 31, 2009.[2] The rate of interest applicable to the lease is 14% compounded annually.

> **? FYI**
>
> Many companies structure their lease agreements so as not to meet the lease capitalization criteria. In these cases, the companies must still disclose their expected future lease payments in the notes to the financial statements.

Assuming the lease meets the criteria for a capital lease, Malone Corporation will record the computer and the related liability at the present value of the future lease payments. From Table II, on page 485, the factor for the present value of an annuity for 10 payments at 14% is 5.2161. This factor is multiplied by the annual lease payment to determine the present value. The entry to record the lease on Malone's books is:

```
2008
Dec. 31   Leased Computer  ...................................   52,161
             Lease Liability  ...................................            52,161
             Leased a computer from Macro Data, Inc., for
             $10,000 a year for 10 years discounted at 14%
             ($10,000 × 5.2161 = $52,161).
```

---

[2] Readers should be aware that the illustration of a capital lease presented here assumes that lease payments are made at the end of each year, with the present values based on an ordinary annuity. Usually, lease payments are made at the beginning of each lease period, which requires present value calculations using the concept of an annuity in advance or "annuity due." These calculations are explained in intermediate accounting texts.

A construction company may choose to lease large equipment rather than purchase such an asset.

If Malone Corporation uses a calendar year for financial reporting, the December 31, 2009, balance sheet will report the leased asset in the property, plant, and equipment section and the lease liability in the liabilities section.

A schedule of the computer lease payments is presented in Exhibit 4. Each year the lease liability account balance is multiplied by 14% to determine the amount of interest included in each of the annual $10,000 lease payments.

Note that this is the same procedure used with a mortgage when determining the amount of each payment that is applied to reduce the principal and the amount that is considered interest expense. As you can see, in the table the interest expense is first calculated by multiplying the interest rate times the lease account balance; the principle amount of the payment is calculated by deducting the interest expense from the payment and the lease account balance for the subsequent year is determined by subtracting the principal amount of the payment from the previous years' lease account balance.

The remainder of the payment is a reduction in the liability. For example, the first lease payment is recorded as follows:

```
2009
Dec. 31   Interest Expense ......................................   7,303
            Lease Liability ........................................   2,697
              Cash ........................................................          10,000
                Paid annual lease payment for computer
                ($52,161 × 0.14 = $7,303; $10,000 − $7,303 = $2,697).
```

Similar entries would be made in each of the remaining nine years of the lease, except that the principal payment (reduction in Lease Liability) would increase while the interest expense would decrease. Interest expense decreases over the lease term because a constant rate (14%) is applied to a decreasing principal balance.

EXHIBIT 4	**Schedule of Computer Lease Payments**			
Year	Annual Payment	Interest Expense (0.14 × Lease Liability)	Principal	Lease Liability
				$52,161
1	$10,000	(0.14 × $52,161) = $7,303	$2,697	49,464
2	10,000	(0.14 × 49,464) = 6,925	3,075	46,389
3	10,000	(0.14 × 46,389) = 6,494	3,506	42,883
4	10,000	(0.14 × 42,883) = 6,004	3,996	38,887
5	10,000	(0.14 × 38,887) = 5,444	4,556	34,331
6	10,000	(0.14 × 34,331) = 4,806	5,194	29,137
7	10,000	(0.14 × 29,137) = 4,079	5,921	23,216
8	10,000	(0.14 × 23,216) = 3,250	6,750	16,466
9	10,000	(0.14 × 16,466) = 2,305	7,695	8,771
10	10,000	(0.14 × 8,771) = 1,229*	8,771	0

*Rounded.

Although the asset and liability accounts have the same balance at the beginning of the lease term, they seldom remain the same during the lease period. The asset and the liability are accounted for separately, with the asset being depreciated using one of the methods discussed in Chapter 9.

Operating Leases

When a lease is accounted for as a capital lease, the lease obligation (and an associated leased asset) will appear on the balance sheet of the company using the leased asset. If, on the other hand, a company is able to classify a lease as an operating lease according to the criteria outlined in Chapter 9, *nothing will appear on the balance sheet.* Neither the leased asset nor the lease liability will be recognized. For this reason, an operating lease is often referred to as a form of "off-balance-sheet financing"—the economic obligation associated with the financing arrangement entered into to secure the use of an asset is not reported on the balance sheet.

Because operating leases are not reported on the balance sheet, accounting rules require companies to disclose operating lease details in the financial statement notes so that financial statement users will be aware of these off-balance-sheet obligations. The information from the operating lease note from **Disney's** 2005 financial statements is reproduced below.

Contractual commitments for broadcast programming rights, future minimum lease payments under non-cancelable operating leases and creative talent and other commitments totaled $23.3 billion at October 1, 2005, payable as follows:

	Broadcast Programming	Operating Leases	Other	Total
2006	$ 4,174	$ 279	$ 887	$ 5,340
2007	2,836	253	484	3,573
2008	2,445	204	324	2,973
2009	1,944	171	196	2,311
2010	2,093	149	92	2,334
Thereafter	6,065	580	96	6,741
	$19,557	$1,636	$2,079	$23,272

Recall that the obligation to make this $23.3 billion in operating lease payments is not reported as a liability on Disney's balance sheet.

REMEMBER THIS...

- A lease is a contract whereby the lessee makes periodic payments to the lessor for the use of an asset.
- A simple short-term rental agreement, or operating lease, involves only the recording of rent expense by the lessee and rent revenue by the lessor.
- A capital lease is accounted for as a debt-financed purchase of the leased asset. Both the asset and the liability are initially recorded by the lessee at the present value of the future lease payments discounted at the applicable interest rate. The asset is subsequently depreciated. The liability is recorded as being repaid, with interest.
- Operating leases are a form of off-balance-sheet financing because the obligation to make future operating lease payments is not recognized as a liability on the balance sheet.
- Companies are required to disclose the amount of their future operating lease payments in the notes to the financial statements.

The Nature of Bonds

A **bond** is a contract between the borrowing company (issuer) and the lender (investor) in which the borrower promises to pay a specified amount of interest at the end of each period the bond is outstanding and to repay the principal at the maturity date of the bond contract. Bonds generally have maturity dates exceeding 10 years and, as a result, are another example of a long-term liability.

Types of Bonds

Bonds can be categorized on the basis of various characteristics. The following classification system considers three characteristics:

1. The extent to which bondholders are protected.
    a. **Debentures** (or **unsecured bonds**). Bonds that have no underlying assets pledged as security, or collateral, to guarantee their repayment.
    b. **Secured bonds**. Bonds that have a pledge of company assets, such as land or buildings, as a protection for lenders. If the company fails to meet its bond obligations, the pledged assets can be sold and used to pay the bondholders. Bonds that are secured with the issuer's assets are often referred to as "mortgage bonds."
2. How the bond interest is paid.
    a. **Registered bonds**. Bonds for which the issuing company keeps a record of the names and addresses of all bondholders and pays interest only to those whose names are on file.
    b. **Coupon bonds**. Unregistered bonds for which the issuer has no record of current bondholders but instead pays interest to anyone who can show evidence of ownership. Usually, these bonds have a printed coupon for each interest payment. When a payment is due, the bondholder clips the coupon from the certificate and sends it to the issuer as evidence of bond ownership. The issuer then sends an interest payment to the bondholder.
3. How the bonds mature.
    a. **Term bonds**. Bonds that mature in one single sum on a specified future date.
    b. **Serial bonds**. Bonds that mature in a series of installments.
    c. **Callable bonds**. Term or serial bonds that the issuer can redeem at any time at a specified price.
    d. **Convertible bonds**. Term or serial bonds that can be converted to other securities, such as stocks, after a specified period, at the option of the bondholder. (The accounting for this type of bond is discussed in advanced accounting texts.)

Two other types of bonds that are often encountered are zero-coupon bonds and junk bonds. **Zero-coupon bonds** are issued with no promise of interest payments. The company issuing the bonds promises only to repay a fixed amount at the maturity date. While the idea of having to make no interest payments might be initially appealing to the issuer, remember that the present value of the bond is affected by both the single payment at the end of the bond's life and the annuity payment. If this annuity (interest) payment will not be part of the bond, potential buyers will pay much less for the bond. For this reason, zero-coupon bonds are often referred to as *deep-discount bonds.*

Junk bonds are high-risk bonds issued by companies in weak financial condition or with large amounts of debt already outstanding. These bonds typically

---

bond

A contract between a borrower and a lender in which the borrower promises to pay a specified rate of interest for each period the bond is outstanding and repay the principal at the maturity date.

debentures (unsecured bonds)

Bonds for which no collateral has been pledged.

secured bonds

Bonds for which assets have been pledged in order to guarantee repayment.

registered bonds

Bonds for which the names and addresses of the bondholders are kept on file by the issuing company.

coupon bonds

Unregistered bonds for which owners receive periodic interest payments by clipping a coupon from the bond and sending it to the issuer as evidence of ownership.

term bonds

Bonds that mature in one single sum at a specified future date.

serial bonds

Bonds that mature in a series of installments at specified future dates.

callable bonds

Bonds for which the issuer reserves the right to pay the obligation before its maturity date.

convertible bonds

Bonds that can be traded for, or converted to, other securities after a specified period of time.

zero-coupon bonds

Bonds issued with no promise of interest payments; only a single payment will be made.

junk bonds

Bonds issued by companies in weak financial condition with large amounts of debt already outstanding; these bonds yield high rates of return because of high risk.

yield returns of at least 12%, but some may return in excess of 20%. Of course, with these high returns comes greater risk.

Characteristics of Bonds

When an organization issues bonds, it usually sells them to underwriters (brokers and investment bankers), who in turn sell them to various institutions and to the public. At the time of the original sale, the company issuing the bonds chooses a trustee to represent the bondholders. In most cases, the trustee is a large bank or trust company to which the company issuing the bonds delivers a contract called a bond indenture, deed of trust, or trust indenture. The **bond indenture** specifies that in return for an investment of cash by investors, the company promises to pay a specific amount of interest (based on a specified, or stated, rate of interest) each period the bonds are outstanding and to repay the **principal** (also called **face value** or **maturity value**) of the bonds at a specified future date (the **bond maturity date**) (see page 470 for definitions). It is the duty of the trustee to protect investors and to make sure that the bond issuer fulfills its responsibilities.

The total value of a single "bond issue" often exceeds several million dollars. A bond issue is generally divided into a number of individual bonds, which may be of varying denominations. The principal, or face value, of each bond is usually $1,000 or a multiple thereof. Note that the price of bonds is quoted as a percentage of $1,000 face value. Thus, a bond quoted at 98 is selling for $980 (98% × $1,000), and a bond quoted at 103 is selling for $1,030 (103% × $1,000). By issuing bonds in small denominations, a company increases the chances that a broad range of investors will be able to compete for the purchase of the bonds. This increased demand usually results in the bonds selling for a higher price.

In most cases, the market price of bonds is influenced by (1) the riskiness of the bonds and (2) the interest rate at which the bonds are issued. The first factor, riskiness of the bonds, is determined by general economic conditions and the financial status of the company selling the bonds, as measured by organizations (**Moody's** or **Standard and Poor's**, for instance) that regularly assign a rating, or a grade, to all corporate bonds.

Companies strive to earn as high a bond rating as possible because the higher the rating, the lower the interest rate they will have to pay to attract buyers. For example, using the widely cited Moody's bond rating, an Aaa bond is a bond of the highest quality with the least risk of nonpayment. As of May 2006, bonds with this rating were paying interest of approximately 5.9%. A high-risk bond, on the other hand, will have a low rating, which means the company will have to offer a higher rate of interest to attract buyers. For example, as of March 2006, the bonds of financially troubled **General Motors** were rated B by Moody's, a rating indicating that the bonds were "highly speculative."

Determining a Bond's Issuance Price

When a company issues bonds, it is generally promising to make two types of payments: (1) a payment of interest of a fixed amount at equal intervals (usually semiannually but sometimes quarterly or annually) over the life of the bond and (2) a single payment—the principal, or face value, of the bond—at the maturity date. For example,

 FYI

Another type of bond that has arisen in recent years is the "Yankee bond." A Yankee bond is a bond issued by a non-U.S. company with all bond-related payments made in U.S. dollars. Non-U.S. companies sometimes choose to pay principal and interest on bonds in U.S. dollars because U.S. dollar amounts are associated with less risk of currency exchange fluctuations than are payments in less stable currencies such as the Indonesian rupiah. Lower risk means that the company can pay a lower interest rate to lenders.

bond indenture

A contract between a bond issuer and a bond purchaser that specifies the terms of a bond.

assume that Denver Company issues 10%, five-year bonds with a total face value of $800,000. Interest is to be paid semiannually. This information tells us that Denver Company agrees to pay $40,000 ($800,000 × 0.10 × ½ year) in interest every six months and also agrees to pay to the investors the principal amount of $800,000 at the end of five years. The following diagram reflects this agreement between Denver Company and the bond investors:

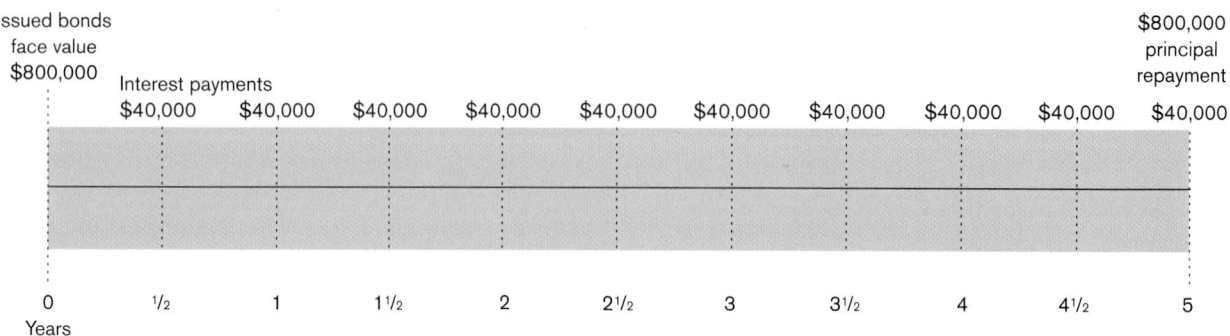

Issued bonds face value $800,000

Interest payments

$40,000 $40,000 $40,000 $40,000 $40,000 $40,000 $40,000 $40,000 $40,000 $40,000

$800,000 principal repayment

| 0 | ½ | 1 | 1½ | 2 | 2½ | 3 | 3½ | 4 | 4½ | 5 |

Years

principal (face value or maturity value)

The amount that will be paid on a bond at the maturity date.

bond maturity date

The date at which a bond principal or face amount becomes payable.

In this example, we assumed that the bonds were issued at their face value of $800,000. However, bonds are frequently issued at a price that is more or less than their face value. The actual price at which bonds are issued is affected by the interest rate investors are seeking at the time the bonds are sold in relation to the interest rate specified by the borrower in the bond indenture. How, then, is the issuance price of bonds determined?

Essentially, present value concepts are used to measure the effect of time on the value of money. The price should equal the present value of the interest payments (an annuity) plus the present value of the bond's face value at maturity. These present values are computed using the **market rate of interest** (also called the **effective rate** or **yield rate**), which is the rate investors expect to earn on their investment. It is contrasted with the **stated rate of interest**, which is the rate printed on the bond (10% in the Denver Company example).

FYI

Bonds are bought and sold on trading markets just like stocks. The New York Bond Exchange is the largest exchange of this type.

STOP & THINK

If the market rate of interest is higher than the rate of interest stated on the bonds, will the bonds sell at a price higher or lower than the face value? Think about the question this way: Is the higher rate more attractive to investors, and if it is, what would investors do as a result?

If the effective rate is equal to the stated rate, the bonds will sell at face value (that is, at $800,000). If the effective rate is higher than the stated rate, the bonds will sell at a **bond discount** (at less than the face value) because the investors desire a higher rate than the company is promising to pay. Likewise, if the effective rate is lower than the stated rate, the bonds will sell at a **bond premium** (at more than face value) because the company is promising to pay a higher rate than the market is paying at that time.

Consider the following scenario: If Company A is issuing bonds with a stated rate of 12% and the market rate for similar

market rate (effective rate or yield rate) of interest

The actual interest rate earned or paid on a bond investment.

bonds is 10%, what will happen to the price of Company A's bonds? Investors, eager to receive a 12% return, will bid the price of the bonds up until the price at which the bonds sell yields a 10% return. The amount paid for the bonds over and above the maturity value is the bond premium. If Company A were issuing bonds with a stated rate of 8%, no one would buy the bonds until the price was lowered sufficiently to allow investors to earn a return of 10%. The

stated rate of interest

The rate of interest printed on the bond.

bond discount

The difference between the face value and the sales price when bonds are sold below their face value.

bond premium

The difference between the face value and the sales price when bonds are sold above their face value.

difference between the selling price and the maturity value would be the amount of the bond discount.

We will use the Denver Company bonds example (from page 470) to explain how the price is computed in each situation.

Bonds Issued at Face Value Denver Company has agreed to issue $800,000 bonds and pay 10% interest, compounded semiannually. Assume that the effective interest rate demanded by investors for bonds of this level of risk is also 10%. Using the effective interest rate, which happens to be the same as the stated rate, the calculation to determine the price at which the bonds will be issued is shown below. (Note that because the interest is compounded semiannually, the interest rate is halved and the five-year bond life is treated as 10 six-month periods.)

The calculation shows why the bonds sell at face value. At the effective rate, the sum of the present value of the interest payments and the payment at maturity is $800,000, which is the issuance price at the stated rate. This equality of present values will occur only when the effective rate and the stated rate are the same.

1. Semiannual interest payments . . . . $ 40,000
   Present value of an annuity of
       10 payments of $1 at 5% (Table II) . . . . × 7.7217
   Present value of interest payments $308,868

2. Maturity value of bonds $800,000
   Present value of $1 received 10 periods
       in the future discounted at 5% (Table I) . . . . × 0.6139
   Present value of principal amount 491,132*

3. Issuance price of bonds (total present value) $800,000

*Difference is due to the rounding of the present value factor.

The value of the bonds can also be computed using a business calculator as follows:

Hewlett-Packard Keystrokes:
a. **CLEAR ALL**.
b. Set **P/YR** to 1.

1. 800,000   Press **FV**.
2. 40,000   Press **PMT**.
3. 10   Press **N**.
4. 5   Press **I/YR**.
5. Press **PV** for the answer of $800,000.

Bonds Issued at a Discount Denver Company will sell its bonds at less than the face value of $800,000 (at a discount) if the stated rate of interest is less than the effective rate that investors are seeking. To illustrate the issuance of bonds at a discount, assume that the effective rate is 12% compounded semiannually; the stated rate remains 10% compounded semiannually. In this case, the bonds will be issued at a price of $741,124, as shown here:

1. Semiannual interest payments	$ 40,000	
Present value of an annuity of		
10 payments of $1 at 6% (Table II)	× 7.3601	
Present value of interest payments		$294,404
2. Maturity value of bonds	$800,000	
Present value of $1 received		
10 periods in the future discounted at 6% (Table I)	× 0.5584	
Present value of principal amount		446,720
3. Issuance price of bonds (total present value)		$741,124

CAUTION

The most common mistake made in computing bond values is to use the stated rate of interest in calculating the present value of the cash flows. The stated rate of interest is used *only* to compute the amount of the semiannual interest payments. The present value computations are done using the current market rate (i.e., effective or yield rate) of interest.

Denver Company will receive less than the $800,000 face value because the stated rate of interest is lower than the effective rate. In this case, there is a discount of $58,876 ($800,000 − $741,124).

The following keystrokes are used to compute the value of the bonds using a business calculator:

Hewlett-Packard Keystrokes:
a. **CLEAR ALL**.
b. Set **P/YR** to 1.

1. 800,000   Press **FV**.
2. 40,000   Press **PMT**.
3. 10   Press **N**.
4. 6   Press **I/YR**.
5. Press **PV** for the answer of $741,119.30. This answer differs slightly from the value computed using the tables because of rounding.

Bonds Issued at a Premium   The Denver Company bonds will be issued for more than $800,000 (at a premium) when the stated interest rate is higher than the effective rate. Let us now assume that the effective rate is 8% compounded semiannually and that the stated rate is still 10% compounded semiannually. In this case, the bonds will be issued at $864,916, as shown here:

1. Interest payments	$ 40,000	
Present value of an annuity of		
10 payments of $1 at 4% (Table II)	× 8.1109	
Present value of interest payments		$324,436
2. Maturity value of bonds	$800,000	
Present value of $1 received		
10 periods in the future discounted at 4% (Table I)	× 0.6756	
Present value of principal amount		540,480
3. Issuance price of bonds (total present value)		$864,916

Denver Company will receive more than the $800,000 face value when the bonds are issued because the company has agreed to pay the investors a higher rate of interest than the market rate.

The same calculation can be done using a business calculator as follows:

Hewlett-Packard Keystrokes:
a. **CLEAR ALL.**
b. Set **P/YR** to 1.

1. 800,000   Press **FV**.
2. 40,000   Press **PMT**.
3. 10   Press **N**.
4. 4   Press **I/YR**.
5. Press **PV** for the answer of $864,887.17. This answer differs slightly from the value computed using the tables because of rounding.

In all three situations, the 10% stated rate determined the amount of each interest payment. The price of the bonds was determined by discounting the $40,000 of interest payments and the $800,000 face amount at maturity by the effective rate of interest, which may vary from day to day, depending on market conditions. In essence, the issuance price depends on four factors: (1) face value of the bonds, (2) periodic interest payments (face value × stated interest rate), (3) time period, and (4) effective interest rate. Although the bond price is the exact amount that allows investors to earn the interest rate they are seeking, it also reflects the real cost of money to the borrowing company.

Now that you know how to calculate bond values, you may feel ready to move to New York City and become a Wall Street bond trader. Not so fast. There are four steps to computing bond values, as outlined below.

1. Determine the market interest rate.
2. Compute the present value of the maturity amount (using the market interest rate as the discount rate).
3. Compute the present value of the annuity of annual interest payments (using the market interest rate as the discount rate).
4. Add the quantities computed in (2) and (3).

Three of these steps—2, 3, and 4—are very straightforward. These are the steps that you have learned in this chapter. The initial step of determining the market interest rate is where the art and analysis of bond trading are brought to bear. For example, how can you tell whether a company's riskiness requires that the market interest rate on its bonds should be 7.2% or 7.3%? This is an extremely difficult determination to make, and yet it is exactly the type of decision that bond traders must make many times each day.

Accounting for Bonds Payable Issued at Face Value

When a company issues bonds, it must account for the issuance (sale) of the bonds, for the interest payments, and for the amortization of any bond premium or discount. Then, at or before maturity, the company must account for the bond's retirement.

The accounting for these four elements depends on the issuance price of the bonds and on the date of issuance in relation to the date on which interest is paid. In the following sections, we explain the accounting for bonds when the issue price is equal to face value. The accounting for bonds issued at a premium or at a discount is discussed in the expanded material section of the chapter. For most of this discussion, we will use the following data:

Issuing company	Central Trucking Company
Accounting year	Calendar year ending December 31
Face value of bonds issued	$100,000
Stated interest rate	12%
Effective interest rate when issued	12%
Initial date of issuance	January 1, 2009
Date of maturity	January 1, 2019
Interest payment dates	January 1 and July 1

Central Trucking Company issued $100,000 bonds with a stated interest rate of 12% on January 1, 2009. The bonds were issued at face value because 12% is the effective, or market, rate of interest for similar bonds. The journal entry to record their issuance on January 1, 2009, is as follows:

Cash	100,000	
Bonds Payable		100,000
Issued $100,000, 12%, 10-year bonds at face value.		

The entry to record the first semiannual payment of interest on July 1, 2009, is:

Bond Interest Expense	6,000	
Cash		6,000
Paid semiannual interest on the $100,000, 12%,		
10-year bonds ($100,000 × 0.12 × ½ year).		

Because Central Trucking operates on a calendar-year basis, it will need to make the following adjusting entry on December 31, 2009, to account for the interest expense between July 1 and December 31, 2009:

Bond Interest Expense	6,000	
Bond Interest Payable		6,000
To recognize expense for the six months July 1 to		
December 31, 2009 ($100,000 × 0.12 × ½ year).		

At the end of the accounting period (December 31, 2009), the financial statements will report the following:

Income Statement

Bond interest expense ($6,000 × 2)	$ 12,000

Balance Sheet

Current liabilities:	
Bond interest payable	$ 6,000
Long-term liabilities:	
Bonds payable (12%, due January 1, 2019)	$100,000

On January 1, 2010, when the semiannual interest is paid, the bond interest payable account is eliminated. The January 1 entry is:

```
Bond Interest Payable ...........................................  6,000
    Cash ......................................................         6,000
        Paid semiannual bond interest.
```

The entries to record the interest expense payments during the remaining nine years will be the same as those made during 2009 and on January 1, 2010. The only other entry required in accounting for these bonds is the recording of their retirement on January 1, 2019. That entry, assuming that all interest has been accounted for, will be:

```
Bonds Payable ...........................................  100,000
    Cash ......................................................         100,000
        Retired the $100,000, 10-year, 12% bonds.
```

As the preceding entries illustrate, accounting for the issuance of bonds, the payment of the interest, and the retirement of the bonds is relatively simple when the bonds are issued at face value.

Bond Retirements before Maturity

Bond issues are, by definition, an inflexible form of long-term debt. The issuing company has a set schedule of interest payments and a specified maturity date, usually at least 5 or 10 years from the issuance date. In many cases, however, a company may want to pay off (redeem) and retire its bonds before maturity. This situation might occur when interest rates fall—a company uses the money obtained by issuing new bonds at a lower interest rate to retire the older, higher-interest bonds. As a result, the company retains the money it needs for expansion or other long-range projects but pays less interest for using that money.

As noted earlier, callable bonds are issued with an early redemption provision. Although the company usually has to pay a premium (penalty) for the privilege of redeeming (calling) the bonds, the amount of the penalty will probably be less than the amount gained by paying a lower interest rate. With bonds that are not callable, the company simply purchases the bonds in the open market, as available, at the going price.

To illustrate the retirement of bonds before maturity, assume that the Central Trucking Company bonds are now selling in the bond market at 109 and are callable at 110. The company decides to take advantage of the lower interest rate (8%) by issuing new bonds and using the proceeds to pay off the outstanding bonds. Given that the bonds were issued at their face value, the penalty (the call premium) is $10,000. The entry to record the retirement of the bonds at 110 is:

```
Bonds Payable ...........................................  100,000
Loss on Bond Retirement .......................................   10,000
    Cash ($100,000 × 1.10) ....................................         110,000
        To retire $100,000 of bonds at a call price of 110.
```

In this case, the bonds were retired at a loss of $10,000. The loss is probably tolerable because the company expects to pay significantly less interest over the life of the new bond issue than it would have had to continue to pay on the old bonds. Gains and losses on the early retirement of bonds are reported on the income statement.

> **R E M E M B E R   T H I S . . .**
>
> - Bonds are certificates of debt issued by companies or government agencies, guaranteeing a stated interest rate and repayment of the principal at a specified maturity date.
> - Bonds can be classified by their level of security (debentures versus secured bonds), by the way interest is paid (registered versus coupon bonds), and by the way they mature (term bonds, serial bonds, callable bonds, and convertible bonds).
> - The bond's face value, or principal, and future interest payments (face value × stated interest rate) are discounted by the interest rate desired by investors (the effective yield or market rate) to arrive at the issuance price of the bonds.
> - Bonds will sell at their face value if the stated interest rate is equal to the effective rate. If the effective rate is higher than the stated rate, the bonds will sell at a discount. If the effective rate is lower than the stated rate, the bonds will sell at a premium.
> - Accounting for bonds involves three steps: (1) accounting for their issuance, (2) accounting for the periodic interest payments, and (3) accounting for their retirement.
> - When bonds are retired at maturity, there is no gain or loss because the amount paid is equal to the face value of the bonds. When bonds are retired before maturity, a gain or loss often results because the price paid to retire the bonds can be different from the carrying value of the bonds.

Using Debt-Related Financial Ratios

Use debt-related financial ratios to determine the degree of a company's financial leverage and its ability to repay loans.

(5) As illustrated earlier in the chapter in Exhibit 2, an important business issue associated with long-term debt is the determination of how a company wishes to obtain the money it needs to buy necessary assets. A company's leverage is the degree to which the company has borrowed the funds needed for asset acquisitions. This section describes the financial ratios that are commonly used to evaluate the level of a company's financial leverage.

Debt Ratio and Debt-to-Equity Ratio

The **debt ratio** measures the amount of assets supplied by lenders. It is calculated as follows:

debt ratio

A measure of leverage, computed by dividing total liabilities by total assets.

$$\text{Debt ratio} = \frac{\text{Total liabilities}}{\text{Total assets}}$$

The computed value of the debt ratio indicates the percentage of a company's funding that has come through borrowing.

The debt ratio for **Disney** for 2005 is calculated as follows (the numbers are in millions):

debt-to-equity ratio

The number of dollars of borrowed funds for every dollar invested by owners; computed as total liabilities divided by total stockholders' equity.

$$\text{Debt ratio} = \frac{\$26,948}{\$53,158} = 50.7\%$$

Thus, 51% of Disney's assets are provided by lenders and 49% by stockholders and company earnings that have been retained.

The **debt-to-equity ratio** also measures the balance of funds being provided by creditors and stockholders. This ratio is calculated by dividing total liabilities by total stockholders' equity. The higher the debt-to-equity ratio, the more debt the company has. The debt-to-equity ratio for Disney is calculated as follows:

$$\text{Debt-to-equity ratio} = \frac{\text{Total liabilities}}{\text{Total stockholders' equity}}$$

$$\text{Debt-to-equity ratio} = \frac{\$26,948}{\$26,210} = 1.03$$

In this case, the debt-to-equity ratio indicates that Disney's debt is about 3% higher than its equity. Note that the debt ratio and the debt-to-equity ratio both indicate the same thing—that Disney has acquired just a little bit more of its total financing from borrowing than from stockholders and retained earnings. It doesn't matter which of these two ratios you use to measure a company's leverage; the important thing is that you are consistent and that any ratios you use for comparison have been computed using the same formula.

Times Interest Earned Ratio

times interest earned

A measure of a borrower's ability to make required interest payments; computed as income before interest and taxes divided by annual interest expense.

Lenders like to have an indication of the borrowing company's ability to meet the required interest payments. **Times interest earned** is the ratio of the income that is available for interest payments to the annual interest expense. Times interest earned is computed as follows:

$$\text{Times interest earned} = \frac{\text{Income before interest and taxes (operating profit)}}{\text{Annual interest expense}}$$

To illustrate the computation of this ratio, we will return to Disney. For year-end 2005, Disney's interest expense was $597 million, and its operating profit was $4,584 million. This results in times interest earned of 7.7 times, computed as follows:

$$\text{Times interest earned} = \frac{\$4,584}{\$597} = 7.7 \text{ times}$$

Disney's times interest earned value of 7.7 times means that its operations in 2005 generated enough profit to be able to pay Disney's interest expense for the year 7.7 times. This suggests that Disney's creditors have a substantial cushion before they need to be concerned about Disney's ability to meet its required periodic interest payments.

REMEMBER THIS...

- Both the debt ratio and the debt-to-equity ratio measure the level of a company's leverage.
  - Debt ratio = Total liabilities divided by total assets
  - Debt-to-equity ratio = Total liabilities divided by total stockholders' equity
- The times interest earned ratio (operating income divided by interest expense) measures how much cushion a company has in terms of being able to make its periodic interest payments.

EXPANDED
material

The present value techniques discussed in this chapter are useful in determining the value of obligations due at some future time. The computations and accounting are similar for interest-bearing notes, mortgages, capital leases, and bonds. However, there are certain complexities associated with these liabilities that deserve additional attention. In this section of the chapter, we discuss the procedures associated with the amortization of a bond discount or premium.

Bonds Issued at a Discount or at a Premium

Amortize bond discounts and bond premiums using either the straight-line method or the effective-interest method.

⑥ As we have explained, bonds may be issued at a discount or a premium because their stated interest rate may be (and often is) lower or higher than the effective rate. The two rates often differ because economic conditions in the marketplace change between the date the stated interest is set and the date the bonds are actually sold. Various factors determine this second date—for example, the time it takes to print the bonds and the investment banker's decision regarding the best time to offer the bonds. Because the cost to the company for the use of the bond money is really the effective interest rate rather than the stated rate, the discount or premium must be written off (amortized) over the period the bonds are outstanding, and the amortization is treated as an adjustment to bond interest expense.

straight-line amortization

A method of systematically writing off a bond discount or premium in equal amounts each period until maturity.

There are two methods of amortizing bond discounts and bond premiums: straight-line amortization and effective-interest amortization. With **straight-line amortization**, a company writes off the same amount of discount or premium each period the bonds are held. For example, with a $4,000 discount on a 10-year bond, $400 is amortized each year. **Effective-interest amortization** takes the time value of money into consideration. The amount of discount or premium amortized is the difference between the interest actually incurred (based on the effective rate) and the interest actually paid (based on the stated rate). The straight-line amortization method will be used to explain the accounting for the amortization of discounts and premiums; then the effective-interest method will be explained and illustrated.

effective-interest amortization

A method of systematically writing off a bond premium or discount that takes into consideration the time value of money and results in an equal interest rate being used for amortization for each period.

Accounting for Bonds Issued at a Discount

When bonds are issued at a discount, a contra-liability account is used to keep a separate record of the discounted amount. To illustrate, we will assume that the $100,000, 10-year, 12% bonds issued by Central Trucking on January 1, 2009, sold for $98,000. The entry to record the issuance of the bonds is:

Cash	98,000	
Discount on Bonds	2,000	
Bonds Payable		100,000
Issued $100,000, 12%, 10-year bonds at 98.		

The discount on bonds account represents the difference between the face value of the bonds and the issuance price. This discount is accounted for as additional bond interest expense over the life of the bonds. In other words, if the company receives only $98,000 when the bonds are issued and is required to pay $100,000 at maturity, the $2,000 difference is additional interest. The following analysis shows that total interest on the bonds is $122,000, comprised of the periodic interest payments ($120,000) plus the $2,000 discount.

Amount to be paid to bondholders:	
Interest paid each year for 10 years ($100,000 × 0.12 × 10)	$120,000
Face value to be paid at maturity	100,000
Total amount to be paid to bondholders	$220,000
Proceeds received from sale of bonds ($100,000 × 0.98)	98,000
Total interest expense	$122,000
Average annual interest expense ($122,000/10 years)	$ 12,200

Although the $2,000 of additional interest arising from the discount will not be paid until the bonds mature, interest accrues, or accumulates, over time. Thus, each year that the bonds are outstanding, Central Trucking will record bond interest expense for the amount paid at the stated rate ($100,000 × 0.12 = $12,000) and will also recognize a portion of the discount as bond interest expense. In recording the additional bond interest expense, the contra account Discount on Bonds is amortized or written off over the life of the bonds. Using straight-line amortization, an even amount is amortized each period. In the Central Trucking Company example, the semiannual amortization would be $100 ($2,000 discount/10 years × ½). Bond amortization is recorded when interest payments are made, and the entry on July 1, 2009, is:

Bond Interest Expense	6,100	
Discount on Bonds		100
Cash		6,000

Paid semiannual interest on the $100,000, 12%, 10-year bonds ($100,000 × 0.12 × ½ year) and amortized the bond discount ($2,000/10 years × ½ year).

As illustrated, amortization of a discount increases bond interest expense. In this case, the bond interest expense is $6,100, or the sum of the semiannual interest payment and the semiannual amortization of the bond discount. Over the 10-year life of the bonds, the bond interest expense will be increased by $2,000 (20 periods × $100), the amount of the discount. Thus, these bonds pay an effective interest rate of approximately 12.45%[3] per year ($12,200 interest/$98,000 received on the bonds).

The adjusting entry to record the bond interest expense on December 31, 2009, is:

Bond Interest Expense	6,100	
Discount on Bonds		100
Bond Interest Payable		6,000

To recognize bond interest expense for the six months July 1 to December 31, 2009.

The financial statements prepared at December 31, 2009, would report the following:

Income Statement

Bond interest expense ($6,100 × 2)	$12,200

Balance Sheet

Current liabilities:		
Bond interest payable		$ 6,000
Long-term liabilities:		
Bonds payable (12%, due January 1, 2019)	$100,000	
Less unamortized discount ($2,000 – $200)	1,800	$98,200

The entries to account for the bond interest expense and bond discount amortization during the remaining nine years will be the same as those illustrated. And because the bond discount will be completely amortized at the end of the 10 years, the entry to record

[3] Because straight-line amortization was used, this effective rate of 12.45% is only an approximation that will change slightly each period. An accurate effective rate can be calculated only if the effective-interest method of amortization is used.

the retirement of the bonds will be the same as that for bonds issued at face value. That entry is:

Bonds Payable	100,000	
Cash		100,000
Retired the $100,000, 12%, 10-year bonds.		

Accounting for Bonds Issued at a Premium

Like discounts, premiums must be amortized over the life of the bonds. To illustrate the accounting for bonds sold at a premium, we will assume that Central Trucking was able to sell its $100,000, 12%, 10-year bonds at 103 (that is, at 103% of face value). The entry to record the issuance of these bonds on January 1, 2009, is:

Cash	103,000	
Premium on Bonds		3,000
Bonds Payable		100,000
Sold $100,000, 12%, 10-year bonds at 103.		

Premium on Bonds is added to Bonds Payable on the balance sheet and, like Discount on Bonds, is amortized using either the straight-line method or the effective-interest method. Thus, if Central Trucking uses the straight-line method, the annual amortization of the premium will be $300 ($3,000/10 years), or $150 every six months. The entry to record the first semiannual interest payment and the premium amortization of July 1, 2009, is:

Bond Interest Expense	5,850	
Premium on Bonds	150	
Cash		6,000
Paid semiannual interest on the $100,000, 12%, 10-year bonds		
($100,000 × 0.12 × ½ year) and amortized the bond premium		
($3,000/10 years × ½).		

The amortization of a premium on bonds reduces the actual bond interest expense. The following analysis shows why bond interest expense is reduced when bonds are sold at a premium:

Amount to be paid to bondholders:	
[($12,000 interest × 10 years) + $100,000 face value]	$220,000
Proceeds received from sale of bonds	103,000
Total interest to be paid	$117,000
Average annual interest expense ($117,000/10 years)	$ 11,700

CAUTION

If bonds issued at a premium or discount are retired before maturity, remember that the bond payable and any associated premium or discount would have to be eliminated from the books.

In this case, the annual payments of $12,000 include interest of $11,700 and $300, which represents a partial repayment (one-tenth) of the bond premium. Thus, the effective interest rate is approximately 11.36% ($11,700/$103,000), which is less than the stated rate of 12%.

The adjusting entry to record the accrual of the interest expense on December 31, 2009, is:

Bond Interest Expense	5,850	
Premium on Bonds	150	
Bond Interest Payable		6,000
To recognize bond interest expense for the six months		
July 1 to December 31, 2009.		

The financial statements prepared at December 31, 2009, would report the following:

Income Statement

Bond interest expense ($5,850 × 2)	$ 11,700

Balance Sheet

Current liabilities:		
Bond interest payable		$ 6,000
Long-term liabilities:		
Bonds payable (12%, due January 1, 2019)	$100,000	
Plus unamortized premium ($3,000 − $300)	2,700	$102,700

Effective-Interest Amortization

Companies can often justify use of the straight-line method of amortizing bond premiums and discounts on the grounds that its results are not significantly different from those of the theoretically more accurate effective-interest method. Nevertheless, because the effective-interest method considers the time value of money, it is required by generally accepted accounting principles if it leads to results that differ significantly from those obtained by the straight-line method.

The effective-interest method amortizes a varying amount each period, which is the difference between the interest actually incurred and the cash actually paid. The amount actually incurred is the changing **bond carrying value** (the face value of the bond minus the unamortized discount or plus the unamortized premium) multiplied by a constant rate, the effective-interest rate.

bond carrying value

The face value of bonds minus the unamortized discount or plus the unamortized premium.

To illustrate the effective-interest method, let's continue with the Central Trucking Company example we have used previously. We will assume that the Central Trucking Company $100,000, 12%, 10-year bonds were issued on January 1, 2009, for $112,463. The bonds pay interest semiannually on January 1 and July 1, so their effective interest rate is approximately 10%[4] a year, or 5% every six months. Because the actual bond interest expense for each interest period is equal to the effective rate of 5% multiplied by the bond carrying value, the amortization (rounded to the nearest $1) for the 10 years is calculated as shown in the following table.

F Y I

Note that the table on the next page looks a lot like the mortgage amortization schedule on page 464 and the schedule of computer lease payments on page 466. The reason is that these other schedules also use the effective-interest amortization method.

---

[4] The 10% rate is the rate that will discount the face value of the bonds and the semiannual interest payments to a present value that equals the issuance price of the bonds, computed as follows:

Present value of $100,000 at 5% for 20 periods	$100,000 × 0.3769 = $ 37,690
Present value of $6,000 at 5% for 20 payments	$ 6,000 × 12.4622 = 74,773
Total present value = issuance price of the bonds	$112,463

Period	1 Cash Paid for Interest	2 Semiannual Interest Expense (0.05 × Bond Carrying Value)	3 Premium Amortization (1) − (2)	4 Carrying Value
Issuance date				$112,463
Year 1, first six months	$6,000	$5,623	$377	112,086
Year 1, second six months	6,000	5,604	396	111,690
Year 2, first six months	6,000	5,585	415	111,275
Year 2, second six months	6,000	5,564	436	110,839
Year 3, first six months	6,000	5,542	458	110,381
Year 3, second six months	6,000	5,519	481	109,900
Year 4, first six months	6,000	5,495	505	109,395
Year 4, second six months	6,000	5,470	530	108,865
Year 5, first six months	6,000	5,443	557	108,308
Year 5, second six months	6,000	5,415	585	107,723
Year 6, first six months	6,000	5,386	614	107,109
Year 6, second six months	6,000	5,355	645	106,464
Year 7, first six months	6,000	5,323	677	105,787
Year 7, second six months	6,000	5,289	711	105,076
Year 8, first six months	6,000	5,254	746	104,330
Year 8, second six months	6,000	5,217	783	103,547
Year 9, first six months	6,000	5,177	823	102,724
Year 9, second six months	6,000	5,136	864	101,860
Year 10, first six months	6,000	5,093	907	100,953
Year 10, second six months	6,000	5,047	953	100,000

In this computation, the $6,000 in column (1) is the actual cash paid each six months. Column (2) shows the interest expense for each six months, which is the amount that will be reported on the income statement. Column (3), which is the difference between columns (1) and (2), represents the amortization of the premium. Column (4) shows the carrying, or book, value of the bonds (that is, the total of the bonds payable and the unamortized bond premium), which is the amount that will be reported on the balance sheet each period. Using the effective-interest method, the bond carrying value is always equal to the present value of the bond obligation. As the carrying value decreases, while the effective rate of interest remains constant, the interest expense also decreases from one period to the next, as illustrated in column (2) of the amortization schedule.

To help you translate this table into the entries for the interest payments and premium amortization at the end of each six-month period, we have provided the semiannual journal entries for year 3.

Year 3, End of First Six Months

Bond Interest Expense	5,542	
Bond Premium	458	
Cash		6,000

To record effective-interest expense on Central Trucking Company bonds for the first six months of year 3.

Year 3, End of Second Six Months

Bond Interest Expense	5,519	
Bond Premium	481	
Bond Interest Payable		6,000

To record effective-interest expense on Central Trucking Company bonds for the second six months of year 3.

Because the straight-line method would show a constant amortization ($12,463/20 = $623.15 per six-month period) on a decreasing bond balance, the straight-line interest rate cannot be constant. When the straight-line results differ significantly from the effective-interest results, generally accepted accounting principles require use of the effective-interest method.

The effective-interest method of amortizing a bond discount is essentially the same as amortizing a bond premium. The main difference is that the bond carrying value is increasing instead of decreasing.

REMEMBER THIS...

- When bonds are issued at a premium or a discount, the premium or discount must be amortized over the life of the bond.

- When a bond premium or discount exists, bond interest expense recognized on the income statement is not equal to the amount of cash paid for interest.

- Two methods of amortization are available—the straight-line method and the effective-interest method.

- The straight-line method amortizes an equal amount of premium or discount every period.

- When the effective-interest method is used, the amount of discount or premium amortized each period is equal to the market rate of interest multiplied by the bond's carrying value.

| TABLE I | The Present Value of $1 Due in n Periods* |

Period	1%	2%	3%	4%	5%	6%	7%	8%	9%	10%	12%	14%	15%	16%	18%	20%
1	.9901	.9804	.9709	.9615	.9524	.9434	.9346	.9259	.9174	.9091	.8929	.8772	.8696	.8621	.8475	.8333
2	.9803	.9612	.9426	.9246	.9070	.8900	.8734	.8573	.8417	.8264	.7972	.7695	.7561	.7432	.7182	.6944
3	.9706	.9423	.9151	.8890	.8638	.8396	.8163	.7938	.7722	.7513	.7118	.6750	.6575	.6407	.6086	.5787
4	.9610	.9238	.8885	.8548	.8227	.7921	.7629	.7350	.7084	.6830	.6355	.5921	.5718	.5523	.5158	.4823
5	.9515	.9057	.8626	.8219	.7835	.7473	.7130	.6806	.6499	.6209	.5674	.5194	.4972	.4761	.4371	.4019
6	.9420	.8880	.8375	.7903	.7462	.7050	.6663	.6302	.5963	.5645	.5066	.4556	.4323	.4104	.3704	.3349
7	.9327	.8706	.8131	.7599	.7107	.6651	.6227	.5835	.5470	.5132	.4523	.3996	.3759	.3538	.3139	.2791
8	.9235	.8535	.7894	.7307	.6768	.6274	.5820	.5403	.5019	.4665	.4039	.3506	.3269	.3050	.2660	.2326
9	.9143	.8368	.7664	.7026	.6446	.5919	.5439	.5002	.4604	.4241	.3606	.3075	.2843	.2630	.2255	.1938
10	.9053	.8203	.7441	.6756	.6139	.5584	.5083	.4632	.4224	.3855	.3220	.2697	.2472	.2267	.1911	.1615
11	.8963	.8043	.7224	.6496	.5847	.5268	.4751	.4289	.3875	.3503	.2875	.2366	.2149	.1954	.1619	.1346
12	.8874	.7885	.7014	.6246	.5568	.4970	.4440	.3971	.3555	.3186	.2567	.2076	.1869	.1685	.1372	.1122
13	.8787	.7730	.6810	.6006	.5303	.4688	.4150	.3677	.3262	.2897	.2292	.1821	.1625	.1452	.1163	.0935
14	.8700	.7579	.6611	.5775	.5051	.4423	.3878	.3405	.2992	.2633	.2046	.1597	.1413	.1252	.0985	.0779
15	.8613	.7430	.6419	.5553	.4810	.4173	.3624	.3152	.2745	.2394	.1827	.1401	.1229	.1079	.0835	.0649
16	.8528	.7284	.6232	.5339	.4581	.3936	.3387	.2919	.2519	.2176	.1631	.1229	.1069	.0930	.0708	.0541
17	.8444	.7142	.6050	.5134	.4363	.3714	.3166	.2703	.2311	.1978	.1456	.1078	.0929	.0802	.0600	.0451
18	.8360	.7002	.5874	.4936	.4155	.3503	.2959	.2502	.2120	.1799	.1300	.0946	.0808	.0691	.0508	.0376
19	.8277	.6864	.5703	.4746	.3957	.3305	.2765	.2317	.1945	.1635	.1161	.0829	.0703	.0596	.0431	.0313
20	.8195	.6730	.5537	.4564	.3769	.3118	.2584	.2145	.1784	.1486	.1037	.0728	.0611	.0514	.0365	.0261
25	.7798	.6095	.4776	.3751	.2953	.2330	.1842	.1460	.1160	.0923	.0588	.0378	.0304	.0245	.0160	.0105
30	.7419	.5521	.4120	.3083	.2314	.1741	.1314	.0994	.0754	.0573	.0334	.0196	.0151	.0116	.0070	.0042
40	.6717	.4529	.3066	.2083	.1420	.0972	.0668	.0460	.0318	.0221	.0107	.0053	.0037	.0026	.0013	.0007
50	.6080	.3715	.2281	.1407	.0872	.0543	.0339	.0213	.0134	.0085	.0035	.0014	.0009	.0006	.0003	.0001
60	.5504	.3048	.1697	.0951	.0535	.0303	.0173	.0099	.0057	.0033	.0011	.0004	.0002	.0001	†	†

*The formula used to derive the values in this table was $PV = F \dfrac{1}{(1 + i)^n}$ where PV = present value, F = future amount to be discounted, i = interest rate, and n = number of periods.

†The value of 0 to four decimal places.

TABLE II **The Present Value of an Annuity of $1 per Number of Payments***

Number of Payments	1%	2%	3%	4%	5%	6%	7%	8%	9%	10%	12%	14%	15%	16%	18%	20%
1	0.9901	0.9804	0.9709	0.9615	0.9524	0.9434	0.9346	0.9259	0.9174	0.9091	0.8929	0.8772	0.8596	0.8621	0.8475	0.8333
2	1.9704	1.9416	1.9135	1.8861	1.8594	1.8334	1.8080	1.7833	1.7591	1.7355	1.6901	1.6467	1.6257	1.6052	1.5656	1.5278
3	2.9410	2.8839	2.8286	2.7751	2.7232	2.6730	2.6243	2.5771	2.5313	2.4869	2.4018	2.3216	2.2832	2.2459	2.1743	2.1065
4	3.9820	3.8077	3.7171	3.6299	3.5460	3.4651	3.3872	3.3121	3.2397	3.1699	3.0373	2.9137	2.8550	2.7982	2.6901	2.5887
5	4.8884	4.7135	4.5797	4.4518	4.3295	4.2124	4.1002	3.9927	3.8897	3.7908	3.6048	3.4331	3.3522	3.2743	3.1272	2.9906
6	5.7985	5.6014	5.4172	5.2421	5.0757	4.9173	4.7665	4.6229	4.4859	4.3553	4.1114	3.8887	3.7845	3.6847	3.4976	3.3255
7	6.7282	6.4720	6.2303	6.0021	5.7864	5.5824	5.3893	5.2064	5.0330	4.8684	4.5638	4.2883	4.1604	4.0386	3.8115	3.6046
8	7.6517	7.3255	7.0197	6.7327	6.4632	6.2098	5.9713	5.7466	5.5348	5.3349	4.9676	4.6389	4.4873	4.3436	4.0776	3.8372
9	8.5660	8.1622	7.7861	7.4353	7.1078	6.8017	6.5152	6.2469	5.9952	5.7590	5.3282	4.9464	4.7716	4.6065	4.3030	4.0310
10	9.4713	8.9826	8.5302	8.1109	7.7217	7.3601	7.0236	6.7101	6.4177	6.1446	5.6502	5.2161	5.0188	4.8332	4.4941	4.1925
11	10.3676	9.7868	9.2526	8.7605	8.3064	7.8869	7.4987	7.1390	6.8052	6.4951	5.9377	5.4527	5.2337	5.0286	4.6560	4.3271
12	11.2551	10.5733	9.9540	9.3851	8.8633	8.3838	7.9427	7.5361	7.1607	6.8137	6.1944	5.6603	5.4206	5.1971	4.7932	4.4392
13	12.1337	11.3484	10.6350	9.9856	9.3936	8.8527	8.3577	7.9038	7.4869	7.1034	6.4235	5.8424	5.5831	5.3423	4.9095	4.5327
14	13.0037	12.1062	11.2961	10.5631	9.8986	9.2950	8.7455	8.2442	7.7862	7.3667	6.6282	6.0021	5.7245	5.4675	5.0081	4.6106
15	13.8651	12.8493	11.9379	11.1184	10.3797	9.7122	9.1079	8.5595	8.0607	7.6061	6.8109	6.1422	5.8474	5.5755	5.0916	4.6755
16	14.7179	13.5777	12.5611	11.6523	10.8378	10.1059	9.4466	8.8514	8.3126	7.8237	6.9740	6.2651	5.9542	5.6685	5.1624	4.7296
17	15.5623	14.2919	13.1661	12.1657	11.2741	10.4773	9.7632	9.1216	8.5436	8.0216	7.1196	6.3729	6.0472	5.7487	5.2223	4.7746
18	16.3983	14.9920	13.7535	12.6593	11.6896	10.8276	10.0591	9.3719	8.7556	8.2014	7.2497	6.4674	6.1280	5.8178	5.2732	4.8122
19	17.2260	15.6785	14.3238	13.1339	12.0853	11.1581	10.3356	9.6036	8.9501	8.3649	7.3658	6.5504	6.1982	5.8775	5.3162	4.8435
20	18.0456	16.3514	14.8775	13.5903	12.4622	11.4699	10.5940	9.8181	9.1285	8.5136	7.4694	6.6231	6.2593	5.9288	5.3527	4.8696
25	22.0232	19.5235	17.4131	15.6221	14.0939	12.7834	11.6536	10.6748	9.8226	9.0770	7.8431	6.8729	6.4641	6.0971	5.4669	4.9476
30	25.8077	22.3965	19.6004	17.2920	15.3725	13.7648	12.4090	11.2578	10.2737	9.4269	8.0552	7.0027	6.5660	6.1772	5.5168	4.9789
40	32.8347	27.3555	23.1148	19.7928	17.1591	15.0463	13.3317	11.9246	10.7574	9.7791	8.2438	7.1050	6.6418	6.2335	5.5482	4.9966
50	39.1961	31.4236	25.7298	21.4822	18.2559	15.7619	13.8007	12.2335	10.9617	9.9148	8.3045	7.1327	6.6605	6.2463	5.5641	4.9995
60	44.9550	34.7609	27.6756	22.6235	18.9293	16.1614	14.0392	12.3766	11.0480	9.9672	8.3240	7.1401	6.6651	6.2482	5.5553	4.9999

*The formula used to derive the values in this table was $PV = F\left(\dfrac{1 - \dfrac{1}{(1+i)^n}}{i}\right)$ where PV = present value, F = periodic payment to be discounted, i = interest rate, and n = number of payments.

TABLE III	Amount of $1 Due in *n* Periods													
Period	1%	2%	3%	4%	5%	6%	7%	8%	9%	10%	12%	14%	15%	16%	18%	20%
1	1.0100	1.0200	1.0300	1.0400	1.0500	1.0600	1.0700	1.0800	1.0900	1.1000	1.1200	1.1400	1.1500	1.1600	1.1800	1.2000
2	1.0201	1.0404	1.0609	1.0816	1.1025	1.1236	1.1449	1.1664	1.1881	1.2100	1.2544	1.2996	1.3225	1.3456	1.3924	1.4400
3	1.0303	1.0612	1.0927	1.1249	1.1576	1.1910	1.2250	1.2597	1.2950	1.3310	1.4049	1.4815	1.5209	1.5609	1.6430	1.7280
4	1.0406	1.0824	1.1255	1.1699	1.2155	1.2625	1.3108	1.3605	1.4116	1.4641	1.5735	1.6890	1.7490	1.8106	1.9388	2.0736
5	1.0510	1.1041	1.1593	1.2167	1.2763	1.3382	1.4026	1.4693	1.5386	1.6105	1.7623	1.9254	2.0114	2.1003	2.2878	2.4883
6	1.0615	1.1262	1.1941	1.2653	1.3401	1.4185	1.5007	1.5869	1.6771	1.7716	1.9738	2.1950	2.3131	2.4364	2.6996	2.9860
7	1.0721	1.1487	1.2299	1.3159	1.4071	1.5036	1.6058	1.7138	1.8280	1.9487	2.2107	2.5023	2.6600	2.8262	3.1855	3.5832
8	1.0829	1.1717	1.2668	1.3686	1.4775	1.5938	1.7182	1.8509	1.9926	2.1436	2.4760	2.8526	3.0590	3.2784	3.7589	4.2998
9	1.0937	1.1951	1.3048	1.4233	1.5513	1.6895	1.8385	1.9990	2.1719	2.3579	2.7731	3.2519	3.5179	3.8030	4.4355	5.1598
10	1.1046	1.2190	1.3439	1.4802	1.6289	1.7908	1.9672	2.1589	2.3674	2.5937	3.1058	3.7072	4.0456	4.4114	5.2338	6.1917
11	1.1157	1.2434	1.3842	1.5395	1.7103	1.8983	2.1049	2.3316	2.5804	2.8531	3.4785	4.2262	4.6524	5.1173	6.1759	7.4031
12	1.1268	1.2682	1.4258	1.6010	1.7959	2.0122	2.2522	2.5182	2.8127	3.1384	3.8960	4.8179	5.3502	5.9360	7.2876	8.9161
13	1.1381	1.2936	1.4685	1.6651	1.8856	2.1329	2.4098	2.7196	3.0658	3.4523	4.3635	5.4924	6.1528	6.8858	8.5994	10.699
14	1.1495	1.3195	1.5126	1.7317	1.9799	2.2609	2.5785	2.9372	3.3417	3.7975	4.8871	6.2613	7.0757	7.9875	10.147	12.839
15	1.1610	1.3459	1.5580	1.8009	2.0789	2.3966	2.7590	3.1722	3.6425	4.1772	5.4736	7.1379	8.1371	9.2655	11.973	15.407
16	1.1726	1.3728	1.6047	1.8730	2.1829	2.5404	2.9522	3.4259	3.9703	4.5950	6.1304	8.1372	9.3576	10.748	14.129	18.488
17	1.1843	1.4002	1.6528	1.9479	2.2920	2.6928	3.1588	3.7000	4.3276	5.0545	6.8660	9.2765	10.761	12.467	16.672	22.186
18	1.1961	1.4282	1.7024	2.0258	2.4066	2.8543	3.3799	3.9960	4.7171	5.5599	7.6900	10.575	12.375	14.462	19.673	26.623
19	1.2081	1.4568	1.7535	2.1068	2.5270	3.0256	3.6165	4.3157	5.1417	6.1159	8.6128	12.055	14.231	16.776	23.214	31.948
20	1.2202	1.4859	1.8061	2.1911	2.6533	3.2071	3.8697	4.6610	5.6044	6.7275	9.6463	13.743	16.366	19.460	27.393	38.337
30	1.3478	1.8114	2.4273	3.2434	4.3219	5.7435	7.6123	10.062	13.267	17.449	29.959	50.950	66.211	85.849	143.37	237.37
40	1.4889	2.2080	3.2620	4.8010	7.0400	10.285	14.974	21.724	31.409	45.259	93.050	188.88	267.86	378.72	750.37	1469.7
50	1.6446	2.6916	4.3839	7.1067	11.467	18.420	29.457	46.901	74.357	117.39	289.00	700.23	1083.6	1670.7	3927.3	9100.4
60	1.8167	3.2810	5.8916	10.519	18.679	32.987	57.946	101.25	176.03	304.48	897.59	2595.9	4383.9	7370.1	20555.	56347.

TABLE IV — Amount of an Annuity of $1 per Number of Payments

Number of Payments	1%	2%	3%	4%	5%	6%	7%	8%	9%	10%	12%	14%	15%	16%	18%	20%
1	1.0000	1.0000	1.0000	1.0000	1.0000	1.0000	1.0000	1.0000	1.0000	1.0000	1.0000	1.0000	1.0000	1.0000	1.0000	1.0000
2	2.0100	2.0200	2.0300	2.0400	2.0500	2.0600	2.0700	2.0800	2.0900	2.1000	2.1200	2.1400	2.1500	2.1600	2.1800	2.2000
3	3.0301	3.0604	3.0909	3.1216	3.1525	3.1836	3.2149	3.2464	3.2781	3.3100	3.3744	3.4396	3.4725	3.5056	3.5724	3.6400
4	4.0604	4.1216	4.1836	4.2465	4.3101	4.3746	4.4399	4.5061	4.5731	4.6410	4.7793	4.9211	4.9934	5.0665	5.2154	5.3680
5	5.1010	5.2040	5.3091	5.4163	5.5256	5.6371	5.7507	5.8666	5.9847	6.1051	6.3528	6.6101	6.7424	6.8771	7.1542	7.4416
6	6.1520	6.3081	6.4684	6.6330	6.8019	6.9753	7.1533	7.3359	7.5233	7.7156	8.1152	8.5355	8.7537	8.9775	9.4420	9.9299
7	7.2135	7.4343	7.6625	7.8983	8.1420	8.3938	8.6540	8.9228	9.2004	9.4872	10.8090	10.7305	11.0668	11.4139	12.1415	12.9159
8	8.2857	8.5830	8.8923	9.2142	9.5491	9.8975	10.2598	10.6366	11.0285	11.4359	12.2997	13.2328	13.7268	14.2401	15.3270	16.4991
9	9.3685	9.7546	10.1591	10.5828	11.0266	11.4913	11.9780	12.4876	13.0210	13.5795	14.7757	16.0853	16.7858	17.5185	19.0859	20.7989
10	10.4622	10.9497	11.4639	12.0061	12.5779	13.1808	13.8164	14.4866	15.1929	15.9374	17.5487	19.3373	20.3037	21.3215	23.5213	25.9587
11	11.5668	12.1687	12.8078	13.4864	14.2068	14.9716	15.7836	16.6455	17.5603	18.5312	20.6546	23.0445	24.3493	25.7329	28.7551	32.1504
12	12.6825	13.4121	14.1920	15.0258	15.9171	16.8699	17.8885	18.9771	20.1407	21.2843	24.1331	27.2707	29.0017	30.8502	34.9311	39.5805
13	13.8093	14.6803	15.6178	16.6268	17.7130	18.8821	20.1406	21.4953	22.9534	24.5227	28.0291	32.0887	34.3519	36.7862	42.2187	48.4966
14	14.9474	15.9739	17.0863	18.2919	19.5986	21.0151	22.5505	24.2149	26.0192	27.9750	32.3926	37.5811	40.5047	43.6720	50.8180	59.1959
15	16.0969	17.2934	18.5989	20.0236	21.5786	23.2760	25.1290	27.1521	29.3609	31.7725	37.2797	43.8424	47.5804	51.6595	60.9653	72.0351
16	17.2579	18.6393	20.1569	21.8248	23.6575	25.6725	27.8881	30.3243	33.0034	35.9497	42.7535	50.9804	55.7178	60.9250	72.9390	87.4421
17	18.4304	20.0121	21.7616	23.6975	25.8404	28.2129	30.8402	33.7502	36.9737	40.5447	48.8837	59.1176	65.0751	71.6730	87.0680	105.9306
18	19.6147	21.4123	23.4144	25.6454	28.1324	30.9057	33.9990	37.4502	41.3013	45.5992	55.7497	68.3941	75.8364	84.1407	103.7403	128.1167
19	20.8190	22.8406	25.1169	27.6712	30.5390	33.7600	37.3790	41.4463	46.0185	51.1591	63.4397	78.9692	88.2118	98.6032	123.4135	154.7400
20	22.0190	24.2974	26.8704	29.7781	33.0660	36.7856	40.9955	45.7620	51.1601	57.2750	72.0524	91.0249	102.4436	115.3797	146.6280	186.6880
30	34.7849	40.5681	47.5754	56.0849	66.4388	79.0582	94.4608	113.2832	136.3075	164.4940	241.3327	356.7868	434.7451	530.3117	790.9480	1181.8816
40	48.8864	60.4020	75.4013	95.0255	120.7998	154.7620	199.6351	259.0565	337.8824	442.5926	767.0914	1342.0251	1779.0903	2360.7572	4163.2130	7343.8578
50	64.4632	84.5794	112.7969	152.6671	209.3480	290.3359	406.5289	573.7702	815.0836	1163.9085	2400.0182	4994.5213	7217.7163	10435.6488	21813.0937	45497.1908
60	81.6697	114.0515	163.0534	237.9907	353.5837	533.1282	813.5204	1253.2133	1944.7921	3034.8164	7471.6411	18535.1333	29219.9916	46057.5085	114189.6665	281732.5718

REVIEW OF LEARNING OBJECTIVES

 Use present value concepts to measure long-term liabilities.

- Long-term liabilities are recorded at their present value.
- Terms associated with the time value of money include the following:
  - Present value—amount of money right now to which a future lump sum or annuity is economically equivalent.
  - Future value—amount to which a lump sum or annuity will accumulate in the future.
  - Annuity—a series of equal payments to be made or received in the future.
  - Lump sum—one payment to be made or received in the future.
  - Compounding—adding interest to the principal amount so that subsequent interest is computed on the original principal plus accumulated interest.

② **Account for long-term liabilities, including notes payable and mortgages payable.**

- Interest-bearing notes are recorded on the books of the issuer at face value.
  - Interest expense is incurred based on the rate of interest, the carrying value of the note, and the passage of time.
  - Interest Expense is debited for the amount of interest incurred and Cash or Interest Payable is credited.
- Mortgage liabilities are paid by a series of regular payments that include interest expense and a reduction of the principal of the mortgage note.
  - The balance sheet liability at any given time is the present value of the remaining mortgage payments.

③ **Account for capital lease obligations and understand the significance of operating leases being excluded from the balance sheet.**

- A lease is a contract whereby the lessee makes periodic payments to the lessor for the use of an asset.

Operating Lease	Capital Lease
Accounted for as a rental agreement	Accounted for as a debt-financed purchase of an asset.
Leased asset: Not on the balance sheet	Leased asset: Initially recorded at the present value of the future lease payments, subsequently depreciated.
Lease liability: Not on the balance sheet	Lease liability: Initially recorded at the present value of the future lease payments, subsequently recorded as being repaid, with interest.

 Account for bonds, including the original issuance, the payment of interest, and the retirement of bonds.

Accounting for bond issuance	<ul><li>If bonds are sold at face value, Cash is debited and Bonds Payable is credited.</li><li>If bonds are sold at a discount, the discount is debited and subtracted from Bonds Payable on the balance sheet.</li><li>If bonds are sold at a premium, the premium is credited and added to Bonds Payable on the balance sheet.</li></ul>

(continued)

Accounting for bond interest payments	• When interest is paid, Bond Interest Expense is debited and Cash is credited. • An adjustment is made to bond interest expense if the bond is sold at a premium or discount.
Accounting for bond retirement	• At the date a bond matures, the borrowing company pays the face value to the investors, and the bonds are canceled. • If the bonds are retired before maturity, a gain or loss will be recognized when the carrying value of the bonds differs from the amount paid to retire the bonds.

(5) Use debt-related financial ratios to determine the degree of a company's financial leverage and its ability to repay loans.

• Both the debt ratio and the debt-to-equity ratio measure the level of a company's leverage.
  • Debt ratio = Total liabilities divided by total assets
  • Debt-to-equity ratio = Total liabilities divided by total stockholders' equity
• The times interest earned ratio (operating income divided by interest expense) measures how much cushion a company has in terms of being able to make its periodic interest payments.

(6) Amortize bond discounts and bond premiums using either the straight-line method or the effective-interest method.

• When bonds are issued at a premium or a discount, the premium or discount must be amortized over the life of the bond.
• When a bond premium or discount exists, bond interest expense recognized on the income statement is not equal to the amount of cash paid for interest.
• The straight-line method amortizes an equal amount of premium or discount every period.
• When the effective-interest method is used, the amount of discount or premium amortized each period is equal to the market rate of interest multiplied by the bond's carrying value.

KEY TERMS & CONCEPTS

annuity, 459
bond, 468
bond discount, 471
bond indenture, 470
bond maturity date, 470
bond premium, 471
callable bonds, 469
compounding
  period, 458
convertible bonds, 469
coupon bonds, 468

debentures (unsecured
  bonds), 468
debt ratio, 476
debt-to-equity ratio, 476
junk bonds, 469
long-term liabilities, 455
market rate (effective
  rate or yield rate) of
  interest, 470
mortgage amortization
  schedule, 464

mortgage payable, 463
present value of $1, 455
present value of an
  annuity, 459
principal (face value or
  maturity value), 470
registered bonds, 468
secured bonds, 468
serial bonds, 469
stated rate of
  interest, 471

term bonds, 469
times interest earned, 477
zero-coupon bonds, 469

bond carrying value, 481
effective-interest
  amortization, 478
straight-line
  amortization, 478

REVIEW PROBLEMS

Accounting for Long-Term Liabilities

Energy Corporation had the following transactions relating to its long-term liabilities for the year:

a. Issued a $30,000, three-year, 8% note payable to White Corporation for a truck purchased on January 2. Interest is payable annually on December 31 of each year.

b. Issued $300,000 of 12%, 10-year bonds on July 1. The market rate on the date of issuance was 12%. Interest payments are made on June 30 and December 31 of each year.

c. Purchased a warehouse on December 1 by borrowing $250,000. The terms of the mortgage call for monthly payments of $2,194 for 30 years to be made at the end of each month. The interest rate on the mortgage is 10%.

Required:

Make all journal entries required during the year to account for the above liabilities. Energy Corporation reports on a calendar-year basis.

Solution

Jan. 2 Truck	30,000	
Note Payable		30,000
Purchased a truck by issuing a note.		
July 1 Cash	300,000	
Bonds Payable		300,000
Issued 12%, 10-year bonds with a face value of $300,000.		
Dec. 1 Warehouse	250,000	
Mortgage Payable		250,000
Purchased a warehouse by issuing a 10%, 30-year mortgage.		
31 Interest Expense	2,400	
Cash		2,400
Paid yearly interest on the 3-year, 8% note ($30,000 × 8% = $2,400).		
31 Bond Interest Expense	18,000	
Cash		18,000
Paid semiannual interest payment on 12%, 10-year bonds ($300,000 × 0.12 × $^{6}/_{12}$ = $18,000).		
Interest Expense	2,083	
Mortgage Payable	111	
Cash		2,194
Paid first monthly payment on 30-year mortgage (interest: $250,000 × 0.10 × $^{1}/_{12}$ = $2,083; reduction in principal: $2,194 − $2,083 = $111).		

EXPANDED
material

Bonds Payable

Scientific Engineering Company received authorization on July 1, 2009, to issue $300,000 of 12% bonds. The maturity date of the bonds is July 1, 2029. Interest is payable on January 1 and July 1 of each year. The bonds were sold for $289,200 on July 1, 2009 (the same day as authorized). Scientific Engineering uses straight-line amortization.

Required:

1. Compute the approximate effective interest rate for the bonds.

(continued)

2. Record the journal entries on:
   a. July 1, 2009.
   b. December 31, 2009.
   c. January 1, 2010.
   d. July 1, 2010.
   e. December 31, 2010.
3. Record the journal entries on July 1, 2029, for the final interest payment and the retirement of the bonds.

Solution

1. Effective Interest Rate

Because the bonds sold at a discount, the actual or effective rate of interest is higher than the stated interest rate of 12%. The effective interest rate can be approximated as follows:

Bond discount amortized per year = $10,800/20 periods = $540
Annual interest expense = ($300,000 $\times$ 12%) + $540 = $36,540
Effective interest rate = $36,540/$289,200 = 12.63%

2. Journal Entries

a. 2009

July	1	Cash		289,200	
		Discount on Bonds		10,800	
		Bonds Payable			300,000
		To record the sale of $300,000 of 12% bonds			
		due on July 1, 2029.			

b. 2009

Dec. 31		Bond Interest Expense		18,270	
		Discount on Bonds			270
		Bond Interest Payable			18,000
		To record semiannual bond interest expense			
		on $300,000, 12%, 20-year bonds			
		($300,000 $\times$ 0.12 $\times$ ½ year) and amortize bond			
		discount ($10,800 ÷ 20 years $\times$ ½ year).			

c. 2010

Jan.	1	Bond Interest Payable		18,000	
		Cash			18,000
		Paid semiannual interest on $300,000 bonds.			

d. 2010

July	1	Bond Interest Expense		18,270	
		Discount on Bonds			270
		Cash			18,000
		Paid semiannual interest on $300,000 bonds			
		and amortized bond discount.			

e. 2010

Dec. 31		Bond Interest Expense		18,270	
		Discount on Bonds			270
		Bond Interest Payable			18,000
		To record semiannual bond interest expense on			
		$300,000 bonds and amortize bond discount.			

3. Retirement of the Bonds

2029

July 1		Bond Interest Expense		18,270	
		Discount on Bonds			270
		Bond Interest Payable			18,000
		To record the bond interest expense and discount			
		amortization up to the date of maturity.			

(continued)

Bonds Payable	300,000	
Bond Interest Payable	18,000	
Cash		318,000

*To record the payment of interest for six months
and retire the bonds at maturity.*

The first entry on July 1, 2029, updates the amortization of the bond discount to the retirement date and reflects the cash owed for interest for the period January 1–July 1, 2029. The second entry reflects payment for retiring the bonds plus payment of the interest owed. Alternatively, Cash could have been credited for $18,000 in the first entry. If Cash had been credited, the second entry would have included only a debit to Bonds Payable and a credit to Cash for $300,000.

DISCUSSION QUESTIONS

1. The higher the interest rate, the lower the present value of a future amount. Why?
2. What is an annuity?
3. When does the stated amount of a liability equal its present value?
4. What is the difference between a note payable and a mortgage payable?
5. When a mortgage payment is made, a portion of it is applied to interest, and the balance is applied to reduce the principal. How is the amount applied to reduce the principal computed?
6. If a lease is recorded as a capital lease, what is the relationship of the lease payments and the lease liability?
7. Why do companies prefer to classify leases as operating leases rather than as capital leases?
8. To whom do companies usually sell bonds?
9. What are two important characteristics that determine the issuance price of a bond?
10. Identify four different ways in which bonds can mature or be eliminated as liabilities.
11. If a bond's stated interest rate is below the market interest rate, will the bond sell at a premium or at a discount? Why?
12. If you think the market interest rate is going to drop in the near future, should you invest in bonds?

13. When do you think bonds will sell at or near face value?
14. Explain why bonds retired before maturity may result in a gain or loss to the issuing company.
15. What does the debt ratio measure?
16. From the standpoint of a lender, which is more attractive: a high times interest earned ratio or a low times interest earned ratio? Explain.

EXPANDED *material*

17. What type of account is Discount on Bonds?
18. Why does the amortization of a bond discount increase the book value of bonds?
19. Why is the effective-interest amortization method more theoretically appropriate than the straight-line amortization method?
20. What is the carrying value of a bond?
21. How does the carrying value of a bond affect the accounting for bonds payable under the effective-interest method?
22. If the effective rate of interest for a bond is greater than its stated rate of interest, explain why the annual bond interest expense will be different from the periodic cash interest payments to the bondholders.

PRACTICE EXERCISES

PE 10-1   **Present Value of a Single Amount**
LO1   The company will receive $20,000 in five years when the interest rate is 8%. Compute the present value of this payment.

PE 10-2   **Future Value of a Single Amount**
LO1   The company invests $61,000 today in a savings account that earns 10% compounded annually. What will be the balance in the savings account ten years from today (e.g., future value)?

PE 10-3 **Interest Rate per Compounding Period**

LO1 The interest rate is 16% compounded quarterly for six years. Compute the interest rate per compounding period.

PE 10-4 **Number of Interest Periods**

LO1 The interest rate is 12% compounded monthly for seven years. Compute the number of interest periods.

PE 10-5 **Future Value of Single Amount Compounded Monthly**

LO1 Compute the future value of $10,000 invested today at 24% interest compounded monthly for five years.

PE 10-6 **Computing the Present Value of an Annuity**

LO1 The company will receive $1,600 every six months for eight years. The company's interest rate is 10% compounded semiannually. Compute the present value of this annuity payment.

PE 10-7 **Computing Periodic Payment Amount**

LO1 The company borrowed $50,000 to be repaid in equal monthly installments at 12% interest over five years. Compute the periodic payment amount.

PE 10-8 **Interest-Bearing Notes**

LO2 The company borrowed $20,000 at 8% interest by issuing a note payable. The terms of the note require yearly interest payments for seven years and repayment of the principal at the end of seven years. Make the necessary journal entries to record the following transactions:

1. Issuance of the note payable.
2. Payment of the first interest expense.

PE 10-9 **Mortgages Payable Issuance and First Payment**

LO2 On January 1, the company borrowed $500,000 to purchase a new building and signed a mortgage agreement pledging the building as collateral on the loan. The mortgage is at 12% for 30 years, and the monthly payment is $5,143 payable on January 31 with subsequent payments due at the end of each month thereafter. Make the necessary journal entries to record the following transactions:

1. Acquisition of the mortgage.
2. January 31 (first month) payment on mortgage.

PE 10-10 **Mortgages Payable Second Payment**

LO2 Refer to the data in PE 10-9. Make the necessary journal entry(ies) to record the second month's mortgage payment on February 28. Round to the nearest penny.

PE 10-11 **Capital Lease Acquisition**

LO3 The company leased a delivery truck on January 1, 2009. The lease requires annual payments of $7,500 for seven years at a 12% rate of interest payable at the end of each year. The company classifies this lease as a capital lease. Make the necessary journal entry(ies) to record the lease of this asset.

PE 10-12 **Capital Lease Payment**

LO3 Refer to the data in PE 10-11. Make the necessary journal entry(ies) to record the first lease payment on December 31, 2009. Round amounts to the nearest penny.

PE 10-13 **Types of Bonds**

LO4 Which one of the following statements is false?

a. Debentures are bonds that have no underlying assets pledged as collateral to guarantee their payment.

(continued)

b. Serial bonds mature in one single sum on a specified future date.

c. Callable bonds can be redeemed by the issuer at any time at a specified price.

d. Companies keep a record of the names and addresses of all registered bondholders and pay interest only to those whose names are on file.

PE 10-14
LO4

Bonds Issued at Face Value

The company issued 15-year, $100,000 bonds with a stated rate of interest of 12%, compounded quarterly. The effective interest rate demanded by investors for bonds of this level of risk is also 12%. Calculate the issuance price of the bond (e.g., the total present value).

PE 10-15
LO4

Bonds Issued at a Discount

The company issued five-year, $25,000 bonds with a stated rate of interest of 8%, compounded semiannually. The effective interest rate demanded by investors for bonds of this level of risk is 12%. Calculate the issuance price of the bond (e.g., the total present value).

PE 10-16
LO4

Bonds Issued at a Premium

The company issued seven-year, $100,000 bonds with a stated rate of interest of 8%, compounded semiannually. The effective interest rate demanded by investors for bonds of this level of risk is 6%. Calculate the issuance price of the bond (e.g., the total present value).

PE 10-17
LO4

Accounting for Bonds Payable Issued at Face Value

The company issued 20-year, $450,000 bonds with a stated rate of interest of 11%, compounded semiannually. The effective interest rate demanded by investors for bonds of this level of risk is also 11%. Since these bonds are issued at face value (i.e., the stated rate of interest is equal to the interest rate demanded by investors for bonds of this level of risk), the issuance price is also $450,000. Make the necessary journal entries for:

1. The issuance of the bonds.
2. The first interest payment.

PE 10-18
LO4

Accounting for Retirement of Bonds Payable Issued at Face Value

Refer to the data in PE 10-17. Assuming all interest has been accounted for, make the necessary journal entry(ies) to record the retirement of the bonds at the end of 20 years.

PE 10-19
LO4

Bond Retirements before Maturity

The company had $300,000 in callable bonds in the open market. The company's bonds were selling in the open market at 106 and were callable at 107. The company decided to retire the bonds early. Make the necessary journal entry(ies) to record the retirement of these bonds.

PE 10-20
LO5

Debt Ratio

Using the following information, compute the debt ratio.

Total liabilities	$247,500
Annual interest expense	5,204
Total assets	542,850
Income before interest and taxes	62,030

PE 10-21
LO5

Debt-to-Equity Ratio

Refer to the data in PE 10-20. Compute the debt-to-equity ratio.

PE 10-22
LO5

Times Interest Earned Ratio

Refer to the data in PE 10-20. Compute the times interest earned ratio.

EXERCISES

E 10-23
LO1

Computing the Present Value of a Single Sum

Find the present value (rounded to the nearest dollar) of:
1. $20,000 due in 4 years at 6% compounded annually.
2. $40,000 due in 6½ years at 4% compounded semiannually.
3. $15,000 due in 5 years at 16% compounded quarterly.
4. $11,000 due in 25 years at 10% compounded semiannually.

E 10-24
LO1

Computing the Future Value of a Single Sum

Compute the future value (rounded to the nearest dollar) of the following investments:
1. $15,842 invested to earn interest at 6% compounded annually for 4 years.
2. $30,920 invested to earn interest at 4% compounded semiannually for 6½ years.
3. $6,846 invested to earn interest at 16% compounded quarterly for 5 years.
4. $959 invested to earn interest at 10% compounded semiannually for 25 years.

E 10-25
LO1

Computing the Present Value of an Annuity

What is the present value (rounded to the nearest dollar) of an annuity of $12,000 per year for seven years if the interest rate is:
1. 9% compounded annually.
2. 12% compounded annually.

E 10-26
LO1

Computing the Amount of Periodic Payments

Howard Company has just borrowed $250,000. The loan is to be repaid in regular annual payments made at the end of each year. What is the amount of each annual payment under the following sets of terms:
1. Interest rate of 8% compounded annually; repayment in four annual payments.
2. Interest rate of 7% compounded annually; repayment in eight annual payments.

E 10-27
LO2

Accounting for Long-Term Note Payable

Maloney Company borrowed $60,000 on a two-year, 8% note dated October 1, 2008. Interest is payable annually on October 1, 2009, and October 1, 2010, the maturity date of the note. The company prepares its financial statements on a calendar-year basis. Prepare all journal entries relating to the note for 2008, 2009, and 2010.

E 10-28
LO2

Accounting for Long-Term Note Payable

Silmaril, Inc., borrowed $25,000 from First National Bank by issuing a three-year, 10% note dated July 1, 2008. Interest is payable semiannually on December 31 and June 30. The principal amount is to be repaid in full on June 30, 2011. Silmaril, Inc., reports on a calendar-year basis. Prepare all journal entries relating to the note during 2008, 2009, 2010, and 2011.

E 10-29
LO2

Accounting for a Mortgage

Kohler Kleaners borrowed $50,000 on June 1, 2009, to finance the purchase of a building. The mortgage requires payments of $525 to be made at the end of every month for 12 years with the first payment being due on June 30, 2009. The interest rate on the mortgage is 8%.
1. Prepare a mortgage amortization schedule for 2009.
2. How much interest will be paid in 2009?
3. By how much will the principal amount of the mortgage be reduced by the end of 2009?

E 10-30
LO2

Accounting for a Mortgage

On January 1, 2009, Paik, Inc., borrowed $75,000 to finance the purchase of machinery. The terms of the mortgage require payments to be made at the end of every month with the first payment being due on January 31, 2009. The length of the mortgage is five years, and the mortgage carries an interest rate of 24%.

(continued)

1. Compute the amount of the monthly payment.
2. Prepare a mortgage amortization schedule for 2009.
3. Prepare the journal entry to be made on January 31, 2009, when the first payment is made.
4. For the remainder of the year, how will the journal entries relating to the mortgage differ from the one made on January 31?

E 10-31
LO3

Lease Accounting

Logan Electronics signed a lease to use a machine for five years. The annual lease payment is $14,200 payable at the end of each year.

1. Record the lease, assuming that the lease should be accounted for as a capital lease and the applicable interest rate is 12%. (Round to the nearest dollar.)
2. For the initial year, record the annual lease payment.

E 10-32
LO3

Lease Accounting

Digital, Inc., leased computer equipment from Young Leasing Company on January 2, 2009. The terms of the lease required annual payments of $4,141 for five years beginning on December 31, 2009. The interest rate on the lease is 14%.

1. Assuming the lease qualifies as an operating lease, what journal entry would be made on January 2 to record the leased asset?
2. If the lease qualifies as an operating lease, what journal entry would be made when the first payment is made on December 31, 2009?
3. Provide the journal entry made on January 2, 2009, assuming the lease qualifies as a capital lease.
4. Provide the journal entry made on December 31, 2009, to record the first lease payment, assuming a capital lease.

E 10-33
LO4

Issuance Price of Bonds

Neukoelln Company issued seven-year bonds on January 1. The face value of the bonds is $72,000. The stated interest rate on the bonds is 12%. The market rate of interest at the time of issuance was 10%. The bonds pay interest semiannually. Calculate the issuance price of the bonds.

E 10-34
LO4

Issuance Price of Bonds

Hopeful Company issued seven-year bonds on January 1. The face value of the bonds is $80,000. The stated interest rate on the bonds is 7%. The market rate of interest at the time of issuance was 10%. The bonds pay interest semiannually. Calculate the issuance price of the bonds.

E 10-35
LO4

Accounting for Bonds Issued at Face Value

Romulus, Inc., issued $500,000 of 10%, five-year bonds at face value on July 1, 2009. Interest on the bonds is payable semiannually on December 31 and June 30.

1. Provide the journal entry to record the issuance of the bonds on July 1, 2009.
2. Provide the journal entry made on December 31, 2009, to account for these bonds.
3. On September 30, 2010, Romulus elected to retire the bonds early. The market price of the bonds on this date was $486,000. Provide the journal entries to record the early retirement.
4. Why do you think Romulus elected to retire the bonds early?

E 10-36
LO4

Accounting for Bonds Issued at Face Value

Schwedt Company issued $280,000 of 9%, 10-year bonds at face value on September 1, 2009. The bonds pay interest on March 1 and September 1. Schwedt uses the calendar year for financial reporting purposes.

1. Provide the journal entry to record the bond issuance on September 1, 2009.
2. Provide the journal entry to record interest expense on December 31, 2009.

(continued)

3. Provide the journal entries made during 2010 relating to the bond.

4. On February 20, 2011, Schwedt elected to retire the bond issue early. The market price on the day of retirement was $300,000. Provide the journal entries to record the bond retirement.

5. Why do you think Schwedt elected to retire the bonds early?

E 10-37

LO5

Computation of Debt-Related Financial Ratios

The following information comes from the financial statements of Gwynn Company:

Long-term debt	$50,000
Total liabilities	78,000
Total stockholders' equity	40,000
Operating income	16,000
Interest expense	6,000

Compute the following ratio values:

1. Debt ratio.
2. Debt-to-equity ratio.
3. Times interest earned.

E 10-38

LO3, LO5

Impact of Capitalizing the Value of Operating Leases

The following information comes from the financial statements of Karlla Peterson Company:

Total liabilities	$100,000
Total stockholders' equity	80,000

In addition, Karlla Peterson has a large number of operating leases. The payments on these operating leases total $20,000 per year for the next 15 years. The present value of the economic obligation associated with these operating leases is $150,000. Of course, because these are operating leases, this economic obligation is off the balance sheet.

Compute the following ratio values:

1. Debt ratio. *Hint:* Remember the accounting equation.
2. Debt-to-equity ratio.
3. Debt-to-equity ratio assuming that Karlla Peterson's operating leases are accounted for as capital leases.
4. Debt ratio assuming that Karlla Peterson's operating leases are accounted for as capital leases.

EXPANDED *material*

E 10-39

LO4, LO6

Accounting for Bonds Issued at a Discount

Kontiki Alarm Company issued $250,000 of 10%, five-year bonds at 98 on June 30, 2009. Interest is payable on June 30 and December 31. The company uses the straight-line method to amortize bond premiums and discounts. The company's fiscal year is from February 1 through January 31.

Prepare all necessary journal entries to account for the bonds from the date of issuance through June 30, 2010. Also record the retirement of the bonds on June 30, 2014, assuming that all interest has been paid and that the discount has been fully amortized.

E 10-40

LO4, LO6

Accounting for Bonds Issued at a Premium

Sealon Corporation issued $100,000 of 10%, 10-year bonds at 102 on April 1, 2009. Interest is payable semiannually on April 1 and October 1. Sealon Corporation uses the calendar year for financial reporting.

(continued)

1. Record the necessary entries to account for these bonds on the following three dates. (Use the straight-line method to amortize the bond premium.)
   a. April 1, 2009.
   b. October 1, 2009.
   c. December 31, 2009.
2. Show how the bonds would be reported on the balance sheet of Sealon Corporation on December 31, 2009.

E 10-41   **Effective-Interest Calculation**

LO6   Determine the *approximate* effective rate of interest for $300,000, 8%, five-year bonds issued at 95. (Assume straight-line amortization.)

E 10-42   **Bond Amortization Schedule**

LO6   The following is a partially completed amortization schedule prepared for the Liggett Company to account for its three-year bond issue with a face value of $50,000. The schedule covers the first three semiannual interest payment dates. Amounts are rounded to the nearest dollar. Compute the missing numbers.

Year	Interest Paid	Bond Expense	Premium Amortized	Bonds Payable Carrying Value
0				$52,537
½	(1)	$2,627	(2)	52,164
1	$3,000	(3)	$392	(4)
1½	(5)	(6)	(7)	(8)

E 10-43   **Accounting for Bonds**

LO4, LO6   Brown & Co., a calendar-year firm, is authorized to issue $500,000 of 11%, 15-year bonds dated May 1, 2009, with interest payable semiannually on May 1 and November 1.

Amortization of bond premiums or discounts is recorded using the straight-line amortization method. Prepare journal entries to record the following events, assuming that the bonds are sold at 97 on May 1, 2009.

1. The bond issuance on May 1, 2009.
2. Payment of interest on November 1, 2009.
3. Adjusting entry on December 31, 2009.
4. Payment of interest on May 1, 2010.

PROBLEMS

P 10-44   **Present and Future Value Computations**

LO1   *Required:*

1. Determine the present value in each of the following situations:
   a. A $9,000 loan to be repaid in full at the end of five years. Interest on the loan is payable quarterly. The interest rate is 8% compounded quarterly.
   b. A six-year note for $12,000 bearing interest at an annual rate of 12%, compounded semiannually. Interest is payable semiannually.
   c. A one-year mortgage to be paid in monthly installments of $6,000. The interest rate is 12% compounded monthly.
2. Determine the future value in each of the following situations:
   a. An investment of $20,000 today to earn interest at 8% compounded semiannually to provide for a down payment on a house four years from now.
   b. An investment of $40,000 today to earn interest at 12% compounded quarterly that is designated for a charitable contribution 15 years from now when the donor retires.

P 10-45   **Present and Future Value Computations**

LO1   *Required:*

1. Compute the present value for each of the following situations, assuming an interest rate of 10% compounded annually. (Round amounts to the nearest dollar.)
   a. A single payment of $30,000 due on a mortgage five years from now.
   b. A series of payments of $5,000 each, due at the end of each year for five years.
   c. A five-year, 10% loan of $25,000, with interest payable annually, and the principal due in five years.
2. Compute the future value amounts (rounded to the nearest dollar) in each of the following situations:
   a. A $20,000 lump-sum investment today that will earn interest at 10% compounded annually over five years.
   b. A $5,000 lump-sum investment today that will earn interest at 8%, compounded quarterly to provide money for a child's college education 15 years from now.

P 10-46   **Computing the Amount of Periodic Payments**

LO1   Nathan Smith has just purchased a new car for $28,000. He paid $8,000 down and signed a note for the remaining $20,000. The interest rate on the note is 12% compounded monthly, or 1% per month.

Required:

1. Compute the amount of Mr. Smith's monthly payment if he plans to pay off the $20,000 note in 30 monthly payments. Remember: The interest rate is 1% per month.
2. Repeat part (1) assuming that Mr. Smith wishes to repay the note in 60 monthly payments.
3. Assume that Mr. Smith decides to repay the note in 60 monthly payments. What is the balance remaining on the note immediately after he makes the 30th payment? *Hint:* Compute the present value of the remaining 30 payments.

P 10-47   **Accounting for Notes Payable**

LO2   Sweet's Candy Company needed cash for its current business operations. On January 1, 2008, the company borrowed $8,000 on a two-year, interest-bearing note from Peterson Bank at an annual interest rate of 10%. Interest is payable annually on January 1, and the note matures January 1, 2010. Sweet's Candy Company also borrowed $4,500 from Laurence National Bank on January 1, 2008, signing a three-year, 11% note due on January 1, 2011, with interest payable annually on January 1.

Required:

Prepare all journal entries relating to the two notes for 2008, 2009, 2010, and 2011. Assume that Sweet's Candy Company uses the calendar year for financial reporting. (Round all amounts to the nearest dollar.)

P 10-48   **Accounting for Notes Payable**

LO2   During 2008, Schmaal Corporation had the following transactions relating to long-term liabilities:

May 1   Purchased a machine costing $600,000 from Kretschmar Corporation. Issued a three-year, interest-bearing note with interest payable on May 1 of each year. The note matures on May 1, 2011, and carries an interest rate of 7%.

July 1   Borrowed $25,000 from South-Central National Bank. The terms of the note require semiannual payments of interest on December 31 and June 30. The note matures in two years and carries an interest rate of 6%.

Required:

1. Prepare the journal entries made on May 1 and July 1 to record the issuance of these two notes.
2. Prepare all journal entries made on December 31, 2008.
3. Prepare all journal entries made during 2009.

P 10-49   **Accounting for a Mortgage**

LO2   On November 1, 2009, Nydegger Company arranges with an insurance company to borrow $400,000 on a 30-year mortgage to purchase land and a building to be used in its operations. The land and the building are pledged as collateral for the loan, which has an annual interest rate of 12%, compounded monthly. The monthly payments of $4,114 are made at the end of each month, beginning on November 30, 2009.

Required:

1. Prepare the journal entry to record the purchase of the land and building, assuming that $75,000 of the purchase price is assignable to the land.
2. Prepare the journal entries on November 30 and December 31 for the monthly payments on the mortgage.
3. **Interpretive Question:** Explain generally how the remaining liability at December 31, 2009, will be reported on the company's balance sheet dated December 31, 2009.

P 10-50   **Lease Accounting**

LO3   On January 1, 2008, Linda Lou Foods, Inc., leased a tractor. The lease agreement qualifies as a capital lease and calls for payments of $7,000 per year (payable each year on January 1, starting in 2009) for eight years. The annual interest rate on the lease is 8%. Linda Lou Foods uses a calendar-year reporting period.

Required:

1. Prepare the journal entries for the following dates:
   a. January 1, 2008, to record the leasing of the tractor.
   b. December 31, 2008, to recognize the interest expense for the year 2008.
   c. January 1, 2009, to record the first lease payment.
2. Prepare the appropriate journal entries at December 31, 2009, and January 1, 2010.
3. **Interpretive Question:** Explain briefly how the leased asset is accounted for annually.

P 10-51   **Lease Accounting**

LO3   Empire, Inc., leased a starship on January 2, 2009. Terms of the lease require annual payments of $135,746 per year for 14 years. The interest rate on the lease is 10%, and the first payment is due on December 31, 2009.

Required:

1. Compute the present value of the lease payments.
2. Assuming the lease qualifies as a capital lease, prepare the journal entry to record the lease.
3. Prepare the journal entry to record the first lease payment on December 31, 2009, and to depreciate the leased asset. Empire, Inc., uses the straight-line method for depreciating all long-term assets.
4. **Interpretive Question:** How would the leased asset, and its associated liability, be disclosed on the balance sheet prepared on December 31, 2009?

P 10-52   **Issuance Price of Bonds**

LO4   Patterson Company issued 30-year bonds on June 30. The face value of the bonds was $750,000. The stated interest rate on the bonds was 6%. The market rate of interest at the time of issuance was 4%. Patterson also issued another set of bonds on August 31. These bonds were 20-year bonds and had a face value of $556,000. The stated rate of interest on these bonds was 5%. The market rate of interest at the time these bonds were issued was 8%. Both sets of bonds pay interest semiannually.

Required:

Calculate the issuance price of these bonds.

P 10-53   **Accounting for Bonds**

LO4   On July 1, 2009, Paramount, Inc. issued $500,000, 8%, 30-year bonds with interest paid semiannually on January 1 and July 1. The bonds were sold when the market rate of interest

(continued)

was 8%. On October 1, 2012, the bonds were retired when their fair market value was $495,000.

Required:

1. Demonstrate, using the present value tables, that the bonds were sold for $500,000.
2. Provide the journal entry made on July 1 to record the issuance of the bonds.
3. Provide the journal entry made on December 31, 2009, relating to interest.
4. Provide the journal entries to record the retirement of the bonds.

P 10-54 **Accounting for Bonds**

LO4 Lihue Enterprises issued $1.5 million, 9%, 20-year bonds on November 1, 2008. Interest payment dates are May 1 and November 1. The bonds were sold at face value.

Required:

1. Provide the journal entry to record the initial issuance of the bonds.
2. Provide the required journal entry on December 31, 2008.
3. Provide all journal entries relating to the bonds made during 2009.

P 10-55 **Reporting Liabilities on the Balance Sheet**

LO5 The following list of accounts is taken from the adjusted trial balance of Goforth Company.

Accounts Payable	$45,000
Notes Payable (due in 6 months)	24,000
Income Taxes Payable	18,000
Unearned Sales Revenue	27,500
Notes Payable (due in 2 years)	40,000
Prepaid Insurance	6,200
Accounts Receivable	53,000
Current Portion of Mortgage Payable	12,300
Mortgage Payable (due beyond 1 year)	93,000
Retained Earnings	91,400
Property Taxes Payable	8,700
Salaries & Wages Payable	15,200
Sales Tax Payable	3,100

Required:
Prepare the liabilities section of the company's balance sheet.

P 10-56 **Reporting Liabilities on the Balance Sheet**

LO5 The following amounts are shown on Plymouth Company's adjusted trial balance for the year 2009:

Accounts Payable	$ 36,000
Property Taxes Payable	6,300
Short-Term Notes Payable	44,000
Mortgage Payable (due within 1 year)	28,000
Mortgage Payable (due after 1 year)	300,000
Accrued Interest on Mortgage Payable	3,000
Lease Liability (current portion)	58,000
Lease Liability (long term)	414,000
Rent Payable	70,000
Income Taxes Payable	50,000
Federal & State Unemployment Taxes Payable	16,000

Required:
Prepare the liabilities section of Plymouth Company's balance sheet at December 31, 2009.

P 10-57

LO5

Computation of Debt-Related Financial Ratios

The following information comes from the financial statements of Walker Company:

Long-term debt	$430,000
Total liabilities	490,000
Total stockholders' equity	360,000
Current assets	140,000
Earnings before income taxes	28,000
Interest expense	50,000

Required:

Compute the following ratio values. State any assumptions that you make.
1. Debt ratio.
2. Debt-to-equity ratio.
3. Times interest earned.
4. **Interpretive Question:** You are a bank manager considering making a new $35,000 loan to Walker that would replace part of the existing long-term debt. You expect Walker to repay your loan in two years. Which of the ratios computed in parts (1) through (3) would be most useful to you in evaluating whether to make the loan to Walker?

P 10-58

LO5

Impact of Capitalizing the Value of Operating Leases

The following information comes from the financial statements of Travis Campbell Company:

Total liabilities	$100,000
Total stockholders' equity	80,000
Property, plant, and equipment	110,000
Sales	500,000
Earnings before income taxes	11,000
Interest expense	23,000

In addition, Travis Campbell has a large number of operating leases. The payments on these operating leases total $30,000 per year for the next 10 years. The present value of the economic obligation associated with these operating leases is $180,000. Of course, because these are operating leases, this economic obligation is off the balance sheet.

Required:

Compute the following ratio values:
1. Debt ratio. *Hint:* Remember the accounting equation.
2. Debt ratio assuming that Travis Campbell's operating leases are accounted for as capital leases.
3. Asset turnover (sales/total assets).
4. Asset turnover assuming that Travis Campbell's operating leases are accounted for as capital leases.
5. **Interpretive Question:** You are Travis Campbell's banker. You are concerned that the times interest earned ratio is not accurately reflecting the risk that Travis Campbell will not meet its fixed annual payments because most of those fixed payments are operating lease payments, not interest payments. Design an alternative ratio that will reflect the fact that, like interest payments, operating lease payments are fixed obligations that must be covered through operating profits each year. Compute the value for the ratio that you have designed.

P 10-59

LO4, LO6

Accounting for Bonds

Nemo Company authorized and sold $90,000 of 10%, 15-year bonds on April 1, 2009. The bonds pay interest each April 1, and Nemo's year-end is December 31.

Required:

1. Prepare journal entries to record the issuance of Nemo Company's bonds under each of the following three assumptions:
   a. Sold at 97.
   b. Sold at face value.
   c. Sold at 105.
2. Prepare adjusting entries for the bonds on December 31, 2009, under all three assumptions. (Use the straight-line amortization method.)
3. Show how the bond liabilities would appear on the December 31, 2009, balance sheet under each of the three assumptions.
4. **Interpretive Question:** What condition would cause the bonds to sell at 97? At 105?

P 10-60

LO4, LO6

Accounting for Bonds Issued at a Premium

On March 1, 2009, Roger Corporation issued $90,000 of 12%, five-year bonds at 110. The bonds were dated March 1, 2009, and interest is payable on March 1 and September 1. Roger records amortization using the straight-line method. Roger's financial reporting year ends on December 31.

Required:

Provide all necessary journal entries on each of the following dates:
1. March 1, 2009.
2. September 1, 2009.
3. December 31, 2009.
4. March 1, 2014.

P 10-61

LO4, LO6

Bonds Retired at Maturity

Stottard Company issued $450,000 of 10%, 10-year bonds on June 1, 2008, at 103. The bonds were dated June 1, and interest is payable on June 1 and December 1 of each year.

Required:

1. Record the issuance of the bonds on June 1, 2008.
2. Record the interest payment on December 1, 2008. Stottard uses the straight-line method of amortization.
3. Record the interest accrual on December 31, 2008, including amortization.
4. Record the journal entries required on June 1, 2018, when the bonds mature.

P 10-62

LO4, LO6

Straight-Line versus Effective-Interest Amortization

Cyprus Corporation issued $150,000 of bonds on January 1, 2009, to raise funds to buy some special machinery. The maturity date of the bonds is January 1, 2014, with interest payable each January 1 and July 1. The stated rate of interest is 10%. When the bonds were sold, the effective rate of interest was 12%. The company's financial reporting year ends December 31.

Required:

1. Determine the price at which the bonds would be sold.
2. Prepare the amortization schedule using the effective-interest method.
3. Prepare a comparative schedule of interest expense for each year (2009–2014) for the effective-interest and straight-line methods of amortization.
4. Record the journal entry for the last payment using the amortization schedule in part (2).
5. Record the journal entry for the retirement of the bonds.

(continued)

6. **Interpretive Question:** Is the difference between the interest expense each year between the straight-line and effective-interest methods sufficient to require the use of the effective-interest method? How do you think this question would be answered in practice?

P 10-63

LO4, LO6

Effective-Interest Amortization

Royce Corporation issued $200,000 of three-year, 12% bonds on January 1, 2008. The bonds pay interest on January 1 and July 1 each year. The bonds were sold to yield a 10% return, compounded semiannually.

Required:

1. At what price were the bonds issued?
2. Prepare a schedule to amortize the premium or discount on the bonds using the effective-interest amortization method.
3. Use the information in the amortization schedule prepared for part (2) to record the interest payment on July 1, 2010, including the appropriate amortization of the premium or discount.
4. **Interpretive Question:** Explain why these bonds sold for more or less than face value.

P 10-64

LO4, LO6

Accounting for Bonds

Bell Company sold $200,000 of 10-year bonds on January 1, 2008, to Brown Corporation. The bond indenture included the following information:

Face value	$200,000
Date of bonds	January 1, 2008
Maturity date	January 1, 2018
Stated rate of interest	14%*
Effective (market) rate of interest	12%*

*Compounded semiannually

Required:

1. Prepare the journal entry to record the issuance of the bonds.
2. What is the interest expense on the Bell Company books for the years ending December 31, 2008, and December 31, 2009, using straight-line amortization?
3. Show how the bonds would be presented on Bell's balance sheet at December 31, 2009.

P 10-65

LO4, LO6

Straight-Line versus Effective-Interest Amortization

Foster Corporation issued three-year bonds with a $180,000 face value on March 1, 2008, in order to pay for a new computer system. The bonds mature on March 1, 2011, with interest payable on March 1 and September 1. The contract rate of interest is 10%. (Interest is compounded semiannually.) When the bonds were sold, the effective rate of interest was 12%. The company's fiscal year ends on February 28.

Required:

1. At what price were the bonds issued based on the information presented?
2. Prepare an amortization schedule using the effective-interest method.
3. Prepare a schedule of interest expense for each year (2008–2011), comparing the annual interest expense for straight-line and effective-interest amortization.
4. Using the amortization schedule prepared in part (2), prepare the journal entry to record the interest payment on September 1, 2008.
5. Prepare the adjusting journal entry to record accrued interest on February 28, 2009.
6. Prepare the journal entry to retire the bonds on March 1, 2011, assuming all interest has been paid prior to retirement.

P 10-66

LO4, LO6

Bonds Retired before Maturity

Amity Construction Company issued $100,000 of 10% bonds on January 1, 2009. The maturity date of the bonds is January 1, 2019. Interest is payable January 1 and July 1. The bonds

(continued)

were sold at 111.4 on July 1, 2009. The company uses the straight-line method of amortizing bond premiums and discounts.

Required:

1. Make the required journal entries for each of the following dates:
   a. July 1, 2009.
   b. December 31, 2009.
   c. January 1, 2010.
   d. July 1, 2010.
2. Because of a substantial decline in the market rate of interest, Amity Construction Company purchased all the bonds on the open market at face value (100) on July 1, 2012. The following entry had just been made on that day:

Bond Interest Expense	4,400	
Premium on Bonds	600	
Cash		5,000
Made semiannual interest payment on the bonds		
and amortized bond premium for six months.		

Prepare the journal entry to record the retirement of the bonds on July 1, 2012.

P 10-67

LO4, LO6

Unifying Concepts: Accounting for Bonds Payable

Gonzalez Corporation was authorized to issue $100,000 of 7%, four-year bonds, dated May 1, 2009. All the bonds were sold on that date when the effective interest rate was 8%. Interest is payable on May 1 and November 1 each year. The company follows a policy of amortizing premium or discount using the effective-interest method. The company closes its books on December 31 of each year.

Required:

1. Calculate the issuance price of the bonds.
2. Prepare an amortization schedule that covers the life of the bond.
3. Prepare journal entries at the following dates based on the information shown in the amortization schedule prepared for part (2).
   a. December 31, 2009.
   b. May 1, 2010.
   c. November 1, 2010.
   d. December 31, 2010.
4. Based on the journal entries prepared for part (3), how much interest expense related to this bond issue did the company report on its income statement for the year 2010?
5. What was the carrying value of this bond issue on the balance sheet of the company at December 31, 2010?
6. **Interpretive Question:** Explain why another company in the same industry, which issued bonds with the same amount of face value, the same date of issuance, and the same stated rate of interest, might have had an issuance price of more or less than the price you computed for the issuance of the Gonzalez Corporation bonds.

P 10-68

LO4, LO6

Analysis of Bonds

Bonds with a face value of $200,000 and a stated interest rate of 12% were issued on March 1, 2009. The bonds pay interest each February 28 and August 31 and mature on March 1, 2019. The issuing company uses the calendar year for financial reporting.

Required:

Using these data, complete the following tables for each of the conditions listed. (Show computations and assume straight-line amortization.)

1. The bonds sold at face value.
2. The bonds sold at 97.
3. The bonds sold at 103.

(continued)

	Case 1	Case 2	Case 3
Cash received at issuance date	_____	_____	_____
Total cash paid to bondholders through maturity	_____	_____	_____
Income statement for 2009:			
Bond interest expense	_____	_____	_____
Balance sheet at December 31, 2009:			
Long-term liabilities:			
Bonds payable, 12%	_____	_____	_____
Unamortized discount	_____	_____	_____
Unamortized premium	_____	_____	_____
Bond carrying value	_____	_____	_____
Approximate effective interest rate*	_____	_____	_____

*Round to the nearest tenth of a percent.

ANALYTICAL ASSIGNMENTS

AA 10-69
DISCUSSION

Present Value Concepts

Hamburg Company recently began business and purchased a large facility to make beach clothing. Hamburg Company managed to make a small profit in its initial year of operations, although it used all its cash to purchase inventory and equipment. After preparing its tax return for the year, Hamburg's managers realized that they could pay less taxes than they thought. Because IRS accelerated depreciation methods allow for higher depreciation expense than the straight-line method the company is using for financial-reporting purposes, Hamburg can claim more depreciation expense than it thought it could and can reduce taxable income by $30,000. However, Hamburg's managers know that the two depreciation methods will eventually even out because the difference is only temporary and will create a deferred income tax liability, which must be recorded on the books. The managers are very conservative, though, and would rather pay the additional taxes now than record a liability that must be paid in the future, even if they must borrow the money from a bank to pay the extra taxes. They have come to you for advice. What would you tell them?

AA 10-70
DISCUSSION

Debt and Equity Financing

Berlin Company is in a world of hurt. For the past 15 years, the company has been the exclusive toy supplier to Infants-R-Us toy stores. Unfortunately for Berlin Company, Infants-R-Us just declared bankruptcy and went out of business. Berlin is the supplier for a few local toy stores, but Infants-R-Us was by far its largest customer. Berlin's managers believe that they can save the company if they can raise enough money to develop a new product line of a popular toy, "Nano Babies." Developing the new product line will require a considerable investment, however. Berlin is trying to decide the best way to finance the investment. It has found a bank that will loan it the money at 18%, a very high rate but the only one it can get because of its precarious financial position. Berlin can also issue bonds to raise the money, but because of investors' concerns about the future viability of the company, the only kind of bonds investors will buy are high-interest junk bonds at an interest rate of 17%. Even then, there is concern that the bonds will be discounted when they are marketed. Which financing alternative would you recommend to the company? If you were an investor, would you buy Berlin Company's bonds?

AA 10-71
JUDGMENT CALL

You Decide: Should the following bonds be classified as debt or equity on the balance sheet?

A company has recently issued bonds that are convertible into stock at the bondholder's request. The interest rate on the bonds is ridiculously low because it is expected that most holders will exercise the conversion options! How should the bonds be reported?

AA 10-72
JUDGMENT CALL

You Decide: **If a young company has a negative "times interest earned" ratio, should the company be refused or given a loan by lenders?**

Design Arts Inc. is a young computer game design company that has been in business for two years. The company has been working on a computer game that is scheduled for release in six months. However, it has exhausted all its financial resources and needs one last loan of $100,000 to help it meet its deadline. The company has not had any revenues up to this point but knows that once the game hits the market, it will be extremely profitable. Would you make a loan to this company?

AA 10-73
REAL COMPANY
ANALYSIS

Wal-Mart

The 2006 Form 10-K for **Wal-Mart** is included in Appendix A. Locate that Form 10-K and consider the following questions:

1. Examine Wal-Mart's balance sheet as of January 31, 2006. What percent of the increase in Wal-Mart's total assets from 2005 to 2006 was financed with an increase in the company's long-term debt?
2. Compute Wal-Mart's debt ratio for 2006 and 2005. Is the ratio increasing or decreasing? Identify the primary reason for the change.

AA 10-74
REAL COMPANY
ANALYSIS

IBM

International Business Machines (IBM) included the following information in Note K to its 2005 financial statements:

Long-Term Debt
At December 31, 2005
(dollars in millions)

At December 31:	Maturities	2005	2004
U.S. dollars:			
Debentures:			
5.875%	2032	$ 600	$ 600
6.22%	2027	469	469
6.5%	2028	313	313
7.0%	2025	600	600
7.0%	2045	150	150
7.125%	2096	850	850
7.5%	2013	532	532
8.375%	2019	750	750
3.43% convertible notes	2007	238	278
Notes: 5.4% average	2006–2013	2,713	2,724
Medium-term note program: 4.4% average	2006–2018	5,620	3,627
Other: 4.1% average	2006–2011	1,833	1,555
		$14,668	$12,448
Other currencies (average interest rate at December 31, 2005, in parentheses):			
Euros (3.1%)	2006–2010	$ 1,280	$ 1,095
Japanese yen (1.4%)	2006–2015	1,450	3,435
Canadian dollars (7.7%)	2008–2011	5	9
Swiss francs (1.5%)	2008	378	220
Other (6.1%)	2006–2011	406	513
		$18,187	$17,720

1. IBM lists eight different issues of debentures. What is a debenture?
2. What is unusual about the 7.125% debentures?
3. IBM has borrowed the equivalent of $3.519 billion in the form of foreign currency loans. Why would IBM get loans denominated in foreign currencies rather than get all of its loans in U.S. dollars?

(continued)

4. The average interest rates on the foreign currency loans range from a low of 1.4% for loans of Japanese yen to 7.7% for loans of Canadian dollars. What factors would cause IBM to pay a higher interest rate when it borrows Canadian dollars than when it borrows Japanese yen?

AA 10-75

REAL COMPANY
ANALYSIS

Citigroup

The **City Bank of New York** was chartered on June 16, 1812, just two days before the start of the War of 1812 between the United States and Great Britain. To get around twentieth-century bank holding laws, a holding company was organized to own the bank. This holding company took the name of **Citicorp** in 1974. In 1998, **Citicorp** and **Travelers Group** merged to become **Citigroup Inc.**

A simplified balance sheet for Citigroup as of December 31, 2005, and a schedule outlining the interest rate on Citigroup's outstanding long-term debt are given below.

Citigroup
Balance Sheet
December 31, 2005

	(millions of dollars)
Cash	$ 28,373
Investment securities	180,597
Loans receivable	573,721
Other assets	711,346
Total	$1,494,037
Deposit liabilities	$ 592,595
Other liabilities	571,406
Long-term debt	217,499
Stockholders' equity	112,537
Total	$1,494,037

Interest Rates Prevailing on Parent and Subsidiary Loans
for Loans Outstanding on December 31, 2005

Type of Loan	Average Interest Rate
Parent Company	
Senior notes	4.42%
Subordinated notes	5.45%
Parent Company and Subsidiaries	
Senior notes	4.75%
Subordinated notes	5.71%

1. Citigroup's simplified balance sheet is representative of most banks' balance sheets. Using the information about relative sizes of assets and liabilities given in that balance sheet, write a brief description of the primary operating activity of a bank.
2. Compute Citigroup's debt ratio (total liabilities divided by total assets). Comment on whether the value seems high or low to you.
3. In its long-term debt of $217.5 billion, Citigroup has both fixed-rate loans and floating-rate (or variable-rate) loans. What is the advantage of borrowing with a fixed-rate loan? What is the advantage of borrowing with a variable-rate loan?
4. Citigroup states that some of the subsidiary long-term debt is guaranteed by Citigroup. When Citigroup guarantees the long-term debt of one of its subsidiaries, does that raise or lower the interest rate that the subsidiary must pay on the debt? Explain. Is the interest rate on a loan higher when it is secured by assets or when it is unsecured? Explain.

AA 10-76

INTERNATIONAL

British Petroleum

In May 1901, William Knox D'Arcy convinced the Shah of Persia (present-day Iran) to allow him to hunt for oil. The oil discovered in Persia in 1908 was the first commercially significant amount of oil found in the Middle East. The company making the discovery called itself the **Anglo-Persian Oil Company**, later named **British Petroleum**, or BP. Today, BP is one of the largest oil and gas exploration and refining companies in the world.

The information below comes from Note 39 (Finance debt) of British Petroleum's 2005 financial statements.

(millions of dollars)	Loans	Finance Leases
Payments due within:		
1 year	$ 5,418	$ 78
2 to 5 years	8,421	320
Thereafter	4,542	838
	$18,381	$1,236
Less finance charge	0	455
Net obligation	$18,381	$ 781

1. In Great Britain, a finance lease is what we in the United States would call a capital lease. According to Note 39, British Petroleum expects to make total lease payments of $1.236 billion under finance leases. However, a liability of only $781 million is reported. Why is there a difference between the two amounts?

2. The $1.236 billion payment amount for the finance leases reflects the total of all lease payments that will be made under the agreements. Does the $18.381 billion amount reported for loans reflect the amount of all payments that will be made under the loan agreements? Explain.

3. The future loan and finance lease payments are separated into amounts to be repaid within one year, within two to five years, and after five years. How would a financial statement user find this payment timing information to be useful?

AA 10-77

ETHICS

Hiding an Obligation By Calling It a Lease

You and your partner own Miss Karma's Preschool, which provides preschool and day care services for about 100 children per day. Business is booming, and you are right in the middle of expanding your operation. Three months ago you took your financial statements to the local bank and applied for a five-year, $145,000 loan. The bank approved the loan, but it included as part of the loan agreement a condition that you would incur no other long-term liabilities during the five-year loan period. You cheerfully agreed to this condition because you didn't anticipate any further financing needs.

Two weeks ago a state government inspector came to your facility and said that your square footage was not enough for the number of children enrolled in your programs. The inspector gave you one month to find another facility, or else you would have to shut down. Luckily, you were able to find another building to use. However, the owner of the building insists on having you sign a 20-year lease. Alternatively, you can buy the building for $220,000. To buy the building, you would have to get a mortgage, which would, of course, violate the agreement on your five-year bank loan.

Your partner suggests that the lease is the way to solve all of your problems. Your partner has studied some accounting and reports that you can sign the lease but carefully construct the lease contract so that the lease will be accounted for as an operating lease. In this way, the lease obligation will not be reported as an accounting liability, the loan agreement will not be violated, and you can move to the new facility without any problem.

Is your partner right? Is it possible to avoid reporting the 20-year lease contract as an accounting liability? By signing the lease, are you violating the debt bank loan agreement? What do you think is the best course of action?

AA 10-78
WRITING

My Contract's Bigger Than Your Contract!

You are an agent for professional athletes. One of your clients is a superstar in the NBA. Last month you negotiated a new deal for your client that pays him $22 million per year for each of the next six years. Your client was very pleased with this $132 million contract, especially because it was a bigger contract than any of the other players on his team received.

This morning, while you were relaxing in your Jacuzzi, you got an angry cellular call from your client. It seems that one of his teammates just signed a $150 million deal, paying him $15 million per year for each of the next 10 years. Your client is outraged because you guaranteed that no one on his team would be receiving a bigger contract this season. Your client has threatened to terminate his agreement with you and also to spread the word among all his friends that you are not trustworthy.

Write a one-page memo to your client explaining that the actual value of his $132 million contract is greater than the $150 million contract signed by his teammate. Your client has a marketing degree from an ACC school, so he has had some exposure to the concept of the time value of money.

AA 10-79
CUMULATIVE
SPREADSHEET
PROJECT

Preparing New Forecasts

This spreadsheet assignment is a continuation of the spreadsheet assignments given in earlier chapters. If you completed those spreadsheets, you have a head start on this one.

1. Handyman wishes to prepare a forecasted balance sheet and income statement for 2010. Use the original financial statement numbers for 2009 [given in part (1) of the Cumulative Spreadsheet Project assignment in Chapter 2] as the basis for the forecast, along with the following additional information:

   a. Sales in 2010 are expected to increase by 40% over 2009 sales of $700.
   b. Cash will increase at the same rate as sales.
   c. The forecasted amount of accounts receivable in 2010 is determined using the forecasted value for the average collection period. For simplicity, do the computations using the end-of-period accounts receivable balance instead of the average balance. The average collection period for 2010 is expected to be 14.08 days.
   d. The forecasted amount of inventory in 2010 is determined using the forecasted value for the number of days' sales in inventory (computed using the end-of-period inventory balance). The number of days' sales in inventory for 2010 is expected to be 107.6 days.
   e. The forecasted amount of accounts payable in 2010 is determined using the forecasted value for the number of days' purchases in accounts payable (computed using the end-of-period accounts payable balance). The number of days' purchases in accounts payable for 2010 is expected to be 48.34 days.
   f. The $160 in operating expenses reported in 2009 breaks down as follows: $5 depreciation expense, $155 other operating expenses.
   g. See item (l) for the assumption concerning the amount of new long-term debt that will be acquired in 2010.
   h. No cash dividends will be paid in 2010.
   i. New short-term loans payable will be acquired in an amount sufficient to make Handyman's current ratio in 2010 exactly equal to 2.0.
   j. The forecasted amount of property, plant, and equipment (PP&E) in 2010 is determined using the forecasted value for the fixed asset turnover ratio. For simplicity, compute the fixed asset turnover ratio using the end-of-period gross PP&E balance. The fixed asset turnover ratio for 2010 is expected to be 3.518 times.
   k. In computing depreciation expense for 2010, use straight-line depreciation and assume a 30-year useful life with no residual value. Gross PP&E acquired during the year is depreciated for only half the year. In other words, depreciation expense for 2010 is the sum of two parts: (1) a full year of depreciation on the beginning balance in PP&E, assuming a 30-year life and no residual value and (2) a half-year of depreciation on any new PP&E acquired during the year, based on the change in the gross PP&E balance.

(continued)

Note: These statements were constructed as part of the spreadsheet assignment in Chapter 9; you can use that spreadsheet as a starting point if you have completed that assignment. *Clearly state any additional assumptions that you make.*

For this exercise, add the following additional assumptions:

l. New long-term debt will be acquired (or repaid) in an amount sufficient to make Handyman's debt ratio (total liabilities divided by total assets) in 2010 exactly equal to 0.80.

m. Assume an interest rate on short-term loans payable of 6.0% and on long-term debt of 8.0%. Only a half-year's interest is charged on loans taken out during the year. For example, if short-term loans payable at the end of 2010 are $15 and given that short-term loans payable at the end of 2009 were $10, total short-term interest expense for 2010 would be $0.75 [($10 × 0.06) + ($5 × 0.06 × 1/2)].

Clearly state any additional assumptions that you make.

2. Repeat (1), with the following changes in assumptions:
    a. The debt ratio in 2010 is exactly equal to 0.70.
    b. The debt ratio in 2010 is exactly equal to 0.90.
3. Prepare a table displaying the forecasted values of long-term debt and paid-in capital in 2010 under each of the following assumptions about the debt ratio: 0.70, 0.80, and 0.90. The sum of these two items can be viewed as the total amount of long-term financing (both debt and equity) received from outsiders. Comment on why the total of these two items is not the same under each debt ratio assumption.

11

Equity Financing

After studying this chapter, you should be able to:

(1) Distinguish between debt and equity financing, and describe the advantages and disadvantages of organizing a business as a proprietorship or a partnership. *Equity financing entitles the investor to share in the profits of the company; debt financing only entitles the lender to a fixed repayment amount. A business can be organized as a sole proprietorship, a partnership, or a corporation. Both proprietorships and partnerships can be easily formed; they both have the disadvantage of exposing the owner or owners to unlimited liability.*

(2) Describe the basic characteristics of a corporation and the nature of common and preferred stock. *Two advantages of the corporate form are the ease in transferability of ownership and the limited liability of the shareholders. The common stockholders of a corporation collectively choose the board of directors who then choose managers to conduct the day-to-day operation of the corporation. Preferred stockholders give up some of the advantages of ownership in exchange for some of the protection enjoyed by lenders.*

(3) Account for the issuance and repurchase of common and preferred stock. *When a company issues shares of stock, a portion of the proceeds is typically reported as the par value of the stock, with the remainder being called paid-in capital in excess of par. Treasury stock is shares of a company's own stock that have been repurchased. The amount spent to repurchase treasury stock is shown as a reduction in stockholders' equity.*

(4) Understand the factors that affect retained earnings, describe the factors determining whether a company can and should pay cash dividends, and account for cash dividends. *Cash dividends represent a distribution of accumulated profits to shareholders. Cash dividends reduce retained earnings. Preferred stock dividends must be paid before any dividends can be paid to common stockholders.*

(5) Describe the purpose of reporting comprehensive income in the equity section of the balance sheet, and prepare a statement of stockholders' equity. *Accumulated other comprehensive income is the portion of the balance sheet equity section where the equity impact of certain unrealized gains and losses is summarized.*

In 1882, two young newspaper reporters, Charles Dow and Edward Jones, teamed up to provide the Wall Street financial community with handwritten news bulletins. In 1889, when the staff of **Dow Jones & Company** had grown to 50, they decided to convert the bulletin service into a daily newspaper. The first issue of *The Wall Street Journal* appeared on July 8, 1889. Clarence Barron, who operated a financial news service in Boston, was the paper's first out-of-town reporter. Barron purchased Dow Jones & Company in 1902 for $130,000, and his heirs still hold majority control of the company today.

The Wall Street Journal is the flagship of the company, but the name "Dow Jones" is best known because of the Dow Jones Industrial Average that is cited in the news every day. "The Dow" is widely used to reflect the general health of the U.S. economy. So, what is it? Simply put, the Dow Jones Industrial Average measures the average movement of the stock prices of selected U.S. companies. The very first value of the average was 40.94 on May 26,

1896. Charles Dow computed this value by adding the share prices of 12 important companies chosen by him (**General Electric** was one of them) and then dividing by 12. Thus, the average price per share for these 12 companies was $40.94. Since 1928, the average has included 30 companies selected by the editors of *The Wall Street Journal*. The average is no longer computed by simply averaging share prices, but the underlying concept remains the same. Changes in the companies included in the average are rare. Nevertheless, since 1990, 14 companies have been replaced to reflect the decreasing importance of manufacturing in the U.S. economy. For example, **Bethlehem Steel**, which had been in "The Dow" since 1928, was replaced in March 1997 by **Wal-Mart**. In 1999, the first two NASDAQ companies were added to "The Dow"– **Microsoft** and **Intel**. The 30 companies included in the average as of June 1, 2006, are listed in Exhibit 1. The 30 companies in the average are listed every day in *The Wall Street Journal*, often on page C3.[1]

EXHIBIT 1	**The 30 Firms Included in the Dow Jones Industrial Average (as of June 1, 2006)**

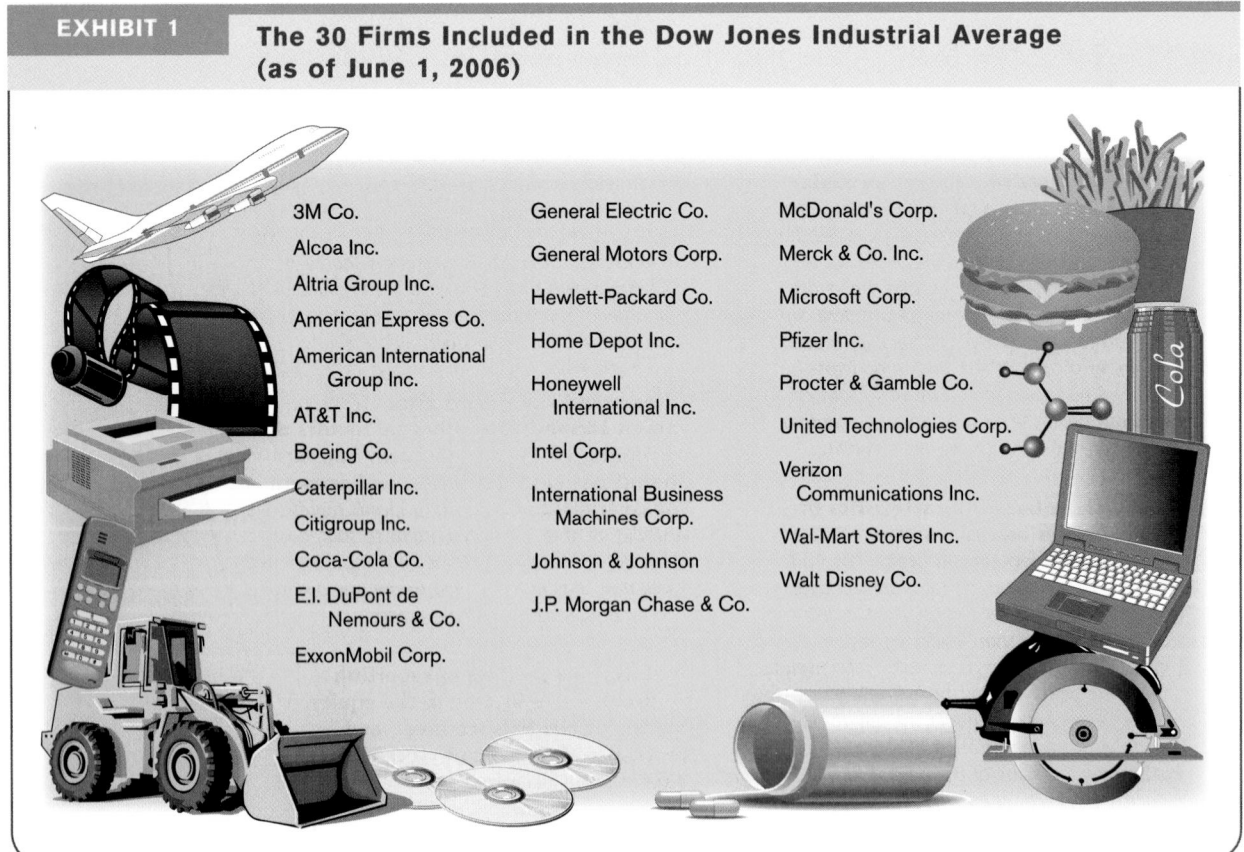

3M Co.
Alcoa Inc.
Altria Group Inc.
American Express Co.
American International Group Inc.
AT&T Inc.
Boeing Co.
Caterpillar Inc.
Citigroup Inc.
Coca-Cola Co.
E.I. DuPont de Nemours & Co.
ExxonMobil Corp.

General Electric Co.
General Motors Corp.
Hewlett-Packard Co.
Home Depot Inc.
Honeywell International Inc.
Intel Corp.
International Business Machines Corp.
Johnson & Johnson
J.P. Morgan Chase & Co.

McDonald's Corp.
Merck & Co. Inc.
Microsoft Corp.
Pfizer Inc.
Procter & Gamble Co.
United Technologies Corp.
Verizon Communications Inc.
Wal-Mart Stores Inc.
Walt Disney Co.

---

[1] This description is based on information obtained from Dow Jones & Company History at **http://dowjones.com**; Dow Jones & Company, *International Directory of Company Histories*, vol. 19 (Detroit: St. James Press, 1998), pp. 128–131.

ow Jones & Company is an appropriate symbol of capitalism–a corporation that has done business in and around the spiritual heart of capitalistic finance, the New York Stock Exchange, for over one hundred years. With the disintegration of the former Soviet Union and the rapid conversion of China into a "socialist market" economy, it seems that the economic battle of capitalism and communism has been won by capitalism. As the history of many of the companies profiled in earlier chapters (Microsoft, Sears, Yahoo!, General Electric) illustrates, the true story of capitalism is not the story of rich "capitalists" exploiting the masses, but rather the story of unknown individuals using a free market to find outside investor financing that will turn their ideas into reality. Accounting for investor financing is the topic of this chapter.

This is the second chapter on financing activities. In the previous chapter, financing through borrowing (debt) was discussed. Another way

organizations raise money to finance operations is from investments by owners. In corporations, those investments take the form of stock purchases. In proprietorships and partnerships, they take the form of capital investments in the business. Exhibit 2 shows the financial statement items that will be covered in this chapter.

Certain basic characteristics are common to all investor financing, no matter what the form of business. The first is that owner investments affect the equity accounts of the business. Second, together with the liabilities, these owners' equity accounts show the sources of the cash that was used to buy the assets. There are three primary ways to bring money into a business: borrowing (debt financing), selling owners' interests (equity financing), and earning profits (also reflected in the equity accounts through the retained earnings account). In this chapter, we illustrate the accounting for equity financing in the context of corporations.

SETTING THE STAGE

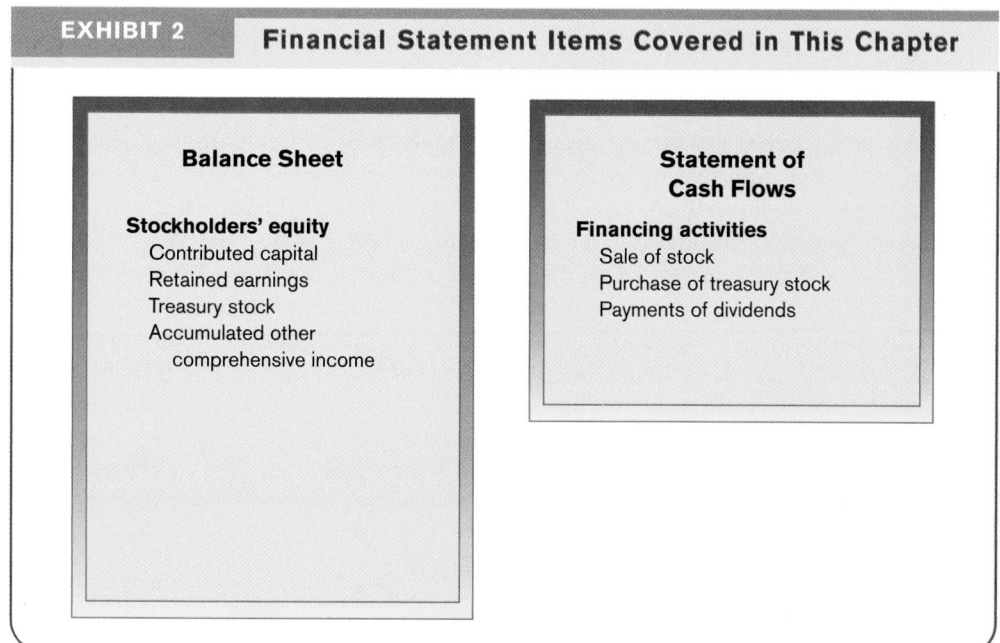

EXHIBIT 2 **Financial Statement Items Covered in This Chapter**

Balance Sheet

Stockholders' equity
Contributed capital
Retained earnings
Treasury stock
Accumulated other
    comprehensive income

**Statement of
Cash Flows**

Financing activities
Sale of stock
Purchase of treasury stock
Payments of dividends

Raising Equity Financing

Distinguish between debt and equity financing, and describe the advantages and disadvantages of organizing a business as a proprietorship or a partnership.

(1) Most business owners do not have enough excess personal cash to establish and expand their companies. Therefore, they eventually need to look for money from outsiders, either in the form of loans or as funds contributed by investors. The business issues associated with investor financing are summarized in the time line in Exhibit 3.

The factors affecting the choice between borrowing and seeking additional investment funds are described in this section of the chapter. This section also outlines the advantages and disadvantages of organizing a business as a proprietorship or a partnership. The decision to incorporate and the process that a corporation follows in soliciting investor funds are described in the next section. The bulk of the chapter is devoted to the accounting procedures used to give a proper reporting of stockholders' equity to the investors. Of course, proper financial reporting to current and potential investors is one of the primary reasons for the existence of financial accounting.

Difference between a Loan and an Investment

Imagine that you own a small business and need $40,000 for expansion. What is the difference between borrowing the $40,000 and finding a partner who will invest the $40,000? If you borrow the money, you must guarantee to repay the $40,000 with interest. If you fail to make these payments, the lender can haul you into court and use the power of the law to force repayment. On the other hand, if your company does very well and you generate more than enough cash to repay the $40,000 plus interest, the lender does not get to share in your success. You owe the lender $40,000 plus interest and not a penny more. So, a loan is characterized by a fixed, legal obligation to repay a specified amount, whether the borrowing company performs poorly or performs well.

If you receive $40,000 in investment funds from a new partner, the partner now shares in your company's failures and successes. If business is bad and the investor is never able to recover his or her $40,000 investment—well, that's the way it goes. The law will not help the investor recover the investment because the very nature of an investment is that the investor accepts the risk of losing everything. However, in exchange for accepting this risk, the investor also gets to share in the success if the company does well. For example, if you had loaned $40,000 to Sam Walton for **Wal-Mart**'s expansion back in 1970, you would have been repaid the $40,000 plus a little interest. If you had invested that same $40,000 in Wal-Mart, however, your investment would have grown in value to $240.5 million by June 2006. Thus, an investment is characterized by a higher

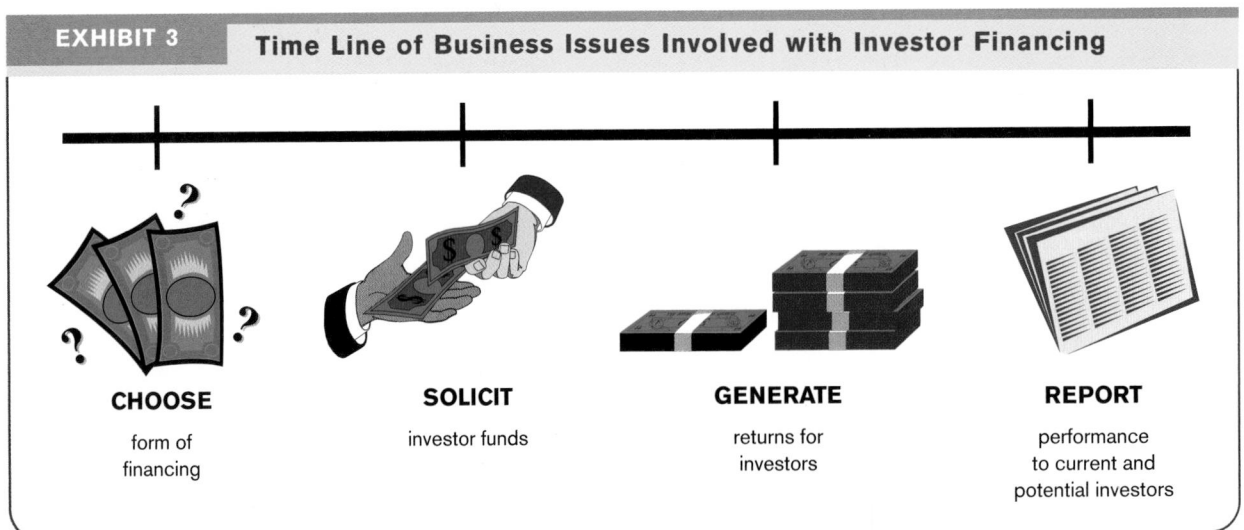

EXHIBIT 3   **Time Line of Business Issues Involved with Investor Financing**

CHOOSE
form of financing

SOLICIT
investor funds

GENERATE
returns for investors

REPORT
performance to current and potential investors

risk of losing your money, balanced by the chance of sharing in the wealth if the company does well.

Proprietorships and Partnerships

As explained in Chapter 2, a business can be organized as a proprietorship, a partnership, or a corporation. These three types of organization are merely different types of legal contracts that define the rights and responsibilities of the owner or owners of the business. The advantages and disadvantages of proprietorships and partnerships are discussed below. Corporations are discussed in the next section.

proprietorship

A business owned by one person.

partnership

An association of two or more individuals or organizations to carry on economic activity.

A **proprietorship** is a business owned by one person. A **partnership** is a business owned by two or more persons or entities. In most respects, proprietorships and partnerships are similar to each other but very different from corporations. Both a proprietorship and a partnership are characterized by ease of formation, limited life, and unlimited liability.

Ease of Formation Proprietorships and partnerships can be formed with few legal formalities. When a person decides to establish a proprietorship, he or she merely acquires the necessary cash, inventory, equipment, and other assets; obtains a business license; and begins providing goods or services to customers. The same is true for a partnership, except that because two or more persons are involved, they must decide together which assets will be acquired and how business will be conducted.

Limited Life Because proprietorships and partnerships are not legal entities that are separate and distinct from their owners, they are easily terminated. In the case of a proprietorship, the owner can decide to dissolve the business at any time. For a partnership, anything that terminates or changes the contract between the partners legally dissolves the partnership. Among the events that dissolve a partnership are:

1. the death or withdrawal of a partner,
2. the bankruptcy of a partner,
3. the admission of a new partner,
4. the retirement of a partner, or
5. the completion of the project for which the partnership was formed.

The occurrence of any of these events does not necessarily mean that a partnership must cease business; rather, the existing partnership is legally terminated, and another partnership must be formed.

Unlimited Liability Proprietorships and partnerships have unlimited liability, which means that the proprietor or partners are personally responsible for all debts of the business. If a partnership is in poor financial condition, creditors first attempt to satisfy their claims from the assets of the partnership. After those assets are exhausted, creditors may seek payment from the personal assets of the partners. In addition, because partners are responsible for one another's actions (within the scope of the partnership), creditors may seek payment for liabilities created by a departed or bankrupt partner from the personal assets of the remaining partners. This unlimited liability feature is probably the single most significant disadvantage of a proprietorship or partnership. It can deter a wealthy person from joining a partnership for fear of losing personal assets. (For more information relating to proprietorship and partnership accounting, access this book's Web site at **http://www.thomsonedu.com/accounting/albrecht.**)

> **REMEMBER THIS...**
>
> - A loan is a fixed, legal obligation to repay a specified amount, whether the borrowing company performs poorly or performs well.
> - With an investment, the investor risks losing the investment funds if the company performs poorly but shares in the wealth if the company does well.
> - A proprietorship is a business owned by one person.
> - A partnership is a business owned by two or more persons.
> - Both a proprietorship and a partnership are easy to start and easy to terminate.
> - A major disadvantage of proprietorships and partnerships is the unlimited liability of the owner or partners.

Corporations and Corporate Stock

② Describe the basic characteristics of a corporation and the nature of common and preferred stock.

Corporations are the dominant form of business enterprise in the United States. Established as separate legal entities, **corporations** are legally distinct from the persons responsible for their creation. In many respects, they are accorded the same rights as individuals; they can conduct business, be sued, enter into contracts, and own property. Firms are incorporated by the state in which they are organized and are subject to that state's laws and requirements.

Characteristics of a Corporation

Corporations have several characteristics that distinguish them from proprietorships and partnerships. These characteristics are discussed below.

corporation

A legal entity chartered by a state; ownership is represented by transferable shares of stock.

Limited Liability   **Limited liability** means that in the event of corporate bankruptcy, the maximum financial loss any stockholder can sustain is his or her investment in the corporation (unless fraud can be proved). Because a corporation is a separate legal entity and is responsible for its own acts and obligations, creditors usually cannot look beyond the corporation's assets for satisfaction of their claims. This limited liability feature is probably the main reason for the phenomenal growth of the corporate form of business because it protects investors from sustaining losses beyond their investments. In most cases of bankruptcy, however, stockholders will lose most of their investment because the claims of creditors must be satisfied before stockholders receive anything.

limited liability

The legal protection given stockholders whereby they are responsible for the debts and obligations of a corporation only to the extent of their capital contributions.

Easy Transferability of Ownership   Shares of stock in a corporation can be bought, sold, passed from one generation to another, or otherwise transferred without affecting the legal or economic status of the corporation. In other words, most corporations have perpetual existence—the life of the corporation continues by the transfer of shares of stock to new owners.

Ability to Raise Large Amounts of Capital   Raising large amounts of capital can be easier for a corporation than for a proprietorship or a partnership because a corporation can sell shares of its stock. The sale of shares of stock permits many investors, both large and small, to participate in ownership of the business. Some corporations actually have thousands of individual stockholders. In its 2005 annual report, **Dow Jones & Company** reports that it has approximately 14,000 stockholders of record. Because of this widespread ownership, large corporations are said to be publicly owned.

© RYAN MCVAY/PHOTODISC RED/ GETTY IMAGES INC.

Corporations are the dominant form of business in the United States. A corporation is a legal entity, and its ownership is represented by transferable shares of stock.

Double Taxation   Because corporations are separate legal entities, they are taxed independently of their owners. This often results in a disadvantage, however, because the portion of corporate profits that is paid out in dividends is taxed twice. First, the profits are taxed to the corporation; second, the owners, or stockholders, are taxed on their dividend income.

Close Government Regulation

Because large corporations may have thousands of stockholders, each with only a small ownership interest, the government has assumed the task of monitoring certain corporate activities. For example, the government requires that all major corporations be audited and that they issue periodic financial statements. As a result, in certain respects, major corporations often enjoy less freedom than do partnerships and proprietorships.

Starting a Corporation

Suppose that you want to start a corporation. First, you should study your state's corporate laws (usually with the aid of an attorney). Then you must apply to the appropriate state official for a charter. Your application will include the intended name of your corporation, its purpose (that is, the type of activity it will engage in), the type and amount of stock you plan to have authorized for your corporation, and, in some cases, the names and addresses of the potential stockholders. Finally, if the state approves your application, you will be issued a "charter" (also called "articles of incorporation"), giving legal status to your corporation.

 F Y I

There are some hybrid organizations that have characteristics of both partnerships and corporations. For example, several of the large international accounting firms are organized as limited liability partnerships (LLPs). An LLP offers the advantages of a partnership structure but also provides each partner with limited liability for the costs of lawsuits caused by the actions of his or her partners.

F Y I

An LLC (limited liability company) offers the limited liability legal protection of a corporation as well as the favorable partnership treatment for income tax purposes.

prospectus

A report provided to potential investors that represents a company's financial statements and explains its business plan, sources of financing, and significant risks.

stockholders

Individuals or organizations that own a portion (shares of stock) of a corporation.

Of course, one of the purposes of forming a corporation is to then sell stock in the corporation in order to obtain business financing. If the business you intend to establish will operate across state lines and if you intend to seek investment funds from the general public, then you must register your intended stock issue with the Securities and Exchange Commission in Washington, D.C. You are required to provide a **prospectus** to each potential investor; the prospectus outlines your business plan, sources of financing, significant risks, and the like. Finally, you can sell your shares to the public in what is called an "initial public offering" (IPO). You will receive the proceeds from the IPO, minus the commission charged by the investment banker sponsoring the issue.

When an investor buys stock in a corporation, he or she receives a stock certificate as evidence of ownership. For convenience, these stock certificates are frequently held by the stockbroker through whom the investor purchased the shares. The investors in a corporation are called **stockholders**, and they govern

board of directors

Individuals elected by the stockholders to govern a corporation.

the corporation through an elected **board of directors**. In most corporations, the board of directors then chooses a management team to direct the daily affairs of the corporation. In smaller companies, the board of directors is usually made up of members of that management team.

Several types of stock can be authorized by the charter and issued by the corporation. The most familiar types are common stock and preferred stock, and the major difference between them concerns the degree to which their holders are allowed to participate in the rights of ownership of the corporation.

Common Stock

common stock

The most frequently issued class of stock; usually, it provides a voting right but is secondary to preferred stock in dividend and liquidation rights.

Certain basic rights are inherent in the ownership of **common stock**. These rights are as follows:

1. The right to vote in corporate matters such as the election of the board of directors or the undertaking of major actions such as the purchase of another company.
2. The preemptive right, which permits existing stockholders to purchase additional shares whenever stock is issued by the corporation. This allows common stockholders to maintain the same percentage of ownership in the company if they choose to do so.
3. The right to receive cash dividends if they are paid. As explained later, corporations do not have to pay cash dividends, and the amount received by common stockholders is sometimes limited.
4. The right to ownership of all corporate assets once obligations to everyone else have been satisfied. This means that once all loans have been repaid and the claims of the preferred stockholders have been met (as discussed below), all the excess assets belong to the common stockholders.

 F Y I

Occasionally, a corporation will have more than one class of common stock. For example, Dow Jones & Company has common stock and Class B common stock. Each Class B share gets 10 votes in corporate matters, and most of the Class B shares are owned by the descendants of Clarence Barron.

In essence, the common stockholders of a corporation are the true owners of the business. They delegate their decision-making authority to the board of directors, who in turn delegate authority for day-to-day operations to managers hired for that purpose. Thus, a distinguishing characteristic of business ownership as a common stockholder of a corporation is a clear separation between owning the business and operating the business.

Preferred Stock

preferred stock

A class of stock that usually provides dividend and liquidation preferences over common stock.

The term "preferred stock" is somewhat misleading because it gives the impression that **preferred stock** is better than common stock. Preferred stock isn't better; it's different. A good way to think of preferred stock is that preferred stockholders usually give up some of the ownership rights of the common stockholders in exchange for some of the protection enjoyed by lenders.

In most cases, preferred stockholders are not allowed to vote for the corporate board of directors. In addition, preferred stockholders are usually allowed to receive only a fixed cash dividend, meaning that if the company does well, preferred stockholders do not get to share in the success. In exchange for these limitations, in the event that the corporation is liquidated, preferred stockholders are entitled to receive their cash dividends and have their claims fully paid before any cash is paid to common stockholders.

convertible preferred stock

Preferred stock that can be converted to common stock at a specified conversion rate.

Preferred stock may also include other types of privileges, the most common of which is convertibility. **Convertible preferred stock** is preferred stock that can be converted to common stock at a specified conversion rate. For example, in the notes to **Microsoft**'s 1999 financial statements, Microsoft detailed the terms of 12.5 million shares of Microsoft convertible preferred stock that was sold in December 1996. Holders of those shares of preferred stock were able to exchange them for Microsoft common stock beginning in December 1999. On December 15, 1999, each preferred share was converted into 1.1273 common shares. Convertible preferred stock can be very appealing to investors. They can enjoy the dividend privileges of the preferred stock while having the option to convert to common stock if the market value of the common stock increases significantly. By issuing shares of stock with varying rights and privileges, companies can appeal to a wider range of investors.

REMEMBER THIS...

- The five major features of a corporation are:
  1. limited liability for stockholders,
  2. easy transferability of ownership,
  3. the ability to raise large amounts of capital,
  4. separate taxation, and
  5. for large corporations, closer regulation by government.
- Common stock confers four basic rights upon its owners:
  1. the right to vote in corporate matters,
  2. the right to maintain proportionate ownership,
  3. the right to receive cash dividends, and
  4. the ownership of all excess corporate assets upon liquidation of the corporation.
- Preferred stock typically carries preferential claims to dividend and liquidation privileges but has no voting rights.

Accounting for Stock

③ In this section we focus on the accounting for the issuance of stock as well as the accounting for stock repurchases.

Account for the issuance and repurchase of common and preferred stock.

Issuance of Stock

Each share of common stock usually has a **par value** printed on the face of the stock certificate. For example, the common stock of **Dow Jones & Company** has a $1 par value. This par value has little to do with the market value of the shares. In May 2006, each Dow Jones common share with a $1 par value was selling for about $34 per share. When par-value stock sells for a price above par, it is said to sell at a premium. In most states it is illegal to issue stock for a price below par value. If stock were issued at a discount (below par), stockholders could later be held liable to make up the difference between their investment and the par value of the shares they purchased. The par value multiplied by the total number of shares outstanding is usually equal to a company's "legal capital," and it represents the amount of the invested funds that cannot be returned to the investors as long as the corporation is in existence. This legal capital requirement was originally intended to protect a company's creditors; without it, excessive dividends could be paid, leaving nothing for creditors. The par value really was of more importance a hundred years ago and is something of a historical oddity today. These days, most states allow the sale of no-par stock.

par value

A nominal value assigned to and printed on the face of each share of a corporation's stock.

When par-value stock is issued by a corporation, usually Cash is debited, and the appropriate stockholders' equity accounts are credited. For par-value common stock, the equity accounts credited are Common Stock, for an amount equal to the par value, and Paid-In Capital in Excess of Par, Common Stock, for the premium on the common stock.

To illustrate, we will assume that the Boston Lakers Basketball Team (a corporation) issued 1,000 shares of $1 par-value common stock for $50 per share. The entry to record the stock issuance is:

```
Cash (1,000 shares × $50) ...........................................   50,000
    Common Stock (1,000 shares × $1 par value) ......................           1,000
    Paid-In Capital in Excess of Par,
    Common Stock (1,000 shares × $49) ...............................          49,000
        Issued 1,000 shares of $1 par-value common stock at $50 per share.
```

contributed capital

The portion of owners' equity contributed by investors (the owners) in exchange for shares of stock.

A similar entry would be made if the stock being issued were preferred stock. The total par value of the common and preferred stock, along with the associated amounts of paid-in capital in excess of par, constitutes a corporation's **contributed capital**.

This illustration points out two important elements in accounting for the issuance of stock: (1) the equity accounts identify the type of stock being issued (common or preferred), and (2) the proceeds from the sale of the stock are divided into the portion attributable to its par value and the portion paid in excess of par value. These distinctions are important because the owners' equity section of the balance sheet should correctly identify the specific sources of capital so that the respective rights of the various stockholders can be known.

If the stock being issued has no par value, only one credit is included in the entry. To illustrate, assume that the Lakers' stock does not have a par value and that the corporation issued 1,000 shares for $50 per share. The entry to record this stock issuance would be:

```
Cash ...............................................................   50,000
    Common Stock ...................................................          50,000
        Issued 1,000 shares of no-par stock at $50 per share.
```

Although stock is usually issued for cash, other considerations may be involved. To illustrate the kinds of entries made when stock is issued for noncash considerations, we will assume that a prospective stockholder exchanged a piece of land for 5,000 shares of the Boston Lakers' $1 par-value common stock. Assuming the market value of the stock at the date of the exchange was $40 per share, the entry is:

```
Land (5,000 shares × $40) ..........................................  200,000
    Common Stock (5,000 shares × $1) ...............................           5,000
    Paid-In Capital in Excess of Par,
    Common Stock (5,000 shares × $39) ..............................         195,000
        Issued 5,000 shares of $1 par-value common stock for land
        (5,000 shares × $40 per share = $200,000).
```

When noncash considerations are received in payment for stock, the assets or services received should be recorded at the current market value of the stock issued. If the market value of the stock cannot be determined, the market value of the assets or services received should be used as the basis for recording the transaction.

Accounting for Stock Repurchases

treasury stock

Issued stock that has subsequently been reacquired by the corporation.

Sometimes, when a company has excess cash or needs some of its shares of stock back from investors, it may purchase some of its own outstanding stock. This repurchased stock is called **treasury stock** by accountants. There are many reasons for a firm to buy its own stock. Five of the most common are that management:

1. wants the stock for a profit-sharing, bonus, or stock-option plan for employees,
2. feels that the stock is selling for an unusually low price and is a good buy,
3. wants to stimulate trading in the company's stock,
4. wants to remove some shares from the market in order to avoid a hostile takeover, or
5. wants to increase reported earnings per share by reducing the number of shares of stock outstanding.

Many successful U.S. companies have ongoing stock repurchase plans. For example, **Wal-Mart** disclosed in its 2006 Form 10-K (Appendix A) that it spent $3.580 billion in 2006 to repurchase 74 million of its own shares. **Coca-Cola** spent $5.255 billion in the years 2003–2005 repurchasing its own shares. The most aggressive stock buyback program is **General Electric**'s—a number of years ago GE announced its intention to buy back its own shares. In December 2004, GE's board of directors authorized a three-year $15 billion share repurchase program. Subsequently in 2005, the board increased the authorized repurchase amount to $25 billion. As of the end of 2005, GE had spent a cumulative total of $17.3 billion on net stock repurchases, $5.3 billion of which occurred in 2005.

When a firm purchases stock of another company, the investment is included as an asset on the balance sheet. However, a corporation cannot own part of itself, so treasury stock is not considered an asset. Instead, it is a contra-equity account and is included on the balance sheet as a deduction from stockholders' equity. Think of it this way: when a corporation issues shares, its equity is increased; when the corporation buys those shares back, its equity is reduced. The reporting of treasury stock is illustrated in the stockholders' equity section of the balance sheet for General Electric in Exhibit 4.

Notice that the $17.326 billion spent by General Electric to buy back its own shares as of December 31, 2005, is shown as a subtraction from total share owners' equity. By the way, the "other capital" included in GE's equity section is primarily composed of paid-in capital in excess of par. Also, the "accumulated nonowner changes other than earnings" item is quite interesting and controversial, as will be explained in a later section.

Treasury stock is usually accounted for on a cost basis; that is, the stock is debited at its cost (market value) on the date of repurchase. To illustrate, we assume that 100 shares

EXHIBIT 4	Share Owners' Equity for General Electric

General Electric Company
December 31, 2005 and 2004
Share Owners' Equity
(in millions of U.S. dollars)

	2005	2004
Common stock	$ 669	$ 669
Accumulated nonowner changes other than earnings	2,667	7,238
Other capital	25,227	24,265
Retained earnings	98,117	91,411
Less common stock held in treasury	(17,326)	(12,762)
Total share owners' equity	$109,354	$110,821

of the $1 par-value common stock were reacquired by the Boston Lakers for $60 per share. The entry to record the repurchase is:

Treasury Stock, Common	6,000	
Cash (100 shares × $60)		6,000
Purchased 100 shares of treasury stock at $60 per share.		

FYI

An alternative way to account for stock repurchases is called the par-value method. This method, though not used as frequently as the cost method illustrated in this section, is the method of choice for a number of large U.S. companies including **Microsoft**, **Intel**, and **Wal-Mart**. The par-value method of accounting for stock repurchases is covered in intermediate accounting courses.

The effect of this entry is to reduce both total assets (Cash) and total stockholders' equity by $6,000.

When treasury stock is reissued, the treasury stock account must be credited for the original amount paid to reacquire the stock. If the treasury stock's reissuance price is greater than its cost, an additional credit must be made to an account called Paid-In Capital, Treasury Stock. Together, these credits show the net increase in total stockholders' equity. At the same time, the cash account is increased by the total amount received upon reissuance of the treasury stock.

To illustrate, we assume that 40 of the 100 shares of the treasury stock that were originally purchased for $60 per share are reissued at $80 per share. The entry to record that reissuance is:

Cash (40 shares × $80)	3,200	
Treasury Stock, Common (40 shares × $60 cost)		2,400
Paid-In Capital, Treasury Stock [40 × ($80 − $60)]		800
Reissued 40 shares of treasury stock at $80 per share.		

The company now has a balance of $3,600 in the treasury stock account (60 shares at $60 per share).

CAUTION

Do not credit a gain when treasury stock is reissued at a price greater than its cost. Gains are associated with a company's operations, not with a company buying and selling its own shares.

Sometimes the reissuance price of treasury stock is less than its cost. As before, the entry involves a debit to Cash for the amount received and a credit to Treasury Stock for the cost of the stock. However, because an amount less than the repurchase cost has been received, an additional debit is required. The debit is to Paid-In Capital, Treasury Stock if there is a balance in that account from previous transactions, or to Retained Earnings if there is no balance in the paid-in capital, treasury stock account.

To illustrate, we will consider two more treasury stock transactions. First, we assume that another 30 shares of treasury stock are reissued for $40 per share, $20 less than their cost. Because Paid-In Capital, Treasury Stock has a balance of $800, the entry to record this transaction is:

Cash (30 shares × $40)	1,200	
Paid-In Capital, Treasury Stock	600	
Treasury Stock, Common (30 shares × $60 cost)		1,800
Reissued 30 shares of treasury stock at $40 per share; original cost was $60 per share.		

Note that after this transaction is recorded, the balance in Paid-In Capital, Treasury Stock is $200 ($800 − $600).

Next, we assume that the company reissues 20 additional shares at $45 per share. The entry to record this transaction is:

Cash (20 shares × $45)	900	
Paid-In Capital, Treasury Stock	200	
Retained Earnings	100	
Treasury Stock (20 shares × $60 cost)		1,200
Reissued 20 shares of treasury stock at $45 per share; original cost		
was $60 per share.		

In this transaction, the selling price was $300 less than the cost of the treasury stock. Because the paid-in capital, treasury stock account had a balance of only $200, Retained Earnings was debited for the remaining $100.

Balance Sheet Presentation

We have discussed the ways in which stock transactions affect owners' equity accounts. We will now show how these accounts are summarized and presented on the balance sheet. The following data, with the addition of the preferred stock information in (1), summarize the stock transactions of the Boston Lakers shown earlier:

1. $40 par-value preferred stock: issued 1,000 shares at $45 per share.
2. $1 par-value common stock: issued 1,000 shares at $50 per share.
3. $1 par-value common stock: issued 5,000 shares for land with a fair market value of $200,000.
4. Treasury stock, common: purchased 100 shares at $60; reissued 40 shares at $80; reissued 30 shares at $40; reissued 20 shares at $45.

With these data, and assuming a Retained Earnings balance of $100,000, the stockholders' equity section would be as shown in Exhibit 5.

EXHIBIT 5	Stockholders' Equity for Boston Lakers

Boston Lakers Basketball Team
Stockholders' Equity

Preferred stock ($40 par value, 1,000 shares issued and outstanding)	$ 40,000
Common stock ($1 par value, 6,000 shares issued, 5,990 shares outstanding)*	6,000
Paid-in capital in excess of par, preferred stock	5,000
Paid-in capital in excess of par, common stock	244,000
Total contributed capital	$295,000
Retained earnings (to be discussed)	100,000
Total contributed capital and retained earnings	$395,000
Less treasury stock (10 shares of $1 par common at cost of $60 per share)	(600)
Total stockholders' equity	$394,400

*Treasury shares are described as being issued but not outstanding. Thus, 6,000 common shares have been issued, but only 5,990 are outstanding because 10 are held by the Boston Lakers as treasury shares.

REMEMBER THIS...

- When a company issues stock, it debits Cash or a noncash account (Property, for example) and credits various stockholders' equity accounts.
- Shares typically are assigned a par value, which is usually small in relation to the market value of the shares. Amounts received upon issuance of shares are divided into par value and paid-in capital in excess of par.
- A company's own stock that is repurchased is known as treasury stock and is included in the financial statements as a contra-stockholders' equity account.

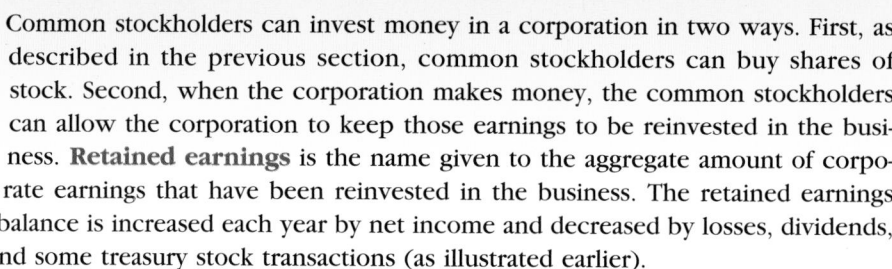

Retained Earnings

(4) Common stockholders can invest money in a corporation in two ways. First, as described in the previous section, common stockholders can buy shares of stock. Second, when the corporation makes money, the common stockholders can allow the corporation to keep those earnings to be reinvested in the business. **Retained earnings** is the name given to the aggregate amount of corporate earnings that have been reinvested in the business. The retained earnings balance is increased each year by net income and decreased by losses, dividends, and some treasury stock transactions (as illustrated earlier).

> **Understand the factors that affect retained earnings, describe the factors determining whether a company can and should pay cash dividends, and account for cash dividends.**

Remember, retained earnings is not the same as cash. In fact, a company can have a large Retained Earnings balance and be without cash, or it can have a lot of cash and a very small Retained Earnings balance. For example, on December 31, 2005, **Dow Jones & Company** had a Cash balance of $11 million but a Retained Earnings balance of $817 million. Although both Cash and Retained Earnings are usually increased when a company has earnings, they typically are increased by different amounts. This occurs for two reasons: (1) the company's net income, which increases Retained Earnings, is accrual-based, not cash-based; and (2) cash from earnings may be invested in productive assets such as inventories, used to pay off loans, or spent in any number of ways, many of which do not affect net income or retained earnings. In summary, cash is an asset; retained earnings is one source of financing (along with borrowing and direct stockholder investment) that a corporation can use to get funds to acquire assets.

> **retained earnings**
>
> The portion of a corporation's owners' equity that has been earned from profitable operations and not distributed to stockholders.

Cash Dividends

If you had your own business and wanted to withdraw money for personal use, you would simply withdraw it from the company's checking account or cash register. In a corporation, a formal action by the board of directors is required before money can be distributed to the owners. In addition, such payments must be made on a pro rata basis. That is, each owner must receive a proportionate amount on the basis of ownership percentage. These pro rata distributions to owners are called **dividends**. When paid in the form of cash, they are called **cash dividends**. The amount of dividends an individual stockholder receives depends on the number of shares owned and on the per-share amount of the dividend.

> **dividends**
>
> Distributions to the owners (stockholders) of a corporation.

> **cash dividend**
>
> A cash distribution of earnings to stockholders.

Should a Company Pay Cash Dividends? Note that a company does not have to pay cash dividends. Theoretically, a company that does not pay dividends should be able to reinvest its earnings in assets that will enable it to grow more rapidly than its dividend-paying competitors. This added growth will presumably be reflected in increases in the per-share price of the stock. In practice, most public companies pay regular cash dividends, but some well-known companies do not. For example, **Berkshire Hathaway** has never paid cash dividends to its common stockholders.

So, should a corporation pay cash dividends or not? Well, the surprising answer is that no one knows the answer to that question. Ask your finance professor what he or she thinks. Although no one knows the theoretically best dividend policy, three general observations can be made:

- Stable companies pay out a large portion of their income as cash dividends.
- Growing companies pay out a small portion of their income, if any, as cash dividends. They keep the funds inside the company for expansion.
- Companies are very cautious about raising dividends to a new level because once investors come to expect a certain level of dividends, they see it as very bad news if the company reduces the dividends back to the old level.

STOP & THINK

If you were a **Microsoft** shareholder, would you want to receive a high level of cash dividends, or would you prefer that Microsoft use your share of the profits for business expansion?

Although cash dividends are the most common type of dividend, corporations can distribute other types of dividends as well. A stock dividend is a distribution of additional shares of stock to stockholders. A property dividend is a distribution of corporate assets (for example, the stock of another firm) to stockholders. Property dividends are quite rare. In this section, only the accounting for cash dividends will be discussed.

declaration date

The date on which a corporation's board of directors formally decides to pay a dividend to stockholders.

Accounting for Cash Dividends Three important dates are associated with dividends: (1) declaration date, (2) date of record, and (3) payment date. The first is when the board of directors formally declares its intent to pay a dividend. On this **declaration date**, the company becomes legally obligated to pay the dividend. Assuming that the board of directors votes on December 15, 2009, to declare an $8,000 dividend, this liability may be recorded as follows:

Dividends	8,000	
Dividends Payable		8,000
Declared dividend on December 15, 2009.		

At the end of the year, the dividends account is closed to Retained Earnings by the following entry:

Retained Earnings	8,000	
Dividends		8,000
To close Dividends to Retained Earnings.		

From this entry, you can see that a declaration of dividends reduces Retained Earnings and, eventually, the amount of cash on hand. Thus, though not considered to be an expense, dividends do reduce the amount a company could otherwise invest in productive assets.

date of record

The date selected by a corporation's board of directors on which the stockholders of record are identified as those who will receive dividends.

Alternatively, a declaration of dividends can be recorded by debiting Retained Earnings directly. However, using the dividends account instead of Retained Earnings allows a company to keep separate records of dividends paid to preferred and common stockholders. Whichever method is used, the end result is the same: a decrease in Retained Earnings.

The second important dividend date is the **date of record**. Falling somewhere between the declaration date and the payment date, this is the date selected by the board of directors on which the stockholders of record are identified as those who will receive dividends. Because many corporate stocks are in flux—being bought and sold daily—it is important that the stockholders who will receive the dividends be identified. No journal entry is required on the date of record; the date of record is simply noted in the minutes of the directors' meeting and in a letter to stockholders.

dividend payment date

The date on which a corporation pays dividends to its stockholders.

As you might expect, the third important date is the **dividend payment date**. This is the date on which, by order of the board of directors, dividends will be paid. The entry to record a dividend payment would typically be:

Dividends Payable	8,000	
Cash		8,000
Paid dividends declared on December 15, 2009.		

The following press release, made by **Ford Motor Company** on March 8, 2006 (declaration date), identifies both the date of record and the dividend payment date:

> The Board of Directors of Ford Motor Company (NYSE: F) today declared a second quarter dividend of 10 cents a share on the company's Class B and common stock. This is the same level of dividend paid in the first quarter of 2006. The second quarter dividend is payable on June 1, 2006 to shareholders of record on May 2, 2006.

As mentioned earlier, once a dividend-paying pattern has been established, the expectation of dividends is built into the per-share price of the stock. A reduction in the dividend usually produces a sharp drop in the price. Similarly, an increased dividend usually triggers an increase in the stock price. Dividend increases are usually considered to set a precedent, indicating that future dividends will be at this per-share amount or more. With this in mind, boards of directors are careful about increasing or decreasing dividends.

Dividend Preferences   When cash dividends are declared by a corporation that has both common and preferred stock outstanding, how the dividends are allocated to the two classes of investors depends on the rights of the preferred stockholders. These rights are identified when the stock is approved by the state. Two "dividend preferences," as they are called, are (1) current-dividend preference and (2) cumulative-dividend preference.

Current-Dividend Preference.   Preferred stock has a dividend percentage associated with it and is typically described as follows: "5% preferred, $40 par-value stock, 1,000 shares outstanding." The first figure—"5%" in this example—is a percentage of the par value and can be any amount, depending on the particular stock. So, $2 per share (0.05 × $40 par) is the amount that will be paid in dividends to preferred stockholders each year that dividends are declared. The fact that preferred stock dividends are fixed at a specific

current-dividend preference

The right of preferred stockholders to receive current dividends before common stockholders receive dividends.

percentage of their par value makes them somewhat similar to the interest paid to bondholders. The **current-dividend preference** requires that when dividends are paid, this percentage of the preferred stock's par value be paid to preferred stockholders before common stockholders receive any dividends.

To illustrate the payment of different types of dividends, the following data from the Boston Lakers Basketball Team will be used throughout this section. (The various combinations of dividend preferences illustrated over the next few pages are summarized in Cases 1 to 4 in Exhibit 6.) As a reminder, the outstanding stock includes:

- Preferred stock: 5%, $40 par value, 1,000 shares issued and outstanding.
- Common stock: $1 par value, 6,000 shares issued, 5,990 shares outstanding.

To begin, note that, as with all preferred stock, the Lakers' 5% preferred stock has a current-dividend preference: Before any dividends can be paid to common stockholders, preferred stockholders must be paid a total of $2,000 ($40 × 0.05 × 1,000 shares). Thus, if only $1,500 of dividends are declared (Case 1), preferred stockholders will receive the

EXHIBIT 6		**Dividend Preferences: Summary of Cases 1 to 4**			
Case	**Preferred Dividend Feature**	**Years in Arrears**	**Total Dividend**	**Preferred Dividend**	**Common Dividend**
1	5%, Noncumulative	Not applicable	$ 1,500	$1,500	$ 0
2	5%, Noncumulative	Not applicable	3,000	2,000	1,000
3	5%, Cumulative	2	5,000	5,000	0
4	5%, Cumulative	2	11,000	6,000	5,000

entire dividend payment. If $3,000 are declared (Case 2), preferred stockholders will receive $2,000 and common stockholders, $1,000.

cumulative-dividend preference

The right of preferred stockholders to receive current dividends plus all dividends in arrears before common stockholders receive any dividends.

dividends in arrears

Missed dividends for past years that preferred stockholders have a right to receive under the cumulative-dividend preference if and when dividends are declared.

Cumulative-Dividend Preference. The cumulative-dividend preference can be quite costly for common stockholders because it requires that preferred stockholders be paid current dividends plus all unpaid dividends from past years before common stockholders receive anything. If dividends have been paid in all previous years, then only the current 5% must be paid to preferred stockholders. But if dividends on preferred stock were not paid in full in prior years, the cumulative deficiency must be paid before common stockholders receive anything.

With respect to the cumulative feature, it is important to repeat that companies are not required to pay dividends. Any past unpaid dividends are called **dividends in arrears.** Because they do not have to be paid unless dividends are declared in the future, dividends in arrears do not represent actual liabilities and thus are not recorded in the accounts. Instead, they are reported in the notes to the financial statements.

To illustrate the distribution of dividends for cumulative preferred stock, we will assume that the Boston Lakers Basketball Team has not paid any dividends for the last two years but has declared a dividend in the current year. The Lakers must pay $6,000 in dividends to preferred stockholders before they can give anything to the common stockholders. The calculation is as follows:

Dividends in arrears, 2 years	$4,000
Current-dividend preference	
($40 × 0.05 × 1,000 shares)	2,000
Total	$6,000

Therefore, if the Lakers pay only $5,000 in dividends (Case 3), preferred stockholders will receive all the dividends, common stockholders will receive nothing, and there will still be dividends in arrears of $1,000 the next year. If $11,000 in dividends are paid (Case 4), preferred stockholders will receive $6,000, and common stockholders will receive $5,000. The entries to record the declaration and payment of dividends in Case 4 are:

Date of Declaration

Dividends, Preferred Stock	6,000	
Dividends, Common Stock	5,000	
Dividends Payable		11,000
Declared dividends on preferred and common stock.		

Date of Payment

Dividends Payable	11,000	
Cash		11,000
Paid dividends on preferred and common stock.		

Constraints on Payment of Cash Dividends

Earlier in this section, the question was asked whether a company should pay cash dividends. A related question is: Can the company legally pay cash dividends? To illustrate, consider the following exaggerated scenario. Tricky Company obtains a corporate charter, borrows $1 million from Naïve Bank, pays out a $1 million cash dividend to the stockholders, and all the stockholders disappear to the Bahamas. Is this a legal possibility? No, it isn't, because the corporate right to declare cash dividends is regulated by state law in order to protect creditors. The right to declare cash dividends is often linked to a company's Retained Earnings balance.

In many states, a company is not allowed to pay cash dividends in an amount that would cause the retained earnings balance to be negative. Thus, if the retained earnings balance of the Boston Lakers were $8,500, the $11,000 dividend in Case 4 discussed previously could not be paid, even if the Lakers had the available cash to make the payment. The incorporation laws in many states are less restrictive and allow the payment of cash dividends in excess of the retained earnings balance if, for example, current earnings are strong or the market value of the assets is high.

Frequently, lenders do not rely on state incorporation laws to protect them from excess cash dividend payments by corporations to which they lend money. Instead, the loan contract itself includes restrictions on the payment of cash dividends during the period that the loan is outstanding. In this way, lenders are able to prevent cash that should be used to repay loans from being paid to stockholders as dividends.

Dividend Payout Ratio

dividend payout ratio

A measure of the percentage of earnings paid out in dividends; computed by dividing cash dividends by net income.

A ratio of interest to stockholders is the **dividend payout ratio**. This ratio indicates the percentage of net income paid out during the year in the form of cash dividends and is computed as follows:

$$\text{Dividend payout ratio} = \frac{\text{Cash dividends}}{\text{Net income}}$$

Dividend payout ratio values for Dow Jones, Microsoft, and General Electric for 2005 are computed below. The numbers are in millions.

	Dow Jones	Microsoft	General Electric
Cash dividends	$81.59	$36,968.00	$9,647.00
Net income	$60.40	$12,254.00	$16,353.00
Dividend payout ratio	135.08%	301.68%	58.99%

Both Dow Jones and Microsoft paid out more in dividends than they earned in income for the year. This is not typical. Microsoft's high ratio was as a result of a one-time large cash dividend. General Electric's payout ratio of 59% is at the high end of what corporation's typically pay out. Most large U.S. corporations pay out approximately 40 to 60% of their annual income as dividends.

REMEMBER THIS...

- The retained earnings account reflects the total undistributed earnings of a business since incorporation. It is increased by net income and decreased by dividends, net losses, and some treasury stock transactions.
- The important dates associated with a cash dividend are:
  - the date of declaration,
  - the date of record, and
  - the payment date.
- Preferred stockholders can be granted a current and a cumulative preference for dividends over the rights of common stockholders.
- In some states, the payment of cash dividends is limited to an amount not to exceed the existing Retained Earnings balance.
- The dividend payout ratio (cash dividends divided by net income) reveals the percentage of net income that is paid out as cash dividends.

Other Equity Items

Describe the purpose of reporting comprehensive income in the equity section of the balance sheet, and prepare a statement of stockholders' equity.

⑤ In addition to the two major categories of contributed capital and retained earnings, the equity section of a balance sheet often includes a number of miscellaneous items. These items are gains or losses that bypass the income statement when they are recognized. A further discussion of these items is given below.

Equity Items That Bypass the Income Statement

Since 1980, the equity sections of U.S. balance sheets have begun to fill up with a strange collection of items, each the subject of an accounting controversy. Two of these items are summarized below.

- *Foreign currency translation adjustment.* The foreign currency translation adjustment arises from the change in the equity of foreign subsidiaries (as measured in terms of U.S. dollars) that occurs as a result of changes in foreign currency exchange rates. For example, if the Japanese yen weakens relative to the U.S. dollar, the equity of Japanese subsidiaries of U.S. firms will decrease, in dollar terms. Before 1981, these changes were recognized as losses or gains on the income statement. Multinational firms disliked this treatment because it added volatility to reported earnings. The FASB changed the accounting rule, and now these changes are reported as direct adjustments to equity on the balance sheet, insulating the income statement from this aspect of foreign currency fluctuations.
- *Unrealized gains and losses on available-for-sale securities.* As will be explained in Chapter 12, available-for-sale securities are securities that a company purchased without intending to resell them immediately but also not necessarily planning to hold them forever. When the FASB was considering requiring securities to be reported at their market values on the balance sheet, companies complained about the income volatility that would be caused by recognizing these changes as gains or losses on the income statement. The FASB made the standard more acceptable to businesses by allowing unrealized gains and losses on available-for-sale securities to bypass the income statement and go straight to the equity section of the balance sheet.

The hodgepodge of direct equity adjustments described above is conceptually unsatisfying. These adjustments have arisen on a case-by-case basis as part of the FASB's effort to establish accounting standards that are accepted by the business community. As mentioned, many businesspeople are opposed to including these categories on the income statement because, they say, the income statement would become cluttered with gains and losses from market value changes, distracting from the purpose of the income statement, which is to focus on reporting profits from the activities of the business. The compromise that allows market values in the balance sheet while keeping the income statement uncluttered is the creation of a separate category of equity called **accumulated other comprehensive income**. Accumulated other comprehensive income is composed of certain market-related gains and losses that are not included in the computation of net income. It is important to remember that accumulated other comprehensive income is not income at all, but an equity category that summarizes the changes in equity that result during the period from market-related increases and decreases in the reported values of assets and liabilities. The reporting of accumulated other comprehensive income is illustrated in the 2005 equity section of **Dow Jones & Company**, shown in Exhibit 7.

accumulated other comprehensive income

Certain market-related gains and losses that are not included in the computation of net income; for example, foreign currency translation adjustments and unrealized gains or losses on investments.

EXHIBIT 7	Equity Section for Dow Jones & Company

Dow Jones & Company's Equity Section
(amounts in million of dollars)

	2005	2004
Common stock, par value $1.00 per share	$ 81,738	$ 81,572
Class B common stock, convertible, par value $1.00 per share	20,443	20,609
	$ 102,181	$ 102,181
Additional paid-in capital	137,290	124,082
Retained earnings	817,168	839,446
Accumulated other comprehensive income:		
Unrealized gain on investments	2,636	4,949
Unrealized (loss) gain on hedging	(198)	227
Foreign currency translation adjustment	3,430	6,826
Minimum pension liability, net of deferred taxes	(28,861)	(13,942)
	$1,033,646	$1,063,769
Less, treasury stock	871,381	913,226
Total stockholders' equity	$ 162,265	$ 150,543

statement of comprehensive income

A statement outlining the changes in accumulated comprehensive income that arose during the period.

A **statement of comprehensive income** provides a place, outside the regular income statement, for reporting all the unrealized gains and losses that are reported as equity adjustments. The appeal of comprehensive income is that this approach preserves the traditional income statement (calming the fears of the business community) but allows unrealized gains and losses to be reported. In essence, comprehensive income makes it possible to recognize unrealized gains and losses so that current market values can be reported on the balance sheet without having those unrealized gains and losses affect the income statement.

 STOP & THINK

Which will have a greater impact on a company's stock price: net income of $100 million or a $100 million unrealized gain from a change in exchange rates or securities prices? Explain your answer.

The statement of comprehensive income is very new; U.S. companies have been required to present it starting December 31, 1998. Dow Jones & Company's comprehensive income presentation for 2005 is shown in Exhibit 8. Note that net income is one component in the computation of comprehensive income. For Dow Jones, 2005 was a particularly bad year, with all five of the reported elements of comprehensive income being negative.

EXHIBIT 8	Statement of Comprehensive Income for Dow Jones & Company

(in thousands)	2005	2004	2003
Net income	$60,395	$ 99,548	$170,599
Unrealized gain (loss) on investments	(254)	(734)	4,118
Unrealized gain (loss) on hedging	(198)	227	453
Foreign currency translation adjustments	(1,179)	3,009	3,551
Minimum pension liability	(14,919)	(13,719)	9,756
Other	(4,503)	(453)	(2,059)
Comprehensive income (loss)	$39,342	$ 87,878	$186,418

Statement of Stockholders' Equity

statement of stockholders' equity

A financial statement that reports all changes in stockholders' equity.

Companies that have numerous changes in their stockholders' equity accounts during the year usually include a **statement of stockholders' equity** (also called a statement of changes in stockholders' equity) with their financial statements. This statement reconciles the beginning and ending balances for all stockholders' equity accounts reported on the balance sheet.

An illustrative statement of stockholders' equity from the 2005 annual report of Dow Jones & Company is presented in Exhibit 9. Note the following items in the statement:

- As mentioned earlier in the chapter, Dow Jones has two classes of common stock. Class B common shares with a par value of $166,000 were converted into ordinary common shares during the year.
- Dow Jones paid a dividend during the year of $82.673 million.
- The company reissued $41.8 million of its treasury shares during the year.

The last column in the statement reflects the total beginning and ending stockholders' equity account balances and all increases and decreases. Both the individual account

Exhibit 9	Statement of Stockholders' Equity for Dow Jones & Company

Consolidated Statement of Stockholders' Equity
Dow Jones & Company, Inc.
For the Year Ended December 31, 2005
(amounts in thousands of U.S. dollars)

	Common Stock	Class B Common Stock	Additional Paid-In Capital	Retained Earnings	Accumulated Other Comprehensive Income (Loss)	Treasury Stock Shares	Treasury Stock Amount	Total
Balance, December 31, 2004	$81,572	$20,609	$124,082	$839,446	$ (1,940)	(20,136,426)	$(913,226)	$150,543
Net income–2005				60,395				$ 60,395
Adjustment for realized gain on investments in income					(1,101)			(1,101)
Reclassification Adjustment					(958)			(958)
Unrealized loss on investment					(254)			(254)
Unrealized loss on hedging					(198)			(198)
Adjustment for realized gain on hedging included in net income					(227)			(227)
Translation adjustment, net of deferred taxes of $635					(1,179)			(1,179)
Adjustment for realized translation adjustment in net income					(2,217)			(2,217)
Minimum pension liability, net of deferred taxes of $8,377					(14,919)			(14,919)
Comprehensive income								$ 39,342
Dividends, $1.00 per share				(82,673)				$ (82,673)
Conversion of class B common stock into common stock	166	(166)						
Issuance of stock options related to acquisition of MarketWatch			24,902					24,902
Sales under stock compensation plans			(11,694)			1,061,785	41,845	30,151
Balance, December 31, 2005	$81,738	$20,443	$137,290	$817,168	$(22,993)	(19,074,641)	$(871,381)	$162,265

balances and total Stockholders' Equity at December 31, 2005, are reported on the balance sheet of Dow Jones & Company.

REMEMBER THIS...

- Accumulated other comprehensive income is not income at all, but an equity category that summarizes the effect on equity of certain market-related gains and losses.

- Two examples of items giving rise to accumulated other comprehensive income are:

  1. market fluctuations in the value of some investment securities and

  2. changes in the value of assets and liabilities held by foreign subsidiaries that are caused by exchange rate changes.

- A statement of stockholders' equity summarizes the changes affecting all the different categories of equity during the year.

REVIEW OF LEARNING OBJECTIVES

(1) Distinguish between debt and equity financing, and describe the advantages and disadvantages of organizing a business as a proprietorship or a partnership.

- A lender receives a fixed repayment amount.
- An investor receives a variable amount, depending on whether the company does well.

Proprietorship	Partnership
Owned by one person	Owned by two or more persons
Easy to start, easy to terminate	Easy to start, easy to terminate
Unlimited liability	Unlimited liability

(2) Describe the basic characteristics of a corporation and the nature of common and preferred stock.

Features of a corporation	(1) limited liability for stockholders,
	(2) easy transferability of ownership,
	(3) the ability to raise large amounts of capital,
	(4) separate taxation, and
	(5) for large corporations, closer regulation by government.
Basic rights of common stockholders	(1) the right to vote in corporate matters,
	(2) the right to maintain proportionate ownership,
	(3) the right to receive cash dividends, and
	(4) the ownership of all excess corporate assets upon liquidation of the corporation.

- Preferred stock typically carries preferential claims to dividend and liquidation privileges but has no voting rights.

(3) **Account for the issuance and repurchase of common and preferred stock.**

- When a company issues stock, it debits Cash or a noncash account (Property, for example) and credits various stockholders' equity accounts.
- Shares typically are assigned a par value, which is usually small in relation to the market value of the shares. Amounts received upon issuance of shares are divided into par value and paid-in capital in excess of par.
- A company's own stock that is repurchased is known as treasury stock and is included in the financial statements as a contra-stockholders' equity account.

(4) **Understand the factors that affect retained earnings, describe the factors determining whether a company can and should pay cash dividends, and account for cash dividends.**

- The retained earnings are:
  - increased by net income,
  - decreased by dividends, net losses, and some treasury stock transactions.
- The important dates associated with a cash dividend are:
  - the date of declaration,
  - the date of record, and
  - the payment date.
- Preferred stockholders can be granted a current and a cumulative preference for dividends over the rights of common stockholders.
- The dividend payout ratio (cash dividends divided by net income) reveals the percentage of net income that is paid out as cash dividends.

(5) **Describe the purpose of reporting comprehensive income in the equity section of the balance sheet, and prepare a statement of stockholders' equity.**

- Accumulated other comprehensive income is an equity account.
- Two examples of items giving rise to accumulated other comprehensive income are:
  - market fluctuations in the value of some investment securities, and
  - changes in the value of assets and liabilities held by foreign subsidiaries that are caused by exchange rate changes.
- A statement of stockholders' equity summarizes the changes affecting all the different categories of equity during the year.

KEY TERMS & CONCEPTS

REVIEW PROBLEM

Stockholders' Equity

Clarke Corporation was organized during 1979. At the end of 2009, the equity section of the balance sheet was:

Contributed capital:	
Preferred stock (8%, $30 par, 6,000 shares authorized,	
5,000 shares issued and outstanding)	$150,000
Common stock ($5 par, 50,000 shares authorized,	
20,000 shares issued, 17,000 shares outstanding)	100,000
Paid-in capital in excess of par, common stock	80,000
Total contributed capital	$330,000
Retained earnings	140,000
Total contributed capital plus retained earnings	$470,000
Less treasury stock (3,000 shares of common stock	
at cost, $10 per share)	(30,000)
Total stockholders' equity	$440,000

During 2009, the following stockholders' equity transactions occurred in chronological sequence:

a. Issued 800 shares of common stock at $11 per share.
b. Reissued 1,200 shares of treasury stock at $12 per share.
c. Issued 300 shares of preferred stock at $33 per share.
d. Reissued 400 shares of treasury stock at $9 per share.
e. Declared and paid a dividend large enough to meet the current-dividend preference on the preferred stock and to pay the common stockholders $1.50 per share.
f. Net income for 2009 was $70,000, which included $400,000 of revenues and $330,000 of expenses.
g. Closed the dividends accounts for 2009.

Required:

1. Journalize the transactions.
2. Set up T-accounts with beginning balances and post the journal entries to the T-accounts, adding any necessary new accounts. (Assume a beginning balance of $20,000 for the cash account.)
3. Prepare the stockholders' equity section of the balance sheet as of December 31, 2009.

Solution
1. Journalize the Transactions

a.	Cash	8,800	
	Common Stock		4,000
	Paid-In Capital in Excess of Par, Common Stock		4,800
	Issued 800 shares of common stock at $11 per share.		

Cash received is $11 × 800 shares; common stock is par value times the number of shares ($5 × 800); paid-in capital is the excess.

b.	Cash	14,400	
	Treasury Stock		12,000
	Paid-In Capital, Treasury Stock		2,400
	Reissued 1,200 shares of treasury stock at $12 per share.		

Cash is $12 × 1,200 shares; treasury stock is the cost times the number of shares sold ($10 × 1,200 shares); paid-in capital is the excess.

c.	Cash	9,900	
	Preferred Stock		9,000
	Paid-In Capital in Excess of Par, Preferred Stock		900
	Issued 300 shares of preferred stock at $33 per share.		

(continued)

Cash is 33×300 shares; preferred stock is par value times the number of shares issued (30×300); paid-in capital is the excess.

d.	Cash	3,600	
	Paid-In Capital, Treasury Stock	400	
	Treasury Stock		4,000
	Reissued 400 shares of treasury stock at $9 per share.		

Cash is 9×400 shares; treasury stock is the cost times the number of shares sold (10×400); paid-in capital is decreased for the difference. If no Paid-In Capital, Treasury Stock balance had existed, Retained Earnings would have been debited.

e.	Dividends, Preferred Stock	12,720	
	Dividends, Common Stock	29,100	
	Cash		41,820
	Declared and paid cash dividend.		

Calculations:

Preferred Stock	Number of Shares	Par-Value Amount
Original balance	5,000	$150,000
Entry (c)	300	9,000
Total	5,300	$159,000
		$\times 0.08$
		$ 12,720

Common Stock	Number of Shares
Original balance (excludes treasury stock)	17,000
Entry (a)	800
Entry (b)	1,200
Entry (d)	400
Total	19,400 shares
	$\times$ $1.50
	$29,100
Total preferred stock dividend	$12,720
Total common stock dividend	29,100
Total dividend	$41,820

f.	Revenues (individual revenue accounts)	400,000	
	Expenses (individual expense accounts)		330,000
	Retained Earnings		70,000
	To close net income to Retained Earnings.		

g.	Retained Earnings	41,820	
	Dividends, Preferred Stock		12,720
	Dividends, Common Stock		29,100
	To close the dividends accounts for 2009.		

2. Set up T-Accounts and Post to the Accounts

Cash

Beg.			
Bal.	20,000	(e)	41,820
(a)	8,800		
(b)	14,400		
(c)	9,900		
(d)	3,600		
Bal.	14,880		

Preferred Stock

		Beg.	
		Bal.	150,000
		(c)	9,000
		Bal.	159,000

Paid-In Capital in Excess of Par, Preferred Stock

		(c)	900
		Bal.	900

(continued)

Common Stock

		Beg.	
		Bal.	100,000
		(a)	4,000
		Bal.	104,000

Paid-In Capital in Excess of Par, Common Stock

		Beg.	
		Bal.	80,000
		(a)	4,800
		Bal.	84,800

Treasury Stock

Beg.			
Bal.	30,000	(b)	12,000
		(d)	4,000
Bal.	14,000		

Paid-In Capital, Treasury Stock

(d)	400	(b)	2,400
		Bal.	2,000

Retained Earnings

		Beg.	
(g)	41,820	Bal.	140,000
		(f)	70,000
		Bal.	168,180

Dividends, Preferred Stock

(e)	12,720	(g)	12,720
Bal.	0		

Dividends, Common Stock

(e)	29,100	(g)	29,100
Bal.	0		

Revenues

		Beg.	
(f)	400,000	Bal.	400,000
		Bal.	0

Expenses

Beg.			
Bal.	330,000	(f)	330,000
Bal.	0		

3. Prepare Stockholders' Equity Section of the Balance Sheet

Clarke Corporation
Partial Balance Sheet
December 31, 2009

Stockholders' Equity

Contributed capital:

Preferred stock (8%, $30 par, 6,000 shares authorized, 5,300 shares issued and outstanding)	$159,000
Common stock ($5 par, 50,000 shares authorized, 20,800 shares issued, 19,400 outstanding)	104,000
Paid-in capital in excess of par, preferred stock	900
Paid-in capital in excess of par, common stock	84,800
Paid-in capital, treasury stock	2,000
Total contributed capital	$350,700
Retained earnings	168,180
Total contributed capital plus retained earnings	$518,880
Less treasury stock (1,400 shares of common stock at cost, $10 per share)	(14,000)
Total stockholders' equity	$504,880

Transaction	Common Stock Issued	Common Stock Authorized	Treasury Stock
Number of shares originally issued	20,000	50,000	3,000
Entry (a)	800		
Entry (b)			(1,200)
Entry (d)			(400)
Total	20,800	50,000	1,400

DISCUSSION QUESTIONS

1. What are the primary differences between debt financing and equity financing?
2. What are the major differences between a partnership and a corporation?
3. How is a proprietorship or partnership established?
4. Does the death of a partner legally terminate a partnership? If so, does it mean that the partnership must cease operating?
5. Are partners legally liable for the actions of other partners? Explain.
6. In which type of business entity do all owners have limited liability?
7. In what way are corporate profits subject to double taxation?
8. How do common and preferred stock differ?
9. What is the purpose of having a par value for stock?
10. Why would a company repurchase its own shares of stock that it had previously issued?
11. Is treasury stock an asset? If not, why not?
12. How is treasury stock usually accounted for?
13. In what way does the stockholders' equity section of a balance sheet identify the sources of the assets?
14. What factors affect the Retained Earnings balance of a corporation?
15. Is it possible for a firm to have a large Retained Earnings balance and no cash? Explain.
16. When is a company legally barred from paying cash dividends?
17. Why should a potential common stockholder carefully examine the dividend preferences of a company's preferred stock?
18. The dividend payout ratio for Deedle Company is 40%. What does this mean?
19. What is accumulated other comprehensive income? Why was this concept adopted by accounting standard-setters?
20. Give two examples of other equity items (items that bypass the income statement and go directly to the equity section of the balance sheet).

PRACTICE EXERCISES

PE 11-1
LO1
Characteristics of Proprietorships and Partnerships
Which one of the following is *not* a usual characteristic of either a proprietorship or a partnership?
a. Limited size.
b. Limited life.
c. Ease of formation.
d. Unlimited liability.

PE 11-2
LO2
Characteristics of Corporations
Which one of the following is *not* a usual characteristic of a corporation?
a. Limited liability.
b. Limited life.
c. Close government regulation.
d. Easy transferability of ownership.
e. Ability to raise large amounts of capital.

PE 11-3
LO2
Characteristics of Common Stock and Preferred Stock
Which one of the following statements is true regarding common stock and preferred stock?
a. Preferred stockholders always have the right to vote in corporate matters.
b. Common stockholders are the residual owners of the business after all other obligations have been paid.
c. Preferred stock is better than common stock.
d. Common stockholders receive dividends before preferred stockholders.
e. Preferred stock can never be converted into common stock.

PE 11-4
LO3
Issuance of No-Par Common Stock
The company issued 5,000 shares of no-par common stock at $25 per share for cash. Make the necessary journal entry(ies) to record this transaction.

PE 11-5   **Issuance of Common Stock for Cash**

LO3   The company issued 3,000 shares of $1 par-value common stock for $40 per share for cash. Make the necessary journal entry(ies) to record this transaction.

PE 11-6   **Issuance of Common Stock for Other Assets**

LO3   The company issued 7,200 shares of $1 par-value common stock in exchange for a building. The market value of the stock at the date of the exchange was $30 per share. Make the necessary journal entry(ies) to record this transaction.

PE 11-7   **Accounting for Stock Repurchases**

LO3   The company repurchased 1,500 shares of $1 par-value common stock for $32 per share from the open market. Make the necessary journal entry(ies) to record this transaction.

PE 11-8   **Accounting for Sale of Treasury Stock at Price Higher than Cost**

LO3   Refer to the data in PE 11-7. The company resells 400 shares of treasury stock for $40 per share. Make the necessary journal entry(ies) to record this transaction.

PE 11-9   **Accounting for Sale of Treasury Stock at Price Lower than Cost**

LO3   Refer to the data in PE 11-7 and PE 11-8. The company resells 300 shares of treasury stock for $28 per share. Make the necessary journal entry(ies) to record this transaction.

PE 11-10   **Accounting for Sale of Treasury Stock at Price Lower than Cost**

LO3   Refer to the data in PE 11-7 through PE 11-9. The paid-in capital, treasury stock account currently has a $2,500 credit balance. The company resells 800 shares of treasury stock for $26 per share. Make the necessary journal entry(ies) to record this transaction.

PE 11-11   **Dividend Declaration Accounting**

LO4   The company has the following two types of stock:
1. 2,000 shares of 10% cumulative preferred stock with a $20 par value.
2. 5,000 shares of common stock with a $1 par value.

The company declared a $21,000 cash dividend. Make the necessary journal entry(ies) to record this event.

PE 11-12   **Dividend Payment Accounting**

LO4   Refer to the data in PE 11-11. Make the necessary journal entry(ies) to record the payment of the cash dividend.

PE 11-13   **Dividend Closing Entry(ies)**

LO4   Refer to the data in PE 11-11. Make the necessary journal entry(ies) to close the dividend accounts to retained earnings at the end of the year.

PE 11-14   **Dividend Payout Ratio**

LO4   Using the following data, compute the dividend payout ratio.

Cash dividends	$ 19,000
Sales	512,000
Net income	76,000

PE 11-15   **Balance Sheet Preparation**

LO5   Using the following data, prepare a statement of stockholders' equity for the company.

(continued)

Paid-in capital in excess of par, common stock	$492,000
Retained earnings	200,000
Common stock ($1 par value, 8,400 shares issued, 8,000 outstanding)	8,000
Treasury stock (400 shares of $1 common at cost of $45)	18,000
Preferred stock ($20 par value, 2,500 shares issued and outstanding)	50,000

PE 11-16
LO5

Statement of Comprehensive Income

Using the following items, compute the company's comprehensive income.
1. The company's investment in a foreign subsidiary increased by $4,000 because the Euro strengthened relative to the U.S. dollar during the year.
2. Net income for the year was $52,000.
3. Unrealized loss on investments for the year was $11,000.

EXERCISES

E 11-17
LO3

Issuance of Stock

Brockbank Corporation was organized on July 15, 2009. Record the journal entries for Brockbank to account for the following:
a. The state authorized 30,000 shares of 7% preferred stock ($20 par) and 100,000 shares of no-par common stock.
b. The company gave 6,000 shares of common stock to its attorney in return for her help in incorporating the business. Fees for this work are normally about $18,000. (*Note:* The debit is to Legal Expense.)
c. Brockbank Corporation gave 15,000 shares of common stock to an individual who contributed a building worth $50,000.
d. Brockbank Corporation issued 5,000 shares of preferred stock at $25 per share.
e. Peter Brockbank paid $70,000 cash for 30,000 shares of common stock.
f. Another individual donated a $15,000 machine and received 4,000 shares of common stock.
g. The attorney sold all her shares to her brother-in-law for $18,000.

E 11-18
LO3

No-Par Stock Transactions

Harmsen Maintenance Corporation was organized in early 2009 with 60,000 shares of no-par common stock authorized. During 2009, the following transactions occurred:
a. Issued 31,000 shares of stock at $24 per share.
b. Issued another 3,900 shares of stock at $28 per share.
c. Issued 3,000 shares for a building appraised at $90,000.
d. Declared dividends of $1.50 per share.
e. Earned net income of $187,000 for the year, including $405,000 of revenues and $218,000 of expenses, and closed these accounts.
f. Closed the dividends accounts.

Given this information:
1. Journalize the transactions.
2. Present the stockholders' equity section of the balance sheet as it would appear on December 31, 2009.

E 11-19
LO3

Treasury Stock Transactions

Provide the necessary journal entries to record the following:
a. Washington Corporation was granted a charter authorizing the issuance of 200,000 shares of $10 par-value common stock.

(continued)

b. The company issued 50,000 shares of common stock at $15 per share.

c. The company reacquired 3,000 shares of its own stock at $19 per share, to be held in treasury.

d. Another 1,500 shares of stock were reacquired at $21 per share.

e. Of the shares reacquired in (c), 1,200 were reissued for $24 per share.

f. Of the shares reacquired in (d), all 1,500 were reissued for $16 per share.

g. Given the preceding transactions, what is the balance in the treasury stock account?

E 11-20

LO3, LO4

Stock Issuance and Cash Dividends

Lindstrom Corporation was organized in January 2009. The state authorized 200,000 shares of no-par common stock and 75,000 shares of 8%, $24 par, preferred stock. Record the following transactions that occurred in 2009:

a. Issued 20,000 shares of common stock at $35 per share.

b. Issued 3,500 shares of preferred stock for a building appraised at $100,000.

c. Declared a cash dividend sufficient to meet the current-dividend preference on preferred stock and pay common shareholders $3.50 per share.

E 11-21

LO3, LO4

Stock Issuance, Treasury Stock, and Dividends

On January 1, 2009, Vaness Corporation was granted a charter authorizing the following capital stock: common stock, $5 par, 200,000 shares; preferred stock, $10 par, 7%, 50,000 shares. Record the following 2009 transactions:

a. Issued 95,000 shares of common stock at $22 per share.

b. Issued 18,000 shares of preferred stock at $13 per share.

c. Bought back 10,000 shares of common stock at $30 per share.

d. Reissued 1,000 shares of treasury stock at $27 per share.

e. Declared cash dividends of $27,400 to be allocated between common and preferred stockholders. (The preferred stock, which has a current-dividend preference, is noncumulative.)

f. Paid dividends of $27,400.

E 11-22

LO3, LO4

Stock Issuance, Treasury Stock, and Dividends

On January 1, 2009, Snow Company was authorized to issue 100,000 shares of common stock, par value $10 per share and 10,000 shares of 8% preferred stock, par value $20 per share. Record the following transactions for 2009:

a. Issued 70,000 shares of common stock at $25 per share.

b. Issued 8,000 shares of preferred stock at $30 per share.

c. Reacquired 5,000 shares of common stock at $20 per share.

d. Reissued 2,000 shares of treasury stock for $46,000.

e. Declared a cash dividend sufficient to meet the current-dividend preference on preferred stock and pay common shareholders $1 per share.

E 11-23

LO3, LO4

Stock Transactions and Dividends

Fowler Corporation was organized in January 2009. The state authorized 150,000 shares of no-par common stock and 50,000 shares of 12%, $8 par, preferred stock. Record the following transactions that occurred in 2009:

a. Issued 28,000 shares of common stock at $32 per share.

b. Issued 15,000 shares of preferred stock for a piece of land appraised at $200,000.

c. Declared a cash dividend sufficient to meet the current-dividend preference on preferred stock and paid common shareholders $2 per share.

d. How would your answer to (c) change if the dividend declared were not sufficient to meet the current-dividend preference on preferred stock?

E 11-24

LO4

Dividend Calculations

On January 1, 2009, Oldroyd Corporation had 130,000 shares of common stock issued and outstanding. During 2009, the following transactions occurred (in chronological order):

(continued)

a. Oldroyd issued 10,000 new shares of common stock.

b. The company reacquired 2,000 shares of stock for use in its employee stock option plan.

c. At the end of the option period, 1,200 shares of treasury stock had been purchased by corporate officials.

Given this information, compute the following:

1. After the foregoing three transactions have occurred, what amount of dividends must Oldroyd Corporation declare in order to pay 50 cents per share? To pay $1 per share?

2. What is the dividend per share if $236,640 is paid?

3. If all 2,000 treasury shares had been purchased by corporate officials through the stock option plan, what would the dividends per share have been, again assuming $236,640 in dividends were paid? (Round to the nearest cent.)

E 11-25

LO4

Dividend Calculations

Churchill Corporation has the following stock outstanding:

Preferred stock (6%, $20 par value, 40,000 shares)	$800,000
Common stock ($2 par value, 400,000 shares)	800,000

For the two independent cases that follow, compute the amount of dividends that would be paid to preferred and common shareholders. Assume that total dividends paid are $200,000. No dividends have been paid for the past three years.

Case A, Preferred is noncumulative.
Case B, Preferred is cumulative.

E 11-26

LO3, LO4

Stock Issuance, Treasury Stock, and Dividends

During 2009, Doxey Corporation had the following transactions and related events:

Jan. 15 Issued 6,500 shares of common stock at par ($16 per share), bringing the total number of shares outstanding to 121,300.

Feb. 6 Declared a 50-cent-per-share dividend on common stock for stockholders of record on March 6.

Mar. 6 Date of record.

8 Pedro Garcia, a prominent banker, purchased 20,000 shares of Doxey Corporation common stock from the company for $346,000.

Apr. 6 Paid dividends declared on February 6.

June 19 Reacquired 800 shares of common stock as treasury stock at a total cost of $9,350.

Sept. 6 Declared dividends of 55 cents per share to be paid to common stockholders of record on October 15, 2009.

Oct. 6 The Dow Jones Industrial Average plummeted 300 points, and Doxey's stock price fell $3 per share.

15 Date of record.

Nov. 16 Paid dividends declared on September 6.

Dec. 15 Declared and paid a 6% cash dividend on 18,000 outstanding shares of preferred stock (par value $32).

Given this information:

1. Prepare the journal entries for these transactions.

2. What is the total amount of dividends paid to common and preferred stockholders during 2009?

E 11-27   **Dividend Payout Ratio**

LO4   The following numbers are for three different companies:

	A	B	C
Total assets	$3,100	$3,500	$2,900
Cash dividends	30	200	340
Total liabilities	2,600	1,600	2,000
Net income	310	420	460

For each company, compute the dividend payout ratio.

E 11-28   **Analysis of Stockholders' Equity**

LO5   The stockholders' equity section of Kay Corporation at the end of the current year showed:

Preferred stock (6%, $40 par, 10,000 shares authorized, 6,000 shares issued and outstanding)	$?
Common stock ($6 par, 80,000 shares authorized, 53,000 issued, 52,650 shares outstanding)	318,000
Paid-in capital in excess of par, preferred stock	?
Paid-in capital in excess of par, common stock	129,000
Retained earnings	86,000
Less treasury stock (350 shares at cost)	(2,000)
Total stockholders' equity	$?

1. What is the dollar amount to be reported for preferred stock?
2. What is the average price for which common stock was issued? (Round to the nearest cent.)
3. If preferred stock was issued at an average price of $43 per share, what amount should appear in the paid-in capital in excess of par, preferred stock account?
4. What is the average cost per share of treasury stock? (Round to the nearest cent.)
5. Assuming that the preferred stock was issued for an average price of $43 per share, what is total stockholders' equity?
6. If net income for the year were $67,000 and if only dividends on preferred stock were paid, by how much would retained earnings increase?

E 11-29   **Preparing the Stockholders' Equity Section**

LO5   The following account balances, before any closing entries, appear on the books of Spring Company as of December 31, 2009:

Retained Earnings (balance at Jan. 1, 2009)	$240,000
Dividends, Preferred Stock	15,000
Dividends, Common Stock	35,000
Common Stock ($5 par, 100,000 shares authorized, 70,000 issued and outstanding)	350,000
Paid-In Capital in Excess of Par, Common Stock	350,000
Preferred Stock (6%, $50 par, 50,000 shares authorized, 5,000 issued and outstanding)	250,000
Paid-In Capital in Excess of Par, Preferred Stock	25,000

Based on these account balances, and assuming net income for 2009 of $80,000, prepare the stockholders' equity section of the December 31, 2009, balance sheet for Spring Company.

E 11-30   **Comprehensive Income**

LO5   The following information relates to Larkin Company:

a. Larkin Company's net income for the year was $23,000.

(continued)

b. Larkin Company has an investment portfolio for long-term investment purposes. That portfolio decreased in value by $2,600 during the year.

c. Larkin Company has several foreign subsidiaries. The currencies in the countries where those subsidiaries are located increased in value (relative to the U.S. dollar) during the year. Accordingly, the computed value of the equity of those subsidiaries, in U.S. dollars, decreased by $1,700.

Compute Larkin's comprehensive income for the year.

E 11-31

LO5

Other Equity Items

Red Rider Company has the following stockholders' equity section on its balance sheet as of December 31, 2009 and 2008.

Red Rider Company (in millions)		
	2009	**2008**
Stockholders' Equity		
Preferred stock	$ 2.0	$ 2.0
Common stock	32.0	32.0
Paid-in capital–various	12.4	11.2
Retained earnings	24.5	24.6
Subtotal	$ 70.9	$69.8
Accumulated foreign currency translation adjustments	5.2	4.5
Net unrealized gains on investments in certain debt and equity securities	25.6	20.0
Total stockholders' equity	$101.7	$94.3

Based on this stockholders' equity section, answer the following questions:

1. At the end of 2009, what was the total amount of equity financing provided by Red Rider's investors?
2. At the end of 2009, how much of Red Rider's earnings had not been distributed to investors?
3. What is the total amount of "other equity items" contained in the 2009 stockholders' equity section?
4. What contributed most to the increased equity from 2008 to 2009?

PROBLEMS

P 11-32

LO3, LO4

Stock Transactions and Analysis

The following selected items and amounts were taken from the balance sheet of Quale Company as of December 31, 2009:

Cash	$ 93,000
Property, plant, and equipment	850,000
Accumulated depreciation	150,000
Liabilities	50,000
Preferred stock (7%, $100 par, noncumulative, 10,000 shares authorized, 5,000 shares issued and outstanding)	500,000
Common stock ($10 par, 100,000 shares authorized, 80,000 shares issued and outstanding)	800,000
Paid-in capital in excess of par, preferred stock	1,000
Paid-in capital in excess of par, common stock	125,000
Paid-in capital, treasury stock	1,000
Retained earnings	310,000

(continued)

Required:

For each of parts (1) to (5), (a) prepare the necessary journal entry (or entries) to record each transaction, and (b) calculate the amount that would appear on the December 31, 2009, balance sheet as a consequence of this transaction only for the account given. (*Note:* In your answer to each part of this problem, consider this to be the only transaction that took place during 2009.)

1. Quale Company issued 200 shares of common stock in exchange for cash of $4,000.
   a. Entry
   b. Paid-In Capital in Excess of Par, Common Stock
2. The company issued 200 shares of preferred stock at a price of $102 per share.
   a. Entry
   b. Paid-In Capital in Excess of Par, Preferred Stock
3. The company issued 500 shares of common stock in exchange for a building. The common stock is not actively traded, but the building was recently appraised at $11,000.
   a. Entry
   b. Property, Plant, and Equipment
4. The company reacquired 1,000 shares of common stock from a stockholder for $23,000 and subsequently reissued the shares to a different investor for $21,500. (*Note:* Make two entries.)
   a. Entries
   b. Paid-In Capital, Treasury Stock
5. The board of directors declared dividends of $75,000. This amount includes the current-year dividend preference on preferred stock, with the remainder to be paid to common shareholders.
   a. Entry
   b. Retained Earnings

P 11-33   **Stock Transactions and the Stockholders' Equity Section**

LO3, LO4, LO5   The following is Saratoga Springs Company's stockholders' equity section of the balance sheet on December 31, 2008:

Preferred stock (7%, $50 par, noncumulative, 22,000 shares authorized, 9,000 shares issued and outstanding)	$450,000
Common stock ($8 par, 110,000 shares authorized, 94,000 shares issued and outstanding)	752,000
Paid-in capital in excess of par, preferred stock	125,000
Paid-in capital in excess of par, common stock	326,000
Retained earnings	540,000

Required:

1. Journalize the following 2009 transactions:
   a. Issued 3,000 preferred shares at $62 per share.
   b. Reacquired 2,500 common shares for the treasury at $17 per share.
   c. Declared and paid a $1.50-per-share dividend on common stock in addition to paying the required preferred dividends. (*Note:* Debit Retained Earnings directly.)
   d. Reissued 900 treasury shares at $20 per share.
   e. Reissued the remaining treasury shares at $16 per share.
   f. Earnings for the year were $83,000, including $350,000 of revenues and $267,000 of expenses.
2. Prepare the stockholders' equity section of the balance sheet for the company at December 31, 2009.

P 11-34   **Recording Stockholders' Equity Transactions**

LO3   Zina Corporation was organized during 2008. At the end of 2008, the stockholders' equity section of the balance sheet appeared as follows:

(continued)

Contributed capital:	
Preferred stock (5%, $30 par, 15,000 shares authorized,	
8,000 shares issued and outstanding)	$240,000
Common stock ($22 par, 36,000 shares authorized, 18,000 issued,	
15,000 outstanding)	396,000
Paid-in capital in excess of par, preferred stock	56,000
Total contributed capital	$692,000
Retained earnings	244,000
Total contributed capital plus retained earnings	$936,000
Less treasury stock (3,000 shares at cost of $28 per share)	(84,000)
Total stockholders' equity	$852,000

During 2009, the following transactions occurred in the order given:

a. Issued 1,200 shares of common stock at $25 per share.

b. Reissued 1,600 shares of treasury stock at $30 per share.

c. Reissued 750 shares of treasury stock at $21 per share.

Required:

Record the transactions.

P 11-35

LO3, LO4, LO5

Stock Transactions and Stockholders' Equity Section

The balance sheet for Lakeland Corporation as of December 31, 2008, is as follows:

Assets		$750,000
Liabilities		$410,000
Stockholders' equity:		
Preferred stock, convertible (5%, $20 par)	$ 50,000	
Common stock ($10 par)	150,000	
Paid-in capital in excess of par, common stock	30,000	
Retained earnings	116,000	
	$346,000	
Less treasury stock, common (500 shares at cost)	(6,000)	340,000
Total liabilities and stockholders' equity		$750,000

During 2009, the following transactions were completed in the order given:

a. The company reacquired 750 shares of outstanding common stock at $7 per share.

b. The company reacquired 150 shares of common stock in settlement of an account receivable of $1,500.

c. Semiannual cash dividends of 75 cents per share on common stock and 50 cents per share on preferred stock were declared and paid.

d. Each share of preferred stock is convertible into three shares of common stock. Five hundred shares of preferred stock were converted into common stock. (*Hint:* Shares are converted at par values, and any excess reduces Retained Earnings.)

e. The 900 shares of common treasury stock acquired during 2009 were sold at $13. The remaining treasury shares were exchanged for a machine with a fair market value of $6,300.

f. The company issued 3,000 shares of common stock in exchange for land appraised at $39,000.

g. Semiannual cash dividends of 75 cents per share on common stock and 50 cents per share on preferred stock were declared and paid.

h. Closed net income of $35,000 to Retained Earnings, which included $135,000 of revenues and $100,000 of expenses.

i. Closed dividends accounts to Retained Earnings.

(continued)

Required:

1. Give the necessary journal entries to record the transactions listed.
2. Prepare the stockholders' equity section of the balance sheet as of December 31, 2009.

P 11-36

LO3, LO4, LO5

Stockholders' Equity, Dividends, and Treasury Stock

The stockholders' equity section of Nielsen Corporation's December 31, 2008, balance sheet is as follows:

Stockholders' equity:	
Preferred stock (10%, $50 par, 10,000 shares authorized,	
1,000 shares issued and outstanding)	$ 50,000
Common stock ($15 par, 100,000 shares authorized,	
5,000 shares issued and outstanding)	75,000
Paid-in capital in excess of par, preferred stock	2,000
Paid-in capital in excess of par, common stock	25,000
Total contributed capital	$152,000
Retained earnings	102,000
Total stockholders' equity	$254,000

During 2009, Nielsen Corporation had the following transactions affecting stockholders' equity:

Jan.	20	Paid a cash dividend of $2 per share on common stock. The dividend was declared on December 15, 2008.
Aug.	15	Reacquired 1,000 shares of common stock at $20 per share.
Sept.	30	Reissued 500 shares of treasury stock at $21 per share.
Oct.	15	Declared and paid cash dividends of $3 per share on the common stock.
Nov.	1	Reissued 200 shares of treasury stock at $18 per share.
Dec.	15	Declared and paid the 10% preferred cash dividend.
	31	Closed net income of $40,000 to Retained Earnings. (Revenues were $260,000; expenses were $220,000.) Also closed the dividends accounts to Retained Earnings.

Required:

1. Journalize the transactions.
2. Prepare the stockholders' equity section of Nielsen Corporation's December 31, 2009, balance sheet.
3. **Interpretive Question:** What is the effect on earnings per share when a company purchases treasury stock?

P 11-37

LO4

Dividend Calculations

Snowy Peaks Corporation was organized in January 2006 and issued shares of preferred and common stock as shown. As of December 31, 2009, there have been no changes in outstanding stock.

Preferred stock (10%, $15 par, 10,000 shares issued and outstanding)	$150,000
Common stock ($20 par, 15,000 shares issued and outstanding)	300,000

Required:

For each of the following independent situations, compute the amount of dividends that would be paid for each class of stock in 2008 and 2009. Assume that total dividends of $8,000 and $92,000 are paid in 2008 and 2009, respectively.

1. Preferred stock is noncumulative.
2. Preferred stock is cumulative, and no dividends are in arrears in 2008.
3. Preferred stock is cumulative, and no dividends have been paid during 2006 and 2007.

P 11-38

LO4

Dividend Calculations

Lowe Corporation had authorization for 80,000 shares of 8% preferred stock, par value $20 per share, and 24,000 shares of common stock, par value $120 per share, all of which are issued and outstanding. During the years beginning in 2008, Lowe Corporation maintained a policy of paying out 50% of net income in cash dividends. One-half the net income for the three years beginning in 2008 was $50,000, $280,000, and $340,000. There are no dividends in arrears for years prior to 2008.

Required:

Compute the amount of dividends paid to each class of stock for each year under the following separate cases:

1. Preferred stock is noncumulative.
2. Preferred stock is cumulative.
3. **Interpretive Question:** Why is it important that a common stockholder know about the dividend privileges of the preferred stock?

P 11-39

LO3, LO4

Dividend Transactions and Calculations

As of December 31, 2008, Nibley Corporation has 300,000 shares of $12 par-value common stock authorized, with 120,000 of these shares issued and outstanding.

Required:

1. Prepare journal entries to record the following 2009 transactions:

Jan. 1 Received authorization for 150,000 shares of 5%, cumulative preferred stock with a par value of $15.

2 Issued 14,000 shares of the preferred stock at $20 per share.

June 1 Reacquired 30% of the common stock outstanding for $25 per share.

2 Declared a cash dividend of $20,000. The date of record is June 15.

30 Paid the previously declared cash dividend of $20,000.

2. Determine the proper allocation to preferred and common stockholders of a $150,000 cash dividend declared on December 31, 2009. (This dividend is in addition to the June 2 dividend.)

3. **Interpretive Question:** Why didn't the preferred stockholders receive their current-dividend preference of $10,500 in part (2)?

P 11-40

LO4

Dividend Payout Ratio

The following numbers are for three different companies:

	A	B	C
Cash	$ 300	$ 500	$ 700
Retained earnings	900	1,000	4,100
Cash dividends	0	100	600
Paid-in capital	3,200	2,000	2,500
Total liabilities	800	900	700
Sales	8,000	6,000	7,000
Net income	400	700	900

Required:

1. For each company, compute the dividend payout ratio.
2. **Interpretive Question:** Which of the three companies is most likely to be a high-growth Internet company? Which is most likely to be an old, stable company? Explain.

P 11-41

LO4, LO5

Preparing the Stockholders' Equity Section and Recording Dividends

In 2007, Lee Ann Adams and some college friends organized The Candy Jar, a gourmet candy company. In 2007, The Candy Jar issued 150,000 of the 300,000 authorized shares of

(continued)

common stock, par value $15, for $3,000,000 and all the 50,000 authorized shares of 10%, $20 par, cumulative preferred stock for $1,100,000. Combined earnings for 2007, 2008, 2009, and 2010 amounted to $1,250,000. Dividends paid in the four years were as follows: 2007—$100,000; 2008—$300,000; 2009—$0; 2010—$150,000.

Required:

1. Prepare the stockholders' equity section of the balance sheet as of December 31, 2010, for The Candy Jar.
2. Prepare the journal entry that would be necessary to record the dividends paid in 2010.

P 11-42

LO3, LO4, LO5

Stockholders' Equity Calculations

A computer virus destroyed important financial information pertaining to Paseo Company's stockholders' equity section. Your expertise is needed to compute the missing account balances. The only information you can recover from the computer's backup system is as follows:

a. During 2009, 7,000 shares of common stock with a par value of $1 were issued when the market price per share was $12.
b. Cash dividends of $25,000 were paid to preferred shareholders.
c. Paseo Company acquired 3,000 shares of common stock at $14 to hold as treasury stock.
d. Paseo Company reissued 2,500 shares of treasury stock for $16.

	December 31, 2008	December 31, 2009
Preferred stock	$ 3,000	$ 3,000
Common stock	8,000	?
Paid-in capital in excess of par, preferred stock	1,500	1,500
Paid-in capital in excess of par, common stock	12,000	?
Paid-in capital, treasury stock	0	?
Retained earnings	18,200	7,400
Treasury stock	0	(7,000)
Total stockholders' equity	42,700	?

Required:

1. Calculate the account balances for the following accounts:
   a. Common Stock
   b. Paid-In Capital in Excess of Par, Common Stock
   c. Paid-In Capital, Treasury Stock
   d. Stockholders' Equity
2. How much net income did Paseo Company report for 2009?

P 11-43

LO3, LO5

Stock Calculations and the Stockholders' Equity Section

The following account balances appear on the books of World Corporation as of December 31, 2009:

Preferred stock (7%, $40 par, 70,000 shares authorized, 50,000 shares issued and outstanding)	$2,000,000
Common stock ($3 par, 500,000 shares authorized, 300,000 shares issued and outstanding)	900,000
Paid-in capital in excess of par, preferred stock	310,000
Paid-in capital in excess of par, common stock	490,000
Net income for 2009	130,000
Dividends paid during 2009	70,000
Retained earnings, January 1, 2009	1,360,000

(continued)

Required:

1. If the preferred stock is selling at $45 per share, what is the maximum amount of cash that World Corporation can obtain by issuing additional preferred stock given the present number of authorized shares?
2. If common stock is selling for $12 per share, what is the maximum amount of cash that can be obtained by issuing additional common stock given the present number of authorized shares?
3. Given the account balances at December 31, 2009, and ignoring parts (1) and (2), prepare, in good form, the stockholders' equity section of the balance sheet.

P 11-44

LO3, LO5

Unifying Concepts: Stock Transactions and the Stockholders' Equity Section

Richard Corporation was founded on January 1, 2009, and entered into the following stock transactions during 2009:

a. Received authorization for 100,000 shares of $20 par-value common stock, 50,000 shares of 6% preferred stock with a par value of $5, and 50,000 shares of no-par common stock.
b. Issued 25,000 shares of the $20 par-value common stock at $24 per share.
c. Issued 10,000 shares of the preferred stock at $8 per share.
d. Issued 5,000 shares of the no-par common stock at $22 per share.
e. Reacquired 1,000 shares of the $20 par-value common stock at $25 per share.
f. Reacquired 500 shares of the no-par common stock at $20 per share.
g. Reissued 250 of the 1,000 reacquired shares of $20 par-value common stock at $23 per share.
h. Reissued all the 500 reacquired shares of no-par common stock at $23 per share.
i. Closed the $14,000 net income to Retained Earnings. Revenues and expenses for the year were $90,000 and $76,000, respectively.

Required:

1. Prepare journal entries to record the 2009 transactions in Richard Corporation's books.
2. Prepare the stockholders' equity section of Richard Corporation's balance sheet at December 31, 2009. Assume that the transactions represent all the events involving equity accounts during 2009.

P 11-45

LO3, LO5

Unifying Concepts: Stock Transactions, the Stockholders' Equity Section, and the Statement of Stockholders' Equity

The condensed balance sheet of JCB Corporation at December 31, 2008, is shown below.

JCB Corporation
Balance Sheet
December 31, 2008

Assets

Cash	$ 550,000
All other assets	828,000
	$1,378,000

Liabilities and Stockholders' Equity

Current liabilities	$ 145,000
Long-term liabilities	220,000
	$ 365,000
Contributed capital:	
Common stock ($10 par, 150,000 shares authorized,	
70,000 shares outstanding)	$ 700,000
Paid-in capital in excess of par, common stock	140,000
Retained earnings	173,000
	$1,013,000
	$1,378,000

(continued)

During 2009, the following transactions affected stockholders' equity:

Feb. 15   Purchased 6,000 shares of JCB outstanding common stock at $18 per share.
May 21   Sold 3,500 of the shares purchased on February 15 at $21 per share.
Sept. 15   Issued 12,000 shares of previously unissued common stock at $22 per share.
Dec. 21   Sold the remaining 2,500 shares of treasury stock at $23 per share.
    31   Closed net income of $91,600 to Retained Earnings. Revenues were $291,600; expenses were $200,000.

Required:

1. Prepare the journal entries to record the 2009 transactions.
2. Prepare the stockholders' equity section of the balance sheet at December 31, 2009.
3. Prepare a statement of stockholders' equity for the year ended December 31, 2009.

P 11-46   **Unifying Concepts: Stockholders' Equity**

LO3, LO4, LO5   Icon Corporation was organized during 2007. At the end of 2008, the equity section of its balance sheet appeared as follows:

Contributed capital:	
Preferred stock (6%, $20 par, 10,000 shares authorized,	
5,000 shares issued and outstanding)	$100,000
Common stock ($10 par, 50,000 shares authorized,	
11,000 shares issued, 10,000 outstanding)	110,000
Paid-in capital in excess of par, preferred stock	20,000
Total contributed capital	$230,000
Retained earnings	100,000
Total contributed capital plus retained earnings	$330,000
Less treasury stock (1,000 shares of common at cost)	(12,000)
Total stockholders' equity	$318,000

During 2009, the following stockholders' equity transactions occurred (in chronological sequence):

a. Issued 500 shares of common stock at $13 per share.
b. Reissued 500 shares of treasury stock at $13 per share.
c. Issued 1,000 shares of preferred stock at $25 per share.
d. Reissued 500 shares of treasury stock at $10 per share.
e. Declared a dividend large enough to meet the current-dividend preference of the preferred stock and to pay the common stockholders $2 per share. Dividends are recorded directly in the retained earnings account.
f. Closed net income of $65,000 to Retained Earnings. Revenues were $400,000; expenses were $335,000.

Required:

1. Journalize the transactions.
2. Prepare the stockholders' equity section of the balance sheet at December 31, 2009.

P 11-47   **Comprehensive Income**

LO5   The following information relates to Loveland Company:

Sales	$60,000
Cost of goods sold	36,000
Other operating expenses	8,000
Interest expense	500
Income tax expense	5,400

(continued)

In addition, the following events occurred during the year:

a. Loveland Company has an investment portfolio for long-term investment purposes. That portfolio decreased in value by $9,000 during the year.

b. Loveland Company owns a substantial amount of land. During the year, the land increased in value by $34,000.

c. Loveland Company has several foreign subsidiaries. The currencies in the countries where those subsidiaries are located declined in value (relative to the U.S. dollar) during the year. Accordingly, the computed value of the equity of those subsidiaries, in U.S. dollars, decreased by $3,700.

Required:

1. Compute Loveland's comprehensive income for the year.
2. **Interpretive Question:** Is comprehensive income a good measure of the change in a company's value during the year?

P 11-48

LO5

Stockholders' Equity Section with Selected "Other Information"

The stockholders' equity section of Glory Company's balance sheet was as follows as of December 31, 2009, and December 31, 2008:

Glory Company Stockholders' Equity Sections of Balance Sheet December 31, 2009 and 2008 (in millions)		
	2009	**2008**
Preferred stock	$ 21.4	$ 21.4
Common stock	48.4	43.2
Paid-in capital, various types	22.6	15.3
Retained earnings	51.8	41.2
Subtotal	$144.2	$121.1
Accumulated foreign currency translation adjustments	21.4	57.3
Net unrealized gains (losses) on investments in		
certain debt and equity securities	(46.4)	(8.8)
Total stockholders' equity	$119.2	$169.6

Required:

Based on the stockholders' equity section for Glory Company, answer the following questions:

1. Do you believe Glory Company made a profit during the year 2009? Assuming that only net income and dividends changed the retained earnings balance from 2008 to 2009, by how much did net income exceed dividends?

2. What was the total amount of money raised during 2009 from the selling of stock? (Assume that only the selling of stock affected the contributed capital accounts.)

3. Did the market value of Glory Company's securities that affect the equity section increase or decrease in 2009? By how much?

4. **Interpretive Question:** The board of directors believes it should fire the current management of the company because total stockholders' equity decreased substantially. Do you agree? Why or why not?

ANALYTICAL ASSIGNMENTS

AA 11-49

DISCUSSION

Does Stockholders' Equity Tell the Real Story?

Last year, Shades International (a hypothetical company) invented the famous Shades Sunglasses that are widely popular around the world and especially in Japan and the Far East. Citizens of these countries love the new-age sunglasses and are buying them as fast as they can. Shades International owns the patent but contracts out to other companies to

(continued)

manufacture the glasses. Shades International also leases its research and development facility, the only building it occupies. Royalties from the glasses exceeded $10 million last year and are expected to increase dramatically this year. Selected data (in millions of dollars) from Shades International's financial statements are as follows:

Patent	$ 0.3
Other assets	0.9
Total liabilities	4.5
Total stockholders' equity	(3.3)

In the next two months, Shades International will be offering stock for sale to the public. Your friend is encouraging you to buy some of the stock. You are leery about the negative stockholders' equity balance. Is Shades International worth even considering as a possible investment?

AA 11-50
DISCUSSION

To Pay or Not To Pay Dividends

Assume Lenny Company manufactures specialized computer peripheral parts such as speakers and modems. It is a new company that has been in operation for just two years. During those two years, Lenny Company's stock price has increased over 400%. Lenny Company does not pay dividends nor does the company plan to do so in the future. However, the company's stock seems to be heavily traded. Why do you think there is so much interest in buying Lenny Company's stock if stockholders do not receive dividends?

AA 11-51
JUDGMENT CALL

You Decide: **Should partners of a business be held personally liable for the debts of the business, or should their business activities and debts be kept separate from their personal activities?**

John and Jeff formed a partnership and started selling cookies based on a secret recipe they created. After one year of strong sales, Jeff left the company with $30,000 cash and was never heard of again. Now, the creditors are requesting payment from John to satisfy a loan Jeff signed. If John can't make the payments from what is left in the business, who will the bank look to for payment?

AA 11-52
JUDGMENT CALL

You Decide: **Should the U.S. government change the current corporate tax system from double to single taxation, or is the present system (taxing corporate profits and then dividends to shareholders) adequate?**

You were recently at a family gathering when the topic of conversation turned political. Your father, a retired CEO of a regional grocery chain, commented on his dissatisfaction with the current corporate tax system. He said, "It was very frustrating to see profits of my company taxed once at the corporate level and then again when the shareholders receive dividends. Something should be done about that!" Do you agree with your father?

AA 11-53
JUDGMENT CALL

You Decide: **Should companies be required to pay cash dividends on their stock to shareholders, or should it be left up to the companies' discretion whether they pay dividends or reinvest those funds back in the company?**

Your father asked you why his investment in a publicly-traded stock is not paying him any dividends. He said, "As far as I know, they never have. I invested in the company to get something back and so far, I haven't received anything. Shouldn't the company be looking after its shareholders?" Should all companies be required to pay dividends?

AA 11-54
REAL COMPANY
ANALYSIS

Wal-Mart

The 2006 Form 10-K for Wal-Mart is included in Appendix A. Wal-Mart's stockholders' equity statements provide details of equity transactions of the company during the 2006 fiscal year. Locate the statements and consider the following questions:

1. What was the major reason that stockholders' equity increased for the year?
2. How much did common stockholders receive in dividends during the year?
3. Did Wal-Mart issue more shares than it repurchased during the year or vice versa? How can you tell?

AA 11-55

REAL COMPANY
ANALYSIS

Union Pacific Corporation

Union Pacific's statement of shareholders' equity for the year 2005 is reproduced below.

Millions of Dollars / Thousands of Shares	Common Shares	Treasury Shares	Common Shares	Paid-In-Surplus	Retained Earnings	Treasury Stock	Minimum Pension Liability Adj.	Foreign Currency Trans. Adj.	Derivative Adj.	Total
Balance at Jan. 1, 2003	275,579	(21,920)	$ 689	$ 3,946	$ 7,597	$ (1,347)	$ (232)	$ (9)	$ 7	$ 10,651
Comprehensive income/(loss):										
Net income			–	–	1,585	–	–	–	–	1,585
Other comp. income/(loss) from continuing operations [a]			–	–	–	–	39	(9)	(4)	26
Other comp. income/(loss) from discontinued operations [b]			–	–	–	–	84	–	–	84
Total comprehensive income/(loss)			–	–	1,585	–	123	(9)	(4)	1,695
Conversion, exercises of stock options, forfeitures, and other	114	4,388	–	(10)	–	270	–	–	–	260
Dividends declared ($0.99 per share)	–	–	–	–	(252)	–	–	–	–	(252)
Balance at Dec. 31, 2003	275,693	(17,532)	$ 689	$ 3,936	$ 8,930	$ (1,077)	$ (109)	$ (18)	$ 3	$12,354
Comprehensive income/(loss):										
Net income			–	–	604	–	–	–	–	604
Other comp. income/(loss) [a]			–	–	–	–	(103)	–	(10)	(113)
Total comprehensive income/(loss)			–	–	604	–	(103)	–	(10)	491
Conversion, exercises of stock options, forfeitures, and other	2	2,357	–	(19)	–	141	–	–	–	122
Dividends declared ($1.20 per share)	–	–	–	–	(312)	–	–	–	–	(312)
Balance at Dec. 31, 2004	275,695	(15,175)	$ 689	$ 3,917	$ 9,222	$ (936)	$ (212)	$ (18)	$ (7)	$12,655
Comprehensive income/(loss):										
Net income			–	–	1,026	–	–	–	–	1,026
Other comp. income/(loss) [a]			–	–	–	–	1	5	1	7
Total comprehensive income/(loss)			–	–	1,026	–	1	5	1	1,033
Conversion, exercises of stock options, forfeitures, and other	104	6,011	–	(2)	–	337	–	–	–	335
Dividends declared ($1.20 per share)	–	–	–	–	(316)	–	–	–	–	(316)
Balance at Dec. 31, 2005	275,799	(9,164)	$ 689	$ 3,915	$ 9,932	$ (599)	$ (211)	$ (13)	$ (6)	$13,707

(continued)

1. Based on the dividends paid during 2005, how many shares of stock were outstanding when the dividends were paid?
2. Why isn't the number of shares receiving dividends exactly the same as the number of shares outstanding on December 31 as indicated in the statement?
3. Compute Union Pacific's dividend payout ratio for each year. Has that number increased or decreased over time?

AA 11-56

INTERNATIONAL

The EMI Group

The shareholders' equity section of the balance sheet of **The EMI Group**, a company based in the United Kingdom, is reproduced below. Review this information and answer the questions below.

<table>
<thead>
<tr><th colspan="3">The EMI Group
Balance Sheets
at 31 March 2005</th></tr>
<tr><th></th><th colspan="2">Group</th></tr>
<tr><th></th><th>2005
£m</th><th>2004
£m</th></tr>
</thead>
<tbody>
<tr><td>**Capital and reserves**</td><td></td><td></td></tr>
<tr><td>Called-up share capital</td><td>110.6</td><td>110.4</td></tr>
<tr><td>Share premium account</td><td>447.3</td><td>445.8</td></tr>
<tr><td>Capital redemption reserve</td><td>495.8</td><td>495.8</td></tr>
<tr><td>Other reserves</td><td>252.2</td><td>255.7</td></tr>
<tr><td>Profit and loss reserve (including goodwill previously written off)</td><td>(2,101.3)</td><td>(2,091.7)</td></tr>
<tr><td>Equity shareholders' funds</td><td>(795.4)</td><td>(784.0)</td></tr>
<tr><td>Minority interests (equity)</td><td>48.3</td><td>67.6</td></tr>
<tr><td></td><td>(747.1)</td><td>(716.4)</td></tr>
</tbody>
</table>

1. What do you think the term "called-up share capital" means?
2. What do you think the term "share premium account" means?
3. What does the term "profit and loss reserve" mean?

AA 11-57

ETHICS

Buying Your Own Shares Back

You are the chief financial officer for Esoteric, Inc., a company whose stock is publicly traded. The stock market has recently experienced an overall downturn, and the price of your company's stock has decreased by about 15%. This significantly affects the compensation of the executives of your company as their bonuses are based on the company's stock price. The bonus plan rewards company executives who take actions to increase the value of the company to shareholders. The reasoning is that if management increases the value of the company to shareholders, management should be rewarded.

As you consider ways to increase the value of the company, when the market itself is slumping, the following idea pops into your head: We will buy back our own stock. That will cause the remaining outstanding stock to increase in value, which is good for those individuals holding that stock. And it will also result in you and the other corporate executives receiving sizable bonuses.

Do you think this plan of action to increase stock price was what the designers of the compensation plan had in mind when they linked executive bonuses to company stock price? Does buying back the company's own stock add value to the company as a whole? Should the compensation plan prohibit activities like buying stock back? Consider these issues and be prepared to discuss them.

AA 11-58

WRITING

Other Comprehensive Income

In this chapter you learned that certain transactions that changed a company's net assets were not reflected on the income statement but instead were reflected on the statement of stockholders' equity under the heading of accumulated other comprehensive income. Prepare a two-page memo summarizing the following points:

1. Why aren't all items included under accumulated other comprehensive income simply disclosed on the income statement? What is it about these transactions that keep their effects off the income statement?

2. In your opinion, do you think there should be a separate accumulated other comprehensive income statement or is disclosing the amount in the statement of stockholders' equity sufficient to get investor's attention?

AA 11-59

CUMULATIVE
SPREADSHEET
PROJECT

Preparing New Forecasts

This spreadsheet assignment is a continuation of the spreadsheet assignments given in earlier chapters. If you completed those spreadsheets, you have a head start on this one.

1. Handyman wishes to prepare a forecasted balance sheet and income statement for 2010. Use the original financial statement numbers for 2009 [given in part (1) of the Cumulative Spreadsheet Project assignment in Chapter 2] as the basis for the forecast, along with the following additional information:

    a. Sales in 2010 are expected to increase by 40% over 2009 sales of $700.

    b. Cash will increase at the same rate as sales.

    c. The forecasted amount of accounts receivable in 2010 is determined using the forecasted value for the average collection period. For simplicity, do the computations using the end-of-period accounts receivable balance instead of the average balance. The average collection period for 2010 is expected to be 14.08 days.

    d. The forecasted amount of inventory in 2010 is determined using the forecasted value for the number of days' sales in inventory (computed using the end-of-period inventory balance). The number of days' sales in inventory for 2010 is expected to be 107.6 days.

    e. The forecasted amount of accounts payable in 2010 is determined using the forecasted value for the number of days' purchases in accounts payable (computed using the end-of-period accounts payable balance). The number of days' purchases in accounts payable for 2010 is expected to be 48.34 days.

    f. The $160 in operating expenses reported in 2009 breaks down as follows: $5 depreciation expense, $155 other operating expenses.

    g. New long-term debt will be acquired (or repaid) in an amount sufficient to make Handyman's debt ratio (total liabilities divided by total assets) in 2010 exactly equal to 0.80.

    h. No cash dividends will be paid in 2010.

    i. New short-term loans payable will be acquired in an amount sufficient to make Handyman's current ratio in 2010 exactly equal to 2.0.

    j. The forecasted amount of property, plant, and equipment (PP&E) in 2010 is determined using the forecasted value for the fixed asset turnover ratio. For simplicity, compute the fixed asset turnover ratio using the end-of-period gross PP&E balance. The fixed asset turnover ratio for 2010 is expected to be 3.518 times.

    k. In computing depreciation expense for 2010, use straight-line depreciation and assume a 30-year useful life with no residual value. Gross PP&E acquired during the year is depreciated for only half the year. In other words, depreciation expense for 2010 is the sum of two parts: (1) a full year of depreciation on the beginning balance in PP&E, assuming a 30-year life and no residual value and (2) a half-year of depreciation on any new PP&E acquired during the year, based on the change in the gross PP&E balance.

    l. Assume an interest rate on short-term loans payable of 6.0% and on long-term debt of 8.0%. Only a half-year's interest is charged on loans taken out during the year.

(continued)

For example, if short-term loans payable at the end of 2010 are $15 and given that short-term loans payable at the end of 2009 were $10, total short-term interest expense for 2010 would be $0.75 [($10 × 0.06) + ($5 × 0.06 × ½)].

Note: These statements were constructed as part of the spreadsheet assignment in Chapter 10; you can use that spreadsheet as a starting point if you have completed that assignment.

For this exercise, add the following additional assumptions:

- In addition to preparing forecasted financial statements for 2010, Handyman also wishes to prepare forecasted financial statements for 2011. All assumptions applicable to 2010 are also assumed to be applicable to 2011. Sales in 2011 are expected to be 40% higher than sales in 2010.

Clearly state any additional assumptions that you make.

2. For each forecasted year, 2010 and 2011, state whether Handyman is expected to issue new shares of stock or to repurchase shares of stock.
3. Repeat (2), with the following changes in assumptions:
   a. The debt ratio in 2010 and 2011 is exactly equal to 0.70.
   b. The debt ratio in 2010 and 2011 is exactly equal to 0.95.
4. Comment on how it is possible for a company to have negative paid-in capital.

Investments in Debt and Equity Securities

After studying this chapter, you should be able to:

(1) Understand why companies invest in other companies. *Companies sometimes make investments in securities in order to provide a safety cushion of available funds or to store a temporary excess of cash. Companies also invest in other companies in order to earn a return, to secure influence, or to gain control.*

(2) Understand the different classifications for securities. *For accounting purposes, stocks and bonds purchased as investment securities are classified as trading, available-for-sale, or held-to-maturity investments, or as equity investments. These classifications, and the associated accounting treatment, reflect the underlying reasons for the investment.*

(3) Account for the purchase, recognition of revenue, and sale of trading and available-for-sale securities. *The cost of an investment includes the purchase price plus any brokerage fees. Interest and dividends received on trading and available-for-sale securities are reported as revenue. When a security is sold, the gain or loss on the sale is called a realized gain or loss.*

(4) Account for changes in the value of securities. *Both trading and available-for-sale securities are reported in the balance sheet at market value. Unrealized gains and losses are reported in the income statement for trading securities and as an equity adjustment for available-for-sale securities.*

EXPANDED *material*

(5) Account for held-to-maturity securities. *Held-to-maturity securities are reported in the balance sheet at amortized cost, which reflects the gradual adjustment of the book value of the investment from its original cost to its ultimate maturity value.*

(6) Account for securities using the equity method. *When a company owns between 20% and 50% of another company, the equity method is used to account for the investment. Income from the investment is computed as the investing company's share of the net income of the investee. Dividends received are viewed as a partial return of the original amount invested.*

(7) Understand the basics of consolidated financial statements. *Consolidated financial statements are prepared when a parent owns more than 50% of one or more subsidiaries. All of the assets, liabilities, revenues, and expenses of the parent and the majority-owned subsidiaries are added in preparing the consolidated financial statements.*

Warren Buffett, who has been called "the world's greatest investor," has lived most of his life not far from the house in which he grew up in Omaha, Nebraska.[1] He attended the Wharton School at the University of Pennsylvania (but dropped out because he thought he wasn't learning anything); received a bachelor's degree from the University of Nebraska; applied for admission to do graduate work at Harvard but was rejected; and instead earned a master's degree in economics at Columbia.

Buffett began his professional career as a stock trader and eventually created an investment fund called the Buffett Partnership, which earned a 32% average annual return over its life from 1956 to 1969. Buffett also began purchasing shares in a small textile manufacturer called **Berkshire Hathaway**. His first 2,000 shares of Berkshire Hathaway stock cost $7.50 per share (plus $0.10 per share in commissions). Buffett transformed Berkshire Hathaway from a textile manufacturer into a holding company that invests in the stock of other companies. A selection of the companies controlled by Berkshire Hathaway, along with some of Berkshire Hathaway's major investments, is shown in Exhibit 1.

How has Berkshire Hathaway's stock performed under Warren Buffett's leadership? Well, on September 1, 2006, the company's stock closed at $96,000 per share! How has Warren Buffett done personally? He receives a salary of only $100,000 per year (making him the lowest paid CEO among the nation's top

EXHIBIT 1   **Berkshire Hathaway's Operations and Investments**

Companies Owned by Berkshire Hathaway*

	Industry
GEICO	Property and casualty insurance
FlightSafety	Aviation training
See's Candy	Candy
Nebraska Furniture Mart, R.C. Willey, Star Furniture, and Jordan's Furniture	Home furnishings
Helzberg Diamonds, Borsheim's Fine Jewelry, and Ben Bridge Jeweler	Retail jewelry stores
International Dairy Queen	Fast food and dairy desserts
Fruit of the Loom	Underwear
Acme Building Brands	Bricks and concrete masonry products
Pampered Chef	Kitchen tools

Companies in Which Berkshire Hathaway Has Invested*

Company Name	Ownership Percentage
American Express Company	12.2%
Ameriprise Financial, Inc. (a spin off of American Express)	12.1%
Anheuser-Busch Cos., Inc.	5.6%
The Coca-Cola Company	8.4%
Moody's Corporation	16.2%
PetroChina "H" shares (or equivalents)	1.3%
The Procter & Gamble Company	3.0%
Wal-Mart Stores, Inc.	0.5%
The Washington Post Company	18.0%
Wells Fargo & Company	5.7%

*This information is as of the end of 2005.

---

[1] Janet Lowe, *Warren Buffett Speaks: Wit and Wisdom from the World's Greatest Investor* (New York: John Wiley & Sons, 1997).

200 companies). But don't feel sorry for Mr. Buffett. He was smart enough to purchase a large number of Berkshire Hathaway shares when the price was low. With a personal worth of approximately $42 billion, he ranks second on the list of the world's richest people.[2]

In this chapter we focus on why companies invest in other companies and how to account for those investments. When a company purchases the debt or equity securities of another company, several accounting issues are raised: how to account for the initial purchase, how to account for the receipt of dividends or interest, how to account for any subsequent changes in value of the security, and how to account for the security if it is sold or matures. The remainder of this chapter focuses on each of these issues. First, we examine how securities are classified and the different accounting implications of these classifications. We then introduce proper accounting for the purchase, receipt of revenue, sale, and valuation of securities. In the expanded material section of the chapter, we review the computations and accounting for a bond premium or discount from the point of view of the purchaser (we focused on the seller's perspective in Chapter 10). We also introduce the equity method of accounting and discuss when its application is appropriate. Exhibit 2 highlights the financial statement accounts that will be discussed in this chapter.

SETTING THE STAGE

Why Companies Invest in Other Companies

Understand why companies invest in other companies.

(1) Companies invest in the debt and equity securities of other companies for a variety of reasons. A major reason is to earn a return on their excess cash. Most businesses are cyclical or seasonal; that is, their cash inflows and outflows vary significantly throughout the year. At certain times (particularly when inventories are being purchased), a company's cash supply is low. At other times (usually during or shortly after heavy selling seasons), there is excess cash on hand. A typical cash flow pattern for a retail firm is illustrated in Exhibit 3. The time line shows that the company has insufficient cash for inventory buildup for the Christmas rush, followed by large amounts of accounts receivable (from credit sales), and then an excess of cash immediately after Christmas.

When a company needs cash to meet current obligations, funds can be obtained through such means as borrowing from financial institutions or selling (factoring) accounts receivable or other assets. During those periods of time when excess cash exists, firms usually prefer to invest that money and earn a return. One possibility is to place the money in a bank and earn a fixed return. Most firms, however, are not satisfied with the low interest rates offered by financial institutions and have turned to other investment alternatives. Investing in the stocks (equity) and bonds (debt) of other companies allows a firm to earn a higher rate of return by accepting a higher degree of risk. **Berkshire Hathaway** is perhaps the most famous example of a company whose sole purpose is to invest in the debt and equity securities of other companies.

---

[2] If you have never had the pleasure of reading one of Warren Buffett's "Chairman's Letter to the Shareholders," you should take the opportunity now. No one writes a funnier, more insightful letter than Mr. Buffett. The company's Internet address is **http://www.berkshirehathaway.com**.

EXHIBIT 2   **Financial Statement Items Covered in This Chapter**

Balance Sheet

Current assets
Investments

Long-term investments

Stockholders' equity
Unrealized increase/decrease
in value of securities

**Statement of
Cash Flows**

Operating activities
Purchase of trading securities
Sale of trading securities

Investing activities
Purchase of debt and equity
securities other than
trading securities
Sale of debt and equity
securities other than
trading securities

**Income
Statement**

Other revenues and expenses
Gains and losses on sales
of securities
Unrealized gains and losses
on securities
Interest revenue
Dividend revenue

EXHIBIT 3   **A Cash Flow Pattern**

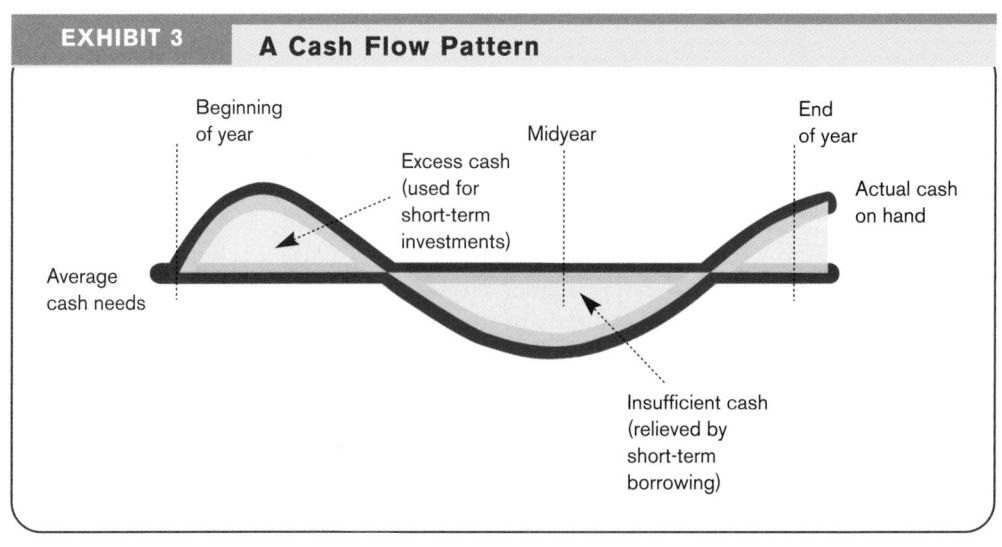

© JACK ANDERSEN/GETTY IMAGES INC.

The Coca-Cola Company owns significant stakes in companies that bottle its products. Such investments allow Coca-Cola to ensure that its bottling facilities remain available and that its soft-drink products consistently meet the company's quality standards.

Firms also invest in other companies for reasons other than to earn a return. The desire to purchase strategic resources, to influence the board of directors, or to diversify its product offerings are additional reasons for a company to invest in other companies. For example, **The Coca-Cola Company** owns 36% of **Coca-Cola Enterprises**, 40% of **Coca-Cola Femsa**, and 32% of **Coca-Cola Amatil Ltd**. These three companies bottle many of Coke's products, and The Coca-Cola Company maintains a significant ownership percentage to ensure that the bottling facilities remain available. As indicated in Exhibit 1, Berkshire Hathaway owns a number of companies outright and has significant investments in other companies. These investments allow Berkshire Hathaway to significantly influence or even control the operating decisions of those companies.

Rather than investing in the research and development required to develop a product or an area of expertise, many companies find it cheaper to purchase all or part of another company that has already expended the effort and the time to develop the desired product or know-how. As an example, to complement its existing software, **Novell** (a computer company specializing in networking) purchased WordPerfect and Quattro Pro, word-processing and spreadsheet software packages, respectively. This purchase then allowed Novell to assemble a menu of software packages to compete with **Microsoft's** Word, Excel, PowerPoint, and Access software packages. Novell's attempt to compete with Microsoft failed, however, and the company eventually sold WordPerfect to **Corel**.

STOP & THINK

Can you think of additional reasons why companies would purchase interests in other companies?

REMEMBER THIS...

- Companies invest in other companies for a variety of reasons. In most cases, the objective is to earn a return on the investment, either through the receipt of interest or dividends, or through an increase in the value of the investment.
- A firm may also invest in other companies so that it will be able to influence their operating decisions.
- In some cases, companies find it cheaper to buy another company to gain access to its assets than to expend the resources necessary to develop the assets on their own.

Classifying a Security

Understand the different classifications for securities.

② Two general types of securities are purchased by companies—debt securities and equity securities. **Debt securities** are financial instruments that carry with them the promise of interest payments and the repayment of the principal amount. Bonds are the most common type of debt security. Debt securities are issued by companies when the need for cash arises. These securities are often traded on public exchanges such as the New York Bond Exchange. Investors often prefer debt securities to equity securities because of the certainty of the income stream (interest) and the relative safety (low risk) of debt as an investment. Investors in corporate debt securities have priority over investors in equity securities, both for the yearly interest payments and for the return of principal if the issuing corporation gets into financial difficulty. Bonds issued by corporations are the most common type of debt securities (recall from Chapter 10 that bonds are typically issued in multiples of $1,000). Once the bonds are issued, ownership of the entire bond issuance, or just a portion, can change hands frequently.

Unlike bonds, **equity securities** (or **stock**), which are also traded on public exchanges, represent actual ownership interest in a corporation. The owner of equity securities is allowed to vote on such corporate matters as executive compensation policies, who will serve on the board of directors of the corporation, and who will be the outside auditor. In addition to voting, the owner of stock often receives a return on that investment in the form of a dividend. A second type of return often accumulates to the stockholder as well—appreciation in stock price. Many investors invest in a company not for the dividend but for the potential increase in stock price. With the potential for increased stock price also comes a risk—the stock price could fall. Holders of debt securities, barring extreme financial difficulties by the issuer, will always receive the face amount of the bond upon maturity. Equity holders do not have that same promise. Stock can greatly increase in value or become worthless.

As mentioned earlier, investors can purchase both debt and equity securities with different goals in mind. Some may purchase to receive interest or dividend payments or to realize quick gains on price changes, while others may invest for more long-term reasons. Accounting standard-setters have developed different methods of accounting for investments depending on the intentions of the holder of the security. Exhibit 4 outlines the major classifications of debt and equity securities.

debt securities

Financial instruments issued by a company that carry with them a promise of interest payments and the repayment of principal.

equity securities (stock)

Shares of ownership in a corporation that can change significantly in value and that provide for a return to investors in the form of dividends.

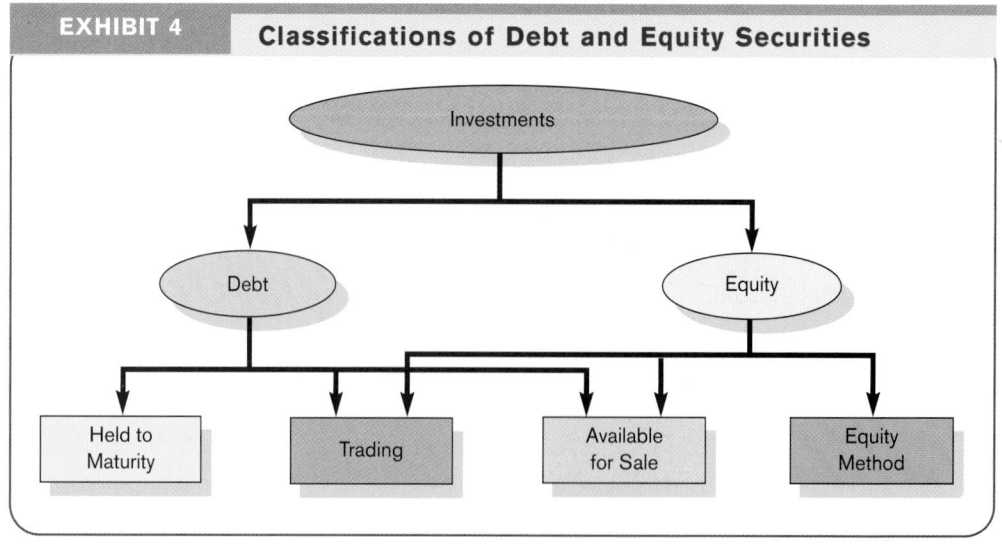

EXHIBIT 4 — **Classifications of Debt and Equity Securities**

Held-to-Maturity Securities

held-to-maturity security

A debt security purchased by an investor with the intent of holding the security until it matures.

If an investor purchases a debt security with the intent of holding the security until it matures, it is classified as a **held-to-maturity security** and is accounted for using techniques similar to those discussed in Chapter 10 for the bond issuer. The investor and the issuer record the same amounts but in a different way. With bond liabilities, the face value of the bonds is recorded in Bonds Payable, and a separate contra account is maintained for any discount or premium. Amortization of the discount or premium is then recorded in these contra accounts. With bond investments, the actual amount paid for the bonds (the cost of the asset), not the face value, is originally debited to the investment account. The amortization of any bond premium or discount is then recorded directly in the investment account. Thus, if you recall the accounting for Bonds Payable as presented in Chapter 10, you already know most of the accounting for a bond investment that is expected to be held to maturity. The procedures relating to amortizing premiums and discounts for the investors are discussed in the expanded material section of this chapter. Note that equity securities cannot be classified as held-to-maturity securities; equity securities typically do not mature.[3]

F Y I

Equity securities cannot be classified as held-to-maturity securities.

Equity Method Securities

equity method

A method used to account for an investment in the stock of another company when significant influence can be imposed (presumed to exist when 20 to 50% of the outstanding voting stock is owned).

consolidated financial statements

Statements that report the combined operating results, financial position, and cash flows of two or more legally separate but affiliated companies as if they were one economic entity.

In the case of equity securities, accounting standard-setters have determined that if securities are held with the objective of significantly influencing the operations of the investee, then the securities should be accounted for using the **equity method**. The equity method records changes in the value of the investment as the net assets of the investee change. The assumption underlying the equity method is that if the investor can influence the operating decisions of the investee, then any change in the net assets of the investee should be reflected on the books of the investor. In determining what constitutes significant influence, the Accounting Principles Board suggests that, unless evidence exists to the contrary, ownership of at least 20% of the outstanding common stock of a company, but less than 50%, indicates the existence of significant influence. Because accounting for a security using the equity method can get complicated, details of the equity method are presented in the expanded material section of this chapter. If ownership exceeds 50%, then a controlling interest is assumed, and the accounting becomes far more complex. The FASB is examining the issue of control and has suggested that companies look beyond ownership percentage and examine other factors that may indicate control.[4] Two factors the FASB has highlighted are (1) ownership of a large minority voting interest (approximately 40%) with no other group owning a significant interest and (2) a company's domination of the process for electing the investee's board of directors. In cases where it is determined that control exists, the parent company (the acquiring company) and the subsidiary company (the acquired company) are required to combine their financial statements into one set of statements as if they were one economic entity. Such combined statements are called **consolidated financial statements**. The preparation of consolidated financial statements is briefly covered in the expanded material of this chapter.

---

[3] There are exceptions to this rule, as in the case of "mandatorily redeemable preferred stock," but the accounting for these types of securities is beyond the scope of this text.

[4] Exposure Draft: Consolidated Financial Statements, Including Accounting and Reporting of Noncontrolling Interests in Subsidiaries—a replacement of ARB No. 51 (Norwalk: Financial Accounting Standards Board, 2005).

F Y I

Debt securities cannot be classified as equity method securities.

trading securities

Debt and equity securities purchased with the intent of selling them should the need for cash arise or to realize short-term gains.

available-for-sale securities

Debt and equity securities not classified as trading, held-to-maturity, or equity method securities.

Trading and Available-for-Sale Securities

In those instances where securities are not being held to maturity (in the case of debt) or to control or significantly influence an investee (in the case of equity), the Financial Accounting Standards Board has developed two other classes of securities—trading and available-for-sale. **Trading securities** are those debt and equity securities held with the intent of selling the securities should the need for cash arise or to realize gains arising from short-term changes in price. These types of securities are purchased simply to earn a return on excess cash. **Available-for-sale securities** are publicly-traded securities that are classified as neither held-to-maturity nor trading (in the case of debt securities). In the case of equity securities, they represent securities that are not classified as trading securities or accounted for using the equity method.

Why the Different Classifications?

Why are there different classifications for debt and equity securities? Why not simply classify all securities as "investments"? The reason for the distinction lies in the different treatments of accounting for changes in market value. In the case of securities classified as held-to-maturity, changes in the securities' value between the date of purchase and the maturity date do not affect the amount to be received at maturity. That amount is fixed on the day the bonds are issued. Thus, temporary changes in the value of securities classified as held-to-maturity are not recognized on the investor's books. Similar reasoning applies to securities accounted for under the equity method. These securities are purchased, not with the intent of selling them in the future, but instead to be able to exercise influence over a corporation. Again, temporary changes in the value of these securities are not recognized on the investor's books.

Trading securities are purchased with the intent of earning a return—through interest or dividends and through short-term resale of the securities. Firms are required to recognize these two types of returns on the income statement. For example, assume that XYZ Company purchases 100 shares of ABC, Inc. stock for $5 per share. During the year, ABC pays a $1 dividend per share, and the value of the stock increases to $7 per share. XYZ will recognize, as income, $100 in dividend income as well as $200 in unrealized market gains. While the $100 in dividends was actually received, the $200 gain was not.

F Y I

Many companies avoid the issue of what to include on the income statement by classifying all their investment securities as being available-for-sale. Berkshire Hathaway and **Microsoft** are examples of companies that use this classification scheme.

The securities would have to have been sold in order to actually receive the $200 increase in value. Recognizing this gain, even though it was not realized through an arm's-length transaction, represents a major departure from the historical cost principle that has guided accounting for centuries. In 1994, the FASB determined that because the fair market value of many debt and equity securities can be objectively determined (via market quotes) and they can easily be sold (one phone call to a broker), it would be appropriate to include any unrealized gains or losses on changes in value of trading securities on the income statement.

Changes in the value of securities classified as available-for-sale are recorded on the balance sheet. However, no gain or loss is realized on the income statement. Instead, an adjustment is made directly to a stockholders' equity account—Unrealized Increase/Decrease in Value of Available-for-Sale Securities-Equity. The obvious question is "Why aren't changes in the value of these securities reflected on the income statement?"

The answer lies in the intent behind holding the securities. Trading securities will probably be sold sooner rather than later. We cannot make that same assumption with available-for-sale securities. We are less certain they will be sold. Because of this uncertainty as to when the change in value will actually be realized, the FASB elected to go around the income statement in reporting changes in value relating to available-for-sale securities. Whatever the classification used, companies disclose their classification in the notes to the financial statements. For example, **Berkshire Hathaway** provides the following note disclosure relating to its investments:

> Berkshire's management determines the appropriate classifications of investments in fixed maturity securities and equity securities at the acquisition date and re-evaluates the classifications at each balance sheet date. Berkshire's investments in fixed maturity and equity securities are primarily classified as available-for-sale, except for certain securities held by finance businesses which are classified as held-to-maturity. Held-to-maturity investments are carried at amortized cost, reflecting Berkshire's intent and ability to hold the securities to maturity. Available-for-sale securities are stated at fair value with net unrealized gains or losses reported as a component of accumulated other comprehensive income.

As you can see, Berkshire Hathaway classifies virtually every security as available-for-sale and is very specific as to what this classification means for the financial statements: current values go on the balance sheet, with unrealized gains and losses disclosed in stockholders' equity, while realized gains and losses are reported on the income statement.

Exhibit 5 summarizes the classification and disclosure issues relating to investments in debt and equity securities.

EXHIBIT 5	Classification and Disclosure of Securities		
Classification of Securities	**Types of Securities**	**Disclosed at**	**Reporting of Temporary Changes in Fair Value**
Trading	Debt and equity	Fair value	Income statement
Available-for-sale	Debt and equity	Fair value	Stockholders' equity
Held-to-maturity	Debt	Amortized cost	Not recognized
Equity method	Equity	Cost adjusted for changes in net assets of investee	Not recognized

REMEMBER THIS...

- Securities are classified depending upon the intent of management. If management's intent is to hold the investment until maturity (debt) or to influence the decisions of an investee (equity), then the held-to-maturity (debt) and equity method (equity) classifications are appropriate.

- If the securities are being held for other reasons, then management may classify them as either trading or available-for-sale. The importance of the classification becomes apparent when accounting for changes in value.

Accounting for Trading and Available-for-Sale Securities

(3) Four issues are associated with accounting for securities: (1) accounting for the purchase, (2) accounting for the revenue earned, (3) accounting for the sale, and (4) accounting for the changes in value. The first three issues are fairly straightforward and are presented in this section. Accounting for changes in the value of securities is discussed in the following section. The time line in Exhibit 6 illustrates the important business issues associated with buying and selling investment securities.

Accounting for the Purchase of Securities

Investments in securities, like all other assets, are recorded at cost when purchased. This is the case whether the security being purchased is debt or equity or whether it is being held with the intent to sell it quickly or hold it for the long term. Cost includes the market price of the security plus any extra expenditures required in making the purchase (such as a stockbroker's fee).

To illustrate the accounting for securities, we will use the following information throughout the chapter. On July 1, 2009, Far Side, Inc., purchased the following securities:

Security	Type	Classification	Cost (including Broker's Fees)
1	Debt	Trading	$ 5,000
2	Equity	Trading	27,500
3	Debt	Available-for-sale	17,000
4	Equity	Available-for-sale	9,200

The initial entry to record the investments is as follows:

Investment in Trading Securities	32,500	
Investment in Available-for-Sale Securities	26,200	
Cash		58,700

EXHIBIT 6 | **Time Line of Business Issues Associated with Buying and Selling Investment Securities**

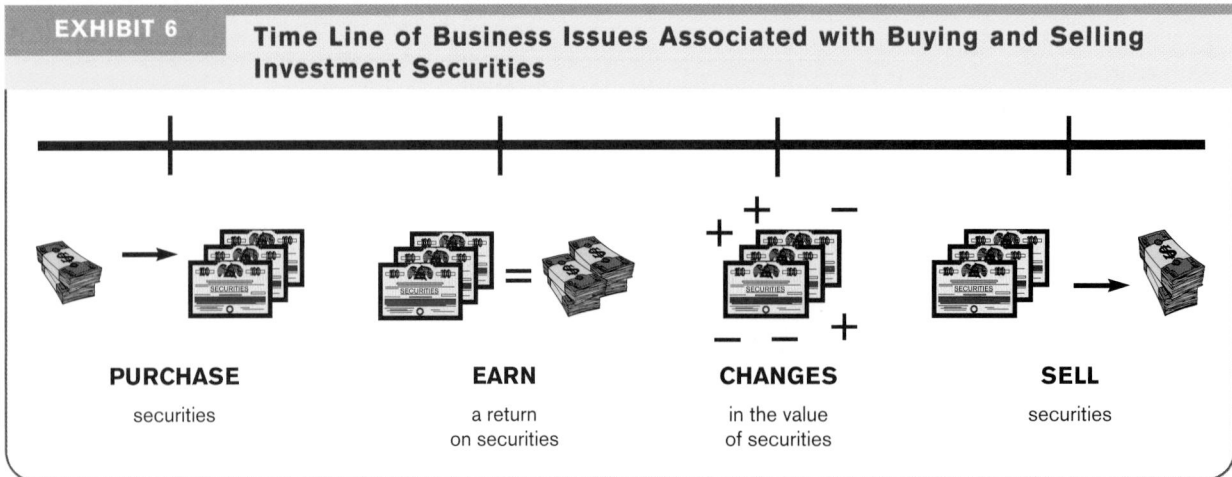

PURCHASE	**EARN**	**CHANGES**	**SELL**
securities	a return on securities	in the value of securities	securities

Berkshire Hathaway purchased with cash over $21.9 billion of securities in 2005.

Though investments in securities are all recorded at cost, each of the four classifications of securities is accounted for differently subsequent to purchase. As a result, separate accounts are used to record the initial purchase. Management purchased Securities 1 and 2 with the intent of earning a return on the investment and selling the securities should the need for cash arise. Therefore, those securities are classified as "trading." Securities 3 and 4 were also purchased to earn a return on excess cash, but management has classified them as "available-for-sale." While the journal entry illustrated above combines all securities of the same classification into one account, subsidiary records will be kept for each individual security purchased.

Accounting for the Return Earned on an Investment

When a firm invests in the debt or equity of another firm with the intent of earning a return on its investment, how that return is accounted for varies depending on the classification of the investment. Recall from Chapter 10 that when debt securities are sold, a premium or discount can arise as a result of differences between the stated rate of interest and the market rate of interest. The resulting premium or discount must then be amortized over the life of the investment, thereby affecting the amount of interest expense recorded by the issuer. Theoretically, the purchaser of that debt security must also account for the difference between the purchase price and the eventual maturity value. In the discussion that follows, however, we are assuming that the time for which the investor anticipates holding debt securities classified as "trading" or as "available-for-sale" is not long enough for any amortization of premium or discount to materially affect interest expense. Amortization of premiums and discounts on debt securities is illustrated for "held-to-maturity" securities in the expanded material section of this chapter.

With this caveat in mind, the accounting for dividends and interest received on trading and available-for-sale securities becomes relatively straightforward. Cash received relating to interest and dividends is credited to Interest Revenue and Dividend Revenue, respectively. Interest earned but not yet received or dividends that have been declared but not paid are also recorded as revenue with a corresponding receivable. Continuing our example, interest and dividends received during 2009 relating to Far Side's securities investments were as follows:

Berkshire Hathaway reported interest, dividends, and other investment income earned of $3.5 billion during 2005.

Security	Interest	Dividends
1	$225	
2		$825
3	850	
4		644

The appropriate journal entry to record the receipt of interest and dividends is:

Cash	2,544	
Interest Revenue		1,075
Dividend Revenue		1,469

Accounting for the Sale of Securities

Suppose that Far Side sells all of its investment in Security 2 for $28,450 on October 31, 2009. As Security 2 was purchased for $27,500, the security has increased in value and that increase must be recorded. The journal entry to record the sale is:

Cash	28,450	
Investment in Trading Securities		27,500
Realized Gain on Sale of Trading Securities		950

If Security 2 had been sold for less than $27,500, a loss would have been recorded. If a broker's fee had been charged on the transaction, the fee would reduce the amount of cash received and decrease the gain recognized. If the broker's fee exceeded $950, a loss would be recorded on the books of the seller.

At the end of the accounting period, any gain or loss on the sale of securities must be included on the income statement. In the above example, the "Realized Gain on Sale of Trading Securities" would be included with Other Revenues and Expenses on the income statement. Note the term *realized*. **Realized gains and losses** indicate that an arm's-length transaction has occurred and that the securities have actually been sold. This distinction is important because in the next section we focus on accounting for unrealized gains and losses—those gains and losses that occur while a security is still being held and no arm's-length transaction has taken place.

realized gains and losses

Gains and losses resulting from the sale of securities in an arm's-length transaction.

On its statement of cash flows, **Berkshire Hathaway** reported proceeds of $4,872 million from the sale of debt securities and equity securities. On its income statement, the company reported net realized gains of $427 million from the sale of securities. With this information, we can compute the historical cost of the securities sold during the period. Proceeds of $4,872 million less a gain of $427 million indicate that the cost of the securities was $4,445 million. A summary journal entry indicating the effects of these transactions for Berkshire Hathaway is as follows:

Cash	4,872	
Available-for-Sale Securities		4,445
Realized Gain on Sale of Securities		427

> **REMEMBER THIS...**
>
> - Investments in debt and equity securities are recorded at cost, which includes the fair value of the securities plus any other expenditures required to purchase the securities.
> - When purchased, the securities are classified into one of four categories: held-to-maturity, equity method, trading, or available-for-sale securities.
> - Revenues from securities take the form of interest, dividends, or gains or losses from selling the securities and are included under Other Revenues and Expenses on the income statement.

Accounting for Changes in the Value of Securities

Account for changes in the value of securities.

(4) Investments in debt and equity securities are initially recorded at cost. If the value of a security changes after it is purchased, should that change in value be recorded on the investor's books? As stated previously in the chapter, the answer is "it depends." It depends on management's intent regarding that security. In the case of trading and available-for-sale securities, changes in market value are recorded on the books of the investor. For held-to-maturity securities and equity method securities, changes in value are not recorded unless they are considered permanent. To illustrate the accounting for changes in value of securities, we will continue the Far Side example. On December 31, 2009, the following market values were available:[5]

Security	Classification	Historical Cost	Market Value (December 31, 2009)
1	Trading	$ 5,000	$ 5,200
3	Available-for-sale	17,000	16,700
4	Available-for-sale	9,200	9,250

Changes in the Value of Trading Securities

At the end of 2009, Far Side computes the market value of its trading securities portfolio and compares it to the historical cost of the portfolio. In this instance, market value is $200 greater than historical cost. The journal entry to record this increase in value is:

Market Adjustment–Trading Securities	200	
Unrealized Gain on Trading Securities–Income		200

unrealized gains and losses

Gains and losses resulting from changes in the value of securities that are still being held.

market adjustment— trading securities

An account used to track the difference between the historical cost and the market value of a company's portfolio of trading securities.

This journal entry recognizes the $200 increase in the value of the trading securities and records the unrealized gain on the income statement. **Unrealized gains and losses** indicate that the securities have changed in value and are still being held. This journal entry also introduces a new account—**Market Adjustment—Trading Securities**. This account is combined with the trading securities account and reported on the balance sheet. Thus, the balance sheet will reflect the trading securities at their fair market value. Why not adjust the trading securities account directly instead of creating this market adjustment account? The reason is that the use of a valuation account, Market Adjustment— Trading Securities, allows a record of historical cost to be maintained. With this approach, a company can easily determine realized and unrealized gains. Perhaps the most important reason for keeping a record of historical cost is that, for tax purposes, only realized gains and losses are relevant. Other decisions made within a firm also rely on this historical cost information.

Changes in the Value of Available-for-Sale Securities

A market adjustment account is also employed when adjusting available-for-sale securities to their fair market value. However, the change in value is not recorded on the income statement but is instead recorded in the account "Unrealized

---

[5] Remember that Security 2 was sold on October 31, 2009.

STOP & THINK

In Chapter 7, we were not to write inventory up if its value increased, though we were to write it down if its value declined. In Chapter 9, we were not to write property, plant, and equipment up if its value increased, though we were to write it down if its value declined. Why can we write up the value of securities if their price increases above the original cost?

Increase/Decrease in Value of Available-for-Sale Securities—Equity." The "equity" used in the account title refers to the fact that this account is disclosed in the stockholders' equity section of the balance sheet, and its balance is carried forward from year to year. To illustrate, the available-for-sale portfolio of Far Side has a fair market value of $25,950 at year-end and a historical cost of $26,200. The appropriate adjustment is:

Unrealized Increase/Decrease in Value of Available-for-Sale Securities–Equity	250	
Market Adjustment–Available-for-Sale Securities		250

This journal entry adjusts the portfolio of available-for-sale securities to its fair market value at year-end and records the difference in the equity account.

Subsequent Changes in Value

Assume that no securities were bought or sold by Far Side, Inc., during 2010. At the end of 2010, its portfolio of securities had the following fair market values:

Security	Classification	Historical Cost	Market Value (December 31, 2010)
1	Trading	$ 5,000	$ 4,850
3	Available-for-sale	17,000	16,900
4	Available-for-sale	9,200	9,150

The value of the trading securities has declined to $4,850. Since the market adjustment account relating to trading securities should reflect the difference between historical cost and market, an entry is made to adjust the balance in Market Adjustment—Trading Securities from its previous $200 debit balance to the required $150 credit balance ($5,000 – $4,850). Where did this $200 debit balance come from? It came from the adjusting entry made on December 31, 2009. Remember that the market adjustment account is a real (balance sheet) account and is not closed at the end of an accounting period. Its balance carries forward from year to year. The required adjusting entry is:

Unrealized Loss on Trading Securities–Income	350	
Market Adjustment–Trading Securities		350

When this entry is posted, the Market Adjustment—Trading Securities T-account will appear as follows:

Market Adjustment–Trading Securities

12/31/09	200		
		Adjustment	350
		12/31/10	150

CAUTION

The amount of the adjustment for the current period depends on the balance in the market adjustment account. Don't forget to factor that balance into your calculations.

The $150 credit balance will be netted against the $5,000 balance in the trading securities account and disclosed on the balance sheet as "Investment in Trading Securities (net)" for $4,850. The $350 unrealized loss will be included in the current period's net income and reported on the income statement. This adjustment procedure ensures that changes in the value of the trading securities portfolio are reflected in the period in which those changes in value occurred.

A similar procedure is employed in valuing the available-for-sale securities portfolio, except that the stockholders' equity account is used instead of the income statement account. For Far Side, the market value of the available-for-sale securities portfolio is $26,050. In comparing this to the historical cost of $26,200, a $150 credit balance in the market adjustment account is required. Take a moment and read the information again. An adjustment *to* get to a $150 credit balance is required—not an adjustment *of* $150. Given the previous credit balance in Market Adjustment—Available-for-Sale Securities of $250, the following adjusting entry is required:

Market Adjustment–Available-for-Sale Securities	100	
Unrealized Increase/Decrease in Value of Available-for-Sale		
Securities–Equity		100

Once this entry is posted, Market Adjustment—Available-for-Sale Securities will have the required $150 credit balance as follows:

**Market Adjustment–
Available-for-Sale Securities**

		12/31/09	250
Adjustment	100		
		12/31/10	150

When individual securities from a portfolio are sold, a realized gain or loss is recognized for the difference between the original cost of the securities and the selling price, without regard to previous adjustments made to a market adjustment account. At the end of the period, the cost of the remaining securities is compared to the fair market value of the remaining securities, and the market adjustment account is updated to account for the difference.

As mentioned earlier, **Berkshire Hathaway** classifies all of its securities as available-for-sale. To determine how well Warren Buffett has managed the portfolio during the year, the financial statement reader must review both the income statement and the statement of stockholders' equity. Comparing the performance of the company's portfolio of securities for the years 2003 through 2005 results in the following (in millions):

	2003	2004	2005
Realized investment gains (from the income statement)	$ 2,914	$1,746	$5,728
Unrealized appreciation of investments			
(from the statement of shareholders' equity)	10,842	2,599	2,081
Total portfolio performance	$13,756	$4,345	$7,809

> **REMEMBER THIS...**
>
> - When the value of a trading or available-for-sale security changes, that change is reflected on the balance sheet using a market adjustment account.
> - For trading securities, the unrealized gain or loss is reflected on the income statement for the period.
> - For available-for-sale securities, the unrealized increase or decrease is recorded in a stockholders' equity account.

EXPANDED *material*

In this section of the chapter, we turn our attention to some of the complexities associated with purchasing debt and equity securities. First, we examine held-to-maturity securities and how any associated premium or discount associated with these securities is amortized. We also address the issue of purchasing a debt security between interest payment dates. The accounting issues associated with an equity security accounted for under the equity method are also presented, and the chapter concludes with a brief discussion of consolidated financial statements.

Account for held-to-maturity securities.

Accounting for Held-to-Maturity Securities

⑤   Held-to-maturity securities are debt securities issued by companies to raise needed funding for expansion, acquisitions, or other business reasons. Bonds (discussed in Chapter 10 from the point of view of the issuer) are by far the most common type of debt instrument that can be readily bought and sold. Because bonds represent the most common type of publicly-traded debt instrument, the following discussion will focus on bonds purchased as investments to be held to maturity.

Accounting for the Initial Purchase

Bonds can be purchased at amounts either above face value (at a premium), below face value (at a discount), or at face value. Regardless of the purchase price, like all other assets, bonds are initially recorded at cost. The cost is the total amount paid to acquire the bonds; this includes the actual price paid for the bonds and any other purchasing expenditures, such as commissions or broker's fees.

To illustrate, assume that Far Side, Inc., purchased a fifth security and classified it as held-to-maturity. Security 5 consists of twenty $1,000 bonds of Chicago Company. The bonds were issued on July 1, 2009, and will mature five years from the date of issuance. The bonds will pay interest at a stated annual rate of 12%, with payments to be made semiannually on June 30 and December 31. In determining the value of the bonds, the present value of these future cash flows must be determined at the market rate on the date of the purchase. Assuming the market rate on bonds of similar risk is 16%, the purchase price of the bonds is obtained by adding the present value of $20,000 (received 10 periods in the future and discounted at 8%) to the present value of the annuity of the 10 interest payments of $1,200 each (discounted at 8%). The reason 8% is used is that interest is received semiannually; recall that in calculating present value, you must halve the interest rate (16%/2) for semiannual compounding periods. Likewise, you must double the number of years to determine the number of periods (5 years × 2 periods per year = 10 periods). The calculations are:

1.	Semiannual interest payment	$ 1,200
	Present value of an annuity of 10 payments	
	of $1 at 8% (Table II, page 485)	× 6.7101
	Present value of interest payments	$ 8,052
2.	Principal (face value) of bonds	$20,000
	Present value of $1 received 10 periods in the	
	future discounted at 8% (Table I, page 484)	× 0.4632
	Present value of principal	9,264
3.	Total present value of investment	$17,316

In this example, 16% is the effective rate of interest because that is the amount of interest actually earned; 12% is the stated, or nominal, rate of interest on Chicago Company's bonds. Note that the 12% stated rate determines the size of the annuity payments ($20,000 × 0.12 × ½ year) but not the purchase price of the bonds; the purchase price varies according to market conditions. The 16% effective rate depends on three amounts: the purchase price, the interest payments, and the face value of the bonds. The $17,316 bond price is the amount that earns Far Side exactly 16%. The journal entry to record the acquisition is:

Investment in Held-to-Maturity Securities	17,316	
Cash		17,316

Note that the investment account is debited for the cost of the bonds with no separate amount shown for the discount of $2,684 ($20,000 – $17,316). Although the discount could be recorded in a separate contra-asset account, in practice it is more common for investors to record the asset cost in the investment account as shown.

Accounting for Bonds Purchased between Interest Dates

The preceding entry assumes that the investing company purchased the bonds on the issuance date, which was also the beginning date for the first interest period. In many cases, however, the date bonds are actually issued does not coincide with an interest date. Further, investors often acquire bonds in the "secondary market"; that is, they purchase bonds from other investors rather than from the issuing company. The secondary market for bonds includes the New York Bond Exchange. Since bonds are traded actively in this market each weekday, investors often acquire bonds between interest dates.

An investor who buys bonds between interest dates, either from the issuing company or in the secondary market, has to pay for the interest that has accrued since the last interest payment date. As explained in Chapter 10, this is necessary because whoever owns the bonds at the time interest is paid receives interest for one full interest period, usually six months, regardless of how long the bonds have been held.

To illustrate, we will assume that Far Side purchased the Chicago Company bonds in the secondary market for $17,316 on November 1, 2009. Semiannual interest of $1,200 ($20,000 × 0.12 ×½) is paid on the bonds on June 30 and December 31 of each year. On December 31, 2009, Far Side will receive $1,200 even though the bonds were purchased only two months earlier. Since the previous owner is entitled to 4 months' interest on November 1, Far Side will have to pay that individual or company the interest for the period July 1 to October 31. This is illustrated in Exhibit 7.

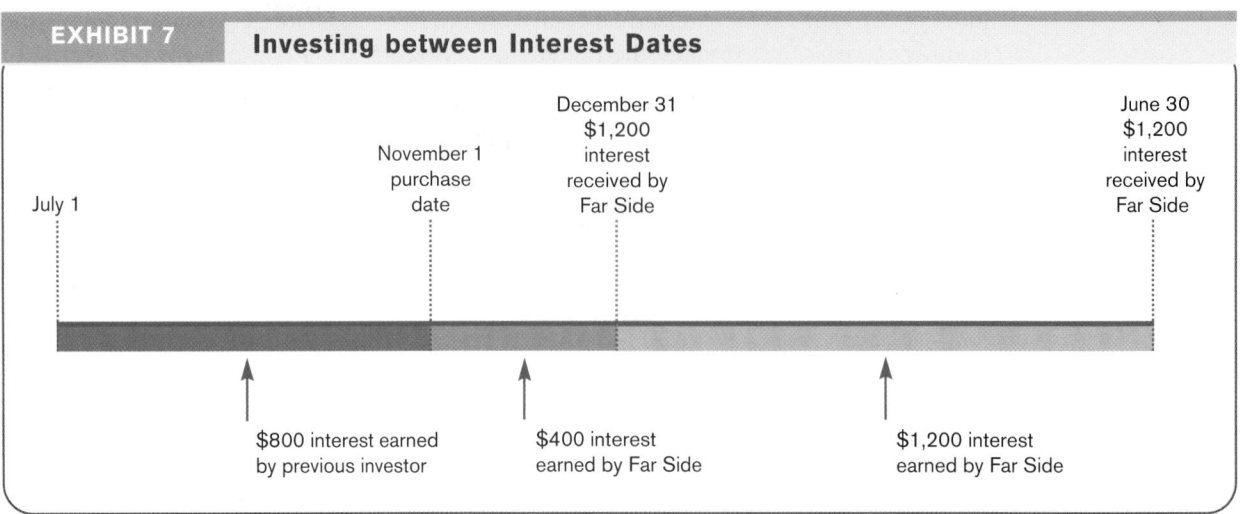

EXHIBIT 7   **Investing between Interest Dates**

The entry to record the investment in bonds on November 1 (between interest dates) is:

Investment in Held-to-Maturity Securities	17,316	
Bond Interest Receivable	800	
Cash		18,116
Purchased $20,000 of Chicago Company bonds for $17,316		
and paid four months' accrued interest.		

When Far Side receives $1,200 in interest on December 31, it will make the following entry:

Cash	1,200	
Interest Receivable		800
Interest Revenue		400
Received interest on Chicago Company bonds.		

Accounting for the Amortization of Bond Discounts and Premiums

Only in those rare instances when the stated interest rate of a bond is exactly equivalent to the prevailing market (or yield) rate for similar investments is a bond purchased at face value. At all other times, bonds are purchased either at a discount (below face value) or at a premium (above face value). Because the face amount of a bond is received at maturity, discounts and premiums must be written off (amortized) over the period that a bond is held.

As you learned in Chapter 10, there are two common methods of amortizing bond discounts and premiums: the straight-line method and the effective-interest method. Because straight-line amortization is simpler, it will be used first to illustrate the amortization process; then the effective-interest method will be described.

straight-line amortization

A method of systematically writing off a bond discount or premium in equal amounts each period until maturity.

Straight-Line Amortization
To illustrate the **straight-line amortization** of a bond discount, we will assume again that Far Side purchased the Chicago Company $20,000, 12%, five-year bonds for $17,316 on the issuance

date, July 1, 2009. The entry to record this investment was given on page 575. Far Side will record amortization of $268.40 ($2,684/5 years $\times^1/_2$) on each interest date. Thus, every six months, beginning on December 31, 2009, Far Side will make the following entry:

Cash	1,200.00	
Investment in Held-to-Maturity Securities	268.40	
Bond Interest Revenue		1,468.40
Received semiannual bond interest and amortized		
bond discount.		

At the end of five years, the investment in the held-to-maturity securities account will have a balance of $20,000.

The discount amortization is revenue earned on the bonds; when the bonds mature, Far Side will receive $20,000 (the face value) in return for an original investment of $17,316. It is this additional revenue of $2,684 that increases the return the investor actually earns from the 12% stated interest rate to the effective interest rate of 16%. The following analysis shows how this works:

Maturity value to be received	$20,000
Interest to be received ($1,200 $\times$ 10 payments)	12,000
Total amount to be received	$32,000
Investment	17,316
Total interest revenue to be earned	$14,684

Interest earned per year:

Stated amount of interest ($20,000 $\times$ 0.12)	$2,400.00	12%
Additional interest from discount ($2,684/5 years)	536.80	4%*
Total	$2,936.80	16%

*This is an approximation; with the straight-line method, the actual interest earned each year changes.

When accounting for the amortization of a bond discount, a company must be careful to amortize the discount only over the period the bonds are actually held. For example, if Far Side had purchased the Chicago Company bonds four months after the issuance date, the discount would have been amortized over a period of 56 months (4 full years plus 8 months of the first year). The amortization for the first year would then have been approximately $383.43 ($2,684 $\times$ $^8/_{56}$), and the amortization for each of the succeeding four years would be approximately $575.14 ($2,684 $\times$ $^{12}/_{56}$).

Accounting for the amortization of a premium on investments is essentially the opposite of accounting for a discount. Amortization of a premium decreases revenue earned, and the effect of the amortization entry is to reduce Investment in Held-to-Maturity Securities to the face value of the bonds by the maturity date.

To illustrate the amortization of a bond premium by the investor, assume that Far Side acquired the $20,000, 12%, five-year Chicago Company bonds for $21,540 on July 1, 2009, the date of issuance. The entry to record the purchase is:

Investment in Held-to-Maturity Securities	21,540	
Cash		21,540
Purchased $20,000 of Chicago Company bonds for $21,540.		

At each interest payment date, beginning December 31, 2009, Far Side will make the following entry:

Cash	1,200	
Investment in Held-to-Maturity Securities		154
Bond Interest Revenue		1,046
Received semiannual bond interest and amortized bond premium		
($1,540/5 years $\times$ $\frac{1}{2}$).		

The effect of the amortization entries is to reduce the return earned on the bonds from the stated annual interest rate of 12% to the rate actually earned on the investment (approximately 10%).

effective-interest amortization

A method of systematically writing off a bond premium or discount that takes into consideration the time value of money and results in an equal rate of amortization for each period.

Effective-Interest Amortization   To illustrate the computations involved in using the **effective-interest amortization** method, we will again consider Far Side's purchase of the 12%, five-year, $20,000 bonds of Chicago Company for $17,316 on the issuance date. The amount of discount amortized in each of the five years using the effective-interest method is computed as shown in Exhibit 8.

In the computation, column (2) represents the cash received at the end of each interest period; column (3) shows the amount of effective interest earned, which is the amount that will be reported on the income statement each period; column (4) is the difference between columns (3) and (2) and so represents the amortization; and column (5) shows the investment balance that will be reported on the balance sheet at the end of each period. Note that the interest rate used to compute the actual interest earned is the effective rate of 8% (16%/2) and not the stated rate of 12%. Also note that the total discount is the same as it was when the straight-line method was used, $2,684.

When bonds are purchased at a discount, the amount of amortization increases each successive period. This is so because the investment balance of the bonds increases, and a constant interest rate times an increasing balance results in an increasing amount of interest income. If bonds are purchased at a premium, the effective-interest amortization method will involve a constant interest rate being multiplied by a declining investment balance each period. The result will be a decline in actual interest earned each period.

EXHIBIT 8	**Amortization Table for Chicago Company Bonds**

(1)	(2)	(3)	(4)	(5)
			Amount of	
	Cash	**Interest Actually Earned**	**Amortization**	**Investment**
Time Period	**Received**	**(0.16 $\times$ 1/2 $\times$ Investment Balance)**	**(3) – (2)**	**Balance**
Acquisition date				$17,316
Year 1, first six months	$1,200	(0.08 $\times$ $17,316) = $1,385	$ 185	17,501
Year 1, second six months	1,200	(0.08 $\times$ $17,501) = 1,400	200	17,701
Year 2, first six months	1,200	(0.08 $\times$ $17,701) = 1,416	216	17,917
Year 2, second six months	1,200	(0.08 $\times$ $17,917) = 1,433	233	18,150
Year 3, first six months	1,200	(0.08 $\times$ $18,150) = 1,452	252	18,402
Year 3, second six months	1,200	(0.08 $\times$ $18,402) = 1,472	272	18,674
Year 4, first six months	1,200	(0.08 $\times$ $18,674) = 1,494	294	18,968
Year 4, second six months	1,200	(0.08 $\times$ $18,968) = 1,517	317	19,285
Year 5, first six months	1,200	(0.08 $\times$ $19,285) = 1,543	343	19,628
Year 5, second six months	1,200	(0.08 $\times$ $19,628) = 1,572*	372	20,000
			$2,684	

*Difference due to rounding.

Note the similarities between this table and the amortization tables prepared in Chapter 10. The computations are identical—the only difference is that in Chapter 10, we were paying cash, whereas in Chapter 12, we are receiving cash.

Since the effective-interest amortization method takes into account the time value of money, and thus shows the true revenue earned each period (whereas the straight-line method represents only approximations), companies normally should use the effective-interest amortization method. As an exception to this rule, companies are allowed to use the straight-line method when the two methods produce amortization amounts that are not significantly different. Because that is often the case, both methods continue to be used.

Accounting for the Sale or Maturity of Bond Investments

If bonds are held until their maturity date, the accounting for the bond proceeds at maturity includes a debit to Cash and a credit to the investment account for the principal amount. For example, if Far Side, Inc., holds the $20,000, 12% bonds from Chicago Company to maturity, the entry to record the receipt of the bond principal on the maturity date will be:

Cash	20,000	
Investment in Held-to-Maturity Securities		20,000
Received the principal of Chicago Company bonds at maturity.		

This entry assumes, of course, that all previous receipts of interest and bond amortizations have been properly recorded.

Because held-to-maturity securities are usually traded on major exchanges, thus providing a continuous and ready market, they can be sold to other investors prior to their maturity. When these securities are sold prior to their maturity, the difference between the sales price and the investment balance is recognized as a gain or loss on the sale of the investment.

To illustrate, we will assume that Sawyer Company purchased ten $1,000, 8%, five-year bonds of REX Company. We will also assume that the bonds were originally purchased on January 1, 2009, at 101% of their face value; on January 1, 2010, Sawyer showed a balance of $10,040 for these bonds. If the bonds are sold on that day for $10,300, the entry to record the sale and recognize the gain is (assuming no sales commission):

Cash	10,300	
Gain on Sale of Bonds		260
Investment in Held-to-Maturity Securities		10,040
Sold the REX bonds for $10,300.		

If held-to-maturity securities are sold prior to their maturity date, it is important that the amortization of the bond premium or discount be recorded up to the date of sale. If the amortization of the discount or premium is not updated, the gain or loss recognized on the sale will be incorrect.

REMEMBER THIS...

- Accounting for investments in held-to-maturity securities involves four steps:
    1. accounting for the purchase of the securities,
    2. accounting for interest received on the securities,
    3. accounting for amortization of the premium or discount, and
    4. accounting for the sale or maturity of the securities.
- Amortization of premiums and discounts is usually accounted for by the simple straight-line amortization method or the theoretically more correct effective-interest method. The amortization adjusts the interest earned on the bonds from the stated to the effective rate.
- Investments in held-to-maturity securities are generally reported at cost (adjusted for premium or discount amortization), regardless of whether the current market value is less than or greater than their historical cost.
- When held-to-maturity securities are sold before maturity, the premium or discount must be amortized to the date of sale; a gain or loss would be reflected in the income statement for the difference between the selling price and the carrying value on the date of sale.
- Debt securities held until maturity result in no gain or loss on retirement because the carrying value after amortization of a premium or discount should be equal to the face value of the securities.

Account for securities using the equity method.

(6)

Accounting for Equity Investments Using the Equity Method

When enough of the outstanding common stock of a company is purchased by another company, the acquiring company may have the ability to significantly influence the operating decisions of the investee. If the ability to influence is present, then accounting standards require the use of the equity method in accounting for the investment. As stated previously, significant influence is presumed if a company owns between 20 and 50% of a company. Keep in mind that the percentage ownership criterion serves only as a guideline. The ability to influence is the key criterion. For example, assume that a company owns 35% of a firm that is headquartered in a foreign country whose government is undergoing a period of volatility. Some of the radical leaders in that country are calling for more internal investment and less outside interference from U.S. corporations. These leaders, if able to gain positions of power, have threatened to expropriate (take over all operations owned by U.S. companies). Even though the U.S. company meets the percentage ownership criterion, it may not be able to significantly influence the operations of the foreign subsidiary. Consider another example of a firm whose ownership is widespread, with no single shareholder owning more than 2% of the corporation. If one stockholder were able to acquire 15% of the outstanding common stock, that investor might be able to influence the decisions of the investee simply because of the size of the ownership percentage relative to that of all other stockholders. The important point is that the ability to influence is the key criterion for using the equity method of accounting.

Under the equity method, dividend payments represent a return of investment; they do not represent revenue, as they do when accounting for trading or available-for-sale securities. Revenue is recognized when the investee company has earnings. When earnings

FYI
Although temporary changes in the value of equity method securities are not accounted for, permanent changes are recognized.

CAUTION

A common mistake in accounting for equity method securities is to debit or credit the investment account for the entire amount of the investee's income or dividends. Remember, the investor accounts only for its share of the investee's income and dividends.

FYI

Coca-Cola, a company in which **Berkshire Hathaway** owns over 8%, has a number of subsidiaries that it accounts for using the equity method. In 2005, Coca-Cola reported equity income from those subsidiaries of $680 million accounted for using the equity method.

are announced, the carrying (book) value of the investment is increased because the investor owns a fixed percentage of a company that is worth more now than it was when the investment was originally made.

In accounting for investments with the equity method, the original investment is first recorded on the books at cost and is subsequently modified to reflect the investor's share of the investee's reported income, losses, and dividends. In this way, book value is increased to recognize the investor's share of earnings and decreased by the dividends received or to recognize the investor's share of losses. Temporary changes in value of investments accounted for using the equity method are not recorded.

There are two reasons why the procedures employed under the equity method are preferred over those used when accounting for trading or available-for-sale securities. First, the equity method assumes that significant influence can be exerted. Thus, the accounting procedures prevent the investing company from manipulating earnings by dictating the dividend policy of the investee. For a trading or available-for-sale security, where dividend payments are reported as revenue, an influential investor could increase its income by putting pressure on the investee to pay larger and more frequent dividends. With the equity method, dividends do not affect earnings. Second, the equity method provides more timely recognition of the investee's earnings and losses than do the procedures employed for trading or available-for-sale securities.

Illustrating the Equity Method

To illustrate the accounting for the equity method, we will use the following information: Kimball, Inc. purchases 20% (2,000 shares) of Holland Enterprises outstanding common stock (10,000 shares), paying $100 per share. Later in the year, Kimball receives a dividend of $2.50 per share; at year-end, Kimball receives Holland's income statement showing that the company earned $50,000 for the year. To ensure that you understand how the equity method differs from the accounting demonstrated earlier in the chapter, we will proceed with two scenarios: (1) Kimball is not able to exercise significant influence on Holland and, as a result, classifies the security as available-for-sale, and (2) Kimball is able to exercise significant influence and uses the equity method.

The accounting for this purchase of stock and subsequent events is shown in Exhibit 9. Column 1 shows the journal entries assuming that the Holland stock is considered an available-for-sale security. Column 2 illustrates the equity method. It is assumed that the Holland stock is selling for $102 per share at year-end.

Although accounting for the holding of equity method securities is different from the accounting for available-for-sale or trading securities, accounting for the sale of a stock investment is the same regardless of the classification. If the selling price exceeds the balance in the investment account, the difference is recognized as a gain. If the selling price is less than the recorded investment balance, the difference is recognized as a loss. To illustrate, assume that Kimball sells its 2,000 shares of Holland Enterprises stock (previously accounted for under the equity method) for $225,000 shortly after the year-end recognition of its $10,000 share def Holland's earnings. The entry to record the sale is:

EXHIBIT 9	**Accounting for Equity Securities**			
	(1) **Available-for-Sale Security**		**(2)** **Equity Method Security**	

Accounting for the
initial purchase of
the stock
	Investment in Available-for-Sale
	Securities 200,000
	    Cash ....
		200,000	Investment in Equity Method
			Securities 200,000
			    Cash ....
				200,000

Payment of a $2.50
per share dividend by
Holland Company
	Cash 5,000
	    Dividend Revenue ....
		5,000	Cash 5,000
			    Investment in Equity
			    Method Securities ....
				5,000

Announcement by Holland of net income for the year of $50,000	No entry		Investment in Equity Method Securities .... 10,000 Revenue from Investments.....	10,000

Holland stock is
selling at $102 per
share at year-end
	Market Adjustment–
	Available-for-Sale Securities 4,000
	    Unrealized Increase
	    in Available-for-Sale
	    Securities–Equity ....
		4,000	No entry	

Cash 225,000		
Investment in Equity Method Securities	205,000	
Realized Gain on Sale of Investment	20,000	

The $205,000 is obtained by adding Kimball's share of Holland's reported net income to the original investment cost and subtracting the dividends received from Holland ($200,000 + $10,000 − $5,000).

REMEMBER THIS...

- When the percentage of outstanding voting common stock owned is sufficient to exercise influence (as is usually true with ownership of 20 to 50%), the equity method is used.

- This method involves increasing the book value of the investment for earnings and decreasing it for dividends and losses.

Understand the basics of consolidated financial statements.

Consolidated Financial Statements

⑦ The equity method is used when an investor is able to exercise significant influence over an investee's operations. If the investor is able to control decisions made by the investee, then consolidated financial statements are appropriate. The objective with consolidated financial statements is to reflect in one set of financial statements the results of all companies owned or controlled by the parent corporation.

To show how consolidation works, a simple example of a parent company owning part or all of three other companies will be used. The income statement and balance sheet data for the four companies are given at the top of the next page.

		Percentage of the Parent's Ownership		
	Parent	**100% Sub1**	**80% Sub2**	**30% Sub3**
Assets				
Cash	$ 48	$ 20	$ 20	$ 20
Accounts receivable	200	80	80	80
Plant and equipment	500	100	100	100
Investment in Sub 1 ($120 × 1.00)	120			
Investment in Sub 2 ($120 × 0.80)	96			
Investment in Sub 3 ($120 × 0.30)	36			
Total assets	$ 1,000	$ 200	$ 200	$ 200
Liabilities	$ 600	$ 80	$ 80	$ 80
Equity	400	120	120	120
Total liabilities and stockholders' equity	$ 1,000	$ 200	$ 200	$ 200
Revenues				
Sales	$ 4,790	$ 2,000	$ 2,000	$ 2,000
Income from Sub 1 ($100 × 1.00)	100			
Income from Sub 2 ($100 × 0.80)	80			
Income from Sub 3 ($100 × 0.30)	30			
Expenses	(3,000)	(1,900)	(1,900)	(1,900)
Net income	$ 2,000	$ 100	$ 100	$ 100

Note that in the parent company's books, ownership of all three subsidiaries has been accounted for using the equity method. So, in each case the parent reports an investment asset equal to its share of the net assets, or equity, of the subsidiary, and investment income equal to its share of the net income of the subsidiary.

The objective of consolidation is to create financial statements for the parent and its controlled subsidiaries to report their performance as if they were one company. Operationally, this means that the individual assets, liabilities, revenues, and expenses of the parent and all subsidiaries of which it owns more than 50% are added together and included in the consolidated financial statements. Companies of which the parent owns less than 50% but more than 20% are accounted for using the equity method, as described in the preceding section. The consolidated balance sheet and income statement for the parent company and its subsidiaries are shown in Exhibit 10.

You should note four things concerning these consolidated results:

1. The consolidated balance sheet and income statement include *all* assets, liabilities, revenues, and expenses of the parent and the subsidiaries it controls. Thus, even though the parent owns only 80% of Sub 2, all of that subsidiary's assets, liabilities, revenues, and expenses are included in the consolidated total. An example of the intuition here is that the parent, with its 80% ownership, completely *controls* the assets of Sub 2 even though it doesn't own them completely.

2. *None* of the individual assets, liabilities, revenues, and expenses of Sub 3 are included in the consolidated financial statements because that subsidiary is not controlled by the parent. Instead, the parent's ownership of 30% of Sub 3 is accounted for using the equity method.

3. The fact that all of the assets, liabilities, revenues, and expenses of Sub 2 have been included in the consolidated total and yet the parent owns only 80% of that subsidiary is reflected in the minority interest items. In the consolidated balance sheet, **minority interest** is the amount of equity investment made by outside shareholders to consolidated subsidiaries that are not 100% owned by the parent. In the consolidated income statement, minority interest income (shown as a subtraction) reflects the amount of

minority interest

The amount of equity investment made by outside shareholders to consolidated subsidiaries that are not 100% owned by the parent.

EXHIBIT 10	**Consolidated Financial Statements**

Parent Company and Subsidiaries
Consolidated Balance Sheet

Assets

Cash ($48 + $20 + $20)	$ 88
Accounts receivable ($200 + $80 + $80)	360
Plant and equipment ($500 + $100 + $100)	700
Investment in Sub 3 ($120 × 0.30)	36
Total assets	$ 1,184
Liabilities ($600 + $80 + $80)	$ 760
Minority interest ($120 × 0.20)	24
Equity	400
Total liabilities and equities	$ 1,184

Parent Company and Subsidiaries
Consolidated Income Statement

Revenues

Sales ($4,790 + $2,000 + $2,000)	$ 8,790
Income from Sub 3 ($100 × 0.30)	30
Expenses ($3,000 + $1,900 + $1,900)	(6,800)
Minority interest income ($100 × 0.20)	(20)
Net income	$ 2,000

income belonging to outside shareholders of consolidated subsidiaries that are not 100% owned.

4. Total consolidated equity of $400 in this example is the same as total equity reported by the parent. Consolidated equity can be thought of as the amount invested by the group of shareholders who control the entire consolidated economic entity; this group of shareholders is the shareholders of the parent company. Of course, some of this equity investment, along with some funds borrowed by the parent, has been used to purchase 100% of Sub 1, 80% of Sub 2, and 30% of Sub 3. But to add portions of the equity of each of those subsidiaries in computing consolidated equity would essentially result in double counting the original investment made by the parent shareholders.

REMEMBER THIS...

- Consolidated financial statements are prepared when a parent owns more than 50% of one or more subsidiaries.
- All of the assets, liabilities, revenues, and expenses of the parent and the majority-owned subsidiaries are added in preparing the consolidated financial statements.

REVIEW OF LEARNING OBJECTIVES

(1) Understand why companies invest in other companies. Companies usually invest in other companies for one of the following reasons:

- To earn a return on excess cash.
- To gain influence, or even control, over the other company.

(2) Understand the different classifications for securities.

Classification of Securities	Types of Securities	Disclosed at	Reporting of Temporary Changes in Fair Value
Trading	Debt and equity	Fair value	Income statement
Available-for-sale	Debt and equity	Fair value	Stockholders' equity
Held-to-maturity	Debt	Amortized cost	Not recognized
Equity method	Equity	Cost adjusted for changes in net assets of investee	Not recognized

(3) Account for the purchase, recognition of revenue, and sale of trading and available-for-sale securities.

- Investments in debt and equity securities are recorded at cost, which includes the fair value of the securities plus any other expenditures required to purchase the securities.
- Revenues from securities take the form of:
  - interest,
  - dividends, or
  - gains or losses from selling the securities.

(4) Account for changes in the value of securities.

- Changes in value of trading or available-for-sale securities are reflected on the balance sheet using a market adjustment account.
- For trading securities, the unrealized gain or loss is reflected on the income statement for the period.
- For available-for-sale securities, the unrealized increase or decrease is recorded in a stockholders' equity account.

EXPANDED *material*

(5) Account for held-to-maturity securities.

- Amortization of premiums and discounts on held-to-maturity securities is accounted for by:
  - the straight-line amortization method or
  - the effective-interest method.
- The amortization adjusts the interest earned on the bonds from the stated to the effective rate.
- Investments in held-to-maturity securities are generally reported at cost (adjusted for premium or discount amortization), regardless of whether the current market value is less than or greater than their historical cost.

![badge]

(6) Account for securities using the equity method.

- When the percentage of outstanding voting common stock owned is sufficient to exercise influence (as is usually true with ownership of 20 to 50%), the equity method is used.
- This method involves:
  - increasing the book value of the investment for a percentage share of earnings and
  - decreasing it for a percentage share of dividends and losses.

(7) Understand the basics of consolidated financial statements.

- Consolidated financial statements are prepared when a parent owns more than 50% of one or more subsidiaries.
- All of the assets, liabilities, revenues, and expenses of the parent and the majority-owned subsidiaries are added in preparing the consolidated financial statements.

KEY TERMS & CONCEPTS

available-for-sale securities, 566
consolidated financial statements, 565
debt securities, 564
equity method, 565

equity securities (stock), 564
held-to-maturity security, 565
Market Adjustment— Trading Securities, 571

realized gains and losses, 570
trading securities, 566
unrealized gains and losses, 571

effective-interest amortization, 578
minority interest, 583
straight-line amortization, 576

REVIEW PROBLEM

Investments in Debt and Equity Securities

On January 1, 2009, Schultz, Inc., purchased the following securities:

Security	Type	Classification	Cost
1	Debt	Trading	$2,500
2	Debt	Trading	1,500
3	Equity	Trading	1,750
4	Debt	Available-for-sale	4,300
5	Equity	Available-for-sale	2,750

On March 31, one-half of Security 2 was sold for $900. During the year, interest and dividends were received as follows:

Security	Interest	Dividends
1	$200	
2	85	
3		none
4	435	
5		$200

(continued)

The following fair market values are available on December 31, 2009. Schultz had no balance in its market adjustment accounts on January 1, 2009.

Security	Market Value
1	$2,400
2	950
3	1,600
4	4,250
5	2,900

Required:

Record all necessary journal entries to account for these investments during 2009.

Solution

To account for these investments, four events must be accounted for:

1. The initial purchase on January 1.
2. The sale of one-half of Security 2 on March 31.
3. The receipt of interest and dividends during the year.
4. The changes in value as of December 31.

The initial purchase

Jan. 1	Investment in Trading Securities		5,750	
	Investment in Available-for-Sale Securities		7,050	
	Cash			12,800
	To record the purchase of trading and available-for-sale securities.			

The sale of one-half of Security 2 on March 31

Mar. 31	Cash		900	
	Realized Gain on Sale of Securities			150
	Investment in Trading Securities			750
	Sold one-half of Security 2 ($750 book value) for $900.			
	Recorded the $150 realized gain ($900 − $750).			

The receipt of interest and dividends during the year

Cash		920	
Interest Revenue			720
Dividend Revenue			200
Received $720 in interest during the year and $200 in dividends.			

Note: Even if cash were not received by year-end, the interest and dividends earned would need to be recorded, with the offsetting debit to a receivable account(s).

The changes in value as of December 31, 2009

Dec. 31	Unrealized Loss on Trading Securities		50	
	Market Adjustment–Trading Securities			50
	To account for the difference between book value			
	($5,000) and fair market value ($4,950) of trading securities.			

Note: Remember that one-half of Security 2 was sold during the year.

Dec. 31	Market Adjustment–Available-for-Sale Securities		100	
	Unrealized Increase/Decrease in Value of			
	Available-for-Sale Securities–Equity			100
	To account for the difference between book value ($7,050) and			
	fair market value ($7,150) of available-for-sale securities.			

DISCUSSION QUESTIONS

1. Why do firms invest in assets that are not directly related to their primary business operations?
2. Describe the risk and return trade-off of investments.
3. What are the four different classifications of debt and equity securities?
4. When will a security be classified as "trading"?
5. What types of securities can be classified as "held-to-maturity"?
6. To be classified as an equity method security, the investor must typically own at least a certain percentage of the outstanding common stock of the investee. What is that minimum percentage? That percentage of ownership represents the investor's ability to do what?
7. Identify the different types of returns an investor can realize when investing in debt and equity securities.
8. When a security is sold, what information must be known to account for that transaction?
9. What is the difference between a realized gain or loss and an unrealized gain or loss?
10. What does the account "Market Adjustment" represent?
11. How are changes in the value of trading securities accounted for on the books of the investor?
12. How are changes in the value of available-for-sale securities accounted for on the books of the investor?
13. What is the process for adjusting the value of a trading or available-for-sale security after a valuation account has been established?
14. Why aren't premiums and discounts on available-for-sale securities amortized?
15. Why aren't changes in the value of held-to-maturity and equity method securities accounted for on the books of the investor?

16. How does the accounting for changes in the value of trading and available-for-sale securities differ?

EXPANDED *material*

17. What future cash inflows is a company buying when it purchases a held-to-maturity security?
18. When would a company be willing to pay more than the face amount (a premium) for a held-to-maturity security?
19. Why does the amortization of a discount increase the amount of interest revenue earned on a held-to-maturity security?
20. Why must an investor purchasing held-to-maturity securities between interest payment dates pay the previous owner for accrued interest on those securities?
21. Why is the effective-interest amortization method theoretically superior to the straight-line method?
22. What is the key criterion for using the equity method of accounting for equity securities?
23. What guidelines have been provided to determine if the ability to significantly influence the decisions of an investee exists?
24. How does the equity method of accounting for securities differ from the procedures employed for a trading security?
25. Under what circumstances should consolidated financial statements be prepared?
26. What financial statement accounts are shown only in consolidated financial statements and never in the financial statements of individual companies?

PRACTICE EXERCISES

PE 12-1 **Why Companies Invest in Other Companies**
LO1   Which one of the following is *not* a primary reason companies invest in other companies?
a   To earn return on excess cash.
b. To eliminate risk in other investments.
c. To gain influence over another company.
d. To gain control over another company.

PE 12-2 **Classifying a Security**
LO2   Which one of the following types of investments is *always* an example of a debt security?
a. Available-for-sale securities.   b. Trading securities.
c. Held-to-maturity securities.   d. Equity method securities.

PE 12-3

LO2

Equity Method Securities

What is the general rule for what percentage an entity must own in another company to account for the investment using the equity method?

a. The entity should own 20 to 50% of the other company's outstanding voting stock.
b. The entity should own 5 to 10% of the other company's outstanding voting stock.
c. The entity should own 50 to 90% of the other company's outstanding voting stock.
d. The entity should own 10 to 20% of the other company's outstanding voting stock.

PE 12-4

LO2

Disclosure of Securities

Which two of the following classifications of securities are valued at fair value on a company's balance sheet?

a. Available-for-sale securities.
b. Equity method securities.
c. Trading securities.
d. Held-to-maturity securities.

PE 12-5

LO3

Accounting for the Purchase of Trading and Available-for-Sale Securities

The company purchased the following securities with cash:

Security	Type	Classification	Cost (including Broker's Fees)
1	Equity	Trading	$28,000
2	Equity	Available-for-sale	61,000
3	Debt	Available-for-sale	18,600
4	Debt	Trading	37,400

Make the necessary journal entry(ies) to record the purchase of these securities.

PE 12-6

LO3

Accounting for the Return Earned on an Investment

Refer to the data in PE 12-5. The company received the following interest and dividends from its securities investments during the year:

Security	Interest	Dividends
1		$340
2		560
3	$154	
4	305	

Make the necessary journal entry(ies) to record the receipt of interest and dividends during the year.

PE 12-7

LO3

Accounting for the Sale of Securities

Refer to the data in PE 12-5. Near the end of the year, the company sold Security 1 for $25,200. Make the necessary journal entry(ies) to record the sale.

PE 12-8

LO4

Changes in Value of Trading Securities

At the end of the year, the company had the following securities:

Security	Classification	Historical Cost	Market Value (December 31)
1	Available-for-sale	$52,000	$52,400
2	Available-for-sale	12,300	11,500
3	Trading	23,500	24,250

Make the necessary journal entry(ies) to record the change in value of the company's trading security (Security 3).

PE 12-9   **Changes in Value of Available-for-Sale Securities**

LO4   Refer to the data in PE 12-8. Make the necessary journal entry(ies) to record the change in value of the company's available-for-sale securities.

PE 12-10   **Subsequent Changes in Value of Trading Securities**

LO4   At the end of year 2, the company owned the following security (which was originally purchased for $41,600 and had a market value at the end of year 1 of $42,700).

Classification	Historical Cost	Market Value (December 31, Year 2)
Trading	$41,600	$40,800

Make the necessary journal entry(ies) to record the change in value of the security in the second year.

EXPANDED
material

PE 12-11   **Computing the Value of Held-to-Maturity Securities**

LO5   On January 1, 2009, the company purchased thirty $1,000 held-to-maturity bonds of another company. The bonds mature in four years from the date of issuance and pay interest at a stated annual rate of 8%, with payments to be made quarterly on March 31, June 30, September 30, and December 31. The market rate on bonds of similar risk is 12%. Compute the present value of this investment.

PE 12-12   **Accounting for the Initial Purchase of Held-to-Maturity Securities**

LO5   Using the information from PE 12-11, make the necessary journal entry to record the purchase of this held-to-maturity security.

PE 12-13   **Straight-Line Amortization of Bond Discounts**

LO5   The company purchased $40,000, 10%, three-year bonds for $35,939. Interest on the bonds is payable semiannually. Using straight-line amortization of the bond discounts, make the necessary journal entry(ies) to be made at each interest payment date to record the semiannual interest payment.

PE 12-14   **Straight-Line Amortization of Bond Premiums**

LO5   The company purchased $65,000, 10%, three-year bonds for $68,407.39. Interest on the bonds is payable semiannually. Using straight-line amortization of the bond premiums, make the necessary journal entry(ies) to be made at each interest payment date to record the semiannual interest payment.

PE 12-15   **Effective-Interest Amortization of Bond Premiums**

LO5   Refer to the data in PE 12-14. Using the effective-interest method of bond premium amortization, make the necessary journal entries to record the first two interest payments received on the bonds.

PE 12-16   **Accounting for the Sale of Bond Investments**

LO5   Refer to the data in PE 12-14 and 12-15. The company decided to sell the bonds for $67,000 immediately after receiving the second interest payment. Make the necessary journal entry(ies) to record the sale of these bonds.

PE 12-17

LO6

Accounting for Investments Using the Equity Method

Manwill Company owns 40% (30,000 shares) of Hall Company's voting stock. Since Manwill has a significant interest in Hall Company, it uses the equity method of accounting for the investment. Hall Company reported the following information for the year:

1. Hall reported net income of $80,000.
2. Hall paid dividends of $20,000.
3. Hall's stock value increased from $40 to $45.

Make the necessary journal entry(ies) to record the change in value of Manwill Company's investment in Hall Company.

PE 12-18

LO7

Consolidated Financial Statements

Parent Company owns 90% of the outstanding stock of Sub Company. At the end of the year, Sub Company reports revenues of $1,000 and expenses of $850. What will Parent Company report on its own financial statements as "Income from Sub"? On the consolidated financial statements, how much of Sub Company's revenues and expenses will be reported?

EXERCISES

E 12-19

LO3, LO4

Investment in Trading Securities–Journal Entries

Prepare the journal entries to account for the following investment transactions of Samuelson Company:

2008

July   1   Purchased 350 shares of Bateman Company stock at $22 per share plus a brokerage fee of $600. The Bateman stock is classified as trading.

Oct. 31   Received a cash dividend of $2.00 per share on the Bateman Company stock.

Dec. 31   At year-end, Bateman Company stock had a market price of $19 per share.

2009

Feb. 20   Sold 175 shares of the Bateman Company stock for $26 per share.

Oct. 31   Received a cash dividend of $2.20 per share on the Bateman Company stock.

Dec. 31   At year-end, Bateman Company stock had a market price of $29 per share.

E 12-20

LO3, LO4

Investment in Trading Securities–Journal Entries

In June 2009, Hatch Company had no investment securities but had excess cash that would not be needed for nine months. Management decided to use this money to purchase trading securities as a short-term investment. The following transactions relate to the investments:

July 16   Purchased 4,000 shares of Eli Corporation stock. The price paid, including brokerage fees, was $41,880.

Sept. 23   Received a cash dividend of $0.90 per share on the Eli stock.

28   Sold 2,000 shares of Eli Corporation stock at $11 per share. Paid a selling commission of $160.

Dec. 31   The market value of Eli's stock was $11.25 per share.

Given these data, prepare the journal entries to account for Hatch's investment in Eli Corporation stock.

E 12-21

LO3, LO4

Investment in Available-for-Sale Securities–Journal Entries

Bird Beak Corporation made the following available-for-sale securities transactions:

Jan. 14   Purchased 4,000 shares of Pinegar Corporation common stock at $20.80 per share.

Mar. 31   Received a cash dividend of $0.25 per share on the Pinegar Corporation stock.

Aug. 28   Sold 1,600 shares of Pinegar Corporation stock at $22.60 per share.

Dec. 31   The market value of the Pinegar Corporation stock was $24 per share.

Prepare journal entries to record the transactions.

E 12-22   **Investment in Securities**

LO3, LO4   In January 2007, Solitron, Inc., determined that it had excess cash on hand and decided to invest in Horner Company stock. The company intends to hold the stock for a period of three to five years, thereby making the investment an available-for-sale security. The following transactions took place in 2007, 2008, and 2009:

2007

Jan.	17	Purchased 2,750 shares of Horner Company stock for $89,500.
May	10	Received a cash dividend of $1.30 per share on Horner Company stock.
Dec.	31	The market value of the Horner Company stock was $30 per share.

2008

May	22	Purchased 750 shares of Horner Company stock at $40 per share.
July	18	Received a cash dividend of $0.90 per share on the Horner Company stock.
Dec.	31	The market value of the Horner Company stock was $42 per share.

2009

June	7	Received a cash dividend of $1 per share on the Horner Company stock.
Oct.	5	Sold the Horner Company stock at $27 per share for cash.
Dec.	31	The market value of the Horner Company stock was $25 per share.

Prepare the journal entries required to record each of these events.

E 12-23   **Investment in Equity Securities**

LO4   During 2007, Riverbend Company purchased trading securities as a short-term investment. The costs of the securities and their market values on December 31, 2009, are listed below.

Security	Cost	Market Value (December 31, 2009)
A	$250,000	$130,000
B	160,000	169,000
C	315,000	350,000

Riverbend had no trading securities in the years before 2009. Before any adjustments related to these trading securities, Riverbend had net income of $630,000 in 2009.

1. What is net income (ignoring income taxes) after making any necessary trading security adjustments?
2. What would net income be if the market value of Security A were $240,000?

E 12-24   **Investment in Debt and Equity Securities**

LO3, LO4   In February 2009, Packard Corporation purchased the following securities. Prior to these purchases, Packard had no portfolio of investment securities.

Security	Type	Classification	Cost
1	Debt	Trading	$11,500
2	Equity	Trading	9,000
3	Equity	Available-for-sale	7,250
4	Debt	Available-for-sale	12,300

During 2009, Packard received $2,400 in interest and $1,800 in dividends. On December 31, 2009, Packard's portfolio of securities had the following market values:

Security	Fair Market Value
1	$12,000
2	8,750
3	7,500
4	12,500

Prepare the journal entries required to record each of these transactions.

E 12-25

LO3, LO4

Investment in Debt and Equity Securities

Andrews, Inc., purchased the following securities during 2009:

Security	Type	Classification	Cost
1	Debt	Trading	$ 2,400
2	Equity	Trading	3,500
3	Debt	Available-for-sale	4,200
4	Equity	Available-for-sale	1,800
5	Debt	Held-to-maturity	11,000

During 2009, Andrews received interest of $1,400 and dividends of $600 on its investments. On September 29, 2009, Andrews sold one-half of Security 1 for $1,600. On December 31, 2009, the portfolio of securities had the following fair market values:

Security	Fair Market Value
1	$ 1,700
2	3,600
3	4,000
4	1,900
5	12,000

Andrews had no balance in its market adjustment accounts at the beginning of the year. Prepare the journal entries required to record the purchase of the securities, the receipt of interest and dividends, the sale of securities, and the adjustments required at year-end.

E 12-26

LO4

Investment in Securities–Changes in Value

Sharp, Inc., had the following portfolio of investment securities on January 1, 2009:

Security	Type	Classification	Historical Cost	Fair Market Value (1/1/09)
1	Debt	Trading	$1,000	$ 800
2	Equity	Trading	1,250	1,100
3	Debt	Trading	1,700	1,650
4	Debt	Available-for-sale	2,200	2,150
5	Debt	Held-to-maturity	1,800	1,750

Appropriate adjustments have been made in prior years. No securities were bought or sold during 2009. On December 31, 2009, Sharp's portfolio of securities had the following fair market values:

Security	Fair Market Value (12/31/09)
1	$ 650
2	1,200
3	1,700
4	2,250
5	1,850

Prepare the necessary adjusting entry(ies) on December 31, 2009.

E 12-27

LO4

Investment in Securities–Changes in Value

Indonesia, Inc., held the following portfolio of securities on December 31, 2008 (the end of its first year of operations):

	Cost	Market Value (12/31/08)
Trading securities	$16,300	$14,800
Available-for-sale securities	24,100	25,000
Held-to-maturity securities	19,000	20,300

No additional securities were bought or sold during 2009. On December 31, 2009, Indonesia's securities had a fair market value of:

Trading securities	$15,900
Available-for-sale securities	25,200
Held-to-maturity securities	18,900

Prepare the entries required at the end of 2008 and 2009 to properly adjust Indonesia's portfolio of securities.

E 12-28

LO3, LO5

Accounting for the Purchase of Securities

The Running Store is a chain of sporting goods stores. The Running Store is interested in using some of its excess cash to invest in securities. It decides to buy the following securities:

Security	Type	Price
Steven Company	Available-for-sale	$ 2,750
Nick, Inc.	Trading	11,040
Ryan Company	Available-for-sale	6,830
Jacob Company	Held-to-maturity	15,000

Prepare the journal entry to record the purchase of these securities.

E 12-29

LO3, LO5

Accounting for the Sale of Securities

Shay Company owns the following securities, which it is interested in selling:

Security	Type	Cost	Market Adjustments	Market Price
London Company	Available-for-sale	$5,000	$ 600 increase	$6,400
Brown Company	Trading	6,100	800 decrease	6,300
Shaw Company	Available-for-sale	8,400	1,000 increase	8,700
Robbins Company	Held-to-maturity	7,200	None	9,800

Prepare the journal entry to record the sale of these securities.

EXPANDED material

E 12-30

LO5

Held-to-Maturity Security Price Determination

1. How much should an investor pay for $100,000 of debenture bonds that pay interest every six months at an annual rate of 8%, assuming that the bonds mature in 10 years and that the effective interest rate at the date of purchase is also 8%?
2. How much should an investor pay for $100,000 of debenture bonds that pay $5,000 of interest every six months, have a maturity date in 10 years, and are sold to yield 8% interest, compounded semiannually?

E 12-31

LO5

Held-to-Maturity Security Price Determination

McMinville Corporation has decided to purchase bonds of La Verkin Corporation as a long-term investment. The 10-year bonds have a stated rate of interest of 12%, with interest payments being made semiannually. How much should McMinville be willing to pay for $150,000 of the bonds if:

1. A rate of return of 14% is deemed necessary to justify the investment?
2. A rate of return of 10% is considered to be an adequate return?

E 12-32

LO5

Investments in Held-to-Maturity Securities

Control Group purchased thirty $1,000, 10%, 20-year bonds of Natchez Corporation on January 1, 2009, as a long-term investment. The bonds mature on January 1, 2029, and interest is payable every January 1 and July 1. Control Group's reporting year ends December 31, and the company uses the straight-line method of amortizing premiums and discounts.

Make all necessary journal entries relating to the bonds for 2009, assuming:

1. The purchase price is 104% of face value.
2. The purchase price is 94% of face value.

E 12-33

LO5

Straight-Line Amortization of Premium

On their issuance date, Salina Company purchased thirty-five $1,000, 10%, six-year bonds of AF Corporation as a long-term investment for $38,285. Interest payments are made semiannually. Prepare a schedule showing the amortization of the bond premium over the six-year life of the bonds. Use the straight-line method of amortization.

E 12-34

LO5

Effective-Interest Amortization of Premium

Assume the same facts as in E 12-33. Prepare a schedule showing the amortization of the bond premium over the six-year life of the bonds. Use the effective-interest method of amortization. (*Hint:* The effective rate of interest earned on the bonds is 8% compounded semiannually.)

E 12-35

LO6

Investments in Stock–Equity Method

On January 3, 2009, Jorgenson, Inc., purchased 30,000 shares of the outstanding common stock of Horace Corporation. At the time of this transaction, Horace has 100,000 shares of common stock outstanding. The cost of the purchase (including brokerage fees) was $19 per share. During the year, Horace reported income of $32,000 and paid dividends of $4,000. On December 31, 2009, Horace's stock was valued at $23 per share.

Provide the entries necessary to record the above transactions.

E 12-36

LO6

Equity Method

Foster Enterprises purchased 20% of the outstanding common stock of Novelties, Inc., on January 2, 2009, paying $150,000. During 2009, Novelties, Inc., reported net income of $20,000 and paid dividends to shareholders of $15,000. On December 31, 2009, Foster's investment in Novelties stock had a fair market value of $158,000. Assuming this is the only security owned by Foster, prepare all journal entries required by Foster in 2009 assuming:

1. The security is classified as a trading security.
2. The security is classified as an available-for-sale security.
3. The equity method is applied to the investment.

E 12-37

LO6

Investments in Stock–Equity Method

During 2009, Genco Corporation purchased 10,000 shares of Wiener Company stock for $85 per share. Wiener had a total of 40,000 shares of stock outstanding.

1. Prepare journal entries for the following transactions:

Jan. 1   Purchased 10,000 shares of common stock at $85.

Dec. 31   Wiener Company declared and paid a $4.60-per-share dividend.

      31   Wiener Company reported net income for 2009 of $360,000.

(continued)

2. On December 31, 2009, the market price of Wiener's stock was $79 per share. Show how this investment would be reported on Genco's balance sheet at December 31, 2009, assuming that this is the only stock investment owned by Genco.

E 12-38   **Consolidated Financial Statements–Balance Sheet**

LO7   Ecotec Inc. purchased 70% of the outstanding common stock of Beatrix Co. on January 1, 2007, paying $875,000. On that day, the balance sheets of the two companies immediately after the purchase are as follows:

(in thousands)	Ecotec	Beatrix
Cash	$ 410	$ 260
Other current assets	1,875	1,240
Property, plant, & equipment	1,100	850
Investment in Beatrix	875	0
Total assets	$4,260	$2,350
Current liabilities	$1,225	$ 800
Long-term liabilities	775	300
Common stock	800	500
Retained earnings	1,460	750
Total liabilities & equities	$4,260	$2,350

1. Compute the amount that will be disclosed on the consolidated balance sheet as "Minority Interest."
2. Prepare a consolidated balance sheet as of January 1, 2007.

E 12-39   **Consolidated Financial Statements–Income Statement**

LO7   On January 1, 2007, Limbo Inc. purchased 80% of the outstanding common stock of Euphoria Co. at a price of $960,000. At the end of 2007, each company prepared separate income statements, which are presented below.

(in thousands)	Limbo	Euphoria
Sales	$3,650	$1,245
Income from Euphoria	112	0
Interest revenue	108	15
	$3,870	$1,260
Cost of goods sold	1,900	640
Other operating expenses	1,020	450
Interest expense	210	30
Net income	$ 740	$ 140

1. Compute the amount that will be reported on the consolidated income statement as "Minority Interest Income."
2. Prepare a consolidated income statement.
3. Compare Limbo's reported net income with consolidated net income. Explain the relationship.

PROBLEMS

P 12-40   **Investment in Securities–Recording and Analysis**

LO3   The following data pertain to the securities of Linford Company during 2009, the company's first year of operations:

a. Purchased 400 shares of Corporation A stock at $40 per share plus a commission of $200. This security is classified as trading.

(continued)

b. Purchased $6,000 of Corporation B bonds. These bonds are classified as trading.

c. Received a cash dividend of $0.50 per share on the Corporation A stock.

d. Sold 100 shares of Corporation A stock for $46 per share.

e. Received interest of $240 on the Corporation B bonds.

f. Purchased 50 shares of Corporation C stock for $3,500. Classified the stock as available-for-sale.

g. Received interest of $240 on the Corporation B bonds.

h. Sold 150 shares of Corporation A stock for $28 per share.

i. Received a cash dividend of $1.40 per share on the Corporation C stock.

j. Interest receivable at year-end on the Corporation B bonds amounts to $60.

Required:

Prepare journal entries to record the preceding transactions. Post the entries to T-accounts, and determine the amount of each of the following for the year:

1. Dividend revenue.
2. Bond interest revenue.
3. Net gain or loss from selling securities.

P 12-41

LO3, LO4

Buying and Selling Trading Securities

Iron Company incurred the following transactions relating to the common stock of Bronze Company:

July 14, 2007	Purchased 12,000 shares at $41 per share.
Sept. 4, 2008	Sold 2,100 shares at $46 per share.
Aug. 24, 2009	Sold 1,500 shares at $40 per share.

The end-of-year market prices for the shares were as follows:

Dec. 31, 2007	$38 per share
Dec. 31, 2008	$49 per share
Dec. 31, 2009	$36 per share

Iron Company classifies the Bronze stock as trading securities.

Required:

1. Determine the amount of (a) realized gain or loss and (b) unrealized gain or loss to be reported on the income statement each year relating to the Bronze stock.
2. How would your answer to part (1) change if the securities were classified as available-for-sale? Explain.

P 12-42

LO3, LO4

Trading and Available-for-Sale Securities

Lorien Technologies, Inc., purchased the following securities during 2008:

Security	Classification	Cost	Market Value (12/31/08)
A	Trading	$ 5,000	$ 4,000
B	Trading	7,000	10,000
C	Available-for-sale	10,000	8,000
D	Available-for-sale	6,000	3,500

The following transactions occurred during 2009:

a. On January 1, 2009, Lorien purchased Security E for $12,000. Security E is classified as available-for-sale.

b. On March 23, 2009, Security B was sold for $4,700.

c. On July 23, 2009, Security C was sold for $19,500.

(continued)

The remaining securities had the following market values as of December 31, 2009:

Security	Market Value
A	$ 4,500
D	5,000
E	13,000

Required:

1. Determine the amount of (a) realized gain or loss and (b) unrealized gain or loss to be reported relating to Lorien's trading securities for 2009.
2. Determine the amount of (a) realized gain or loss and (b) unrealized gain or loss to be reported relating to Lorien's available-for-sale securities for 2009. Which amounts will appear on the income statement?

P 12-43

LO3

Investments in Trading Securities

In December 2009, the treasurer of Toth Company concluded that the company had excess cash on hand and decided to invest in Soren Corporation stock. The company intends to hold the stock for a period of 6 to 12 months and classifies the security as trading. The following transactions took place:

Jan.	1	Purchased 7,600 shares of Soren Corporation stock for $152,000.
Apr.	24	Received a cash dividend of $1.20 per share on the Soren Corporation stock.
May	5	Sold 2,000 shares of the Soren Corporation stock at $23 per share for cash.
July	21	Received a cash dividend of $1.30 per share on the Soren Corporation stock.
Aug.	9	Sold the balance of the Soren Corporation stock at $15 per share for cash.

Required:

Prepare the appropriate journal entries to record each of these transactions.

P 12-44

LO3, LO4

Investments in Debt and Equity Securities

Wilbur Company often invests in the debt and equity securities of other companies as short-term investments. During 2009, the following events occurred:

July   1   Wilbur purchased the securities listed here:

Security	Type	Classification	Cost
1	Debt	Trading	$41,200
2	Equity	Trading	23,940
3	Equity	Trading	51,250
4	Equity	Available-for-sale	21,300

Sept.	30	Wilbur received a cash dividend of $2,460 on Security 2.
Dec.	1	Wilbur sold Security 4 for $18,300.
	31	Wilbur received interest of $4,300 on Security 1.
	31	The market prices were quoted as follows: Security 1, $40,900; Security 2, $25,550; Security 3, $44,000.

Required:

1. Prepare journal entries to record the events.
2. Illustrate how these investments would be reported on the balance sheet at December 31.
3. What items and amounts would be reported on the income statement for the year?

P 12-45

LO3, LO4

Unifying Concepts: Short-Term Investments in Stocks and Bonds

JAG Manufacturing Company produces and sells one main product. There is significant seasonality in demand, and the unit price is quite high. As a result, during the heavy selling season, the company generates cash that is idle for a few months. The company

(continued)

uses this cash to acquire investments. The following transactions relate to JAG's investments during 2009:

Mar. 15   Purchased 1,200 shares of Gates Corporation stock at $21 per share, plus broker-
           age fees of $815. This stock is classified as trading.

Apr.   1   Purchased $39,000 of 10% bonds of Micro Company. This investment is classi-
           fied as available-for-sale.

June   3   Received a cash dividend of $0.75 per share on the Gates Corporation stock.

Oct.   1   Received a semiannual interest payment of $1,950 on the Micro Company bonds.

      10   Sold 400 shares of the Gates Corporation stock at $26 per share less a $295 bro-
           kerage fee.

Dec. 31   Recorded $975 of interest earned on the Micro Company bonds for the period
           October 1, 2009, through December 31, 2009.

      31   The market price of the Gates Corporation stock was $19 per share; the market
           price of the Micro Company bonds was $38,560.

Required:
Prepare journal entries to record these transactions.

P 12-46

LO3, LO4

Recording Investment Transactions

The following data pertain to the investments of Sumner Company during 2009, the company's first year of operations:

a. Purchased 200 shares of Corporation A stock at $40 per share, plus brokerage fees of
    $100. Classified as trading.
b. Purchased $10,000 of Corporation B bonds at face value. Classified as trading.
c. Received a cash dividend of $0.50 per share on the Corporation A stock.
d. Received interest of $600 on the Corporation B bonds.
e. Purchased 50 shares of Corporation C stock for $3,500. Classified as available-for-sale.
f. Received interest of $600 on the Corporation B bonds.
g. Sold 80 shares of Corporation A stock for $32 per share due to a significant decline in
    the market.
h. Received a cash dividend of $1.40 per share on the Corporation C stock.
i. Interest receivable at year-end on the Corporation B bonds amounts to $200.
j. Market value of securities at year-end: Corporation A stock, $42 per share; Corporation B
    bonds, $10,200; Corporation C stock, $3,450.

Required:
Enter these transactions in T-accounts, and determine each of the following for the year:
1. Dividend revenue.
2. Bond interest revenue.
3. Net gain or loss from selling securities.
4. Unrealized gain or loss from holding securities.

P 12-47

LO3, LO4

Investments in Available-for-Sale Securities

Lindorf Company often purchases common stocks of other companies as long-term investments. At the end of 2008, Lindorf held the common stocks listed. (Assume that Lindorf
Company exercises no significant influence over these companies; that is, they are classified
as available-for-sale securities.)

Corporation	Number of Shares	Cost per Share
A	2,500	$ 40
B	2,000	26
C	2,300	153
D	750	75

(continued)

Additional information for 2008:

Sept. 30   Lindorf received a cash dividend of $1.15 per share on Corporation A stock.

Dec. 31   The market prices were quoted as follows:
Corporation A stock, $35; Corporation B stock, $28;
Corporation C stock, $154; Corporation D stock, $70.

Required:
1. Illustrate how these investments would be reported on the balance sheet at December 31, 2008, and prepare the adjusting entry at that date.
2. What items and amounts would be reported on the income statement for 2008?
3. Prepare the journal entry for the sale of Corporation D stock for $71 per share in 2009.
4. **Interpretive Question:** Why are losses from the write-down of available-for-sale securities not included in the current year's income, whereas similar losses for trading securities are included?

P 12-48

LO3

Unifying Concepts: Investments in Debt and Equity Securities

On January 1, Heiress Company had surplus cash and decided to make some long-term investments. The following transactions occurred during the year:

Jan.   1   Purchased thirty $1,000, 11% bonds of McComb Corporation at face value. Semiannual interest payment dates are January 1 and July 1 each year. The bonds are classified as available-for-sale.

Feb. 15   Purchased 3,000 shares of Gordon Corporation stock at $28 per share, plus brokerage fees of $1,100. The stock is classified as available-for-sale.

July   1   Received a semiannual interest payment on the McComb Corporation bonds.

Sept. 30   Received an annual cash dividend of $1.00 per share on Gordon Corporation stock.

Oct. 15   Sold 1,000 shares of the Gordon Corporation stock at $33 per share.

Dec. 31   Adjusted the accounts to accrue interest on the McComb Corporation bonds.

Required:
1. Prepare journal entries for these transactions.
2. The market quote for McComb Corporation's bonds at closing on December 31 was 103. The Gordon Corporation stock closed at $32 per share. Prepare a partial balance sheet showing all the necessary data for these securities. Assume that Heiress exercises no significant influence over its investees.

P 12-49

LO3, LO4

Investments in Equity Securities

On March 15, 2009, Boston Company acquired 5,000 shares of Richfield Corporation common stock at $45 per share as a long-term investment. Richfield has 50,000 shares of outstanding voting common stock. Boston does not own any other stocks. The following additional events occurred during the fiscal year ended December 31, 2009:

Dec.   1   Boston received a cash dividend of $2.50 per share from Richfield Corporation.

31   Richfield Corporation announced earnings for the year of $150,000.

31   Richfield common stock had a closing market price of $42 per share.

Required:
1. What accounting method should be used to account for this investment? Why?
2. Prepare journal entries for the above transactions.
3. Prepare a partial income statement and balance sheet to show how the investments accounts would be shown on the financial statements.

P 12-50 **Investment Portfolio**

LO4 General Corporation has the following investments in equity securities at December 31, 2008 (there are no existing balances in the market adjustment account):

Company	Classification	Shares	Percentage of Shares Owned	Cost	Market Price at 12/31/05
Clarke Corporation	Trading	1,000	2%	$75	$78
Marlin Company	Available-for-sale	4,000	15	34	32
Air Products, Inc.	Available-for-sale	3,000	10	46	43

Required:

1. Prepare any adjusting entries required at December 31, 2008.
2. Illustrate how these investments would be presented on General Corporation's balance sheet at December 31, 2008. The available-for-sale securities are expected to be held for two to five years.
3. Prepare the journal entry on April 10, 2009, when General Corporation sold the Clarke Corporation investment for $72 per share.
4. Assume that General Corporation still owns its investment in Marlin Company and Air Products at December 31, 2009; the market prices on that date are $37 for Marlin and $44 for Air Products. Prepare all adjusting journal entries needed at December 31, 2009.

P 12-51 **Investments in Held-to-Maturity Securities**

LO5 Eysser Corporation purchased $50,000 of Hillside Construction Company's 10% bonds at $103\frac{1}{3}$ plus accrued interest on February 1, 2008. The bonds mature on April 1, 2015, and interest is payable on April 1 and October 1. Eysser Corporation uses the straight-line method of amortizing bond premiums and discounts.

Required:

1. Record all journal entries to account for this investment during the years 2008 and 2009, assuming that Eysser closes its books annually on December 31.
2. **Interpretive Question:** At the time these bonds were purchased (February 1, 2008), was the market rate of interest above or below 10%? Explain.

P 12-52 **Investments in Held-to-Maturity Securities**

LO5 On January 1, 2009, Eurowest Company purchased a $25,000, 12% bond at 104 as a long-term investment. The bond pays interest annually on each December 31 and matures on December 31, 2011.

Assuming straight-line amortization, answer the following questions:

Required:

1. What will be the net amount of cash received (total inflows minus total outflows) from this investment over its life?
2. How much cash will be collected each year?
3. How much premium will be amortized each year?
4. By how much will Investment in Held-to-Maturity Securities decrease each year?
5. How much revenue will be reported on the income statement each year relating to this security?

P 12-53 **Determining the Purchase Price of Held-to-Maturity Securities and Effective-Interest Amortization**

LO5 Corbett Corporation decided to purchase twenty $1,000, 10%, six-year bonds of Texas Manufacturing Company as a long-term investment on February 1, 2008. The bonds mature

(continued)

on February 1, 2014, and interest payments are made semiannually on February 1 and August 1.

Required:

1. How much should Corbett Corporation be willing to pay for the bonds if the current interest rate on similar bonds is 8%?
2. Prepare a schedule showing the amortization of the bond premium or discount over the remaining life of the bonds, assuming that Corbett Corporation uses the effective-interest method of amortization.
3. How much bond interest revenue would be recorded each year if the straight-line method of amortization were used? Show how these amounts differ from the annual interest recognized using the effective-interest method. (Assume a fiscal year ending July 31.)
4. **Interpretive Question:** Which of the two amortization methods is preferable? Why?

P 12-54

LO5

Investments in Held-to-Maturity Securities

Walsh Equipment Company made the following purchases of debt securities during 2009. All are classified as held-to-maturity, and all pay interest semiannually.

Purchase Date	Corp.	Face Amount	Cost	Interest Rate, %	Maturity Date	Last Interest Payment Date
10/15/09	A	$10,000	97	8	1/1/14	7/1/09
11/30/09	B	15,000	103	10	4/1/12	10/1/09
12/15/09	C	20,000	99	14	6/1/13	12/1/09
12/31/09	D	16,000	105	12	5/1/10	11/1/09

Required:

1. Prepare journal entries for the purchases.
2. Show all adjusting entries relating to the bonds on December 31, 2009, assuming that Walsh Equipment Company closes its book on that date and uses the straight-line amortization method.

P 12-55

LO3, LO4, LO6

Long-Term Investments in Equity Securities

Century Corporation acquired 8,400 common shares of Fidelity Company on January 10, 2009, for $12 per share and acquired 15,000 common shares of Essem Corporation on January 25, 2009, for $22 per share. Fidelity has 60,000 shares of common stock outstanding, and Essem has 50,000 shares outstanding. At December 31, 2009, the following information was obtained about the operations of Fidelity and Essem:

	Fidelity	Essem
Net income	$36,000.00	$100,000.00
Dividends paid per share	0.40	1.00
Market value per share at December 31, 2009	10.00	20.00

Assume that Century Corporation exerted significant influence over the policies of Essem Corporation, but influenced the policies of Fidelity Corporation only to a very limited extent. Century classified its investment in Fidelity as an available-for-sale security.

Required:

1. How should Century account for its investments in Essem Corporation?
2. Prepare the journal entries for each investment for the year 2009 using the method or methods you selected in part (1).

P 12-56

LO6

Investments in Stocks–Equity Method

On March 20, 2009, Reeder Company acquired 80,000 shares of Needed Industries common stock at $32 per share as a long-term investment. Needed has 200,000 shares of outstanding voting common stock. The following additional information is presented for the calendar year ended December 31, 2009:

Nov. 15   Reeder received a cash dividend of $1.50 per share from Needed Industries.
Dec. 31   Needed announced earnings for the year of $250,000.
    31   Needed Industries common stock had a closing market price of $28 per share.

Required:
1. **Interpretive Question:** What accounting method should be used by Reeder Company to account for this investment? Why?
2. Prepare journal entries for the transactions and events described.

P 12-57

LO3, LO4, LO6

Long-Term Investments in Stock–Available-for-Sale and Equity Method

The following activities relate to Merrill Company during the years 2008 and 2009:

2008
Feb. 15   Merrill purchased 10,000 shares of Hendershot Equipment stock for $40 per share.
Dec. 1   Merrill received an $0.80-per-share cash dividend from Hendershot Equipment.
    31   Hendershot Equipment common stock had a closing market price of $37 per share. Hendershot's 2008 net income was $120,000.

2009
July 1   Merrill sold all 10,000 shares of Hendershot Equipment stock for $42 per share.

Additional information: Hendershot Equipment had 50,000 shares of common stock outstanding on January 1, 2008.

Required:
1. Prepare journal entries to record the transactions assuming:
   a. The securities are classified as available-for-sale.
   b. The equity method is used.
2. Show the amounts that would be reported on the financial statements of Merrill Company at December 31, 2008, under each assumption.
3. **Interpretive Question:** What is the minimum number of shares of stock that Hendershot could have outstanding in order for Merrill to use the equity method?

P 12-58

LO3, LO4, LO6

Long-Term Investments in Equity Securities

During January 2009, Danbury, Inc., acquired 40,000 shares of Corporation A common stock for $24 per share. In addition, it purchased 5,000 shares of Corporation B preferred (nonvoting) stock for $112 per share. Corporation A has 160,000 shares of common stock outstanding, and Corporation B has 12,000 shares of nonvoting stock outstanding. Danbury anticipates holding both securities for at least five years.

The following data were obtained from operations during 2009:

	2009
Net income:	
Corporation A	$190,000
Corporation B	80,000
Dividends paid (per share):	
Corporation A	$0.60
Corporation B	2.50
Market value per share at December 31:	
Corporation A	$ 25
Corporation B	109

(continued)

Required:

1. **Interpretive Question:** What method should Danbury, Inc., use in accounting for the investment in Corporation A stock? Why? What accounting method should be used in accounting for Corporation B nonvoting stock? Why?
2. Prepare the journal entries necessary to record the transactions for 2009.

P 12-59

LO5, LO6

Unifying Concepts: Long-Term Investments in Stocks and Bonds

On January 2, 2009, Drexello, Inc., purchased $75,000 of 10%, five-year bonds of Greasy Trucking as a held-to-maturity security at a price of $77,610 plus accrued interest. The bonds mature on November 1, 2013, and interest is payable semiannually on May 1 and November 1. Drexello uses the straight-line method of amortizing bond premiums and discounts.

In addition to the bonds, Drexello purchased 30% of the 50,000 shares of outstanding common stock of Mellon Company at $42 per share, plus brokerage fees of $450, on January 10, 2009. On December 31, 2009, Mellon announced that its net income for the year was $150,000 and paid an annual dividend of $2 per share as advised by the board of directors of Drexello. The closing market price of Mellon common stock on December 31 was $38 per share.

Required:

1. Record all the 2009 transactions relating to these two investments in general journal form.
2. Show how the long-term investments and the related revenues would be reported on the financial statements of Drexello at December 31, 2009.

P 12-60

LO7

Consolidated Financial Statements

Parent Company owns parts of three different subsidiaries. The balance sheets and income statements for these four companies are listed below. Note that, in the financial statements of Parent Company, its ownership interest in the three subsidiaries has been accounted for using the equity method.

		Percentage of the Parent's Ownership		
	Parent	**90% Sub 1**	**60% Sub 2**	**40% Sub 3**
Assets				
Cash	$ 120	$ 40	$ 30	$ 60
Accounts receivable	500	120	90	50
Plant and equipment	1,050	400	160	300
Investment in Sub 1	288			
Investment in Sub 2	78			
Investment in Sub 3	84			
Total assets	$2,120	$ 560	$ 280	$ 410
Liabilities	$ 900	$ 240	$ 150	$ 200
Equity	1,220	320	130	210
Total liabilities and stockholders' equity	$2,120	$ 560	$ 280	$ 410
Sales	$6,420	$3,000	$3,000	$8,000
Income from Sub 1	360			
Income from Sub 2	480			
Income from Sub 3	160			
Expenses	(4,200)	(2,600)	(2,200)	(7,600)
Net income	$3,220	$ 400	$ 800	$ 400

Required:

1. Prepare a consolidated balance sheet for Parent Company and its subsidiaries.
2. Prepare a consolidated income statement for Parent Company and its subsidiaries.
3. **Interpretive Question:** Return on sales is net income divided by total sales. Without doing any computations, state what would happen to consolidated return on sales if Sub 3 were consolidated rather than accounted for using the equity method. Explain.

ANALYTICAL ASSIGNMENTS

AA 12-61

DISCUSSION

Which Investment Should We Make?

Pentron Data Corporation has a significant amount of excess cash on hand and has decided to make a long-term investment in either debt or equity securities. After a careful analysis, the investment committee has recommended to the company treasurer that Pentron purchase either one of the following two investments. The first investment involves purchasing sixty $1,000, 8% bonds issued by Andrea Company. The bonds mature in four years, pay interest semiannually, and are currently selling at 92. The second investment alternative involves purchasing 3,000 shares of Franklin Corporation common stock at $30 per share (including brokerage fees). The investment committee believes that the Franklin stock will pay an annual dividend of $3.50 per share and is likely to be salable at the end of four years for $36 per share.

Discuss the following questions:

1. If Pentron wants to earn 12% per year, should it make either investment?
2. Which of the two investments would you advise the treasurer to invest in assuming the inherent risk is approximately equal? Your decision should be based on which investment provides the more attractive return, ignoring income tax effects.

AA 12-62

DISCUSSION

Classification of Securities

Memphis Company has just purchased five securities; it intends to hold the stock until the price increases to a sufficiently high level, at which time it plans to sell the stock. In fact, it is unlikely that the company will hold the securities for more than a few months. Nevertheless, Memphis's management has decided to classify the securities as available-for-sale rather than as trading securities. Why is Memphis choosing this type of classification, and would you allow it if you were the auditor?

AA 12-63

JUDGMENT CALL

You Decide: **Should the trading securities that companies own be left on the books at historical cost, or should they be adjusted annually to their current market price (as is now required by GAAP)?**

When physical assets are purchased, they are recorded on the balance sheet at cost and left there until the asset is sold. For example, when land is purchased, the cost of the land is recorded on the books. If the land increases in value, no adjustment is made. The company realizes the gain in value when it sells the land at a gain. Why don't we do this for marketable securities? Why should the assets for land and securities be different?

AA 12-64

REAL COMPANY
ANALYSIS

Microsoft

(Since **Wal-Mart** doesn't report investments activity, we will refer to **Microsoft**'s 2005 annual report for the case.) Locate Microsoft's 2005 annual report at **http://www.microsoft.com** to answer the following questions:

1. Find Microsoft's note on accounting policies. Using the information in that note (under the heading "Financial Instruments"), determine what fraction of Microsoft's investment securities are classified as "available-for-sale."
2. In its note on "Cash and short-term investments," Microsoft lists the general types of investments that make up its $60.592 billion portfolio. Certificates of deposit are listed both as "cash and cash equivalents" and as "short-term investments." What is the difference between these two categories? *Hint:* Go back to the note you looked at to answer (1).
3. Look at Microsoft's stockholders' equity statement. Where in the equity section does Microsoft report the unrealized gains and losses from available-for-sale securities?

AA 12-65

REAL COMPANY
ANALYSIS

Berkshire Hathaway

The following note comes from the 2005 annual report of **Berkshire Hathaway**:

(6) Investments in equity securities

Data with respect to investments in equity securities are shown below.
Amounts are in millions.

December 31, 2005	Cost	Unrealized Gains	Fair Value
Common stock of:			
American Express Company	$ 1,287	$ 6,515	$ 7,802
The Coca-Cola Company	1,299	6,763	8,062
The Procter & Gamble Company*	5,963	(175)	5,788
Wells Fargo & Company	2,754	3,221	5,975
Other equity securities	10,036	9,058	19,094
	$21,339	$25,382	$46,721

December 31, 2004	Cost	Unrealized Gains	Fair Value
Common stock of:			
American Express Company	$ 1,470	$ 7,076	$ 8,546
The Coca-Cola Company	1,299	7,029	8,328
The Gillette Company*	600	3,699	4,299
Wells Fargo & Company	463	3,045	3,508
Other equity securities	5,505	7,531	13,036
	$ 9,337	$28,380	$37,717

*The Gillette Company was acquired by The Procter & Gamble Company during 2005.

Berkshire Hathaway also discloses that it classifies each of these investments as an available-for-sale security.

1. All securities included in the tables in Berkshire Hathaway's Note 6 are classified as available-for-sale. Make all journal entries that were required in 2005 to account for Berkshire Hathaway's investments in:
    a. **The Coca-Cola Company**.
    b. Other equity securities.
2. Did the performance of Berkshire Hathaway's portfolio of equity securities have any bright spots in 2005?
3. How has Berkshire Hathaway's portfolio of equity securities performed over time?

AA 12-66

INTERNATIONAL

Sony

Sony Corporation was organized in 1946 under the name **Tokyo Tsushin Kogyo**. The name "Sony" is a combination of the Latin word sonus (sound) and the English word sonny; it was given to a small transistor radio sold by the company in the United States, starting in 1954. The radio was so popular that the entire company changed its name to Sony in 1958.

In its 2006 annual report, Sony included the note to its financial statements shown on the following page.

(continued)

8. Marketable securities and securities investments and other

	Yen in millions							
	March 31, 2005				March 31, 2006			
	Cost	Gross unrealized gains	Gross unrealized losses	Fair value	Cost	Gross unrealized gains	Gross unrealized losses	Fair value
Available-for-sale:								
Debt securities	¥2,090,605	¥ 58,161	¥(2,464)	¥2,146,302	¥2,522,864	¥ 17,021	¥(22,810)	¥2,517,075
Equity securities	107,126	49,350	(814)	155,662	227,079	171,921	(1,589)	397,411
Held-to-maturity securities	27,431	530	(13)	27,948	33,193	132	(221)	33,104
Total	¥2,225,162	¥108,041	¥(3,291)	¥2,329,912	¥2,783,136	¥189,074	¥(24,620)	¥2,947,590

	Dollars in millions			
	March 31, 2006			
	Cost	Gross unrealized gains	Gross unrealized losses	Fair value
Available-for-sale:				
Debt securities	$21,563	$ 145	$(195)	$21,513
Equity securities	1,941	1,470	(14)	3,397
Held-to-maturity securities	283	1	(1)	283
Total	$23,787	$1,616	$(210)	$25,193

1. In the notes to its English-language financial statements, Sony states that those statements "conform with accounting principles generally accepted in the United States." However, Sony's official accounting records are maintained using Japanese accounting principles. Why would Sony go to the trouble of preparing a separate set of English-language financial statements using U.S. accounting principles?

2. Assuming that approximately the same available-for-sale securities were on hand in both 2005 and 2006, how well did Sony's investments perform in 2006?

3. What journal entries did Sony make during the year to record the revaluation of available-for-sale securities? Use only the total amounts (that is, don't use the separate amounts for debt and equity securities), and ignore the fact that securities were bought and sold during the year.

AA 12-67

ETHICS

Is It OK to Strategically Classify Securities?

You have recently been hired as a staff assistant in the office of the chairman of the board of directors of Clefton, Inc. Because you have some background in accounting, the chairman has asked you to review the preliminary financial statements that have been prepared by the company's accounting staff. After the financial statements are approved by the chairman of the board, they will be audited by external auditors. This is the first year that Clefton has had its financial statements audited by external auditors.

In examining the financial statement note on investment securities, you notice that all of the securities that had unrealized gains for the year have been classified as trading, whereas all of the securities that had unrealized losses have been classified as available-for-sale. You realize that this has the impact of placing all the gains on the income statement and hiding all the losses in the equity section of the balance sheet. You call the chief accountant who confirms that the securities are not classified until the end of the year and that the classification depends on whether a particular security has experienced a gain or

(continued)

a loss during the year. The chief accountant states that this policy was adopted, with the approval of the chairman of the board, in order to maximize the reported net income of the company. The chief accountant tells you that investment security classification is based on how management intends to use those securities; therefore, management is free to classify the securities in any way it wishes.

You are uncomfortable with this investment security classification strategy. You are also dismayed that the chief accountant and the chairman of the board seem to have agreed on this scheme to maximize reported income. You are also worried about what the external auditors will do when they find out about this classification scheme. You have been asked to report to the chairman of the board this afternoon to give your summary of the status of the preliminary financial statements. What should you do?

AA 12-68

WRITING

Why Doesn't the Gain Go on the Income Statement?

You are the controller for Chong Lai Company. You just received a very strongly worded e-mail message from the president of the company. The president has learned that a $627,000 gain on a stock investment made by the company last year will not be reported in the income statement because you have classified the security as available-for-sale. With the gain, the company would report a record profit for the year. Without the gain, profits are actually down slightly from the year before. The president wants an explanation—now.

It has been your policy for the past several years to routinely classify all investments as available-for-sale. Your company is not in the business of actively buying and selling stocks and bonds. Instead, all investments are made to strengthen relationships with either suppliers or major customers. As such, your practice is to buy securities and hold them for several years.

Write a one-page memo to the president explaining the rationale behind your policy of security classification.

AA 12-69

CUMULATIVE
SPREADSHEET
PROJECT

Adding an Investment Portfolio

This spreadsheet assignment is a continuation of the spreadsheet assignments given in earlier chapters. If you completed those spreadsheets, you have a head start on this one.

This assignment is based on the spreadsheet prepared in part (1) of the spreadsheet assignment for Chapter 9. Review that assignment for a summary of the assumptions made in preparing a forecasted balance sheet, income statement, and statement of cash flows for 2010 for Handyman Company. Using those financial statements, complete the following exercise.

Handyman has decided that, in 2010, it will create an available-for-sale investment portfolio. Handyman plans to invest $20 million in a variety of stocks and bonds. (Recall that the numbers in the Handyman spreadsheet are in millions.) As of the end of 2009, Handyman has no investment portfolio. Adapt your spreadsheet to include this expected $20 million investment portfolio as a current asset in 2010. Ignore the possibility of any interest, dividends, gains, or losses on this portfolio. Answer the following questions:

1. With the assumptions built into your spreadsheet, where will Handyman get the $20 million in funding necessary to acquire these investment securities?
2. Where in the statement of cash flows did you put the cash outflow associated with the acquisition of these investment securities? Explain your placement.

Warner Company started business on January 1, 2009. The following transactions and events occurred in 2009 and 2010. For simplicity, information for sales, inventory purchases, collections on account, and payments on account is given in summary form at the end of each year.

2009

Jan. 1   Issued 150,000 shares of $1-par common stock to investors at $15 per share.

1   Purchased a building for $720,000. The building has a 25-year expected useful life and a $70,000 expected salvage value. Warner uses the straight-line method of depreciation.

1   Leased equipment under a ten-year lease. The five lease payments of $20,000 each are to be made on December 31 of each year. The cash price of the equipment is $134,202. This lease is accounted for as a capital lease with an implicit interest rate of 8%. The equipment has a ten-year useful life and zero expected salvage value; Warner uses straight-line depreciation with all of its equipment.

Feb. 1   Borrowed $1.8 million from Foley Bank. The loan bears a 9% annual interest rate. Interest is to be paid each year on February 1. The principal on the loan will be repaid in four years.

Mar. 1   Purchased 50,000 shares of Ryan Company for $30 per share. Warner classifies this as an investment in trading securities. These securities are reported as a current asset.

July 15   Purchased 55,000 shares of Anson Company for $23 per share. Warner classifies this as an investment in available-for-sale securities. These securities are reported as a long-term asset.

Nov. 17   Declared a cash dividend of $0.30 per share, payable on January 15, 2010.

Dec. 31   Made the lease payment.

31   The Ryan Company shares had a market value of $26 per share. The Anson Company shares had a market value of $28 per share.

Summary:

a. Sales for the year (all on credit) totaled $900,000. The cost of inventory sold was $480,000.

b. Cash collections on credit sales for the year were $420,000.

c. Inventory costing $540,000 was purchased on account. (Warner Company uses the perpetual inventory method.)

d. Payments on account totaled $500,000.

2010

Jan. 1   Issued $400,000 in bonds at par value. The bonds have a stated interest rate of 10%, payable semiannually on July 1 and January 1.

1   The estimated useful life and salvage value for the building were changed. It is now estimated that the building has a remaining life (as of January 1, 2010) of 20 years. Also, it is now estimated that the building will have no salvage value. These changes in estimate are to take effect for the year 2010 and subsequent years.

15   Paid the cash dividend declared in November 2009.

Feb.	1	Warner Company repurchased 15,000 shares of its own common stock to be held as treasury stock. The price paid was $32 per share.
	1	Paid the interest on the loan from Foley Bank.
Apr.	10	Sold all 50,000 shares of the Ryan Company stock. The shares were sold for $25 per share.
July	1	Paid the interest on the bonds.
Oct.	1	Retired the bonds that were issued on January 1. Warner had to pay $380,000 to retire the bonds. This amount included interest that had accrued since July 1.
Nov.	20	Declared a cash dividend of $0.30 per share. The dividend applies only to outstanding shares, not to treasury shares.
Dec.	31	Made the lease payment.
	31	After recording depreciation expense for the year, the building was evaluated for possible impairment. The building is expected to generate cash flows of $18,000 per year for its 19-year remaining life. The building has a current market value of $320,000.
	31	The Anson Company shares had a market value of $19 per share.

Summary:

a. Sales for the year (all on credit) totaled $1.8 million. The cost of inventory sold was $950,000.
b. Cash collections on credit sales for the year were $1.54 million.
c. Inventory costing $1,000,000 was purchased on account.
d. Payments on account totaled $970,000.

Required:

1. Prepare all journal entries to record the information for 2009. Also prepare any necessary adjusting entries.
2. Prepare a trial balance as of December 31, 2009. There is no need to show your ledger T-accounts; however, preparing and posting to T-accounts may aid in the preparation of the trial balance.
3. Prepare an income statement for the year ended December 31, 2009, and a balance sheet as of December 31, 2009.
4. Prepare all journal entries to record the information for 2010. Also prepare any necessary adjusting entries.
5. Prepare a trial balance as of December 31, 2010. (As you compute the amounts to include in the trial balance, don't forget the beginning balances left over from 2009.)
6. Prepare an income statement for the year ended December 31, 2010, and a balance sheet as of December 31, 2010.

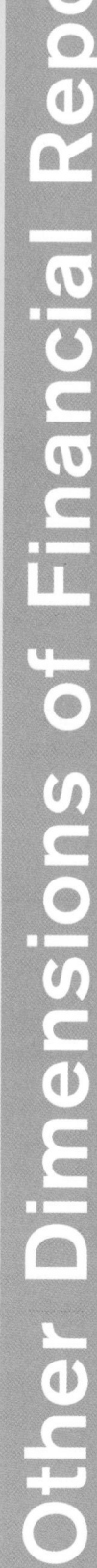

PART

4

Other Dimensions of Financial Reporting

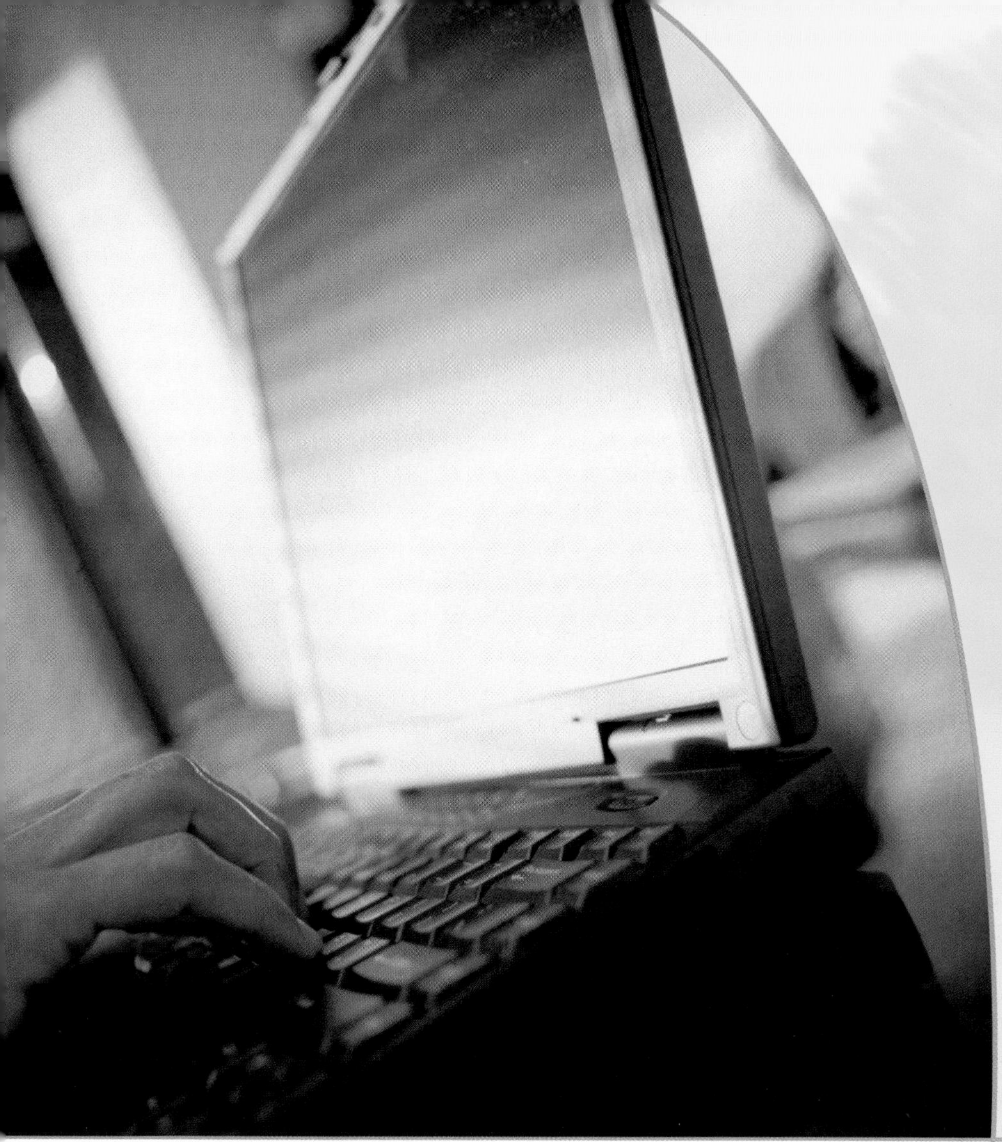

© DUNCAN SMITH/PHOTODISC GREEN/GETTY IMAGES INC.

The Statement of Cash Flows

After studying this chapter, you should be able to:

(1) Understand the purpose of a statement of cash flows. *The statement of cash flows provides information that is not readily apparent by looking at just the balance sheet and the income statement. Operating cash flow is particularly useful in selected cases when net income does not give an accurate refection of a company's performance.*

(2) Recognize the different types of information reported in the statement of cash flows. *Cash flows are partitioned into three categories—operating, investing, and financing. In normal circumstances, a company has positive cash from operations and negative cash from investing activities. Whether cash from financing activities is positive or negative typically depends on how fast a company is growing.*

(3) Prepare a simple statement of cash flows. *Preparing a statement of cash flows is a simple process if one has access to the record of a company's detailed cash transactions. One simply scans the list of cash transactions and sorts them into operating, investing, and financing items.*

(4) Analyze financial statements to prepare a statement of cash flows. *When detailed cash flow information is not available, a statement of cash flows can be prepared using knowledge of how the three primary financial statements articulate. Operating cash flow can be reported using either the direct or the indirect method.*

(5) Use information from the statement of cash flows to make decisions. *Knowledge of how the three primary financial statements tie together allows one to forecast how interactions among management decisions might affect a company's future financial position.*

Home Depot is the leading retailer in the "do-it-yourself" home handyman market. In January 2006, Home Depot had 1,984 stores in the United States, Canada, and Mexico. With each store averaging 105,000 square feet (and an additional 23,000 square feet in the outside garden center), a lot of shelf space is filled with paint, lumber, hardware, and plumbing fixtures. If plumbing fixtures don't seem very exciting to you, consider this: Home Depot is the 14th largest company in the United States (in terms of revenues), with 2006 revenues of $81.5 billion and market value of $91.1 billion.[1] And if lumber and hardware seem obsolete in this high-tech world, consider that, for the past 10 years, Home Depot's earnings per share (EPS) has grown an average of 23.1% per year. In fiscal 2006, Home Depot's net income reached $5.8 billion.[2]

But Home Depot's prospects weren't always so rosy. Back in 1985, when sales were only $700 million, Home Depot experienced cash flow problems, in large part due to rapid increases in the level of inventory. Part of this inventory increase was the natural result of Home Depot's expansion. But Home Depot stores were also starting to fill up with excess inventory because of lax inventory management. In 1983, the average Home Depot store contained enough inventory to support average sales for 75 days.

By 1985, the number of days' sales in inventory had increased to 83 days. Combined with Home Depot's rapid growth, this inventory inefficiency caused total inventory to increase by $69 million in 1985. This increase in inventory was instrumental in Home Depot's negative cash flow from operations of $43 million. Concerns about this declining profitability and negative cash flow caused Home Depot's stock value to take a dive in 1985, and the beginning of 1986 found Home Depot wondering where it would find the investors and creditors to finance its aggressive expansion plans. Exhibit 1 summarizes the differences between Home Depot's reported net income and the company's cash flow from operations for the fiscal years 1984 through 1986 and the company's recent performance.

Home Depot's current success is the result of an incredible operating cash flow turnaround that began in fiscal 1987. Operating income almost tripled in 1987 compared to fiscal 1986, and net income increased from $8.2 million to $23.9 million. A computerized inventory management program was instituted, and the number of days' sales in inventory dropped to 80 days. Improved profitability and more efficient management of inventory combined to transform the negative $43 million operating cash flow in fiscal 1986 into positive cash from operations of $66 million in fiscal 1987.

EXHIBIT 1	Home Depot's Net Income and Cash Flows from Operations		
	Fiscal Year Ended		
(in thousands)	**February 2, 1986**	**February 3, 1985**	**January 29, 1984**
Net earnings	$ 8,219	$14,122	$ 10,261
Net cash provided by operations	(43,120)	(3,056)	(10,574)
	Fiscal Year Ended		
(in thousands)	**January 29, 2006**	**January 30, 2005**	**February 1, 2004**
Net earnings	$5,838,000	$5,001,000	$4,304,000
Net cash provided by operations	6,484,000	6,904,000	6,545,000

[1] See the Fortune 500 listing at **http://www.fortune.com**.
[2] January 30, 2006, 10-K filing of The Home Depot, Inc.

n this chapter, we will study the statement of cash flows. You will learn that this statement provides one of the earliest warning signs of cash concerns of the type experienced by Home Depot. The statement of cash flows alerts financial statement readers to increases and decreases in cash as well as to the reasons and trends for the changes.

In today's business environment, it is not enough simply to monitor earnings and earnings per share measurements. An entity's financial position and especially its inflows and outflows of cash are also critical to its financial success.

The three primary financial statements were introduced and illustrated in Chapter 2. In subsequent chapters, we examined in detail the components of the balance sheet and income statement. For our discussion of the statement of cash flows, we will first describe the purpose and general format of a statement of cash flows. We will then show how easy it is to prepare a statement of cash flows if detailed cash flow information is available. A statement of cash flows can also be prepared based on an analysis of balance sheet and income statement accounts. We will also distinguish between the direct and indirect methods of reporting operating cash flows and discuss the usefulness of the statement of cash flows. Finally, we will explain how the statement of cash flows can be used to make investment and lending decisions.

What's the Purpose of a Statement of Cash Flows?

Understand the purpose of a statement of cash flows.

(1) The **statement of cash flows**, as its name implies, summarizes a company's cash flows for a period of time. The statement of cash flows explains how a company's cash was generated during the period and how that cash was used.

You might think that the statement of cash flows is a replacement for the income statement, but the two statements have very different objectives. The income statement, as you know, measures the results of operations for a period of time. Net income is the accountant's best estimate at reflecting a company's economic performance for a period. The income statement provides details as to how the retained earnings account changes during a period and ties together, in part, the owners' equity sections of comparative balance sheets.

statement of cash flows

The financial statement that shows an entity's cash inflows (receipts) and outflows (payments) during a period of time.

The statement of cash flows, on the other hand, provides details as to how the cash account changed during a period. The statement of cash flows reports the period's transactions and events in terms of their impact on cash. In Chapter 4, we compared the cash-basis and accrual-basis methods of measuring income and explained why accrual-basis income is considered a better measure of periodic income. The statement of cash flows provides important information from a cash-basis perspective that complements the income statement and balance sheet, thus providing a more complete picture of a company's operations and financial position. It is important to note that the statement of cash flows does not include any transactions or accounts that are not already reflected in the balance sheet or the income statement. Rather, the statement of cash flows simply provides information relating to the cash flow effects of those transactions.

Users of financial statements, particularly investors and creditors, need information about a company's cash flows in order to evaluate the company's ability to generate positive net cash flows in the future to meet its obligations and to pay dividends. In some cases, careful analysis of cash flows can provide early warning of impending financial problems, as was the case with **Home Depot**.

Before moving on, it is important to reiterate that the statement of cash flows does not replace the income statement. The income statement summarizes the results of a company's operations, whereas the statement of cash flows summarizes a company's inflows and outflows of cash. Information contained in the income statement can be used to facilitate the preparation of a statement of cash flows; information in the statement of cash flows sheds some light on the company's ability to generate income in the future. The statement of cash flows and the income statement provide complementary information about different aspects of a business.

> **REMEMBER THIS...**
>
> - The statement of cash flows, one of the three primary financial statements, provides information about the cash receipts and payments of an entity during a period.
> - The statement of cash flows provides important information that complements the income statement and balance sheet.

What Information Is Reported in the Statement of Cash Flows?

Recognize the different types of information reported in the statement of cash flows.

(2) Accounting standards include specific requirements for the reporting of cash flows. The general format for a statement of cash flows, with details and dollar amounts omitted, is presented in Exhibit 2. As illustrated, the inflows and outflows of cash must be divided into three main categories: operating activities, investing activities, and financing activities. Further, the statement of cash flows is presented in a manner that reconciles the beginning and ending balances of cash and cash equivalents. **Cash equivalents** are short-term, highly liquid investments that can easily be converted into cash. Generally, only investments with maturities of three months or less qualify as cash equivalents. Examples are U.S. Treasury bills, money market funds, and commercial paper (short-term debt issued by corporations). In this chapter, as is common in practice, the term *cash* will be used to include cash and cash equivalents.

cash equivalents

Short-term, highly liquid investments that can easily be converted into cash.

Major Classifications of Cash Flows

Exhibit 3 shows the three main categories of cash inflows and outflows—operating, investing, and financing. Exhibit 4 summarizes the specific activities included in each category. Beginning with operating activities, each of the cash flow categories will be explained. We will also discuss the reporting of significant noncash transactions and events.

operating activities

Transactions and events that enter into the determination of net income.

Operating Activities **Operating activities** include those transactions and events that enter into the calculation of net income. Cash receipts from

EXHIBIT 2	General Format for a Statement of Cash Flows

Cash provided by (used in):	
Cash from operating activities	$XXX
+ Cash from investing activities	XXX
+ Cash from financing activities	XXX
= Net increase (decrease) in cash and cash equivalents	$XXX
+ Cash and cash equivalents at beginning of year	XXX
= Cash and cash equivalents at end of year	$XXX

EXHIBIT 3 **The Flow of Cash**

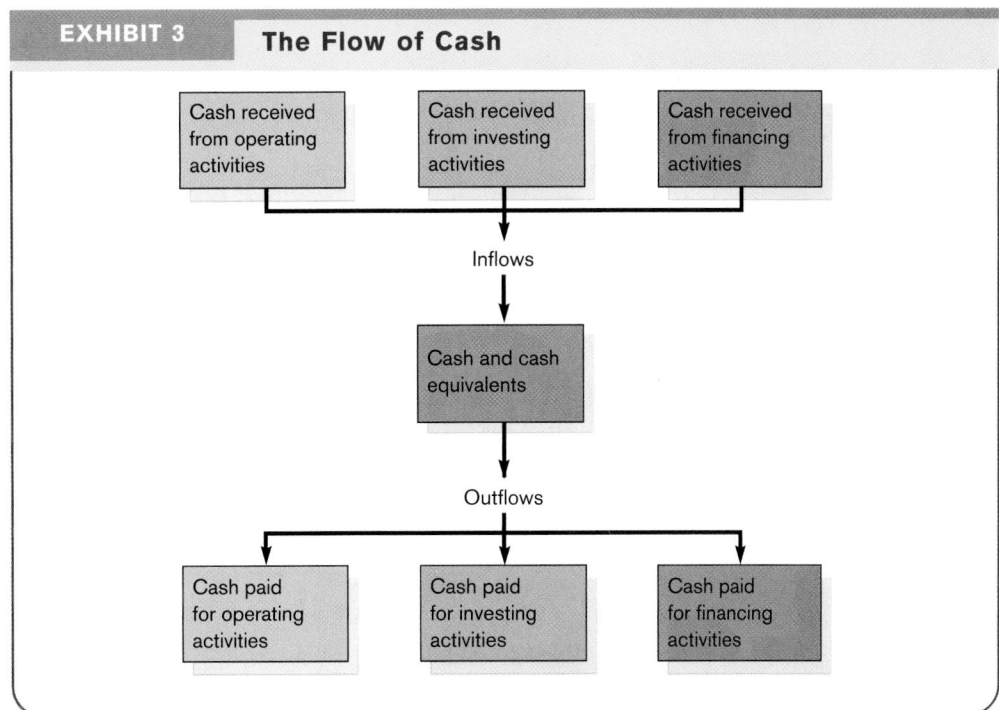

EXHIBIT 4 **Major Classifications of Cash Flows**

Operating Activities
Cash receipts from:
  Sale of goods or services
  Interest revenue
  Dividend revenue
  Sale of investments in trading securities
Cash payments to:
  Suppliers for inventory purchases
  Employees for services
  Governments for taxes
  Lenders for interest expense
  Brokers for purchase of trading securities
  Others for other expenses (e.g., utilities, rent)

Investing Activities
Cash receipts from:
  Sale of property, plant, and equipment
  Sale of a business segment
  Sale of investments in securities other than trading securities
  Collection of principal on loans made to other entities
Cash payments to:
  Purchase property, plant, and equipment
  Purchase debt or equity securities of other entities (other than trading securities)
  Make loans to other entities

Financing Activities
Cash receipts from:
  Issuance of own stock
  Borrowing (e.g., bonds, notes, mortgages)
Cash payments to:
  Stockholders as dividends
  Repay principal amounts borrowed
  Repurchase an entity's own stock (treasury stock)

Operating activities, including the sale of goods, help determine net income and are reported on the statement of cash flows.

the sale of goods or services are the major cash inflows for most businesses. Other inflows include cash receipts for interest revenue, dividend revenue, and similar items. Major outflows of cash are for the purchase of inventory and for the payment of wages, taxes, interest, utilities, rent, and similar expenses. As we will explain later, the amount of cash provided by (or used in) operating activities is a key figure and should be highlighted on the statement of cash flows.

Note that our focus in analyzing operating activities is to determine cash flows from operations. An analysis is required to convert income from an accrual-basis to a cash-basis number.

To do this, we begin with the net income figure, remove all items relating to investing activities (such as depreciation and gains/losses on the sale of equipment) and financing activities (such as gains/losses on retirement of debt), and then adjust for changes in those current assets and current liabilities that involve cash and relate to operations (which are most of the current assets and current liabilities).

? F Y I

Although cash inflows from interest and dividends logically might be classified as financing activities, the FASB has decided to classify them as operating activities, which conforms to their presentation on the income statement.

Investing Activities   Transactions and events that involve the purchase and sale of securities (other than trading securities), property, buildings, equipment, and other assets not generally held for resale, and the making and collecting of loans are classified as **investing activities**. These activities occur regularly and result in cash inflows and outflows. They are not classified under operating activities because they relate only indirectly to the entity's central, ongoing operations, which usually involve the sale of goods or services.

investing activities

Transactions and events that involve the purchase and sale of securities (excluding cash equivalents), property, plant, equipment, and other assets not generally held for resale, and the making and collecting of loans.

The analysis of investing activities involves identifying those accounts on the balance sheet relating to investments (typically long-term asset accounts) and then explaining how those accounts changed and how those changes affected the cash flows for the period.

Financing Activities   Financing activities include transactions and events whereby resources are obtained from or paid to owners (equity financing) and creditors (debt financing). Dividend payments, for example, fit this definition. As noted earlier, the receipt of dividends and interest and the payment of interest are classified under operating activities simply because they are reported as a part of income on the income statement. The receipt or

? F Y I

The purchase and sale of trading securities is classified as an operating activity.

financing activities

Transactions and events whereby resources are obtained from, or repaid to, owners (equity financing) and creditors (debt financing).

payment of the principal amount borrowed or repaid (but not the interest) is considered a financing activity.

Analyzing the cash flow effects of financing activities involves identifying those accounts relating to financing (typically long-term debt and common stock) and explaining how changes in those accounts affected the company's cash flows. Exhibit 5 summarizes the activities reflected on the statement of cash flows and indicates how the balance sheet and income statement accounts relate to the various activities.

 F Y I

On the statement of cash flows, the activities are typically listed in this order: operating, investing, and financing. However, there is no requirement that they be listed in this way. **Microsoft**, for example, uses this order: operating, financing, and investing.

Noncash Investing and Financing Activities

Some investing and financing activities do not affect cash. For example, equipment may be purchased with a note payable, or land may be acquired by issuing stock. These noncash transactions are not reported in the statement of cash flows. However, if a company has significant noncash financing and investing activities, they should be disclosed in a separate schedule or in a narrative explanation. The disclosures may be presented below the statement of cash flows or in the notes to the financial statements.

Cash Flow Patterns

Most U.S. companies (about 60%) report positive cash flows from operations. That shouldn't come as a big surprise because companies need to generate cash from operating activities to survive in the long term. In addition, about 80% of U.S. companies report negative cash flows from investing activities. Again, this is expected as companies must expand, enhance, or replace long-term assets. Predicting whether the sign for cash from financing activities will be positive or negative is more difficult. That sign depends on

EXHIBIT 5	How Balance Sheet and Income Statement Accounts Relate to the Statement of Cash Flows		

Cash Flow Activity	Related Balance Sheet and Income Statement Accounts	Examples	Chapters in Which Accounts Were Covered
Operating	All income statement accounts **except** those income statement items relating to:	Sales, Cost of Goods Sold, Salaries Expense, etc.	Chs. 6–8
	• Investing	Depreciation, Gains/Losses on Sale of Equipment	Ch. 9
	• Financing	Gains/Losses on Retirement of Debt	Ch. 10
	Current assets	Accounts Receivable	Ch. 6
		Inventory	Ch. 7
	Current liabilities	Accounts Payable	Ch. 7
Investing	Long-term assets	Property, Plant, and Equipment	Ch. 9
	Long-term investments	Available-for-Sale and Held-to-Maturity Securities	Ch. 12
Financing	Long-term debt	Bonds and Mortgages	Ch. 10
	Stockholders' equity (except for	Common Stock	Ch. 11
	net income in Retained Earnings)	Dividends	Ch. 11

F Y I

Many companies report positive cash flows from operations even though they have net losses. This is primarily because depreciation and amortization are added to net income when calculating cash flow from operations. In fact, many companies focus on a number called EBITDA which is earnings before income taxes, depreciation, and amortization.

whether the company is young, growing, and in need of cash, or mature, stable, and flush with cash. As a company proceeds through the normal life cycle of a business, cash from financing typically will vary between positive and negative. As an example, in fiscal 2005 Home Depot reported positive cash flows from operations ($6.5 billion), negative cash flows from investing ($4.6 billion), and negative cash flows from financing ($1.6 billion).

REMEMBER THIS...

- The statement of cash flows is presented in a manner that highlights three major categories of cash flows:
  - operating activities,
  - investing activities, and
  - financing activities.
- Any significant noncash investing and financing activities should be disclosed separately, either below the statement of cash flows or in the notes to the financial statements.

Prepare a simple statement of cash flows.

Preparing a Statement of Cash Flows–A Simple Example

Now that we have reviewed the three types of cash flow activities disclosed on the statement of cash flows, let's start with a simple example to see how easy (conceptually) a statement of cash flows is to prepare. For this example, we will begin with the following trial balance information for Silmaril, Inc.

Silmaril, Inc.

Trial Balance

January 1, 2009

	Debit	Credit
Cash	$ 300	
Accounts Receivable	2,500	
Inventory	1,900	
Property, Plant, and Equipment	4,000	
Accumulated Depreciation		$1,200
Accounts Payable		1,700
Taxes Payable		40
Long-Term Debt		2,200
Common Stock		1,000
Retained Earnings		2,560
Totals	$8,700	$8,700

The following transactions were conducted by Silmaril, Inc., during 2009:

1. Sales on account, $13,500.
2. Collections on account, $14,000.
3. Purchased inventory on account, $7,900.
4. Cost of goods sold, $8,000.
5. Paid accounts payable, $8,100.
6. Purchased property, plant, and equipment for cash, $1,700.
7. Sold property, plant, and equipment for cash, $500 (original cost, $1,200; accumulated depreciation, $800).
8. Paid long-term debt, $200.
9. Issued stock at par value, $450.
10. Recorded depreciation expense, $500.
11. Paid interest on debt, $180.
12. Recorded interest owed (accrued) but not paid, $20.
13. Paid miscellaneous expenses (e.g., wages, supplies, etc.) for the period, $3,200.
14. Recorded tax expense for the period, $450.
15. Paid taxes during the period, $440.

With this information, we can reconstruct the journal entries made by Silmaril, Inc., during the year:

		Debit	Credit
1.	Accounts Receivable	13,500	
	Sales		13,500
2.	Cash	14,000	
	Accounts Receivable		14,000
3.	Inventory	7,900	
	Accounts Payable		7,900
4.	Cost of Goods Sold	8,000	
	Inventory		8,000
5.	Accounts Payable	8,100	
	Cash		8,100
6.	Property, Plant, and Equipment	1,700	
	Cash		1,700
7.	Cash	500	
	Accumulated Depreciation	800	
	Property, Plant, and Equipment		1,200
	Gain on Sale of Equipment		100
8.	Long-Term Debt	200	
	Cash		200
9.	Cash	450	
	Common Stock		450
10.	Depreciation Expense	500	
	Accumulated Depreciation		500
11.	Interest Expense	180	
	Cash		180
12.	Interest Expense	20	
	Interest Payable		20
13.	Miscellaneous Expenses	3,200	
	Cash		3,200
14.	Tax Expense	450	
	Taxes Payable		450
15.	Taxes Payable	440	
	Cash		440

When these journal entries are posted, the following trial balance results:

Silmaril, Inc.
Trial Balance
December 31, 2009

	Debit	Credit
Cash	$ 1,430	
Accounts Receivable	2,000	
Inventory	1,800	
Property, Plant, and Equipment	4,500	
Accumulated Depreciation		$ 900
Accounts Payable		1,500
Interest Payable		20
Taxes Payable		50
Long-Term Debt		2,000
Common Stock		1,450
Retained Earnings		2,560
Sales		13,500
Gain on Sale of Equipment		100
Cost of Goods Sold	8,000	
Depreciation Expense	500	
Interest Expense	200	
Tax Expense	450	
Miscellaneous Expenses	3,200	
Totals	$22,080	$22,080

To this point, this is all a review—journalizing transactions, posting journal entries, and preparing a trial balance. From this trial balance, we can easily prepare an income statement and a balance sheet; but our objective here is to prepare a statement of cash flows. With information from the Cash T-account, we can prepare a statement of cash flows. The Cash T-account would contain the following information (journal entry reference numbers are in parentheses):

Cash

Beg. Bal.	300		
(2)	14,000	(5)	8,100
(7)	500	(6)	1,700
(9)	450	(8)	200
		(11)	180
		(13)	3,200
		(15)	440
End. Bal.	1,430		

Our task at this point is simply to categorize each cash inflow and outflow as an operating, investing, or financing activity. The inflows and outflows break down as follows:

Operating Activities:

Collections on account (2)		$ 14,000
Payments for inventory (5)	$ 8,100	
Payments for miscellaneous expenses (13)	3,200	
Payment for interest (11)	180	
Payment for taxes (15)	440	(11,920)
Cash flows from operating activities		$ 2,080

Investing Activities:

Sold equipment (7)	$ 500	
Purchased equipment (6)	(1,700)	
Cash flows from investing activities		(1,200)

Financing Activities:

Issued stock (9)	$ 450	
Paid debt (8)	(200)	
Cash flows from financing activities		250
Net increase in cash		$ 1,130
Beginning cash balance		300
Ending cash balance		$ 1,430

As you can see, if we have access to the detailed transaction data from the Cash T-account, preparing a statement of cash flows involves determining the proper cash flow category (operating, investing, or financing) for each inflow or outflow and then properly formatting the statement. More advanced accounting software programs allow financial statement preparers to categorize each cash inflow and outflow as an operating, investing, or financing activity and to prepare a statement of cash flows with the press of a key. Once considered one of the most difficult parts of accounting, preparing a statement of cash flows has been greatly simplified as a result of computer technology.

If information is properly coded when input into a computerized accounting system, the preparation of a statement of cash flows is easy. As mentioned, the more advanced accounting software facilitates this process. But what happens if an accounting system does not classify cash transactions according to their activities? In the next section, we discuss how a statement of cash flows is prepared if one does not have ready access to detailed cash inflow and outflow information.

REMEMBER THIS...

- If transactions are properly classified when input into the accounting system, the preparation of a statement of cash flows is straightforward.
- Cash inflows and outflows are segregated according to type of activity (operating, investing, or financing), and a statement of cash flows is prepared based on that information.

Analyze financial statements to prepare a statement of cash flows.

Analyzing the Other Primary Financial Statements to Prepare a Statement of Cash Flows

(4) If detailed cash flow information is not accessible, the preparation of a statement of cash flows is more difficult. The income statement and comparative balance sheets must be analyzed to determine how cash was generated and how cash was used by a business. How can we determine a company's cash inflows and outflows by looking at balance sheets and an income statement? The secret lies in remembering the basics of double-entry accounting: each journal entry has two parts—a debit and a credit. In the case of the cash account, every time Cash is debited, some other account is credited; every time Cash is credited, some other account is debited. If we don't have access to the details of the cash account, we can infer those details based on our knowledge of accounting and by analyzing changes in accounts other than Cash.

For example, consider the accounts receivable account. A debit to that account means what? Ninety-nine percent of the time, a debit to Accounts Receivable is associated with a sale on account. A credit to Accounts Receivable means what? Most likely, cash was collected. If we have the beginning and ending balances for the accounts receivable account (from comparative balance sheets) and sales for the period (from the income statement), we can infer the cash collected for the period. Consider the information taken from Silmaril's beginning trial balance and the year-end trial balance relating to Accounts Receivable (remember, we are assuming that the detailed journal entries are not available to us, only the resulting financial statements):

Accounts Receivable

Beg. Bal.	2,500		
Sales	13,500	Collections	?
End. Bal.	2,000		

To reconcile the accounts receivable account, we can only assume that cash collections of $14,000 occurred. With any other amount the account will not reconcile.[3] In other words, we can infer that the following journal entry must have been made:

| Cash .... | 14,000 | |
| Accounts Receivable .... | | 14,000 |

As you can see from this analysis, we don't necessarily need the detailed cash account information to prepare a statement of cash flows. We can use our knowledge of double-entry accounting to infer those details.

CAUTION

Every balance sheet account (except Cash) must be analyzed to determine any cash flow effects. Then those effects must be classified by activity.

A similar analysis is conducted for every balance sheet account (except Cash). The analyses draw on our knowledge of the relationship between the income statement and balance sheet accounts and of what accounts are associated with operating, investing, and financing activities. Consider another example—Common Stock. First of all, we know that changes in the common stock account are considered financing activities. Second, what do we know about credits to the common stock account? They typically are associated with the issuance (sale) of stock. What about debits to the common stock account? They are associated with the retirement of common stock. Assume we are given comparative balance sheet information (transactions in a company's own stock are not reflected on the income statement) relating to the common stock account of Silmaril, Inc., as follows:

	Beginning Balance	Ending Balance
Common stock	$1,000	$1,450

What would you infer about Silmaril's cash flow activities relating to its common stock account? Without any additional information, it would be safe to assume that the company sold stock for $450. If something out of the ordinary happened in the common stock account (like the retirement of stock), that information would generally be available in the notes to the financial statements and would be used to modify the analysis.

As an illustration of this type of complexity, consider Silmaril's property, plant, and equipment (PP&E) account. First of all,

FYI

Buying and using PP&E would be considered common activities. Selling PP&E would be considered less common.

---

[3] Some of you may be thinking that Accounts Receivable can be credited when accounts are written off. This is true, and write-offs would affect our analysis. However, our purpose here is to understand the concepts. A more complicated analysis including write-offs will be covered in an intermediate accounting class.

the PP&E account is associated with what type of cash flow activity? Investing. Increases in property, plant, and equipment correspond to purchases of PP&E, and decreases relate to the sale of PP&E. Because the sale of PP&E is typically an out-of-the-ordinary type of transaction, we could look at the notes to the financial statements for information relating to any sales. In the case of Silmaril, Inc., we find that equipment costing $1,200, with accumulated depreciation of $800, was sold for $500. Based on this information, and using information from the comparative balance sheets, we can infer the purchases made during the period as follows:

Property, Plant, and Equipment

Beg. Bal.	4,000		
Purchases	?	Sold	1,200
End. Bal.	4,500		

How much PP&E was purchased during the period? The only amount that will reconcile the PP&E account is $1,700. The journal entry would have been a debit to PP&E and a credit to Cash. Again, we find that we don't need the details of the cash account to be able to infer the cash inflows and outflows for the company. Our knowledge of double-entry accounting allows us to do a little detective work and infer what went on in the cash account.

A Six-Step Process for Preparing a Statement of Cash Flows

Is there a systematic method for analyzing the income statement and comparative balance sheets to prepare a statement of cash flows? Yes, the following six-step process can be used in preparing a statement of cash flows:

1. Compute the change in the cash and cash-equivalent accounts for the period of the statement. Seldom is one handed a check figure in real life, but such is the case when preparing a statement of cash flows. The statement of cash flows is not complete until you have explained the change from the beginning balance in the cash account to the balance at year-end.

2. Convert the income statement from an accrual-basis to a cash-basis summary of operations. This is done in three steps: (1) eliminate from the income statement those expenses that do not involve cash (such **noncash items** would include depreciation expense that does not involve an outflow of cash in the current period even though income was reduced); (2) eliminate from the income statement the effects of nonoperating activity items (such items include gains and losses on the sale of long-term assets and gains and losses associated with the retirement of debt); and (3) identify those current asset and current liability accounts associated with the income statement accounts, and adjust those income statement accounts for the changes in the associated current assets and current liabilities. For example, Sales will be adjusted for the change between the beginning and ending balance in Accounts Receivable to derive the cash collections for the period. The final result will be cash flows from operating activities.

3. Analyze the long-term assets to identify the cash flow effects of investing activities. Changes in property, plant, and equipment and in long-term investments may indicate that cash has either been spent or been received.

4. Analyze the long-term debt and stockholders' equity accounts to determine the cash flow effects of any financing transactions. These transactions could be borrowing or repaying debt, issuing or buying back stock, or paying dividends.

noncash items

Items included in the determination of net income on an accrual basis that do not affect cash; for example, depreciation and amortization.

STOP & THINK

Why must gains (losses) on the sale of equipment be subtracted (added) when computing cash flows from operations?

> **⚠ CAUTION**
>
> Make sure that the total net cash flows from the statement (the sum of net cash flows from operating, investing, and financing activities) are equal to the net increase (decrease) in cash as computed in step 1.

5. Prepare a formal statement of cash flows by classifying all cash inflows and outflows according to operating, investing, and financing activities. The net cash flows provided by (used in) each of the three main activities of an entity should be highlighted. The net cash flows amount for the period is then added (subtracted) from the beginning Cash balance to report the ending Cash balance.

6. Report any significant investing or financing transactions that did not involve cash in a narrative explanation or in a separate schedule to the statement of cash flows. This would include such transactions as the purchase of land by issuing stock or the retirement of bonds by issuing stock.

An Illustration of the Six-Step Process

We will illustrate this six-step process for preparing the statement of cash flows using the information from the Silmaril, Inc., example presented earlier. Remember that in this case we are assuming that we do not have access to the detailed cash flow information. Thus, we are going to have to make inferences about cash flows by examining all other balance sheet and income statement accounts other than the cash account.

Step 1. Compute the Change in the Cash and Cash-Equivalent Accounts for the Period of the Statement
Recall that Silmaril began the year with a Cash balance of $300 and ended with a Cash balance of $1,430. Thus, our objective in preparing the statement of cash flows is to explain why the cash account changed by $1,130 during the year.

Step 2. Convert the Income Statement from an Accrual Basis to a Cash Basis
From the trial balance prepared at the end of the year, we can prepare the following income statement for Silmaril, Inc.:

Sales	$13,500
Cost of goods sold	8,000
Gross margin	$ 5,500
Miscellaneous expenses	3,200
Depreciation expense	500
Income from operations	$ 1,800
Interest expense	(200)
Gain on sale of equipment	100
Income before taxes	$ 1,700
Tax expense	450
Net income	$ 1,250

Our objective at this point is to convert the income statement to cash flows from operations. Recall that this involves three steps: (1) eliminating expenses not involving cash, (2) eliminating the effects of nonoperating activities, and (3) adjusting the remaining figures from an accrual basis to a cash basis. We will use a work sheet to track the adjustments that will be made. The first two adjustments involve removing depreciation expense (because it does not involve an outflow of cash) and eliminating the gain on the sale of the equipment (because the sale of equipment is an investing activity, the effect of which will be disclosed in the investing activities section of the statement). The following work sheet reflects these adjustments:

	Income Statement	Adjustments	Cash Flows from Operations
Sales	$13,500		
Cost of goods sold	(8,000)		
Miscellaneous expenses	(3,200)		
Depreciation expense	(500)	**+ 500 (not a cash flow item)**	0
Interest expense	(200)		
Gain on sale of equipment	100	**– 100 (not an operating activity)**	0
Tax expense	(450)		
	$ 1,250		

Note that because depreciation expense was initially subtracted to arrive at net income, our adjustment involves adding $500 back because no cash actually flowed out of the company relating to depreciation. The cash flow effect of the sale of the equipment should be reflected in the investing activities section of the statement of cash flows. Therefore, the effect of the gain must be removed from the operating activities section.

CAUTION

When equipment is initially purchased, the cash outflow is reported as an investing activity. When the equipment is used, this use is recorded as depreciation and does not involve any cash flow even though it is reported as an expense on the income statement.

Because the gain was initially added, we must subtract $100 as an adjustment to remove the effects of this investing activity from the operating activities section.

The adjustments now involve converting the remaining revenue and expense items from an accrual basis to a cash basis. Recall from our analysis earlier in this section that the amount of cash collected from customers differed from sales for the period. In fact, collections exceeded sales by $500 (explaining how the accounts receivable account declined by $500). An adjustment must be made to increase the accrual-basis sales figure to its cash-basis counterpart. We add $500 as illustrated below.

	Income Statement	Adjustments	Cash Flows from Operations
Sales	$13,500	**+ 500 (decrease in accounts receivable)**	$14,000
Cost of goods sold	(8,000)		
Miscellaneous expenses	(3,200)		
Depreciation expense	(500)	**+ 500 (not a cash flow item)**	0
Interest expense	(200)		
Gain on sale of equipment	100	**– 100 (not an operating activity)**	0
Tax expense	(450)		
	$ 1,250		

Next, we turn our attention to Cost of Goods Sold. The statement of cash flows should reflect the amount of cash paid for inventory during the period. We can compute that amount by adjusting Cost of Goods Sold to reflect the inventory used this period but purchased last period, as well as inventory that was purchased last period and paid for this period.

Because Inventory declined for the period from a beginning balance of $1,900 to an ending balance of $1,800, we must adjust Cost of Goods Sold to reflect that it includes inventory that was purchased last period and used this period (explaining how the inventory balance declined). To reduce Cost of Goods Sold, our adjustment involves adding $100. The resulting number represents the amount of inventory purchased during the year. A similar adjustment is made for the change in the balance in Accounts Payable and reflects

> **CAUTION**
>
> Remember that Cost of Goods Sold is sub-tracted from Sales. Adding $100 serves to re-duce the negative number, and subtracting $200 makes the cost of goods sold figure a larger negative number.

the amount of inventory paid for during the year. What event would cause Accounts Payable to decline? Obviously, Accounts Payable would most likely decline because more was paid for this period than was purchased this period. If more was paid for this period, we are required to subtract an additional $200 to reflect the additional cash outflow. The net effect of these two adjustments is to convert the accrual-basis Cost of Goods Sold figure to the amount of inventory paid for during the year. The following T-account analysis shows the net effect of these two adjustments:

Cash	Inventory	Accounts Payable	Cost of Goods Sold
8,100^C	Beg. Bal. 1,900 8,000^A 7,900^B	8,100^C Beg. Bal. 1,700 7,900^B	8,000^A
	End. Bal. 1,800	End. Bal. 1,500	

^{A} Cost of inventory sold during the period (from the income statement).
^{B} Inventory purchased during the period [solved for based on the beginning and ending inventory balances and the cost of goods sold (A)].
^{C} Inventory paid for during the period [solved for based on the beginning and ending Accounts Payable balances and the inventory purchased during the period (B)].

Updating our work sheet results in the following:

	Income Statement	Adjustments	Cash Flows from Operations
Sales	$13,500	+500 (decrease in accounts receivable)	$14,000
Cost of goods sold	(8,000)	**+100 (decrease in inventory)**	(8,100)
		−200 (decrease in accounts payable)	
Miscellaneous expenses	(3,200)		
Depreciation expense	(500)	+500 (not a cash flow item)	0
Interest expense	(200)		
Gain on sale of equipment	100	−100 (not an operating activity)	0
Tax expense	(450)		
	$ 1,250		

Because neither a miscellaneous expenses payable account nor a prepaid expenses account exists, we can safely assume that all the miscellaneous expenses were paid for in cash. Therefore, there would be no adjustment.

Both Interest Expense and Tax Expense require adjustments similar to that done for Accounts Payable and/or Inventory. Let's first adjust Interest Expense from an accrual basis to a cash basis. Note that Interest Payable increased from $0 at the beginning of the period to $20 at the end of the period. How would that happen? Obviously, if a payable account increases, the company owes for products and services it has purchased or used. In this case what was used is money. Interest expense for the period was $200, of which Silmaril has yet to pay $20. Thus, the cash flow related to interest must be $180—requiring an adjustment of $20.

Tax Expense is adjusted in a similar fashion. Because the amount of taxes owed increased from the beginning to the end of the period, Silmaril must have paid a lesser amount relating to taxes than is reflected on the income statement. Reviewing the T-account for Taxes Payable helps us see how that can be:

Taxes Payable

		Beg. Bal.	40
Taxes paid during the period	?	Amount related to tax expense	450
		End. Bal.	50

As you can determine, the only amount that will balance the above T-account is $440—the amount paid for taxes during the period. Because the income statement reflects expense of $450 related to taxes, yet the cash outflow was only $440, we must make an adjustment of $10. The work sheet, with these final adjustments, appears as follows:

	Income Statement	Adjustments	Cash Flows from Operations
Sales	$13,500	+500 (decrease in accounts receivable)	$14,000
Cost of goods sold	(8,000)	+100 (decrease in inventory)	(8,100)
		−200 (decrease in accounts payable)	
Miscellaneous expenses	(3,200)	+0	(3,200)
Depreciation expense	(500)	+500 (not a cash flow item)	0
Interest expense	(200)	**+20 (increase in interest payable)**	(180)
Gain on sale of equipment	100	−100 (not an operating activity)	0
Tax expense	(450)	**+10 (increase in taxes payable)**	(440)
	$ 1,250	+830 net adjustment	$ 2,080

Note that the cash flows from operations figure obtained through an analysis of the income statement accounts and current asset and current liability accounts is the same figure obtained previously when we assumed access to the detailed cash account information. We should always get the same answer when the question is the same—"What were cash flows from operations?"

The Direct and Indirect Methods. Our final task relating to cash flows from operations relates to preparing the operating activities section of the statement of cash flows. At this point, we have two alternatives—the indirect method or the direct method.

indirect method

A method of reporting net cash flows from operations that involves converting accrual-basis net income to a cash basis.

The **indirect method** begins with net income as reported on the income statement and then details the adjustments made to arrive at cash flows from operations. For Silmaril, Inc., it involves beginning with the net income figure and then listing the adjustments from the work sheet. In other words, the following highlighted portions of the work sheet are used.

	Income Statement	Adjustments	Cash Flows from Operations
Sales	$13,500	+500 (decrease in accounts receivable)	$14,000
Cost of goods sold	(8,000)	+100 (decrease in inventory)	(8,100)
		−200 (decrease in accounts payable)	
Miscellaneous expenses	(3,200)	+0	(3,200)
Depreciation expense	(500)	+500 (not a cash flow item)	0
Interest expense	(200)	+20 (increase in interest payable)	(180)
Gain on sale of equipment	100	−100 (not an operating activity)	0
Tax expense	(450)	+10 (increase in taxes payable)	(440)
	$ 1,250	+830 net adjustment	$ 2,080

The operating activities section is formatted as follows:

Operating Activities:		
Net income		$1,250
Add: Depreciation expense	$ 500	
Decrease in accounts receivable	500	
Decrease in inventory	100	
Increase in interest payable	20	
Increase in taxes payable	10	
Less: Gain on sale of equipment	(100)	
Decrease in accounts payable	(200)	830
Cash flows from operations		$2,080

direct method

A method of reporting net cash flows from operations that shows the major classes of cash receipts and payments for a period of time.

Using the **direct method**, the operating activities section of a statement of cash flows is, in effect, a cash-basis income statement. Unlike the indirect method, the direct method does not start with net income. Instead, this method directly reports the major classes of operating cash receipts and payments of an entity during a period. This information is obtained from the last column of the work sheet as follows:

	Income Statement	Adjustments	Cash Flows from Operations
Sales	$13,500	+500 (decrease in accounts receivable)	$14,000
Cost of goods sold	(8,000)	+100 (decrease in inventory)	(8,100)
		−200 (decrease in accounts payable)	
Miscellaneous expenses	(3,200)	+0	(3,200)
Depreciation expense	(500)	−500 (not a cash flow item)	0
Interest expense	(200)	+20 (increase in interest payable)	(180)
Gain on sale of equipment	100	−100 (not an operating activity)	0
Tax expense	(450)	+10 (increase in taxes payable)	(440)
	$ 1,250	+830 net adjustment	$ 2,080

The resulting operating activities section, given below, looks a lot like the operating activities section we prepared when we had access to the detailed cash flow information.

Operating Activities:		
Collections from customers		$ 14,000
Payments for inventory	$8,100	
Payments for miscellaneous expenses	3,200	
Payments for interest	180	
Payments for taxes	440	(11,920)
Cash flows from operating activities		$ 2,080

STOP & THINK

Now that you have seen both methods for preparing the operating activities section of the statement of cash flows, which method do you prefer? Which method do you think is used most often by companies?

Note that the same amount of cash flows from operating activities is derived using either the indirect method or the direct method.

Why Two Methods? You may be wondering, "Why are there two methods for preparing a statement of cash flows when both methods always result in the same answer?" Good question. Each method has advantages and disadvantages. Most companies prefer and use the indirect method because it is relatively easy to apply and reconciles the difference between net income and the net cash flows provided by operations. Many users of financial statements favor the direct method because it reports the sources of cash inflows and outflows directly without the potentially confusing adjustments to net income. The accounting standard-setters considered the arguments for both methods, and although they preferred the clarity of the direct method, they permitted either method to be used. Because they can choose either method and already have to compute net income, approximately 95% of large U.S. corporations use the indirect method when preparing a statement of cash flows.

Some Rules of Thumb. Although all this analysis may seem complex, the guidelines below will help you as you analyze accounts and prepare a statement of cash flows.

Accounts	Direction of Change during the Period	Adjustment to Be Made
Current assets	Increase	Subtracted
Current assets	Decrease	Added
Current liabilities	Increase	Added
Current liabilities	Decrease	Subtracted

When current assets increase (decrease) during the period, the difference between the beginning and ending balances is subtracted (added) from the appropriate income statement account to arrive at cash flows for the period. As an example, if accounts receivable increase during the period, that means sales exceed collections and Sales on the income statement must be reduced to reflect the cash collected for the period. The reverse would be true when accounts receivable decrease.

In the case of current liabilities, an increase (decrease) requires that an adjustment be made to add (subtract) the difference between the beginning and ending balances. For example, when interest payable increases from the beginning to the end of the period, interest expense exceeds the cash paid during the period. Interest Expense must be reduced (by adding back) to reflect the cash paid during the period. Again, the reverse would be true if interest payable were to decrease during the period. Exhibit 6 summarizes the procedures for converting selected accounts from an accrual to a cash basis.

CAUTION

These guidelines will help you to understand how certain adjustments are made, but they will not help you understand why the adjustments are being made. To understand why, you must use your knowledge of accounting.

Step 3. Analyze the Long-Term Assets to Identify the Cash Flows Effect of Investing Activities

The only long-term asset account for Silmaril, Inc., is the property, plant, and equipment (PP&E) account with its associated accumulated depreciation. The balance in the PP&E account increased by $500 during the period. What does an increase in the PP&E account indicate? Obviously, something was purchased. If we had no additional information, we would assume that PP&E was purchased by paying $500. But we do have additional information. We know that PP&E was purchased during the period by paying $1,700. With that information, we can prepare the following PP&E T-account:

Property, Plant, and Equipment

Beg. Bal.	4,000		
Purchased	1,700	Sold	?
End. Bal.	4,500		

EXHIBIT 6		Guidelines for Converting from Accrual to Cash Basis		

Accrual Basis	±	Adjustments Required	=	Cash Basis
Net sales	+	Beginning accounts receivable*		Cash receipts
	−	Ending accounts receivable*	=	from customers
Other revenues (e.g., rent and interest):				
Rent revenue	+	Ending unearned rent		Cash received
	−	Beginning unearned rent	=	for rent
Interest revenue	+	Beginning interest receivable		Cash received
	−	Ending interest receivable	=	for interest
Cost of goods sold	+	Ending inventory		
	−	Beginning inventory		Cash paid
	+	Beginning accounts payable	=	for inventory
	−	Ending accounts payable		
Operating expenses** (e.g., insurance and wages): Insurance				
expense	+	Ending prepaid insurance		Cash paid
	−	Beginning prepaid insurance	=	for insurance
Wages expense	+	Beginning wages payable		Cash paid
	−	Ending wages payable	=	for wages
Income tax	+	Beginning income taxes payable		Cash paid for
expense	−	Ending income taxes payable	=	income taxes
				Net cash flows provided by (used in) operating activities

*Net of allowance for uncollectible accounts.
**Excluding depreciation and other noncash items.

To make the T-account balance, equipment must have been sold. What was the original cost of the equipment that was sold? It must have been $1,200 (that is the only number that will make the T-account balance). What was the accumulated depreciation associated with the sold equipment? Let's take a look at the accumulated depreciation T-account. Entries on the debit side of that account track the accumulated depreciation associated with equipment that has been sold. Entries to the credit side are associated with depreciation expense for the period. Because we know depreciation expense for the period (from the income statement), and we know the beginning and ending balances in the account (from the balance sheet), we can infer the accumulated depreciation associated with the equipment that was sold.

Accumulated Depreciation

		Beg. Bal.	1,200
		Depreciation	
Sold	?	Expense	500
		End. Bal.	900

The accumulated depreciation associated with the equipment that was sold must have been $800. In addition, we know from the income statement that the sale resulted in a gain of $100. With this information, we can infer that the following journal entry was made relating to the sale of PP&E:

Cash	500	
Accumulated Depreciation	800	
Property, Plant, and Equipment		1,200
Gain on Sale of Equipment		100

As you can see, we can determine the amount of cash received from the sale of PP&E by monitoring the change in other related accounts on the income statement and balance sheet.

As Silmaril's only investing activity related to the PP&E account, we have analyzed all the changes in that account and are now ready to prepare the investing activities section of the statement of cash flows. Had Silmaril bought or sold available-for-sale or held-to-maturity securities during the year, we would need to analyze these accounts to determine any cash flow effects. The investing activities section of the statement of cash flows for Silmaril, Inc., would be as follows:

Investing Activities:		
Proceeds from the sale of property, plant, and equipment	$ 500	
Purchased property, plant, and equipment	(1,700)	
Cash flows from investing activities		(1,200)

Step 4. Analyze the Long-Term Debt and Stockholders' Equity Accounts to Determine the Cash Flow Effects of any Financing Transactions

Consider long-term debt accounts. What would make them increase? What would make them decrease? Obviously, these debt accounts would increase when a company borrows more money (an inflow of cash) and decrease when the company pays back the debt (an outflow of cash). In the case of Silmaril, we observe that the company's long-term debt account declined from $2,200 to $2,000. Unless something unusual happened (such as additional debt was issued and then some debt was repaid), we assume that the reason for the decrease was that cash was used to reduce the liability.

In the case of stockholders' equity accounts, we examine both the common stock and retained earnings accounts for increases and decreases resulting from cash flows. The common stock account will increase as a result of the sale of stock and decrease if any stock is repurchased and retired. Because the common stock account increased by $450 during the period, we assume that the increase resulted from the sale of stock. Again, if an unusual transaction had occurred, information relating to the transaction would be available in the notes. Retained Earnings increases from the recognition of net income (an operating activity) and decreases as a result of net losses (also an operating activity) or through the payment of dividends (a financing activity). In the case of Silmaril, Inc., because no dividends are disclosed on the trial balance, the entire change in Retained Earnings results from net income; the cash flow effect has already been included in operating activities.

Silmaril, Inc., would prepare the following information relating to its financing activities:

Financing Activities:		
Proceeds from the sale of stock		$ 450
Repayment of long-term debt		(200)
Cash flows from financing activities		250

Step 5. Prepare a Formal Statement of Cash Flows   Based on our analysis of all income statement and balance sheet accounts, we have identified all inflows and out-flows of cash for Silmaril, Inc., and categorized those cash flows based on the type of activity. The resulting statement of cash flows (prepared using the direct method)[4] would be as follows:

Operating Activities:		
Collections from customers		$ 14,000
Payments for inventory	$ 8,100	
Payments for miscellaneous expenses	3,200	
Payments for interest	180	
Payments for taxes	440	(11,920)
Cash flows from operating activities		$ 2,080
Investing Activities:		
Proceeds from the sale of property, plant, and equipment	$ 500	
Purchased property, plant, and equipment	(1,700)	
Cash flows from investing activities		(1,200)
Financing Activities:		
Proceeds from the sale of stock	$ 450	
Repayment of long-term debt	(200)	
Cash flows from financing activities		250
Net increase in cash		$ 1,130
Beginning cash balance		300
Ending cash balance		$ 1,430

Additional disclosure is required in the notes to the financial statements depending on the method used. Other disclosures required by FASB Statement No. 95 include the amounts paid for interest and income taxes. When the indirect method is used to report cash flows from operating activities, cash paid for interest and income taxes is disclosed as supplemental. When the direct method is used to report cash flows from operating ac-tivities, these amounts are included in the statement of cash flows.

An additional disclosure required when the direct method is used is a schedule rec-onciling net income with net cash flows provided by (used in) operating activities. This schedule is, in effect, the same as the operating activities section of a statement of cash flows prepared using the indirect method.

noncash transactions

Investing and financing activities that do not affect cash; if significant, they are disclosed below the statement of cash flows or in the notes to the financial statements.

Step 6. Report Any Significant Investing or Financing Transactions That Did Not Involve Cash   If Silmaril had any significant **noncash trans-actions**, such as purchasing PP&E by issuing debt or trading Silmaril stock for that of another company, these transactions would be disclosed in the notes to the financial statements or in a separate schedule below the statement of cash flows. In this example, no such transactions occurred.

[4] A statement of cash flows prepared using the indirect method is shown in the Review Problem on pages 639–641. The state-ment of cash flows for **Wal-Mart**, shown in Appendix A, was also prepared using the indirect method.

> ### REMEMBER THIS...
>
> - Operating activities include those transactions that enter into the determination of net income.
> - The direct or the indirect method may be used to show the net cash flows provided by (used in) operating activities.
> - The indirect method starts with net income, as reported on the income statement, and adds or subtracts adjustments to convert accrual net income to net cash flows from operations.
> - When using the indirect method, adjustments to net income are made for increases and decreases in operating account balances, noncash items such as depreciation, and gains and losses from the sale of assets.
> - The direct method shows the major classes of operating cash receipts and payments. The direct method requires analysis of cash transactions or an analysis of accrual revenues and expenses in order to convert them to cash receipts and payments.
> - Investing activities involve the purchase or sale of long-term assets such as property, plant, and equipment or investment securities.
> - Financing activities include transactions in which cash is obtained from or paid to owners and creditors.

Using Information from the Statement of Cash Flows to Make Decisions

Use information from the statement of cash flows to make decisions.

(5) To this point in the text, we have reviewed numerous financial statement analysis techniques involving the income statement and the balance sheet. We have used numerous ratios that were computed using numbers from the income statement and the balance sheet. We can also use information from the statement of cash flows for analysis purposes.

Analysis using cash flow information is often restricted to examining the relationships among the categories in the statement of cash flows. Although the statement of cash flows, like the other financial statements, reports information about the past, careful analysis of this information can help investors, creditors, and others assess the amounts, timing, and uncertainty of future cash flows. Specifically, the statement helps users answer questions such as how a company is able to pay dividends when it had a net loss, or why a company is short of cash despite increased earnings. A statement of cash flows may show, for example, that external borrowing or the issuance of capital stock provided the cash from which dividends were paid even though a net loss was reported for that year. Similarly, a company may be short on cash, even with increased earnings, because of increased inventory purchases, plant expansion, or debt retirement.

Trends are often more important than absolute numbers for any one period. Accordingly, cash flow statements usually are presented on a comparative basis. This enables users to analyze a company's cash flows over time.

Because companies are required to highlight cash flows from operating, investing, and financing activities, a company's operating cash flows and investing and financing policies can be compared with those of other companies. We can learn much about a company by examining patterns that appear among the three cash flow categories in the statement of cash flows. Exhibit 7 shows eight possible cash flow patterns and provides some insight into what each cash flow pattern indicates about the company.

Positive cash flows from operations are necessary if a company is to succeed over the long term (patterns 1 through 4). The most common cash flow pattern is 2. Companies

	CF from Operating	CF from Investing	CF from Financing	General Explanation
EXHIBIT 7				**Analysis of Cash Flows Statement: Patterns**
#1	+	+	+	Company is using cash generated from operations, from sale of assets, and from financing to build up pile of cash—very liquid company—possibly looking for acquisition.
#2	+	−	−	Company is using cash flows generated from operations to buy fixed assets and to pay down debt or pay owners.
#3	+	+	−	Company is using cash from operations and from sale of fixed assets to pay down debt or pay owners.
#4	+	−	+	Company is using cash from operations and from borrowing (or from owner investment) to expand.
#5	−	+	+	Company's operating cash flow problems are covered by sale of fixed assets, by borrowing, or by stock-holder contributions. The negative cash flow from operations could cause long-term problems if it persists.
#6	−	−	+	Company is growing rapidly, but has shortfalls in cash flows from operations and from purchase of fixed assets financed by long-term debt or new investment.
#7	−	+	−	Company is financing operating cash flow shortages and payments to creditors and/or stockholders via sale of fixed assets.
#8	−	−	−	Company is using cash reserves to finance operation shortfall and pay long-term creditors and/or investors.

Source: Michael T. Dugan, Benton E. Gup, and William D. Samson, "Teaching the Statement of Cash Flows," *Journal of Accounting Education*, Vol. 9, 1991, p. 36.

use cash flows from operations to purchase fixed assets or to pay down debt. Growing companies follow cash flow pattern 6. Cash is being borrowed to cover a shortage of cash from operations as well as to purchase fixed assets. Most (about 80%) of the publicly-traded companies in the United States follow patterns 2, 4, and 6.

REMEMBER THIS...

- An analysis of the relationships among the categories on the statement of cash flows can provide insight into a company's performance.
- Positive cash flows from operations are necessary if a company is to succeed over the long term.

REVIEW OF
LEARNING OBJECTIVES

(1) Understand the purpose of a statement of cash flows.

- The statement of cash flows is one of the three primary financial statements presented by companies in their annual reports.
- The primary purpose of the statement of cash flows is to provide information about the cash receipts and payments of an entity during a period.
- The statement of cash flows also explains the changes in the balance sheet accounts and the cash effects of the accrual-basis amounts reported in the income statement.

(2) Recognize the different types of information reported in the statement of cash flows.

Operating activities	• Receipts from the sale of goods or services and from interest, and the payments for inventory, wages, utilities, taxes, and interest.
Investing activities	• Purchase and sale of land, buildings, or equipment.
	• Purchase and sale of certain investment securities.
Financing activities	• Selling stock, paying cash dividends, and borrowing money and repaying loans.
Significant noncash transactions	• One example is the purchase of land by the issuance of stock.

(3) Prepare a simple statement of cash flows.

- If transactions are properly classified when input into the accounting system, the preparation of a statement of cash flows is straightforward.
- Cash inflows and outflows are segregated according to type of activity (operating, investing, or financing), and a statement of cash flows is prepared based on that information.

(4) Analyze financial statements to prepare a statement of cash flows. A six-step process can be employed to assist in the analysis of balance sheet and income statement data to prepare a statement of cash flows.

(1) Compute the change in the cash balance for the period.
(2) Convert the income statement from an accrual basis to a cash basis. The result is cash flows from operating activities.
(3) Analyze long-term assets to determine the cash flow effects of investing activities.
(4) Analyze long-term liabilities and stockholders' equity accounts to determine the cash flow effects of financing activities.
(5) Prepare a formal statement of cash flows.
(6) Disclose significant noncash transactions in the notes to the financial statements or in a separate schedule at the bottom of the statement of cash flows.

(5) Use information from the statement of cash flows to make decisions.

- A statement of cash flows helps investors and creditors observe trends related to a company's use of operating income and its use of external sources of capital.
- Used with the income statement and the balance sheet, the statement of cash flows is a valuable source of information.

KEY TERMS & CONCEPTS

cash equivalents, 616

direct method, 630

financing activities, 619

indirect method, 629

investing activities, 618

noncash items, 625

noncash

transactions, 634

operating activities, 616

statement of cash

flows, 615

REVIEW PROBLEMS

Classifying Cash Flows

Anna Dimetros is the bookkeeper for Russia Imports, Inc. (RII), a New York City–based company. Anna has collected the following cash flow information about RII for the most current year of operations. The cash balance at the beginning of the year was $105,000.

Cash receipts:	
Cash received from issuance of stock	$ 50,000
Cash received from customers	252,300
Cash received from interest at bank	4,600
Cash received from borrowing at bank	25,000
Total cash receipts	$331,900
Cash payments:	
Cash paid for wages of employees	$134,600
Cash paid to stockholders as dividends	5,500
Cash paid to bank for interest	7,200
Cash paid to bank to repay earlier loan	10,000
Cash paid for taxes	23,500
Cash paid for operating expenses	128,100
Cash paid for equipment	15,000
Total cash payments	$323,900

Required:

1. From the information provided, classify the cash flows for Russia Imports, Inc., according to operating, investing, and financing activities.
2. Determine the ending cash balance.

Solution

Russia Imports, Inc.

Cash Flows

20XX

1.	*Cash flows from operating activities:*		
	Cash receipts from:		
	Customers	$252,300	
	Bank (interest)	4,600	$256,900
	Cash payments to:		
	Employees (wages)	$134,600	
	Bank (interest)	7,200	
	Government (taxes)	23,500	
	Various entities (operating expenses)	128,100	293,400
	Net cash flows used in operating activities		$ (36,500)

(continued)

Cash flows from investing activities:		
Cash payments to:		
Purchase equipment	$(15,000)	
Net cash flows used in investing activities		$ (15,000)
Cash flows from financing activities:		
Cash receipts from:		
Issuance of stock	$ 50,000	
Borrowing at bank	25,000	$ 75,000
Cash payments to:		
Stockholders (dividends)	$ (5,500)	
Repay earlier loan	(10,000)	(15,500)
Net cash flows provided by financing activities ...		$ 59,500
Total net cash flows for period		$ 8,000

2. Beginning cash balance .... $ 105,000
Total net cash flows for period 8,000
Ending cash balance .... $ 113,000*

*Alternatively, beginning balance ($105,000) + receipts ($331,900) − payments ($323,900) = ending balance ($113,000).

Preparing a Statement of Cash Flows

Snow Corporation produces clock radios. Comparative income statements and balance sheets for the years ended December 31, 2009 and 2008, are presented.

Snow Corporation
Comparative Income Statements
For the Years Ended December 31, 2009 and 2008

	2009	2008
Net sales revenue	$600,000	$575,000
Cost of goods sold	500,000	460,000
Gross margin	$100,000	$115,000
Operating expenses	66,000	60,000
Operating income	$ 34,000	$ 55,000
Interest expense	4,000	3,000
Income before taxes	$ 30,000	$ 52,000
Income taxes	12,000	21,000
Net income	$ 18,000	$ 31,000

Snow Corporation
Comparative Balance Sheets
December 31, 2009 and 2008

	2009	2008
Assets		
Current assets:		
Cash and cash equivalents	$ 11,000	$ 13,000
Accounts receivable (net)	92,000	77,000
Inventory	103,000	92,000
Prepaid expenses	6,000	5,000
Total current assets	$ 212,000	$ 187,000

(continued)

	2009	2008
Property, plant, and equipment:		
Land	$ 69,000	$ 66,000
Machinery and equipment	172,000	156,000
Accumulated depreciation, machinery and equipment	(113,000)	(102,000)
Total property, plant, and equipment	$ 128,000	$ 120,000
Total assets	$ 340,000	$ 307,000
Liabilities and Stockholders' Equity		
Current liabilities:		
Accounts payable	$ 66,000	$ 78,000
Dividends payable	2,000	0
Income taxes payable	3,000	5,000
Total current liabilities	$ 71,000	$ 83,000
Long-term debt	75,000	42,000
Total liabilities	$ 146,000	$ 125,000
Stockholders' equity:		
Common stock, no par	$ 26,000	$ 26,000
Retained earnings	168,000	156,000
Total stockholders' equity	$ 194,000	$ 182,000
Total liabilities and stockholders' equity	$ 340,000	$ 307,000

The following additional information is available.

a.   Dividends declared during 2009 were $6,000.

b.   The market price per share of stock on December 31, 2009, was $14.50.

c.   Equipment worth $16,000 was acquired by the issuance of a long-term note ($10,000) and by paying cash ($6,000).

d.   Land was acquired for $3,000 cash.

e.   Depreciation of $11,000 was included in operating expenses for 2009.

f.   There were no accruals or prepaid amounts for interest.

Required:

Analyze the data provided to prepare a statement of cash flows. Use (1) the indirect method and (2) the direct method to report cash flows from operating activities.

Solution

1. Indirect Method

Snow Corporation
Statement of Cash Flows (Indirect Method)
For the Year Ended December 31, 2009

Cash flows from operating activities:		
Net income	$ 18,000	
Add (deduct) adjustments to cash basis:		
Depreciation expense	11,000	
Increase in accounts receivable	(15,000)	
Increase in inventory	(11,000)	
Increase in prepaid expenses	(1,000)	
Decrease in accounts payable	(12,000)	
Decrease in income taxes payable	(2,000)	
Net cash flows used in operating activities		$(12,000)

(continued)

Cash flows from investing activities:

Cash payments for:

Land	$ (3,000)	
Machinery and equipment	(6,000)	
Net cash flows used in investing activities		(9,000)

Cash flows from financing activities:

Cash receipts from long-term borrowing	$ 23,000	
Cash payments for dividends	(4,000)*	
Net cash flows provided by financing activities		19,000
Net decrease in cash		$ (2,000)
Cash and cash equivalents at beginning of year		13,000
Cash and cash equivalents at end of year		$ 11,000

*Cash dividends declared ($6,000) less increase in dividends payable ($2,000)

Supplemental disclosure:

Cash payments for:

Interest	$ 4,000
Income taxes	14,000

Noncash transaction:

Equipment was purchased by issuing a long-term note for $10,000.

The statement of cash flows for Snow Corporation shows that although reported net income was positive for 2009, the net cash flows generated from operating activities were negative. Only by borrowing cash was Snow Corporation able to pay dividends and purchase land and equipment. Even then the cash account decreased by $2,000 during the period.

2. Direct Method

Snow Corporation

Statement of Cash Flows (Direct Method)

For the Year Ended December 31, 2009

Cash flows from operating activities:

Cash receipts from customers		$ 585,000

Cash payments for:

Inventory	$523,000	
Operating expenses	56,000	
Interest expense	4,000	
Income tax expense	14,000	(597,000)
Net cash flows used in operating activities		$ (12,000)

Cash flows from investing activities:

Cash payments for:

Land	$ (3,000)	
Machinery and equipment	(6,000)	
Net cash flows used in investing activities		(9,000)

Cash flows from financing activities:

Cash receipts from long-term borrowing	$ 23,000	
Cash payments for dividends	(4,000)	
Net cash flows provided by financing activities		19,000
Net decrease in cash		$ (2,000)
Cash and cash equivalents at beginning of year		13,000
Cash and cash equivalents at end of year		$ 11,000

*Supplemental Disclosure**

Equipment was purchased by issuing a long-term note for $10,000.

*A schedule reconciling net income with net cash flow used by operating activities would also be presented, either with the statement of cash flows or in the notes to the financial statements. The information provided in the schedule is the same as the operating activities section of the statement of cash flows prepared using the indirect method (see part 1).

DISCUSSION QUESTIONS

1. What is the main purpose of a statement of cash flows?
2. What are cash equivalents, and how are they treated on a statement of cash flows?
3. Distinguish among cash flows from operating, investing, and financing activities, providing examples for each type of activity.
4. How are significant noncash investing and financing transactions to be reported?
5. Describe the process of converting from accrual revenues to cash receipts.
6. Describe the six-step process that can be used to prepare a statement of cash flows by analyzing the income statement and comparative balance sheets.

7. Distinguish between the indirect and direct methods of reporting net cash flows provided by (used in) operating activities.
8. How are depreciation and similar noncash items treated on a statement of cash flows?
9. What supplemental disclosures are likely to be required in connection with a statement of cash flows?
10. How might investors and creditors use a statement of cash flows?

PRACTICE EXERCISES

PE 13-1   **Categories of Cash Inflows and Outflows**
LO2   Which one of the following is *not* one of the three main sections in the statement of cash flows for a company?
   a. Earning activities.
   b. Financing activities.
   c. Operating activities.
   d. Investing activities.

PE 13-2   **Identifying Operating Activities**
LO2   Which one of the following is an example of an operating activity?
   a. Cash payments to repay principal amounts borrowed.
   b. Cash payments to suppliers for inventory purchases.
   c. Cash receipts from sale of a business segment.
   d. Cash receipts from issuance of own stock.

PE 13-3   **Identifying Investing Activities**
LO2   Which one of the following is an example of an investing activity?
   a. Cash payments to lenders for interest expense.
   b. Cash receipts from borrowing notes.
   c. Cash receipts from sale of goods or services.
   d. Cash payments to purchase property, plant, and equipment.

PE 13-4   **Identifying Financing Activities**
LO2   Which one of the following is an example of a financing activity?
   a. Cash payments to purchase debt or equity securities of other entities (other than trading securities).
   b. Cash payments to stockholders as dividend.
   c. Cash receipts from dividend revenue.
   d. Cash receipts from collection of principal on loans made to other entities.

PE 13-5   **Computing Net Change in Cash for the Period**
LO3   The company had a beginning cash balance of $215. In addition, the company reported the following amounts of cash provided by (used in) each category of the statement of cash flows:

(continued)

Operating activities	$ 3,460
Investing activities	(3,730)
Financing activities	298

Using the above information, compute the company's ending cash balance.

PE 13-6
LO3

Computation of Cash from Operating Activities

Using the following information, compute the amount of cash provided by operating activities.

Payments for miscellaneous expenses	$1,031
Payment to stockholders as dividends	350
Payment for taxes	135
Payment for interest	43
Collections on account	4,286
Payments for inventory	2,874

PE 13-7
LO3

Solving for Cash from Investing Activities

Using the following information, compute the amount of cash provided by (used in) investing activities:

Cash from operating activities	$136,190
Cash from financing activities	86,340
Beginning cash balance	12,540
Ending cash balance	13,405

PE 13-8
LO4

Using Accounts Receivable to Compute Cash Collections

Assume all of the company's sales are on account. The accounts receivable balance at the beginning of the year was $512, and the ending balance was $481. During the year, the company had sales of $4,526. Compute the amount of cash collections on sales.

PE 13-9
LO4

Identifying Noncash Flow Items and Nonoperating Activity Items

Using the following income statement accounts, identify the items that are noncash items and/or should not be included in the operating activities section of the statement of cash flows. (These items will be added to or subtracted from net income to compute cash flow from operating activities.)

Sales revenues	$23,236
Gain on sale of land	540
Cost of goods sold	(15,304)
General and administrative expenses	(2,634)
Depreciation expense	(1,785)
Interest expense	(429)
Tax expense	(1,450)

PE 13-10
LO4

Using Inventory and Accounts Payable to Compute Cash Paid for Inventory

Using the following information and assuming that all inventory is purchased on account, compute cash paid for inventory:

Cost of goods sold	$36,843
Inventory, beginning balance	3,110
Inventory, ending balance	2,982
Accounts payable, beginning balance	2,576
Accounts payable, ending balance	2,718

PE 13-11   **Using Taxes Payable to Compute Cash Paid for Taxes**

LO4   Using the following information, compute cash paid for taxes.

Income tax expense	$3,464
Taxes payable, beginning balance	237
Taxes payable, ending balance	276

PE 13-12   **Indirect Method**

LO4   Using the following information, prepare the operating activities section of the statement of cash flows using the indirect method.

	Income Statement	Adjustments		Cash Flows from Operations
Sales	$ 32,840	−340	(increase in accounts receivable)	$ 32,500
Cost of goods sold	(21,352)	−103	(increase in inventory)	(21,310)
		+145	(increase in accounts payable)	
Miscellaneous expenses	(4,670)	+130	(decrease in prepaid expenses)	(4,540)
Depreciation expense	(4,503)	+4,503	(not a cash flow item)	0
Interest expense	(362)	−24	(decrease in interest payable)	(386)
Loss on sale of land	(1,030)	+1,030	(not an operating activity)	0
Income tax expense	(369)	+14	(increase in taxes payable)	(355)
Net income	$ 554	+5,355	(net adjustment)	$ 5,909

PE 13-13   **Direct Method**

LO4   Refer to the data in PE 13-12. Prepare the operating activities section of the statement of cash flows using the direct method.

PE 13-14   **Computing Cash Paid for Property, Plant, and Equipment**

LO4   The company reported the following information related to its long-term assets:

Property, plant, and equipment, beginning balance	$195,410
Property, plant, and equipment, ending balance	210,850
Accumulated depreciation, beginning balance	74,330
Accumulated depreciation, ending balance	73,680
Depreciation expense	8,240

In addition, the company disclosed that it sold equipment with a historical cost of $18,700 for $14,270.

Using this information, compute cash paid for property, plant, and equipment.

PE 13-15   **Computing Gain on Sale of Property, Plant, and Equipment**

LO4   Refer to the data in PE 13-14. Compute the realized gain on the sale of equipment.

PE 13-16   **Computing Cash from Financing Activities**

LO4   Using the following information, compute the amount of cash from financing activities:
1. The company purchased $12,000 of its own common stock to be held in the treasury.
2. The company paid cash dividends of $2,350 to its stockholders.
3. The company repaid $25,000 of long-term debt.

PE 13-17   **Using Information from the Statement of Cash Flows to Make Decisions**

LO5   Using the following information about a company, decide whether you would want to loan money to the company.

(continued)

	2007	2008	2009
Net income	$ 2,045	$ 1,295	$ 2,540
Cash provided by (used in) operating activities	121	(2,023)	(6,843)
Cash provided by (used in) investing activities	(6,300)	(1,450)	(2,460)
Cash provided by (used in) financing activities	4,010	5,300	9,200

EXERCISES

E 13-18

LO2

Classification of Cash Flows

Indicate whether each of the following items would be associated with a cash inflow (I), cash outflow (O), or noncash item (N) and under which category each would be reported on a statement of cash flows: Operating Activities (OA); Investing Activities (IA); Financing Activities (FA); or not on the statement (NOS). An example is provided.

Item	Classified as	Reported under
Example: Sales Revenue	I	OA

1. Fees collected for services
2. Interest paid
3. Proceeds from sale of equipment
4. Cash (principal) received from bank on long-term note
5. Purchase of treasury stock for cash
6. Collection of loan made to company officer
7. Cash dividends paid
8. Taxes paid
9. Depreciation expense
10. Wages paid to employees
11. Cash paid for inventory purchases
12. Proceeds from sale of common stock
13. Interest received on loan to company officer
14. Purchase of land by issuing stock
15. Utility bill paid

E 13-19

LO2

Classification of Cash Flows

The following items summarize certain transactions that occurred during the past year for Alta Inc. Show in which section of the statement of cash flows the information would be reported by placing an X in the appropriate column. (Assume the direct method is used to report operating cash flows.)

Transaction	Reported in Statement of Cash Flows			Not Reported in Statement of Cash Flows
	Operating	Investing	Financing	
a. Collections from customers				
b. Depreciation expense				
c. Wages and salaries paid				
d. Cash dividends paid				
e. Taxes paid				
f. Utilities paid				
g. Building purchased in exchange for stock				
h. Stock of Western Co. purchased				
i. Inventory purchased for cash				
j. Interest on Alta's note to local bank paid				
k. Interest received from a note with a customer				
l. Delivery truck sold at no gain or loss				

E 13-20

LO2

Transaction Analysis

Following are the transactions of McKinley Company:

a. Sold equipment for $3,600. The original cost was $11,100; the book value is $3,050.
b. Purchased equipment costing $77,000 by paying cash of $27,000 and signing a $50,000 long-term note at 10% interest.
c. Received $8,200 of the principal and $490 in interest on a long-term note receivable.
d. Received $6,300 in cash dividends on stock held as a trading security.
e. Purchased treasury stock for $2,400. (Assume that the cost method is used.)

Complete the following:

1. Prepare journal entries for each of the transactions. (Omit explanations.)
2. For each transaction, indicate the amount of cash inflow or outflow. Then, note how each transaction would be classified on a statement of cash flows.

E 13-21

LO3

Transaction Analysis

The Vikon Company had the following selected transactions during the past year:

a. Sold (issued) 1,000 shares of common stock, $10 par, for $25 per share.
b. Collected $100,000 of accounts receivable.
c. Paid dividends to current stockholders in the amount of $50,000 (assume dividends declared earlier establishing a dividends payable account).
d. Received $1,500 interest on a note receivable from a company officer.
e. Paid the annual insurance premium of $1,200.
f. Recorded depreciation expense of $5,000.

Complete the following:

1. Prepare appropriate journal entries for each of the above transactions. (Omit explanations.)
2. For each transaction, indicate the amount of cash inflow or outflow and also how each cash flow would be classified on a statement of cash flows.

E 13-22

LO3

Preparing a Simple Cash Flow Statement

Assume you have access to the ledger (specifically, the detail of the cash account) for Stern Company, represented by the following T-account:

Cash

Beg. Bal.	29,870	(2)	60,000
(1)	145,500	(3)	64,000
(4)	4,750	(5)	4,000
(6)	45,000	(7)	10,500
(8)	17,000	(9)	25,000
End. Bal.	78,620		

The transactions that are represented by posting entries (1) through (9) in the cash account are as follows:

1. Collections on account
2. Payments for wages and salaries
3. Payments for inventory
4. Proceeds from sale of equipment
5. Payments of dividends
6. Proceeds from new bank loan
7. Payments for other cash operating expenses
8. Proceeds from sale of nontrading securities
9. Payments for taxes

From these data, prepare a statement of cash flows for Stern Company for the year ended December 31, 2008.

E 13-23

LO4

Determining Cash Receipts and Payments

Assuming the following data, compute:
1. Cash collected from customers.
2. Cash paid for wages and salaries.
3. Cash paid for inventory purchases.
4. Cash paid for taxes.

	Income Statement Amount for Year	Balance Sheet	
		Beg. of Year	End of Year
Sales revenue	$450,000		
Accounts receivable (net)		$28,000	$33,000
Wages and salaries expense	95,000		
Wages and salaries payable		11,000	8,000
Cost of goods sold	220,000		
Accounts payable		23,500	21,000
Inventory		22,000	25,000
Income tax expense	40,000		
Income taxes payable		19,000	20,500

E 13-24

LO4

Adjustments to Cash Flows from Operations (Indirect Method)

Assume that you are using the indirect method of preparing a statement of cash flows. For each of the changes listed, indicate whether it would be added to or subtracted from net income in computing net cash flows provided by (used in) operating activities. If the change does not affect net cash flows provided by (used in) operating activities, so indicate.
1. Increase in Accounts Receivable (net)
2. Decrease in Accounts Payable
3. Increase in securities classified as cash equivalents
4. Gain on sale of equipment
5. Decrease in Inventory
6. Increase in Prepaid Insurance
7. Depreciation
8. Increase in Wages Payable
9. Decrease in Dividends Payable
10. Decrease in Interest Receivable

E 13-25

LO4

Cash Flows from Operations (Direct Method)

Neil Brown is the proprietor of a small company. The results of operations for last year are shown, along with selected balance sheet data. From the information provided, determine the amount of net cash flows provided from operations, using the direct method.

Sales revenue	$510,000	
Cost of goods sold	320,000	
Gross margin		$190,000
Operating expenses:		
Wages expense	$ 75,000	
Utilities expense	2,500	
Rent expense	35,400	
Insurance expense	6,900	119,800
Net income		$ 70,200

(continued)

	Beginning of Year	End of Year
Accounts receivable (net)	$42,000	$39,000
Inventory	38,000	39,000
Prepaid insurance	2,200	1,800
Accounts payable	16,000	19,000
Wages payable	10,000	8,800

E 13-26

LO4

Cash Flows from Operations (Indirect Method)

Given the data in E 13-25, show how the amount of net cash flows from operating activities would be calculated using the indirect method.

E 13-27

LO4

Cash Flows Provided by Operations (Direct Method)

The following information was taken from the comparative financial statements of Imperial Corporation for the years ended December 31, 2008 and 2009:

Net income for 2009	$ 90,000
Sales revenue	500,000
Cost of goods sold	300,000
Depreciation expense for 2009	60,000
Amortization of goodwill for 2009	10,000
Interest expense on short-term debt for 2009	3,500
Dividends declared and paid in 2009	65,000

	Dec. 31, 2009	Dec. 31, 2008
Accounts receivable (net)	$30,000	$43,000
Inventory	50,000	42,000
Accounts payable	56,000	59,400

Use the direct method to compute cash flows provided by operating activities in 2009. (*Hint:* You need to calculate cash paid for operating expenses.)

E 13-28

LO4

Cash Flows Provided by Operations (Indirect Method)

Given the data in E 13-27, show how the amount of cash provided by operations for 2009 is computed using the indirect method.

E 13-29

LO4

Cash Flows Provided by Operations (Direct Method)

The following information was taken from the comparative financial statements of Dougal Industries, Inc., for the years ended December 31, 2008 and 2009:

Net income for 2009	$ 60,000
Sales revenue	900,000
Cost of goods sold	720,000
Depreciation expense for 2009	50,000
Interest expense on short-term debt for 2009	7,400
Dividends declared and paid in 2009	20,000
Utilities expense	4,100

(continued)

	Dec. 31, 2009	Dec. 31, 2008
Accounts receivable (net)	$51,000	$46,000
Inventory	83,100	72,400
Accounts payable	65,200	68,700

Use the direct method to compute cash flows provided by operating activities in 2009. (*Hint:* You need to calculate cash paid for operating expenses.)

E 13-30 **Cash Flows Provided by Operations (Indirect Method)**

LO4   Given the data in E 13-29, show how the amount of cash flows provided by operations for 2009 is computed using the indirect method.

E 13-31 **Net Cash Flows (Indirect Method)**

LO4   Given the following selected data for Milton Corporation, using the indirect method to report cash flows from operating activities, determine the net increase (decrease) in cash for the year ended December 31, 2009.

Net income	$ 95,000
Depreciation	25,000
Other operating expenses	140,000
Cost of goods sold	240,000
Sales revenue	500,000
Increase in accounts receivable (net)	10,000
Decrease in accounts payable	5,000
Decrease in inventory	3,000
Increase in prepaid assets	7,000
Increase in wages payable	15,000
Equipment purchased for cash	40,000
Increase in bonds payable	100,000
Dividends declared and paid	40,000
Decrease in dividends payable	2,000

E 13-32 **Net Cash Flows (Direct Method)**

LO4   Based on the following information, determine the net increase (decrease) in cash for Luther Corp. for the year ended December 31, 2009. Use the direct method to report cash flows from operating activities.

Cash received from interest revenue	$ 16,000
Cash paid for dividends	80,000
Cash collected from customers	712,000
Cash paid for wages	476,000
Depreciation expense for the period	65,000
Cash received from issuance of common stock	350,000
Cash paid for retirement of bonds at par	150,000
Cash received on sale of equipment at book value	13,000
Cash paid for land	210,000

E 13-33 **Statement of Cash Flows (Indirect Method)**

LO4   North Western Company provides the following financial information. Prepare a statement of cash flows for 2009, using the indirect method to report cash flows from operating activities.

(continued)

North Western Company
Comparative Balance Sheets
December 31, 2009 and 2008

	2009	2008
Assets		
Cash and cash equivalents	$ 4,500	$ 9,000
Accounts receivable (net)	33,000	36,000
Inventory	75,000	60,000
Plant and equipment (net)	262,500	225,000
Total assets	$375,000	$330,000
Liabilities and Stockholders' Equity		
Accounts payable	$ 60,000	$ 54,000
Capital stock	225,000	217,500
Retained earnings	90,000	58,500
Total liabilities and stockholders' equity	$375,000	$330,000

North Western Company
Income Statement
For the Year Ended December 31, 2009

Sales	$412,500
Cost of goods sold	225,000
Gross margin	$187,500
Operating expenses	135,000
Net income	$ 52,500

Note: Dividends of $21,000 were declared and paid during 2009. Depreciation expense for the year was $22,500.

E 13-34   **Statement of Cash Flows (Direct Method)**

LO4   By analyzing the information in E 13-33, prepare a statement of cash flows. Use the direct method to report cash flows from operating activities.

E 13-35   **Cash Flow Patterns**

LO5   Below are recent financial statement data for the following companies:
- Amazon.com
- Coca-Cola
- ExxonMobil
- Microsoft

Use the financial statement data to match each company with its numbers. All numbers are in millions.

		Cash Flow from		
	Net Income	**Operating Activities**	**Investing Activities**	**Financing Activities**
1	$ (720)	$ (91)	$ (922)	$ 1,104
2	7,910	15,013	(10,985)	(4,779)
3	7,785	10,030	(11,191)	2,245
4	2,431	3,883	(3,421)	(471)

(continued)

Consider the following information as you match the companies:
1. Start-ups have high positive financing cash flows relative to investing cash flows.
2. Companies with lots of property, plant, and equipment have cash from operations that is greater than net income because of lots of depreciation expense.
3. Old cash cows are spending money on investing but still have plenty left over for a net cash outflow from financing activities.

E 13-36

LO5

Analyzing Cash Flows

Study the comparative cash flow statements for **Wal-Mart** in Appendix A. What observations do you have about Wal-Mart's cash flow position? From a liquidity standpoint, is the trend over the last few years positive or negative? Explain.

PROBLEMS

P 13-37

LO4

Transaction Analysis

Klein Corporation reports the following summary data for the current year:
a. Sales revenue totaled $125,750.
b. Interest revenue for the period was $1,100.
c. Interest expense for the period was $400.
d. Cost of goods sold for the period was $78,000.
e. Operating expenses, all paid in cash (except for depreciation of $7,500), were $24,000.
f. Income tax expense for the period was $4,000.
g. Accounts receivable (net) increased by $5,000 during the period.
h. Accounts payable increased by $2,500 during the period.
i. Inventory at the beginning and end of the period was $17,500 and $12,500, respectively.
j. Cash increased during the period by $2,500.

Assume all other current asset and current liability accounts remained constant during the period.

Required:
1. Compute the amount of cash collected from customers.
2. Compute the amount of cash paid for inventory.
3. Compute the amount of cash paid for operating expenses.
4. Compute the amount of cash flows provided by (used in) operations.
5. **Interpretive Question:** What must have been the combined amount of cash flows provided by (used in) investing and financing activities?

P 13-38

LO3, LO4

Analysis of the Cash Account

The following information, in T-account format, is provided for Mars Company for the year 2009:

Cash Account

Beg. Bal.	16,300	(b)	45,500
(a)	168,000	(c)	29,000
(d)	5,000	(f)	40,800
(e)	22,000	(g)	2,100
		(h)	3,300
End. Bal.	90,600		

(continued)

Additional information:

a. Sales revenue for the period was $164,000. Accounts receivable (net) decreased $4,000 during the period.

b. Net purchases of $48,000 were made during 2009, all on account. Accounts payable increased $2,500 during the period.

c. The equipment account increased by $21,000 during the year.

d. One piece of equipment that cost $8,000, with a net book value of $4,000, was sold for a $1,000 gain.

e. The company borrowed $22,000 from its bank during the year.

f. Various operating expenses were all paid in cash, except for depreciation of $2,400. Total operating expenses were $43,200.

g. Interest expense for the year was $1,800. The interest payable account decreased by $300 during the year.

h. Income tax expense for the year was $4,200. The income taxes payable account increased by $900 during the year.

Required:

1. From the information given, reconstruct the journal entries that must have been made during the year (omit explanations).

2. Prepare a statement of cash flows for Mars Company for the year ended December 31, 2009.

P 13-39   **Analyzing Cash Flows**

LO4   The following information was provided by the treasurer of Surety, Inc., for the year 2009:

a. Cash sales for the year were $50,000; sales on account totaled $60,000.

b. Cost of goods sold was 50% of total sales.

c. All inventory is purchased on account.

d. Depreciation on equipment was $31,000 for the year.

e. Amortization of goodwill was $2,000.

f. Collections of accounts receivable were $38,000.

g. Payments on accounts payable for inventory equaled $39,000.

h. Rent expense paid in cash was $11,000.

i. The company issued 20,000 shares of $10-par stock for $240,000.

j. Land valued at $106,000 was acquired by issuance of a bond with a par value of $100,000.

k. Equipment was purchased for cash at a cost of $84,000.

l. Dividends of $46,000 were declared but not yet paid.

m. The company paid $15,000 of dividends that had been declared the previous year.

n. A machine used on the assembly line was sold for $12,000. The machine had a book value of $7,000.

o. Another machine with a book value of $500 was scrapped and was reported as an ordinary loss. No cash was received on this transaction.

p. The cash account increased $191,000 during the year to a total of $274,000.

Required:

1. Compute the beginning balance in the cash account.

2. How much cash was provided by (or used in) operating activities?

3. How much cash was provided by (or used in) investing activities?

4. How much cash was provided by (or used in) financing activities?

5. Would all the above items, (a) through (p), be reported on a cash flow statement? Explain.

P 13-40 **Cash Flows from Operations (Indirect Method)**

LO4 Gardner Enterprises reported a net loss of $40,000 for the year just ended. Relevant data for the company follow.

	Beginning of Year	End of Year
Cash and cash equivalents	$ 50,000	$ 20,000
Accounts receivable (net)	80,000	65,000
Inventory	123,000	130,000
Prepaid expenses	7,500	4,500
Accounts payable	55,000	60,000
Accrued liabilities	10,000	4,000
Dividends payable	25,000	35,000
Depreciation for the year, $43,000		
Dividends declared, $35,000		

Required:

1. Using the indirect method, determine the net cash flows provided by (used in) operating activities for Gardner Enterprises.
2. **Interpretive Question:** Explain how Gardner Enterprises can pay cash dividends during a year when it reports a net loss.

P 13-41 **Cash Flows from Operations (Direct Method)**

LO4 Saturday Shoppers, Inc., shows the following information in its accounting records at year-end:

Sales revenue	$740,000
Interest revenue	24,000
Cost of goods sold	380,000
Wages expense	190,000
Depreciation expense	42,000
Other (cash) operating expenses	68,000
Dividends declared	30,000

Selected balance sheet data are as follows:

	Beginning of Year	End of Year
Accounts receivable (net)	$ 63,000	$ 74,000
Interest receivable	9,000	6,000
Inventory	210,000	219,000
Accounts payable	41,000	44,000
Wages payable	32,000	34,000
Dividends payable	25,000	30,000

Required:

1. Using the direct method, compute the net cash flows provided by (used in) operating activities for Saturday Shoppers, Inc.
2. **Interpretive Question:** Explain the main differences between the net amount of cash flows from operations and net income (loss).

P 13-42 **Cash Flows from Operations (Indirect and Direct Methods)**

LO4 The following combined income and retained earnings statement, along with selected balance sheet data, are provided for McDuffie Company:

McDuffie Company
Combined Income and Retained Earnings Statement
For the Year Ended December 31, 2009

Net sales revenue		$105,000
Other revenues		3,000*
Total revenues		$108,000
Expenses:		
Cost of goods sold	$55,000	
Selling and administrative expenses	15,200	
Depreciation expense	5,400	
Interest expense	1,200	
Total expenses		76,800
Income before taxes		$ 31,200
Income taxes		9,360
Net income		$ 21,840
Retained earnings, January 1, 2009		33,500
		$ 55,340
Dividends declared and paid		4,000
Retained earnings, December 31, 2009		$ 51,340

*Gain on sale of equipment (cost, $8,400; book value, $6,000; sales price $9,000).

	Beginning of Year	End of Year
Accounts receivable (net)	$12,300	$11,000
Inventory	16,800	18,000
Prepaid expenses	950	1,100
Accounts payable	7,200	7,000
Interest payable	750	1,000
Income taxes payable	2,200	2,500

Required:

1. Using the indirect method, compute the net cash flows from operations for McDuffie Company for 2009.
2. Using the direct method, compute the net cash flows from operations for McDuffie Company for 2009.
3. What is the impact of dividends paid on net cash flows from operations? Explain.

P 13-43 **Computation of Net Income from Cash Flows from Operations (Direct Method)**

LO4 The following partially completed work sheet is provided for ATM Corporation, which uses the direct method in computing net cash flows from operations:

(continued)

ATM Corporation
Partial Work Sheet–Cash Flows from Operations
(Direct Method)
For the Year Ended December 31, 2009

	Accrual Basis	Adjustments Debits	Adjustments Credits	Cash Basis
Net sales revenue				$150,000
Expenses:				
Cost of goods sold				$ 75,000
Depreciation				0
Loss on sale of equipment				0
Other (cash) expenses				26,000
Total expenses				$101,000
Net income (net cash flows from operations)				$ 49,000

Key:

1. Decrease in Accounts Receivable (net), $4,500.
2. Loss on sale of equipment, $1,500.
3. Increase in Inventory, $10,000.
4. Increase in Accounts Payable, $3,000.
5. Depreciation for the year, $8,000.
6. Decrease in Prepaid Expenses, $1,000.
7. Increase in Accrued Liabilities, $2,500.

Required:
Complete the work sheet with the key items above and compute the net income (loss) to be reported by ATM Corporation on its income statement for 2009.

P 13-44
LO4

Income Statement from Cash Flow Data

Parker Corporation computed the amount of cash flows from operations using both the direct and indirect methods, as follows:

Direct method:	
Collections from customers	$ 525,000
Payments to suppliers	(170,000)
Payments for operating expenses	(198,000)
Cash flows provided by operating activities	$ 157,000
Indirect method:	
Net income	$ 95,000
Depreciation	62,100
Gain on sale of equipment	(4,000)
Decrease in inventory	2,400
Decrease in accounts receivable (net)	3,600
Decrease in accounts payable	(6,800)
Increase in miscellaneous accrued payable	4,700
Cash flows provided by operating activities	$ 157,000

Required:
Using the data provided, prepare an income statement for Parker Corporation for the year 2009.

P 13-45   **Statement of Cash Flows (Indirect Method)**

LO4   JEM Company's comparative balance sheets for 2008 and 2009 are provided.

JEM Company
Comparative Balance Sheets
December 31, 2009 and 2008

	2009	2008
Assets		
Cash and cash equivalents	$ 30,500	$ 10,000
Accounts receivable (net)	64,500	51,000
Inventory	100,000	115,000
Equipment	55,000	30,000
Accumulated depreciation–equipment	(21,500)	(14,000)
Total assets	$228,500	$192,000
Liabilities and Stockholders' Equity		
Accounts payable	$ 52,500	$ 46,000
Long-term notes payable	70,000	50,000
Capital stock	60,000	60,000
Retained earnings	46,000	36,000
Total liabilities and stockholders' equity	$228,500	$192,000

The following additional information is available:

a. Net income for the year 2009 (as reported on the income statement) was $50,000.

b. Dividends of $40,000 were declared and paid.

c. Equipment that cost $8,000 and had a book value of $1,000 was sold during the year for $2,500.

Required:

Based on the information provided, prepare a statement of cash flows for JEM Company for the year ended December 31, 2009. Use the indirect method to report cash flows from operating activities.

P 13-46   **Statement of Cash Flows (Direct Method)**

LO4   Financial statement data for Bankhead, Inc., are provided. (All numbers are shown rounded to the nearest thousand, with 000's omitted.)

Bankhead, Inc.
Income and Retained Earnings Statements
For the Year Ended December 31, 2009

Sales revenue	$1,450
Cost of goods sold	1,030
Gross margin	$ 420
Operating expenses:	
Sales and administrative expenses	$ 110
Depreciation expense	17
Other expenses	81
Total operating expenses	$ 208
Income before taxes	$ 212
Income taxes	53
Net income	$ 159
Dividends paid	25
Increase in retained earnings	$ 134

(continued)

Bankhead, Inc.

Comparative Balance Sheets

December 31, 2009 and 2008

	2009	2008
Assets		
Cash and cash equivalents	$ 783	$ 612
Accounts receivable (net)	456	448
Inventory	245	980
Land	1,450	1,300
Store fixtures	255	255
Accumulated depreciation, store fixtures	(72)	(55)
Total assets	$3,117	$3,540
Liabilities and Stockholders' Equity		
Liabilities:		
Accounts payable	$ 170	$ 366
Short-term notes payable	574	735
Long-term debt	824	1,024
Total liabilities	$1,568	$2,125
Stockholders' equity:		
Common stock	$ 145	$ 145
Paid-in capital in excess of par	550	550
Retained earnings	854	720
Total stockholders' equity	$1,549	$1,415
Total liabilities and stockholders' equity	$3,117	$3,540

Required:

1. Compute the net cash flows from operations using the direct method.
2. **Interpretive Question:** Comment on the difference between net income and net cash flows from operations.
3. Prepare a statement of cash flows for Bankhead, Inc., for the year ended December 31, 2009.

P 13-47

LO4

Statement of Cash Flows (Indirect Method)

1. Using the data from P 13-46, prepare a statement of cash flows. Use the indirect method to report cash flows from operating activities.
2. **Interpretive Question:** What are the main differences between a statement of cash flows prepared using the indirect method and one prepared using the direct method?

P 13-48

LO4, LO5

Unifying Concepts: Analysis of Operating, Investing, and Financing Activities

Jonathan Beecher is the manager and one of three brothers who own the Mile High Sporting Goods Company in Denver, Colorado. Jonathan is pleased that sales were up last year and that his new, small company has been able to expand and open a second store in Denver. After reviewing the balance sheet, however, Jonathan is concerned that Cash shows a negative balance. He can't understand how his company can show net income, based on increased sales, yet have a negative Cash position. He is concerned about what his banker is going to say when they meet next month to discuss a loan for the company to expand to a third store. Jonathan provides the following financial information and asks for your help.

(continued)

Mile High Sporting Goods Company
Income Statement
For the Year Ended December 31, 2009

Sales		$210,000
Less cost of goods sold		96,000
Gross margin		$114,000
Operating expenses:		
Salary and wages	$41,000	
Depreciation	6,800	
Other operating expenses	14,200	62,000
Operating income		$ 52,000
Income taxes		12,300
Net income		$ 39,700

Mile High Sporting Goods Company
Comparative Balance Sheets
As of December 31, 2009 and 2008

	2009	2008
Assets		
Current assets:		
Cash	$ (2,900)	$ 4,300
Accounts receivable (net)	3,800	3,100
Inventory	60,000	51,000
Total current assets	$ 60,900	$ 58,400
Other assets:		
Property, plant, and equipment	$ 94,800	$ 46,300
Less accumulated depreciation	(19,200)	(12,400)
Total other assets	$ 75,600	$ 33,900
Total assets	$136,500	$ 92,300
Liabilities and Stockholders' Equity		
Current liabilities:		
Accounts payable	$ 8,200	$ 10,400
Wages payable	1,300	3,200
Taxes payable	1,000	2,400
Total current liabilities	$ 10,500	$ 16,000
Other liabilities:		
Notes payable	35,000	25,000
Total liabilities	$ 45,500	$ 41,000
Stockholders' equity:		
Capital stock	$ 40,000	$ 40,000
Retained earnings	51,000	11,300
Total stockholders' equity	$ 91,000	$ 51,300
Total liabilities and stockholders' equity	$136,500	$ 92,300

Required:

1. Using the direct method, compute the net cash flows from operations. Also determine net cash flows for investing and financing activities.
2. **Interpretive Question:** Is Mile High Sporting Goods Company in a good liquidity position? As Mr. Beecher's banker, would you loan him more money to fund the company's expansion?

AA 13-49
DISCUSSION

Should We Make the Loan?

Save More, Inc., a discount department store, has applied to its bankers for a loan. Although the company has been profitable, it is short of cash. The loan application includes the following information about current assets, current liabilities, net income, depreciation expense, and dividends for the past five years. (All numbers are rounded to the nearest thousand, with the 000's omitted.)

	Dec. 31, 2004	Dec. 31, 2005	Dec. 31, 2006	Dec. 31, 2007	Dec. 31, 2008
Cash and cash equivalents	$ 5	$ 73	$ 10	$158	$ (189)
Accounts receivable (net)	403	555	516	576	654
Inventory	253	142	383	385	1,022
Accounts payable	19	17	281	253	52
Net income	454	492	467	440	481
Depreciation expense	50	50	55	60	60
Dividends paid	177	197	208	211	211

As a bank loan officer, you have been asked to review these figures in order to determine whether the bank should loan money to Save More, Inc.

1. Compute the net cash flows from operations for the last four years.
2. What caused the sudden decrease in cash flows from operations?
3. What factors would you focus on, and what additional information would you need before deciding whether to make the loan?

AA 13-50
DISCUSSION

Analyzing the Cash Position of Good Time, Inc.

The following data show the account balances of Good Time, Inc., at the beginning and end of the company's fiscal year:

	Aug. 31, 2009	Sept. 1, 2008
Debits		
Cash and cash equivalents	$ 88,200	$ 29,000
Accounts receivable (net)	15,000	13,300
Inventory	10,500	12,700
Prepaid insurance	2,800	2,000
Long-term investments (cost equals market)	3,000	8,400
Equipment	40,000	33,000
Treasury stock (at cost)	5,000	10,000
Cost of goods sold	184,000	
Operating expenses	93,500	
Income taxes	18,800	
Loss on sale of equipment	500	
Total debits	$461,300	$108,400

(continued)

	Aug. 31, 2009	Sept. 1, 2008
Credits		
Accumulated depreciation–equipment	$ 9,500	$ 9,000
Accounts payable	3,500	5,600
Interest payable	500	1,000
Income taxes payable	6,000	4,000
Notes payable–long-term	8,000	12,000
Common stock	55,000	50,000
Paid-in capital in excess of par	16,000	15,000
Retained earnings	9,800*	11,800
Sales	352,000	
Gain on sale of long-term investments	1,000	
Total credits	$461,300	$108,400

*Preclosing balance

The following information concerning this year was also available:

a. All purchases and sales were on account.

b. Equipment with an original cost of $5,000 was sold for $1,500; a loss of $500 was recognized on the sale.

c. Among other items, the operating expenses included depreciation expense of $3,500; interest expense of $1,400; and insurance expense of $1,200.

d. Equipment was purchased by issuing common stock and paying the balance ($6,000) in cash.

e. Treasury stock was sold for $2,000 less than it cost; the decrease in stockholders' equity was recorded by reducing Retained Earnings.

f. No dividends were paid this year.

You are to examine Good Time's cash position by:

1. Preparing schedules showing the amount of cash collected from accounts receivable, cash paid for accounts payable, cash paid for interest, and cash paid for insurance.

2. Preparing a statement of cash flows for Good Time for the fiscal year 2009 using the direct method.

3. Identifying the major reasons why Good Time's cash and cash equivalents increased so dramatically during the year.

4. Comment on whether the dividend policy seems appropriate under the current circumstances.

AA 13-51
DISCUSSION

Analyzing Cash Flow Patterns

Paula Dalton is a security analyst for DJM, Inc. She claims that she can tell a great deal about companies by analyzing their cash flow patterns. Specifically, she looks at the negative or positive cash flow trends in the three categories on cash flow statements. Paula thinks this information is even more valuable than net income trend data from income statements. She illustrates her theory with the following patterns of cash flows for Abbott Company over the past three years.

	2009	2008	2007
Net income	−	+	+
Cash flows from:			
Operating activities	−	−	+
Investing activities	+	+	+
Financing activities	+	+	+

How do you think Paula would analyze these results? Do you agree that analyzing cash flow patterns provides superior analytical information?

AA 13-52

JUDGMENT CALL

You Decide: Which method is better at reporting information on the statement of cash flows–the indirect or direct method?

Your finance professor said that the indirect method is a better way to prepare the statement of cash flows because it starts with a known number—net income. However, in your accounting course, your professor teaches that the direct method gives you more information on *how* the cash is used and, therefore, contains more useful information. Which professor do you agree with?

AA 13-53

JUDGMENT CALL

You Decide: Ignoring all other factors, will a company that is generating negative cash flows from operating activities be a good or bad investment?

When evaluating a company, you notice the following on its cash flow statement: negative cash flow from operating activities, negative cash from investing activities, and positive cash flow from financing activities. A fellow student commented, "I wouldn't invest in a company that cannot generate cash from its core business activities!" However, in 1985, **Home Depot** had a very large negative cash flow from operating activities and later turned into a very large, successful company. How would you answer your friend?

AA 13-54

REAL COMPANY
ANALYSIS

Wal-Mart

The 2006 Form 10-K for **Wal-Mart** appears in Appendix A. Locate that Form 10-K and consider the following questions:

1. Does Wal-Mart present the three cash flow statement categories—operating, investing, and financing—in the same order as that illustrated in the chapter?
2. In 2006 Wal-Mart subtracted $456 million in arriving at cash flow from operations relating to an increase in receivables. Why would an increase in receivables be subtracted?
3. In 2006, Wal-Mart spent $14.183 billion on various investing activities. Were the cash flows from operations sufficient to pay for these investments?
4. Did Wal-Mart pay any cash dividends to common stockholders during 2006? Did Wal-Mart make any payments to common stockholders during the year?

AA 13-55

REAL COMPANY
ANALYSIS

The Coca-Cola Company

The 2005 statement of cash flows for **The Coca-Cola Company** is given on page 662. Use the statement to answer the following questions:

1. Compute Coca-Cola's "Net cash provided by operations after reinvestment." This amount is computed by subtracting "Net cash used in investing activities" from "Net cash provided by operating activities." Interpret the results of the calculation for Coca-Cola for the period 2003–2005.
2. In its operating activities section, Coca-Cola subtracts gains on sales of assets in computing net cash provided by operating activities. Why are these gains subtracted?
3. Think of the dealings that The Coca-Cola Company has with its shareholders. The shareholders give money to the company by purchasing new shares of stock. In turn, the company returns cash to shareholders by paying cash dividends and by repurchasing shares of stock. For the three-year period 2003–2005, did The Coca-Cola Company receive more cash from its shareholders than it paid back to them, or did it pay more cash to its shareholders than it received? Show your calculations.
4. Look carefully at the statement of cash flows. Did the U.S. dollar get stronger or weaker during the three-year period 2003–2005?

(continued)

The Coca-Cola Company and Subsidiaries
Consolidated Statements of Cash Flows
For the Years Ended December 31, 2003, 2004, 2005
(in millions)

	2005	2004	2003
Operating activities:			
Net income	$ 4,872	$ 4,847	$ 4,347
Depreciation and amortization	932	893	850
Stock-based compensation expense	324	345	422
Deferred income taxes	(88)	162	(188)
Equity income or loss, net of dividends	(446)	(476)	(294)
Foreign currency adjustments	47	(59)	(79)
Gain on issuances of stock by equity investees	(23)	(24)	(8)
Gains on sales of assets, including bottling interests	(9)	(20)	(5)
Other operating changes	85	480	330
Other items	299	437	249
Net change in operating assets and liabilities	430	(617)	(168)
Net cash provided by operating activities	$ 6,423	$ 5,968	$ 5,456
Investing activities:			
Acquisitions and investments, principally trademarks and bottling companies	$ (637)	$ (267)	$ (359)
Purchases of investments and other assets	(53)	(46)	(177)
Proceeds from disposals of investments and other assets	33	161	147
Purchases of property, plant and equipment	(899)	(755)	(812)
Proceeds from disposals of property, plant and equipment	88	341	87
Other investing activities	(28)	63	178
Net cash used in investing activities	$(1,496)	$ (503)	$ (936)
Financing activities:			
Issuances of debt	$ 178	$ 3,030	$ 1,026
Payments of debt	(2,460)	(1,316)	(1,119)
Issuances of stock	230	193	98
Purchases of stock for treasury	(2,055)	(1,739)	(1,440)
Dividends	(2,678)	(2,429)	(2,166)
Net cash used in financing activities	$(6,785)	$(2,261)	$(3,601)
Effect of exchange rate changes on cash and cash equivalents	$ (148)	$ 141	$ 183
Cash and cash equivalents:			
Net increase during the year	$(2,006)	$ 3,345	$ 1,102
Balance at beginning of year	6,707	3,362	2,260
Balance at end of year	$ 4,701	$ 6,707	$ 3,362

AA 13-56

INTERNATIONAL

GlaxoSmithKline

GlaxoSmithKline, a British company, is one of the largest pharmaceutical firms in the world. The name "Glaxo" comes from the company's first major product line, baby food products that were sold with the slogan, "Builds Bonnie Babies." Growth of the company in recent years has been driven by sales of Zantac, an anti-ulcer drug.

GlaxoSmithKline's 2005 statement of cash flows is shown on the next page. Look at the statement and answer the following questions.

1. International accounting standards treat interest paid and interest received differently than those items are treated in the United States. Interest paid and interest received are classified as operating activities in the United States. Where are they classified on GlaxoSmithKline's statement and cash flow and what do you think is the reasoning behind the classification?

(continued)

2. Note that GlaxoSmithKline includes a reconciliation of operating profit to operating cash flow separate from the operating activities section of the statement of cash flows. Why do you think it would do that?

GlaxoSmithKline plc

Consolidated Statement of Cash Flows

31st December 2005

(in millions of £)

Reconciliation of operating profit to operating cash flows	2005 £m	2004 £m	2003 £m
Operating profit	6,874	5,756	6,050
Depreciation	710	691	704
Impairment and assets written off	193	94	255
Amortization of goodwill and intangible fixed assets	194	168	127
(Profit)/Loss on sale of property, plant and equipment	(19)	2	–
(Profit)/Loss on sales of intangible assets	(203)	1	(7)
Profit on sale of equity investments	(15)	(33)	(89)
Fair value loss on inventory sold	–	13	–
Decrease/(increase) in inventories	47	(33)	(76)
Increase in trade and other receivables	(397)	(235)	(369)
Increase/(decrease) in trade and other payables	491	163	(74)
(Decrease)/increase in pension and other provisions	(453)	(351)	71
Share-based incentive plans	236	333	375
Other	7	(42)	38
Net cash inflow from operating activities	7,665	6,527	7,005
Cash flow statement			
Cash flows from operating activities			
Cash generated from operations	7,665	6,527	7,005
Taxation paid	(1,707)	(1,583)	(1,917)
Net cash inflow from operating activities	5,958	4,944	5,088
Cash flow from investing activities			
Purchase of property, plant and equipment	(903)	(788)	(746)
Proceeds from sale of property, plant and equipment	54	53	46
Proceeds from sale of intangible assets	221	–	–
Purchase of intangible assets	(278)	(255)	(316)
Purchase of equity instruments	(23)	(103)	(63)
Proceeds from sale of equity instruments	35	58	125
Share transactions with minority shareholders	(36)	–	–
Purchase of businesses, net of cash acquired	(1,026)	(297)	(12)
Disposal of businesses and interest in associates	(2)	230	3
Investments in associates and joint ventures	(2)	(2)	(3)
Interest received	290	173	104
Dividends from associates and joint ventures	10	11	1
Net cash outflow from investing activities	(1,660)	(920)	(861)

(continued)

Reconciliation of operating profit to operating cash flows	2005 £m	2004 £m	2003 £m
Cash flow from financing activities			
Decrease/(increase) in liquid investments	550	(53)	(373)
Proceeds from own shares for employee share options	68	23	26
Issue of share capital	252	42	41
Share capital purchased for cancellation	–	(201)	(980)
Purchase of Treasury shares	(999)	(799)	–
Redemption of preference shares issued by subsidiary	–	(489)	–
Increase in long-term loans	982	1,365	1,046
Repayment of long-term loans	(70)	(15)	(23)
Net repayment of short-term loans	(857)	(407)	(442)
Net repayment of obligations under finance leases	(36)	(22)	–
Interest paid	(381)	(350)	(236)
Dividends paid to shareholders	(2,390)	(2,475)	(2,333)
Dividends paid to minority interests	(86)	(73)	(84)
Dividends paid on preference shares	–	(2)	(15)
Other financing cash flows	53	49	82
Net cash outflow from financing activities	(2,914)	(3,407)	(3,291)
Exchange adjustments	233	(93)	(110)
Increase in cash and bank overdrafts	1,617	524	826

AA 13-57

ETHICS

Manipulating the Federal Budget Deficit

Assume that you are the paymaster in charge of all U.S. Department of Defense (DOD) payroll matters. The total amount that you disburse in payroll checks in any given week is in excess of $1 billion.

Assume also that tax receipts have been lower than expected and that a federal budget deficit, and not a surplus, is now projected. Currently, Congress is struggling to reduce the projected budget deficit. It is an election year, and the members of Congress are worried that they will be stuck with a "tax and spend" label if the government runs a deficit this year. Of course, the DOD budget has been scrutinized very carefully to reduce reported expenditures as much as possible.

Yesterday, a congressional leader came to your office with a disturbing proposal. Because the federal budget numbers are reported on a cash basis, rather than on an accrual basis, expenses are reported when they are paid instead of when they are incurred. This year, the final DOD payday of the year happens to fall on the last day of the federal government's fiscal year (September 30). The congressional leader suggested that you delay issuing the payroll checks by one day. This would push the actual payment of the cash into the next fiscal year. Thus, even though the payment would be for services performed in the current fiscal year, the expense wouldn't be reported until next year. With this simple trick, the reported deficit for this year (an election year) can be reduced by $1 billion.

What should you do?

AA 13-58

WRITING

Convincing the Old-Timers of the Need for Cash Flow Data

You are the chief accountant for Harry Monst Company. The president of the company is a former accountant who worked her way up through the management ranks over the course of 30 years. She is a great manager, but her knowledge of accounting is outdated.

Harry Monst Company has a revolving line of credit with Texas Commercial Bank. A new loan officer has just been put in charge of the Harry Monst account. The new loan officer is surprised to see that Harry Monst has not been submitting a statement of cash flows along with the rest of the financial statements that comprise the annual loan review packet. The new loan officer called you and asked for a statement of cash flows.

You were surprised when you took the completed statement of cash flows to the president for her signature. She refused to sign, stating that she had never looked at or prepared a statement of cash flows in her career and she wouldn't start now.

(continued)

Write a one-page memo to the president with the objective of convincing her of the usefulness of the statement of cash flows.

AA 13-59

CUMULATIVE SPREADSHEET PROJECT

Preparing New Forecasts

This spreadsheet assignment is a continuation of the spreadsheet assignments given in earlier chapters. If you completed those spreadsheets, you have a head start on this one.

1. Handyman wishes to prepare a forecasted balance sheet, income statement, and statement of cash flows for 2010. Use the original financial statement numbers for 2009 [given in part (1) of the Cumulative Spreadsheet Project assignment in Chapter 2] as the basis for the forecast along with the following additional information:
   a. Sales in 2010 are expected to increase by 40% over 2009 sales of $700.
   b. In 2010, Handyman expects to acquire new property, plant, and equipment costing $80.
   c. The $160 in operating expenses reported in 2009 breaks down as follows: $5 depreciation expense, $155 other operating expenses.
   d. No new long-term debt will be acquired in 2010.
   e. No cash dividends will be paid in 2010.
   f. New short-term loans payable will be acquired in an amount sufficient to make Handyman's current ratio in 2010 exactly equal to 2.0.

Construction of the forecasted statement of cash flows for 2010 involves analyzing the forecasted income statement for 2010, along with the balance sheets for 2009 (actual) and 2010 (forecasted).

For this exercise, the current assets are expected to behave as follows:
   a. Cash will increase at the same rate as sales.
   b. The forecasted amount of accounts receivable in 2010 is determined using the forecasted value for the average collection period (computed using the end-of-period Accounts Receivable balance). The average collection period for 2010 is expected to be 14.08 days. This is from the *Chapter 6 spreadsheet*.
   c. The forecasted amount of inventory in 2010 is determined using the forecasted value for the number of days' sales in inventory (computed using the end-of-period Inventory balance). The number of days' sales in inventory for 2010 is expected to be 107.6 days. This is from the *Chapter 7 spreadsheet*.
   d. The forecasted amount of accounts payable in 2010 is determined using the forecasted value of the number of days' purchases in accounts payable (computed using the end-of-period Accounts Payable balance). The number of days' purchases in accounts payable for 2010 is expected to be 48.34 days. This is from the *Chapter 7 spreadsheet*.

Clearly state any additional assumptions that you make.

2. Repeat (1), with the following changes in assumptions:
   a. The average collection period is expected to be 9.06 days with days' sales in inventory remaining at 107.6 days and days' purchases in payables remaining at 48.34 days.
   b. The average collection period is expected to be 20 days with days' sales in inventory remaining at 107.6 days and days' purchases in payables remaining at 48.34 days.
   c. Days' sales in inventory are expected to be 66.2 days with the average collection period remaining at 14.08 days and days' purchases in payables remaining at 48.34 days.
   d. Days' sales in inventory are expected to be 150 days with the average collection period remaining at 14.08 days and days' purchases in payables remaining at 48.34 days.

Comment on the forecasted values of cash from operating activities in 2010 under each of the scenarios given in (2).

Introduction to Financial Statement Analysis

After studying this chapter, you should be able to:

(1) Explain the purpose of financial statement analysis. *Analysis of financial statement numbers can be used to diagnose existing problems and to forecast how a company will perform in the future.*

(2) Understand the relationships between financial statement numbers and use ratios in analyzing and describing a company's performance. *Financial ratios are relationships between two financial statement numbers and are often used in analyzing and describing a company's performance.*

(3) Use common-size financial state-ments to perform comparison of financial statements across years and between companies. *Common-size finan-cial statements allow comparison of financial statements across years and between compa-nies and are prepared by dividing all financial statement numbers by sales for the year.*

(4) Understand the DuPont framework and how return on equity can be decomposed into its profitability, efficiency, and leverage components. *The DuPont framework decomposes return on equity into its profitability, efficiency, and leverage components.*

(5) Conduct a focused examination of a company's efficiency by using asset-specific ratios. *Accounts receivable turnover, inventory turnover, and fixed asset turnover can be used to measure how efficiently a company is using those assets.*

(6) Determine the degree of a company's financial leverage and its ability to repay loans using debt-related financial ratios. *Debt-related financial ratios give an indication of the degree of a company's leverage and how much cushion operating profits give in terms of being able to make periodic interest payments.*

(7) Use cash flow information to evaluate cash flow ratios. *Cash flow ratios are frequently overlooked because traditional analysis models are based on the balance sheet and the income statement.*

(8) Understand the limitations of financial statement analysis. *Analysis of financial statements can be misleading if statements are not comparable or if statements exclude significant information. In addition, analysis of historical data can distract one's attention from relevant current information.*

Microsoft was founded in 1975 by Bill Gates and Paul Allen. How successful has the company been? In terms of stock price, Microsoft's per-share stock price (adjusted for stock splits) has gone from $0.07 in 1986 to almost $27 in April of 2006 (see Exhibit 1). But as the graph illustrates, Microsoft's stock price is down from its historic high of $60 per share in 1999. An analysis of Microsoft's financial statements reveals some of the reasons for the declining stock price. That is the topic of this chapter—an introduction to financial statement analysis. With some basic analysis tools (called ratios), we will be able to conduct some fundamental analysis of a company's financial statements. Our analysis will provide us with insights as to a company's performance and will help us identify areas of concern. Keep in mind that this is merely an introduction to financial statement analysis. There are entire textbooks devoted to the analysis of financial statements. Our objective here is to expose you to some of the basic tools to help you start to understand what financial statements can tell us about the operations of a business. To illustrate the analysis techniques introduced in this chapter, we will reference the 2005 financial statements of Microsoft.

EXHIBIT 1   **History of Microsoft's Stock Price per Share**

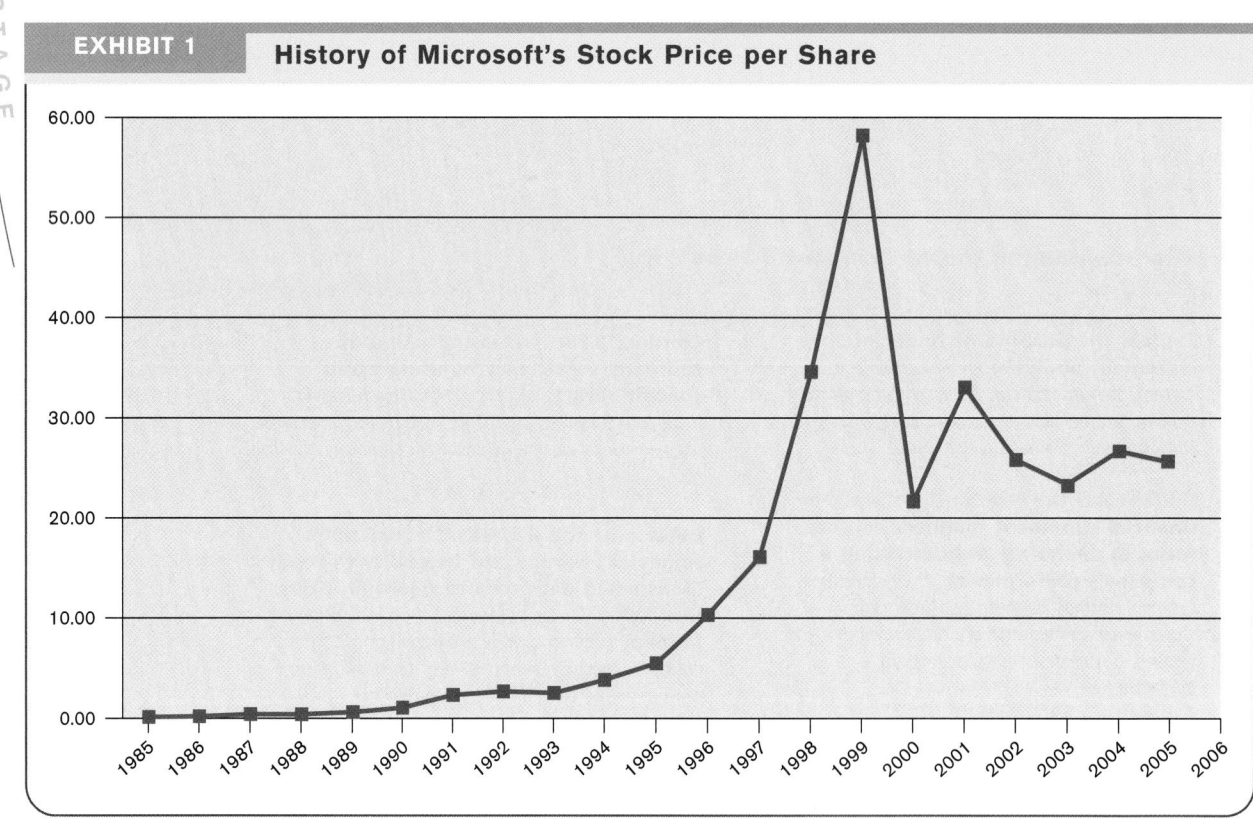

The Need for Financial Statement Analysis

Explain the purpose of financial statement analysis.

(1) Consider the following questions related to financial statement information for **Microsoft** in 2005:

- Microsoft's net income in 2005 was $12.254 billion. That seems like a lot, but does it represent a large amount for a company the size of Microsoft?
- Total assets for Microsoft at the end of 2005 were $70.815 billion. Given the volume of business that Microsoft does, is this amount of assets too much, too little, or just right?
- By the end of 2005, Microsoft's liabilities totaled $22.700 billion. Is this level of debt too much for Microsoft?

financial statement analysis

The examination of both the relationships among financial statement numbers and the trends in those numbers over time.

financial ratios

Relationships between financial statement amounts.

The important point to recognize is that just having the financial statement numbers is not enough to answer the questions that financial statement users want answered. Without further analysis, the raw numbers themselves don't tell much of a story.

Financial statement analysis involves the examination of both the relationships among financial statement numbers and the trends in those numbers over time. One purpose of financial statement analysis is to use the past performance of a company to predict how it will do in the future. Another purpose is to evaluate the performance of a company with an eye toward identifying problem areas. In sum, financial statement analysis is both diagnosis—identifying where a firm has problems—and prognosis—predicting how a firm will perform in the future.

Relationships between financial statement amounts are called **financial ratios**. Net income divided by sales, for example, is a financial ratio called return on sales, which tells you how many pennies of profit a company makes on each dollar of sales. The return on sales for Microsoft is 30.8%, meaning that Microsoft makes almost 31 cents' worth of profit for every dollar of product or service sold. There are hundreds of different financial ratios, each shedding light on a different aspect of the health of a company.

Exhibit 2 illustrates how financial statement analysis fits into the decision cycle of a company's management. Notice that the preparation of the financial statements is just the starting point of the process. After the statements are prepared, they are analyzed using techniques akin to those to be introduced in this chapter. Analysis of the summary information in the financial statements usually doesn't provide detailed answers to management's questions, but it does identify areas in which further data should be gathered. Decisions are then made and implemented, and the accounting system captures the results of these decisions so that a new set of financial statements can be prepared. The process then repeats itself.

 F Y I

Financial information is almost always compared to what was reported in the previous year. For example, when Microsoft publicly announced on January 26, 2006, that its quarterly revenues were $11.84 billion, the press release also stated that this amount represented a 9% increase over the same period in the prior year.

F Y I

Financial statement analysis often points to areas in which additional data must be gathered, including details of significant transactions, market share information, competitors' plans, and customer demand forecasts.

| EXHIBIT 2 | The Need for Financial Statement Analysis |

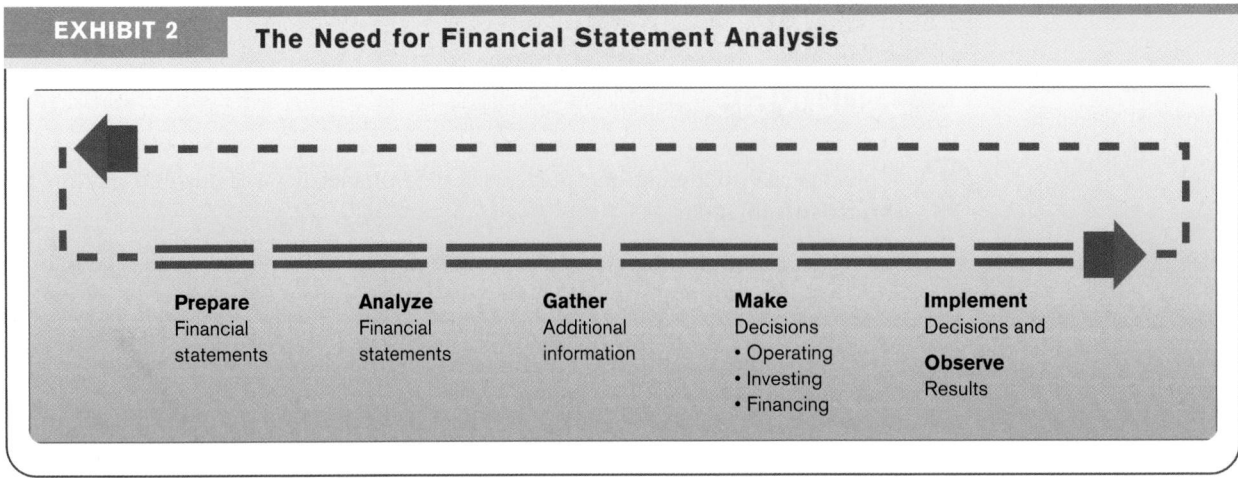

Prepare	Analyze	Gather	Make	Implement
Financial	Financial	Additional	Decisions	Decisions and
statements	statements	information	• Operating	
			• Investing	**Observe**
			• Financing	Results

For external users of financial statements, such as investors and creditors, financial statement analysis plays the same role in the decision-making process. Whereas management uses the analysis to help in making operating, investing, and financing decisions, investors and creditors analyze financial statements to decide whether to invest in, or loan money to, a company.

In analyzing a company's financial statements, merely computing a list of financial ratios is not enough. Most pieces of information are meaningful only when they can be compared with some benchmark. For example, knowing that Microsoft's return on sales in 2005 was 30.8% tells you a little, but you can evaluate the ratio value much better if you know that Microsoft's return on sales was 22.2% and 23.4% in 2004 and 2003, respectively. In short, the usefulness of financial ratios is greatly enhanced when they are compared with past values and with values for other firms in the same industry.

REMEMBER THIS...

- Financial statement analysis is used:
  - to predict a company's future profitability and cash flows from its past performance and
  - to evaluate the performance of a company with an eye toward identifying problem areas.
- The informativeness of financial ratios is greatly enhanced when they are compared:
  - with past values and
  - with values for other firms in the same industry.

Widely Used Financial Ratios

Understand the relationships between financial statement numbers and use ratios in analyzing and describing a company's performance.

(2) Before diving into a comprehensive treatment of financial ratio analysis, we'll first get our feet wet with the most widely used ratios. Familiarity with financial ratios will allow you to hold your own in most casual business conversations and will enable you to understand most ratios used in the popular business press. Data from Microsoft's 2005 financial statements will be used to illustrate the ratio calculations. The data are displayed in Exhibit 3.

Debt Ratio

Comparing the amount of liabilities with the amount of assets indicates the extent to which a company has borrowed money to leverage the owners' investments and increase the size of the company. One frequently used measure of leverage is the **debt ratio**, computed as total liabilities divided by total assets. An intuitive interpretation of the debt ratio is that it represents the proportion of borrowed funds used to acquire the company's assets. For Microsoft, the debt ratio is computed as follows:

debt ratio

A measure of leverage, computed by dividing total liabilities by total assets.

$$\text{Debt Ratio: } \frac{\text{Total Liabilities}}{\text{Total Assets}} = \frac{\$22,700}{\$70,815} = 32.1\%$$

In other words, Microsoft borrowed 32.1% of the money it needed to buy its assets.

Is 32.1% a good or bad debt ratio, or is it impossible to tell? If you are a banker thinking of lending money to Microsoft, you want Microsoft to have a low debt ratio because a smaller amount of other liabilities increases your chances of being repaid. If you are a Microsoft stockholder, you want a higher debt ratio because you want the company to add borrowed funds to your investment dollars to expand the business.

> **! CAUTION**
>
> The debt ratio is often confused with the debt-to-equity ratio and the asset-to-equity ratio. Each of these ratios is a measure of a company's leverage. However, each is computed slightly differently. Make sure when discussing a leverage ratio, it is understood which one is being used.

Thus, there is some happy middle ground where the debt ratio is not too high for creditors but not too low for investors. The general rule of thumb across all industries is that debt ratios should be around 50%, but this benchmark varies widely from one industry to the next. By comparison, **Apple Computer**'s 2005 debt ratio was 35.4%.

Current Ratio

liquidity

A company's ability to pay its debts in the short run.

An important concern about any company is its **liquidity**, or ability to pay its debts in the short run. If a firm can't meet its obligations in the short run, it may

EXHIBIT 3	Selected Financial Data for Microsoft for 2005	
Current assets		$ 48,737*
Total assets		70,815
Current liabilities		16,877
Total liabilities		22,700
Stockholders' equity		48,115
Sales		39,788
Net income		12,254
Market value of shares (as of June 30, 2006)		263,573

*All numbers are in millions of dollars.

current ratio

A measure of the liquidity of a business; equal to current assets divided by current liabilities.

not survive to enjoy the long run. The most commonly used measure of liquidity is the **current ratio**, which is a comparison of current assets (cash, receivables, and inventory) with current liabilities. Current ratio is computed by dividing total current assets by total current liabilities. For Microsoft, the current ratio is computed as follows:

$$\text{Current Ratio: } \frac{\text{Current Assets}}{\text{Current Liabilities}} = \frac{\$48,737}{\$16,877} = 2.888$$

Historically, the rule of thumb has been that a current ratio below 2 suggests the possibility of liquidity problems. However, advances in information technology have enabled companies to be much more effective in minimizing the need to hold cash, inventories, and other current assets. As a result, current ratios for successful companies these days are frequently less than 1. Current ratios for selected U.S. companies are shown in Exhibit 4.

Return on Sales

return on sales

A measure of the amount of profit earned per dollar of sales, computed by dividing net income by sales.

As mentioned earlier, Microsoft makes 30.8 cents of profit on each dollar of sales. This ratio is called **return on sales** and, using Microsoft's numbers, is computed as follows:

$$\text{Return on Sales: } \frac{\text{Net Income}}{\text{Sales}} = \frac{\$12,254}{\$39,788} = 30.8\%$$

As with all ratios, the return-on-sales value for Microsoft must be evaluated in light of the appropriate industry. For example, the 2004 return on sales for Microsoft was 22.2%. At the other end of the spectrum, return on sales in the supermarket industry is frequently between 1% and 2%. These values, because they come from outside Microsoft's industry, do not really provide a useful benchmark against which Microsoft's return on sales can be compared. A better comparison for Microsoft is the 2005 return-on-sales value for Apple Computer, which was 9.6%. So, it appears that return on sales for Microsoft was substantially above the industry average in 2005; why this happened will be examined later in the chapter.

Asset Turnover

asset turnover

A measure of company efficiency, computed by dividing sales by total assets.

Microsoft's balance sheet reveals total assets of $70.815 billion. Are those assets being used efficiently? A financial ratio that gives an overall measure of company efficiency is called **asset turnover** and is computed as follows:

$$\text{Asset Turnover: } \frac{\text{Sales}}{\text{Total Assets}} = \frac{\$39,788}{\$70,815} = 0.56$$

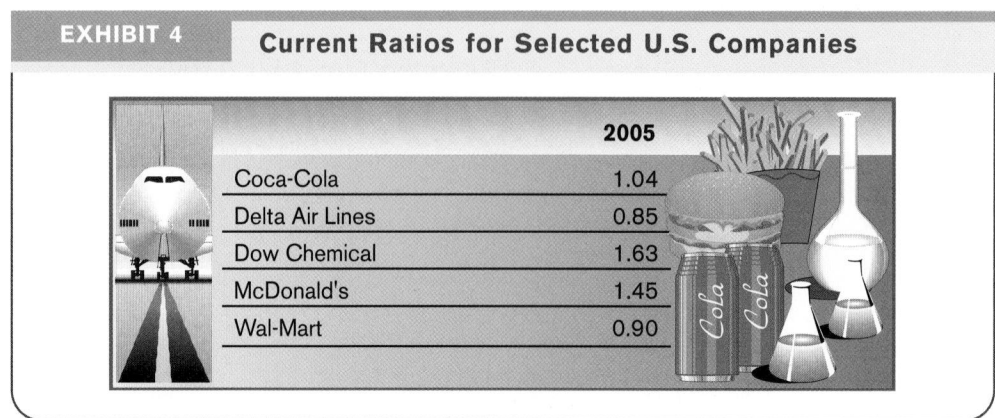

EXHIBIT 4	Current Ratios for Selected U.S. Companies

	2005
Coca-Cola	1.04
Delta Air Lines	0.85
Dow Chemical	1.63
McDonald's	1.45
Wal-Mart	0.90

CAUTION

The computed asset turnover ratio can be misleading, as discussed in the concluding section of this chapter, because not all economic assets are recorded as assets on the balance sheet. Thus, the denominator of the ratio can be understated, sometimes very significantly.

Microsoft's asset turnover ratio of 0.56 means that for each dollar of assets Microsoft is able to generate $0.56 in sales. The higher the asset turnover ratio, the more efficient the company is at using its assets to generate sales. In evaluating Microsoft's asset turnover, note that asset turnover for Apple Computer in 2005 was 1.21, indicating that Microsoft was less efficient than its competitor at using its assets to generate sales.

Return on Equity

return on equity

A measure of the amount of profit earned per dollar of investment, computed by dividing net income by equity.

What investors really want to know is not how many pennies of profit are earned on a dollar of sales or what the current ratio is—they want to know how much profit they earn for each dollar they invest. This amount, called **return on equity**, is the overall measure of the performance of a company. Return on equity for Microsoft is computed as follows:

$$\text{Return on Equity: } \frac{\text{Net Income}}{\text{Stockholders' Equity}} = \frac{\$12,254}{\$48,115} = 25.5\%$$

Microsoft's return on equity of 25.5% means that 25.5 cents of profit were earned for each dollar of stockholder investment in 2005. By comparison, Apple Computer's return on equity in 2005 was 17.9%. Good companies typically have return on equity values between 15% and 25%. Return on equity is the fundamental measure of overall company performance and forms the basis of the DuPont framework discussed later on.

Price-Earnings Ratio

price-earnings ratio

A measure of growth potential, earnings stability, and management capabilities; computed by dividing market value of a company by net income.

If a company earned $100 this year, how much should I pay to buy that company? If I expect the company to make more in the future, I'd be willing to pay a higher price than if I expected the company to make less. Also, I'd probably be willing to pay a bit more for a stable company than for one that experiences wild swings in earnings. The relationship between the market value of a company and that company's current earnings is measured by the **price-earnings ratio**, or PE ratio, and is computed by dividing the market value of the shares outstanding by the company's net income.[1] Microsoft's PE ratio at the end of 2005 was:

$$\text{PE Ratio: } \frac{\text{Market Value of Shares}}{\text{Net Income}} = \frac{\$263,573}{\$12,254} = 21.5$$

In the United States, PE ratios typically range between 5 and 30. High PE ratios are associated with firms for which strong growth is predicted in the future. **Google**, for example, has a high PE ratio, but it is not found on the list of companies with high net income. The reason Google is valued so highly is that it is expected to continue to grow so rapidly in the future that its current income is small compared with what investors are expecting in the future. This expected future growth is reflected in Google's PE ratio of about 80 (in 2006). Sample PE ratios for several companies as of April 14, 2006, are included in Exhibit 5.

A summary of the financial ratios discussed in this section is presented in Exhibit 6.

---

[1] The PE ratio can be equivalently computed using per share amounts: PE ratio = Market price per share/Earnings per share.

EXHIBIT 5	Sample PE Ratios for Several U.S. Companies	

Company Name	Stock Ticker Symbol	PE Ratio
Yahoo!	Yhoo	24.4
Wal-Mart	wmt	17.1
Berkshire Hathaway	brka	15.7
Home Depot	hd	15.1
Sears	shld	24.9

EXHIBIT 6	Summary of Selected Financial Ratios	

1. Debt ratio	$\dfrac{\text{Total liabilities}}{\text{Total assets}}$	Percentage of funds needed to purchase assets that were obtained through borrowing.
2. Current ratio	$\dfrac{\text{Current assets}}{\text{Current liabilities}}$	Measure of liquidity; number of times current assets could cover current liabilities.
3. Return on sales	$\dfrac{\text{Net income}}{\text{Sales}}$	Number of pennies earned during the year on each dollar of sales.
4. Asset turnover	$\dfrac{\text{Sales}}{\text{Total assets}}$	Number of dollars of sales during the year generated by each dollar of assets.
5. Return on equity (ROE)	$\dfrac{\text{Net income}}{\text{Stockholders' equity}}$	Number of pennies earned during the year on each dollar invested.
6. Price-earnings ratio (PE)	$\dfrac{\text{Market value of shares}}{\text{Net income}}$	Amount investors are willing to pay for each dollar of earnings; indication of growth potential.

Note that the PE ratio is different from the other ratios in that it is not the ratio of two financial statement numbers. Instead, the PE ratio is a comparison of a financial statement number to a market value number. The large majority of financial ratios, however, are (1) a comparison of two amounts found in the same financial statement (such as return on sales, which compares two income statement amounts) or (2) a comparison of two amounts from different financial statements (such as asset turnover, which compares an income statement and a balance sheet amount). These two types of ratios are illustrated in Exhibit 7.

In looking at Exhibit 7, you might justifiably conclude that the cash flow statement is completely ignored when computing financial ratios. Unfortunately, that is often true. Relative to the other two primary financial statements, the statement of cash flows is relatively new (the balance sheet and the income statement have been a part of accounting since its invention—the statement of cash flows has only been required since 1988). As a result, ratios involving balance sheet and income statement accounts have been in existence for decades. Given the newness of the statement of cash flows, standardized ratios are still developing. The **Enron** accounting scandal highlighted the usefulness of ratios involving cash flow information (see Analytical Assignment 14-73 in the end-of-chapter material). To make sure you don't fall victim to the oversight of ignoring cash flow ratios, we include a special section on cash flow ratios later in this chapter.

EXHIBIT 7 — **Financial Ratios and the Relationships among the Financial Statements**

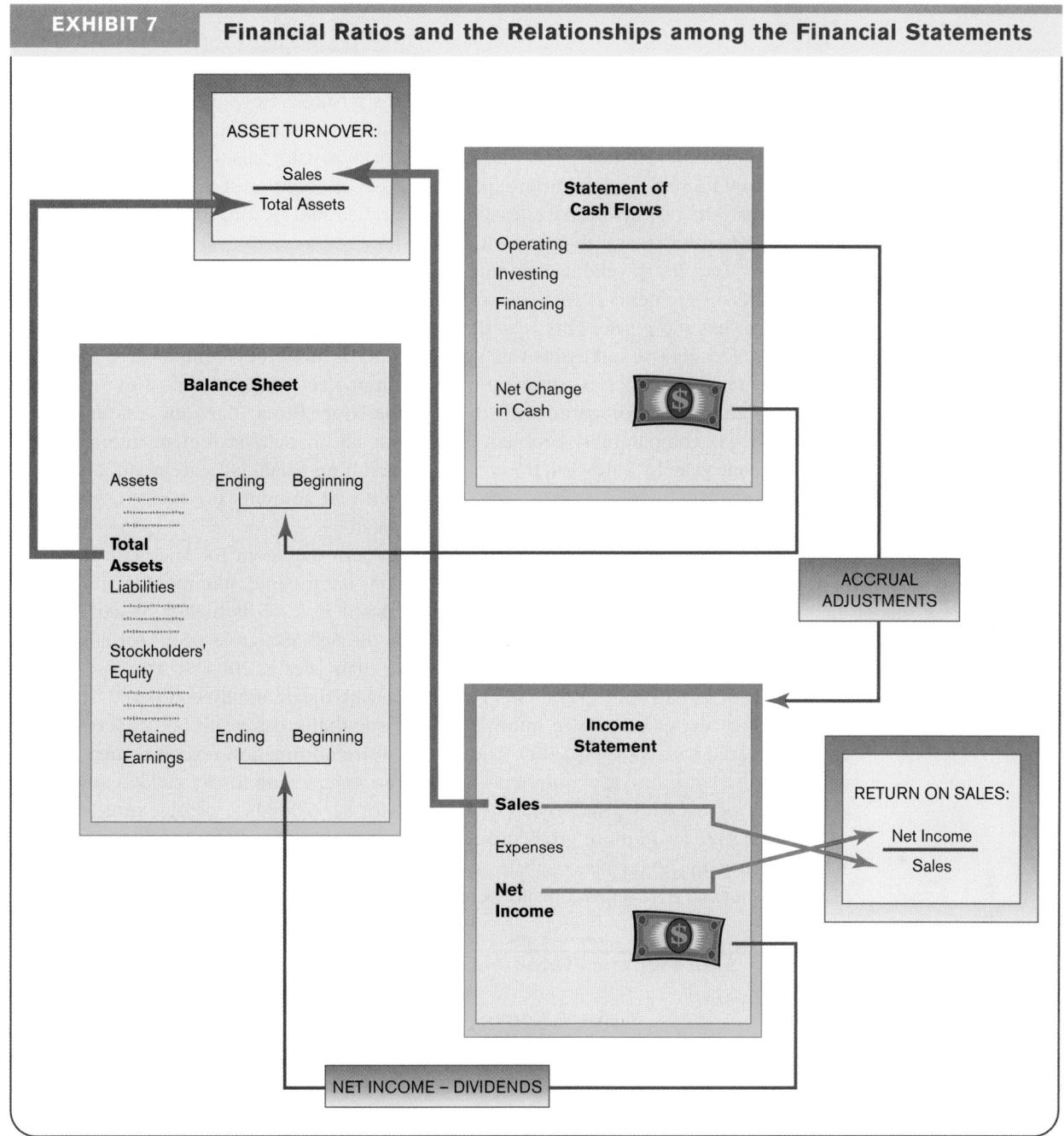

REMEMBER THIS...

Financial ratios result from the relationship between two financial statement numbers.

- **Debt ratio:** Percentage of company funding that is borrowed.
- **Current ratio:** Indication of a company's ability to pay its short-term debts.
- **Return on sales:** Pennies in profit on each dollar of sales.
- **Asset turnover:** Measure of efficiency; number of sales dollars generated by each dollar of assets.
- **Return on equity:** Pennies in profit for each dollar invested by stockholders.
- **Price-earnings ratio:** Number of dollars an investor must pay to "buy" the future rights to each dollar of current earnings.

Common-Size Financial Statements

Use common-size financial statements to perform comparison of financial statements across years and between companies.

③ Financial statement analysis is sometimes wrongly viewed as just the computation of a bunch of financial ratios—divide every financial statement number by every other number. This shotgun approach usually fails to lead to any concrete conclusions. This section explains the use of common-size financial statements that are easy to prepare, easy to use, and should be the first step in any comprehensive financial statement analysis.

The first problem encountered when using comparative data to analyze financial statements is that the scale, or size, of the numbers is usually different. If a firm has more sales this year than last year, it is now a larger company and the levels of expenses and assets this year can't be meaningfully compared to the levels last year. In addition, if a company is of medium size in its industry, how can its financial statements be compared with those of the larger firms? The quickest and easiest solution to this comparability problem is to divide all financial statement numbers for a given year by sales for the year. The resulting financial statements are called **common-size financial statements**, with all amounts for a given year being shown as a percentage of sales for that year.

Exhibit 8 contains a common-size income statement for Microsoft for 2005. To illustrate the usefulness of a common-size income statement, consider the question of whether Microsoft's gross profit in 2005 is higher. In comparison with the gross profit of $30,119 in 2004, the $33,588 gross profit for 2005 looks pretty good. But sales in 2005 are higher than sales in 2004, so the absolute levels of gross profit in the two years cannot be meaningfully compared. But looking at the common-size information, we see that gross profit is 81.8% of sales in 2004 compared with 84.4% in 2005. The common-size information reveals something that was not apparent in the raw numbers—in 2004 an item selling for $1 yielded an average gross profit of just 81.8¢; in 2005 an item selling for $1 yielded an average gross profit of 84.4¢. Microsoft made more gross profit from each dollar of sales in 2005 than in 2004. The news is even better because the 2005 gross profit represents a continuation of the increase from the 81.2% gross profit percentage in 2003.

common-size financial statements

Financial statements achieved by dividing all financial statement numbers by total sales for the year.

EXHIBIT 8	**Common-Size Income Statement for Microsoft**

Microsoft Corporation
Income Statement
For Years Ended June 30
(in millions)

Year Ended June 30	2003	%	2004	%	2005	%
Revenue	32,187	100.0%	36,835	100.0%	**39,788**	100.0%
Cost of revenue	6,059	18.8%	6,716	18.2%	**6,200**	15.6%
Gross profit on sales	26,128	81.2%	30,119	81.8%	**33,588**	84.4%
Operating expenses:						
Research and development	6,595	20.5%	7,779	21.1%	**6,184**	15.5%
Sales and marketing	7,562	23.5%	8,309	22.6%	**8,677**	21.8%
General and administrative	2,426	7.5%	4,997	13.6%	**4,166**	10.5%
Total operating expenses	16,583	51.5%	21,085	57.2%*	**19,027**	47.8%
Operating income	9,545	29.7%	9,034	24.5%*	**14,561**	36.6%
Investment income and other	1,509	4.7%	3,162	8.6%	**2,067**	5.2%
Income before income taxes	11,054	34.3%*	12,196	33.1%	**16,628**	41.8%
Provision for income taxes	3,523	10.9%	4,028	10.9%	**4,374**	11.0%
Net income	7,531	23.4%	8,168	22.2%	**12,254**	30.8%

*Note: Because of rounding, the percentages don't always add up exactly. This is a minor arithmetic problem that shouldn't get in the way of the analysis.

Each item on the income statement can be analyzed in the same way. In 2005, income before income taxes was 41.8% of sales compared with 33.1% in 2004. Operating expenses as a percentage of sales decreased sharply from 2004 to 2005 (57.2% vs. 47.8%) indicating the increase in operating income in 2005 related mainly to a decrease in the operating expense percentage. With a common-size income statement, each of the income statement items can be examined in this way, yielding much more information than just looking at the raw income statement numbers.

At this point, you should be saying to yourself: "Yes, but what is the exact explanation for Microsoft's increase in gross profit percentage in 2005? And why did regular operating expenses decrease?" These questions illustrate the usefulness and the limitations of financial statement analysis. Our quick analysis of Microsoft's income statement has pointed out the major areas in which Microsoft has experienced significant income statement change in the past two years. But the only way to find out why these financial statement numbers changed is to gather information from outside the financial statements—ask management, read press releases, talk to financial analysts who follow the firm, read industry newsletters, and dig into the notes to the financial statements. In short, financial statement analysis usually doesn't tell you the final answers, but it

does suggest which questions you should be asking and where you should look to find the answers.

A common-size balance sheet also expresses each amount as a percentage of sales for the year. As an illustration, a comparative balance sheet for Microsoft with each item expressed in both dollar amounts and percentages is shown in Exhibit 9.

The most informative section of the common-size balance sheet is the asset section, which can be used to determine how efficiently a company is using its assets. For example, looking at total assets for Microsoft in 2004 and 2005, you see the company's total assets were $70,815 in 2005. Did Microsoft manage its assets more efficiently in 2005 than in 2004 when total assets were $94,368? Comparing the raw numbers can't give a clear answer because Microsoft's level of sales is different in the two years. The common-size balance sheet indicates that each dollar of sales in 2004 required assets in place of $2.562, whereas each dollar of sales in 2005 required assets of just $1.780. So in which of the two years was Microsoft more efficient at using its assets to generate sales? Microsoft was more efficient in 2005, when each dollar of sales required a lower level of assets.

Specific ratios related to asset efficiency have been introduced in earlier chapters. Those ratios will be reviewed in a later section of this chapter.

Common-size financial statements are not a sophisticated analytical tool, and they don't constitute a complete analysis. However, they are the easiest, most intuitive, and fastest tool available, and they should be included in the initial stages of any comprehensive analysis of financial statements.

EXHIBIT 9	Common-Size Balance Sheet for Microsoft			
30-Jun	**2004**		**2005**	
Assets				
Current assets:				
Cash and equivalents	14,304	38.8%	4,851	12.2%
Short-term investments	46,288	125.7%	32,900	82.7%
Total cash and short-term investments	60,592	164.5%	37,751	94.9%
Accounts receivable, net	5,890	16.0%	7,180	18.0%
Inventories	421	1.1%	491	1.2%
Deferred income taxes	2,097	5.7%	1,701	4.3%
Other	1,566	4.3%	1,614	4.1%
Total current assets	70,566	191.6%	48,737	122.5%
Property and equipment, net	2,326	6.3%	2,346	5.9%
Equity and other investments	12,210	33.1%	11,004	27.7%
Goodwill	3,115	8.5%	3,309	8.3%
Intangible assets, net	569	1.5%	499	1.3%
Deferred income taxes	3,808	10.3%	3,621	9.1%
Other long-term assets	1,774	4.8%	1,299	3.3%
Total assets	94,368	256.2%*	70,815	178.0%*
Liabilities and stockholders' equity				
Current liabilities:				
Accounts payable	1,717	4.7%	2,086	5.2%
Accrued compensation	1,339	3.6%	1,662	4.2%
Income taxes	3,478	9.4%	2,020	5.1%
Short-term unearned revenue	6,514	17.7%	7,502	18.9%
Other	1,921	5.2%	3,607	9.1%
Total current liabilities	14,969	40.6%	16,877	42.4%*
Long-term unearned revenue	1,663	4.5%	1,665	4.2%
Other long-term liabilities	2,911	7.9%	4,158	10.5%
Total liabilities	19,543	53.1%*	22,700	57.1%
Stockholders' equity:				
Common stock and paid-in capital	56,396	153.1%	60,413	151.8%
Retained earnings, including accumulated other comprehensive income of $1,119 and $1,426	18,429	50.0%	(12,298)	(30.9%)
Total stockholders' equity	74,825	203.1%	48,115	120.9%
Total liabilities and stockholders' equity	94,368	256.2%*	70,815	178.0%

*Note: Because of rounding, the percentages don't always add up exactly. This is a minor arithmetic problem that shouldn't get in the way of the analysis.

REMEMBER THIS...

- Common-size financial statements are generated by dividing all financial statement amounts for a given year by sales for that year.
- A common-size income statement reveals the number of pennies of each expense for each dollar of sales.
- The asset section of a common-size balance sheet tells how many pennies of each asset are needed to generate each dollar of sales.

DuPont Framework

4 As discussed earlier, return on equity (net income ÷ equity) is the single measure that summarizes the financial health of a company. Return on equity can be interpreted as the number of cents of net income an investor earns in one year by investing one dollar in the company. As a very rough rule of thumb, return on equity (ROE) consistently above 15% is a sign of a company in good health; ROE consistently below 15% is a sign of trouble. Return on equity for Microsoft for the years 2005 and 2004 is computed as follows.

Understand the DuPont framework and how return on equity can be decomposed into its profitability, efficiency, and leverage components.

	2005	2004
Net income	$12,254	$8,168
Stockholders' equity	$48,115	$74,825
Return on equity	25.5%	10.9%

What can we say about Microsoft's overall performance in 2005? It was good relative to the rough ROE benchmark of 15%, and it increased significantly when compared to the ROE of 2004. But how do we pin down the exact reason or reasons for any change in a company's ROE? The answer is the focus of this section.

DuPont framework

A systematic approach for breaking down return on equity into three ratios: return on sales, asset turnover, and assets-to-equity ratio.

The **DuPont framework** (named after a system of ratio analysis developed 70 years ago at DuPont by F. Donaldson Brown) provides a systematic approach to identifying general factors causing ROE to deviate from normal. The DuPont system also provides a framework for computation of financial ratios to yield a more in-depth analysis of a company's areas of strength and weakness. The insight behind the DuPont framework is that ROE can be decomposed into three components as shown in Exhibit 10.

For each of the three ROE components—profitability, efficiency, and leverage—there is one ratio that summarizes a company's performance in that area. These ratios are as follows:

assets-to-equity ratio

A measure of the number of dollars of assets a company is able to acquire using each dollar of equity; calculated by dividing assets by equity.

- **Return on sales** is computed as net income divided by sales and is interpreted as the number of pennies in profit generated from each dollar of sales.
- **Asset turnover** is computed as sales divided by assets and is interpreted as the number of dollars in sales generated by each dollar of assets.
- **Assets-to-equity ratio** is computed as assets divided by equity and is interpreted as the number of dollars of assets acquired for each dollar invested by stockholders.

The DuPont analysis of Microsoft's ROE for 2005 and 2004 is as follows:

			Profitability	×	Efficiency	×	Leverage
	Return on Equity	=	$\dfrac{\text{Net Income}}{\text{Sales}}$	×	$\dfrac{\text{Sales}}{\text{Assets}}$	×	$\dfrac{\text{Assets}}{\text{Equity}}$
2005	25.5%	=	$\dfrac{\$12,254}{\$39,788}$	×	$\dfrac{\$39,788}{\$70,815}$	×	$\dfrac{\$70,815}{\$48,115}$
		=	30.8%	×	0.56	×	1.47
2004	10.9%	=	$\dfrac{\$8,168}{\$36,835}$	×	$\dfrac{\$36,835}{\$94,368}$	×	$\dfrac{\$94,368}{\$74,825}$
		=	22.2%	×	0.39	×	1.26

EXHIBIT 10   **Analysis of ROE Using the DuPont Framework**

Return on Equity   =   Profitability   ×   Efficiency   ×   Leverage

=   Return on Sales   ×   Asset Turnover   ×   Assets-to-Equity Ratio

$$= \frac{\text{Net Income}}{\text{Sales}} \times \frac{\text{Sales}}{\text{Assets}} \times \frac{\text{Assets}}{\text{Equity}}$$

Profitability = The company's ability to generate net income per dollar of sales
Efficiency = The ability of the company to generate sales through the use of assets
Leverage = The degree to which a company uses borrowed funds instead of invested funds

The results of the DuPont analysis suggest that Microsoft's ROE was lower in 2004 for the following reasons:

1. In 2004, each sale was less profitable than in 2005: each dollar of sales produced 30.8¢ of profit in 2005, compared to 22.2¢ in 2004.
2. In 2004, assets were used less efficiently to generate sales: each dollar of assets generated $0.39 in sales in 2004 compared to $0.56 in sales in 2005.

In 2005, Microsoft was also slightly more effective at leveraging stockholders' investment. Through the use of liabilties, Microsoft was able to turn each dollar of invested funds in 2005 into $1.47 of assets, more than the $1.26 in assets in 2004.

The DuPont analysis allows a financial statement user to begin to answer the question of "Why?" Why did a company's return on equity increase (or decrease) during a period? What has been the trend over time in each of the three areas of profitability, efficiency, and leverage? Answers to these questions will allow the user to begin to focus attention on those areas of the business that have experienced changes as reflected in the ratios.

This preliminary DuPont analysis is only the beginning of a proper ratio analysis. If a DuPont analysis suggests problems in any of the three ROE components, additional ratios in each area can shed more light on the exact nature of the problem.

One of the insights behind the DuPont framework is that overall company performance is a function of both the profitability of each sale, measured by return on sales, and the ability to use assets to generate sales, measured by asset turnover. For example, comparing Microsoft and Apple indicates that Microsoft is better than Apple Computer in terms of profitability (2005 return on sales of 30.8% for Microsoft compared to just 9.6% for Apple) but is worse in terms of efficiency (2005 asset turnover of 0.56 for Microsoft and 1.21 for Apple).

Profitability Ratios

When the DuPont calculations indicate that a company has a profitability problem, then a common-size income statement can be used to identify which expenses are causing the problem. Referring back to the common-size income statement in Exhibit 8, cost of goods sold as a percentage of sales was higher in 2004 than in 2005 (18.2% vs. 15.6%). In addition, operating expenses were also higher in 2004 (57.2% compared to just 47.8% in 2005). To summarize, the return on sales indicates overall whether a firm has a problem with the profitability of each dollar of sales; the common-size income statement can be used to pinpoint exactly which expenses are causing the problem.

Efficiency Ratios

The asset turnover ratio suggests that Microsoft was less efficient at using its assets to generate sales in 2004 than it was in 2005. But which assets were causing this decreased efficiency? One way to get a quick indication is to review the common-size balance sheet in Exhibit 9, whose numbers indicate that in 2004 Microsoft had a much higher amount of cash and short-term investments as a percentage of sales (164.5%) than in 2005 (94.9%), suggesting that Microsoft was not using a very large part of the company's assets in an income-producing fashion in 2004.

In addition to the common-size balance sheet, specific financial ratios have been developed to indicate whether a firm is holding too much or too little of a particular asset. Some of these additional ratios were introduced earlier in the text. These efficiency ratios are reviewed later in this chapter.

leverage
Borrowing that allows a company to purchase more assets than its stockholders are able to pay for through their own investment.

Leverage Ratios

Leverage ratios are an indication of the extent to which a company is using other people's money to purchase assets. **Leverage** is borrowing that allows a company to purchase more assets than its stockholders are able to pay for through their own investment. The assets-to-equity ratios for Microsoft for 2004 and 2005 indicate that leverage was higher in 2005 (1.26 in 2004; 1.47 in 2005). Higher leverage increases return on equity through the following chain of events:

- More borrowing means that more assets can be purchased without any additional equity investment by stockholders.
- More assets mean that more sales can be generated.
- More sales mean that net income should increase.

STOP & THINK

Company Z has an assets-to-equity ratio of 2.5. Can you compute what its debt ratio would be?

Investors generally prefer high leverage in order to increase the size of their company without increasing their investment, but lenders prefer low leverage to increase the safety of their debt. The field of corporate finance deals with how to optimally balance these opposing tendencies and choose the perfect capital structure for a firm. As mentioned earlier, a general rule of thumb is that large U.S. companies borrow about half of the funds they use to purchase assets. There are specific ratios that allow financial statement users to analyze the leverage of a firm. Those ratios were introduced in the chapter on debt (Chapter 10). Those ratios are reviewed later in this chapter.

Exhibit 11 show the DuPont framework ratios for a number of familiar companies for 2005.

Note that although **Wal-Mart** has the lowest return on sales, it does have one of the highest returns on equity. The reason becomes readily apparent by looking at the components of return on equity. Wal-Mart has the highest asset turnover of the companies

EXHIBIT 11	**DuPont Framework Ratios for Selected U.S. Companies**

	ROE	Return on Sales	Asset Turnover	Assets-to-Equity Ratio
Disney	9.7%	7.9%	0.6	2.0
Wal-Mart	21.1%	3.6%	2.3	2.6
Home Depot	21.7%	7.2%	1.8	1.7
Federal Express	13.0%	4.3%	1.5	2.1
Southwest Airlines	8.2%	7.2%	0.5	2.1

Information for financial analysis comes from many sources. Electronic media offer a wealth of information that can be timelier than print sources of financial information.

© DIGITAL VISION/GETTY IMAGES INC.

included in the list as well as having the highest assets-to-equity ratio. Wal-Mart's efficiency and leverage combine to make for a high return on equity.

Remember, the preparation of financial statements by the accountant is not the end of the process but just the beginning. The statements are then analyzed by investors, creditors, and management to detect signs of existing deficiencies in performance and to predict how the firm will perform in the future. As repeated throughout this section, proper interpretation of a ratio depends on comparing the ratio value to the value for the same firm in the previous year and to values for other firms in the same industry. Finally, ratio analysis doesn't reveal the answers to a company's problems, but it does highlight areas in which further information should be gathered to find those answers.

REMEMBER THIS...

The DuPont framework decomposes return on equity (ROE) into three areas:

- **Profitability.** Return on sales is computed as net income divided by sales and is interpreted as the number of pennies in profit generated from each dollar of sales.

- **Efficiency.** Asset turnover is computed as sales divided by assets and is interpreted as the number of dollars in sales generated by each dollar of assets.

- **Leverage.** Assets-to-equity ratio is computed as assets divided by equity and is interpreted as the number of dollars of assets a company is able to acquire using each dollar invested by stockholders.

More Efficiency Ratios

Conduct a focused examination of a company's efficiency by using asset-specific ratios.

(5) In earlier chapters, we learned how accounts receivable turnover, inventory turnover, and fixed asset turnover can be used to measure how efficiently a company is using those assets. Those discussions are summarized in this section. In the preceding sections of this chapter, we have used the financial numbers for Microsoft to illustrate the computation of ratios. Because Microsoft has a relatively low level of inventory and property, plant, and equipment, different company illustrations are used in this section. The two companies that will be used to illustrate the computation of the asset efficiency ratios are **ExxonMobil** and **Chevron**, both in the oil production, refining, and retailing business. Selected financial statement numbers for these two companies for 2005 are as follows:

(in millions of dollars)	ExxonMobil	Chevron
Sales	$370,680	$198,200
Cost of goods sold	185,219	127,968
Accounts receivable (average)	26,422	14,807
Inventory (average)	7,994	2,962
Property, plant, and equipment (average)	107,825	54,074

Accounts Receivable Efficiency

The accounts receivable turnover ratio is a computation of how many times during the year a company is "turning over" or collecting its receivables. It is a measure of how many times old receivables are collected and replaced by new receivables. Accounts receivable turnover is calculated as follows:

$$\text{Accounts Receivable Turnover} = \frac{\text{Sales Revenue}}{\text{Average Accounts Receivable}}$$

The accounts receivable turnover ratios for ExxonMobil and Chevron for 2005 are computed as follows:

$$\text{ExxonMobil} = \frac{\$370,680}{\$26,422} = 14.03 \text{ times}$$

$$\text{Chevron} = \frac{\$198,200}{\$14,807} = 13.39 \text{ times}$$

It appears that ExxonMobil turns its receivables over slightly more frequently than does Chevron.

Accounts receivable turnover can be converted into the number of days it takes to collect receivables by computing average collection period. Average collection period is computed by dividing 365 (or the number of days in a year) by the accounts receivable turnover as follows:

$$\text{Average Collection Period} = \frac{365}{\text{Accounts Receivable Turnover}}$$

The average collection periods for ExxonMobil and Chevron for 2005 are computed as follows:

$$\text{ExxonMobil} = \frac{365}{14.03 \text{ times}} = 26.0 \text{ days}$$

$$\text{Chevron} = \frac{365}{13.39 \text{ times}} = 27.3 \text{ days}$$

The computation of average collection period allows us to more easily see that there really isn't much difference between the receivables collection practices of ExxonMobil and Chevron—ExxonMobil collects its receivables just 1.3 days sooner, on average.

Inventory Efficiency

Inventory turnover provides a measure of how many times a company turns over, or replenishes, its inventory during a year. The calculation is similar to the calculation for accounts receivable turnover.

$$\text{Inventory Turnover} = \frac{\text{Cost of Goods Sold}}{\text{Average Inventory}}$$

The inventory turnover ratios for ExxonMobil and Chevron for 2005 are computed as follows:

$$\text{ExxonMobil} = \frac{\$185,219}{\$7,994} = 23.17 \text{ times}$$

$$\text{Chevron} = \frac{\$127,968}{\$2,962} = 43.20 \text{ times}$$

From these computations we can see that Chevron is managing its level of inventory much more aggressively than is ExxonMobil. Inventory turnover can also be converted into the number of days' sales in inventory. This ratio is computed by dividing 365 by the inventory turnover, as follows:

$$\text{Number of Days' Sales in Inventory} = \frac{365}{\text{Inventory Turnover}}$$

The number of days' sales in inventory for ExxonMobil and Chevron for 2005 are computed as follows:

$$\text{ExxonMobil} = \frac{365}{23.17 \text{ times}} = 15.8 \text{ days}$$

$$\text{Chevron} = \frac{365}{43.20 \text{ times}} = 8.4 \text{ days}$$

ExxonMobil has a level of inventory that is almost twice as large, in terms of the number of days' sales that the inventory level represents, as Chevron's inventory. A deeper understanding of the underlying reasons for this substantial difference would require an in-depth analysis of the specific inventory management practices of the two companies.

Property, Plant, and Equipment Efficiency

Fixed asset turnover can be used to evaluate the appropriateness of the level of a company's property, plant, and equipment. Fixed asset turnover is computed as sales divided by average property, plant, and equipment (fixed assets) and is interpreted as the number of dollars in sales generated by each dollar of fixed assets. This ratio is also often called PP&E turnover. The computations of the fixed asset turnover for ExxonMobil and Chevron are shown below.

$$\text{ExxonMobil} = \frac{\$370,680}{\$107,825} = 3.44 \text{ times}$$

$$\text{Chevron} = \frac{\$198,200}{\$54,074} = 3.67 \text{ times}$$

These fixed asset turnover calculations suggest that Chevron is slightly more efficient at using its property, plant, and equipment to generate sales than is ExxonMobil. However, unlike what we found in our analysis of the two companies' inventory management practices, the difference in fixed asset turnover is relatively small.

REMEMBER THIS...

Ratios to assess the level of accounts receivable:
- Accounts receivable turnover (Sales Revenue ÷ Average Accounts Receivable)
- Average collection period (365 ÷ Accounts Receivable Turnover)

Ratios to assess the level of inventory:
- Inventory turnover (Cost of Goods Sold ÷ Average Inventory)
- Number of days' sales in inventory (365 ÷ Inventory Turnover)

Ratio to assess the level of property, plant, and equipment:
- Fixed asset turnover (Sales Revenue ÷ Average Property, Plant, and Equipment)

More Leverage Ratios

(6) As we saw in our consideration of the DuPont framework earlier in this chapter, the amount of a company's financial leverage has a direct impact on that company's return on equity—the higher the leverage, the higher the return on equity. One leverage-related ratio, the debt ratio, was discussed earlier in this chapter in the section on widely-used ratios. This section reviews the debt-to-equity ratio and the times interest earned ratio which were first introduced in Chapter 10. As with the preceding section on efficiency ratios, 2005 financial statement information for ExxonMobil and Chevron will be used to illustrate the computation of these ratios. That information is given below.

(in millions of dollars)	ExxonMobil	Chevron
Total assets	$208,335	$125,833
Total liabilities	97,149	63,157
Total stockholders' equity	111,186	62,676
Operating profit	59,928	25,679
Interest expense	496	482

Debt-to-Equity Ratio

The debt-to-equity ratio reflects the mix of sources of financing for a company. This ratio is calculated by dividing total liabilities by total stockholders' equity. The ratio has a value of 1.0 if the amount of borrowing is exactly equal to the amount of stockholder investment. The higher the debt-to-equity ratio, the more debt the company has. The debt-to-equity ratios for ExxonMobil and Chevron for 2005 are computed as follows:

$$\text{ExxonMobil} = \frac{\$97,149}{\$111,186} = 0.87$$

$$\text{Chevron} = \frac{\$63,157}{\$62,676} = 1.01$$

Chevron's liabilities are a little higher than its stockholders' equity yielding a debt-to-equity ratio of 1.01. Another way to view this is that Chevron has borrowed a little bit more than half of its total financing needs which is a somewhat higher proportion than what ExxonMobil has borrowed.

Students are frequently confused about the differences among the debt ratio, the debt-to-equity ratio, and the assets-to-equity ratio. All three of these ratios represent the same thing—the relationship between the amount of a company's borrowing and the amount of a company's stockholder investment. However, because each of the ratios is computed a little differently, the resulting numbers are not comparable. This is exactly analogous to the interpretation of temperatures from different scales. A temperature of 0° on the Celsius scale corresponds to 32° on the Fahrenheit scale. If someone tells you that the temperature is 40°, in order to interpret that information you first need to know what temperature scale is being used—40° on the Celsius scale is a lot different from 40° on the Fahrenheit scale. Similarly, a debt-related ratio of 1.00 (or 100%) means the following very different things for each of the three debt-related ratios mentioned above.

- Debt-to-equity ratio—A ratio value of 1.00 means that total liabilities and total stockholders' equity are equal.
- Debt ratio—A ratio value of 1.00, or 100%, means that ALL of the company's financing has come from debt and that there is no stockholder investment at all.
- Assets-to-equity ratio—A ratio value of 1.00 means that total assets and total stockholders' equity are equal to each other, implying that there are no liabilities.

Whenever you see a computed value for a debt-related ratio, make sure that you first know what formula was used in computing the ratio before you start to interpret the meaning of the ratio value.

Times Interest Earned Ratio

Lenders like to have an indication of the borrowing company's ability to meet the required interest payments. Times interest earned is the ratio of the income that is available for interest payments to the annual interest expense. Times interest earned is computed as follows:

$$\text{Times Interest Earned} = \frac{\text{Income Before Interest and Taxes (Operating Profit)}}{\text{Annual Interest Expense}}$$

The times interest earned ratios for ExxonMobil and Chevron for 2005 are computed as follows:

$$\text{ExxonMobil} = \frac{\$59,928}{\$496} = 120.8 \text{ times}$$

$$\text{Chevron} = \frac{\$25,679}{\$482} = 53.3 \text{ times}$$

Both of these ratio values are very high indicating that the lenders who have loaned money to ExxonMobil or to Chevron have no reason to doubt that the two companies will be able to continue to make their interest payments in the future.

REMEMBER THIS...

- The debt ratio, the debt-to-equity ratio, and the assets-to-equity ratio all measure the level of a company's leverage.
  - Debt ratio = Total liabilities divided by total assets
  - Debt-to-equity ratio = Total liabilities divided by total stockholders' equity
  - Assets-to-equity ratio = Total assets divided by total stockholders' equity
- The times interest earned ratio (operating income divided by interest expense) measures how much cushion a company has in terms of being able to make its periodic interest payments.

Cash Flow Ratios

Use cash flow information to evaluate cash flow ratios.

7 The requirement that companies provide a cash flow statement is very recent (since 1988), especially when you remember that double-entry accounting itself is over 500 years old. Because the cash flow statement is relatively new, it often fails to get the emphasis it deserves as one of the three primary financial statements. Most of the age-old tools of financial statement analysis, such as the DuPont framework, do not incorporate cash flow data. Accordingly, information from the cash flow statement is not yet ingrained in the analytical tradition, but it will be. In fact, one way to impress others that you are a modern, well-trained, future-looking professional is to become proficient in analyzing cash flow data.

Usefulness of Cash Flow Ratios

Analysis of cash flow information is especially important in those situations in which net income does not give an accurate picture of the economic performance of a company. Three such situations are discussed briefly below.

Large Noncash Expenses When a company reports large noncash expenses, such as write-offs and depreciation, earnings may give a gloomier picture of current operations than is warranted. In fact, a company may report record losses in the same years it is reporting positive cash flow from operations. In such cases, cash flow from operations is a better indicator of whether the company can continue to honor its commitments to creditors, customers, employees, and investors in the near term. Don't misunderstand this to mean that a reported loss is nothing to worry about so long as cash flow is positive: the positive cash flow indicates that business can continue for the time being, but the reported loss may hint at looming problems in the future. As an example, consider the case of **AOL Time Warner** (now called just **Time Warner**). In 2002, the company reported the largest net loss in the history of American business—$98.7 billion. However, much of that loss related to the impairment of certain assets—a noncash expenditure for the year. For 2002, AOL Time Warner reported a positive cash flow from operations of $7 billion.

F Y I

Although net income may sometimes paint a misleading picture of a company's performance, in most cases net income is the single best measure of a firm's economic performance.

Rapid Growth Cash flow analysis is also a valuable tool for evaluating rapidly growing companies that use large amounts of cash to expand inventory. In addition, cash collections on growing accounts receivable often lag behind the need to pay creditors. In these cases, reported earnings may be positive but operations are actually consuming rather than generating cash. For example, **Pixar**, the company that has produced such films as *Toy Story* and *Monsters, Inc.*, experienced revenue growth in 2002 of 77%. The company reported record net income in 2002 of $90 million. However, cash flow from operations was a negative $4.5 million. The message: For high-growth companies, positive earnings are no guarantee that sufficient cash flows are there to service current needs.

Window Dressing Time Cash flow analysis offers important insights into companies that are striving to present a stellar financial record. Accrual accounting involves making assumptions in order to adjust raw cash flow data into a better measure of economic performance—net income. For companies entering phases in which it's critical that reported earnings look good, accounting assumptions and adjustments can be stretched—sometimes to the breaking point. Such phases include the period just before a company applies for a large loan, just before an initial public offering of stock (when founding entrepreneurs cash in all those years of struggle and sweat), and just before a company is being bought out by another company. In these cases, cash flow from operations, which is not impacted by accrual assumptions, provides an excellent reality check for reported earnings.

To illustrate the computation of selected cash flow ratios, the data in Exhibit 12 from Microsoft's 2005 and 2004 financial statements are used.

cash flow-to-net income ratio

A ratio that reflects the extent to which accrual accounting assumptions and adjustments have been included in computing net income.

Cash Flow to Net Income

Perhaps the most important cash flow relationship is that between cash from operations and reported net income. The **cash flow-to-net income ratio** reflects the extent to which accrual accounting assumptions and adjustments have been

EXHIBIT 12	Selected Cash Flow Data for Microsoft for 2005 and 2004*	
	2005	**2004**
Net income	$12,254	$ 8,168
Cash from operations	16,605	14,626
Cash paid for capital expenditures	1,019	1,113
*All amounts are in millions of dollars.		

included in computing net income. For Microsoft, computation of the cash flow-to-net income ratio (in millions of dollars) is as follows:

	2005	**2004**
Cash from operations	$16,605	$14,626
Net income	$12,254	$8,168
Cash flow-to-net income ratio	1.36	1.79

STOP & THINK

Can you think of some accrual accounting adjustments that might cause a difference between net income and cash from operations?

In general, the cash flow-to-net income ratio will have a value greater than one because of significant noncash expenses (such as depreciation) that reduce reported net income but have no impact on cash flow. For a given company, the cash flow-to-net income ratio should remain fairly stable from year to year. A significant change in the ratio indicates that accounting assumptions were instrumental in reducing reported net income.

cash flow adequacy ratio

Cash from operations divided by expenditures for fixed asset additions and acquisitions of new businesses.

Cash Flow Adequacy

A "cash cow" is a business that is generating enough cash from operations to completely pay for all new plant and equipment purchases with cash left over to repay loans or distribute to investors. The **cash flow adequacy ratio**, computed as cash from operations divided by expenditures for fixed asset additions and acquisitions of new businesses, indicates whether a business is a cash cow. Computation of the cash flow adequacy ratio for Microsoft is as follows:

	2005	**2004**
Cash from operations	$16,605	$14,626
Cash paid for capital expenditures	$1,019	$1,113
Cash flow adequacy ratio	16.30	13.14

The calculations indicate that in 2005 and in 2004 Microsoft's cash from operations was sufficient to pay for its capital expansion with something left over. This means that Microsoft could pay for its expansion without incurring any new debt or seeking funds from investors. It would be fair to say that Microsoft could be considered a cash cow. 2005 cash flow ratios for a group of companies are presented in Exhibit 13.

Southwest Airlines reports cash flow from operations as being more than four times its reported net income. In addition, all of the companies in the list each generated

EXHIBIT 13	2005 Cash Flow Ratios for Selected U.S. Companies	
	Cash Flow/ Net Income	Cash Flow Adequacy Ratio
Disney	1.7	2.4
Wal-Mart	1.6	1.2
Home Depot	1.1	1.0
Federal Express	2.0	1.4
Southwest Airlines	4.1	1.8

F Y I

Cash paid for dividends is sometimes added to the denominator of the cash flow adequacy ratio. With this formulation, the ratio indicates whether operating cash flow is sufficient to pay for both capital additions and regular dividends to stockholders.

enough cash flow from operations in 2005 to more than pay for all their capital expenditures for the year.

Remember that cash flow ratios fall outside many financial statement analysis models because the cash flow statement hasn't been around long enough to work its way into traditional models. Rebel against tradition and don't forget cash flow!

REMEMBER THIS...

- Because the statement of cash flows is a relatively recent requirement, time-tested ratios using information from that statement are still developing.
- Cash flow ratios are useful in that they can identify instances where accrual basis accounting measures are not providing a complete picture.
- The ratio of cash flow to net income highlights when there are significant differences between cash from operations and net income.
- The cash flow adequacy ratio demonstrates a company's ability to finance its capital expansion through cash from operations.

Potential Pitfalls

Understand the limitations of financial statement analysis.

8 Financial statement analysis, as emphasized previously, usually does not give answers but instead points in directions where further investigation is needed. This section discusses several reasons why we must be careful not to place too much weight on an analysis of financial statement numbers themselves.

Financial Statements Don't Contain All Information

Accountants, including the authors, should be forgiven for mistakenly thinking that all knowledge in the universe can be summarized in numerical form in financial statements. Accountants love numbers, they love things that balance, and they love condensing and summarizing the complexity of business—in short, accountants love financial statements. Businesspeople don't have this emotional relationship with financial statements and therefore should be able to take a more detached view. Businesspeople should remember that financial statements represent just one part of the information spectrum. Microsoft's financial statements, for example, tell nothing about the morale of Microsoft's employees, about new products being developed in Microsoft's research laboratories, or about the strategic plans of Microsoft's competitors. In addition, as discussed in Chapter 2, many valuable economic assets, such as the value of a company's own homegrown reputation, brand recognition, and customer loyalty, are not recognized in financial statements. The danger in financial statement analysis is that, in computing dozens of ratios and comparing common-size financial statements across years and among competitors, we can forget there is lots of decision-relevant information to be found *outside* financial statements. Don't let the attractiveness of the apparent precision of financial statement numbers distract you from searching for all relevant information, no matter how imprecise and nonquantitative.

Lack of Comparability

Ratio analysis is most meaningful when ratios can be benchmarked to comparable values for the same company in prior years and to ratio values for other companies in the same industry. A problem arises when reported financial statement numbers that seem to be comparable are actually measurements of different things. For example, some companies list depreciation expense separately and include advertising expense as part of selling, general, and administrative expense whereas others do not list depreciation expense separately but do report a separate line for advertising expense. This classification difference makes it more difficult to compare the income statements of the two companies.

conglomerates

A company comprised of a number of divisions with those divisions often operating in different industries.

Another benchmarking difficulty arises because many large U.S. companies are **conglomerates**, meaning that they are composed of divisions operating in different industries, sometimes quite unrelated to one another. Throughout this chapter **Apple Computer**, for example, was used as a benchmark competitor for **Microsoft**, but in addition to operating in the software industry, Apple is also heavily involved in the computer hardware business. Thus, a true benchmark firm for Microsoft would be to use (if available) only the results for the software segment of Apple Computer.

Finally, comparison difficulties arise because all companies don't use the same accounting practices. Companies can choose different methods of computing depreciation expense, cost of goods sold, and bad debt expense. Some companies report leased assets as part of property, plant, and equipment in the balance sheet, and some companies don't report leased assets anywhere at all on the balance sheet.

Search for the Smoking Gun

Financial case studies are very useful and fun because they allow students to discover key business insights for themselves in the context of real situations. When analyzing a case, one feels a bit like Sherlock Holmes scouring financial statements to see whether a company's problems are caused by poor inventory management, short-sighted tax planning, or growing difficulties collecting receivables. This detective mentality can be counterproductive, however, because not every company you analyze is going to be a candidate for a Harvard Business School case that illustrates one particular management principle. For example, not every company suffering from poor profitability has one stupendous flaw that will leap out at you as you do your ratio analysis. If you focus too much on trying to "solve" the case and find the smoking gun, you may overlook indications of a collection of less spectacular problems.

Anchoring, Adjustment, and Timeliness

Financial statements are based on historical data. A large part of the value of this historical data lies in its ability to indicate how a company will perform in the future. The danger in performing ratio analysis on several years of past data is that we might then tend to focus on the company's past performance and ignore current year information. All of the analysis performed in this chapter using historical data for Microsoft for 2005 and before may tell us less about Microsoft's operating position than the news that Microsoft and the U.S. Department of Justice had reached an agreement on a three-year-old antitrust dispute. The careful analyst must balance what he or she learns from an analysis of historical financial statement data with more current data available from different sources.

REMEMBER THIS . . .

- There is more to a company and its future than just the information contained in the financial statements.
- Care must be taken to ensure that when comparing financial statement information across time or across companies at the same point in time, that similar accounting practices have been used.
- Care must be taken to ensure that current information is included when analyzing past data.

REVIEW OF LEARNING OBJECTIVES

(1) Explain the purpose of financial statement analysis.

- Financial statement analysis is used:
  - to predict a company's future profitability and cash flows from its past performance and
  - to evaluate the performance of a company with an eye toward identifying problem areas.
- The informativeness of financial ratios is greatly enhanced when they are compared:
  - with past values and
  - with values for other firms in the same industry.

(2) Understand the relationships between financial statement numbers and use ratios in analyzing and describing a company's performance. Six of the most commonly used financial ratios are as follows:

- **Debt ratio:** Percentage of company funding that is borrowed.
- **Current ratio:** Indication of a company's ability to pay its short-term debts.
- **Return on sales:** Pennies in profit on each dollar of sales.
- **Asset turnover:** Measure of efficiency; number of sales dollars generated by each dollar of assets.
- **Return on equity:** Pennies in profit for each dollar invested by stockholders.
- **Price-earnings ratio:** Number of dollars an investor must pay to "buy" the future rights to each dollar of current earnings.

(3) Use common-size financial statements to perform comparison of financial statements across years and between companies.

- Common-size financial statements are the easiest, most intuitive, and fastest tool available for starting an analysis of a company's financial statements.

- A common-size income statement reveals the number of pennies of each expense for each dollar of sales.

- The asset section of a common-size balance sheet tells how many pennies of each asset are needed to generate each dollar of sales.

(4) Understand the DuPont framework and how return on equity can be decomposed into its profitability, efficiency, and leverage components. The DuPont framework decomposes return on equity (ROE) into three areas:

- **Profitability:** Return on sales is computed as net income divided by sales and is interpreted as the number of pennies in profit generated from each dollar of sales.

- **Efficiency:** Asset turnover is computed as sales divided by assets and is interpreted as the number of dollars in sales generated by each dollar of assets.

- **Leverage:** Assets-to-equity ratio is computed as assets divided by equity and is interpreted as the number of dollars of assets a company is able to acquire using each dollar invested by stockholders.

(5) Conduct a focused examination of a company's efficiency by using asset-specific ratios.

	Ratios	Formulas
Accounts Receivable	• Accounts Receivable Turnover • Average Collection Period	• Sales ÷ Average Accounts Receivable • 365 ÷ Accounts Receivable Turnover
Inventory	• Inventory Turnover • Number of Days' Sales in Inventory	• Cost of Goods Sold ÷ Average Inventory • 365 ÷ Inventory Turnover
Property, Plant, and Equipment	• Fixed Asset Turnover	• Sales ÷ Average Property, Plant, and Equipment

(6) Determine the degree of a company's financial leverage and its ability to repay loans using debt-related financial ratios.

- The debt ratio, the debt-to-equity ratio, and the assets-to-equity ratio all measure the level of a company's leverage.

  - Debt ratio = Total liabilities divided by total assets
  - Debt-to-equity ratio = Total liabilities divided by total stockholders' equity
  - Assets-to-equity ratio = Total assets divided by total stockholders' equity

- The times interest earned ratio (operating income divided by interest expense) measures how much cushion a company has in terms of being able to make its periodic interest payments.

(7) Use cash flow information to evaluate cash flow ratios.

- Cash flow ratios are particularly useful:

  - when net income is impacted by large noncash expenses,
  - when rapid growth causes cash from operations to be much less than reported net income, and
  - when company management has a strong incentive to bias reported net income in order to get a loan or issue shares at a favorable price.

- The ratio of cash flow to net income highlights when there are significant differences between cash from operations and net income.

- The cash flow adequacy ratio demonstrates a company's ability to finance its capital expansion through cash from operations.

⑧ **Understand the limitations of financial statement analysis.** Financial statement analysis usually does not provide answers but only points out areas in which more information should be gathered.

We must be careful not to base a decision solely on an analysis of financial statement numbers because:

- financial statements don't contain all the relevant information;

- financial statements sometimes can't be properly compared among companies because of differences in classification, industry mix, and accounting methods;

- most sets of financial statements will not reveal a smoking gun that, if fixed, will solve all of a company's problems; and

- focusing on historical financial statement data may cause us to overlook important current information.

KEY TERMS & CONCEPTS

asset turnover, 672
assets-to-equity ratio, 679
cash flow adequacy
  ratio, 688
cash flow-to-net income
  ratio, 687

common-size
  financial
  statements, 676
conglomerates, 690
current ratio, 672
debt ratio, 671

DuPont
  framework, 679
financial ratios, 669
financial statement
  analysis, 669
leverage, 681

liquidity, 671
price-earnings
  ratio, 673
return on equity, 673
return on sales, 672

REVIEW PROBLEM

Financial Statement Analysis

The comparative income statements and balance sheets for Montana Corporation for the years ending December 31, 2009 and 2008, are given here.

Montana Corporation Income Statements For the Years Ended December 31, 2009 and 2008		
	2009	**2008**
Net sales	$600,000	$575,000
Cost of goods sold	500,000	460,000
Gross margin	$100,000	$115,000
Expenses:		
Selling and administrative expenses	$ 66,000	$ 60,000
Interest expense	4,000	3,000
Total expenses	$ 70,000	$ 63,000
Income before taxes	$ 30,000	$ 52,000
Income taxes	12,000	21,000
Net income	$ 18,000	$ 31,000
Earnings per share	$1.80	$3.10

(continued)

Montana Corporation
Balance Sheets
December 31, 2009 and 2008

	2009	2008
Assets		
Current assets:		
Cash	$ 11,000	$ 13,000
Accounts receivable (net)	92,000	77,000
Inventory	103,000	92,000
Prepaid expenses	6,000	5,000
Total current assets	$212,000	$187,000
Property, plant, and equipment:		
Land and building	$ 61,000	$ 59,000
Machinery and equipment	172,000	156,000
Total property, plant, and equipment	$233,000	$215,000
Less accumulated depreciation	113,000	102,000
Net property, plant, and equipment	$120,000	$113,000
Other assets	$ 8,000	$ 7,000
Total assets	$340,000	$307,000
Liabilities and Stockholders' Equity		
Current liabilities:		
Accounts payable	$ 66,000	$ 55,000
Notes payable	–	23,000
Dividends payable	2,000	–
Income taxes payable	3,000	5,000
Total current liabilities	$ 71,000	$ 83,000
Long-term debt	75,000	42,000
Total liabilities	$146,000	$125,000
Stockholders' equity:		
Common stock ($1 par)	$ 10,000	$ 10,000
Paid-in capital in excess of par	16,000	16,000
Retained earnings	168,000	156,000
Total stockholders' equity	$194,000	$182,000
Total liabilities and stockholders' equity	$340,000	$307,000
Additional information:		
Dividends declared in 2009		$6,000
Market price per share, December 31, 2009		$14.50
Cash Flow Information:		
Cash from operations for 2009		$11,000
Cash paid for capital expenditures for 2009		$19,000

Required:

Prepare a comprehensive financial statement analysis of Montana Corporation for 2009. Note that though financial statement analysts usually compare data from two or more years, we are more concerned here with the methods of analysis than the results, so we will use only one year, 2009.

(continued)

Solution

1. Key Relationships

The computation of the four key ratios for 2009 provides the analyst with an overall view of the company's performance and gives an indication of how well management performed with respect to operations, asset turnover, and debt-equity management.

Computation of Key Ratios (2009)

Operating Performance		Asset Turnover		Debt-Equity Management		Return on Stockholders' Equity
$\dfrac{\text{Net Income}}{\text{Net Sales}}$	$\times$	$\dfrac{\text{Net Sales}}{\text{Average Total Assets}}$	$\times$	$\dfrac{\text{Average Total Assets}}{\text{Average Stockholders' Equity}}$	$=$	$\dfrac{\text{Net Income}}{\text{Average Stockholders' Equity}}$
$\dfrac{\$18,000}{\$600,000}$	$\times$	$\dfrac{\$600,000}{\$323,500}$	$\times$	$\dfrac{\$323,500}{\$188,000}$	$=$	$\dfrac{\$18,000}{\$188,000}$
3.00%	$\times$	1.85 times	$\times$	1.72 times	$=$	9.57%*

*The factors do not multiply to the product because of rounding.

2. Analysis of Operating Performance

Operating performance is measured by means of vertical and horizontal analyses of the income statement.

Vertical analysis of the income statement: When the income statement is analyzed vertically, net sales is set at 100%, and each expense and net income are shown as percentages of net sales.

Montana Corporation
Vertical Analysis of Income Statement
For the Year Ended December 31, 2009

Net sales	$600,000	100.0%
Cost of goods sold	500,000	83.3
Gross margin	$100,000	16.7%
Expenses:		
Selling and administrative expenses	$ 66,000	11.0%
Interest expense	4,000	0.7
Total expenses	$ 70,000	11.7%
Income before taxes	$ 30,000	5.0%
Income taxes	12,000	2.0
Net income	$ 18,000	3.0%

(continued)

3. Analysis of Asset Turnover and Utilization

Asset turnover and utilization are analyzed by performing vertical analysis of the balance sheet.

Montana Corporation Vertical Analysis of the Balance Sheet (as a % of sales) December 31, 2009		
Assets		
Current assets:		
Cash	$ 11,000	1.8%
Accounts receivable (net)	92,000	15.3
Inventory	103,000	17.2
Prepaid expenses	6,000	1.0
Total current assets	$212,000	35.3%
Property, plant, and equipment:		
Land and building	$ 61,000	10.2%
Machinery and equipment	172,000	28.7
Total property, plant, and equipment	$233,000	38.8%*
Less accumulated depreciation	113,000	18.8
Net property, plant, and equipment	$120,000	20.0%
Other assets	$ 8,000	1.3%
Total assets	$340,000	56.7%*
Liabilities and Stockholders' Equity		
Current liabilities:		
Accounts payable	$ 66,000	11.0%
Dividends payable	2,000	0.3
Income taxes payable	3,000	0.5
Total current liabilities	$ 71,000	11.8%
Long-term debt	75,000	12.5
Total liabilities	$146,000	24.3%
Stockholders' equity	194,000	32.3
Total liabilities and stockholders' equity ...	$340,000	56.7%*

*Note: Because of rounding, the percentages don't always add up exactly.

4. Common Ratios

a. Debt Ratio:

$$\frac{\text{Total Liabilities}}{\text{Total Assets}} = \frac{\$146,000}{\$340,000} = 42.9\%$$

b. Current Ratio:

$$\frac{\text{Current Assets}}{\text{Current Liabilities}} = \frac{\$212,000}{\$71,000} = 2.99$$

c. Return on Sales:

$$\frac{\text{Net Income}}{\text{Net Sales}} = \frac{\$18,000}{\$600,000} = 0.03$$

d. Asset Turnover Ratio:

$$\frac{\text{Net Sales}}{\text{Average Total Assets}} = \frac{\$600,000}{\dfrac{\$340,000 + \$307,000}{2}} = \frac{\$600,000}{\$323,500} = 1.85$$

(continued)

e. Return on Stockholders' Equity:

$$\frac{\text{Net Income}}{\text{Average Stockholders' Equity}} = \frac{\$18,000}{\dfrac{\$194,000 + \$182,000}{2}} = \frac{\$18,000}{\$188,000} = 9.6\%$$

f. Price-Earnings Ratio:

$$\frac{\text{Market Price per Share}}{\text{Earnings per Share}} = \frac{\$14.50}{\$1.80} = 8.1$$

DISCUSSION QUESTIONS

1. Financial statement analysis can be used to identify a company's weak areas so that management can work toward improvement. Can financial statement analysis be used for any other purpose? Explain.
2. "An analysis of a company's financial ratios reveals the underlying reasons for the company's problems." Do you agree or disagree? Explain.
3. What benchmarks can be used to add meaning to a computed financial ratio value?
4. What characteristic of a company does current ratio measure?
5. Company A has a return on sales of 6%. Is this a high value for return on sales?
6. How does the price-earnings ratio differ from most other financial ratios?
7. What is a common-size financial statement? What are its advantages?
8. What other types of information should be gathered if an analysis of common-size financial statements suggests that a company has problems?
9. What is the most informative section of the common-size balance sheet? Explain.
10. What is the purpose of the DuPont framework?
11. Identify the three ROE components represented in the DuPont framework and tell what ratio

summarizes a company's performance in each area.
12. What further analysis can be done if the DuPont calculations suggest that a company has a profitability problem?
13. What can the inventory turnover ratio tell us?
14. How is fixed asset turnover calculated, and what does the resulting ratio value mean?
15. What does the debt-to-equity ratio measure?
16. From the standpoint of a lender, which is more attractive: a high times interest earned ratio or a low times interest earned ratio? Explain.
17. Why are cash flow ratios often excluded from financial analysis models?
18. Why is it especially important to look at cash flow data when examining a firm that is preparing to make an application for a large loan?
19. What does it mean when the value of a company's cash flow adequacy ratio is less than one?
20. What factors can reduce comparability among financial statements?
21. What is the danger in focusing a financial analysis solely on the data found in the historical financial statements?

PRACTICE EXERCISES

PE 14-1   **What Is a Financial Ratio?**
LO1   Choose the letter of the correct answer. A financial ratio is a
    a. key source of external financing for most publicly-traded companies.
    b. relationship between financial statement amounts.
    c. stockbroker who performs financial statement analysis.
    d. trend in a number over time.
    e. complete set of the three primary financial statements.

PE 14-2   **Usefulness of Financial Ratios**

LO1   Choose the letter of the correct answer. The usefulness of financial ratios is greatly enhanced when the values are
a. computed by the SEC.
b. compared to values for companies in different industries.
c. compared to past values of the same ratio for the same company.
d. compared to the retained earnings balance.
e. included in the body of the statement of cash flows.

PE 14-3   **Financial Ratios Defined**

LO2   Write the formula for computing each of the following financial ratios.
a. Debt ratio
b. Current ratio
c. Return on sales
d. Asset turnover
e. Return on equity
f. Price-earnings ratio

PE 14-4   **Debt Ratio**

LO2   Using the following data, compute the debt ratio.

Accounts Payable	$ 2,400
Accounts Receivable	6,750
Building	65,000
Cash	2,100
Capital Stock	26,150
Inventory	4,100
Land	14,000
Long-Term Notes Payable	32,000
Market Value of Equity	103,000
Net Income	9,000
Retained Earnings (ending)	24,000
Sales	86,000
Short-Term Notes Payable	5,700
Stockholders' Equity	50,150
Unearned Revenue	1,700

PE 14-5   **Current Ratio**

LO2   Refer to the data in PE 14-4. Compute the current ratio.

PE 14-6   **Return on Sales**

LO2   Refer to the data in PE 14-4. Compute return on sales.

PE 14-7   **Asset Turnover**

LO2   Refer to the data in PE 14-4. Compute asset turnover.

PE 14-8   **Return on Equity**

LO2   Refer to the data in PE 14-4. Compute return on equity.

PE 14-9   **Price-Earnings Ratio**

LO2   Refer to the data in PE 14-4. Compute the price-earnings ratio.

PE 14-10 **Common-Size Income Statement**

LO3 Using the following data, prepare a common-size income statement.

Sales		$75,000
Cost of goods sold		40,000
Gross profit		$35,000
Operating expenses:		
Sales and marketing	$3,000	
General and administrative	8,000	
Total operating expenses		11,000
Operating income		$24,000
Interest expense		4,000
Income before income taxes		$20,000
Income tax expense		3,500
Net income		$16,500

PE 14-11 **Comparative Common-Size Income Statements**

LO3 Using the following data, (1) prepare comparative common-size income statements for Years 1 and 2 and (2) briefly outline why return on sales is lower in Year 2 (1.8%) compared to Year 1 (7.0%).

	Year 2	Year 1
Sales	$100,000	$80,000
Cost of goods sold	70,000	50,000
Gross profit	$ 30,000	$30,000
Operating expenses	25,000	20,000
Operating income	$ 5,000	$10,000
Interest expense	2,000	2,000
Income before income taxes	$ 3,000	$ 8,000
Income tax expense	1,200	2,400
Net income	$ 1,800	$ 5,600

PE 14-12 **Common-Size Balance Sheet**

LO3 Using the following data, prepare a common-size balance sheet. Sales for the year were $75,000.

Assets		
Current assets:		
Cash	$4,800	
Accounts receivable	9,300	
Inventory	6,000	
Total current assets		$20,100
Property, plant, and equipment (net)		33,000
Goodwill		5,700
Total assets		$58,800
Liabilities and stockholders' equity		
Current liabilities:		
Accounts payable	$7,200	
Unearned revenue	3,800	
Total current liabilities		$11,000
Long-term debt		18,000
Total liabilities		$29,000
Capital stock		15,000
Retained earnings		14,800
Total liabilities and stockholders' equity		$58,800

PE 14-13

LO3

Common-Size Balance Sheet Standardized Using Total Assets

Refer to the data in PE 14-12. Prepare a common-size balance sheet using total assets to standardize each amount instead of using total sales.

PE 14-14

LO3

Comparative Common-Size Balance Sheets

Using the following data, (1) prepare comparative common-size balance sheets for Years 1 and 2 (standardized by sales) and (2) briefly outline any significant changes from Year 1 to Year 2. Sales for Year 1 were $80,000, and sales for Year 2 were $100,000.

	Year 2	Year 1
Assets		
Cash	$ 4,000	$ 3,200
Accounts receivable	8,000	6,400
Inventory	17,000	15,000
Property, plant, and equipment (net)	25,000	25,000
Total assets	$54,000	$49,600
Liabilities and stockholders' equity		
Accounts payable	$ 9,000	$ 7,200
Long-term debt	20,000	20,000
Total liabilities	$29,000	$27,200
Capital stock	15,000	15,000
Retained earnings	10,000	7,400
Total liabilities and stockholders' equity	$54,000	$49,600

PE 14-15

LO4

DuPont Framework Defined

(1) List the three ratios that combine to form the DuPont framework. Also list the formulas used to compute each ratio. (2) Give a brief intuitive explanation of the interpretation of the values of each of the three ratios.

PE 14-16

LO4

Computation of Return on Equity Using the DuPont Framework

Using the following DuPont framework ratios, compute return on equity for Year 1, Year 2, and Year 3.

	Year 3	Year 2	Year 1
Return on sales	25.9%	23.4%	22.5%
Asset turnover	0.71	0.67	0.60
Assets-to-equity ratio	1.52	1.45	1.20

PE 14-17

LO4

Analysis of Return on Equity Using the DuPont Framework

Refer to the data in PE 14-16. Briefly explain why the company's return on equity increased from Year 1 to Year 3.

PE 14-18

LO4

DuPont Framework Computations

Using the following data, compute return on equity, return on sales, asset turnover, and the assets-to-equity ratio.

Total assets	$120,000
Interest expense	$5,000
Total stockholders' equity	$70,000
Sales	$190,000
Net income	$17,000
Total liabilities	$50,000
Market value of equity	$112,000
Current ratio	2.48

PE 14-19   **DuPont Framework Computations**

LO4   Using the following data, compute return on equity, return on sales, asset turnover, and the assets-to-equity ratio.

Sales	$450,000
Cash flow from operating activities	$12,000
Net income	$20,000
Total assets	$300,000
Total liabilities	$120,000
Price-earnings ratio	17.4

PE 14-20   **DuPont Framework Intuition Test**

LO4   Return on equity can be computed by dividing net income by stockholders' equity. It can also be computed by multiplying return on sales, asset turnover, and the assets-to-equity ratio. Using the definitions of the various ratios, show why both of these approaches yield the same answer.

PE 14-21   **Accounts Receivable Turnover**

LO5   Using the following data, calculate the company's accounts receivable turnover.

Accounts receivable balance, December 31	$ 54,000
Inventory balance, December 31	59,000
Sales revenue	520,000
Cost of goods sold	310,000
Accounts receivable balance, January 1	46,000

PE 14-22   **Average Collection Period**

LO5   Refer to the data in PE 14-21. Calculate the company's average collection period.

PE 14-23   **Inventory Turnover**

LO5   Using the following data, compute inventory turnover.

Inventory, December 31, year 1	$ 82,000
Cost of goods sold	342,000
Sales	694,000
Inventory, January 1, year 1	74,000

PE 14-24   **Number of Days' Sales in Inventory**

LO5   Refer to the data in PE 14-23. Compute number of days' sales in inventory.

PE 14-25   **Fixed Asset Turnover**

LO5   Using the following data, compute the fixed asset turnover.

Current assets, end of year	$ 35,000
Fixed assets, end of year	180,000
Fixed assets, beginning of year	195,000
Sales during the year	595,000

PE 14-26   **Debt Ratio**

LO6   Using the following information, compute the debt ratio.

Total liabilities	$247,500
Annual interest expense	5,204
Total assets	542,850
Income before interest and taxes	62,030

PE 14-27   **Debt-to-Equity Ratio**

LO6   Refer to the data in PE 14-26. Compute the debt-to-equity ratio.

PE 14-28   **Times Interest Earned Ratio**

LO6   Refer to the data in PE 14-26. Compute the times interest earned ratio.

PE 14-29   **When Operating Cash Flow Information Is Particularly Valuable**

LO7   Which one of the following is *not* a situation in which cash flow data can provide a better picture of a company's economic performance than does net income?

a.   A company preparing for an initial public offering.

b.   A company experiencing rapid growth.

c.   A company reporting large noncash expenses.

d.   A company with high asset turnover.

e.   A company preparing to apply for a large loan.

PE 14-30   **Cash Flow-to-Net Income Ratio**

LO7   Using the following data, compute the cash flow-to-net income ratio.

Total revenues	$225,000
Cash expenses	98,000
Noncash expenses	111,000
Cash paid for capital expenditures	48,000
Cash from operations	25,000

PE 14-31   **Cash Flow Adequacy Ratio**

LO7   Refer to the data in PE 14-30. Compute the cash flow adequacy ratio.

PE 14-32   **Potential Pitfalls of Financial Statement Analysis**

LO8   Which one of the following statements is true with respect to financial statement analysis?

a.   All aspects of a business can be summarized neatly into the three primary financial statements.

b.   Comparing the financial statements of different companies is relatively easy because all companies are required to use the same financial statement formats and classifications.

c.   Every company examined using financial statement analysis will be found to have at least one prominent flaw.

d.   Analysts should use only historical ratio analysis, rather than information about current events, in deciding how to rate a company's future prospects.

e.   Financial statement analysis usually does not give answers but instead points in directions where further investigation is needed.

EXERCISES

E 14-33   **Computation of Ratios**

LO2   The balance sheet for Tony Corporation is as follows:

Tony Corporation	
Balance Sheet	
December 31, 2009	

Assets	
Current assets:	
Cash	$ 11,000
Accounts receivable	18,000
Total current assets	$ 29,000
Long-term investments	25,000
Property, plant, and equipment	55,000
Total assets	$109,000

(continued)

Liabilities and stockholders' equity
Current liabilities:

Accounts payable	$ 15,000
Salaries payable	5,000
Total current liabilities	$ 20,000
Long-term liabilities	17,500
Total liabilities	$ 37,500
Stockholders' equity:	
Paid-in capital	$ 50,000
Retained earnings	21,500
Total stockholders' equity	$ 71,500
Total liabilities and stockholders' equity	$109,000

In addition, the following information for 2009 has been assembled:

Sales	$265,000
Net income	33,000
Market value at December 31, 2009	150,000

Compute the following ratios:

1. Debt ratio
2. Current ratio
3. Return on sales
4. Asset turnover
5. Return on equity
6. Price-earnings ratio

E 14-34　　**Ratios and Computing Missing Values**

LO2　　The balance sheet for Rodman Company is as follows:

Rodman Company
Balance Sheet
December 31, 2009

Assets	
Current assets:	
Cash	$ (a)
Accounts receivable	55,000
Total current assts	$ (b)
Long-term investments	35,000
Property, plant, and equipment	120,000
Total assets	$ (c)
Liabilities and stockholders' equity	
Current liabilities:	
Account payable	$ 64,000
Income taxes payable	(d)
Total current liabilities	$ 80,000
Long-term liabilities	(e)
Total liabilities	$ (f)
Stockholders' equity:	
Paid-in capital	$ (g)
Retained earnings	78,500
Total stockholders' equity	$ (h)
Total liabilities and stockholders' equity	$ (i)

(continued)

In addition, the following information for 2009 has been assembled:

Debt ratio	50%
Current ratio	1.2

Compute the missing values (a) through (i).

E 14-35

LO2

Computations Using Ratios

The following information for Chong Lai Company for 2009 has been assembled:

Market value at December 31, 2009	$600,000
Total liabilities	$100,000
Debt ratio	40%
Return on sales	10%
Asset turnover	2.0

Compute the following:
1. Total assets
2. Sales
3. Net income
4. Price-earnings ratio

E 14-36

LO3

Common-Size Income Statement

Comparative income statements for King Engineering Company for 2009 and 2008 are given below.

	2009	2008
Sales	$ 885,000	$ 545,000
Cost of goods sold	(570,000)	(305,000)
Gross profit on sales	$ 315,000	$ 240,000
Selling and general expenses	(106,000)	(84,000)
Operating income	$ 209,000	$ 156,000
Interest expense	(35,000)	(20,000)
Income before income tax	$ 174,000	$ 136,000
Income tax expense	(52,000)	(41,000)
Net income	$ 122,000	$ 95,000

1. Prepare common-size income statements for King Engineering Company for 2009 and 2008.
2. Return on sales for King Engineering is lower in 2009 than in 2008. What expense or expenses are causing this lower profitability?

E 14-37

LO3

Common-Size Balance Sheet

The following data are taken from the comparative balance sheet prepared for Warren Road Company:

	2009	2008
Cash	$ 34,000	$ 25,000
Accounts receivable	43,000	40,000
Inventories	68,000	30,000
Property, plant, and equipment	91,000	55,000
Total assets	$236,000	$150,000

(continued)

Sales for 2009 were $1,000,000. Sales for 2008 were $800,000.

1. Prepare the asset section of a common-size balance sheet for Warren Road Company for 2009 and 2008.
2. Overall, Warren Road is less efficient at using its assets to generate sales in 2009 than in 2008. What asset or assets are responsible for this decreased efficiency?

E 14-38

LO3

Common-Size Balance Sheet

The following data are taken from the comparative balance sheet prepared for Elison Company:

	2009	2008
Cash	$ 68,000	$ 50,000
Accounts receivable	86,000	80,000
Inventories	136,000	60,000
Property, plant, and equipment	182,000	110,000
Total assets	$472,000	$300,000

Sales for 2009 were $2,000,000. Sales for 2008 were $1,600,000.

1. Prepare the asset section of a common-size balance sheet for Elison Company for 2009 and 2008.
2. Overall, Elison is less efficient at using its assets to generate sales in 2009 than in 2008. What asset or assets are responsible for this decreased efficiency?

E 14-39

LO3

Common-Size Income Statement

Comparative income statements for Callister Company for 2009 and 2008 are given below.

	2009	2008
Sales	$1,600,000	$900,000
Cost of goods sold	1,020,000	480,000
Gross profit	$ 580,000	$420,000
Selling and administrative expenses	200,000	160,000
Operating income	$ 380,000	$260,000
Interest expense	80,000	60,000
Income before taxes	$ 300,000	$200,000
Income tax expense	90,000	60,000
Net income	$ 210,000	$140,000

1. Prepare common-size income statements for Callister Company for 2009 and 2008.
2. The profit margin for Callister is lower in 2009 than in 2008. What expense or expenses are causing this lower profitability?

E 14-40

LO3

Income Statement Analysis

You have obtained the following data for Lindsey Garns Company:

Sales	$230,000
Gross profit (as a percentage of sales)	30%
Return on sales	10%
Operating expenses (as a percentage of sales)	15%

Based on the above data, determine the following:

1. Cost of goods sold
2. Net income
3. Operating expenses
4. Income taxes (assume there are no other expenses or revenues)

E 14-41   **Income Statement and Balance Sheet Analysis**

LO2   Answer each of the following independent questions:

1. Nicholas Toy Company had a net income for the year ended December 31, 2009, of $72,000. Its total assets at December 31, 2009, were $1,860,000. Its total stockholders' equity at December 31, 2009, was $910,000. Calculate Nicholas Toy's return on equity.

2. On January 1, 2009, Andrew's Bookstore had current assets of $293,000 and current liabilities of $185,000. By the end of the year, its current assets had increased to $324,000 and its current liabilities to $296,000. Did the current ratio change during the year? If so, by how much?

3. The total liabilities and stockholders' equity of Ryan James Corporation is $750,000. Its current assets equal 40% of total assets and the current ratio is 1.5. Further, the ratio of stockholders' equity to total liabilities is 3 to 1. Determine (a) the amount of current liabilities and (b) the debt ratio.

E 14-42   **DuPont Framework**

LO4   The following information is for Calle Concordia Company:

	2009	2008	2007
Current assets	$ 30,000	$ 25,000	$ 35,000
Total assets	100,000	80,000	90,000
Current liabilities	20,000	15,000	15,000
Total liabilities	45,000	40,000	50,000
Stockholders' equity	55,000	40,000	40,000
Sales	400,000	300,000	300,000
Net income	20,000	10,000	5,000

For the years 2007, 2008, and 2009, compute:

1. Return on equity
2. Return on sales
3. Asset turnover
4. Assets-to-equity ratio

E 14-43   **DuPont Framework**

LO4   The numbers below are for Iffy Company and Model Company for the year 2009:

	Iffy	Model
Cash	$ 120	$ 900
Accounts receivable	600	4,500
Inventory	480	6,000
Property, plant, and equipment	3,440	15,000
Total liabilities	3,190	18,150
Stockholders' equity	1,450	8,250
Sales	10,000	75,000
Cost of goods sold	9,200	66,750
Wage expense	700	5,250
Net income	100	3,000

1. Compute return on equity, return on sales, asset turnover, and the assets-to-equity ratio for both Iffy and Model.
2. Briefly explain why Iffy's return on equity is lower than Model's.

E 14-44

LO4

DuPont Framework

The numbers for Faulty Company and Benchmark Company for the year 2009 are as follows:

	Faulty	Benchmark
Cash	$ 140	$ 500
Accounts receivable	900	2,740
Inventory	2,200	6,100
Property, plant, and equipment	1,800	6,300
Total liabilities	3,780	11,730
Stockholders' equity	1,260	3,910
Sales	12,000	45,000
Cost of goods sold	7,650	32,100
Wage expense	1,300	4,200
Other expenses	2,940	7,760
Net income	110	940

1. Compute return on equity, return on sales, asset turnover, and the assets-to-equity ratio for both Faulty and Benchmark.
2. Briefly explain why Faulty's return on equity is lower than Benchmark's.

E 14-45

LO4

DuPont Framework

The following information is for Ina Company:

	2009	2008	2007
Total assets	$200,000	$160,000	$180,000
Total liabilities	90,000	80,000	100,000
Stockholders' equity	110,000	80,000	80,000
Sales	800,000	600,000	600,000
Net income	40,000	20,000	10,000

For the years 2007, 2008, and 2009, compute:
1. Return on equity
2. Profit margin
3. Asset turnover
4. Assets-to-equity ratio

E 14-46

LO4

DuPont Framework for Analyzing Financial Statements

The income statement and balance sheet for Rollins Company are provided below. Using the DuPont framework, compute the profit margin, asset turnover, assets-to-equity ratio, and resulting return on equity for the year 2009.

Rollins Company

Income Statement

For the Year Ended December 31, 2009

Revenue from services		$151,920
Operating expenses:		
Insurance expense	$ 5,480	
Rent expense	500	
Office supplies expense	2,960	
Salaries expense	55,000	63,940
Net income		$ 87,980

(continued)

Rollins Company

Balance Sheet

December 31, 2009

Assets		Liabilities and Owners' Equity	
Cash	$ 22,000	Accounts payable	$ 54,800
Accounts receivable	40,000	Capital stock	50,000
Notes receivable	12,800	Retained earnings	150,000
Machinery	180,000	Total liabilities	
Total assets	$254,800	and owners' equity	$254,800

E 14-47   **DuPont Framework for Analyzing Financial Statements**

LO4   Using the income statement and balance sheet for Kau and Sons Company, compute the three components of return on equity—profitability, efficiency, and leverage—based on the DuPont framework, for the year 2009.

Kau and Sons Co.

Income Statement

For the Year Ended December 31, 2009

Revenues		$320,000
Expenses:		
Supplies expense	$124,000	
Salaries expense	33,200	
Utilities expense	7,100	
Rent expense	29,000	
Other expenses	7,700	201,000
Net income		$119,000

Kau and Sons Co.

Balance Sheet

December 31, 2009

Assets		Liabilities and Owners' Equity	
Cash	$ 52,100	Accounts payable	$ 29,800
Accounts receivable	34,900	Notes payable	56,200
Supplies	46,700	Capital stock	80,000
Land	70,000	Retained earnings	304,800
Buildings	267,100	Total liabilities	
Total assets	$470,800	and owners' equity	$470,800

E 14-48   **DuPont Framework**

LO4   DuPont framework data for four industries are presented below.

	Assets-to-Equity Ratio	Asset Turnover	Return on Sales
Retail jewelry stores	1.578	1.529	0.050
Retail grocery stores	1.832	5.556	0.014
Electric service companies	2.592	0.498	0.069
Legal services firms	1.708	3.534	0.083

(continued)

For the four industries, compute:
1. Return on assets
2. Return on equity

E 14-49

LO2

Financial Statement Analysis

You have obtained the following data for the Jacob Company for the year ended December 31, 2009. (Some income statement items are missing.)

Cost of goods sold	$485,000
General and administrative expenses	80,000
Interest expense	8,500
Net income	12,000
Sales	790,000
Tax expense	8,000

Answer each of the following questions:
1. What is the total gross profit?
2. What is the amount of operating income?
3. What is the amount of other operating expenses (in addition to general and administrative expenses)?
4. What is the gross profit percentage (that is, gross profit as a percentage of sales)?
5. If the return on assets is 4%, what are the total assets?
6. If the return on stockholders' equity is 8%, what is the stockholders' equity?
7. What is the return on sales?
8. What is the income tax rate? (Tax Expense/Income before Taxes)

E 14-50

LO5

Accounts Receivable Efficiency

The following are summary financial data for Parker Enterprises, Inc., and Boulder, Inc., for three recent years:

	Year 3	Year 2	Year 1
Net sales (in millions):			
Parker Enterprises, Inc.	$ 3,700	$ 3,875	$ 3,882
Boulder, Inc.	17,825	16,549	15,242
Net accounts receivable (in millions):			
Parker Enterprises, Inc.	1,400	1,800	1,725
Boulder, Inc.	5,525	5,800	6,205

1. Using the above data, compute the accounts receivable turnover and average collection period for each company for years 2 and 3.
2. Which company appears to be managing its accounts receivable more efficiently?

E 14-51

LO5

Inventory Ratios

The following data are available for 2009, regarding the inventory of two companies:

	Atkins Computers	Burbank Electronics
Beginning inventory	$ 40,000	$ 80,000
Ending inventory	48,000	95,000
Cost of goods sold	690,000	910,000

Compute inventory turnover and number of days' sales in inventory for both companies. Which company is managing its inventory more efficiently?

E 14-52   **Fixed Asset Turnover**

LO5   The Store Next Door reported the following asset values in 2008 and 2009:

	2009	2008
Cash	$ 45,000	$ 27,000
Accounts receivable	500,000	430,000
Inventory	550,000	480,000
Land	300,000	280,000
Buildings	800,000	660,000
Equipment	150,000	110,000

In addition, The Store Next Door had sales of $3,200,000 in 2009. Cost of goods sold for the year was $1,900,000.

Compute The Store Next Door's fixed asset turnover ratio for 2009.

E 14-53   **Computation of Debt-Related Financial Ratios**

LO5, LO6   The following information comes from the financial statements of Gwynn Company:

Long-term debt	$50,000
Total liabilities	78,000
Total stockholders' equity	40,000
Operating income	16,000
Interest expense	6,000

Compute the following ratio values:

1. Debt ratio
2. Debt-to-equity ratio
3. Times interest earned

E 14-54   **Cash Flow Ratios**

LO7   Below are data extracted from the financial statements for Pagoda Company.

Pagoda Company		
Selected Financial Statement Data		
For the Years Ended December 31, 2009 and 2008		
	2009	2008
Net income	$51,000	$ 63,500
Cash from operating activities	38,200	205,000
Cash paid for purchase of fixed assets	47,000	215,000
Cash paid for interest	21,000	26,000
Cash paid for income taxes	23,000	50,100

Compute the following for both 2008 and 2009:

1. Cash flow-to-net income ratio
2. Cash flow adequacy ratio

PROBLEMS

P 14-55

LO2

Computing and Using Common Ratios

The following information is for the year 2009 for Millard Company and Grantsville Company, which are in the same industry:

	Millard	Grantsville
Current assets	$20,000	$75,000
Long-term assets	$40,000	$140,000
Current liabilities	$8,000	$60,000
Long-term liabilities	$15,000	$110,000
Sales	$200,000	$850,000
Net income	$4,000	$10,000
Market price per share	$15	$50
Number of shares outstanding	6,000 shares	3,000 shares

Required:

Compute the following:

1. Current ratio
2. Debt ratio
3. Return on sales
4. Asset turnover
5. Return on equity
6. Price-earnings ratio

P 14-56

LO2

Financial Ratios

The following information for SuperStar Company is provided:

Current assets	$215,000
Long-term assets	$780,000
Current liabilities	$120,000
Long-term liabilities	$330,000
Owners' equity	$545,000
Sales for year	$1,875,000
Net income for year	$178,000
Average market price per share	$90.00
Average number of shares outstanding	50,000

Required:

1. Compute the current ratio, debt ratio, return on sales, return on equity, asset turnover, and price-earnings ratio.
2. **Interpretive Question:** What do these ratios show for SuperStar Company?

P 14-57

LO2

Working Backwards Using Common Ratios

The following information for Steven Benjamin Company for 2009 has been assembled:

Price-earnings ratio	39.0
Stockholders' equity	$150,000
Debt ratio	80%
Net income	$41,000
Asset turnover	0.75
Current liabilities	$135,000
Long-term assets	$280,000

Required:

Compute the following:

1. Return on equity
2. Total assets
3. Sales
4. Return on sales
5. Current ratio
6. Total market value of shares

P 14-58   **Common-Size Income Statement**

LO3   Operations for Janelle Company for 2008 and 2009 are summarized below.

	2009	2008
Net sales	$600,000	$560,000
Cost of goods sold	430,000	300,000
Gross profit on sales	$170,000	$260,000
Selling and general expenses	130,000	150,000
Operating income	$ 40,000	$110,000
Interest expense	50,000	45,000
Income (loss) before income tax	$ (10,000)	$ 65,000
Income tax (refund)	3,000	20,000
Net income (loss)	$ (7,000)	$ 45,000

Required:

1. Prepare common-size income statements for 2009 and 2008.
2. What caused Janelle's profitability to decline so dramatically in 2009?

P 14-59   **Common-Size Financial Statements**

LO3   Below are financial statement data for Wong Shek Company for the years 2008 and 2009.

Wong Shek Company Financial Statements For 2008 and 2009		
Cash	$ 14	$ 10
Receivables	35	27
Inventory	230	153
Property, plant, and equipment	221	190
Total assets	$ 500	$ 380
Accounts payable	$ 106	$ 74
Long-term debt	217	217
Total liabilities	$ 323	$ 291
Paid-in capital	$ 113	$ 50
Retained earnings	64	39
Total liabilities and equity	$ 500	$ 380
Sales	$1,000	$ 700
Cost of goods sold	(700)	(500)
Gross profit	$ 300	$ 200
Operating expenses	(240)	(160)
Operating profit	$ 60	$ 40
Interest expense	(22)	(22)
Income before taxes	$ 38	$ 18
Income tax expense	(13)	(6)
Net income	$ 25	$ 12

Required:

1. Prepare common-size financial statements for Wong Shek for 2008 and 2009.
2. Did Wong Shek do better or worse in 2009 compared with 2008? Explain your answer.

P 14-60   **Common-Size Financial Statements**

LO3   The comparative income statements and balance sheets for Clarksville Corporation for the years 2007, 2008, and 2009 are given below.

(continued)

Clarksville Corporation
Comparative Income Statements
For the Years Ended December 31

	2009	2008	2007
Net sales	$5,700,000	$6,600,000	$3,800,000
Cost of goods sold	4,000,000	4,800,000	2,520,000
Gross profit on sales	$1,700,000	$1,800,000	$1,280,000
Selling expense	$1,120,000	$1,200,000	$ 960,000
General expense	400,000	440,000	400,000
Total operating expenses	$1,520,000	$1,640,000	$1,360,000
Operating income (loss)	$ 180,000	$ 160,000	$ (80,000)
Other revenue (expense)	80,000	130,000	160,000
Income before taxes	$ 260,000	$ 290,000	$ 80,000
Income tax	80,000	85,000	20,000
Net income	$ 180,000	$ 205,000	$ 60,000

Clarksville Corporation
Comparative Balance Sheets
December 31

	2009	2008	2007
Assets:			
Current assets	$ 855,000	$ 955,500	$ 673,500
Land, building, and equipment	1,275,000	1,075,000	925,000
Intangible assets	100,000	100,000	100,000
Other assets	48,000	60,500	61,500
Total assets	$2,278,000	$2,191,000	$1,760,000
Liabilities:			
Current liabilities	$ 410,000	$ 501,000	$ 130,000
Long-term liabilities	400,000	600,000	400,000
Total liabilities	$ 810,000	$1,101,000	$ 530,000
Stockholders' equity:			
Paid-in capital	$1,100,000	$ 800,000	$1,000,000
Retained earnings	368,000	290,000	230,000
Total stockholders' equity	$1,468,000	$1,090,000	$1,230,000
Total liabilities and stockholders' equity	$2,278,000	$2,191,000	$1,760,000

Required:

1. Prepare common-size income statements and balance sheets for Clarksville Corporation for the years 2007, 2008, and 2009.
2. Summarize any trends you see in Clarksville's numbers from 2007 to 2009.

P 14-61

LO4

DuPont Analysis

Financial information (in thousands of dollars) relating to three different companies follows.

	Company A	Company B	Company C
Net sales	$ 60,000	$28,000	$21,000
Net income	9,600	1,850	360
Total assets	155,400	21,500	3,200
Total equity	61,000	11,300	1,690

(continued)

Required:

1. Compute the following ratios:
   a. Return on sales
   b. Asset turnover
   c. Assets-to-equity ratio
   d. Return on equity

2. **Interpretive Question:** Assume the three companies are (a) a large department store, (b) a large supermarket, and (c) a large electric utility. Based on the above information, identify each company. Explain your answer.

P 14-62   **DuPont Analysis**

LO4   Refer to the financial statement information in P 14-60 for Clarksville Corporation.

Required:

For the years 2007, 2008, and 2009, compute the following ratios:

1. Return on sales
2. Asset turnover
3. Assets-to-equity ratio
4. Return on equity

P 14-63   **Ratio Analysis**

LO2   The following financial data are taken from the records of Big Brother Company.

Big Brother Company Comparative Balance Sheet December 31		
	2009	**2008**
Assets:		
Cash	$ 38,000	$ 23,000
Accounts receivable	11,000	15,000
Inventory	220,000	195,000
Property, plant, and equipment	70,000	70,000
Total assets	$339,000	$303,000
Liabilities and stockholders' equity:		
Current liabilities	$ 52,000	$ 36,000
Noncurrent liabilities	175,000	170,000
Stockholders' equity	112,000	97,000
Total liabilities and stockholders' equity	$339,000	$303,000

Big Brother Company Comparative Income Statement For the Years Ended December 31		
	2009	**2008**
Sales	$463,000	$345,000
Cost of goods sold	240,000	182,000
Gross margin on sales	$223,000	$163,000
Operating expenses	133,000	121,000
Interest expense	15,000	10,000
Income tax expense	30,000	12,000
Net income	$ 45,000	$ 20,000

(continued)

Required:

1. Compute the following ratios for 2008 and 2009:
    a. Current ratio
    b. Debt ratio
    c. Asset turnover
    d. Return on sales
    e. Return on equity
2. Have the firm's performance and financial position improved from 2008 to 2009? Explain.

P 14-64 **Ratio Analysis**

LO2 The following data are taken from the records of John Spencer Corporation.

John Spencer Corporation Comparative Balance Sheet December 31		
	2009	**2008**
Assets:		
Cash	$ 4,000	$ 6,000
Accounts receivable	16,000	14,000
Inventory	40,000	20,000
Property, plant, and equipment	100,000	100,000
Other assets	16,000	20,000
Total assets	$176,000	$160,000
Liabilities and stockholders' equity:		
Current liabilities	$ 44,000	$ 50,000
Long-term liabilities	24,000	10,000
Paid-in capital	60,000	60,000
Retained earnings	48,000	40,000
Total liabilities and stockholders' equity	$176,000	$160,000

John Spencer Corporation Comparative Income Statement For the Years Ended December 31		
	2009	**2008**
Sales	$530,000	$448,000
Cost of goods sold	372,000	338,000
Gross margin on sales	$158,000	$110,000
Operating expense	102,000	68,000
Operating income	$ 56,000	$ 42,000
Interest expense	4,000	2,000
Income before taxes	$ 52,000	$ 40,000
Income taxes	13,000	12,000
Net income	$ 39,000	$ 28,000

Required:

1. Compute the following ratios for 2008 and 2009:
    a. Current ratio
    b. Debt ratio
    c. Asset turnover

(continued)

    d. Return on sales

    e. Return on equity

2. Have the firm's performance and financial position improved from 2008 to 2009? Explain.

P 14-65

LO5

Analysis of Accounts Receivable Management

The following accounts receivable information is for Rouge Company:

	2009	2008	2007
Accounts receivable	$ 98,000	$ 50,000	$ 70,000
Sales revenue	190,000	175,000	165,000

Required:

Is there any cause for alarm in the accounts receivable data for 2009? Explain.

P 14-66

LO5

Calculating and Interpreting Inventory Ratios

Captain Geech Boating Company sells fishing boats to fishermen. Its beginning and ending inventories for 2009 are $462 million and $653 million, respectively. It had cost of goods sold of $1,578 million for the year ended December 31, 2009. Merchant Marine Company also sells fishing boats. Its beginning and ending inventories for the year 2009 are $120 million and $90 million, respectively. It had cost of goods sold of $1,100 million for the year ended December 31, 2009.

Required:

1. Calculate the inventory turnover and number of days' sales in inventory for the two companies.
2. **Interpretive Question:** Are the results of these ratios what you expected? Which company is managing its inventory more efficiently?

P 14-67

LO5

Fixed Asset Turnover Ratio

Waystation Company reported the following asset values in 2008 and 2009:

	2009	2008
Cash	$ 40,000	$ 30,000
Accounts receivable	500,000	400,000
Inventory	700,000	500,000
Land	300,000	200,000
Buildings	800,000	600,000
Equipment	400,000	300,000

In addition, Waystation had sales of $4,000,000 in 2009. Cost of goods sold for the year was $2,500,000.

As of the end of 2008, the fair value of Waystation's total assets was $2,500,000. Of the excess of fair value over book value, $50,000 resulted because the fair value of Waystation's inventory was greater than its recorded book value. As of the end of 2009, the fair value of Waystation's total assets was $3,500,000. As of December 31, 2009, the fair value of Waystation's inventory was $100,000 greater than the inventory's recorded book value.

Required:

1. Compute Waystation's fixed asset turnover ratio for 2009.
2. Using the fair value of fixed assets instead of the book value of fixed assets, recompute Waystation's fixed asset turnover ratio for 2009. State any assumptions that you make.

(continued)

3. **Interpretive Question:** Waystation's primary competitor is Handy Corner. Handy Corner's fixed asset turnover ratio for 2009, based on publicly available information, is 2.8 times. Is Waystation more or less efficient at using its fixed assets than is Handy Corner? Explain your answer.

P 14-68
LO6

Computation of Debt-Related Financial Ratios

The following information comes from the financial statements of Walker Company:

Long-term debt	$430,000
Total liabilities	490,000
Total stockholders' equity	360,000
Current assets	140,000
Earnings before income taxes	28,000
Interest expense	50,000

Required:

Compute the following ratio values. State any assumptions that you make.

1. Debt ratio.
2. Debt-to-equity ratio.
3. Times interest earned.
4. **Interpretive Question:** You are a bank manager considering making a new $35,000 loan to Walker that would replace part of the existing long-term debt. You expect Walker to repay your loan in two years. Which of the ratios computed in parts (1) through (3) would be most useful to you in evaluating whether to make the loan to Walker?

P 14-69
LO7

Cash Flow Analysis

Below are data extracted from the financial statements for Mushu Company.

Mushu Company		
Selected Financial Statement Data		
For the Years Ended December 31, 2009 and 2008		
(in millions of dollars)		
	2009	**2008**
Total assets	$112,000	$103,000
Stockholders' equity	24,000	22,000
Sales	96,000	78,000
Net income	8,100	5,400
Cash from operations	10,300	14,800
Cash paid for capital expenditures	7,500	6,400
Cash paid for acquisitions	3,400	1,100
Cash paid for interest	2,100	1,200
Cash paid for income taxes	3,400	3,200

Required:

1. Compute the following for 2008 and 2009:
   a. Return on sales
   b. Return on equity
   c. Cash flow-to-net income ratio
   d. Cash flow adequacy ratio
2. In which year did Mushu Company perform better: 2008 or 2009? Explain your answer.

ANALYTICAL ASSIGNMENTS

AA 14-70

DISCUSSION

Analyzing Earnings

Roger Donahoe owns two businesses: a drug store and a retail department store.

	Drug Store	Department Store
Net sales	$1,050,000	$670,000
Cost of goods sold	1,000,000	600,000
Average total assets	50,000	200,000
Other expenses	39,500	36,500

Which business is more profitable? Which business is more efficient? Overall, which business would you consider to be a more attractive investment?

AA 14-71

DISCUSSION

Can a Ratio Be Too Good?

Tony Christopher is analyzing the financial statements of Shaycole Company and has computed the following ratios:

	Shaycole	Industry Comparison
Current ratio	4.7	1.9
Asset turnover	1.8 times	1.4 times
Debt ratio	0.317	0.564

Andy Martinez, Tony's colleague, tells Tony that Shaycole looks great. Andy points out that, although Shaycole's ratios deviate significantly from the industry norms, all the deviations suggest that Shaycole is doing better than other firms in its industry. Is Andy right?

AA 14-72

DISCUSSION

Evaluating Alternative Investments

Judy Snow is considering investing $10,000 and wishes to know which of two companies offers the better alternative.

The Hoffman Company earned net income of $63,000 last year on average total assets of $280,000 and average stockholders' equity of $210,000. The company's shares are selling for $100 per share; 6,300 shares of common stock are outstanding.

The McMahon Company earned $24,375 last year on average total assets of $125,000 and average stockholders' equity of $100,000. The company's common shares are selling for $78 per share; 2,500 shares are outstanding.

Which stock should Judy buy?

AA 14-73

JUDGMENT CALL

You Decide: **Could we see Enron coming?**

Sherron Watkins, the whistle-blower at **Enron**, made the following statement at a conference that one of the authors attended: "If anyone would have been watching the cash flows of Enron, they could have figured out that there were problems." While traditional ratios don't reveal the problems, the following ratio provides some interesting results when looked at on a quarterly basis:

$$\frac{\text{Net Income from Operations} - \text{Cash Flows from Operations}}{\text{Net Income from Operations}}$$

(continued)

During the period 1998 and 2001, this ratio revealed the following:

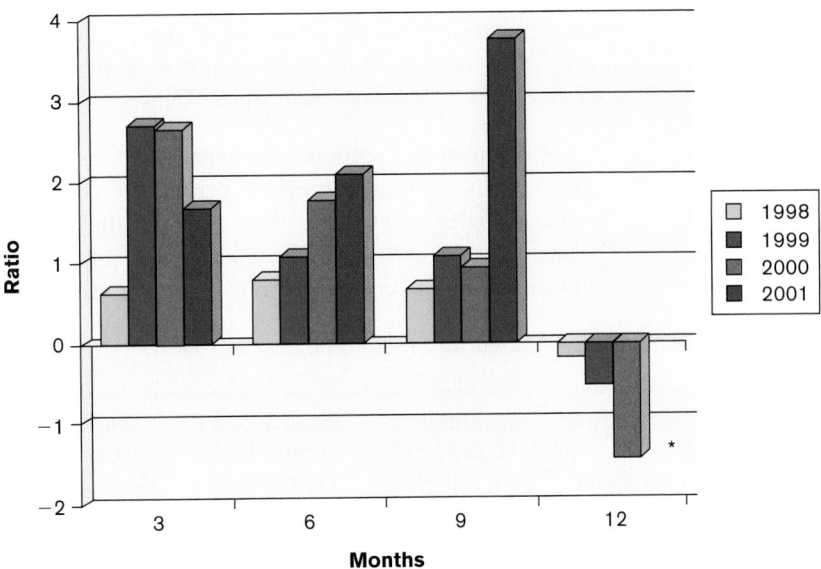

*Note:** The Enron fraud was discovered in the 4th quarter of 2001. As a result, comparable 12-month numbers are not available.

Does this ratio look normal or as expected for a nonfraud committing company? What would you expect this ratio to look like? Why do the yearly results look so different than the quarterly results?

AA 14-74

JUDGMENT CALL

You Decide: Ratios and debt covenants

XYZ Company has some leases on buildings that are structured so they do not have to be reported on the balance sheet as assets and liabilities (synthetic leases). However, as a term of the agreement, the lessor—a financial institution—requires that the company maintain an amount of cash in its institution so that the buildings could be purchased if the company misses some restrictive covenant agreements (i.e., certain ratio requirements, such as a current ratio of 2:1, etc.). The total amount of cash required to be held by the bank is $60 million. So far, XYZ has been including the $60 million in its cash account when calculating its current ratio. Your auditor has suggested that since the $60 million is restricted for a certain purpose, it should be reported as a long-term investment rather than as cash. Reclassifying the $60 million from cash to long-term investments would throw all kinds of ratios in default and you definitely don't want to do it. What is the appropriate accounting?

AA 14-75

REAL COMPANY ANALYSIS

Wal-Mart

Using **Wal-Mart**'s 2006 Form 10-K contained in Appendix A, answer the following questions:

1. Compute the following ratios for Wal-Mart for 2005 and compare those results to the 2006 results—debt ratio, current ratio, return on sales, asset turnover, and return on equity. For which of these ratios did Wal-Mart improve from 2005 to 2006?

2. Wal-Mart's fiscal 2006 inventory represents what percentage of sales? What percentage of total assets does this line item represent? Why do you think Wal-Mart has so much money tied up in inventory?

DuPont

In this chapter, you were introduced to the DuPont framework. Let us take a moment and apply that framework to the **DuPont Company**. DuPont is a company made up of many business segments and has the challenge of how to manage the diverse set of businesses operating under the control of the DuPont management team. In its 2005 annual report, DuPont described its business segments as follows:

> The company has six reporting segments. Five of the segments constitute the company's growth platforms: Agriculture & Nutrition; Coatings & Color Technologies; Electronic & Communication Technologies; Performance Materials; and Safety & Protection. The Pharmaceuticals segment is limited to income from the company's interest in two drugs, Cozaar and Hyzaar.

Summary segment results for 2005 are as follows:

2005	Agriculture & Nutrition	Coatings & Color Technologies	Electronic & Communication Technologies	Per-formance Materials	Pharma-ceuticals	Safety & Protection	Others
Total segment sales	$6,394	$6,234	$3,506	$6,750	$ –	$5,230	$ 52
Pretax operating income (loss)	862	564	532	523	751	980	(78)
Segment net assets	6,084	3,633	2,189	3,563	169	2,686	148

1. Using segment pretax operating income as a substitute for total company net income, tell which segment has the highest return on sales? The lowest?
2. Which segment has the highest asset turnover? The lowest?

The Walt Disney Company

Information from the 2005 financial statements of **The Walt Disney Company** is listed below. This information reports Disney's performance, by geographic area.

	United States and Canada	Europe	Asia Pacific	Latin America and Other
Sales	$24,806	$5,207	$1,451	$480
Operating income	3,512	688	377	77
Identifiable assets	45,809	5,120	2,110	119

1. Disney divides its worldwide operations into four geographic areas: the United States and Canada, Europe, Asia Pacific, and Latin America and Other. Which of these four has the best 2005 profitability as measured by return on sales?
2. Which of Disney's four geographic areas has the best overall asset efficiency in 2005 as measured by asset turnover?
3. Discuss why return on equity cannot be computed for each geographic area.

Which Is the Stronger Partner in the Merger?

In May 1998, **Daimler-Benz** and **Chrysler** announced their intention to merge. Daimler-Benz was the largest industrial company in Europe, and Chrysler was Number 3 of the Big Three automakers in the United States. The merger resulted in **DaimlerChrysler** becoming (at the time) the second largest automobile company in the world with 2000 sales exceeding $150 billion (**General Motors** reported sales in 2000 of $160 billion).

An interesting question is, "At the time of the merger, which of the two companies was the stronger?" Below are summary data for the two companies, both overall and for their respective automotive divisions.

(continued)

	Daimler-Benz		Chrysler	
	Overall	**Automotive**	**Overall**	**Automotive**
Sales	DM 124,050	DM 91,632	$61,147	$58,662
Net income	8,042	3,501	2,805	4,238
Total assets	137,099	46,955	60,418	44,483

The amounts are in millions of Deutsche marks for Daimler-Benz and millions of U.S. dollars for Chrysler.

For the automotive segment information, net income is the operating income for the segment and total assets are the assets that are identifiable with the segment.

1. Compute the following for both companies for overall results and automotive division results:
   a. Return on sales
   b. Asset turnover
2. In comparing the ratios calculated in (1), why don't you have to make adjustments for currency differences?
3. Which company had more worldwide automotive sales in 1997? *Note:* Don't forget the currency difference.

AA 14-79

ETHICS

Does the Bonus Plan Reward the Right Thing?

Roaring Springs Booksellers is an Internet book company. Customers choose their purchases from an online catalog and make their orders online. Roaring Springs then assembles the books from its warehouse inventory, packs the order, and ships it to the customer within three working days. The rapid turnaround time on orders requires Roaring Springs to have a large warehouse staff; wage expense averages almost 20% of sales.

Each member of Roaring Springs's top management team receives an annual bonus equal to 1% of his or her salary for every 0.1% that Roaring Springs's return on sales exceeds 5.0%. For example, if return on sales is 5.3%, each top manager would receive a bonus of 3% of salary. Historically, return on sales for Roaring Springs has ranged between 4.5% and 5.5%.

The management of Roaring Springs has come up with a plan to dramatically increase return on sales, perhaps to as high as 6.5% to 7.0%. The plan is to acquire a sophisticated, computerized packing machine that can receive customer order information, mechanically assemble the books for each order, box the order, print an address label, and route the box to the correct loading dock for pickup by the delivery service. Acquisition of this machine will allow Roaring Springs to lay off 100 warehouse employees, resulting in a significant savings in wage expense. Top management intends to acquire the machine by using new investment capital from stockholders and thus avoid an increase in interest expense. Because the depreciation expense on the new machine will be much less than the savings in reduced wage expense, return on sales will increase.

All the top managers of Roaring Springs are excited about the new plan because it could increase their bonuses to as much as 20% of salary. As assistant to the chief financial officer of Roaring Springs, you have been asked to prepare a briefing for the board of directors explaining exactly how this new packing machine will increase return on sales. As part of your preparation, you decide to examine the impact of the machine acquisition on the other two components of the DuPont framework—efficiency and leverage. You find that even with the projected increase in return on sales, the decrease in asset turnover and in the assets-to-equity ratio will cause total return on equity to decline from its current level of 18% to around 14%.

Your presentation is scheduled for the next board of directors meeting in two weeks. What should you do?

AA 14-80
WRITING

Who Should Get a Holiday Loan?

You are head of the loan department at Wilshire National Bank and have been approached by two firms in the retail toy business. Each firm is requesting a nine-month term loan to purchase inventory for the holiday season. You must make your recommendations to the loan committee and have gathered the following data in order to make your analysis. Fun Toy Company was organized in early 2008. The first year of operations was fairly successful, as the firm earned net income of $45,000. Total sales for the year were $600,000, and total assets at year-end December 31, 2008, were $350,000. A condensed balance sheet at September 30, 2009, follows. The firm is requesting a $100,000 loan.

Assets:		Liabilities and stockholders' equity:	
Cash	$ 60,000	Accounts payable	$ 70,000
Accounts receivable	65,000	Note payable, due 10/5/09	100,000
Inventory	125,000	Stockholders' equity	240,000
Prepaid expenses	5,000		
Furniture and fixtures	155,000	Total liabilities and	
Total assets	$410,000	stockholders' equity	$410,000

The Toy Store, the other firm, has been in business for many years. The firm's net income was $100,000 on total sales of $2,000,000 in the most recent fiscal year. A balance sheet as of September 30, 2009, is given below. The firm is seeking a $200,000 loan.

Assets:		Liabilities and stockholders' equity:	
Cash	$ 60,000	Accounts payable	$ 350,000
Accounts receivable	100,000	Current bank loan payable	150,000
Inventory	400,000	Long-term debt	400,000
Supplies	10,000	Stockholders' equity	500,000
Prepaid expenses	5,000		
Property, plant, and			
equipment	825,000	Total liabilities and	
Total assets	$1,400,000	stockholders' equity	$1,400,000

Write a one-page memo to the loan committee containing your recommendation about making loans to Fun Toy Company and to The Toy Store. You should use selected financial ratios in making your recommendation. Remember, your memo is only one page, so you can't just present a list of every possible ratio computation. Build your recommendation around a few key numbers.

AA 14-81
CUMULATIVE
SPREADSHEET
PROJECT

Projecting Financial Performance

The financial statement numbers and ratio assumptions used in constructing this series of cumulative spreadsheet projects in the text, starting in Chapter 2, are based on the actual experience of **Home Depot**. The original financial statement numbers in the spreadsheet project are adapted from Home Depot's actual 1985 financial statements. The projected financial statements that you will prepare in (1) below are a projection of how Home Depot would have performed in the years after 1985 if Home Depot had not made significant changes to its operations.

1. Handyman wishes to prepare forecasted balance sheets, income statements, and statements of cash flows for five years—2010, 2011, 2012, 2013, and 2014. Use the original financial statement numbers for 2009 (given in part (1) of the Cumulative Spreadsheet Project assignment in Chapter 2) as the basis for the forecast, along with the following additional information:
   a. Sales in 2010 are expected to increase by 40% over 2009 sales of $700. Sales are expected to increase 40% in each year thereafter.
   b. Cash will increase at the same rate as sales.

(continued)

c. The forecasted amount of accounts receivable is determined using the forecasted value for the average collection period. The average collection period is expected to be 14.08 days. To make the calculations simpler, this value of 14.08 days is based on forecasted end-of-year accounts receivable rather than on average accounts receivable.

d. The forecasted amount of inventory is determined using the forecasted value for the number of days' sales in inventory. The number of days' sales in inventory is expected to be 107.6 days. To make the calculations simpler, this value of 107.6 days is based on forecasted end-of-year inventory rather than on average inventory.

e. The forecasted amount of accounts payable is determined using the forecasted value for the number of days' purchases in accounts payable. The number of days' purchases in accounts payable is expected to be 48.34 days. To make the calculations simpler, this value of 48.34 days is based on forecasted end-of-year accounts payable rather than on average accounts payable.

f. The $160 in operating expenses reported in 2009 breaks down as follows: $5 depreciation expense, $155 other operating expenses.

g. New long-term debt will be acquired (or repaid) in an amount sufficient to make Handyman's debt ratio (total liabilities divided by total assets) in each year exactly equal to 0.80.

h. No cash dividends will be paid in any year.

i. New short-term loans payable will be acquired in an amount sufficient to make Handyman's current ratio exactly equal to 2.0 in each year.

j. The forecasted amount of property, plant, and equipment (PPE) is determined using the forecasted value for the fixed asset turnover ratio. For simplicity, compute the fixed asset turnover ratio using the end-of-period Gross PPE balance. The fixed asset turnover ratio is expected to be 3.518 times.

k. In computing depreciation expense, use straight-line depreciation and assume a 30-year useful life with no residual value. Gross PPE acquired during the year is only depreciated for half the year. In other words, depreciation expense is the sum of two parts: (1) a full year of depreciation on the beginning balance in PPE, assuming a 30-year life and no residual value and (2) a half year of depreciation on any new PPE acquired during the year, based on the change in the Gross PPE balance.

l. Assume an interest rate on short-term loans payable of 6.0% and on long-term debt of 8.0%. Only a half year's interest is charged on loans taken out during the year. For example, if short-term loans payable at the end of 2010 is $15 and given that short-term loans payable at the end of 2009 were $10, total short-term interest expense for 2010 would be $0.75 [($10 × .06) + ($5 × .06 × 1/2)].

2. Repeat (1), with the following changes in assumptions:

- Average Collection Period   9.06 days
- Number of Days' Sales in Inventory   66.23 days
- Fixed Asset Turnover   3.989 times
- Gross Profit Percentage   27.55%
- Other Operating Expenses/Sales   19.86%
- Number of Days' Purchases in Accounts Payable   50.37 days

Note: After making these changes in ratio values, your spreadsheet may have negative amounts for Short-Term Loans Payable. This is impossible. Adjust your spreadsheet so that Short-Term Loans Payable is never less than zero. This will require a relaxation of the requirement that the current ratio be at least 2.0.

3. Discuss why Handyman has a projected current ratio of less than 2.0 in some years when using the ratios in (2).

4. Which company would you rather loan money to—a company with the projected financial statements prepared in (1) or a company with the projected financial statements prepared in (2)? Explain your answer.

© DUNCAN SMITH/PHOTODISC RED/GETTY IMAGES INC.

Management Accounting and Cost Concepts

After studying this chapter, you should be able to:

(1) Explain how management accounting is a competitive tool. *The primary purpose of management accounting is to provide superior information to those running a company so that they can make better decisions and more successfully compete for customers, suppliers, employees, and so forth.*

(2) Understand the essential differences between management accounting and financial accounting. *Management accounting is intended for the use of the internal managers who run a company. Financial accounting is primarily intended to provide summary information to outsiders such as lenders and investors.*

(3) Recognize and understand the common terms and concepts used in management accounting. *One useful way to view costs for decision making is to separate them into fixed costs (those that stay the same as the level of production changes) and variable costs (those that increase as the level of production increases). Other useful classifications of costs are product/period, direct/indirect, differential/sunk, and out-of-pocket/opportunity.*

(4) Discuss the need for ethics in management accounting and describe the Standards of Ethical Conduct that apply to this profession. *Management accountants have access to a company's most important and sensitive internal competitive information. Accordingly, it is absolutely critical that management accountants conduct their work professionally and with the utmost integrity.*

DuPont was established in 1802 near Wilmington, Delaware, by a French immigrant, Eleuthére Irénée du Pont de Nemours, to produce black blasting powder. Three of E. I. du Pont's great-grandsons, Alfred, Coleman, and Pierre, purchased the firm's assets from the family in 1902. The three cousins decided to make the company even bigger by purchasing many of the company's suppliers of raw materials (such as charcoal, sodium nitrate, and crude glycerin) used in DuPont's explosive products. In addition, instead of wholesaling the products through traditional retailers, DuPont's new managers decided to create their own network of branch sales offices scattered across the United States.

Alfred, Coleman, and Pierre knew how to run a manufacturing business, but now they were in the mining, shipping, and sales business as well. How were they going to be able to effectively plan schedules, control operations, and evaluate the profitability of each of their diverse business segments? Essentially, Alfred, Coleman, and Pierre had an accounting problem.

Enter the management accountant, Donaldson Brown (DuPont's chief financial officer or CFO). Mr. Brown, along with other executives at DuPont, realized that every division required an investment in assets in order to be in business. The overall goal of every business should be to effectively use its assets to make a profit. For example, an explosives plant using assets worth $10 million and earning $500,000 in profit is not performing as well as a major sales division that also creates a $500,000 profit but only requires $5 million in assets. The sales division is earning a 10% return ($500,000 ÷ $5,000,000) on the DuPont investment in inventory, equipment, and buildings. The explosives plant is earning only a 5% ($500,000 ÷ $10,000,000) **return on investment**, or **ROI**. Obviously, additional investment would first go to the sales division in order to earn a 10% return rather than a mere 5% return. The ROI tool allowed the DuPont cousins to be hugely successful in managing the country's first integrated company by combining cost management with asset management and raising it to an art form! It's likely that few management accounting techniques have had as great an impact on business management as the DuPont ROI formula.[1]

return on investment (ROI)

A measure of operating performance and efficiency in utilizing assets; computed in its simplest form by dividing net income by average total assets. This measure is also known as ROA (return on assets).

 F Y I

Donaldson Brown took the ROI approach with him when he followed Pierre du Pont to help rescue another company in the midst of an inventory crisis in 1920. The name of the company was **General Motors**.

This chapter introduces management accounting and distinguishes it from financial accounting. The key purpose of management accounting is fulfilling the competitive needs of the company. DuPont had a competitive need to manage a very large and diverse organization and so invented new accounting measurements to serve as important management tools. A company's management accounting system is used to support the management processes of planning, controlling, and evaluating.

Business professionals who are in a position to use management accounting data to make important decisions must take care to make the best decisions possible on behalf of the organization, its owners, its employees, the surrounding community, and the public at large. As a result, it is critical that these decision makers understand the ethics of good business and are committed to perform ethically.

---

[1] Historical sources: H. T. Johnson and R. S. Kaplan, *Relevance Lost* (Boston: HBS Press, 1987); the DuPont Heritage Web site at **http://heritage.dupont.com/**.

In summary, this chapter has four purposes.

1. To demonstrate how management accounting can be a competitive tool.

2. To distinguish management accounting from financial accounting.

3. To introduce management accounting terminology in the context of several key management tools.

4. To explain the need for business ethics in management accounting.

Explain how management accounting is a competitive tool.

Management Accounting as a Competitive Tool

① An important facet of the DuPont story is that no government regulations or accounting rules were needed to prompt DuPont to develop the ROI analysis. Instead, the managers of DuPont were motivated by a desire to run their business better. Their hope was that the ROI measurements would help them make better decisions than their competitors were making. In short, good management accounting is a competitive tool.

Consider another example: two soup-and-salad restaurants are competing for business in a college community. One of the restaurants has a traditional pricing structure and offers coupons and special discounts for holidays, back-to-school week, and so forth. This restaurant's accounting system is centered on getting the bills paid on time and accurately accounting for payroll. The other restaurant has a management accounting system that carefully tracks the cost of each item on the menu, the time of day that each order is made, the server who takes each order, the demographics of the customers (as reported by the server), and the items that appear to be ordered in combinations. These data are used to design special offers targeted to certain types of customers for certain days and times of day. The order combination and cost data are used to cut prices on some popular items knowing that this will attract customers who will then order related items at regular prices. Now, the bottom line is if the second restaurant doesn't serve good food in an attractive atmosphere, then its fancy management accounting system can't make the business a success. But if the essential quality of the food and service is good, then the improved decision making using a superior management accounting system will, in the long run, give the second restaurant the competitive edge over its rival.

Because management accounting is a competitive tool, the practice of management accounting involves innovation, experimentation, diversity, success, and failure as businesses tinker with their management accounting systems to create superior information for decision making. Certainly there are "best practices" in management accounting; you will learn about them in the succeeding chapters. But remember that a good business is always re-examining its internal information system to see whether it can be coaxed into providing better, timelier data.

REMEMBER THIS...

- Good management accounting is a competitive tool.
- Good companies experiment with their internal information systems in order to generate better data allowing them to make better decisions than their competitors are making.

Understand the essential differences between management accounting and financial accounting.

Management Accounting and Financial Accounting

(2) The DuPont story is an example of how management accounting evolves within organizations. This development pattern has been playing out across companies for a long time. Since the first days of the Industrial Revolution, business owners and managers have generally adopted the best accounting ideas available from other companies and then created their own new accounting system to provide a competitive edge. In fact, a company often regards a good management accounting system as a valuable company secret—and rarely discloses its details to the public.

> **! CAUTION**
>
> Don't think management accounting is not important just because it is not defined as precisely as financial accounting. Management accounting is critical to the success of businesses throughout the world.

In contrast, financial accounting has effectively developed in the United States to provide a *common reporting platform* to the public. The purpose of financial accounting, as defined by generally accepted accounting principles (GAAP), is to satisfy the needs of outside investors, creditors, and regulators for fair and consistent reports of financial position and operations. Accordingly, all companies are required to apply the same general financial accounting rules so that outsiders can compare financial reports coming from many different companies. These financial accounting rules are established by the Financial Accounting Standards Board (FASB) and are enforced by the Securities and Exchange Commission (SEC).

In contrast to the rules and regulations surrounding financial accounting, no government regulator or auditor is going to insist that a company implement a good management accounting system; the choice of how to collect and use information within a company is part of a company's competitive strategy. For example, no one forced the DuPont cousins to use the ROI formula to better manage their business; however, because the ROI evaluation framework worked well for DuPont, it was subsequently mimicked by many (but not all) of DuPont's competitors. Remember, the only reason a company does management accounting is to satisfy a competitive need, and competitive need often dictates that one organization's management accounting system will *not* look like another's!

The differences between management accounting and financial accounting can be summarized as follows:

Source:
- Management accounting *evolves* from best practices.
- Financial accounting is *legislated and governed* by regulatory agencies and professional institutions.

Purpose:
- Management accounting exists to serve the *competitive needs* of organizations.
- Financial accounting exists to serve the need for organizations to *periodically report* results to outside investors and lenders.

Outcome:
- Management accounting results in both *financial and nonfinancial data* that are *proprietary* (i.e., guarded from becoming available to competitors and the general public).
- Financial accounting results in *only financial data* that are *public* and reported to investors and creditors.

EXHIBIT 1   **The Management Process**

- Recognize needs
- Identify alternatives
- Evaluate choices
- Implement decisions

Planning

Decision Making

Evaluating

Controlling

- Reward performance
- Provide feedback
- Analyze results
- Identify problems

- Establish expectations
- Create performance measures
- Gather results
- Compute variances

STOP & THINK

We have described some differences in financial and management accounting. Why is it important for an accounting system to provide *both* types of accounting information?

Managers are always making choices using the available management accounting information. What should be produced? What should be sold? How should the service be delivered? What does this client need? Which supplier should be used? Who should be promoted? How should financing be obtained? Exhibit 1 illustrates the central role that decision making, using management accounting data, plays in the general management process.

The three management functions of planning, controlling, and evaluating generally follow a natural order—at least in theory. In practice, managers are often required to work with processes, customers, and employees requiring all three decision-making functions at once. For example, the manager of a campus copy center must simultaneously plan the week's work flow, control the production process by balancing the needs of student customers and faculty copy requests, and evaluate the performance of both the employees and the copy machines.

planning

Outlining the activities that need to be performed for an organization to achieve its objectives.

Planning

Management **planning** involves a process of identifying problems or opportunities, identifying alternatives, evaluating alternatives, then choosing and implementing the best alternative(s). There are two basic types of planning:

1. Long-run planning, which includes:
   a. Strategic planning
   b. Capital budgeting

2. Short-run planning, which includes:
   a. Production and process prioritizing
   b. Operational budgeting (profit planning)

Long-run planning involves making decisions with effects that extend several years into the future—usually three to five years, but sometimes longer. This includes broad-based decisions about products, markets, productive facilities, and financial resources. Long-run planning is often called strategic planning. **Strategic planning**, likely the most critical decision-making process that takes place at the executive level in any organization today, usually involves identifying an organization's mission, the goals flowing from that mission, and strategies and action steps to accomplish those goals. Successful executives, such as Bill Gates (**Microsoft**) or Warren Buffett (**Berkshire Hathaway**), have always displayed great skill in studying the market, identifying customer needs, evaluating competitors' strengths and weaknesses, and defining the right investments and processes their organization needs for success. Good management accounting supports good strategic planning by providing the internal information needed by executives to evaluate and adjust their strategic plans.

strategic planning

Broad, long-range planning usually conducted by top management.

capital budgeting

Systematic planning for long-term investments in operating assets.

With strategic planning in place (or in process), the company can then plan for the purchase and use of major assets such as buildings or equipment to help the company meet its long-range goals. For example, if part of a university's long-run strategic plan is to increase the competitive level of its football team, then the university probably should consider improving, or even replacing, its existing football stadium and practice facility. This type of long-run planning of the acquisition of assets is called **capital budgeting**. We will cover capital budgeting in detail in a later chapter.

Colleges and universities often conduct "capital" campaigns. These are fundraising campaigns targeted at generating funds for the construction of long-term assets such as academic buildings and athletic facilities.

Short-run planning is divided into two categories. Once the organization has made long-term resource commitments (e.g., land, buildings, equipment, management personnel, etc.), then managers need to determine how to best use those committed resources to maximize the return on their capital investments—a process often referred to as **production prioritizing**.[2] Did you catch the phrase "return on capital investment" in the last sentence? Sound familiar? The DuPont ROI concept is one way to establish priorities on products, service processes, or divisions that make the largest contributions to the goals of the organization. For example, you can view your study of accounting as a production process; production prioritizing involves analysis to determine how you should best spend your time in preparing for the next exam—reading the chapters, doing homework problems, studying in a group, or catching up on your sleep.

production prioritizing

Management's continual evaluation of the profitability of the various product lines and divisions within an organization so that products or divisions that are performing below expectations can be analyzed to identify problems and potential solutions.

Once the organization has determined what to provide to the marketplace in order to maximize its goals, then managers are ready to go on to the next phase of short-run planning—**operational budgeting**. Sometimes known as profit plans, operational budgets are used by managers to establish and communicate daily, weekly, and monthly goals (also known as "standards") for the organization. Many individuals—young, middle-aged, and old—face severe personal financial problems because they fail to use even the most basic

---

[2] Production prioritizing includes the process of prioritizing what services will be created and delivered to the marketplace (e.g., airlines, consulting, and banking).

F Y I

In the next section, we'll introduce another popular method of prioritizing the production potential of an organization—cost-volume-profit analysis.

techniques of regular operational budgeting. We will discuss operational budgets in a later chapter.

Controlling

operational budgeting

Managerial planning decisions regarding current operations and those of the immediate future (typically one year or less) that are characterized by regularity and frequency.

Controlling involves a process of tracking actual performance. These data are then used subsequently in the evaluating process to compare against the budgets previously prepared in the planning process to measure deviations from the original goals or standards. Controlling also involves the real-time, day-to-day management of all of a company's business processes. A good example of a control device is the radar gun used by major league baseball teams to measure the speed the pitcher is throwing his pitches. These measurements can be used at the end of the season in evaluating which pitchers are most valuable to the team. But these measurements can also be used by the manager during the course of a game to indicate when a pitcher is getting tired and should be replaced. The radar gun measurements are useful for evaluating individual performance after the fact but are also useful in effectively managing the team.

controlling

Implementing management plans and identifying how plans compare with actual performance.

Evaluating

Evaluating involves analyzing results, providing feedback to managers and other employees, rewarding performance, and identifying problems. Evaluating is typically a process of comparing actual performance against expected inputs of costs, expected outputs of quality, and expected timelines. This comparison typically results in information called *variances,* which tell management how well the organization is achieving its plans. If performance is in accordance with the plan, the variances signal that operations are in control and no unusual management action is necessary. If performance is substantially different from the plan, management needs to decide how to alter operations in order to improve future performance. For example, most students in college classes are asked to evaluate their instructors near the end of the term. These evaluation results can be used by conscientious faculty members who are trying to improve their teaching, and the results can also be used by department heads in deciding which teachers should be retained or replaced.

evaluating

Analyzing results, rewarding performance, and identifying problems.

This third function in the management process, evaluating, brings us back to the point where we started, planning. The information gained through the evaluating function is used in planning for the following period. Remember that as managers *evaluate* performance in the last period, they may also be making *planning* decisions to improve operations for the next period while gathering and receiving results to control the current period.

REMEMBER THIS...

Management Accounting:
- Competitive tool
- Both financial and nonfinancial data
- Data usually kept secret within the company
- Used for internal planning, control, and evaluation

Financial Accounting:
- Uniform across companies (generally accepted accounting principles)
- Restricted to financial data
- Data often made public
- Used primarily by investors and creditors in deciding whether to provide capital to the company

Managerial Accounting Terminology

Recognize and understand the common terms and concepts used in management accounting.

(3) In this section you will be introduced to the common terms and concepts used in management accounting. This introduction is meant as an overview; you will get detailed practice in each of these areas in subsequent chapters.

Terms Used in Planning and Cost-Volume-Profit Analysis

This section introduces **cost-volume-profit (C-V-P) analysis**, which is a management tool primarily used in the planning process. The basic objective of C-V-P analysis is determining how the level of a company's sales impacts profits. For example, before opening a new Thai restaurant, the would-be restaurateur should calculate how many customers a day, on average, must be served in order to pay the rent and generate a reasonable profit. If the necessary number of customers to "break even" seems unreasonably high, the business plan must be revised or abandoned.

F Y I

C-V-P analysis is often referred to as break-even analysis.

This sounds like an obvious planning exercise, but too many small business owners neglect doing even this basic analysis.

To use C-V-P analysis successfully, a manager must categorize costs as either fixed or variable costs. The concept of fixed and variable costs is fairly simple. Total **variable costs** change in *direct proportion* to changes in some particular activity level, such as production or sales volumes. One example of a variable cost is the costs of materials (such as bolts of cloth in a clothing factory), which vary proportionately with the number of units produced. Sales commissions, which vary proportionately with sales volume, are another example of a variable cost. Another way to think of a variable cost is that the cost is a set amount per unit—$3.50 per meal or $2,000 per car or $12 per book. The more meals or cars or books that are sold, the higher the total variable cost.

In contrast, **fixed costs** remain constant in total, regardless of activity level, at least over a certain range of activity. Examples of fixed costs are rent, insurance, equipment depreciation, and supervisors' salaries. Regardless of changes in sales or production output, these costs typically remain constant. For example, think back on the Thai restaurant example mentioned earlier. The rent on the restaurant location is a fixed cost because, no matter how many customers are attracted to the restaurant during the month, the monthly rent is typically still the same amount.

Obviously, to be successful, a business must first be able to cover, or pay for, all of its costs. However, a good understanding of variable and fixed costs provides the organization with a clear view of how it can make a profit using C-V-P analysis. The basic C-V-P concept is that the difference, or margin, between sales and variable costs must first be used to cover fixed costs. Once the organization achieves that breakeven point, then the remaining margin becomes profit. For example, if the average variable cost to create a meal at a restaurant is $3 and the average price of a meal is $9, then each meal on average

cost-volume-profit (C-V-P) analysis

Techniques for determining how changes in revenues, costs, and level of activity affect the profitability of an organization.

variable costs

Costs that change in total in direct proportion to changes in activity level.

fixed costs

Costs that remain constant in total, regardless of activity level, at least over a certain range of activity.

CAUTION

In theory, distinguishing between variable and fixed costs sounds simple. If the activity, such as production volume or sales volume, increases and the cost in question increases, then it must be a variable cost. Otherwise, it is a fixed cost. In reality, however, identifying and managing variable and fixed costs can involve many complexities. Subsequent chapters will focus more on identifying and using variable and fixed costs.

The cost of bolts of cloth used in a clothing factory is classified as a variable cost because it varies proportionately by the number of units produced. The more cloth used in production, the more the total amount of this cost.

© MONTY RAKUSEN/DIGITAL VISION/GETTY IMAGES INC.

contributes $6 to cover the fixed costs of running the restaurant. If monthly fixed costs (such as rent, insurance, and so forth) at the restaurant are $9,000, then the owner needs to sell 1,500 meals ($9,000 ÷ $6) each month in order to break even. As you will see in a subsequent chapter, cost-volume-profit analysis is a simple but powerful tool that is core to the planning process in organizations.

Terms Related to Controlling Product Cost Flows

product costs

Costs associated with products or services offered.

Imagine a trip to your favorite fast-food restaurant. Now consider all of the costs incurred by that entire fast-food organization, from the president's salary down to the cost of the lettuce for the sandwiches. For management accounting purposes, we can divide these costs into two groups, product costs and period costs. Costs closely associated with the products or services offered are called **product costs**. Examples in a fast-food setting are the cost of the food, the wages of the food preparers, the salary of the store manager, and the rent on the store location. As you sit there, ready to bite into your sandwich, you can look around and see all of these costs. In this sense, they are closely associated with the product (the sandwich) and are classified as product costs. In a manufacturing company such as **DuPont**, for example, product costs (often referred to as manufacturing costs) are all costs necessary to create finished goods ready for sale. They include all costs related to production: the factory manager's salary, depreciation and taxes on the factory building, wages of the factory workers, and the materials that go into the product. In a merchandising company such as **Wal-Mart** or **Home Depot**, product costs are the costs incurred to purchase goods and get them ready for resale to customers. In a service company such as the **Union Pacific Railroad** or **Kelly Services** (which provides temporary employees), product costs (sometimes called cost of services) involve labor, supplies, and other costs directly related to providing services to customers.

> ⬡ **STOP & THINK**
>
> A major difference between Kelly Services and manufacturers or merchandisers is inventory. Kelly sells services. Can we put service labor into inventory?

period costs

Costs not directly related to a product, service, or asset. These costs are charged as expenses to the income statement in the period in which they are incurred.

Period costs are all costs incurred that are not closely associated with a specific product or service. In the fast-food setting we considered earlier, examples of period costs are the president's salary, advertising, and office costs incurred in the corporate headquarters. These are costs that are not directly associated with the sandwich that you are eating or the environment in which you are eating it. In general, the most common period costs are selling and administrative costs. Examples of selling costs are sales salaries, advertising, and delivery costs. Examples of administrative costs are salaries of the president and controller, depreciation or rent on office buildings, taxes on assets used in administration, and other office expenditures such as postage, supplies, and utilities.

The labels "product" and "period" stem from the procedure followed in reporting these costs as expenses on the income statement. For product costs, these costs are associated with specific products or services and are expensed when those products are sold. For example, if Wal-Mart sells two-thirds of the inventory it purchased during November, only the cost of the inventory sold (i.e., Cost of Goods Sold) becomes an expense on that month's income statement. The other third of the inventory cost remains an asset (i.e., Inventory) on the balance sheet. In contrast, period costs are reported as an expense *immediately* in the period in which they are incurred. So, regardless of how many products are sold during the month, the president's entire salary for November is recognized as an expense on the November monthly income statement. Thus, these costs are called period costs because they are always expensed in the period (e.g., month) in which they are incurred.

Types of Product Costs

Now let's consider how you might measure and control product and period costs in a variety of organizations. How would you measure product costs for a merchandiser? Actually, that is a fairly easy question. The resources Home Depot spends to acquire store inventory for resale to customers clearly are product costs. As products are sold, these inventory costs become an expense on the income statement. What about the wages and salaries of Home Depot's cashiers, sales associates, and managers? Home Depot will likely categorize these costs as part of its selling and administrative expenses and treat them as a period cost on the income statement. That's not too difficult.

Now consider the same question for **Ernst & Young LLP**, one of the largest certified public accounting (CPA) firms in the world. What are the products sold by this service firm? Ernst & Young sells the time of its tax accountants, auditors, and consultants. The salaries of these professionals represent the costs of its "product." These costs are reported as the expense "cost of services sold" in the same period in which Ernst & Young reports the corresponding service revenue. Thus, if the consulting revenue from a specific job is reported in January 2009, any product costs associated with that job which were incurred in 2008 are not expensed until January 2009. As of the end of 2008, these costs are given a label such as "consulting projects in progress" or "unbilled services" and reported as inventory on the December 2008 balance sheet. Ernst & Young also employs many other people (such as clerks, secretaries, and office managers) to support the professionals and to administer office needs. The costs of these people are not closely associated with specific consulting jobs. Accordingly, the wages and salaries of these clerks and office managers, along with costs of office rent, desk supplies, and computers, are likely treated as period costs and recognized as selling and administrative expenses on the income statement in the period in which they are incurred.

When identifying product costs for control purposes, the most challenging organization to analyze is a manufacturing business. Does DuPont purchase inventory for resale? Actually, it does purchase some inventory, such as basic chemicals. But it doesn't simply turn around and resell these basic chemicals to customers. Significant processing has to take place before these raw materials become a finished product ready for sale. DuPont must employ laborers to work with these chemicals. In addition, DuPont builds factory buildings and purchases manufacturing equipment. DuPont must also employ managers and other support personnel (such as engineers and custodians) to support the line workers' efforts to convert basic chemicals into finished products. These are all product costs. Basically, any cost required to get the product manufactured and ready for sale is a product cost.

direct materials

Materials that become part of the product and are traceable to it.

indirect materials

Materials that are necessary to a manufacturing or service business but are not directly included in or are not a significant part of the actual product.

To help management analyze the manufacturing cost of its products, product costs are divided into three components: (1) direct materials, (2) direct labor, and (3) manufacturing overhead. **Direct materials** are materials that become part of the product and are traceable to it. Some materials, however, such as the glue and nails in a finished piece of furniture, are so minor and their use so difficult to trace to a specific product that they are not considered direct materials, but rather **indirect materials**. Indirect materials also include the materials and

direct labor

Wages that are paid to those who physically work on direct materials to transform them into a finished product and are traceable to specific products.

indirect labor

Labor that is necessary to a manufacturing or service business but is not directly related to the actual production of the manufactured or service product.

manufacturing overhead

All costs incurred in the manufacturing process other than direct materials and direct labor.

direct costs

Costs that are specifically traceable to a unit of business or segment being analyzed.

supplies used in nonproduction activities such as maintenance and custodial processes. **Direct labor** consists of the wages that are paid to those who physically work on the direct materials to transform them into a finished product. Conversely, wages and salaries paid to factory supervisors and management, maintenance staff, and factory security guards are treated as **indirect labor**. **Manufacturing overhead** includes all other costs incurred in the manufacturing process not specifically identified as direct materials or direct labor. Both indirect materials and indirect labor are included in manufacturing overhead. Exhibit 2 summarizes the relationship between product costs and period costs in various types of organizations. A solid understanding of product and period costs helps managers better understand and control costs of providing services, purchasing merchandise, or producing goods.

Terms Related to Evaluation and Decision Making

Managers are paid to make hard decisions as markets for particular products change based on developments in technology, new fads and trends in consumer taste, and increased pressure from new and existing competitors. Occasionally, the situation requires a serious look at the potential need to exit from a particular market or to drop a specific product line. Sometimes these decisions are motivated by the opportunity to enter a new market or add a new product line. For example, airlines are constantly evaluating whether to cut service on less-traveled routes, to increase or cut back the number of first-class seats, and so forth. The decision to drop a product line is critical because subsequently reversing the decision can be difficult or impossible. Good management accounting can do much to facilitate the process of evaluating divisions, personnel, processes, and products. Conversely, a poor understanding of some critical management accounting concepts can lead to painful, if not potentially lethal, company problems. To illustrate how accounting supports this evaluation process, we need to extend your vocabulary of key management accounting terms.

Direct and Indirect Costs   So far we have identified fixed and variable costs as a method of cost classification that provides good support to the planning process. We've also defined product and period costs and used those classifications to demonstrate the management controlling process. Now we introduce some new ways to classify costs that are useful for evaluating performance. One of these classifications is direct costs and indirect costs. **Direct costs** are costs that can be obviously and physically traced to a business unit or segment being analyzed. The unit may be a sales territory, product line, division, plant, or any other subdivision for which performance needs to be analyzed. Direct costs are often described as those costs that could be saved if the segment were to be discontinued. Typically, many

EXHIBIT 2	Product Costs and Period Costs in Business Organizations	
Type of Company	**Product Costs**	**Period Costs**
Service company	Costs of providing services	Selling costs Administrative costs
Merchandising company (wholesale or retail)	Costs incurred in purchasing goods from suppliers	Selling costs Administrative costs
Manufacturing company	All manufacturing costs including direct materials, direct labor, and manufacturing overhead	Selling costs Administrative costs

types of direct costs are variable, but some direct costs are fixed. For example, if the business segment being considered is a branch sales office, the cost of inventory and labor to run the store would be direct costs that are variable, while the cost to rent the building would be a direct cost that is fixed.

indirect costs

Costs normally incurred for the benefit of several segments within the organization; sometimes called common costs or joint costs.

Indirect costs—sometimes referred to as common costs or joint costs—are costs that are normally incurred for the benefit of several segments. Indirect costs can also be either fixed or variable, although these costs are nearly always fixed. Sometimes these costs are allocated in order to be assigned to a segment. For example, consider a sales manager's salary. If a segment is defined as a branch sales office and a sales manager supervises only one segment, the manager's salary is likely a direct cost of that sales office. If the manager is responsible for several segments, however, the salary would then be an indirect cost to any one of the sales offices. Total indirect costs, such as the manager's salary, normally do not change if one or more of the segments (in this case, the sales offices) are discontinued. Another example of an indirect cost may be manufacturing overhead. In most large organizations, many (but not all) types of manufacturing overhead costs are not directly identifiable with a specific product or product line. Hence, manufacturing overhead costs are typically classified as indirect costs to these products or product lines because they are incurred as a consequence of general or overall operating activities.

F Y I

Activity-based costing (ABC) is a relatively new method of cost assignment that we will fully discuss in a later chapter on activity-based costing. A major emphasis of ABC is to connect costs directly with certain activities. One result of ABC is an increase in the number of costs that can be classified as direct costs.

Costs are designated as either direct or indirect so that a business segment such as a division or product line can be evaluated on the basis of only those costs *directly* traceable or chargeable to it. Although companies sometimes allocate indirect costs among segments, such allocations often confuse the analysis of the segment's operations. By focusing only on direct costs, management can both identify segments where performance needs to be improved and recognize segments where performance is outstanding and should be rewarded.

Differential Costs and Sunk Costs   The difference between direct costs and indirect costs is similar to the difference between another set of cost terms—differential costs and sunk costs. The **differential costs** of a decision—sometimes called avoidable costs, incremental costs, or relevant costs—are the future costs that change as a result of that decision. In the context of making a decision as to whether to drop a product line, there is likely little difference between the terms *differential cost* and *direct cost*. (The term *differential* is also commonly applied to future *revenues* that will be affected by the decision.) **Sunk costs**, on the other hand, are past costs that cannot be changed as the result of a future decision. You should note that the definition of sunk costs is not quite the same as that of indirect costs. Indirect costs are those costs that are not affected by a *particular* decision. For example, whether **DuPont** decides to continue or discontinue a product line will likely not affect its general and administrative costs. These costs are indirect to a particular product line. This does not mean that management cannot change any of DuPont's general and administrative costs. It just means that a different management decision process is required to change these costs than the process used in evaluating the viability of a particular product line. If this sounds as though a cost could be indirect to one evaluation situation or focus and direct to another, you're right. Defining a cost as direct or indirect depends on the object of the decision. On the other hand, sunk costs are not dependent at all on any decision object.

differential costs

Future costs that change as a result of a decision; also called incremental or relevant costs.

sunk costs

Costs, such as depreciation, that are past costs and do not change as a result of a future decision.

out-of-pocket costs

Costs that require an outlay of cash or other resources.

opportunity costs

The benefits lost or forfeited as a result of selecting one alternative course of action over another.

A sunk cost is exactly what it sounds like—sunk! There is nothing a company can reasonably do to change a sunk cost.

As an example of sunk costs, assume you have season tickets to a school's basketball game. On the night of a game, a friend asks you to go to a movie with her. You have wanted to see the movie for a long time. If you decline because you have already purchased the basketball tickets and believe you must therefore go to the game, you may have made the wrong decision. The cost of the basketball tickets is a sunk cost. The only costs that are relevant to your decision are the costs associated with going to the movie, such as the ticket price and popcorn and other goodies you might buy, as well as any out-of-pocket costs you might spend at the basketball game.

Out-of-Pocket Costs and Opportunity Costs

At the most general level, costs can be separated into out-of-pocket costs and opportunity costs. **Out-of-pocket costs** require an outlay of cash or other resources. Many of the costs discussed thus far in this chapter could be called out-of-pocket costs. If a company is deciding whether to accept a special order, the costs of materials needed to produce that order are out-of-pocket costs. If a fast-food restaurant is considering installing a drive-up window, the cost of construction is an out-of-pocket cost. Naïve individuals and organizations usually consider only out-of-pocket costs when making decisions. For example, an individual deciding whether to attend a movie might consider only the $9 cost of the ticket required to gain admittance. On the other hand, opportunity costs do not require an outlay of resources. Nevertheless, they are as important as out-of-pocket costs to good management decision making. **Opportunity costs** are the benefits lost or forfeited as a result of selecting one alternative course of action over another. For example, choosing to go to a movie instead of working two hours at $8 per hour has an opportunity cost of $16, as well as an out-of-pocket cost of $9 for the ticket. Installing a drive-up window at a fast-food outlet may have several opportunity costs, such as lost seating or lost parking available to customers.

STOP & THINK

Which of the following costs are typically recorded in a traditional accounting system: product costs, fixed costs, indirect costs, out-of-pocket costs, sunk costs, opportunity costs?

CAUTION

It is important to understand that opportunity costs are very important costs that are not formally tracked in the company's accounting system.

REMEMBER THIS...

Costs can be categorized in a variety of ways depending on the decision that is being made. The most important categorizations are as follows:

Fixed/Variable   Fixed—A cost that doesn't change based on changes in the level of sales or production. Examples are building rent and executive salaries.

Variable—A cost that changes directly with changes in the level of sales or production. Examples are materials costs and sales commissions.

Product/Period   Product—A cost incurred as part of the production process. Operationally, you can think of these as the costs incurred in the factory. These costs are first reported as an

(continued)

asset (inventory) and then as an expense (cost of goods sold) when the product is sold.

Period—A cost incurred outside the factory or production facility. These costs are reported as an expense in the period in which they are incurred.

Types of Product Cost	Direct materials—The cost of the primary raw materials used in production. For example, in the production of french fries, the direct materials cost is the cost of the potatoes.
	Direct labor—The cost of the wages of the workers who are assembling the direct materials into the finished product. For example, in the production of an automobile, the direct labor cost is the compensation cost of the auto workers on the assembly line.
	Manufacturing overhead—All factory costs that are not direct materials or direct labor. Examples are factory foremen salaries, factory building depreciation, and miscellaneous indirect materials such as glue, screws, and so forth.
Direct/Indirect	Direct—The costs that are created by a particular product or segment that is being analyzed. If a product or segment is dropped, the direct costs created by that product or segment will disappear.
	Indirect—The costs that are assigned to a particular product or segment but that are not actually caused by that product or segment. Importantly, if a product or segment is dropped, the indirect costs assigned to that product or segment will remain.
Differential/ Sunk	Differential—A future cost that can be changed by a decision made now. For example, the monthly rent that you will pay on the apartment you choose to live in next year is a differential cost.
	Sunk—A past cost that cannot be changed by any decision made now. For example, the rent that you paid for your apartment last month is a sunk cost.
Out-of-pocket/ Opportunity	Out-of-pocket—Costs that involve the outlay of cash or the use of some other asset (such as equipment).
	Opportunity—The benefits not received because of actions NOT taken. For example, the opportunity cost of going to a basketball game is the increased points that you could have received on the next day's accounting exam if you had spent that time studying.

The Role of Ethics in Management Accounting

(4) The function of management accounting in the organization is to support competitive decision making by collecting, processing, and communicating information that helps managers plan, control, and evaluate business processes and company strategy. The top accountant in most large organizations is usually called the controller. In most organizations, professionals responsible for accounting systems and other critical decision-support data report to the controller. The controller usually reports to a vice president of finance or perhaps the chief finance officer (CFO). This individual, in turn, reports to the organization's president or chief executive officer (CEO).

As the chief accounting officer, the controller is ultimately responsible for what information is created to manage the organization, as well as how that information is used. This individual, as well as all others who work with him or her, are in a position of significant power. Those who manage the management accounting process have access to the organization's most important and sensitive competitive information used to make operational and strategic decisions. Hence, it is absolutely critical that these individuals conduct their work professionally and with utmost integrity. Otherwise, the consequences of unethical behavior in the practice of management accounting can ruin (and, on occasion, has ruined) individuals, companies, and communities.

Unfortunately, ethical dilemmas in both large and small organizations are not rare. As white-collar crime continues to rise, those who work in management accounting are often confronted with ethical issues on the job and need to be prepared to deal with them on a rational basis. A sampling of some of the ethical dilemmas that business professionals may be exposed to are listed in Exhibit 3. If your career path leads you to a position that involves management accounting (and most management positions in an organization do somehow involve management accounting processes), you will find that dealing with these types of ethical indiscretions is often not easy. The situation is often complicated by the fact that violators are frequently people you know and work with.

Your role as a member of the management team requires that as far as possible you work to handle questions of ethics *within* the organization. However, some occasions may require you to involve outside authorities. The Institute of Management Accountants (IMA) is the leading professional organization in North America devoted exclusively to

---

EXHIBIT 3	**Ethical Dilemmas Faced by Management Accountants**

Ethical internal dilemmas
- Padding expense accounts
- Theft in the workplace
- Inflating profits on financial reports
- Violating a firm's purchasing policies
- Understating or postponing recognition of costs to achieve higher bonuses or make the financial statements look better
- Using company assets for personal use

Ethical issues involving third-party transactions
- Bid rigging to give business to favored suppliers
- Taking kickbacks on purchase contracts
- Adjusting inspection reports to reflect higher quality of product
- Withholding unfavorable information

management accounting. Its goals are to help those working in management accounting to develop themselves both personally and professionally, by means of education, certification, and association with other business professionals. As a respected leader within the global financial community, the IMA's ethical standards provide guidance to practitioners for maintaining the highest levels of ethical conduct. Essentially, the IMA notes that its members are ethically required to (1) be competent in their profession, (2) not disclose confidential information, (3) act with both actual and apparent integrity in all situations, and (4) maintain objectivity when communicating information to decision makers. If confronted with situations that may involve ethical conflicts, the business professional should consider the following courses of action: (1) Discuss the problem with the immediate supervisor (only when the supervisor is involved should higher management levels be involved). (2) Confidentially use an objective advisor to help clarify the issues. (3) Resign from the organization and submit an informative report to an appropriate representative of the organization (after exhausting all levels of internal communication).[3]

FYI

Those who work in management accounting can obtain a professional certificate that is much like the CPA certification. The Certificate in Management Accounting (CMA) is sponsored by the Institute of Management Accountants. The CMA certification focuses on a broad range of topics that are key to management performance. In addition to management accounting topics that we will study in this textbook, the CMA exam topics include economics, business finance, situational analysis, and decision making with a strong emphasis on ethics.

Although the IMA has a formal code of ethics, there really isn't a perfect set of rules you can follow to help you resolve every conflict. Therefore, you need to be developing values and skills right now in order to prepare for future challenges. To help you, we have included at the end of each chapter at least one ethics case. Perhaps more than anything else you do, developing a commitment to and an understanding of good ethics will develop you into a great business professional and will help improve our society.

REMEMBER THIS...

- The chief accountant in most organizations is the controller.
- Those persons involved with creating management accounting information will occasionally confront ethical issues inside the organization.
- The Institute of Management Accountants (IMA) provides standards of ethical conduct to help guide professionals involved in management accounting processes.

---

[3] A more complete description of the IMA's "Standards of Ethical Conduct" can be viewed at the following URL: **http://www.imanet.org/pdf/981.pdf**.

REVIEW OF LEARNING OBJECTIVES

(1) **Explain how management accounting is a competitive tool.** Good companies experiment with their internal information systems in order to generate better data allowing them to make better decisions than their competitors are making.

(2) **Understand the essential differences between management accounting and financial accounting.**

	Management Accounting	Financial Accounting
Variability Across Companies	Unique competitive tool	Uniform across companies (generally accepted accounting principles)
Type of Data	Both financial and nonfinancial data	Restricted to financial data
Availability of Data	Data usually kept secret within the company	Data often made public
Use of Data	Used for internal planning, control, and evaluation	Used primarily by investors and creditors in deciding whether to provide capital to the company

(3) **Recognize and understand the common terms and concepts used in management accounting.**

Decision Context

Given the cost structure, will sales be high enough to break even? How much will profits change with a given change in sales?	**Fixed cost**–A cost that doesn't change based on changes in the level of sales or production.	**Variable cost**–A cost that changes directly with changes in the level of sales or production.
What is the cost per unit to make a product?	**Product cost**–A cost incurred as part of the production process. Operationally, these are the costs incurred in the factory. These costs are first reported as an asset (inventory) and then as an expense (cost of goods sold) when the product is sold.	**Period cost**–A cost incurred outside the factory or production facility. These costs are reported as an expense in the period in which they are incurred.
Should we stop making a certain product? Should we close down a certain business segment?	**Direct cost**–A cost that is created by a particular product or segment that is being analyzed. If a product or segment is dropped, the direct costs created by that product or segment will disappear.	**Indirect cost**–A cost that is assigned to a particular product or segment but that is not actually caused by that product or segment. If a product or segment is dropped, the indirect costs assigned to that product or segment will remain.
Should we do Action A (where Action A can be dropping a product line, firing an employee, taking a special order, and so forth)?	**Differential cost**–A future cost that can be changed by a decision made now.	**Sunk cost**–A past cost that cannot be changed by any decision made now.
Should we do Action A (where Action A can be dropping a product line, firing an employee, taking a special order, and so forth)?	**Out-of-pocket cost**–Cost that involves the outlay of cash or the use of some other asset (such as equipment).	**Opportunity cost**–The benefits not received because of actions NOT taken.

Types of Product Cost:
- Direct materials–The cost of the primary raw materials used in production. For example, in the production of french fries, the direct materials cost is the cost of the potatoes.
- Direct labor–The cost of the wages of the workers who are assembling the direct materials into the finished product. For example, in the production of an automobile, the direct labor cost is the cost of the auto workers on the assembly line.
- Manufacturing overhead–All factory costs that are not direct materials or direct labor. Examples are factory foremen salaries, factory building depreciation, and miscellaneous indirect materials such as glue, screws, and so forth.

(4) Discuss the need for ethics in management accounting and describe the Standards of Ethical Conduct that apply to this profession.

- The chief accountant in most organizations is the controller.
- Those persons involved with creating management accounting information will occasionally confront ethical issues inside the organization.
- The Institute of Management Accountants (IMA) provides standards of ethical conduct to help guide professionals involved in management accounting processes.

KEY TERMS & CONCEPTS

capital budgeting, 732
controlling, 733
cost-volume-profit (C-V-P) analysis, 734
differential costs, 738
direct costs, 737
direct labor, 737
direct materials, 736

evaluating, 733
fixed costs, 734
indirect costs, 738
indirect labor, 737
indirect materials, 736
manufacturing overhead, 737

operational budgeting, 733
opportunity costs, 739
out-of-pocket costs, 739
period costs, 735
planning, 731
product costs, 735

production prioritizing, 732
return on investment (ROI), 728
strategic planning, 732
sunk costs, 738
variable costs, 734

DISCUSSION QUESTIONS

1. What exactly did Donaldson Brown, the chief financial officer for **DuPont**, develop, and why was it so revolutionary?
2. The chapter states that the focus of management accounting is to create information to fill a competitive need. Explain how management accounting can provide a competitive edge in business.
3. How can management accounting information help companies to be competitive and profitable?
4. Management accounting and financial accounting provide different information for different purposes. Explain what this means and provide an example that illustrates the differences between management and financial accounting.
5. Managers need not be concerned about external financial statements. Do you agree or disagree with this statement? Explain.

6. Why is GAAP so important for external financial reporting but not for internal management reporting?
7. Identify the three management functions relating to the decision-making process. Briefly define each function.
8. How is strategic planning related to capital budgeting?
9. How do variable costs and fixed costs differ? Give an example of each.
10. Analyze your personal expenses on a variable and fixed basis. What are some of your personal fixed costs and variable costs? What would cause them to change?
11. What is C-V-P analysis used for? In the process of using C-V-P analysis, what does it mean to "break even"?
12. Explain the difference between a product cost and a period cost.

13. What are the three components of manufacturing costs? Briefly describe them.
14. How do nonmanufacturing costs and indirect costs differ?
15. What classification determines whether materials used in the production of a product are direct materials or indirect materials? Is the classification always simple to determine? What are some examples of direct materials and indirect materials used in the production of a chair?
16. What is the difference between a direct cost and an indirect cost? Give an example of each in the context of teaching an accounting class at your school.
17. What is the difference between sunk costs and differential costs? Give an example of each.
18. How can out-of-pocket costs and opportunity costs be applied to your personal financial decisions?

PRACTICE EXERCISES

PE 15-1 **DuPont's Development of ROI (Return on Investment)**

LO1 Which one of the following statements best describes the reason **DuPont** developed return on investment (ROI) into an important management technique?
  a. A bankruptcy court trustee required DuPont to improve its management practices.
  b. Antitrust legislation passed at the turn of the twentieth century required all corporations to adopt ROI.
  c. DuPont was concerned about competition from low-cost foreign imports.
  d. DuPont needed a technique for comparing the operating performance of its different business divisions.
  e. DuPont needed a technique for evaluating the performance of its stock market investment portfolio.

PE 15-2 **Management Accounting and Financial Accounting**

LO2 Which one of the following is correct?
  a. Management accounting reports are usually available to the public.
  b. Management accounting is legislated and governed by regulatory agencies.
  c. Financial accounting focuses primarily on qualitative company data.
  d. Financial accounting exists to serve the competitive needs of an organization.
  e. Management accounting evolves from the best practices of managers working within their companies.

PE 15-3 **Management Accounting and Financial Accounting**

LO2 Which one of the following is *incorrect*?
  a. Management accounting is not as important as financial accounting for the competitive success of a company.
  b. Governments do not require a company to implement a good management accounting system.
  c. Management accounting systems evolve over time to adapt to the needs of a company.
  d. Financial accounting provides a common reporting platform to the public.
  e. A company often regards a good management accounting system as a valuable company secret.

PE 15-4 **Primary Management Functions**

LO2 The three primary management functions are:
  a. Planning, surveying, and competing.
  b. Planning, evaluating, and aerating.
  c. Planning, controlling, and evaluating.
  d. Planning, controlling, and competing.
  e. Planning, competing, and evaluating.

PE 15-5   **Planning**

LO2   Which one of the following is correct?

a.   Short-run planning includes capital budgeting and operational budgeting.

b.   Long-run planning includes production and process prioritizing.

c.   Long-run planning includes strategic planning and capital budgeting.

d.   Short-run planning includes strategic planning and production and process prioritizing.

e.   Long-run planning includes capital budgeting and operational budgeting.

PE 15-6   **Controlling**

LO2   Which one of the following is a correct description of "controlling" in a management accounting context?

a.   Deciding on the acquisition of long-term assets

b.   The real-time, day-to-day management of a company's business processes

c.   Identifying a company's mission and the goals flowing from that mission

d.   Prioritizing the production potential of an organization through cost-volume-profit analysis

e.   Communicating daily, weekly, and monthly goals

PE 15-7   **Evaluating**

LO2   Which of the following is *not* an example of evaluating?

a.   Comparing actual costs and budgeted costs

b.   Budgeting costs between various departments

c.   Assessing the performance of products and services

d.   Analyzing profitability of different products

e.   Identifying problems in the production process

PE 15-8   **Fixed Costs and Variable Costs**

LO3   Which of the following is an example of a variable cost?

a.   Insurance premium for fire insurance on the factory building

b.   The salary of the company president

c.   Wood used to make custom tables

d.   Rent for use of a storage warehouse

e.   Depreciation on the factory building

PE 15-9   **Product and Period Costs**

LO3   Which one of the following is an example of a product cost for a manufacturing company?

a.   Office supplies at corporate headquarters

b.   Wages paid to office staff

c.   Fire insurance premium on office building

d.   Wages paid to factory workers

e.   Commissions paid to salespeople

PE 15-10   **Types of Product Costs**

LO3   Which one of the following statements is *incorrect*?

a.   Manufacturing overhead includes all direct material and direct labor costs.

b.   Indirect materials include those materials that become part of the product but cannot be traced to specific products.

c.   Direct labor includes the wages paid to factory workers who do the actual assembly of a product.

d.   Direct materials include those materials that become part of the product and can be traced to specific products.

e.   Indirect labor includes the salaries of manufacturing supervisors.

PE 15-11

LO3

Computing the Cost of a Manufactured Product

The company manufactures filing cabinets. The company's costs are as follows:

Direct materials	$25.13 per unit
Direct labor	$49.25 per unit
Variable manufacturing overhead	$9.34 per unit
Fixed manufacturing overhead	$1,000,000 per year
Administrative costs	$750,000 per year

In an average year, the company manufactures 40,000 units.

What is the variable cost to manufacture each filing cabinet?

PE 15-12

LO3

Direct and Indirect Costs

Which one of the following statements best explains why companies want to distinguish between direct and indirect costs?

a. To evaluate business segments on the basis of only those costs directly traceable to each segment
b. To better determine whether a company is a large organization or a small organization
c. To determine the sales prices necessary to break even
d. To better distinguish between variable and fixed costs for each product
e. To better distinguish between materials costs and labor costs

PE 15-13

LO3

Differential Costs and Sunk Costs

Which one of the following statements is *incorrect*?

a. Sunk costs should be irrelevant in decision making.
b. Differential costs are the costs a company should consider when making decisions.
c. Differential costs cannot be reasonably avoided by a company.
d. Sunk costs are costs made in the past or committed in the future that do not pertain to future decisions.
e. Differential costs are sometimes called avoidable costs.

PE 15-14

LO3

Out-of-Pocket Costs and Opportunity Costs

Which one of the following is an example of an opportunity cost?

a. Revenue lost from sale of cakes by deciding to sell only cookies
b. Wages paid to construction workers
c. Materials used to assemble computers
d. Ordering costs related to a customer's special order of guitar strings
e. Rent paid for the use of a factory building

PE 15-15

LO4

Ethics in Management Accounting

Which one of the following statements is correct?

a. The Institute of Management Accountants has implemented a perfect set of rules to resolve every conflict.
b. The top accountant in most large organizations is usually called the controller.
c. Upon discovering an ethical dilemma in an organization, a management accountant's first responsibility is to notify outside authorities and government officials.
d. Ethical dilemmas in both large and small organizations are rare.
e. The chief executive officer (CEO) in a company typically reports to the company's chief financial officer (CFO).

EXERCISES

E 15-16
LO1

Changes in Business Affecting Management Accounting

You are at the student union having lunch with a friend who is attending law school. In the course of your conversation, you tell your friend that, in contrast to financial accounting or tax accounting, management accounting has "competitive value" and is highly proprietary. Further, management accounting is more important in business today than ever before, and only those organizations that best control costs and improve quality are competitive. Your friend asks you two questions:

1. What do you mean by "competitive value"?
2. Why is it more important for accountants to provide useful information to management today than it was before?

E 15-17
LO2

Characteristics of Accounting Reports

Indicate whether each of the following is characteristic of financial accounting reports, management accounting reports, or both.

1. They are used primarily by creditors and investors.
2. They aid management in identifying problems.
3. They are based on generally accepted accounting principles.
4. They are standardized across companies.
5. They provide information for decision making by management.
6. They measure performance and isolate differences between planned and actual results.
7. They are created based on competitive needs that are unique to the organization.

E 15-18
LO2

Financial and Management Accounting

A friend who is thinking about majoring in accounting has asked you to distinguish between the work of financial accounting and management accounting. What is your response?

E 15-19
LO3

Period Costs and Product Costs

Balls, Hoops, and Bats, Inc., a producer of sports equipment, incurs the following types of costs:
a. Depreciation on the production plant
b. Depreciation on the corporate offices
c. Wages of production-line employees
d. Paper, toner, and miscellaneous supplies for the office copy machines
e. Raw materials used in the production of sports equipment
f. Wages of the corporate headquarters' secretarial staff
g. Maintenance costs on the production equipment
h. Advertising costs
i. Shipping costs for products sold
j. Salaries of plant supervisors
k. Interest on bank loans
l. Property tax on the production plant
m. Property tax on the corporate offices
n. Commissions paid to sales personnel
o. Administrative salaries of corporate executives

Classify each cost as a period cost or a product cost. For each item classified as a product cost, indicate whether it would usually be included in direct materials, direct labor, or manufacturing overhead.

E 15-20
LO3

Manufacturing Costs

Jordan Industries is a manufacturing company that produces solid oak office furniture. During the year, the following costs were incurred. The building depreciation and the utilities are allocated three-fourths to production and one-fourth to administration. The cost of furniture parts can be traced to specific production runs.

(continued)

Oak wood	$ 50,000
Miscellaneous supplies (glue, saw blades, varnish, etc.)	10,000
Furniture parts (wheels, locks, etc.)	5,500
Payroll–plant manager's salary	25,000
Payroll–administrative salaries	100,000
Payroll–production-line employees' wages	45,500
Building depreciation	28,000
Maintenance–plant and equipment	5,000
Utilities	16,000
Income taxes	8,500

1. Classify the costs into the following four categories: direct materials, direct labor, manufacturing overhead, and period costs.
2. Calculate the total amount of cost for each category.

E 15-21
LO3

Manufacturing and Nonmanufacturing Costs

The Benson Manufacturing Company produces rides for amusement parks. Parts for the rides are purchased from other suppliers. Rides are then assembled in various company plants.

Recently, Benson Manufacturing hired two new employees. One will be working in an assembly plant, and the other will be working in the marketing division of the corporate offices as a sales representative.

The assembly plant employee will be paid an annual salary of $34,000, or $17.00 per hour. Her time will be charged to the individual rides that she assembles. The marketing division employee will receive an annual salary of $30,000 plus commission. He will be responsible for both advertising and selling. His salary is for advertising responsibilities, and he will be paid a commission on sales of amusement rides.

1. Should the salary of the assembly plant employee be classified as a manufacturing or a nonmanufacturing cost? Should the salary of the marketing division employee be classified as a manufacturing or a nonmanufacturing cost? How is this classification made?
2. After classifying the salaries as manufacturing or nonmanufacturing costs, determine how the salary costs will affect the cost of assembling the amusement rides. Classify the employee costs as direct, indirect, fixed, variable, product, or period. (Each cost can be classified in more than one way.)

E 15-22
LO2

Performance Measurement

The president of Radkline Corporation, Karen Pinkus, has asked you, the company's controller, to advise her on whether Radkline should develop a new inventory management system. Is the decision facing Karen Pinkus an example of a strategic planning decision, a capital budgeting decision, a production prioritization decision, or an operational budgeting decision? Be sure to defend your answer.

E 15-23
LO3

Cost Classifications

The following are costs associated with manufacturing firms, merchandising firms, or service firms:
a. Miscellaneous materials used in production
b. Salesperson's commission in a real estate firm
c. Administrators' salaries for a furniture wholesaler
d. Administrators' salaries for a furniture manufacturer
e. Freight costs associated with acquiring inventories for a grocery store
f. Office manager's salary in a doctor's office
g. Utilities for the corporate offices of a toy manufacturer
h. Line supervisor's salary for a clothing manufacturing firm
i. Training seminar for sales staff of a service firm
j. Fuel used in a trucking firm

(continued)

  k. Paper used at a printing business
  l. Oil for machinery at a plastics manufacturing firm
  m. Food used at a restaurant
  n. Windshields used for a car manufacturer

Classify the costs as (1) product or period; (2) variable or fixed; and (3) for those that are product costs, as direct materials, direct labor, or manufacturing overhead. Write "not applicable (N/A)" if a category doesn't apply.

E 15-24   **Cost Classifications**

LO3   The following are costs associated with manufacturing firms, merchandising firms, or service firms:

  a. Legal services for an accounting firm
  b. Car leases for company management
  c. Oil used to service manufacturing equipment
  d. Office supplies for a grocery store
  e. Entertainment expense for clients
  f. Travel expenses for doctors in a medical firm
  g. Plastic used in making computers
  h. Collection costs of accounts receivable
  i. Electricity to run saws at a lumber yard
  j. Food for a company banquet
  k. Advertising expense
  l. Continuing education for a doctor
  m. Commissions paid to salespersons
  n. Depreciation on sports equipment by a professional football team
  o. Calculators used by office employees
  p. Fuel used in baggage transporters at an airport
  q. Toll charges incurred because of business travel
  r. Fuel used in manufacturing equipment

Classify the costs as (1) product or period; (2) variable or fixed; and (3) for those that are product costs, as direct materials, direct labor, or manufacturing overhead. Write "not applicable (N/A)" if a category doesn't apply.

E 15-25   **C-V-P Analysis**

LO3   Jesse, Inc., located in Mesa, Arizona, manufactures high-end baby chairs. The firm's cost accountant, Lisa, has been assigned by the CEO to determine how many baby chairs Jesse, Inc., needs to make and sell in order to break even. She is given the following data:

Baby chair sales price	$ 15
Variable cost per baby chair	9
Production worker salary	1,350

Determine how many baby chairs Jesse, Inc., needs to make and sell in order to break even.

E 15-26   **C-V-P Analysis**

LO3   The **Dallas Mavericks** basketball team has hired you as its new accountant. On your first day on the job, Mavericks' owner, Mark Cuban, comes to you and asks, "How many tickets must we sell to pay for Dirk Nowitzki's salary?" He then hands you a sheet of paper with the following information:

Dirk Nowitzki's salary	$12,000,000
Average ticket price	80
Printing cost of one ticket	1

(continued)

1. Prepare your response to Mark's question.
2. How many tickets would the Mavericks have to sell to pay for the entire Mavericks team if the total team salary (including Finley) is $80,000,000?

E 15-27
LO3

Product Costing

The total manufacturing cost data on **DuPont**'s Teflon product line are provided below.

Direct materials	$60.00 per gallon
Direct labor	$1.80 per gallon
Manufacturing overhead:	
Variable	$3.20 per gallon
Fixed	$3,200,000 per month
General corporate sales and administrative costs	$6,400,000 per month

Assuming that DuPont expects to produce 100,000 gallons in the next month, what appears to be the total manufacturing cost on average to produce one gallon of Teflon?

E 15-28
LO3

Product Costing

BatsRUs, Inc., has created a unique line of aluminum baseball bats that, while illegal for league use, are designed to nearly double the average length of a batted ball. They are a great "hit" in the personal and family use market. Recently, a new competitor, Awesome Bats, Inc., has introduced a competing bat to the market. Suddenly, BatsRUs is experiencing severe market pressure to significantly lower its normal market price of $175. The problem is that management is not very confident about the actual production cost per bat. With some effort, the following data have been developed for management to use in setting a new market price and, more importantly, beginning an effort to better control costs.

Standard Variable Costs to Produce One Batch of 10 Bats (600 batches are typically produced each week)

	Average Cost per Pound	Average Pounds per Batch	Total Costs
Direct materials	$ 3	16	$ 48
	Average Rate per Hour	**Average Hours per Batch**	
Direct labor	$15	2	30
Variable manufacturing overhead	20	2	40
Total variable costs			$118

Standard Weekly Fixed Costs

Manufacturing overhead	$240,000
Sales and administrative costs	180,000
Total fixed costs	$420,000

1. What appears to be the average cost for BatsRUs to manufacture a single baseball bat?
2. Do you have any questions or concerns about how the data are being used to determine the cost of manufacturing a baseball bat at BatsRUs?

E 15-29
LO3

Product Costing and C-V-P Analysis

Wakefield, Inc., offers a CPA review course in cities throughout the eastern United States. Wakefield hires local CPAs to do the teaching. Each instructor is paid $115 an hour to teach the course; a course consists of 12 weeks of instruction with sessions taking place four evenings a week for two hours at each session. The other instruction costs to Wakefield are to pay for hotel conference rooms to host the course. Generally, Wakefield pays the hotel

(continued)

$800 per evening to rent a conference room. Also, tuition for the course includes all course materials, which cost the company $210 for each student.

1. What is the product cost of providing one evening of instruction for all students?
2. What is the product cost of training a student over the entire course (there are 75 students in this particular course)?
3. Assuming that Wakefield charges each student $1,500 for the course, how many students would be required to break even on this course?

E 15-30

LO3

Decisions about Business Segments

You are the accountant for the largest manufacturer of sheet steel. The company's hottest product is the RX-6, which provides most of the firm's revenue. Management is considering dropping the RX-5 product line, which hasn't turned a profit for two consecutive years. The CFO comes to you and asks what you would do given the following data:

Operating Statements	RX-6	RX-5	Total
Batches produced and sold	200	240	
Sales revenue	$30,000	$43,200	$ 73,200
Direct materials	(2,000)	(8,400)	(10,400)
Direct labor	(4,000)	(7,680)	(11,680)
Variable manufacturing overhead	(1,000)	(4,800)	(5,800)
Fixed manufacturing overhead	(2,000)	(17,400)	(19,400)
Sales and general administrative costs	(2,000)	(6,000)	(8,000)
Operating profit	$19,000	$ (1,080)	$ 17,920

Note: Approximately 20% of the fixed manufacturing overhead is directly related to (i.e., created within) each segment; if the segment is eliminated, 20% of the fixed manufacturing overhead currently allocated to the segment can be eliminated. None of the sales and general administrative costs are directly affected by either product line.

1. Distinguish between direct and indirect costs and find the segment profit for each product.
2. Determine the gain or loss that the firm would incur if it dropped the RX-5 product line. What figure would you provide the CFO?
3. Explain your recommendation to continue or discontinue product line RX-5.

E 15-31

LO3

Opportunity Costs

Clark is employed by a company that currently pays him $90,000 per year. He owns a new car that he bought for cash of $39,000. Clark is thinking about returning to school to obtain a law degree. Tuition for the school he wants to attend is $29,000 per year, books cost an average $1,400 per year, and room and board is $17,980 per year.

Determine the total sunk cost and the total opportunity cost for Clark if he decides to go back to law school for three years.

E 15-32

LO3

Segment Analysis and Opportunity Costs

Assume that sales of Kevlar at **DuPont** have dropped significantly. DuPont reported the following results for this product line for the past month and expects this sales pattern to continue into the future.

Operating Statements	Kevlar
Sales revenue	$7,500,000
Variable manufacturing costs	(2,700,000)
Fixed manufacturing overhead	(1,500,000)
Sales and administrative costs	(4,100,000)
Operating profit	$ (800,000)

(continued)

1. Assume that approximately 30% of the fixed manufacturing overhead and none of the sales and administrative costs can be avoided if Kevlar is dropped. In order to determine the "true performance" of the Kevlar product line, what is its incremental segment profit or loss?
2. If DuPont were to drop the Kevlar product line and use the available resources to produce another product that provided an incremental profit of $3,500,000, what is the overall economic profit or loss of the Kevlar product line?

ANALYTICAL ASSIGNMENTS

AA 15-33
DISCUSSION

Developing Management Accounting Information (DuPont)

The story of **E. I. Du pont de Nemours and Company** detailed at the beginning of this chapter provides key insights into the development of management accounting. In particular, we see how the structure of a business affects the kinds of information required for planning, controlling, and evaluating purposes. Consider the decision to expand and diversify the company by acquiring its suppliers and creating its own network of sales offices. What were the potential risks to **DuPont** of this decision? What accounting information would have been required to determine if the decision to diversify was successful? Does the traditional accounting system designed to produce external financial reports provide the required information in an easily obtainable fashion?

AA 15-34
DISCUSSION

Supporting the Management Process (IBM)

International Business Machines Corporation (IBM) has faced challenges this last decade due to increased competition in the home-consumer segment of the personal computer (PC) market. When IBM introduced the PC in the early 1980s, it was a huge success. Over time, however, the PC market grew immensely, and competition began to rise.

Although the PC was initially marketed toward businesses, a home-consumer market emerged as well. In 1995, IBM, under the direction of then-CEO Louis Gerstner, set up a home-consumer PC division to augment its business PC division. IBM hoped that with the two divisions, each employing its own design, manufacturing, and marketing personnel, it could better focus on the needs of its various customers and increase total sales.

IBM's consumer division quickly developed PCs that had high customer appeal. In early 1996, the division released its "Aptiva" PC in a sleek, dark gray color. The model was equipped with many high-tech features. Also, IBM's reputation for quality allowed the consumer division to charge a higher price for the PCs. (In December 1996, IBM PCs sold for an average of $1,880, whereas other companies charged as little as $1,300 to $1,400.)

Initially, the manufacturing department in IBM's consumer division could not keep up with consumer demand. Soon, however, IBM began losing market share to companies such as **Dell**, **Compaq**, and **Gateway**. These companies discovered that consumers prefer low price to the extra "frills" that IBM offers in its computers. Furthermore, IBM found that many consumers were no longer willing to pay higher prices for IBM's reputation. IBM, the company that originally created and dominated the PC market, began losing market share in the PC business very fast. IBM's PC division lost almost $1 billion in 1998. In 1999, IBM reduced its PC workforce from 10,000 to approximately 9,000 employees and cut its losses down to $360 million. In early 2000, IBM unveiled a new line of sleek, stylish machines that it branded as the NetVista line of products. With these and a number of other changes in place, business finally began growing in the second half of 2000. By the fourth quarter of 2000, IBM regained enough market share to be listed as No. 5 for PC shipments in the United States.

1. Did IBM make a good decision in setting up its consumer division? How so?
2. Analyze IBM's decisions and actions involving the consumer division. Try to categorize these decisions and actions following the threefold management process of planning, controlling, and evaluating.

(continued)

3. Based on the threefold management process of planning, controlling, and evaluating, where do you think IBM was weakest in its decision-making practice with respect to the consumer division? Where do you think it was strongest?

4. If you were Sam Palmisano (IBM's current CEO), what information would you want from your accountants in order to effectively plan, control, and evaluate the decision to either shut down or continue to operate the division? *Note:* In 2005, IBM sold its personal computer division to Lenovo, a Chinese company.

Source: Raju Narisetti, "IBM to Revamp Struggling Home-PC Business," *The Wall Street Journal*, October 14, 1997; Lisa Smith, "IBM's Personal Computer Unit Makes Turnaround," *The Herald-Sun*, March 22, 2001.

AA 15-35

JUDGMENT CALL

You Decide: When allocating costs, if you don't know where costs should be allocated, should you take time to figure out if the costs relate to materials or labor, or should you allocate all the costs as manufacturing overhead?

It is your first day on the job at a bicycle manufacturing company. Your first job is to determine the cost of a new line of bikes. After reviewing all the cost information, your boss says, "If you don't know how to allocate a cost, just put it in manufacturing overhead. Whether it is a direct or indirect material, it will end up in the same place." Do you agree with your boss? Why or why not?

AA 15-36

JUDGMENT CALL

You Decide: Should sunk costs be considered in a planning decision or ignored?

You currently work part time at a flower shop. You split your time between keeping the books and making deliveries. The van you use to make these deliveries has been in and out of the repair shop over the past two months. In addition to the engine, the transmission was just replaced. The mechanic said that the van is old enough to require constant repair. Your boss isn't too happy about all this repair work and was heard saying, "I would like to get a new van, but I can't afford it. I have invested too much money in the one we have now!" What should you tell your boss?

AA 15-37

REAL COMPANY ANALYSIS

Wal-Mart

Wal-Mart employs 1.8 million people worldwide through more than 3,800 stores in the United States and more than 2,600 stores in other countries. The March 22, 2006, grand opening of the new Supercenter in Beaumont, California, was a milestone for Wal-Mart, marking 2,000 Supercenters officially open across the United States. The first Supercenter, featuring a complete grocery department along with the 36 departments of general merchandise, opened in 1988. In addition to having more than 2,000 Supercenters today, Wal-Mart has approximately 1,200 general merchandise stores, nearly 600 SAM's CLUBS (membership warehouse clubs), and has recently launched over 100 small neigbhorhood grocery markets.

1. What business factors does Wal-Mart need to consider in deciding to launch a new store?

2. How can management accounting information be used to help plan, control, and evaluate the new store?

AA 15-38

REAL COMPANY ANALYSIS

DuPont

As described in the chapter, the challenge facing **DuPont** in the early twentieth century was how to manage the diverse set of businesses operating under the control of the DuPont management team. This diversity still exists today. In its 2005 annual report, DuPont notes that its strategic business units (operating segments) are organized by product line. For purposes of financial reporting, these have been aggregated into eight reportable segments: Agriculture & Nutrition, Coatings & Color Technologies, Electronic & Communication Technologies, Performance Materials, Pharmaceuticals, Safety & Protection, and Other.

(continued)

Summary segment results for 2005 for five of these eight segments are as follows (dollars in millions):

	Agriculture & Nutrition	Coatings & Color Technologies	Electronic & Communication Technologies	Performance Materials	Safety & Protection
Total revenue	$6,318	$6,150	$3,165	$5,882	$5,072
After-tax operating income	506	331	312	307	575
Identifiable assets at December 31, 2005	6,084	3,633	2,189	3,563	2,686

1. Which segment has the highest return on investment? The lowest?
2. How could the segment with the lowest return on investment improve its financial performance?

AA 15-39

INTERNATIONAL

Toyota

Toyota Motor Corporation was started in 1918 by Sakichi Toyoda as the **Toyota Spinning and Weaving Company**; in fact, a subsidiary of Toyota still makes spinning and weaving equipment today. By 1995, Toyota was the third-largest motor vehicle producer in the world, manufacturing 4,512,076 vehicles (behind **General Motors** at 7,997,794 and **Ford** at 6,401,495). In January 1997, Toyota made its 100 millionth vehicle. Despite a difficult world economy since 2000, Toyota has continued to prosper. In 2005, Toyota reported its consolidated net income at 1.17 trillion yen ($10.91 billion). In the 2005 annual report, Katsuaki Watanabe, president of Toyota, noted three main factors behind his company's strong financial performance in 2005. First, the Japanese economy recovered mildly due to an increase in employment. Second, Toyota claimed a larger share of the Japanese market with a 44.5% market share. Finally, Toyota's hybrid cars were successful throughout the world; Toyota shipped 151,000 units in 2005, 2.5 times higher than in 2004.

Toyota attributes its constant growth in net income to three factors: improvement in the Japanese economy, increase in market share, and the increase in sales of hybrid vehicles. Consider conducting a performance evaluation on the following people, and decide which of the three factors should be considered in the evaluation of:

a. an assembly-line worker
b. a factory manager
c. a sales manager
d. the company president

AA 15-40

ETHICS

Whom to Tell about Medicare Overbilling

Professor Mary Allen is sitting in her office one day when Mark Sullivan, an accounting graduate from five years ago, knocks on her door. Mark had been an exceptionally good student and had started with the CPA firm Peat & Price upon graduation. After three years with that firm, he joined MiniCare Health Company as the chief accountant and is now serving as its controller. Mark asks if he can talk with Professor Allen in confidence and then tells her that he has a problem: "Two years ago, I started working for MiniCare. Not long after I was promoted to controller, I noticed that the officers of the company were doing things that I didn't think were right. They have overbilled Medicare on several occasions, and senior management executives are misusing their positions by taking company perks that are against the company code of ethics. I have talked to my superior, the financial vice president, and he has, in essence, told me to mind my own business—that accountants are to report results and assist management, not question them."

Mark informs Professor Allen that he is making $110,000 a year, far more than he could earn in another company at this stage in his career. He asks for her advice. What should

(continued)

Professor Allen recommend that he do? Should Mark quit his job? Should he talk to someone else? If so, to whom? Should he go public with his information?

AA 15-41   **Costs May Be Sunk, but They Aren't Forgotten**

WRITING   You are the manager of the tire manufacturing subdivision of Uniyear Diversified Products. Last year, you were successful in convincing corporate executives that your division needed to purchase a new warehouse facility costing $40 million to house raw materials. You argued at the time that you could be much more productive if delays in getting materials from suppliers could be eliminated.

During the past 18 months, your company has worked hard to implement a number of innovative programs to improve its production operations. One of the improvements includes placing online terminals at key supplier locations. As a result, the lag time in getting the raw materials the company needs has dropped from an average of four weeks to six hours.

Your problem now is that you no longer need the $40 million warehouse. It is a sunk cost. However, you are afraid that if you reveal that fact to the corporate executives, they will penalize or even fire you for being so shortsighted.

Draft a one-page memo to the president of Uniyear Diversified Products that explains why the $40 million warehouse is no longer needed. Remember that the memo has two purposes: to inform the president that the warehouse is no longer needed and to do so in a way that doesn't cost you your job.

16

Cost Flows and Business Organizations

After studying this chapter, you should be able to:

① Explain the flow of products and costs in a manufacturing organization. *The cost of direct materials is combined with the cost of direct labor and manufacturing overhead in the work-in-process inventory account; this account is a symbolic representation of the factory. When goods are completed, their cost is transferred to Finished Goods Inventory, and then to Cost of Goods Sold when the goods are sold.*

② Understand the traditional procedure of accounting for overhead. *Manufacturing overhead costs are temporarily accumulated in the manufacturing overhead account. These costs are systematically applied, or added, to Work-in-Process Inventory using a rate that is determined at the beginning of the period. Any manufacturing overhead cost left over at the end of the period (called underapplied overhead) is usually added directly to Cost of Goods Sold; overapplied overhead is subtracted from Cost of Goods Sold.*

③ Create a Cost of Goods Manufactured schedule and understand how it is used to calculate cost of goods sold. *Cost of Goods Manufactured is the total production cost of goods completed in the factory (i.e., the work-in-process inventory account) and transferred to Finished Goods Inventory during the period. Cost of Goods Sold is then simply the total value of goods sold out of the finished goods inventory account.*

④ Explain the flow of products and costs in a service organization and in a merchandising organization. *The flow of costs in a service organization is very similar to the flow in a manufacturing organization. In essence, a service organization "manufactures" a service. In a merchandising organization, the flow of inventory costs is simple: inventory ready for sale is purchased, and when that inventory is sold, its cost is reported as Cost of Goods Sold.*

EXPANDED material

⑤ Compute product costs using process costing. *Process costing is used when the production process involves the continuous production of similar units. The flow of costs is the same as with job order costing. The challenge in process costing is figuring out the quantity of "equivalent units" produced during the period, factoring in the work done to complete the units in beginning Work-in-Process Inventory and the work done on uncompleted units still sitting in ending Work-in-Process Inventory.*

On May 10, 1869, the **Union Pacific Railroad** from the East and the **Central Pacific Railroad** from the West were joined at Promontory Point, Utah. Railroad companies soon grew to sizes that dwarfed the scale of the largest factories, and the names of railroad tycoons such as J. P. Morgan and Edward Henry Harriman became famous (or infamous, depending on your perspective).

Managing these huge administrative entities required special record-keeping systems that captured enormous numbers of daily transactions and summarized essential information for frequent internal reports to management. The challenge for railroads was that employees and processes were literally spread all over the map! Senior managers needed some means of assessing the performance of station managers at terminals and yards across the country. Management accounting expanded as "costs per ton-mile" (the average cost to move a ton of material one mile) and "operating ratio" (a ratio of operating expenses to revenues) began providing competitive information to indicate how the performance of various station managers would affect the railroad's total financial performance. These performance measures were used to delegate responsibilities and to control and evaluate the business from a distance, facilitating the spread of the railroads.

Managers need accurate product cost information to plan for the future, to control current operations, and to evaluate past performance. They also need accurate product cost information so that they can deliver high-quality products to customers at the lowest price and at the fastest speed. For most companies, accurately determining product costs is a surprisingly difficult challenge. Regardless of the difficulty, however, having accurate product cost information is critical for a business. Without knowledge of accurate product costs, managers could easily over- or underprice products and make other poor decisions.

What if, for example, Toyota sells its 2006 Camry SE V6 for $25,500 (its intended sales price), but the actual cost of producing the car is $30,000? How long could Toyota stay in business losing $4,500 ($30,000 − $25,500) per car? In this case, buyers will probably rush to buy Camrys because they will likely be priced much lower than other comparable cars (assuming Toyota's competitors have more accurate cost information and have priced their cars to cover their total manufacturing costs). Not only will Toyota lose money on every car it sells, but the more cars Toyota sells, the greater its losses will be.

Management accounting is the result of the efforts of many individuals and organizations to create information that has a competitive value in the marketplace. To really understand management accounting, you need to grasp the flow of costs in manufacturing, service, and merchandising organizations. The foundation of management accounting is cost control. Understanding cost flows is a useful way to understand how a business is structured or organized. Without accurate cost information, it is difficult to set appropriate prices, evaluate performance, reward employees, or make production decisions. It is even difficult to know whether a company should be competing in a specific market.

In this chapter, you will learn how goods and services flow in manufacturing, service, and merchandising companies and how product costs incurred in these organizations are tracked and accumulated. In subsequent chapters you will learn how to use product costs to manage manufacturing, service, and merchandising companies.

manufacturing organizations

Organizations that focus on using labor and/or machinery to convert raw materials into marketable products.

service organizations

Organizations that focus on delivery of marketable services, such as legal advice or education, to individuals or other organizations.

merchandising organizations

Organizations that focus on buying products from manufacturers, then distributing those products to customers.

The Flow of Products and Costs in Manufacturing Firms

Explain the flow of products and costs in a manufacturing organization.

Costs of manufacturing products can be broken down into three elements: (1) direct materials, (2) direct labor, and (3) manufacturing overhead. Direct materials include the cost of raw materials that are used directly in the manufacture of products. Direct materials are kept in the raw materials warehouse until used and include such things as rubber used in making tires, steel used to make cars, wood used to make tables, and plastic used to make eyeglasses. Direct labor includes the wages and other payroll-related expenses of factory employees who work directly on products. Direct labor includes the cost of wages and benefits for assembly-line workers, but it does not include the wages and benefits of the factory custodians or the factory controller because, even though they work in the factory, they don't work directly on making products. Manufacturing overhead includes all manufacturing costs that are not classified as direct materials or direct labor. This includes miscellaneous materials used in production, such as glue or nails; wages for the factory supervisor, controller, and custodians who work in the factory, but not directly on products; and other manufacturing costs such as utilities, depreciation of manufacturing facilities, insurance, and property taxes.

> **CAUTION**
>
> Product costs are only one element management must consider when establishing prices for its products. Pricing is a complex issue, and management usually looks to its own strategy and to the market to set prices (also considering competitors' prices, market's ability to pay, and so forth). It would be wrong to assume that management simply sets the price of products on the basis of product cost information.

One of the best ways to understand how an organization works is to "follow the money"; in other words, observe how costs flow through the organization. We'll use cost flows to introduce you to manufacturing, merchandising, and service organizations. For a long time, manufacturing was the basis of the U.S. economy. Today, relative to other industries, manufacturing is much smaller. Nevertheless, management accounting systems were originally built to support the manufacturing process, so we'll start there.

Consider the layout for a simple, hypothetical manufacturing company shown in Exhibit 1. This floor plan is for a hypothetical manufacturer of furniture, Broyman Furniture Company. The floor plan shows a building that is partitioned into two sections. The administrative offices include office space for various vice presidents, the sales staff, the president, and the administrative staff. The manufacturing facility encompasses the offices of the vice president of manufacturing, the plant manager, and the controller; the raw materials and finished goods warehouses; and the factory floor, where production takes place.

The manufacturing process for Broyman is not very complicated as illustrated in the following sequence.

raw materials inventory

The inventory of raw materials that have not yet begun the production process.

work-in-process inventory

Inventory that is partly completed in the production process, but not yet ready for sale to customers.

Step 1: Raw materials are purchased and delivered to the **raw materials inventory** warehouse where they are stored until needed.

Step 2: When requested, raw materials are moved out onto the factory floor for the actual manufacturing process; there all material is referred to as **work-in-process inventory** until the process is completed. In this example, the factory floor includes three different manufacturing departments: cutting, machining, and finishing.

EXHIBIT 1	**Broyman Furniture Company (A Manufacturing Firm's Layout)**

finished goods inventory

Inventory that has completed the production process and is ready for sale to customers.

Step 3: On the factory floor, factory employees combine materials with their labor to produce finished products.

Step 4: The finished products are then moved into the **finished goods inventory** warehouse and stored until sold.

You remember from Chapter 15 that product costs include all costs necessary to create the product: essentially, the costs of all people and processes within Broyman's manufacturing facility. Product costs are associated with specific inventory items, and this inventory cost is reported as an expense (Cost of Goods Sold) when the inventory is sold. On the other hand, the costs of people and processes in Broyman's administrative offices, which are not associated with the production of furniture, are period costs. Period costs are reported as an expense in the period in which they occur.

A simple rule of thumb is that all costs that occur in or are associated with the factory are product costs. Accordingly, all of the following are product costs:

- Cost of the raw materials used in production
- Wages of factory employees who work on the factory floor
- Salaries of the vice president of manufacturing and the plant manager

- Utility bills to heat and light the factory building
- Depreciation or rent on the factory building
- Wages of maintenance personnel and custodians who work in the factory

Period costs are those costs associated with activities or facilities outside the factory. For example, because the individuals working in the administrative offices work outside the factory, their salaries should not be classified as product costs but instead as period costs. Likewise, the costs to pay for electricity, heat, and other expenses for the administrative offices are period costs.

The following section will give you practice in accounting for product costs.

The Product Costing System

Most accounting systems that track product costs are based on a few key procedures.

- First, identify the product or project that needs cost measurement and track this project through the production process.[1]
- Second, specifically trace the direct costs (costs of direct materials and direct labor) to each product or project.
- Finally, allocate an appropriate amount of overhead costs to each product or project.

job order costing

A method of product costing whereby each job, product, or batch of products is costed separately.

This accounting approach is called **job order costing**. As we discuss the mechanics of this product costing system, keep in mind the overall procedure—identify the product or service (the "job"), trace the direct costs, and allocate the overhead. Also be sure to remember the big picture. In other words, why are we doing this? Product cost information is used to plan future operations (e.g., what will be the costs of future levels of production?), to control current operations (e.g., are our costs too high?), and to evaluate performance (e.g., were our costs and performance last year good or bad?).

In our example, we will track product costs as we follow an order for a mahogany table that is manufactured by Broyman Furniture Company. The production of the table is a custom job requiring two operations: machining (preparing the mahogany) and finishing (assembling, staining, and packaging the table). (You will recall that there were three manufacturing areas in Exhibit 1. To keep things simple, we will assume that the materials used in this table come "pre-cut" to the factory, and so this product does not require work in the cutting department.)

Before we work through the specifics of the cost accounting, take a moment to review the flows of product costs in Exhibit 1. Notice that these costs represent very closely the flow of product and work on the factory floor. The work-in-process inventory account symbolically represents the factory itself. As raw materials move onto the factory floor, costs move out of the raw materials inventory account and into the work-in-process inventory account. As employees work directly on Broyman's products, their labor costs are recognized in the work-in-process inventory account. As the manufacturing process

---

[1] In some organizations, it is not reasonable or possible to specifically track the product being produced. For example, a lumber mill that continuously processes timber into planks may not specifically track individual products. Instead, the mill would track the total production costs expended for a particular period of time (e.g., a day), then assign those costs to the total amount of timber processed during that same period of time. This management accounting approach is called process costing and will be discussed in the expanded material section of this chapter.

goes forward, the indirect costs related to manufacturing overhead are allocated to Work-in-Process Inventory. As furniture is completed and moved off of the factory floor and into the finished goods warehouse, the materials, labor, and overhead costs of that product are moved out of work-in-process inventory and into the finished goods inventory account. Finally, as furniture is sold to customers, the costs of those goods are moved out of the finished goods inventory account and into the cost of goods sold account. Be sure to keep this overall view of the cost accounting in mind as we work through the detail below of costing a specific mahogany table, which Broyman will track as Job #117.

Exhibit 2 shows that the mahogany table costs $959 to make. This amount includes $375 of direct materials, $202 of direct labor, and $382 of manufacturing overhead (which includes supervisor and production staff salaries, insurance, utilities, depreciation on plant and machinery, and so on). Looking at the cost summary in Exhibit 2, we can see that the

manufacturing overhead rate

The rate at which manufacturing overhead costs are assigned to products; equals estimated manufacturing overhead costs for the period divided by the number of units of the activity base being used.

hourly wage rate for direct labor is $14 per hour in machining and $18 per hour in finishing; the manufacturing overhead rate is $32 per machine hour in machining and $38 per direct labor hour in finishing. The **manufacturing overhead rate** is an estimate of the overhead that will be incurred for each unit (in this case, allocated on the basis of machine hours and direct labor hours). In this example, the company incurs an average of $32 of overhead costs for every hour the machine is run in the machining department. Thus, each table that requires the use of the machine is allocated a portion of the overhead costs. The use of different manufacturing overhead rates is common. Each department will allocate manufacturing overhead to products on the basis of the most meaningful activity in that department. The machining department is more automated, so activity is

---

EXHIBIT 2	**Total Product Costs for Job #117–One Mahogany Table**

Machining Department Costs

Direct Materials Requisitioned	Direct Labor			Manufacturing Overhead (based on machine hours)		
	Hours	Wage Rate	Amount	Hours	Overhead Rate	Amount
$300	8	$14	$112	6	$32	$192

Finishing Department Costs

Direct Materials Requisitioned	Direct Labor			Manufacturing Overhead (based on direct labor hours)		
	Hours	Wage Rate	Amount	Hours	Overhead Rate	Amount
$50	3	$18	$54	3	$38	$114
25	2	$18	36	2	$38	76
$75			$90			$190

Final Product Cost for Mahogany Table

	Machining	Finishing	Total
Direct materials	$300	$ 75	$375
Direct labor	112	90	202
Manufacturing overhead	192	190	382
Total cost	$604	$355	$959

tied more closely to machine hours; the finishing department requires more handwork, so activity is tied more closely to direct labor hours.

With these "finished costs" in mind, let's talk about how Broyman Furniture Company actually created these data on the mahogany table. (*Note:* Don't worry if you are still a little confused about how Broyman creates and uses manufacturing overhead rates. We're going to discuss these concepts in detail later in this chapter.)

Direct Materials Costs To illustrate the accounting for direct materials costs, we will assume that Broyman purchased a supply of mahogany and placed it in a materials storeroom. The entry to record this purchase is:[2]

Raw Materials Inventory	30,000	
Accounts Payable		30,000
Purchased 5,000 board feet of mahogany materials at $6 per foot.		

When raw materials are needed (such as for the manufacture of the table), the machining department sends a request (i.e., a requisition) to the storeroom (usually via computer) identifying the quantity and type of materials needed. When the raw materials warehouse fills the requisition, it records the transfer of goods to the factory floor by making an entry (usually by computer) that serves as the basis for the accounting records. The storeroom manager sends the requisition information to the accounting department, where the unit cost is entered and the total cost of direct materials calculated. The accounting entry made to record the transfer of mahogany from storage to machining is provided below. In addition, the finishing department requisitioned some packaging material to prepare mahogany tables for shipping.

Work-in-Process Inventory	300	
Raw Materials Inventory		300
Job #117: Issued direct materials to production–50 board feet		
of mahogany at $6 per foot.		
Work-in-Process Inventory	75	
Raw Materials Inventory		75
Job #117: Issued direct materials to production–packaging material.		

The mahogany and packaging material were used directly in the production and shipping preparation of the table; the cost is assigned as direct materials for this particular job. Indirect materials and supplies used in production (classified as manufacturing overhead costs), such as glue, nails, and varnish, are ordered from the storeroom in the same manner. Although some inexpensive materials, such as glue, are used directly in the manufactured products and others are used to support production, it is generally not cost-beneficial to trace such miscellaneous items to a particular job. These miscellaneous items are treated as indirect materials costs and recorded in the manufacturing overhead account (explained later in the chapter). Manufacturing overhead consists of numerous expenditures such as indirect labor, indirect materials, utilities, rent, and the like. The sum of these various expenditures provides the balance in the manufacturing overhead account. The following entry records a requisition for cleaning supplies for the factory custodial crew:

Manufacturing Overhead	124	
Raw Materials Inventory		124
Issued indirect materials to production–cleaning supplies.		

---

[2] In this chapter, we will use a *normal* costing system based on actual direct materials and labor costs. We will discuss standard cost accounting systems in a later chapter on budgeting.

Before we talk about how to account for direct labor costs, let's look at how the detailed accounting entries for the raw materials inventory account will flow through Broyman's accounting system (compare this detailed accounting system to the "flow diagram" on the right side of Exhibit 1). Note that at the end of each reporting period, the amount of materials and supplies that remain on hand in the raw materials warehouse will be shown on the balance sheet as Raw Materials Inventory.

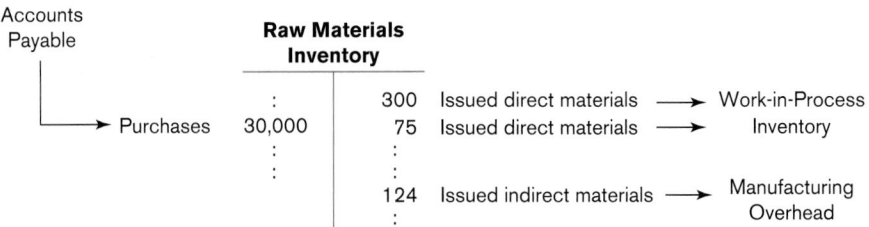

Direct Labor Costs

The method of charging direct labor costs to production jobs is similar to that for direct materials costs. Most factories have a time clock where employees punch in and record their hourly activities. These time clocks often allow workers to identify specific jobs worked on. When the time clocks do not capture specific job information, the information is noted by making entries in the computer or on manual time tickets. The product costs, shown in Exhibit 2, reveal that machining employees worked on the mahogany table for 8 hours. Because the wage rate was $14 per hour in machining, the total direct labor cost in machining was $112 ($14 per hour × 8 hours). Similar calculations provide the entry to record the direct labor costs in the finishing department. The entries to record all the direct labor costs (ignoring payroll taxes and benefits) for the mahogany table are:

Work-in-Process Inventory	112	
Salaries & Wages Payable		112
Job #117: To record direct labor costs–machining department.		
Work-in-Process Inventory	90	
Salaries & Wages Payable		90
Job #117: To record direct labor costs–finishing department.		

Like materials, labor costs can be either direct or indirect. Indirect labor costs include the wages of employees who perform functions not related to a specific job, such as maintenance and custodial. Although these employees may also punch time clocks, their wages become part of the indirect labor costs that are included in manufacturing overhead, as discussed in the next section. The following entry records the cost of the production supervisor's salary for the month:

Manufacturing Overhead	3,700	
Salaries & Wages Payable		3,700
To record indirect labor costs–supervisor salary.		

Now let's look at the detailed accounting entries for the salaries & wages payable account in Broyman's accounting system (again, compare this detailed accounting system to the "flow diagram" on the right side of Exhibit 1). We will next discuss how Broyman accounts for manufacturing overhead costs.

Salaries & Wages Payable

112	Incurred direct labor ⟶	Work-in-Process
90	Incurred direct labor ⟶	Inventory
⋮		
⋮		
3,700	Incurred indirect labor ⟶	Manufacturing Overhead
⋮		

Manufacturing Overhead Costs In contrast to direct materials and direct labor, manufacturing overhead (the third type of product cost) involves more complex accounting procedures and estimation problems. As we've discussed earlier, usually direct materials and direct labor can be readily assigned to specific jobs or products. However, manufacturing overhead costs are difficult to trace directly to the production of a single item. For example, think about the cost of driving your car (if you have one) from your house or apartment to the nearest supermarket and back. It is unlikely that your tires will wear out or that you will need an engine overhaul or an oil change on this short trip. However, over the life of the car, you will spend substantial amounts of money on maintenance and repair costs. It would be a challenging accounting issue to compute how much of the overhead maintenance and repair cost should be included in the calculation of the cost of your short trip to the store and back. And yet this cost information is essential as you decide whether it is better to use your car or to sell your car and ride a bicycle.

By definition, most manufacturing overhead costs benefit all products made in a department or a company during a period. The depreciation on equipment and the wages paid for maintenance in the machining department, for example, ensure the smooth operation of the entire department during the production period; however, these costs cannot be traced directly to individual items produced during the period. Some manufacturing overhead costs, such as property taxes and repairs, are not known until the end of a production period. However, managers need current product cost information (for pricing similar jobs, estimating costs for next year, and so forth), so each job is assigned a share of *estimated* (i.e., budgeted) manufacturing overhead costs. In accounting terminology, manufacturing overhead costs are applied to (or absorbed by) jobs or products. Overall, knowing how to set up and handle the accounting for overhead costs at Broyman Company is a tricky business, which we'll talk further about later in this chapter.

STOP & THINK

In our example, the company makes a mahogany table using two operations: machining and finishing. When making a real table, how many separate operations do you think would be necessary? Can you envision how complicated it can be to track product costs in a "real-world" production setting?

As *actual* manufacturing overhead costs for Broyman are incurred, the management accounting system needs to recognize and record the costs. During the current production period, these costs include $1,200 for repairs to equipment, $6,450 for monthly rent allocated to the production facility, $850 for liability insurance, and $2,900 in depreciation of manufacturing equipment. The total of these costs is debited to Manufacturing Overhead, and the individual amounts are credited to their respective accounts, as shown here.

Manufacturing Overhead	11,400	
Accounts Payable		1,200
Rent Payable		6,450
Prepaid Insurance		850
Accumulated Depreciation		2,900
To record actual manufacturing overhead costs.		

CAUTION

Many students will make the mistake of debiting manufacturing overhead costs to an expense account. Although these costs eventually do become an expense, first they are debited to Manufacturing Overhead, then allocated to Work-in-Process Inventory, then transferred to Finished Goods Inventory, and finally expensed in Cost of Goods Sold.

In addition to recording the actual costs of manufacturing overhead, Broyman's accountants need to allocate overhead costs to the mahogany table in production. As you can see in Exhibit 2, the Broyman management accountants follow a traditional approach of assigning manufacturing overhead costs by taking the expected annual costs of overhead for each department and dividing this estimated amount by the selected activity base (in this case, machine hours for the machining department and direct labor hours for the finishing department).

predetermined overhead rate

A rate at which estimated manufacturing overhead costs are assigned to products throughout the year; equals total estimated manufacturing overhead costs divided by a suitable allocation base, such as number of units produced, direct labor hours, direct materials used, or direct labor costs.

Estimated overhead costs typically come from the company's annual budgets. Selection of the activity base is the result of experience and analysis. The result is an allocation rate for each department that is used to uniformly assign a "fair share" of manufacturing overhead costs to production volume throughout the year. This allocation rate is called the **predetermined overhead rate**. In this case, Broyman's accountants allocate $192 to the mahogany table based on activity in the machining department ($32 predetermined overhead rate × 6 machine hours) and allocate $190 based on activity in the finishing department ($38 rate × 5 direct labor hours). The entries to record these allocations are:

Work-in-Process Inventory	192	
Manufacturing Overhead		192
Job #117: To apply manufacturing overhead in the		
machining department.		
Work-in-Process Inventory	190	
Manufacturing Overhead		190
Job #117: To apply manufacturing overhead in the		
finishing department.		

Notice in the detailed accounting entries in Broyman's accounting system that as *actual* overhead costs are incurred, the manufacturing overhead account is debited. As overhead costs are *applied* to products on the factory floor, the manufacturing overhead account is credited. Be sure to compare the detail of these accounting entries to the overall flow of overhead costs on the right side of Exhibit 1. We will spend a little more time on accounting for manufacturing overhead later in this chapter.

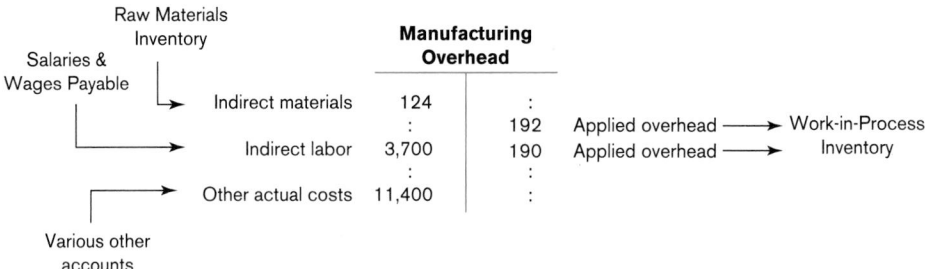

Transferring the Costs of Completed Jobs and Computing Unit Costs

While a job is in process, the costs of direct materials, direct labor, and manufacturing overhead are accounted for separately. When the job is completed, however, these costs (in total) are transferred together from Work-in-Process Inventory to Finished Goods Inventory. In the Broyman Furniture Company example, the total cost assigned to the mahogany table is $959, as illustrated in Exhibit 2. The entry to transfer the completed cost of the table to Finished Goods Inventory is:

Finished Goods Inventory	959	
Work-in-Process Inventory		959
Job #117: To record the completion of the mahogany table.		

It's important that you keep your eye on Exhibit 1. Can you see that how the flow of product costs through the accounts closely resembles how the product is created and moves through the manufacturing facility? The product costs assigned to the table literally follow that table as it moves through the factory floor (and through the work-in-process inventory account) until the table is completed and moves into the finished goods warehouse (and into the finished goods inventory account). The detailed accounting demonstrating the costs flowing in and out of the work-in-process inventory account is shown below.

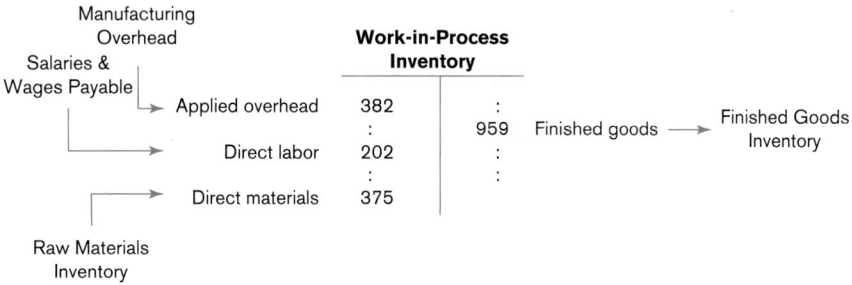

Once completed, cost data for the mahogany table are used in pricing similar jobs, estimating costs for the next year, and measuring income. Note that this cost accounting process would be no different if, instead of representing a single table, Job #117 represented an entire batch of mahogany tables. In this case, at the completion of the job, the average unit cost of each table could be determined by adding the direct materials, direct labor, and manufacturing overhead costs for the batch and dividing the total by the number of tables produced in the batch (i.e., the job).

Transferring the Costs of Products That Are Sold

When a product is sold, the costs assigned to it are transferred to Cost of Goods Sold. For example, when the mahogany table, which cost $959 to make, is shipped to a customer, the table is loaded from the warehouse onto the truck, and the cost of the table is transferred from finished goods inventory to Cost of Goods Sold, using the following entry:

Cost of Goods Sold	959	
Finished Goods Inventory		959
Job #117: To record the cost of goods sold for the mahogany table.		

With this entry, costs have been traced all the way through the production cycle and expensed onto the income statement. The flow of product costs through the finished goods inventory account is shown below.

Return once more to Exhibit 1 and be sure that you clearly see how all the costs flow through the manufacturing process for Broyman. Note that direct labor, when incurred, and direct materials, when used, are debited directly to Work-in-Process Inventory. Actual manufacturing overhead costs, on the other hand, are entered first as debits to

STOP & THINK

Now that you've worked through the cost accounting details for the mahogany table example (Job #117), return to Exhibit 1 and visualize how the table product physically moved through Broyman's manufacturing facility and how the product costs flowed through Broyman's accounting system.

Manufacturing Overhead and then are allocated to Work-in-Process Inventory by crediting Manufacturing Overhead. As goods are completed, the costs are then credited out of the work-in-process inventory account and debited into the cost of goods sold account where they remain until the goods are sold. You should also note that at the end of the period, the company will usually have three inventory balances: Raw Materials Inventory, Work-in-Process Inventory, and Finished Goods Inventory.

REMEMBER THIS...

The "action" in a product costing system (whether job order costing or process costing is used) centers around the work-in-process inventory account which is a symbolic representation of the factory. Make sure you understand the cost flows into and out of the T-account below.

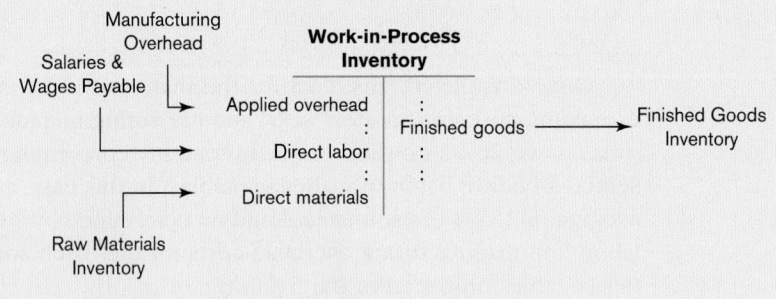

Accounting for Overhead

Understand the traditional procedure of accounting for overhead.

2 In the Broyman Company example of producing a mahogany table and tracking its production costs, you can see that accounting for manufacturing overhead costs is not the same process as accounting for direct materials and direct labor costs. Because manufacturing overhead costs generally do not coincide with the flow of production, a few extra steps are required to handle the accounting. These steps are:

1. Before the year begins, budget the *estimated* manufacturing overhead, estimate the allocation activity, and establish the predetermined overhead rate.
2. During the year, as costs are incurred, record *actual* manufacturing overhead as debits to the manufacturing overhead account.
3. During the year, as activity takes place, record *applied* manufacturing overhead as credits to the manufacturing overhead account and debits to the work-in-process account.
4. At the end of the year, compare *actual* and *applied* overhead balances and close out the difference (i.e., the over- and underapplied overhead) in the manufacturing overhead account.

Estimated Manufacturing Overhead

As you can see, the list above includes three different classifications of manufacturing overhead costs—estimated, actual, and applied. It is critical that you understand the differences among these numbers. **Estimated manufacturing overhead** is the amount of overhead costs that management has budgeted for the upcoming production period. The predetermined overhead rate is created by dividing estimated manufacturing overhead by the estimate of the expected level of activity (e.g., direct labor hours) to be used to allocate overhead during the year.

> **estimated manufacturing overhead**
>
> Budgeted manufacturing overhead costs that are used to establish the predetermined overhead rate.

To illustrate the use of estimated manufacturing overhead to create the predetermined overhead rate for the machining department at Broyman Company, assume that at the beginning of the year the accountants and production personnel estimated that 8,400 machine hours would be used on the factory floor. Budgeted (estimated) overhead costs for the machining department are shown below.

Indirect labor	$ 47,000
Indirect materials	13,000
Repairs	3,500
Rent	105,000
Depreciation	85,000
Insurance	15,300
Total expected manufacturing overhead cost for the year (machining department)	$268,800

Using these data, the accountants then computed the predetermined overhead rate in the machining department to be $32 per machine hour, as follows:

$$\frac{\text{Total estimated manufacturing overhead cost for the year}}{\text{Total estimated machine hours for the year}} = \frac{\$268{,}800}{8{,}400 \text{ hours}} = \$32 \text{ per machine hour}$$

Similar calculations were used to calculate the predetermined overhead rate of $38 per direct labor hour in the finishing department.

Actual Manufacturing Overhead

After studying financial accounting, some students have a difficult time with the accounting for actual manufacturing overhead. For example, in financial accounting, we accounted for salaries by debiting Salaries Expense and crediting Salaries Payable, which is the correct entry when the salaries are for sales or other nonmanufacturing personnel. However, as you saw in tracking production costs for Broyman's mahogany table, when the wages are related to manufacturing, the debit is to Work-in-Process Inventory for direct labor and to Manufacturing Overhead for indirect labor. Thus, in management accounting, it is important to determine first whether salaries are for manufacturing or for nonmanufacturing personnel. Then, for manufacturing personnel, it must be determined whether the individuals worked directly on the product (Work-in-Process Inventory) or indirectly on the product (Manufacturing Overhead). The same is true for other costs such as

 FYI

One useful way to think about the manufacturing overhead account is to consider it to be simply a temporary holding tank for overhead costs that we don't immediately know how to assign to production. By the end of the period, however, we will have sorted out how much was actually spent on overhead and how much estimated overhead was applied as actual production took place. At that point, we can clear out the "holding tank" and start over the process of tracking and applying overhead costs in the next period.

depreciation and rent. If these costs relate to manufacturing, they are debited to Manufacturing Overhead; costs not related to manufacturing are debited to Depreciation Expense, Rent Expense, and so forth. The manufacturing costs will eventually become expenses when the products are sold (Cost of Goods Sold).

Applied Manufacturing Overhead

It is important to understand that the debit side of the manufacturing overhead account is used to record actual overhead expenses. Conversely, the credit side of this account is used to record applied manufacturing overhead that is simultaneously debited to the work-in-process inventory account, as illustrated below.

Manufacturing Overhead

Actual manufacturing overhead costs are entered as debits on a regular basis as they are incurred.	Applied overhead costs are entered as credits as production takes place; costs are applied (debited) to Work-in-Process on the basis of a predetermined overhead rate.

Manufacturing Overhead is effectively a temporary holding account that simultaneously records actual overhead costs as they occur *irregularly* throughout the year while *regularly* transferring allocated overhead costs into the asset account called Work-in-Process Inventory. Hence, Manufacturing Overhead is a very important account to help deal with the fact that actual costs, including actual manufacturing overhead costs, are needed for accurate reporting of annual income and for computing a company's income tax liability at the end of the year. However, the management process of controlling and evaluating costs and prices cannot wait until the end of the year. Hence, while both actual and applied manufacturing overhead costs are accounted for constantly throughout the year, actual overhead costs are too sporadic to be effectively used as prices and costs are constantly evaluated throughout the year. This is why predetermined overhead rates are used to apply overhead throughout the year.

Disposition of Over- and Underapplied Manufacturing Overhead

If the beginning-of-the-year estimates of both manufacturing overhead costs and the activity basis (e.g., machine hours) are perfect, then at the end of the year the accountants at the Broyman Company will have applied exactly as much overhead to Work-in-Process as was actually incurred, and the ending balance in the manufacturing overhead account will be $0 (this rarely happens). Typically, though, the ending balance in the manufacturing overhead account is not very large. Nevertheless, the manufacturing overhead account is a temporary account that must be closed out at the end of the year. Handling any balance left in Manufacturing Overhead is the process of disposing of over- and underapplied manufacturing overhead.

In our earlier example, while accounting for the costs of producing one mahogany table at Broyman (Job #117), we debited a total of $15,224 in actual costs to the manufacturing overhead account. To illustrate the accounting for the difference between actual and applied manufacturing overhead costs, we will assume another $26,376 in actual manufacturing overhead costs were recognized and recorded in the manufacturing overhead account during the month of March 2009. Further, including the work done on the mahogany table in our example, the machining department at Broyman used a total of 650 machine hours and applied $20,800 to Work-in-Process Inventory, and the finishing department employed 275 direct labor hours and applied $10,450. Finally, we will assume that the cutting department (using a similar overhead allocation procedure) applied $9,600. At the end of March, the manufacturing overhead account would appear as follows:

Manufacturing Overhead

(Actual costs)	(Applied costs)	
15,224	20,800	Applied in machining dept.
26,376	10,450	Applied in finishing dept.
	9,600	Applied in cutting dept.
41,600	40,850	
Balance (underapplied) 750		

STOP & THINK

What would it mean if the debit (actual overhead) and credit (applied overhead) amounts in the manufacturing overhead account were vastly different?

overapplied manufacturing overhead

The excess of applied manufacturing overhead (based on a predetermined application rate) over the actual manufacturing overhead costs for a period.

underapplied manufacturing overhead

The excess of actual manufacturing overhead costs over the applied overhead costs for a period (based on a predetermined application rate).

A comparison of the debit and credit sides of the manufacturing overhead account shows that actual manufacturing overhead costs incurred were $750 higher than applied costs (which indicates that overhead was underapplied for the month). This difference is usually ignored until year-end because management is concerned with immediate decisions, for which current estimates are adequate. At year-end, however, this difference must be accounted for, not only to balance the books, but also to show actual costs in measuring income.

If, at the end of the year, total actual manufacturing overhead is less than the amount applied, the account will have a credit balance. This result is referred to as **overapplied manufacturing overhead**. Conversely, if applied manufacturing overhead is less than actual costs, the account will have a debit balance representing **underapplied manufacturing overhead**.

Which is better to have at the end of the year—under- or overapplied overhead? If overhead is underapplied, then the total cost of jobs will be understated. If a company were to allow the price on its products to fall based on this understated cost, the company could lose money because it might not cover its actual manufacturing overhead costs. On the other hand, overapplied manufacturing overhead indicates that jobs were overcharged for overhead and costs were overstated. If future pricing decisions were made based on these overstated costs, the company would soon find customers looking elsewhere for more reasonably priced products. Neither over- nor underapplied overhead is desirable. A company's objective is to attempt to anticipate overhead costs and accurately charge those costs to the various jobs.

There are two methods of treating over- and underapplied manufacturing overhead in the accounting system:

1. Close over- or underapplied manufacturing overhead directly to Cost of Goods Sold.
2. Allocate over- or underapplied manufacturing overhead to Work-in-Process Inventory, Finished Goods Inventory, and Costs of Goods Sold on the basis of the ending balances in these three accounts.

The first method is easier and more commonly used, especially if the over- or underapplied amount is small, because it requires only a single entry to correct the amount of manufacturing overhead applied. Let's assume that at year-end, when total actual and applied manufacturing overhead have been recorded, manufacturing overhead for Broyman was overapplied by $1,900. The entry to assign this overapplied manufacturing overhead to Cost of Goods Sold would be:

Manufacturing Overhead	1,900	
Cost of Goods Sold		1,900

    *To recognize the excess of applied manufacturing overhead
    costs over actual manufacturing overhead.*

Note: The entries for *underapplied* manufacturing overhead would be opposite from what
is shown above—debit Cost of Goods Sold and credit Manufacturing Overhead.

This entry will decrease the cost of goods sold account for the year by $1,900 and will close out the manufacturing overhead account.

    The second method is more accurate because, theoretically, any difference between applied and actual manufacturing overhead should be allocated proportionately to all items in production during the year. The items that were in production during the year include those produced and sold (Cost of Goods Sold), those produced and not sold (Finished Goods Inventory), and those still being produced (Work-in-Process Inventory). If the estimate had been accurate, manufacturing overhead costs would have been allocated proportionately to all products. Therefore, those products actually sold should not be burdened with, or relieved of, the entire amount of the estimation error. This alternative is more complicated, however, and requires detailed calculations and several journal entries, so it will not be illustrated here. When differences between actual and applied overhead are small, or when the ending balances in the work-in-process and finished goods inventory accounts are small, this more accurate method is usually not worth the extra effort.

REMEMBER THIS...

Manufacturing Overhead

Actual	Applied

- When ACTUAL overhead is more than APPLIED overhead (underapplied), the remaining debit balance is traditionally added to Cost of Goods Sold.

Cost of Goods Sold	XXX	
Manufacturing Overhead		XXX

- When APPLIED overhead is more than ACTUAL overhead (overapplied), the remaining credit balance is subtracted from Cost of Goods Sold.

Manufacturing Overhead	XXX	
Cost of Goods Sold		XXX

The Cost of Goods Manufactured Schedule

(3) In this section we will examine a single report, the Cost of Goods Manufactured schedule, that summarizes the cost flows in a manufacturing organization during a given period. As you will see, the Cost of Goods Manufactured schedule is really just a report that details what happened in the work-in-process inventory account during the period. We will also see how this cost information is used to then compute cost of goods sold.

If needed, be sure that you review the mahogany table example to see again how manufacturing costs (materials, labor, and overhead) are accumulated in the Work-in-Process Inventory account, then flow to Finished Goods Inventory, and finally to the Cost of Goods Sold account. These cost flows are summarized on a **Cost of Goods Manufactured schedule**, which supports the cost of goods sold calculation on the income statement.

The purpose of the Cost of Goods Manufactured schedule is to report the total costs that have been incurred to manufacture goods during a period. In our example, Exhibit 3 shows the Cost of Goods Manufactured schedule for Broyman Furniture Company. You will note that the numbers used in Exhibit 3 cannot be specifically traced back to the mahogany table example. This is because the costs used in that example are focused on the manufacture of a single table whereas the manufacturing costs in Exhibit 3 are for an entire year. The important thing for you to focus on in Exhibit 3 is the format for summarizing and reporting manufacturing cost flows. Note how the calculation for raw materials used in production is actually based on using the raw materials inventory account to calculate (or "plug") the number that flows into the work-in-process account as shown below.

Cost of Goods Manufactured schedule

A schedule supporting the income statement that summarizes the total cost of goods manufactured and transferred out of the work-in-process inventory account during a period. These costs include direct materials, direct labor, and applied manufacturing overhead.

Raw Materials Inventory

Beginning balance	50,000		
Purchases	270,000	*290,000*	Transferred to Work-in-Process
Ending balance	30,000		

Plug this number

EXHIBIT 3	**Cost of Goods Manufactured Schedule**

Broyman Furniture Company
Cost of Goods Manufactured Schedule
For the Year Ended December 31, 2009

Raw materials:		
Beginning raw materials inventory	$ 50,000	
Add: Raw materials purchased	270,000	
Total raw materials available	$320,000	
Less: Ending raw materials inventory	30,000	
Raw materials used in production		$290,000
Direct labor		300,000
Applied manufacturing overhead		174,000
Total manufacturing costs		$764,000
Add: Beginning work-in-process inventory		90,000
Less: Ending work-in-process inventory		(80,000)
Cost of goods manufactured		$774,000

The Cost of Goods Manufactured schedule provides the calculations that support the flow of costs for a manufacturing firm. In our example, the schedule shows that materials costing $290,000 were combined with direct labor costs of $300,000 and *applied* manufacturing overhead costs of $174,000 to transfer $764,000 of manufacturing costs to Work-in-Process Inventory. This $764,000 amount of total manufacturing costs represents the new manufacturing costs incurred during the period and is a good representation of the level of production activity carried out during the period. The $764,000 was then adjusted for the beginning and ending work-in-process inventories to determine the $774,000 cost of goods manufactured for the period. The amount of cost of goods manufactured represents the total cost of items for which production was completed during the period; this cost includes some costs incurred in prior periods (from beginning work-in-process inventory) and most costs incurred during this period. Effectively, cost of goods manufactured is simply the flow of costs out of the work-in-process account as shown below.

Work-in-Process Inventory

Beginning balance	90,000		
Direct materials costs	290,000		
Direct labor costs	300,000		
Applied manuf. overhead costs	174,000	774,000	Transferred to Finished Goods
Ending balance	80,000		

Plug this number

Knowing the total cost of goods manufactured makes it easy to determine the total cost of goods sold. The cost of goods manufactured amount is added to beginning finished goods inventory (assume $60,000) to arrive at cost of goods available for sale of $834,000. The ending finished goods inventory (assume $40,000) is then subtracted to determine the *unadjusted* cost of goods sold ($794,000). Finally, this number is adjusted for any over- or underapplied manufacturing overhead (assume $6,000 overapplied) to arrive at the adjusted costs of goods sold ($788,000). This calculation of cost of goods sold is shown below.

Cost of Goods Sold

Beginning finished goods inventory	$ 60,000
Add: Cost of goods manufactured	774,000
Cost of goods available for sale	$834,000
Less: Ending finished goods inventory	(40,000)
Unadjusted cost of goods sold	$794,000
Less: Overapplied manufacturing overhead	(6,000)
Adjusted cost of goods sold	$788,000

This calculation can also be shown using the finished goods inventory and cost of goods sold accounts as shown below.

Finished Goods Inventory

Beginning balance	60,000		
Cost of goods manufactured	774,000	794,000	Transferred to Cost of Goods Sold
Ending balance	40,000		

Plug this number

Cost of Goods Sold

Unadjusted cost of goods sold	*794,000	6,000	Overapplied manuf. overhead costs
Adjusted cost of goods sold	788,000		

*Cost of goods sold	794,000
Finished goods inventory	794,000
Sale of inventory valued using the applied manufacturing	
overhead rate.	

CAUTION

Remember that over- or underapplied overhead is usually charged to the cost of goods sold account. Thus, in the cost of goods sold calculation, underapplied overhead is added to, and overapplied overhead is subtracted from, the costs transferred from the finished goods inventory account.

Total cost of goods manufactured should include only those costs that have gone through the work-in-process inventory account during the period. Thus, as shown in Exhibit 3, applied (rather than actual) overhead costs are included in the Cost of Goods Manufactured schedule. As illustrated, the cost of goods sold account is then adjusted for the amount of over- or underapplied overhead. Cost of goods sold, while an important number for reporting on the income statement for investors and creditors, is not particularly useful for management purposes. More detailed information that is useful for managing the manufacturing process is provided in the details of the Cost of Goods Manufactured schedule.

REMEMBER THIS...

	Total Manufacturing Costs (Direct Materials, Direct Labor, and **Applied** Overhead)
+	Beginning Work-in-Process Inventory
−	Ending Work-in-Process Inventory
=	Cost of Goods Manufactured

	Cost of Goods Manufactured
+	Beginning Finished Goods Inventory
−	Ending Finished Goods Inventory
=	Unadjusted Cost of Goods Sold
+/−	Under- or Overapplied Overhead
=	Adjusted Cost of Goods Sold

The Flow of Products and Costs in Service and Merchandising Firms

Explain the flow of products and costs in a service organization and in a merchandising organization.

So far in this chapter we have defined and discussed the nature of manufacturing businesses. However, arguably the most import type of business in the United States is service. What is a service business? For our purposes, we'll use a simple definition of a service business as follows:

> A service business is any organization whose main economic activity involves producing a nonphysical product that provides value to a customer.

As you'll see in the list in Exhibit 4, there is a lot of variety in the specific types of organizations that fit in the category of a service business. As you study Exhibit 4, try to apply our definition of a service business to each of these categories and see if the definition fits.

EXHIBIT 4	Categories of Service Businesses

- Accounting/legal
- Architectural/engineering
- Communications (e.g., television, radio, etc.)
- Banking/financial (including insurance, investment brokers, consulting, etc.)
- Health care
- Software/systems integration (e.g., programming, installation, service, consulting, etc.)
- Marketing/advertising
- Public utilities
- Research and development
- Transportation
- Entertainment
- Education and training (not including state-owned schools and universities)

Comparing Service and Manufacturing Business Activities

It is important that we spend time understanding how costs are accounted for in a service industry because these types of businesses are the largest and fastest-growing sector in our economy (which means it is more likely that your career will involve working with service businesses than any other business type). Service companies actually share a lot of similarities with manufacturing companies. Like manufacturers, most service companies perform a significant number of activities to prepare their service products for sale and delivery to their customers. Typically, a lot of direct labor and overhead is involved in a service business. Service work is a very real production activity. However, what service firms provide is not nearly as tangible as the product provided by manufacturers. Yes, an architect or engineer does provide a tangible set of drawings or blueprints. But what is really being sold is the knowledge and customized advice that is represented by the drawings.

Consider the organizational effort required for a CPA firm to provide an audit service to a client. This organization is depicted in Exhibit 5. As you can see, there is direct labor (the auditing staff) involved in this audit that is supported by a complex system of supervisors, supplies, equipment, capital assets, computer network and databases, and so forth. This support system essentially forms the overhead costs of the audit product, and these overhead costs will need to be appropriately allocated as part of the product cost of the audit. You can see, then, that there are many similarities between the process of manufacturing and service companies.

CAUTION

When trying to decide whether a company is in the service business, consider the following old joke:

A plumber is called out to fix a clogged pipe. The plumber examines the situation for a few seconds, then pulls out a hammer and taps on the offending pipe. The problem is solved. However, the customer is a bit upset upon receiving the bill for $100.17. "All you did was tap on the pipe. I demand an itemized bill!" the customer complains. So, the plumber sends the following itemized bill:

Tapping on pipe	$ 0.17
Knowing where to tap	100.00
Total	$100.17

Remember that expertise is a significant component of most service companies.

© ANDREAS POLLOK/GETTY IMAGES INC.

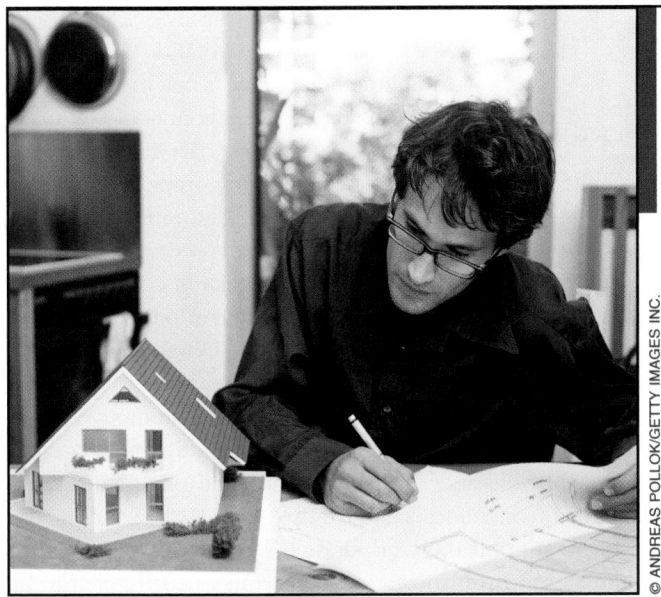

An architect creates a product, but the product being created and sold really is not a set of blueprints or a scale model of a building. The architect is a service provider who creates and sells an intangible product—the expertise required to provide a solution to a design problem.

Product Cost Accumulation in Service Organizations

There are a number of accounting similarities between manufacturing and service organizations. One important similarity is that both manufacturing and service organizations use a significant amount of direct labor in producing their products. In addition, large amounts of overhead costs typically are allocated to individual products. Similar to many

EXHIBIT 5 **The Service Process at a CPA Firm**

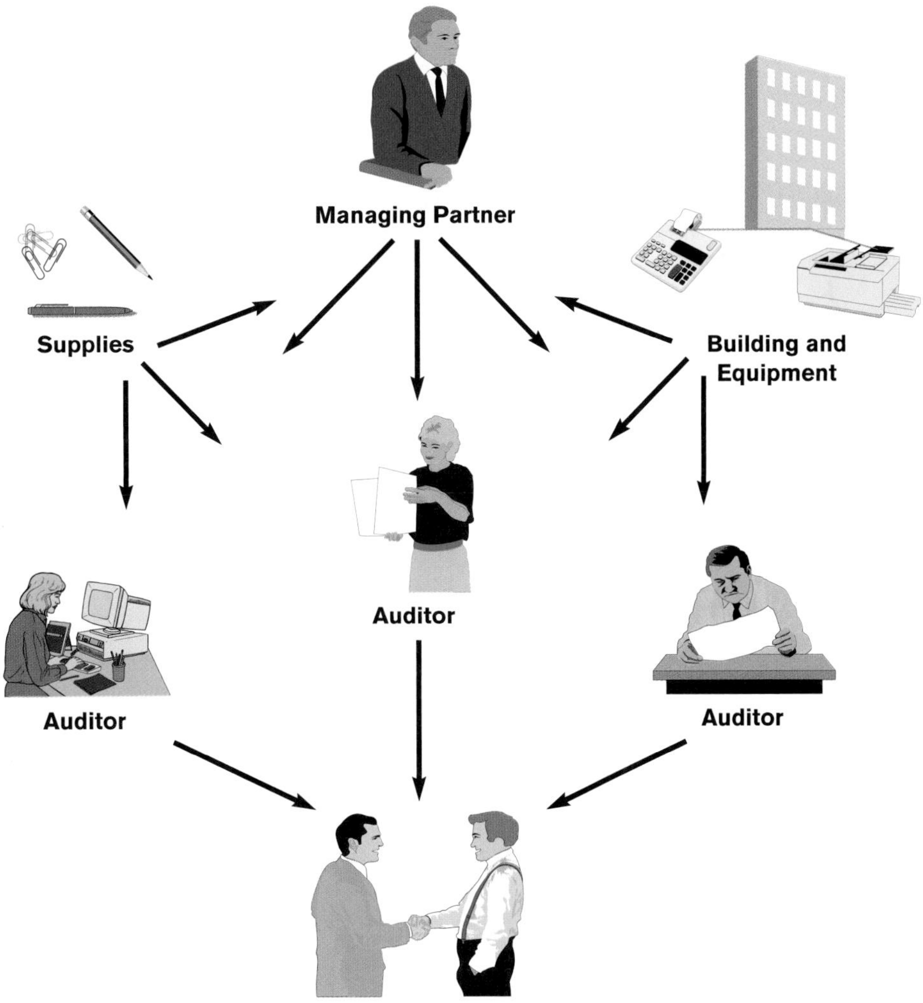
Managing Partner
Supplies
Building and Equipment
Auditor
Auditor
Auditor
Client

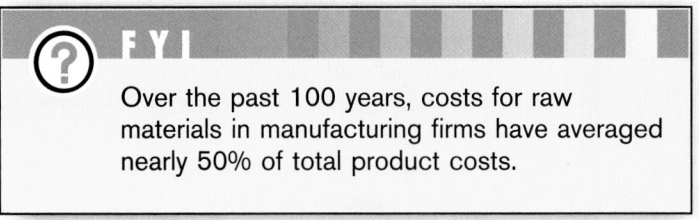

manufacturers, service businesses often allocate overhead on the basis of direct labor hours. One important difference is that manufacturers must also manage large amounts of raw materials costs, while the materials included in the services sold by service companies are typically limited to insignificant amounts of supplies used in the service process.

The overhead for service firms can involve nearly any kind of management cost. Allocating overhead to service activities generally involves factoring an overhead rate into the billing rate used to charge customers. Think about all the services you buy and use. Often, some type of a billing rate per hour or per event is used to determine the price you pay for the service. For example, accountants, lawyers, consultants, computer programmers, and automotive repair shops often charge by the hour. When you get the bill, you understand that the huge rate per hour does not represent solely the wage or salary of the professional who provided the service to you. This rate has been enhanced (sometimes significantly!) in order to cover all the overhead and supplies costs necessary to support the work done by the service professional. Similarly, doctors, trainers, entertainers, and transportation companies usually charge by event. You understand that the doctor isn't paid the full $175 charge when he or she gives you a physical exam. Much of that amount goes to pay for the costs of staff, equipment, and building occupancy necessary to support the actual service provided by your doctor.

Assigning overhead costs to a service event follows a pattern that should be familiar to you now that you've worked through the cost accounting for manufacturing firms. Total overhead for the service organization is estimated for a period of time, generally a year. This estimated overhead is then divided by an appropriate activity measure. For an accountant, this activity measure may be billable hours. The measure for a bank could be the number of teller transactions or number of accounts. For a cable TV company, it could be the average number of accounts expected for the year or the total billable months of service. The activity measure for an electric company might be the expected number of kilowatts produced during the next year. Other examples of possible overhead rate calculations for several types of service companies are shown below.

	Law Firm	**Radio Station**	**Trucking Firm**
Estimated overhead for the upcoming year	$\dfrac{\$770,000}{11,000 \text{ billable hours}} = \$70.00/\text{hour}$	$\dfrac{\$138,400}{34,600 \text{ advertising events}} = \$4.00/\text{event}$	$\dfrac{\$602,000}{8,600,000 \text{ trucking miles}} = \$0.07/\text{mile}$
Estimated activity level for the upcoming year			

Exhibit 6 provides a basic comparison of the flow of product costs in manufacturing, service, and merchandising organizations (we'll discuss merchandising organizations in the next section). As you can see, the overhead account for a service company is used in much the same manner as in a manufacturing firm. As actual overhead costs are incurred, they are debited to the overhead account rather than being debited to an expense account. Then, as the appropriate overhead activities actually take place (e.g., consulting hours, teller transactions, and kilowatts), overhead costs are allocated to Work-in-Process Services.[3] As services are actually billed, these overhead costs are combined with the direct labor costs of the service professionals (if any) and any incidental costs of supplies are debited to Cost of Services (an account very similar to the cost of goods sold account used by

---

[3] Some service organizations refer to this work-in-process account as Unbilled Services.

| EXHIBIT 6 | Comparing Manufacturing, Service, and Merchandising Product Cost Flows |

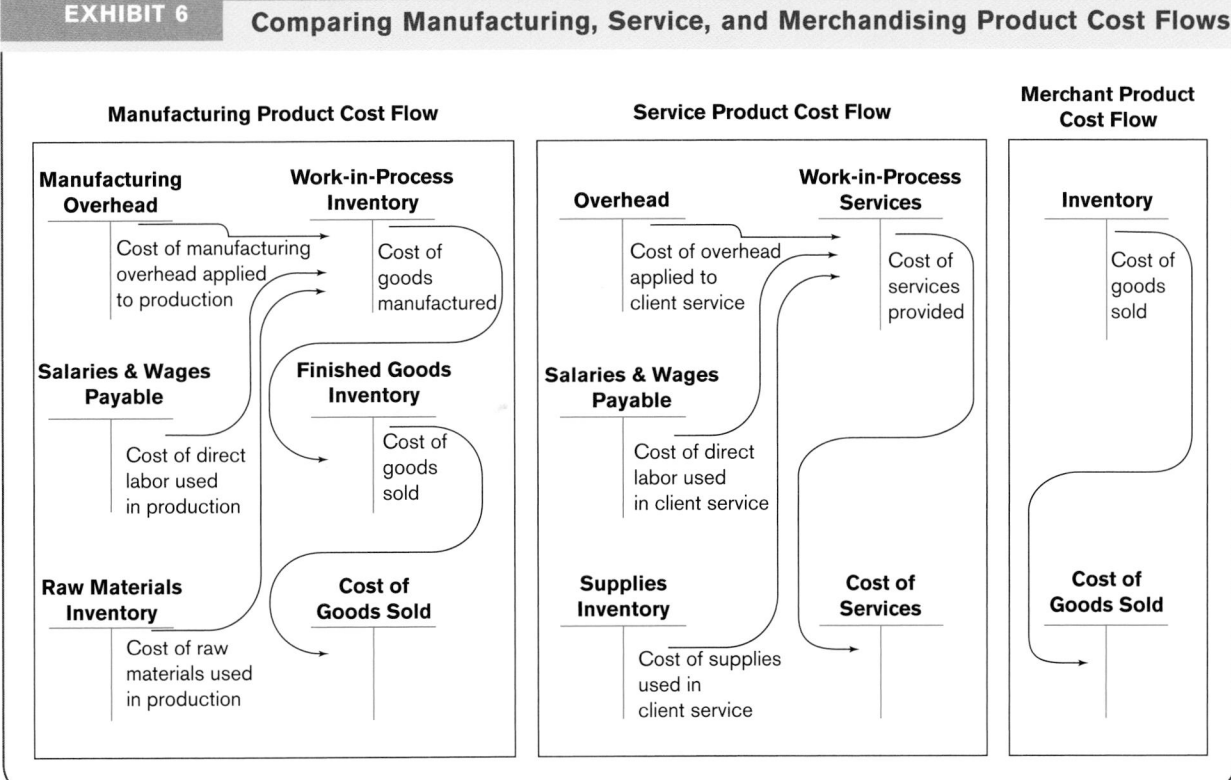

STOP & THINK

The selection of the activity base that is used to allocate overhead is a very important management decision because any particular activity base could have a significant impact on how much cost is assigned to one product or service versus another. For example, suppose that the academic advisement center at your college is trying to determine what it costs to provide advisement services to a specific student each semester. What are some possible activity bases this department might use to allocate the costs of the office equipment, supervisor salary, and other overhead items? Would your choice of a base have an effect on which students are then identified as "high-cost-to-serve" students?

manufacturers and merchants). Any underapplied or overapplied overhead at the end of the year is handled in the same way as illustrated previously for a manufacturing company.

The following are some examples of work in process that are likely to exist at the end of an accounting period for various types of service companies:[4]

- Accounting/legal—An audit that will take three months to complete is in its initial stage.
- Architectural/engineering—The blueprints for a large construction project are only partially completed.
- Banking/financial—The fieldwork has been completed and the lending documents are being finalized for a large loan that will be closed next month.
- Marketing/advertising—Three weeks of effort have been expended on the development of a new advertising campaign that will not be ready for presentation to the client for another three weeks.
- Transportation—A large shipment of coal is being held in a midwestern freight yard en route to its shipping point on the East Coast.

---

[4] O. B. Martinson, *Cost Accounting in the Service Industry: A Critical Assessment* (Montvale, N.J.: Institute of Management Accountants, 1989), pp. 47–48.

In each of these examples, resources have been invested in creating a service that the customer has not yet received. As a result, a work-in-process inventory asset exists and should be recognized on the balance sheet. As you can see in Exhibit 6, as supplies and labor costs are directly invested in the process of creating a service for customers, these amounts are debited to Work-in-Process Services. As overhead costs such as utilities, rent, taxes, and support staff salaries are incurred, these costs are debited to the overhead account and are subsequently allocated to Work-in-Process Services using an overhead rate. When the service is completed and delivered to the customer, then the revenue earning process is complete and the service costs are transferred out of Work-in-Process Services and into Cost of Services.[5]

Product Cost Accumulation in Merchandising Organizations

retailers

Second-tier merchants who typically purchase products from wholesalers to distribute to end-user customers. Many large retailers, however, often bypass wholesalers to purchase products directly from the original manufacturers.

wholesalers

Top-tier merchants who typically deal directly with the original manufacturers to distribute products to retailers.

The business process for merchants is probably quite familiar to you. Most retail merchants or **retailers** place orders with and receive shipments from whole-sale merchants or **wholesalers**. As shown in the floor plan in Exhibit 7, many retail merchants have a receiving dock and a breakdown area used to prepare goods for display on their sales floor. Some retailers also keep a stock room for holding excess inventory. However, the cost of holding inventory in today's competitive environment is causing retailers to demand that wholesalers provide smaller and more frequent shipments. As a result, many retailers are able to avoid having a stock room. Inventory in these companies can then be moved directly from the breakdown area onto the sales floor.

As you can see in Exhibit 6 on page 779, in contrast to accounting for manufacturing and service businesses, the flow of costs through the merchandising accounting system is relatively simple. Essentially, accounting for inventory in merchandising organizations is a fairly straightforward process. There are no overhead accounts, and no raw materials and work-in-process accounts. Merchandise inventory, by definition, is essentially complete and ready for sale when purchased. Hence, the cost of purchased inventory is debited to Merchandise Inventory throughout the year as it is acquired.[6] As inventory is sold, the cost of inventory is credited from Merchandise Inventory and debited to Cost of Goods Sold. The accounting transaction is simply reversed when customers return merchandise that can be resold, and the cost of goods sold account is credited and the inventory account is debited (if the returned merchandise cannot be resold, then nothing happens in either of these particular accounts).

Conceptually, the inventory costs for a merchant should also include all costs required to purchase the inventory, transport it to the merchant's place of business, and prepare it for sale (unpacking, displaying, etc.). Hence, the inventory cost should include the purchase price, shipping costs (freight in), insurance while in transit, administrative costs incurred by the merchant related to purchasing and handling activities, and storage costs prior to sale. In practice, though, most of these overhead-related costs, other than freight in costs, are difficult to allocate to specific inventory items. As a result, overhead costs related to merchandise inventory are often expensed as a period cost and included in Selling and General Administrative Expenses on the income statement.

---

[5] Some fairly large long-term service contracts are sometimes designed to allow the provider to bill and receive partial payments as the contract is completed. In these cases, as the revenue process is partially completed, some service costs can be transferred out of Work-in-Process Services and into Cost of Services. Learning about this type of accounting, called percentage-of-completion accounting, is reserved for more advanced accounting courses.

[6] You may recall from your studies in financial accounting that this method of continuously debiting and crediting Merchandise Inventory as inventory is purchased and sold (and debiting Cost of Goods Sold as inventory is sold) is called the perpetual inventory method of accounting. The alternative to the perpetual method is the periodic inventory method. There are several more accounts involved with the periodic inventory method, including Purchases, Purchase Discounts, and Purchase Returns. A significant difference between the perpetual and periodic inventory methods is that the periodic inventory method adjusts Merchandise Inventory only at the end of each period when cost of goods sold is calculated for the income statement.

EXHIBIT 7 **A Typical Floor Plan for a Merchant Retailer**

Retailer's Floor Plan

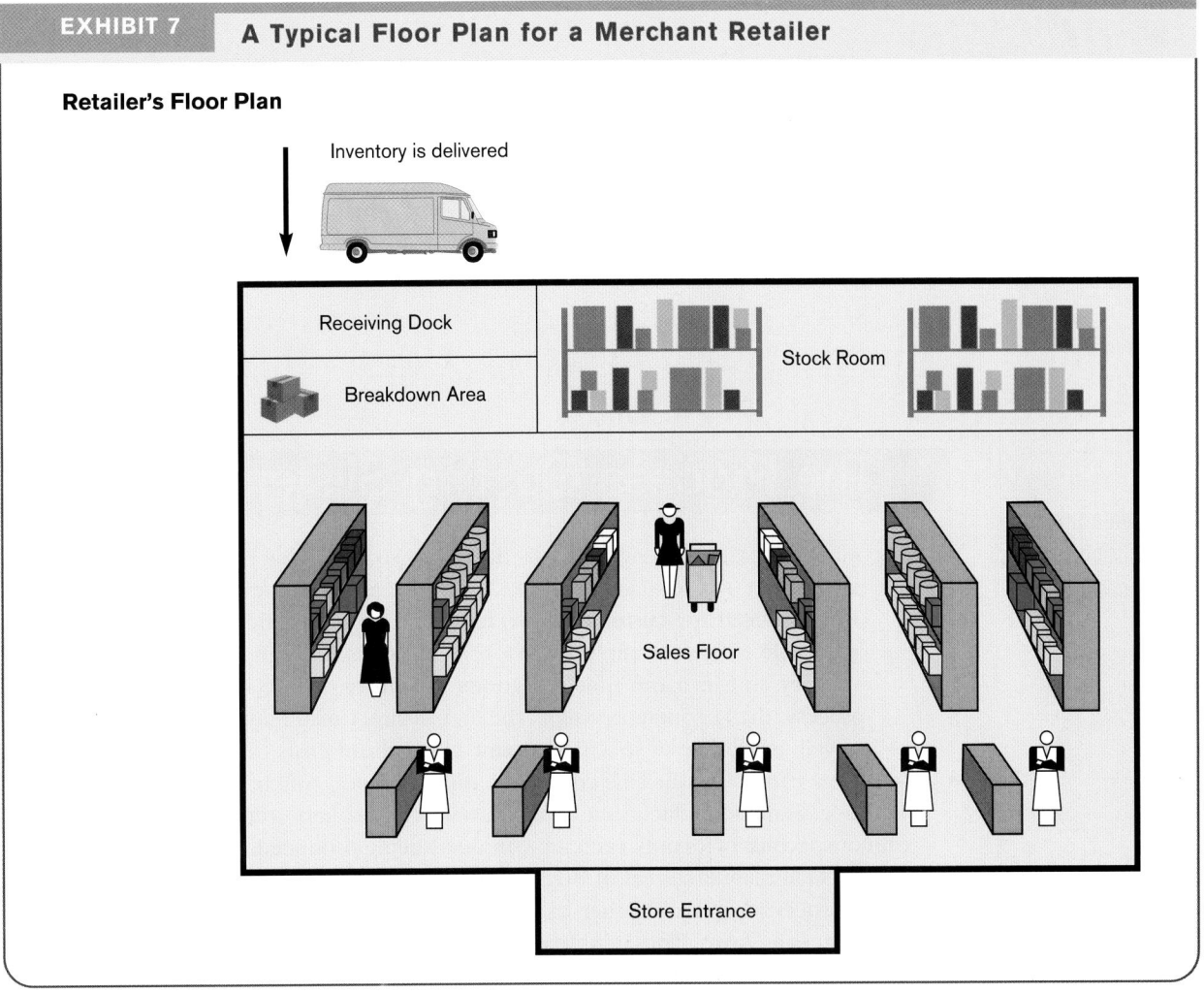

As we wrap up this part of the chapter, you may feel that tracking inventory costs in a merchant's accounting system is a fairly easy conceptual process. However, developing useful information on merchandise inventory for managers who need to plan, control, and evaluate inventory and inventory costs is very involved. Think about your last trip to **Wal-Mart**. There is an awful lot of inventory in a Wal-Mart store. Getting the product cost accounting right is critical for a merchant this big and complex!

REMEMBER THIS...

- Costs flow through a service firm in a manner very similar to a manufacturing firm. Costs of supplies (usually insignificant in size) and direct labor (usually very significant in size) accumulate in an account called Work-in-Process Services. This account performs much the same function as the work-in-process inventory account in a manufacturing firm. Overhead is applied to Work-in-Process Services as service activities take place.

- The process of accounting for inventory in a merchandising business is not nearly as complicated as it is in a manufacturing or service business. Purchasing costs of merchant inventory are debited to the inventory account, while inventory sales are credited out of the inventory account and debited to Cost of Goods Sold.

In the first part of the chapter we illustrated product costing using the job order costing method. This method is commonly used in both manufacturing and service organizations. In this expanded material section, we discuss how companies (largely manufacturers) use process costing when it is difficult to specifically identify unique jobs during the production process.

The Process Costing System

Compute product costs using process costing.

(5) All the product costing methods described so far in this chapter assume that the accountant is able to specifically identify the job (i.e., the product or service) being produced for customers. By identifying each specific job, the accountant is then able to specifically track a job as it moves through the work-in-process inventory and into the finished goods inventory. While it is in the production process, the accountant assigns the actual direct materials and direct labor costs, as well as allocates a specific amount of overhead costs, that are required to produce a particular job. This cost accounting method is often referred to as job order costing. Some manufacturing companies cannot use job order costing because they cannot specifically identify each job (product) being produced. Examples of such companies include manufacturers of bricks, lumber, paint, soft drinks, and newspapers and most food processing plants. Other examples include large-scale tax preparation or loan processing firms. These companies produce large volumes of products or services using a series of uniform processes. For these companies, **process costing** is the appropriate product cost accounting method. Because these companies can't focus on costing a particular job, they focus on costing the amount of work done for a particular *period of time*. We'll talk more about this concept of work done in a particular time period below. For now, remember that for process costing to be appropriate, two general conditions typically exist:

process costing

A method of product costing whereby costs are accumulated by process or work centers and averaged over all products manufactured in a center or department during a particular production period. There are two methods of process costing: The FIFO method and the weighted-average method.

1. The activities performed in each process center are identical for all units.
2. The units produced as a result of passing through the process centers are basically the same.

Steps in Process Costing

A firm whose products and processes meet the preceding conditions would employ process costing using five steps:

1. Identify units that went into the process and identify where those units are at the end of the production period. Determine the amount of "work done" (equivalent units of production) during the production period.
2. Determine the amount of production costs that went into the process and compute the product costs per unit for the production period.
3. Compute the total cost of units completed and transferred out (cost of goods manufactured) during the production period.
4. Compute the total cost of units remaining in process (ending work-in-process inventory) at the end of the production period.
5. Prepare the production cost report.

equivalent units of production

A method used in a process costing system to measure the production output during a period. Equivalent units of production essentially measures the "work done" by the center or department in terms of units of output.

Step 1. Compute Equivalent Units of Production

The first step in process costing is to track the flow of units and compute the **equivalent units of production**. The concept of equivalent units of production essentially means to calculate the amount of work actually done during any particular period of time in terms of units of output. It's really a very simple concept. For example, let's assume that you are being paid by the hour to hand paint porcelain figurines for a small local art shop. It's an arduous process, taking several hours to paint a single figurine. On average, you can do only three or four figurines per day. At the end of your first day on the job, you have painted three figurines and have another one nearly complete. If your boss were to ask you how much work you did for the day, are you going to reply that you painted only three figurines? Of course not! Instead, you'll likely tell her that you completely painted three figurines and that you have another one nearly done (let's say it is 90% done). So, did you paint four figurines? Not really. The amount of work done on your first day is 3.9 figurines (three whole units plus 90% of a fourth unit), right? In other words, you did 3.9 equivalent units of production. The work that you have done includes one unit in ending work-in-process inventory (the figurine that is 90% done).

The more interesting measure of equivalent units of production is what happens on your second day on the job. When you come back to the shop the next day, the first thing you will do is work on that day's beginning work-in-process inventory, which is the figurine that is 90% done from the day before.[7] Let's assume that you then start and complete three more figurines. Before it's time to go home, you are able to start one more figurine and get it about 30% done. Now how do you answer the boss's question about how much work was done on your second day? You completed a total of four figurines (the figurine that was work-in-process when you came to work plus three more that were both started and completed this same day), but to say that you did the work of four figurines isn't quite accurate, is it? To be accurate, you completed 10% of one figurine, 100% of three figurines, and 30% of a final figurine that is still work-in-process. In other words, the work done for the day was 3.4 figurines, computed as follows:

	Physical Units	Percent Completed (i.e., "work done")	Equivalent Units of Production
Beginning work-in-process	1	× 10%	= 0.1
Started and completed	3	× 100%	= 3.0
Ending work-in-process	1	× 30%	= 0.3
Total equivalent units of production			3.4

With this example of equivalent units of production in mind, let's now use an example that's more representative of manufacturers that follow the process costing approach to accounting for product costs. Exhibit 8 shows how products and costs move through the two process centers (mixing and bagging) of the Allied Cement Company. For now, we will focus on the process costing for the mixing center at Allied Cement. Production units at Allied are measured in pounds of finished cement. When the mixing machines are shut down at the end of a production period (let's assume a production period at Allied is one month), not all pounds of cement started the last day of the month in the mixing center will have been completed. In fact, as at most manufacturers, units are usually in process at both the beginning and the end of a period. Were it not for these beginning and ending work-in-process inventories, the number of units actually produced in

---

[7] This is the reason we call this particular method of process costing the FIFO (first in, first out) method. It is based on the assumption that all beginning work-in-process inventory is completed before any new units are started.

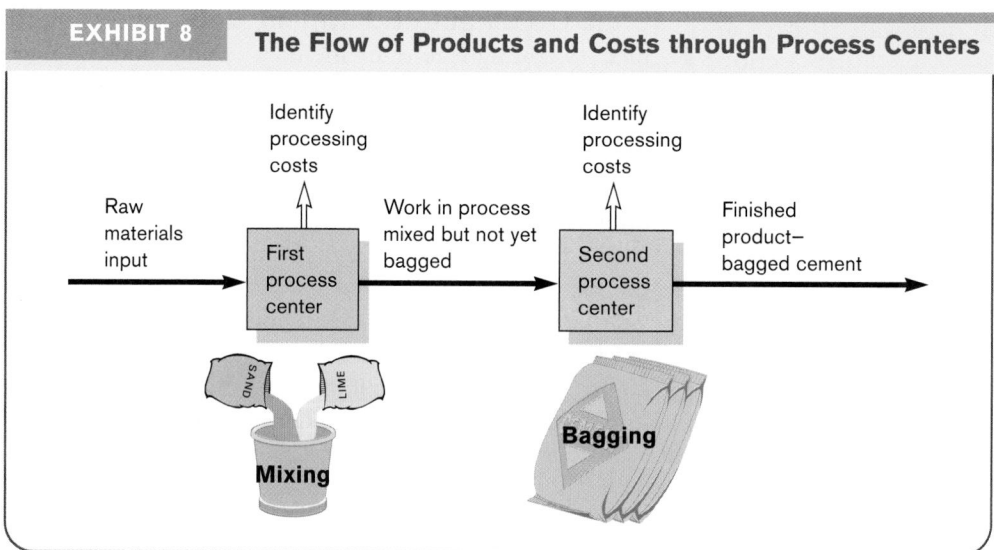

| EXHIBIT 8 | The Flow of Products and Costs through Process Centers |

the mixing center for the period could be determined merely by counting all pounds of cement that were transferred out of the mixing center and into the bagging center. However, as you saw in our earlier example of hand painting figurines, the amount of work actually done in the mixing center for the period also includes how much work was done in the beginning and ending work-in-process inventories.

With this in mind, look at the report below on equivalent units of production for the mixing center.

Step 1: Compute equivalent units of production.

	Physical Units (pounds)	Direct Materials Costs		Conversion Costs	
		Percent Done	Equivalent Units	Percent Done	Equivalent Units
Beginning work-in-process	4,000	× 0%	= 0	× 80%	= 3,200
Started and completed	44,000	× 100%	= 44,000	× 100%	= 44,000
Ending work-in-process	2,000	× 100%	= 2,000	× 60%	= 1,200
Equivalent units of production			**46,000**		**48,400**
Transferred out (to bagging)	48,000				

The "Physical Units" column reports that the mixing center had 4,000 pounds of cement in beginning work-in-process when the month started. The department finished mixing these 4,000 pounds and mixed an additional 44,000 pounds before the end of the month, allowing the mixing center to transfer a total of 48,000 pounds to the bagging center. At the end of the month, 2,000 pounds of cement remained in ending work-in-process.

Now look at the "Equivalent Units" column for the Direct Materials Costs. In this case, all of the materials necessary to mix a pound of cement are put in place at the beginning of the mixing process. In other words, when the month began, the 4,000 pounds of cement in beginning work-in-process were already 100% complete in terms of materials. Similarly, at the end of the month, the 2,000 pounds of cement in ending work-in-process were 100% complete in terms of materials. As a result, the equivalent units of production (i.e., "work done") to be used when accounting for costs of direct materials for Allied is simply the number of pounds of cement *started* into production during the month, or

conversion costs

The costs of converting raw materials to finished products; includes direct labor and manufacturing overhead costs.

100% of units started and completed plus 100% of units in ending work-in-process (and 0% of units in beginning work-in-process).[8]

Finally, look at the "Equivalent Units" column under "Conversion Costs." **Conversion costs** is the term we use to describe all product costs necessary to "convert" raw materials into finished goods. Hence, conversion costs include all costs of direct labor and manufacturing overhead.[9] In this example, at the beginning of the month, the beginning work-in-process inventory was 20% complete in terms of costs of direct labor and manufacturing overhead. As a result, the first work done in the mixing center for the current production period was to finish the remaining 80% of the effort required to complete these 4,000 pounds of cement. In other words, the mixing center did 3,200 equivalent units of production (4,000 × 80%) on beginning work-in-process. At the end of the month, there were 2,000 pounds in ending work-in-process that were 60% complete in terms of direct labor and manufacturing overhead costs, which means that the mixing center did 1,200 equivalent units of production (2,000 × 60%) on ending work-in-process. When combined with the work done on units started and completed, the mixing center's "work done" in terms of direct labor and manufacturing overhead was 48,400 equivalent units (3,200 + 44,000 + 1,200).

> ⊘ **CAUTION**
>
> When computing the equivalent units of work done on beginning work-in-process inventory, remember that the key question we are asking is "how much work was done in the *current* production period?" Hence, if the beginning work-in-process inventory was 20% complete at the beginning of the month, then in a "First In First Out" manufacturing process, the first thing to do in the current month is finish the remaining 80% of the beginning work-in-process inventory. Look at the "Percent Done" column in the table "Step 1: Compute Equivalent Units of Production." This column might make more sense to you if you think of it as the "Percent Done in the Current Month."

Step 2. Compute the Product Costs per Unit With Step 1 completed, we know how much work was done in terms of production output for the mixing center. Now, to compute the product cost per unit, we need to determine how much was spent on production. For the mixing center, we will assume that the beginning work-in-process of 4,000 pounds includes $800 in direct materials and $1,200 in direct labor and manufacturing overhead (i.e., conversion costs). Further, Allied spent $9,660 for direct materials and $70,180 for conversion costs in the current production period. Computing the product costs per unit (pound) for the mixing department is then a simple matter of dividing the product costs by the appropriate equivalent units of production, reported as follows:

Step 2: Compute the product costs per unit.

	Total Costs	Equivalent Units	Cost per Unit
Beginning work-in-process			
Direct materials costs	$ 800	÷ 4,000	= $0.20
Conversion costs	1,200	÷ 800	= 1.50
Total	$ 2,000		**$1.70**
Current period			
Direct materials costs	$ 9,660	÷ 46,000	= $0.21
Conversion costs	70,180	÷ 48,400	= 1.45
Total	$79,840		**$1.66**

---

[8] When discussing equivalent units in this chapter, we will always assume that direct materials are all added at the beginning of the process. However, this assumption is not always the case in actual companies.

[9] Because we assume in this example that costs of manufacturing overhead are being allocated on the basis of direct labor, we can combine the equivalent units calculation for direct labor and for manufacturing overhead costs into one calculation for conversion costs. This is the assumption that we will follow for all subsequent equivalent units calculations in this chapter.

CAUTION

When using beginning work-in-process in the calculation of equivalent units of production for the current production period, remember to use the percentage yet to be done. In other words, the "work done" in the current period on beginning work-in-process is:

$$\begin{array}{c}\text{Number of}\\ \text{physical units}\\ \text{in inventory}\end{array} \times \begin{array}{c}(1 - \text{Percent}\\ \text{completed})\end{array}$$

The "work done" on ending work-in-process for the current period is:

$$\begin{array}{c}\text{Number of}\\ \text{physical units}\\ \text{in inventory}\end{array} \times \begin{array}{c}\text{Percent}\\ \text{completed}\end{array}$$

As you can see in the report above on product costs per unit, Allied spent $0.21 per pound for direct materials in the mixing center in the current production period. This cost is based on dividing the total equivalent units of 46,000 for work done on direct materials into the total direct materials costs of $9,660. Bearing in mind that beginning work-in-process came from the previous production period, Allied can compare the current direct materials cost to the direct materials cost in the previous production period, which was $0.20 per pound. This cost is obtained by dividing the costs of direct materials in beginning work-in-process by the equivalent units in beginning work-in-process (remember that when the day begins, all 4,000 pounds in inventory are 100% done with respect to direct materials). The current-period conversion cost per unit is $1.45, based on dividing the total equivalent units of 48,400 for work done in terms of direct labor and manufacturing overhead into the total conversion costs of $70,180. Again, Allied's management can check their efforts to control conversion costs by comparing the current-period costs with the previous month's cost of $1.50 per pound, which is calculated by dividing conversion costs in beginning work-in-process by the work already done in beginning work-in-process when the month begins (800 equivalent pounds = 4,000 physical pounds × 20% "work done" last month).

Step 3. Compute the Costs Transferred Out   Allied has spent a total of $79,840 this month in the mixing center. In addition, when the month began, there was work-in-process inventory in the mixing center that had a total value of $2,000. Hence, as you can see in the report above on product costs per unit, the mixing center needs to account for $81,840. Assuming that there has been no waste or pilferage in the mixing process, at the end of the month all costs have either been transferred out to the bagging center or remain in ending work-in-process. To compute the costs transferred out to the bagging center, the mixing center needs to account for the costs of completing the cement in beginning work-in-process, as well as the cement that was started and completed during the month. The following report shows the costs transferred out:

Step 3: Compute the costs transferred out.

	Cost per Unit	Equivalent Units		
Beginning work-in-process				
Initial direct materials costs				$ 800
Initial conversion costs				1,200
Costs to complete materials	$0.21	×	0	= 0
Costs to complete conversion	$1.45	×	3,200	= 4,640
Total				$ 6,640
Started and completed	$1.66	×	44,000	= 73,040
Total costs transferred out				**$79,680**

As you can see in the above report, the mixing center did not need to add any more direct materials costs to complete the beginning work-in-process. However, there were

3,200 equivalent units of work in terms of direct labor and manufacturing overhead that needed to be completed during the month before the 4,000 pounds of cement in beginning work-in-process could be transferred out to the bagging center. Hence, the mixing department spent $4,640 in conversion costs ($1.45 per unit × 3,200 equivalent units) to complete the mixing on beginning work-in-process. When added to the initial beginning work-in-process costs of $2,000 ($800 + $1,200), the first 4,000 pounds of cement transferred to the bagging center carried total production costs of $6,640.

Of the total 48,000 pounds transferred to the bagging center, 44,000 pounds were started and completed during the month. At a total cost per unit of $1.66 ($0.21 per unit for direct materials + $1.45 per unit for direct labor and manufacturing overhead), the mixing department spent $73,040 to mix the remaining units transferred out of its operations during the month.

Step 4. Compute Costs of Ending Work-in-Process Inventory

The fourth step in the mixing center's process costing effort is to determine the costs of the 2,000 pounds of cement remaining in work-in-process inventory at the end of the current production period. These calculations are reported below.

Step 4: Compute costs of ending work-in-process inventory.

	Cost per Unit	Equivalent Units	
Costs for direct materials	$0.21	× 2,000	= $ 420
Conversion costs	$1.45	× 1,200	= 1,740
Cost of ending work-in-process			**$2,160**

Because all 2,000 pounds are 100% complete in terms of direct materials, this inventory represents $420 ($0.21 per unit × 2,000 pounds × 100%) in direct materials costs. On the other hand, because these 2,000 pounds are only 60% complete in terms of direct labor and manufacturing overhead, there are $1,740 ($1.45 per unit × 2,000 pounds × 60%) in conversion costs residing in ending work-in-process inventory. In total, ending work-in-process contains $2,160 ($420 + $1,740) in product costs.

production cost report

A document that compiles all the costs of a manufacturing center for a particular production period. The information on this report is used to control and evaluate production costs, as well as transfer costs and units of output from one manufacturing center to another.

Step 5. Prepare the Production Cost Report

All the data calculated so far are combined into the **production cost report** for the mixing center. This report is shown in Exhibit 9. As you can see, this report includes a large number of calculations. However, we've carefully worked through all the calculations in this report together, so you should feel fairly comfortable understanding how it all fits together. (You'll feel more comfortable once you've worked through the review problem at the end of this chapter and a few homework problems!) Remember that the report is composed of four overall steps, each of which should make sense to you.

When a lot of calculations are involved, as in the production cost report in Exhibit 9, a good check figure can be a wonderful tool. Notice in Exhibit 9 that the arrows point to a very good check figure—$81,840. This amount represents the total dollars that have gone into the mixing center in the current period ($2,000 in beginning work-in-process + $79,840 in current production costs), as well as the total dollars that have come out of the mixing process ($79,680 transferred out + $2,160 in ending work-in-process). If the production cost report can balance out to this check figure, you have good (though not perfect) assurance that all of your work on the production cost report has been done correctly.

EXHIBIT 9   **A Production Cost Report**

Allied Cement Company
Mixing Center
Production Cost Report
For the Month of October 2009

Equivalent Units of Production

		Direct Materials Costs		Conversion Costs	
	Physical Units (pounds)	**Percent Done**	**Equivalent Units**	**Percent Done**	**Equivalent Units**
Beginning work-in-process..............	4,000	× 0%	= 0	× 80%	= 3,200
Started and completed	44,000	× 100%	= 44,000	× 100%	= 44,000
Ending work-in-process................	2,000	× 100%	= 2,000	× 60%	= 1,200
Equivalent units of production			**46,000**		**48,400**
Transferred out	48,000				

Product Costs per Unit

	Total Costs	**Equivalent Units**	**Cost per Unit**
Beginning work-in-process			
Direct materials costs	$ 800	÷ 4,000	= $0.20
Conversion costs	1,200	÷ 800	= 1.50
Total	$ 2,000		**$1.70**
Current period			
Direct materials costs	$ 9,660	÷ 46,000	= $0.21
Conversion costs	70,180	÷ 48,400	= 1.45
Total	$79,840		**$1.66**
TOTAL DOLLARS IN	**$81,840** ←		

Costs Transferred Out

	Cost per Unit	**Equivalent Units**	
Beginning work-in-process			
Initial direct materials costs			$ 800
Initial conversion costs................................			1,200
Costs to complete materials............................	$0.21	× 0	= 0
Costs to complete conversion	$1.45	× 3,200	= 4,640
Total...			$ 6,640
Started and completed	$1.66	× 44,000	= 73,040
Total costs transferred out			**$79,680**

Costs of Ending Work-in-Process

	Cost per Unit	**Equivalent Units**	
Costs for direct materials................................	$0.21	× 2,000	= $ 420
Conversion costs.......................................	$1.45	× 1,200	= 1,740
Cost of ending work-in-process			**$ 2,160**
TOTAL DOLLARS OUT			**$81,840** ←

REMEMBER THIS...

Process costing involves five steps:

1. Determine the amount of "work done" (equivalents units of production) during the processing time period,
2. Compute the product costs per unit by dividing total costs during the processing period by "work done,"
3. Compute the total cost of units completed and transferred out,
4. Compute the total cost of units in ending work-in-process inventory, and
5. Prepare the production cost report.

REVIEW OF LEARNING OBJECTIVES

① Explain the flow of products and costs in a manufacturing organization.

Inflows to Work-in-Process Inventory (debits):

- Direct materials (from Raw Materials Inventory)
- Direct labor (from payroll records)
- Applied manufacturing overhead (based on the predetermined overhead rate)

Outflows from Work-in-Process Inventory (credits):

- Cost of Goods Manufactured (to Finished Goods Inventory)

Inflows to Finished Goods Inventory (debits):

- Cost of Goods Manufactured (from Work-in-Process Inventory)

Outflows from Finished Goods Inventory (credits):

- Cost of Goods Sold (to the customer)

② Understand the traditional procedure of accounting for overhead.

- Compute a predetermined overhead rate based on estimated overhead and an estimated level of activity (such as direct labor hours) at the beginning of the period.
- Accumulate *actual* manufacturing overhead costs as debits in the manufacturing overhead account.
- Apply *applied* manufacturing overhead to Work-in-Process Inventory based on the level of activity. Do this by crediting the manufacturing overhead account and debiting the work-in-process inventory account.
- Close any end-of-period balance in the manufacturing overhead account to cost of goods Sold—add (i.e., debit) underapplied overhead to cost of goods sold and subtract (i.e., credit) overapplied overhead from cost of goods sold.

③ Create a Cost of Goods Manufactured schedule and understand how it is used to calculate cost of goods sold.

Computation of Cost of Goods Manufactured:

    Total Manufacturing Costs (Direct Materials, Direct Labor, *Applied* Overhead)
+ Beginning Work-in-Process Inventory
− Ending Work-in-Process Inventory
= Cost of Goods Manufactured

Computation of Cost of Goods Sold:

	Cost of Goods Manufactured
+	Beginning Finished Goods Inventory
−	Ending Finished Goods Inventory
=	Unadjusted Cost of Goods Sold
+/−	Under- or Overapplied Overhead
=	Adjusted Cost of Goods Sold

(4) **Explain the flow of products and costs in a service organization and in a merchandising organization.**

- Costs flow through a service firm in a manner very similar to a manufacturing firm. Costs of supplies and direct labor accumulate in an account called Work-in-Process Services. Overhead is applied to Work-in-Process Services as service activities take place.
- The process of accounting for inventory in a merchandising business is not nearly as complicated as it is in a manufacturing or service business. Purchases of merchant inventory are debited to the inventory account while inventory sales are credited out of the inventory account and debited to Cost of Goods Sold.

(5) **Compute product costs using process costing.**

Process costing involves five steps:

(1) determine the amount of "work done" (equivalents units of production) during the production period,

(2) compute the product costs per unit by dividing total costs during the production period by "work done,"

(3) compute the total cost of units completed and transferred out,

(4) compute the total cost of units in ending work-in-process inventory, and

(5) prepare the production cost report.

KEY TERMS & CONCEPTS

Cost of Goods
  Manufactured
  schedule, 773
estimated
  manufacturing over-
  head, 769
finished goods
  inventory, 760
job order
  costing, 761

manufacturing
  organizations, 758
manufacturing overhead
  rate, 762
merchandising
  organizations, 758
overapplied manufactur-
  ing overhead, 771
predetermined overhead
  rate, 766

raw materials
  inventory, 759
retailers, 780
service organizations, 758
underapplied
  manufacturing
  overhead, 771
wholesalers, 780
work-in-process
  inventory, 759

conversion costs, 785
equivalent units of
  production, 783
process costing, 782
production cost
  report, 787

REVIEW PROBLEMS

Job Order Costing

Salem Manufacturing Company applies manufacturing overhead costs on the basis of direct materials costs. The year 2009 estimates are:

Direct materials costs	$300,000
Manufacturing overhead	180,000

For every dollar of direct materials costs, 60 cents of overhead is applied ($180,000 ÷ $300,000 = $0.60).

Following are the Salem Manufacturing Company transactions for 2009 (entries rounded to the nearest dollar):

a. Purchased materials for cash, $500,000.
b. Issued $400,000 of materials to production (80% direct, 20% indirect).
c. Incurred direct labor costs of $250,000.
d. Incurred indirect labor costs of $70,000.
e. Incurred costs for administrative and sales salaries of $70,000 and $60,000, respectively.
f. Incurred manufacturing overhead costs: property taxes on manufacturing plant, $6,000; plant utilities, $14,000; insurance on plant and equipment, $3,000. (Assume these expenses have not yet been paid.)
g. Recorded depreciation on manufacturing plant and equipment of $18,000 and $6,000, respectively.
h. Applied manufacturing overhead to Work-in-Process Inventory.
i. Transferred 65% of Work-in-Process Inventory to Finished Goods Inventory. Beginning Work-in-Process Inventory was $13,000.
j. Sold 90% of finished goods on account at a markup of 60% of cost. There was no beginning inventory of finished goods.
k. Closed the balance in Manufacturing Overhead to Cost of Goods Sold.

Required:
Prepare a journal entry for each transaction.

Solution

a.	Raw Materials Inventory	500,000	
	Cash		500,000
	Purchased raw materials.		
b.	Manufacturing Overhead	80,000	
	Work-in-Process Inventory	320,000	
	Raw Materials Inventory		400,000
	Issued materials to production.		
c.	Work-in-Process Inventory	250,000	
	Wages Payable (or Cash)		250,000
	Incurred direct labor costs.		
d.	Manufacturing Overhead	70,000	
	Wages Payable (or Cash)		70,000
	Incurred indirect labor costs.		
e.	Salaries Expense, Administrative	70,000	
	Salaries Expense, Sales	60,000	
	Salaries Payable (or Cash)		130,000
	Incurred sales and administrative salaries expense.		
f.	Manufacturing Overhead	23,000	
	Property Taxes Payable		6,000
	Utilities Payable		14,000
	Insurance Payable		3,000
	Incurred manufacturing overhead costs.		

(continued)

g. Manufacturing Overhead 24,000

    Accumulated Depreciation–Plant 18,000

    Accumulated Depreciation–Equipment 6,000

    Recorded depreciation on plant and equipment.

h. Work-in-Process Inventory 192,000

    Manufacturing Overhead 192,000*

    Applied manufacturing overhead to Work-in-Process Inventory.

* The predetermined overhead rate is equal to estimated total manufacturing overhead divided by estimated direct materials costs ($180,000 ÷ $300,000), or 60% of direct materials costs. In this case, $192,000 ($320,000 × 0.60) is applied because direct materials costs were $320,000 ($400,000 × 0.80).

i. Finished Goods Inventory 503,750

    Work-in-Process Inventory 503,750*

    Transferred Work-in-Process Inventory to
    Finished Goods Inventory (0.65 × $775,000).

* The amount transferred is determined as follows:

Work-in-Process Inventory

Beginning balance	13,000		
(b)	320,000		
(c)	250,000		
(h)	192,000		
	775,000	(i)	503,750
Ending balance	271,250		

j. Accounts Receivable 725,400

    Sales 725,400*

    Cost of Goods Sold 453,375*

        Finished Goods Inventory 453,375

    Sold 90% of Finished Goods Inventory.

* Because Finished Goods Inventory is $503,750 (i), Cost of Goods Sold is $453,375 ($503,750 × 0.90). Because Finished Goods Inventory is marked up 60%, Sales are $725,400 ($453,375 × 1.6).

k. Cost of Goods Sold 5,000

    Manufacturing Overhead 5,000*

    Closed underapplied manufacturing overhead.

* The amount of underapplied manufacturing overhead is determined as follows:

Manufacturing Overhead

	(b)	80,000	(h)	192,000	}	Applied Overhead
Actual	(d)	70,000				
Overhead	(f)	23,000				
	(g)	24,000				
	Balance	5,000				

Accounting for Overhead in a Service Business

Columbus & Hercules, a public accounting firm, is computing the overhead rates to use when billing customers and bidding on jobs. Columbus & Hercules provides the following estimates relating to overhead costs for the year 2009:

Utilities	$ 12,000
Rent	30,000
Equipment depreciation	22,000
Office supplies	20,000
Support staff salaries	120,000
Total estimated overhead costs	$204,000

(continued)

In addition, Columbus & Hercules offers the following annual estimates (based on a 50-week work year) regarding the salaries and estimated hours associated with the professionals employed by the firm:

Position	Total Estimated Salaries	Total Estimated Billable Hours
Partners (2 × $100,000)	$200,000	4,400
Managers (3 × $70,000)	210,000	6,600
Seniors (6 × $50,000)	300,000	13,200
Staff auditors (10 × $25,000)	250,000	22,000

Columbus & Hercules computes a chargeable hourly rate for each position that is the sum of the following: (1) each position's hourly rate (based on salary), (2) an overhead rate, and (3) a markup of 20% of (1) and (2). The overhead rate allocates estimated overhead costs to each position, then relates the allocated costs to the hours expected to be worked by each position. Travel and materials costs are directly traceable and billed to each job.

Columbus & Hercules has no client projects in process on January 1, 2009. During January of 2009, Columbus & Hercules worked on several auditing and accounting jobs and incurred the following costs:

Jan. 1   Paid rent for January, $2,500.
      4   Purchased office supplies on account, $1,200.
      9   Paid $4,500 for payables from last year.
      15   Paid office support salaries, $5,000.
      15   Paid biweekly salaries of professionals: partners, $8,000; managers, $8,400; seniors, $12,000; staff, $10,000.
      15   Applied overhead costs based on billable hours: partners, 170 hours; managers, 270 hours; seniors, 500 hours; staff, 900 hours.
      18   Used office supplies totaling $800 to prepare client materials.
      21   Purchased office supplies on account, $1,100.
      25   Received and paid invoice from office supply store for purchase on January 4.
      27   Billed clients for the following jobs using the computed hourly rate for each position:

	Job #1	Job #2
Partner	90 hours	80 hours
Manager	150 hours	140 hours
Senior	320 hours	200 hours
Staff	560 hours	400 hours

      27   Transferred costs from Work-in-Process Services to Cost of Services based on information from January 27.
      31   Estimated utility costs for the month of January to be $1,000.
      31   Paid office support salaries, $5,400.
      31   Recognized depreciation of office equipment, $1,900.
      31   Paid biweekly salaries of professionals: partners, $8,000; managers, $8,400; seniors, $12,000; staff, $10,000.
      31   Applied overhead costs based on billable hours: partners, 180 hours; managers, 280 hours; seniors, 525 hours; staff, 950 hours.

Required:
1. Compute the billing rate to be used for each position.
2. Provide the journal entries made by Columbus & Hercules for January.
3. Compute the ending balance in Work-in-Process Services.
4. Compute the ending balance in Overhead.

(continued)

Solution

1. **Billing rate**

Overhead allocation rate: $204,000 ÷ $960,000 = $0.2125 per dollar of salary.

Position	Estimated Salaries	Preliminary Rate	Allocated Overhead	Billable Hours	Overhead Rate per Hour
Partner	$200,000	$0.2125	$ 42,500	4,400	$9.66
Manager	210,000	0.2125	44,625	6,600	6.76
Senior	300,000	0.2125	63,750	13,200	4.83
Staff	250,000	0.2125	53,125	22,000	2.41
Total	$960,000		$204,000		

Billable Rate for Each Position				
Position	Hourly Rate (1)	Overhead Rate (2)	Markup [(1) + (2)] × 0.20 = (3)	Billable Rate (1) + (2) + (3)
Partner	$45.45[1]	$9.66	$11.02	$66.13
Manager	31.82[2]	6.76	7.72	46.30
Senior	22.73[3]	4.83	5.51	33.07
Staff	11.36[4]	2.41	2.75	16.52

[1]$200,000 ÷ 4,400 hours = $45.45 per hour
[2]$210,000 ÷ 6,600 hours = $31.82 per hour
[3]$300,000 ÷ 13,200 hours = $22.73 per hour
[4]$250,000 ÷ 22,000 hours = $11.36 per hour

2. **Journal entries**

Jan. 1	Overhead	2,500	
	Cash		2,500
	Paid rent for the month of January.		
4	Office Supplies	1,200	
	Accounts Payable		1,200
	Purchased office supplies on account.		
9	Accounts Payable	4,500	
	Cash		4,500
	Paid accounts payable from prior period.		
15	Overhead	5,000	
	Cash		5,000
	Paid office support salaries.		
15	Work-in-Process Services	38,400	
	Cash		38,400
	Paid salaries of professionals.		

Partners	$ 8,000
Managers	8,400
Seniors	12,000
Staff	10,000
Total	$38,400

(continued)

Jan. 15   Work-in-Process Services   8,051

       Overhead   8,051

Allocated overhead based on billable hours.

Partners–170 hours × $9.66	$1,642
Managers–270 hours × $6.76	1,825
Seniors–500 hours × $4.83	2,415
Staff–900 hours × $2.41	2,169
Total	$8,051

18   Work-in-Process Services   800

       Office Supplies   800

Used office supplies on behalf of clients.

21   Office Supplies   1,100

       Accounts Payable   1,100

Purchased office supplies on account.

25   Accounts Payable   1,200

       Cash   1,200

Paid for supplies purchased on January 4.

27   Accounts Receivable   57,724

       Service Revenue   57,724

Billed clients for Jobs #1 and #2.

Partners–170 hours × $66.13	$11,242
Managers–290 hours × $46.30	13,427
Seniors–520 hours × $33.07	17,196
Staff–960 hours × $16.52	15,859
Total	$57,724

27   Cost of Services   48,107

       Work-in-Process Services   48,107

Transferred completed work in process to cost of services;
comprised of each position's hourly rate and overhead rate.

Partners–170 hours × ($45.45 + $9.66)	$ 9,369
Managers–290 hours × ($31.82 + $6.76)	11,188
Seniors–520 hours × ($22.73 + $4.83)	14,331
Staff–960 hours × ($11.36 + $2.41)	13,219
Total	$48,107

31   Overhead   1,000

       Utilities Payable   1,000

To record estimated utilities expense for the month.

31   Overhead   5,400

       Cash   5,400

Paid office support salaries.

31   Overhead   1,900

       Accumulated Depreciation–

         Office Equipment   1,900

To record depreciation expense for the month.

31   Work-in-Process Services   38,400

       Cash   38,400

Paid salaries of professionals.

Partners	$ 8,000
Managers	8,400
Seniors	12,000
Staff	10,000
Total	$38,400

(continued)

| Jan. 31 | Work-in-Process Services | 8,458 | |
| | Overhead | | 8,458 |

Allocated overhead based on billable hours.

Partners—180 hours × $9.66	$1,739
Managers—280 hours × $6.76	1,893
Seniors—525 hours × $4.83	2,536
Staff—950 hours × $2.41	2,290
Total	$8,458

3. Ending balance in Work-in-Process Services

Work-in-Process Services

1/15	38,400	1/27	48,107
1/15	8,051		
1/18	800		
1/31	38,400		
1/31	8,458		
End. bal.	46,002		

4. Ending balance in Overhead

Overhead

1/1	2,500	1/15	8,051
1/15	5,000	1/31	8,458
1/31	1,000		
1/31	5,400		
1/31	1,900		
		End. bal.	709
		(overapplied)	

Process Costing

Cleveland Enterprises produces flour in a continuous manufacturing process. The flour is mixed in one step and transferred to the finished goods department. At the beginning of September, Cleveland had 1,600 bags of flour in process (100% complete as to materials and 20% complete as to processing) that held $2,800 in costs of direct materials and $800 in conversion costs. During September, 20,000 bags of flour were placed into production, and by the end of the month, only 2,000 bags of flour remained in process (100% complete as to materials and 30% complete as to processing). Production costs for September are as follows:

Direct materials	$36,000
Conversion costs	47,712

Required:
1. Prepare the production cost report for September.
2. Prepare the journal entries required to record the production of flour and the transfer of the finished bags to finished goods inventory. Assume that the processing costs are 75% direct labor and 25% manufacturing overhead.

(continued)

Solution
1. Production cost report

Cleveland Enterprises					
Production Cost Report					
For the Month of September					

EQUIVALENT UNITS OF PRODUCTION

		Direct Materials Costs		Conversion Costs	
	Physical Units	**Percent Done**	**Equivalent Units**	**Percent Done**	**Equivalent Units**
Beginning work-in-process	1,600	0%	0	80%	1,280
Started and completed	18,000	100%	18,000	100%	18,000
Ending work-in-process	2,000	100%	2,000	30%	600
Equivalent units of production			**20,000**		**19,880**
Transferred out	19,600				

PRODUCT COSTS PER UNIT

	Total Costs	Equivalent Units	Cost per Unit
Beginning work-in-process			
Direct materials costs	$ 2,800	1,600	$1.75
Conversion costs	800	320	2.50
Total	$ 3,600		**$4.25**
Current period			
Direct materials costs	$36,000	20,000	$1.80
Conversion costs	47,712	19,880	2.40
Total	$83,712		**$4.20**
TOTAL DOLLARS IN	**$87,312**		

COSTS TRANSFERRED OUT

	Cost per Unit	Equivalent Units	
Beginning work-in-process			
Initial direct materials costs			$ 2,800
Initial conversion costs			800
Costs to complete materials	$1.80	0	0
Costs to complete conversion	$2.40	1,280	3,072
Total			$ 6,672
Started and completed	$4.20	18,000	75,600
Total costs transferred out			**$82,272**

COSTS OF ENDING WORK-IN-PROCESS

	Cost per Unit	Equivalent Units	
Costs for direct materials	$1.80	2,000	$ 3,600
Conversion costs	$2.40	600	1,440
Cost of ending work-in-process			**$ 5,040**
TOTAL DOLLARS OUT			**$87,312**

(continued)

2. Journal entries

Work-in-Process Inventory	36,000	
Direct Materials Inventory		36,000
Transferred direct materials to work-in-process inventory.		
Work-in-Process Inventory	47,712	
Wages Payable		35,784
Manufacturing Overhead		11,928
To record the department's payroll costs and applied manufacturing		
overhead ($47,712 × 75% = $35,784; $47,712 × 25% = $11,928).		
Finished Goods Inventory	82,272	
Work-in-Process Inventory		82,272
Transferred finished goods to the finished goods inventory.		

DISCUSSION QUESTIONS

1. Why do managers need accurate product cost information?
2. For financial reporting, which costs are usually included as product costs in a manufacturing company?
3. Why should a firm know how much it costs to produce its goods and services?
4. Describe some possible resources that organizations can use to help in the effort to improve quality while also reducing product costs.
5. Why is it difficult to track the costs of manufactured products?
6. What is the difference in the accounting treatment for direct materials and indirect materials?
7. Why are actual manufacturing overhead costs *not* assigned directly to products as they are incurred?
8. What is the normal flow of costs in a job order costing system?
9. What are some common bases for applying manufacturing overhead costs to products?
10. Why might Manufacturing Overhead be referred to as a "clearing account"?
11. How does a firm dispose of over- or underapplied overhead costs?
12. Cost of goods manufactured represents the costs being transferred out of the work-in-process account into the finished goods inventory account. Does the cost of goods manufactured calculation include actual manufacturing overhead costs or applied manufacturing overhead costs?

13. What is the difference between a manufacturing company and a merchandising company? Between a merchandising company and a service company?
14. What is a service organization?
15. Name three ways in which the service industry differs from the manufacturing industry.
16. What is the principal "product cost" for a service company?
17. Which three costs go into the work-in-process services account for a service company? How does this account differ between service and manufacturing firms?
18. What similarities and differences exist among the costs of merchandising, manufacturing, and service firms?
19. Should managers concentrate only on the costs of production (e.g., the cost of goods sold), or should they also consider other costs and factors?

EXPANDED *material*

20. What is the major difference between job order costing and process costing?
21. What two conditions generally exist for process costing to be appropriate?
22. What are the five steps involved in employing process costing?
23. What is meant by the term "equivalent units of production"?

PRACTICE EXERCISES

PE 16-1   **Importance of Accurately Identifying Product Costs**
LO1   Which one of the following statements is *false?*

a. A company wishing to enter a new market may decide not to enter the market because the prices charged by potential competitors are too low to allow the company to cover its costs.

(continued)

b. Because gathering accurate cost data is so difficult, the benefits rarely outweigh the costs.

c. Having accurate cost information helps companies identify and eliminate costly processes or products.

d. Comparing budgeted costs with actual costs helps companies identify progress and problems of current projects.

PE 16-2
LO1

Manufacturing Overhead Components

Which one of the following is *not* an example of manufacturing overhead?

a. Tires used in the assembly of cars
b. Production supervisor's salary
c. Utilities for production plant
d. Staples used in assembling furniture
e. Insurance on assembly equipment

PE 16-3
LO1

Cost Flow Sequence

Which one of the following sequences is the *correct* sequence for the flow of costs through a production process?

a. Raw materials inventory, work-in-process inventory, cost of goods sold, finished goods inventory

b. Raw materials inventory, cost of goods sold, work-in-process inventory, finished goods inventory

c. Raw materials inventory, work-in-process inventory, finished goods inventory, cost of goods sold

d. Cost of goods sold, raw materials inventory, work-in-process inventory, finished goods inventory

e. Raw materials inventory, finished goods inventory, cost of goods sold, work-in-process inventory

PE 16-4
LO1

Purchasing Raw Materials

The company purchased plastic costing $23,000 and sheet metal costing $92,000. The company paid cash. Both of these materials are used in the production process. Make the necessary journal entry or entries to record these transactions.

PE 16-5
LO1

Direct Materials

The company transferred plastic costing $4,000 and sheet metal costing $22,000 to the factory floor to be used as direct materials in production. Make the necessary journal entry or entries to record these transactions.

PE 16-6
LO1

Indirect Materials

The company transferred plastic costing $1,700 and sheet metal costing $3,200 to the factory floor to be used in general maintenance projects. Because these materials will not be used in the production process itself, they are classified as indirect materials. Make the necessary journal entry or entries to record these transactions.

PE 16-7
LO1

Direct Labor

Two workers worked six hours each to build a custom entertainment center. Each worker earns $12 per hour. Make the necessary journal entry to record this transaction. *Note:* The wages have not yet been paid in cash.

PE 16-8
LO1

Indirect Labor

The company paid $5,000 in April to its production supervisor for her monthly salary. Make the necessary journal entry to record this transaction.

PE 16-9
LO1
Recording Actual Manufacturing Overhead

The cost of certain overhead items for the month was as follows:

Rent for production facility	$3,900
Insurance premium for the month	2,250
Monthly depreciation on equipment	4,750
Repairs on equipment	5,200

Payment for these items was as follows:

a. The company is required to pay for one year's rent in advance. The total for one year is $46,800; this amount was paid three months ago. The $3,900 amount represents the rent applicable for this month.

b. The company is required to pay for six months' insurance in advance. The total for six months is $13,500; this amount was paid two months ago. The $2,250 amount represents the insurance applicable for this month.

c. Depreciation is recognized on a straight-line basis.

d. The repairs were performed in the current month. The company will pay for the repairs next month.

Make the necessary journal entries to record these items.

PE 16-10
LO1
Applying Manufacturing Overhead

The company used 130 direct labor hours to complete a certain job. The company applies manufacturing overhead based on direct labor hours at a rate of $6.80 per hour. Make the necessary journal entry to record the application of manufacturing overhead to this job.

PE 16-11
LO1
Transferring the Cost of Completed Jobs

The total cost of materials, labor, and overhead assigned to a job was $563. The company transferred this job to its finished goods warehouse. Make the necessary journal entry to record this transaction.

PE 16-12
LO1
Transferring the Costs of Products That Are Sold

Refer to the data in PE 16-11. The company sold for $1,250 the inventory produced in this job. Make the journal entry to record this transaction. The sale was on account. The company uses a perpetual inventory system.

PE 16-13
LO1
Costs Transferred out of Work-in-Process Inventory

The company spent a total of $102,340 in the current period in one of its production centers. In addition, when the production period began, there was work-in-process inventory in the production center that had a total value of $3,820. If the costs of the inventory at the end of the period are $4,190, what are the total costs of the inventory transferred out of the production center?

PE 16-14
LO1
Costs of Ending Work-in-Process Inventory

The company spent a total of $309,203 in the current period in one of its production centers. In addition, when the production period began, there was work-in-process inventory in the production center that had a total value of $18,802. If the total costs of the inventory transferred out of the production center are $311,214, what are the costs of the inventory at the end of the period?

PE 16-15
LO2
Calculating Predetermined Overhead Rates

The company reports the following information from the budget for the coming year:

(continued)

Estimated total amount of manufacturing overhead	$1,600,000
Average wage for production employees	$13.50
Estimated direct labors hours	250,000
Estimated machine hours	145,000

The company allocates manufacturing overhead based on direct labor hours. Compute the company's predetermined overhead rate.

PE 16-16

LO2

Over- and Underapplied Manufacturing Overhead

The company incurred $32,056 in manufacturing overhead and applied $32,537. The company uses the most common and simple method of handling differences between actual and applied overhead. Make the necessary journal entry to dispose of the difference.

PE 16-17

LO3

Computing Cost of Goods Manufactured

Using the following information, compute cost of goods manufactured, which is the cost of inventory transferred to Finished Goods Inventory.

Work-in-process inventory, beginning balance	$132,425
Work-in-process inventory, ending balance	126,300
Direct materials costs	350,080
Direct labor costs	365,225
Actual manufacturing overhead costs	287,200
Applied manufacturing overhead costs	285,900

PE 16-18

LO3

Cost of Goods Manufactured Schedule

Using the following information, prepare a Cost of Goods Manufactured schedule.

Work-in-process inventory, beginning balance	$160,000
Work-in-process inventory, ending balance	180,000
Raw materials inventory, beginning balance	100,000
Raw materials inventory, ending balance	60,000
Raw materials purchased	540,000
Direct labor cost	600,000
Depreciation on factory building	100,000
Indirect labor	150,000
Other manufacturing overhead costs	86,000
Applied manufacturing overhead costs	330,000

PE 16-19

LO3

Computing Cost of Goods Sold

Using the following information, compute cost of goods sold. Make sure to consider all necessary adjustments. Any over- or underapplied manufacturing overhead is closed and adjusted to cost of goods sold.

Finished goods inventory, beginning balance	$115,000
Finished goods inventory, ending balance	105,000
Cost of goods manufactured	350,000
Actual manufacturing overhead costs	170,000
Applied manufacturing overhead costs	190,000

Note: The $350,000 amount of cost of goods manufactured includes the $190,000 in applied manufacturing overhead.

PE 16-20   **The Flow of Services and Costs in Service Companies**
LO4   Which one of the following statements is *false?*
a. Service companies use predetermined overhead rates.
b. Regarding the accounting for cost of "goods" sold, service companies are more similar to merchants than to manufacturers.
c. Service companies use work-in-process inventory accounts to accumulate costs such as direct labor and manufacturing overhead.
d. A service business is any organization whose main economic activity involves producing a nonphysical product.

EXPANDED
material

PE 16-21   **Units Started and Completed**
LO5   At the beginning of the month, the company had 80 units that were 35% complete in inventory. At the end of the month, the company had 70 units that were 95% complete in inventory. During the month, the company completed and transferred 1,400 units out of inventory. Compute the number of units started and completed during the month.

PE 16-22   **Equivalent Units of Production**
LO5   Given the following information, compute the equivalent units of production.

	Physical Units	Percent Complete
Beginning work-in-process	25	20%
Started and completed	430	100
Ending work-in-process	35	40

PE 16-23   **Product Costs per Unit**
LO5   Using the following information, compute the total product costs per unit for both beginning work-in-process inventory and for current period production.

	Total Costs	Equivalent Units
Beginning work-in-process direct materials costs	$ 3,250	6,000
Current period direct materials costs	8,000	14,700
Beginning work-in-process conversion costs	2,600	2,000
Current period conversion costs	22,000	16,000

EXERCISES

E 16-24   **Work-in-Process Analysis in a Manufacturing Organization**
LO1   Steven James, a recently hired internal auditor, is currently auditing the work-in-process inventory account. Steven has forgotten some basic cost accounting concepts and asks for your assistance. Identify the four types of transactions or events that affect the work-in-process inventory account in a manufacturing organization. Prepare and explain a sample journal entry for each type of transaction.

E 16-25

LO1

Flow of Manufacturing Costs

Post the following cost data to the appropriate T-accounts to trace the flow of costs from the time they are incurred until the product is completed and sold. (Assume that purchases and expenses are credited to Cash or Accounts Payable.)

a. Direct materials purchased	$ 60,000
b. Direct materials used	50,000
c. Indirect materials purchased	9,000
d. Indirect materials used	7,000
e. Wages payable, direct	60,000
f. Wages payable, indirect	12,000
g. Selling and administrative expenses	32,000
h. Actual manufacturing overhead costs other than indirect materials and indirect labor	25,000
i. Manufacturing overhead applied	40,000
j. Work-in-process completed	120,000
k. Finished goods sold	135,000

Raw Materials Inventory

Beg. bal. 9,000

Manufacturing Overhead

Work-in-Process Inventory

Beg. bal. 30,000

Finished Goods Inventory

Beg. bal. 20,000

Cash (Accounts Payable)

Wages Payable

Cost of Goods Sold

Selling and Administrative Expenses

E 16-26

LO1

Assigning Manufacturing Costs to Jobs

Farrer Manufacturing Company uses a job order costing system. All relevant information for Jobs #203 and #204, which were completed during May, is provided here. No other jobs were in process during the month of May.

	Job #203	Job #204
Direct materials cost	$10,000	$13,000
Direct labor cost	$7,800	$10,800
Direct labor hours on job	800	1,400
Units produced	1,000	1,750

A predetermined overhead rate of $12 per direct labor hour is used to apply manufacturing overhead costs to jobs. Actual manufacturing overhead for the month of May totaled $25,000. All completed products are delivered to customers immediately after completion, so costs are transferred directly to Cost of Goods Sold without going through Finished Goods Inventory.

1. How much manufacturing overhead will be assigned to each job completed during May?
2. Compute the total cost of each job.
3. Compute the unit cost for each job.
4. Compute the over- or underapplied manufacturing overhead for May.
5. Prepare the journal entries to transfer the cost of direct materials, direct labor, and manufacturing overhead to Work-in-Process Inventory and to transfer the cost of completed jobs to Cost of Goods Sold. (Omit explanations.)

(continued)

6. **Interpretive Question:** How would the company have computed its predetermined overhead rate of $12 per direct labor hour? Explain.

E 16-27   **Analyzing Manufacturing Costs**

LO1   The following T-accounts represent inventory costs as of December 31, 2009:

Raw Materials Inventory		
Bal. 12/31/05 70,000		200,000
175,000		
Bal. 12/31/06 45,000		

Finished Goods Inventory		
Bal. 12/31/05 39,500		336,500
350,000		
Bal. 12/31/06 53,000		

Work-in-Process Inventory		
Bal. 12/31/05 12,500		350,000
200,000		
124,500		
86,000		
Bal. 12/31/06 73,000		

Manufacturing Overhead		
24,500		124,500
26,000		
30,000		
36,000		

1. Determine the direct labor costs for 2009.
2. Determine the cost of goods manufactured for 2009.
3. Determine the cost of goods sold for 2009.
4. Compute over- or underapplied manufacturing overhead for 2009.
5. Determine actual indirect manufacturing costs for 2009.

E 16-28   **Predetermined Manufacturing Overhead Rates**

LO2   The Boise Manufacturing Company uses a job order costing system. For Job #221, the production manager requisitioned $1,350 of direct materials and used 50 hours of direct labor at $19 per hour. Manufacturing overhead is applied on the basis of direct labor hours, using a predetermined overhead rate. At the beginning of the year, $956,250 of manufacturing overhead costs were estimated based on a forecast of 225,000 direct labor hours. Prepare a summary of the costs for Job #221. (*Note:* You have to calculate the predetermined overhead rate.)

E 16-29   **Predetermined Manufacturing Overhead Rates**

LO2   The Make-It-Right Company manufactures special wheelchairs for handicapped athletes. The company uses a job order costing system. Partial data for a particular job include:

Direct materials	$450
Direct labor	375
Manufacturing overhead	?
Total cost	$?

The company allocates manufacturing overhead on the basis of direct labor hours. The estimated total manufacturing costs for the year are $750,000, and the total estimated direct labor hours are 150,000. Factory workers are paid $15 per hour.

1. Compute the predetermined manufacturing overhead rate.
2. What is the allocated manufacturing overhead cost and the total cost of the above referenced job?

E 16-30   **Predetermined Manufacturing Overhead Rates**

LO2   Chicago Corporation uses a job order costing system. Thus, management must establish a predetermined overhead rate for applying manufacturing overhead. During the past three years, the following data have been accumulated:

(continued)

	2007	2008	2009
Direct labor hours	45,000	53,000	68,000
Machine hours	90,000	75,000	55,000
Direct materials costs	$450,000	$300,000	$410,000
Total budgeted manufacturing overhead	$90,000	$75,000	$55,000

1. What would the predetermined overhead rate be for each of the three years, if based on (a) direct labor hours, (b) machine hours, and (c) direct materials costs?
2. **Interpretive Question:** Which allocation basis would you recommend be used in the future for applying manufacturing overhead? Why?

E 16-31

LO2

Predetermined Manufacturing Overhead Rates

East Lake Corporation uses a job order costing system and applies manufacturing overhead using a predetermined overhead rate. The following data are available for the past two years.

	2008	2009
Direct labor hours	104,000	130,000
Direct materials costs	$500,000	$780,000
Machine hours	100,000	70,000
Total budgeted manufacturing overhead	$130,000	$90,000

1. Compute the predetermined overhead rate for each of the two years, based on (a) direct labor hours, (b) direct materials costs, and (c) machine hours.
2. **Interpretive Question:** Which allocation basis would you recommend for applying manufacturing overhead? Why?

E 16-32

LO2

Applying Manufacturing Overhead

Chris Company has four manufacturing subsidiaries (listed below). Each subsidiary keeps a separate set of accounting records. Manufacturing cost forecasts for 2009 for each subsidiary are:

	Subsidiaries			
	Tulare	Fresno	Kings	Kern
Materials to be used (lbs)	50,000	50,000	40,000	25,350
Direct labor hours	14,000	19,000	13,500	19,000
Direct labor costs	$6,000	$6,000	$1,875	$3,500
Machine hours	13,500	7,500	4,750	20,000
Manufacturing overhead	$30,000	$25,000	$10,000	$50,000

The predetermined overhead rates for each subsidiary are based on the following:

Tulare Subsidiary:	Machine hours
Fresno Subsidiary:	Direct labor costs
Kings Subsidiary:	Materials to be used
Kern Subsidiary:	Direct labor hours

1. Compute the predetermined overhead rate to be used in 2009 by each subsidiary.
2. If the Fresno Subsidiary actually had $4,000 of direct labor costs and $15,750 of manufacturing overhead, will overhead be over- or underapplied and by how much?
3. If the Kings Subsidiary used 33,000 pounds of materials in 2009, what will be the applied manufacturing overhead?
4. **Interpretive Question:** Identify the two most commonly used methods to dispose of under- or overapplied manufacturing overhead. What is the major advantage of each method?

E 16-33

LO2

Applying Manufacturing Overhead

Valtec Company has three manufacturing divisions (listed below). Each division has its own job order costing system and forecasts the following manufacturing costs for the year 2009:

	Division		
	Wayne	**Monroe**	**Yates**
Materials to be used (lbs)	120,000	100,000	80,000
Direct labor hours	45,000	60,000	25,000
Machine hours	40,000	25,000	15,000
Total budgeted manufacturing overhead	$50,000	$70,000	$45,000

The predetermined overhead rates for each division are based on the following:

Wayne Division: Machine hours
Monroe Division: Materials to be used
Yates Division: Direct labor hours

1. Compute the predetermined overhead rate to be used in 2009 by each division.
2. If the Wayne Division actually had 37,000 machine hours and $49,000 of manufacturing overhead, will overhead be over- or underapplied and by how much?
3. If the Monroe Division used 95,000 pounds of materials in 2009, what will be the applied manufacturing overhead?
4. **Interpretive Question:** Of the two commonly used methods to dispose of over- or underapplied manufacturing overhead, which method would you recommend and why?

E 16-34

LO2

Assigning Manufacturing Costs to Jobs

Cedar Company uses predetermined overhead rates in assigning manufacturing overhead costs to jobs. The rates are based on machine hours in the machining department and on direct labor hours in the assembly department. Estimated costs, machine hours, and direct labor hours for the year in each department are:

	Machining	**Assembly**
Direct labor cost	$75,000	$103,000
Manufacturing overhead	$80,000	$48,000
Direct labor hours	13,000	35,000
Machine hours	19,000	3,000

During the month of July, Job #315X had the following data for 60 completed units of product:

	Machining	**Assembly**
Direct materials cost	$400	$700
Direct labor cost	$750	$2,200
Direct labor hours	150	690
Machine hours	900	75

1. What predetermined overhead rates would be used by the company in assigning manufacturing overhead costs to Job #315X in machining and in assembly? (*Note:* You should round all rates you calculate to two decimal places.)
2. Using the overhead rates you calculated in part (1), how much manufacturing overhead is applied to Job #315X?
3. What is the unit cost for Job #315X? (Round the unit cost to two decimal places.)

E 16-35

LO3

Total Manufacturing Costs and Cost of Goods Manufactured

The following information is for Kiev Derrald Company:

Manufacturing overhead (actual)	$125,000
Ending raw materials inventory	10,000
Manufacturing overhead (applied)	155,000
Beginning work-in-process inventory	60,000
Ending work-in-process inventory	42,000
Beginning raw materials inventory	15,000
Direct labor costs	70,000
Raw materials purchases	50,000

1. Compute total manufacturing costs.
2. Compute cost of goods manufactured.

E 16-36

LO3

Total Manufacturing Costs, Cost of Goods Manufactured, and Cost of Goods Sold

The following information is for MTC Harry Company:

Beginning raw materials inventory	$ 25,000
Raw materials *used* in production as direct materials	110,000
Ending raw materials inventory	40,000
Manufacturing overhead (actual)	300,000
Beginning work-in-process inventory	150,000
Ending work-in-process inventory	180,000
Direct labor costs	95,000
Beginning finished goods inventory	71,000
Ending finished goods inventory	86,000
Underapplied manufacturing overhead	19,000

1. Compute total manufacturing costs.
2. Compute cost of goods manufactured.
3. Compute cost of goods sold.

E 16-37

LO4

Service Cost Flows

Xavier & Associates Law Firm estimated its total overhead costs for 2009 to be $1.8 million. It allocates overhead based on direct labor hours. Xavier employs a total of 11 attorneys, each working an average of 2,000 hours per year. The average annual salary for Xavier attorneys is $140,000, or approximately $70 per hour. Xavier attorneys worked a total of 23 hours and used $150 of supplies in doing work for Mr. Bailey, one of Xavier's clients.

1. What is Xavier's overhead rate?
2. Prepare the journal entry to record the overhead for the Bailey job.
3. Prepare the journal entry to record the cost of supplies for the Bailey job.
4. Prepare the journal entry to record the cost of labor for the Bailey job.

E 16-38

LO4

Service Cost Flows

Johnson Engineers incurred (but has not yet paid) the following costs in 2009:

Use of supplies for clients	$ 4,000
Utilities	7,000
Property taxes	10,000
Engineers' salaries	125,000
Support staff salaries	45,000
Applied overhead	60,000

Prepare the journal entries to account for the costs given. Close the overhead account to Cost of Services.

E 16-39   **Predetermined Service Overhead Rates**

LO4   The following data are available for Haul-It-Away Truckers:

	2008	2009
Budgeted direct labor hours	135,000	140,000
Planned number of moving jobs	300	310
Total miles to be driven	450,000	597,000
Total budgeted overhead	$900,000	$1,200,000

1. Compute the predetermined overhead rate for each of the two years, if based on (a) direct labor hours, (b) number of moving jobs, and (c) total miles driven.
2. **Interpretive Question:** Which allocation basis would you recommend for applying overhead? Why?

E 16-40   **Applying Overhead**

LO4   Brown School teaches private accounting courses. It applies overhead based on instructor hours. The following information was forecasted for 2009:

Direct labor	$280,000
Property tax on equipment	$2,500
Supplies	$10,000
Rent	$19,000
Support staff salaries	$130,000
Instructor hours	15,000

1. Calculate the predetermined overhead rate for 2009.
2. If Brown School actually had 18,000 instructor hours and spent $160,000 on overhead, will overhead be under- or overapplied for 2009? By how much?

E 16-41   **Service Costs**

LO4   The following information is available for a particular consulting contract performed by Newland Business Consultants in 2009:

Consulting labor costs	$4,000
Supplies	500
Overhead	?
Total cost	$?

Newland applies overhead on the basis of client consulting hours. The estimated total overhead costs for 2009 are $6.2 million, and the estimated total consulting hours are 150,000. Newland pays its consultants $40 per hour.

1. Compute the predetermined overhead rate.
2. What are the allocated overhead cost and the total cost of this particular contract?

E 16-42   **Equivalent Units–Process Costing**

LO5   Assume that you are the owner and sole employee of a lube, oil, and filter service business that you run out of your home. Currently, you are running a spring special on a "super maintenance service" on cars. The maintenance service you offer is quite comprehensive and includes (among other things) changing the oil, rotating the tires, topping off all fluids, and washing and waxing each car. It takes about one to two hours to complete a car. With

(continued)

the great price you're offering on this service, you immediately find yourself with about five days of customer order backlog. To catch up, you decide to spend the next week working solely on the "super maintenance service." Further, you want to track your output to see if you can improve the amount of maintenance work you do each of the next five days.

When you come to work the following Monday, you have one car that is about 70% complete. At the end of the week, the results are as follows:

	Total Cars Completed Each Day	End-of-Day Car in Process
Monday	5	50% complete
Tuesday	5	80% complete
Wednesday	7	10% complete
Thursday	6	80% complete
Friday	7	10% complete

How much work did you get done each day? In other words, how many equivalent units of production did you have each day?

E 16-43
LO5

Equivalent Units and Unit Costs–Process Costing

A large factory that manufactures wooden furniture has several assembly lines. One of the assembly lines is dedicated to assembly of wooden kitchen tables. All raw materials necessary to complete each table are requisitioned from the raw materials warehouse at the time each table starts production on the assembly line. The following data relate to one week of production:

Beginning Work-in-Process:
48 tables; 75% complete; $432 in direct materials costs; $756 in conversion costs

Ending Work-in-Process:
40 tables; 20% complete

Current Week:
600 tables started and completed; $5,440 requisitioned from raw materials warehouse, $13,640 incurred in conversion costs

1. Compute the equivalent units of production for both direct materials and conversion costs for the week.
2. Compute the total production cost per chair for the week on the assembly line.
3. How does this week's production cost on the assembly line compare to last week's production cost?

E 16-44
LO5

Equivalent Units and Unit Costs–Process Costing

Heidi Corporation began producing quick-drying paper cement in June (i.e., there was no beginning work-in-process inventory on June 1). The manufacturing process involves only one step. In June, the costs were $15,360 for direct materials and $33,512 for conversion costs. During the month, 3,200 pounds of direct materials were placed in production. At the end of June, 600 pounds of direct materials were still being processed and were 40% complete. Assume that all direct materials are added at the beginning of production.

1. Compute the number of equivalent units of output in terms of materials costs and labor and overhead (conversion) costs for June, assuming FIFO cost flow.
2. Determine the total cost of goods transferred to Finished Goods Inventory and the total cost of Work-in-Process Inventory at the end of June.

PROBLEMS

P 16-45

LO1

Job Order Costing in a Manufacturing Organization–Journal Entries

Following are transactions for Itabuna Manufacturing Company. Assume that the company has no beginning work-in-process inventory or finished goods inventory.

1. Itabuna purchased $575,000 of raw materials, paying 12% down, with the remainder to be paid in 10 days.
2. The production manager requisitioned $280,000 of materials (85% for direct use and the remainder for indirect purposes).
3. The liability incurred in (1) was paid in full.
4. 25,000 hours of direct labor and 2,750 hours of indirect labor were incurred. (Assume an average hourly wage rate of $9 for both direct and indirect labor.)
5. The following salaries were paid:

Factory supervisor (a product cost)	$75,000
Administrative executives	65,000
Sales personnel	95,000

6. Rent and utilities for the building of $33,000 and $9,000, respectively, were paid. Three-fourths of these expenses are applicable to manufacturing and the remainder to administration.
7. Depreciation on factory equipment was $17,000.
8. Advertising costs for the year totaled $16,000.
9. Manufacturing overhead is applied at a rate of $6.84 per direct labor hour.
10. All but $35,000 of Work-in-Process Inventory was completed and transferred to Finished Goods Inventory.
11. The sales price of finished goods that were sold was 130% of manufacturing costs. Assume a perpetual inventory system and that all finished goods were sold.
12. Close over- or underapplied overhead directly to cost of goods sold.

Required:

Prepare journal entries for the transactions.

P 16-46

LO1

Accounting for Manufacturing Transactions–Journal Entries

Payson Company uses a job order costing system. The following is a *partial* list of the company's accounts. (*Note:* Additional accounts may be needed.)

Cash
Manufacturing Overhead
Sales
Cost of Goods Sold
Sales Commissions Expense
Administrative Expenses
Accounts Receivable
Commissions Payable

Required:

1. Prepare journal entries for each of the following transactions (omit explanations).
2. Prepare T-accounts and post the journal entries to the T-accounts. Transaction (a) has been completed as an example.
   a. Raw materials previously purchased on account were paid for in cash, $700.

Cash		Accounts Payable	
	(a) 700	(a) 700	

(continued)

b. Raw materials were purchased for $1,500 on account.

c. Direct labor costs of $3,000 were recorded.

d. Direct materials costing $1,100 were issued directly to production.

e. Depreciation of $1,500 on manufacturing equipment was recorded. (Assume this is a product cost.)

f. Property taxes payable of $2,600 were recorded, half to manufacturing and half to administration.

g. Manufacturing overhead costs of $400 were applied to a job in process.

h. Materials previously purchased on account were paid for in cash, $1,500.

i. Sales commissions of $240 were recorded.

j. Goods costing $2,700 were transferred from Work-in-Process Inventory to Finished Goods Inventory.

k. Finished goods costing $2,300 were sold for $3,200 on credit, and the cost of goods sold was recorded.

P 16-47

LO1

Manufacturing Cost Flows

Ogden Corporation uses a job order costing system in its manufacturing operation. For the year 2009, Ogden's predetermined overhead rate was 75% of direct labor costs. For September 2009, the company incurred the following costs:

Purchased raw materials on account	$ 75,000
Issued raw materials to manufacturing process	67,000
Incurred direct labor costs ($10 per hour × 7,800 hrs)	78,000
Actual manufacturing overhead costs	55,000
Cost of goods completed and sold	215,300

The company's inventories at the beginning of September 2009 were as follows:

Raw materials	$11,000
Work-in-process	62,500

The costs of all completed orders are transferred directly from Work-in-Process Inventory to Cost of Goods Sold.

Required:

1. Compute the following amounts.

   a. Work-in-Process Inventory balance at the end of September 2009.

   b. Over- or underapplied manufacturing overhead for the month of September.

2. Prepare journal entries to reflect the flow of costs into and out of Work-in-Process Inventory during September (omit explanations).

P 16-48

LO1

Using T-Accounts: Cost Flows in a Job Order Manufacturing Organization

High Country Furniture Company manufactures custom furniture only and uses a job order costing system to accumulate costs. Actual direct materials and direct labor costs are accumulated for each job, but a predetermined overhead rate is used to apply manufacturing overhead costs to individual jobs. Manufacturing overhead is applied on the basis of direct labor hours. In computing a predetermined overhead rate, the controller estimated that manufacturing overhead costs for 2009 would be $80,000 and direct labor hours would be 20,000. The following information is available for the year 2009:

a. Direct materials purchased, $22,000.

b. Direct materials used in production, $19,500.

c. Wages and salaries paid for the year: direct labor (18,000 hours), $117,000; indirect labor, $12,000; sales and administrative salaries, $21,000.

(continued)

d. Depreciation on machinery and equipment, $9,000.
e. Rent and utilities for building (75% factory), $16,000.
f. Miscellaneous manufacturing overhead, $51,500.
g. Advertising costs, $12,000.
h. Manufacturing overhead is applied to Work-in-Process Inventory.
i. Eighty percent of Work-in-Process Inventory was completed and transferred to Finished Goods Inventory.

Required:

1. Compute the predetermined overhead rate at which manufacturing overhead costs will be applied to jobs.
2. Set up T-accounts and post the transactions.
3. Compute the under- or overapplied manufacturing overhead. Prepare a journal entry to close Manufacturing Overhead and transfer the balance to Cost of Goods Sold.

P 16-49 **Applying Manufacturing Overhead**

LO2 Swenson Corporation has four independent manufacturing divisions. The following data apply to the divisions for the year ended December 31, 2009:

	Cook	**Fulton**	**Pike**	**Fayette**
Direct materials costs	$250,000	$290,000	$130,000	$145,000
Direct labor hours	85,000	55,000	53,000	33,000
Direct labor costs	$250,000	$125,000	$120,000	$74,000
Actual manufacturing overhead	$184,900	$205,400	$140,000	$27,000
Machine hours worked	41,000	11,000	26,000	13,000
Number of units produced	205,000	4,250	31,400	11,000
Predetermined overhead rate	80% of direct labor costs	65% of direct materials costs	$3.30 per direct labor hour	$2.10 per machine hour

Required:

1. For each of the four divisions, calculate:
    a. Applied manufacturing overhead.
    b. Over- or underapplied manufacturing overhead.
    c. Cost of goods manufactured, assuming no work-in-process inventories.
    d. Average cost per unit produced.
2. **Interpretive Question:** How would you recommend that the over- or underapplied manufacturing overhead be disposed of in each division? Why?

P 16-50 **Applying Manufacturing Overhead**

LO2 Openshaw Manufacturing Company made the following estimates at the beginning of the year:

	Machining Department	**Painting Department**
Direct labor costs	$219,000	$166,980
Manufacturing overhead	$86,700	$153,340
Machine hours	17,000	12,500
Direct labor hours	30,000	22,000

Manufacturing overhead is applied on the basis of machine hours in the Machining Department and on the basis of direct labor hours in the Painting Department. During the year, the following two jobs were completed (there were no jobs in process at the beginning or end of the year):

(continued)

Job #29		
	Machining Department	**Painting Department**
Direct materials used	$16,000	$9,200
Direct labor costs	$18,250	$14,420
Direct labor hours	2,500	1,900
Machine hours	1,410	1,080

Job #30		
	Machining Department	**Painting Department**
Direct materials used	$17,500	$8,100
Direct labor costs	$19,710	$13,920
Direct labor hours	2,700	1,800
Machine hours	1,530	1,020

Required:

1. Compute the predetermined overhead rate for each department.
2. Determine the amount of manufacturing overhead to be applied to each job.
3. Determine the total cost of each job.
4. Given that the actual manufacturing overhead costs for the year in the Machining Department and the Painting Department were $88,200 and $152,500, respectively; that the actual machine hours in the Machining Department were 18,100; and that the direct labor hours in the Painting Department were 21,600; compute the amount of over- or underapplied manufacturing overhead.
5. **Interpretive Question:** Why is the predetermined overhead rate based on estimated rather than actual information?

P 16-51
LO1, LO2

Unifying Concepts: Job Order Costing, Cost Flows, Journal Entries, and Predetermined Overhead Rates

Dunn Manufacturing Company applies manufacturing overhead on the basis of direct materials costs. The estimates for 2009 were:

Direct materials costs	$270,000
Manufacturing overhead	$90,000

Following are the transactions of Dunn Manufacturing Company for 2009:

a. Raw materials purchased on account, $265,000 (85% for direct use and 15% for indirect use).
b. Raw materials issued to production, 85% for direct use and 15% for indirect use, for a total of $190,000.
c. Direct labor costs, $230,000.
d. Indirect labor costs, $28,000.
e. Administrative and sales salaries, $75,000 and $40,000, respectively.
f. Utilities, $11,500; plant depreciation, $22,000; maintenance, $8,500. (These costs are allocated on the basis of plant floor space—administrative facilities, 1,000 square feet; manufacturing, 5,000 square feet; sales facilities, 2,000 square feet.)
g. Manufacturing equipment depreciation, $6,500.
h. Additional raw materials issued to production for direct use, $120,000.
i. Manufacturing overhead is applied.
j. Recorded factory foreman's salary, $25,000.

(continued)

k. Ninety percent of existing Work-in-Process Inventory is transferred to Finished Goods Inventory. (Work-in-Process beginning inventory was $10,000.)

l. All finished goods are sold. (Assume no beginning inventory. Sales are marked up an additional 40% of cost.)

m. Over- or underapplied manufacturing overhead is closed entirely to Cost of Goods Sold.

Required:

1. Prepare a journal entry for each of the transactions and show the T-accounts for Manufacturing Overhead and Work-in-Process Inventory.
2. What is the ending balance in the cost of goods sold account?
3. **Interpretive Question:** Comparing actual manufacturing overhead with estimates for 2009, what would you recommend that Dunn Manufacturing Company estimate for manufacturing overhead costs in 2010?

P 16-52

LO1, LO2

Unifying Concepts: Job Order Costing

Jones Custom Furniture Manufacturing, Inc., made the following estimates at the beginning of the year, 2009:

Budgeted direct labor costs	$300,000
Budgeted direct labor hours	20,000
Budgeted manufacturing overhead	$520,000

Jones applies manufacturing overhead to specific job orders on the basis of direct labor hours.

During the month of January, the following transactions occurred for Job #345, an order for 10 custom oak chairs, manufactured in the first week of January 2009:

Jan. 3   Requisitioned direct materials (lumber, fabric, paint), $876; put into production on Job #345.

3   Requisitioned indirect materials (glue, staples, sandpaper, and equipment grease), $154, for use in manufacturing the 10 chairs for Job #345, as well as other subsequent jobs.

7   Processed time card for Employee 214; 25 direct labor hours attributed to Job #345 at wage rate of $15 per hour.

7   Applied manufacturing overhead at the predetermined rate to Job #345, based on the actual direct labor hours.

7   Processed the manufacturing supervisor's weekly salary of $1,000. (This salary is considered indirect labor because the supervisor oversees all jobs in process and does not account for her time on a job-by-job basis.)

7   Job #345 was completed and transferred to the finished goods warehouse to await shipment to the customer.

9   The 10 oak chairs (Job #345) were shipped to the customer. The sales invoice reflects a sales price of $3,000 on account.

In addition to Job #345, Jones completed 47 other job orders in January and had seven others in process at month-end. The following information summarizes additional manufacturing transactions for Jones for the month of January (not relating to Job #345):

a. Raw materials purchased on account, $102,675.

b. Requisitioned raw materials to specific job orders, $90,430; 80% direct materials and the remainder indirect materials not directly attributable to any one specific job.

c. Incurred and paid direct labor wages totaled, $24,600; an average of $15 per hour for 1,640 total direct labor hours for January.

d. Applied manufacturing overhead at the predetermined rate to all jobs in progress on the basis of the actual direct labor hours incurred by job.

e. Incurred and paid supervisor salaries and other indirect manufacturing labor (e.g., maintenance labor) totaled $7,000.

(continued)

f. Incurred and paid the following costs associated with the manufacturing process and facility:

Factory rent	$ 7,600
Factory utilities	2,700
Insurance	1,200
Miscellaneous	1,900
	$13,400

g. Recorded depreciation of manufacturing equipment for the month, $5,500.

h. The cost of the 47 jobs completed during the month totaled $125,446.

i. Shipped all completed jobs to customers by month-end at a total sales price of $200,714 on account.

j. Incurred and paid selling and administrative costs (e.g., administrative salaries, sales commissions, office supplies, office rent, etc.), $46,514.

Required:

1. a. Calculate Jones' predetermined overhead rate for the year 2009.
   b. Prepare journal entries for the first seven transactions (relating to Job #345). Omit explanations.
   c. Determine the total cost of manufacturing each of the 10 oak chairs.
   d. Determine the total gross margin earned on all 10 oak chairs.
2. Prepare the journal entries for transactions (a)–(j). Omit explanations.
3. Close Manufacturing Overhead to Cost of Goods Sold (include all transactions noted for Job #345).
4. Calculate Jones' total gross margin for January, including Job #345.
5. Calculate Jones' total operating income for January.
6. Determine the ending January balances in Raw Materials Inventory, Work-in-Process Inventory, and Finished Goods Inventory (assume no beginning balances).

P 16-53

LO3

Cost of Goods Manufactured

The following data apply to Newton Company and Alexander Company (two independent companies):

	Newton Company	Alexander Company
Raw materials inventory, January 1, 2009	$ 1	$ 4,000
Raw materials purchased	21,000	4
Raw materials inventory, December 31, 2009	6,000	3,000
Manufacturing overhead (actual)	8,000	5
Manufacturing overhead (applied)	2	16,000
Selling and administrative expenses	14,000	25,000
Work-in-process inventory, January 1, 2009	3	20,000
Work-in-process inventory, December 31, 2009	16,000	22,000
Direct (raw) materials used in production	15,000	6
Direct labor costs	25,000	30,000
Cost of goods manufactured	49,000	55,000
Overapplied (or underapplied) manufacturing overhead	(2,000)	4,000

Required:

Fill in the unknowns for the two cases. (*Hint:* Indirect materials are not used in either company.)

P 16-54

LO3

Cost of Goods Manufactured Schedule

(*Note:* This problem is a continuation of P 16-51.) Dunn Manufacturing Company's journal entries and T-accounts for Manufacturing Overhead and Work-in-Process Inventory

(continued)

were completed in P 16-51. Assume that Dunn had the following beginning inventory amounts:

Direct materials inventory	$75,000
Work-in-process inventory	10,000
Finished goods inventory	0

Required:

Prepare a Cost of Goods Manufactured schedule for 2009 for Dunn Manufacturing Company.

P 16-55
LO3
Unifying Concepts: Job Order Costing and the Cost of Goods Manufactured Schedule

Delta Manufacturing Company applies manufacturing overhead to jobs on the basis of machine hours. The 2009 estimates of manufacturing overhead and machine hours were:

Manufacturing overhead	$1,825,000
Machine hours	365,000

Delta had the following transactions for October 2009:

a. Raw materials of $420,000 were purchased on account.
b. Raw materials of $400,000 were issued to production; 90% were direct materials, and the balance was indirect materials.
c. Direct labor costs incurred, $300,000.
d. Indirect labor costs incurred, $55,000.
e. Selling, general, and administrative expenses incurred, $150,000.
f. Manufacturing overhead costs incurred:

Plant depreciation (factory)	$25,000
Equipment depreciation (factory)	14,000
Utilities (factory)	7,000
Factory maintenance	9,000
Factory taxes and insurance	5,000
Miscellaneous manufacturing overhead	6,000

g. Machine hours for the month, 30,400.
h. Eighty-five percent of Work-in-Process Inventory was transferred to Finished Goods Inventory. Assume that beginning Work-in-Process Inventory amounted to $95,000.
i. *All* finished goods are sold for cash at a 20% markup over costs of production. (There is no beginning or ending finished goods inventory.)
j. Over- or underapplied manufacturing overhead is charged to Cost of Goods Sold, and the overhead account is closed.

Required:

1. Prepare journal entries to reflect the flow of costs incurred during October.
2. Assuming that beginning raw materials inventory was $16,000 and beginning work-in-process inventory was $95,000, prepare a Cost of Goods Manufactured schedule for October 2009.

P 16-56
LO1, LO3
Unifying Concepts: Analysis of Manufacturing Cost Flows, the Cost of Goods Manufactured Schedule, and the Cost of Goods Sold Schedule

The following T-accounts represent manufacturing cost flows for Lincoln Manufacturing Company for the year 2009.

(continued)

Direct Materials Inventory		
1/1	60,000	230,000
	200,000	
12/31	30,000	

Work-in-Process Inventory		
1/1	70,000	700,000
	230,000	
	300,000	
	160,000	
12/31	60,000	

Finished Goods Inventory		
1/1	110,000	760,000
	700,000	
12/31	50,000	

Manufacturing Overhead		
	20,000	160,000
	32,000	
	14,000	
	48,000	
	42,000	

Required:

1. Identify the following amounts for 2009 from Lincoln's T-accounts:
   a. Direct labor cost.
   b. Cost of goods manufactured.
   c. Cost of goods sold.
   d. Actual manufacturing overhead costs.
2. Prepare a Cost of Goods Manufactured schedule for 2009.
3. Prepare a Cost of Goods Sold schedule for 2009.
4. **Interpretive Question:** Explain how the over- or underapplied manufacturing overhead is usually accounted for.

P 16-57
LO4

Computing Overhead Rates and Client Billing in a Service Firm

Sutherland Estimating Company employs three professional estimators, each having a different specialty. John Spencer specializes in structural estimating; Steve Ray, electrical estimating; and Dave Eugene, mechanical estimating. The firm expects to incur the following operating costs for 2009; travel and materials costs are billed separately to clients.

Office salaries and wages	$ 54,000
Office supplies	30,000
Utilities and telephone	23,100
Depreciation	24,300
Taxes and insurance	15,450
Miscellaneous expenses	3,150
Total estimated costs for 2009	$150,000

The salaries and billable hours of the three estimators are expected to be as follows:

	Expected Salary	Expected Hours
Spencer	$ 90,000	1,900
Ray	72,000	2,000
Eugene	63,000	1,850
Total	$225,000	5,750

Required:

1. Compute the overhead cost rate that should be used for each of the estimators (based on the expected hours to be billed, with overhead cost rates varying in proportion to each estimator's compensation) to ensure that the total expected operating costs for 2009 will be recovered from clients. (*Hint:* Allocate total estimated overhead costs to

(continued)

each estimator based on relative salaries, then relate the allocated costs to the hours expected to be worked by each estimator.)

2. Using the overhead cost rates determined in part (1), determine the costs associated with the firm's work for Landslide Company with the following estimating services and related costs: Spencer, 150 hours; Ray, 60 hours; Eugene, 15 hours; transportation and supplies costs, $2,400.

P 16-58

LO4

Service Costing–Journal Entries

Following are transactions for Michael Custodial, Inc. Assume the company's beginning work-in-process services account balance is zero.

a. Purchased supplies costing $8,000 for cash.
b. Received and immediately paid a utility bill, $600.
c. Used supplies costing $4,500 in doing work for a customer.
d. Incurred and paid 3,500 hours of direct labor and 1,700 hours of indirect labor. The average hourly wage rate for both direct and indirect labor is $8.
e. Made monthly rent payment, $4,000.
f. Applied overhead at $5.50 per direct labor hour.
g. Michael bills its customers at a rate of $24 per direct labor hour. All work in process was moved to Cost of Services.
h. Closed all under- or overapplied overhead to Cost of Services.

Required:
Prepare the journal entries for the above transactions.

P 16-59

LO4

Service Costing–Journal Entries

Blake Accounting Services has the following transactions. Its beginning work-in-process services account balance is zero.

a. Purchased supplies costing $11,000 on account.
b. Paid property tax, $20,000.
c. Paid rent, $2,000; and utilities, $700.
d. Paid support staff salaries, $35,000.
e. Used supplies costing $9,000.
f. Paid direct labor salaries, $50,000. Average rate was $10 per hour.
g. Applied overhead at $11.50 per direct labor hour.
h. Transferred $100,000 from Work-in-Process to Cost of Services and billed customers for 4,500 hours of work. Blake bills its customers $40 per direct labor hour.
i. Closed under- or overapplied overhead to Cost of Services.

Required:
1. Prepare the journal entries for the above transactions.
2. Determine the ending balance in the work-in-process services account.

P 16-60

LO4

Service Cost Flows

Allee Company had the following balances at the beginning of 2009:

	Debit	Credit
Accounts receivable	$44,000	
Supplies	10,000	
Work-in-process services	30,000	
Accounts payable (related to supplies)		$ 7,000
Salaries & wages payable		70,000
Utilities payable		2,400
Rent payable		3,000

(continued)

Allee estimates that its total 2009 overhead will amount to $400,000. It allocates overhead based on direct labor hours. Allee estimates that its total 2009 direct labor hours will be 100,000 hours. Because it produces monthly financial statements, Allee makes adjusting entries at the end of each month. However, over- or underapplied overhead is not closed to Cost of Services until the end of the year.

During January 2009, Allee had the following transactions:

Jan. 1   Paid rent. Allee has a three-year, $162,000 lease. Rent is payable on the first of each month.

3   Paid for all supplies purchased in 2008.

4   Paid all utilities payable from 2008.

7   Purchased supplies, $1,200.

10   Paid all salaries & wages payable from 2008. $46,000 was for direct labor; $24,000 was for indirect labor.

12   Used supplies, $900.

19   Collected $30,000 from a customer for services performed and billed in December 2008.

27   Used supplies, $2,600.

31   Paid all employees for January labor. Total direct labor costs for the month of January were $50,000, direct labor hours, 8,000. Indirect labor costs were $30,000.

31   Applied overhead for the month.

31   Estimated its January utility expenses to be $2,000.

31   Completed and billed jobs costing $80,000. The company billed customers $140,000.

Required:

1. Prepare all journal entries necessary for the month of January.
2. What is the balance in the work-in-process services account at the end of January?
3. Compute the balance in the overhead account on January 31.

EXPANDED
material

P 16-61   **FIFO Cost Flow–Process Costing**

LO5   The cleaning division of Clark Corn Company had the following data for January:

	Tons	Percentage Completed	Direct Materials Costs	Conversion Costs
Beginning work-in-process inventory	800	75%	$ 15,250	$ 2,000
Units started in production	41,100	–		
Costs added this month			904,200	182,340
Ending work-in-process inventory	1,200	35%		
Units completed during month and transferred to packing	40,700	–		

Required:

1. Using the FIFO cost flow method, compute the per-ton cost of corn processed by the cleaning division in this period (all materials are in place at the beginning of the process).
2. Compute the cost of the 39,900 tons of corn that were started and completed during January.
3. Compute the cost of the ending work-in-process inventory.

P 16-62

LO5

FIFO Cost Flow–Process Costing in a Service Organization

C&H Square Company provides a tax return processing service. C&H essentially has two processing centers—staff and managers. The data that follow show the production and cost results for the staff center for the month of March:

Production data:	
Tax returns in process, March 1 (45% complete)	60
Tax returns started in production	2,730
Tax returns in process, March 31 (60% complete)	90
Cost data:	
Costs in tax returns in process, March 1	$ 1,917
Costs for March	188,163
Total	$190,080

Required:

Costs of direct materials (paper, staples, etc.) are immaterial for C&H. Hence, all production costs are conversion costs (labor and overhead). Prepare the March production cost report for the staff center.

P 16-63

LO5

FIFO Cost Flow–Process Costing with Prior Department Costs

The assembly department of Charles Manufacturing Company reported the following data for the month of August:

	Units	Costs
Beginning inventory (75% complete)	3,000	
Units transferred from prior department	22,500	
Ending inventory (50% complete)	4,500	
Cost of beginning inventory (prior department $18,300;		
assembly materials $11,250; assembly conversion $12,375)		$ 41,925
Cost transferred in from prior department		135,000
Cost of materials used in assembly department		67,500
Conversion costs for August in assembly department		117,600
Total cost		$362,025

(*Note:* Materials used in the assembly department are added at the beginning of the assembly process.)

Required:

Prepare the production cost report for the assembly department. (*Note:* The prior department's manufacturing costs should be included in this department's production cost report.)

P 16-64

LO5

Equivalent Units and FIFO Cost Flow–Process Costing in a Service Center with Partial Materials

Wheelie Electric, Inc. performs tune-ups on automobiles. It has five service bays. During September, Wheelie Electric had the following operating data:

	Cars	Percent of Materials Added	Percent of Labor and Overhead Completed	Direct Materials Costs	Conversion Costs
Beginning work-in-process inventory . . .	4	80%	60%	$128.00	$224.40
Cars started and					
completed this month	360				
Costs added this month				$13,792.20	$34,907.60
Ending work-in-process inventory	6	20%	40%		

(continued)

Required:

Direct materials include spark plugs, wires, ignition parts, etc. Materials are added to each car as needed during the tune-up process (in other words, materials are *not* all added at the beginning of the tune-up process). Assuming a FIFO flow of costs, compute:

1. The "work done" for September (in equivalent units of production) for direct materials and for conversion costs.
2. The total tune-up cost per car in September.
3. The cost of all cars completed during September.
4. The cost of ending work-in-process inventory.

ANALYTICAL ASSIGNMENTS

AA 16-65
DISCUSSION

Packard, Inc.

Packard, Inc., produces and sells mousetraps. The cost of a mousetrap can be broken down as follows:

Direct materials	$0.23
Direct labor	0.09
Manufacturing overhead	0.12
Cost per trap	$0.44

The traps are then sold for 120% of cost, or $0.53 each. The manufacturing overhead is applied based on direct labor costs and was computed at the beginning of the year using the following estimates:

Estimated manufacturing overhead for the period	$540,000
Estimated direct labor costs	405,000
Predetermined overhead rate (per direct labor dollar)	1.33

For the first six months of the year, overhead costs of $272,000 were actually incurred. For that same time period, actual direct labor costs were $204,000. However, during the year several changes in the production process were made. As a result, by the midpoint of the year, expected manufacturing overhead costs have been significantly reduced below the original estimate of $540,000. Hence, for the last six months of the year, overhead costs are expected to be $225,000, and direct labor costs are expected to be $202,500.

1. What changes (if any) should be made in the predetermined manufacturing overhead rate for Packard, Inc.?
2. Assuming that per-unit direct materials and direct labor costs will remain the same for the last six months of the year, determine the new cost of a single mousetrap.
3. Because the cost of producing mousetraps dropped during the second half of the year, Packard can reduce the price of its traps and still earn its 20% markup on cost. Should the company reduce the price of its mousetraps? What factors would affect your decision?

AA 16-66
DISCUSSION

US MacDonald Corporation

You work for US MacDonald Corporation (USMC), an airplane manufacturer. USMC makes airplanes for commercial airlines, such as **United**, **American**, and **Delta**, and for the **U.S. Air Force**. Many parts are common to all planes made by USMC. The market for commercial planes is extremely competitive with **General Dynamics**, **Lockheed**, and European manufacturer **Airbus** often bidding lower than USMC. However, USMC's contract with the Air Force allows it to bill them at cost plus a 9% profit.

Times have been tough lately for USMC. In fact, if you can't find a way to increase profits, the company may have to lay off 5,000 employees.

(continued)

A colleague has just presented you with an idea that he believes will increase profits. He suggests that instead of using direct labor hours to allocate overhead costs among airplanes, you should allocate costs on the basis of the number of each type of airplane made. Because you make far more, smaller, less expensive planes for the Air Force, more of the overhead costs will be allocated to those planes. This action will not only decrease your cost per unit on commercial planes (allowing you to be competitive in that market), but will also increase your profits on Air Force planes because the cost per plane will be higher.

You are not sure about your colleague's suggested action. You do know that your allocation base of direct labor hours is quite arbitrary and probably does not correspond well to the way overhead costs are consumed.

1. What is an appropriate allocation basis? Would adopting the suggestion be ethical?
2. Would you change your mind if you learned that competitors were allocating overhead on the basis of number of each type of plane made?
3. Is your action appropriate, from both a business and an ethical point of view, if direct labor hours is not an accurate allocation base?

AA 16-67	**Service Cost Flows**
DISCUSSION	The CPA firm you work for has just been hired by Phillips Attorneys at Law to perform an audit. In the process of the audit, you notice that Phillips' accountant has been inconsistent in accounting for the company president's salary. You notice that sometimes he has accounted for the company president's salary as follows:

Overhead	20,000	
Salaries & Wages Payable		20,000
To record the company president's salary.		

Other times, the accountant has debited Salaries and Wages Expense instead of Overhead. When you confront the accountant about the inconsistency, he gets somewhat defensive and says that it doesn't matter which method is used because both methods result in an expense, and net income will be the same either way.

1. Assuming that the company president's tasks are exclusively administrative, do you agree with the accountant? Why or why not?
2. Which journal entry is correct? Why?

AA 16-68	***You Decide:*** **With advancements in the Internet and e-commerce, will retailers be**
JUDGMENT CALL	**important to the future success of businesses, or will their services be eliminated in order to decrease costs?**
	Companies such as **Amazon.com** and **eBay** eliminated retailers altogether and have changed the way their customers shop. Amazon.com and eBay have no physical store locations. Customers order their products over the Internet and pay shipping to have goods delivered to any location they choose. Amazon.com and eBay are able to pass the extra savings on to the consumer in the form of lower prices. Will retailers be completely eliminated in 15 years? What do you think?

AA 16-69	***You Decide:*** **Should the costs associated with an uncompleted consulting project**
JUDGMENT CALL	**be classified as a work-in-process asset on the balance sheet, or should the cost be expensed on the income statement as a part of doing business?**
	Your marketing company has been working on a consulting project for a client. Your team has worked on the project for two months, and it is now year-end. The project will be completed by February of the next year, and the client has not yet been billed. For the financial statements, how should the project be classified?

AA 16-70	**Wal-Mart**
REAL COMPANY ANALYSIS	**Wal-Mart**, as the world's largest retailer, is well known for its ability to keep its cost of goods sold very low. However, as pointed out in its Management's Discussion and Analysis

(continued)

for 2006, Wal-Mart's costs are influenced by a number of other factors including interest rates, employment and labor costs, inflation, fuel prices, and weather patterns. Discuss how each of these factors could affect Wal-Mart's cost of goods sold.

AA 16-71
REAL COMPANY ANALYSIS

Pump, Inc.

Acquiring management accounting data on real companies can be a challenge because this information is generally highly proprietary and of significant competitive value. The cost data below are for a medium-size family-owned pump manufacturing business located in the Midwest. (This business chooses to remain anonymous in order to keep its competitors from using these data to compete against it.) We'll refer to this company simply as Pump, Inc.

Pump, Inc., had reorganized much of its production into manufacturing "cells": self-supervising work centers that produce complete products. The cell program was initiated because of a strategic decision (with no management accounting data to support it) to improve customer service. The financial impact of the program was unclear; the operational causes and the financial effects were murky. As a result, the management team at Pump, Inc., was having a difficult time evaluating the effects of its strategic decision to change most of the company to manufacturing cells. (Some of the production process continued to be organized as a typical production line, similar to what is demonstrated in the chapter.) The current year's cost data are presented below in the standard format typically used by the management accountant for Pump, Inc.

Typical Cost Data Format		
Cost Category	**Cost**	**Percent of Cost**
Direct materials	$433,966	54.55%
Direct labor	96,990	12.19
Manufacturing overhead	264,583	33.26
Total costs	$795,539	100.00%

The management team, however, had a difficult time using the cost data in the typical format to effectively control and evaluate its reorganization decision. The management accountant was asked to reformat the data to make them more useful for the management team. After some analysis, the accountant decided to provide more detail by breaking down Manufacturing Overhead into subcategories organized by function: Indirect Materials, Indirect Labor, Factory Support, Occupancy Costs, and Non-Factory Support. The accountant also realized that she could divide all costs into two additional categories: People Costs (represent costs for wages and salaries) and Purchased Costs (represent costs for materials, supplies, and services acquired from outside agencies). The new report format is presented below.

New Cost Data Format			
Cost Category	**People Costs**	**Purchased Costs**	**Total Cost**
Direct materials		$433,966	$433,966
Indirect materials		9,460	9,460
Direct labor	$ 96,990		96,990
Indirect labor (production line supervision)	29,100		29,100
Factory support (material handling, equipment depreciation, utilities, expediting, engineering, etc.)	80,953	71,310	152,263
Occupancy costs (rents, taxes, maintenance, etc.)	15,180	32,550	47,730
Non-factory support (cost accounting, personnel, etc.)	23,390	2,640	26,030
Total costs	$245,613	$549,926	$795,539

Source: Adapted from J. S. McGroarty and C. T. Horngren, "Functional Costing for Better Teamwork and Decision Support," *Journal of Cost Management*, Winter 1993, pp. 24–36. Reprinted with permission.

(continued)

Consider the two reports on cost data for Pump, Inc.

1. Do you think the new report format provides any additional information value for controlling and evaluating the decision to change most of the production process into manufacturing cells?

2. What costs do you think the management team at Pump, Inc., should pay careful attention to in its effort to better control costs in the production plant?

3. Most importantly, if you were on the management team at Pump, Inc., what additional data would you like to see the management accountant provide?

AA 16-72

INTERNATIONAL

Management Accounting in France

France has a well-developed set of financial accounting rules, as embodied in the *Plan Comptable Général (PCG)*. The French PCG is comparable to U.S. GAAP. You may not have realized it, but the cost accounting for manufacturers we have studied in this chapter has a very clear connection to the way financial accounting is reported. Exhibit 1 in the text visibly demonstrates the difference between the production process and the administration process in a manufacturing organization. U.S. cost accounting makes a clear functional distinction between costs related to the production process (e.g., direct materials, direct labor, and manufacturing overhead) versus the administration process (e.g., selling costs and general administration costs). Further, Exhibit 6 in the chapter demonstrates that the flow of direct materials costs and direct labor costs through the accounting system, as well as the allocation of manufacturing overhead costs, allows U.S. companies to determine product costs and easily compute cost of goods sold for financial reporting purposes. However, cost accounting (*comptabilité analytique*) in France is explicitly decoupled from financial accounting, as defined by the PCG. What this means is that the chart of accounts French companies use for cost accounting is completely different from the chart of accounts used for financial accounting. The reason is not necessarily because French companies perform cost accounting differently from U.S. companies, but that the nature of French financial accounting is quite different from financial accounting in the United States. The PCG requires financial accounting reports in France to organize and report costs by their inherent nature (materials, labor, depreciation, etc.). Costs are not assigned to products or to departments. Hence, one wouldn't expect to see a French company report Cost of Goods Sold or Selling and General Administrative Expense.

Think about this for a moment. If costs are not being assigned to products, departments, or operations within the organization, how does the organization perform the management processes of planning, controlling, and evaluating? Actually, French companies do not have a tradition of using costs to manage their companies. In fact, the traditional phrase used in France to describe the techniques and practices of planning, control, and evaluation has been contrôle de gestion, literally, "management control." The absence of the word *comptabilité* (accounting) in this phrase is significant: it indicates that accounting numbers play a limited role in managerial reporting systems in France. Only very recently has the phrase *comptabilité de gestion* become more common. French business has had a long tradition of being led by engineers, not by accountants and financiers. Even today some 50% of managing directors in France are engineers by profession or training.

Costs are not being used as the main tool for managing companies in France. Given that a large number of the management executives of French companies have engineering backgrounds, how do French companies handle the management processes of planning, controlling, and evaluating (e.g., what kinds of numbers and reports might you expect to find in a French company)? Would you expect that French companies reconcile their *comptabilité analytique* systems with their financial accounting systems, as U.S. companies typically do?

Source: Reprinted from A. Roberts, "Management Accounting in France," *Management Accounting (UK)*, March 1995, pp. 44–46, by permission of the publisher Academic Press Limited, London.

AA 16-73

ETHICS

State Home Builders Inc.

You have recently been hired as an accountant for the largest residential construction company in the state. Your primary responsibility is to track costs for each home being

(continued)

constructed. Tracking the costs for direct materials and direct labor is relatively straightforward. Materials requisitioned for each home site are carefully tracked, and the construction workers are very careful about assigning their time to the homes they work on.

Accounting for manufacturing overhead costs, on the other hand, presents quite a problem. In the past, overhead has been allocated on the basis of direct labor hours. As a result, because larger houses require more workers, those houses have been allocated a larger share of the overhead.

Your company was recently selected by the state to build a number of low-income housing complexes. The state has agreed to an arrangement whereby it will pay your costs plus a 10% profit. Construction of these low-income housing units will be relatively simple and will not require a great deal of materials or labor, compared to the average house the company builds.

At a meeting following the granting of the construction contract by the state, the production foreman proposes the following idea:

> Since the state has agreed to pay our costs plus 10%, the higher the costs on the project, the more money we make. What we need to do is to funnel as much of our costs as possible to this low-income housing project. Now I don't want anyone to think I am proposing something unethical. I am not saying that we should charge the state for fictitious costs. What I am saying is that we should allocate as much overhead as possible to the low-income project. Therefore, I propose that we allocate overhead on a per-house basis with each house, regardless of size, being allocated the same amount of overhead.

You have analyzed the activities that drive overhead costs and have found that bigger houses, in addition to requiring more direct materials and direct labor, require more inspections, more supervision, etc. You can see that most in attendance at the meeting are being persuaded by the production foreman's idea. You slowly raise your hand. It takes about 10 seconds before all the voices quiet. You look around the table and see 10 of your colleagues staring at you. You open your mouth and . . .

1. What would you do in this situation? Is the overhead allocation method being proposed by the production foreman illegal? Is it unethical?
2. Suppose you argue that overhead should continue to be allocated on the basis of direct labor hours. After hearing your points, the group votes to go with the production foreman and allocate the overhead on a per-house basis. What would you do next?

AA 16-74
WRITING

Trends in Product Cost Relationships

The ratios among the three types of product costs have changed quite a bit over the last 150 years of business. Generally, costs of direct materials have consistently formed approximately 50% of total product costs for manufacturing firms. However, the ratio of direct labor costs has been decreasing with an offsetting increase in the ratio of manufacturing overhead costs. What kinds of costing challenges does this shift from direct costs to manufacturing overhead costs pose for a manufacturing company? What factors do you think have contributed to this trend? Do you think that the advent of e-business will significantly affect the amount or ratio of direct labor costs in manufacturing products? If so, how? Write a one- to two-page paper on this topic.

Activity-Based Costing

After studying this chapter, you should be able to:

(1) **Explain the fundamentals of activity-based costing (ABC).** *When using an activity-based costing (ABC) system, a company identifies specific business activities that create overhead costs, such as worker turnover or design changes, and then assigns overhead to products or divisions based on the level of those activities.*

(2) **Identify overhead cost activities.** *The first step in implementing an ABC overhead system is for a company to determine exactly what activities cause overhead costs in that company. The four general categories of ABC activities are activities that take place each time a unit is produced, activities that take place with each new batch, activities necessary to support a product line, and activities necessary to keep the production facility open.*

(3) **Determine measurable cost drivers to be used as the basis for assigning overhead costs to products.** *A cost driver is a numerical measure that reflects how much effort has gone into an activity. These cost drivers quantify the amount of overhead activity associated with different aspects of production and are used in assigning overhead costs in an ABC system.*

(4) **Assign overhead to production using ABC cost drivers.** *Overhead costs are assigned to products or divisions based on the level of cost driver use associated with that product or division. These ABC overhead cost allocations reveal that the amount of overhead cost associated with production is not necessarily proportional to the level of some simple measure of activity such as direct labor hours.*

(5) **Use ABC data to make decisions.** *The effort required to design and implement an ABC system pays for itself if the company can use the improved cost information to make better decisions. A properly-designed ABC system yields cost information that better reflects economic reality.*

If you were to take a walking tour of **Boeing's** 747, 767, 777, and 787 plant in Everett, Washington, you would understand how important (and how difficult) it is for Boeing to control its production process. The cavernous plant in Everett is monstrous, able to house 74 football fields. Planes are everywhere in various stages of completion, and with an army of mechanics running around, to an outsider the plant operations look like barely-controlled chaos. And yet this "chaos" produces ten to fifteen massive jets per month, each priced between $130 and $235 million.

Each Boeing jet is tailor-made to the desires of the specific customer. This customization doesn't end with engine specifications and landing systems. It includes choice of paint colors (e.g., if you want white, Boeing offers nearly 110 shades to choose from) and location in the cockpit where the pilot's clipboard will be placed.

Making these customization adjustments is not simple. Every alteration, even a seemingly minor one such as moving the location of an emergency flashlight holder, can consume thousands of hours of engineering time, require hundreds of pages of detailed drawings, and cost hundreds of thousands, if not millions, of dollars to execute.

The increased costs created by the movement of the location of an emergency flashlight holder in a Boeing aircraft are not direct materials costs because the flashlight holder costs the same no matter where it is placed. Those increased costs are not direct labor costs because it probably takes the mechanics about the same amount of time to install the flashlight holder no matter where it is located. No, the increased costs are overhead costs–engineer design time, safety inspector time, cost to generate new technical blueprints, and so forth. And an important insight is that these overhead costs are not created by the use of more direct materials or more direct labor but are created by the design change itself. In other words, without the design change, the total cost generated by the manufacture of the plane would be lower even though the direct materials and direct labor cost would be exactly the same.

Design changes are one source of overhead costs in a Boeing aircraft plant, and one can get a better idea of the amount of overhead cost created by the manufacture of a particular plane by counting the number of design changes associated with that plane. As you will learn in this chapter, a Boeing design change is an example of an overhead cost driver which is a measurable factor that is directly related to the amount of overhead cost associated with the production of a specific item. Cost drivers are a key component of a nontraditional method of overhead cost accounting called activity-based costing which is the focus of this chapter.

Activity-Based Costing

Explain the fundamentals of activity-based costing (ABC).

(1) Product costing has always been a primary purpose of management accounting. However, manufacturing processes of today don't look at all like the manufacturing processes of the late 1800s, when the traditional product costing model was developed. Advances in technology, combined with increasingly intense global competition, have resulted in manufacturing systems that are very complex compared to their 19th-century predecessors. Because the companies that best understand their costs have an advantage over their competitors, product costing has undergone some important changes that we will consider in this chapter.

One major development in product costing is **activity-based costing (ABC)**. With an ABC system, a company identifies business activities that create overhead costs, such as worker turnover or design changes, and then assigns overhead to products or divisions

**activity-based
costing (ABC)**

A method of attributing
overhead costs to
products based on
measurable factors that
relate to activities that
create overhead costs.

based on the level of those activities. For many types of manufacturing and service companies, ABC is a more accurate product costing system than the traditional product costing systems introduced in Chapter 16. However, ABC requires more time and expense to administer than do traditional costing systems.

Introduction to Lily Ice Cream Company

To briefly review what we know about product costing and to introduce activity-based costing, we will use the example of a hypothetical ice cream manufacturer—Lily Ice Cream Company. Lily has traditionally produced and sold just plain vanilla ice cream. Lily has been in business for years and has always reported solid profits. However, with the increased demand for gourmet ice cream flavors, Lily has seen her sales and profits slide. So this year Lily decided to start making and selling her own flavors of gourmet ice cream.

By expanding beyond the production of plain vanilla ice cream, Lily has seen her manufacturing overhead costs increase. Some of the new overhead costs are as follows:

- *Flavor chemist.* With all of these new flavors, Lily has had to hire a highly-qualified flavor chemist to research, develop, and monitor the chemical interactions among the new array of flavor ingredients.
- *Quality control inspections.* Because Lily is now constantly switching her production process among the different flavors, the production supervisor is required to test flavor quality at the start and end of every batch.
- *Machine operators.* The ice cream machinery has to be reconfigured for the production of each different flavor. As a result, Lily has hired additional workers to set up the machines for each flavor batch.
- *Machine maintenance personnel.* With the broad range of flavor ingredients that now flow through the machinery, the machines need to be cleaned more frequently to remove flavor residues so that the vanilla ice cream doesn't get tainted with gingerbread flavoring. Accordingly, more machine maintenance personnel have been hired.
- *Accounting staff.* When Lily made just vanilla ice cream, her accounting needs were simple. Now, she has a much broader set of suppliers and customers requiring a more sophisticated billing and collections system. In addition, internal management reports are now much more complex in an attempt to track the costs and profits of each different flavor. Lily's accounting staff has increased substantially.

Note that these new costs described above are not related to the cost of the direct materials or to the number of hours worked by the skilled technicians who actually operate the ice cream machinery. These new costs are all overhead costs. Traditionally, Lily has had a very simple method of overhead allocation. Total expected overhead cost for a year was divided by the number of gallons of ice cream expected to be produced, and each gallon of ice cream was allocated the same amount of overhead. In the past, this overhead allocation system worked fine because all of the ice cream was one flavor, vanilla. However, Lily is concerned that this simple overhead allocation method may no longer work in her more complex manufacturing setting. Lily's concerns are prompted by two problems she has seen in her most recent profit reports.

- Lily's overall profitability has slipped since the introduction of the new flavors.
- Using the old overhead allocation method, it appears that vanilla ice cream is now being sold at a loss.

Lily is considering whether to stop selling vanilla ice cream altogether, but first wants to do a more detailed overhead cost analysis using the ABC approach. The objective of this overhead cost analysis is to be able to answer one fundamental question for each one of Lily's ice cream flavors—HOW MUCH DOES IT COST TO PRODUCE ICE CREAM? Later in this chapter we'll do the detailed calculations to answer this question.

The Basics of ABC

Because activity-based costing is a method for more accurately assigning overhead costs to the products that create them, let's take a look at Lily's overhead. Total overhead for Lily Ice Cream Company for the most recent year was expected to be $1,740,000. The number of gallons of ice cream expected to be produced during the year was 1,500,000. Under Lily's traditional overhead allocation process, the predetermined overhead rate is computed as follows:

$$\$1,740,000 \text{ overhead cost} \div 1,500,000 \text{ gallons} = \$1.16 \text{ overhead per gallon}$$

This $1.16 amount is the overhead cost assigned to each gallon of ice cream, no matter what the flavor. By the way, to keep this example simple we will assume that the actual amount of overhead cost and the actual number of gallons of ice cream produced were equal to the expected amounts.

The total of $1,740,000 in overhead cost is broken down into the following categories:

	Overhead Costs
Electricity	$ 200,000
Machine depreciation	400,000
Factory cleaners	300,000
Machine repairpersons	100,000
Production supervisor	200,000
Flavor chemist	170,000
Accounting department	150,000
Building depreciation	80,000
Security guards	90,000
Building insurance	50,000
Total	$1,740,000

Consider what it means to assign $1.16 in overhead cost to each gallon of ice cream, regardless of the flavor and the specific production process involved in making that flavor. We are assuming that each gallon of ice cream requires the same amount of electricity to produce. As you think about it, you realize that, as an approximation, this might not be a bad assumption. But we are also assuming that the production of each gallon of ice cream—be it Vanilla, Peanut Butter Swirl, or Marshmallow Caramel Delight—creates the same amount of mess and thus requires the same amount of attention from the factory cleaners. This might not be a good assumption. We are also assuming that the flavor chemist spends the same amount of time testing the five simple ingredients for Vanilla as she does testing the 25 chemically-complex ingredients in Gingerbread Cheesecake Supreme. This almost certainly is not a good assumption.

Activity-based costing involves looking more carefully at what causes overhead costs. For example, the factory cleaners probably have to spend more time cleaning up after a batch of Marshmallow Caramel Delight, so proportionately more of the $300,000 in factory cleaning overhead cost should be assigned to gallons of this flavor of ice cream. Similarly, the flavor chemist spends more of her time testing the 25 ingredients in Gingerbread Cheesecake Supreme, so more of the $170,000 in flavor chemist overhead should be assigned to gallons of this flavor of ice cream.

The focus of activity-based costing is identifying activities that cause overhead costs and then assigning those overhead costs based on reliable measures of those activities. For example, a better way to assign the $170,000 in flavor chemist overhead may be on the basis of the number of ingredients used to make the ice cream flavor—the five-ingredient vanilla flavor would be assigned less flavor chemist overhead cost than the 25-ingredient Gingerbread Cheesecake Supreme.

In the following sections of this chapter, we will illustrate and discuss the five steps in implementing and using an ABC system, which are:

1. Identify overhead cost activities
2. Analyze individual overhead costs in terms of those cost activities
3. Identify measurable cost drivers
4. Assign overhead
5. Use the ABC data to make decisions

REMEMBER THIS...

- Companies that better understand their costs have an advantage over their competitors.
- When using an activity-based costing (ABC) system, a company identifies specific business activities that create overhead costs and then assigns overhead to products or divisions based on the level of those activities.
- The ultimate purpose of an ABC system is to help a company make better decisions.

Overhead Cost Activities

Identify overhead cost activities.

(2) The first step in implementing an ABC overhead system is to do a detailed study of the production process to determine exactly what activities cause overhead costs. With a traditional overhead allocation system, we basically view overhead as a big lump cost generated by the production process as a whole. We then assume that there is a simple relationship between this big lump of cost and a single measure of activity that is based on output volume, such as the number of direct labor hours or machine hours or gallons of ice cream produced.

In the Lily Ice Cream example, we can do better than to simply assume that, no matter what the flavor and the associated production process, the production of each gallon of ice cream creates the same amount of overhead. To do a better job of assigning overhead, we need a better understanding of the key activities involved in the production process that create overhead costs. Lily herself, the owner of the Lily Ice Cream Company, has done this analysis and has created the following list of key activities:

1. Operating the ice cream production process
2. Producing a specific batch of ice cream
3. Servicing the special needs of each individual ice cream flavor
4. Keeping the factory open

1. Operating the ice cream production process Operating the ice cream production process requires electricity to operate the machines and also involves some wear and tear on the machines themselves. In addition, the general production process does create some mess that the factory cleaners must take care of in order to maintain the sanitary standards required by both the government inspectors and Lily herself. Also, the machine repairpersons are constantly doing routine maintenance to keep the machines in working order, and the production supervisor spends part of her time monitoring the overall flow of ice cream through the production process. Finally, some portion of the time of the accounting staff is spent preparing regular production reports, accounting for the costs of the direct labor and direct material costs involved in production, and so forth. Lily has decided to group all of these activities under the heading "operating the ice cream production process." Clearly, as the company produces more gallons of ice cream, the volume of these activities must increase.

2. Producing a specific batch of ice cream

Producing a specific batch of ice cream is another production activity that creates overhead cost. Stopping a production run of Double Dutch Chocolate Brownie to begin a run of Strawberry Banana Surprise means that the factory cleaners must come in and thoroughly clean the machines, removing all of the chocolate residue so that it doesn't contaminate the subtle blend of strawberry and banana flavors. In addition, the more often the machines are stopped and started to begin a new batch, the more likely it is that the machines will break down, requiring more repairs. Also, quality control inspections ensure the quality and flavor of each batch. So, the more batches, the more inspections. Finally, with each batch of ice cream, the accounting department must track a different mix of ingredients, with different costs, as they are inserted into the production process. All of these overhead costs are created by the activity that Lily has decided to call "producing a specific batch of ice cream." It is important to understand that the volume of these activities is much more closely tied to the number of *batches* of ice cream produced by the company than to the number of *gallons* of ice cream produced.

3. Servicing the special needs of each individual ice cream flavor

Servicing the special needs of each individual ice cream flavor is an activity that Lily Ice Cream Company didn't have until production was expanded beyond just the flavor Vanilla. As a result of the expansion, Lily has had to hire a flavor chemist whose job it is to monitor the quality of the ingredients that go into each of Lily's six flavors. In addition, the production supervisor now spends a portion of her time comparing the mix of ingredients put into production for each ice cream flavor with Lily's secret recipe. Finally, the ordering of these new ingredients has required the accounting department to open and maintain accounts with a number of suppliers with which Lily had never before done business. These overhead costs fall under the activity heading "servicing the special needs of each individual ice cream flavor." And the volume of these activities is closely tied to the number of ingredients that Lily now uses in her ice cream flavors. These activities are *not* a function of how much ice cream is actually produced.

4. Keeping the factory open

Keeping the factory open is the final overhead cost activity identified by Lily. Some overhead costs are necessary to keep Lily Ice Cream Company open for business, no matter how much ice cream, of whatever flavor and in however many batches, is produced. For example, Lily needs an accounting department to prepare financial statements, periodic income tax filings, payroll tax reports, and so forth. In addition, Lily's factory building depreciates and requires insurance and security no matter how much production goes on inside. These overhead costs are classified as the cost of "keeping the factory open."

Of course, these four activities are specific to this hypothetical Lily Ice Cream example. However, these four categories for Lily Ice Cream Company correspond to four general categories that have been identified for use in any business setting that uses ABC. The four general categories of ABC activities are:

* Unit
* Batch
* Product line
* Facility support

unit-level activities

Activities that take place each time a unit of product is produced.

Unit-level activities are those overhead activities that are performed each time a unit is produced. In the Lily Ice Cream Company example, the activities associated with "operating the ice cream production process" are unit-level activities. Classic examples of unit-level overhead activities are:

- Machine maintenance
- Machine depreciation
- Electricity and other energy costs

batch-level activities

Activities that take place in order to support a batch or production run, regardless of the size of the batch.

Batch-level activities are those overhead activities that are performed each time a new production batch is started or ended. In the Lily Ice Cream Company example, the activities associated with "producing a specific batch of ice cream" are batch-level activities. Examples of batch-level activities are:

- Inspections
- Machine setups
- Movement of and accounting for materials

product line activities

Activities that take place in order to support a product line, regardless of the number of batches or individual units actually produced.

Product line activities are those overhead activities that are associated with the capability to produce different types of products. In the Lily Ice Cream Company example, the activities associated with "servicing the special needs of each individual ice cream flavor" are product line activities. For companies with a number of separate operating divisions, the product line overhead activities vary based on the number of product lines in a division. For a company such as Lily Ice Cream Company, there is just one operating division, so the product line overhead activities are associated with the complexity of each individual product line, or ice cream flavor in this case. Examples of product line activities are:

- Engineering product design
- Storage in special warehouses
- Managing by a special supervisor of all activities associated with a particular product line
- Ordering, purchasing, and receiving materials unique to a particular product line

facility support activities

Activities necessary to have a facility in place in order to participate in the development and production of products or services. However, these activities are not related to any particular line of products or services.

Facility support activities are those overhead activities that must be in place before any of the other production activities can take place. In the Lily Ice Cream Company example, the activities associated with "keeping the factory open" are facility support activities. It is important to understand that these activities cannot be related to any particular product or product line. Examples of facility support activities are:

- Property taxes
- Factory insurance
- Security
- Landscaping
- General accounting
- General factory administration

Analyze Individual Overhead Costs

Once the activities associated with the creation of overhead costs are identified, implementation of an ABC system continues with an analysis of each of the specific overhead costs to determine which of the overhead activities causes that particular cost. For Lily Ice Cream Company, recall that the total overhead cost is $1,740,000 created by four different activities. The components of the overhead cost, and the four activities, are shown in Exhibit 1. Implementation of the ABC system now requires that each of the overhead costs be analyzed to determine what fraction of that cost is caused by each one of the four overhead cost activities.

| EXHIBIT 1 | Overhead Cost/Activity Matrix for Lily Ice Cream Company |

			Overhead Cost Activities			
Overhead Cost Items	Overhead Costs	‖	Ice Cream Production	Ice Cream Batches	Ice Cream Flavors	Keeping Factory Open
Electricity	$ 200,000	‖	$200,000	$ 0	$ 0	$ 0
Machine depreciation	400,000	‖	400,000	0	0	0
Factory cleaners	300,000	‖	90,000	210,000	0	0
Machine repairpersons	100,000	‖	15,000	85,000	0	0
Production supervisor	200,000	‖	30,000	100,000	70,000	0
Flavor chemist	170,000	‖	0	0	170,000	0
Accounting department	150,000	‖	15,000	45,000	30,000	60,000
Building depreciation	80,000	‖	0	0	0	80,000
Security guards	90,000	‖	0	0	0	90,000
Building insurance	50,000	‖	0	0	0	50,000
Total	$1,740,000	‖	$750,000	$440,000	$270,000	$280,000

For example, consider the first item on the list, electricity cost of $200,000. As discussed earlier, the use of electricity is a good example of a unit-level overhead activity because the more units that are produced, the higher the electricity cost. In terms of Lily's analysis, the electricity cost is part of the cost of "operating the ice cream production process." Accordingly, the $200,000 electricity cost is included as part of the cost of this activity.

As with the electricity cost, many of the specific overhead costs are easily associated with one of the four activities identified by Lily, as follows:

- *Machine depreciation*: a unit-level item associated with the overhead cost activity "operating the ice cream production process."
- *Building depreciation*: a facility support item associated with the overhead cost activity "keeping the factory open."
- *Security guards*: a facility support item associated with the overhead cost activity "keeping the factory open."
- *Building insurance*: a facility support item associated with the overhead cost activity "keeping the factory open."

In Exhibit 1, notice how the costs in the rows representing these overhead costs have been assigned to the associated overhead cost activity column. Our goal is to assign all $1,740,000 in overhead cost to one of the four overhead cost activity columns.

Some overhead costs are split among activities. For example, some of the factory cleaner costs are associated with the number of gallons of ice cream produced, and some are associated with the number of batches. The hard part of implementing an ABC system is analyzing these kinds of overhead costs in terms of what fraction is associated with each overhead cost activity. This analysis requires a detailed understanding of the production process and the underlying causes of all of the individual overhead costs. Many companies do not have this detailed understanding, and gaining such an understanding would involve a long and costly examination of the production process. Not surprisingly, this is where some companies decide to avoid the cost of implementing an ABC system and instead just stay with their traditional overhead allocation approach. For some companies, this makes sense because the cost of implementing the ABC system is higher than the benefit to be gained in improved cost information. But in other cases, as we will see in the Lily Ice Cream Company example, an ABC system can more than pay for itself in terms of better decisions as well as a better understanding of factors creating costs inside the company.

In the Lily Ice Cream Company example, the analysis of the remaining overhead costs requires a determination of what percent of the time the employees spent on each overhead cost activity, as follows.

	Percentage of Time Spent on Each Activity			
	Ice Cream Production	Ice Cream Batches	Ice Cream Flavors	Keeping Factory Open
Factory cleaners	30%	70%	0%	0%
Machine repairpersons	15%	85%	0%	0%
Production supervisor	15%	50%	35%	0%
Flavor chemist	0%	0%	100%	0%
Accounting department	10%	30%	20%	40%

Assembling these data could involve asking the employees to keep a log of their daily activities, assigning someone from the accounting staff to actually watch employees to verify the accuracy of these logs, or simply conducting interviews with the employees to determine approximately how much time is spent in various activities. These percentages are used to assign the overhead costs to the different cost activities. For example, the $300,000 overhead cost associated with the factory cleaners should be assigned 30% (or $90,000) to the "operating the ice cream production process" activity and 70% (or $210,000) to the "producing a specific batch of ice cream" activity. The complete analysis of all of the overhead cost items is summarized in Exhibit 1.

cost pool

Total cost identified as being generated by a specific overhead cost activity.

In Exhibit 1, each of the overhead cost activity columns is called a **cost pool**. The cost pool associated with the "operating the ice cream process" totals $750,000. The ice cream batch cost pool totals $440,000; the ice cream flavor cost pool totals $270,000; and the facility support (or "keeping the factory open") cost pool totals $280,000.

In summary, the table in Exhibit 1 embodies the information gathered in the first two steps in implementing Lily Ice Cream Company's ABC overhead system. We first identified four overhead cost activities, represented by the four columns in the table. Then we analyzed each individual overhead cost item to determine how much of that overhead cost was associated with each of the four overhead cost activities. This analysis led us to the computation of the amounts in the four cost pools.

REMEMBER THIS...

- Four general categories of ABC activities have been identified for use in any business setting.
  - Unit—activities that take place each time a unit of product is produced.
  - Batch—activities that take place in order to support a batch or production run, regardless of the size of the batch.
  - Product line—activities that take place in order to support a product line, regardless of the number of batches or individual units actually produced.
  - Facility support—activities necessary to have a production facility in place. However, these activities are not related to any particular line of products or services.
- The total cost identified as being generated by a specific overhead cost activity is called the cost pool.

Cost Drivers

Determine measurable cost drivers to be used as the basis for assigning overhead costs to products.

(3) Once the overhead cost activities have been identified, the individual overhead items analyzed, and the cost pools computed, it is time to determine the basis to be used to assign the dollars in the overhead cost pools to production. This assignment is done using **cost drivers**. Cost drivers are used to track how costs of activities are related to specific cost objects such as products or divisions.

For example, recall that Lily Ice Cream Company's traditional overhead allocation method uses number of gallons of ice cream produced to allocate overhead cost to production. It turns out that this same measure, number of gallons of ice cream produced, offers a good reflection of how much effort has been expended in the "operating the ice cream production process" activity—the more gallons of ice cream produced, the more ice cream production activity has taken place. The specific overhead cost items that are included in the cost pool for this activity are the costs of electricity and machine depreciation along with a portion of the costs of factory cleaning, machine repair, and production supervision. The analysis done by Lily suggests that these overhead costs are associated with the general level of production. Accordingly, gallons of ice cream produced is an appropriate cost driver for these overhead costs because it is a numerical measure that reflects how much effort has gone into operating the ice cream production process. The pairing of the activity "operating the ice cream production process" with the cost driver "gallons of ice cream produced" is shown in the first row of Exhibit 2.

cost driver

Numerical measure used to reflect the amount of a specific cost that is associated with a particular activity.

The second overhead cost activity identified by Lily is "producing a specific batch of ice cream." The overhead cost items associated with this activity are portions of the costs of factory cleaning, machine repair, production supervision, and accounting. The natural cost driver associated with this overhead cost pool is the number of batches of ice cream produced. In general, Lily can choose to produce its ice cream in lots of small batches, or in a few large batches. As the number of batches increases, the cost associated with stopping, cleaning, and repairing the machines increases. In addition, because the production supervisor must ensure the quality and flavor of each batch, production of many small batches means that the production supervisor must perform more inspections. Also, the accounting department has additional record-keeping functions associated with each new batch. In summary, the more batches, no matter what their size, the more overhead associated with the activity "producing a specific batch of ice cream." So the cost driver associated with this overhead cost pool is the number of production batches, as shown in the second row in Exhibit 2.

The third overhead cost activity identified by Lily is "servicing the special needs of each individual ice cream flavor." As mentioned previously, for many years Lily had a successful business just making and selling vanilla ice cream. Lily's vanilla ice cream includes only five ingredients—cream, milk, sugar, egg yolks, and vanilla extract. The ice cream

---

EXHIBIT 2	**Matching of Cost Drivers with Overhead Cost Activities for Lily Ice Cream Company**

Overhead Cost Activity	**Driver**
Operating the ice cream production process	Gallons of ice cream produced
Producing a specific batch of ice cream	Batches produced
Servicing the special needs of each individual ice cream flavor	Number of ingredients
Keeping the factory open	Not applicable

storage freezer had just one section because all of the vanilla ice cream was kept at the same optimal temperature. Flavor and quality inspections were easy because all of the ice cream was the same flavor, and the ordering of materials by the accounting department was very straightforward.

With the introduction of Lily's gourmet ice cream flavors, Lily Ice Cream Company now makes six flavors of ice cream.

- Vanilla
- Marshmallow Caramel Delight
- Gingerbread Cheesecake Supreme
- Strawberry Banana Surprise
- Double Dutch Chocolate Brownie
- Peanut Butter Swirl

Each flavor requires a slightly different inspection process. Because each flavor requires a different mix of ingredients, the newly-hired flavor chemist has to do a different set of tests for each flavor. Each type of ice cream must be stored at a slightly different temperature, so the storage freezer has been modified. Clearly, the introduction of the new flavors has increased the overhead costs at Lily Ice Cream Company.

After careful consideration, Lily has decided that the one numerical cost driver that best captures the complexity of manufacturing each flavor is the number of ingredients in the ice cream recipe. This number varies from five for Vanilla to 30 for Peanut Butter Swirl. In summary, the more ingredients, no matter what the number of batches or the number of gallons of ice cream produced, the more overhead associated with the activity "servicing the special needs of each individual ice cream flavor." As shown in Exhibit 2, the cost driver associated with this overhead cost pool is the number of ingredients.

The fourth and final overhead cost activity identified by Lily is "keeping the factory open." The overhead costs associated with this activity, such as building insurance, security, and building depreciation, are the same no matter how many gallons of ice cream Lily produces, with whatever number of ingredients and in however many batches. Accordingly, there is no production-related cost driver that matches up with changes in the amount of overhead cost associated with this activity.

How do we then account for the fourth overhead cost activity "keeping the factory open"? We have two choices. First, because there is no cost driver that reasonably corresponds to this facility support activity, we can just select some basis, such as number of gallons of ice cream produced, and arbitrarily allocate these overhead costs to the ice cream produced. This approach is quite unsatisfying because the whole point of the ABC analysis is to carefully match overhead costs with the activity that causes them and with a cost driver that can be used to reasonably assign those overhead costs. Simply allocating the costs of "keeping the factory open" equally across all gallons of ice cream just doesn't feel right.

Our second choice is to just not assign these costs to production. And with an ABC system this is exactly what we do. We will treat these costs as common costs that are not assigned to any specific product, division, or product line because there isn't any clear relationship between these cost objects and the costs of keeping the factory open. What this means is that facility support costs in an ABC system are treated in the same way that period costs are treated in a traditional product costing system. Instead of assigning these facility support costs to specific products, they are simply listed as general expenses on the income statement. The hope is that the sum of the profits from each of the six ice cream flavors, computed using a careful ABC analysis, will be enough to cover the facility support costs.

In summary, our ABC analysis has identified three cost drivers: number of gallons of ice cream produced, number of batches, and number of ingredients. These cost drivers quantify the amount of overhead activity associated with different aspects of production. In the next section we will see how we can use the cost drivers to assign overhead costs to the different ice cream flavors.

Assigning Overhead to Production Using ABC

Assign overhead to production using ABC cost drivers.

(4) Most of the hard work in implementing Lily Ice Cream Company's ABC system is now done. We have identified the key cost activities, analyzed each overhead cost in terms of these activities in order to compute the cost pools, and specified numerical cost drivers that can be used to assign the overhead costs to production. Now all we need to do is to gather the data, do some arithmetic, and assign the overhead using our ABC calculations.

Recall that we summarized our analysis of the individual overhead items in Exhibit 1. For the purpose of assigning overhead to production, we need to know the total of the cost pool associated with each overhead cost activity. This information can be extracted from Exhibit 1 and is shown in the second column in Exhibit 3. For each of the overhead cost activities, we have identified a cost driver. The total numbers of these cost driver events have been extracted from Lily Company's accounting records and are reported in the third column in Exhibit 3. We can now combine the data about the cost pools and the cost driver events to compute the overhead cost per cost driver event as shown in the last column in Exhibit 3.

In Exhibit 3, note that the facility support costs listed under the "keeping the factory open" activity are NOT assigned under the ABC system because, as discussed before, these overhead costs cannot be tied to any specific production actions. The $0.50 per gallon overhead cost computed for the "operating the ice cream production process" activity reflects the cost of the overhead activities that occur with each gallon of ice cream produced, such as electricity, some cleanup, machine depreciation, some maintenance, and some production supervisor oversight. The $880 per batch overhead cost computed for the "producing a specific batch of ice cream" activity reflects the cost of machine cleanup and repair, production supervisor inspection, and accounting procedures associated with starting and stopping each new batch of ice cream. Note that these batch overhead costs are independent of the size of the batch. Finally, the $2,700 per ingredient overhead cost

EXHIBIT 3	**Computation of Cost per Cost Driver Event for Lily Ice Cream Company**		
Overhead cost activity	**Cost Pool Amount**	**Number of Cost Driver Events**	**Overhead Cost per Cost Driver Event**
Ice cream production	$750,000	1,500,000 gallons	$0.50 per gallon
Ice cream batches	440,000	500 batches	$880 per batch
Ice cream flavors	270,000	100 ingredients	$2,700 per ingredient
Keeping the factory open	280,000	not assigned	not assigned

computed for the "servicing the special needs of each individual ice cream flavor" activity reflects the costs associated with the complexities of each ice cream flavor. Recall that we chose to represent this complexity by the number of ingredients needed to make each flavor. These overhead costs include the cost of the flavor chemist, the cost of the time the production supervisor spends making sure that the mix of each ingredient matches the master recipe, and the cost to the accounting department of ordering and accounting for each of the different ingredients. You should also note that these product line costs associated with each flavor are not related to how many batches or how many individual gallons of ice cream are produced.

The reason that Lily Ice Cream Company undertook this ABC analysis was to be able to answer the following question: For each of the six flavors of ice cream that Lily sells, how much does it cost to produce ice cream? To answer this question, we need to know the number of gallons of ice cream, the number of ice cream batches, and the number of ingredients associated with each ice cream flavor. These data are summarized in Exhibit 4.

Using these data on the occurrence of the cost driver events, combined with the cost per cost driver event computed in Exhibit 3, we can compute the overhead cost associated with each flavor of ice cream. Let's illustrate this procedure by doing the calculations for Gingerbread Cheesecake Supreme.

Overhead Cost Assigned to Gingerbread Cheesecake Supreme

Ice cream production: 200,000 gallons × $0.50 per gallon	$100,000
Ice cream batches: 235 batches × $880 per batch.	206,800
Ice cream ingredients: 25 ingredients × $2,700 per ingredient	67,500
Total overhead assigned to Gingerbread Cheesecake Supreme	$374,300

The results of similar calculations for the other five flavors are shown in Exhibit 5. The data in Exhibit 5 reveal a key insight that can arise from an ABC analysis: the amount of overhead cost associated with production is not necessarily proportional to the level of some simple measure of activity such as direct labor hours or, in this case, number of gallons of ice cream produced. For example, more gallons of Vanilla (500,000) are produced than of any other flavor, and yet the amount of manufacturing overhead cost created by production of Vanilla is just $285,500, substantially less than the $374,300 in overhead cost associated with Gingerbread Cheesecake Supreme. The high overhead cost of Gingerbread Cheesecake Supreme is a function of the large number of ingredients (25) and the extremely large number of batches (235). Assigning overhead using a single cost basis such as direct labor hours or gallons produced (as is done in most traditional cost systems) ignores important differences in the overhead-creating activities associated with the production of each different ice cream flavor.

EXHIBIT 4	**Cost Driver Usage for Lily's Six Ice Cream Flavors**		
Flavors	**Number of Gallons**	**Number of Batches**	**Number of Ingredients**
Vanilla	500,000	25	5
Marshmallow Caramel Delight	250,000	50	20
Gingerbread Cheesecake Supreme	200,000	235	25
Strawberry Banana Surprise	50,000	60	10
Double Dutch Chocolate Brownie	400,000	30	10
Peanut Butter Swirl	100,000	100	30
Total	1,500,000	500	100

EXHIBIT 5	Overhead Assigned to Each Ice Cream Flavor Based on Lily's ABC Analysis			
Flavors	**Ice Cream Production**	**Ice Cream Batches**	**Ice Cream Ingredients**	**Total Overhead Assigned**
Vanilla	$250,000	$ 22,000	$ 13,500	$ 285,500
Marshmallow Caramel Delight	125,000	44,000	54,000	223,000
Gingerbread Cheesecake Supreme	100,000	206,800	67,500	374,300
Strawberry Banana Surprise	25,000	52,800	27,000	104,800
Double Dutch Chocolate Brownie	200,000	26,400	27,000	253,400
Peanut Butter Swirl	50,000	88,000	81,000	219,000
Total	$750,000	$440,000	$270,000	$1,460,000

In the next section, we will use these ABC overhead cost computations, along with data about direct materials and direct labor cost, to compute the cost of producing a gallon of ice cream for each of the six different flavors.

REMEMBER THIS...

- The first three steps in implementing an ABC system are:
    1. identify the key cost activities,
    2. analyze each overhead cost in terms of these activities in order to compute the cost pools, and
    3. specify numerical cost drivers that can be used to assign the overhead costs to production.
- To then assign overhead costs to production, the necessary steps are:
    1. gather the overhead cost and numerical cost driver data,
    2. compute the amount of overhead cost per cost driver event, and
    3. use these data to assign overhead to production.

Making Decisions Using ABC Data

Use ABC data to make decisions.

(5) With the ABC analysis now completed, we are ready to use the data to make some decisions regarding the six ice cream flavors that Lily Ice Cream Company is currently producing. Let's begin by looking at the profitability report for each of the six flavors prepared using the traditional method of allocating overhead costs. This report is shown in Exhibit 6.

In looking at Exhibit 6, recall that using the traditional method, all overhead is allocated based solely on the number of gallons of ice cream produced and that the predetermined rate is $1.16 per gallon. Also note that overhead cost is not the only production cost; the total production cost includes direct materials and direct labor as well as overhead.

The traditional profitability report in Exhibit 6 reveals four items of concern for Lily Ice Cream Company.

1. Overall flavor gross profit is actually a loss of $230,000.
2. The historical backbone of the company, Vanilla, generated a loss of $155,000.

| EXHIBIT 6 | Flavor Gross Profit Computations Using Traditional Overhead Allocation for Lily Ice Cream Company |

	Vanilla	Marshmallow Caramel Delight	Gingerbread Cheesecake Supreme	Strawberry Banana Surprise	Double Dutch Chocolate Brownie	Peanut Butter Swirl	Total
Number of gallons	500,000	250,000	200,000	50,000	400,000	100,000	1,500,000
Sales	$750,000	$625,000	$600,000	$125,000	$800,000	$350,000	$3,250,000
Production cost:							
Direct materials	$200,000	$200,000	$250,000	$50,000	$300,000	$150,000	$1,150,000
Direct labor	125,000	100,000	100,000	15,000	200,000	50,000	590,000
Overhead ($1.16 per gallon)	580,000	290,000	232,000	58,000	464,000	116,000	1,740,000
Total flavor production cost	$905,000	$590,000	$582,000	$123,000	$964,000	$316,000	$3,480,000
Flavor gross profit	$(155,000)	$35,000	$18,000	$2,000	$(164,000)	$34,000	$(230,000)

3. One of the new flavors, Double Dutch Chocolate Brownie, also generated a sizeable loss.

4. The two money-losing flavors are also the two flavors with the highest sales volume— 500,000 gallons for Vanilla and 400,000 gallons for Double Dutch Chocolate Brownie.

Based on this profitability report, Lily is considering dropping the Vanilla and Double Dutch Chocolate Brownie flavors. However, before finalizing this decision, Lily would like to look at the results of the ABC analysis. The profitability report based on the ABC analysis is shown in Exhibit 7.

Before we discuss some of the fascinating things revealed in the ABC profitability report in Exhibit 7, let's make sure that we understand where the numbers are coming from. We will illustrate the computations using the numbers given for the Marshmallow Caramel Delight flavor.

Sales. We see in this report that Lily has produced and sold 250,000 gallons of Marshmallow Caramel Delight ice cream. With the total sales amount being $625,000, we

| EXHIBIT 7 | Flavor Gross Profit Computations Using ABC Overhead Assignment for Lily Ice Cream Company |

	Vanilla	Marshmallow Caramel Delight	Gingerbread Cheesecake Supreme	Strawberry Banana Surprise	Double Dutch Chocolate Brownie	Peanut Butter Swirl	Total
Number of gallons	500,000	250,000	200,000	50,000	400,000	100,000	1,500,000
Sales	$750,000	$625,000	$600,000	$125,000	$800,000	$350,000	$3,250,000
Production cost:							
Direct materials	$200,000	$200,000	$250,000	$50,000	$300,000	$150,000	$1,150,000
Direct labor	125,000	100,000	100,000	15,000	200,000	50,000	590,000
Overhead (using ABC):							
Gallons of ice cream	250,000	125,000	100,000	25,000	200,000	50,000	750,000
Number of batches	22,000	44,000	206,800	52,800	26,400	88,000	440,000
Number of ingredients	13,500	54,000	67,500	27,000	27,000	81,000	270,000
Total flavor production cost	$610,500	$523,000	$724,300	$169,800	$753,400	$419,000	$3,200,000
Flavor gross profit	$139,500	$102,000	$(124,300)	$(44,800)	$46,600	$(69,000)	$50,000
Facility support costs							280,000
Company gross profit							$(230,000)

can deduce that the selling price per gallon is $2.50 ($625,000 ÷ 250,000 gallons). *Note:* We are assuming here that the number of gallons produced is equal to the number of gallons sold, thus avoiding any inventory issues. Of course, in a real company the number of units produced is rarely equal to the number of units sold. But we are trying to keep this example simple.

Direct materials.   The total direct materials cost for the Marshmallow Caramel Delight ice cream is $200,000. This works out to be a cost of $0.80 per gallon ($200,000 ÷ 250,000 gallons).

Direct labor.   The total direct labor cost for the Marshmallow Caramel Delight ice cream is $100,000. This works out to be a cost of $0.40 per gallon ($100,000 ÷ 250,000 gallons).

Using the overhead cost per cost driver numbers shown in Exhibit 3, and the cost driver numbers for Marshmallow Caramel Delight shown in Exhibit 4, the amount of overhead assigned to the Marshmallow Caramel Delight flavor is computed as follows.

Ice cream production:	250,000 gallons × $0.50 per gallon	$125,000
Ice cream batches:	50 batches × $880 per batch	$44,000
Ice cream flavors:	20 ingredients × $2,700 per ingredient	$54,000

Total flavor production cost.   The total production cost for the Marshmallow Caramel Delight flavor is the sum of the direct materials ($200,000), direct labor ($100,000), and overhead costs ($223,000 = $125,000 + $44,000 + $54,000). These costs total $523,000.

Flavor gross profit.   The gross profit is the difference between the $625,000 sales amount and the $523,000 production cost. Accordingly, the gross profit for the Marshmallow Caramel Delight flavor is $102,000 ($625,000 − $523,000).

Note that under the ABC system the facility support costs of $280,000 are not assigned to any of the six flavors. Because no reasonable basis can be identified for assigning these costs of keeping the facility open to any of the six flavors, these are common costs which must be covered by the profits generated by the six different ice cream flavors. Unfortunately for Lily, the cumulative gross profit of $50,000 from the six ice cream flavors is not nearly enough to pay for the $280,000 in overhead costs to keep the ice cream factory open.

Now that we understand how the computations were done, let's see what we can learn from the ABC gross profit report in Exhibit 7. First of all, we see that the total loss of $230,000 is the same as was computed using the traditional overhead allocation method. It is important to understand that an ABC system doesn't get rid of a company's costs but instead is a better way of assigning those costs to different areas of production.

By comparing Exhibits 6 and 7, we also see that determining which ice cream flavors are profitable differs depending on whether the ABC or the traditional method of overhead allocation is used. These differences are summarized as follows:

	Flavor Gross Profit	
Flavors	**Traditional**	**ABC**
Vanilla	$(155,000)	$ 139,500
Marshmallow Caramel Delight	35,000	102,000
Gingerbread Cheesecake Supreme	18,000	(124,300)
Strawberry Banana Surprise	2,000	(44,800)
Double Dutch Chocolate Brownie	(164,000)	46,600
Peanut Butter Swirl	34,000	(69,000)

Note: Remember that the flavor gross profits don't add up to the same number under the two systems because with the ABC system the $280,000 in facility support overhead is treated as a common cost and is not allocated to any of the six flavors. However, after subtracting the $280,000 in facility support costs with the ABC system, total gross profit is the same in both cases—negative $230,000—as shown in Exhibits 6 and 7.

Why are the flavor gross profit numbers different in the two cases? The difference in this case must be due to the method of assigning overhead costs to the flavors. With the traditional method, the total amount of overhead ($1,740,000) is spread evenly over the 1,500,000 gallons of ice cream produced, resulting in the allocation of $1.16 ($1,740,000/1,500,000 gallons) in overhead to each gallon of ice cream, no matter what the flavor. Although this may seem "fair" in some abstract egalitarian sense, this equal allocation approach ignores a lot of information that we have about Lily's ice cream production processes. For example, this equal allocation approach ignores the fact that the production of a batch of ice cream, no matter how many gallons are produced, involves a certain amount of bookkeeping cost, machine cleaning and setup cost, supervisor inspection cost, and so forth.

As an example of the usefulness of the ABC data, we learn that one factor that influences the amount of overhead created by the production of a particular ice cream flavor is the average size of a production batch. The table below shows a computation of the average size of the ice cream batches, in gallons, for each of the six flavors of ice cream.

Flavors	Gallons	Batches	Gallons per Batch
Vanilla	500,000	25	20,000
Marshmallow Caramel Delight	250,000	50	5,000
Gingerbread Cheesecake Supreme	200,000	235	851
Strawberry Banana Surprise	50,000	60	833
Double Dutch Chocolate Brownie	400,000	30	13,333
Peanut Butter Swirl	100,000	100	1,000

You can see that Gingerbread Cheesecake Supreme and Strawberry Banana Surprise are made in relatively small batches, substantially increasing the number of batches and thus increasing the batch-related overhead costs associated with these flavors. Similarly, the production of some flavors involves a large number of ingredients which increases the complexity and overhead cost associated with these flavors. For example, the production of Peanut Butter Swirl ice cream, no matter how many gallons and no matter how many batches, involves extra supervisor, flavor chemist, and accounting overhead costs associated with the 30 different ingredients required in the production of Peanut Butter Swirl. By identifying the activities that create overhead costs and then assigning those costs to production using measurable cost drivers, a management accountant using ABC data has a much better idea of the true economic cost of production.

The average size of a production batch can substantially change the overhead created by the production of an ice cream flavor.

© AP PHOTO/BRETT COOMER

Given this discussion, look again at Lily's ABC profitability report in Exhibit 7. The traditional profitability report indicated that the Vanilla flavor had lost $155,000. However, this number is potentially misleading because the traditional overhead allocation approach involves just arbitrarily assigning $1.16 in overhead cost to every gallon of ice cream produced. What would happen to Lily Ice Cream Company's gross profit if this piece of data were used to support a decision to stop making Vanilla ice cream? The ABC profitability report answers this question. Elimination of the Vanilla flavor would drop total company gross profit by $139,500. This $139,500 ABC number is much more informative than is the loss of $155,000 indicated by the traditional system because the ABC number is the result of a careful economic analysis of exactly what factors create the overhead costs.

The ABC profitability report in Exhibit 7 indicates that Gingerbread Cheesecake Supreme, Strawberry Banana Surprise, and Peanut Butter Swirl are all losing money for Lily Ice Cream Company. Lily could increase profits by $124,300 by stopping the production of Gingerbread Cheesecake Supreme, by an additional $44,800 by stopping the production of Strawberry Banana Surprise, and by an additional $69,000 by stopping the production of Peanut Butter Swirl.

What if Lily doesn't want to stop producing these three flavors but instead wants to do something with the production process to reduce the cost of producing these flavors so that they can be sold at a profit? The ABC overhead system highlights actions that can be taken to improve profitability. In fact, two characteristics of a good management accounting measure are that it:

a.   Reflects economic reality and
b.   Motivates correct behavior.

The ABC flavor profitability report reflects economic reality in that it represents the economic cost of producing each flavor of ice cream. And the ABC analysis that went into the computation of these costs can also help Lily identify and perhaps reduce costly activities in her ice cream factory. Refer back to the computation of the cost for each of the cost driver events shown in Exhibit 3 and the report of the number of cost driver events associated with each ice cream flavor as reported in Exhibit 4. From these data, we can see that making the Gingerbread Cheesecake Supreme flavor profitable could involve reducing the number of batches by making each batch larger. Deeper investigation by Lily has revealed that the large number of Gingerbread Cheesecake Supreme batches (235) is the result of one customer, an ice cream retail chain, that insists on having its Gingerbread Cheesecake Supreme ice cream produced fresh daily. Now that the ABC analysis has highlighted the overhead cost created by this practice, Lily can approach the customer and explain that, in order to maintain the same price, Lily will have to cut back and produce Gingerbread Cheesecake Supreme just once a week instead of once a day. Let's say that through this change, Lily were able to reduce the number of Gingerbread Cheesecake Supreme batches from 235 per year to 50 per year. This change would reduce the batch-level overhead created by Gingerbread Cheesecake Supreme from $206,800 to $44,000, computed as follows:

235 batches × $880 per batch $206,800
50 batches × $880 per batch $44,000

With this change in batch-related overhead, the profitability report for the Gingerbread Cheesecake Supreme flavor changes from showing a loss of $124,300 to showing a profit of $38,500 as shown in Exhibit 8.

Similarly, the Peanut Butter Swirl flavor is currently showing a loss of $69,000 according to the ABC analysis. This is in part due to the fact that Peanut Butter Swirl was produced in 100 small batches last year. As with Gingerbread Cheesecake Supreme, the profitability of Peanut Butter Swirl can be improved by manufacturing the ice cream in larger, less frequent, batches. In addition, the Peanut Butter Swirl flavor creates a large amount of overhead because its recipe requires 30 different ingredients, and the ABC analysis has indicated that each different ingredient causes overhead costs $2,700. Can the Peanut Butter Swirl

EXHIBIT 8	Change in Gross Profit of Gingerbread Cheesecake Supreme with a Reduction in the Number of Batches	
	235 Batches Gingerbread Cheesecake Supreme	**50 Batches Gingerbread Cheesecake Supreme**
Number of gallons	200,000	200,000
Sales	$ 600,000	$600,000
Production cost:		
Direct materials	$ 250,000	$250,000
Direct labor	100,000	100,000
Overhead (using ABC):		
Gallons of ice cream	100,000	100,000
Number of batches	206,800	44,000
Number of ingredients	67,500	67,500
Total flavor production cost	$ 724,300	$561,500
Flavor gross profit	$(124,300)	$ 38,500

recipe be revised to include fewer ingredients without any loss in flavor? This may not be possible, but the ABC analysis suggests that it is at least worth investigating.

Now, you may be saying to yourself that a decision to reduce the number of Gingerbread Cheesecake Supreme batches doesn't immediately lower the batch-related overhead costs such as the salary of the factory supervisor or the wages for the factory cleaners and machine repairpersons. This is true. However, lowering the number of batches does reduce the need for these costs and makes it possible for Lily to decide to eliminate some of the costs, such as through hiring fewer machine repairpersons in the future, or by deciding to use these resources for something else, such as allowing the production supervisor to spend more time boosting the production of other flavors.

REMEMBER THIS...

- Designing and operating an ABC system usually costs more than using a simple traditional system based on a single activity measure such as direct labor hours.
- The increased cost of operating an ABC system pays for itself when use of the improved ABC data results in significantly better decisions.
- Two characteristics of a good management accounting measure are that it:
  - reflects economic reality and
  - motivates correct behavior.

Summary

The ABC approach to assigning overhead costs gives a better reflection of the economic cost created in the production of a particular product or service than does the traditional method of allocating overhead cost based on a single rate computed using, say, direct labor hours. As you saw in our Lily Ice Cream example, the implementation of an ABC system involves considerable analysis of a company's production process. For some companies, such as those with only one type of product or with a number of similar products, implementation of an ABC system is more trouble than it is worth because the cost of developing the ABC system outweighs the potential benefit of making better decisions using the system. However, for companies with diverse products involving substantially different production processes, an ABC system yields better cost data and better management decisions.

REVIEW OF LEARNING OBJECTIVES

(1) Explain the fundamentals of activity-based costing (ABC). The five steps in implementing and using an ABC system are:

1. Identify overhead cost activities
2. Analyze individual overhead costs in terms of those cost activities
3. Identify measurable cost drivers
4. Assign overhead
5. Use the ABC data to make decisions

(2) Identify overhead cost activities.

General Cost Activity Category	Definition	Examples
Unit level	Activities that take place each time a unit of product is produced.	• Machine maintenance • Machine depreciation • Electricity and other energy costs
Batch level	Activities that take place in order to support a batch or production run, regardless of the size of the batch.	• Inspections • Machine setups • Movement of and accounting for materials
Product line	Activities that take place in order to support a product line, regardless of the number of batches or individual units actually produced.	• Engineering product design • Storage in special warehouses • Managing by a special supervisor of all activities associated with a particular product line • Ordering, purchasing, and receiving materials unique to a particular product line
Facility support	Activities necessary to have a production facility in place. However, these activities are not related to any particular line of products or services.	• Property taxes • Factory insurance • Security • Landscaping • General accounting • General factory administration

(3) Determine measurable cost drivers to be used as the basis for assigning overhead costs to products.

- A cost driver is a numerical measure used to reflect the amount of a specific overhead cost that is associated with a particular activity.
- Examples of cost drivers in the Lily Ice Cream Company example are:
  - number of gallons of ice cream to reflect the amount of unit-level activity,
  - number of ice cream batches to reflect the amount of batch-level activity, and
  - number of ingredients to reflect the special product line activities associated with each ice cream flavor.
- In an ABC system, facility support overhead costs are treated as common costs that are not assigned to any specific product, division, or product line.

(4) Assign overhead to production using ABC cost drivers. The first three steps in implementing an ABC system are:

- identify the key cost activities,
- analyze each overhead cost in terms of these activities in order to compute the cost pools, and
- specify numerical cost drivers that can be used to assign the overhead costs to production.

To then assign overhead costs to production, the necessary steps are:
- gather the overhead cost and numerical cost driver data,
- compute the amount of overhead cost per cost driver event, and
- use these data to assign overhead to production.

(5) **Use ABC data to make decisions.**

- Designing and operating an ABC system usually costs more than using a simple traditional system based on a single activity measure such as direct labor hours.
- The increased cost of operating an ABC system pays for itself when use of the improved ABC data results in significantly better decisions.
- Two characteristics of a good management accounting measure are that it:
  - reflects economic reality and
  - motivates correct behavior.

KEY TERMS & CONCEPTS

activity-based costing (ABC), 829
batch-level activities, 833
cost driver, 836
cost pool, 835

facility support activities, 833
product line activities, 833
unit-level activities, 833

REVIEW PROBLEM

ABC versus Traditional Product Costing

Willett Company makes two types of products: Product A and Product B. The company's management accountants accumulated the following production cost information for 2009:

	Product A	Product B	Total
Production and sales volume (units)	1,000	500	
Direct labor cost per hour	$6	$12	
Direct materials cost per unit	$5	$7	
Manufacturing overhead costs:			
Total cost of manufacturing utilities			$ 20,000
Total cost of quality inspections			80,000
Total cost of engineering			48,000
Total cost of factory supervision salaries			52,000
Total manufacturing overhead costs			$200,000
Activities cost drivers:			
Direct labor hours per unit	3	2	4,000
Number of production batches per product line	22	18	40
Number of engineering changes per product line	4	8	12

Required:

Assume Product A sells for $140 each and Product B sells for $160 each. If all products are sold, what is the gross margin of each product assuming the following:
1. All manufacturing overhead costs are allocated on the basis of direct labor hours.
2. Costs of manufacturing utilities are assigned on the basis of direct labor hours; costs of quality inspections are assigned on the basis of production batches; costs of engineering are assigned on the basis of engineering changes made; and costs of factory supervision salaries can't be directly assigned to either product.

(continued)

Solution

1. Traditional Cost Allocation

	Product A	Product B	Total
Production and sales volume (units)	1,000	500	1,500
Total manufacturing overhead costs			$ 200,000
Direct labor hours per unit . . . . `. . .`	× 3	× 2	
Total labor hours	3,000	1,000	÷ 4,000
Total manufacturing overhead cost driver rate			$ 50
Sales	$140,000	$80,000	$ 220,000
Production cost:			
Direct labor cost (direct labor rate × labor hours) . . .	$ 18,000	$12,000	$ 30,000
Direct materials cost (direct materials cost			
per unit × production volume)	5,000	3,500	8,500
Manufacturing overhead cost (direct labor hours			
× manufacturing overhead cost rate)	150,000	50,000	200,000
Total production cost	$173,000	$65,500	$ 238,500
Company gross profit	$ (33,000)	$14,500	$ (18,500)

2. Activity-Based Cost Assignment

	Product A	Product B	Total
Production and sales volume (units)	1,000	500	
Manufacturing utilities overhead costs			$ 20,000
Total labor hours	3,000	1,000	÷ 4,000
Manufacturing utilities cost driver rate			$ 5
Quality inspection costs on production batches			$ 80,000
Total production batches	22	18	÷ 40
Quality inspection cost driver rate			$ 2,000
Engineering changes costs			$ 48,000
Total engineering changes	4	8	÷ 12
Engineering changes cost driver rate			$ 4,000
Sales	$140,000	$80,000	$220,000
Production cost:			
Direct labor cost (direct labor rate × labor hours) . . .	$ 18,000	$12,000	$ 30,000
Direct materials cost (direct materials cost			
per unit × production volume)	5,000	3,500	8,500
Manufacturing utilities overhead cost			
(utilities cost driver rate × labor hours)	15,000	5,000	20,000
Quality inspection overhead costs			
(inspection cost driver rate × batches)	44,000	36,000	80,000
Engineering overhead costs (engineering cost			
driver rate × changes)	16,000	32,000	48,000
Total product production costs	$ 98,000	$88,500	$186,500
Product gross profit	$ 42,000	$ (8,500)	$ 33,500
Factory supervision overhead cost			52,000
Company gross profit			$ (18,500)

DISCUSSION QUESTIONS

1. How are overhead costs assigned to products or divisions when an activity-based costing (ABC) system is used?
2. What is the most serious drawback of an ABC system?
3. What are the five steps involved in implementing and using an ABC system?
4. What are the four general categories of ABC activities?
5. Give two examples of unit-level activities.
6. Give two examples of batch-level activities.
7. Give two examples of product line activities.
8. Give two examples of facility support activities.
9. What must a company do in order to be able to assign overhead costs to specific overhead activities?
10. What can a company do to determine what percentage of time employees spend on particular overhead cost activities?
11. What is a cost pool?
12. What is a cost driver?
13. How are facility support overhead costs treated in an ABC system?
14. Why is the amount of overhead cost allocated to a product or division in an ABC system not necessarily proportional to a single measure of activity such as direct labor hours?
15. Compare Exhibits 6 and 7. Why does the total "flavor gross profit" differ in the two exhibits?
16. Using the traditional overhead allocation technique described in the chapter, Lily Ice Cream Company's Vanilla flavor has a gross profit of negative $155,000 (see Exhibit 6). Using the ABC system, Vanilla has a gross profit of positive $139,500 (see Exhibit 7). Why is there so much difference in the gross profits for Vanilla as reported using the two overhead allocation systems?
17. What are the two characteristics of a good management accounting measure?

PRACTICE EXERCISES

PE 17-1 Overhead Allocation Problem in the Lily Ice Cream Company Example

LO1 Which one of the following statements is *true* with respect to the Lily Ice Cream Company example described in the text of this chapter?
  a. The original traditional overhead allocation system ignored the impact of spoiled goods on the calculation of gross profit.
  b. The original materials warehouse requisition system did not include adequate controls to ensure separation of duties.
  c. The original manufacturing overhead application system based on gallons of ice cream did not provide accurate insight on overhead cost behavior.
  d. The original overhead application system overstated cost of goods sold during times of inflation.

PE 17-2 Characteristics of Traditional Overhead Allocation Systems

LO1 Which one of the following statements is *false* with respect to a traditional overhead allocation system?
  a. A traditional overhead allocation system is a good method of cost allocation in the right context.
  b. A traditional overhead allocation system is widely used by many companies.
  c. A traditional overhead allocation system essentially allocates overhead costs based on the number of units produced.
  d. A traditional overhead allocation system usually works well in a company with multiple products and services.

PE 17-3 Traditional Overhead Allocation System

LO1 The company expects to use 500,000 direct labor hours in the production of its only product. Using a traditional overhead allocation system based on direct labor hours and the

(continued)

following manufacturing overhead costs for the year, compute the manufacturing overhead allocation rate.

Electricity	$ 48,000
Depreciation	140,000
Engineering	60,000
Quality testing	173,000
Property tax	53,000
Supervisors' salaries	210,000
Maintenance	110,000

PE 17-4

LO2

Overhead Allocation Problems

Which one of the following statements is *false*?
a. Facility support costs should *not* be allocated over each division.
b. Facility support costs include direct labor and direct materials.
c. Traditional overhead allocation systems can result in application of manufacturing overhead costs that do not reflect economic reality.
d. The development and operation of an ABC accounting system can cost more than the development and operation of a traditional overhead allocation system.

PE 17-5

LO2

Difference between a Traditional System and an ABC System

Which one of the following statements best summarizes the difference between a traditional overhead allocation system and an ABC system?
a. With a traditional system, overhead costs are first allocated to products; with ABC, overhead costs are first allocated to activities.
b. With a traditional system, overhead costs are first allocated to activities; with ABC, overhead costs are first allocated to departments.
c. With a traditional system, overhead costs are first allocated to departments; with ABC, overhead costs are first allocated to divisions.
d. With a traditional system, overhead costs are first allocated to products; with ABC, overhead costs are first allocated to departments.

PE 17-6

LO2

General Categories of ABC Activities

Which one of the following is *not* one of the four general categories of ABC activities?
a. Facility support activities
b. Batch-level activities
c. Unit-level activities
d. Product line activities
e. Manufacturing application activities

PE 17-7

LO2

Batch-Level Activities

Which one of the following would *not* be an example of a batch activity for a manufacturing firm?
a. Purchase orders
b. Special product warehouse manager's salary
c. Number of setups
d. Number of inspections

PE 17-8

LO2

Product Line Activities

Which one of the following is *not* an example of a product line activity?
a. Property taxes on the production facility
b. Costs related to specialized materials warehouses
c. Production process design activities
d. Training activities for specific types of consulting services

PE 17-9 **Facility Support Activities**

LO2 Which one of the following is *not* an example of a facility support activity?

    a. Manufacturing vice president's salary

    b. Property taxes

    c. Accounting

    d. Product engineer's salary

    e. Plant security

PE 17-10 **Identifying Cost Drivers**

LO3 The company manufactures a variety of models of automobile transmissions. Which one of the following is the best cost driver to use with the activity "designing the parts for a new transmission"?

    a. Number of machine hours

    b. Number of production batches used to manufacture transmissions

    c. Number of parts in the transmission

    d. Number of direct labor hours

PE 17-11 **Unit-Level Activities**

LO4 The company has determined that $1,029,600 of its total manufacturing overhead costs related to unit-level activities such as electricity costs for running the manufacturing equipment and equipment maintenance costs. The company allocates these costs over the individual units of production based on machine hours. Using the following expected machine hours for the company's three divisions that all make the same product, (1) determine the manufacturing overhead rate per machine hour and (2) allocate the manufacturing overhead to each division.

Division A	20,000 hours
Division B	40,000
Division C	50,000

PE 17-12 **Unit-Level, Batch-Level, Product Line, and Facility Support Costs**

LO4 The company has determined that its total manufacturing overhead cost of $900,000 is a mixture of unit-level, batch-level, product line, and facility support costs. The company has assembled the following information concerning the manufacturing overhead costs, the annual number of units produced, production batches, and number of product lines in each division.

	Total Overhead Costs	Division A	Division B
Unit-level overhead	$210,000	7,500 units	13,500 units
Batch-level overhead	280,000	50 batches	90 batches
Product line overhead	210,000	10 lines	18 lines
Facility support overhead	200,000	–	–
Total	$900,000		

Compute how much total overhead cost would remain if Division A were eliminated.

PE 17-13 **Resolving Cost Distortions**

LO5 Which one of the following statements is *false*?

    a. In a manufacturing setting with several different types of products, a traditional overhead allocation system can cause a manager to evaluate products incorrectly.

(continued)

b. In a manufacturing setting with several different types of products, the cost allocations done as part of an ABC system can better reflect economic reality.

c. The gross profit for a specific product or division computed using a traditional overhead allocation system can differ from the gross profit computed using an ABC system.

d. Allocating facility support costs to individual product lines is an essential part of an ABC system.

PE 17-14

LO5

Overhead Costs and Dropping a Product Line

The company manufactures three products. Profit computations for these three products for the most recent year are as follows:

	Product X	**Product Y**	**Product Z**	**Total**
Sales	$300,000	$ 700,000	$ 800,000	$1,800,000
Direct materials	(70,000)	(150,000)	(200,000)	(420,000)
Direct labor	(50,000)	(200,000)	(250,000)	(500,000)
Manufacturing overhead	(100,000)	(400,000)	(500,000)	(1,000,000)
Profit	$ 80,000	$ (50,000)	$(150,000)	$ (120,000)

The company traditionally allocates manufacturing overhead based on the level of direct labor cost—$2 of manufacturing overhead are allocated for each $1 of direct labor cost. However, of the company's $1,000,000 in manufacturing overhead costs, $700,000 is directly related to the number of product batches produced during the year. The number of batches of the three products for the year was as follows: Product X, 20 batches; Product Y, 30 batches; Product Z, 50 batches. The remaining $300,000 in overhead is for facility support (property taxes, security costs, general administration, and so forth).

As you can see, the total company loss is $120,000. In an effort to reduce or eliminate this loss, the company has decided to drop Product Z. What would total company profit (or loss) have been in the most recent year if Product Z had been dropped at the beginning of the year?

EXERCISES

E 17-15

LO1

Product Costing Review

Mad Dog Enterprises manufactures computer game control devices such as joysticks and steering wheels. Following is a list of the costs incurred by Mad Dog in 2009:

Wages paid to assembly workers	$100,000
Cost of plastic used in making devices	25,000
Insurance on factory building	12,000
Salary of factory supervisor	57,000
Interest on money borrowed to finance operations	34,000
Wages paid to factory maintenance workers	61,000
Cost of computer/controller boards installed in devices	38,000
Advertising costs	127,000
Cost of electricity used in factory	46,000

Compute the total cost for each of the following categories:
1. Direct materials
2. Direct labor
3. Manufacturing overhead
4. Period costs

E 17-16 **Importance of Manufacturing Overhead Allocation**

LO1

The percentages of product costs comprised by direct materials, direct labor, and manufacturing overhead for three companies are as follows:

	Company A	Company B	Company C
Direct materials	7%	21%	42%
Direct labor	13	42	49
Manufacturing overhead	80	37	9
	100%	100%	100%

Based on this information, which of these three companies would probably improve its product costing accuracy most by converting to activity-based costing (ABC)? Explain your answer.

E 17-17 **Product Cost Hierarchy**

LO2

For the following list of costs, indicate by the appropriate letter which category of activities each cost applies to: unit level (U), batch level (B), product line (P), or facility support (F):
a. Machine fine-tuning adjustment cost (required after the production of each unit)
b. Salary of vice president of finance
c. Machine inspection cost (required after the completion of each day's production)
d. Cost of the external audit firm
e. Direct labor
f. Product testing cost (performed at the start of each day's production)
g. Direct materials
h. Factory security cost
i. Machine straight-line depreciation cost (Generally, machines are dedicated to producing a particular type of product.)
j. Warehousing cost (Each type of product has its own warehouse.)
k. Employee training cost (Training is generally specific to different types of products.)

E 17-18 **Computing Profit Using ABC**

LO4

Cottrell Company manufactures three products. Gross margin computations for these three products for 2009 are given below.

	Product A	Product B	Product C
Sales	$ 300,000	$ 500,000	$ 600,000
Direct materials	(50,000)	(250,000)	(200,000)
Direct labor	(150,000)	(50,000)	(100,000)
Manufacturing overhead*	(225,000)	(75,000)	(150,000)
Gross margin	$(125,000)	$ 125,000	$ 150,000

*Manufacturing overhead is allocated to production based on the amount of direct labor cost.

Cottrell has reexamined the factors that cause its manufacturing overhead costs and has discovered that the annual amount of manufacturing overhead is more closely related to the number of product batches produced during the year than it is to direct labor costs. The number of batches of the three products for 2009 was as follows: Product A, 10 batches; Product B, 60 batches; Product C, 30 batches.
1. Prepare gross margin calculations for Cottrell's three products assuming that manufacturing overhead is allocated based on the number of batches.
2. Under the direct labor cost method of manufacturing overhead allocation, one of Cottrell's products appears profitable but the ABC calculations reveal that it is not. Which product is this?

E 17-19   **Computing Profit Using ABC**

LO4   Halsey, Inc. manufactures two types of baby car seats: standard and deluxe. Information for the year 2009 has been given as follows:

	Standard	Deluxe
Sales price	$50	$80
Units produced and sold	23,400	9,750
Direct materials cost	$195,000	$130,000
Direct labor cost per hour	$10	$10
Direct labor hours	35,100	42,900
Purchase orders	100	25

Manufacturing overhead for the year totals $650,000. Halsey allocates manufacturing overhead by direct labor hour.

1. Prepare gross margin calculations for each product line using direct labor hours as an allocation base.
2. Management has determined that a more correct method of allocating manufacturing overhead is by the number of purchase orders. Prepare new gross margin calculations for management using purchase orders as the allocation base.
3. By how much do the profits of the two types of baby car seats differ between the direct labor hour allocation method and ABC allocation? Assuming that allocating manufacturing overhead by purchase orders is more correct, what can you conclude from this difference?

E 17-20   **Allocating Batch-Level and Product Line Manufacturing Overhead Costs**

LO4   Giles Company has two divisions. Gross margin computations for these two divisions for 2009 are as follows:

	Standard Products	Custom Products
Sales	$1,200,000	$1,800,000
Direct materials	(200,000)	(300,000)
Direct labor	(600,000)	(600,000)
Manufacturing overhead*	(500,000)	(500,000)
Gross margin	$ (100,000)	$ 400,000

*Manufacturing overhead is allocated to production based on the amount of direct labor cost.

Giles has determined that its total manufacturing overhead cost of $1,000,000 is a mixture of batch-level costs and product line costs. Giles has assembled the following information concerning the manufacturing overhead costs, the annual number of production batches in each division, and the number of product lines in each division:

	Total Mfg. Overhead Costs	Standard Products	Custom Products
Batch-level manufacturing overhead	$ 600,000	15 batches	60 batches
Product line manufacturing overhead	400,000	10 lines	30 lines
	$1,000,000		

1. Prepare gross margin calculations for Giles' two divisions assuming that manufacturing overhead is allocated based on the number of batches and number of product lines.
2. By how much do the profits of the two divisions differ between the direct labor cost allocation method and ABC allocation? Assuming that allocating manufacturing overhead using the ABC method is more correct, what can you conclude from this difference?

E 17-21 **Allocating Batch-Level and Product Line Manufacturing Overhead Costs**

LO4   Sundance Skis Company is preparing its end-of-year gross margin computations. Sundance Skis manufactures three types of products: skis, snowboards, and snow skates. The following information, as of the end of the year, is available for these products:

	Skis	Snowboards	Snow Skates
Total sales revenue	$1,250,000	$1,500,000	$750,000
Units produced	4,500	3,750	6,750
Direct materials	$(625,000)	$(500,000)	$(125,000)
Direct labor	$(125,000)	$(250,000)	$(375,000)
Number of setups	9	18	3
Number of product styles	5	7	3

Total manufacturing overhead is $1,125,000, with $506,250 related to batch-level activities and $618,750 related to product line activities.

1. In the past, Sundance Skis has allocated manufacturing overhead based on the number of units produced. Prepare gross margin calculations for Sundance Skis' three divisions allocating manufacturing overhead according to the number of units produced.

2. After investigation, management at Sundance Skis determined that a more accurate allocation of manufacturing overhead would be to assign these costs using batch-level and product line activities. Prepare gross margin calculations for Sundance Skis' three divisions by assigning manufacturing overhead using batch-level and product line activities. Assume that the number of setups is the activity allocation basis for assigning costs of batch-level activities and that the number of product styles is the allocation base for assigning costs of product line activities.

E 17-22 **Problems from Allocating Facility Support Costs**

LO5   Blaine Avenue Company manufactures three products. Gross margin computations for these three products for 2009 are as follows:

	Product X	Product Y	Product Z
Sales	$800,000	$ 700,000	$ 600,000
Direct materials	(50,000)	(150,000)	(200,000)
Direct labor	(50,000)	(200,000)	(250,000)
Manufacturing overhead*	(80,000)	(320,000)	(400,000)
Gross margin	$620,000	$ 30,000	$(250,000)

*Manufacturing overhead is allocated to production based on the amount of direct labor cost.

Blaine Avenue has reexamined the activities that relate to its manufacturing overhead costs and has discovered that $500,000 of the annual amount of manufacturing overhead is directly related to the number of product batches produced during the year. The number of batches of the three products for 2009 was as follows: Product X, 100 batches; Product Y, 100 batches; Product Z, 50 batches. The remaining $300,000 in overhead is for facility support (property taxes, security costs, general administration, etc.) and does not vary at all with the level of activity.

1. Prepare gross margin calculations for Blaine Avenue's three products assuming that manufacturing overhead is allocated based on the number of batches. Also, show a "total" column. Facility support costs are not to be allocated to any of the products, but are to be subtracted in the "total" column in the computation of total company operating profit.

2. Using the gross margin numbers prepared under the direct labor cost method of manufacturing overhead allocation, Blaine Avenue's board of directors has tentatively decided to discontinue the Z product line. Assume that this was done at the beginning of 2009. What would have happened to total company operating profit for the year? Explain.

E 17-23

LO5

Problems from Allocating Facility Support Costs

Wilken Sandwich Shop maintains three separate menus for breakfast, lunch, and dinner. Gross margin computations for the three menu lines for 2009 are as follows:

	Breakfast	**Lunch**	**Dinner**
Sales	$ 880,000	$1,015,000	$ 720,000
Direct materials	(260,000)	(217,500)	(175,000)
Direct labor	(325,000)	(290,000)	(155,000)
Overhead*	(528,000)	(264,000)	(264,000)
Gross margin	$(233,000)	$ 243,500	$ 126,000

*Overhead is allocated to the menu lines based on the number of customers served each day. In 2009, 4,000 breakfast customers, 2,000 lunch customers, and 2,000 dinner customers were served.

Management at Wilken has tentatively decided to stop serving breakfast in its restaurants because of poor financial performance. Before doing so, they have reexamined the costs of all three menu lines in order to verify that they are correct. Management determined that direct materials and direct labor costs are correct. However, using an activity-based costing approach, they discovered that $408,000 of overhead costs are related to facility support activities and the rest of the overhead ($648,000) is related to the kitchen setup activities required to prepare the menu line each day (a batch-level activity). They determined that a good cost allocation base for batch-level kitchen activities is number of setups per business day. Wilken was open for business 360 days in 2009. The number of daily setup activities for each menu line is as follows:

Breakfast	10
Lunch	15
Dinner	5

1. Since management has tentatively decided to stop serving breakfast, they have asked to see gross margin calculations for the lunch and dinner menus. Assuming the breakfast menu was dropped at the beginning of 2009, prepare gross margin calculations for the lunch and dinner menu lines assuming overhead is allocated based on the number of customers served. Be sure to show a "total" column.
2. Prepare gross margin calculations for Wilken's three menu lines assuming that overhead is assigned using activity-based costing. Facility support costs are not to be allocated to any of the menu lines, but are to be subtracted in the "total" column in the computation of total company operating profit.
3. Using the gross margin numbers prepared in parts (1) and (2), what would have happened to total company operating profit for the year 2009 if Wilken would have dropped its breakfast menu at the beginning of the year? Explain.

PROBLEMS

P 17-24

LO2

Identifying Overhead Cost Activities

Below is a list of overhead cost activities. For each activity, determine whether it is a unit-level, batch-level, product line, or facility support activity.

1. *Employee training:* Employees need special training to work with each of the company's different products.
2. *Product inspection:* No inspection is performed on each unit produced. Instead, a sample of units from each production batch is inspected.
3. *Electricity:* The production machines are powered by electricity.
4. *Liability insurance*: Because of hazardous chemicals used throughout the plant, the company is required to buy a liability insurance policy.

(continued)

5. *Product design:* A staff of design engineers generates refinements to the designs of each of the products.

6. *Vice president in charge of production:* The company vice president has specific responsibility for overseeing all aspects of the production facility.

7. *Machine setup:* The production machines must be repositioned and inspected at the beginning of each production batch.

8. *Machine setup:* The production machines must be repositioned and inspected only when production is changed from one type of product to another.

9. *Product inspection:* An inspection is performed on each unit produced.

10. *Machine maintenance:* The production machines need constant preventative maintenance in order to extend their operating lives.

P 17-25

LO2

Computing Cost Pools

MaScare Company produces clothing and has identified five overhead cost activities. These activities are shown as the columns in the table below, along with the percentage of time spent in each activity by various factory employees.

	Percentage of Time Spent on Each Activity				
	Repairing Equipment	Hiring and Training Workers	Inspecting Clothing	Ordering Materials	Creating Clothing Designs
Maintenance people	100%	0%	0%	0%	0%
Production foreman	10%	60%	20%	10%	0%
Accounting department	0%	50%	0%	50%	0%
Design staff	0%	0%	10%	20%	70%
Factory superintendent	0%	30%	40%	10%	20%

The total overhead cost associated with each of the categories of factory employee is as follows:

Maintenance people	$100,000
Production foreman	80,000
Accounting department	150,000
Design staff	200,000
Factory superintendent	120,000

Required:

From these data, compute the amount of the cost pool associated with each of the five overhead cost activities.

P 17-26

LO3

Identifying and Using Volume-Based and Activity-Based Cost Allocation Rates

Rane Company produces electronic fish finders. It makes two different fish finders: the standard model, which is produced in bulk and sells for $150, and the deluxe model, which comes in various configurations and sells for $300. Rane's engineering and design overhead cost for 2009 is $60,000. The following information relates to production in 2009:

Number of different machine setups needed for a standard model production run	4
Number of different machine setups needed for a deluxe model production run	11
Number of standard fish finders produced	22,000
Number of deluxe fish finders produced	8,000
Number of engineering design changes needed on the standard model	6
Number of engineering design changes needed on the deluxe model	2
Average batch size per production run for standard model	400
Average batch size per production run for deluxe model	200

(continued)

Required:

1. Determine the engineering and design costs to be assigned to standard and deluxe fish finders using the following allocation methods:
    a. Number of units produced
    b. Number of setups required
    c. Number of engineering design changes needed
2. Which allocation method do you believe is most equitable?

P 17-27   **Computing Profit Using ABC**

LO4   Rockwell Company has three operating divisions. Gross margin computations for these three divisions for 2009 are given below.

	Division M	Division N	Division O
Sales	$ 600,000	$ 400,000	$ 300,000
Direct materials	(100,000)	(200,000)	(80,000)
Direct labor	(300,000)	(60,000)	(140,000)
Manufacturing overhead*	(210,000)	(42,000)	(98,000)
Gross margin	$ (10,000)	$ 98,000	$ (18,000)

*Manufacturing overhead is allocated to production based on the amount of direct labor cost.

Rockwell has determined that its total manufacturing overhead cost of $350,000 is a mixture of batch-level costs and product line costs. Rockwell has assembled the following information concerning the overhead costs, the annual number of production batches in each division, and the number of product lines in each division:

	Total Mfg. Overhead Costs	Division M	Division N	Division O
Batch-level overhead	$200,000	20 batches	80 batches	100 batches
Product line overhead	150,000	10 lines	30 lines	40 lines
	$350,000			

Required:

1. Prepare gross margin calculations for Rockwell's three divisions assuming that manufacturing overhead is allocated based on the number of batches and the number of product lines.
2. By how much do the profits of the three divisions differ between the direct labor cost allocation method and ABC allocation? Assuming that allocating manufacturing overhead using the ABC method is more correct, what can you conclude from these differences?
3. After preparing the gross margin calculations in part (1), what advice do you have for Rockwell concerning whether it should shut down any of its three divisions? Is this the same advice that would come from looking at the original gross margin calculations using manufacturing overhead allocated according to direct labor cost? Why is there a difference?

P 17-28   **Allocating Unit-Level, Batch-Level, and Product Line Manufacturing Overhead**

LO4   **Costs**

Solar Salt Company has two divisions. Gross margin computations for these two divisions for 2009 are as follows:

(continued)

	Agricultural Products	Retail Products
Sales	$1,600,000	$ 900,000
Direct materials	(100,000)	(50,000)
Direct labor	(900,000)	(500,000)
Manufacturing overhead*	(450,000)	(250,000)
Gross margin	$ 150,000	$ 100,000

*Manufacturing overhead is allocated to production based on the amount of direct labor cost.

Solar Salt has determined that its total manufacturing overhead cost of $700,000 is a mixture of unit-level costs, batch-level costs, and product line costs. Solar Salt has assembled the following information concerning the manufacturing overhead costs, the annual number of units produced, production batches, and number of product lines in each division:

	Total Mfg. Overhead Costs	Agricultural Products	Retail Products
Unit-level overhead	$210,000	13,500 units	7,500 units
Batch-level overhead	280,000	90 batches	50 batches
Product line overhead	210,000	18 lines	10 lines
	$700,000		

Required:

1. Prepare gross margin calculations for Solar Salt's two divisions assuming that manufacturing overhead is allocated based on the number of units, number of batches, and number of product lines.
2. Comment on the comparison between the original overhead allocation done using direct labor cost and the manufacturing overhead allocation done in part (1).
3. Repeat part (1), assuming the following information concerning the number of units, batches, and product lines in each division.

	Total Mfg. Overhead Costs	Agricultural Products	Retail Products
Unit-level overhead	$210,000	13,500 units	7,500 units
Batch-level overhead	280,000	50 batches	90 batches
Product line overhead	210,000	10 lines	18 lines
	$700,000		

P 17-29

Manufacturing Overhead Allocation Using Activity-Based Costing

The following information is given for Greenbaum Manufacturing Company:

	Product A	Product B	Product C	Product D
Units produced	3,000	3,450	2,875	2,400
Direct materials cost	$135,000	$169,050	$149,500	$103,200
Direct labor cost	$75,000	$124,200	$117,875	$93,600

(continued)

Manufacturing Overhead	Mfg. Overhead Costs	Relevant Activities
Engineering	$209,950	Engineering changes
Quality control	129,500	Number of setups
Maintenance	41,065	Maintenance hours worked in each area of production
Manufacturing support	93,800	Production volume (units produced)

Activities	Product A	Product B	Product C	Product D
Engineering changes	300	150	275	125
Number of setups	12	5	9	11
Maintenance hours worked in each area of production	45	49	56	41
Production volume	3,000	3,450	2,875	2,400

Required:

1. Determine the ABC allocation rate for each activity (i.e., each manufacturing overhead cost pool).
2. Determine the manufacturing overhead cost for each product.
3. If Products A, B, C, and D sell for $130, $125, $156, and $166, respectively, determine the gross margin for Greenbaum's four products. Assume all units are sold.

P 17-30
LO4

Manufacturing Overhead Allocation Using Activity-Based Costing

Rick's Crane Company manufactures three different crane engines with 50 horsepower (hp), 60 horsepower, and 70 horsepower engines, respectively. Relevant information for each engine is provided as follows:

	50 hp		60 hp		70 hp	
	Total	Per Unit	Total	Per Unit	Total	Per Unit
Units produced	2,500		2,000		1,500	
Direct materials cost	$425,000	$170	$370,000	$185	$360,000	$240
Direct labor cost	$595,000	$238	$510,000	$255	$472,500	$315
Sales price		$450		$540		$630
Purchases per year	44		52		54	
Number of machine setups per year	60		68		80	
Engineering change orders per year	72		84		100	

Total manufacturing overhead cost pools:

Engineering	$102,400
Quality control	88,400
Purchasing costs	49,200
Machine maintenance costs	81,000
Total costs	$321,000

Required:

1. Determine the gross margin for each product allocating manufacturing overhead costs on the basis of production volume (units produced).

(continued)

2. Identify appropriate allocation bases for each of the four pools of manufacturing overhead costs.

3. Determine the ABC allocation rates for each of the four cost pools suggested in part (2).

4. Using the allocation bases suggested in part (2), determine manufacturing overhead costs per product.

5. a. Determine the gross margin per product using the manufacturing overhead costs determined in part (4).

   b. **Interpretive Question:** Which of the methods (unit-based costing or activity-based costing) is the better method to allocate the manufacturing overhead costs?

P 17-31
LO4

Manufacturing Overhead Allocation with Multiple Products

Schmidt Electronics produces two products: CD105 and HD210. Relevant costing information for each product is as follows:

Per Unit	CD105	HD210
Direct materials	$10.50	$17.25
Direct labor	$10.00	$15.00
Direct labor hours per unit	1	2
Total number of machine setups	400	200
Units produced	6,000	7,000

Manufacturing overhead costs and associated ABC allocation bases are as follows:

	Mfg. Overhead Costs	Allocation Bases
Product inspection	$30,000	Units produced
Materials management	48,000	Number of machine setups
Manufacturing support	16,000	Product lines

Required:

1. If manufacturing overhead is allocated on the basis of direct labor hours, compute the cost per unit for CD105 and HD210.

2. Determine the allocation rate per activity for each ABC allocation basis.

3. Determine the manufacturing overhead cost for each product using your answer to part (2).

4. Using your answer to part (3), compute the cost per unit for CD105 and HD210.

5. Compare your answers to part (1) and part (4). Why the difference in costs?

P 17-32
LO4

Activity-Based Costing and Gross Margin Calculations

Stafford Manufacturing, Inc., produces two different products. Product 1 sells for $950 each, and Product 2 sells for $700 each. Estimated annual production and sales for Product 1 and Product 2 are 2,100 units and 2,900 units, respectively. Direct materials are $350 for Product 1 and $200 for Product 2. Direct labor costs are $300 for Product 1 and $310 for Product 2. Stafford purchases materials for Product 1 every month and for Product 2 every two months. On average, Stafford performs 10 setups each month for Product 1 production and 8 setups each month for Product 2 production. The following are manufacturing overhead costs incurred by Stafford Manufacturing:

Quality control	$150,000
Purchasing costs	74,880
Miscellaneous manufacturing overhead	62,640

Required:

1. Assuming that the allocation bases for the three manufacturing overhead costs are production volume for quality control, number of purchases for purchasing costs, and

(continued)

number of setups for miscellaneous manufacturing overhead, calculate the cost per unit of each allocation basis.

2. Determine total manufacturing overhead costs for each product.

3. Determine the gross margin percent for Stafford Manufacturing for each product it produces.

P 17-33

LO4

Allocation of Manufacturing Overhead with Multiple Products

Geddy, Inc., is a manufacturing firm that manufactures two types of boat engines. The Type A engine is designed for a specific type of cruise ship. Because of a long-term commitment with a cruise company, Type A engines need no modifications. Type B engines are designed for slightly smaller cruise ships. Because the Type B engine is designed for several different models of cruise ships and the mounting hardware is different for each, retooling is regularly required. Costs for the two types of engines are presented here:

	Type A Engine (200 Units Produced)		Type B Engine (90 Units Produced)	
	Total	**Per Unit**	**Total**	**Per Unit**
Direct materials cost	$176,000,000	$880,000	$70,200,000	$780,000
Direct labor cost	147,000,000	735,000	60,300,000	670,000
Manufacturing overhead costs:				
Engineering costs				$144,000,000
Quality control				38,880,000
Utilities and maintenance				1,305,000

Required:

1. Determine the amount of manufacturing overhead to be assigned to each unit of activity assuming the following ABC information:

   Manufacturing overhead costs
   - Engineering costs
   - Quality control
   - Utilities and maintenance

   Allocation Bases
   - Engineering change orders per unit
   - Machine setups per unit
   - Production volume

   Type A Engines
   - 0 engineering change orders per unit
   - 9 machine setups per unit
   - 200 units produced

   Type B Engines
   - 8 engineering change orders per unit
   - 16 machine setups per unit
   - 90 units produced

2. Determine the amount of manufacturing overhead to be assigned to each type of engine.

3. Compute the gross margin on Type A and Type B engines assuming selling prices of $2,000,000 and $2,300,000, respectively.

P 17-34

LO4

Allocation of Manufacturing Overhead with Multiple Products

Macey Sprinkling Company produces two types of pipe: (1) lawn sprinkler pipe and (2) building sprinkler pipe. Relevant information for the production of the two types of pipe for 2009 is as follows:

	Lawn Sprinkler Pipe	Building Sprinkler Pipe
Feet produced	325,000	150,000
Direct materials and direct labor costs	$243,750	$123,000
Manufacturing overhead costs:		
Utilities	$75,000	$40,000
Support staff	63,000	35,750
Quality control	8,000	4,060
Purchasing	19,200	10,250

(continued)

Macey allocates utilities and support staff costs on the basis of production volume, quality control costs on the basis of number of machine setups required, and purchasing department costs on the basis of number of purchase orders. During 2009, volume of these various activities per *product line* was:

	Lawn Sprinkler Pipe	Building Sprinkler Pipe
Production volume	325,000 feet	150,000 feet
Machine setups	12	24
Purchase orders	1	30

Required:

1. Determine the cost per unit for each cost driver.
2. Determine the amount of manufacturing overhead to be assigned to the two types of sprinkler pipe.
3. Determine the total cost for each type of pipe produced for the year.

P 17-35
LO5

Using ABC to Compute Product Cost and Make Decisions

Yosef Company makes two products—guns and butter. Production cost data are as follows:

Production volume	1,000 guns	500,000 pounds
Direct materials	$50,000	$100,000
Direct labor	$120,000	$30,000

Both the guns and the butter are manufactured in the same facility and, surprisingly, using the same equipment. The company manufactures seven different gun models and three different types of butter. Total overhead cost for the production facility was $600,000 for the most recent year. An ABC analysis of these overhead costs revealed the following:

	Overhead Cost Pools	Guns	Butter
Unit-level overhead	$200,000	4,000 hours	1,000 hours
Batch-level overhead	50,000	450 batches	50 batches
Product line overhead	250,000	7 models	3 types
	$500,000		

The hours referred to with respect to the unit-level overhead are direct labor hours. The ABC analysis indicates that direct labors hours is the best basis on which to assign this unit-level overhead. The remaining $100,000 in overhead ($600,000 total − $500,000 assigned to the overhead cost pools) was determined to be related to facility support and therefore cannot be meaningfully assigned to either product.

Total revenue from the sale of guns was $450,000. Total revenue from the sale of butter was $500,000.

Required:

Using the ABC overhead analysis, compute the following three quantities: (1) the gross profit from the sale of guns, (2) the gross profit from the sale of butter, and (3) overall company gross profit. Also, (4) estimate what gun gross profit would be if only two gun models were produced.

P 17-36
LO5

Problems from Allocating Facility Support Costs

Ashlyn Company manufactures three products. Gross margin computations for these three products for 2009 are as follows:

(continued)

	Widgets	Gidgets	Zidgets
Sales	$ 600,000	$ 525,000	$ 450,000
Direct materials	(112,500)	(37,500)	(150,000)
Direct labor	(37,500)	(150,000)	(187,500)
Manufacturing overhead*	(60,000)	(240,000)	(300,000)
Gross margin	$ 390,000	$ 97,500	$ (187,500)

*Manufacturing overhead is allocated to production based on the amount of direct labor cost.

Ashlyn has reexamined the factors that cause its manufacturing overhead costs and has discovered that $225,000 of the annual amount of manufacturing overhead is directly related to the number of product batches produced during the year. The number of batches of the three products for 2009 was as follows: Widgets, 225 batches; Gidgets, 150 batches; Zidgets, 75 batches. The remaining $375,000 in manufacturing overhead is for facility support (property taxes, security costs, general administration, etc.) and does not vary at all with levels of manufacturing activity in the company.

Required:

1. Assume that the Zidget product was eliminated at the start of the year. Estimate what the gross margin for the remaining two products would have been. Use the direct labor cost method of overhead allocation.
2. Now, assume that both the Gidget and Zidget products were eliminated at the start of the year. Estimate what the gross margin for the remaining product, Widgets, would have been. (Note that no manufacturing overhead allocation computation is needed because there is only one product.)
3. In light of your answers in parts (1) and (2), what problems can arise when facility support manufacturing overhead costs are allocated?
4. Prepare gross margin calculations for Ashlyn's three products assuming that manufacturing overhead is allocated based on the number of batches. Also, show a "total" column. Facility support costs are not to be allocated to any of the products, but are to be subtracted in the "total" column in the computation of total company operating profit.

ANALYTICAL ASSIGNMENTS

AA 17-37

DISCUSSION

Stott Knife Company

Stott Knife Company produces three models of kitchen knives: Dicer, Slicer, and CutsAll. Sales and costing information for the three models are as follows:

	Dicer	Slicer	CutsAll
Selling price per unit	$35	$65	$80
Units produced	26,000	16,000	12,000
Direct materials cost	$410,000	$215,000	$125,000
Direct labor cost	$110,000	$45,000	$35,000

In the past, manufacturing overhead has been allocated based on number of units produced. Manufacturing overhead for the period is $810,000, and the predetermined overhead rate is $15 per unit produced.

Based on this information, management has determined that the Dicer is barely breaking even. Because the market for knives is quite competitive, the price for each model is set by the market—not by management. Thus, increasing the price charged for products is not an option. As a result, management is considering discontinuing the Dicer. Before making a

(continued)

final decision, management has come to you for advice. You collect the following information regarding manufacturing overhead:

Manufacturing Overhead	Manufacturing Overhead Costs	Allocation Bases
Engineering	$125,000	Engineering changes
Quality control	375,000	Number of units produced
Manufacturing support	310,000	Number of setups
Total overhead	$810,000	

Allocation Bases	Dicer	Slicer	CutsAll
Engineering changes	2	7	6
Number of units produced	26,000	16,000	12,000
Number of setups	28	77	65

Determine the gross profit for each model under the current manufacturing overhead allocation scheme. Determine the manufacturing overhead cost for each model using the information relating to activities. Determine the gross profit for each model using the ABC allocated manufacturing overhead. What recommendation would you make to management regarding its decision to discontinue the Dicer?

AA 17-38

JUDGMENT CALL

You Decide: **Does cost information provide help in running a business, or is it only useful within the bounds of an accounting system?**

Your friends in the MBA program at your university seem to think that cost information in a company is helpful but that it is rarely used in the decision-making process within a company. One friend said, "You have to know how to work with people and manage what they do on a day-to-day basis. Cost information has its place and time, but is often not relevant. The executives in upper management have more important things to consider in running a business than the cost of products and services!" Do you agree or disagree?

AA 17-39

JUDGMENT CALL

You Decide: **Does activity-based costing (ABC) help a company revamp and improve its business operations, or is it too much of an administrative burden that takes away from the company's primary goals?**

Over the last 20 years, there have been many new developments in the area of activity-based costing (ABC). Companies strive to increase profitability by improving their products and processes. However, you are still a bit skeptical. At your current place of employment, your boss has heard about ABC and tries to meet at least every six weeks to talk about what is being done in implementing ABC and what could be improved. You don't see any benefits from the meetings. Nothing that is brought up in the meetings is ever implemented. It just seems to be an opportunity to meet with your friends and have a free lunch. Are you wasting your time?

AA 17-40

REAL COMPANY ANALYSIS

Microsoft

Microsoft, like most other companies, is continually striving to appropriately allocate costs and to increase the quality of its products. Use your knowledge of Microsoft and your understanding of the computer software industry to answer the following question.

What types of overhead costs might Microsoft incur that would be associated with its software products? Identify several cost drivers that Microsoft might consider in allocating overhead using the ABC method of overhead allocation.

AA 17-41

REAL COMPANY ANALYSIS

Deluxe Corporation

Deluxe Corporation (Deluxe) is the world's largest printer of checks as well as a provider of electronic products and services to financial institutions and retail companies. The

(continued)

company produces more of the nearly 42.5 billion checks written by American consumers and businesses annually than any other check printer. In fact, Deluxe printed enough checks in 2001 that if lined up end to end would stretch to the moon and back. The company serves nearly 1.8 million small businesses annually and provides 2 million products—each with personalized information, most within two days of receiving the order, with 98% order accuracy. Revenues in 2002 were $1.28 billion, with operating income of $214 million. Deluxe was recently ranked by *Fortune* magazine as the 936th largest U.S. company.

Although Deluxe has been profitable in all but one year since it was founded in 1915, market shifts in 1997 from paper-based to electronic transactions were causing margins to erode and revenues to decline in Deluxe's core checkprinting business. These competitive pressures brought about many changes at Deluxe in regards to management and strategy. The centerpiece of all these changes to its management process was a new measure called Deluxe value added (DVA). DVA measures the incremental profits of customers and customer segments after the costs of capital assets required to support these customers are covered. This focus on the profitability of customers was a significant change in view from the company's previous focus on the profitability of its check products.

Measurement of DVA at Deluxe requires accurate cost information. However, at the time that Deluxe adopted DVA, Deluxe's costing system was used primarily to value its check inventory for financial statement purposes. Hence, in 1997 the company decided to implement an activity-based costing (ABC) system to measure the costs of specific customers. A comprehensive project structure was put into place in order to design and implement the new ABC system. An executive sponsor provided focus, resources, and leadership and reviewed performance. A steering committee approved the project plan, established priorities, and approved ongoing progress and results. Two project managers were responsible for quality control, problem resolution, leadership, and training. Field teams consisting of full- and part-time members were responsible for executing the work plan.

A multi-phased project was initiated with a time line of six months. The plan included forming project teams, analyzing activities and linking costs to customers, analyzing customer profitability, and building a sustainable ABC information system that could be updated on a regular basis as activities and customers changed.

Answer the following questions:

1. Deluxe implemented ABC over a time period of six months. Does this time period seem too short, too long, or just right? Explain your answer.
2. Upon implementing ABC, Deluxe involved teams and groups from various departments within the company. Why do you think it was important for Deluxe to involve so many employees in its implementation of ABC?
3. Is Deluxe's approach to implementation likely to increase or decrease management's use of ABC information for decision making? Explain your answer.

Source: Adapted from P. B. B. Turney, "Deluxe Corporation: Activity-Based Costing," University of Virginia Darden School Foundation (1999).

AA 17-42   **Minuteman Enterprises**

ETHICS

You are the controller for Minuteman Enterprises, a manufacturer of rocket booster engines and various aerospace products. Though there are many commercial customers for most of the company's products, the federal government is the only buyer of your rocket booster engines. Because you are the only provider for the engines, the government has agreed to buy these engines at a price equal to your cost plus a 10% markup.

As the controller, you have recently been studying the accuracy of your product costs. Traditionally, manufacturing overhead has been allocated on the basis of direct labor hours. Using this method, rocket boosters have borne a high percentage of manufacturing overhead because they take many more direct labor hours than do the other products.

You have just been presented an analysis by one of your staff members that shows that direct labor hours is not a very relevant base for allocating manufacturing overhead costs.

(continued)

Rather, she has made a very convincing case that manufacturing overhead should be allocated using activity-based costing with multiple cost drivers. Using her suggested approach, however, you discover that the rocket boosters bear a much smaller portion of manufacturing overhead costs, and therefore, the total cost of the boosters is considerably less than the amount you had been using to determine the price charged to the government.

You know that her calculations using ABC are likely more accurate than the current cost allocation method and that the commercial products should bear a larger amount of manufacturing overhead costs. Yet, you also know that by using ABC and the more accurate cost drivers, your profits from both the boosters and the commercial products will be reduced.

1. What should you do?
2. Is it ethical to continue to allocate manufacturing overhead costs on the basis of direct labor hours?
3. Would it be ethical to use direct labor hours if that were the basis used by other government contractors?
4. If you decide to switch to ABC, should you inform the government that you have overcharged it and return the excess profits?

AA 17-43
WRITING

Advantages and Disadvantages of ABC

Your boss recently attended a conference where activity-based costing was discussed. She is intrigued by the ABC concept and wonders if the company is appropriately costing its products. Your company produces and sells four different styles of briefcases. The production process differs for each briefcase, as different features require different equipment. She returns from the conference and asks you to summarize the advantages and disadvantages of ABC. Your assignment is to write a two-page memo addressing these issues.

AA 17-44
DEBATE

ABC or Bust!

As the text indicates, activity-based costing has received much attention from businesses around the world. Yet some firms still resist adopting an ABC system, and others have adopted ABC and then reverted to their more traditional costing systems. Divide your group into two teams and prepare five-minute presentations defending the following positions:

- Team One is "In Support of ABC." Your team's task is to identify the benefits of using an activity-based product costing system. Briefly explain the advantages that a company will realize if it adopts ABC.
- Team Two is "In Support of Tradition." Your team's task is to identify the benefits of using a more traditional product costing system based on, for example, direct labor hours. Explain the advantages of a traditional system that cause many firms to still choose it over ABC.

Management Accounting Topics and Costing

Imagine that one of your parents has traveled across the country to visit you at college. As the two of you have dinner together at one of your favorite restaurants, the discussion turns to your accounting class. You begin describing some of the new ideas and techniques you have been learning lately. Suddenly, your parent wants to talk about the family business. As the discussion goes on, it become clear that your parent is expecting you to provide some specific ideas about how to improve the management process in the family business using current accounting methods. You certainly want to impress your parent with all the detailed knowledge that you have gained since beginning your course work in accounting. However, you are also concerned that you may describe something incorrectly or say something misleading. One day you expect to run the family business, and you would hate to say anything during dinner that might later cause problems in the company!

Required:

You need to respond to your parent using insights gained from the first three management accounting chapters (Chapters 15-17). Further, answering your parent's questions will require you to carefully construct your remarks in light of the exact nature of the family business. Hence, we will assume three separate types of businesses for your family:

1. Computer manufacturing plant
2. Large architectural firm
3. Neighborhood grocery store

Part A

Listed below are a number of topics from Chapters 15 and 16. Briefly describe in three sentences or less how each topic may relate to the family business.

1. Direct materials costs
2. Direct labor costs
3. Overhead costs
4. Inventory
5. Job order costing
6. Process costing

Part B

For only the company types 1 and 2 above (computer manufacturing plant and large architectural firm), describe how activity-based costing (presented in Chapter 17) can be used to better understand the costs associated with the company's products or services. Identify specific production departments for each of these two company types and describe how each department generates costs or revenues for the company. Also, identify specific drivers for those departments that may help to effectively assign overhead costs.

© HISHAM F IBRAHIM/PHOTODISC GREEN/GETTY IMAGES INC.

Budgeting and Control

(1) Describe the importance of personal budgeting. *Personal budgeting is an important activity for those individuals who wish to successfully control their spending and their future. Those who budget have more freedom in how, where, and when they spend their money.*

(2) Explain the budgeting process and its behavioral implications in organizations. *Budgeting is based on long-term strategy and a careful understanding of its behavioral implications in the organization. The budgeting process should be a combination of the efficiency of top-down budgeting and the motivational benefits of bottom-up budgeting.*

(3) Construct an operations budget and its components for manufacturing firms. *The operations budget is at the core of the master budget for a manufacturing company. The budgeting process begins with a forecast of sales. This sales forecast is then used to plan when the units will be produced and when selling and administrative expenses will be incurred. The production plan allows budgeting of raw materials purchases, direct labor costs, and manufacturing overhead.*

(4) Compare the operations budget for a manufacturing firm to that of a merchandising or service firm. *Operations budgets for merchandising firms and service firms differ from manufacturing firms only to the extent that merchants purchase goods to sell instead of manufacturing goods to sell, and service providers can generally combine their sales budgets and production budgets into the same budget.*

EXPANDED material

(5) Distinguish between static and flexible budgets. *Flexible budgeting is a process of adjusting the original static budget to reflect the costs that should have been incurred for the sales and production volumes that actually took place. The idea of variable and fixed costs is important in constructing a flexible budget.*

(6) Create the cash budget. *Information in other budgets is used to forecast the amount and timing of cash receipts and cash payments. Careful comparison of these budgeted amounts allows a company to forecast its financing needs (if any).*

(7) Prepare pro-forma financial statements. *Pro-forma financial statements are budgeted, or forecasted, financial statements. Because financial statements must articulate, or tie together, in a specific way (for example, net income is used to compute retained earnings in the balance sheet), construction of pro-forma financial statements is a good way to ensure that all of the company's budgets are internally consistent.*

Every organization needs to budget. Budgets help allocate resources effectively so that the organization can accomplish its mission. Consider how the federal government budgets, for example. The arrival of the president's budget on Capitol Hill signals the beginning of the annual budget process in Congress—a process that can last more than eight months and require the passage of scores of bills and resolutions.[1] Congress drafts a budget resolution—a spending plan that defines in broad terms how much the government will take in through taxes and other receipts and spend on all government accounts during the coming fiscal year. Both the House and Senate have their own budget committees, and each committee drafts its own version of a budget resolution. The committees bring the drafts to their respective chambers for approval, iron out differences in conference, and return the resulting version to their chambers for adoption. It's a back and forth process that takes a lot of effort! The budget resolution serves as a blueprint for congressional spending decisions. It sets the total levels for budget authority, outlays, incoming revenues, loan obligations, and loan guarantee commitments, as well as the public debt ceiling for the upcoming fiscal year.

For example, the 2007 federal budget is broken down as follows:

Spending Category	Amount*	Percentage of Total
Social Security	$ 581 billion	21.0%
Defense	503	18.2
Other Discretionary (Education, Transportation, etc.)	492	17.8
Medicare	387	14.0
Other Mandatory (Agriculture, Interior, etc.)	320	11.6
Interest on Debt	247	8.9
Health and Human Services	205	7.4
Homeland Security	34	1.2
Total	$2,769 billion	100.0%

*Amounts reflect estimates provided in fiscal year 2007. Available at **http://www.whitehouse.gov/omb/budget**.

As you can see, a significant portion of the budget goes to pay interest on the national debt. However, given that between $200 and $400 billion in budget deficits are predicted in each of the six years beginning with 2006 (see Exhibit 1 on the next page), you can probably expect this cost to grow.

Budgeting probably consumes more congressional time than any other single activity.

However, even though you may argue that Congress and the President have not been as fiscally responsible as they could have been, you should be comforted that the budgeting process instills some discipline in their spending habits and provides a sense of order for governmental expenditures and management of programs.

budget

A quantitative expression of a plan of action that shows how a firm or an organization will acquire and use resources over some specified period of time.

A budget is a quantitative expression of a plan of action that shows how a firm, an organization (such as the government in the opening scenario), or an individual will acquire and use resources over a specified period of time. For a firm, implicit in most budgets is management's expectation of earning sufficient profit to provide a reasonable return on investment. The budget identifies and allocates resources necessary to effectively and efficiently carry out the mission of the organization. Although budgeting may sound to you like an unappealing activity (maybe you have tried budgeting your personal expenditures),

---

[1] Further information on the federal budget process can be obtained from **http://www.rules.house.gov/budget_pro.htm**.

EXHIBIT 1	U.S. Federal Government Estimated Annual Budget*

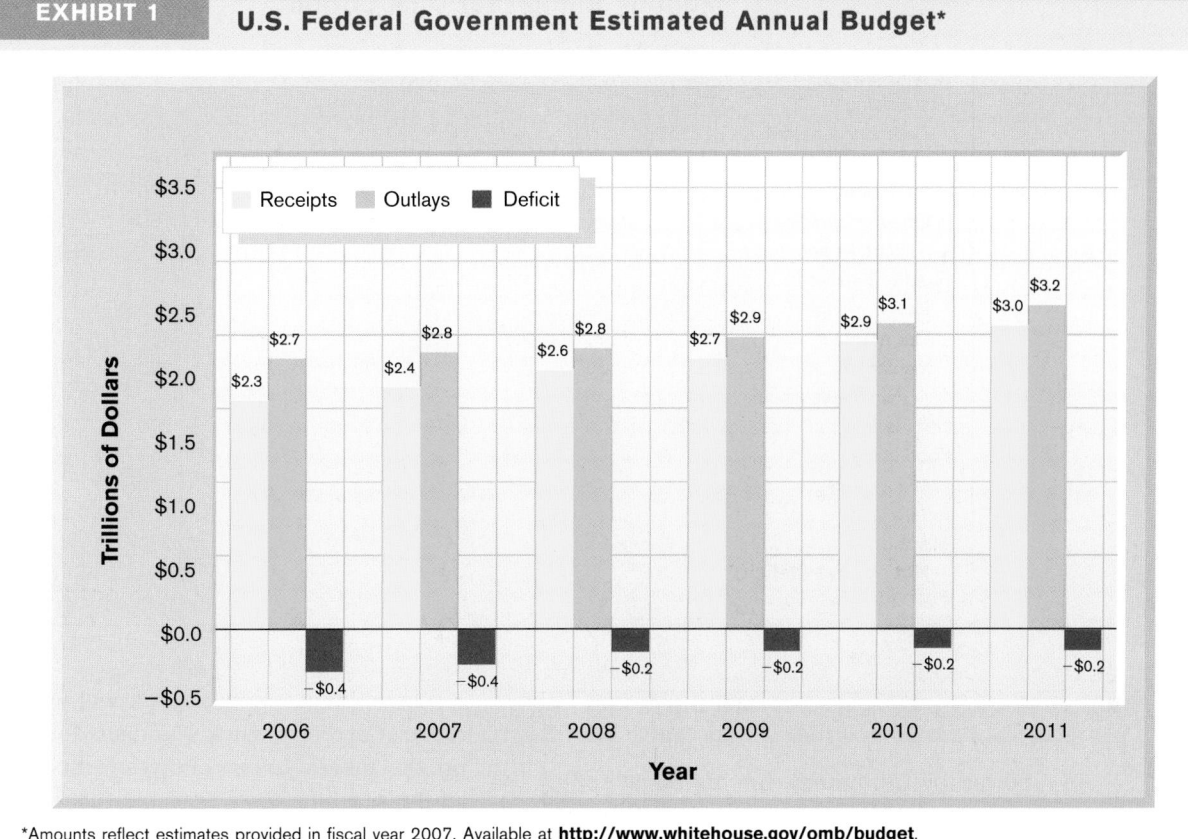

*Amounts reflect estimates provided in fiscal year 2007. Available at **http://www.whitehouse.gov/omb/budget**.

SETTING THE STAGE

successful budgeting is absolutely critical to the success of a business. In this chapter, we will briefly touch on personal budgeting and then cover budgeting for manufacturing, merchandising, and service firms.

Purposes of Personal Budgeting

Describe the importance of personal budgeting.

1 Whether we're talking about an individual, a family, or a large organization, the overall purpose of a budget is to clearly establish a plan so that performance in relation to a goal can be carefully monitored. Thus, budgeting has a twofold purpose. The first purpose is to allow individuals or companies to develop a plan to meet a specified goal. The second purpose is to allow ongoing comparison between actual results and the plan in order to better control operations or activities. To illustrate, let us assume that Dick Cotton earns $3,600 a month (and takes home only $2,390 after taxes) and has prepared a budget of his income and expenses.

The budget in Exhibit 2 contains an important warning that spending is exceeding earnings. The commitment of $1,700 to fixed expenses leaves only $690 to cover all of Dick's necessary expenditures for utilities, food, clothing, and the like. Because Dick cannot cover these expenditures using his **disposable income** of $690 a month, he must revise his plans; perhaps he could ask for a raise, get a second job or a new job that pays more, or decrease his spending. This simple illustration shows that budgeting is extremely important. Unless Dick takes corrective action, he will soon join the growing number of individuals declaring bankruptcy.

disposable income

Income left after withholdings and fixed expenses have been subtracted from gross salary; the amount left to cover variable expenditures.

EXHIBIT 2	Monthly Budget for Dick Cotton		
Gross salary			$ 3,600
Withholdings:			
Federal income taxes		$ 600	
State income taxes		180	
FICA taxes		270	
Other withholdings		160	(1,210)
Net take-home pay			$ 2,390
Fixed expenses:			
House mortgage		$1,100	
Car payment		350	
Insurance		250	(1,700)
Disposable income			$ 690
Utilities		$ 200	
Food		400	
Clothing		100	
Entertainment		100	
Miscellaneous		200	(1,000)
Net surplus (deficit)			$ (310)

FYI

As reported by **CNNMoney.com**, personal consumer bankruptcy filings soared nearly 32% to just over 2 million in 2005. That's one personal bankruptcy filing for every 53 households in the United States.

In addition, someday Dick will want to retire. Currently, Dick's budget does not provide for any savings or investments. With all the planning tools available today, such as tax-sheltered retirement plans, investments, annuities, and so forth, an individual who plans and budgets well can prepare adequately for the future. Unfortunately, at his present rate, Dick will not be one of these individuals.

Indeed, the penalty for not budgeting is severe. Individuals who budget successfully typically find that they can purchase those things that they feel they really want to have. In fact, budgeting does not really limit spending. The only real difference between individuals who budget and those who don't is that those who budget will spend money how, where, and when they want to, and those who do not budget often feel like they never have enough money to purchase those things that they really need.

Are you wondering which category you fall into—those who successfully budget or those who don't? Review these characteristics of good personal budgeters and see how you compare.

- Understand debt and interest
- Disciplined
- Flexible
- Organized
- Good communicator (especially important if married)
- Proactive
- Goal-driven

REMEMBER THIS...

This section of the chapter is simply intended to alert you to the importance of creating and following a personal budget. If you do, you will be able to plan your spending and be better prepared for the future. To be successful with your personal budget, you need to be:

- goal oriented
- organized
- proactive
- disciplined

The Budgeting Process in Organizations

Explain the budgeting process and its behavioral implications in organizations.

(2) Budgeting is critical to the management planning process. There are two basic types of planning: (1) long-run planning, which includes strategic planning and capital budgeting, and (2) short-run planning, which includes production and process prioritizing and operations budgeting or profit planning. Long-run planning involves making strategic decisions where the effects will extend several years into the future. Long-run strategic planning takes place at the executive level in an organization and involves identifying the organization's mission, the goals flowing from that mission, and the strategies and actions that will be taken to accomplish those goals. With strategic planning in place, the company can then plan for the purchase and use of major assets such as buildings or equipment to help the company meet its long-range goals. This type of planning, which you will study in Chapter 22, is called capital budgeting.

Once the organization's strategic decisions involving key products, markets, production facilities, and financial resources are in place, managers are then able to focus on operating plans for the immediate month, quarter, and year. This short-run operational planning can be divided into two categories. First, with the capital structure in place (land, buildings, equipment, management personnel, etc.), managers need to determine how to best use those committed resources to maximize profit. This process will be discussed later in Chapter 21. Once the organization has established its production priorities, managers are ready to go to the second category of short-run planning—operations budgeting. Sometimes known as profit plans, operations budgets are used by managers to establish and communicate daily, weekly, and monthly goals for the organization. We'll use the remainder of this chapter to study the process of operations budgeting for manufacturers, merchants, and service companies. Failure to carefully perform strategic planning, capital budgeting, or budgeting for operations can have adverse consequences for organizations, even to the point of causing bankruptcy. The list of companies that have

FYI

Although budgeting is very helpful for internal decision making, organizations are often required to provide detailed budgets before bankers will loan money. When companies declare bankruptcy and are taken over by court-ordered trustees, one of the trustee's first steps is to prepare detailed budgets. These budgets help to determine whether the company should cease operations and liquidate (known as a Chapter 7 bankruptcy), or whether the trustee should ask the court to give the company time to work through its financial problems so that it can fully or partially repay its debts (known as a Chapter 11 bankruptcy). Overall, 80 public companies filed for Chapter 11 protection in 2005, with combined asset values of nearly $134 billion. By contrast, 2004 saw 92 comparatively smaller public company Chapter 11 cases, with aggregate asset values of only $47.7 billion.

budget committee

A management group responsible for establishing budgeting policy and for coordinating the preparation of budgets.

failed in recent years as a result of poor planning and execution is getting longer each day.

Budgeting is such an important activity that the top executives of most companies coordinate and participate in the process. Large firms usually establish a **budget committee**, which may include among its members the vice presidents for sales, production, purchasing, and finance and the controller or chief financial officer. These executives work to implement the organization's strategy by coordinating the preparation of a detailed budget in their areas of responsibility and then together oversee the integration of a comprehensive master budget for the firm. Two important issues faced by executives in the budgeting process are:

1. Behavioral considerations, and
2. Involvement in preparing the budget.

Behavioral Considerations

Research has shown that several behavioral factors determine how successful the budgeting process will be. First, the process must have the support of top management. Without a clear indication from top management that the budgeting process is important to the organization, managers will not be motivated to devote the time necessary to formulate an effective and efficient budget.

Second, managers and other employees are more motivated to achieve budget goals that they understand and helped design. For this process to work, managers must feel that their opinions are respected and given full consideration. In addition, this communication and participation process should remain open throughout the year. When internal or external circumstances change, all parties involved should discuss the necessary budget adjustments. Generally, the most effective companies are those that involve employees in the decision-making process. However, as you'll see in the next section, involving a lot of employees adds significant time and cost to the budgeting process.

Third, deviations (also known as variances) from the budget must be addressed by managers in a positive and constructive manner. Identifying deviations from the plan is simply a way to focus management's attention on areas needing improvement. Unfortunately, some managers treat these deviations as an opportunity to find fault and assign blame to lower-level managers. The result is usually a loss of motivation, accompanied by such dysfunctional behavior as interdepartmental bickering, defensive attitudes, and overall unethical behavior. One output of such behavior is **budgetary slack** in the budget system; that is, intentionally creating an easy budget target that a manager is certain he or she can meet.

Obviously, all these behaviors waste an organization's resources and do not contribute to meeting its strategic and operational goals. A more useful reaction to deviations is to focus on the action to be taken. As one CEO stated, "I never made a dime for the company by assessing blame or firing a manager. If I can provide help to a manager to solve a problem, though, we can see the benefit." In administering the budget process, it is extremely important that top management not use the budget as a "club" or "whipping stick."

budgetary slack

The process of inflating a department's budget request for resource inputs (e.g., materials, labor, time, etc.) or deflating the department's budget commitment to output (products, services, sales, etc.) so that the department manager can more easily achieve the budget.

Involvement in Preparing the Budget: Top-Down versus Bottom-Up

A firm-wide operations budget could be prepared by top management, distributed to the major segments of the firm, and then further spread out to each lower-level segment manager. This is the top-down approach. Its proponents argue that only top management knows the strategic direction of the firm and is aware of all the external factors influencing its operations. Further, since top management involves only a few people who have risen to positions where they should no longer have special interests to protect, they are in the best position to efficiently coordinate the competing needs of the segments.

participative budgeting

A bottom-up approach to budgeting that involves the full cooperation and participation of managers at all levels of the organization.

The alternative is the bottom-up approach, also known as **participative budgeting**. Essentially, each division manager in a bottom-up approach prepares a budget request for his or her segment. These requests are combined and reviewed as they move up the organization hierarchy, with adjustments being made to coordinate the needs and goals of individual units with the overall organization. Proponents of this approach contend that segment managers have the best information on the products or services they provide, the customers they serve, and the technology that is emerging; they are, therefore, in the best position to identify segment needs and to weigh alternative courses of action. More importantly, as mentioned earlier, managers who have a role in setting segment goals are more motivated to achieve these goals. It is also good training for managers to develop their planning skills in preparation for promotions to positions of greater authority. Naturally, the organization also benefits when its managers are proficient in planning. However, the bottom-up approach is very costly and time-intensive when compared to the top-down approach. In order to achieve personal goals, participants may also engage in political maneuvering that creates budgetary slack and other problems in the budgeting system.

Because both top-down and bottom-up are legitimate approaches, most organizations use some combination of the two. The budget committee members know the strategic direction of the firm and the important external factors that affect it, so they prepare a set of planning guidelines that are communicated to lower-level managers. These guidelines include such things as a forecast of key economic variables and their potential impact on the firm, plans for introducing and advertising new products, and some broad sales targets and resource allocations. With these guidelines in mind, lower-level managers prepare their individual budgets. These budgets are always reviewed to be sure they are consistent with the objectives of other segments and of the company as a whole. The budget committee understands that, from a behavioral point of view, any changes to a manager's budget should be made with great care. This is not to suggest that changes should not be made, only that reasons for those changes should be substantial and should be discussed with the managers involved.

The blending of these two approaches will vary among organizations. A smaller organization with few management levels will rely more on the top-down approach than a larger organization. Top management in smaller organizations tends to be more knowledgeable about and more involved in the operating details.

REMEMBER THIS...

- Budgeting in most organizations is based on that organization's long-term strategic plan and capital budget.
- The behavioral factors that contribute to the success of the operations budgeting process include:
  - The support of top management
  - The participation of all managers in the budgeting process
  - The need to address deviations from the budget in a positive and constructive manner
- Poor budgeting processes create dysfunctional behavior in the organization. One type of dysfunctional behavior is budgetary slack, which represents an effort by employees to build for themselves a "cushion" of higher budgeted costs and lower budgeted revenues.
- With the top-down approach to budgeting, top management prepares the entire budget. With bottom-up budgeting, each segment manager makes budget requests. Most firms use a combination of the two approaches.

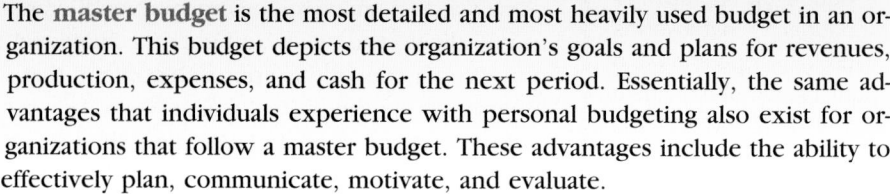

The Master Budget

Construct an
operations budget
and its components
for manufacturing
firms.

(3) The **master budget** is the most detailed and most heavily used budget in an organization. This budget depicts the organization's goals and plans for revenues, production, expenses, and cash for the next period. Essentially, the same advantages that individuals experience with personal budgeting also exist for organizations that follow a master budget. These advantages include the ability to effectively plan, communicate, motivate, and evaluate.

master budget

A network of many
separate schedules and
budgets that together
constitute the overall
operating and financing
plan for the coming
period.

The master budget is an integrated group of detailed budgets that together constitute the overall operating and financing plans for a specific time period. In a manufacturing firm, the master budget begins with a forecast of sales; is followed by detailed budgets for the production, selling, administrative, and financial activities; and culminates in a set of pro-forma (or budgeted) financial statements. The flow of the preparation of the individual budgets within this master budget network is shown in Exhibit 3. Notice that the budgeting process is based on the long-term strategic and short-term operational plans established by top management. Also note how the capital budgeting process fits into the master budget. The final items forming the financial budget include the capital expenditures budget (or the capital budget), the cash budget, and the budgeted or pro-forma financial statements. Preparing the cash budget and the pro-forma statements is discussed in the expanded material of this chapter. (You will study capital budgeting later in Chapter 22.)

STOP & THINK

Review Exhibit 3 carefully because we will follow these budget schedules in sequence in the next sections of this chapter. Consider each budget and think for a moment about how it feeds into the subsequent budget.

To help explain these steps, we will illustrate the budgeting process in a manufacturing firm using an integrated example of budgets for the Sunbird Boat Company, a manufacturer of small fishing boats. Because it is important that you understand the budgeting process, you should work through the calculations of each budget schedule. Be sure to keep in mind that this formalized budgeting activity forces management to make many important decisions that guide

a company toward its goals—decisions involving scheduling, pricing, borrowing, investing, and cost control.

Budgeting for Operations in a Manufacturing Firm

Our first illustration of the budgeting process is for Sunbird Boat Company, a manufacturing company that makes fishing boats. The boats are made of fiberglass and wood. To help us move through this example more quickly, we will assume that Sunbird only makes one type of boat—a 15-foot fishing boat. Exhibit 4 contains Sunbird's actual balance sheet for 2008. This is our beginning point for creating Sunbird's 2009 operations budget. In explaining the budgeting for Sunbird Boat Company, we will begin with the sales budget and then discuss each budget identified in Exhibit 3.

sales budget

A schedule of projected
sales over the budget
period.

Sales Budget The first step in developing a master budget is to prepare a **sales budget**. As shown in Exhibit 3, all the other budgets are developed from this budget. Projecting accurate sales is very difficult, however, because sales are a function of both uncontrollable external variables (customer tastes and economic conditions, for example) and controllable internal variables (such as price, sales effort, and advertising expenditures).

EXHIBIT 3   The Master Budget

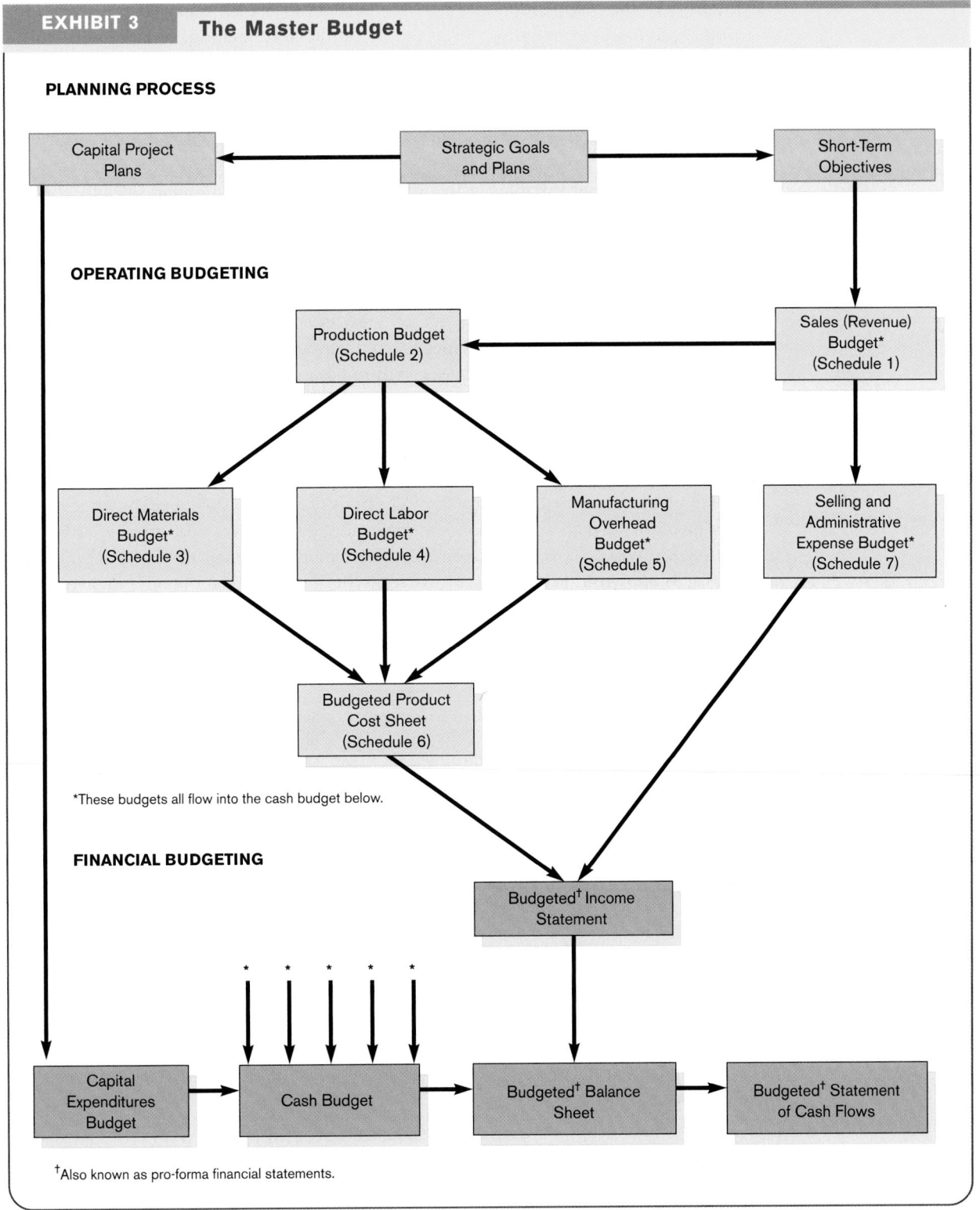

PLANNING PROCESS

Capital Project Plans ← Strategic Goals and Plans → Short-Term Objectives

OPERATING BUDGETING

Production Budget (Schedule 2) ← Sales (Revenue) Budget* (Schedule 1)

Direct Materials Budget* (Schedule 3)

Direct Labor Budget* (Schedule 4)

Manufacturing Overhead Budget* (Schedule 5)

Selling and Administrative Expense Budget* (Schedule 7)

Budgeted Product Cost Sheet (Schedule 6)

*These budgets all flow into the cash budget below.

FINANCIAL BUDGETING

Budgeted† Income Statement

Capital Expenditures Budget → Cash Budget → Budgeted† Balance Sheet → Budgeted† Statement of Cash Flows

†Also known as pro-forma financial statements.

Uncontrollable external factors driving sales include the following:

- The business environment, which includes current government policies and law, the status of the economy, demographics (characteristics of the population such as age, wealth, family status, etc.), and the state of technology.
- Customer needs and tastes with respect to the product or service being analyzed and other substitute products.

- Intensity of the competition and possible barriers to market entry (barriers can include technology copyrights, government contracts, reputation, or large sales volumes that provide economies of scale).
- Seasonal cycles creating abrupt changes in sales demand due to holidays or weather patterns.
- Unexpected events such as droughts, hurricanes, and earthquakes.

Analysis of external variables is accomplished through research and sales forecasting techniques. These techniques may be as simple as having the sales staff ask major customers about their buying plans for the next year or as sophisticated as statistical market research techniques. Some firms use quantitative forecasting models—these range from simple growth rate trends derived from the past year's sales to complex forecasting models that attempt to measure the influence of many economic and industry variables. Data used to drive these analyses are obtained from a variety of sources.

For purposes of this illustration, we will not go further into the details about the development of data for the sales budget. This is an important topic for your coursework in marketing and strategy. At this point, let's assume that Sunbird Boat Company has projected 2009 sales to be 100 boats. The anticipated sales price for each boat is $10,000.

Most organizations divide their yearly sales budget into monthly, weekly, or even daily budgets in order to plan production schedules and cash flows more precisely. For our illustration, we will assume that Sunbird Boat Company projects its boat sales on a quarterly basis, as shown in Schedule 1. However, whether the budget is on a quarterly or a daily basis, the concepts we're going to talk about are the same.

EXHIBIT 4	Sunbird Boat Company 2008 Balance Sheet

Sunbird Boat Company
Balance Sheet (Actual)
December 31, 2008

Assets

Current assets:			
Cash		$ 137,000	
Accounts receivable		60,000	
Direct materials inventory[1]		8,000	
Finished goods inventory[2]		50,000	$ 255,000
Long-term assets:			
Land		$ 231,500	
Building and equipment		1,500,000	
Less accumulated depreciation		(120,000)	1,611,500
Total assets			$1,866,500

Liabilities & Stockholders' Equity

Current liabilities:			
Accounts payable[3]		$ 10,000	
Income taxes payable[3]		96,000	$ 106,000
Stockholders' equity:			
Common stock, $5 par		$1,000,000	
Paid-in capital in excess of par		250,000	
Retained earnings		510,500	1,760,500
Total liabilities & stockholders' equity			$1,866,500

[1]Composed of 600 board feet of lumber and 400 square feet of fiberglass.
[2]Composed of 10 finished boats.
[3]Expected to be paid in the first quarter of 2009.

SCHEDULE 1

Schedule 1
Sunbird Boat Company
2009 Sales Budget

	Q1	Q2	Q3	Q4	Total
Sales volume	20 boats	40 boats	30 boats	10 boats	100 boats
Price	×$ 10,000	×$ 10,000	×$ 10,000	×$ 10,000	×$ 10,000
Revenue earned	$200,000	$400,000	$300,000	$100,000	$1,000,000
Received in current quarter	× 80%	× 80%	× 80%	× 80%	
Current revenue collected	$160,000	$320,000	$240,000	$ 80,000	$ 800,000
Prior revenue collected*	60,000	40,000	80,000	60,000	240,000
Collections from customers	$220,000	$360,000	$320,000	$140,000	$1,040,000

*Prior revenue collected in Q1 (Quarter 1) represents the accounts receivable balance from the 2008 balance sheet. Prior revenue collected in Q2 through Q4 represents the revenue not collected in the prior quarter (i.e., revenue earned in prior quarter times 20%).

As you can see in Schedule 1, the sales budget that we are creating for Sunbird is computing two important numbers. First, we can assume that the marketing department for Sunbird has effectively researched all the relevant variables in order to predict the number of boats that will be sold each quarter. These numbers are used to determine the budgeted sales revenue that Sunbird expects to recognize. However, remember that this revenue still needs to be collected because at least some boats are sold on account. Based on past experience, Sunbird is able to collect approximately 80% of revenue from customers in the quarter in which the sale took place, with the remaining 20% collected in the following quarter. Happily, in this example, Sunbird doesn't expect to have any uncollectible accounts. Using this information, Sunbird is able to budget the level of cash collections from customers for each quarter. Take a moment to study Schedule 1 in order to understand exactly how Sunbird is computing cash collections.

production budget

A schedule of production requirements for the budget period.

STOP & THINK

Sunbird plans to keep its inventory level of boats at 50% of next quarter's sales. That is a lot of inventory! Why do you think that Sunbird follows this kind of an inventory policy?

CAUTION

Note that the entries in the Total column do not always equal the sum of the four quarters. For example, the beginning inventory balance in Schedule 2 is the same for the year as it is for the first quarter. Similarly, the ending inventory balance is the same for the year as it is for the fourth quarter. Be sure to watch for similar patterns in subsequent budget schedules.

Production Budget The second detailed budget (Schedule 2) covers production, the number of units to be produced during the period. Factors to be considered in preparing this **production budget** are projected sales volume for the period, the desired amount of ending inventory, and the amount of inventory already on hand in the beginning inventory.

Ending inventory is an important figure because management wants enough units on hand to meet customer demands, but not so many that unnecessary costs will be incurred because of excessive inventory. For our work in this chapter, the desired ending inventory for any period will be expressed as a percentage of the following period's expected sales volume. Let's assume that Sunbird Boat Company has determined that its desired ending inventory for each quarter should be approximately 50% of projected

STOP & THINK

Using a concept called just-in-time (JIT) inventory management, some companies are able to remove all, or nearly all, of the inventory from their organization. As you work through the operations budget for Sunbird, you may realize that the removal of inventory from this organization would change the budget schedules we're building. In particular, think carefully about Sunbird's production budget (Schedule 2). Would this budget be needed if Sunbird had a JIT inventory system? (We'll discuss JIT management systems in Chapter 23.)

sales for the next quarter. The fourth quarter's ending inventory is 15 boats, which is 50% of the next quarter's (first quarter of 2010) expected sales.

The production budget (Schedule 2) supplies information needed for all manufacturing cost budgets. Only after production quantities are known can management determine the amount of direct materials, direct labor, and manufacturing overhead needed during the period. As you study Schedule 2, do you see how the expected levels of beginning and ending inventory affect the level of production budgeted for each quarter? Hence, budgeted production levels are different from the budgeted levels of sales volumes.

SCHEDULE 2

Schedule 2
Sunbird Boat Company
2009 Production Budget

	Q1	Q2	Q3	Q4	Total
Sales volume (Schedule 1)	20 boats	40 boats	30 boats	10 boats	100 boats
Desired ending inventory[1]	20 boats	15 boats	5 boats	15 boats	15 boats
Total boats needed	40 boats	55 boats	35 boats	25 boats	115 boats
Less beginning inventory[2]	(10 boats)	(20 boats)	(15 boats)	(5 boats)	(10 boats)
Total boats to produce	30 boats	35 boats	20 boats	20 boats	105 boats

[1]Sunbird desires to have ending boat inventory equal to 50% of the expected sales volume for the following quarter. Sunbird's marketing department forecasts sales of 30 boats during the first quarter of 2010.
[2]Sunbird's beginning finished goods inventory for 2009 is 10 boats. Beginning inventory for Q2 through Q4 is equal to the ending inventory for the prior quarter.

direct materials budget

A schedule of direct materials to be used during the budget period and direct materials to be purchased during that period.

Direct Materials Budget   The next detailed budget to be prepared is the **direct materials budget** (Schedule 3). Based on the engineering department's estimates of the materials required to make a boat, this budget helps management schedule purchases from suppliers. Sunbird's engineers estimate that the standard amounts of wood and fiberglass needed per boat are as follows:

	15-Foot Boat
Direct materials requirements:	
Wood	100 board feet
Fiberglass	40 square feet

Sunbird's purchasing agent has been able to purchase wood at $10 per board foot and fiberglass at $5 per square foot. The purchasing agent expects that these prices will continue to be available to Sunbird through 2009.

Based on these requirements for materials, the direct materials budget for Sunbird Boat Company for 2009 is shown in Schedule 3. Similar to the production budget (Schedule

SCHEDULE 3

Schedule 3
Sunbird Boat Company
2009 Direct Materials Budget

Wood	Q1	Q2	Q3	Q4	Total
Production volume (Schedule 2)	30 boats	35 boats	20 boats	20 boats	105 boats
Standard feet per boat	× 100 feet	× 100 feet	× 100 feet	× 100 feet	× 100 feet
Wood needed in production	3,000 feet	3,500 feet	2,000 feet	2,000 feet	10,500 feet
Desired ending inventory[1]	1,050 feet	600 feet	600 feet	900 feet	900 feet
Total wood needed	4,050 feet	4,100 feet	2,600 feet	2,900 feet	11,400 feet
Less beginning inventory[2]	(600) feet	(1,050) feet	(600) feet	(600) feet	(600) feet
Total wood to purchase	3,450 feet	3,050 feet	2,000 feet	2,300 feet	10,800 feet
Standard purchase price	× $10	× $10	× $10	× $10	× $10
Wood purchases	$34,500	$30,500	$20,000	$23,000	$108,000

Fiberglass	Q1	Q2	Q3	Q4	Total
Production volume (Schedule 2)	30 boats	35 boats	20 boats	20 boats	105 boats
Standard feet per boat	× 40 feet	× 40 feet	× 40 feet	× 40 feet	× 40 feet
Fiberglass needed in production	1,200 feet	1,400 feet	800 feet	800 feet	4,200 feet
Desired ending inventory[1]	700 feet	400 feet	400 feet	600 feet	600 feet
Total fiberglass needed	1,900 feet	1,800 feet	1,200 feet	1,400 feet	4,800 feet
Less beginning inventory[2]	(400) feet	(700) feet	(400) feet	(400) feet	(400) feet
Total fiberglass to purchase	1,500 feet	1,100 feet	800 feet	1,000 feet	4,400 feet
Standard purchase price	× $5	× $5	× $5	× $5	× $5
Fiberglass purchases	$ 7,500	$ 5,500	$ 4,000	$ 5,000	$ 22,000

Total	Q1	Q2	Q3	Q4	Total
Total materials purchases	$42,000	$36,000	$24,000	$28,000	$130,000
Paid in current quarter	× 75%	× 75%	× 75%	× 75%	× 75%
Current purchase payments	$31,500	$27,000	$18,000	$21,000	$ 97,500
Prior purchase payments[3]	10,000	10,500	9,000	6,000	35,500
Payments to suppliers	$41,500	$37,500	$27,000	$27,000	$133,000

[1]Sunbird desires to have ending raw materials inventory equal to 30% of the wood and 50% of the fiberglass needed to support production volume for the following quarter. Sunbird's production volume for the first quarter of 2010 is expected to be 30 boats.

[2]Sunbird's beginning raw materials inventory for 2009 is 600 board feet of wood and 400 square feet of fiberglass. Beginning inventory for Q2 through Q4 is equal to the ending inventory for the prior quarter.

[3]Prior purchase payments in Q1 represent the accounts payable balance from the 2008 balance sheet. Prior purchase payments in Q2 through Q4 represent the purchases not paid for in the prior quarter (i.e., total materials purchases in prior quarter times 25%).

 CAUTION

Schedule 3 looks like a big, complicated budget. However, don't be put off by it. One reason for its size is that Sunbird has two types of raw materials in its boats, but the purchases budget is the same for both types of materials. Hence, if you understand the budget for wood purchases, then you understand the budget for fiberglass purchases and you can skip down to the final area of Schedule 3 where cash payments are budgeted.

2), the materials needed are based on production and on ending inventories. Then the materials needed are then adjusted for the beginning inventory expected for each quarter. Like the production budget, the desired level of ending inventory has a big impact on the direct materials budget. If management does not maintain sufficient materials inventory levels, the production process could be held up; if inventories are too high, inventory investment and storage costs can get out of control. Therefore, Sunbird's management has decided to maintain a supply of 30% and 50% of the next quarter's production requirements for wood and fiberglass, respectively.

Finally, as is typical in most supplier relationships, Sunbird does not pay for raw materials at the time of the purchase, which means that Sunbird maintains an accounts payable balance. Sunbird's policy is to pay for 75% of its raw materials purchases in the current quarter, and the remaining 25% in the subsequent quarter. Based on this payment policy, Sunbird is able to adjust the total purchases in Schedule 3 to compute the cash payments made to suppliers in each quarter (similar to the approach used to compute cash payments received from customers in the sales budget in Schedule 1).

direct labor budget

A schedule of direct labor requirements for the budget period.

Direct Labor Budget   The fourth budget in the master budget is the **direct labor budget** (Schedule 4). The direct labor budget for Sunbird Boat Company is based on an average hourly wage rate of $20 per hour for production workers and 80 labor hours to make a 15-foot boat. In our example, the $20 per-hour wage rate includes fringe benefits (i.e., the cost of sick leave, vacation pay, insurance, etc.) and payroll taxes.[2] We will assume in our example that Sunbird's budgeted labor costs for each quarter are all paid in that same quarter. Hence, there is no need to adjust the labor costs in order to budget for labor cash payments each quarter.

SCHEDULE 4

Schedule 4
Sunbird Boat Company
2009 Direct Labor Budget

	Q1	Q2	Q3	Q4	Total
Production volume (Schedule 2)	30 boats	35 boats	20 boats	20 boats	105 boats
Standard hours per boat	× 80 hours	× 80 hours	× 80 hours	× 80 hours	× 80 hours
Budgeted labor hours	2,400 hours	2,800 hours	1,600 hours	1,600 hours	8,400 hours
Standard wage rate per hour[1]	× $20	× $20	× $20	× $20	× $20
Direct labor cost[2]	$48,000	$56,000	$32,000	$32,000	$168,000

[1]Includes fringe benefits and payroll taxes.
[2]These costs are all paid in the quarter incurred.

 FYI

The recent trend in many companies has been to keep a relatively small full-time staff and hire an increasing number of part-time or temporary employees. Not only are these employees much easier to hire and terminate, but the company does not have to pay retirement and other benefits for them. Banks, for example, have replaced many of their full-time customer representatives with part-time employees. As a result of the smaller full-time workforce, companies that provide temporary workers are increasing in both size and number. From management's perspective, both part-time and temporary workers increase workforce flexibility and make direct labor budgeting easier. Unfortunately, these same trends probably mean less stable and secure careers for more and more workers unless, of course, part-time employment agencies take over the role of providing job security, retirement, and other benefits.

Management must plan so that sufficient (but not excessive) labor is always available.[3] Otherwise, the company is likely to suffer the high cost of frequent hiring, firing, layoffs, and overtime work. Probably even more important than the high cost of employee turnover, however, is the feeling of demoralization among employees that such events can cause. If employees lack job security, they usually behave in ways

[2] The inclusion of fringe benefits and payroll taxes into the standard wage rate per hour is a significant decision in the budgeting process. Companies may also choose to include in the standard wage rate some measure of expected overtime pay. Other companies do not include the costs of fringe benefits and payroll taxes into the standard wage rate, but add them to the overhead application rate.

[3] Just how variable labor costs are has aroused significant controversy in the management accounting literature. Some researchers argue that employees cannot easily be hired or terminated and, therefore, labor should be a fixed cost. Other researchers argue that labor is constantly hired and terminated—just read business newspapers where announcements of employee layoffs are printed every day. One thing is certain, though—labor costs are a very large component of the product cost that management needs to carefully budget.

Banks have replaced many of their full-time customer representatives with part-time employees. From management's perspective, the use of part-time workers makes direct labor budgeting easier.

© PHOTODISC BLUE/GETTY IMAGES INC.

that maximize their own personal short-run benefits (e.g., they may slow down production, thus creating the need for more employment or overtime work).

Manufacturing Overhead Budget

The **manufacturing overhead budget** (Schedule 5) includes all production costs other than those for direct materials and direct labor. As noted in earlier chapters, manufacturing overhead is a major element of total manufacturing costs in many organizations. Hence, organizations that are able to effectively plan and control these costs have a significant advantage in the marketplace.

SCHEDULE 5

Schedule 5
Sunbird Boat Company
2009 Manufacturing Overhead (MOH) Budget

Variable MOH costs		Q1	Q2	Q3	Q4	Total
Total labor hours (Schedule 4)		2,400 hours	2,800 hours	1,600 hours	1,600 hours	8,400 hours
Variable MOH rates per hour:						
Indirect materials	$ 1.50	$ 3,600	$ 4,200	$ 2,400	$ 2,400	$ 12,600
Indirect labor	5.00	12,000	14,000	8,000	8,000	42,000
Utilities	1.00	2,400	2,800	1,600	1,600	8,400
Total variable MOH costs	$ 7.50	$18,000	$21,000	$12,000	$12,000	$ 63,000
Fixed MOH costs per quarter		**Q1**	**Q2**	**Q3**	**Q4**	**Total**
Property taxes	$ 2,000	$ 2,000	$ 2,000	$ 2,000	$ 2,000	$ 8,000
Insurance	1,000	1,000	1,000	1,000	1,000	4,000
Depreciation–plant	15,000	15,000	15,000	15,000	15,000	60,000
Supervisors' salaries	24,000	24,000	24,000	24,000	24,000	96,000
Total fixed MOH costs	$42,000	$42,000	$42,000	$42,000	$42,000	$168,000
Total		**Q1**	**Q2**	**Q3**	**Q4**	**Total**
Total MOH costs		$60,000	$63,000	$54,000	$54,000	$231,000
Less depreciation		(15,000)	(15,000)	(15,000)	(15,000)	(60,000)
Total MOH payments*		$45,000	$48,000	$39,000	$39,000	$171,000

*Because depreciation does not represent a cash payment, these costs are removed to determine cash payments made each quarter for manufacturing overhead costs. All other manufacturing overhead costs are paid for in the quarter incurred.

manufacturing overhead budget

A schedule of production costs other than those for direct labor and direct materials.

In preparing this budget, Sunbird's accounting department first estimates the annual variable and fixed manufacturing overhead costs, as shown in the first column of Schedule 5. As you can see, the estimated variable manufacturing overhead costs are based on a cost per direct labor hour. In our example, we assume that volume of direct labor hours is a good predictor of variable manufacturing overhead costs for Sunbird, and that Sunbird uses direct labor hours to allocate these costs to each quarter. These variable cost rates per hour have been estimated

Remember that the budgets being discussed in this chapter are for only one level of expected sales. If the level of sales changes, the budgeted variable costs will also change. This means that all the direct materials and direct labor budgets will change, as will some of the manufacturing overhead and selling and administrative expense budgets. This important issue of changing levels of sales or operations is covered in the expanded material section of the chapter under the topic of flexible budgeting.

previously by Sunbird's accountants. These rates are then multiplied by the number of direct labor hours estimated for each quarter (from Schedule 4) to figure the budgeted variable manufacturing overhead cost for boats for that quarter.[4] Total fixed costs are simply allocated evenly across the four quarters.

To be sure that you understand how the variable manufacturing overhead cost rates are used to create Schedule 5, assume that total indirect materials costs for 2009 were estimated to be $12,600. Dividing that number by 8,400 direct labor hours (the total labor hours from Schedule 4) yields a rate of $1.50 per hour. Multiplying the $1.50 rate by 2,400 direct labor hours produces $3,600 to be assigned to the first quarter as the budgeted cost of indirect materials. With 2,800 direct labor hours in the second quarter, the cost for that quarter is $4,200. The calculation is the same for the remaining quarters, as well as for other variable overhead items.

budgeted product cost sheet

A schedule of all of the product costs (i.e., the costs of direct materials, direct labor, and manufacturing overhead) used to create a single product.

The final computation on the manufacturing overhead budget is to determine the budgeted cash payments for these costs to be made each quarter. We assume that Sunbird stays current with these costs and makes payments as the costs are used in production. However, depreciation does not represent an actual cash outflow. Hence, these costs are removed from the budgeted manufacturing overhead costs to determine the payments expected to be made each quarter related to manufacturing overhead.

Budgeted Product Cost Sheet   The **budgeted product cost sheet** (Schedule 6) accumulates all the budgeted product costs (direct materials, direct

---

SCHEDULE 6

Schedule 6
Sunbird Boat Company
2009 Budgeted Product Cost Sheet

		Total
Direct materials cost per boat (Schedule 3):		
Wood (100 board feet @ $10 per foot)	$ 1,000	
Fiberglass (40 board feet @ $5 per foot)	200	$1,200
Direct labor cost per boat (Schedule 4): 80 hours × $20 per hour		1,600
Variable MOH cost per boat (Schedule 5): 80 hours × $7.50 per hour		600
Total variable cost per boat		$3,400
Total Fixed MOH (Schedule 5)	$168,000	
Divided by production volume (Schedule 2)	÷ 105 boats	
Fixed MOH cost allocated per boat*		1,600
Total production cost per boat		$5,000

*Note that the production costs per boat for Sunbird will actually vary from quarter to quarter because of the change in fixed MOH costs per boat due to changes in quarterly production volume. To avoid these artificial changes in quarterly budgeted boat production costs, Sunbird creates the budgeted product cost sheet on an annual basis only.

---

[4] Earlier in Chapter 16 we used direct labor hours to assign manufacturing overhead cost. This is actually a very simplistic approach to accounting for overhead costs. Remember that we studied an important technique called activity-based costing (ABC) in Chapter 17 that is used by some organizations to more realistically account for and manage overhead costs. Nevertheless, we will use direct labor hours here because using various activity-based cost drivers would unnecessarily complicate our budgeting examples. The budgeting concepts we are working with here are similar in either case.

labor, and manufacturing overhead) to estimate the total production cost of building each boat. The product cost sheet is useful to help us understand that the operations budget serves two different management purposes. First, by comparing actual sales and costs, the master budget data can be used as the basis for controlling costs and evaluating the performance of the managers responsible for those costs. (You'll clearly see how this control process works when we study variance analysis in Chapter 19.)

Second, these budgets are used in product costing. As you will recall from Chapter 16, the manufacturing overhead costs that flow through Work-in-Process Inventory to Finished Goods Inventory (and eventually to Cost of Goods Sold) are standardized costs that are applied based on predetermined overhead rates. Accountants then track the difference between actual overhead costs and applied overhead costs (the over- or under-applied manufacturing overhead amount you studied in Chapter 16) in order to determine if overhead resources are being efficiently used.[5] In our example, this predetermined overhead rate that Sunbird will use during the year to apply overhead costs to products being manufactured is calculated by dividing estimated annual direct labor hours (from Schedule 4) into estimated annual total manufacturing overhead (from Schedule 5). The rate is then computed as $231,000 \div 8,400$ hours $= \$27.50$ per hour.

Using the direct materials, direct labor, and manufacturing overhead budgets (the three elements of a product's cost), we are able to compute Sunbird's budgeted cost of making its 15-foot boats. As you can see in Schedule 6, these costs are largely based on data from the budgets we have been preparing. This information is then used to measure budgeted cost of goods sold for the pro-forma income statement that we will study in the expanded material section of this chapter.

selling and administrative expense budget

A schedule of all nonproduction spending expected to occur during the budget period.

Selling and Administrative Expense Budget The **selling and administrative expense budget** (Schedule 7) includes planned expenditures for all areas other than production. The costs of supplies used by the office staff, the salaries of the sales manager and company president, and the depreciation of administrative office buildings (*not* production facilities) all belong in this category. Because this budget covers several areas, it is usually quite large and may be supported by individual budgets for specific departments within the selling and administrative functions.

The selling and administrative expense budget for Sunbird is prepared in a manner similar to the manufacturing overhead budget. Total selling and administrative expenses are estimated for the year, with each expense then being distributed among the four quarters. As shown in Schedule 7, fixed expenses are assigned equally to each quarter, whereas variable expenses are allocated according to the number of boats to be sold. Variable delivery expenses, for example, are allocated to quarters by first determining the delivery expense rate [$50,000 estimated delivery expenses $\div$ 100 boats expected to be sold during the year (from Schedule 1) = $500 per boat]. This rate is multiplied by the number of boats sold in a quarter to determine the delivery expenses allocated to that quarter. Because Sunbird expects to sell 20 boats in the first quarter at a rate of $500 per boat, the amount of delivery expense budgeted for that quarter is $10,000 ($500 × 20 boats).

Sales commissions are allocated to each quarter in the same way.

Similar to our approach with the manufacturing overhead budget (Schedule 5), depreciation expense is eliminated from the budgeted selling and administrative expense to determine the expected quarterly cash payments for these expenses.

CAUTION

Variable expenses in the sales and administrative expense budget are typically based on the volume of sales, not on the volume of production.

---

[5] In fact, you will learn in Chapter 19 that we can use similar standardized costs of direct materials and direct labor to track and control how efficiently direct materials and direct labor are used to produce goods and services.

SCHEDULE 7

Schedule 7
Sunbird Boat Company
2009 Selling and Administrative (S&A) Expense Budget

Variable S&A expenses		Q1	Q2	Q3	Q4	Total
Sales volume (Schedule 1)		20 boats	40 boats	30 boats	10 boats	100 boats
Variable expense per boat sold:						
Delivery expense	$ 500	$ 10,000	$ 20,000	$ 15,000	$ 5,000	$ 50,000
Sales commissions	1,500	30,000	60,000	45,000	15,000	150,000
Total variable S&A expenses	$ 2,000	$ 40,000	$ 80,000	$ 60,000	$ 20,000	$200,000

Fixed S&A expenses per quarter		Q1	Q2	Q3	Q4	Total
Executives' salaries	$34,000	$ 34,000	$ 34,000	$ 34,000	$ 34,000	$136,000
Depreciation expense	5,000	5,000	5,000	5,000	5,000	20,000
Advertising expense	10,000	10,000	10,000	10,000	10,000	40,000
Miscellaneous expenses	2,500	2,500	2,500	2,500	2,500	10,000
Total fixed S&A expenses	$51,500	$ 51,500	$ 51,500	$ 51,500	$ 51,500	$206,000

Total	Q1	Q2	Q3	Q4	Total
Total S&A expenses	$ 91,500	$131,500	$111,500	$ 71,500	$406,000
Less depreciation	(5,000)	(5,000)	(5,000)	(5,000)	(20,000)
Total S&A payments*	$ 86,500	$126,500	$106,500	$ 66,500	$386,000

*Because depreciation does not represent a cash payment, these expenses are removed to determine cash payments made each quarter for selling and administrative expenses. All other selling and administrative expenses are paid for in the quarter incurred.

REMEMBER THIS...

- Operations budgeting is not hard to do so long as you keep in mind a few key formulas and remember how the individual budgets connect and feed into each other based on the following diagram.

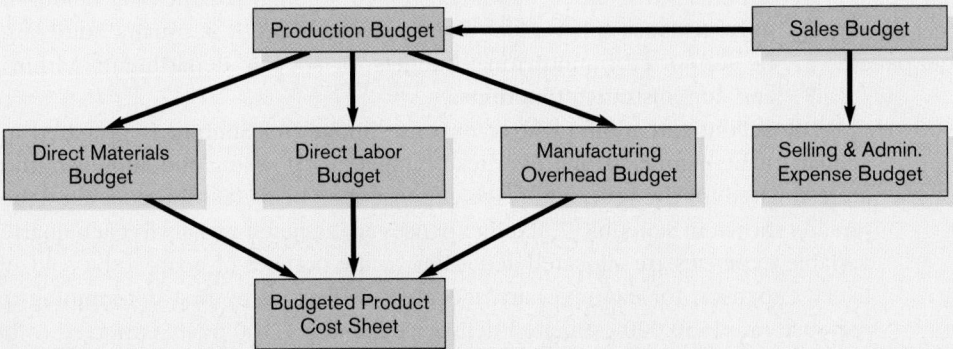

- When computing the production budget and direct materials budget, remember the following formula: Needs of the prior budget + ending inventory − beginning inventory = the current budget. Hence,
  - Sales budget + ending finished goods inventory − beginning finished goods inventory = the production budget.
  - Production budget × direct materials per unit = direct materials production budget;
  - Direct materials production budget + ending direct materials inventory − beginning direct materials inventory = the direct materials purchases budget.
- Fixed budget costs are constant each production period (e.g., each quarter) while the variable budget costs are based on the expected sales or production volume for each production period.
- Revenues ≠ receipts and purchases ≠ payments. Hence,
  - Cash collected from customers = (current period revenue × current period collection rate) + cash collected from previous period sales.
  - Cash payments to suppliers = (current period purchases × current period payment rate) + cash paid on previous period purchases.
- Budgeted expenses ≠ cash outflows. Hence, be sure to add back depreciation and other noncash costs to budgeted expenses when computing cash outflows.

Budgeting and Control **Chapter 18** 889

Although the selling and administrative expense budget in Schedule 7 looks reasonably simple, it is often more complex in actual practice than it appears here. Traditionally, these types of costs have not been a focus of management accounting control efforts. However, selling and administrative costs have become proportionately larger for many organizations and now receive substantial management attention. Hence, rather than classifying these costs based on their function (salaries, depreciation, etc.), we often see in practice that these budgets are divided into multiple categories that may emphasize how costs are related to important functions in the organization such as research and development (R&D), product or service design, marketing, distribution, and customer service.

Budgeting in Merchandising and Service Firms

Compare the operations budget for a manufacturing firm to that of a merchandising or service firm.

(4) We have worked through the operations budget process for a manufacturing firm, Sunbird Boat Company. We will now compare Sunbird Boat Company's operations budget with budgets for merchandising firms (retail and wholesale) by describing the operations budget process for Wind River Boat Company, a company that buys boats for resale from other manufacturers rather than making the boats itself. Then we will illustrate budgeting in service firms by illustrating the operations budget process for a small motel, the Boulder View Inn.

As we examine a merchandise company and a service company, you will see a lot of similarities in the budgeting process for manufacturing businesses. Basically, the budgeting process involves budgeting (or forecasting) revenues and cash that will be generated by those revenues, as well as budgeting expenses and cash that will be paid for those expenses. Managers are always interested in how much revenues and expenses they will have during each budgeted period and how much cash and other assets and liabilities they will have at the end of each budgeted period.

Budgeting for Operations in a Merchandising Firm

We discussed the flow of costs for merchants previously in Chapter 16. Well-known retail companies include **Wal-Mart**, **Sears**, and **Macy's**. Because merchandising companies buy products (rather than make them), their budgeting process is less complicated than the budgeting done by manufacturing companies. For example, if Sunbird Boat Company were a merchandising firm rather than a manufacturing firm, the company would prepare a purchases budget, rather than a production budget, for boats. However, the format of the merchant's purchases budget would be very similar to the format of the manufacturer's production budget (see, for example, Schedule 2 for Sunbird Boat Company). By combining expected sales with desired ending inventory, and subtracting the beginning inventory expected to be on hand, the merchant will arrive at the number of boats to be purchased (rather than produced) for the period.

Exhibit 5 compares the master budgeting process for a merchandising firm with that for a manufacturing firm (from Exhibit 3). You can see in Exhibit 5 that merchandising companies replace four budgets (production budget, direct materials budget, direct labor budget, and manufacturing overhead budget)

STOP & THINK

In this chapter, the emphasis is on budgeting costs and revenues. Remember, though, that management is also interested in managing quality and timeliness. Do you think management performs any budgeting related to the quality or the delivery time of products or services to customers?

A Comparison of the Master Budgets for a Manufacturing and a Merchandising Firm

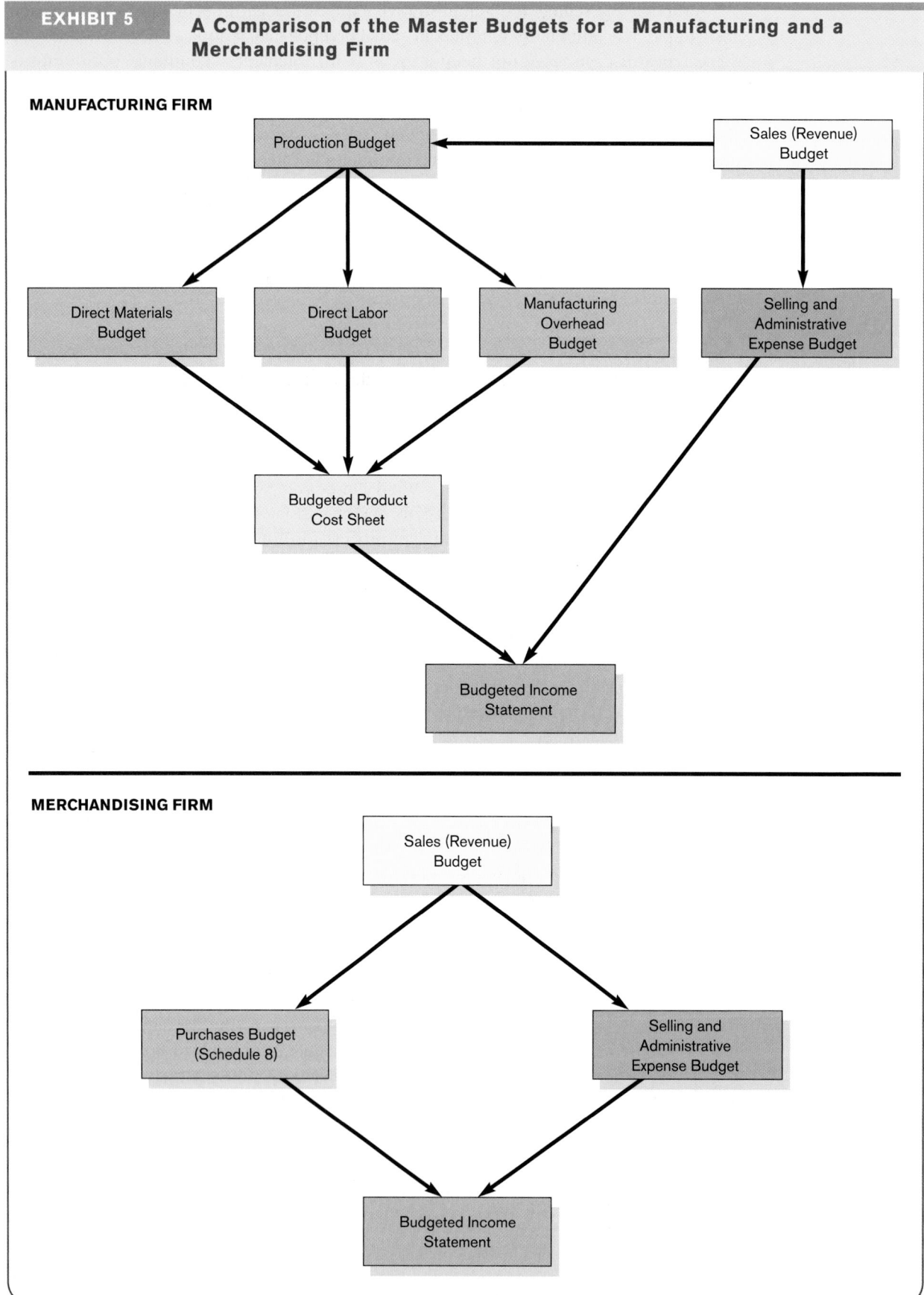

used by manufacturing firms with a single budget, the purchases budget. The sales budget and the selling and administrative expense budget are similar to those prepared for manufacturing firms, and so we won't discuss these budgets again. Instead, we'll focus on the purchases budget for Wind River Boat Company which we described earlier as a retail company that buys boats from manufacturers and sells them to consumers.

purchases budget

A schedule of projected purchases over the budget period.

Purchases Budget Assuming the same level of sales as we did for Sunbird, the **purchases budget** for Wind River Boat Company is shown in Schedule 8. You can see from Schedule 8 that Wind River Boat Company pays its suppliers $8,000 for each 15-foot boat. (If you compare this cost with the total manufacturing cost for Sunbird Boat Company, you will see that it is higher. This is because manufacturing companies also need to make a profit.) As you can see in Schedule 8, Wind River Boat Company begins the year with 4 boats in beginning inventory and has a policy to maintain 20 percent of next quarter's expected sales in ending inventory. Finally, the company plans to pay for 50 percent of its purchases in the month of purchase with the remaining purchases paid for in the following month.

SCHEDULE 8

Schedule 8
Wind River Boat Company
2009 Purchases Budget

15-Foot Boats	Q1	Q2	Q3	Q4	Total
Sales volume (Schedule 1)	20 boats	40 boats	30 boats	10 boats	100 boats
Desired ending inventory[1]	8 boats	6 boats	2 boats	5 boats	5 boats
Total boats needed	28 boats	46 boats	32 boats	15 boats	105 boats
Less beginning inventory[2]	(4 boats)	(8 boats)	(6 boats)	(2 boats)	(4 boats)
Total boats to purchase	24 boats	38 boats	26 boats	13 boats	101 boats
Cost per boat	×$ 8,000	×$ 8,000	×$ 8,000	×$ 8,000	×$ 8,000
Boat purchases	$192,000	$304,000	$208,000	$104,000	$808,000
Paid in current quarter	× 50%	× 50%	× 50%	× 50%	× 50%
Current purchase payments	$ 96,000	$152,000	$104,000	$ 52,000	$404,000
Prior purchase payments[3]	48,000	96,000	152,000	104,000	400,000
Payments to suppliers	$144,000	$248,000	$256,000	$156,000	$804,000

[1]Wind River desires to have ending boat inventory equal to 20% of the expected sales volume for the following quarter. Wind River's marketing department forecasts sales of 25 boats during the first quarter of 2010.
[2]Wind River's beginning finished goods inventory for 2009 is 4 boats. Beginning inventory for Q2 through Q4 is equal to the ending inventory for the prior quarter.
[3]Prior purchase payments in Q1 represent the accounts payable balance from Wind River's 2008 balance sheet (not shown). Prior purchase payments in Q2 through Q4 represent the purchases not paid for in the prior quarter (i.e., total boat purchases in prior quarter times 50%).

Budgeting for Operations in a Service Firm

Each year, a larger and larger percentage of businesses in the United States is service companies. Service companies differ from manufacturing and merchandising companies in that they provide services to customers instead of products. Examples of service organizations are law, accounting, and engineering firms; doctors and dentists; hotels and motels; hunting and fishing guide services; automotive, home, and appliance repair services; and Internet providers. Budgeting for service firms is similar to budgeting for manufacturing firms. As was the case with both manufacturing and merchandising companies, the budgeting process for service firms begins with a sales budget (sometimes called a revenue budget). Exhibit 6 compares the operations budgeting process for a service firm with a manufacturing firm. You can see that the service firm does not require a production budget. If you compare Schedule 1 and Schedule 2 for Sunbird Boat Company, you can see that the production budget starts with the sales volume and makes adjustments

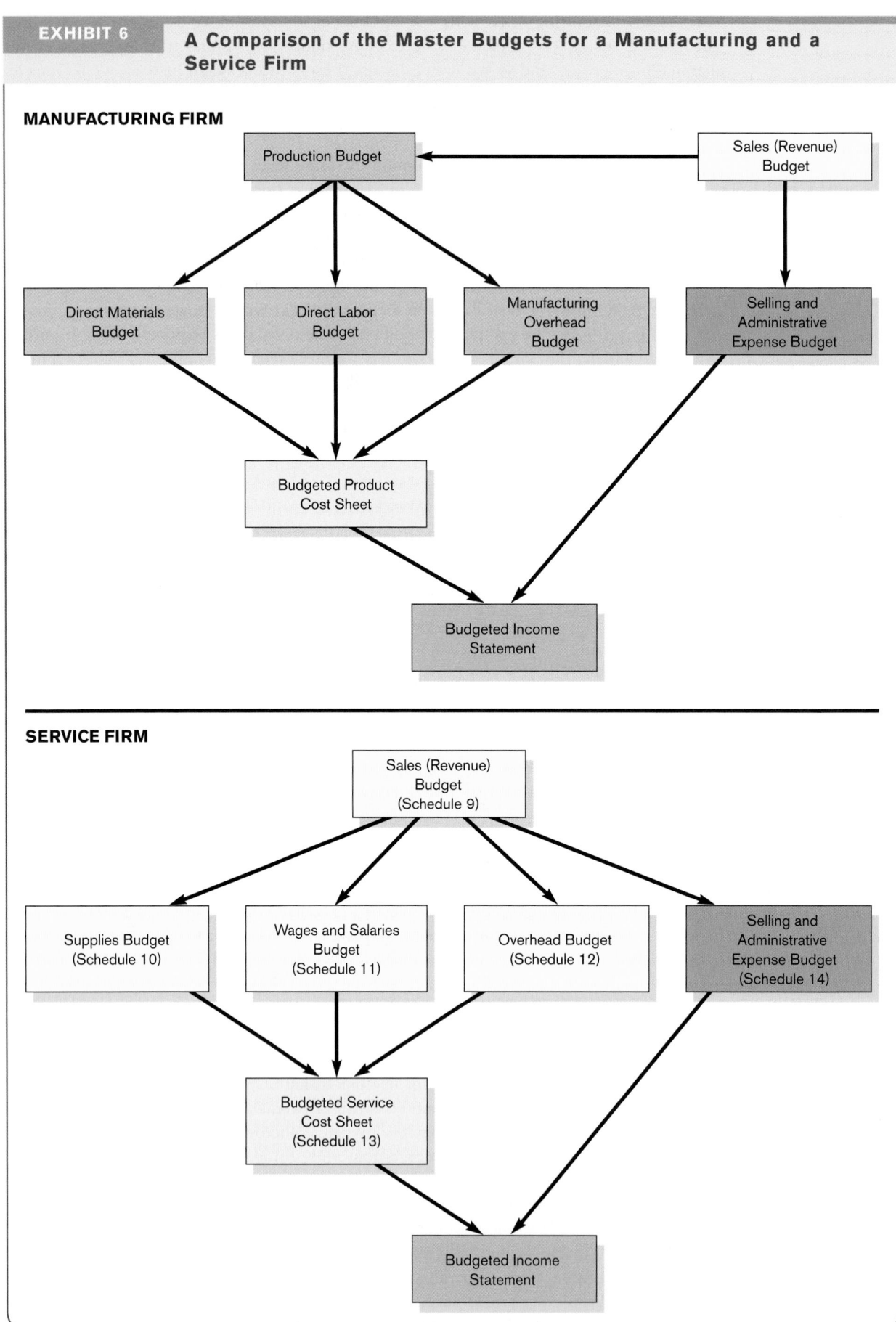

EXHIBIT 6   A Comparison of the Master Budgets for a Manufacturing and a Service Firm

MANUFACTURING FIRM

Production Budget

Sales (Revenue) Budget

Direct Materials Budget

Direct Labor Budget

Manufacturing Overhead Budget

Selling and Administrative Expense Budget

Budgeted Product Cost Sheet

Budgeted Income Statement

SERVICE FIRM

Sales (Revenue) Budget (Schedule 9)

Supplies Budget (Schedule 10)

Wages and Salaries Budget (Schedule 11)

Overhead Budget (Schedule 12)

Selling and Administrative Expense Budget (Schedule 14)

Budgeted Service Cost Sheet (Schedule 13)

Budgeted Income Statement

to it based on expected beginning and ending inventories of finished goods. Service firms sell intangible products (for example, physician appointments, car repairs, room rentals, monthly Internet access) that can't be inventoried. Therefore, the sales volume determined in the revenue budget is the "production" for the operating period.

Revenue Budget To illustrate the budgeting process in service firms, we will use the example of Boulder View Inn, a small motel that has 10 rooms to rent each night. Boulder View Inn is located adjacent to a national park in southern Utah, and its business is highly seasonal, with April through December being busy (peak period) and January through March being very slow. Boulder View Inn rents its rooms for an average rate of $150 per night during the peak period and $100 per night during the slow period. Guests who stay at the hotel either pay cash or use credit cards, such as **Visa**, **Mastercard**, **American**

revenue budget

A service entity's budget that identifies how much revenue (and often cash) will be generated during a period.

Express, or **Discover**. The motel has a direct link with its bank that immediately deposits credit card receipts in Boulder View Inn's bank account after charging a 4 to 5% discount fee, which covers the bank's costs as well as fees charged by the credit card companies. Historically, Boulder View Inn has found that because most customers use credit cards to pay for their rooms, it pays an average of $5 per room per night to the credit card companies to cover the discount fee. Based on past experience, occupancy rates for the coming year are expected to be as follows:

January–March	30%
April–June	90%
July–September	80%
October–December	60%

Using these data, the **revenue budget** for Boulder View Inn is shown in Schedule 9.

SCHEDULE 9

Schedule 9
Boulder View Inn
2009 Revenue Budget

	Q1	Q2	Q3	Q4	Total
Number of rooms	10 rooms	10 rooms	10 rooms	10 rooms	
Number of days in quarter	× 90 days	× 90 days	× 90 days	× 90 days	
Potential rental volume	900 rentals	900 rentals	900 rentals	900 rentals	
Occupancy rate	× 30%	× 90%	× 80%	× 60%	
Rented rooms	270 rentals	810 rentals	720 rentals	540 rentals	2,340 rentals
Room rate	× $100	× $150	× $150	× $150	
Revenue[1]	$27,000	$121,500	$108,000	$81,000	$337,500

[1]These revenues are all collected in the quarter earned.

This budget shows that Boulder View Inn will generate gross revenues of $337,500 during the next year. Because Boulder View Inn collects cash or its equivalent (credit cards) from each guest, the revenue earned is expected to be collected each quarter. Remember that the revenue budget also establishes the expected "production," or number of rooms expected to be rented each quarter. Hence, you can see from the revenue budget that Boulder View Inn expects to rent 2,340 rooms next year. And you can see in Exhibit 6 that this sales volume will be used to determine the supplies, wages and salaries, overhead, and selling and administrative expense budgets.

The revenue budget for Boulder View Inn would be similar for other types of service firms, except that instead of a per-room revenue, the revenue would be based on per patient visit (for doctors and dentists), per contract (for engineers, accountants, and lawyers), or per subscription (for Internet providers). Service companies that do not immediately collect payment, but rather bill clients on a periodic basis (such as lawyers and accountants), would also need to extend the revenue budget to determine when the cash generated from revenues will be collected.

supplies budget

The budget, prepared by service entities, that identifies projected supplies expenses over the budget period.

Supplies Budget Most service businesses need supplies to operate. For a restaurant, supplies include the food used in preparing meals, cleaning materials, and the paper goods needed for menus and customer invoices. For a medical doctor, supplies might include needles, tape, and bandages, as well as office supplies. For Boulder View Inn, supplies include soap and shampoo for the guest rooms, as well as doughnuts, cereal, juice, and milk for the continental breakfast. The **supplies budget** for Boulder View Inn is shown in Schedule 10.

SCHEDULE 10

Schedule 10
Boulder View Inn
2009 Supplies Budget

		Q1	Q2	Q3	Q4	Total
Total rental days (Schedule 9)		270 rooms	810 rooms	720 rooms	540 rooms	2,340 rooms
Supplies needed per room:						
Bathroom supplies cost	$ 2.00	$ 540	$1,620	$1,440	$1,080	$ 4,680
Laundry supplies cost	1.00	270	810	720	540	2,340
Breakfast supplies cost	8.00	2,160	6,480	5,760	4,320	18,720
Total supplies cost per room*	$11.00	$2,970	$8,910	$7,920	$5,940	$25,740

*Because the level of supplies is immaterial, the supplies cost each quarter is essentially paid in cash in each quarter.

wages and salaries budget

The budget, prepared by service entities, that identifies projected labor costs involved directly in providing the service over the budget period.

Wages and Salaries Budget The **wages and salaries budget** is reserved for labor costs involved directly in providing the service (similar to direct labor in a manufacturing firm). Administrative labor costs are not included in this budget; they are part of the selling and administrative expense budget. For a law firm, the wages and salaries budget would include salaries of lawyers; but not of paralegals, photocopy personnel, computer specialists, or office secretaries—these personnel costs would all be part of the selling and administrative expense budget. For Boulder View Inn, the only labor cost included in this budget is the $25 per room that is paid for cleaning the rooms. Schedule 11 is the wages and salaries budget for Boulder View Inn.

SCHEDULE 11

Schedule 11
Boulder View Inn
2009 Wages and Salaries Budget

	Q1	Q2	Q3	Q4	Total
Total rental days (Schedule 9)	270 rooms	810 rooms	720 rooms	540 rooms	2,340 rooms
Cleaning fee[1]	× $25	× $25	× $25	× $25	× $25
Total wages[2]	$6,750	$20,250	$18,000	$13,500	$58,500

[1]Includes fringe benefits and payroll taxes.
[2]These costs are all paid in the quarter incurred.

service overhead budget

The budget, prepared by service entities, that identifies projected costs associated with providing the service.

Overhead Budget As was the case with manufacturing firms, the **service overhead budget** includes all the costs associated with providing the product, or service, in this case. The overhead budget does not include selling and administrative costs not directly associated with providing the service. For Boulder View Inn, overhead costs include utilities, depreciation, TV and telephone service, and miscellaneous expenses. In the case of this particular service provider, all overhead costs are fixed. In other words, regardless of whether or not a room is rented, these overhead costs are incurred. Schedule 12 is the overhead budget for Boulder View Inn.

SCHEDULE 12

Schedule 12
Boulder View Inn
2009 Overhead Budget

	Q1	Q2	Q3	Q4	Total
Utilities	$ 5,000	$ 5,000	$ 5,000	$ 5,000	$20,000
Depreciation expense	10,000	10,000	10,000	10,000	40,000
TV and telephone	2,000	2,000	2,000	2,000	8,000
Miscellaneous costs	550	550	550	550	2,200
Total overhead costs	$17,550	$17,550	$17,550	$17,550	$70,200
Less depreciation	(10,000)	(10,000)	(10,000)	(10,000)	(40,000)
Total overhead payments*	$ 7,550	$ 7,550	$ 7,550	$ 7,550	$30,200

*Because depreciation does not represent a cash payment, these costs are removed to determine cash payments made each quarter for overhead costs. All other overhead costs are paid for in the quarter incurred.

budgeted service cost sheet

A schedule of all of the service costs (i.e., the costs of supplies, wages and salaries, and overhead) used to provide a single service event.

The depreciation in Schedule 12 is calculated by dividing the motel cost of $1,000,000 by its 25-year life to arrive at $40,000 per year (and further divided into quarterly costs of $10,000). The utilities include heat, lights, sewer, and garbage removal.

Budgeted Service Cost Sheet The **budgeted service cost sheet** (Schedule 13) is similar to the budgeted product cost sheet for manufacturing firms. This schedule accumulates all the budgeted service costs (supplies, wages

SCHEDULE 13

Schedule 13
Boulder View Inn
2009 Budgeted Service Cost Sheet

		Total
Annual supplies cost (Schedule 10)	$25,740	
Annual wage cost (Schedule 11)	58,500	
Total annual variable service costs	$84,240	
Annual volume of rental rooms	÷2,340 rooms	
Total variable cost per rental		$36.00
Annual fixed overhead costs (Schedule 12)	$70,200	
Annual volume of rental rooms	÷2,340 rooms	
Fixed MOH cost allocated per rental*		30.00
Total service cost per room rental		$66.00

*Note that the service costs per room rental for Boulder View Inn will actually vary from quarter to quarter because of the change in fixed overhead costs per rental due to changes in occupancy rate each quarter.

and salaries, and overhead) to estimate the total service cost of providing a room to rent at Boulder View Inn. Based on the three service-related budgets (supplies, wages and salaries, and overhead), we know it costs Boulder View Inn approximately $36.00 in variable costs to provide the services needed to rent one room for one night. Because Boulder View Inn expects to rent 2,340 rooms during the year, the overhead cost assigned to each room rental (all of which is fixed) is $30.00 ($70,200 ÷ 2,340 rooms). The calculation of these service costs is shown in Schedule 13.

Selling and Administrative Expense Budget   As was the case for Sunbird Boat Company, the selling and administrative expense budget for Boulder View Inn includes planned expenditures for all selling and administrative expenses. As in manufacturing companies, the selling and administrative expense budget for a service firm can be quite large and is sometimes supported by individual budgets for specific elements included in this budget. The selling and administrative expense budget for Boulder View Inn is shown in Schedule 14.

SCHEDULE 14

Schedule 14
Boulder View Inn
2009 Selling and Administrative (S&A) Expense Budget

Variable S&A expenses	Q1	Q2	Q3	Q4	Total
Total rental days (Schedule 9)	270 rooms	810 rooms	720 rooms	540 rooms	2,340 rooms
Average credit card discount fee	× $5	× $5	× $5	× $5	× $5
Total variable S&A expenses	$ 1,350	$ 4,050	$ 3,600	$ 2,700	$11,700

Fixed S&A expenses per quarter	Q1	Q2	Q3	Q4	Total
Manager's salary	$ 8,500	$ 8,500	$ 8,500	$ 8,500	$34,000
Depreciation expense	1,200	1,200	1,200	1,200	4,800
Advertising expense	800	800	800	800	3,200
Miscellaneous expenses	500	500	500	500	2,000
Total fixed S&A expenses	$11,000	$11,000	$11,000	$11,000	$44,000

Total	Q1	Q2	Q3	Q4	Total
Total S&A expenses	$12,350	$15,050	$14,600	$13,700	$55,700
Less depreciation	(1,200)	(1,200)	(1,200)	(1,200)	(4,800)
Total S&A payments*	$11,150	$13,850	$13,400	$12,500	$50,900

*Because depreciation does not represent a cash payment, these expenses are removed to determine cash payments made each quarter for selling and administrative expenses. All other selling and administrative expenses are paid for in the quarter incurred.

This selling and administration expense budget shows that Boulder View Inn's total selling and administrative expense for the year is budgeted to be $55,700. The selling and administrative expenses include credit card charges, the manager's salary, miscellaneous expenses around the office, and advertising expense (which includes yellow page directory advertisement and Internet listings). This budget also includes the depreciation expense on the cottage provided by Boulder View to the manager who must be available at the inn on a 24-hour, 7-days-a-week basis.

REMEMBER THIS...

- A merchandising firm's purchases budget replaces four of a manufacturing firm's budgets—production, direct materials, direct labor, and manufacturing overhead.
- Because services cannot usually be inventoried, the sales budget for most service firms also serves as the production (i.e., service) budget.
- Other than the two distinctions above, the merchant and service firm budgets used in this section of the chapter differ from the budgeting example in the previous section simply to illustrate how different business processes affect the budgets of different companies.
- Successfully creating operations budgets (whether for a manufacturer, merchant, or service firm) is largely a matter of being able to think logically about specific business processes and accurately represent the flow of expected revenues and costs.

EXPANDED *material*

The budgeting process discussed to this point allows management to plan various operating activities within the firm, such as purchasing, hiring, and overall management of the production or service process. Armed with these budgets, management is now prepared to monitor the firm's performance and compare actual results to budgeted results. If corrective action is needed, management can identify deviations from the budget early and take the appropriate steps to remedy problems. However, management has a problem using budgets to monitor performance and compare results when the budget is based on an outdated sales volume figure. Hence, this section opens with a discussion of static and flexible budgeting and illustrates the advantages of flexible budgeting. In addition, we use the operations budgets from the Sunbird Boat Company to prepare a cash budget, as well as a pro-forma (i.e., budgeted) income statement, balance sheet, and statement of cash flows.

Static versus Flexible Budgeting

Distinguish between static and flexible budgets.

(5) So far, the budgets we've discussed in this chapter are **static budgets**; that is, they are geared to only one level of sales activity. However, as hard as companies try to predict sales volumes, these numbers rarely turn out to be exactly as predicted. In fact, as there are unexpected changes in the economy, technology, or competitors, actual sales can turn out to be very different from planned sales! This is a critical issue since sales budgets are the key input in building the rest of the operations budget. In the next chapter we will compare actual results to budgets in order to control and evaluate performance. However, before we can do this, we will need to adjust budgets to make them relevant to the actual results. To be specific, we will need to recompute the budgets based on the actual sales activity. This is the process of creating a flexible budget.

A **flexible budget** is much more useful for control and performance evaluation because it is not confined to one level of activity. Flexible budgets are dynamic; that is, they can be tailored to any level of activity within the relevant range. Using flexible budgeting, a manager can look at the actual level of activity attained and then determine what costs should have been at that sales level.

static budget

A quantified plan that projects revenues and costs for only one level of activity.

flexible budget

A quantified plan that projects revenues and costs for varying levels of activity.

Weaknesses in Static Budgeting

To illustrate why a static budget is simply inadequate for controlling operations, let's return once more to the Sunbird Boat Company example. In particular, let's look at its budgeted product cost sheet (Schedule 6). Based on the information from that schedule, Sunbird developed the following budgeted per-unit manufacturing costs for 15-foot boats:

Direct materials	$1,200
Direct labor	1,600
Variable manufacturing overhead	600
Fixed manufacturing overhead	1,600
Total cost per boat	**$5,000**

STOP & THINK

Suppose that a production department's budget is based on manufacturing and selling 10,000 widgets at a standard product cost of $10 per widget. The department actually produced 9,000 widgets and spent $95,000. Obviously, it didn't meet its sales goal. However, did it spend more or less than it should have? What if it had actually produced 11,000 widgets and spent $105,000?

As you consider these numbers, you need to be very careful with the fixed manufacturing overhead. The $1,600 represents the *average* fixed manufacturing overhead cost per boat for the year. However, fixed manufacturing overhead is expected to be $42,000 each quarter (for a total of $168,000 for the year, *regardless of the number of boats actually produced.* (You can review these numbers in Schedule 5.) And if you review Schedule 2, you'll see that Sunbird's expected production will vary from quarter to quarter. What this means is that we shouldn't multiply the $1,600 with the expected volume of production in order to determine the budgeted fixed manufacturing overhead for the quarter. Fixed manufacturing overhead is actually what it says—it is fixed! Hence, if you want to predict the level of total manufacturing costs each quarter for Sunbird, you won't multiply the expected production volume by $5,000. The better way to do this is to use the following formula:

Total budget costs = (variable costs per unit × production level) + total fixed costs

Extending this budget formula to establish a total budgeted amount for the first quarter of 2009, Sunbird Boat Company could then prepare a budget as follows:

Sunbird Boat Company
Budgeted Manufacturing Costs
January–March 2009

Budgeted production (boats)		30
Variable manufacturing costs per boat:		
Direct materials	$1,200	
Direct labor	1,600	
Variable manufacturing overhead	600	
Total variable manufacturing costs per boat	$3,400	
Total variable manufacturing costs ($3,400 × 30 boats)		$102,000
Total fixed manufacturing costs		42,000
Total budgeted manufacturing costs		**$144,000**

This simple operations budget for the first quarter of 2009 can be quite useful to Sunbird if it actually produces 30 boats. However, let's assume that sales decreased and Sunbird actually had to produce only 27 boats to support sales in that first quarter. Sunbird's actual costs incurred were $88,000 for direct materials, direct labor, and variable manufacturing overhead, and $42,200 for fixed manufacturing overhead. Comparing actual results with the static budget information, the performance report for the quarter would be as follows:

Sunbird Boat Company
Static Budget Performance Report
January–March 2009

	Budgeted	Actual	Difference
Production (boats)	30	27	3
Manufacturing costs:			
Variable manufacturing costs	$102,000	$ 88,000	$14,000
Fixed manufacturing overhead	42,000	42,200	(200)
Total actual and budgeted manufacturing costs	$144,000	$130,200	$13,800

STOP & THINK

Consider the budget formula used to compute total budgeted manufacturing costs of $144,000 in the first quarter of 2009 for Sunbird Boat Company. Does this formula look familiar to you? It should look familiar if you studied geometry and the basic equation to plot a simple line, which is:

$$y = mx + b.$$

Sunbird Boat Company's equation to budget costs for the first quarter of 2009 is:

Total quarter costs = $3,400(boats produced) + $42,000.

How do these two formulas relate to each other?

According to this report, Sunbird has spent $13,800 less than it should have. However, something is wrong with this performance report. Producing fewer boats than budgeted (27 actual boats versus 30 budgeted boats) has led to less actual costs than were expected. But given the decrease in production, Sunbird *should* have spent less in manufacturing costs (right?). The real question is, should management be rewarded for keeping actual costs at $130,200 or criticized for producing fewer units than budgeted? Using the static budget doesn't help us answer this question. The deficiencies of this static budget performance report can be explained as follows: A production manager is responsible for controlling two things—production (output) and costs (input); that is, he or she must try to meet budgeted production volume and control costs in the process. To measure a manager's performance, the production and cost control functions must be separated. It makes no sense to note that the total actual cost of producing 27 boats is less than the budgeted cost of producing 30 boats. It obviously should be. The manager in our example clearly has not met budgeted production volume, but to determine whether he or she has controlled costs adequately, we must be able to compare actual costs to budgeted costs *based on the same number of units of production*. In other words, how much costs *should have* been incurred given this higher level of production? Answering this question correctly *is* the process of using a flexible budget.

Using the Flexible Budget

Instead of providing budgeted costs for only a single level of production or sales activity that was predicted before the operating period began, the flexible budget effectively adjusts the static budget at the end of the operation period based on the actual activity level. To make it possible to prepare budgeted costs at any possible activity level within the relevant range, per-unit variable costs, and total fixed costs are budgeted at the beginning of the operating period and are then used at the end of the period to create a flexible budget that is useful in measuring and analyzing actual input and output performance. The steps in preparing a flexible operations budget are as follows:

1. Determine a relevant range over which production is expected to vary during the coming operating period.
2. Before the operating period begins, establish the budgeted per-unit variable manufacturing costs and total fixed manufacturing costs.
3. At the conclusion of the operating period, use the per-unit variable costs and total fixed costs to build a flexible budget based on actual output activity.

To illustrate the preparation of a flexible budget, let us assume that Sunbird's relevant range of production activity per quarter is between 20 and 30 boats. This is important because producing outside of this relevant range is likely to result in expected differences in per-unit variable and total fixed costs.[6] As noted earlier, the per-unit variable manufacturing costs are expected to be $3,400, while total fixed manufacturing costs are expected to be $42,000 per quarter. These budgeted costs can now be used at the conclusion of the first quarter of 2009 to prepare a flexible budget that is relevant to assess the actual costs of producing 27 boats. This performance report based on flexible budgeting for the 27 boats actually produced now makes much more sense.

Sunbird Boat Company
Flexible Budget Performance Report
January–March 2009

	Budgeted Costs	Budgeted Costs for 27 Boats	Actual Costs Incurred for 27 Boats	Difference
Actual production (boats)				27
Budgeted production (boats)				30
Difference				3
Variable manufacturing costs	$ 3,400 per boat	$ 91,800	$ 88,000	$3,800
Fixed manufacturing costs	$42,000 in total	42,000	42,200	(200)
Total costs		$133,800	$130,200	$3,600

Notice that the actual variable manufacturing costs are lower than the flexible budget, which is based on how much should have been spent to produce 27 boats. Only the actual fixed manufacturing costs have exceeded the flexible budget. We are now comparing apples with apples, or actual costs of producing 27 boats with expected costs of producing 27 boats. Using the same activity level has revealed that total manufacturing costs were less than budget by $3,600.

Flexible budgets provide management with useful information for investigating problem areas. This flexible budget performance report shows that actual production fell short of planned production, but that the costs incurred were less than those expected at the actual activity level. Assuming that the company actually needed only those 27 boats, the manager appears to be doing well with cost control. Having meaningful cost comparisons as a result of using flexible budgeting is very useful for evaluating performance. We'll spend a lot of time in the next chapter analyzing specific cost variances for Sunbird Boat Company.

---

[6] We'll discuss the relevant range concept further in Chapter 20.

> **REMEMBER THIS...**
>
> - A static budget is a budget that is prepared for only one level of activity.
> - Static budgets are useful for planning purposes, but flexible budgets are much more useful for control and performance evaluation.
> - Flexible budgets allow budgeted and actual costs to be compared at the same level of activity.
> - The formula for a flexible budget is:
>
>   Total budget costs = (variable costs per unit × production level)
>
>   + total fixed costs

Cash Budget

Create the cash budget.

⑥ The **cash budget**, which shows expected cash receipts and disbursements during a period, is impacted by all of the preceding budgets in the master budget (which is demonstrated in Exhibit 3 on p. 879). A detailed cash budget will point out when a company has excess cash to invest and when it has to borrow funds. This allows a firm to earn maximum interest on excess funds and to avoid the costs of unnecessary borrowing.

Typically, a cash budget is divided into three sections:

1. Cash receipts
2. Cash payments
3. Financing

cash budget

A schedule of expected cash receipts and disbursements during the budget period.

The cash receipts section summarizes all cash expected to flow into the business during the budget period. Because many companies generally extend credit to their customers, a lot of their sales are originally recorded as accounts receivable. The collection of accounts receivable is a major source of cash, and its timing is an important consideration in preparing a cash budget.

As we worked through the operations budgeting process for Sunbird Boat Company, we determined the impact on cash flows of this company's management policies regarding its receivables and payables. In fact, you can see this effort illustrated clearly in Schedules 1 and 3 on pages 881 and 883, respectively.

As you can see in Schedule 1, an analysis of how Sunbird's customers pay on accounts receivable shows that total collections during 2009 are budgeted to be $1,040,000. In particular, you should note that based on Sunbird's expectation that the remaining 20% of accounts are collected in the subsequent quarter, we can assume that the entire beginning balance in accounts receivable is collected in the first quarter of 2009. Further, in the Sunbird example, we assumed that all proceeds from credit sales are eventually collected. Usually, however, some customers never pay, and these uncollectible accounts must be considered when analyzing estimated cash collections from accounts receivable. You should recognize that economic factors play a significant role in the timing of collections of accounts receivable. During recessionary periods, customers often drag out their payments much longer than they would in prosperous times.[7]

The cash budget for Sunbird is shown in Schedule 15. Cash receipts for Sunbird

  CAUTION

When preparing a cash budget, be careful not to include expenditures that do not require cash (e.g., depreciation expense from the manufacturing overhead and selling and administrative expense budgets).

---

[7] Although the reality that some customers never pay off their account does complicate the cash collection budget for accounts receivable, the use of a contra account such as "Allowance for Doubtful Accounts" establishes a net balance for accounts receivable on the balance sheet that represents what is realistically expected to be collected. This "net balance" accounting is very helpful when creating a budget for cash receipts.

are composed solely of what the company collects from its customers, and the computation is reasonably straightforward. However, the cash payments section of this schedule is a bit more involved. You can see that the first four items come directly from the operations budgets for purchases of materials, payments for direct labor, and payments for manufacturing overhead and selling and administrative expense. In addition, there are four other payments that Sunbird has scheduled that take place outside of its day-to-day operations.

SCHEDULE 15

Schedule 15
Sunbird Boat Company
2009 Cash Budget

	Q1	Q2	Q3	Q4	Total
Receipts:					
Collections from customers (Schedule 1)[1]	$220,000	$360,000	$320,000	$140,000	$1,040,000
Payments:					
Direct materials (Schedule 3)[2]	$ 41,500	$ 37,500	$ 27,000	$ 27,000	$ 133,000
Direct labor (Schedule 4)	48,000	56,000	32,000	32,000	168,000
Manufacturing overhead (Schedule 5)[3]	45,000	48,000	39,000	39,000	171,000
Selling and admin. expense (Schedule 7)[3]	86,500	126,500	106,500	66,500	386,000
Income tax payment for 2008	96,000				96,000
Interest payments (10% annual rate)[4]		1,500			1,500
Dividends			30,000		30,000
Equipment purchase				100,000	100,000
Total payments	$317,000	$269,500	$234,500	$264,500	$1,085,500
Financing:					
Beginning cash balance	$137,000	$100,000	$130,500	$216,000	$ 137,000
Total receipts (collections from customers)	220,000	360,000	320,000	140,000	1,040,000
Total payments	(317,000)	(269,500)	(234,500)	(264,500)	(1,085,500)
Cash available	$ 40,000	$190,500	$216,000	$ 91,500	$ 91,500
Minimum cash balance desired[5]	(100,000)	(100,000)	(100,000)	(100,000)	(100,000)
Cash excess (deficiency)	$ (60,000)	$ 90,500	$116,000	$ (8,500)	(8,500)
Borrowings	$ 60,000			$ 8,500	$ 68,500
Repayments of principle		$ (60,000)			(60,000)
Total financing inflows (outflows)	$ 60,000	$ (60,000)	$ –	$ 8,500	$ 8,500
Ending cash balance	$100,000	$130,500	$216,000	$100,000	$ 100,000

[1]Q1 = Beginning accounts receivable balance from balance sheet + 80% of Q1 revenue; Q2 thru Q4 = 80% of current quarter revenue + 20% of previous quarter revenue.
[2]Q1 = Beginning accounts payable balance from balance sheet + 75% of Q1 purchases; Q2 thru Q4 = 75% of current quarter purchases + 25% of previous quarter purchases.
[3]MOH and S&A depreciation is not included in the cash cost of these expenses.
[4]Interest expense for Q2 = $60,000 × 10% × ¼ year = $1,500.
[5]Ending cash balance for each quarter must be at least $100,000. Otherwise, the company must borrow on its line of credit at the bank (interest rate is 10% annual).

- First, Sunbird accrued at the end of 2008 a $96,000 payable for income taxes (see Sunbird's 2008 balance sheet in Exhibit 4). This bill from the IRS is expected to be paid during the first quarter of 2009.

- Second, at the end of the first quarter, Sunbird needs to borrow $60,000 from the bank in order to maintain its desired $100,000 cash balance. At the end of the second quarter, Sunbird has enough excess cash to repay this loan and pay the interest outstanding on this loan (the interest calculation is shown as a footnote in this schedule). Sunbird doesn't need to borrow again until the fourth quarter ($8,500). This is perhaps the most complicated item on the cash budget. You should be sure to work through the calculation of the loan amount in the first quarter, as well as the interest calculation in the second quarter.

- Third, Sunbird plans to declare dividends of $30,000 in the first quarter of 2009, which it expects to pay in the third quarter.

- Fourth, based on its capital projects plan, Sunbird is planning to make a capital expenditure of $100,000 for equipment in the final quarter of 2009. You can see how capital expenditure decisions relate to the master budget by reviewing Exhibit 3.

By combining the expected cash payments with the desired ending cash balance, Sunbird can determine its total cash need for each quarter and compare that need with the total amount of cash it expects to have available during the quarter. The final section of this budget reports the cash excess or deficiency as the difference between budgeted cash availability and cash needs.

In addition to the timing and amounts of all projected borrowings and repayments during the period, the financing section of the cash budget is also used to estimate the amount of interest to be paid on borrowed funds. By accurately projecting these amounts and events, firms can give banks and other lending institutions advance notice of their cash needs. Banks appreciate, and sometimes insist, that companies plan their cash needs in advance. Because money has a time value, management always walks a tightrope between having too much or too little cash on hand.

Exhibit 7 shows how a typical company's cash balance and requirements fluctuate constantly. Most of this fluctuation is due to the varying amounts of raw materials and finished goods that are needed in the different seasons of the year. A prosperous firm could, if it desired, maintain enough cash on hand so that short-term borrowing would never be necessary, but such a policy might not be cost-beneficial. Long-term investments in productive assets usually earn considerably more than short-term cash investments; firms are generally better off maintaining lower cash balances, keeping as much capital as possible "at work" in the company's productive assets, and borrowing from time to time for short periods. For this reason, most companies obtain a line of credit from banks. A **line of credit** is a pre-arranged agreement whereby an organization or individual can borrow money on demand, up to a specific amount at specific rates.

line of credit

An arrangement whereby a bank agrees to loan an amount of money (up to a certain limit) on demand for short periods of time, usually less than a year.

FYI

Remember that having income does not mean that the organization will have cash. Revenues don't get collected immediately (which leads to accounts receivable). Expenses don't get paid immediately (which leads to accounts payable). And capital expenditures (which are not reflected on the income statement) use up a lot of cash.

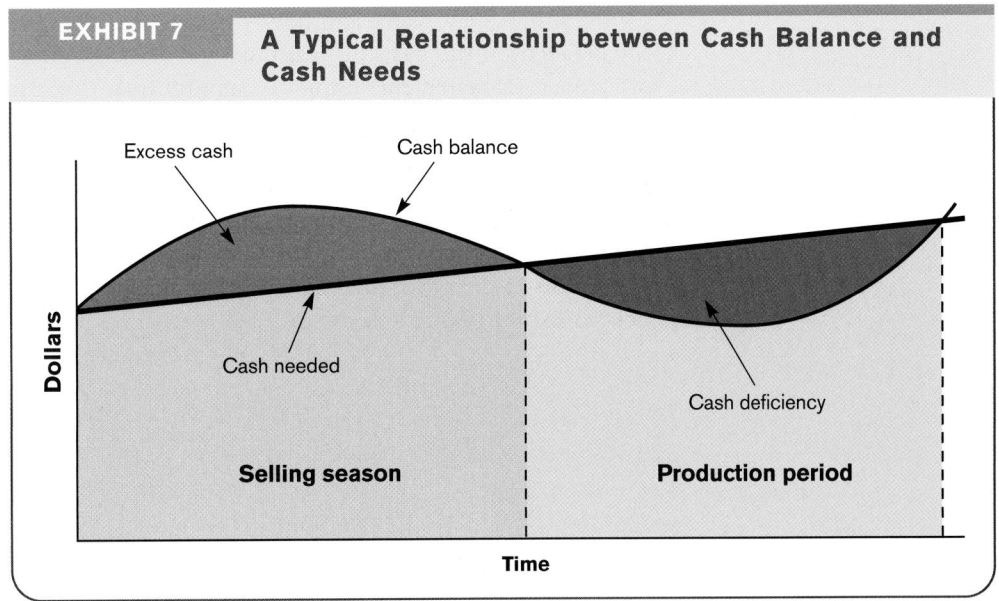

| EXHIBIT 7 | A Typical Relationship between Cash Balance and Cash Needs |

With the cash budget, the company is now able to make planning decisions regarding financing. For example, Sunbird is now aware that there will probably be cash shortages in the first and fourth quarters of 2009. With this knowledge, the company can take steps to deal with these situations. One solution would be to access a line of credit with its bank. The company might also obtain money by attempting to get customers to pay sooner, trying to negotiate with creditors for a longer repayment period, or simply reducing the desired ending cash balance (currently at $100,000). The point is, with knowledge of the coming cash shortfall, Sunbird is able to anticipate and deal with potential problems now rather than waiting until the company actually finds itself in a cash shortage crisis.

> ### REMEMBER THIS...
>
> - The cash budget shows expected cash receipts and disbursements as the result of receipts from customers, payments for inventory, labor, and overhead.
> - Cash budgets must also track expenditures for capital equipment, taxes, interest payments, and various other items.
> - Cash budgets signal when the company can expect a cash shortage, which requires outside financing using a line of credit or another similar finance tool, or a cash excess, which should be temporarily invested in income-producing assets.
> - Cash budgets are typically organized into three sections:
>   - Cash receipts
>   - Cash payments
>   - Financing

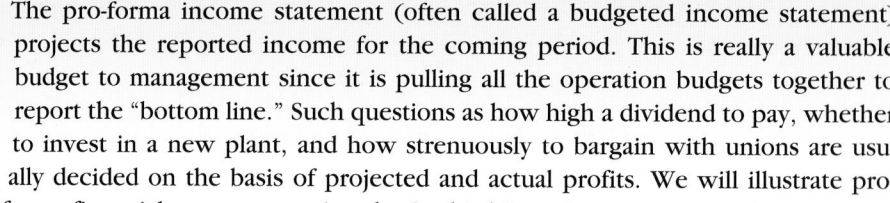

Pro-Forma Financial Statements

Prepare pro-forma financial statements.

(7) The pro-forma income statement (often called a budgeted income statement) projects the reported income for the coming period. This is really a valuable budget to management since it is pulling all the operation budgets together to report the "bottom line." Such questions as how high a dividend to pay, whether to invest in a new plant, and how strenuously to bargain with unions are usually decided on the basis of projected and actual profits. We will illustrate pro-forma financial statements using the Sunbird Boat Company example.

Perhaps the most challenging aspect of determining Sunbird's pro-forma income statement is computing cost of goods sold (shown in Schedule 16). This computation requires a careful assessment of changes in Sunbird's inventory balances. In making this computation, we will assume that Sunbird does not typically have significant work-in-process inventory at the end of a quarter. However, the company does have significant inventory in direct (or raw) materials and finished goods (as shown in Sunbird's balance sheet in Exhibit 4).

Schedule 16

Sunbird Boat Company

Budgeted Cost of Goods Sold

For the Year Ended December 31, 2009

Direct materials purchases (Schedule 3)	$130,000
Direct materials beginning inventory (2008 balance sheet)	8,000
Less direct materials ending inventory (Schedule 3)[1]	(12,000)
Direct materials costs in production	$126,000
Direct labor costs in production (Schedule 4)	168,000
MOH costs in production (Schedule 5)	231,000
Cost of goods manufactured	$525,000
Finished goods beginning inventory (2008 balance sheet)	50,000
Less finished goods ending inventory (Schedules 2 and 6)[2]	(75,000)
Cost of goods sold	$500,000

[1](900 feet of wood × $10 purchase price) + (600 feet of fiberglass × $5 purchase price) = $12,000.
[2]15 boats × $5,000 product cost per boat = $75,000.

Now that we have computed the expected cost of goods sold for 2009, Sunbird is ready to compose its pro-forma income statement, which is shown in Schedule 17. In this income statement, we assume an income tax rate of 40% for Sunbird.

Schedule 17

Sunbird Boat Company

Pro-Forma Income Statement

For the Year Ended December 31, 2009

Sales revenue (Schedule 1)	$1,000,000
Cost of goods sold (Schedule 16)	(500,000)
Gross margin	$ 500,000
Selling and administrative expense (Schedule 7)	(406,000)
Operating income	$ 94,000
Interest expense (Schedule 15)	(1,500)
Net income before tax	$ 92,500
Income taxes (40% average tax rate)	(37,000)
Net income after tax	$ 55,500

The final two items to be projected are the balance sheet and the statement of cash flows. These statements are presented in Schedules 18 and 19. All of the calculations necessary to complete these pro-forma financial statements have been effectively developed all along as we have worked through previous budgets. Be sure to work through each line item in these pro-forma statements to see which schedule is the source of the computation. (This is an excellent way to review everything you've studied in this chapter on computing budgets for manufacturing companies!)

SCHEDULE 18

Schedule 18
Sunbird Boat Company
Pro-Forma Balance Sheet
December 31, 2009

Assets

Current assets:

Cash (Schedule 15)	$ 100,000	
Accounts receivable (Schedule 1)[1]	20,000	
Direct materials inventory[2]	12,000	
Finished goods inventory[2]	75,000	$ 207,000

Long-term assets:

Land	$ 231,500	
Building and equipment (Schedule 15)[3]	1,600,000	
Less accumulated depreciation (Schedules 5 and 7)[4]	(200,000)	1,631,500
Total assets		$1,838,500

Liabilities & Stockholders' Equity

Current liabilities:

Accounts payable (Schedule 3)[5]	$ 7,000	
Income taxes payable (Schedule 16)	37,000	
Short-term loan payable (Schedule 15)	8,500	$ 52,500

Stockholders' equity:

Common stock, $5 par	$1,000,000	
Paid-in capital in excess of par	250,000	
Retained earnings (Schedules 15 and 17)[6]	536,000	1,786,000
Total liabilities & stockholders' equity		$1,838,500

[1]Q4 revenue × 20%.
[2]See the calculation for cost of goods sold in chapter text.
[3]Original account balance ($1,500,000) + equipment purchase ($100,000).
[4]Original account balance ($120,000) + MOH depreciation ($60,000) + S&A depreciation ($20,000).
[5]Q4 purchases × 25%.
[6]Original account balance ($510,500) + income ($55,500) − dividends ($30,000).

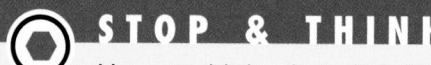

STOP & THINK

How would the three financial statements be different if we assumed Sunbird was a merchandising company instead of a manufacturing company?

The master budget is now complete. It is ready for use to communicate information, coordinate and authorize activities, motivate employees, and measure performance. The decisions to be made on the basis of this budget depend on the answers to such questions as:

1. Is the budgeted net income of $55,500 adequate? If not, how can it be increased?
2. How does the expected financial position at the end of the year fit with long-range objectives and goals?
3. In light of the projected decrease in cash, will the company have enough cash to meet its goals?
4. Are there sufficient liquid assets to purchase needed assets?
5. How should management be rewarded if these budgets are met?
6. Who should be responsible for meeting the goals set for sales, production, and costs?

These are only a few of the questions that management needs to answer. However, these questions should give you a sense of the master budget's usefulness. In fact, it is hard to imagine how a company could be profitable in the long run without such planning.

SCHEDULE 19

Schedule 19

Sunbird Boat Company

Pro-Forma Statement of Cash Flows

For the Year Ended December 31, 2009

Cash flow from operating activities:		
Net income (Schedule 17)		$ 55,500
Adjustments:		
Depreciation (Schedules 5 and 7)	$ 80,000	
Accounts receivable decrease (Schedule 18)*	40,000	
Direct materials inventory increase (Schedule 18)*	(4,000)	
Finished goods inventory increase (Schedule 18)*	(25,000)	
Accounts payable decrease (Schedule 18)*	(3,000)	
Income taxes payable decrease (Schedule 18)*	(59,000)	29,000
Net cash provided by operating activities		$ 84,500
Cash flow from investing activities:		
Purchase of equipment (Schedule 15)	$(100,000)	
Net cash used in investing activities		(100,000)
Cash flow from financing activities:		
Cash obtained from borrowing (Schedule 18)*	$ 8,500	
Payment of dividends (Schedule 15)	(30,000)	
Net cash used in financing activities		(21,500)
Net decrease in cash		$ (37,000)
Beginning cash balance		137,000
Ending cash balance		$100,000

*Compare the relevant ending account balance on these schedules with the beginning account balance on Sunbird's 2008 balance sheet (Exhibit 4).

REMEMBER THIS . . .

- Budgeted cost of goods sold is built using expected changes in inventory balances and the budgeted manufacturing costs. Cost of goods sold is then combined with budgeted revenue, selling and administrative expenses, interest expense, and tax expense to develop the pro-forma income statement.
- Developing the pro-forma balance sheet requires carefully analyzing each budget schedule to identify changes in each account balance.
- Developing the pro-forma statement of cash flows is largely based on assessing the change in beginning and ending balances for each account on the pro-forma balance sheet.
- Once these pro-forma financial statements have been prepared, management can then determine if budgeted sales and production levels will allow the company to achieve its strategic goals.

REVIEW OF LEARNING OBJECTIVES

(1) Describe the importance of personal budgeting.

- To be successful with your personal budget, you need to be goal oriented, organized, proactive, and disciplined.

(2) Explain the budgeting process and its behavioral implications in organizations.

- The behavioral factors that contribute to the success of the operations budgeting process include the support of top management, the participation of all managers in the budgeting process, and the need to address deviations from the budget in a positive and constructive manner.
- Poor budgeting processes create dysfunctional behavior in the organization.
- With the top-down approach to budgeting, top management prepares the entire budget. With bottom-up budgeting, each segment manager makes budget requests. Most firms use a combination of the two approaches.

(3) Construct an operations budget and its components for manufacturing firms.

- Be sure to remember the following diagram:

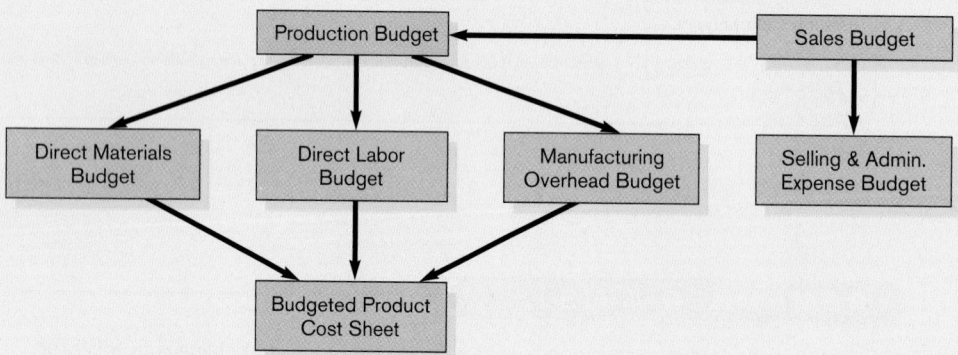

- When computing the production budget and direct materials budget, remember the following formula:

   Needs of the prior budget + ending inventory − beginning inventory = the current budget.

- Fixed budget costs are constant each production period (e.g., each quarter) while the variable budget costs are based on the expected sales or production volume for each production period.
- Also remember the following important facts of budgeting:
  - Revenues ≠ receipts
  - Purchases ≠ payments
  - Budgeted expenses ≠ cash outflows

(4) Compare the operations budget for a manufacturing firm to that of a merchandising or service firm.

- A merchandising firm's purchases budget replaces four of a manufacturing firm's budgets—the production, direct materials, direct labor, and manufacturing overhead budgets.
- Because services cannot usually be inventoried, the sales budget for most service firms also serves as the production (i.e., service) budget.

(5) **Distinguish between static and flexible budgets.**

- A static budget is a budget that is prepared for only one level of activity.
- Flexible budgets allow budgeted and actual costs to be compared at the same level of activity.
- The formula for a flexible budget is:

Total budget costs = (variable costs per unit × production level) + total fixed costs.

(6) **Create the cash budget.**

- Cash budgets are typically organized into three sections:
  - Cash receipts that typically represent collections from customers.
  - Cash payments for inventory, labor, and overhead; and for other expenditures such as for capital equipment, taxes, interest payments, and various other items.
  - Financing when the company expects a cash shortage or has excess cash to repay financing or temporarily invest in income-producing assets.

(7) **Prepare pro-forma financial statements.**

- Budgeted cost of goods sold is built using expected changes in inventory balances and the budgeted manufacturing costs. Cost of goods sold is then combined with budgeted revenue, selling and administrative expenses, interest expense, and tax expense to develop the pro-forma income statement.
- Developing the pro-forma balance sheet requires carefully analyzing each budget schedule to identify changes in each account balance.
- Developing the pro-forma statement of cash flows is largely based on assessing the change in beginning and ending balances for each account on the pro-forma balance sheet.

KEY TERMS & CONCEPTS

REVIEW PROBLEM

Budgeting in a Manufacturing Firm

The following information is available for the Call Company:

Expected sales (units):	
June	840
July	980
August	1,400
Selling price per unit	$15
Accounts receivable balance, June 1	$6,300
Accounts payable balance, June 1	$2,350
Desired finished goods inventory, August 31 (units)	250
Beginning finished goods inventory, June 1 (units)	270
Direct materials needed per unit	11 lbs.
Desired direct materials inventory, August 31	2,800 lbs.
Beginning direct materials inventory, June 1	2,700 lbs.
Total direct labor time per finished unit	3 hours
Direct materials cost per pound	$0.60
Direct labor cost per hour	$8

Additional information:

a. Seventy-five percent of a month's sales is collected by the month's end; the remaining 25% is collected in the following month.
b. Sixty percent of a month's purchases is paid by the month's end; the remaining 40% is paid in the following month.
c. The desired ending finished goods inventory every month is 25% of the next month's sales.
d. The desired ending direct materials inventory every month is 20% of the next month's production needs.

Required:

1. Prepare the sales budget, including cash collections, for June, July, and August (in dollars).
2. Prepare the production budget for June, July, and August (in units).
3. Prepare the direct materials budget, including cash payments, for June, July, and August (in dollars).
4. Prepare the direct labor budget for June, July, and August (in dollars).

Solution
1. Sales Budget

	June	July	August
Expected sales (units)	840	980	1,400
Selling price per unit	× $15	× $15	× $15
Revenue earned	$12,600	$14,700	$21,000
Percent received in current month	× 75%	× 75%	× 75%
Current revenue collected	$ 9,450	$11,025	$15,750
Prior revenue collected*	6,300	3,150	3,675
Collections from customers	$15,750	$14,175	$19,425

*Prior revenue collected in June represents the accounts receivable balance on June 1. Prior revenue collected in July and August represents the revenue not collected in the prior month (i.e., revenue earned in prior month times 25%).

(continued)

2. Production Budget

	June	July	August
Expected sales (units)	840	980	1,400
Add desired ending inventory*	245	350	250
Total needed	1,085	1,330	1,650
Less beginning inventory**	(270)	(245)	(350)
Budgeted production (units)	815	1,085	1,300

*Desired ending inventory for June and July is equal to 25% of next month's sales. Desired ending inventory in August is given.

**Beginning inventory in June is given. Beginning inventory in July and August is based on the desired ending inventory for the previous month.

3. Direct Materials Budget

	June	July	August
Units to be produced	815	1,085	1,300
Direct materials needed per unit	× 11 lbs.	× 11 lbs.	× 11 lbs.
Total production needs	8,965 lbs.	11,935 lbs.	14,300 lbs.
Desired ending direct materials inventory*	2,387	2,860	2,800
Total pounds needed	11,352 lbs.	14,795 lbs.	17,100 lbs.
Less beginning inventory**	(2,700)	(2,387)	(2,860)
Materials to be purchased	8,652 lbs.	12,408 lbs.	14,240 lbs.
Standard cost per pound	×$0.60	× $0.60	× $0.60
Materials purchases (rounded)	$ 5,191	$ 7,445	$ 8,544
Paid in current month	× 60%	× 60%	× 60%
Current purchase payments (rounded)	$ 3,115	$ 4,467	$ 5,126
Prior purchase payments***	2,350	2,076	2,978
Payments to suppliers	$ 5,465	$ 6,543	$ 8,104

*Desired ending direct materials inventory for June and July is equal to 20% of next month's production needs. Desired ending direct materials inventory in August is given.

**Beginning direct materials inventory in June is given. Beginning direct materials inventory in July and August is based on the desired ending direct materials inventory for the previous month.

***Prior purchase payments in June represent the June 1 accounts payable balance. Prior purchase payments in July and August represent the purchases not paid for in the prior month (i.e., material purchases in prior month times 40%—rounded).

4. Direct Labor Budget

	June	July	August
Units to be produced	815	1,085	1,300
Direct labor hours per unit	× 3 hrs.	× 3 hrs.	× 3 hrs.
Total hours needed	2,445 hrs.	3,255 hrs.	3,900 hrs.
Cost per hour	× $8	× $8	× $8
Direct labor cost	$19,560	$26,040	$31,200

DISCUSSION QUESTIONS

1. What are the two general purposes of budgeting?
2. How are strategic planning, capital budgeting, and operations budgeting different?
3. Describe the advantages of the top-down approach and the bottom-up approach to budgeting.
4. Why are budgets usually prepared for one year?

5. Why does the accuracy of the entire master budget depend on a reliable sales forecast?

6. Identify the sequence of schedules used in preparing a master budget for a manufacturing firm.

7. How is the budgeting process for a merchandising firm different from the budgeting process for a manufacturing firm?

8. How is the budgeting process for a service firm similar to the budgeting process for a manufacturing firm? What are any differences?

EXPANDED *material*

9. Describe the three sections of a cash budget.

10. How does a cash budget differ from a pro-forma income statement?

11. How are flexible budgets useful in controlling costs?

PRACTICE EXERCISES

PE 18-1 Personal Budgeting
LO1 Which one of the following is *not* a characteristic of a successful personal budgeter?
a. Goal-driven
b. Flexible
c. Proactive
d. Disciplined
e. Impulsive

PE 18-2 Behavioral Considerations of Budgeting
LO2 Which one of the following is *not* a behavioral consideration of the budgeting process?
a. Top management must support the budgeting process.
b. All managers, and as many employees as possible, should participate in the budgeting process.
c. Deviations from the budget must be addressed by managers in a positive and constructive manner.
d. The budgeting process should remain impersonal in nature.

PE 18-3 Top-Down versus Bottom-Up Budgeting
LO2 Which one of the following statements is *false*?
a. An advantage of top-down budgeting is that upper management knows the strategic objectives of the company.
b. An advantage of bottom-up budgeting is that segment managers have an excellent understanding of products, technology, and current customer needs.
c. An advantage of top-down budgeting is universal acceptance of the final budget from line employees.
d. An advantage of bottom-up budgeting is that lower managers who help prepare the budget are likely to support the final budget.

PE 18-4 Master Budget
LO3 Which one of the following is *not* part of the master budget of a manufacturing firm?
a. Sales budget
b. Depreciation budget
c. Production budget
d. Direct labor budget
e. Selling and administrative expense budget

PE 18-5 Master Budget Information Flow
LO3 Place the following schedules in chronological order from start to finish in the master budgeting process.
a. Cash budget
b. Pro-forma income statement
c. Production budget

(continued)

d. Sales budget

e. Direct materials budget

PE 18-6
LO3
Sales Budget

Is the following statement true or false?

Since external variables (such as customer tastes and economic conditions) cannot be controlled by a company, those inputs are not used when computing a sales budget. Instead, the sales budget is generated using only historical sales data and internal cost information.

PE 18-7
LO3
Production Budget

Using the following information, compute the number of units to be produced.

Desired ending inventory (in units)	3,750
Beginning inventory (in units)	3,450
Expected sales (in units)	24,250

PE 18-8
LO3
Direct Materials Budget

Refer to the data in PE 18-7. Using the following additional information, compute the cost of materials to be used in the coming period. (Assume no beginning nor ending direct materials inventory.)

Wood requirement per unit	10 board feet
Aluminum requirement per unit	7.5 square feet
Cost of wood (per board foot)	$4.60
Cost of aluminum (per square foot)	$5.75

PE 18-9
LO3
Direct Labor Budget

Refer to the data in PE 18-7. Using the following additional information, compute the direct labor cost.

Direct labor hours per unit	6
Rate per direct labor hour	$12

PE 18-10
LO3
Manufacturing Overhead Budget

Using the following information, compute total manufacturing overhead.

Indirect labor rate	$4.00 per unit
Indirect materials rate	$2.50 per unit
Utilities rate	$1.25 per unit
Property tax expense	$29,000
Depreciation expense	$133,600
Insurance expense	$38,000
Supervisor salaries expense	$240,300
Expected production (in units)	21,000

PE 18-11
LO4
Purchases Budget

Using the following information, compute the dollar amount of total purchases to be made in the coming period.

Beginning inventory (in units)	123
Expected sales (in units)	1,240
Desired ending inventory (in units)	128
Cost per unit	$685

PE 18-12   Master Budget for Manufacturing Firms versus Service Firms

LO4   Which one of the following budgets do manufacturing firms and service firms have in common?
a. Direct labor budget
b. Supplies budget
c. Production budget
d. Revenue budget
e. Direct materials budget

PE 18-13   Revenue Budget

LO4   The company performs tune-ups on standard diesel engines. Using the following information, compute the budgeted gross revenue for the period.

Gross revenue per tune-up	$180
Tune-up capacity per day	13
Number of working days in period	76
Historical occupancy rate*	65%

*This refers to the rate at which the companies' service bays are actually occupied compared to their total capacity. It is similar to the concept of hotel room occupancy rate.

EXPANDED material

PE 18-14   Flexible Budgets

LO5   Using the following manufacturing costs per unit, prepare a flexible budget for the company at levels of production of 550, 600, and 650 units.

Direct materials	$6.80
Direct labor	8.90
Manufacturing overhead	5.20

PE 18-15   Flexible Budget Performance Report

LO5   Refer to the data in PE 18-14. Using the flexible budget created in PE 18-14 and the following actual data, prepare a flexible budget performance report.

Actual number of units produced	650
Actual direct materials costs	$4,200
Actual direct labor costs	$5,750
Actual manufacturing overhead costs	$3,430

PE 18-16   Cash Budget

LO6   Using the following information, determine how much external funding will be necessary during the coming period (if any).

Collections from customers	$104,300
Minimum cash balance desired	25,000
Direct labor expense	24,350
Cash balance, beginning	32,000
Manufacturing overhead expense	22,750
Income tax expense	21,680
Selling and administrative expenses	54,140
Direct materials expense	43,200

PE 18-17

LO7

Pro-Forma Financial Statements

Which one of the following statements regarding pro-forma financial statements is *false*?

a. Pro-forma financial statements include an income statement, a balance sheet, and a statement of cash flows.

b. The pro-forma financial statements complete the master budget for a company.

c. Pro-forma financial statements help companies make decisions regarding dividends and management bonus opportunities for the coming year.

d. Most companies do not create pro-forma financial statements because of the many assumptions required.

EXERCISES

E 18-18

LO1

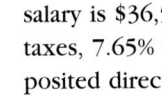

Personal Budgeting

Jennifer Swartz works as an interior decorator for Modern Fashion Corporation. Her annual salary is $36,500. Of that amount, 20% is withheld for federal income taxes, 7.15% for state taxes, 7.65% for FICA taxes, and 2% as a contribution to the United Way. Another 5% is deposited directly into a company credit union for savings. Jennifer has four monthly payments: $225 for her car, $80 for furniture, $410 for rent, and $100 to repay college loans. Jennifer's other monthly expenses are approximately:

Food expense	$250
Clothing expense	100
Entertainment expense	125
Utilities expense	80
Insurance expense	30
Gas and maintenance expenses on car	180
Miscellaneous expenses	200
Total	$965

Prepare both a monthly budget and an annual budget for Jennifer that identifies gross salary, net take-home pay, net disposable income, and net surplus or deficit.

E 18-19

LO1

Personal Budgeting

George Marcus, a recent college graduate, has been hired by Taylor Corporation at a salary of $54,000 per year. In anticipation of his salary, George purchased a $20,000 new ski boat and will pay for it at a rate of $425 per month, including interest, for five years. He also rented a condominium for $600 a month and bought a car on account for $350 a month. In addition, George figures that his other monthly expenses will be:

Food expense	$250
Clothing expense	125
Entertainment expense	250
Insurance expense	150
Gas and other car expenses	200
Utilities expense	130

1. On the assumption that George also pays income and FICA taxes of 25 and 7.65%, respectively, prepare his monthly budget.

2. George plans to save enough money for a down payment on a house. If a $20,000 down payment is needed, how long will it take him to save the needed amount? (For this exercise, ignore interest on savings, and assume that George does not have any savings at the present time.)

E 18-20   **Budgeting Sales Revenue and Collections**

LO3   Fred's Frames mass produces and wholesales wooden picture frames at an average price of $7 per frame. Expected sales volumes over the first six months of 2009 are forecasted as follows:

January	7,800
February	8,600
March	8,100
April	9,200
May	8,600
June	8,200

Fred's Frames expects to collect 85% of its revenues in the month of the sale, with the remaining 15% collected in the following month.

1. Compute the expected balance in Accounts Receivable as of February 1, 2009. (*Hint:* It is based solely on sales in January 2009.)
2. Budget the expected monthly revenue and collections for the five months of February through June.

E 18-21   **Production Budgeting**

LO3   Daytona Electric makes and sells two kinds of portable music players—a CD player and an MP3 player. The sales forecasts for these players for the next four quarters are as follows:

	CD Player	MP3 Player
First quarter	170	130
Second quarter	178	139
Third quarter	166	127
Fourth quarter	190	145
Totals	704	541

At the beginning of the first quarter, Daytona has 140 CD players and 120 MP3 players in stock. Experience has shown that Daytona must maintain an inventory equal to two-thirds of the next quarter's sales.

How many players of each type must be produced during each of the first three quarters to meet sales and inventory demands?

E 18-22   **Production Budgeting**

LO3   Jim Seagal is the CEO of Seagal Monitor Company, a manufacturer of computer monitors. Seagal manufactures three types of flat panel LCD computer monitors: 15-inch, 17-inch, and 19-inch. The sales projections (in units) for 2009 and the first quarter of 2010 are:

	15-inch	17-inch	19-inch
First quarter, 2009	3,100	5,100	2,200
Second quarter, 2009	2,450	4,700	2,050
Third quarter, 2009	2,800	4,950	1,900
Fourth quarter, 2009	3,150	4,870	2,100
First quarter, 2010	2,850	5,150	2,000

Beginning inventory for 15-inch, 17-inch, and 19-inch monitors are 1,300, 1,500, and 1,250, respectively. Seagal requires that half of the next quarter's sales be maintained in inventory.

How many monitors must be manufactured for each quarter of 2009 to meet sales and inventory demand?

E 18-23

LO3

Direct Materials Budgeting

Shaver Bicycle Shop assembles and sells tricycles and bicycles. The frames are purchased from one supplier and the wheels from another. The following materials are required:

Bicycles	Tricycles
One 22-inch frame, $35	One 12-inch frame, $15
Two 22-inch wheels, $10 each	Two 4-inch wheels, $10 each
	One 12-inch wheel, $7.50

Management anticipates that 150 bicycles and 160 tricycles will be assembled during the first quarter of 2009. On December 31, 2008, the following assembly parts are on hand:

22-inch frames	12
22-inch wheels	20
12-inch frames	8
4-inch wheels	24
12-inch wheels	10

Management also decides that, beginning in January, the inventory of parts on hand at the end of each month should be sufficient to make 10 bicycles and 10 tricycles.

Prepare a budget for direct materials purchases for the first quarter of 2009. (*Note:* You are not required to extend the budget to determine the budget for cash payments to suppliers.)

E 18-24

LO3

Direct Materials Budgeting

Shanahan Corporation produces three types of videocassettes: VHS, S-VHS, and 8 millimeter. Shanahan purchases tape for the videocassettes from a firm in Mexico and purchases the cases from another supplier in Brazil. The following materials are required for production:

	VHS	S-VHS	8MM
Tape	$1.75	$2.30	$3.05
Cases	2.50	2.50	2.00

Beginning inventory for Shanahan Corporation is 5,000, 7,000, and 3,500 tapes for VHS, S-VHS, and 8 MM, respectively. Management wants to have 5,000 VHS and 8 MM tapes and 2,500 S-VHS tapes in ending inventory. Projected sales for the first half of 2009 are 40,000 VHS tapes, 14,000 S-VHS tapes, and 21,000 8 MM tapes.

Shanahan's policy is to pay 80% of its accounts with suppliers by the end of each half year. The balance in accounts payable on January 1, 2009, is $55,000.

1. Prepare a budget for direct materials purchases for the first half of 2009.
2. Prepare a budget for payments to direct materials suppliers for the first half of 2009.

E 18-25

LO3

Direct Labor Budgeting

Super Rich Chocolate Company makes and sells two kinds of candy: chocolate peanut bars and caramel bars. The production budget for the next three months for each of the bars is as follows:

(continued)

	Boxes of Chocolate Peanut Bars	Boxes of Caramel Bars
January	690	720
February	860	490
March	910	640

From experience, Super Rich's management knows that it takes approximately 20 minutes to make a box of chocolate peanut bars and 30 minutes to make a box of caramel bars. Super Rich pays its direct labor employees $8 per hour.

Prepare a direct labor budget for each of the two products in both hours and costs for January, February, and March.

E 18-26

LO3

Direct Labor Budgeting

Sanford Shoe Company makes three shoe styles: loafers, work boots, and tennis shoes. The production budget for the next three months for each type of shoe is:

	Loafers	Work Boots	Tennis Shoes
January	2,900	5,400	3,160
February	3,100	6,000	5,400
March	2,750	6,600	4,300

From experience, Sanford's management knows that it takes 15 minutes of direct labor to make a pair of loafers, 20 minutes to make a pair of work boots, and 12 minutes to make a pair of tennis shoes. At Sanford, direct labor employees are paid $10 per hour.

Prepare a direct labor budget in both hours and costs for each of the three months.

E 18-27

LO3

Production Overhead Cost Budget

Linden Nursery grows and sells potted perennial plants, as well as ornamental and fruit trees. The owner of Linden Nursery has determined that variable overhead costs are largely a function of direct labor hours spent growing and tending the plants and trees. Variable overhead costs include supervisory costs, indirect materials, and utilities (power and water) and are estimated to be $0.75, $0.40, and $0.55 per direct labor hour, respectively. Fixed overhead costs for property taxes, equipment depreciation, and night security are expected to be $1,500, $900, and $1,100, respectively, each quarter. Linden keeps a minimal staff during the winter season and then expands its workforce substantially during the gardening season. The direct labor hours budgeted for 2009 are as follows:

First quarter	1,000 hours
Second quarter	9,500
Third quarter	6,100
Fourth quarter	800

Prepare a production overhead budget for Linden Nursery.

E 18-28

LO3

Budgeted Product Costs

Home Run Bat Company makes two types of baseball bats: aluminum and wood. During the past several years, management has kept accurate records of costs and resource requirements and has determined that the following is needed to make the baseball bats:

(continued)

Wood Bat	Production Requirements	Unit Cost
Wood	4 board feet	$ 5.75
Paint and protective finish	1 pint	6.50
Direct labor	3 hours	11.00
Manufacturing overhead	3 hours	5.75
Aluminum Bat		
Aluminum	7 pounds	$ 4.00
Paint and protective finish	½ pint	6.50
Direct labor	2½ hours	11.00
Manufacturing overhead	2½ hours	5.75

Compute the budgeted product costs for both the wood and aluminum baseball bats.

E 18-29

LO4

Operations Budgeting (Service Company)

Dr. Dawn Gifford is a new dentist specializing in treating children under the age of 18. Dr. Gifford has two primary sources of revenues: (1) fees from regular dental work (checkups, cleanings, fillings, etc.) and (2) fees from specialized dental reconstructive surgery. Last year, Dr. Gifford earned an average of $75 per patient visit from regular customers and $800 per surgery. The following operating expenses were incurred last year in running the office:

Variable operating expenses:	
Dental supplies (per patient)	$ 10
Hospital surgery room rental (per surgery)	200
Annual fixed operating expenses:	
Office manager's salary	$18,000
Dental hygienist's salary	26,000
Utilities	3,600
Rental of office space	12,000
Depreciation expense on office equipment*	20,000
Liability insurance	48,000
Other expenses	9,600

*Total equipment cost, $200,000; depreciated over 10 years on a straight-line basis.

Last year, Dr. Gifford treated an average of 200 patients per month and performed an average of eight surgeries per month. She expects to increase the number of patients serviced by 10% this coming year and the number of surgeries to ten per month. She also expects the average patient fee to be $80 and the average surgical fee to be $850. Dr. Gifford expects the variable expenses to remain constant this year, but is expecting to raise the manager's salary by 5% and the hygienist's by 15%. She thinks the other expenses will stay about the same. All revenues are expected to be collected and all payable expenses are expected to be paid during the year.

Based on these data (and ignoring payroll and income taxes):

1. What was the operating profit (loss) for last year?
2. Prepare a revenue budget and an operating expense budget for this coming year.

E 18-30

LO5

Static versus Flexible Budgeting–Performance Reports (Service Firm)

Flannery Muffler Shop has budgeted to repair 10,000 mufflers during 2009. Each repair job takes 1½ hours, and employees are paid $12 per hour. During 2009, Flannery actually repaired 9,425 mufflers, and the salary expense amounted to $179,000.

(continued)

1. Assuming a static budget, use the information to prepare a performance report for Flannery Muffler Shop for 2009.
2. Assuming a flexible budget, use the information to prepare a performance report for Flannery Muffler Shop for 2009.
3. **Interpretive Question:** The manager of the muffler shop believes he deserves a bonus because the actual wage expense ($179,000) was less than budgeted. Do you agree? Explain.

E 18-31   **Flexible Budgets (Service Firm)**

LO5   Outdoors Unlimited operates a fishing lodge in northern Canada. The following cost information has been developed by the company's accountant:

Fixed costs:	
Salaries	$68,000
Mortgage payments	24,000
Taxes	4,000
Other	3,000
Variable costs (per guest):	
Fishing tackle	$20
Food	80
Other	16

1. In planning for its 2009 summer season, Outdoors Unlimited does not know exactly how many guests to expect and, hence, how much to charge per guest. Prepare a flexible budget showing expected total costs at 200, 300, 400, and 500 guests.
2. Assume that Outdoors Unlimited conservatively estimates 300 guests for the year. If it wants to earn profits of $100,000 for the 300 guests, how much should it charge per guest?

E 18-32   **Cash Budgeting–Hospital**

LO6   The management of Table Rock Memorial Hospital needs to prepare a cash budget for July 2009. The following information is available:

a. The cash balance on July 1, 2009, is $245,000.
b. Actual services performed during May and June and projected services for July are:

	May	June	July
Cash services (bills paid by individuals as they leave the hospital)	$115,000	$ 98,000	$115,000
Credit services (bills paid by insurance companies and Medicare)	950,000	1,075,000	950,000

Credit sales are collected over a 2-month period, with 60% collected during the month the service is performed and 40% in the following month.
c. Hospital personnel plan to purchase $70,000 of supplies during July on account. Accounts payable are usually paid one-half in the month of purchase and one-half in the following month. The accounts payable balance on July 1, 2009, is $30,000.
d. Salaries and wages paid during July will be approximately $650,000. (Ignore income and other tax withholdings.)
e. Depreciation on the hospital and equipment for July will be $120,000.
f. A short-term bank loan of $90,000 (including interest) will be repaid in July.
g. All other cash expenses for July will total $86,000.

Prepare the hospital's July cash budget.

E 18-33

LO6

Cash Budgeting

Medical Supplies, Inc., purchases first-aid items from large wholesalers. Medical Supplies then assembles and sells first-aid kits to businesses and contracts to maintain the first-aid kits. You have been asked to prepare a cash budget for January. The following information is provided:

a. Cash in the bank on January 1 is $33,000.

b. Actual sales for October, November, December, and projected sales for January are as follows:

	October	November	December	January
Cash	$12,000	$11,500	$ 8,200	$12,500
Credit	31,000	29,400	32,000	28,000

Payments on credit sales are received 50% in the month of sale, 31% in the month following the sale, and 15% and 4% in the second and third months, respectively, following the sale.

c. Total administrative and selling expenses (all cash) are $25,000.

d. Purchases are always paid 30 days after delivery. Purchases for October, November, and December were $28,000, $39,000, and $29,500, respectively.

e. Cash dividends of $22,000 are paid.

f. Any cash excess is used to purchase 30-day government securities, and any cash deficiency is compensated by short-term borrowing.

g. Management desires a minimum balance of $9,000 in the bank.

Prepare a cash budget for the month of January.

E 18-34

LO6

Cash Budgeting (Merchandising Company)

Whitlock, Inc., buys hardware parts from various manufacturers and sells them to retail stores. Management is currently trying to prepare a cash budget for August and has the following information available:

a. The cash balance on August 1 is $25,000.

b. Actual sales for June and July and projected sales for August are as follows:

	June	July	August
Cash sales	$ 30,000	$ 45,000	$ 50,000
Credit sales	100,000	120,000	130,000

Credit sales are collected 63% during the month of sale, 26% during the month following the sale, and 11% during the second month following the sale.

c. Whitlock's actual purchases for June and July and its projected purchases for August are as follows:

	June	July	August
Cash purchases	$10,000	$20,000	$25,000
Credit purchases	40,000	50,000	60,000

All accounts payable are paid in the month following the purchase.

d. Total administrative and selling expenses (including $14,000 depreciation) for August are expected to be $105,000.

e. Whitlock expects to pay a $26,000 dividend to stockholders and to purchase, for cash, a $25,000 piece of land during August.

f. Cash on hand should never drop below $25,000.

1. Prepare Whitlock's August cash budget, assuming that the company borrows any amounts needed to meet its minimum desired balance.

2. **Interpretive Question:** What types of expenses other than depreciation would be excluded from a cash budget?

E 18-35   **Pro-Forma Income Statement**

LO7   Gamma Manufacturing, Inc., is a manufacturer of electric pencil sharpeners. The following is information regarding Gamma Manufacturing for the fiscal year-end, May 31, 2009:

Beginning finished goods inventory	$ 51,000
Ending finished goods inventory	48,000
Interest expense	29,000
Selling and administrative expenses	69,000
Sales revenue	445,000
Direct materials used	57,000
Direct labor	62,000
Manufacturing overhead	33,000

Assume a tax rate of 33%. Prepare a pro-forma income statement for the year ended May 31, 2009, for Gamma Manufacturing, Inc. (Note that Gamma Manufacturing does not have work-in-process inventory.)

E 18-36   **Pro-Forma Income Statement**

LO7   Silver Company has asked you to prepare a pro-forma income statement for the coming year. The following information is available:

Expected sales revenue	$1,240,000
Manufacturing costs:	
Variable cost of goods sold	625,000
Fixed overhead	125,000
Selling expenses:	
Variable expenses	140,000
Fixed expenses	45,000
Administrative expenses:	
Variable expenses	45,000
Fixed expenses	160,000
Other:	
Interest expense	28,000
Income tax rate	35%

Prepare a pro-forma contribution margin income statement for Silver Company.

E 18-37   **Pro-Forma Statement of Cash Flows**

LO7   The accountants at Karl's Fish Hatchery are currently preparing the pro-forma statement of cash flows for May. In getting ready to prepare the statement, they have the following information available:

Dividends to be paid in May	$ 1,500
Bonds to be issued in May	8,000
Equipment to be purchased in May	15,000
Repayment of short-term loans in May	3,000
Depreciation expense during May	2,500
Expected May net income	10,000
Expected changes in current assets and	
liabilities during May:	
Accounts receivable decrease	1,200
Accounts payable decrease	1,730
Increase in inventory	2,580
Increase in income taxes payable	2,550

Prepare Karl's pro-forma statement of cash flows (using the indirect method).

E 18-38

LO7

Pro-Forma Income Statement and Balance Sheet (Service Industry)

Bel-Air, Inc., is a small engineering corporation that surveys land for development. The company has grown rapidly over the past few years, and management has to decide whether to hire new engineers and open new offices. To assess future growth, the company's accountant has gathered budgeted information for the coming year, 2009:

Ending common stock balance	$ 36,000
Beginning retained earnings balance	37,000
Ending accounts payable balance	8,500
Ending equipment balance	154,000
Ending accumulated depreciation balance	25,000
Ending accounts receivable balance	21,500
Ending cash balance	35,000
Interest expense	5,000
Salary expense	125,000
Other expenses (including depreciation)	41,000
Service revenue	350,000
Income tax rate	40%

Income taxes due on the coming year's net income will be paid during 2010. Dividends of $75,000 are to be declared and paid during 2009.

1. Prepare a pro-forma income statement and balance sheet for 2009 from which the company president can make expansion decisions.
2. **Interpretive Question:** On the basis of this information, is the company very profitable? How should this level of profits affect its expansion plans?

PROBLEMS

P 18-39

LO1

Personal Budgeting

Ben Fleming has just received a job offer of $35,000 salary per year plus overtime pay, which will amount to 10% of his salary. Ben estimates his living costs as follows:

Federal, state, and FICA taxes amount to	35% of income
Rent	$550/month
Car payment	$210/month
IRA	$1,500/year
Long-term savings for retirement	4% of net take-home pay
Utilities	$90/month
Gas and maintenance–automobile	$130/month
Insurance	$75/month
Food	$240/month
Entertainment	$170/month
Clothing	$80/month

Required:

1. Prepare a budget for the year. Assume Ben starts his job on January 1.
2. Is Ben's offer sufficient to meet his projected expenses?
3. Ben has always dreamed of going to Africa to photograph wildlife. The trip will cost $5,000. How long will it take Ben to save for the trip? (Ignore interest earnings, and assume that Ben will not use his retirement savings for this trip.)

P 18-40

LO1

Personal Budgeting

Kathy Bourne is an advertising specialist for Success Advertising, Inc. Her annual salary is $42,000, of which 20% is withheld for federal income taxes, 7% for state income taxes, 7.65% for FICA taxes, and 5% for a tax-sheltered annuity. She estimates that her monthly expenses are approximately as follows:

(continued)

Rent	$ 500
Automobile payment	250
Food	240
Automobile gasoline and maintenance	140
Utilities	80
Clothing	90
Entertainment	140
Miscellaneous	150
Total monthly expenses	$1,590

Required:

1. Prepare Kathy's monthly budget, assuming that the car payments will continue for about three years.
2. Assume that Kathy would like to accumulate savings of $12,000 in order to take an extended leave from her job. This will allow her to travel and take courses as a way of generating some fresh ideas she can use in creating new approaches to advertising. How long will it take her to save the needed amount? (Ignore interest earnings, and assume that she has no savings at the present time.)
3. **Interpretive Question:** If Kathy asked you for advice on how she might reduce her expenses, what would you suggest?

P 18-41   **Sales Revenue Budgeting (Service Firm)**

LO3   Six-Peak Pools in Montana is open May through September. It has the capability of serving approximately 600 patrons each day. July is the peak month for Six-Peak Pools. With kids being in school, May and September are its slowest months. For the upcoming 2009 season, Six-Peak's management projects the following usage rates:

May	30%
June	80
July	90
August	75
September	20

The pool admission fees for Six-Peak are as follows:

Adults (12 years and up)	$5
Children (3 to 11 years)	$3
Babies (2 and under)	Free

On a typical day, 40% of the patrons are adults, 50% are children, and 10% are babies. Because Six-Peak only accepts cash and credit cards, its daily admission revenue and daily cash collections are the same.

Required:
Budget the expected monthly sales in admission fees for Six-Peak Pools.

P 18-42   **Sales Collections**

LO3   Rocky Peak Company plans on the following collection pattern on its sales:

Collected in month of sale	70%
Collected in the first month after sale	15
Collected in the second month after sale	10
Collected in the third month after sale	4
Uncollectible	1

(continued)

Budgeted sales for the last six months of 2009 are shown below.

July	$ 60,000
August	70,000
September	80,000
October	90,000
November	100,000
December	85,000

Required:

1. What are the estimated total cash collections during October 2009?
2. How much of the third quarter sales (i.e., July, August, and September) are expected to be collected during the third quarter?
3. What is the expected 2009 ending balance in accounts receivable, net of allowance for doubtful accounts?

P 18-43

LO3

Production Budgeting

Carry-It-All Company makes and sells two products: leather and vinyl briefcases. The sales forecasts for these briefcases for the next four quarters are as follows:

	Leather Briefcases	Vinyl Briefcases
First quarter	120	110
Second quarter	160	170
Third quarter	240	220
Fourth quarter	280	250
Total	800	750

On January 1, Carry-It-All has a stock of 90 completed leather briefcases and 80 vinyl briefcases. Experience indicates that Carry-It-All must maintain an inventory equal to one-half of the next quarter's sales.

Required:

1. How many leather and vinyl briefcases must be produced during each of the first three quarters to meet sales and inventory demands?
2. **Interpretive Question:** Assume Carry-It-All is a wholesale merchandising company instead of a manufacturing company. How would the budget information provided in part (1) change?

P 18-44

LO3

Production and Direct Materials Budget

Chandler Manufacturing Company makes two products: widgets and gidgets. The following information is available on May 1:

a. Direct materials needed to make a widget: six units of X, three units of Y. Direct materials needed to make a gidget: two units of X, six units of Y.
b. Number of units available at beginning of May:

Direct material X	72 units
Direct material Y	43 units
Finished widgets	12
Finished gidgets	15

c. Expected sales during May:

Widgets	100
Gidgets	95

(continued)

d. Desired levels of ending inventory:

Direct material X	70 units
Direct material Y	35 units
Widgets	11
Gidgets	13

e. Cost of direct materials:

Direct material X	$3 per unit
Direct material Y	$2 per unit

Chandler has a $1,300 balance in accounts payable on May 1 and expects to pay for half of its May purchases by the end of the month. All accounts are paid in full within 30 days.

Required:
Prepare a production budget and a direct materials budget for Chandler Company for the month of May.

P 18-45
LO3

Manufacturing Overhead Cost Budget

World-Wide Gym, Inc. makes weight lifting equipment. It designs and manufactures its own weight plates, as well as home gym sets such as workout towers, strength cages, and universal stations. Its variable manufacturing overhead (MOH) costs are determined as a result of either the pounds of weight plates or the number of gym sets manufactured. The variable MOH rates are as follows: $0.05 and $0.02 per pound of weight plates for materials handling and storage costs, respectively; and $45 and $12 per gym set for insurance and inspection work, respectively. The fixed MOH costs each month are $2,200 for property taxes, $3,200 for plant depreciation, $450 for utilities, and $17,000 for research and development.

The following monthly manufacturing volumes are expected for the second quarter of 2009:

	Pounds of Weight Plates	Number of Gym Sets
April	10,000	775
May	11,500	650
June	11,000	700
Total	32,500	2,125

Required:
Prepare a monthly manufacturing overhead budget for World-Wide Gym, Inc.

P 18-46
LO3

Budgeted Product Cost Sheet

New Harbour Candy Company makes and sells two kinds of candy bars: chocolate almond and coconut. During the past several years, the company has kept accurate records of costs and resource requirements and has determined that the following are needed to make the candy bars:

One Box of 24 Chocolate Almond Bars	Cost
Chocolate (1½ pounds)	$2.00/pound
Almonds (1 pound)	$6.00/pound
Sugar (2 pounds)	$0.75/pound
Direct labor (20 minutes)	$12.00/hour
Manufacturing overhead (20 minutes)	$6.00/direct labor hour

(continued)

One Box of 24 Coconut Bars	Cost
Chocolate (1 pound)	$2.00/pound
Coconut (1¼ pounds)	$4.00/pound
Sugar (1¾ pounds)	$0.75/pound
Direct labor (30 minutes)	$12.00/hour
Manufacturing overhead (30 minutes)	$6.00/direct labor hour

Required:

1. Establish the budgeted product cost sheet for each type of candy bar.
2. If New Harbour management wants to mark up each box of candy 30% to cover other costs and earn a profit, how much should be charged for a box of each type of candy bar?

P 18-47

LO3

Unifying Concepts: Sales, Cash Collections, and Purchases Budgets

The following information is available for Laurel Company, a wholesale company:

Expected sales volume:	
October	6,200 units
November	6,700 units
December	7,100 units
Selling price per unit	$45
Accounts receivable balance, October 1	$55,000
Desired ending inventory, December 31	1,800 units
Beginning inventory, October 1	2,000 units

Additional information:

a. Each month 75% of sales is collected by month-end; the remaining 25% is collected in the following month.
b. The desired inventory every month is 30% of the next month's sales.

Required:

1. Prepare sales budgets for October, November, and December (in dollars).
2. Prepare cash collection budgets for October, November, and December (in dollars). Assume that all sales are on credit.
3. Prepare purchases budgets for October, November, and December (in units).

P 18-48

LO3

Unifying Concepts: Production, Direct Materials, Direct Labor, and Manufacturing Overhead Budgets; and Budgeted Product Cost Sheets

San Antonio Furniture Company makes two products: bookshelves and rocking chairs. The following information is available for September:

a. Production requirements:

	Bookshelves	Rocking Chairs
Materials needed:		
Wood	100 board feet at $0.90 per foot	90 board feet at $0.90 per foot
Stain	2 gallons at $9 per gallon	3 gallons at $9 per gallon
Bolts, nuts, etc.	1 dozen at $1.50 per dozen	1½ dozen at $1.50 per dozen
Direct labor	12 hours at $8.50 per hour	10 hours at $8.50 per hour
Variable manufacturing overhead	12 hours at $4 per direct labor hour	10 hours at $4 per direct labor hour
Fixed manufacturing overhead*	$1,521 per month	

*Fixed manufacturing overhead is assigned to products using direct labor hours.

(continued)

b. Levels of inventories:

	Actual Beginning Inventory	Desired Ending Inventory
Wood	1,100 board feet	1,000 board feet
Stain	11 gallons	12 gallons
Bolts, nuts, etc.	15 dozen	9 dozen
Finished bookshelves	3	5
Finished rocking chairs	6	7

Required:

1. Prepare the production budget, assuming that the company expects to sell 40 bookshelves and 50 rocking chairs in September.
2. Based on the production budget and the desired ending inventory level, prepare the direct materials usage and purchases budget for September. (*Note:* Direct materials purchases are paid for at the time of the purchase.)
3. Based on the production budget, prepare the direct labor budget for September.
4. Based on the production budget, prepare the manufacturing overhead budget for September.
5. Based on the operations budgets prepared above, prepare the budgeted product cost sheets for bookshelves and rocking chairs for September.

P 18-49

LO3

Unifying Concepts: Sales, Cash Collections, Production, Direct Materials, and Direct Labor Budgets

The following information is available for Raleigh Company:

Expected sales volume:	
April	1,600 units
May	1,500 units
June	1,750 units
Selling price per unit	$12
Accounts receivable balance, April 1	$6,000
Accounts payable balance, April 1	$796
Desired finished goods inventory, June 30	200 units
Beginning finished goods inventory, April 1	210 units
Direct materials needed per unit	5 pounds
Desired direct materials inventory, June 30	550 pounds
Beginning direct materials inventory, April 1	420 pounds
Total direct labor time per finished product	2 hours
Direct materials cost per pound	$0.50
Direct labor cost per hour	$8

Additional information:

a. Each month 70% of sales are collected by month-end; the remaining 30% are collected in the following month.
b. The desired finished goods inventory every month is 20% of the next month's sales.
c. The desired direct materials inventory every month is 10% of the next month's production needs.
d. Each month 80% of direct materials purchases are paid by month-end; the remaining 20% are paid in the following month.

Required:

1. Prepare sales budgets for April, May, and June (in dollars).

(continued)

2. Prepare cash collection budgets for April, May, and June (in dollars). Assume that all sales are on credit.
3. Prepare production budgets for April, May, and June (in units).
4. Prepare direct materials budgets for April, May, and June (in dollars).
5. Prepare direct labor budgets for April, May, and June (in dollars).

P 18-50

LO4

Budgeting for a Service Company

Lakeside Country Club has 425 members at the end of 2008 (including 20 new members who joined during the year). Each member has paid a $10,000 initiation fee and pays $100 a month in dues to remain an active member of the club (new members do not pay monthly dues during the first calendar year of their membership). The club offers golf, tennis, and food and beverage services. The club is essentially run on a cash basis. Operating data for 2008 are as follows:

Lakeside Country Club Annual Budget For the Year 2008		
Revenues:		
Dues[1]	$686,000	
Guest fees[2]	6,500	
Golf revenues	450,000	
Tennis revenues	175,000	
Food and beverage	310,000	
Miscellaneous	2,500	$1,630,000
Expenses:		
Golf course	$390,000	
Tennis courts	190,000	
Food and bar	275,000	
Administration and maintenance[3]	525,000	
Interest on debt[4]	50,000	
Miscellaneous	27,000	(1,457,000)
Net operating profit		$ 173,000

[1]Dues (405 × $1,200 = $486,000; 20 new members × $10,000 = $200,000).
[2]Guest fees (130 × $50 = $6,500).
[3]Maintenance includes $125,000 depreciation on facilities.
[4]Interest ($500,000 × 0.10 × 1 year).

Assume the following additional facts for the year 2009:
a. There are 425 members paying dues, as well as 15 additional new members.
b. Guest fees are 120% of 2008 fees.
c. Golf revenues are 115% of 2008 revenues.
d. Tennis revenues are 90% of 2008 revenues (due to courts being closed for one month).
e. Food and beverage revenues are the same as 2008.
f. Operating expenses (golf, tennis, and food and beverage) are up 5%.
g. Administration and maintenance will increase $45,000 due to expected repairs.
h. Principal payment of $50,000 during 2009 will reduce interest expense by 10% for 2009.
i. Miscellaneous revenues will stay the same; miscellaneous expenses are expected to be $20,000.

Required:
1. Using the same format as the Annual Budget for 2008, prepare an annual budget for Lakeside for the year 2009.
2. **Interpretive Question:** Is Lakeside in better shape financially in 2009 as compared to 2008? What areas of concern do you see?

P 18-51   **Static versus Flexible Budgeting (Service Firm)**

LO5   Wasatch Medical Clinic has three doctors on staff. The clinic's budget for 2009 is as follows:

Wasatch Medical Clinic		
Budget for the Year Ended December 31, 2009		
Expected number of patient visits		26,000
Average charge per patient		× $25
Total revenues		$650,000
Budgeted costs:		
Variable costs:		
Supplies for each patient ($2 × 26,000)		$ 52,000
Fixed costs:		
Utilities	$ 2,400	
Rent	9,600	
Nurses' salaries	90,000	
Malpractice insurance	150,000	
Equipment leases	25,000	
Other	30,000	
Total fixed costs		307,000
Total budgeted costs		$359,000
Expected income		$291,000
Number of doctors on staff		÷ 3
Expected income per doctor		$ 97,000

Required:

1. Is this a static or flexible budget?
2. Prepare a flexible budget showing expected income per doctor at 22,000, 26,000, 30,000, and 34,000 total patient visits.
3. **Interpretive Question:** Why does the expected income per doctor increase so dramatically as the number of patient visits increases?

P 18-52   **Static versus Flexible Budgeting (Service Firm)**

LO5   Peterson Management, Inc., is a small firm that sponsors time-management seminars in hotels throughout the country. It sponsors 20 two-day seminars during the year for a tuition fee of $200 per student. The following is a budget for a single seminar:

Peterson Management, Inc.	
Budget per Seminar	
Expected enrollment	40
Tuition per person	× $200
Revenue per seminar	$8,000
Variable costs:	
Catering ($25 per person)	$1,000
Books and handouts ($10 per person)	400
Fixed costs:	
Airfare	425
Hotel rental fee	600
Advertising	1,000
Other	300
Total costs	$3,725
Expected income	$4,275

(continued)

Required:

Bruce Peterson, owner of the company and the speaker at the seminars, would be pleased with an income of $4,275 per seminar. With 20 seminars per year, the company's annual income would be $85,500. He is concerned, however, that every seminar may not have 40 participants. Prepare a flexible budget, showing what annual income would be if 10, 20, 40, or 50 people enroll in each seminar.

P 18-53

LO6

Cash Budgeting (Manufacturing Company)

Hare Manufacturing Company makes wax for automobiles. As part of overall planning, a cash budget is prepared quarterly each year. You have been asked to assist in preparing the cash budget for the fourth quarter of the company's fiscal year. The following information is available:

a. Sales:

Third quarter (actual)	$180,000
Fourth quarter (expected)	175,000

All sales are made on account, with 70% collected in the quarter in which the sales are made and 30% collected during the following quarter.

b. Materials purchases are scheduled as follows:

Third quarter (actual)	$90,000
Fourth quarter (expected)	80,000

Materials are purchased on account and paid for at the rate of 80% in the quarter of purchase and 20% in the following quarter.

c. Direct labor and manufacturing overhead costs (including $6,000 of depreciation) are expected to be $45,000 and $21,000, respectively, during the fourth quarter.

d. Selling and administrative expenses are expected to total $27,000 during the fourth quarter, including $2,000 of depreciation.

e. Plans have been made to purchase, for cash, $15,000 of equipment during the fourth quarter.

f. The cash balance at the beginning of the quarter is $16,000. The company can borrow money in $1,000 multiples at 12% interest from a local bank. The bank assesses interest for a full quarter, both for the quarter in which the money is borrowed and for the quarter in which it is repaid. All interest is paid at the time of note repayment. Hare ran short of cash during the third quarter and had to borrow $8,000 from the bank. Hare wishes to maintain a minimum cash balance of $16,000.

Required:

Prepare a schedule showing the cash budget and financing needs of Hare Manufacturing Company for the fourth quarter.

P 18-54

LO6

Cash Budgeting (Merchandising Company)

Jim Henry, owner of Henry's Retail, is negotiating a $100,000, 15%, four-month loan from the Garfield County Bank, effective October 1, 2009. The bank loan officer has requested that Henry's prepare a cash budget for each of the next four months as evidence of its ability to repay the loan. The following information is available as of September 30, 2009:

Cash on hand	$ 9,000
Accounts receivable	97,500
Inventory	64,000
Accounts payable	144,500

(continued)

a. The accounts payable are for September merchandise purchases and operating expenses and will all be paid in October. Sales forecasts for the next few months are October, $220,000; November, $300,000; December, $400,000; January, $200,000; February, $140,000.

b. Collections on sales are usually made at the rate of 20% during the month of the sale, 60% during the month following the sale, and 15% during the second month after the sale. Five percent of accounts receivable are written off as uncollectible. Of the $97,500 of accounts receivable at September 30, $65,000 will be collected in October, and $32,500 will be collected in November. Cost of goods sold is 55% of sales, with all purchases paid for in the month following purchase. Ending inventory should always equal the cost of the goods that will be sold during the next month. Operating expenses are $18,000 a month plus 5% of sales, all paid in the month following their incurrence.

Required:

Prepare a cash budget showing receipts and disbursements for October, November, December, and January. Also prepare supporting schedules for cash collections, purchases, and operating expenses. Assume that the loan plus interest will be paid on January 31.

P 18-55 **Cash Budgeting**

LO6   Athletic World is a sporting goods store. The following data are for use in preparing its forecast of cash needs for June:

a. Current assets (May 31):

Cash	$25,000
Inventory	18,500
Accounts receivable	30,000
Property, plant, and equipment	92,000
Accounts payable (merchandise purchases only)	14,400
Recent and estimated future sales:	
May	50,000
June	56,000
July	54,000

b. Sales are made 60% on credit and 40% for cash. All credit sales are collected in the month following the sale.

c. Athletic World's June expenses are estimated to be:

Salaries and wages expense	20% of sales
Rent expense	4% of sales
All other cash expenses	6% of sales
Depreciation expense	$600
Gross margin	40% of sales

d. Athletic World buys all its inventory from companies on the West Coast and wants to maintain an inventory level equal to one-half of the next month's sales. Payments for merchandise are made 50% during the month of purchase and 50% in the next month.

e. Other cash expenditures planned for June are:

(1) The purchase of $7,000 of furniture.

(2) The payment of $9,000 of dividends.

(continued)

f. Athletic World desires to maintain a minimum cash balance of $10,000. The store has an arrangement with a local bank whereby it can borrow money in multiples of $1,000. Interest is charged on all loans at an annual rate of 10% and is assessed for a full quarter both in the quarter in which the money is borrowed and in the quarter in which the money is repaid. Interest is paid when the loan is repaid.

Required:

Prepare Athletic World's cash budget for June.

P 18-56
LO7

Unifying Concepts: The Pro-Forma Income Statement, Balance Sheet, and Statement of Cash Flows

Pun Corporation makes construction cranes. During the past few days, the company's accountants have been preparing the master budget for 2009. To date, they have gathered the following projected data:

For the Year Ended December 31, 2009:	
Sales revenue	$20,254,400
Variable selling expenses	896,000
Variable administrative expenses	1,344,000
Interest expense	134,400
Cost of goods sold (variable costs only)	11,200,000
Fixed manufacturing expenses	1,568,000
Fixed administrative expenses	984,000
Fixed selling expenses	672,000

Account Balances at December 31, 2009:	
Cash	$ 896,000
Accounts receivable	336,000
Land	834,400
Buildings	1,008,000
Equipment	716,800
Accumulated depreciation—equipment	179,200
Accumulated depreciation—buildings	160,000
Direct materials inventory	212,800
Finished goods inventory	235,200
Accounts payable	90,480
Common stock	1,400,000
Retained earnings	?
Paid-in capital in excess of par	80,000
Income taxes payable	400,000

Other Information:	
Dividends to be declared and paid during 2009	$ 1,303,680
Income tax rate	30%

(continued)

In addition, last year's balance sheet was as follows:

Pun Corporation
Balance Sheet
December 31, 2008

Assets

Cash		$ 379,200
Accounts receivable		90,800
Direct materials inventory		180,000
Finished goods inventory		246,400
Land		672,000
Buildings	$ 896,000	
Less accumulated depreciation	(100,000)	796,000
Equipment	$ 649,600	
Less accumulated depreciation	(120,000)	529,600
Total assets		$2,894,000

Liabilities and Stockholders' Equity

Liabilities:

Accounts payable	$ 150,000	
Income taxes payable	450,000	
Total liabilities		$ 600,000

Stockholders' Equity:

Common stock	$1,400,000	
Paid-in capital in excess of par, common stock	80,000	
Retained earnings	814,000	
Total stockholders' equity		2,294,000
Total liabilities and stockholders' equity		$2,894,000

Required:

1. Prepare a pro-forma income statement for 2009 (contribution margin approach).
2. Prepare a pro-forma balance sheet as of December 31, 2009.
3. Prepare a pro-forma statement of cash flows for 2009 (indirect method).

P 18-57
LO7

Pro-Forma Income Statement and Balance Sheet

Style Right Company makes hair dryers. During the past few days, its accountants have been preparing the master budget for the coming year, 2009. To date, they have gathered the following projected data:

Sales revenue (at $20 per unit)	$281,750
Variable selling expenses	17,250
Variable administrative expenses	40,250
Interest expense (not included in selling and administrative expenses)	1,725
Cost of goods sold (includes only variable costs)	103,500
Ending cash balance	30,475
Ending accounts receivable balance	47,150
Ending land balance	24,150
Ending buildings balance	71,300
Ending equipment balance	24,150
Ending accumulated depreciation–buildings balance	47,150
Ending accumulated depreciation–equipment balance	9,200
Ending direct materials inventory balance	16,100
Ending finished goods inventory balance	25,300
Ending accounts payable balance	6,900
Ending common stock balance	32,200
Retained earnings balance, January 1	64,050
Balance in paid-in capital in excess of par account	23,000
Fixed selling expenses	23,000
Fixed administrative expenses	28,750
Fixed manufacturing overhead	11,150
Income tax rate	35%

(continued)

Required:

1. Prepare a pro-forma income statement (contribution margin approach) and balance sheet for the coming year. Any income taxes owed on the coming year's net income will be paid the following year.
2. By approximately how much would Style Right's profits increase if another 3,000 units were produced and sold for $20 each?

P 18-58
LO7

Pro-Forma Statement of Cash Flows

The accountants at Boise Department Store are preparing the pro-forma statement of cash flows for 2009. The following information is available:

Expected net income	$80,000
Dividends to be paid	20,000
Equipment to be purchased	39,000
Expected short-term borrowing	6,000
Expected long-term borrowing	15,000
Expected depreciation expense for 2009	12,000
Expected issuance of common stock	85,000
Expected purchase of a new plant	73,000
Expected changes in current assets and liabilities during 2009:	
Increase in accounts receivable	$ 800
Increase in accounts payable	1,200
Increase in inventory	1,500
Decrease in income taxes payable	1,900

Required:

Prepare the pro-forma statement of cash flows for Boise Department Store (indirect method).

ANALYTICAL ASSIGNMENTS

AA 18-59
DISCUSSION

West Mountain Canning Company

West Mountain Canning Company produces several food items, including certain tomato-based products. For about nine months during the year, the company is able to purchase tomatoes from various parts of the country. The tomatoes are then processed and canned for sale in grocery stores.

The processing department employs three highly skilled workers, who are paid an average of $15 per hour. Between January and March, tomatoes are not available, and the processing and canning departments are shut down. Rather than lay off these three specialists, who have excellent alternative job opportunities, the company transfers them to the shipping department, at the same $15 pay rate. The shipping department manager is not happy, however, because his five regular employees are paid only $9 per hour. His unhappiness has become particularly acute since he was told he was $9,000 over budget for wages during the January-to-March quarter (budget was $36,000; actual was $45,000). Note that the actual amount includes 1,500 hours (3 employees × 500 hours) at $15 per hour, and that each employee works 2,000 hours in a year.

The shipping department manager feels that he is being unduly penalized for two reasons: (1) $15 is too much to pay even a good shipping clerk, and (2) the three skilled workers do not work as hard as his regular employees because they know they are needed for tomato processing and will not be fired. Therefore, he has suggested to his boss that the wages in excess of the $9 he normally pays be assigned elsewhere or that he be allowed to hire his own temporary employees (if needed) during this part of the year.

(continued)

Answer the following questions:

1. Does the shipping department manager have a legitimate complaint? Explain.
2. Explain how management arrived at the budgeted figure of $36,000 for shipping wages.
3. How might the quarterly figures be reported to satisfy the shipping department manager?
4. How would you recommend that the problem be solved?

AA 18-60

DISCUSSION

Tip Top Company

Tip Top Company recently hired a new hot-shot CEO. Traditionally, the budgeting process at Tip Top has been pretty relaxed, with the executive vice president for sales providing "best-guess" sales projections and the controller providing "ballpark" cost estimates. Although the budget has been due each year 30 days prior to the new fiscal year, it generally is not finalized until two or three months into the new fiscal year. One of the first actions of the new CEO is to institute a formalized top-down budgeting process, complete with fairly sophisticated sales projections and cost data based on benchmark statistics from industry competitors.

Discuss the issues involved in the new budgeting process for Tip Top Company.

AA 18-61

DISCUSSION

New Age Budgeting

Manes.com is an Internet company that searches out job listings on corporate home pages, organizes them by type of job, and lists them so that individuals seeking jobs can see the kinds of jobs that are available. The Internet site is free to all users. Manes.com hopes that by providing a job-matching service, its site will attract substantial traffic, and advertisers will be willing to pay large sums of money to advertise. The company has a $20 million investment from a venture capitalist to get started but must provide budget projections to secure additional funding. Assume you are the controller for the company. How would you go about forecasting revenues and preparing budgets and profit projections to show potential investors?

AA 18-62

DISCUSSION

Disagreements over the Value of Budgets

Tueller Enterprises is a large manufacturer of airplane parts for commercial and military aircraft. In addition to making parts, it also serves as a distributor for other, smaller manufacturers. Traditionally, the company has spent large amounts of time preparing operations budgets, only to find that they are rarely useful and often outdated. Some managers have even argued that because they are evaluated on the basis of how well they meet the budget, they have been unable to react to changing markets and take advantage of new opportunities that have become available. The managers argue that the entire budgeting process is too constraining and should be scrapped. The new controller agrees that the traditional budgeting process has been flawed but argues that with the availability of new computer technology and up-to-date performance information, budgets can now be revised more frequently and will be much more useful than in the past. The company is trying to decide what to do. Should it scrap the entire budgeting process? Or, should it work to make the budgeting process more relevant and useful?

AA 18-63

JUDGMENT CALL

You Decide: **Is budgeting a necessary tool to help a fast-growing company plan and prepare for the future, or is budgeting too complicated and subjective for a growing company?**

A budget is a good tool for a company to use to determine how it will secure the necessary finances to accomplish its business goals. However, a fast-growing company does not always know how its needs will grow or change over a short time frame. In addition, often a new company has no history to use in guiding budgets and, as a result, budgeting often involves substantial guesswork.

AA 18-64
JUDGMENT CALL

You Decide: **Should pro-forma financial statements be prepared in a manner consistent with GAAP, or do pro-forma statements provide enough useful information to investors in their current form?**

Most financial statements prepared by companies and filed with the Securities and Exchange Commission are prepared using generally accepted accounting principles. However, pro-forma financial statements are often not prepared in accordance with these standards. Many of the numbers included by companies in these "pro-forma" statements are based on assumptions that are not recognized as appropriate for SEC filings. Sometimes, companies highlight positive information and leave out information about certain costs or charges, such as stock-based compensation, interest, and taxes. The real question is whether or not investors are being misled.

AA 18-65
REAL COMPANY
ANALYSIS

Wal-Mart

Auditors are extremely reluctant to publish any projections of future financial performance for the companies they are auditing. **Ernst & Young LLP** obviously has made no such predictions in its audit of **Wal-Mart's** 2006 financial performance (see the "Report of Independent Registered Public Accounting Firm" in Appendix A). However, the Management's Discussion and Analysis of Results of Operations and Financial Condition, in the section titled "Forward-Looking Statements," provides some important guidance about statements made by management regarding expectations about future financial performance at Wal-Mart. Elsewhere in the management discussion are insights useful in predicting future operating expenses, interest income, and income taxes. These discussions can be extremely important to investors who are trying to understand what Wal-Mart plans to do in in its 2007 fiscal year. Essentially, these investors need to put together their own pro-forma financial statements on Wal-Mart for use in planning, controlling, and evaluating their investment decisions in this company.

Consider the 2006 income statement below and use the information provided in Wal-Mart's Management Discussion of "Forward-Looking Statements," as well as any other comments in the management's discussion that you might find useful, to prepare your own pro-forma 2007 income statement for Wal-Mart. Be sure to read and consider each item in the management discussion relating to Wal-Mart's income statement provided in the annual report in Appendix A. You may also want to consider the 2004 and 2005 revenue and cost trends from the income statement published in this same annual report. For each line item (i.e., for each revenue and cost category), briefly defend the budget number you chose to use.

	2006
(amounts in millions)	
Revenue	$315,654
Cost of sales	(240,391)
Gross margin	$ 75,263
Operating, selling, general and administrative expense	(56,733)
Operating income	$ 18,530
Interest expense	(1,172)
Income before income taxes	$ 17,358
Provision for income taxes	(5,803)
Minority interest	(324)
Net income	$ 11,231

AA 18-66
REAL COMPANY
ANALYSIS

Participative Living, Inc.

Participative Living, Inc. (a fictitious name) is an actual charitable organization in a medium-size community in Canada. It was organized by parents of disabled adults to provide accommodation and training for severely disabled adults in the community. With the help of the Ministry of Community and Social Services, the parents eventually organized six different

(continued)

homes, each with two to four residents. In addition to the six homes, Participative Living also had an employment and education program that provided training and assistance for residents seeking employment or educational opportunities. Overall, the organization had eight divisions composed of six homes, the employment and education program, and an administrative program. A supervisor who reports to the Participative Living executive team staffs each division. The executive team, in turn, reports to a volunteer board of directors composed of 12 people from the community.

Participative Living is a not-for-profit organization. Hence, while surpluses and deficits are occasionally expected, each division is expected to break even each operating period. Seven of the eight divisions are established as break-even operations, with responsibility for both revenues and expenses. The main revenue source is the Ontario government, through the Ministry of Community and Social Services, which provides all funding necessary to support each home as well as the employment and education program. All costs of Participative Living's administrative division in excess of any donations from the community are allocated to its other seven divisions. The Ministry follows a procedure of disbursing operating funds for all social service agencies under its direction based on annual operations budgets submitted to the Ministry. Generally, the Ministry is not concerned about whether an individual budget item was overspent as long as the overall spending is within the approved budget. As a result, it became a common practice among agencies to transfer expenses from one budget line to another and, in the case of Participative Living, to transfer expenses from one division to another depending on which division had excess budgeted funds. As with most government organizations, the Ministry's administrative process of reviewing and approving a new home for Participative Living is often quite slow. As long as the Ministry is holding up the establishment of a proposed new home, it provides significant interest payments to Participative Living. The Ministry was making large interest payments during the first few months of Participative Living's 2009 fiscal year (which ended on March 31, 2009) while the organization waited for government approval and funding of the sixth group home.

In November 2008, Mr. Brad Dunford, the executive director of Participative Living, Inc., was reviewing the financial statements for the first seven months of the 2009 fiscal year. He was puzzled about how the agency could suddenly be $50,000 over budget in salaries and benefits when just last month the statements indicated that spending was slightly under budget.

1. As you review operating results for the last seven months at Participative Living, Inc., what problems do you foresee?
2. Consider the style of management and management accounting in this not-for-profit organization, as well as its relationship with the Ministry of Community and Social Services. What aspects of the way business is conducted here do you think have led to the current situation?

(continued)

Participative Living, Inc.

Operating Results

For the Seven Months Ended October 31, 2008

YTD	Admin. Costs	Admin. Budget	Employ. and Edu. Costs	Employ. and Edu. Budget	Group Homes Costs	Group Homes Budget	Total Actual	Total Budget*	% of Budget
Revenues:									
Ministry**	$ –	$ –	$206,315	$297,675	$521,841	$476,714	$728,156	$774,389	94.0%
Interest	20,943	–	–	–	–	–	20,943	–	0%
Donations	1,567	–	–	–	–	–	1,567	–	0%
Total revenues	$ 22,510	$ –	$206,315	$297,675	$521,841	$476,714	$750,666	$774,389	96.9%
Expenses:									
Salaries	$ 59,029	$ 61,754	$141,034	$197,386	$434,014	$327,789	$634,077	$586,929	108.0%
Occupancy costs	10,392	12,264	39	2,205	61,598	68,761	72,029	83,230	86.5%
Services, supplies, and food	4,375	7,000	3,643	14,147	16,812	35,301	24,830	56,448	44.0%
Personal needs	–	–	3,077	–	35	26,327	3,112	26,327	11.8%
New furnishing and equip.	5	350	60	2,765	6,548	19,236	6,613	22,351	29.6%
Other expenses	1,176	4,669	197	7,707	15,681	7,868	17,054	20,244	84.2%
Travel and training	436	875	1,972	8,792	1,992	4,900	4,400	14,567	30.2%
Specific reimbursements	–	–	–	–	(32,119)	(35,707)	(32,119)	(35,707)	90.0%
Allocated admin. costs	(75,417)	(86,912)	56,293	64,673	19,123	22,239	(1)	–	0.0%
Total expenses	$ (4)	$ –	$206,315	$297,675	$523,684	$476,714	$729,995	$774,389	94.3%
Net surplus (deficit)	$ 22,514	$ –	$ –	$ –	$ (1,843)	$ –	$ 20,671	$ –	N/A

*Budget columns represent the total annual budget. Note that Participative Living is now seven months into its fiscal year.

**Ministry revenues are based on actual payments made by the Ministry. Total payments limited to maximum of total annual budget approved.

Source: Adapted from M. Heisz, "Participative Living, Inc.," *Journal of Accounting Case Research* 2(3), 1995, pp. 87–91. Permission to use has been granted by Captus Press, Inc. and the Accounting Education Resource Centre of The University of Lethbridge. [Journal Subscription: Captus Press Inc., York University Campus, 4700 Keele Street, North York, Ontario, M3J1P3, by calling (416) 736-5537, or by fax at (416) 736-5793, E-mail: info@captus.com, Internet: **http://www.captus.com**]

AA 18-67

INTERNATIONAL

It's Not Easy Being an Accountant in Poland (Applying U.S-Type Budgeting in a Different Country)

The late 1980s and early 1990s were a very significant time for Eastern Europe. Several national boundaries and political ideologies, as well as the names of a few countries, changed during this period. Poland, like its neighbors, experienced tremendous upheaval in its political and economic climate during this time. In 1989, Poland changed to a non-Communist government and a free market economy. Since the end of World War II in 1945, Poland had been a centrally planned economy with government-enforced economic rules based on Marxism-Leninism. A Polish accountant's professional life during the 1945–1989 period was not very exciting. Most university-trained accountants worked in a state-owned enterprise, earning a reasonable salary. The work was not complicated, generally entailing only basic bookkeeping. Performing the accounting work essentially required simple mathematical operations. In addition, the nature of Poland's history since the fifteenth century had generally created disdain for business and profiteering in general. These traditions, coupled with the social environment engendered by a Marxist government, resulted in a serious lack of respect (sometimes bordering on distrust) for accountants, economists, and business managers from 1945 to 1989.

The failure of the Communist system in 1989 was the beginning of a new career stage for most accountants in Poland. The accounting profession suddenly became prestigious. It also became very challenging. Past accounting knowledge and skills were simply inadequate for the new economic situation, particularly for accountants moving out of state-owned enterprises and into the private sector. Business terminology, performance measures, and goals changed. Before 1989, the Communist regime promoted a view that everything a "capitalist"

(continued)

did was wrong and everything a Communist did was right. After the change in the political system, a lot of people began to see things in an opposite way; they expected that life in a capitalist country would be completely just and everyone would be employed with plenty of money. Obviously, life in a capitalist country is not perfect. There are problems, including injustice and unemployment. Complicating this reality, many people also carried over into the 1990s some of the prevailing pre-1989 attitudes that accountants and for-profit businesses were not trustworthy. Today Poland is making steady progress, but the accounting profession continues to face a number of challenges as attitudes and business processes are still in transition.

Assume that you have just been transferred by your U.S.-based company to an accounting or management position in the company's Poland division. Your assignment is to implement a traditional budgeting system (similar to the budget systems described in this chapter) in a large-scale manufacturing plant. Based on your understanding of Polish history and attitudes, what specific challenges would you expect to encounter in this new assignment? Do you have any ideas on how to handle these challenges?

Source: Adapted from P. Stec, "Mr. Kowalski: A Man Against All Odds," *The Journal of Accounting Case Research* 2(3), 1995, pp. 52–54. Permission to use has been granted by Captus Press, Inc. and the Accounting Education Resource Centre of The University of Lethbridge. [Journal Subscription: Captus Press Inc., York University Campus, 4700 Keele Street, North York, Ontario, M3J 1P3, by calling (416) 736-5537, or by fax at (416) 736-5793, E-mail: info@captus.com, Internet: **http://www.captus.com**]

AA 18-68

ETHICS

Skipper Enterprises (Manipulated Revenues)

You are the management accountant for Skipper Enterprises, a manufacturer of screen doors. Recently, one of the commissioned salespersons (your close personal friend) confided in you that a problem with the budgets is hurting the company's profitability.

Your friend explained that salespersons are paid a straight commission of $15 for every screen door they sell. If a salesperson meets the budgeted sales of 3,000 screen doors per year, he or she is paid an annual bonus of $5,000. Your friend stated that it is actually quite easy to reach budgeted sales of 3,000 doors by October or early November. Because there is no financial incentive to sell additional doors once the 3,000 sales level is met and the $5,000 bonus is earned, salespersons only "line up" sales for next year during the last couple of months of each year. In other words, instead of selling additional doors during November and December, they commit customers to buy during January of next year. This way, the doors count as next year's sales, ensuring that the commissioned salespersons are well on their way to meeting the sales budget for next year.

You realize the current bonus plan is causing two problems. First, valuable sales are being deferred each year because there is less incentive to sell near the end of the year. Second, customers are receiving less than optimum service because it can take as long as two months for customers to get their desired doors.

You don't know what to do with your new information.

1. Should you inform management that the sales plan is hurting company profits, or should you keep the information confidential as your friend requested?
2. If it becomes known that you had this information and didn't come forward, you could lose your job. On the other hand, you hate to lose a good friend. What should you do?

AA 18-69

WRITING

Preparing a Personal Budget

Most people have the ability to spend more than they make. As a student, you probably fit in that category. This writing assignment requires you to prepare a personal budget for a one-month period. Forecast your income and expenses to determine what your cash position will be at the end of the month. If you forecast a cash shortage, what actions can you take to address the problem (e.g., increase income, reduce expenses, borrow money, etc.)? If you forecast a cash surplus, what are your options for the surplus?

Controlling Cost, Profit, and Investment Centers

(1) Describe the responsibility accounting concept and identify the three types of organizational control units. *The idea behind responsibility accounting is that the performance of a manager should be based only on those items (costs, revenues, or assets) over which that manager exercises some control.*

(2) Describe standard costing and use materials and labor cost variance analysis to explain how performance is controlled in cost centers. *In order to evaluate the performance of a manager, there must be a standard to which the performance of the manager can be compared. In a cost center, where the manager has control only over the costs, the actual amount paid for and used in materials and labor is compared to the amount that should have been paid for and used; any difference is called a cost variance.*

(3) Use segment margin statements and revenue variance analysis to explain how performance is controlled in profit centers. *Manager performance in profit centers should be evaluated solely on expenses and revenues that are directly related to that business segment. Revenue variances can be combined with cost variances to control and evaluate performance in profit centers.*

(4) Use ROI and residual income analysis to explain how performance is controlled in investment centers. *A manager of an investment center has responsibility to effectively manage costs, revenues, and assets. Computation of return on investment (ROI) and residual income incorporates cost, revenue, and asset performance.*

EXPANDED *material*

(5) Compute and interpret variable overhead cost variances. *In addition to managing the cost of materials and labor, the manager of a cost center is also responsible for managing variable manufacturing overhead costs. The actual variable overhead cost incurred is compared to the cost that should have been incurred given the level of activity.*

(6) Compute and interpret fixed overhead cost variances. *Many cost center managers are responsible for fixed manufacturing overhead costs. Fixed overhead variances occur both because of a difference between actual and budgeted spending and because of a difference between the actual and budgeted levels of activity.*

SETTING THE STAGE

Before Randy Curran was appointed CEO, **ICG Communications** was losing $34 million a month. That was in September 2000. On November 14, 2000, ICG filed for Chapter 11 bankruptcy. *BusinessWeek* reported that ICG's survival was unlikely. However, ICG recovered from hard times to become a smaller but prosperous company and was finally purchased by **Level 3 Communications** in 2006 for $163 million. ICG's story is about how a company gone awry can be saved through fiscal responsibility and good management control.[1]

ICG provides voice, data, and Internet communications services in targeted cities. During the heyday of the Internet explosion in the late 1990s, ICG became the poster child for the failed "build it and they will come" business model. During this time, ICG quickly burned through $2 billion raised through Wall Street investors. Randy Curran, the current CEO, is largely responsible for recovering ICG after the previous CEO went on a spending spree hosting elaborate parties and building excessive facilities in an apparent effort to put himself and his company in the spotlight of trade and business publications and the society pages. Randy Curran faced a difficult task in carefully controlling a turnaround of ICG's financial position. A high level view of the company revealed numerous problems that needed immediate attention. Curran realized that a poor-performing network would kill the business, regardless of the impressive size and scale of the network operation. He identified a large number of unprofitable products, services, and customers.

ICG emerged from Chapter 11 protection on October 10, 2002, after its employee head count had dropped from 3,000 to 1,000. Randy Curran and his management team had to carefully refocus the company on controlling costs, managing revenues, and effectively using its assets. It took a lot of work to bring ICG through the next three and half years to eventually negotiate a successful acquisition. Companies such as ICG provide good outlines for other tech companies on how to control and manage a successful (sometimes smaller) business in the post-Internet bubble era.

I n Chapter 18, we created the master budget, which is a major planning tool for management. In this chapter, we will examine how managers create and maintain an effective system of control within their organizations. Traditional control systems are initially based on using the standard cost and revenue data created in the master budget. These data are used to assess business processes throughout the year in order to identify performance in various organization units that require management attention.

In the process of establishing effective management control within an organization, it is critical to clearly define each division's and each person's specific responsibility within the organization. Because it is often difficult to separate the performance of a unit from the performance of its managers, managers are most often evaluated on how well their units perform. If managers are responsible for costs only, they are usually evaluated on how well they control costs. If they are responsible for revenues and costs, they are usually evaluated on the profitability of their units. And, if they are responsible for costs, revenues, and investments, managers are most frequently evaluated on the return their division investments generate. In the case of ICG, the new CEO was responsible for doing a better job than had the previous CEO of controlling costs, revenues, and investments. Because the company initially lost large sums of money, one may fairly question the effectiveness of cost, revenue, and asset controls at ICG prior to 2000. On the other hand, ICG's turnaround since 2000 is largely attributable to Randy Curran's fiscal responsibility and his efforts to bring ICG's operations under control.

---

[1] Paul M. Sherer and Gary McWilliams, "How a Brash Provider of Internet Services Became Unplugged," *The Wall Street Journal*, November 13, 2000, p. A1; Paul M. Sherer, "ICG Files for Protection from Creditors," *The Wall Street Journal*, November 15, 2000, p. A1; Peter Elstrom, "Dead Companies Walking," *BusinessWeek Online*, January 22, 2001; John Sullivan and Tom Cross, "A New Day at ICG," *Boardwatch Magazine*, April 2002, Vol. 16, Issue 4, pp. 42–44; "ICG out of Bankruptcy," *Denver Business Journal*, October 10, 2002, **http://denver.bizjournals.com**, accessed September 5, 2003; Client Interview with ICG, **http://www.gapinter.com/ClientProfiles**, accessed September 5, 2003. Level 3 Communications, Inc. news release, May 31, 2006.

Control of Divisions and Personnel in Different Types of Operating Units

Describe the responsibility accounting concept and identify the three types of organizational control units.

(1) Most companies are made up of a number of relatively independent **segments** or subunits, sometimes called groups, divisions, or subsidiaries. As an example, Exhibit 1 shows an organizational chart for a hypothetical company that we will call International Manufacturing Corporation (IMC). IMC has three operating (subsidiary) companies: Acme Computer, Edison Automobile, and Jennifer Cosmetics. Although each of these companies has several divisions and other sub-segments, only a few of those for Edison Automobile are shown. Edison has three geographic bases: the United States, the Far East, and Europe. The making and selling of automobiles in the Far East division is further broken down into the Japan and Korea units. The Japan unit is separated into its sales, manufacturing, and service functions. Edison Automobile's other geographic divisions have similar subsegments.

segments

Parts of an organization requiring separate reports for evaluation by management.

EXHIBIT 1   **An Organizational Chart**

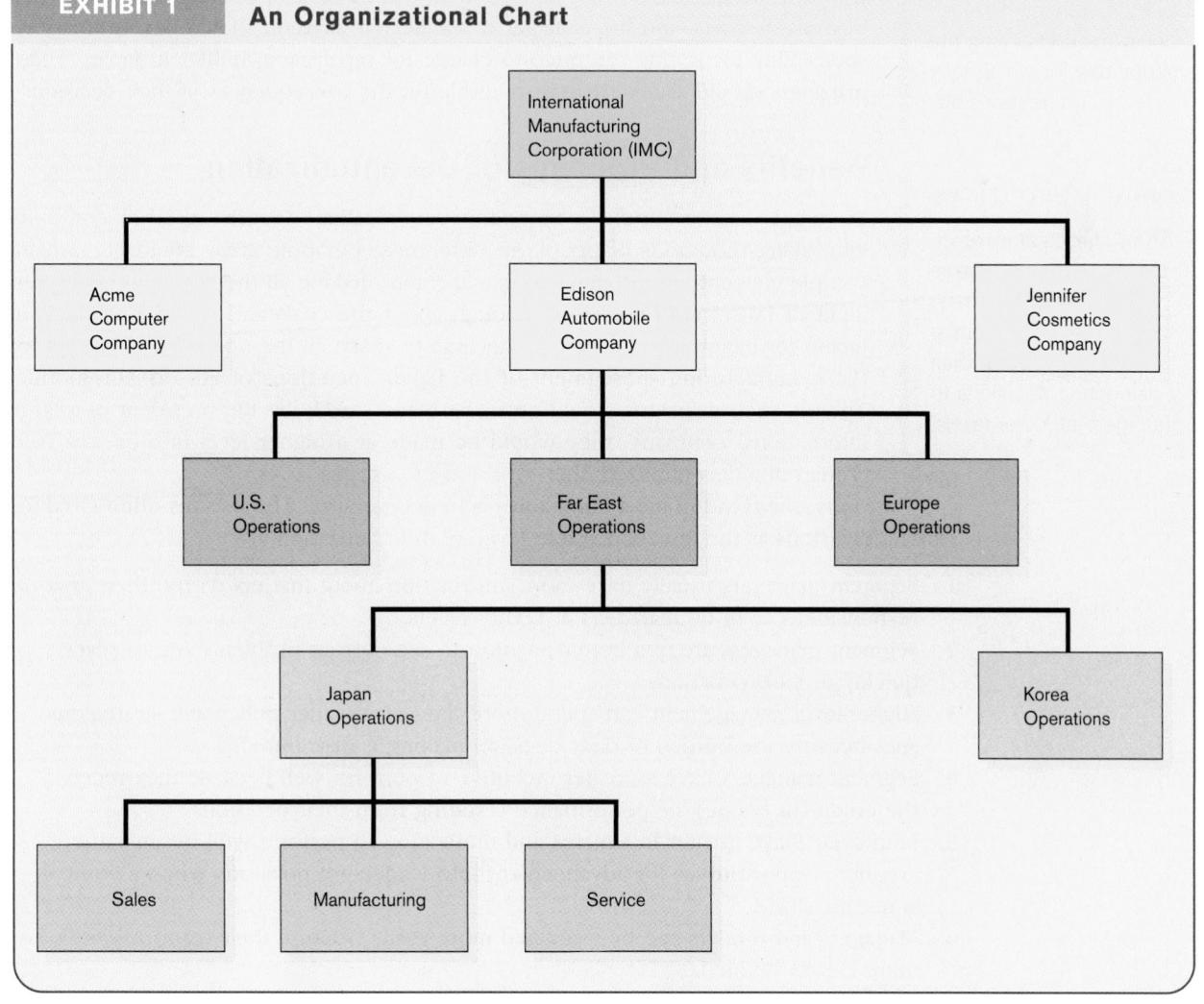

You will notice that IMC uses different criteria to define its segments at each level. At the highest level, product group (computers, autos, cosmetics) is used, probably because there is a significant difference in the business knowledge needed to produce and sell these products. At the middle level, segments are defined geographically because of the unique needs of each market and the distances involved. At the lowest level, each country unit is subdivided by business function—sales, manufacturing, and service.

Given the organizational chart in Exhibit 1, how much autonomy should the executives of each division be granted by corporate management? If each company (Acme, Edison, and Jennifer) has its own president, vice presidents, and other officers, should these executives be allowed to operate independently of one another? If Acme, for example, is the most profitable company, should it be given more **operating capital** than Edison and Jennifer, or less? Should a decision for Acme to expand into hand-held computers be made by Acme's executives or by IMC's corporate officers? Within Edison Automobile, how much autonomy should each of the geographic offices have? Should a decision to double the advertising budget or offer consumer rebates in the Far East operations be made by the manager of that division, by the president of Edison Automobile, or by the CEO of IMC?

> **operating capital**
>
> Funds available for use in financing the day-to-day activities of a business.

These are challenging questions. In fact, it would probably be difficult to find two companies that would answer them the same way. Assuming that IMC is basically a **decentralized company**, managers at all levels will have the authority to make decisions concerning the operations for which they are directly responsible. Regarding the question of rebates in the Far East, for example, the operating manager of that geographic division should probably decide whether to offer them. Likewise, the manager of the Japan Manufacturing division should decide where to buy engine parts, and the manager of the Service division should have primary responsibility for setting the price to charge for repairing a muffler in Japan. These managers should also be held responsible for the consequences of their decisions.

> **decentralized company**
>
> An organization in which managers at all levels have the authority to make decisions concerning the operations for which they are responsible.

Benefits and Problems of Decentralization

> **centralized company**
>
> An organization in which top management makes most of the major decisions for the entire company rather than delegating decisions to managers at lower levels.

To what degree should a company decentralize? Clearly, a large company employing thousands of people in different geographic areas could not remain completely centralized, with top management making all the decisions. The president of IMC would not know enough about the costs and varieties of paint in Japan, for example, or have enough time to make all the operating decisions for the manufacturing subsegment of the Japan operations of Edison Automobile. Though such decisions would never be made strictly by the president of a large international company, they would be made at a higher level in a **centralized company** than in a decentralized one.

Currently, the trend in most companies is to decentralize. The reasons often cited for making decisions at the lowest possible level in an organization are:

1. Segment managers usually have more information about matters within their area of responsibility than do managers at higher levels.
2. Segment managers are in a better position to see current problems and to react quickly to local situations.
3. Higher-level management can spend more time on broader policy and strategic issues because the burden of daily decision making is distributed.
4. Segment managers have a greater incentive to perform well because they receive the credit (or blame) for performance resulting from their decisions.
5. Employees have greater incentives and motivation to perform well because there are more opportunities for advancement into leadership positions when a company is decentralized.
6. Managers and officers can be evaluated more easily because their responsibilities are more clearly defined.

Decentralization has its drawbacks as well. Decisions made by managers of decentralized units are sometimes not consistent with the overall objectives of the firm. For example, Edison Automobile might find it less expensive to buy computer parts for its automobiles from an outside source than from Acme Computer, or the Service division of Japan operations may find it cheaper to buy repair parts from outsiders rather than from the Manufacturing division. Such decisions would allow the buying divisions to report lower costs, but the decisions might decrease the company's overall profitability (depending on whether or not costs in other division can actually be avoided when Edison Automobile decides to purchase computer parts from an outside vendor).

goal congruence

The selection of goals for responsibility centers that are consistent, or congruent, with those of the company as a whole.

There are two ways to prevent such problems. First, certain decisions should be centralized. For example, all decisions related to insurance coverage, which benefits the entire company, should probably be made at the corporate level. Second, an effective system of responsibility accounting should be established so that a manager's decisions will benefit not only the segment but also the firm as a whole. This **goal congruence**, whereby the goals of the company and all its segments are in harmony, can be achieved only if the responsibility accounting system is well designed.

Responsibility Accounting

responsibility accounting

A system of evaluating performance; managers are held accountable for the costs, revenues, assets, or other elements over which they have control.

Responsibility accounting is a system in which managers are assigned and held accountable for certain costs, revenues, and/or assets. There are two important behavioral considerations in assigning responsibilities to managers.

- First, the responsible manager should be involved in developing the plan for the unit over which the manager has control. Current research indicates that people are more motivated to achieve a goal if they participate in setting it. Such participation assures that the goals will be reasonable and, perhaps more importantly, that they will be *perceived* to be reasonable by the managers.
- Second, a manager should be held accountable only for those costs, revenues, or assets over which the manager has substantial control. Some costs may be generated within a segment, but control over them lies outside that unit. The manager of the Japan Manufacturing division, for example, may be held responsible for labor costs, but employee wages may be determined by a union scale controlled elsewhere. Admittedly, determining "substantial control" requires a judgment based on the circumstances, but if all relevant factors are considered, careful and fair judgments can be made.

Responsibility Accounting Reports Regardless of the degree of autonomy given to managers at various operating levels, performance reports based on responsibility accounting are needed at all levels of the organization. At the lowest levels, these reports tell managers where corrective action must be taken to control their segments' operations. At top levels, these reports keep management informed of the activities of all segments. The reports are then used to reward past performance and set incentives for future performance.

Exhibit 2 illustrates the kind of responsibility accounting reports a company might use. Note that reporting begins at the bottom and "rolls" upward, with each manager receiving information on the operations for which that manager is responsible, as well as summary information on the performance of lower-level managers. Note also that these reports are **exception reports**, meaning that variances from, or exceptions to, the budget are highlighted. In the report, unfavorable variances are labeled "U" while favorable variances are labeled "F." Such reports direct management immediately to the areas requiring their attention. Note that Exhibit 2 reports only on cost management. In this chapter, we'll also discuss reporting performance on revenue and asset management.

exception reports

Reports that highlight variances from, or exceptions to, the budget.

EXHIBIT 2	**Responsibility Accounting Reports for Edison Automobile Company of IMC (in thousands of dollars)**

President, Edison Automobile	Responsibility Centers	Budgeted Costs	Actual Costs	Variance*
The president receives from each geographic area of operations a report summarizing its performance. The president can see where further investigation needs to be done by tracing the differences between budget and actual downward to their sources.	General Administration	$ 89,000	$ 81,000	$ 8,000 F
	United States	145,000	151,000	6,000 U
	Far East	58,000	65,000	7,000 U
	Europe	111,000	99,000	12,000 F
	Total costs	$403,000	$396,000	$ 7,000 F

Far East Operations	Responsibility Centers	Budgeted Costs	Actual Costs	Variance
The manager of Far East operations receives a report from each country segment's head. These reports are then summarized and passed on to the president of Edison Automobile.	Japan Operations	$ 21,000	$ 23,000	$ 2,000 U
	Korea Operations	18,000	17,000	1,000 F
	China Operations	11,000	13,000	2,000 U
	Thailand Operations	8,000	12,000	4,000 U
	Total costs	$ 58,000	$ 65,000	$ 7,000 U

Japan Operations	Responsibility Centers	Budgeted Costs	Actual Costs	Variance
The manager of Japan operations receives from each unit a report summarizing its performance. These reports are combined and sent up to the next level, the manager of Far East operations.	Sales	$ 2,800	$ 1,700	$ 1,100 F
	Manufacturing	9,000	10,200	1,200 U
	Service	5,800	6,500	700 U
	Administration	3,400	4,600	1,200 U
	Total costs	$ 21,000	$ 23,000	$ 2,000 U

Japan Manufacturing Division	Variable Costs of Manufacturing	Budgeted Costs	Actual Costs	Variance
The Manufacturing division supervisor receives a performance report on the supervisor's center of responsibility. The totals from these reports are then communicated to the manager of Japan operations, the next level of responsibility.	Direct materials	$ 2,000	$ 2,500	$ 500 U
	Direct labor	6,000	6,400	400 U
	Manufacturing overhead	1,000	1,300	300 U
	Total costs	$ 9,000	$ 10,200	$ 1,200 U

*U means unfavorable.

responsibility center

An organizational unit in which a manager has control over and is held accountable for performance.

cost center

An organizational unit in which a manager has control over and is held accountable for cost performance.

Responsibility Centers   In our example, the president of IMC is responsible for the entire organization and should be held accountable for the company's overall successes and failures. At lower levels, the president of Edison Automobile Company, the manager of Edison's operations in the Far East, the manager in charge of Japan operations in Edison's Far East operations, and the manager of the Japan Manufacturing division, for example, would be held responsible for operations within their respective units.

Each unit is referred to as a **responsibility center**, and, depending on the operation, it may be a cost, profit, or investment center. As the name implies, a **cost center** is any organizational unit in which the manager of that unit has control only over the costs incurred. The manager of a cost center has no responsibility for revenues or assets, either because revenues are not generated in

profit center

An organizational unit in which a manager has control over and is held accountable for both cost and revenue performance.

investment center

An organizational unit in which a manager has control over and is held accountable for cost, revenue, and asset performance.

the center or because revenues and assets are under the control of someone else. The manufacturing unit of Japan operations of IMC, for example, could be designated a cost center. A **profit center** manager, however, has responsibility for both costs and revenues. Profit centers are usually found at higher levels in an organization than are cost centers. The geographic regions (United States, Far East, and Europe, as well as various country operations within the Far East region) of Edison Automobile could be profit centers (though they could also be designated as investment centers).

In an **investment center**, the manager is responsible for costs, revenues, and assets. This means that the manager is responsible not only for operating costs and revenues, but also for determining the amount of funds to be invested in the center's plant and equipment and for the rate of return earned on those investments. Investment centers are usually found at relatively high levels in organizations. The different companies in IMC (Acme Computer, Edison Automobile, and Jennifer Cosmetics) would probably be investment centers.

REMEMBER THIS...

- Decentralized companies delegate decisions and responsibility to lower-level managers, while centralized companies retain decisions and responsibility to run the business at higher levels of management.

- In order for managers to operate effectively in decentralized companies, a system of responsibility accounting should be established.

- Responsibility accounting is based on carefully identifying business units in the organization and classifying those business units as:

  - cost centers,

  - profit centers, or

  - investment centers.

- Generally, cost centers are found at lower levels of the organization, while profit and investment centers are found at higher levels of the organization.

Standard Cost Systems

Describe standard costing and use materials and labor cost variance analysis to explain how performance is controlled in cost centers.

(2) If managers are to be held responsible for the costs incurred in their centers, they must have control over those costs, have relevant information about those costs, and have a system that focuses on and supports effective cost controls. Traditionally, companies have used a *standard costing* system that isolates differences between actual and standard (or budgeted) costs to determine whether costs are too high or too low, as well as whether costs are improving (decreasing) or getting worse (increasing). This is critical information if the organization expects to be competitive. In a standard cost management system, standard costs are compared to actual costs, and variances are computed.

Service, merchandising, and manufacturing firms that use standard costing will design their accounting systems to incorporate standard costs and variances. This type of system, called a **standard cost system**, is a cost-accumulation process based on costs that *should have been* incurred rather than costs that *were actually* incurred (see page 950 for definition). The steps in establishing and operating a standard cost system are:

Step	Step	Step	Step	Step	Step	Step
Develop standard costs.	Collect actual costs.	Compare actual costs to standard costs and identify variances.	Journalize actual costs and standard costs and record the variances.	Report results including variances to managers responsible for variances.	Analyze causes of significant controllable variances.	Take action to eliminate variances or revise standard costs.

standard cost system

A cost-accumulation system in which standard costs are used as product costs instead of actual costs. The standard costs are then adjusted to actual costs when financial reports are created. This adjustment creates variances that are reported to management.

These steps describe a typical standard cost system. You are likely to find an extensive standard cost system in most manufacturing firms, which usually have standard costs for direct materials, direct labor, and manufacturing overhead. However, many service and merchandising firms also use a standard cost system to effectively manage critical costs in their organizations. Standard costs usually are often stored in a computer. In Chapter 18 we created an operating budget for Sunbird Boat Company. A critical part of creating this budget was establishing the standard costs to produce a 15-foot fishing boat. These costs are reported in Chapter 18, although they are spread across a number of budget schedules that we created in that chapter. The management team and accountants at Sunbird Boat Company can compile all of these standard cost data for 15-foot fishing boats. The standard costs for Sunbird Boat Company are shown in Exhibit 3. We will use the data in Exhibit 3 to illustrate how variances are calculated and analyzed.

 CAUTION

All of the cost variances we compute in this chapter are based on Sunbird's standard cost card. Be sure to return to Exhibit 3 to review these standards as you work through the remainder of this chapter. (Note that these are the same standard costs and quantities we used to build budgets for Sunbird Boat Company in Chapter 18.)

Determining Standard Costs

In a manufacturing firm, standard costs are determined on the basis of careful analysis and the experience of many people, including accountants, industrial engineers, purchasing agents, and the managers of the departments to be judged. Accountants play an important role in developing standard costs because they have the data needed to determine how costs have changed in the past in relation to levels of activity. This is not an easy task. Changes in methods of production, technology, worker efficiency, and plant layout, for example, can affect the behavior

EXHIBIT 3	Standard Cost Card

Sunbird Boat Company
Standard Cost Card–15-Foot Fishing Boats

	(1) Standard Quantity	(2) Standard Price or Rate	(3) Standard Cost (1) × (2)
Inputs:			
Direct materials:			
Wood	100 feet	$10.00	$1,000.00
Fiberglass	40 feet	5.00	200.00
Direct labor	80 hours	20.00	1,600.00
Manufacturing overhead:			
Variable	80 hours	7.50	600.00
Fixed	80 hours	20.00	1,600.00
Total standard cost per boat			$5,000.00

of costs. Before using standard costs to create the annual budget, past cost data often have to be adjusted to take changes in operating conditions into account. These changes sometimes occur gradually and may not be easily noticeable, making it difficult for accountants to identify cost characteristics that will be useful in setting standards for the future.

Engineers are often involved in setting standard costs because of their knowledge of the most efficient way of performing each task in relation to the existing technology of the operation. Managers who will be judged by the standard costs should be involved in the standard-setting process; they are more likely to be motivated to meet standards if they have participated in setting the standards and have accepted them. In addition, managers' experience and judgment can be quite valuable in establishing appropriate cost standards.

Once management has established a standard price for each resource (direct materials, direct labor, and manufacturing overhead) and has determined the standard input quantity allowed, the standard price is multiplied by the standard quantity to arrive at a standard dollar cost for the product or service. Actual costs are then compared with these standards to calculate the **variance**, the amount by which the actual cost differs from the standard. This variance, if significant, is a signal to management that costs may be "out of control" and that corrective action should be taken to eliminate the variance. This process of using variances from a standard to isolate problem areas is called **management by exception** and is the basis for establishing control in a management accounting system.

Let's review Exhibit 3 again. You can see in the third column that the standard costs to produce boats at Sunbird Boat Company are composed of both a price (or rate) for the input and a quantity (or usage) of the input. Hence, comparing actual costs with standard costs results in two variances: a price (or rate) variance and a quantity (or usage) variance. These variances are usually computed for direct materials, direct labor, and variable manufacturing overhead.

variance

Any deviation from standard.

management by exception

The strategy of focusing attention on significant deviations from standard costs or expectations.

> ### STOP & THINK
> Is it possible for a company to have positive variances (actual costs are less than standard costs) and still have problems? Can you think of an example?

We're going to explain how direct materials variances are computed and analyzed by using the Sunbird Boat Company as an example. Then, we will explain the computation and analysis of direct labor variances. The more complex variances for manufacturing overhead will be discussed and illustrated in the expanded material section of this chapter.

Controlling Performance in Cost Centers

You should understand that managers of cost centers are responsible for costs incurred, and most cost centers usually have one type of cost that is more significant than any other. In service organizations, salaries are generally the major cost. In wholesale and retail businesses, the cost of merchandise purchased for resale is often the most significant cost. In manufacturing firms, costs incurred to make products (direct materials, direct labor, and manufacturing overhead) are usually most significant. The standard cost system we're presenting here is an effective method of controlling these kinds of costs.

Direct Materials Variances

To illustrate the computation of the price and quantity variances for direct materials, let's assume that, while Sunbird Boat Company originally planned to produce 105 boats, it actually only had manufactured 100 boats by the end of the year. The actual results for the year on the 100 fishing boats made by Sunbird Boat Company are as follows:

Direct materials purchased	
Wood	9,800 feet at $9.60 per foot
Fiberglass	5,400 feet at $5.20 per foot
Direct materials used	
Wood	10,150 feet
Fiberglass	3,925 feet
Boats produced	100

Keep in mind throughout the following discussion that the standard costs in Exhibit 3 specify that wood materials should cost $10 per foot, fiberglass materials should cost $5 per foot, and each boat produced should require 100 feet of wood and 40 feet of fiberglass. (Obviously, many different kinds of raw materials are required to make boats. To keep the example simple, we are assuming only two materials are used.)

materials price variance

The extent to which the standard price varies from the actual price for the quantity of materials purchased or used; computed by multiplying the difference between the standard and actual prices by the quantity purchased or used.

Materials Price Variance   The materials price variance reflects the extent to which the actual price varies from the standard price for the actual quantity of materials purchased or used. Although the price variance can be calculated either when materials are purchased or when they are used, it is generally best to isolate the variance at purchase and report the variance to the purchasing manager who has responsibility for controlling the purchase price. If management waits until the materials are used before calculating variances, the information needed by the purchasing managers to take corrective action is delayed.

In calculating the materials price variance, the standard price per unit of materials should reflect the final, delivered cost of materials, net of any discounts taken. For example, Sunbird Boat Company may have determined its standard materials price per foot of wood as follows:

Purchase price	$ 9.84
Freight	0.17
Handling costs	0.04
Less purchase discounts	(0.05)
Standard wood materials cost per foot	$10.00

The standard cost above assumes that the materials were purchased in certain lot sizes (for example, 100-foot quantities) and delivered a certain way (by rail, for example). Handling costs and purchase discounts have also been included.

Assume that variances are determined when materials are purchased. Based on the fact given above that 9,800 feet of wood are purchased by Sunbird during the year, the price variance for wood is computed as follows:

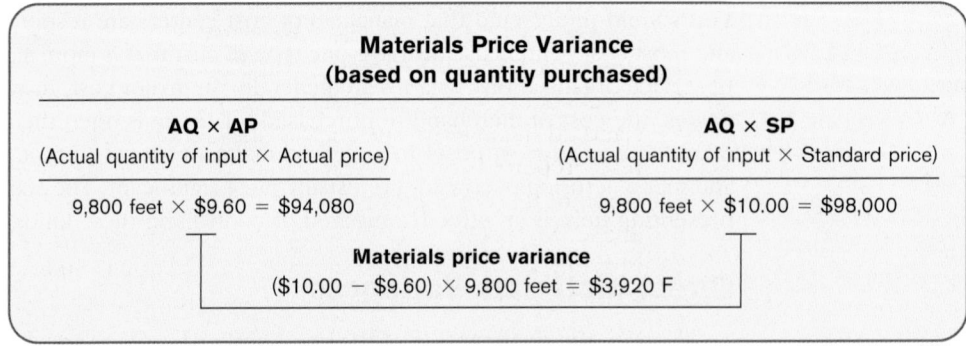

This variance indicates that the company spent $3,920 less than the total standard cost for the wood purchased. Because less money was spent than the standard cost, the variance is labeled "F," meaning "favorable." If the amount expended had been more than the standard cost, the variance would have been "unfavorable," designated with a "U." Rather than using columns of data, another way of mathematically computing the price variance is to simply subtract the actual price from the standard price and multiply the difference by the actual quantity purchased or:

(Standard price − Actual price) × Actual quantity purchased

Now before you start to memorize these computations, think about what a price variance is signaling—that the actual price is different than the standard or expected price.[2] Essentially, if the actual price is more than the expected price, then we have an unfavorable variance. And if the actual price is less than the expected price, then the variance is favorable. It then makes sense to multiply the difference between these two prices by the actual quantity in order to measure the total financial impact on the organization of paying a price or rate that was more or less than was expected. It's really much better to *understand* what the price variance is signaling than it is to focus on memorizing a formula.

Isolating materials price variances at the time of purchase has the advantage of providing immediate information on purchasing decisions. This also allows companies to carry inventory in the accounting records at the standard cost. Some companies, however, prefer to compute materials price variances at the time the materials are transferred to Work-in-Process Inventory (i.e., when these materials are actually used in production). The facts stated above indicate that 10,150 feet were used in production (Sunbird used everything it purchased, plus some of its wood inventory). If materials price variances are computed when materials are transferred to Work-in-Process, the 10,150 feet would be used in the calculation rather than the 9,800 feet purchased. In this case, a favorable price variance of $4,060 would result, as shown below.

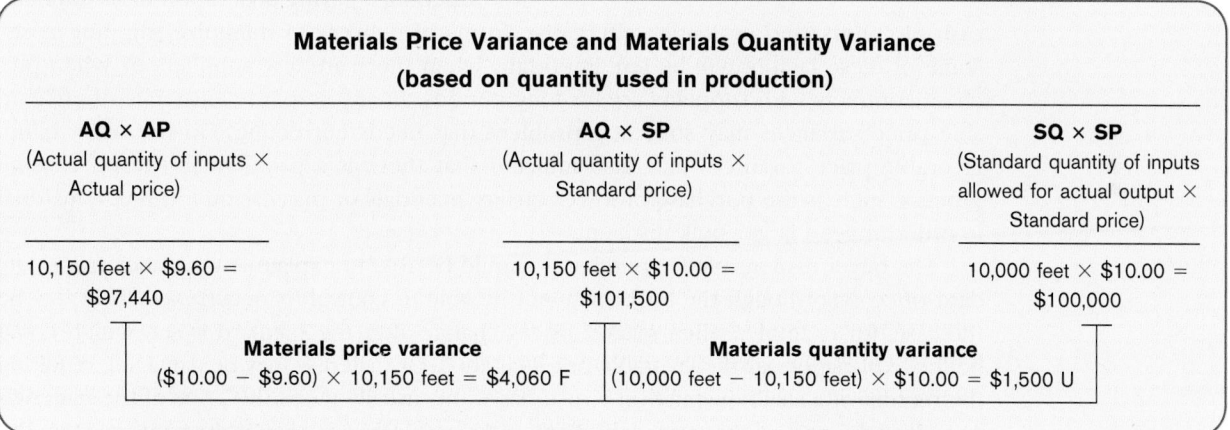

Materials Price Variance and Materials Quantity Variance
(based on quantity used in production)

AQ × AP (Actual quantity of inputs × Actual price)	**AQ × SP** (Actual quantity of inputs × Standard price)	**SQ × SP** (Standard quantity of inputs allowed for actual output × Standard price)
10,150 feet × $9.60 = $97,440	10,150 feet × $10.00 = $101,500	10,000 feet × $10.00 = $100,000

Materials price variance   Materials quantity variance
($10.00 − $9.60) × 10,150 feet = $4,060 F   (10,000 feet − 10,150 feet) × $10.00 = $1,500 U

materials quantity variance

The extent to which the actual quantity of materials varies from the standard quantity; computed by multiplying the difference between the standard quantity of materials allowed and actual quantity of materials used by the standard price.

Materials Quantity Variance   The standard quantity of materials should reflect the amount needed for each completed unit of product but should allow for normal waste, spoilage, and other unavoidable inefficiencies. The standard cost card indicates that 100 feet of wood is allowed for each 15-foot fishing boat produced. Because Sunbird Boat Company produced 100 of these boats last year, the standard quantity of wood allowed is 10,000 feet (100 feet × 100 boats). As already reported above, actual use of wood amounted to 10,150 feet. The computation of the **materials quantity variance** for wood is shown in the illustration above. As you can see, the company used 150 more feet of wood than expected, resulting in an unfavorable quantity variance of $1,500 (150 feet × $10 per foot).

It's important that we make an important concept very clear before we leave the materials quantity variance. As you can see in the second and third columns above, the materials quantity variance compares the actual quantity of inputs to

---

[2] In this discussion, the terms *standard* and *expected* are often used interchangeably. Some people refer to prices and quantities as standard; others refer to them as expected because they aren't under the complete control of the company.

the standard quantity of inputs allowed for actual output. The important concept is *quantity allowed for actual output*. This concept refers to the quantity of materials that should have been used to produce the actual output and relates back to the principle of flexible budgeting that we discussed in the expanded material section of Chapter 18. Simply put, Sunbird management must wait until the end of the year to determine how many feet of wood it should have used during the year. At the end of the year, the accountant for Sunbird Boat Company will multiply the *standard quantity* of materials per boat by the *actual volume* of boats produced to determine the *standard quantity allowed* or:

$$\text{Standard quantity per unit} \times \text{Actual units produced} = \text{Standard quantity allowed}$$

CAUTION

As you can see in the illustration on the previous page, when the actual quantity used is the basis for the materials price variance, the materials price variance and the materials quantity variance share some of the same computations, making these calculations somewhat easier. However, remember that basing the materials price variance on the actual quantity used will delay the recognition of price problems from the time that the materials are purchased until the time they are transferred to production.

This number is then compared to the actual quantity of wood used to determine if there is a favorable or unfavorable quantity variance for materials. The accountant will multiply this variance by the standard price for wood in order to account for this variance in Sunbird's accounting system (which we discuss later in this section).

Controlling Materials Variances

Materials price variances are usually under the control of the purchasing department. The purchasing function involves getting a variety of price quotations, buying in economic lot sizes to take advantage of quantity discounts, paying on a timely basis to obtain cash discounts, and evaluating alternative forms of delivery to minimize shipping costs. Some of these factors will be less important when there are few suppliers or when purchase contracts with suppliers are for long periods. In any case, the existence of unfavorable price variances may suggest a problem that needs correcting. On the other hand, favorable price variances may also indicate that there is a problem in the purchasing process, such as the purchase of lower quality materials or purchasing too much material in order to get a larger bulk discount.

The buyer responsible for purchases should be able to explain any variance from standard price even though the buyer may not be able to control its occurrence. This may be the case, for example, when market prices change after the standard is set, which could be the explanation for the favorable price variance. Or materials may be damaged, requiring the reorder of a small quantity on a rush basis; this usually raises the price of the materials as well as the cost of shipping, causing an unfavorable price variance. The point is that the cause of any significant variance (whether favorable or unfavorable) must be explained and steps taken to avoid such variances in the future. The purpose of variance analysis is not to browbeat employees for failing to meet impossible expectations, but rather to provide information that will help management identify ways of improving the production process.

Materials quantity variances may be caused by quality defects, poor workmanship, poor choice of materials, inexperienced workers, machines that need repair, or an inaccurate materials quantity standard. Just as the purchasing manager must explain significant price variances, generally the production manager must analyze significant quantity variances to determine their cause. If the material is of inferior quality, the purchasing manager, rather than the production manager, may be responsible for the variance. Again, the point is that the cause of the variance must be determined; only then can it be decided what action, if

FYI

In the fast-food arena, for example, franchises, such as **McDonald's** and **Baskin-Robbins**, have standard quantities for meat in hamburgers, ice cream in cones, and the amount of time it should take to serve a customer.

any, to take to prevent its recurrence. Further, production managers should constantly receive reports on these variances in order to maintain good control of costs and usage. If this is done, production managers can then take quick corrective action before problems become significant in size. Corrective action, for example, may involve being careful to return excess materials to the storeroom rather than being careless about control in the production area, which could lead to waste or theft.

Accounting for Materials Variances

The journal entries for recording the purchase and use of materials, as well as the materials price variance (isolated at purchase) and the quantity variance (isolated when materials are used), are:

Materials Price Variance:

Direct Materials Inventory ($10.00 × 9,800 feet)	98,000	
Materials Price Variance [($10.00 − $9.60) × 9,800 feet]		3,920
Cash (or Accounts Payable) ($9.60 × 9,800 feet)		94,080

    Purchased 9,800 feet of wood at $9.60 per foot and entered the materials in inventory at the standard price of $10.00 per foot.

Materials Quantity Variance:

Work-in-Process Inventory (10,000 feet × $10.00)	100,000	
Materials Quantity Variance [(10,000 feet − 10,150 feet) × $10.00]	1,500	
Direct Materials Inventory (10,150 feet × $10.00)		101,500

    Transferred 10,150 feet of wood out of inventory and recorded standard usage on the factory floor of 10,000 feet of wood to produce 100 boats.

Note that the $100,000 debit to Work-in-Process Inventory is based on the standard amount of wood allowed for 100 boats actually produced, which is 10,000 feet (100 boats × 100 standard feet per boat).

As you can see, Materials Price Variance and Materials Quantity Variance are debited when the variances are unfavorable; they are credited when the variances are favorable. A good way to remember that unfavorable variances are debited is to think of an unfavorable variance as an expense, which is also debited. Conversely, a favorable variance, which is credited, can be considered an expense reduction or savings. The actual cost deviations from the standard costs are now recorded in variance accounts. Similar to the approach used to close over- or underapplied manufacturing overhead (discussed previously in Chapter 16), the variance accounts are usually closed and the amounts transferred to Cost of Goods Sold at the end of the period. Thus, Cost of Goods Sold as reported on the income statement is based on actual costs, while inventory accounts on the balance sheet include only the standard costs of materials.

 FYI

When variances are significant in amount, variance account balances at the end of a period should be allocated among Cost of Goods Sold, Raw Materials Inventory, Work-in-Process Inventory, and Finished Goods Inventory instead of simply transferred entirely to Cost of Goods Sold.

Now that we've worked through the accounting for variances on Sunbird's wood materials, see if you can correctly compute and account for the variances on Sunbird's fiberglass materials (compute the price variance using the amount purchased). As you make the variance computations, try to understand the *meaning* of each calculation. To help you, consider the following three-step conceptual approach to variance analysis.

1. First, determine whether the variance is favorable or unfavorable.

    In the case of the wood price variance, the fact that the actual price ($9.60) is less than the standard price ($10.00) is obviously a favorable situation. And the fact that the actual quantity of wood used (10,150 feet) is more than the standard quantity allowed (10,000 feet) is clearly an unfavorable situation.

2. Next, compute the underlying difference that actually determines the variance calculation.

> What we mean here is that the "real" price variance is $0.40 (the difference between $9.60 and $10.00) and the "real" quantity variance is 150 feet (the difference between 10,150 feet and 10,000 feet).

3. Finally, calculate the financial impact of the underlying difference on the company. This is the variance that must be accounted for in the company's accounting system.

> Given a "real" price variance of $0.40 per foot that is favorable, the impact of this difference on Sunbird is a function of the number of board feet actually purchased; that is, $0.40 favorable × 9,800 feet = $3,920 F. Similarly, the financial impact on Sunbird of a "real" quantity variance of 150 feet that is unfavorable is a function of the standard price of $10 per foot; that is, 150 feet unfavorable × $10 = $1,500 U.

The correct computations and journal entries for Sunbird's fiberglass variances are provided in the footnote below.[3]

STOP & THINK

When computing the quantity (usage) variance, do you understand why it is important to compare actual quantity of inputs to the standard quantity of inputs allowed for actual output? Is the standard quantity budgeted (determined at the beginning of the operating period) different from the standard quantity allowed for actual output (determined at the end of the operating period)? If so, what is the difference?

Direct Labor Variances

Typically when a standard cost system is being used in a manufacturing or service firm, a direct labor rate variance and a direct labor efficiency variance are determined for personnel directly involved in the creation of the organization's product or service. These variances are computed in a manner very similar to the materials price and quantity variances.

Labor Rate Variance   A labor rate variance is a price variance; it shows the difference between standard and actual wage rates. Unfavorable labor rate variances may occur when skilled workers with high hourly pay rates are placed in jobs intended for less skilled or lower-wage-rate employees. Unfavorable labor rate variances may also occur when employees work overtime at premium pay (such as time and a half or double time). Conversely, favorable labor rate variances occur when less skilled or lower-wage-rate employees perform duties intended for higher-paid workers.

For Sunbird Boat Company, the standard cost card (Exhibit 3) indicates that the standard direct labor rate per boat is 80 hours at $20 per hour. Actual labor used during the year to make 100 boats was 7,880 hours at an average rate of $20.50 per hour. Therefore, the labor rate variance is $3,940 unfavorable, computed as follows:

labor rate variance

The extent to which the standard labor rate varies from the actual rate for the quantity of labor used; computed by multiplying the difference between the standard rate and the actual rate by the quantity of labor used.

---

[3] The actual fiberglass price was $5.20 and the standard price is $5.00. Hence, the price variance is unfavorable based on an underlying difference of $0.20. Because 5,400 feet of fiberglass were actually purchased, the total financial impact of the underlying unfavorable price difference is a price variance of $1,080 U ($0.20 × 5,400 feet).

Now turning to the quantity variance, the actual fiberglass used was 3,925 feet and the standard quantity allowed is 4,000 feet (40 standard feet per boat × 100 boats actually produced). Hence, the quantity variance is favorable based on the underlying difference of 75 feet (4,000 feet − 3,925 feet). Using a standard price per foot of $5, the total financial impact of the underlying favorable quantity difference is a quantity variance of $375 F (75 feet × $5).

The journal entries to account for the price and quantity variances, respectively, are:

Direct Materials Inventory ($5.00 × 5,400 feet)	27,000	
Materials Price Variance [($5.00 − $5.20) × 5,400 feet]	1,080	
Cash (or Accounts Payable) ($5.20 × 5,400 feet)		28,080
Work-in-Process Inventory (4,000 feet × $5.00)	20,000	
Materials Quantity Variance [(4,000 feet − 3,925 feet) × $5.00]		375
Direct Materials Inventory (3,925 feet × $5.00)		19,625

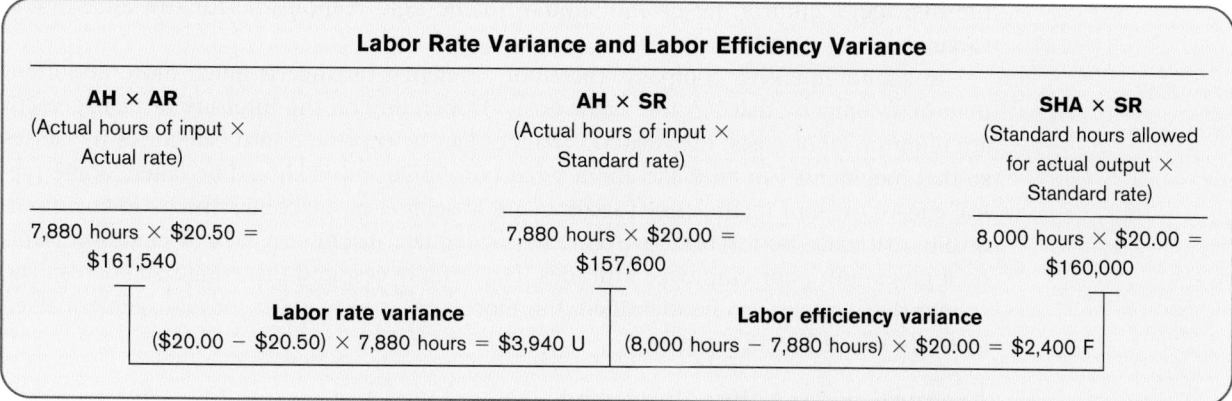

As this variance indicates, the $0.50 difference between the standard wage rate and actual average wage rate results in $3,940 more spent than expected for the actual number of direct labor hours used. Sunbird's management now needs to determine whether the variance should be investigated. Depending on the company's hiring policies, and the degree of authority given to the operating manager in setting wage rates and assigning workers to particular jobs, the operating manager may or may not be responsible for this labor rate variance. In general, labor rates are the responsibility of the personnel manager who makes hiring and staffing decisions.

labor efficiency variance

The extent to which the actual labor used varies from the standard quantity; computed by multiplying the difference between the actual quantity of labor used and the standard quantity of labor allowed by the standard rate.

Labor Efficiency Variance The labor efficiency variance is a quantity variance. It measures the cost (or benefit) of using labor for more (or fewer) hours than prescribed by the standard. Computed in the same manner as the materials quantity variance, the labor efficiency variance computation is also illustrated in the schedule above for Sunbird Boat Company. Note that total standard hours are computed by multiplying the standard hours per boat by the actual number of boats produced (80 hours × 100 boats = 8,000 standard hours allowed). The manufacturing division used 120 less direct labor hours than the standard allowed for actual production output, which generates a favorable efficiency variance of $2,400 (120 hours × $20).

The labor efficiency variance shows how efficiently the workers performed, which is an important measure of the productivity of the department. This variance might be unfavorable for a variety of reasons, including poorly trained employees, poor-quality materials that require extra processing time, old or faulty equipment, and improper supervision of employees. The labor efficiency variance is usually watched very closely by most organizations.

CAUTION

When computing variances, be careful not to confuse actual and standard hours and actual and standard rates. The rate variance is always the difference between the standard and actual rate multiplied by the actual hours. (To multiply it by standard hours would not tell you how much the rate increase actually cost or saved the company in total.) On the other hand, the efficiency variance is a time-based variance; therefore, it is the difference between the standard hours allowed and actual hours multiplied by the standard rate.

Controlling Labor Variances Labor rate variances are normally the responsibility of either the production manager who is responsible for employees' work assignments or the individuals responsible for hiring employees. As indicated, rate variances are likely to be due to (1) certain tasks being performed by workers with different pay rates or (2) working overtime at rates higher than the normal wage rate. These variances may be manageable if care is taken in assigning workers to jobs that are consistent with their skills and pay scales. Deviations may be necessary in certain situations because of vacations, sickness, or absences of other employees. If these variances are caused by factors beyond the manager's control, he or she should not be held responsible for the unfavorable variance.

In a labor-intensive company, the labor efficiency variance is much more important than in a company that has low labor costs. Depending on the intensity of management attention on labor costs, the related variances can be separated into categories by causes so that judgments can be made about what corrective action should be taken. Some typical causes of labor inefficiency variances are absenteeism, machinery breakdowns, poor-quality materials, poor work environment, inadequate machinery, lack of employee skills on a given job, poor employee attitudes, lazy employees, and inaccurate standards. The sooner these causes can be identified, the more opportunity exists for management to effectively take corrective action.

Accounting for Labor Variances Because the labor rate and labor efficiency variances are both computed for a given period of time or for a given amount of production, the labor costs and variances for Sunbird Boat Company can be accounted for in a single journal entry.

Work-in-Process Inventory (8,000 hours × $20.00)	160,000	
Labor Rate Variance		
[($20.00 − $20.50) × 7,880 hours]	3,940	
Labor Efficiency Variance		
[(8,000 hours − 7,880 hours) × $20.00]		2,400
Wages Payable (7,880 hours × $20.50)		161,540

To charge Work-in-Process Inventory for standard labor hours at the standard wage rate to produce 100 boats; to set up unfavorable labor rate and favorable efficiency variances to reflect the use of 120 hours below standard at an average wage rate that was $0.50 above standard.

REMEMBER THIS...

- Standard costs are budgeted costs that serve as benchmarks for judging what actual costs should be.
- The formula for the materials price variance is:

    (Standard price − Actual price) × Actual quantity.

    The actual quantity can be either the quantity purchased or the quantity used in production.
- The formula for the materials quantity variance is:

    (Standard quantity allowed − Actual quantity used) × Standard price.
- Quantity variances are based on the standard quantity allowed, which is:

    Standard input quantity per unit of production ×
    Total actual production volume.
- The formula for the labor rate variance and for the labor efficiency variance is essentially the same as the formula for the materials price variance and for the materials quantity variance, respectively.
- The managers responsible for the variances should determine their causes and, if the variances are outside an acceptable range, take corrective action.
- Each variance is recorded in an individual account when resources (either materials or labor) are acquired and used. Unfavorable variances are recognized as debits, similar to an expense account. Hence, favorable variances are recognized as credits.
- The accounts for variances are generally closed into Cost of Goods Sold in order to adjust this account to actual costs. As a result, the inventory accounts on the balance sheet include only standard costs.

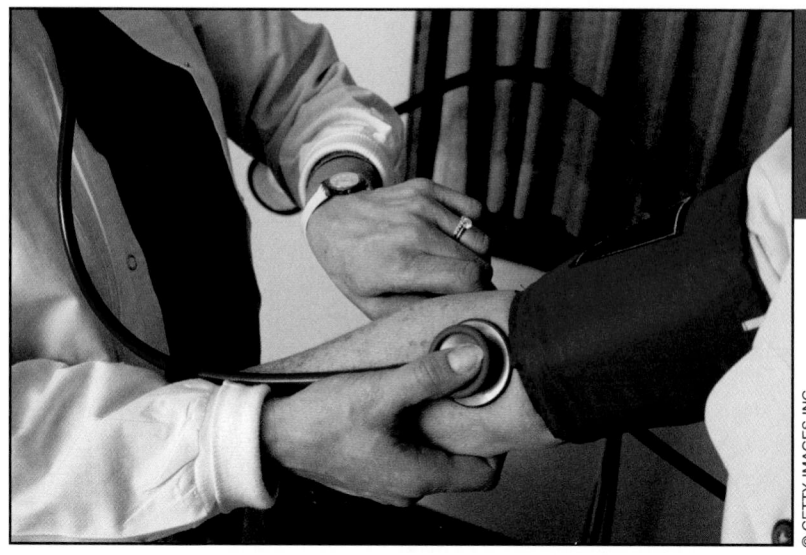

A service organization, much like a manufacturing organization, can express standards in quantitative terms. For example, a hospital might have standard times for activities such as taking blood pressure readings.

As with all production variances, labor variances are generally closed to Cost of Goods Sold at the end of the period. By closing variances into Cost of Goods Sold, actual cost of goods sold will be reported on the income statement, and Work-in-Process Inventory and Finished Goods Inventory will include only the standard costs of labor.

Controlling Performance in Profit Centers

Use segment margin statements and revenue variance analysis to explain how performance is controlled in profit centers.

(3) As defined earlier, a profit center is an organizational unit (segment) in which a manager has responsibility for both costs and revenues. Profit centers both produce and market goods or services. For example, the U.S., Far East, and Europe operations of the Edison Automobile Company of IMC, illustrated in Exhibit 1 on page 945, might be profit centers.

The Segment Margin Statement

To evaluate the performance of profit centers and to decide how limited resources will be divided among profit centers, management needs a report that compares the revenues and costs of the profit centers being evaluated. One report that is often used is the **segment margin statement**, such as the one presented in Exhibit 4 for IMC on pages 960–961.

segment margin statement

A profit and loss statement that identifies costs directly chargeable to a segment and further divides them into variable and fixed cost behavior patterns.

To keep Exhibit 4 reasonably simple, we have limited the report to only two divisions for IMC: Acme Computer and Edison Automobile. Further, we have included only the regions of Edison Automobile. You will note that it includes three geographic regions; the Far East Region has operations in two countries—Japan and Korea. As you read across, note that the segment focus becomes narrower: from divisions to geographic regions to countries within geographic regions.

direct costs

Costs that are specifically traceable to a unit of business or segment being analyzed.

Before reviewing specific aspects of this segment margin statement, we want to remind you of that very important management accounting principle called *responsibility accounting*. Following this principle, segment managers should be evaluated on only the items they can control or influence. As was the case with cost centers, in evaluating profit centers it is important that managers be held responsible only for the controllable costs; the costs over which they have control are usually called **direct costs**. In Exhibit 4, we apply responsibility accounting to IMC by including in each segment report only the revenues and costs controlled by that segment manager. This implies

A Segment Margin Statement

International Manufacturing Corporation (IMC)
Segment Margin Statement
September 2009
(in millions of dollars)

	IMC	Segments	
		Acme Computers	Edison Automobile
Net sales revenue	$ 25,000	$ 15,000	$ 10,000
Variable costs:			
Cost of goods sold	$(16,000)	$(10,000)	$ (6,000)
Selling and administrative costs	(3,300)	(2,000)	(1,300)
Total variable costs	$(19,300)	$ (12,000)	$ (7,300)
Contribution margin	$ 5,700	$ 3,000	$ 2,700
Less fixed costs controllable by segment manager	(1,900)	(1,200)	(700)
Segment margin	$ 3,800	$ 1,800	$ 2,000
Less indirect costs to segments (common costs)	(1,500)		
Operating profit	$ 2,300		
Segment-margin ratio	9.2%	12.0%	20.0%

indirect costs

Costs normally incurred for the benefit of several segments or activities; sometimes called common costs or joint costs.

that some costs, **indirect costs**, will not be assigned to a particular segment because the manager cannot control them. As you can observe in Exhibit 4, when we break IMC down into smaller and smaller segments, more and more costs are considered to be indirect or common. For example, the $1.5 million indirect costs listed in the IMC column are not assigned to the Acme Computer and Edison Automobile segments. These costs might include the IMC president's salary and interest on company-wide debt. As you can imagine, these costs are not controlled by Acme Computer and Edison Automobile. Therefore, these costs are not assigned to these segments.

Similarly, when Edison Automobile is broken down into smaller segments for analysis, we see an additional $200,000 of indirect costs that are not assigned to Edison Automobile's three regions. Costs such as the division manager's salary and advertising for all regions are not controlled by the region manager and so are not allocated to the regions. You will note that as we move down the organizational hierarchy, from divisions to geographic regions to countries, indirect costs increase in total; managers at the lower levels have the narrowest range of responsibility and the fewest costs to control. The manager of manufacturing in Japan, for example, will be responsible for the items ordered for that unit but not for setting the salary of the manager of Far East operations; this is the responsibility of the manager of Edison Automobile. The salary of the manager of Far East operations is thus a direct and controllable cost of Edison Automobile and is an indirect and noncontrollable cost to Japan operations.

CAUTION

Many students confuse the terms *variable* and *fixed costs, controllable* and *noncontrollable costs,* and *direct* and *indirect costs*. Costs are variable if they fluctuate with a specific activity. If they don't fluctuate with activity, costs are fixed. Costs are controllable if they can be changed by the activity manager. If they can't be changed by the activity manager, costs are noncontrollable. Costs are direct if removing the activity results in the costs being eliminated. Costs that remain after an activity is eliminated are indirect to that activity and should be treated as common costs.

International Manufacturing Corporation (IMC)
Segment Margin Statement
September 2009
(in thousands of dollars)

Edison Automobile	Segments			Far East Operations	Segments	
	U.S. Operations	Far East Operations	Europe Operations		Japan Operations	Korea Operations
$10,000	$ 5,000	$ 2,000	$ 3,000	$ 2,000	$1,200	$ 800
$ (6,000)	$(2,900)	$(1,100)	$(2,000)	$ (1,100)	$ (700)	$ (400)
(1,300)	(700)	(300)	(300)	(300)	(170)	(130)
$ (7,300)	$(3,600)	$(1,400)	$(2,300)	$ (1,400)	$ (870)	$ (530)
$ 2,700	$ 1,400	$ 600	$ 700	$ 600	$ 330	$ 270
(500)	(250)	(100)	(150)	(70)	(60)	(10)
$ 2,200	$ 1,150	$ 500	$ 550	$ 530	$ 270	$ 260
(200)				(30)		
$ 2,000				$ 500		
20.0%	23.0%	25.0%	18.3%	25.0%	22.5%	32.5%

Interpreting Profit Center Performance Results

Given that the segment margin statement in Exhibit 4 was prepared in light of the principles of controllable and direct costs, how does management use the information it contains? First, the operating profit figure provides management with concrete information for evaluating the performance of the company as a whole. Second, the **segment margins** enable management to analyze company results by evaluating the performance of each segment.

We are now ready to examine the operations of IMC segments in detail. In absolute terms, Edison Automobile has a larger segment margin than Acme Computer ($2 million versus $1.8 million). U.S. operations have earned more than the Far East and Europe operations; the Japan operations have a larger segment margin than do the Korea operations. Absolute profits, however, often favor those segments with a larger asset base—with larger manufacturing facilities, for example. A larger facility with more manufacturing capacity should naturally have higher production and higher sales and, hence, a higher segment margin. A more equitable way to assess performance is to compare **segment-margin ratios** (segment margin divided by net sales), because ratios focus on relationships rather than absolute dollar amounts. For example, though the segment margin of Europe operations is larger than that of Far East operations, the latter has a higher segment-margin ratio (25% versus 18.3%).

In using segment margin statements to evaluate profit centers, it is important to review performance over several periods or months. A single period or month may not be typical of overall performance. In our example, September might have been an unusually bad profitability month for the Korea unit of Far East operations because of a slump in the Korean economy or a labor strike. In fact, the performance can be evaluated only by looking at cost and profit trends over several periods, and by comparing the results of these units with those of other similar units.

segment margins

The difference between segment revenue and direct segment costs; a measure of the segment's contribution to cover indirect fixed costs and provide profits. In effect, segment margins are the operating profit created by the segment.

segment-margin ratios

The segment margin divided by the segment's net sales revenue; a measure of the efficiency of the segment's operating performance and, therefore, of its profitability.

Managing Revenues in Profit Centers

Profit center managers manage their costs the same way cost center managers evaluate and manage costs. That is, they use the standard costing concepts that we have already discussed. Unlike cost center managers, however, profit center managers are also responsible for managing revenues because the segment profit they are evaluated on is a function of both costs and revenues. In the next section, we examine how variance analysis is used to manage revenues.

Managing Revenues and Revenue Variances   A segment's actual and expected revenues may differ for several reasons including the following:

The sales volume variance is often broken down into several important subcomponents. These subcomponent variances include the sales mix variance, the market share variance, and the industry volume variance. These are complex variances that we'll reserve for more advanced textbooks.

- Sales prices were higher or lower than expected → a sales price variance.
- Sales volume was higher or lower than expected → a sales volume variance.

Because management is interested in knowing which of these factors contributed to differences between actual and expected or standard[4] revenues, variances that help isolate these factors are calculated. To illustrate how revenue variances are calculated, let's return to our Sunbird Boat Company example. Sales data for Sunbird's 15-foot boat line are as follows:

	Expected (Standard) Sales Data	
	Sales Price	Boat Sales
15-foot boats	$10,000	100

	Actual Sales Data	
	Sales Price	Boat Sales
15-foot boats	$10,500	90

Now take a moment and study these data. In terms of Sunbird's revenue performance, what do you see? You should see both positive (favorable) and negative (unfavorable) results on sales-related issues. For instance, the sales price is higher than expected. If Sunbird can sell the same volume of boats at a higher sales price, then revenue is going to increase. This would mean that Sunbird had a favorable sales price variance. On the other hand, Sunbird actually sold fewer boats than expected, which means that it had an unfavorable sales volume variance. After working through the materials and labor variances for Sunbird, these two variances on revenue performance should make sense to you. If so, then you're getting a good feel for how variances are computed and what they signal to management. All that we need to do now is determine the total dollar value (i.e., size) of these revenue variances. The calculations for these two revenue variances are shown below.

sales price variance

The difference between the expected or standard price and the actual price multiplied by the actual quantity sold; measures that part of the variance between expected and actual sales revenue that is due to differences between expected and actual prices of goods.

Sales Price Variance.   The **sales price variance** indicates the impact of a different price than expected on the organization's revenues. Hence, the sales price variance is a function of the difference between the actual sales price and the

---

[4] Again remember that the terms *standard* and *expected* are being used interchangeably in this analysis work.

expected (or standard) sales price. This difference is then multiplied by the actual quantity of goods or services sold in order to determine the financial impact of this variance on the company. Therefore, Sunbird's favorable price variance of $500 ($10,500 − $10,000) is multiplied by the 90 boats actually sold to determine a total sales price variance of $45,000 F.

sales volume variance

The difference between the expected quantity and the actual quantity sold multiplied by the expected or standard price; measures that part of the variance between expected and actual sales revenue that is due to the difference between expected and actual volume of goods sold.

Sales Volume Variance.   As the organization sells more or less than what was expected, this results in a **sales volume variance** that has an important and immediate effect on the organization's revenues. Sunbird has an unfavorable sales volume variance of ten boats. What is the economic impact on Sunbird of selling ten fewer boats? We need to be careful here. If you understand economics, then you understand one important factor that determines the volume of sales is the sales price (e.g., higher prices typically result in lower volumes and vice-versa). However, there are other factors that affect the volume of sales (effort, advertising, competitors, technology, etc.). Nevertheless, in variance analysis it is important to isolate the effect of sales volume on revenues from the effect of sale prices on revenues. Therefore, similar to the approach used with materials quantity and labor efficiency variances, we multiply the underlying "real" volume variance of ten boats by the expected (or standard) sales price to calculate the financial impact on Sunbird of selling fewer boats; in other words, 10 boats × $10,000 = $100,000 U.

You can see how the calculations of the sales price variance and the sales volume variance are related in the illustration below.

Sales Price Variance and Sales Volume Variance

Actual quantity × Actual price	**Actual quantity × Standard price**	**Expected quantity × Standard price**
90 boats × $10,500 = $945,000	90 boats × $10,000 = $900,000	100 boats × $10,000 = $1,000,000

Sales price variance	**Sales volume variance**
($10,500 − $10,000) × 90 boats = $45,000 F	(90 boats − 100 boats) × $10,000 = $100,000 U

In summary, the sales price variance informs users whether actual sales prices were higher or lower than expected. The sales volume variance informs users whether the number of units sold was more or less than expected. As you work through these calculations, be sure to keep in mind that you already know which variances are favorable and unfavorable even before you make the calculations. In fact, it's usually best to determine the nature of the variance (favorable versus unfavorable) before you calculate the actual size of the variance.

Controlling Revenue Variances   Typically, sales prices are under the control of the marketing executives in the organization. These are the people who carefully establish the strategy of setting prices. On the other hand, the sales volume is largely under the control of the sales executives and sales teams in the organization. These are the people who work closely with customers to sell the product. As we've discussed above, it's an economic fact for most products and services that sales price impacts sales volume. Hence, although responsibility accounting is focused on clearly assigning responsibility for each variance to specific people and segments in the organization, the nature of revenue variances may challenge the effort to separate the responsibility for sales prices and sales volumes. Revenue is often the responsibility of many people and segments across the organization.

STOP & THINK

Is it possible that a manager could be doing a poor job of managing revenues and revenue growth even though revenues were increasing from period to period?

```
┌─────────────────────────────────────────────────────────┐
│  REMEMBER THIS...                                         │
```

- Profit centers and their managers are usually evaluated on both costs and revenues.

- The most common profit center measurement tool is the segment margin statement. This statement identifies both direct and indirect costs and charges only the direct costs to segments.

- Costs in profit centers are analyzed and managed the same way they are in cost centers—using standard costing. But because profit center managers are also held responsible for revenues, actual and expected revenues are used to compute sales price variances and sales volume variances.

- The formula for the sales price variance is:

  (Actual price − Standard price) × Actual quantity sold.

- The formula for the sales volume variance is:

  (Actual quantity sold − Expected quantity sold) × Standard price.

Evaluating Performance in Investment Centers

Use ROI and residual income analysis to explain how performance is controlled in investment centers.

(4) An investment center was defined earlier as an organizational unit in which a manager has responsibility for costs, revenues, and assets. Overall, companies are considered to be investment centers, as are some independent segments of decentralized companies. For example, the Acme Computer and Edison Automobile subsidiaries of IMC (see Exhibit 1) would probably both be investment centers. Officers of such segments are responsible for acquiring and managing the assets required to manufacture and market their products, as well as for managing the revenues and costs related to those products. The assets include inventory, accounts receivable, and long-term operating assets such as equipment and delivery trucks. On the other hand, Edison's Japan Operations could be considered a profit center if all asset management decisions are handled by Far East operations. (If Japan Operations handles its own asset management decisions, then it would be an investment center.) Further, the Manufacturing center for Japan Operations is likely a cost center since it doesn't control sales.

The bottom line is that when a segment essentially operates as a separate company with responsibility for all of its assets, then it is considered to be an investment center. There are several methods of evaluating the performance of an investment center. Two of the most common methods used are the rate of return on invested assets and the residual income.

return on investment (ROI)

A measure of operating performance and efficiency in utilizing assets; computed in its simplest form by dividing operating profit by average total assets.

Return on Investment (ROI)

You may recall that we introduced management accounting in Chapter 15 by describing how the management team at **DuPont** used **return on investment (ROI)** (sometimes called return on total assets) to manage their company to success in the early 1900s. ROI is a measure of how much has been earned on the assets of a company; it is equal to operating profit divided by total assets. For example, if a company earned $1,000 on $10,000 of assets[5] for one year, its ROI would be $1,000 ÷ $10,000, or 10%.

─────────────────────────────

[5] In this chapter, we will use the term *ROI* instead of *return on total assets* because it is more commonly used in management decision making. In this text we will use average total assets instead of ending total assets to calculate ROI (although in actual practice, management teams in some organizations may choose to use ending total assets). Average total assets is generally computed by adding the assets balances at the beginning and end of the year, and then dividing the sum in half.

Because an investment center operates as if it were an independent company, its performance can be evaluated using ROI. In calculating the ROI for an investment center, however, management must be sure to consider only the assets, revenues, and costs controlled by that center. In other words, assets used and costs incurred for the benefit of several investment centers should not be included in the calculation. To stress this concept, we will restate the basic ROI formula as:

$$\text{Investment center ROI} = \frac{\text{Investment center operating profit}}{\text{Investment center average assets}}$$

Generally, when an investment center's ROI is analyzed, this formula is divided into its components—the profit margin (sometimes called operating performance) and asset turnover ratios—as follows:

$$\text{Profit margin} \times \text{Asset turnover} = \text{ROI}$$

$$\frac{\text{Operating profit}}{\text{Revenue}} \times \frac{\text{Revenue}}{\text{Average total assets}} = \frac{\text{Operating profit}}{\text{Average total assets}}$$

CAUTION

Dividing the ROI formula into its two components "profit margin" and "asset turnover" creates a more complex formula. You may be tempted to simplify the formula by eliminating the two revenue figures because they cancel each other out. However, including revenue draws attention to the important concept that ROI is a function of both profit margin and asset turnover.

Operating profit (which is a function of both expenses and revenues) and revenues were considered earlier in our discussion on controlling profit centers. The ROI formula expands the use of cost and revenue measures to also include measures of assets. Thus, when combined with cost and revenue variance analysis, ROI is an effective tool in evaluating investment centers where management has responsibility for assets as well as profits. It is this ROI calculation that investors commonly use to evaluate companies in which they are considering investing.

profit margin (operating performance) ratio

An overall measure of the profitability of operations during a period; computed by dividing operating profit by revenue.

asset turnover ratio

An overall measure of how effectively assets are used during a period; computed by dividing revenue by average total assets.

The expanded formula shown above helps us identify the three ways an investment center can improve its ROI: (1) it can decrease costs to increase its **profit margin (operating performance) ratio** (operating profit divided by revenue), (2) it can decrease assets to increase its **asset turnover ratio** (revenue divided by average total assets), or (3) it can increase revenue with a corresponding increase in operating profit. An investment center requiring a major investment in assets (such as a steel mill) will necessarily have a low asset turnover and will therefore have to rely primarily on a higher profit margin to increase its return. An investment center with few operating assets (such as a grocery store) has a more rapid asset turnover and can sustain a lower profit margin ratio while still earning an attractive ROI. For example, a grocery store might make only 2 cents profit per dollar of product sold, but its asset turnover of 12 times a year makes its ROI 24%. A steel mill with an asset turnover of 3 times a year would have to earn a profit margin of 8 cents per dollar of sales to produce an ROI of 24%.

To illustrate the three ways of increasing ROI, we will assume that Acme Computer has revenue of $10,000,000, segment operating profit of $1,000,000, and average total assets of $5,000,000. The ROI is:

$$\text{Profit margin} \times \text{Asset turnover} = \text{ROI}$$

$$\frac{\$1,000,000}{\$10,000,000} \times \frac{\$10,000,000}{\$5,000,000} = \text{ROI}$$

$$10\% \times 2 = 20\%$$

The following examples show how each of the three alternatives increases ROI:

1. Increase ROI by reducing expenses by \$400,000, providing a segment operating profit of \$1,400,000:

$$\frac{\$1,400,000}{\$10,000,000} \times \frac{\$10,000,000}{\$5,000,000} = \text{ROI}$$

$$14\% \times 2 = 28\%$$

2. Increase ROI by reducing average total assets to \$4,000,000:

$$\frac{\$1,000,000}{\$10,000,000} \times \frac{\$10,000,000}{\$4,000,000} = \text{ROI}$$

$$10\% \times 2.5 = 25\%$$

3. Increase ROI by increasing revenue to \$12,000,000 (assume that operating profit increases proportionately):[6]

$$\frac{\$1,200,000}{\$12,000,000} \times \frac{\$12,000,000}{\$5,000,000} = \text{ROI}$$

$$10\% \times 2.4 = 24\%$$

Although ROI is an effective way of evaluating managers of investment centers, it has certain drawbacks. For example, assume that an investment center currently has an ROI of 22%, but the company has an overall ROI of only 16%. If a new project or investment that promises a return of 19% becomes available to the investment center manager, it might be rejected because the investment center's overall ROI would be reduced, even though the company's overall ROI would be increased.

Residual Income

residual income

The amount of operating profit earned above a specified minimum rate of return on assets; used to evaluate investment centers.

Although ROI is widely used to evaluate investment centers, because of its drawbacks, some companies use a closely related measure called **residual income**, which is the amount of operating profit an investment center is able to earn above a certain minimum rate of return on assets. The formula for residual income is as follows:

Operating profit − (Minimum required rate of return × Average total assets) = Residual income

To illustrate, let's return to Acme Computer and calculate its residual income. Assuming that the specified minimum rate of return on assets at IMC is 15%, Acme Computer needs to earn at least \$750,000 (15% × \$5,000,000 average total assets) before it can report any residual income. We then compute Acme Computer's residual income as follows:

\$1,000,000 segment margin − \$750,000 minimum return on assets = \$250,000 residual income

To further illustrate why many companies prefer to use residual income over ROI for evaluating investment center performance, assume that Acme Computer has an opportunity to invest \$1,200,000 in a new project that will generate a return of 16% (\$192,000 per year). If Acme Computer's manager is being evaluated on ROI, she would probably reject this investment opportunity because, as the following analysis shows, it would reduce the division's overall ROI from 20% to 19.2%.

---

[6] As will be discussed in Chapter 20, operating profit is likely to increase more than proportionately when revenue rises. Because some costs (such as rent) are fixed in amount, operating profit should increase to more than 10% when revenue increases 10%. As a result, the ROI in this example should actually increase to more than 24%.

	Without the New Investment	The New Investment	With the New Investment
Segment margin	$1,000,000	$ 192,000	$1,192,000
Total assets	÷$5,000,000	÷$1,200,000	÷$6,200,000
ROI	20%	16%	19.2%

On the other hand, if the manager is being evaluated on residual income (with a minimum rate of return of 15%), she would probably be more positive about the project because it increases residual income from $250,000 to $262,000.

	Without the New Investment	The New Investment	With the New Investment
Total assets	$5,000,000	$1,200,000	$6,200,000
Segment margin	$1,000,000	$ 192,000	$1,192,000
Less the minimum rate of return	(750,000)*	(180,000)**	(930,000)
Residual income	$ 250,000	$ 12,000	$ 262,000

*$5,000,000 × 15% = $750,000
**$1,200,000 × 15% = $180,000

Whether or not the investment should actually be made also depends on several other factors, including what other alternatives are or will be available. The advantage of residual income is that it encourages managers to make as much profit as possible rather than merely maintaining a certain ROI; this means making investments that benefit not only their centers but also the company as a whole.

REMEMBER THIS...

- Managers of investment centers are usually held responsible for costs, revenues, and assets.
- The most common performance measures used in investment centers are ROI (return on investment) and residual income.
- The formula for ROI is:

$$\text{Investment center ROI} = \frac{\text{Investment center income}}{\text{Investment center average assets}}$$

- ROI is a function of both the profit margin ratio and the asset turnover ratio. The formulas for these two ratios are:

$$\text{Profit margin} \times \text{Asset turnover} = \text{ROI}$$

$$\frac{\text{Operating profit}}{\text{Revenue}} \times \frac{\text{Revenue}}{\text{Average total assets}} = \frac{\text{Operating profit}}{\text{Average total assets}}$$

- Residual income helps avoid some ROI decisions by segment managers that are not in the best interest of the company. The formula for residual income is:

$$\text{Operating profit} - (\text{Minimum required rate of return} \times \text{Average total assets}) = \text{Residual income}$$

EXPANDED *material*

Earlier in the chapter, you were introduced to standard costing as a way to evaluate performance in cost centers and you were shown how standard costing can be used to compute variances for materials and labor. Information relating to these material and labor variances can be used by decision makers to evaluate the acquisition and use of these important resources. In this expanded material section, we introduce you to the variances associated with manufacturing overhead costs. Although several of the computations associated with overhead variances are similar to those used for materials and labor, they are generally more complicated. As a result, interpreting the results and assigning responsibility for manufacturing overhead variances must be done with caution.

Variable Manufacturing Overhead Variances in Cost Centers

Compute and interpret variable overhead cost variances.

(5)   Manufacturing overhead is the third type of product cost that must be controlled and accounted for. In this section we will cover variable overhead. Fixed overhead will be covered in the next section.

Measuring and Controlling Variable Manufacturing Overhead Costs

Variable manufacturing overhead includes such costs as indirect materials, indirect labor, utilities, and repairs and maintenance. Like direct materials and direct labor, variable manufacturing overhead is measured and controlled by establishing standard costs, measuring actual costs, analyzing variances from standard, and reporting the variances to managers so they can take necessary corrective action.

Identifying Variable Overhead Elements, Cost Drivers, and Per-Unit Costs
The first step in controlling variable manufacturing overhead is to study the behavior of each overhead cost to determine whether it is fixed, variable, or mixed.[7] The second step is to identify a cost driver for each variable manufacturing overhead element that relates the variable manufacturing overhead cost to specific activities or volume changes. For simplicity in illustrating variable overhead variances, we will assume that variable manufacturing overhead costs vary with direct labor hours. However, you should be aware that, where possible, costs are assigned to activities based on cost drivers that reflect the actual usage of costs for each activity. Thus, instead of using one cost driver, such as direct labor hours, a company might identify different cost drivers for each type of variable overhead cost.[8]

To illustrate the calculation of variable manufacturing cost variances using direct labor hours as the cost driver, we will return again to our Sunbird Boat Company example. Assume for Sunbird that direct labor hours worked fluctuate between 7,000 and 9,000 hours each year. At the beginning of the year, Sunbird's management team and accountants analyzed the company's cost behavior patterns over this relevant range to create an annual budget. Based on their sales budget, they also established a production budget to produce 105 15-foot boats.[9] As you recall from its standard costs (Exhibit 3 on page 950), Sunbird allows 80 standard direct labor hours for each 15-foot boat produced. This means that 8,400 direct labor hours (105 boats × 80 standard hours) were originally forecasted to be used in the current year. These data were then used to establish standard variable manufacturing overhead rates as shown below.

	Annual Budgeted Costs		**Divided by the Total Standard Direct Labor Hours Allowed**		**Variable Manufacturing Overhead Rate**
Indirect materials	$12,600	÷	8,400 hours	=	$1.50 per hour
Indirect labor	42,000	÷	8,400 hours	=	5.00 per hour
Utilities	8,400	÷	8,400 hours	=	1.00 per hour
Variable manufacturing overhead . . .	$63,000				$7.50 per hour

---

[7] We will study issues related to cost behavior and mixed costs in Chapter 20.

[8] Chapter 17 on activity-based costing provided important insight on the need to intelligently select cost drivers that effectively impact overhead costs. In most organizations, effective analysis of overhead costs requires the use of multiple cost drivers. For simplicity, we will assume in this chapter that all variable overhead costs can be analyzed using a single cost driver. Although this is rarely the case, the variable overhead variances discussed here are equally relevant to organizations with multiple overhead cost drivers.

[9] These are the same production and sales numbers we created in Chapter 18 to illustrate operational budgeting. In fact, all standard costs and budgets used in the Sunbird Boat Company example in this chapter are based on data established in Chapter 18. You're encouraged to review the previous chapter if needed to better understand these standard (or budgeted) cost data.

CAUTION

Be sure you understand that in our Sunbird example overhead costs are applied on the basis of *standard direct labor hours allowed*, and not on the actual direct labor hours used. Hence, regardless of how many hours are actually used to produce a boat, variable manufacturing overhead of $600 is applied ($7.50 × 80 hours). This is the approach used by most companies that follow a standard cost accounting system.

As you can see, by summing these amounts, Sunbird developed a total standard variable manufacturing overhead rate of $7.50 per direct labor hour. Because Sunbird allows 80 standard direct labor hours for each 15-foot boat produced, the company applies $600.00 to each boat produced ($7.50 × 80 hours).

Variable Manufacturing Overhead Variances Let's now illustrate how variances are calculated for variable manufacturing overhead costs. You'll recall from our work with direct labor variances that the Sunbird Boat Company actually used 7,880 direct labor hours to produce 100 15-foot boats during the year. Given that only 100 boats were actually produced (rather than the 105 boats originally budgeted to be produced), Sunbird Boat Company should have used 8,000 direct labor hours (as calculated in the table below). Sunbird's end-of-year results, including the total variable manufacturing overhead costs actually incurred, are summarized as follows:

Boats produced	100
Direct labor hours used	7,880
Standard direct labor hours for boats produced (80 hours × 100 boats)	8,000
Standard variable manufacturing overhead allowed for boats actually produced (8,000 hours × $7.50)	$60,000
Actual variable manufacturing overhead costs incurred:	
Indirect materials	$11,259
Indirect labor	43,654
Utilities	8,127
Total variable manufacturing overhead costs	$63,040

CAUTION

The 8,400 direct labor hours *budgeted* at the beginning of the year to build the planned production of 105 boats are not to be confused with the 8,000 hours *allowed for actual production* of 100 boats by the end of the year of 100 boats. Similarly, do not confuse the $63,000 variable manufacturing overhead costs *budgeted* at the beginning of the year with the $60,000 variable manufacturing overhead costs *allowed for actual production* by the end of the year.

As you can see in the table above, on the basis of 8,000 standard direct labor hours allowed to produce an actual output of 100 boats, the standard cost allowed for variable manufacturing overhead is $60,000 (8,000 hours × $7.50 per hour). The difference between the $63,040 actually incurred and the $60,000 standard cost allowed is the amount of over- or underapplied variable overhead. In this example, variable manufacturing overhead has been underapplied by $3,040 ($63,040 − $60,000). As with direct materials and direct labor, the total variable manufacturing overhead variance is separated into two major variances: spending and efficiency. The spending and efficiency variances are computed as follows:

Variable Manufacturing Overhead Variances		
Actual amount spent	**AH × SR** Actual hours of input × Standard rate	**SHA × SR** Standard hours allowed for actual output × Standard rate
$63,040	7,880 hours × $7.50 = $59,100	8,000 hours × $7.50 = $60,000
	Variable overhead spending variance $59,100 − $63,040 = $3,940 U	**Variable overhead efficiency variance** ($8,000 hours − 7,880 hours) × $7.50 = $900 F

Variable Manufacturing Overhead Spending Variance.   The **variable manufacturing overhead spending variance** ($3,940 U) is the difference between the amount predicted by the actual activity level, $59,100 (7,880 actual direct labor hours × $7.50 standard rate) and the actual variable manufacturing overhead costs incurred ($63,040).

Because manufacturing overhead contains several different cost items, it is possible to compute a spending variance for each variable overhead item. This analysis helps managers determine which costs are largely responsible for creating the variances. For Sunbird Boat Company, the analysis would be as follows:

	Actual Costs	Actual Hours of Input × Standard Rate	Spending Variance
Indirect materials	$11,259	7,880 hours × $1.50 = $11,820	$ 561 F
Indirect labor	43,654	7,880 hours × $5.00 = 39,400	4,254 U
Utilities	8,127	7,880 hours × $1.00 = 7,880	247 U
	$63,040	$59,100	$3,940 U

Looking at the spending variance column, we see a $561 favorable variance for indirect materials, a $4,254 unfavorable variance for indirect labor, and a $247 unfavorable variance for utilities. The favorable variance for indirect materials means that less was spent than was expected for the actual hours worked; however, the $561 is probably not a significant difference and likely isn't worth the effort to investigate further. Similarly, the $247 unfavorable variance for utilities is not a large difference either. On the other hand, the $4,254 unfavorable variance for indirect labor costs indicates either that spending is out of control or that the standards are unreasonably low. In any case, managers and others responsible for any significant variances (favorable or unfavorable) should be asked to explain the reason for these variances. Of course, this example assumes that variable overhead is a function of direct labor hours. If direct labor hours is not a good cost driver of (i.e., does not influence) variable overhead costs, then the variances are highly suspect.

Variable Manufacturing Overhead Efficiency Variance.   The $900 favorable variable manufacturing overhead efficiency variance is based on the difference between the standard and actual activity levels times the standard variable overhead rate [(8,000 standard direct labor hours allowed - 7,880 actual direct labor hours) × $7.50]. When direct

variable manufacturing overhead efficiency variance

The difference between the standard variable manufacturing overhead allowed for the standard activity level and the standard variable manufacturing overhead predicted based on the actual activity level. This difference is then multiplied by the standard variable overhead cost rate. This variance effectively measures the efficiency of the underlying activity used to assign variable manufacturing overhead costs.

labor hours are used as the basis for assigning manufacturing overhead, the **variable manufacturing overhead efficiency variance** simply indicates whether the standard number of hours allowed for production are more (favorable) or less (unfavorable) than the actual hours used for production. As you will recall, the same relationship was used on page 957 in computing the direct labor efficiency variance. Hence, because Sunbird's direct labor efficiency variance is favorable ($2,400), the variable manufacturing overhead efficiency variance is also favorable ($900). Conversely, of course, an unfavorable direct labor efficiency variance would have produced an unfavorable variable manufacturing overhead efficiency variance. The only difference between the value for the direct labor efficiency variance and the variable manufacturing overhead efficiency variance is the rate used in computing each variance (standard labor rate of $20 versus the standard variable overhead rate of $7.50). What this means (*and this is important*) is that the variable manufacturing overhead efficiency variance really doesn't describe the efficiency of using variable manufacturing overhead; rather, it reports the efficiency of how the manufacturing allocation basis is being used. Because Sunbird is using direct labor hours to assign manufacturing overhead, the variable manufacturing overhead variance doesn't really provide any additional information for management beyond that already provided by the direct labor efficiency variance. As a result, the manager responsible for the control of direct labor hours is responsible for Sunbird's favorable manufacturing overhead efficiency variance because the variance is a measure of the efficiency with which direct labor is used. (Again, it is important to note that we are assuming that direct labor hours is an appropriate cost driver at Sunbird Boat Company for variable manufacturing overhead costs.)

The only reason for computing the variable manufacturing overhead efficiency variance at Sunbird Boat Company is to be able to completely account for over- or underapplied manufacturing overhead and close the amount to Cost of Goods Sold. We'll talk more about over- or underapplied manufacturing overhead in the next section.

REMEMBER THIS...

- Variable manufacturing overhead costs and activities can be analyzed using two variances: spending and efficiency.
- The formula for the spending variance for variable manufacturing overhead is:

    (Actual activity level × Standard overhead rate) − Actual overhead costs.

- The formula for the efficiency variance for variable manufacturing overhead is:

    (Standard level of activity allowed − Actual activity level)
    × Standard overhead rate.

- Remember that the variable manufacturing overhead efficiency variance does not provide insight on how well overhead costs are being used; rather, this variance captures the efficiency of the activity (i.e., the cost driver) used to assign standard overhead costs.

Compute and
interpret fixed
overhead cost
variances.

Fixed Manufacturing Overhead Variances in Cost Centers

(6) The final product cost to control is fixed manufacturing overhead. Fixed manufacturing overhead includes such costs as rent, insurance, depreciation, staff and supervisor salaries, and property taxes. This cost is unique among the product costs. Because direct materials and direct labor are generally characterized as variable costs similar to variable manufacturing overhead, the process of "controlling" fixed manufacturing overhead is different from the other costs we've studied in this chapter. Nevertheless, fixed manufacturing overhead is a very significant cost in most organizations.[10]

Measuring and Controlling Fixed Manufacturing Overhead Costs

Reporting on how well fixed manufacturing overhead costs are controlled is actually a fairly straightforward process. Because these costs are fixed in total, measuring variances around these costs is simply a matter of comparing the original budget with the total fixed overhead costs that were actually spent. To demonstrate, let's return once more to our Sunbird Boat Company example. Similar to the variable manufacturing overhead budget established at the beginning of the year, Sunbird's management team and accountants also created a fixed manufacturing overhead budget. Then, in order to subsequently allocate these costs to boats as they are produced during the year, Sunbird created standard fixed manufacturing overhead rates using an approach similar to that used to create standard variable manufacturing overhead rates. This process is shown below.

	Annual Budgeted Costs		Divided by the Total Standard Direct Labor Hours Allowed		Fixed Manufacturing Overhead Rate
Property taxes	$ 8,000	÷	8,400 hours	=	$ 0.95 per hour
Insurance	4,000	÷	8,400 hours	=	0.48 per hour
Depreciation on the plant	60,000	÷	8,400 hours	=	7.14 per hour
Supervisors' salaries	96,000	÷	8,400 hours	=	11.43 per hour
Fixed manufacturing overhead	$168,000				$20.00 per hour

As you compare this chart to the similar chart we created earlier for variable manufacturing overhead, be sure to bear in mind that we're dealing with fixed costs here. Similar to the $7.50 variable manufacturing overhead rate created earlier, the $20.00 fixed manufacturing overhead rate above will be used by Sunbird's accountants to allocate manufacturing overhead to production (again, remember that we discussed the overhead allocation process previously in Chapter 16). Hence, Sunbird applies $1,600 ($20.00 × 80 hours) in fixed manufacturing overhead costs to each 15-foot boat produced. In addition, as you remember from the previous section, Sunbird uses the variable manufacturing overhead rate of $7.50 to apply $600 ($7.50 × 80 hours) to each boat produced. Sunbird also uses the $7.50 rate to measure expected variable

---

[10] Sometimes students are confused by the idea that fixed costs need to be controlled or managed. Fixed costs should not change, right? Wrong. Fixed costs are not constant; they are simply fixed with respect to operating activity in the organization as measured by cost drivers such as production volume or direct labor hours. Fixed costs can, and often do, change due to issues unrelated to levels of operating activity.

STOP & THINK

Remember that fixed costs can still change. The reason these costs are fixed is because they are not expected to change based strictly on changes in production activity. Consider each of the four categories of fixed costs for Sunbird Boat Company. Can you think of some good business reasons why some of the actual fixed costs are different than originally planned?

manufacturing overhead costs based on the actual activity level. On the other hand, Sunbird's accountants don't use the $20.00 rate to measure expected fixed manufacturing overhead costs. These costs are fixed and are expected to be $168,000, regardless of the level of boats actually produced.

Fixed Manufacturing Overhead Variances During the year, Sunbird incurred the following costs:

Actual fixed manufacturing overhead costs incurred:	
Property taxes	$ 9,115
Insurance	4,000
Depreciation on the plant	65,533
Supervisors' salaries	94,712
Total actual fixed manufacturing overhead costs	$173,360

These costs, combined with Sunbird's fixed manufacturing overhead budget and the standard fixed manufacturing overhead rate (also known as the predetermined manufacturing overhead rate), are used by Sunbird's accountants to create the two variances in this illustration.

Fixed Manufacturing Overhead Variances

Actual amount spent	Budgeted amount (used to establish the predetermined allocation rate)	SHA × SR Standard hours allowed for actual output × Standard rate
$173,360	$168,000; ($168,000 ÷ 8,400 hours = $20.00 per hour)	8,000 hours × $20.00 = $160,000

Fixed overhead budget variance
$168,000 − $173,360 = $5,360 U

Volume variance
(8,000 hours − 8,400 hours) × $20.00 = $8,000 U

Fixed Manufacturing Overhead Budget Variance. The $5,360 unfavorable **fixed manufacturing overhead budget variance** is the difference between what was actually spent and the original budget. Hence, it is a simple matter to create a detailed budget variance report for each fixed overhead item. This analysis helps managers determine which costs have the biggest impact on the budget variance. For Sunbird Boat Company, the analysis would be as follows:

fixed manufacturing overhead budget variance

The difference between the standard (or budgeted) fixed manufacturing overhead established at the beginning of the reporting period and the actual fixed manufacturing overhead incurred.

	Actual Costs	Budgeted Costs	Budget Variance
Property taxes	$ 9,115	$ 8,000	$1,115 U
Insurance	4,000	4,000	0
Depreciation on the plant	65,533	60,000	5,533 U
Supervisors' salaries	94,712	96,000	1,288 F
	$173,360	$168,000	$5,360 U

Generally, one would expect little change in fixed costs unless a decision is made by management to make a direct change to a cost item. Hence, buying or selling property, changing the insurance contract, adjusting the depreciation schedule, or personnel changes will affect the actual fixed costs incurred. Apparently, Sunbird's insurance contract didn't change. There were some differences in property taxes (likely due to a tax rate increase by the local government) and salaries (perhaps a shift in personnel serving in management roles). It also appears that Sunbird saved a little money on supervisor salaries, perhaps due to staff changes in the company. The largest impact on the fixed overhead budget variance came from depreciation. This variance should be investigated. Perhaps the company accountant made a change to the depreciation method, or perhaps more expensive equipment was acquired during the year. It's important to understand that variances do not provide answers in the management process. Variances signal questions that need to be asked by management.

volume variance

The difference between the expected (or budgeted) production output established at the beginning of the reporting period and the actual production output. This difference is then converted into a dollar number by multiplying it by the standard fixed manufacturing overhead costs per unit.

Volume Variance.   The $8,000 unfavorable **volume variance** shown in the illustration above is a variance unlike any other we've studied in this chapter. Every variance studied thus far has been an *input* variance; that is, it has been either a variance on how much was spent on the input (materials price, labor rate, variable overhead spending, fixed overhead budget) or a variance on how much of the input was used (materials quantity, labor efficiency, variable overhead efficiency). The volume variance is an *output* variance and measures the difference between expected and actual production volumes.

In the case of Sunbird Boat Company, you will recall that at the beginning of the year management expected to produce 105 15-foot boats. However, at the end of the year the company had only produced 100 boats. This is an unfavorable volume variance, and the amount of that variance is five boats. The problem in a standard costing system is that you can't debit or credit "five boats" into the accounting system. To record this variance requires that the difference between expected and actual output volume be changed into a dollar amount. This is done using the fixed manufacturing overhead rate of $20.00 per direct labor hour. Based on the production standards used to establish its standard costs, Sunbird allocates $1,600 (80 standard direct labor hours allowed × $20.00 per direct labor hour) in fixed manufacturing overhead to each boat produced. (Remember that Sunbird established the $20.00 rate based on an expectation of producing 105 boats and uses the rate to allocate the budgeted fixed costs of $168,000.) Because Sunbird only produced 100 boats, it only allocated $160,000 ($1,600 × 100 boats). In other words, Sunbird underapplied its fixed manufacturing overhead costs by $8,000 ($168,000 − $160,000), which results in an unfavorable volume variance of $8,000. Another way of calculating this volume variance would be to simply multiply the unfavorable volume difference of five boats by the $1,600 per-boat application rate. This fixed overhead volume variance can be thought of, roughly speaking, as underapplied fixed manufacturing overhead costs (we discussed this concept earlier in Chapter 16). Because Sunbird actually produced fewer boats than originally expected when it set up the $1,600 application rate, not enough fixed costs were applied to production during the year.

CAUTION

Remember that overhead costs are applied on the basis of *standard direct labor hours allowed*, and not on the actual direct labor hours used. Sunbird will apply $1,600 in fixed manufacturing overhead to each boat produced *regardless* of how many hours are actually used to produce the boat.

FYI

Managers who understand how to use the volume variance as a performance measure know that this dollar figure doesn't really indicate the volume of costs flowing into or out of their organization. They know that if they divide this number by the predetermined fixed manufacturing overhead rate per unit, they can then see exactly how many units were actually produced above or below the expected level of production.

Accounting for Manufacturing Overhead Variances. The four manufacturing overhead variances we've described in the expanded material section of this chapter all combine together to form the total over- or underapplied manufacturing overhead in the organization. At the end of the current year, Sunbird's manufacturing overhead account appears as shown below.

Manufacturing Overhead

(Actual costs)		(Applied costs)
Indirect materials	11,259	60,000 applied variable costs
Indirect labor	43,654	160,000 applied fixed costs
Utilities	8,127	
Property taxes	9,115	
Insurance	4,000	
Depreciation–plant	65,533	
Supervisors' salaries	94,712	
	236,400	220,000
Balance (underapplied)	16,400	

In a simple cost system, we would close out the underapplied overhead directly to Cost of Goods Sold with the following journal entry:

Cost of Goods Sold	16,400	
Manufacturing Overhead		16,400
To close the balance in Manufacturing Overhead and adjust		
the balance in Cost of Goods Sold up to the actual amount.		

However, because Sunbird uses a standard cost system, it recognizes variances in its accounting system and then uses those variances to adjust standard costs and revenues to actual costs and revenues for the income statement. Consistent with the accounting for variances we've done in this chapter, Sunbird will use the underapplied overhead to recognize the four manufacturing overhead variances as shown below.

Variable Overhead Spending Variance	3,940	
Fixed Overhead Budget Variance	5,360	
Volume Variance	8,000	
Variable Overhead Efficiency Variance		900
Manufacturing Overhead		16,400
To close the balance in Manufacturing Overhead and recognize		
the manufacturing overhead variances.		

These overhead variances are subsequently closed to Cost of Goods Sold, which will result in an adjustment that increases Cost of Goods Sold by $16,400.

STOP & THINK

As you have worked through the accounting for manufacturing overhead variances, do you see that the applied manufacturing overhead cost number is the same number as standard overhead costs allowed for actual output? A rule of thumb to use in accounting for overhead variances is that when overhead is underapplied, the total of the four overhead variances will be unfavorable (and vice versa). What kind of adjustment to Cost of Goods Sold is required when manufacturing overhead is underapplied? When manufacturing overhead is overapplied? Do you see why managers and accountants think of underapplied overhead as unfavorable and overapplied overhead as favorable?

> ## REMEMBER THIS...
>
> - The fixed manufacturing overhead budget variance simply measures the difference between the original budget amount and what was actually spent for fixed manufacturing overhead.
> - The volume variance doesn't really report at all on how fixed manufacturing overhead costs are being used. Instead, the volume variance is an output measure that reports on the difference between expected production volume and actual production volume.
> - The formula for the volume variance is based on whatever activity (for example, direct labor hours) that the company chooses to use to apply fixed overhead costs to production. The formula for the volume variance is:
>
>   (Standard level of activity allowed − Original activity level planned)
>   × Standard overhead rate per activity unit.
> - An alternative, and more direct, formula for the volume variance is:
>
>   (Actual production volume − Original production volume planned)
>   × Standard overhead rate per unit of production.
> - The volume variance is combined with the fixed manufacturing overhead budget variance and the variable manufacturing overhead spending and efficiency variances to account for over- or underapplied overhead.

REVIEW OF LEARNING OBJECTIVES

① Describe the responsibility accounting concept and identify the three types of organizational control units.

- Decentralized companies delegate decisions and responsibility to lower-level managers while centralized companies retain decisions and responsibility to run the business at higher levels of management.
- In order to support a responsibility accounting system, business units may be classified as cost centers, profit centers, or investment centers.

② Describe standard costing and use materials and labor cost variance analysis to explain how performance is controlled in cost centers.

- Standards are budgeted costs and budgeted usage that serve as benchmarks to compare against actual costs and actual usage. Differences between standard and actual are called "variances."
- Actual materials cost performance can be assessed separately as materials price variances and materials quantity (or usage) variances.
- The materials price variance formula is:

  (Standard price − Actual price) × Actual quantity.
- The materials quantity variance formula is:

  (Standard quantity allowed − Actual quantity used) × Standard price.
- Actual labor cost performance can be assessed separately as labor rate variances and labor efficiency (or usage) variances. The formula for labor rate variance and for labor efficiency variance is very similar to the formula for materials price and materials quantity, respectively.

(3) Use segment margin statements and revenue variance analysis to explain how performance is controlled in profit centers.

- The most common profit center measurement tool is the segment margin statement. This statement identifies both direct and indirect costs and charges only the direct costs to segments.
- In addition to cost variances, revenue variances are also used to manage performance in profit centers.
- The two revenue variances are based on sales price and sales volume.
- The formula for the sales price variance is:

$$(\text{Actual price} - \text{Standard price}) \times \text{Actual quantity sold.}$$

- The formula for the sales volume variance is:

$$(\text{Actual quantity sold} - \text{Expected quantity sold}) \times \text{Standard price.}$$

(4) Use ROI and residual income analysis to explain how performance is controlled in investment centers.

- Managers of investment centers are usually held responsible for costs, revenues, and assets.
- The most common performance measures used in investment centers are ROI (return on investment) and residual income.
- The formula for ROI is:

$$\text{Investment center ROI} = \frac{\text{Investment center operating profit}}{\text{Investment center average assets}}$$

- The formula for residual income is:

$$\text{Operating profit} - (\text{Minimum required rate of return} \times \text{Average total assets}) = \text{Residual income}$$

- The ROI formula can be broken down into two subcomponents. The formulas for these two subcomponent ratios are:

$$\text{Profit margin} \times \text{Asset turnover} = \text{ROI}$$

$$\frac{\text{Operating profit}}{\text{Revenue}} \times \frac{\text{Revenue}}{\text{Average total assets}} = \frac{\text{Operating profit}}{\text{Average total assets}}$$

(5) Compute and interpret variable overhead cost variances.

- Variable manufacturing overhead costs and activities can be analyzed using two variances: spending and efficiency.
- The formula for the variable overhead spending variance is:

$$(\text{Actual activity level} \times \text{Standard overhead rate}) - \text{Actual overhead costs.}$$

- The formula for the variable overhead efficiency variance is:

$$(\text{Standard level of activity allowed} - \text{Actual activity level}) \times \text{Standard overhead rate.}$$

(6) Compute and interpret fixed overhead cost variances.

- Fixed manufacturing overhead costs are analyzed using a single variance called the fixed manufacturing overhead budget variance.
- The formula for the fixed manufacturing overhead budget variance is:

$$\text{Budgeted fixed overhead costs} - \text{Actual fixed overhead costs.}$$

- The volume variance does not report on how fixed manufacturing overhead costs. Instead, the volume variance reports on the difference between expected production volume and actual production volume.

- The formula for the volume variance is either:

  (Standard level of activity allowed – Original activity level planned)
  × Standard overhead rate per activity unit

  or

  (Actual production volume – Original production volume planned)
  × Standard overhead rate per unit of production.

- All four manufacturing overhead variances can be combined to account for over- or under-applied manufacturing overhead in the standard cost accounting system.

KEY TERMS & CONCEPTS

asset turnover ratio, 965

centralized company, 946

cost center, 948

decentralized
   company, 946

direct costs, 959

exception reports, 947

goal congruence, 947

indirect costs, 960

investment
   center, 949

labor efficiency
   variance, 957

labor rate variance, 956

management by
   exception, 951

materials price
   variance, 952

materials quantity
   variance, 953

operating capital, 946

profit center, 949

profit margin (operating
   performance) ratio, 965

residual income, 966

responsibility
   accounting, 947

responsibility center, 948

return on investment
   (ROI), 964

sales price
   variance, 962

sales volume
   variance, 963

segment margins, 961

segment margin
   statement, 959

segment-margin
   ratios, 961

segments, 945

standard cost
   system, 950

variance, 951

fixed manufacturing
   overhead budget
   variance, 973

variable manufacturing
   overhead efficiency
   variance, 971

variable manufacturing
   overhead spending
   variance, 970

volume variance, 974

REVIEW PROBLEMS

Materials, Labor, and Revenue Variances

The standard cost sheet for Kendra Box Company shows the following unit costs for direct materials and direct labor for each box made:

Direct materials (4 board feet of lumber @ $2)	$ 8
Direct labor (2 standard hours @ $6)	12
Total standard materials and labor costs per box	$20

During the month of October, 83,000 board feet of lumber were used to produce 20,000 boxes, and the following actual costs were incurred:

Lumber purchased (100,000 board feet @ $2.20)	$220,000
Direct labor (39,600 hours @ $6.05)	$239,580

The standard selling price per box is $52. Kendra expects to sell 50,400 boxes during October. Actual revenue results for October are as follows:

Actual revenue (47,355 boxes sold at $53 per box)	$2,509,815

(continued)

Required:
Compute the materials, labor, and revenue variances.

Solution
Materials Variances

The price variance is computed when the lumber is purchased, and the quantity variance is computed when the lumber is used.

Materials price variance:		
Standard price per board foot	$	2.00
Purchase price per board foot for 100,000 feet		(2.20)
Difference	$	0.20 U
Feet of lumber purchased	×	100,000
Total price variance	$	20,000 U

Materials quantity variance:		
Standard lumber allowed (20,000 boxes × 4 feet)	80,000	feet
Actual lumber used	(83,000)	feet U
Difference	3,000	feet U
Standard cost per board foot	× $2.00	
Total quantity variance	$ 6,000	U

Labor Variances

The labor rate and labor efficiency variances are both based on direct labor hours used; thus, they are computed at the same point in time.

Labor rate variance:		
Standard rate	$	6.00
Actual rate		(6.05)
Difference	$	0.05 U
Actual direct labor hours used	×	39,600
Total labor rate variance	$	1,980 U

Labor efficiency variance:		
Standard direct labor hours allowed	40,000	hours
Actual direct labor hours	(39,600)	hours
Difference	400	hours F
Standard direct labor rate	× $6.00	
Total labor efficiency variance	$ 2,400	F

Revenue Variances

Sales price variance:		
Actual price	$	53.00
Standard price		(52.00)
Difference	$	1.00 F
Actual quantity of boxes sold	×	47,355
Total sales price variance	$	47,355 F

(continued)

Sales volume variance:		
Actual quantity of boxes sold	47,355	boxes
Expected (budgeted) quantity	(50,400)	boxes
Difference	3,045	boxes U
Standard price	× $52.00	
Total sales volume variance	$158,340	U

Variable and Fixed Manufacturing Overhead Variances

Use the information given in the previous problem, plus the following information, to address issues associated with Kendra Box Company's manufacturing overhead variances.

The company's budget shows the following monthly variable manufacturing overhead costs at several production levels:

	Percent of Standard Capacity		
	80%	90%	100%
Expected number of boxes	20,000	22,500	25,000
Expected direct labor hours	40,000	45,000	50,000
Variable manufacturing overhead costs	$80,000	$90,000	$100,000
Fixed manufacturing overhead costs	$125,000	$125,000	$125,000

The company normally produces at 100% of capacity and uses this production level to establish its predetermined manufacturing overhead rates. The following actual information for October is available:

Variable manufacturing overhead	$83,000	
Fixed manufacturing overhead	$133,000	
Production	20,000 boxes	

Required:

1. Compute the variable manufacturing overhead cost rate (a) per box and (b) per direct labor hour assuming Kendra Box Company produces at normal capacity.
2. Compute the variable manufacturing overhead spending and efficiency variances for October assuming that Kendra produces at normal capacity and that variable manufacturing overhead costs vary with direct labor hours.
3. Compute the fixed manufacturing overhead cost rate (a) per box and (b) per direct labor hour.
4. Compute the fixed manufacturing overhead budget and volume variances for October using direct labor hours to establish the predetermined overhead rate.

Solution

1. Variable Manufacturing Overhead Cost Rates

		Rate per Box	Rate per Hour
Flexible budget at normal capacity:			
Boxes produced per month	25,000		
Labor hours per month	50,000		
Variable manufacturing overhead costs	$100,000	$4	$2

(continued)

2. Variable Manufacturing Overhead Variances

The following diagram shows the computation of the variable overhead spending and efficiency variances:

Actual amount spent	**AH × SR** Actual hours of input × Standard rate	**SHA × SR** Standard hours allowed for actual output × Standard rate
$83,000	39,600 hours × $2.00 = $79,200	40,000 hours × $2.00 = $80,000

Variable overhead spending variance
$79,200 − $83,000 = $3,800 U

Variable overhead efficiency variance*
(40,000 hours − 39,600 hours) × $2.00 = $800 F

*Be sure to compare this calculation to the labor efficiency variance calculated earlier for Kendra Box Company. Do you see how similar these calculations are? Both are based on the efficiency in labor hour usage.

3. Fixed Manufacturing Overhead Cost Rates

		Rate per Box	Rate per Hour
Flexible budget at normal capacity:			
Boxes produced per month	25,000		
Labor hours per month	50,000		
Fixed manufacturing overhead costs	$125,000	$5	$2.50

4. Fixed Manufacturing Overhead Variances

The following diagram shows the computation of the fixed overhead budget and volume variances:

Actual amount spent	Budgeted amount (used to establish the predetermined allocation rate)	**SHA × SR** Standard hours allowed for actual output × Standard rate
$133,000	$125,000 ($125,000 ÷ 50,000 hours = $2.50 per hour)	40,000 hours × $2.50 = $100,000

Fixed overhead budget variance
$125,000 − $133,000 = $8,000 U

Volume variance**
(40,000 hours − 50,000 hours) × $2.50 = $25,000 U

**Alternative calculation: (Actual production − Expected production) × Rate per box = (20,000 boxes − 25,000 boxes) × $5 = $25,000 U.

DISCUSSION QUESTIONS

1. Why is it practically impossible for a large firm to be completely centralized, that is, to have top management making all operating decisions?
2. Why is a system of responsibility accounting necessary in most businesses?
3. What are some important behavioral factors that must be considered when responsibilities are assigned to managers?
4. Why are most performance reports called exception reports?
5. What is the difference between a cost center and a profit center? Between a profit center and an investment center?
6. What is a standard cost?
7. What is the purpose of a standard cost system?
8. Who is responsible for the development of the standards to be used in a standard cost system?
9. What is a variance from standard?
10. What is the relationship of a standard cost system to the principle of management by exception?
11. What are the steps in establishing and operating a standard cost system?
12. Why are two variances, rather than one, used to measure and control materials and labor costs?
13. Who is usually responsible for each of the following variances?
    a. Direct materials price variance
    b. Direct materials quantity variance
    c. Direct labor rate variance
    d. Direct labor efficiency variance

14. If a profit center has a net loss, does that always mean it is not making a contribution to the company as a whole?
15. What are the variances used to analyze revenues in profit and investment centers?
16. What is the major disadvantage of using ROI to evaluate the performance of investment centers?
17. What is the major advantage of using residual income to evaluate the performance of investment centers?

EXPANDED *material*

18. What are the two steps in developing a management system for use in controlling variable manufacturing overhead?
19. What is a variable manufacturing overhead spending variance, and what does it indicate about variable manufacturing overhead costs?
20. What is a variable manufacturing overhead efficiency variance, and how does it relate to the labor efficiency variance?
21. What does the fixed manufacturing overhead budget variance measure?
22. What does the volume variance measure, and how is this variance different from the other cost variances studied in this chapter?

PRACTICE EXERCISES

PE 19-1 **Centralization versus Decentralization**

LO1 Which one of the following statements is *not* an advantage of decentralization?
   a. Segment managers usually have more information regarding matters within their segments than do managers at higher levels.
   b. Segment managers' decisions are always consistent with the overall objectives of the firm.
   c. Managers can be evaluated more easily because their responsibilities are more clearly defined.
   d. Higher-level management has more time to consider strategic goals when daily decision making is distributed throughout the organization.
   e. Segment managers can spot problems and react more quickly than can managers at higher levels.

PE 19-2 **Responsibility Accounting**

LO2 The company is producing an exception report. One division had $47,500 in budgeted costs, but it actually spent $45,000. How would this variance appear on the exception report?

PE 19-3   **Responsibility Centers**

LO2   Which one of the following is *not* an example of a responsibility center in an organization?

a. Profit center

b. Asset center

c. Cost center

d. Investment center

PE 19-4   **Standard Cost Card**

LO2   Using the following standard quantities and standard rates, calculate the standard costs of direct materials, direct labor, and variable and fixed manufacturing overhead and determine the total standard cost per unit.

	Standard Quantity	Standard Price or Rate
Direct materials	4 pounds	$ 1.25
Direct labor	2.5 hours	15.00
Variable manufacturing overhead (based on direct labor hours)	2.5 hours	1.70
Fixed manufacturing overhead (based on direct labor hours)	2.5 hours	0.50

PE 19-5   **Materials Price Variance**

LO2   The company purchased 10,000 pounds of raw materials at $2.75 per pound. The company's standard cost per pound is $2.50. Calculate the materials price variance for this purchase.

PE 19-6   **Accounting for Materials Price Variances**

LO2   Refer to the data in PE 19-5. Make the necessary journal entry to record the cash purchase of the raw materials inventory at standard cost.

PE 19-7   **Materials Quantity Variance**

LO2   The company used 5,500 board feet of raw materials with a standard cost of $6.00 per board foot to make 400 tables. The company's standard is 14 board feet per table. Calculate the company's materials quantity variance.

PE 19-8   **Accounting for Materials Quantity Variance**

LO2   Refer to the data in PE 19-7. Make the necessary journal entry to record the transfer of these raw materials into work-in-process inventory.

PE 19-9   **Labor Rate Variance**

LO2   Using the following information, compute the labor rate variance.

Number of nightstands produced	150
Actual hours used to produce nightstands	720
Actual labor rate per hour	$15.30
Standard labor rate per hour	$15.00
Standard labor hours per nightstand	5

PE 19-10   **Labor Efficiency Variance**

LO2   Refer to the data in PE 19-9. Compute the labor efficiency variance.

PE 19-11   **Accounting for Labor Variances**

LO2   Refer to the data in PE 19-9 and PE 19-10. Make the necessary journal entry to record direct labor at the standard rates.

PE 19-12   **Segment Margin Statement**

LO3   The company reports the following costs and revenues for one of its segments:

Net sales revenue	$728,000
Cost of goods sold	416,000
Selling and administrative costs	104,000
Advertising cost	62,400
Insurance cost	82,000

Of these costs, cost of goods sold and selling and administrative costs are variable, advertising is a direct fixed cost, and insurance is an indirect fixed cost. Using this information, prepare a segment margin statement for this segment.

PE 19-13   **Segment-Margin Ratio**

LO3   Refer to the data in PE 19-12. Compute the segment-margin ratio.

PE 19-14   **Revenue Variances**

LO3   Which of the following are *not* examples of revenue variances (you may select more than one)?
    a. Sales price variance
    b. Spending variance
    c. Materials price variance
    d. Sales volume variance
    e. Labor rate variance

PE 19-15   **Computing Revenue Variances**

LO3   The company sells one product, which is called Product A. Actual and expected sales data for the most recent year are as follows:

	Company Sales	Sales Price
Actual	500 units	$15
Expected	600	13

Using these data, compute the following:
    1. Sales price variance
    2. Sales volume variance

PE 19-16   **Return on Investment**

LO4   The company's profit margin is 12%, and its asset turnover is 3.1. Compute the company's return on investment (ROI).

PE 19-17   **Residual Income**

LO4   The company had $360,000 in total assets and $94,000 in operating profit this year, and the company requires at least a 12% return on assets. Compute the company's residual income.

PE 19-18   **Variable Manufacturing Overhead Spending Variance**

LO5   Using the following data, compute the variable manufacturing overhead spending variance.

Number of nightstands produced	150
Actual hours used to produce nightstands	720
Total actual variable overhead costs incurred	$8,352
Standard variable overhead rate per direct labor hour	$11.00
Standard labor hours per nightstand	5

PE 19-19

LO5

Variable Manufacturing Overhead Efficiency Variance

Refer to the data in PE 19-18. Compute the variable manufacturing overhead efficiency variance.

PE 19-20

LO6

Fixed Manufacturing Overhead Budget and Volume Variances

The company spent $80,000 on fixed manufacturing overhead during the year. As of the beginning of the year, the company had budgeted to spend $76,000 on fixed manufacturing overhead and to work 2,000 direct labor hours (based on expected production of 500 units at four direct labor hours per unit). The actual number of units produced during the year was 400. Fixed manufacturing overhead is applied to production based on direct labor hours. Compute (1) the fixed manufacturing overhead budget variance, (2) the fixed manufacturing overhead volume variance, and (3) the total amount of under- or overapplied fixed manufacturing overhead.

PE 19-21

LO5, LO6

Accounting for Manufacturing Overhead Variances

The company has the following manufacturing overhead variances:

Variable manufacturing overhead spending variance	$ 300 F
Variable manufacturing overhead efficiency variance	425 U
Fixed manufacturing overhead budget variance	1,000 U
Fixed manufacturing overhead volume variance	740 F

Make the journal entry necessary to close the manufacturing overhead account and recognize these variances.

EXERCISES

E 19-22

LO1

Responsibility Accounting Reports

Lorlily Company is an agricultural supply firm. The management of the company is decentralized, with division managers heading the two operating divisions: Machinery and Seed/Fertilizer. Within each division, the sales are split between the two states of Indiana and Illinois.

The following data are applicable to revenue in 2009:

	Budget	Actual
Machinery–Indiana	$800,000	$750,000
Seed/Fertilizer–Illinois	500,000	580,000
Seed/Fertilizer–Indiana	400,000	530,000
Machinery–Illinois	350,000	250,000

1. Prepare a responsibility accounting report for the head of the Machinery division. For each of the two geographic areas (Indiana and Illinois), show whether the variance between budgeted and actual machinery revenue is favorable or unfavorable.
2. Prepare a responsibility accounting report for the head of the entire company. The company head wants to see only the overall results for each of the two operating divisions (Machinery and Seed/Fertilizer); a detailed breakdown by geographic area is not requested.

E 19-23

LO2

Materials Price Variance

Hogan Manufacturing Company has just adopted a standard cost system. You have been asked to analyze the materials purchases and usage for the month of August to determine the materials price variance to be recorded at the end of the month. During August, 5,000 gallons of a chemical were purchased at $3.10 per gallon. Only 4,600 gallons

(continued)

were put into production. The standard price per gallon is $3.20. Compute the following variances:

1. The materials price variance if the chemical is carried in inventory at standard price (i.e., the price variance is accounted for at the time of purchase).
2. The materials price variance if the chemical is carried in inventory at actual price and is charged to Work-in-Process Inventory at the standard price (i.e., the price variance is accounted for at the time of use in production).

E 19-24   **Materials Price and Quantity Variances–Journal Entries**

LO2   Genesis Enterprises produces one product—MX4. The following information relating to raw materials is available for the month of March:

Beginning direct materials inventory	1,500 pounds @ $3.10 per unit
Purchases made during the month	11,000 pounds @ $3.10 per unit
Direct materials placed in production	11,750 pounds

The standard materials usage for one unit of MX4 is 2 pounds with a standard price per pound of $3. Genesis produced 6,000 units of Product MX4 during the month.

1. Compute the materials price and quantity variances for Genesis assuming the materials price variance is computed at the time of purchase.
2. Provide the journal entries required to record:
   a. The purchase of direct materials and the materials price variance.
   b. Placing the direct materials in production and the materials quantity variance.

E 19-25   **Direct Materials Purchased and Used**

LO2   Mary Clarke is concerned about her performance as a recently employed purchasing agent. The accounting department has provided her with the following performance data for the month of August:

Units produced	2,000
Materials used	1,078 tons
Materials purchased	1,400 tons at $43 per ton

The standard materials usage set by management for one unit of product is half a ton of materials per unit, at $45 per ton. Her performance report shows the following variances:

Used (1,078 tons − 1,000 tons standard) × $45 per ton	$3,510 U
Purchased ($45 per ton standard − $43 per ton actual) × 1,400 tons	2,800 F

If you were Mary Clarke, how would you explain this report?

E 19-26   **Analyzing Materials Cost**

LO2   Mr. Rogers, the production manager, has received a report showing a $10,800 unfavorable total materials variance (materials price variance plus materials quantity variance). He knows that production used 20,000 pounds less than the budgeted amount of direct materials allowed for actual output. Mr. Rogers also knows that the standard price for direct materials was determined to be 90 cents per pound.

What was the actual cost of direct materials used during the period if the standard amount allowed was estimated to be 500,000 pounds?

E 19-27   **Materials Price and Quantity Variances**

LO2   Daniel Smith, production manager, has just received a report stating that the total materials variance (materials price variance plus materials quantity variance) for last month was $6,710 unfavorable. However, he is not certain whether the production foremen are

(continued)

overdrawing from inventory or the purchasing department has been unable to acquire materials at reasonable prices. The information he needs is contained in the following report:

Budgeted production	125,000 units
Actual production	122,000 units
Standard materials per unit	1.5 pounds
Materials used in March	193,000 pounds
Standard price for materials	$1.25 per pound
Actual price for materials	$1.22 per pound

1. Compute the materials price and quantity variances for the month. (*Note:* Mr. Smith's company computes the materials price variance at the time that materials are issued to production.)
2. **Interpretive Question:** What was the cause of the unfavorable variance, and what recommendation would you make to Mr. Smith?

E 19-28   Materials Price and Quantity Variances–Journal Entries

LO2   Starship Enterprises produces and sells calibrators. The company began the period with the following inventory of raw material:

200 units at $5.50 per unit (the materials price variance is recorded at the time of purchase)

A standard of four units of material for each calibrator produced has been established. During the period, Starship purchased an additional 1,500 units of material at a total cost of $8,220. The dollar amount of materials transferred to Work-in-Process Inventory during the period was $8,800. At the end of the period, Starship had an ending materials inventory of 50 units.

1. Provide the journal entry required to record the materials price variance.
2. Provide the journal entry required to record the materials quantity variance.

E 19-29   Labor Rate and Efficiency Variances

LO2   To produce one unit of Product CD requires eight hours of labor at a standard cost per hour of $21.00. During the month of September, 5,000 units were produced. Actual hours and costs for the month are as follows:

Actual direct labor hours	38,400
Actual direct labor costs	$844,800

1. Compute the actual cost per hour of direct labor for the month of September.
2. Compute the labor rate variance.
3. Compute the labor efficiency variance.

E 19-30   Responsibilities for Labor Costs

LO1, LO2   Raymond Stone, a recent business school graduate, has taken a job with Farben Corporation as production manager. His job is to see that production is efficient. After his first month, he is given this memo.

Performance Report	
Raymond Stone:	$32,000 Unfavorable

The following data are also known for Raymond Stone's first month:

Units produced	750 units
Direct labor used	7,600 hours at $20
Standard direct labor hours per unit	10 hours at $16

(continued)

1. What explanation would you give for the total unfavorable variance (which combines both labor rate and labor efficiency variances) if you were in Raymond Stone's position? Be sure to keep in mind that he is not responsible for hiring and firing employees, nor is he responsible for wage rates. These decisions are handled by the personnel department.
2. What might be theoretically wrong with a conclusion that Raymond Stone is not at all responsible for labor rates?

E 19-31
LO2

Labor Variances

During the year, Thompson Plastics was in negotiation with the local union over wages. A settlement was finally reached, and the average wage per hour was increased to $32. Production fell to 130,000 units, and 205,000 hours were incurred. Production had been budgeted at 150,000 units. 1.5 hours of labor were expected to produce one unit at a standard labor cost of $48 per unit. Actual labor cost for the period was $6,601,000.

1. Calculate the labor variances at Thompson Plastics.
2. Prepare the journal entry to enter labor costs in Work-in-Process Inventory and set up the rate and efficiency variances for labor.
3. **Interpretive Question:** Are these variances significant in light of the new wage agreement?

E 19-32
LO2

Labor Variances

Compute the missing amounts.

Total labor variance (efficiency plus rate variances)	$ 47,500 U
Labor efficiency variance	42,000 U
Actual labor hours incurred	110,000
Units produced	50,000
Standard hours allowed per unit	2
Total actual labor costs	$467,500
Standard labor hours allowed for actual output	(a)
Actual labor cost per hour	(b)
Actual labor cost per unit	(c)
Standard labor cost per hour	(d)
Labor rate variance	(e)
Standard labor cost per unit	(f)

E 19-33
LO3

Segment Margin Statements

Professional Management, Inc., is a company that sponsors seminars for executives. It has two profit centers, or divisions: a time-management group and a money-management group. Financial information for the two divisions for the year just ended follows:

	Time Management	Money Management
Revenue	$842,000	$965,000
Mailing costs	48,000	102,000
Printing costs	146,000	98,000
Hotel rental costs	425,000	501,000
Travel expenses	72,000	60,000
Advertising costs	108,000	106,000

Of these costs, printing and advertising are direct fixed costs, whereas mailing, hotel rental, and travel are variable costs. Using this information, prepare segment margin statements for the two divisions. Include in your statements the computation for contribution margin.

E 19-34   **Evaluating Performance with Segment and Contribution Margins**

LO3   Sunshine Center's three profit centers had the following operating data during 2009:

	Harrisburg	Scranton	Albany
Revenue (at $21.50 per unit)	$322,500	$215,000	$430,000
Fixed costs:			
Costs unique to the division	131,150	64,500	150,500
Costs allocated by corporate headquarters	45,150	30,100	60,200
Variable costs per unit	13	14	10

Sunshine's management is concerned because the company is losing money. They ask you to:

1. Calculate each profit center's contribution and segment margins, and overall company profits.
2. Determine, on the basis of these calculations, which center(s), if any, should be discontinued. (Assume that the 2009 performance is indicative of all future years. Ignore all nonfinancial factors.)

E 19-35   **Measuring Performance Using Segment and Contribution Margins**

LO3   El Pico Company has two divisions: Maya and Aztec. During 2009, they had the following operating data:

	Maya Division	Aztec Division
Revenue	$100,000	$120,000
Fixed costs:		
Costs unique to the division	50,000	45,000
Costs allocated by corporate headquarters	11,000	10,000
Variable costs per unit	4	4
Unit sales price of division's product	10	8

1. Compute each division's contribution and segment margins, and the contribution each makes to overall company profits.
2. **Interpretive Question:** Based on only the financial information given, should either division be discontinued? Why?

E 19-36   **Revenue Variances**

LO3   Fabulous Fragrances makes two products: lotion and shampoo. Actual and expected revenue data for the two products are as follows:

	Actual Data	
	Units Sold	Sales Price
Lotion	3,400 bottles	$11
Shampoo	4,800 bottles	9

	Expected Data	
	Units Sold	Sales Price
Lotion	3,000 bottles	$12
Shampoo	5,600 bottles	8

Using the above data, compute the sales price and sales volume variances for lotion and shampoo for Fabulous Fragrances.

E 19-37

LO3

Revenue Variances

Telling Time is a watch retailer. It sells two types of watches: digital and analog. The results for the third quarter for Telling Time are as follows:

	Digital	Analog
Expected sales in units	400	500
Expected sales price	$50	$75
Actual sales in units	375	530
Actual total sales revenue	$19,500	$38,955

1. Calculate the sales price variance and the sales volume variance for digital watches.
2. Calculate the sales price variance and the sales volume variance for analog watches.

E 19-38

LO4

Return on Investment

Compute the missing data, items (a) through (i), in the following table:

	Pittsburgh	Cecil	Monroeville
Revenue	$600,000	$500,000	(g)
Operating profit	$30,000	$25,000	(h)
Total assets	(a)	$100,000	$200,000
Profit margin ratio	(b)	(d)	10%
Asset turnover ratio	(c)	(e)	4 times
ROI	12%	(f)	(i)

E 19-39

LO4

Return on Investment

During 2009, the Hopewell and Hamilton divisions of Granger Company reported the following:

	Hopewell Division	Hamilton Division
ROI	12%	24%
Profit margin ratio	3%	4%
Revenue	$72,000	$90,000
Total assets	$18,000	$15,000

1. What was each division's asset turnover ratio in 2009?
2. What profit margin ratio would each division need in order to generate an ROI of 25%?

E 19-40

LO4

Measuring Performance: Residual Income and ROI

McCormick Corporation measures the performance of its divisions by using the residual income approach, with a minimum accepted rate of return of 16%. In 2009, the printing division, which has total assets of $250,000, generated an operating profit of $48,000, or 8% of sales. The operating results are expected to be the same in 2010. In early 2010, the printing division receives a proposal for a $50,000 investment that would generate an additional $9,000 of income per year.

1. Should the manager of the printing division make the investment?
2. Would your answer to part (1) be different if McCormick Corporation used the ROI approach to evaluate the performance of its various divisions? Why or why not?

E 19-41
LO4

Measuring Performance: Residual Income and ROI

An investment center of Southwick Corporation made three investment proposals. Details of the proposals follow.

	Proposals		
	1	**2**	**3**
Required investment	$80,000	$50,000	$65,000
Annual return	13,000	9,000	9,500

Southwick Corporation uses the residual income method to evaluate all investment proposals. Its minimum rate of return is 15%.

1. As president of Southwick Corporation, which of the investments, if any, would you make? Why?
2. Assuming that Southwick Corporation uses the ROI approach to evaluate investment proposals, which investments, if any, would you make? (Southwick Corporation's current return on assets is 20%.)

E 19-42
LO5, LO6

Variable and Fixed Manufacturing Overhead Variances

Lauder Company manufactures one product. The standard capacity is 20,000 units per month. Manufacturing overhead costs are budgeted and applied on the basis of two machine hours per unit. At standard capacity, the monthly variable overhead budget is $500,000 and the monthly fixed overhead budget is $900,000. During February, 18,000 units of product were actually manufactured, $460,000 of variable manufacturing overhead was incurred, and $975,000 of fixed manufacturing overhead was incurred. Actual machine hours were 35,000.

1. Compute the variable manufacturing overhead spending and efficiency variances.
2. Compute the fixed manufacturing budget and volume variances.

E 19-43
LO5, LO6

Manufacturing Overhead Variances

Rollins Manufacturing Company estimates variable manufacturing overhead for the month of November to be $80,000. Fixed manufacturing overhead is estimated to be $195,000. All manufacturing overhead is estimated on the basis of 10,000 budgeted direct labor hours. At standard production output capacity, each unit of finished product requires two direct labor hours to complete. During November, 5,900 units of finished product were produced. Actual variable and fixed manufacturing overhead costs incurred were $81,500 and $189,000, respectively. Actual direct labor hours during the month were 12,000.

1. Compute the total amount of manufacturing overhead applied during November.
2. Compute the amount of under- or overapplied overhead for the month.
3. Compute the variable manufacturing overhead spending and efficiency variances.
4. Compute the fixed manufacturing budget and volume variances.

PROBLEMS

P 19-44
LO1

Responsibility Accounting Reports

Ryhan Company is a multinational computer services firm. The management of the company is decentralized, with division managers heading the following three divisions: Europe, Asia, and the Americas. Within each division, the three sources of revenue are software sales, service contracts, and consulting fees.

(continued)

The following data are applicable to revenue in 2009:

	Budget	Actual
Europe–software sales	$200,000	$230,000
Asia–software sales	200,000	130,000
Americas–software sales	350,000	420,000
Europe–service contracts	120,000	90,000
Asia–service contracts	70,000	80,000
Americas–service contracts	250,000	190,000
Europe–consulting fees	40,000	90,000
Asia–consulting fees	50,000	35,000
Americas–consulting fees	100,000	60,000

Required:
1. Prepare a responsibility accounting report for the head of the Europe division. For each of the three revenue sources (software sales, service contracts, and consulting fees), show whether the variance between budget and actual is favorable or unfavorable.
2. Prepare a responsibility accounting report for the head of the entire company. The company head wants to see only the overall results for each of the three geographic divisions (budget versus actual); a detailed breakdown by revenue source is not requested.

P 19-45

LO2

Materials and Labor Variances

The standard cost data for Madison Machinery Company show the following costs for producing one of its machines:

Direct materials	400 pounds at $8 = $3,200
Direct labor	150 hours at $15 = $2,250

During April, four machines were built, with actual total costs as follows:

Materials purchased	2,000 pounds at $8.20 = $16,400
Materials used	1,700 pounds
Direct labor incurred	625 hours at $14.80 = $9,250

Required:
1. Compute the following variances:
   a. Materials price variance (raw materials inventory is carried at standard cost)
   b. Materials quantity variance
   c. Labor rate variance
   d. Labor efficiency variance
2. Record the standard materials and labor costs in Work-in-Process Inventory, and enter the variances in appropriate journal entries.

P 19-46

LO2

Materials and Labor Variances

Mayhem Manufacturing provides the following standard cost data for one of its products:

Direct materials	15 feet at $3.00 per foot
Direct labor	2 hours at $12.50 per hour

During the month of February, the following actual cost data were accumulated:

Materials purchased	120,000 feet at $2.85 per foot
Materials used	118,750 feet
Direct labor incurred	17,000 hours at a total cost of $215,560
Units produced	7,800 units

(continued)

Required:

Compute the following variances:

1. Materials price variance (this variance is computed at the time of purchase)
2. Materials quantity variance
3. Labor rate variance
4. Labor efficiency variance

P 19-47
LO2

Materials and Labor Variances

Actual materials	2,000 tons
Actual hours used	1,500 hours
Standard materials for output (tons)	(a)
Standard hours for output	(b)
Actual cost per ton of material	(c)
Standard cost per ton of material	$ 4
Actual cost per direct labor hour	$ 4
Standard cost per direct labor hour	(d)
Total direct labor variance*	$1,625 U
Total direct materials variance**	$ 400 F
Direct materials price variance	(e)
Direct materials quantity variance	$ 0
Direct labor rate variance	$ 750 U
Direct labor efficiency variance	(f)

*Total direct labor variance = Labor rate variance + Labor efficiency variance
**Total direct materials variance = Materials price variance + Materials usage variance (Materials price variance is computed at the time of use in production.)

Required:

Compute the missing amounts.

P 19-48
LO2

Materials and Labor Variances

Sports Manufacturing, Inc., produces and sells footballs. The standard cost for materials and labor for one regulation-size football is as follows:

Direct materials	2 feet of leather at $5.50 per foot
Direct labor	½ hour at $9.00 per hour

During the period, Sports Manufacturing recorded a materials price variance of $100 U and a materials quantity variance of $380 F. In addition, the company recorded a labor rate variance and a labor efficiency variance of $1,200 U and $450 U, respectively. Seven thousand footballs were produced during the period, and the materials inventory did not change during the period.

Required:

1. Compute the actual costs for materials and labor during the period.
2. Provide the journal entries to record the materials price and quantity variances. (*Hint:* The amount of materials purchased and used is the same.)
3. Provide the journal entries to record the labor rate and efficiency variances.

P 19-49
LO2

Materials and Labor Variances

The following information was taken from the records of Liberty Tool Manufacturing Company for its production of jack-hammers in the month of July:

(continued)

Materials (actual):
    Purchases of wood: 1,300 pounds × $2.25
    Purchases of steel: 2,750 pounds × $4.95
    Used 900 pounds of wood
    Used 2,525 pounds of steel

Direct labor (actual):
    Manufacturing Division: 1,650 hours × $13.70
    Assembly Division: 920 hours × $12.45

Standard cost per unit:
    Wood: 1 pound at $2.20 per pound .... $ 2.20
    Steel: 3 pounds at $4.80 per pound 14.40
    Direct labor–manufacturing: 2 hours at $14.00 .... 28.00
    Direct labor–assembly: 1 hour at $12.25 .... 12.25
    Standard cost per unit $56.85

Units produced: 875

Required:

1. Calculate the materials price and quantity variances, assuming that the materials price variance is recognized at the time of purchase.
2. Calculate the labor rate and labor efficiency variances.
3. **Interpretive Question:** What is the advantage, if any, of calculating the materials price variance at the time of purchase rather than at the time of use in production?

P 19-50

LO2

Materials and Labor Variance Analysis

Cooke Manufacturing Company produces high-quality men's pajamas for several large retail stores. The standard costs for each dozen pairs of pajamas is as follows:

Direct materials, 30 yards at $0.80 .... $24
Direct labor, 4 hours at $5.00 20
Manufacturing overhead:
    Variable cost: 4 direct labor hours at $2.00 8
    Fixed cost: 30% of direct labor cost 6
    Total product cost per dozen pairs $58

During the month of September, the company filled three orders of pajamas at the following costs:

Order	Number of Dozens	Yards Used	Labor Hours
8	400	12,200	1,500
9	900	26,750	3,750
10	500	15,450	2,140
	1,800	54,400	7,390

The following additional information involving materials and labor was supplied by the accounting department:

a. Purchases of materials during the month amounted to 60,000 yards at $0.82 per yard.
b. Total direct labor cost for the month was $37,689.

Required:

1. Compute the materials price variance for September. (Materials are carried in Direct Materials Inventory at standard.)
2. Compute the materials quantity variance for September.
3. Compute the labor rate and labor efficiency variances for September.

P 19-51

LO2

Determining How Variances Are Computed

Helon Company uses a standard cost system in its accounting for the manufacturing costs of its only product. The standard cost information for materials and labor is as follows:

Direct materials: 5 pounds at $7	$35
Direct labor: 3 hours at $8	24

During April of its first year of operation, the company completed 2,300 units and had the following materials and labor variances:

Materials price variance	$1,400 F
Materials quantity variance	2,100 F
Labor rate variance	2,115 U
Labor efficiency variance	1,200 U

There was no work-in-process inventory at the beginning or end of April.

Required:

Compute the following amounts:

1. The amount of materials and labor debited to Work-in-Process Inventory during April.
2. The pounds of materials used in production.
3. The actual hours of labor used in production.
4. The actual labor rate per hour.

P 19-52

LO3

Evaluation of Profit Centers–Segment Margin

Della Brown is the manager of one of the stores in the nationwide EatRite supermarket chain. The following information has been gathered about the performance of Della's store in the most recent quarter:

Operating Departments	Revenue	Contribution-Margin Ratio
Groceries	$500,000	30%
Fresh produce	300,000	40%
Dry goods	600,000	35%
Fixed costs controllable by:		
Manager of grocery department	$110,000	
Manager of fresh produce department	75,000	
Manager of dry goods department	130,000	
Store manager	50,000	
Corporate headquarters	100,000	
Total	$465,000	

Required:

Prepare a segment margin statement for corporate headquarters' use in evaluating the store manager, Della Brown, and which Della can use to evaluate the managers of the three departments within the store.

P 19-53

LO3

Evaluation of Profit Centers–Segment Margin

Derrald Pearl Company has two divisions, Computer Consulting and Construction. During the most recent year, the two divisions had the following operating data:

(continued)

	Computer Consulting	Construction
Revenue	$600,000	$250,000
Contribution-margin percentage	45%	15%
Fixed costs controllable by division managers	$200,000	$30,000
Fixed costs allocated by corporate headquarters	$100,000	$100,000

Required:

1. Prepare a segment margin statement for Derrald Pearl Company. Include three columns—one for the company total and one for each of the two divisions.
2. Based on the segment margin statement prepared in part (1), what would happen to overall company profits if the Construction Division were to be discontinued?
3. Should either of the divisions be discontinued? Explain.

P 19-54
LO3

Revenue Variances

Menendez Company is a merchandiser that sells three products: Salsa, Tortillas, and Queso. The following are the actual and expected (standard) data for the three products:

Actual Data			
	Units	Sales Price	Total Actual Market
Salsa	530	$5.00	2,500 units
Tortillas	760	4.00	10,000
Queso	660	7.00	2,500

Standard Data			
	Units	Sales Price	Total Market Share
Salsa	500	$6.00	25%
Tortillas	900	3.00	10
Queso	600	5.00	20

Required:

1. Compute the sales price variance and the sales volume variance for Salsa.
2. Compute the sales price variance and the sales volume variance for Tortillas.
3. Compute the sales price variance and the sales volume variance for Queso.

P 19-55
LO3

Revenue Variances

Family Friendly Photography has just finished its first year of business. It specializes in group portraits, though the company also handles individual portraits. Revenue is determined per photo shooting. Family Friendly Photography has divided prices into three different groups: groups of 15 or more, groups of 2 to 15, and individuals. The following information is for its first year of operation:

	Number of Photo Shoots	Price per Photo Shoot
Groups of 15+	330	$280.00
Groups of 2–15	475	180.00
Individuals	175	105.00

(continued)

At the first of the year, Family Friendly Photography created a budget of expectations for the first year of business. Following are the expectations for the first year of business:

	Number of Photo Shoots	Price per Photo Shoot
Groups of 15+	300	$275.00
Groups of 2–15	450	200.00
Individuals	200	115.00

Required:

Compute the sales price variance and the sales volume variance for each of the three groups listed above.

P 19-56

LO3, LO4

ROI and Contribution-Margin Analysis

Macro Data Corporation's three divisions had the following operating data during 2009:

	Fax Machine	Calculator	Computer
Revenue	$100,000	$150,000	$200,000
Variable costs	50,000	90,000	135,000
Fixed costs	45,000	56,000	53,000
Total assets	50,000	38,000	120,000

Required:

1. Compute the contribution margin for each division.
2. Compute the segment margin for each division (assume that all fixed costs are direct to each division).
3. Compute the ROI for each division.
4. Which division had the highest profit margin ratio?
5. **Interpretive Question:** Which division had the best performance in 2009 Why?

P 19-57

LO4

ROI

Frank's Fixtures has two divisions: the Plumbing Division and the Electrical Division. Following are their operating data for 2009:

	Plumbing Division	Electrical Division
Revenue	$150,000	$180,000
Operating profit	15,000	16,200
Total assets	75,000	72,000
Stockholders' equity	36,000	20,800
Long-term debt	34,500	26,000

Required:

1. Calculate the ROI for each division.
2. **Interpretive Question:** On the basis of this return, which division appears to have the better performance? Why?

P 19-58

LO4

ROI

The following information for 2009 applies to the two sales divisions of Ward Enterprises:

	Joliet	Wheaton
Total inventory	$75,000	$60,000
Profit margin ratio	12%	15%
Operating profit	$24,000	$18,000

(continued)

Required:

1. Calculate each division's revenue.
2. Calculate each division's asset turnover ratio assuming that controllable assets include inventory only.
3. **Interpretive Question:** Which division had the better performance for the period? Why?

P 19-59

LO4

ROI and Residual Income

Pacific Corporation has a number of autonomous divisions. Its real estate division has recently reviewed a number of investment proposals.

a. A new office building would cost $450,000 and would generate yearly operating profit of $80,000.
b. A computer system would cost $350,000 and would reduce bookkeeping and clerical costs by $50,000 annually.
c. A new apartment house would cost $900,000 and would generate yearly operating profit of $150,000.

The real estate division currently has total assets of $1.8 million and operating profit of $350,000.

Required:

1. Assuming that the performance of the manager of the real estate division is evaluated on the basis of the division's ROI, evaluate each of the independent proposals, and determine whether it should be accepted or rejected.
2. Assuming that the manager's performance is evaluated on a residual income basis, determine whether each of the proposals should be accepted or rejected. (The division's minimum accepted rate of return is 15%.)

P 19-60

LO4

ROI and Residual Income

Albertson Furniture Company is a retailer of home furnishings. It currently has stores in three cities—San Francisco, Los Angeles, and Phoenix. Operating data for the three stores in 2009 were as follows:

	San Francisco	Los Angeles	Phoenix
Revenue	$1,500,000	$1,900,000	$1,800,000
Variable costs	900,000	1,200,000	1,200,000
Fixed costs (all direct)	300,000	350,000	250,000
Total assets	1,800,000	2,500,000	1,300,000

Required:

1. Compute the segment margin for each store.
2. Compute the profit margin ratio for each store.
3. Compute the asset turnover for each store.
4. Compute the ROI for each store.
5. Compute the residual income for each store. (The minimum rates of return for the stores are San Francisco, 15%; Los Angeles, 13%; and Phoenix, 18%.)

P 19-61 **ROI and Residual Income**

LO4

	San Jose	Cupertino	Los Altos	Saratoga
Revenue	$180,000	$750,000	$ (i)	$950,000
Operating profit	$ (a)	$175,000	$ (j)	$ (m)
Total assets	$150,000	$ (e)	$333,333	$ (n)
Profit margin ratio	20%	(f)	12%	(o)
Asset turnover ratio	(b)	0.75	(k)	3.0
ROI	(c)	(g)	(l)	18%
Minimum accepted rate of return	15%	(h)	16%	14%
Residual income	$ (d)	$ 15,000	$ 16,000	$ (p)

Required:
Compute the missing data, labeled (a) through (p).

P 19-62 **Measuring Performance: Residual Income and ROI**

LO4

The gaming division of Nevada Corporation had income of $550,000 and total assets of $3 million in 2009. The figures are expected to be similar in 2010. The manager of the gaming division has an opportunity to purchase some new gambling machines for $250,000. He concludes that the new machines would increase annual operating profit by $44,000.

Required:
1. Calculate the current ROI and the expected return on the proposed investment.
2. Calculate the gaming division's current residual income and the expected residual income on the proposed investment. (Assume that the division's minimum accepted rate of return is 17%.)
3. Should the new machines be purchased:
   a. If the division uses the ROI method?
   b. If the division uses the residual income method?

P 19-63 **ROI and Residual Income**

LO4

The manager of the manufacturing division of Minolta Company is evaluated on a residual income basis. He is in the process of evaluating three investment proposals.
a. Pay $500,000 for a new machine that will increase production substantially. This will result in an increased income of $80,000 annually.
b. Pay $350,000 for a new machine that will reduce labor costs by $70,000 annually.
c. Pay $800,000 for a new machine that will increase annual operating profit by $115,000.

The manufacturing division currently has total assets of $1.2 million and operating profit of $200,000. Its minimum accepted rate of return is 15%.

Required:
1. Evaluate the three investment proposals independently, and determine which should be accepted.
2. Assuming that the division manager is evaluated on the basis of the division's ROI, determine whether each of the proposals should be accepted or rejected.

EXPANDED
material

P 19-64 **Manufacturing Overhead Variances**

LO5, LO6

Engraph Manufacturing Company uses standard direct labor hours as a basis for charging manufacturing overhead to Work-in-Process Inventory. The following data were taken from the records:

(continued)

Data for August:

Actual variable manufacturing overhead	$ 217,000
Actual fixed manufacturing overhead	$ 265,700
Actual units produced	8,000
Actual direct labor hours	33,000

Annual budget data:

Budgeted variable manufacturing overhead cost	$2,611,200
Budgeted fixed manufacturing overhead cost	$3,304,800
Budgeted units of production	102,000
Budgeted direct labor hours	408,000

Required:

1. Compute the annual variable manufacturing overhead rate and annual fixed manufacturing overhead rate to be used to apply overhead to Work-in-Process Inventory.
2. Determine the variable overhead spending variance and the variable overhead efficiency variance for August.
3. Determine the fixed overhead budget variance and the volume variance for August.
4. Prepare the journal entry to transfer standard variable and fixed overhead costs to Work-in-Process Inventory.

P 19-65
LO5

Variable Manufacturing Overhead Variances

Grover Glove Company attempts to control manufacturing overhead costs through the use of a flexible budget. Standards are set by studying historical overhead cost data, which are shown here. Actual total overhead costs for each month of the second quarter are also shown.

Standard variable overhead: $2.20 per direct labor hour

Months	Actual Direct Labor Hours	Actual Variable Overhead Costs	Standard Hours Allowed
April	76,000	$155,500	74,500
May	83,000	172,000	80,000
June	63,500	148,000	65,000

Required:

1. Compute the variable overhead spending variance and the variable overhead efficiency variance for each month.
2. **Interpretive Question:** Give several reasons why the variable overhead spending variances might be unfavorable.

P 19-66
LO6

Fixed Manufacturing Overhead Variances

Standard and actual cost data for Willey Corporation for the first three quarters of the year are shown below.

Standards:

Machine hours per unit produced	5.0 machine hours
Units produced per quarter	25,000 units
Fixed manufacturing overhead per quarter	$325,000

	Actual Direct Machine Hours	Actual Fixed Overhead Costs	Actual Number of Units Produced
First quarter	126,000	$321,000	25,500
Second quarter	120,000	330,000	23,000
Third quarter	124,000	324,500	26,500

(continued)

Required:

1. Compute the fixed overhead budget variance for each quarter.
2. Compute the volume variance for each quarter.
3. **Interpretive Question:** At the end of the third quarter, the production manager at Willey Corporation believes that favorable volume variance in the third quarter means that he has more money to spend in production. Explain to the production manager what the volume variance represents and why it does not indicate that there is more money to spend in production.

P 19-67

LO5, LO6

Variable Manufacturing Overhead Spending and Efficiency Variances

The following production information is available for Porter Corporation:

Budgeted production	150,000 units
Actual production	145,000 units
Actual variable manufacturing overhead	$175,000
Variable manufacturing overhead applied	$0.80 per machine hour
Actual fixed manufacturing overhead	$88,500
Budgeted fixed manufacturing overhead	$90,000
Actual machine hours	220,000 hours
Standard machine hours per unit produced	1.5 machine hours

Required:

1. Calculate the following variances for Porter Corporation:
   a. Variable manufacturing overhead spending variance
   b. Variable manufacturing overhead efficiency variance
   c. Fixed manufacturing overhead budget variance
   d. Volume variance
2. **Interpretive Question:** Explain how the spending variance and the efficiency variance are used to control overhead costs.
3. Identify cost drivers other than machine hours that might be better measures of spending and efficient use of variable manufacturing overhead costs.
4. Can machine hours be considered a good cost driver for fixed manufacturing overhead costs?

ANALYTICAL ASSIGNMENTS

AA 19-68

DISCUSSION

Continuous Improvement Needed

One evening after a strenuous day at the office, Janis Walker, president of Western Mills, Inc., a leading textile manufacturing firm, was out jogging to help relieve the tensions of that day's work. While jogging, she focused her thinking on the firm's commercial carpeting division. The major customers of the division are companies that are building new office buildings, hotels, and motels and need quality carpet in their buildings. The carpet division is doing quite well, but Walker has a nagging feeling that the division could be doing better. She decided to discuss the performance of the division with the division manager. When she arrived home after jogging, Walker called the division manager and arranged a meeting for the next day.

At the meeting, Walker asked the division manager how long it took to deliver an order to the building site after production started. The manager's answer was 17 days. Walker then asked what the industry average was for delivery. The answer was 15 days. Walker wanted to know why Western Mills took longer than competitors to meet order requirements. The manager answered that its product was of a higher quality, so customers were willing to wait longer for the order to be filled. With this information in hand and without hesitation, Walker said, "I will give you six months to reduce the delivery time to 10 days!

(continued)

You study the problem and tell me what resources you need to meet this 10-day delivery goal. I want a report from you as soon as possible."

1. Assuming that the division already has a standard cost system, what limitations of that system resulted in two more days of delivery time than its competitors?

2. Assuming this company has a standard cost system, what changes is the division manager likely to make in order to meet the president's 10-day delivery mandate?

AA 19-69
DISCUSSION

What Are My Costs Anyway?

You have recently been promoted to be the manager of the camera division of a large corporation. Your most profitable product is a thin, pocket-sized digital camera. Historically, the pictures taken by the camera were of a poor quality, but due to large investments in research and new breakthroughs in technology, the digital pictures are of increasingly higher quality. You have just received your segment financial statements for the period, which report the following:

Revenue	$81,000,000
Cost of products sold	(40,000,000)
Gross margin	$41,000,000

On the basis of this performance you are due to receive a $300,000 bonus. The top executives of the company are ecstatic about your performance because you have increased quality, reduced defects, and dramatically increased the productivity of your segment. Having studied management accounting, however, you know that the manufacturing costs are not the only ones that add value to your products. In fact, in your heart, you believe that were it not for the fact that you've pushed very hard this last year for more research and development, aggressive marketing, and good customer service subsequent to sales, your segment would not be nearly so profitable. Yet, these costs are tracked in other departments and are not your responsibility.

As a manager who is benefiting from traditional performance evaluation methods, you wonder whether you should inform management that they are actually giving you a bonus that is too high. Apparently, you are the only one in your company that is aware that these other value-adding costs should be included in your performance evaluation. What should you do? Do you let well enough alone, or should you go to management and let them know that some of your bonus should probably be shared with other departments?

AA 19-70
JUDGMENT CALL

You Decide: **Which is more conducive to a successful organization: a centralized or decentralized company?**

With the improvements in technology and communication, many companies are able to decentralize their operations and still work effectively. Many segment managers have been given the responsibility to make decisions and react quickly to problems for their respective department without consulting upper management. Although the trend has been towards decentralization for some time, is this the best solution for today's companies? Many people believe that by decentralizing operations, the overall goals and objectives of the company are forgotten. What one segment manager does for his or her department may not be in the best interest of the company as a whole.

AA 19-71
JUDGMENT CALL

You Decide: **Can a company make a conscious decision and set the prices of its products, or does the supply and demand of the market automatically dictate the price?**

You were talking to your good friend in the economics department about companies and their pricing strategies. You mentioned a number of models used in accounting, such as variance analysis and ROI, and how these accounting models are helping companies accurately price their products, leading to better financial results. However, your friend disagreed. He

(continued)

believes that all the analysis in the world won't help a company price its products because that is left to the consumer. He said, "The consumer dictates what prices you will charge. It is the law of supply and demand. If you have a product that people want but it is priced too high, they won't buy it!"

AA 19-72
REAL COMPANY
ANALYSIS

Wal-Mart

In the 2006 Annual Report for **Wal-Mart** (provided in Appendix A), you will find Segment Information in Note 11 in the Notes to the Financial Statements.

	Wal-Mart Stores	SAM'S CLUB	International	Other	Consolidated
Notes to Financial Statements continued (in millions) **Segment Information** **Year Ended January 31**					
2004					
Revenue	$170,270	$33,804	$46,762	$1,641	$252,477
Operating profit (loss)	12,916	1,126	2,370	(1,387)	15,025
2005					
Revenue	$187,511	$36,332	$55,358	$1,757	$280,958
Operating profit (loss)	14,163	1,280	2,988	(1,340)	17,091
2006					
Revenue	$204,534	$38,955	$61,676	$2,545	$307,710
Operating profit (loss)	15,324	1,385	3,330	(1,509)	18,530

1. As you can see, Wal-Mart has four different segments: Wal-Mart Stores; SAM'S CLUB; International; and Other (that is, all other segments combined). How do you think Wal-Mart primarily evaluates these segments—as cost centers, as profit centers, or as investment centers?

2. Compute the profit margin ratio for the four segments for 2004, 2005, and 2006. Which segment is the most profitable? Which is growing the fastest in terms of revenues?

AA 19-73
REAL COMPANY
ANALYSIS

Petersen Pottery

Just outside Elkins, West Virginia, Clive Petersen has been making ceramic bathroom fixtures (sinks, toilets, and bathtubs) since 1960. Petersen's fixtures had become known over the years for their distinctive customer features, their high quality, and their long life. **Petersen Pottery** started out as a two-man operation. By 1980 it had grown to 20 master potters. By this time, Clive Petersen felt that he had expanded to a point that he needed to institute a formal accounting control system. The insistence of his banker that he get a "real" management accounting system in place was also compelling. As a result, Petersen hired a formally trained management accountant who began working with his most experienced master potters to design cost standards. After some research, Petersen's accountant arrived at the following cost standards for a toilet (note that manufacturing overhead is allocated based on direct labor hours):

Direct materials:	
Raw clay	25 lbs. × $0.95 per lb. = $23.75
Glazing mix	5 lbs. × $0.75 per lb. = 3.75
Direct labor:	
Molding	1.0 hr. × $15.00 per hour = 15.00
Glazing	0.5 hr. × $15.00 per hour = 7.50
Variable manufacturing overhead	1.5 hrs. × $3.00 per hour = 4.50
Fixed manufacturing overhead*	2.0 hrs. × $4.00 per hour = 8.00
Total per fixture	$62.50

*Based on budgeted production of 1,200 toilets.

(continued)

After six months of operations, Petersen was disturbed over the lack of attention paid to the standards by his potters. He felt that the potters were just too set in their ways to adhere to the new system. Many of the potters told Petersen that the new system was "confusing" and didn't help them in their work. In reviewing the June production results, the following actual costs were noted in connection with manufacturing 1,145 toilets:

Materials used:	
Raw clay	28,900 lbs. @ $0.92 per lb.
Glazing mix	5,900 lbs. @ $0.78 per lb.
Direct labor:	
Molding	1,200 hrs. @ $15.25 per hour (average)
Glazing	600 hrs. @ $15.00 per hour (average)
Actual variable manufacturing overhead	$5,120
Actual fixed manufacturing overhead	$9,700

1. Compute all cost variances for the month of June.
2. What suggestions do you have for Mr. Petersen regarding his new standard cost system?

Source: Adapted from J. K. Shank, "Petersen Pottery" case, *Cases in Cost Management: A Strategic Emphasis* (Cincinnati: South-Western, 1996).

AA 19-74
INTERNATIONAL

Target Costing in Japan

Japan is always a good place for useful insight on innovative management accounting practice and technique. From early on, the Japanese recognized that the most efficient way to keep costs down was to *design* them out of their products, not to reduce them after the products entered production. This realization reflects a fundamental reality of cost management in Japan; the majority of a product's costs (as much as 90 to 95% according to some experts) are "designed in." Consequently, effective cost control programs in a Japanese business typically focus heavily on the design process for a particular product. This is done primarily using a concept known as target costing, as well as value engineering (VE). Target costing is used to determine what the market is willing to pay for a product. Using the target market price (i.e., the price required to win the customer's business), the manager then subtracts the target profit to arrive at the target cost. After the target cost is determined, VE then is used to design the product in order to achieve the prespecified targeted level of costs. Thus, target costing manages costs by effectively designing into the products and processes the required costs in order to achieve the desired profit.

What do you think is the effect of target costing and VE on the use of variances? Specifically, will materials usage variances and labor efficiency variances be more or less important to a firm that strictly uses target costing and VE versus a traditional firm that is more focused on controlling daily production processes?

AA 19-75
ETHICS

Cool Air, Inc.

Jack Lear, an internal auditor for Cool Air, Inc., met with Paul Marsh, the manager of the cost accounting department, to discuss a concern about a possible "glitch" in the standard cost system. Jack explained that he had been reviewing the employee time cards in the company division where air-conditioning units and refrigerators were assembled. The time cards reflected how much employee time was devoted to the assembly of air-conditioning units and how much time applied to refrigerators. Jack's concern was that the hours actually charged for each of these operations always seemed to be right on target with the standard labor times for each air-conditioning unit and each refrigerator unit assembled; yet Jack had been told a number of times by employees in the assembly department that the standard hours for assembling air-conditioning units were too low. The employees felt that they could not meet these standards without "fudging" their time cards or sacrificing some quality work in the assembly process. Since company policy emphasized product quality, Jack suspected that time sheets were being modified by shifting hours worked on air-conditioning units to the time sheets for assembling refrigerators.

(continued)

Paul Marsh, the cost manager, thought for a minute about what Jack was telling him and then made an interesting observation. He said that he had been concerned about the fact that the company's prices for its air-conditioning units were generally lower than its competitors' prices for the same size and quality of units, whereas its prices for refrigerators were generally higher than those of its competitors. He wondered if the company's pricing structure, which was tied to its standard costs, was out of line with competition. This position was reinforced when Paul and Jack looked at the company's sales of each of these products. Over the past year or so, the company had gained market share in air-conditioner sales and had lost market share in refrigerators! Based on this information, Paul asked Jack to do some "detective" work on the time cards in the assembly division and report back his findings.

A few days later, Jack reported that he had found convincing evidence that the foremen in the assembly division had been in collusion to "doctor" employee time sheets in order to more closely meet the time standards for both air-conditioner and refrigerator assembly.

1. Who are the stakeholders affected by the "doctoring" of time sheets?
2. What are the ethical issues in this situation?
3. What should Paul do?

AA 19-76

WRITING

Qualitative Variance Analysis

With the push for continuous improvement, stable standards may become a thing of the past. As companies strive for and achieve zero defects and no waste, variances quantifiable in terms of dollars become more and more difficult to obtain. To determine variances from a standard, firms are now turning their attention to qualitative measures such as the number of customer complaints or the number of machine setups. In a one- to two-page paper, identify three standards that might be used in a manufacturing environment and three standards that might be used in a service environment that cannot be readily quantifiable in dollars. Discuss how each of those standards would be measured, as well as how variances from those standards would be measured.

PART

7

Making Decisions Using Management Accounting

Cost Behavior and Decisions Using C-V-P Analysis

After studying this chapter, you should be able to:

(1) **Understand the key factors involved in cost-volume-profit (C-V-P) analysis and why it is such an important tool in management decision making.** *C-V-P analysis involves studying the interrelationships among revenues, fixed and variable costs, levels of activity, and profits.*

(2) **Explain and analyze the basic cost behavior patterns—variable, fixed, and mixed.** *Variable costs increase as the level of sales increases. Food cost in a restaurant is a good example. Fixed costs remain the same regardless of the level of sales. Rent is a good example. A mixed cost is a combination of a fixed cost and a variable cost.*

(3) **Analyze mixed costs using the scattergraph and high-low methods.** *A collection of costs can be mathematically analyzed to determine how much of the total cost is fixed and how much is variable.*

(4) **Perform C-V-P analyses, and describe the effects potential changes in C-V-P variables have on company profitability.** *The basic insight of C-V-P*

analysis is that some things change when the level of sales changes (sales revenue and total variable cost), and some things don't change (total fixed cost). This simple idea can be used to forecast the impact on profit of changes in the level of sales, changes in selling price, changes in cost structure, and so forth.

(5) **Visualize C-V-P relationships using graphs.** *C-V-P analysis reveals that as sales climb higher, losses in a company can turn into profits. The exact pattern in which losses turn to profits as sales increase can be easily and effectively displayed in graphs.*

EXPANDED *material*

(6) **Explain the effects of sales mix on profitability.** *Some goods and services have a very low variable cost per dollar of sales, which means that the contribution margin is high for these products. Other products have a much higher variable cost ratio and lower contribution margin ratio on sales. A company's profits are impacted by the mix of high and low contribution margin products that it sells.*

(7) **Describe how higher fixed costs increase a company's operating leverage leading to increased variability in profits as sales fluctuate.** *A company frequently has to choose between high fixed costs (such as salaries for salespersons) and high variable costs (such as sales commissions). Choosing a high level of fixed costs (and low level of variable costs) makes it more likely that the company will lose a lot of money when sales are low, but also more likely that the company will make a lot of money when sales are high.*

Professional soccer has been launched several times in the United States amid much fanfare, but so far each attempt has failed. The high-profile failure of the **North American Soccer League (NASL)**–which brought Pelé, Cruyff, Best, and Beckenbauer to the United States in the early 1970s–was especially painful because, with the big names, professional soccer looked so promising. One of the major reasons previous efforts failed is that fixed costs were too high for the small number of fans and meager TV revenues. Each attempt ended up with the team owners losing money. To better manage player salaries, which are a significant part of the fixed costs of running a soccer team, **Major League Soccer (MLS)** set up an unusual single-entity structure in 1996, under which the league owns all the teams as well as all player contracts, and investors buy operating rights rather than setting up franchises. The purpose of this structure is to eliminate the financial disparities between large and small markets and to control player salaries and other fixed costs. This approach has successfully kept players' salaries low; so low in fact that a number of players have filed class action lawsuits arguing the MLS structure is holding down salaries in violation of U.S. antitrust laws.

The efforts to contain the fixed cost of players' salaries, along with other efforts by the MLS to save costs and increase revenues, may be working. Most MLS teams continue to lose money, largely due to another significant fixed cost, the cost of the leases on the football or baseball stadiums in which they play their games. To combat the high cost of lease payments and the fact that soccer teams forced to rent their facilities are only able to keep the revenue from ticket sales and are generally cut off from the all-important ancillary revenue that accompanies each game–revenue from concessions, parking, merchandise, stadium signage and naming rights, and luxury boxes, MLS is now building soccer-specific stadiums. Ten teams are expected to have their own facilities by 2010, by which point MLS expects the overall league to finally be profitable. Two MLS teams expected to show a profit in 2006 (the Los Angeles Galaxy and FC Dallas) already have their own stadiums.[1]

Some costs, such as direct materials and direct labor costs in a manufacturing firm, increase in direct proportion to the number of products or services produced. These are called variable costs. Other costs, such as factory rent, remain the same no matter what the level of production is. This characterization of costs allows one to perform cost-volume-profit (C-V-P) analysis, a critical tool in the management process. C-V-P analysis allows a manager to answer the very important question: How much do I need to sell in order to earn a profit?

In this chapter, you will learn that successful managers must think carefully about cost behavior–how costs change in relation to changes in activity levels, such as the number of patients in a hospital or the pounds of ore processed in a copper smelter. An understanding of how costs behave in relation to levels of activity helps managers predict the effects of their plans on future performance.

As you work through this chapter making calculations that will determine how profits will change in relation to changes in sales volume, fixed costs, and variable costs, be sure to think about how these calculations reflect the process of managing actual organizations. For instance, since the 9/11 attacks, the airline industry continues to struggle to be profitable in light of the heavy fixed costs of owning and operating commercial aircraft. Many owners of retail outlets in a mall breathe a sigh of relief each month on the day when enough profit has been generated to allow them to pay the monthly fixed cost of the lease payment to the mall. The owner of a baseball team will look out over a half-filled stadium on game day and worry that the ticket sales may not have been enough to cover the costs of

cost-volume-profit (C-V-P) analysis

Techniques for determining how changes in revenues, costs, and level of activity affect the profitability of an organization.

cost behavior

The way a cost is affected by changes in activity levels.

[1] John McLaughlin, *Sky*, October 1997, pp. 27-31; Ridge Mahoney, "Homes of Their Own," *Sports Illustrated*, July 30, 2001; **http://sportsillustrated.cnn.com**; Tim Lenke, "MLS: Franchises to Be Profitable by 2010," *The Washington Times*, May 11, 2006, **http://washingtontimes.com**.

paying the players and running the stadium. Every business owner must carefully plan how he or she is going to generate enough money to cover the fixed costs of the business. Those who have a clear idea of exactly how many airline seats, or pairs of pants, or hot dogs must be sold to break even will be in a better position to create and maintain profitability in the organization.

Understanding Why C-V-P Analysis Is Important

Understand the key factors involved in cost-volume-profit (C-V-P) analysis and why it is such an important tool in management decision making.

(1) Management must make many critical operating decisions that affect a firm's profitability. With respect to planning, management is often interested in the impact a particular action will have on profitability. C-V-P analysis can help managers assess that impact. The following are examples of questions that can be answered with C-V-P analysis:

- When planning whether or not to open a scuba shop in the mall, how many customers will need to be served each month in order to break even and be able to pay the monthly store rental fee?
- How will the profits of a bookstore be affected if the store raises its prices by 10%, resulting in a reduction of 2% in the number of books sold?
- How many carpets must a fledgling entrepreneur clean in a month in order to generate a net profit of $3,000 each month?
- By how much will the profits of a discount electronics store change if a $100,000 advertising campaign increases the number of computers sold by 13%?
- How will the profits of a fast-food restaurant change if the restaurant stops selling milk shakes and instead focuses on raising the volume of soft drink sales by 25%?

It should be clear to you from these examples that C-V-P analysis involves studying the interrelationships among revenues, costs, levels of activity, and profits. However, quality of products and services and speed of production and delivery must also be considered as managers use C-V-P analysis to determine product prices, the mix of products, market strategy, appropriate sales commissions, advertising budgets, production schedules, and a host of other important planning decisions. Although C-V-P analysis is most useful for planning, it can also be used to assist with controlling decisions (e.g., are the costs too high for the level of sales?) and evaluating decisions (e.g., should we reward employees for holding costs down or be concerned that sales growth has slowed?). In fact, a lot of what is done in management accounting involves some aspect of C-V-P analysis because of the tremendous potential it has to help management increase the profitability and effectiveness of an organization. For this reason, as you use this chapter to learn the mechanics of C-V-P analysis, be sure to see how important it is to be able to understand and manage costs.

REMEMBER THIS...

Key factors involved in C-V-P analysis are:
- the revenues from the sales prices charged for goods and services,
- the fixed and variable costs,
- the sales volume,
- the mix of products, and
- the resulting profits.

Basic Cost Behavior Patterns

Explain and analyze the basic cost behavior patterns—variable, fixed, and mixed.

(2) The two basic cost behavior patterns—variable and fixed—were introduced in Chapter 15. Other cost behavior patterns, such as mixed costs, are variations of these two. Mixed costs exhibit characteristics of both variable and fixed costs. In this section, we will review both variable and fixed costs. We will also introduce stepped costs and mixed costs.

A quick example of what we're talking about may be helpful before we dive into all the details of working with cost behavior. A cost may be classified as either fixed or variable by the way it reacts to changes in level of activity. Think of a doughnut shop such as **Krispy Kreme** or **Winchell's**. It seems logical that as more doughnuts are sold, the total cost of doughnut ingredients will increase. This is a variable cost. On the other hand, we probably wouldn't expect the cost of property taxes to increase as more doughnuts are sold. This is a fixed cost. However, there are costs that have both variable and fixed components. For instance, the electricity costs to run the doughnut shop will increase as we sell more doughnuts because of the cost of the power to make the additional doughnuts. However, even if we don't sell any doughnuts, we will have to pay some utility costs just to keep the shop open. Utility costs are a mixed cost. The cost of a supervisor's salary isn't normally going to increase as we sell more doughnuts *until* we have so many customers that we need to hire an additional supervisor to help with the higher volume. At this point, the fixed cost of salaries will *jump* to a new level. This is an example of a stepped cost.

Overall, once we have defined the activity, measurements of changes in activity level can be used to determine cost behavior patterns.

Measuring Level of Activity

Before we can manage an organization, we need to identify exactly what it is that we intend to manage. In other words, what is the activity upon which we intend to focus our planning, controlling, and evaluating efforts? In the doughnut shop example, it makes sense for management to focus on increasing the number of doughnuts sold. Activity is often measured in terms of output, input, or a combination of the two. Some of the most common activity bases used are number of units sold and number of units produced in manufacturing firms, number of units sold in merchandising firms, and number of contract hours paid for or billed in service firms. We will generally use production volume or sales volume as the activity basis in this chapter to demonstrate the use of C-V-P analysis.

Manufacturing and merchandising companies with a single product generally measure volume of activity in terms of output, for example, number of cars, television sets, or desks produced. However, many companies produce or sell several different products (refrigerators, toasters, and irons, for example), and a simple total of all the products manufactured or sold during a given period may not provide a good activity measure for C-V-P analysis. This is particularly true for manufacturing firms. For example, **General Electric** manufactures a wide variety of products, ranging from light bulbs to locomotives. It obviously takes more effort (and consequently costs more) to produce a locomotive than a light bulb; accordingly, it wouldn't make any sense to state that total production for a given day was 1,000,001—1,000,000 light bulbs and 1 locomotive. In multiproduct situations, these manufacturing firms usually use input measures, such as direct labor hours worked, machine time used, or the time needed to set up a job, as the activity base. In these cases, such specific input measures are often more useful than general output measures.

variable costs

Costs that change in total in direct proportion to changes in activity level.

Variable Costs

Total **variable costs** change in direct proportion to changes in activity level. Examples are costs of direct materials, which vary proportionately with the number of units produced, and sales commissions, which vary proportionately with

EXHIBIT 1	An Example of Variable Costs

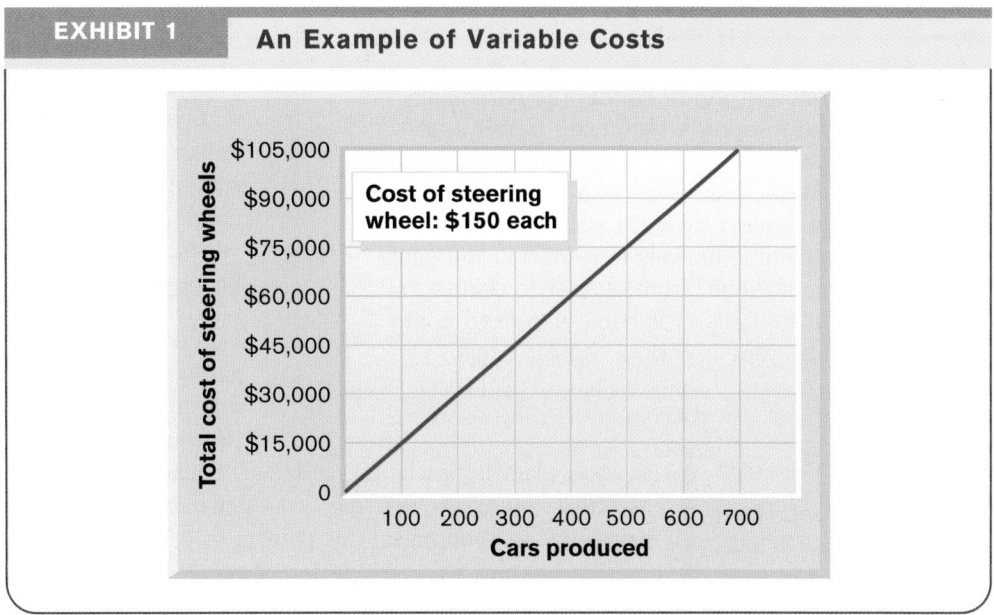

the sales volume. For instance, as an automobile manufacturer, you might define the activity of focus as the number of cars produced. If engines, tires, axles, and steering wheels are purchased from suppliers, the cost of direct materials would be variable because the total cost of purchasing steering wheels, for example, would vary proportionately with the number of cars produced. If no cars are produced, there are no steering wheel costs; if 1,000 cars are manufactured during a period, the total cost for steering wheels and other purchased parts is 1,000 times the unit cost of each item. As more cars are produced, the total cost of each item increases. The unit cost, however, remains constant. For example, if an auto company pays $150 per steering wheel, the total cost of steering wheels for 200 cars is $30,000; for 500 cars, it is $75,000. At both levels of activity, however, the unit cost is still $150. This relationship between variable costs and level of activity is shown graphically in Exhibit 1, which relates the number of cars produced to the total cost of the steering wheels used in production.

In addition to sales commissions and materials, many other costs (such as labor) have a variable cost behavior pattern. For example, if it takes four hours of labor to assemble a frame and each hour costs $25, a unit labor cost of $100 per frame is a variable cost; the total labor cost would be $100 times the number of frames produced.

> ### STOP & THINK
>
> In a manufacturing plant, are direct labor costs variable or fixed? Does your answer change if the direct labor employees belong to a powerful union?

Relevant Range and the Linearity of Variable Costs

Our definition of the variable cost behavior pattern specifies that variable costs have a linear relationship to the level of activity; that is, when the level of activity increases, total variable costs rise at a directly proportional rate. For example, if the level of activity doubles, the total variable costs will also double; this is a called a linear relationship. While this is never exactly true, it is usually safe to assume that variable costs are approximately linear within a certain range of production, called the **relevant range**.

relevant range

The range of operating level, or volume of activity, over which the relationship between total costs (variable plus fixed) and activity level is approximately linear.

Relevant range is an important concept. If activity increases or decreases significantly, cost relationships will probably change. If production volume soars, for example, such factors as overtime work and bulk-purchase discounts may cause direct labor and materials costs per unit to change. That is why we say that

The relevant range concept is particularly difficult to apply when using C-V-P analysis in companies in very high growth situations, such as high-tech start-ups. If a company's sales are increasing by 60% each quarter, for example, it is unlikely to remain in the same "relevant range" from quarter to quarter; so careful analysis of variable and fixed costs must be repeated on a regular basis.

fixed costs

Costs that remain constant in total, regardless of activity level, at least over a certain range of activity.

While total variable costs increase as production increases, the per-unit variable cost is constant across activity levels within the relevant range. In contrast, while total fixed costs are constant over the relevant range, the per-unit fixed cost changes with increases or decreases in production. Many introductory students of management accounting become confused and forget that per-unit variable costs are fixed and per-unit fixed costs will vary over the relevant range!

Have you ever wondered why you always wait so long and why there are so many patients at one time in a dentist's office? Think about the nature of the dentist's costs. Most costs are fixed—dentists' salaries, rent or depreciation, and so forth. When costs are mostly fixed, seeing a high volume of patients is important to cover the fixed costs. Then, once fixed costs are covered, almost all additional patient revenue becomes profit. Thus, by squeezing in only a few additional patients, dentists can increase their profits substantially.

the definition of variable costs—costs that are constant per unit of activity—is applicable only within relevant ranges. The important point to remember is that whenever we define a particular variable cost, we are assuming that the cost is within the relevant range of activity.

Fixed Costs

Fixed costs remain constant in total, regardless of activity level, at least within the relevant range of activity. Examples include property taxes, insurance, executives' salaries, plant depreciation, and rent. Because total fixed costs remain constant as activity increases, the fixed cost per unit (total fixed cost ÷ level of activity) decreases. In economics, this pattern of decreasing costs per unit as volume increases is known as *economies of scale*. Similarly, as the level of activity decreases, the fixed cost per unit increases. This is in contrast to variable costs, where the costs per unit are assumed to remain constant through changes in the level of activity within the relevant range.

In an actual company, the fixed and variable costs are very challenging to identify. That is why it is important that you understand the nature of cost behavior and how to classify costs as either fixed or variable.

Stepped Fixed Costs Let's consider an example of an ice cream manufacturer. The graph in Exhibit 2 shows the relationship between the production line supervisor cost and the total number of gallons of ice cream produced. In this case, until weekly ice cream production reaches 1,000 gallons a week, the manufacturing manager is able to oversee all line workers. At 1,000 gallons a week production, however, the manager expects to hire a production line supervisor at $500 per week to provide more supervision of the workers. Further, the manager expects that she'll need to hire an additional supervisor each time weekly production is increased another 2,000 gallons. Although the production line supervisor cost is changing as the scale of ice cream production changes, we still consider this cost to be fixed within the relevant range. Hence, as shown in Exhibit 2, within a relevant range of activity of between 3,000 and 5,000 gallons of ice cream, the total fixed manufacturing supervisor cost of $1,000 does not change. On the other hand, the per-unit supervisor cost will drop considerably as production increases. For

STOP & THINK

If the "steps" in a stepped cost are wide compared to the relevant range (in other words, the costs essentially are unchanged within the relevant range), the costs are usually treated as fixed. This would be the case with the production line supervisor costs in Exhibit 2. On the other hand, how would you treat a stepped cost with very narrow steps?

example, when the fixed supervisor cost is $1,000 and 3,000 gallons of ice cream are being produced, the supervisor cost per gallon of ice cream is $0.33 ($1,000 ÷ 3,000 gallons). With production of 4,000 gallons, however, this fixed cost is only $0.25 ($1,000 ÷ 4,000 gallons) per gallon.

As you can see in Exhibit 2, the fixed cost of the production line supervision "steps up" as the volume of ice cream production increases. **Stepped costs** are costs that change in total in a stair-step fashion with changes in volume of activity. Another example of a stepped cost might be the la-

stepped costs

Costs that change in total in a stair-step fashion (in large amounts) with changes in volume of activity.

bor charges for the maintenance of the tools and machinery in a small manufacturing plant. One maintenance worker can handle the upkeep of all the equipment during normal levels of activity. However, when there is a significant increase in activity, a second worker must be hired, and the maintenance cost approximately doubles.

EXHIBIT 2 | **Stepped Fixed Costs**

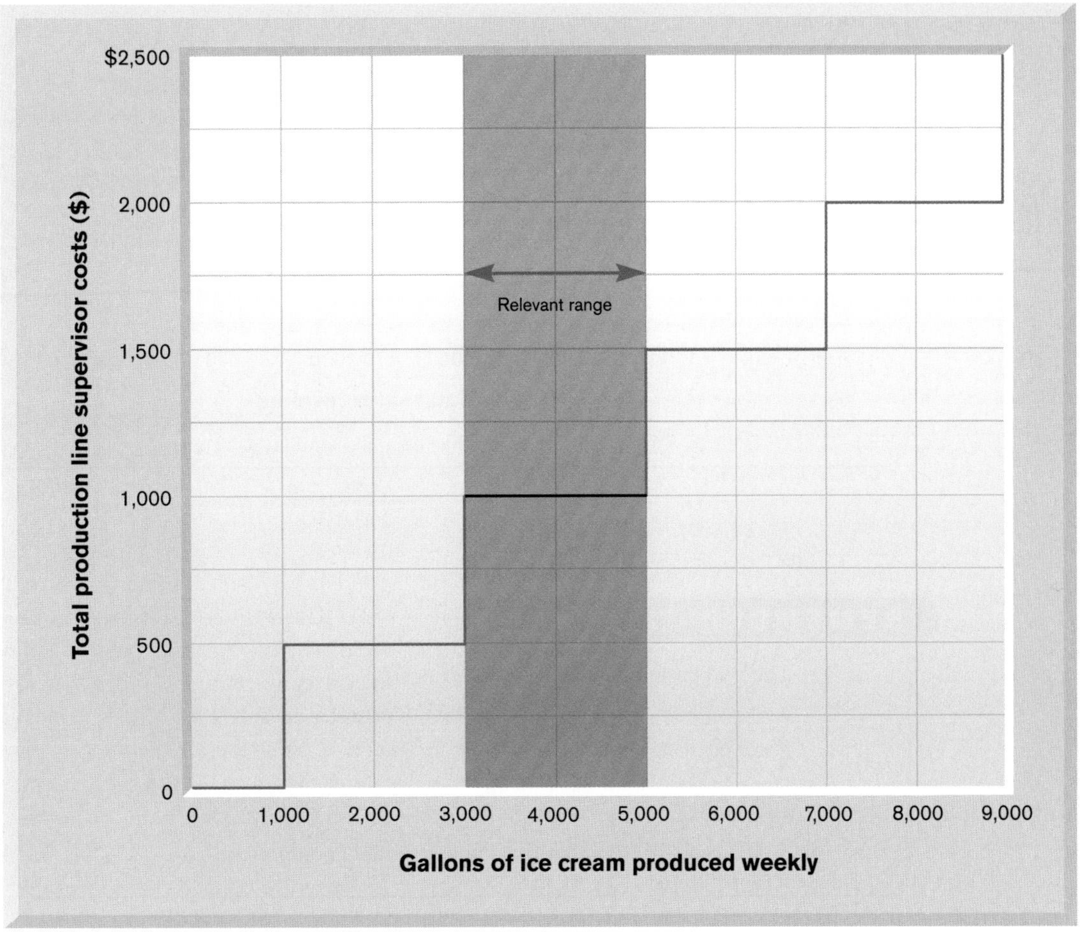

Relevant range

Total production line supervisor costs ($)

Gallons of ice cream produced weekly

Mixed Costs

mixed costs

Costs that contain both variable and fixed cost components.

Mixed costs, like stepped costs, are variations of the basic fixed and variable cost behavior patterns. Specifically, mixed costs are costs that contain both variable and fixed components. An example is rent that is based on a fixed fee plus a percentage of total sales. Thus, the rental terms for an automobile dealer's showroom might include a flat payment of $4,000 per month plus 1% of each month's sales revenue. The 1% of sales revenue is the variable portion, and the $4,000 is the fixed cost. The total rent, therefore, would be considered a mixed cost and could be diagrammed as shown in Exhibit 3. As this exhibit shows, the cost of renting the showroom increases as sales increase. The total rent is $4,000 when there are no sales; $6,000 when sales are $200,000 [$4,000 + (0.01 × $200,000)]; and $8,000 when sales are $400,000 [$4,000 + (0.01 × $400,000)]. This increase is directly due to the variable cost element, which increases in total as activity level (car sales) increases.

One of the important challenges in using C-V-P analysis in the planning process is the need to effectively separate mixed costs into their fixed and variable cost components. Over the years several management accounting techniques have been developed by organizations for this purpose. We will explore these mixed cost analysis methods in the next section of this chapter.

EXHIBIT 3 **An Example of a Mixed Cost**

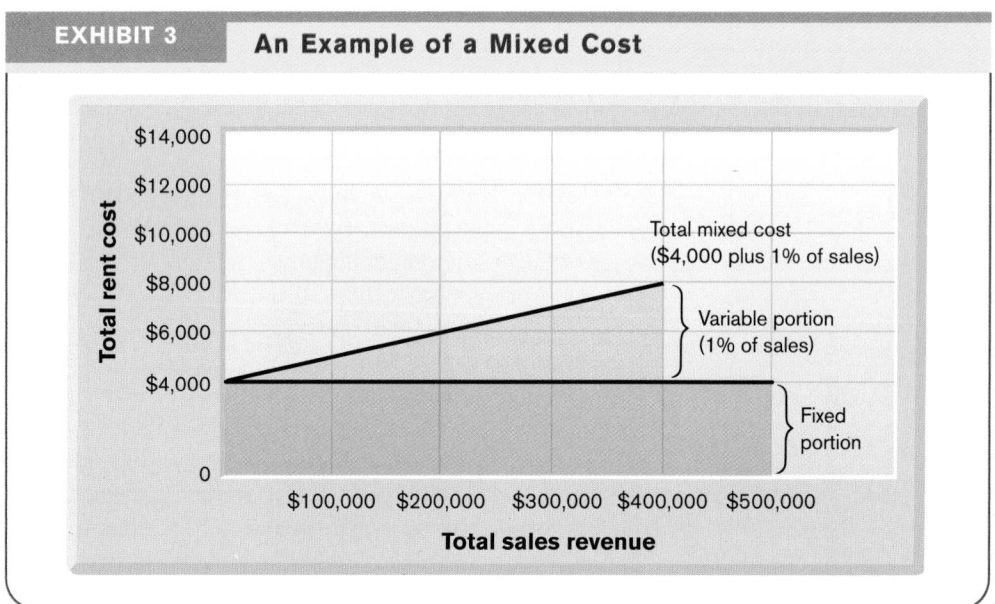

REMEMBER THIS...

- The two basic cost behavior patterns are:
  - variable → variable in total, fixed per unit
  - fixed → fixed in total, variable per unit
- Stepped costs increase with the level of activity but in steps instead of smoothly.
- Mixed costs have both a fixed and a variable component.

Analysis of Mixed Costs

Analyze mixed
costs using the
scattergraph and
high-low methods.

③ With an understanding of the different types of cost behavior, we can discuss how to identify and separate mixed costs into variable and fixed components. This separation is essential because we have to clearly classify all costs as fixed or variable before doing C-V-P analysis. When it comes to mixed costs, remember that the fixed portion represents the cost necessary to maintain a service (such as a telephone) or a facility (such as a building), and the variable portion is based on actual use. Recall the example of the automobile showroom's rental cost, part of which was a flat monthly fee and part a percentage of sales. Other common mixed costs are such overhead costs as electricity and repairs.

One very accurate way to separate the actual fixed and variable components of mixed costs may be to analyze each invoice. Most electricity or telephone bills, for example, include a flat monthly service charge that would be classified as a fixed cost. Additional variable costs are those based on the amount of electricity or minutes actually used during the month. This approach could be very time consuming, however, and may not be cost effective (that is, it would cost more to do the analysis than the detailed information is worth). An alternative approach to classifying costs as fixed or variable is to analyze the historical trend in past costs and activity levels. There are several methods of doing this. In this section, we will introduce you to two methods: the scattergraph method and the high-low method.

**scattergraph
(visual-fit) method**

A method of segregating the fixed and variable components of a mixed cost by plotting on a graph total costs at several activity levels and drawing a regression line through the points.

regression line

On a scattergraph, the straight line that most closely expresses the relationship between the variables.

variable cost rate

The change in cost divided by the change in activity; the slope of the regression line.

The Scattergraph, or Visual-Fit, Method

Probably the simplest method of separating mixed costs into their variable and fixed components is the **scattergraph** (or **visual-fit**) method. Essentially, we're talking here about simply looking at a graph of mixed cost points over time and learning how to "see" a trend of fixed and variable cost components. To do this, the total mixed cost for each level of activity is plotted on a graph, and a straight line (called the **regression line**) is visually fitted through the points. The idea is to position the line through the set of plotted data points in a way that minimizes the average distance between all the data points and the fitted regression line. With the regression line inserted into the graph, the fixed portion of the mixed cost is estimated to be the amount on the cost (vertical) axis at the point where it is intercepted by the regression line. The variable cost per unit (referred to as the **variable cost rate**) is equal to the slope of the regression line, which is simply the change in cost divided by the change in activity (sometimes described as "the rise over the run").

To illustrate the scattergraph method, let's use the example of electricity costs for an automobile manufacturer. In the analysis and calculations that follow, all costs are assumed to fall within the relevant range of activity. In this example, we use direct labor hours as a measure of the activity level.

Exhibit 4 shows a scattergraph on which electricity costs and direct labor hours have been plotted. The regression line has been visually fitted to minimize the distance between data points. It appears that the total fixed portion of electricity cost is about $40,000 per month, which is where the regression line intersects the cost axis. The variable cost rate is approximately $4.29 per direct labor hour, which is the slope of the regression line. To calculate the slope, we use the following formula and the data points of zero and 7,000 direct labor hours, respectively.

> ⓘ **CAUTION**
>
> When making these cost graphs, remember that the dollars go on the vertical axis (or *y axis*) and the level of activity goes on the horizontal axis (or *x axis*).

EXHIBIT 4	Total Electricity Costs

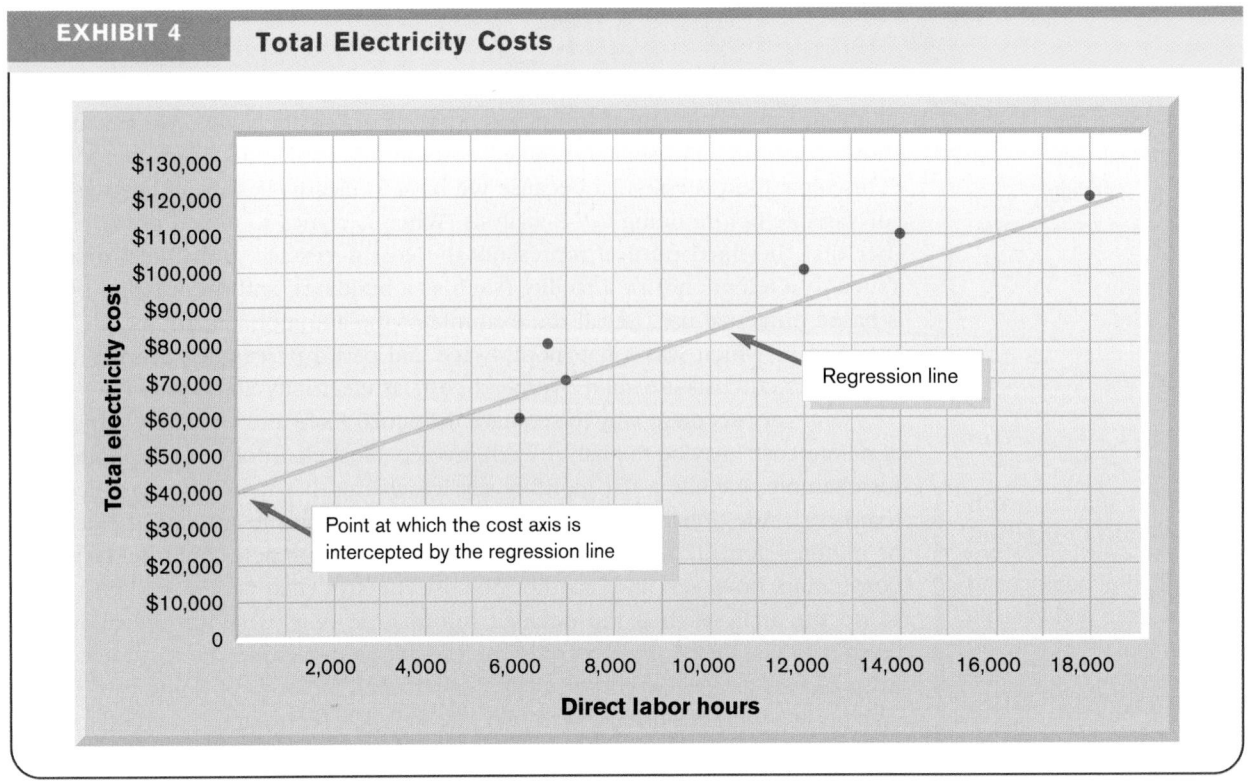

$$\text{Variable} = \frac{\text{Change in (electricity) cost}}{\text{Change in activity (direct labor hours)}}$$

$$X = \frac{\$70,000 - \$40,000}{7,000 - 0}$$

$$X = \frac{\$30,000}{7,000}$$

$$X = \$4.29 \text{ (rounded)}$$

Obviously, the scattergraph method has some limitations as a cost estimation tool. Perhaps the most critical limitation is that how the user fits the regression line through the data points is entirely subjective. Consider Exhibit 4 once more. If you were the one fitting the regression line to these data points, would you have set the line exactly where it is in this graph? Hopefully, your line would have been quite close to the current line.

Still, it probably wouldn't have been exactly the same, resulting in some small differences in your own estimations of fixed and variable costs. Hence, the scattergraph method is a classic "quick and dirty" management accounting technique. Yet, although the scattergraph provides only subjective estimates of the fixed and variable portions of mixed costs, it can be an extremely useful tool to describe and discuss cost behavior in the planning process. It is also useful for thinking about how to control operating costs. For instance, it shows at a glance any trends and abrupt changes in cost behavior patterns. As such, it can be used as a preliminary step before using more sophisticated methods of cost evaluation.

 CAUTION

Once the regression line has been fitted through the data points, the scattergraph method does not depend any longer on the data points to estimate fixed and variable costs. Cost estimations are entirely based on points along the regression line. For instance, notice that in this case we used the points 0 and 7,000 along the visually fitted regression line. However, we could have used any two points on the regression line (such as 2,000 direct labor hours and 10,000 direct labor hours) to calculate the variable costs per direct labor hour.

high-low method

A method of segregating the fixed and variable components of a mixed cost by analyzing the costs at the highest and the lowest activity levels within a relevant range.

The High-Low Method

A second approach to identifying fixed and variables costs is the **high-low method**, which analyzes mixed costs on the basis of total costs incurred at both the highest and the lowest levels of activity. To illustrate this method, we refer again to the electricity costs of the automobile manufacturer. This time, however, we will focus on the following table of reported electricity costs and direct labor hours worked. (The numbers in this table correspond exactly to the points plotted in the scattergragh in Exhibit 4.)

Month	Direct Labor Hours Worked	Total Electricity Cost
January	7,000	$ 70,000
February	6,000	60,000
March	12,000	100,000
April	6,600	80,000
May	18,000	120,000
June	14,000	110,000

Although these two columns of figures do not visually show trends as clearly as the scattergraph does, they do suggest that as the activity level (direct labor hours) increases, total electricity costs increase. Given this relationship, the high-low method can be used to determine the fixed and variable portions of the electricity cost as follows:

1. Identify the highest and lowest activity levels (18,000 hours in May and 6,000 hours in February). As you can see, these two months also represent the highest and lowest levels of electricity costs, or $120,000 and $60,000, respectively (although this may not always be the case).
2. Determine the differences between the high and low activity points.

	Total Electricity Cost	Direct Labor Hours
High point (May)	$120,000	18,000
Low point (February)	60,000	6,000
Difference	$ 60,000	12,000

3. Calculate the variable cost rate (variable cost per unit). The formula is the same as the one used to compute the slope of the regression line in the scattergraph method. The results are different because the scattergraph method is based on a regression line that is plotted, as much as possible, using all the data points, whereas the high-low method uses only the highest and lowest data points.

$$\text{Variable cost rate} = \frac{\text{Change in costs}}{\text{Change in activity}}$$

$$= \frac{\$60,000}{12,000}$$

$$= \$5 \text{ per direct labor hour}$$

4. Determine fixed costs based on the variable cost rate ($5 in this case). The formula for this computation is:

Fixed costs = Total costs − Variable costs

At the high level of activity, the calculation is as follows:

$X = \$120,000 - (18,000 \times \$5)$
$X = \$120,000 - \$90,000$
$X = \$30,000$

You get the same result if you calculate fixed costs at the low level of activity as follows:

$X = \$60,000 - (6,000 \times \$5)$
$X = \$60,000 - \$30,000$
$X = \$30,000$

CAUTION

Once you have selected the high and low activity levels to use in the high-low method, don't use any other activity levels or costs than these two data points to calculate the fixed costs.

In summary, using the high-low method of analyzing mixed costs, the variable portion of the total electricity cost is estimated to be $5 per direct labor hour, and the fixed portion is $30,000 per month. This means that $30,000 appears to be the amount the company pays each month just to have electricity available, and $5 is the average additional electricity cost for each hour of direct labor worked.

A Comparison of the Scattergraph and High-Low Methods

As we have illustrated, the scattergraph and high-low methods may produce different results.

Method	Variable Cost Rate	Fixed Cost
Scattergraph	$4.29	$40,000
High-low	5.00	30,000

FYI

What if the highest and lowest levels of activity do not correspond to the highest and lowest levels of costs? This could easily (and often does) happen in real-life companies. Remember that the high-low method is a method that determines approximately the fixed and variable costs. Hence, companies must then choose to base the estimate on either the highest and lowest activities or the highest and lowest costs. For simplicity, this textbook will always present data such that the highest and lowest levels of activity do correspond to the highest and lowest levels of costs.

Both methods are useful for a quick approximation. The scattergraph method takes all the data into account. Therefore, this method tends to be more accurate, although it is somewhat subjective and inconsistent because different people might draw the line through the points differently. On the other hand, anyone using the high-low method will consistently get the same results. However, because only two data points are used, the high-low method may not be representative of the costs incurred at all levels of activity. It is important that you realize that the math used in the high-low method essentially plots the regression line through the two most extreme points in a scattergraph. To understand what we mean, look at the scattergraph of the electricity cost data in Exhibit 4. Notice that the low point lies below the scattergraph regression line and the high point lies above the scattergraph regression line. Now, if you were to draw a straight line through the high and low points, that line would not be the same line created using the scattergraph (visual-fit) method, and may not necessarily represent all six data points plotted. Nevertheless, you can use either method or both methods to predict future costs. If, for example, management wants to know how much electricity will cost next month with 10,000 direct labor hours budgeted, the following calculations would be made:

Method	Formula	Estimated Cost
Scattergraph	$40,000 + 10,000($4.29) =	$82,900
High-low	$30,000 + 10,000($5.00) =	$80,000

As you can see, the total estimated costs resulting from these two methods, in this case, are reasonably close to each other (although this may not necessarily be the case with sets of actual cost and activity data in some real-life companies).

REMEMBER THIS...

- Two common techniques for analyzing mixed costs are:
  - scattergraph method
  - high-low method
- With both methods, where the line intercepts the cost axis represents the fixed cost, and the slope of the line represents the variable cost per unit.
- The scattergraph method involves visually fitting a straight line (the regression line) through data points plotted on a graph.
- With the high-low method, the high and the low levels of activity are used to define an estimate of the total cost line.

Methods of C-V-P Analysis

Perform C-V-P analyses, and describe the effects potential changes in C-V-P variables have on company profitability.

 Now that you have a better understanding of cost behaviors and can separate mixed costs into their fixed and variable cost elements, you are ready to use your knowledge of cost behaviors to make planning decisions.

If you haven't done so already, now is a good time to think of an actual business organization that is familiar to you, perhaps one by which you've been employed or are now employed. Think about the product or service this organization creates and the costs and processes it uses. Now, as you study the C-V-P analysis method below, be sure to consider how this tool would be used in your own organization to plan and manage costs and activities in order to obtain desired results.

Contribution Margin

contribution margin

The difference between total sales and variable costs; the portion of sales revenue available to cover fixed costs and provide a profit.

In order to effectively use C-V-P analysis, we first need to spend some time working with the concept of contribution margin. **Contribution margin** is equal to sales revenue less variable costs; it is the amount of revenue that remains to cover fixed costs and provide a profit for an organization. For example, the contribution margin from the sale of one order of French fries by a fast-food restaurant is the selling price less the variables costs (potatoes, salt, container, cooking oil, wages of the cook) of producing the fries. Any contribution margin generated by the sale of an order of French fries can be used to pay the fixed costs of the fast-food outlet, such as the monthly rent, the insurance, the supervisor's salary, and so forth. Contribution margin is one of the most important management accounting concepts you will learn because many operating decisions are made on the basis of how contribution margin will be affected. A company may decide, for example, to advertise one product more than others because that product has a higher contribution margin.

The contribution margin generated by the sale of an order of French fries can be used to pay fixed costs such as rent, insurance, and salaries. Now you know why you often hear that ever popular question "Would you like fries with that?" at fast-food restaurants.

© GETTY IMAGES INC.

The Contribution Margin Income Statement To illustrate the concept of contribution margin, let's use the following format of a contribution margin income statement. The statement data for Jewels Corporation, a producer of high-quality baseball gloves, follow.[2]

Jewels Corporation

Contribution Margin Income Statement

For the Month Ended November 30, 2009

	Total	Per Unit
Sales revenue (1,000 gloves)	$200,000	$200
Less variable costs	110,000	110
Contribution margin	$ 90,000	$ 90
Less fixed costs	63,000	
Profit*	$ 27,000	

* In this chapter, "profit" means pretax income; the terms *income* and *profit* are interchangeable.

As this contribution margin income statement shows, for internal decision-making purposes, Jewels Corporation computes its contribution margin on a per-unit (glove) and total-dollar basis. During November, Jewels' **per-unit contribution margin** is $90; the total contribution margin at a sales volume of 1,000 baseball gloves is $90,000.

The per-unit contribution margin tells us that $90 is available from each glove sold to cover fixed costs and provide a profit. By showing the $63,000 of fixed costs separately, this income statement also tells us that Jewels must generate sufficient contribution margin to cover these costs before a profit can be earned. With $200,000 of sales revenue, the contribution margin ($90,000) is sufficient to cover the fixed costs and provide a profit of $27,000.

This type of contribution margin income statement is particularly useful as a planning tool. The statement helps a company to project profits at any level of activity within the relevant range. For example, if Jewels Corporation forecasts sales of 1,200 baseball gloves next month, the company can prepare a forecasted (or pro-forma) income statement (in contribution margin format) as follows:

per-unit contribution margin

The excess of the sales price of one unit over its variable costs.

---

[2] In this example, we assume that there is only one model of baseball glove, which sells for $200.

Jewels Corporation
Pro-Forma Contribution Margin Income Statement
For the Month Ended December 31, 2009

Sales revenue (1,200 gloves × $200)	$240,000
Less variable costs (1,200 gloves × $110)	132,000
Contribution margin	$108,000
Less fixed costs	63,000
Profit	$ 45,000

Notice that with an increase in sales of 200 baseball gloves, the contribution margin increases $18,000 ($108,000 − $90,000). You can confirm this by multiplying the per-unit contribution margin by the increase in volume ($90 per unit × 200 gloves = $18,000). Because we assume that the increase in volume is still within the relevant range of activity (which is a *very* important assumption!), the fixed costs remain at $63,000, and profit increases by the $18,000 increase in contribution margin. The critical thing you should see here is that once the fixed costs are covered, each subsequent dollar in contribution margin goes straight to profit! In other words, when Jewels Corporation hits its break-even point (which is the point where all fixed costs are covered), each additional glove sold will generate $90 in profit.

Notice the importance of accurately determining cost behavior when forecasting profit levels. If one ignores cost behavior, then the $27,000 profit generated by November sales of 1,000 gloves may lead to the conclusion that each glove creates $27 ($27,000 profit/1,000 gloves) in profit. With this *incorrect* information, the forecasted level of profit for December sales of 1,200 gloves is $32,400 ($27 per glove × 1,200 gloves). This forecast differs significantly from the $45,000 profit forecast above that stems from a *correct* consideration of the behavior (fixed or variable) of Jewels Corporation's costs.

F Y I

French fries and soft drinks are good examples of products with a high contribution margin. A $2 order of French fries might have a contribution margin in excess of $1.50. That's why fast-food employees are told to specifically ask customers if they want fries and a drink with their order!

contribution margin ratio

The percentage of net sales revenue left after variable costs are deducted; the contribution margin divided by net sales revenue.

The Contribution Margin Ratio Knowing the **contribution margin ratio**, which is the percentage of sales revenue left after variable costs are deducted, will help you compare the profitability of various products. For example, if product A has a 60% contribution margin ratio and the contribution margin ratio of product B is only 20%, the company should emphasize product A, assuming that other factors are equal. As a concrete example, in a supermarket the prepared foods (baked goods, squeezed juices, ready-to-eat barbecued chicken) generally have high contribution margin ratios whereas the staples such as milk and eggs have lower contribution margin ratios.

To illustrate the calculation of contribution margin ratios, let's look again at the initial Jewels Corporation example. The ratio is computed as follows:

	Total	Per Unit	Ratio (Percentage)
Sales revenue (1,000 gloves)	$200,000	$200	100%
Less variable costs	110,000	110	55
Contribution margin	$ 90,000	$ 90	45%
Less fixed costs	63,000		
Profit	$ 27,000		

The contribution margin ratio is 45% of sales revenue ($90 ÷ $200), which means that for every $1.00 increase in sales revenue, the contribution margin increases by $0.45 (45% of $1.00). If fixed costs are already covered, profit will also increase by $0.45 for every $1.00 increase in sales. As you can see, there is another ratio presented in these calculations—the variable cost ratio. These two ratios are complements of each other. Hence, the variable cost ratio ($110 ÷ $200 = 55%) plus the contribution margin ratio (45%) will always equal 100%. This is important because whether we're describing contribution margin ratios or variable cost ratios, we are really talking about the same basic issue—the relationship of variable costs to sales revenue.

With contribution margin or variable cost ratios, it is easy to analyze the impact of changes in sales on the contribution margin. For example, if you estimate that Jewels' sales will increase by $20,000, you can apply the contribution margin ratio of 45% or the variable cost ratio of 55% and estimate that the contribution margin will increase by $9,000, which is equal to $20,000 × 0.45 or $20,000 × (1 − 0.55). The higher the contribution margin ratio, the larger the share of each additional dollar of sales that goes toward covering fixed costs and increasing profit.

The C-V-P Equation

As you can see, contribution margin calculations will be very useful to you when analyzing cost-volume-profit relationships in the management planning process. Doing C-V-P analysis using contribution margin calculations is a straightforward process. C-V-P analysis does require some simple algebra (here is where you reap the benefits of paying attention during your junior high school math class).

We began this chapter with the assumption that all costs can be described as either fixed or variable. To highlight the important idea that C-V-P analysis depends on dividing costs into fixed and variable behavior patterns, we will develop the C-V-P equation as follows:[3]

1. Because all costs can be classified as either variable or fixed, we can express the calculation of profit with the following basic formula:

   Sales revenue − Variable costs − Fixed costs = Profit

2. We can specify the formula more precisely by expressing the equation in units:

   (Sales price × Units) − (Variable cost × Units) − Fixed costs = Profit

3. Or, we can express the equation using ratios:

   Sales revenue − (Variable cost ratio × Sales revenue) − Fixed costs = Profit

These equations are quick and useful methods for examining the financial aspects of C-V-P analysis problems. To illustrate, see if you can use the C-V-P equation based on units and the data from the Jewels Corporation example to determine profit assuming that sales of 1,200 baseball gloves are expected.

(Sales price × Units) − (Variable cost × Units) − Fixed costs = Profit
($200 × 1,200) − ($110 × 1,200) − $63,000 = Profit
$240,000 − $132,000 − $63,000 = Profit
$45,000 = Profit

Alternatively, you could calculate Jewels' profits using the equation based on ratios.

Sales revenue − (Variable cost ratio × Sales revenue) − Fixed costs = Profit
$240,000 − [($110 ÷ $200) × $240,000] − $63,000 = Profit
$240,000 − (0.55 × $240,000) − $63,000 = Profit
$240,000 − $132,000 − $63,000 = Profit
$45,000 = Profit

---

[3] Granted, fixed and variable costs often get "mixed together" and can be difficult (and sometimes impossible) to separate. The fact that C-V-P analysis is based on an assumption that all costs can be divided clearly into fixed and variable is one of the limitations of this technique.

Note that we calculated the same profit of $45,000 using both formula approaches. This result is no surprise because these are simply alternative routes to the same destination. Both methods are commonly used in business, depending on the data available for the analysis. So, although there may appear to be many alternative ways to write the C-V-P formula, there is really only one formula, and it is not hard to remember:

Sales revenue − Variable costs − Fixed costs = Profit

Once you understand this fact, C-V-P analysis using the equation approach is basic math; you merely insert the known elements into the formula and solve for the one unknown element.

Break-Even Point In many cases, as a manager you will want to know how many units need to be sold to break even. The **break-even point** is defined as the volume of activity at which total revenues equal total costs, or where profit is zero. The break-even point may also be thought of as the volume of activity at which the contribution margin equals the fixed costs.

break-even point

The amount of sales at which total costs of the number of units sold equal total revenues; the point at which there is no profit or loss.

Although the goal of business planning is to make a profit, not just to break even, knowing the break-even point can be useful in assessing the risk of selling a new product, setting sales goals and commission rates, deciding on marketing and advertising strategies, and other similar operating decisions. Because the break-even point is, by definition, that activity level at which no profit or loss is earned, the basic C-V-P equation can be modified to calculate the break-even point as follows:

Sales revenue − Variable costs − Fixed costs = $0

As you can see, to compute the break-even point, all that you need to do is simply set income equal to zero and then solve for the unknown—such as the number of units to be sold or the total revenues to be achieved.

Let's again use the Jewels Corporation example. How many units must Jewels sell to break even? (Note that we will use "X" to represent the unknown element, in this case, the number of baseball gloves.)

(Sales price × Units) − (Variable cost × Units) − Fixed costs = $0
[Sales price × (X)] − [Variable cost × (X)] − Fixed costs = $0
$200X − $110X − $63,000 = $0
$90X = $63,000
X = $63,000 ÷ $90 = 700 units (baseball gloves)

In this case, if Jewels sells 700 baseball gloves, the company will generate enough revenues to cover its variable and fixed costs, earning zero profit [($200 × 700) − ($110 × 700) − $63,000 = $0]. Once you understand the basic C-V-P formula, you just set it up and solve for whatever unknown you're interested in planning. Think you've got it? Then try this one as a check on yourself: Assuming that Jewels can sell only 600 baseball gloves, what price per glove would the company have to use in order to break even?[4]

Determining Sales Volume to Achieve Target Income Another way we can use C-V-P analysis in the planning process is to determine what level of activity is necessary to reach a target level of income. Instead of setting profit at $0 to do a break-even analysis, we can just as easily set income in the formula at the targeted level and then use the formula to plan or predict what fixed costs, variable costs, sales prices, and sales volumes are needed to achieve the target level of income. **Target income** is usually defined as the amount of income that will enable

target income

A profit level desired by management.

---

[4] **(Sales price × Units) − (Variable cost × Units) − Fixed costs = $0**
[(X) × Units] − (Variable cost × Units) − Fixed costs = $0
[(X) × 600] − ($110 × 600) − $63,000 = $0
600X − $66,000 − $63,000 = $0
600X = $129,000
X = $215 (new baseball glove price)

management to reach its objectives—paying dividends, meeting analysts' predictions, purchasing a new plant and equipment, or paying off existing loans. Target income can be expressed as either a percentage of revenues or as a fixed amount.

To illustrate target income, suppose that we want to know how many baseball gloves must be sold by Jewels Corporation to achieve a target income of $36,000, assuming no changes in per-unit variable costs or total fixed costs. The calculation is as follows:

(Sales price × Units) − (Variable cost × Units) − Fixed costs = Target income
$$\$200X - \$110X - \$63,000 = \$36,000$$
$$\$90X = \$99,000$$
$$X = 1,100 \text{ units (baseball gloves)}$$

Thus, we can see that if Jewels sells 1,100 baseball gloves at a contribution margin of $90 each, and assuming that fixed costs are $63,000, the company will earn a pretax profit of $36,000 [($90 × 1,100 units) − $63,000 = $36,000].

A fixed dollar amount of income, such as the $36,000 that would be earned by selling 1,100 baseball gloves, is probably the most typical way of expressing a target income goal for many companies. However, because investors often evaluate companies partially on the basis of the **return on sales revenue** (or simply "return on sales"), management may want to state its goal as a percentage return as opposed to a fixed amount of income. For example, if Jewels Corporation set a target income of a 20% return on sales, the computation would be:

> **return on sales revenue**
>
> A measure of operating performance; computed by dividing net income by total sales revenue. Similar to profit margin.

Sales revenue − Variable costs − Fixed costs = 0.20 × Sales revenue
$$\$200X - \$110X - \$63,000 = 0.2(\$200X)$$
$$\$200X - \$110X - \$63,000 = \$40X$$
$$\$200X - \$110X - \$40X = \$63,000$$
$$\$50X = \$63,000$$
$$X = \$63,000 \div \$50 = 1,260 \text{ gloves}$$

As we can see in this calculation, Jewels Corporation can earn a 20% return on sales by selling 1,260 baseball gloves.

Short-Cut Formulas for C-V-P Analysis Notice that in the C-V-P analysis examples that we've worked through so far, the basic C-V-P equation remains constant. That's what makes this formula so powerful. Once you're comfortable with it, you can use it to manage any number of factors in planning for profits. You can also quickly calculate break-even sales in units using the following formula:

$$\frac{\text{Total fixed costs}}{(\text{Sales price per unit} - \text{Variable cost per unit})} = \text{Break-even sales (in units)}$$

This formula is a "short-cut" version of the C-V-P formulas above. You can see that it is simply the last step in the C-V-P calculation above for Jewels' break-even point of 700 baseball gloves. So, if you understand the basic C-V-P equation, you can simply skip to the last step of the calculation. There are short cuts for computing the level of sales for both break-even volume and target income volume. The short-cut formula for both the break-even volume and the target income volume in units is:[5]

$$\frac{\text{Fixed costs} + \text{Target income}}{\text{Contribution margin per unit}}$$

Note that if you use this formula to determine the break-even volume, then you will assume that target income is $0, giving you:

$$\frac{\text{Fixed costs}}{\text{Contribution margin per unit}}$$

---

[5] Remember that per-unit contribution margin is the sales price per unit less the variable cost per unit.

Plugging in the numbers for Jewels Corporation, the results are the same as shown earlier. As you can see, the short-cut calculation for both the break-even volume and the target income volume is really the same formula. For target income volume:

$$\frac{\$63,000 + \$36,000}{\$90} = 1,100 \text{ units}$$

For the break-even volume:

$$\frac{\$63,000 + \$0}{\$90} = 700 \text{ units}$$

Always remember, though, that short cuts are useful, but they should not be applied until you fully understand the basic C-V-P relationships. In addition, managing some aspects of the C-V-P relationships can be tricky when you use short cuts. So if you ever get confused in solving a C-V-P analysis problem, just put the problem back in the original C-V-P equation:

Sales revenue − Variable costs − Fixed costs = Target income

Computation in Dollar Amounts versus Units Before we finish with C-V-P equations, you should note that a variable cost ratio is sometimes used instead of a per-unit variable cost. In such cases, the basic C-V-P equation is modified as follows:

Sales revenue − (Variable cost ratio × Sales) − Fixed costs = Profit

CAUTION

If you want to use C-V-P analysis to calculate the necessary sales volume in terms of dollars, the per-unit variable cost is not used. Rather, use the variable cost ratio times sales to determine total variable costs. Many students make the mistake of multiplying the per-unit variable cost times sales instead of the variable cost ratio times sales to get total variable costs.

Because the variable costs are stated as a percentage of sales dollars rather than on a per-unit basis, this approach expresses activity in terms of sales dollars, not units. This is still the same basic C-V-P equation, but setting up the equation using the variable cost ratio will result in a break-even point in dollars instead of units. For example, the break-even point for Jewels Corporation would then be expressed as $140,000 in sales revenue ($200 per unit × 700 units) instead of 700 units as previously illustrated. This may be verified using the preceding equation and a 55% variable cost ratio as follows:

Sales revenue − (0.55)Sales revenue − $63,000 = $0
(0.45)Sales revenue = $63,000
Sales revenue = $140,000

(Remember the following: Contribution margin ratio = 1 − Variable cost ratio.)

Measuring the Effect of Potential Changes in C-V-P Variables

The basic techniques of C-V-P analysis that you have worked with in this chapter are used almost daily by organizations in the management processes of planning, controlling, and evaluating. As a result of understanding C-V-P analysis, you will be adept at evaluating the effects on profitability of the following common changes in C-V-P variables: (1) the amount of fixed costs, (2) the variable cost rate, (3) the sales price, (4) the sales volume or the number of units sold, and (5) combinations of these variables.

Changes in Fixed Costs Many factors, such as an increase in property taxes or an increase in management's salaries, for example, will cause an increase in fixed costs. (Recall also from the opening scenario for this chapter that building a new facility such as a soccer stadium can also increase fixed costs.) If all other factors remain constant, an increase in fixed costs always increases the number of units needed to break even. Obviously, the number of units needed to reach a target income will also increase. To illustrate, let's return again to the Jewels Corporation and assume that we need to analyze the effect on profits if fixed costs increase from $63,000 to $81,000. How many more baseball gloves must be sold to maintain Jewels' income goal of $36,000?

$$\text{Sales revenue} - \text{Variable costs} - \text{Fixed costs} = \text{Target income}$$
$$\$200X - \$110X - \$81,000 = \$36,000$$
$$\$90X = \$117,000$$
$$X = 1,300 \text{ gloves}$$

Because of the added fixed costs, Jewels must now sell 1,300 baseball gloves, instead of 1,100, to earn a target income of $36,000. The computations are quite simple. In fact, you may have found them unnecessary, realizing that if fixed costs increase by $18,000 ($81,000 − $63,000), and if the unit contribution margin remains $90 per glove, 200 additional gloves ($18,000 ÷ $90) will have to be sold in order to reach the $36,000 target income (1,100 + 200 = 1,300 gloves).

Changes in the Variable Cost Rate   Like an increase in fixed costs, an increase in the variable cost rate also increases the number of units needed to break even or to reach target income levels, when all other factors remain constant. Suppose that the variable cost rate increased from $110 per baseball glove to $130 per glove because of higher wages for factory personnel, increased costs of direct materials, or other factors. How does this cost increase affect the number of gloves needed to reach the target income, assuming that fixed costs are again $63,000?

$$\text{Sales revenue} - \text{Variable costs} - \text{Fixed costs} = \text{Target income}$$
$$\$200X - \$130X - \$63,000 = \$36,000$$
$$\$70X = \$99,000$$
$$X = 1,415 \text{ gloves*}$$

*Technically, if the C-V-P analysis results in a fractional answer, you should always round the answer *up* to the next digit. In this case, if you round the calculated answer of 1,414.29 to 1,414 gloves, you won't quite achieve the target income of $36,000.

The increase in the variable cost rate reduces the unit contribution margin (from $90 to $70), which means that more gloves must be sold to maintain the same target income. With a unit contribution margin of $90, the company would make a $36,000 target income by selling 1,100 baseball gloves; with a unit contribution margin of only $70, an additional 315 gloves (1,415 − 1,100) must be sold to earn a target income of at least $36,000.

Changes in Sales Price   If all other variables remain constant, an increase in the sales price decreases the sales volume needed to reach a target income. This is because an increase in sales price increases the contribution margin per baseball glove, thereby decreasing the number of gloves that must be sold to earn the same amount of target income.

To illustrate, assume that the demand for baseball gloves is overwhelming and that Jewels cannot produce gloves fast enough. Hence, a decision is made to increase the price from $200 to $230 per glove. As a result of the price increase, the number of gloves that must be sold to reach the target income of $36,000 decreases:

$$\text{Sales revenue} - \text{Variable costs} - \text{Fixed costs} = \text{Target income}$$
$$\$230X - \$110X - \$63,000 = \$36,000$$
$$\$120X = \$99,000$$
$$X = 825 \text{ gloves}$$

With the sales price increase of $30 per glove, the contribution margin also increases $30 per glove to $120; and with a $120 contribution margin per glove, only 825 gloves need to be sold to reach the $36,000 target income. Obviously, a decrease in the sales price would have the opposite effect; it would increase the number of units needed to reach the target income.

Changes in Sales Volume As you have seen, the sales volume (the number of gloves to be sold) for the target income has varied with each change in one of the other variables. When other variables remain constant, an increase in the sales volume will result in an increase in income. Very simply, the more gloves sold, the higher the income (as long as the contribution margin is positive!). The degree of change in profits resulting from volume change depends on the size of the unit contribution margin. To be specific, the change in income will be equal to the change in sales volume units multiplied by the contribution margin per unit. So, when the unit contribution margin is high, a slight change in volume results in a dramatic change in profit. With a lower unit contribution margin, the change in profit is less.

Simultaneous Changes in Several Variables Thus far, we have examined changes in only one variable at a time. However, in your work in actual business organizations, you will find that individual changes are quite rare. More often, a decision will affect several variables, all at the same time. For example, should Jewels Corporation increase fixed advertising costs by $20,000 and reduce the sales price by 10% if the result would increase sales volume by 500 units? The impact on the target income from these proposed changes is as follows:

	Initial Data	Proposed Changes
Sales price per glove	$200	$180 (= $200 × 90%)
Sales volume	1,100 gloves	1,600 gloves (= 1,100 + 500)
Variable costs per glove	$110	$110
Fixed costs	$63,000	$83,000 (= $63,000 + $20,000)
Target income	$36,000	X

Computations and Result:

$$\text{Sales revenue} - \text{Variable costs} - \text{Fixed costs} = \text{Target income}$$
$$(\$180 \times 1,600) - (\$110 \times 1,600) - \$83,000 = X$$
$$\$288,000 - \$176,000 - \$83,000 = X$$
$$\$29,000 = X \text{ (target income)}$$

The analysis shows that target income would drop by $7,000 ($36,000 − $29,000) as a result of these changes. So, our decision should be to *not* implement the proposed changes.

Consider another possible decision: Should Jewels automate part of its production, thereby reducing (by $10) variable costs to $100 per unit and increasing (by $5,000) fixed costs to $68,000? The computation is as follows:

$$\text{Sales revenue} - \text{Variable costs} - \text{Fixed costs} = \text{Target income}$$
$$(\$200 \times 1,100) - (\$100 \times 1,100) - \$68,000 = X$$
$$\$220,000 - \$110,000 - \$68,000 = X$$
$$\$42,000 = X \text{ (target income)}$$

CAUTION

Remember, any change that affects the number of units sold changes both the total sales revenue and total variable costs.

This analysis shows that implementing these proposed changes would be beneficial because they would increase target income by $6,000 ($42,000 − $36,000). Obviously, this is true only if the assumptions can be relied on—that is, if fixed costs will rise by no more than $5,000 and unit variable costs will decrease by a full $10.

Consider another example. Suppose Jewels Corporation could use part of the excess capacity of its operating facilities to make baseball bats. These bats would sell for $90 per unit, increase fixed costs by $40,000, and have a variable cost per unit of $45. Jewels wants to add this new product line only if it can increase income by $25,000. How many baseball bats must Jewels sell to reach this target income? The computation follows:

$$\text{Sales revenue} - \text{Variable costs} - \text{Fixed costs} = \text{Target income}$$
$$\$90X - \$45X - \$40,000 = \$25,000$$
$$\$45X = \$65,000$$
$$X = 1,445 \text{ baseball bats (rounded up)}$$

Now that we have completed the C-V-P calculations, we must determine whether the company can produce and sell 1,445 baseball bats. If that sales goal seems attainable, the facilities should be used to make the bats. Don't forget that making C-V-P calculations is the easy part of managing an organization. It takes an excellent manager to successfully implement the results of a C-V-P analysis into a real business process.

REMEMBER THIS...

- Contribution margin = Sales revenue − Variable costs
- Sales revenue − Variable costs − Fixed costs = Target income
- At break-even, Target income = 0
- Sales revenue = Sales price × Number of units
- Variable costs = Variable cost per unit × Number of units
- Variable costs = Variable cost ratio × Sales revenue

Visualize C-V-P relationships using graphs.

Using Graphs to "See" C-V-P Relationships

(5) Earlier in this chapter, we talked about using scattergraph methods as a way to analyze cost behavior. Recall that once we have plotted the history of costs on a graph and visually fitted a regression line through the data, we can then essentially "see" how the cost can be separated into its fixed and variable cost components. Now, by simply adding a line to the cost chart to represent revenue, we can graphically work with cost-volume-profit relationships. In fact, using graphs may be the most effective way to manage and communicate C-V-P information. This graphical approach allows you to visually examine cost and revenue data over a range of activity rather than at a single volume. Sometimes, though, reading precise information from a graph can be difficult. Hence, when analyzing specific proposals in the future, you will typically combine the C-V-P equations discussed in the preceding section with the graphs discussed in this section.

On a C-V-P graph, volume or activity level usually is shown on the horizontal axis, and total dollars of sales and costs are shown on the vertical axis. Lines are then drawn to represent total fixed costs, total costs, and total revenues. Exhibit 5 shows a C-V-P graph for Jewels Corporation.

Remember that fixed and variable cost relationships are valid only for the relevant range of activity (assumed to be the screened area on the graph in Exhibit 5). In this case, fixed costs are $63,000, and variable costs are $110 per glove over the range of activity

| EXHIBIT 5 | **A Cost-Volume-Profit Graph** |

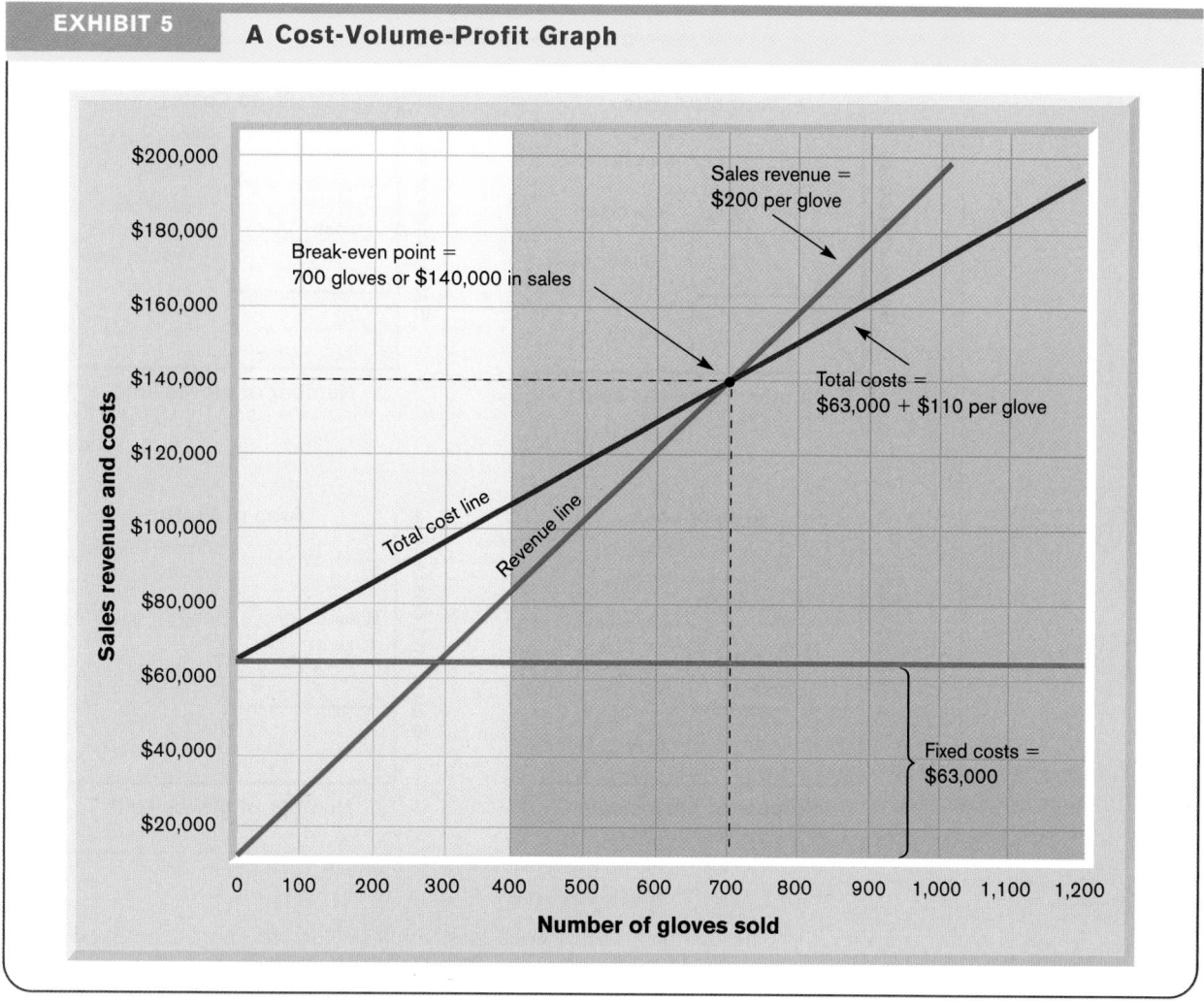

between 400 and 1,200 gloves sold. Total costs are $118,000 at 500 gloves [$63,000 + ($110 × 500 gloves)], $129,000 at 600 gloves [$63,000 + ($110 × 600 gloves)], and so on. Similarly, total revenues are $100,000 at 500 gloves ($200 × 500 gloves), $120,000 at 600 gloves, and so forth. The break-even point, the point at which total revenues equal total costs, is 700 gloves, or $140,000 in sales.

As shown in Exhibit 6, we can use the graphic format to isolate such items of interest as total variable costs, total fixed costs, the area in which losses occur, the area in which profits will be realized, and the break-even point. Because C-V-P graphs illustrate a wide range of activity, this tool can help in quickly determining approximately how much profit or loss will be realized at various levels of sales.

The Profit Graph

profit graph

A graph that shows how profits vary with changes in volume.

With a few adjustments to a standard C-V-P graph, we can create what is called a **profit graph**, which plots only profits and losses and omits costs and revenues. A profit graph is another useful way to visualize how decisions regarding costs and revenues will impact profit. Exhibit 7 shows a profit graph for Jewels Corporation based on the same underlying data used in Exhibit 5.

Notice that, though the horizontal axis of the profit graph is the same as those of the previous graphs, the vertical axis represents only profits and losses. As long as the contribution margin is positive, the maximum amount of losses that can occur is

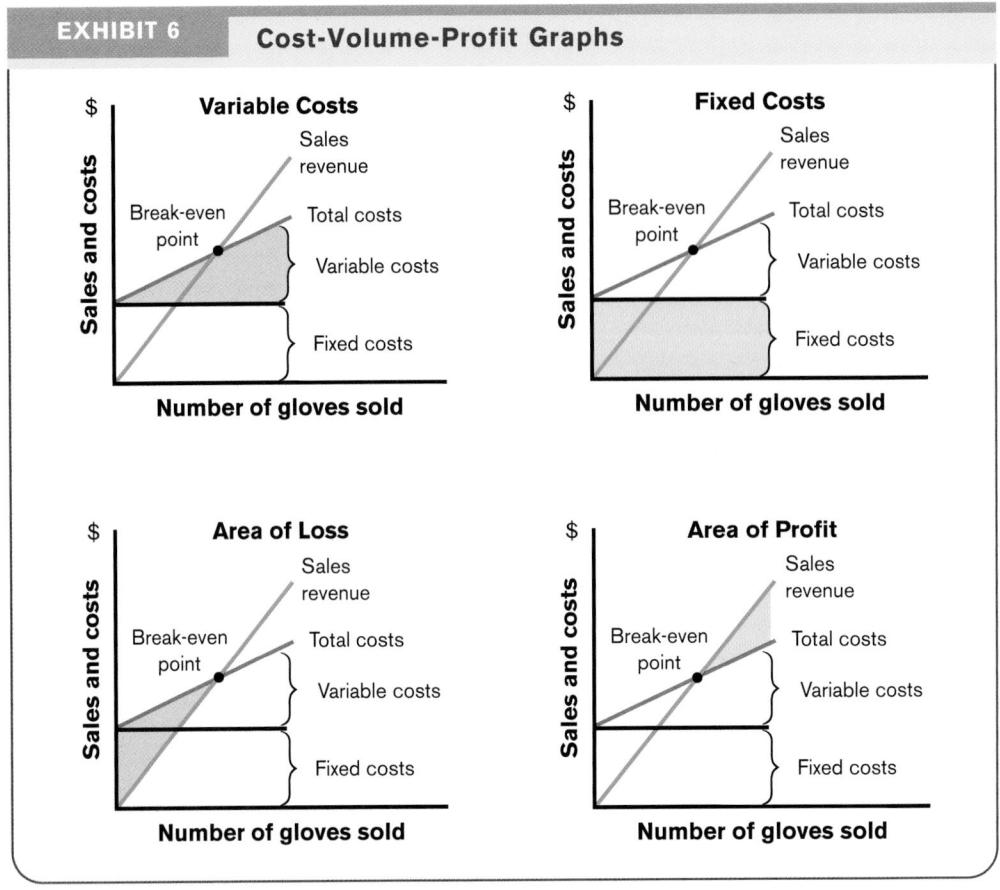

at a zero level of sales. With no sales, total losses will be the amount of the fixed costs. With the axes properly labeled, we can draw the profit line as follows:

1. Locate the loss for zero sales volume on the vertical axis. This is the total fixed cost, or negative $63,000 in this case.
2. Locate the profit or loss at another sales volume. For example, at sales of 700 gloves, profits are zero [$140,000 − ($63,000 + $77,000)], or at sales of 1,000 gloves, profits are $27,000 [$200,000 − ($63,000 + $110,000)].
3. After the two profit or loss points have been identified, draw a line through them back to the vertical axis.

Because of how simple it is to create, the profit graph is widely used for comparing competing projects. It has the disadvantage, however, of not showing explicitly how revenues and costs vary with changes in sales volume.

A Comparison of C-V-P Graphs with C-V-P Equations

C-V-P graphs are very useful in understanding contribution margin income statements and C-V-P equations. To illustrate this point, let's again explore the question of what volume of activity Jewels Corporation needs to reach a target income of $36,000. This was illustrated earlier with the equation approach, but it is repeated here to show that the graph approach will produce the same quantitative results. As you can see in Exhibit 8, Jewels Corporation must sell 1,100 baseball gloves to reach a target income of $36,000.

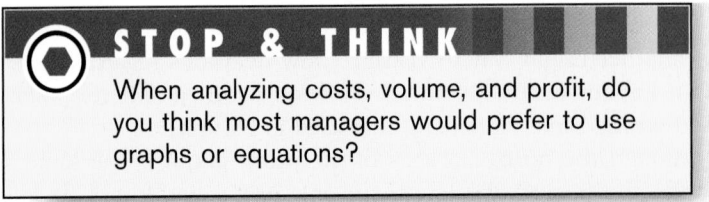

STOP & THINK

When analyzing costs, volume, and profit, do you think most managers would prefer to use graphs or equations?

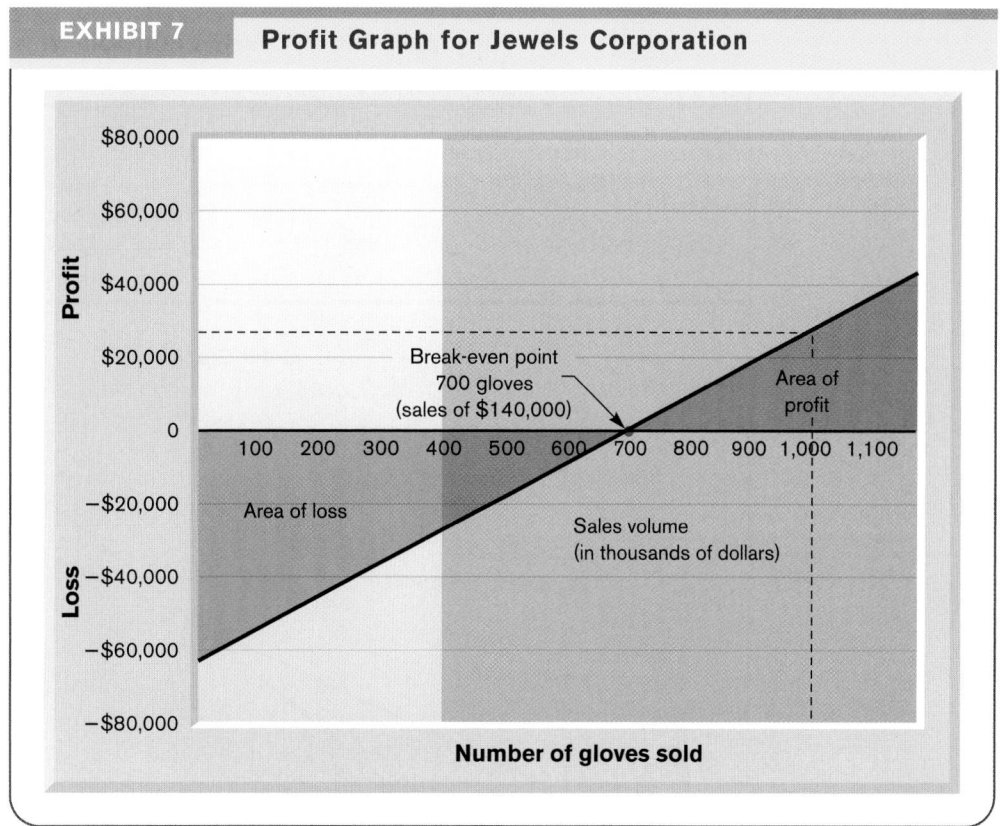

EXHIBIT 7 | **Profit Graph for Jewels Corporation**

REMEMBER THIS...

- In both a cost-volume-profit (CVP) graph and a profit graph, the dollars (sales revenue or costs) are shown on the vertical (or Y) axis and the volume of units is shown on the horizontal (or X) axis.
- A CVP graph is constructed as follows:
  - Draw the two axes, dollars on the vertical axis and units on the horizontal axis.
  - Draw the fixed cost line which is a horizontal line indicating the total amount of fixed cost.
  - Draw the total cost line. This line starts at the vertical axis at the amount of fixed cost, and the upward slope of the line is equal to the variable cost per unit.
  - Draw the total revenue line. This line starts at the origin ($0, 0 units), and the upward slope of the line is equal to the selling price per unit.
  - Label the break-even point. This is the point where the total revenue and total cost lines intersect.
- A profit graph is constructed as follows:
  - Draw the two axes, dollars on the vertical axis and units on the horizontal axis.
  - Place a point on the vertical axis equal to the loss the company will experience if it has no sales. This loss is equal to the amount of fixed cost.
  - Place a second point, this time on the horizontal axis, indicating the number of units the company needs to sell to break even.
  - Draw a line passing through these two points. This is the profit line.

EXHIBIT 8	Comparison of C-V-P Equation with C-V-P Graph

C-V-P Equation

$$(\text{Sales price} \times \text{Units}) - (\text{Variable costs} \times \text{Units}) - \text{Fixed costs} = \text{Profit}$$
$$\$200X - \$110X - \$63,000 = \$36,000$$
$$\$90X = \$99,000$$
$$X = 1,100 \text{ gloves}$$

C-V-P Graph

Sales revenue and costs

- Sales revenue
- $36,000 Profit
- Total costs
- Break-even point
- Variable costs
- Fixed costs

Number of gloves sold

Profit Graph

Profit / Loss

- Target profit point
- Profits
- Losses
- Break-even point

Number of gloves sold

EXPANDED material

Thus far, we have covered various types of costs, simple methods of analyzing mixed costs, and the basics of C-V-P analysis. In this expanded section, we cover the effect of the sales mix on profitability and use the concept of operating leverage to explore differences in cost structures among different types of companies.

Sales Mix

Explain the effects of sales mix on profitability.

(6) As a manager using C-V-P, you need to be aware of what this tool can and cannot do. One important issue is that C-V-P analysis must be adjusted when a company starts changing the mix of products that it sells. **Sales mix** is the proportion of sales revenue represented by each of a company's products. To keep our discussions simple, in previous sections of the chapter we used examples of companies with only one product. Many companies have more than one product, however, so you need to understand how sales mix issues are resolved. To illustrate how a change in sales mix can affect a company's C-V-P relationships, let's assume that Multi-Product, Inc., sells three different products. Following are the monthly revenues and costs for each type of product:

	Product A		Product B		Product C		Total	
	Amount	Percent	Amount	Percent	Amount	Percent	Amount	Percent
Sales revenue	$25,000	100%	$45,000	100.00%	$30,000	100%	$100,000	100%
Less variable costs	20,000	80	30,000	66.67	21,000	70	71,000	71
Contribution margin	$ 5,000	20%	$15,000	33.33%	$ 9,000	30%	$ 29,000	29%
Sales mix in sales dollars	25%		45%		30%		100%	

sales mix

The relative proportion of total sales dollars (or total units sold) that is represented by each of a company's products.

Total sales are $100,000, which in this example includes $25,000 in sales of Product A, $45,000 of Product B, and $30,000 of Product C. Therefore, the sales mix in sales dollars is 25% Product A ($25,000 ÷ $100,000), 45% Product B ($45,000 ÷ $100,000), and 30% Product C ($30,000 ÷ $100,000). With this sales mix, the average variable cost ratio is 71%, which is determined by dividing total variable costs of $71,000 by total sales of $100,000. If Multi-Product, Inc., had fixed costs of $17,400 and desired a target income of $40,000, the necessary sales volume (in dollars) would be:

$$\text{Sales revenue} - (0.71)\text{Sales revenue} - \$17,400 = \$40,000$$
$$(0.29)\text{Sales revenue} = \$57,400$$
$$\text{Sales revenue} = \$57,400 \div 0.29$$
$$\text{Sales revenue} = \$197,932 \text{ (rounded up)}$$

$197,932 is the total sales dollars necessary for Multi-Product, Inc., to break even. However, it's important to note that in order for Multi-Product to actually break even, 25% of these sales must come from Product A, 45% from Product B, and 30% from Product C.

Alternatively, you could calculate the average contribution margin ratio by subtracting the total variable costs from total sales and dividing the result (total contribution margin of $29,000) by total sales of $100,000. The company could then divide the average contribution margin ratio (29%) into fixed costs plus target income ($17,400 + $40,000). This revised, more compact formula is simply a restatement of the preceding equation.

? FYI

A computer can make sales mix and other C-V-P analysis computations easier to do. Using simulation or other programs, you can quickly calculate the financial effects of changes in the sales of one product or simultaneous changes in sales of several products.

$$\frac{\text{Fixed costs} + \text{Target income}}{\text{Average contribution margin ratio}} = \frac{\$57,400}{0.29} = \$197,932 \text{ (rounded up)}$$

Remember, though, that $197,932 in sales will achieve the target income only if the average variable cost and contribution margin ratios, and therefore the sales mix, do not change. In order for you to better understand this fact, assume that the total sales revenue and the sales price of each product remain the same but that the sales mix changes as follows:

	Product A		Product B		Product C		Total	
	Amount	Percent	Amount	Percent	Amount	Percent	Amount	Percent
Sales revenue	$50,000	100%	$30,000	100.00%	$20,000	100%	$100,000	100%
Less variable costs	40,000	80	20,000	66.67	14,000	70	74,000	74
Contribution margin	$10,000	20%	$10,000	33.33%	$ 6,000	30%	$ 26,000	26%
Sales mix in sales dollars	50%		30%		20%		100%	

As you can see in this example, the variable cost and contribution margin ratios for each product remain the same, but the sales mix changes. Product A now comprises 50% of total sales instead of 25%. Because Product A has a lower contribution margin ratio than Products B and C, the average contribution margin ratio decreases from 29% to 26% (stated another way, the average variable cost ratio increases from 71% to 74%). Now think about how this change in the sales mix would affect profit and the volume of sales revenue needed to break even. Would you expect the necessary sales volume to increase or decrease?

Let's use the more compact formula based on the average contribution margin ratio to calculate the new sales volume. When we run the new C-V-P calculation, the sales volume needed to generate $40,000 of target income increases to $220,770, computed as follows:

> **STOP & THINK**
>
> Before moving on, can you calculate the necessary sales volume of $220,770 in the second sales mix example using the familiar C-V-P equation: Sales revenue − Variable costs − Fixed costs = Target income?

$$\frac{\text{Fixed costs} + \text{Target income}}{\text{Average contribution margin ratio}} = \frac{\$57,400}{0.26} = \$220,770 \text{ (rounded up)}$$

The important thing that we've learned from these sales mix calculations is that one sensible profit-maximizing strategy for management would be to maintain as large a contribution margin as possible on all products and then to emphasize those products with the largest contribution margin ratios. In the remaining chapters of this text, we discuss procedures that management can use to control costs and, hence, maintain high contribution margins. The second part of this strategy—emphasizing the products with the highest contribution margin ratios—is a marketing function. Multi-Product, Inc., for example, should promote Product B more aggressively than Product A. With other factors being equal, a company should spend more advertising dollars and pay higher sales commissions on its products with higher contribution margin ratios. In fact, instead of paying commissions based on total sales, a good strategy might be to base sales commissions on the total contribution margin generated. This way, the mix of products

> **STOP & THINK**
>
> Would maximizing the sales of the highest contribution margin products still be the best profit-maximizing strategy if the company experienced production constraints such that producing more of the highest contribution margin products severely limited the quality or production speed of other products?

that maximizes the sales staff's commissions will be the mix that provides the company with the greatest overall profit.[6]

REMEMBER THIS...

- Sales mix is the proportion of sales revenue represented by each of a company's products.
- Changes in sales mix can affect profits because not all products have the same contribution margin.
- Other things being equal, to maximize profits, management should put greater emphasis on the sale of products with higher contribution margin ratios.

Cost Structure and Operating Leverage

Describe how higher fixed costs increase a company's operating leverage leading to increased variability in profits as sales fluctuate.

⑦ Now that we have nearly completed this chapter, we have developed a lot of insight into how to think about and manage costs in the process of making profit-planning decisions. This chapter is actually a lot about the strategy—the strategy of how a company works with its specific types of costs and activities to create a profit. Overall, we now basically understand how cost-volume-profit relationships and contribution margins highlight the different effects that variable and fixed costs have on profitability. As we close this chapter, an important management issue to be understood has to do with the amount of fixed costs a company has in its cost structure. The amount of fixed costs an organization commits itself to often has a lot to do with its type of business, e.g., merchandising, manufacturing, or service. In addition, the arrival of e-commerce into the economy is having an impact on cost structures of organizations. We'll illustrate the differences among these organizations by applying the concept of **operating leverage** to illustrate how a company can manage risk (in terms of profits) by the way it organizes its cost structure—in other words, how much the company is committed to using fixed costs versus variable costs to do business.

operating leverage

The extent to which fixed costs replace variable costs as part of a company's cost structure; the higher the proportion of fixed costs to variable costs, the faster income increases or decreases with changes in sales volume.

Imagine that you have worked with two of your college friends to design a new computer software game that you expect to market to college campuses across the nation. You and your partners have identified three ways to approach the market. First, you can take on the role of the merchant by contracting with a software manufacturing company to handle all the production of the packaged software. You can then concentrate on the sales and marketing of their new game. This approach won't require an expensive production facility, but the reality is that you will have to pay a high price per unit to the company that handles the production of the packaged software. In the second approach, you can take on the role of manufacturer by setting up your own production facilities. In this case, because all of your effort will be dedicated to producing the game, you will need to wholesale the software product to another merchant company that will then resell the product to the actual customers. Finally, you can "virtually" sell the game to other college students by contracting with an e-commerce company that will host your software download site

---

[6] In this chapter we focus on sales mix in sales dollars rather than in units of sales. In either case, the concept of C-V-P analysis is the same. However, there are some important, though subtle, differences in the calculations when a constant sales mix in unit of sales is assumed. These calculation issues will be reserved for more advanced texts.

for a significant fixed fee per month. In any case, regardless of whether you and your partners will wholesale the game to another merchant or retail the game directly to the college student market, you have determined that you can sell the game for $100. The costs of each of these methods of structuring your business are as follows:

Business Structure	Variable Cost per Unit to Manufacture or to Purchase from a Manufacturer	Fixed Cost per Year for the Merchandising, Manufacturing, or E-Commerce Facility
Traditional retail merchant	$80	$100,000
Manufacturer	25	375,000
E-commerce merchant	0	500,000

CAUTION

Don't confuse the concept of operating leverage with the concept of financial leverage, though there is a lot of similarity in these concepts. While both concepts focus on risk and the sensitivity of profit to changes in sales volume, financial leverage has to do with the use of debt versus equity to provide financing for a company. In general, the financial leverage (and risk) of a company increases as management chooses to use debt, rather than equity, to raise funds for the company. Similarly, the operating leverage (and risk) of a company increases as management chooses to emphasize fixed cost, rather than variable cost, to create or obtain the product for sale to the marketplace.

STOP & THINK

Think about the level of operating leverage you would expect to find in a service organization such as a consulting company or a law firm. Would these kinds of organizations typically have high or low levels of operating leverage?

As you can see, one of the issues that you must decide when selecting your company's business structure is whether you and your partners want to commit to high fixed costs in order to have low variable costs, or vice versa. This trade-off of fixed versus variable costs is what we mean when we talk about operating leverage. As total fixed costs increase and variable costs per unit decrease, the operating leverage of the organization increases. In the example above, the operating leverage of your company will be very high if you choose to structure your company as an e-commerce merchant. So, the question you should be asking yourself is whether it is good or bad to have high operating leverage? The answer is that it depends on whether the company is operating above or below the break-even point.

The C-V-P graphs in Exhibit 9 show us the impact of operating leverage for these three types of companies. The break-even point (which is the same for all three companies) is at a sales volume of 5,000 games sold each year. At this point, all three companies would generate the same level of profit—zero. As sales move above or below the break-even point, however, there are significant differences in profit (i.e., the distance between the revenue line and the total costs line) between the company structures. If sales are below the break-even point, then structuring the company as an e-commerce merchant will generate a lot of losses. If the company can sell more than 5,000 games per year, however, then the e-commerce merchant structure will generate the most profit per year. Essentially, operating leverage is a measure of risk. With high levels of operating leverage, the company is at risk of losing a lot of money if sales go down. But business risk often has an upside. In the case of operating leverage, the risk of loss is balanced by the potential for large gains in income as sales go up. So your decision on how to structure your company partly depends on the impact on operating leverage and on how much risk you are willing to accept.

EXHIBIT 9   "Seeing" Operating Leverages

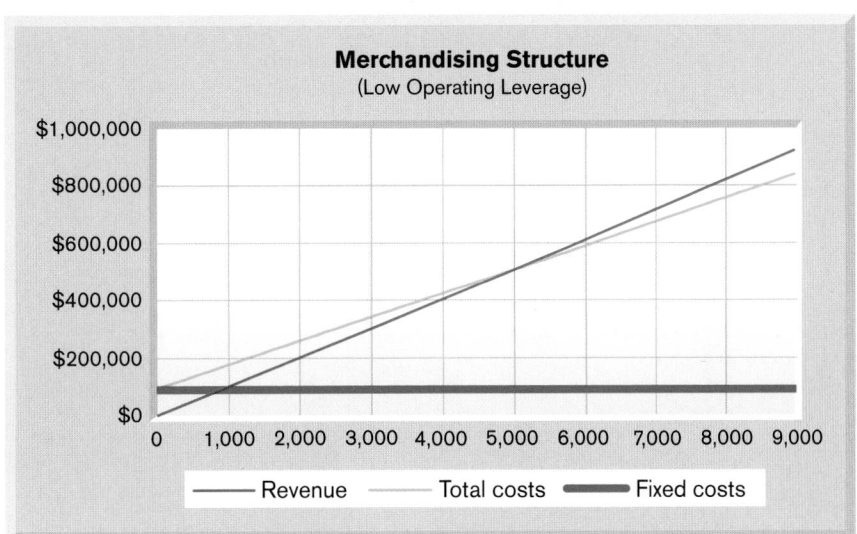

		Sales in Units	Revenue	Total Variable Costs	Contribution Margin	Total Fixed Costs	Operating Income
Price per unit	$ 100	3,000	$300,000	$(240,000)	$ 60,000	$(100,000)	$(40,000)
Variable cost per unit	80	5,000	500,000	(400,000)	100,000	(100,000)	–
Total fixed costs	100,000	7,000	700,000	(560,000)	140,000	(100,000)	40,000

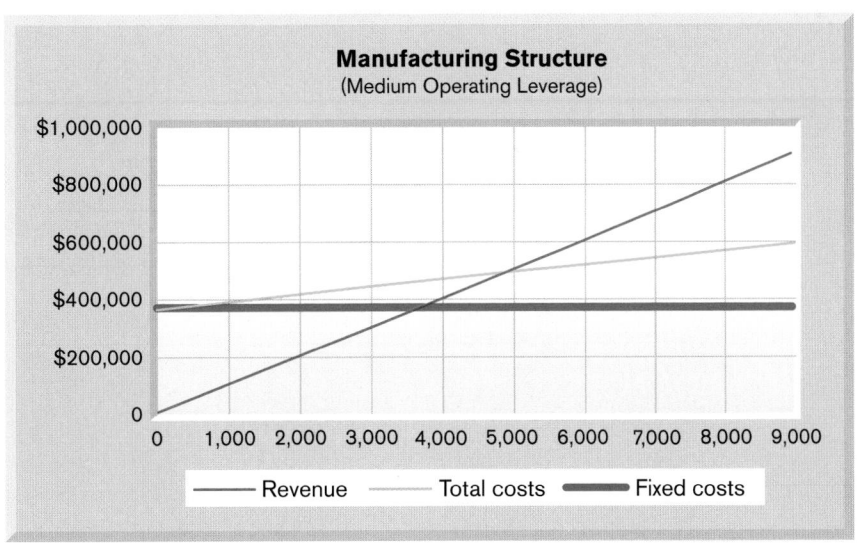

		Sales in Units	Revenue	Total Variable Costs	Contribution Margin	Total Fixed Costs	Operating Income
Price per unit	$ 100	3,000	$300,000	$ (75,000)	$225,000	$(375,000)	$(150,000)
Variable cost per unit	25	5,000	500,000	(125,000)	375,000	(375,000)	–
Total fixed costs	375,000	7,000	700,000	(175,000)	525,000	(375,000)	150,000

EXHIBIT 9   **(continued)**

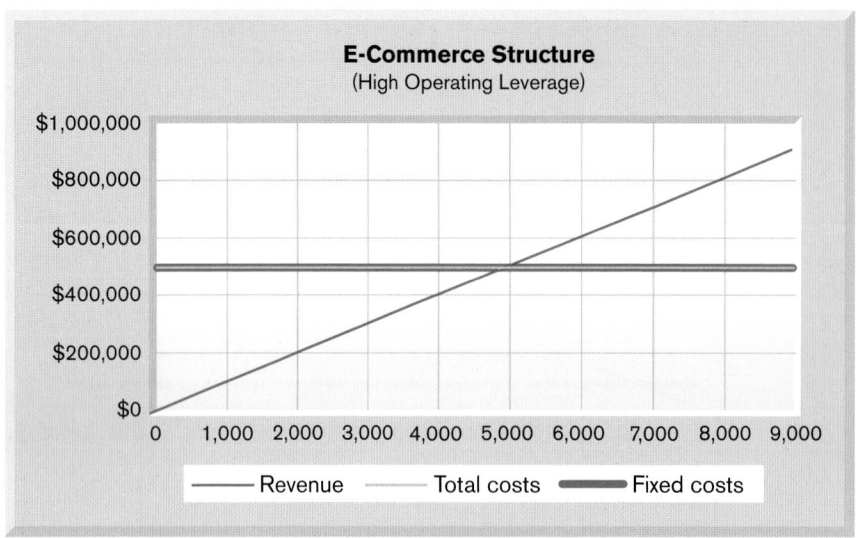

E-Commerce Structure
(High Operating Leverage)

		Sales in Units	Revenue	Total Variable Costs	Contribution Margin	Total Fixed Costs	Operating Income
Price per unit	$ 100	3,000	$300,000	$ –	$300,000	$(500,000)	$(200,000)
Variable cost per unit	0	5,000	500,000	–	500,000	(500,000)	–
Total fixed costs	500,000	7,000	700,000	–	700,000	(500,000)	200,000

REMEMBER THIS...

- Operating leverage relates to the amount of fixed costs a company has in its cost structure. High fixed costs mean high operating leverage; low fixed costs indicate low operating leverage.

- The higher the operating leverage, the more money a company loses if sales are bad, but the more money it makes if sales are good.

REVIEW OF
LEARNING OBJECTIVES

(1) Understand the key factors involved in cost-volume-profit (C-V-P) analysis and why it is such an important tool in management decision making.

Key Factors in CVP Analysis	Depends on . . .
Sales Revenue	• Number of units sold • Selling price per unit • Mix of items sold
Variable Cost	• Number of units sold • Variable cost per unit • Mix of items sold
Fixed Cost	• Management choice of the level of fixed costs; does NOT depend on the number of units sold
Profit	• Sales revenue − Variable cost − Fixed cost

(2) Explain and analyze the basic cost behavior patterns—variable, fixed, and mixed.

- Variable cost: variable in total, fixed per unit
- Fixed cost: fixed in total, variable per unit
- Stepped cost: increases with the level of activity but in steps instead of smoothly. If the steps are wide, the cost is treated as a fixed cost; if the steps are narrow, the cost is approximated as a variable cost.
- Mixed costs have both a fixed and a variable component.

(3) Analyze mixed costs using the scattergraph and high-low methods.

- Before mixed costs can be analyzed and used in decision making, they must be divided into their fixed and variable components.
- The scattergraph and high-low methods are commonly used to analyze mixed costs.
- The scattergraph method involves visually plotting a straight line (the regression line) through points on a graph of cost data at various activity levels.
- With the high-low method, the highest and lowest levels of activity and their associated costs are used to calculate the variable cost rate and the total fixed costs.

(4) Perform C-V-P analyses, and describe the effects potential changes in C-V-P variables have on company profitability.

- Contribution margin = Sales revenue − Variable costs
- Sales revenue − Variable costs − Fixed costs = Target income
- At break-even, Target income = 0
- Sales revenue = Sales price × Number of units
- Variable costs = Variable cost per unit × Number of units
- Variable costs = Variable cost ratio × Sales revenue

(5) Visualize C-V-P relationships using graphs.

Constructing a CVP graph	1. Draw the two axes, dollars on the vertical axis and units on the horizontal axis.
	2. Draw the fixed cost line which is a horizontal line indicating the total amount of fixed cost.

3. Draw the total cost line. This line starts at the vertical axis at the amount of fixed cost, and the upward slope of the line is equal to the variable cost per unit.

4. Draw the total revenue line. This line starts at the origin ($0, 0 units), and the upward slope of the line is equal to the selling price per unit.

5. Label the break-even point. This is the point where the total revenue and total cost lines intersect.

Constructing a profit graph

1. Draw the two axes, dollars on the vertical axis and units on the horizontal axis.

2. Place a point on the vertical axis equal to the loss the company will experience if it has no sales. This loss is equal to the amount of fixed cost.

3. Place a second point, this time on the horizontal axis, indicating the number of units the company needs to sell to break even.

4. Draw a line passing through these two points. This is the profit line.

(6) Explain the effects of sales mix on profitability.

- Sales mix is the proportion of revenue dollars represented by each of a company's products.
- Because all products do not have the same contribution margin ratios, changes in the sales mix of products sold can significantly affect total profits.
- When you are working as a manager to maximize profits, it is best to maintain as large a contribution margin as possible on all products and then emphasize those products with the largest individual contribution margin ratios.

(7) Describe how higher fixed costs increase a company's operating leverage leading to increased variability in profits as sales fluctuate.

- Operating leverage relates to the amount of fixed costs versus variable costs that a company has in its cost structure. High fixed costs (and low variable costs) indicate high operating leverage; low fixed costs (and high variable costs) indicate low operating leverage.
- The higher the operating leverage, the more money a company loses if sales are below the break-even point, but the more money it makes if sales are above the break-even point.

KEY TERMS & CONCEPTS

break-even point, 1025

contribution margin, 1021

contribution margin
  ratio, 1023

cost behavior, 1010

cost-volume-profit
  (C-V-P) analysis, 1010

fixed costs, 1014

high-low method, 1019

mixed costs, 1016

per-unit contribution
  margin, 1022

profit graph, 1031

regression line, 1017

relevant range, 1013

return on sales
  revenue, 1026

scattergraph (visual-fit)
  method, 1017

stepped costs, 1015

target income, 1025

variable cost rate, 1017

variable costs, 1012

EXPANDED *material*

operating leverage, 1037

sales mix, 1035

REVIEW PROBLEMS

Variable and Fixed Costs Analyses

Blade Corporation manufactures two types of inline skates—a basic model and a racing model. During the year 2009, Blade accumulated the following summary information about its two products:

	Racing Model	Basic Model
Selling price	$130	$65
Number of units manufactured and sold	14,000	9,000

	Racing Model		Basic Model	
	Units	Costs	Units	Costs
January	1,200	$ 112,000	800	$ 39,600
February	900	91,000	600	30,000
March	800	76,400	450	25,800
April	1,400	124,800	900	36,900
May	950	92,650	1,000	47,000
June	1,600	146,800	1,200	57,300
July	1,400	134,600	1,300	60,600
August	1,700	154,500	650	32,195
September	1,550	140,200	850	44,250
October	1,500	134,500	500	27,000
November	600	62,500	350	20,700
December	400	44,000	400	22,000
Totals	14,000	$1,313,950	9,000	$443,345

Required:

1. Use the high-low method to estimate the variable and fixed production costs of both the racing model and the basic model skates.
2. All selling costs are fixed, and they total $200,000 for the racing model and $80,000 for the basic model. Prepare a contribution margin income statement for each model at sales of 10,000 racing and 10,000 basic skates.

Solution

1. Variable and Fixed Costs

The high-low method involves finding the variable and fixed costs at the high and low levels of production. In this case:

	Racing Model	Basic Model
High-production month	1,700 (Aug.)	1,300 (July)
Low-production month	400 (Dec.)	350 (Nov.)
Difference	1,300	950
Total production costs of high month	$154,500	$60,600
Total production costs of low month	44,000	20,700
Difference	$110,500	$39,900

(continued)

Once the differences are known, the change in units (production) is divided into the change in costs to determine the variable cost rate.

$$\frac{\text{Change in costs}}{\text{Change in units}} = \text{Variable cost rate}$$

$$\text{Racing model: } \frac{\$110,500}{1,300} = \$85$$

$$\text{Basic model: } \frac{\$39,900}{950} = \$42$$

Because total variable costs equal unit variable cost times number of units produced, and total costs equal total variable costs plus total fixed costs, fixed costs can now be calculated.

$$\text{Total costs} - (\text{Variable cost per unit} \times \text{Number of units}) = \text{Total fixed costs}$$

	Racing Model	**Basic Model**
High production level (X) =	$154,500 - $85(1,700)	$60,600 - $42(1,300)
	$X = $154,500 - $144,500	$X = $60,600 - $54,600
	$X = $10,000	$X = $6,000
Low production level (X) =	$44,000 - $85(400)	$20,700 - $42(350)
	$X = $44,000 - $34,000	$X = $20,700 - $14,700
	$X = $10,000	$X = $6,000

Thus, we have the following:

	Racing Model	**Basic Model**
Variable cost rate	$ 85	$ 42
Total fixed costs	10,000	6,000

2. Contribution Margin Income Statements

Blade Corporation
Contribution Margin Income Statements
For the Year Ended December 31, 2009

	Racing Model	**Basic Model**
Sales revenue (at 10,000 units)	$1,300,000	$ 650,000
Less variable cost of goods sold*	(850,000)	(420,000)
Contribution margin	$ 450,000	$ 230,000
Less fixed cost of goods sold	(10,000)	(6,000)
Less fixed selling costs	(200,000)	(80,000)
Income	$ 240,000	$ 144,000

*$85 per unit for racing model; $42 per unit for basic model.

Assessing the Effects of Changes in Costs, Prices, and Volume on Profitability

K&D Company plans the following for the coming year:

Sales volume	100,000 units
Sales price	$2.50 per unit
Variable costs	$1.30 per unit
Fixed costs	$60,000

(continued)

Required:

1. Determine K&D's target income.
2. Compute what the target income would be under each of the following independent assumptions:
   a. The sales volume increases 20%.
   b. The sales price decreases 20%.
   c. Variable costs increase 20%.
   d. Fixed costs decrease 20%.

Solution

1. Target Income

Basic C-V-P equation: Sales revenue − Variable costs − Fixed costs = Target income

$$(\text{Units sold} \times \text{Sales price}) - (\text{Units sold} \times \text{Variable unit cost}) - \text{Fixed costs} = \text{Target income}$$
$$(100,000 \times \$2.50) - (100,000 \times \$1.30) - \$60,000 = X$$
$$\$250,000 - \$130,000 - \$60,000 = X$$
$$\$60,000 = X$$

This answer can be validated by dividing fixed costs by the per-unit contribution margin to find the break-even point and then multiplying the excess units to be sold above the break-even point by the per-unit contribution margin of $1.20 ($2.50 − $1.30).

$$\frac{\text{Fixed costs}}{\text{Per-unit contribution margin}} = \text{Break-even point}$$

$$\frac{\$60,000}{\$1.20} = 50,000 \text{ units}$$

Units sold	100,000
Less break-even point (units)	50,000
Excess	50,000
Per-unit contribution margin	× $1.20
Target income	$60,000

2a. The sales volume increases 20%.

$$(100,000 \times 1.2 \times \$2.50) - (100,000 \times 1.2 \times \$1.30) - \$60,000 = X$$
$$\$300,000 - \$156,000 - \$60,000 = X$$
$$\$84,000 = X$$

In this case, the contribution margin does not change. Therefore, the answer can be validated by multiplying the units to be sold in excess of the break-even point by the per-unit contribution margin of $1.20 to find the target income.

Units sold	120,000
Less break-even point (units)	50,000
Excess	70,000
Per-unit contribution margin	× $1.20
Target income	$84,000

2b. The sales price decreases 20%.

$$(100,000 \times \$2.50 \times 0.8) - (100,000 \times \$1.30) - \$60,000 = X$$
$$\$200,000 - \$130,000 - \$60,000 = X$$
$$\$10,000 = X$$

In this case, the contribution margin changes. Therefore, the answer can be validated by dividing fixed costs by the new per-unit contribution margin of $0.70 ($2.00 − $1.30) to find the new break-even point and then multiplying the units to be sold in excess of the break-even point by the new per-unit contribution margin.

$$\frac{\$60{,}000 \text{ (fixed costs)}}{\$0.70 \text{ (new per-unit contribution margin)}} = 85{,}715 \text{ units (new break-even point, rounded up)}$$

Units sold	100,000
Less break-even point (units)	85,715
Excess	14,285
Per-unit contribution margin	× $0.70
Target income	$10,000 (rounded)

2c. Variable costs increase 20%.

$$(100{,}000 \times \$2.50) - (100{,}000 \times \$1.30 \times 1.2) - \$60{,}000 = X$$
$$\$250{,}000 - \$156{,}000 - \$60{,}000 = X$$
$$\$34{,}000 = X$$

In this case, the contribution margin changes. Therefore, the answer can be validated by dividing fixed costs by the new per-unit contribution margin of $0.94 ($2.50 − $1.56) to find the new break-even point and then multiplying the units to be sold in excess of the break-even point by the new per-unit contribution margin.

$$\frac{\$60{,}000 \text{ (fixed costs)}}{\$0.94 \text{ (new per-unit contribution margin)}} = 63{,}830 \text{ units (new break-even point, rounded up)}$$

Units sold	100,000
Less break-even point (units)	63,830
Excess	36,170
Per-unit contribution margin	× $0.94
Target income	$34,000 (rounded)

2d. Fixed costs decrease 20%.

$$(100{,}000 \times \$2.50) - (100{,}000 \times \$1.30) - (\$60{,}000 \times 0.8) = X$$
$$\$250{,}000 - \$130{,}000 - \$48{,}000 = X$$
$$\$72{,}000 = X$$

In this case, the contribution margin does not change, but fixed costs, and hence the break-even point, do. Therefore, the answer can be validated by dividing the per-unit contribution margin of $1.20 into the new fixed costs to find the break-even point and then multiplying the units to be sold in excess of the break-even point by the per-unit contribution margin.

$$\frac{\$48{,}000 \text{ (new fixed costs)}}{\$1.20 \text{ (per-unit contribution margin)}} = 40{,}000 \text{ units (new break-even point)}$$

Units sold	100,000
Less break-even point (units)	40,000
Excess	60,000
Per-unit contribution margin	× $1.20
Target income	$72,000

DISCUSSION QUESTIONS

1. Explain how understanding cost behavior patterns can assist management.
2. Discuss how level of activity is measured in manufacturing, merchandising, and service firms.
3. What is meant by the relevant range?
4. How should stepped costs be treated in the planning process?
5. Why must all mixed costs be segregated into their fixed and variable components?
6. What is the major weakness of the scattergraph, or visual-fit, method of analyzing mixed costs?
7. What is the major limitation of the high-low method of analyzing mixed costs?
8. What is the basic C-V-P equation? What is a more detailed version of this equation?

9. What is the contribution margin, and why is it important for managers to know the contribution margins of their products?
10. How much will profits increase for every unit sold over the break-even point?
11. What is the major advantage of using C-V-P graphs?
12. When other factors are constant, what is the effect on profits of an increase in fixed costs? Of a decrease in variable costs?

13. What effect is a change in the sales mix likely to have on a firm's overall contribution margin ratio?

PRACTICE EXERCISES

PE 20-1 **Measuring Level of Activity**
LO1 Which one of the following is *not* an activity base used by a company?
   a. Number of defects per hour in an assembly plant
   b. Number of units sold for a merchandising firm
   c. Number of units produced for a manufacturing firm
   d. Number of client hours billed for an accounting firm
   e. Number of hours a retail store is open

PE 20-2 **Variable Costs**
LO1 Which one of the following would *not* be a variable cost for a construction company?
   a. Cost of trusses used to construct a roof for a house
   b. Cost of windows to be installed in a house
   c. Salary paid to overall project supervisor
   d. Cost of drywall to be installed in house
   e. Cost of exterior house paint

PE 20-3 **Linearity of Variable Costs within the Relevant Range**
LO1 The company has assembled the following data about its variable costs:

Level of Activity	Total Variable Cost
2,000 units	$ 46,000
3,000 units	72,000
4,000 units	96,000
5,000 units	120,000
6,000 units	150,000

The company is currently producing 3,300 units. According to these data, what is the relevant range over which the company can assume that the variable cost per unit is constant?

PE 20-4 **Fixed Costs**
LO2 If the level of activity increases during the month, does the fixed cost per unit increase, decrease, or remain constant?

PE 20-5   **Break-Even Computation**

LO4   B&B company reports the following items:

Direct materials per unit	$ 2.25
Direct labor per unit	3.95
Variable overhead per unit	1.80
Monthly rent	2,200.00
Monthly depreciation	680.00
Other monthly fixed costs	2,400.00
Sales price per unit	14.00

Using the above information, compute the company's monthly break-even point (in units).

PE 20-6   **Stepped Fixed Costs**

LO2   The company pays $3,000 per month to each of its four production supervisors. Each supervisor can handle the workload associated with up to 2,400 units of production per month; the current level of production is 9,000 units. If the company increases its level of production to 12,800 units per month, how much will the company pay, in total, for the salaries of the necessary production supervisors?

PE 20-7   **Mixed Costs**

LO2   The company's president receives a $100,000 base salary and a bonus of 0.5% of sales for the year. How much will the president earn at a sales level of $2,750,000 for the year?

PE 20-8   **Scattergraph Method**

LO3   Which one of the following statements is incorrect?
a. The scattergraph method can be somewhat subjective depending on where one visually places the regression line.
b. The scattergraph method is the most accurate method of analyzing mixed costs.
c. When graphing mixed costs, the dollars go on the vertical axis, and the level of activity goes on the horizontal axis.
d. Regression lines attempt to minimize the average distance between all the data points and the fitted regression line.
e. The slope of the regression line is equal to the variable cost per unit of activity.

PE 20-9   **Using the High-Low Method to Estimate the Variable Cost Rate**

LO3   The company reports the following utility costs for different levels of activity during the first half of the year:

Month	Machine Hours	Total Utility Costs
January	470	$14,900
February	500	15,350
March	570	16,450
April	625	17,300
May	610	16,800
June	525	15,800

Using the high-low method, estimate the variable cost rate.

PE 20-10   **Using the High-Low Method to Estimate Fixed Costs**

LO3   Refer to the data in PE 20-9. Using the high-low method, estimate the fixed costs per month based on the variable cost rate (computed in PE 20-9).

PE 20-11
LO4
Contribution Margin Income Statement
The company sells desks for $550 each. The variable cost per desk is $385. The company's monthly fixed costs are $72,000. Prepare a contribution margin income statement for a month in which the company sells 500 desks.

PE 20-12
LO4
Contribution Margin Ratio and Variable Cost Ratio
Refer to the data in PE 20-11. Compute the contribution margin ratio and the variable cost ratio.

PE 20-13
LO4
The C-V-P Equation
The company sells riding lawnmowers for $2,395 each. The variable cost per lawnmower is $1,645. The company's monthly fixed costs are $141,000. Using the C-V-P equation, compute the amount of profit the company will have for a month in which the company sells 275 lawnmowers.

PE 20-14
LO4
Break-Even Units
The company sells shovels for $27.75 each. The variable cost per shovel is $14.25. The company's monthly fixed costs are $2,538. Compute the number of shovels the company must sell to break even.

PE 20-15
LO4
Determining Sales Volume to Achieve Target Income
Refer to the data in PE 20-14. How many shovels must the company sell to achieve a profit of $10,000?

PE 20-16
LO4
Determining Sales Volume to Achieve Target Return on Sales
The company sells pianos for $7,000 each. The variable cost per piano is $5,500. The company has fixed costs per month of $45,000. Compute the number of units the company must sell in a month to achieve a 15% return on sales.

PE 20-17
LO4
Break-Even Sales Revenue
The company has a variable cost ratio of 55% and monthly fixed costs of $144,000. What is the company's break-even point in terms of sales dollars?

PE 20-18
LO4
C-V-P Analysis with Simultaneous Changes in Several Variables
The company currently sells 50,000 feet of cable each month for $3.50 per foot. The variable cost of the cable is $1.10 per foot, and monthly fixed costs are $75,000. The company is considering whether to raise the sales price for the cable to $4.00 per foot. The marketing team has determined that such an increase in sales price will discourage some customers from purchasing the cable, so the company will be able to sell only 40,000 feet of cable per month. Calculate the profit for the company under both of the following scenarios:
1. 50,000 feet of cable at $3.50 per foot.
2. 40,000 feet of cable at $4.00 per foot.

In terms of profit maximization, should the company raise the price per foot?

PE 20-19
LO4
C-V-P Analysis with Simultaneous Changes in Several Variables
Refer to the data in PE 20-18. The company is considering whether to change its production process to reduce the variable cost per foot to $0.80 by raising fixed costs $10,000 per month to $85,000. This change will have no impact on selling price ($3.50) or sales volume (50,000 feet). In terms of profit maximization, should the company change its production process?

PE 20-20
LO5
Interpreting a C-V-P Graph
Look at the given C-V-P graph. Which one of the following sets of labels correctly labels items A, B, and C in the C-V-P graph?

(continued)

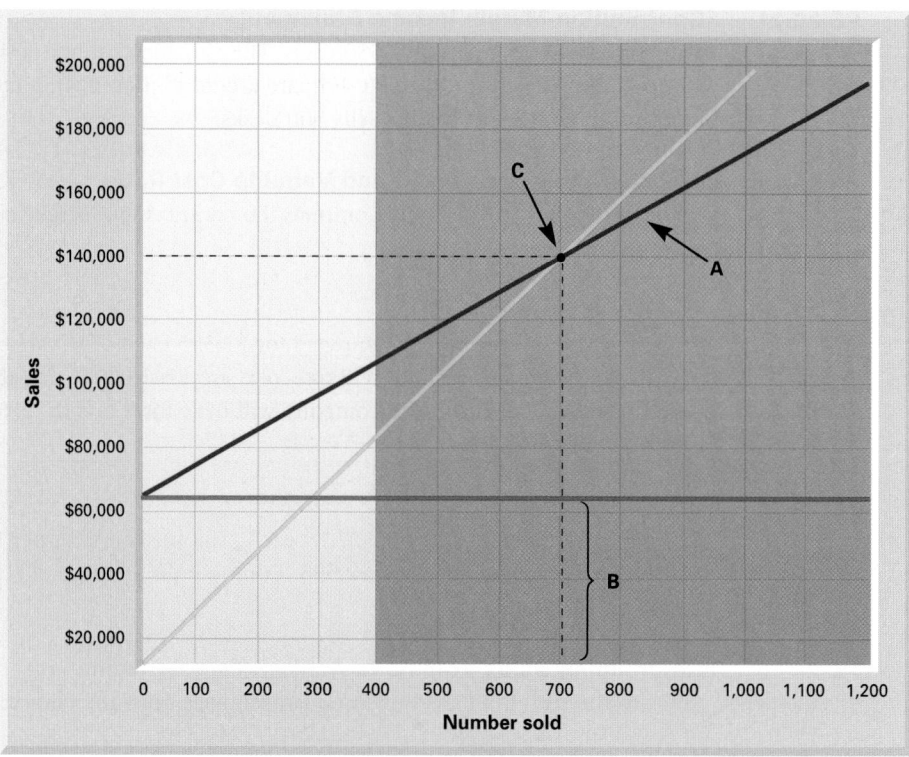

a. A: Total cost line; B: Fixed costs; C: Break-even point
b. A: Revenue line; B: Variable costs; C: Fixed costs
c. A: Fixed cost line; B: Break-even point; C: Fixed costs
d. A: Revenue line; B: Break-even point; C: Fixed costs
e. A: Total cost line; B: Break-even point; C: Fixed costs

PE 20-21 **Interpreting a Profit Graph**

LO5 Look at the given profit graph. Which one of the following sets of labels correctly labels items A, B, and C in the profit graph?

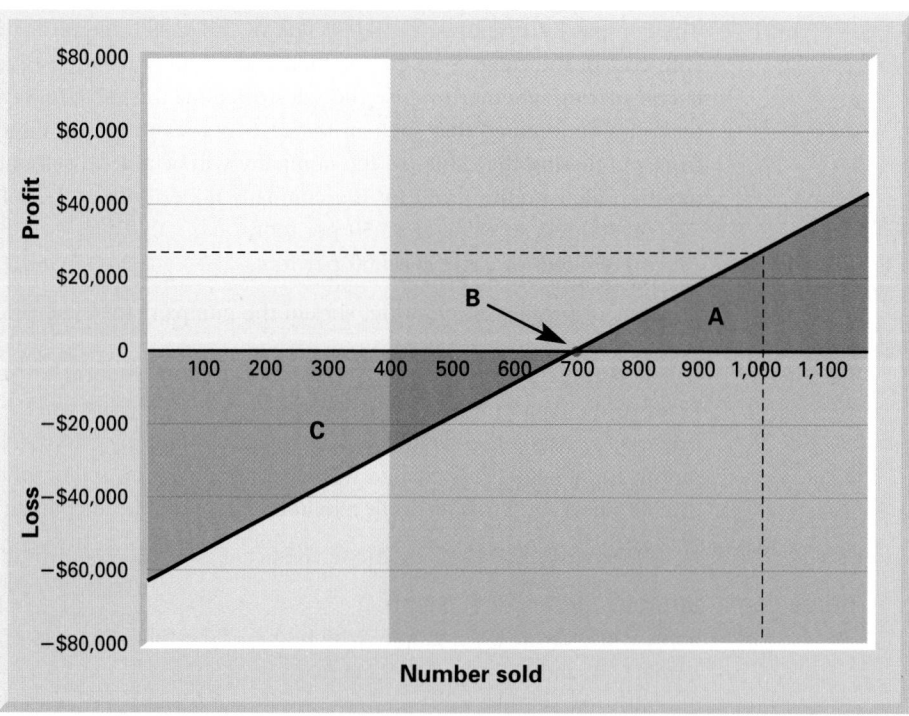

(continued)

a. A: Area of loss; B: Break-even point; C: Area of profit
b. A: Area of loss; B: Area of profit; C: Break-even point
c. A: Break-even point; B: Area of loss; C: Area of profit
d. A: Area of profit; B: Break-even point; C: Area of loss
e. A: Area of profit; B: Area of loss; C: Break-even point

PE 20-22 **Limiting Assumptions of C-V-P Analysis**
LO5 Which one of the following is *not* an assumption of C-V-P analysis?
a. Fixed costs are always greater than variable costs.
b. All costs can be divided into fixed and variable categories.
c. C-V-P analysis is valid only for a relevant range.
d. The mix of a company's products does not change over the relevant range.

PE 20-23 **Sales Mix**
LO6 The company has fixed costs of $43,000 and the following sales mix:

	Product A	Product B	Product C
Sales revenue	$25,000	$85,000	$40,000
Less variable costs	20,000	55,000	33,000
Contribution margin	$ 5,000	$30,000	$ 7,000

Using this same sales mix, calculate the required sales (in dollars) to earn a target income of $50,000.

PE 20-24 **Cost Structure**
LO7 If you experience much higher sales than expected this year, which kind of operating leverage would you like to have in your company for profit maximization?
a. High operating leverage
b. Low operating leverage
c. Medium operating leverage
d. Operating leverage does not affect profitability.

EXERCISES

E 20-25 **Variable and Fixed Costs over the Relevant Range**
LO2 Cook Corporation manufactures plastic garbage cans. In a typical year, the firm produces between 40,000 and 50,000 cans. At this level of production, fixed costs are $10,000 and variable costs are $2 per can.
 1. Graph the cost of producing cans, with cost as the vertical axis and production output as the horizontal axis.
 2. Indicate on the graph the relevant range of the $10,000 in fixed costs, and explain the significance of the relevant range.
 3. What would total production costs be if 46,000 cans were produced?

E 20-26 **Fixed Costs–The Relevant Range**
LO2 Sabrina Company manufactures large leisure boats. The following schedule shows total fixed costs at various levels of boat production:

(continued)

Units Produced	Total Fixed Costs
0–100	$150,000
101–400	250,000
401–900	400,000

1. What is the fixed cost per unit when 75 boats are produced?
2. What is the fixed cost per unit when 300 boats are produced?
3. What is the fixed cost per unit when 750 boats are produced?
4. Plot total fixed costs on a graph similar to that shown in Exhibit 2.

E 20-27   **Scattergraph Method of Analyzing Mixed Costs**

LO3   Wyoming Company makes windmills. The company has the following total costs at the given levels of windmill production:

Units Produced	Total Costs
20	$16,000
30	22,000
40	20,000
50	28,000

1. Use the scattergraph method to estimate the fixed and variable elements of Wyoming's total costs.
2. Compute the total cost of making 64 windmills, assuming that total fixed costs are $10,000 and that the variable cost rate computed in part (1) does not change.

E 20-28   **Scattergraph Method of Analyzing Mixed Costs**

LO3   Given the following mixed costs at various levels of production, complete the requirements.

Month	Units Produced	Mixed Costs
January	2	$24.00
February	3	28.00
March	1	21.00
April	5	30.00
May	4	25.00

1. Plot the data on a scattergraph, and visually fit a straight line through the points.
2. Based on your graph, estimate the monthly fixed cost and the variable cost per unit produced.
3. Compute the total cost of producing eight units in a month, assuming that the same relevant range applies.
4. **Interpretive Question:** Why is it so important to be able to determine the components of a mixed cost?

E 20-29   **Scattergraph Method and High-Low Method of Analyzing Mixed Costs**

LO3   Sailmaster makes boats and has the following costs and production levels for the last eight quarters:

(continued)

Quarter	Boats Produced	Total Costs
1	108	$101,250
2	128	168,750
3	185	189,000
4	245	200,145
5	311	276,200
6	352	255,250
7	389	305,700
8	428	376,500

1. Plot the data on a scattergraph, and visually fit a straight line through the points.
2. Based on your graph, estimate the quarterly fixed cost and the variable cost per unit produced.
3. Use the high-low method to compute the variable and fixed elements of Sailmaster's total costs, and then draw a straight line through the high and low data points on the scattergraph.
4. Compute the total cost of making 500 boats using first the scattergraph results and then using the high-low method results.
5. Comment on the differences between these two methods. Which method appears to most accurately represent the actual variable and fixed costs for Sailmaster?

E 20-30
LO3

High-Low Method of Analyzing Mixed Costs

The *Stamford Times* has determined that the annual printing of 850,000 newspapers costs 13 cents per copy. If production were to be increased to 1,250,000 copies per year, the per-unit cost would drop to 11 cents per copy.

1. Using the high-low method, determine the total fixed and variable costs of printing 850,000 newspapers.
2. Using the fixed and variable costs you determined in part (1), what would be the total cost of producing 1,000,000 copies?

E 20-31
LO4

Contribution Margin Calculations

Jerry Stone owns and operates a small beach shop in a mall on Sanibel Island, Florida. For the last six months, Jerry has had a display of sunglasses in the front window. Largely because of the display, Jerry has sold 100 pairs of sunglasses per month at an average cost of $26 and selling price of $50. The sales volume has doubled since the display was put in the window. One-fourth of Jerry's storage space is occupied by 190 ice coolers. The coolers have not been selling as well as Jerry hoped, but he is convinced that a front window display of coolers would increase sales by 50%. The coolers cost Jerry a total of $2,280 and have been selling at a rate of 100 per month at $28 each.

1. Assuming that cost of goods sold is the only variable cost, compute the contribution margin per unit for sunglasses and ice coolers.
2. Compute the total contribution margins for both sunglasses and ice coolers assuming window displays and no window displays for both items.
3. What are the economic costs associated with keeping the sunglass display in the store window?
4. What are the economic costs associated with replacing the sunglass display with an ice cooler display?

E 20-32
LO4

Contribution Margin Income Statement

The following data apply to Gordon Company for 2009:

(continued)

Sales revenue (100 units at $35 each)	$3,500
Variable selling expenses	630
Variable administrative expenses	350
Fixed selling expenses	420
Fixed administrative expenses	210
Direct labor	700
Direct materials	840
Fixed manufacturing overhead	70
Variable manufacturing overhead	42

1. Prepare a contribution margin income statement. Assume there were no beginning or ending inventories in 2009.
2. How much would Gordon Company have lost if only 70 units had been sold during 2009?

E 20-33

LO4

Analysis of a Contribution Margin Income Statement

Fill in the missing amounts for the following three cases. *Note:* There is no manufacturing overhead in this exercise.

	Case I	Case II	Case III
Sales revenue	$50,000	$60,000	$ (G)
Variable cost of goods sold:			
Direct materials	$12,500	$ (D)	$ 20,000
Direct labor	(A)	15,000	20,000
Variable selling and administrative costs	3,500	(E)	10,000
Contribution margin	$ (B)	$20,000	$ (H)
Fixed selling and administrative costs*	5,500	10,000	(I)
Rent expense on office building	(C)	5,000	2,000
Depreciation expense on delivery trucks	5,000	2,500	8,000
Profit	$ 4,000	$ (F)	$ 0
Gross margin	20,000	30,000	40,000

*Except rent and depreciation.

E 20-34

LO4

Analysis of the Contribution Margin

Dr. Hughes and Dr. Hawkins, owners of the Spanish Fork Care Clinic, have $350,000 of fixed costs per year. They receive 30,000 patient visits in a year, charging each patient an average of $25 per visit; variable costs average $3 per visit (needles, medicines, and so on).

1. What is the contribution margin per patient visit?
2. What is the total contribution margin per year?
3. What is the total pretax profit for a year?
4. Drs. Hughes and Hawkins can bring in another doctor at a salary of $100,000 per year. If this new doctor can handle 5,000 patient visits per year, should the new doctor be hired? (Assume no additional fixed costs will be incurred.)

E 20-35

LO4

Contribution Margin Analysis

Compute the missing amounts for the following independent cases. (Assume zero beginning and ending inventories.)

	Case I	Case II	Case III
Sales volume (units)	24,000	(E)	16,000
Sales price per unit	$10	$8	(I)
Variable costs (total)	(A)	$200,000	$100,000
Contribution margin (total)	(B)	(F)	$60,000
Contribution margin per unit (rounded)	$4	$3	(J)
Fixed costs (total)	(C)	(G)	(K)
Fixed costs per unit (rounded)	(D)	$2	(L)
Profit	$20,000	(H)	$40,000

E 20-36

LO4

Break-Even Point and Target Income

Detienne Company manufactures and sells one product for $10 per unit. The unit contribution margin is 30% of the sales price, and fixed costs total $90,000.

1. Using the equation approach, compute:
   a. The break-even point in sales dollars and units.
   b. The sales volume (in units) needed to generate a profit of $30,000.
   c. The break-even point (in units) if variable costs increase to 80% of the sales price and fixed costs increase to $100,000.
2. See if you can recompute the solutions to 1(a), 1(b), and 1(c) in one equation step using either the contribution margin ratio or the contribution margin dollars per unit.

E 20-37

LO4

Break-Even Point and Target Income

Steven Newman, Inc., estimates 2009 costs to be as follows:

Direct materials	$5 per unit
Direct labor	$8 per unit
Variable manufacturing overhead	$3 per unit
Variable selling and administrative expenses	$2 per unit
Fixed expenses	$80,000

1. Assuming that Newman will sell 55,000 units, what sales price per unit will be needed to achieve a $75,000 profit?
2. Assuming that Newman decides to sell its product for $23 per unit, determine the break-even sales volume in dollars and units.
3. Assuming that Newman decides to sell its product for $23 per unit, determine the number of units it must sell to generate a $100,000 profit.

E 20-38

LO5

Break-Even Point—Graphic Analysis

Using the graph below, answer the following questions:

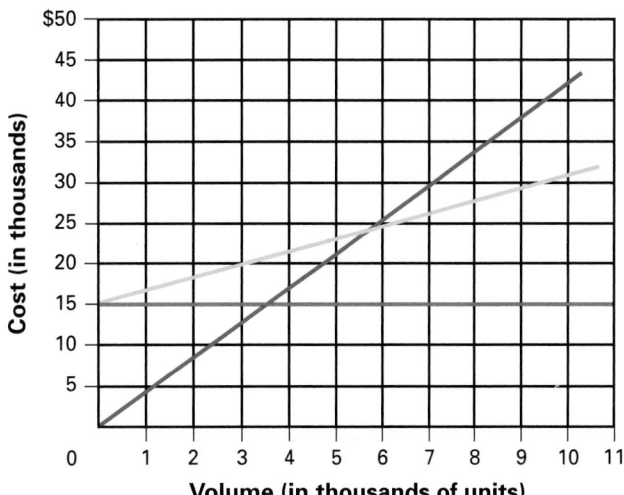

1. Copy the graph and identify (label) fixed costs, variable costs, total revenues, the total cost line, and the break-even point.
2. Determine the break-even point in both sales dollars and volume.
3. Suppose that as a manager you forecast sales volume at 7,000 units. At this level of sales, what would be your total fixed costs, approximate variable costs, and profit (or loss)?
4. At a sales volume of 3,000 units, what would be the level of fixed costs, variable costs, and approximate profit (or loss)?

E 20-39   **The Profit Graph**

LO5   Using the graph below, answer the following questions:

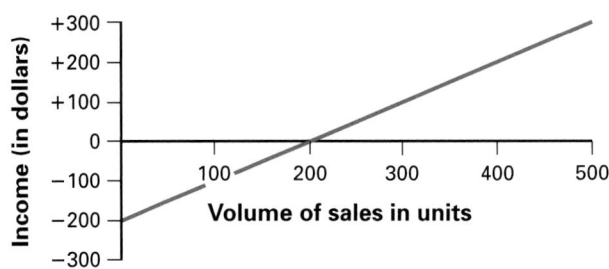

1. What is the break-even point in sales volume (in units)?
2. Approximately what volume of sales (in units) must this company have to generate an income of $300?
3. How much are the fixed costs?

E 20-40   **Graphing Revenues and Costs**

LO5   Montana Company manufactures chocolate candy. Its manufacturing costs are as follows:

Annual fixed costs	$15,000
Variable costs	$2 per box of candy

1. Plot variable costs, fixed costs, and total costs on a graph for activity levels of 0 to 30,000 boxes of candy.
2. Plot a revenue line on the graph, assuming that Montana sells the chocolates for $5 a box.

E 20-41   **C-V-P Analysis**

LO4   The Last Outpost is a tourist stop in a western resort community. Kerry Yost, the owner of the shop, sells hand-woven blankets for an average price of $30 per blanket. Kerry buys the blankets from weavers at an average cost of $21. In addition, he has selling expenses of $3 per blanket. Kerry rents the building for $300 per month and pays one employee a fixed salary of $500 per month.

1. Determine the number of blankets Kerry must sell to break even.
2. Determine the number of blankets Kerry must sell to generate a profit of $1,000 per month.
3. Assume that Kerry can produce and sell his own blankets at a total variable cost of $16 per blanket, but that he would need to hire one additional employee at a monthly salary of $600.
   a. Determine the number of blankets Kerry must sell to break even.
   b. Determine the number of blankets Kerry must sell to generate a profit of $1,000 per month.

E 20-42   **C-V-P Analysis–Changes in Variables**

LO4   Tracy, Inc., estimates that next year's results will be:

Sales revenue (75,000 units)	$ 900,000
Less variable costs	(375,000)
Less fixed costs	(300,000)
Profit	$ 225,000

Recompute profit, assuming each of the following independent conditions:
1. A 9% increase in the contribution margin.
2. An 8% increase in the sales volume.

(continued)

3. A 4% decrease in the sales volume.
4. A 6% increase in variable costs per unit.
5. A 5% decrease in fixed costs.
6. A 5% increase in fixed costs.
7. A 12% increase in the sales volume and a 6% increase in fixed costs.

E 20-43

LO4

C-V-P Analysis–Changes in Variables

Modern Fun Corporation sells electronic games. Its five salespersons are currently being paid fixed salaries of $30,000 each; however, the sales manager has suggested that it might be more profitable to pay the salespersons on a straight commission basis. He has suggested a commission of 15% of sales. Current data for Modern Fun Corporation are as follows:

Sales volume	20,000 units
Sales price	$40 per unit
Variable costs	$29 per unit
Fixed costs	$200,000

1. Assuming that Modern Fun Corporation has a target income of $50,000 for next year, which alternative is more attractive?
2. The sales manager believes that by switching to a commission basis, sales will increase 20%. What is the estimated profit under this assumption?

E 20-44

LO6

Sales Mix

Klein Brothers sells products X and Y. Because of the nature of the products, Klein sells two units of product X for each unit of product Y. Relevant information about the products is as follows:

	X	Y
Sales price per unit	$10	$30
Variable cost per unit	8	18

1. Assuming that Klein's fixed costs total $140,000, compute Klein's break-even point in sales dollars.
2. Assuming that Klein sells one unit of product X for each unit of product Y, and fixed costs remain at $140,000, compute Klein's break-even point in sales dollars.
3. Explain any differences in your answers to parts (1) and (2).

E 20-45

LO6

C-V-P Analysis

Mower Manufacturing's income statement for January 2009 is given below.

Sales (25,000 units × $25)	$625,000
Less variable costs	468,750
Contribution margin	$156,250
Less fixed costs	125,000
Profit	$ 31,250

1. Calculate the company's break-even point in sales dollars and units.
2. The company is contemplating the purchase of new production equipment that would reduce variable costs per unit to $16.25. However, fixed costs would increase to

(continued)

$175,000 per month. Assuming sales of 26,000 units next month, prepare an income statement for both the current and the proposed production methods. Calculate the break-even point (in dollars and units) for the new production method.

3. Comment on the difference (if any) in the break-even point for the new production method. What explains the difference in income at sales of 26,000 units between the two production methods?

E 20-46   **Operating Leverage**

LO7   Ludlam Company and Kassandra Company both make school desks. They have the same production capacity, but Ludlam is more automated than Kassandra. At an output of 2,500 desks per year, the two companies have the following costs:

	Ludlam	Kassandra
Fixed costs	$137,500	$ 37,500
Variable costs at $20 per desk	50,000	
Variable costs at $60 per desk		150,000
Total cost	$187,500	$187,500
Unit cost (2,500 desks)	$ 75	$ 75

Assuming that both companies sell desks for $100 each and that there are no other costs or expenses for the two firms, complete the following:

1. Which company will lose the least money if production and sales fall to 1,000 desks per year?

2. What would be each company's profit or loss at production and sales levels of 1,000 desks per year?

3. What would be each company's profit or loss at production and sales levels of 4,000 desks per year?

PROBLEMS

P 20-47   **Graphing Revenues and Costs**

LO5   Cloward and Hawkins, CPAs, took in $350,000 of gross revenues this year. Besides themselves, they have two professional staff (one manager and one senior) and a full-time secretary. Fixed operating expenses for the office were $50,000 last year. This year the volume of activity is up 5%, and fixed operating expenses are still $50,000. Total variable operating costs, except for bonuses, average $5 per billable hour. The billable time for all professionals is as follows:

Partners: 3,000 hours at $75/hour
Manager: 1,800 hours at $40/hour
Senior: 2,120 hours at $25/hour

Salaries for the professional staff are $40,000 and $28,000, respectively; the secretary is paid $18,000. The partners each draw salaries of $60,000; plus they share a 5% bonus based on gross revenues. The manager is given a 2% bonus, also based on gross revenues.

Required:

1. Plot the data on a graph clearly showing (a) fixed costs, (b) variable costs, (c) total costs, and (d) total revenues.

2. How much profit did the CPA firm make this year (after partners' salaries)?

P 20-48   **High-Low and Scattergraph Methods of Analysis**

LO3   Woodfield Company makes bed linens. During the first six months of 2009, Woodfield had the following production costs:

(continued)

Month	Units Produced	Total Costs
January	10,000	$ 68,000
February	20,000	100,000
March	15,000	90,000
April	8,000	52,000
May	17,000	94,000
June	12,000	74,000

Required:

1. Use the high-low method to compute the monthly fixed cost and the variable cost rate.
2. Plot the costs on a scattergraph.
3. **Interpretive Question:** Based on your scattergraph, do you think the fixed costs and the variable cost rate determined in part (1) are accurate? Why?

P 20-49

LO4

Contribution Margin Income Statement

Early in 2010, Lili H Company (a retailing firm) sent the following income statement to its stockholders:

Lili H Company

Income Statement

For the Year Ended December 31, 2009

Sales revenue (8,000 units)	$600,000	
Less cost of goods sold (variable)	450,000	
Gross margin		$150,000
Operating expenses:		
Selling	$ 60,000	
Administrative	40,000	
Depreciation (fixed)	10,000	
Insurance (fixed)	500	
Utilities ($200 fixed and $300 variable)	500	111,000
Profit		$ 39,000

Required:

1. Prepare a contribution margin income statement. (Assume that the fixed components of the selling expenses and administrative expenses are $20,000 and $20,000, respectively.)
2. **Interpretive Question:** Why is a contribution margin income statement helpful to management?
3. **Interpretive Question:** How would the analysis in part (1) be different if the depreciation expense was considered a stepped cost with wide steps compared to the relevant range?

P 20-50

LO4

Contribution Margin Income Statement

Susan Young is an attorney for a small law firm in Arizona. She is also a part-time inventor and an avid golfer. One day Susan's golf foursome included a man named Henry Jones, a manufacturer of Christmas ornaments. Henry explained to Susan that he manufactures an ornament everyone loves, but stores will not carry the ornaments because they are very fragile and often break during shipping. Susan told Henry about a plastic box she had developed recently that would protect such fragile items during shipping. After crash testing the plastic box, Henry offered Susan a contract to purchase 100,000 of the boxes for $2.20 each. Susan is convinced that the box has many applications and that she can obtain future orders. Production of the plastic boxes will take one year. Estimated costs for the first year are as follows:

(continued)

Lease payments on building	$800 per month
Lease payments on machine	$2,200 per month
Cost to retool machine	$10,000
Depreciation on machine	$9,600
Direct materials	$0.70 per box
Direct labor	$0.30 per box
Indirect materials and other manufacturing overhead	$0.10 per box
Interest on loan	$2,500
Administrative salaries	$15,000

Required:
1. Using the information provided, determine Susan's contribution margin and projected profit at a sales level of 100,000 boxes.
2. If Susan's salary as an attorney is $44,500, determine how many boxes Susan must sell to earn profits equal to her salary.

P 20-51 **Functional and Contribution Margin Income Statements**

LO4 Bassically Jammin', Inc. (BJI) is a retail outlet for customized bass guitars. The average cost of a bass guitar to the company is $1,000. BJI includes a markup of 50% of cost in the sales price. In 2009, BJI sold 380 bass guitars and finished the year with the same amount of inventory it had at the beginning of the year. Additional operating costs for the year were as follows:

Selling expenses:
Advertising (fixed)	$ 700 per month
Commissions (mixed)	3,000 per month plus 2% of sales
Depreciation (fixed)	400 per month
Utilities (fixed)	125 per month
Freight on delivery (variable)	20 per bass guitar

Administrative expenses:
Salaries (fixed)	$4,200 per month
Depreciation (fixed)	330 per month
Utilities (fixed)	200 per month
Clerical (variable)	12 per sale

Required:
1. Prepare a traditional income statement using the functional approach.
2. Prepare an income statement using the contribution margin format.
3. **Interpretive Question:** Which statement is more useful for decision making? Why?

P 20-52 **Contribution Margin and Functional Income Statements**

LO4 The following information is available for Dabney Company for 2009:

Sales revenue (at $20 per unit)	$151,200
Fixed manufacturing costs	24,000
Variable manufacturing costs (at $8 per unit)	60,480
Fixed selling expenses	70,000
Variable selling expenses (at $2 per unit)	15,120

Required:
1. Prepare a contribution margin income statement.
2. Prepare a functional income statement.
3. Calculate the number of units sold.
4. Calculate the contribution margin per unit.
5. **Interpretive Question:** Why is a knowledge of the contribution margin more useful than a knowledge of the markup per unit when management has to make a decision about profitability?

P 20-53

LO3, LO4

Unifying Concepts: High-Low Method, Contribution Margins, and Analysis

Press Publishing Corporation has two major magazines: *Star Life* and *Weekly News*. During 2009, *Star Life* sold 3 million copies at $1.00 each, and *Weekly News* sold 2.1 million copies at $1.10 each. Press Publishing accumulated the following cost information:

	Star Life		Weekly News	
Month	Copies Produced	Manufacturing Cost	Copies Produced	Manufacturing Cost
January	400,000	$170,000	300,000	$170,000
February	300,000	150,000	150,000	105,000
March	400,000	180,000	130,000	100,000
April	200,000	120,000	120,000	90,000
May	250,000	140,000	200,000	130,000
June	200,000	125,000	250,000	150,000
July	240,000	130,000	150,000	110,000
August	200,000	130,000	200,000	135,000
September	180,000	110,000	150,000	105,000
October	230,000	130,000	150,000	108,000
November	200,000	125,000	150,000	115,000
December	200,000	126,000	150,000	112,500

Required:

1. Use the high-low method to estimate the per-unit variable and total fixed manufacturing costs of each magazine. (Round the variable cost rate to three decimal places.)
2. If all selling expenses are fixed and they total $500,000 for *Star Life* and $400,000 for *Weekly News*, prepare contribution margin income statements for the two magazines at sales of 3 million copies each.
3. Which magazine is more profitable at sales of 2 million copies?
4. **Interpretive Question:** If the same total dollar amount spent on either magazine will result in the same number of new subscriptions, which magazine should be advertised?

P 20-54

LO4

Contribution Margin Analysis

Clearview Company is a manufacturer of blown glass vases. The following information pertains to Clearview's 2009 sales:

Sales price per unit	$ 65
Variable costs per unit	52
Total fixed costs	500,000

Required:

1. Determine Clearview Company's per-unit contribution margin and contribution margin ratio.
2. Using the per-unit contribution margin and the contribution margin ratio, compute:
   a. The break-even point in sales dollars and units.
   b. The sales volume (in dollars and units) needed to generate a target income of $75,000.
3. Using the equation approach of C-V-P analysis, compute:
   a. The break-even point in sales dollars and units.
   b. The sales volume (in dollars and units) needed to generate a 15% return on sales.

P 20-55

LO4

Break-Even Analysis

Jane Tamlyn paid $225 to rent a carnival booth for four days. She has to decide whether to sell doughnuts or popcorn. Doughnuts cost $1.80 per dozen and can be sold for $3.60 per dozen. Popcorn will require a $113 rental fee for the popcorn maker and $0.08 per bag of popcorn for the popcorn, butter, salt, and bags; a bag of popcorn could sell for $0.45.

(continued)

Required:

1. Compute the break-even point in dozens of doughnuts if Jane decides to sell doughnuts exclusively and the break-even point in bags of popcorn if she decides to sell popcorn exclusively.
2. Jane estimates that she can sell either 75 doughnuts or 45 bags of popcorn every hour the carnival is open (10 hours a day for four days). Which product should she sell?
3. Jane can sell back to the baker at half cost any doughnuts she fails to sell at the carnival. Unused popcorn must be thrown away. If Jane sells only 70% of her original estimate, which product should she sell? (Assume that she bought or produced just enough to satisfy the demands she originally estimated.)

P 20-56   **Graphic Analysis**

LO5   Using the graph below, complete the requirements.

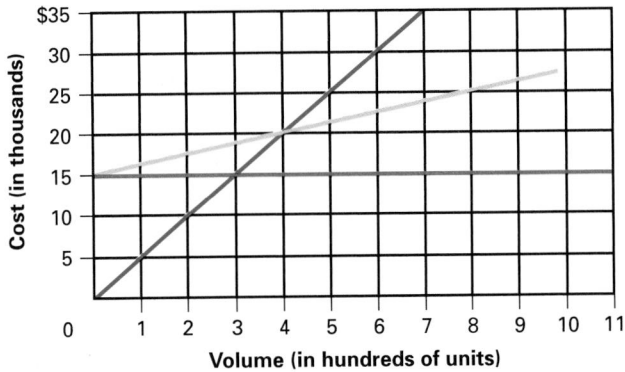

Required:

1. Determine the following:
   a. The break-even point in sales dollars and volume.
   b. The sales price per unit.
   c. Total fixed costs.
   d. Total variable costs at the break-even point.
   e. The variable cost per unit.
   f. The unit contribution margin.
2. What volume of sales must the company generate to reach a target income of $7,500?

P 20-57   **Contribution Margin Analysis–Changes in Variables**

LO4   SMC, Inc., is a producer of hand-held electronic games. Its 2009 income statement was as follows:

SMC, Inc.		
Contribution Margin Income Statement		
For the Year Ended December 31, 2009		
	Total	**Per Unit**
Sales revenue (150,000 games)	$5,250,000	$35
Less variable costs	3,750,000	25
Contribution margin	$1,500,000	$10
Less fixed costs	900,000	
Profit	$ 600,000	

In preparing its budget for 2010, SMC is evaluating the effects of changes in costs, prices, and volume on profit.

(continued)

Required:

1. Evaluate the following independent cases, and determine SMC's 2010 budgeted profit or loss in each case. (Assume that 2009 figures apply unless stated otherwise.)
   a. Fixed costs increase $150,000.
   b. Fixed costs decrease $100,000.
   c. Variable costs increase $3 per unit.
   d. Variable costs decrease $4 per unit.
   e. Sales price increases $5 per unit.
   f. Sales price decreases $5 per unit.
   g. Sales volume increases 25,000 units.
   h. Sales volume decreases 15,000 units.
   i. Sales price decreases $4 per unit, sales volume increases 40,000 units, and variable costs decrease by $2.50 per unit.
   j. Fixed costs decrease by $100,000, and variable costs increase $4 per unit.
   k. Sales volume increases 30,000 units, with a decrease in sales price of $2 per unit. Variable costs drop $1.50 per unit, and fixed costs increase $50,000.

2. What sales volume in units would be needed to realize $1,000,000 in profit if SMC reduces its price to $30?

P 20-58

LO4

Income Statement and Break-Even Analysis

Zimmerman Company records the following costs associated with the production and sale of a steel slingshot:

Selling expenses:	
Fixed	$20,000
Variable	$0.50 per unit sold
Administrative expenses:	
Fixed	$4,500
Variable	$0.25 per unit sold
Manufacturing costs:	
Fixed	$35,000
Variable	$7.50 per unit produced

Required:

Assume that in 2009 the beginning and ending inventories were the same. Also assume that 2009 sales were 25,000 units at $11 per slingshot.

1. Prepare a contribution margin income statement.
2. Determine the break-even point in sales dollars.
3. **Interpretive Question:** Zimmerman believes that sales volume could be improved 20% if an additional commission of $0.50 per unit were paid to the salespeople. Zimmerman also believes, however, that the same percentage increase could be achieved through an increase of $3,000 in annual advertising expense. Which action, if either, should Zimmerman take? Why?

P 20-59

LO4

C-V-P Analysis–Changes in Variables

Wonder T Manufacturing Company produces lanterns. The firm has not been as profitable as expected in the past three years. As a result, it has excess capacity that could be used to produce an additional 20,000 lanterns per year. However, any production above that amount would require a capital investment of $100,000. Operating results for the previous year are shown here. Assume that there is never any ending inventory.

Sales revenue (31,250 lanterns × $40)		$1,250,000
Variable costs (31,250 lanterns × $25)	$781,250	
Fixed costs	400,000	1,181,250
Profit		$ 68,750

(continued)

Required:

Respond to the following independent proposals, and support your recommendations:

1. The production manager believes that profits could be increased through the purchase of more automated production machinery, which would increase fixed costs by $100,000 and reduce the variable costs by $2.00 per lantern. Is she correct if sales are to remain at 31,250 lanterns annually?

2. The sales manager believes that a 10% discount on the sales price would increase the sales volume to 40,000 units annually. If he is correct, would this action increase or decrease profits?

3. Would the implementation of both proposals be worthwhile?

4. The sales manager believes that an increase in sales commissions could improve the sales volume. In particular, he suggests that an increase of $2.50 per lantern would increase the sales volume 30%. If he is correct, would this action increase profits?

5. The accountant suggests another alternative: Reduce administrative salaries by $15,000 so that prices can be reduced by $0.50 per unit. She believes that this action would increase the volume to 35,000 units annually. If she is correct, would this action increase profits?

6. The corporate executives finally decide to spend an additional $42,000 on advertising to bring the sales volume up to 34,050 units. If the increased advertising can bring in these extra sales, is this a good decision?

P 20-60   **C-V-P Analysis–Return on Sales**

LO4   The federal government recently placed a ceiling on the selling price of sheet metal produced by MOB Company. In 2009, MOB was limited to charging a price that would earn a 20% return on gross sales. On the basis of this restriction, MOB had the following results for 2009:

Sales revenue (1,150,000 feet at $2.00 per foot)		$2,300,000
Variable costs (1,150,000 feet × $1.40)	$1,610,000	
Fixed costs	230,000	1,840,000
Profit		$ 460,000

In 2010, MOB predicted that the sales volume would decrease to 900,000 feet of sheet metal. With this level of sales, however, the company anticipated no changes in the levels of fixed and variable costs.

Required:

1. Determine MOB's profit for 2010 if all forecasts are realized. Compute both the dollar amount of profit and the percentage return on sales.

2. MOB plans to petition the government for a price increase so that the 2009 rate of return on sales (20%) can be maintained. What sales price should the company request, based on 2010 projections? (Round to the nearest cent.)

3. How much profit (in dollars) will MOB earn in 2010 if this sales price, as determined in part (2), is approved?

4. **Interpretive Question:** What other factors must be considered by MOB and the government?

P 20-61

LO4

Unifying Concepts: C-V-P Analysis and Changes in Variables

The 2009 pro-forma income statement for Grover Company is as follows (ignore taxes):

Grover Company

Pro-Forma Income Statement

For the Year Ended December 31, 2009

Sales (20,000 units)		$170,000
Cost of goods sold:		
Direct materials	$16,000	
Direct labor	27,000	
Variable manufacturing overhead	6,000	
Fixed manufacturing overhead	2,000	
Total cost of goods sold		51,000
Gross margin		$119,000
Selling expenses:		
Variable	$20,000	
Fixed	45,000	
Administrative expenses:		
Variable	8,000	
Fixed	32,000	
Total selling and administrative expenses		105,000
Profit		$ 14,000

Required:

1. Compute how many units must be sold to break even.
2. Compute the increase (decrease) in profit under the following independent situations:
   a. Sales increase 25%.
   b. Fixed selling and administrative expenses decrease 5%.
   c. Contribution margin decreases 20%.
3. Compute sales in units and dollars at the break-even point if fixed costs increase from $79,000 to $85,000.
4. Compute the number of units that must be sold if expected profit is $1 million.

P 20-62

LO6

Unifying Concepts: High-Low and Scattergraph Methods

You have been hired as a consultant for Jones Inc. The company manufactures high-density compact disks and sells them to a wide variety of business clients. Management is eager to learn more about the company's cost behavior. You have been provided the following data. Assume all production falls within the relevant range.

Month	Machine Hours	Utility Costs
January	290	$10,700
February	280	10,400
March	320	11,600
April	340	12,100
May	350	12,400
June	290	10,750
July	300	10,800
August	300	10,900
September	310	11,200
October	340	12,200
November	290	10,600
December	310	11,000

(continued)

Required:

1. Using the high-low method, compute the variable and fixed elements of Jones' utility costs.
2. Plot the information on a scattergraph. Based on your graph, determine the unit variable cost and monthly fixed costs.
3. **Interpretive Question:** Why are the variable cost per unit and fixed costs different for each of these methods of analysis? Which method is the most accurate for determining variable and fixed cost components?

P 20-63 **Sales Mix**

LO6

Mike's Ice Cream Company produces and sells ice cream in three sizes: quart, half-gallon, and gallon. Relevant information for each of the sizes is as follows:

	Quart	Half-Gallon	Gallon
Average sales price	$1.00	$1.85	$3.60
Less variable cost	0.80	1.40	2.40
Unit contribution margin	$0.20	$0.45	$1.20
Sales mix (% of sales UNITS)	15%	60%	25%

Mike anticipates sales of $500,000 and fixed costs of $120,000 in 2009.

Required:

1. Determine the break-even sales volume in units and dollars for 2009.
2. Determine Mike's 2009 projected profit.
3. Assume that Mike's sales mix changes to 10% quarts, 40% half-gallons, and 50% gallons. Determine Mike's break-even sales volume in units and dollars.

P 20-64 **Unifying Concepts: Break-Even Point and Operating Leverage**

LO4, LO7

The following summary data are provided for Spencer Mercantile Corporation and James Service, Inc. During the year for which these data are reported, Spencer sold 50,000 units and James sold 100,000 units.

(000's omitted)	Spencer Mercantile Corporation	James Service, Inc.
Sales revenue	$1,040	$2,100
Less variable costs	520	630
Contribution margin	$ 520	$1,470
Less fixed costs	200	600
Income	$ 320	$ 870

Required:

1. Determine the break-even point for Spencer and James in both sales dollars and units.
2. **Interpretive Question:** Which company has a higher operating leverage? Why?
3. **Interpretive Question:** Based on your analysis of the cost structures of Spencer and James, which company's cost structure is better? What factors are important to consider in answering such a question?

ANALYTICAL ASSIGNMENTS

AA 20-65

DISCUSSION

Colorado Outdoors Federation

The Colorado Outdoors Federation sponsors an annual banquet. This year the guest speaker is a noted wildlife photographer and lecturer. In planning for the event, the group's treasurer has determined the following costs:

Rental of meeting facility	$1,250
Honorarium for speaker	800
Tickets and advertising	300
Cost of dinner (per person)	20
Door prizes	800

Last year, tickets were sold at $25 per person, and 350 people attended the banquet. This year the planning committee is hoping for an attendance of 450 at a price of $30 each.

1. a. At $30 per person, how many people must attend the banquet for the Federation to break even?
   b. How much profit (loss) will occur if 450 people attend?
2. Should the Federation increase its advertising costs by $200 and its door prizes by $300 if it can expect 500 people to attend the banquet?
3. If the Federation maintains its original expected costs but reduces the price per ticket from $30 to $27, it can expect 500 people to attend the banquet. Should the Federation reduce the price of its tickets to $27 per person?

AA 20-66

DISCUSSION

Entertainment Enterprises

Entertainment Enterprises, a firm that sells magazine subscriptions, is experiencing increased competition from a number of companies. The president, Betty Kincher, has asked you, the controller, to prepare an income statement that will highlight the fixed and variable costs; this will provide more useful information for planning and control purposes. Sales revenues are $25 per subscription. An analysis of company costs for the past six months reveals the following:

Administrative salaries	$10,000 per month
Advertising expense	$2,000 per month
Cost of goods sold	$12.50 per subscription
Rent expense	$5,000 per month
Sales commissions	15% of sales

In addition, the company makes most sales contacts through an extensive telephone network. Consequently, the telephone expense is significant and has both fixed and variable components. Relevant data concerning the telephone expense for the past six months follow:

Month	Unit Sales	Telephone Expense
July	4,000	$10,200
August	5,000	12,300
September	3,500	9,150
October	4,500	11,250
November	5,200	12,720
December	5,500	13,350

Prepare a management report for the president that:
1. Computes the fixed and variable portions of the telephone expense using the high-low method. (*Note:* A scattergraph may be used to visually check your answer.)

(continued)

2. Presents a budgeted (pro-forma) contribution margin income statement for Entertainment Enterprises for the next six months (January through June), assuming that it expects to sell 30,000 subscriptions at a price of $25 each.

3. Explains how the information provided in part (2) might help the president make better management decisions.

AA 20-67
JUDGMENT CALL

You Decide: **Should the management of a company consider fixed costs in the decision-making process, or should they ignore fixed costs and base their decision on what makes the most business sense?**

Recently, the board of directors for a television manufacturing company was considering a change in products from TVs to computers. The board claims, after performing a C-V-P analysis of a new computer manufacturing plant facility, that the computer industry is more profitable and would increase the bottom line immediately. However, just six months earlier, the company built a state-of-the-art television manufacturing plant. The overhead costs on the television plant represent a sizable portion of the company's fixed costs. If the board voted to begin computer manufacturing, a new plant would need to be constructed. What should the board do?

AA 20-68
JUDGMENT CALL

You Decide: **Should companies have large amounts of inventory on hand for customers, or should companies keep inventory at a minimum to free up cash for other parts of the business?**

Your uncle, Tim, started a very successful "home improvement" business 10 years ago. He wanted to create a place where people could go to get anything they needed to complete their "do-it-yourself" home building projects. Coupled with excellent service, Tim believes that he can gain and retain customers by having a large assortment of inventory from which to choose. In addition, he can obtain significant purchase discounts by buying the inventory in large bulk. You argue that maintaining amounts of inventory requires significant commitments to fixed warehousing and other costs that could be avoided by setting up an e-commerce Web site and taking customer orders that are then acquired and delivered one customer at a time. Although this approach will increase the overall variable costs as a result of not receiving bulk discounts on the smaller individual orders, you are able to demonstrate with C-V-P analysis that there is less risk in your approach to selling home improvement products. Your uncle strongly argues that, "Having the inventory on hand for your customers is the key to success. If I don't have what they are looking for, they will just go down the street to **Home Depot**! I have got to have inventory in the stores. There is no other way!"

AA 20-69
REAL COMPANY ANALYSIS

Microsoft

Annual revenues, as well as sales and marketing expenses, for the 1991–2002 years are provided below for **Microsoft Corporation:**

	Microsoft Corporation (millions)	
Year	**Sales and Marketing Expenses**	**Annual Revenue**
1991	$ 490	$ 1,847
1992	758	2,777
1993	1,086	3,786
1994	1,135	4,714
1995	1,564	6,075
1996	2,185	9,050
1997	2,411	11,936
1998	2,887	15,262
1999	3,238	19,747
2000	4,126	22,956
2001	4,885	25,296
2002	5,407	28,365

(continued)

1. Operating output data, such as the number of software products sold each year, are not provided in Microsoft's Form 10-K. However, while it is a little odd to use revenues to predict marketing expense (instead of the other way around), it seems sensible that changes in revenues can serve as an approximate measure of changes in the number of products sold by Microsoft. Use the high-low method to analyze the data above to determine if there is a relationship between revenues and sales and marketing expenses. (*Hint:* Don't round off the value you calculate for variable costs per revenue dollar.) What appears to be the amount of fixed costs in these expenses? Does this fixed cost amount make sense? (*Note:* Remember that the data are in millions of dollars!)

2. The Management's Discussion in Microsoft's 2002 Form 10-K generally uses the following language to describe changes to sales and marketing expenses: "Sales and marketing expenses increased due to higher relative headcount-related costs, higher marketing and sales expenses associated with MSN (Microsoft's popular portal destination on the Web), the Microsoft Agility advertising campaign, and other new sales initiatives." Does this statement provide any help in understanding the analysis?

AA 20-70
REAL COMPANY
ANALYSIS

Star Video

It is likely that a number of grocery stores in your town have video rental departments. Generally, however, grocery stores do not focus much management attention on their small video rental businesses. The main purpose of having a video department is to encourage more customers to come into the store and purchase groceries! Nevertheless, a grocery store cannot simply buy a large selection of videotapes, corner off a section of floor space, and start renting tapes. Successfully managing a rental business requires being aware of an unimaginably large number of video titles. Obviously, new movies are constantly being released, while old movies gradually lose their appeal and are eventually scrapped. Further, large-scale video rental chains such as **Blockbuster** constantly track shifting consumer tastes for certain titles and movie categories. These consumer preferences differ based on demographic data like geographic location, average age, ethnicity, average income, etc. A grocery store really can't manage all these data without losing focus on its main business. Hence, most grocery stores contract out their video rental business to a large-scale video management company. These management companies can purchase huge quantities of tapes, maintain large distribution warehouses, and track demographic data that allow them to manage and move specific inventories to the appropriate grocery store locations. In 1992, one such video management company, Star Video (not its real name), was managing 86 stores representing three supermarket chains in five states—Arizona, California, Montana, Washington, and Wyoming. Total revenue in 1992 for Star Video was $3.6 million. Star Video made all the inventory investments and handled all management activities involved in providing video rentals at each of the 86 stores. Video rental revenue was then split between Star Video and each grocery store, with Star Video keeping the lion's share. Stores liked this arrangement because they made most of their money on grocery sales to customers who came to rent videotapes. Star Video needed to carefully manage revenue and costs at each store in order to stay profitable. Following are the data for six stores located in Washington:

Store Name	Monthly Revenue	Monthly Operating Expenses
Moses Lake	$ 6,408	$ 3,295
W. Kennewick	4,264	2,289
Pasco	4,038	2,270
S. Kennewick	3,692	2,142
E. Wenatchee	1,395	1,316
Richland	2,104	1,516
Total	$21,901	$12,828

(continued)

Use the high-low method to analyze the operating expenses at these six stores. Determine if operating expenses are related to store revenue. What appear to be the fixed costs of operating each store? Create a graph and plot these costs using revenue on the horizontal axis and operating expenses on the vertical axis. Does the scattergraph agree or disagree with the results of your high-low analysis?

AA 20-71

INTERNATIONAL

The Paper Company

The **Ghanata Group of Companies (GGC)** is a locally owned and controlled company in Ghana, West Africa. One of its principal operating divisions, **The Paper Company**, is one of Africa's most modern and largest manufacturers/distributors of paper products. For both operating and reporting purposes, The Paper Company is organized into product lines: scholastic, envelope, and stationery. During the 1980s, the economy in Ghana was stagnant. The country faced severe economic problems as a result of unfavorable trade terms with other countries. The official exchange rate of U.S. $1.00 to the local currency, the cedi, was about 39.00 as of the end of 1984. (The unofficial rate, e.g., the black market rate, was at least five times worse!) As a result of the economy, it became very difficult for GGC to secure direct materials for its divisions. If a division could secure direct materials, it could sell almost everything it produced. Hence, in terms of being able to predict sales volumes, there was a great deal of risk for GGC divisions. The 1985 budgeted operating data for the three departments in The Paper Company were as follows:

The Paper Company 1985 Budgeted Operations Data (*Cedi* 000's)			
	Scholastic	**Envelope**	**Stationery**
Budgeted sales	$ 1,785,000	$ 984,000	$ 3,334,050
Budgeted variable costs	(410,550)	(442,800)	(2,200,473)
Contribution margin	$ 1,374,450	$ 541,200	$ 1,133,577
Budgeted fixed costs	(1,267,350)	(482,160)	(933,534)
Income	$ 107,100	$ 59,040	$ 200,043

Using these operating data, create C-V-P graphs for each department. (*Note:* Since you don't have per-unit prices and costs, you may assume that the product sales price for each department is $1 per unit, and then plot your graphs at 0, 2 million, and 4 million units.) Given the high-risk business environment in Ghana at this time, which department presents the highest risk to GGC? The lowest risk? Be sure to explain your answer in terms of operating leverage. You may also want to consider each department's break-even point compared to budgeted (expected) operations.

Source: A. Oppong, "The Paper Company," *The Journal of Accounting Case Research*, Vol. 3, No. 2 (1996), pp. 80–88. Permission to use has been granted by Captus Press, Inc. and the Accounting Education Resource Centre of The University of Lethbridge. [Journal Subscription: Captus Press, Inc., York University Campus, 4700 Keele Street, North York, Ontario, M3J 1P3, by calling (416) 736-5537, or by fax at (416) 736-5793, E-mail: info **http://www.captus.com**]

AA 20-72

ETHICS

Pickmore International

Joan Hildabrand is analyzing some cost data for her boss, Ross Cumings. The data relate to a special sales order that Pickmore International is considering from a large customer in Singapore. The following data are applicable to the product being ordered:

Normal unit sales price	$49.95
Variable unit manufacturing costs	10.50
Variable unit selling and administrative expenses	18.25

(continued)

The customer is requesting that the sales order be accepted on the following terms:

a. The unit sales price would equal the normal unit contribution margin plus 10%.

b. Freight would be paid by the customer.

c. Pickmore International would pay a $5,000 "facilitating payment" to a "friend of the customer" to get the product through customs more quickly.

In considering the order, Ross has indicated to Joan that this is a very important customer. Furthermore, this work would help some employees earn a little extra Christmas money with overtime.

1. What are the accounting and ethical issues involved in this case?

2. Should Joan recommend acceptance of the sales terms proposed for this special order?

AA 20-73

WRITING

Issues of Quality and Time on C-V-P Analysis Decisions

This chapter described how to analyze whether the difference between sales price and variable costs, as well as the volume of sales, is sufficient to pay for all fixed costs in an organization and provide a sufficient profit. A number of methods have been presented for analyzing these costs, volume, and price relationships. These methods all focus on *quantitative* issues that affect how a company manages its resources to maximize overall profits. However, there are a number of *qualitative* issues involving quality and time that should also affect decisions about what sales prices to set, how to manage fixed and variable costs, and which products should be emphasized within the organization. One way to trade off fixed costs for variable costs is to consider making large fixed cost investments in technology that result in automated production, merchandising, and service processes. These kinds of investments allow some variable costs, such as direct labor, to be reduced. Managing this cost trade-off often has strong implications on the quality of the product or service, as well as the timeliness with which it can be delivered. Both of these qualitative issues eventually affect the quantitative issues of costs, volume, and price. Go to your library and find an article describing one organization's effort to invest in automation or other technologies in order to reduce costs. Determine what quality and time issues are affected by the investment. Write a one- to two-page memo describing what you found.

Budgeting, Control, and C-V-P Analysis

Livingston, Padden, & Company (LPC) makes specialized compact discs that are used for high-density data storage. LPC forecasts an increase of 300 units per month in sales for the first two quarters of the year. The following data are available for the company:

Expected sales in units:	
January	3,200 discs
February.	3,500 discs
March	3,800 discs
April.	4,100 discs
Selling price	$9.00 per disc
Beginning accounts receivable balance, January 1	$9,500.00
Beginning direct materials inventory, January 1	1,500 ounces*
Beginning finished goods inventory, January 1	600 discs*
Desired direct materials inventory, March 31	2,050 ounces
Desired finished goods inventory, March 31.	820 discs
Standard direct materials needed per disc.	5 ounces
Standard direct labor time per finished product	6 minutes
Standard direct materials cost per ounce.	$0.40
Standard direct labor cost per hour	$20.00

*The beginning inventory numbers for January were based on the best estimate of January sales in December. The expectations changed in January, and the new expected sales numbers should be used to estimate beginning inventory on hand for February and March.

Additional information:

- Of a month's sales, 60% is collected by month-end; the remaining 40% is collected the following month.
- The desired finished goods inventory each month is 20% of the next month's sales.
- The desired direct materials inventory every month is 10% of next month's production needs.

Required:

1. Using the standard costs for making the discs, prepare the following:
   a. Sales budgets for January, February, and March (in dollars).
   b. Cash collections budgets for January, February, and March (in dollars). Assume that all sales are on credit.
   c. Production budgets for January, February, and March (in units).
   d. Direct materials usage budgets for January, February, and March (in ounces).
   e. Direct materials purchases budgets for January, February, and March (in ounces).
   f. Direct labor budgets for January, February, and March (in dollars).
2. Assume that actual usage of direct materials to make the discs was 4½ ounces at a cost of $0.50 per ounce. Compute the materials price and quantity variances for each month (compute the quantity variance based on the amount of direct materials used).
3. Assume that actual labor costs to make the discs were 5 minutes of labor at a cost of $22 per hour. Compute labor rate and efficiency variances for each month. (*Note:* round calculations to the nearest whole dollar.)

4. Assume that Gonzales is able to make the discs at the standard costs for materials and labor and that the standard fixed costs per month are $15,000 (there are no variable overhead costs). How many compact disks (CDs) will Gonzales need to sell each month in order to break even? If Gonzales raised its price per CD from $9 to $10, how many CDs will need to be sold in order to break even?

5. Assuming again that Gonzales is able to make the discs at its standard costs, if sales decrease by 500 discs during the three months at the increased price of $10 per disc, should Gonzales raise its price?

Relevant Information and Decisions

After studying this chapter, you should be able to:

(1) Understand the concepts of sunk costs and differential costs and revenues, and be able to identify those costs and revenues that are relevant to making product and process decisions. *Differential costs are future costs that will change as a result of a decision. Differential costs may be variable, fixed, or both. Past costs and future costs that do not change as a result of a decision are not relevant to the decision and are called sunk costs.*

(2) Decide whether to accept or reject a special order. *In deciding whether or not to accept a special order in situations where there is excess capacity, the price should be high enough to provide a positive contribution toward covering normal fixed costs and increasing profit.*

(3) Determine whether a company should make a product itself or whether it should outsource the production to a supplier. *In choosing whether to make or buy a component or service, management must compare the differential costs of making the part or providing the service (including the opportunity cost of alternative uses of the facilities or labor) with the cost of purchasing the part or service.*

(4) Identify when a company should drop a product line or exit or enter a market. *A product or product line should not be dropped or a market exited unless that unit does not make a positive contribution toward covering indirect fixed costs or an alternative product or line of products can be added that will contribute more toward covering indirect fixed costs. Similarly, a market should be entered only if it contributes to the overall profitability of the firm.*

(5) Determine whether to sell a joint product as it is or to process it further before selling it. *It will always be profitable to continue processing a joint product after the split-off point as long as the incremental revenue from the extra processing exceeds the incremental processing costs incurred after the split-off point. Joint costs that have been incurred up to the point of split-off are always irrelevant to the decision.*

(6) Select the best use of a scarce resource. *In deciding how to use a scarce resource, management should choose the item that provides the greatest contribution margin per unit of the most critical input resource.*

(7) Use cost information in setting normal selling prices. *For normal pricing, management should consider all costs, not just differential costs.*

Consider the following three scenarios:

- You are the general manager of a professional basketball team. You have decided to keep a player on your team who has a multi-year, multi-million dollar salary contract even though the player is not playing well. To make room for this fading star, you cut a young, promising, inexpensive player. You make this decision because of the high committed cost of the veteran player who will have to be paid whether or not he is cut. You also instruct the coach to give the veteran player more time on the court to justify the high salary he is being paid.
- You and your family have driven halfway to a mountain resort. Responding to a reduced-rate advertisement, you have previously made a nonrefundable $500 deposit to spend the weekend at the resort, which is at an elevation of 10,000 feet. Every member of the family is starting to get headaches and is feeling nauseous; you suspect this is because of mild altitude sickness. You say it's too bad that you have already paid for the room because you all would much rather spend the time at home; however, you can't afford to waste $500. Everyone agrees.
- You are a theater aficionado and have traveled to New York City for the express purpose of watching as many Broadway plays as possible. On your first night in town, you realize upon arrival at the theater that you've lost your ticket which cost $100. You check in your wallet, and you do have another $100 with which you can replace the ticket. Instead, you decide to go back to your hotel and watch TV because you believe that although the play is worth seeing for $100, it is not worth seeing for $200.

In each of these cases, you are making irrational decisions because you are not recognizing past costs as sunk costs. No matter how much a player is being paid, it is the future performance you should be interested in as long as you can afford to pay the young, promising player. The past contract that was signed with the veteran player is irrelevant because that contract amount must be paid whether you keep the veteran player or not. Similarly, the $500 you and your family spent to reserve the weekend at the resort is irrelevant. The $500 is a sunk cost, and you should do what will benefit you the most in the future. Similarly, in the Broadway play example, the lost ticket and the $100 you paid for it are irrelevant. The new cost of seeing the play is $100, not $200, and to sit around in your hotel room watching TV because you bought and lost a ticket is irrational.

The legendary country music singing star Kenny Rogers once sang, "You gotta know when to hold 'em and know when to fold 'em . . ." A singing accountant would add, "Once you fold 'em, forget 'em." In each of the three opening scenarios, you should have "folded" or "forgotten" the past costs and not considered them in the decision process. When individuals don't understand the relevance or irrelevance of various costs in decision making, they make bad decisions. It doesn't matter whether you are a family making a decision to spend the weekend in a resort, or a business making a major, multi-million dollar decision.

In this chapter, we will consider several types of business decisions that are routinely made by business managers. If you become skilled in differentiating between differential costs, sunk costs, and opportunity costs, you will be a much better business decision maker.

Differential Costs, Sunk Costs, and Decision Making

① In order to make good decisions, organizations must understand the nature of their costs and how those costs will change in the future based on actions taken. Earlier in Chapter 15 and in the opening scenario to this chapter, you were introduced to cost concepts that are critical for making future decisions. To help you remember these cost concepts, consider the following definitions of three cost terms:

- **Sunk cost**: A cost that has already been incurred or a future cost that cannot be avoided, regardless of what a manager decides to do. These costs are always the same, no matter what alternatives are being considered and are, therefore, always irrelevant to a decision.
- **Differential cost**: A cost that differs between alternatives. These costs are sometimes referred to as avoidable or incremental costs. Because differential costs differ between alternatives, they are always relevant for decision making. Differential costs can be eliminated in whole or in part by choosing one alternative over another.
- **Opportunity cost**: The maximum available contribution to profit foregone (or passed up) by using limited resources for a particular purpose. For example, part of the cost of choosing to sell a particular product is the profit you could have made using the same resources to sell a different product. Opportunity costs are always relevant for decision making.

Evaluation of products and processes usually leads to consideration of alternative courses of action. For example, the evaluation of a particular product may lead a company to believe that it must expand capacity, outsource production, or even drop the product in favor of an alternative product. It may also result in the company deciding to buy a competitor. In this chapter we provide examples of how products and processes are evaluated to make better decisions. These concepts are probably best understood by examining examples of decisions to change, add, or drop products or processes. Before you can understand how evaluation can lead to better product and process decisions, however, a framework is necessary. In making decisions about products and processes, the costs and revenues that are different for, and hence relevant to, various alternative courses of action must be identified. You must be able to distinguish among sunk costs, opportunity costs, and differential costs.

To illustrate, assume that you own Speedy Print Shop. A customer wants you to print 500 copies of a one-page flyer immediately. To price the job, you need to know what it will cost. Exhibit 1 includes both an incorrect and a correct analysis of the available cost data. The left column (the incorrect analysis) includes all costs; the right column (the correct analysis) includes only the differential costs. We will explain each cost and how to determine whether the cost is relevant to the pricing decision.

1. *Paper.* The cost of the paper for the printing job is differential because it is a future expenditure that must be made as a result of the decision to accept the order. In a sense, therefore, it is a cost that changes as a result of the decision. If we do not accept the order, we do not need to purchase the paper. Note also that paper is a variable cost—its total cost increases proportionately to the size of the order.

2. *Printing labor.* Accepting the order will require a future expenditure for additional labor to operate the press. This again obviously represents a change from the existing situation—without the order, we would not incur the cost of labor. Also, this example illustrates another important point about measuring future costs. Because

---

Learning Objective Sidebar:

Understand the concepts of sunk costs and differential costs and revenues, and be able to identify those costs and revenues that are relevant to making product and process decisions.

sunk costs

Either past costs, such as already-purchased equipment, or unchangeable future costs, such as committed lease payments, that do not change as the result of a future decision.

differential costs

Future costs that change as a result of a decision; also called incremental or relevant costs.

opportunity cost

The benefits lost or forfeited as a result of selecting one alternative course of action over another.

Deciding whether to accept a special print order involves comparing the special order price to the differential costs of filling the order.

this rush order will have to be printed during overtime hours, the appropriate labor rate is time and a half. (Given a normal hourly rate of $16, the labor rate for this job would be $24.) It is easy to overlook this and assume that the normal labor cost per hour ($16) applies. The differential cost of $24 per hour that will be incurred as a result of the decision, however, is the appropriate cost to use. Like paper, printing labor is a variable cost that increases in total proportionately to the size of the order.

3. *Printing plates.* New printing plates must be prepared for this order, so it is a future expenditure that changes as a result of the decision to accept the order. The important point here is that printing plates are a fixed cost (you can print as many copies as you want from the same set of plates), but the cost is still differential because it is an additional expenditure for this order. A common but incorrect assumption is that only variable costs are relevant and that fixed costs do not have to be taken into account. This is not the case. All future costs that change as a result of accepting the order, whether fixed or variable, are differential.

4. *Printing press depreciation.* This is not a differential cost because it is not a future cost (depreciation is an allocation of a past cost), and it does not change as a result of the decision to accept the order. Costs such as depreciation, which are past costs and do not change, are sunk costs. No decision can change past, or sunk, costs; they are never relevant to a decision.

5. *Manager's salary.* Although the manager's salary is a future cost (we will be paying for future services), it will be paid whether or not the order is accepted. Consequently, despite being a future cost, the manager's salary is a sunk cost because it must be paid regardless of whether or not the printing job is accepted.

The differential costs for this rush order total $270. This means that in pricing the job, Speedy Print Shop will be losing money unless it charges at least this much. Similarly, if Speedy Print Shop declines the job at an offered price of $300 because that price is less than

EXHIBIT 1	**Speedy Print Shop Rush Order Analysis**		
		Incorrect Analysis (all costs)	**Correct Analysis (differential costs)**
Variable costs:			
Paper (500 at 10¢)		$ 50	$ 50
Printing labor (5 hours at $16; 5 hours at $24)		80	120
Fixed costs:			
Printing plates		100	100
Printing press depreciation (5 hours at $10)		50	
Manager's salary (5 hours at $20)		100	
Totals		$380	$270

the incorrectly calculated differential cost of $380, the company will experience an opportunity cost (loss) of $30 ($300 − $270).

Speaking of opportunity costs, Speedy Print Shop must also carefully consider any other opportunity costs associated with accepting this order. If Speedy Print Shop accepts this order, it may not be able to accept another order that already exists or one that might arrive tomorrow. The lost contribution to profit from not being able to accept alternative jobs is an opportunity cost that must be considered. Obviously, if there is plenty of printing capacity available to accept all jobs that are received, the opportunity cost of this rush order is zero.

To further illustrate the role of differential and sunk costs in making a product or process decision, we assume that Dixon Wholesale Company is thinking of purchasing a delivery truck with an estimated useful life of five years. Following are the costs of acquiring and operating a truck:

Original cost		$20,000
Variable costs per mile:		
Gasoline and oil	$ 0.50	
Repairs and maintenance	0.06	
Tires	0.04	
Total variable costs per mile		$ 0.60
Fixed costs per year:		
Insurance	$1,000	
Licenses	220	
Depreciation expense ($20,000 ÷ 5 years)	4,000	
Total fixed costs per year		$ 5,220

These variable and fixed operating costs are incurred each year the truck is used. However, they are not all differential costs; they are not all relevant to every decision made about the truck. For the following decisions, we identify the differential costs, the sunk costs, and the reason for the classifications.

Decision 1 Should the truck be purchased? Whether to purchase the truck is really a capital budgeting decision, a topic we will discuss in Chapter 22 on capital investment decisions. But the decision is based on differential (future) costs to be incurred if the truck is purchased.

- **Differential costs:** All variable costs (60 cents per mile driven); all fixed costs except depreciation (which is already included in the purchase cost); and the purchase cost ($20,000).
- **Sunk costs:** None.
- **Comment:** All costs except depreciation are differential costs because the truck has not yet been purchased; all costs can be avoided by an alternative decision.

Decision 2 Let's now jump forward in time two years. The truck has now been owned and used for two years, but it has not been licensed or insured for the current (third) year. Should it be licensed and insured, or should some other means of transportation be used? (Assume for now that the truck will not be sold, even if not used.)

- **Differential costs:** All variable costs (60 cents per mile driven) and some fixed costs (insurance, $1,000; licenses, $220).
- **Sunk costs:** The original purchase price and the deprecation costs, which are represented by the remaining book value of the truck ($12,000 at the beginning of the year).
- **Comment:** As soon as the truck is purchased, its cost becomes a sunk cost. During its estimated life, its remaining book value is a sunk cost if we assume, for simplicity, that the truck has no resale value. The company must absorb the cost of the truck either by using the truck (and depreciating its cost each year) or by writing off the entire cost. All costs except depreciation and the remaining book value are, therefore, differential costs.

Decision 3   The truck has been owned and used for two years and has been licensed and insured for the current (third) year. Should the truck be used for transporting inventory this year? Should other means be arranged?

- **Differential costs:** All variable costs (60 cents per mile driven) and no fixed costs.
- **Sunk costs:** Insurance ($1,000); licenses ($220); remaining book value ($12,000 at the beginning of the year).
- **Comment:** If insurance and license fees are not refundable, these are sunk costs, as is the remaining book value.

Analysis of the costs that are relevant in making these three decisions should help you understand how differential costs are determined. As you can see, variable costs are *usually* differential; fixed costs are *sometimes* differential; and past costs and committed future costs are *never* differential.

Qualitative Considerations

The effect of product or process decisions on the time and quality with which products or services can be delivered must be considered. In deciding whether to accept the rush print job, for example, Speedy Print Shop must consider the possibility that while accepting the job might lead to additional business, this decision could affect the quality of printing services to other customers. Likewise, if accepting the rush print job will slow down service to other customers, accepting the job may not be a good decision, no matter how financially attractive it seems to be.

In making a final decision, the cost and qualitative factors may lead you to the same conclusion. If they do not, you must decide what to do to enhance your company's overall profitability in the future. You might decide, for example, to accept the rush print job for an amount near or even below your differential cost to ensure that you get the order and establish a relationship with the customer. On the other hand, due to concerns about a reduced ability to service your regular customers, you may decide to not accept the job even though it does contribute to immediate profits.

The concepts of differential, sunk, and opportunity costs apply to all evaluation decisions covered in this chapter. In the remainder of this chapter, we will apply differential costing to several examples of short-term product and process evaluation decisions. We will consider five separate examples: (1) accepting or rejecting special orders, (2) making or buying products, (3) exiting or entering a market, (4) determining at what stage of production to sell products, and (5) selecting the best use of a scarce resource. We will also consider the impact of differential, opportunity, and sunk costs on setting selling prices for products.

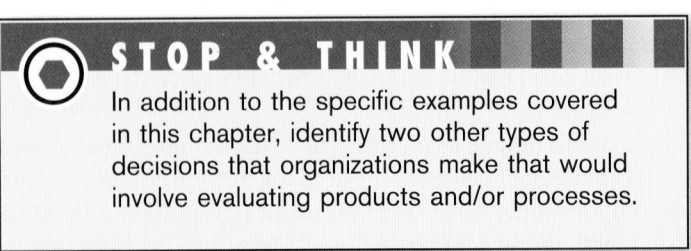

STOP & THINK

In addition to the specific examples covered in this chapter, identify two other types of decisions that organizations make that would involve evaluating products and/or processes.

> **REMEMBER THIS...**
>
> - Differential costs are the future costs that change as a result of a decision.
>   - Only **differential** costs and revenues are relevant to decisions.
>   - Some future costs may not be differential because they do not change as a result of a decision.
>   - Both variable and fixed costs may be differential.
> - Sunk costs are never relevant because they are either past costs or future costs that cannot be changed.
> - Once the quantitative analysis has been completed, qualitative factors must be considered.

Accepting or Rejecting Special Orders

Decide whether to accept or reject a special order.

② A **special order** is an order that may be priced below the normal price in order to utilize excess capacity, thus contributing to company profits. We will look at special orders from the perspective of the seller. (A special order from the perspective of the buyer is really a make or buy decision that will be covered later in this chapter.) Many Internet services are run by companies that specialize in "special orders." That is, these online services specialize in matching customers who insist on paying less than standard market prices with companies that have excess capacity to sell. In a sense, **Priceline.com**, **Hotels.com**, and other similar e-commerce companies are special order matchmakers.

special order

An order that may be priced below the normal selling price in order to utilize excess capacity and thereby contribute to company profits.

Special orders can involve products or services. For example, in manufacturing companies, the special order might involve buying or selling parts on a one-time basis to or from other companies because of a sudden surge in demand. Another example is the one-time outsourcing of the preparation of quarterly payroll tax reports to a local CPA firm. When parts are involved, both the buying and selling companies are manufacturing firms. When a service (such as payroll accounting) is involved, the buyer may be a manufacturing, merchandising, or service company, but the provider is always a service company.

Special Orders–The Seller's Decision

If a seller can sell its products or services profitably at normal market prices, the decision is an easy one—provide the product or the service. After all, that is the purpose of being in business. Where the difficulty comes is in deciding whether to reduce the normal price of a product or service in order to obtain a special order. Typical situations involving a possible price reduction when idle capacity exists are as follows:

1. A manufacturer sells products under its own brand name, as well as to retail chain stores for sale under the chain's in-store generic brand name (this practice is called "private labeling").
2. A firm, such as a building contractor or an equipment manufacturer, sells its products or services in a competitive bidding situation.
3. A firm sells a product under distress conditions, for instance, when there has been a sharp decline in demand for its products because of a new product offered by a competitor.
4. A product has significant sales potential with a foreign distributor, whose market demands lower prices than those in the United States.
5. A provider of a product or service has extra capacity and has the opportunity to sign a large contract, at a lower-than-normal price, that would consume the excess capacity.

In each of these situations, we assume that a firm has available capacity that can be used to fill the special order. The relevant costs for this decision are the additional, or incremental, costs necessary to produce and deliver the special order. Management must therefore know the incremental costs. This information will indicate the lowest price at which the special order will begin to contribute to the firm's profits.

To illustrate, we will assume that Kent Electronics, which usually sells business calculators for a wholesale price of $29, receives an order from a large department store chain for 10,000 calculators at a price of $23 each. The requested calculators are to be sold under the store's brand name. Kent currently has excess capacity that could be used in producing enough calculators to fill the order. Should the company accept the order?

The answer to this question does not, of course, depend on cost and price factors alone. An obvious consideration, for example, would be whether the order would result in a significant loss of sales of the company's own brand of calculators. Let's assume that this is not a problem.

If the accounting department presents the data on a total-cost basis, the manager might erroneously reject the order. It appears from the schedule below that the firm would have a loss if it accepted the special order.

Special Order for Calculators–Total-Cost Approach

Sales price		$ 23
Manufacturing costs:		
Direct materials	$ 8	
Direct labor	4	
Manufacturing overhead	14	
Total manufacturing costs		26
Loss per unit		$ (3)
Number of units in order		×10,000
Expected loss exclusive of selling and administrative expenses		$(30,000)

It is not unusual for managers to base decisions on total-cost information because the data are readily available, having been collected in order to prepare financial statements and income tax returns. Unfortunately, such information may lead management to the wrong conclusion—in this case, to reject the order.

The only differential costs, however, are those future costs that change if the order is accepted. These include the variable product costs as well as the direct fixed costs. Fixed costs that are incurred regardless of whether the order is accepted should not be considered. The following analysis, prepared on a differential-cost basis, shows that Kent Electronics should accept the order:

Special Order for Calculators–Differential-Cost Approach

Sales price		$ 23
Variable and differential fixed costs:		
Direct materials	$8	
Direct labor	4	
Variable manufacturing overhead costs	5	
Variable selling and administrative expenses	1	
Total variable costs		18
Contribution margin per unit		$ 5
Number of units in order		×10,000
Total contribution margin		$50,000
Differential fixed overhead costs*		(30,000)
Remaining margin to cover indirect fixed costs and provide profit		$20,000

*Average differential fixed costs per unit (= $30,000 ÷ 10,000 units)	$3

These data assume that additional fixed costs of $30,000 will be incurred if the order is accepted. If no additional fixed costs would be incurred, then all of the contribution margin of $50,000 would be available to cover Kent's other fixed costs and help provide a profit for the company. The analysis clearly suggests that, from a financial point of view, management should accept the order. This approach identifies not only the differential costs but provides a price floor of $21, which is equal to the total variable costs per unit of $18 plus the average differential fixed costs per unit of $3. The management should probably not accept an order at a price below $21. So long as the price exceeds total variable and differential fixed costs, the firm will increase its profits by accepting the order. This analysis assumes that the company has no better alternative uses for its excess capacity and that special sales by the chain will have no adverse effect on Kent's normal sales. But what if regular customers hear about this special order and insist on lower prices, thus disrupting the normal pricing structure? Or, what if filling the special order will have an adverse effect on the quality of current products or the speed with which products can be offered to regular customers? These and other qualitative factors must also be considered.

The differential-cost approach to pricing can also be used in explaining why theater tickets are less expensive for matinees than for evening performances and why it is cheaper to make telephone calls at night and on weekends than on weekdays. If there is excess capacity that can be used to provide a service or make a product that will generate more revenue than the differential cost of providing the service or making the product, the firm will increase its profits by the amount of the margin remaining after deducting differential costs. This is exactly the rationale for the existence of Internet brokers for theater tickets, last-minute cruises, hotel rooms, and the like.

A few words of caution are in order when making these special order decisions.

1. In some situations, there may also be some additional fixed costs that are relevant to the pricing decision.
2. A company must not accept too many orders that barely cover variable costs, or it will not be able to cover all its fixed costs.
3. Using all extra capacity to fill a special order at a lower-than-normal price may prevent a company from being able to accept additional work at higher prices in the future; this is an example of an opportunity cost.
4. Accepting a special order may force a company to cut corners with normal customers, resulting in lower-quality products or services to those customers or decreasing the speed at which other customers are served.

REMEMBER THIS...

- When excess capacity exists, the relevant costs in determining whether to take a special order are the incremental costs. These costs are:
  - Variable costs and
  - Direct fixed costs.
- Management should also consider the impact that the special order pricing may have on its normal pricing.

Making or Buying Products

Determine whether a company should make a product itself or whether it should outsource the production to a supplier.

③ In the previous section, we looked at special orders from the perspective of the seller. Obviously, whenever there is a special order, there is also a buyer. Many times buyers requesting a special purchase order actually have the ability to make the product or provide the service for themselves. However, just because companies can provide their own goods or services doesn't always mean that they should. Sometimes the cost of making is more than the cost of purchasing, and differential-cost analysis is used to help companies intelligently understand the tradeoffs between making or buying products or services.

outsourcing

An arrangement in which one company provides services for another company which has historically performed those services for itself.

Outsourcing is an important process, and represents a very important decision, for many companies. Many companies outsource virtually everything. For example, a food packaging plant might outsource to an employment agency the task of hiring, firing, training, and paying its production line employees. The plant might also outsource its custodial and bookkeeping services to local providers of those services. The plant might even outsource key management tasks by asking a consulting or professional services firm to provide a top-level manager to run the plant. As another example, many Internet businesses are "virtual outsourcers." They take orders from customers and relay those orders to manufacturers, which, in turn, ship the products directly to the customers. In contrast, other organizations make or provide most of their products and services internally. In the following section, we describe the factors companies must consider when deciding whether to buy products and services from outsiders or to produce these products and services themselves.

Making or Buying Manufactured Parts

Companies, such as automobile manufacturers, must decide which products and services they will produce and offer internally and which ones they will outsource to or buy from outsiders. With respect to manufactured products, if a product consists of a number of parts, management must decide for each component whether to produce it or purchase it from an outside supplier. Over time, and based on a consideration of the relevant quantitative and qualitative factors, management develops a long-term policy regarding what components it will produce for its products and what components it will outsource.

The fact that a long-term policy about make versus buy has been established by a particular company does not mean that the issue is permanently closed. In fact, management should always be reconsidering its decisions and looking for new ways to save money, improve quality, or speed up manufacturing and delivery processes. If a firm has idle facilities, for example, management may wish to find a use for those facilities. One possibility is to manufacture components that are normally outsourced. Whether this decision is wise depends not only on cost considerations but also on a number of qualitative factors, such as the likely effect on the normal supplier, the company's ability to produce a high-quality component, speed of production and delivery, and management's interest in keeping workers on the payroll. Thus, even though a firm has a long-term policy of producing some components and outsourcing others, certain situations may require decisions that alter that policy.

Assuming that the qualitative factors favor the use of idle facilities to produce the part, what costs are relevant to a make-or-buy decision? In general, the purchase cost and all other costs that can be avoided if the part is manufactured are differential costs. Any cost that will be incurred regardless of whether the part is purchased or manufactured is a sunk cost and is irrelevant.

To illustrate how the differential costs in such a decision are identified, assume that Ritter Manufacturing Company has excess capacity that could be used in producing wheel bearings. The accounting department has compiled the following projected total-cost figures for producing the bearings:

	Cost per Unit	Costs for 1,000 Units
Direct materials	$ 3.00	$ 3,000
Direct labor	8.00	8,000
Variable manufacturing overhead	4.00	4,000
Fixed manufacturing overhead, direct	2.50	2,500
Fixed manufacturing overhead, indirect	5.00	5,000*
Total costs	$22.50	$22,500

*Total indirect fixed costs are the same under both alternatives.

The company has been buying this bearing from a regular supplier in 1,000-unit quantities at a price of $19 per unit. Should Ritter continue to buy or start making the bearings? To answer this question, management must identify the differential costs of each alternative, taking into account any additional resources that may be needed, as well as alternative uses for the currently idle facilities. Two possible situations are presented here.

Situation 1   The currently idle facilities have no alternative uses. If the idle facilities do not have any practical alternative use, the opportunity cost is zero. With no opportunity cost, the differential costs would be the costs strictly associated with manufacturing (direct labor, direct materials, and so on).

The costs of the two alternatives should be analyzed on a differential-cost basis, as shown in Exhibit 2. The analysis demonstrates that the firm would save $1,500 per 1,000 units ($1.50 per unit) by making the component rather than buying it. The company's final decision would depend, of course, on whether there were negative qualitative factors that would, in the opinion of management, more than offset the $1.50 unit-cost advantage of making the part. One negative qualitative factor might be that the supplier may not be interested in a long-term business relationship if it can't depend on a steady flow of sales to the company.

Situation 2   The idle facilities can be rented for $4,000 if they are not used to manufacture bearings. Management estimates that, if the facilities are used for manufacturing, 1,000 wheel bearings could be manufactured during this time.

EXHIBIT 2	Analyses of the Costs of Using Idle Facilities (Situation 1)

	Differential-Cost Analysis (per 1,000 Units)	
	Buy	Make
Purchase cost	$19,000	
Direct materials		$ 3,000
Direct labor		8,000
Variable manufacturing overhead		4,000
Fixed manufacturing overhead:		
Direct		2,500
Indirect*		
Total cost	$19,000	$17,500
Difference	$1,500	

*The indirect manufacturing overhead costs of $5,000 are irrelevant because these costs will be incurred whether Ritter chooses to make the component itself or continue to buy the component from its supplier. In other words, this cost is not differential.

EXHIBIT 3	The Effect of an Opportunity Cost on Analyses (Situation 2)	

	Differential-Cost Analysis (per 1,000 Units)	
	Buy	**Make**
Purchase cost	$19,000	
Direct materials		$ 3,000
Direct labor		8,000
Variable manufacturing overhead		4,000
Fixed manufacturing overhead:		
Direct		2,500
Indirect		
Opportunity cost, rental		4,000
Total cost	$19,000	$21,500
Difference	$2,500	

In this case, the opportunity cost of producing the bearings is $4,000, or an average cost of $4 per unit ($4,000 ÷ 1,000 units). This opportunity cost is an important consideration in the firm's decision whether to buy or make the part, as shown in Exhibit 3. When the opportunity cost is considered, the cost of producing the part is $2,500 more than the cost of buying it. Unless there are quality, time, or other qualitative factors that override this cost, Ritter should buy the bearing and rent the idle facilities. Remember, the essence of the make-or-buy problem is management's desire to achieve the best utilization of existing facilities in the short term.

Because opportunity costs do not represent actual transactions, they are not recorded in the accounts. Yet they are always significant in the decision-making process because each situation has at least two alternatives. Thus, opportunity costs provide a good illustration of why a manager cannot rely solely on the data collected for external financial reports.

Purchasing Services or Providing Them Internally

In recent years, companies have not only outsourced product parts, but more and more they are also outsourcing services such as cafeteria service, garbage removal, payroll accounting, legal services, and even basic accounting. In deciding whether to acquire services or provide them internally, companies go through the same kind of analysis as if they were buying products. That is, they consider the differential costs of each alternative, as well as qualitative factors, such as the quality of the service, whether space exists to house the service, whether services can be delivered on a timely basis, and management's interest in keeping workers on the payroll. Assuming management believes it can acquire high-quality services both within and outside the company, what costs are relevant to the make-or-buy decisions (in other words, the provide-or-purchase decisions)? Costs that will be incurred regardless of whether the service is provided internally or purchased externally are sunk costs and are irrelevant to the decision.

To illustrate how the differential costs are identified, assume that Ritter Manufacturing Company is considering outsourcing its payroll function. The following annual cost information relating to payroll accounting is available:

Annual Costs of Payroll Accounting Department

Salaries of payroll accounting employees	$2,600,000
Other payroll costs for accounting employees	75,000
Training costs	100,000
Depreciation on payroll accounting offices	50,000
Utilities for payroll accounting offices	40,000
Computers, software, and supplies	150,000
Total costs of payroll accounting	$3,015,000

A CPA firm has offered to perform the payroll accounting services for $3,100,000 per year. You have determined that if payroll accounting services were contracted out to the CPA firm, the space currently used by the payroll department could be used by the purchasing department, which is currently occupying rented space in a nearby city. The rent paid for offices used by the purchasing department is $10,000 per month.

Should Ritter continue to have its own payroll department, or should it outsource its payroll accounting function to a CPA firm? From a strictly financial point of view, Ritter should not outsource, as shown below.

	Differential-Cost Analysis	
	Purchase	**Provide**
CPA firm cost	$3,100,000	
Salaries of payroll accounting employees		$2,600,000
Other payroll costs for accounting employees		75,000
Training costs		100,000
Depreciation on payroll accounting offices*		
Utilities for payroll accounting offices*		
Computers, software, and supplies		150,000
Opportunity cost, rental for purchasing department		120,000
Total cost	$3,100,000	$3,045,000
Difference	$55,000	

*The cost of depreciation and utilities on the payroll accounting offices will continue after the purchasing department moves in. Therefore, these costs are not differential (i.e., these costs are sunk) and are irrelevant to the analysis.

Of course, the one-year cost analysis is really an incomplete analysis. In making the decision, management must determine what the future costs of each alternative will be. If, for example, management can lock into a five-year commitment of $3,100,000 annually and it believes costs of keeping the payroll department will rise $100,000 per year, from a cost perspective, the company may want to outsource now even though the cost of outsourcing is higher in the current year.

CAUTION

Be careful to consider all differential costs and revenues in making evaluation decisions and to exclude the nondifferential costs. For example, in this payroll accounting example, if depreciation and utilities (which will be incurred whether or not payroll accounting services are outsourced) are considered, an incorrect decision will be made.

In addition to costs, management must consider many other factors. For example, will the CPA firm provide payroll services of the same or higher quality as those provided by the internal accountants? Quality of services is very important in an area like payroll accounting, where it is difficult for management to judge whether the company is getting value for its money. Management would also want to consider other factors: (1) Will the CPA firm be able to provide the services in the long run? (2) Can the company use the displaced payroll accounting employees in other positions, or is the company willing to lay off employees? (3) Will outsourcing the payroll accounting services affect the cost of other services received by the company? (4) If payroll accounting was used as a trainee development area (as it is in many companies), are there other efficient and effective ways to train future company accountants?

REMEMBER THIS...

- Compare the differential costs of making the part or providing the service to the cost of purchasing (outsourcing) the part or service.
- The differential costs are:
  - Variable cost,
  - Direct fixed cost, and
  - Opportunity cost of alternative uses of the facilities.
- Qualitative factors must also be considered.

Exiting or Entering a Market

Identify when a company should drop a product line or exit or enter a market.

 The decision of whether to exit or enter a market is usually based on careful evaluation, although companies seem to be buying and selling businesses quite often these days. We will first consider the decision of whether to exit a market and then the decision of whether to enter a market (which in both cases involves the same basic analysis).

Exiting a Market

When a segment (product or line of products) appears to be losing money, management must decide whether to drop it. Such decisions are particularly difficult because the differential costs are not easy to identify, and this can lead to analyses based on invalid assumptions, as the following example demonstrates.

To illustrate, assume that Augusta Retail Company is thinking of closing one of its stores. The question of the store's continuing viability arose because of the July financial results for the company's three stores (amounts are in thousands):

	Athens Store	Brooks Store	Clinch Store	Total
Sales revenue	$250,000	$90,000	$60,000	$400,000
Cost of goods sold	170,000	40,000	30,000	240,000
Gross margin	$ 80,000	$50,000	$30,000	$160,000
Operating expenses	55,000	30,000	35,000	120,000
Net income (or loss)	$ 25,000	$20,000	$ (5,000)	$ 40,000

If the Clinch Store is closed, it would seem reasonable to assume that Augusta Retail Company's profits will increase by $5 million, as shown here.

	Athens Store	Brooks Store	Total
Sales revenue	$250,000	$90,000	$340,000
Cost of goods sold	170,000	40,000	210,000
Gross margin	$ 80,000	$50,000	$130,000
Operating expenses	55,000	30,000	85,000
Net income	$ 25,000	$20,000	$ 45,000

This analysis is based on three assumptions:

1. That all costs shown are differential and therefore relevant to the decision. In other words, there are no **common costs** (costs that are common across the company and not directly related to any specific store).
2. That the sales of the other stores will not be affected by dropping the Clinch Store.
3. That no qualitative factors have a bearing on the decision.

common costs

Overhead costs such as executive salaries or property taxes that cannot be attributed to and are not the responsibility of, specific products, departments, or business segments.

Before closing the Clinch Store, the company's general manager should check the validity of these assumptions. For simplicity, suppose that the second and third assumptions are valid, and that only the first assumption needs verification. First, the accounting department must separate the total costs of each store into variable costs, direct fixed costs, and common (or unavoidable) fixed costs. With this new information, the accounting department might prepare the following modified report for July (amounts are in thousands).

	Athens Store	Brooks Store	Clinch Store	Total
Sales revenue	$250,000	$90,000	$60,000	$400,000
Variable costs	190,000	50,000	40,000	280,000
Contribution margin	$ 60,000	$40,000	$20,000	$120,000
Direct fixed costs	20,000	15,000	18,000	53,000
Segment margin	$ 40,000	$25,000	$ 2,000	$ 67,000
Common fixed costs (not allocated)				27,000
Net income				$ 40,000

The manager can use this modified report to determine whether the Clinch Store made a positive contribution toward covering the common (indirect) fixed costs. In looking at this modified report, the manager would immediately see that the segment margin for the Clinch Store is a positive $2 million. This means that the Clinch Store is contributing $2 million to the company's overall profit. Thus, if the Clinch Store is dropped, profits will decrease by $2 million unless another store with greater profit potential is added. To illustrate the potential decline in profits if the Clinch Store is dropped, the manager might ask the accounting department to prepare a report to indicate what the company's July financial results would show without the Clinch Store. This pro-forma report would show the following information (amounts are in thousands):

	Athens Store	Brooks Store	Total
Sales revenue	$250,000	$90,000	$340,000
Variable costs	190,000	50,000	240,000
Contribution margin	$ 60,000	$40,000	$100,000
Direct fixed costs	20,000	15,000	35,000
Segment margin	$ 40,000	$25,000	$ 65,000
Common fixed costs (not allocated)			27,000
Net income			$ 38,000

Although the original report suggested that profits would increase by $5 million if the Clinch Store were dropped, total profits would actually decrease by $2 million ($40 million − $38 million). The reason is that the Clinch Store is generating revenues that are $2 million greater than differential costs (variable costs and avoidable fixed costs). This analysis suggests that the Clinch Store should not be dropped, unless it can be replaced by another store or business that will contribute more than $2 million to cover unavoidable indirect fixed costs. (Obviously, we have not considered any sales price Augusta could receive from selling the Clinch Store. Any money received from selling the Clinch Store would need to be weighed against the $2 million annual contribution the Clinch Store is making toward covering indirect costs.)

Entering a Market

The considerations involved in deciding whether to enter a market are quite similar to those when deciding whether or not to exit a market. From a financial perspective, if adding a product line (segment) will contribute to the income of a firm, it is generally a good decision. The contribution can come in several forms. First, entering a new market can reduce the current cost of doing business. For example, assume that Augusta is considering purchasing a wholesale distribution company that will allow the company to buy directly from manufacturers, rather than from other wholesalers, when acquiring merchandise for its stores. Even if the new wholesale company is not profitable on its own, if it could reduce Augusta's costs enough so that overall profits are higher, the decision to buy might be a good one. Buying a new company or entering a new market could increase overall company profits by having the new segment cover some of the common fixed costs now being borne entirely by existing businesses.

In addition to the financial considerations, organizations consider the effects on quality and time to deliver products to customers when deciding whether to enter a market. For example, suppose a small company has superior-quality products, manufacturing knowledge, or other attributes that could enhance the quality of the organization's products. Would it be wise to buy this smaller company even if the purchase doesn't increase overall short-term profits? Probably so. Or, what if a company

FYI

Pick up practically any business newspaper or periodical and you'll read about companies exiting or entering markets. For example, the front page of the March 20, 2003, *Wall Street Journal* carried stories about **Continental Airlines** exiting certain markets it serves; **USA Interactive** agreeing to buy **Expedia**, an online discount site; five different companies making bids to purchase the **Safeway** supermarket chain; **Enron**'s plans to spin off its natural gas pipeline business; **Schwab** exiting the U.K. securities market; **Bank of America** scaling back its European investment banking business; and China's **Huawei** and **3Com** entering into a joint venture to sell computer networking gear to businesses in China.

occupies a strategic location for serving an organization's customers and buying the company would allow the organization to deliver its products more quickly to customers? Would buying the strategically located company be a good decision even if short-term overall profits aren't increased? Again, probably so. Both purchases would allow the organization to serve its customers better by increasing quality and decreasing delivery time. Hopefully, the result of both purchases would be a larger market share and higher profits in the long run. Unfortunately, it is hard to quantify by how much quality and/or delivery time must improve before a purchase is a good one. Because quality and time decisions are subjective, we will focus on the short-term financial considerations in deciding whether to enter a market. You should realize, however, that quality and time considerations are very important, and in considering some purchases, they may be the overriding factors that outweigh short-term financial considerations.

To illustrate entering a new market, assume that Augusta Retail Company now has only two stores. Further, assume that it is considering purchasing the wholesale company just discussed. The following data are available for Augusta Retail Company prior to making the purchase (amounts are in thousands):

	Athens Store	Brooks Store	Total
Sales revenue	$250,000	$90,000	$340,000
Cost of goods sold	170,000	40,000	210,000
Other variable costs	20,000	10,000	30,000
Contribution margin	$ 60,000	$40,000	$100,000
Direct fixed costs	20,000	15,000	35,000
Segment margin	$ 40,000	$25,000	$ 65,000
Common fixed costs (not allocated)			27,000
Net income			$ 38,000

As these data show, Augusta currently makes a net income of $38 million. Now, assume that Augusta can purchase a wholesale company that will allow Augusta to buy directly from manufacturers, thus decreasing its cost of goods sold by 30%. However, the wholesale company is currently losing $10 million per year. Should Augusta buy the wholesale company? The following analysis shows that, from a financial perspective, buying the wholesale company would be a good decision (again, amounts are in thousands):

	Effect on Current Stores							
	Athens Store		**Brooks Store**		**Total (before and after purchase)**		**Wholesale Company**	**Total (including wholesale company)**
	Before	**After**	**Before**	**After**	**Before**	**After**		
Sales revenue	$250,000	$250,000	$90,000	$90,000	$340,000	$340,000	$110,000	$450,000
Cost of goods sold	170,000	119,000[1]	40,000	28,000[2]	210,000	147,000	70,000	217,000
Other variable costs	20,000	20,000	10,000	10,000	30,000	30,000	15,000	45,000
Contribution margin	$ 60,000	$111,000	$40,000	$52,000	$100,000	$163,000	$ 25,000	$188,000
Direct fixed costs	20,000	20,000	15,000	15,000	35,000	35,000	35,000	70,000
Segment margin	$ 40,000	$ 91,000	$25,000	$37,000	$ 65,000	$128,000	$ (10,000)	$118,000
Common fixed cost (not allocated)					27,000	27,000		27,000
Net income					$ 38,000	$101,000	$ (10,000)	$ 91,000

[1]$170,000 − (0.3 × $170,000) = $119,000.
[2]$40,000 − (0.3 × $40,000) = $28,000.

This analysis shows that even though the wholesale company is losing $10 million per year, purchasing the wholesale company will increase overall company profits by $53 million ($91 million – $38 million). Of course, this elaborate analysis really wasn't necessary since many costs (other variable costs, direct fixed costs, and indirect fixed costs) stayed the same. In fact, the only differential costs were the decrease in cost of goods sold (facilitated by being able to buy directly from manufacturers instead of wholesalers) and the $10 million loss the wholesale company incurs. Focusing only on the differential costs, you can see that the net income of the company would be increased by $53 million upon buying the wholesale company (numbers are in thousands).

Differential Costs of Deciding to Enter a Market	
Decrease in cost of goods sold of the Athens Store	$ 51,000
Decrease in cost of goods sold of the Brooks Store	12,000
Loss incurred by wholesaler	(10,000)
Increase in income from buying wholesaler	$ 53,000

This analysis suggests that, from a financial perspective, the wholesale company should be purchased. The decreases in cost of goods sold that will result in the Athens Store and the Brooks Store more than compensate for the losses currently being incurred by the wholesaler.

REMEMBER THIS...

- Compute the differential profit (or loss) generated by the segment or product line.
- The differential costs are:
  - Variable cost,
  - Direct fixed cost, and
  - Opportunity cost of alternative uses of the resources.
- Qualitative factors must also be considered.

Determining at What Stage of Production to Sell Products

Determine whether to sell a joint product as it is or to process it further before selling it.

⑤ In some companies, all the products evolve out of a **joint manufacturing process**, meaning that one material input is used to produce more than one product. Gasoline, oil, and kerosene, for example, are all produced from refining crude oil; various cuts of beef are provided from butchering a steer; and different qualities and types of lumber are available from processing timber. In all these cases, the products are produced simultaneously and are not individually identifiable until the split-off point in the process. When this is the case, management must decide whether a particular product from the joint manufacturing process should be sold as is at the split-off point, or processed further at additional cost, with the expectation of obtaining a higher price.

In choosing the best time to stop processing a product, management basically compares the additional costs that would be incurred from further processing with the additional revenues. If the incremental revenues are greater than the incremental costs, net income is increased, and additional processing is

joint manufacturing process

When one material input is used to produce more than one product.

worthwhile (unless qualitative factors dictate otherwise). If the incremental revenues are less than the incremental costs, the product should probably be sold without further processing. The costs that a firm incurs before the point at which the different products are separated for further processing or immediate sale are called **joint product costs**. These costs are incurred whether the separate products are sold at the point of separation or after further processing. Thus, they are not relevant to a choice between the two alternatives.

joint product costs

The costs that a firm incurs before the point at which the different products are separated for further processing or immediate sale.

To illustrate the decision-making process related to further processing, we will assume that Armaco Oil Company derives two products, jet fuel and reformate gas, from crude oil. Although crude oil cannot be sold independently, both jet fuel and reformate gas can be sold either at the point of separation or after further processing. Further processing jet fuel results in a petrochemical product called xylene, while further processing of reformate gas results in a petrochemical called tolulene. The cost of refining 375,000 gallons of crude oil up to the point of separation is $300,000. Crude oil is then separated into 200,000 gallons of jet fuel and 150,000 gallons of reformate gas. The remaining 25,000 gallons are lost in the process of refining. The selling prices of jet fuel and reformate gas at the point of separation, the costs of processing further, and the selling prices after this further processing are estimated by the accounting department to be as follows:

	Gallons	Net Selling Prince per Gallon at Separation	Additional Processing Costs	Net Selling Price of Xylene and Tolulene per Gallon After Processing
Jet fuel	200,000	$1.20	$80,000	$1.70 (xylene)
Reformate gas	150,000	1.00	90,000	1.50 (tolulene)

To help management decide whether to sell jet fuel or reformate gas at the point of separation or to process them further, the following analysis can be prepared:

Product: Jet Fuel/Xylene

Sales revenue after further processing (200,000 gallons @ $1.70)	$340,000
Sales revenue at point of separation (200,000 gallons @ $1.20)	240,000
Additional revenue from further processing	$100,000
Additional processing costs	80,000
Additional profit from further processing	$ 20,000

Product: Reformate Gas/Tolulene

Sales revenue after further processing (150,000 gallons @ $1.50)	$225,000
Sales revenue at point of separation (150,000 gallons @ $1.00)	150,000
Additional revenue from further processing	$ 75,000
Additional processing costs	90,000
Additional loss from further processing	$(15,000)

This analysis shows that further processing of jet fuel into xylene will contribute an additional $20,000 to net income because the additional revenues generated exceed the additional processing costs by $20,000. On the other hand, further processing of reformate gas into tolulene will reduce net income by $15,000 because the additional processing costs are greater than the additional revenues by that amount. Therefore, reformate gas should be sold at the point of separation. However, should the Armaco Oil Company sell both products after further processing, the increase to net income would be only $5,000 ($20,000 – $15,000). Hence, the best choice is to sell reformate gas at the point of separation and to process jet fuel into xylene before it is sold.

In deciding whether to sell products at the point of separation or after further processing, management must also consider qualitative factors. For example, management will need to consider quality and time issues, as well as the hiring or firing of employees and customers' demands for particular products.

> **REMEMBER THIS...**
>
> - Differential-cost analysis can help determine whether joint products should be sold at the point where they become recognized as separate products or processed further.
> - It will always be profitable to continue processing a joint product after the split-off point as long as the incremental revenue from the extra processing exceeds the incremental processing costs incurred after the split-off point.
> - Joint costs that have been incurred up to the point of split-off are always irrelevant to the additional processing decision.

Selecting the Best Use of a Scarce Resource

Select the best use of a scarce resource.

6 Organizations are often faced with the decision of how to best use scarce resources. In a manufacturing company, the scarce resource might be limited raw materials or limited production capacity. For a retail merchandising firm, such as **Wal-Mart**, the scarce resource might be limited shelf space. For a service firm, the scarce resource might be the limited expertise of the trained professionals. We will illustrate the concept of scarce resources using limited shelf space for a retail merchandising firm.

When a retail merchandising firm sells more than one product and store shelves are inadequate to display all products equally, management has to decide to which products the store should allocate shelf space and how much space should be allocated to each product. With limited shelf space, stocking one product means that another product cannot be stocked or will have to be stocked on a more limited basis. In deciding which products to stock, management needs to know which products and how much of each product to stock in order to maximize net income. A retail store will normally maximize net income by stocking those products that contribute the most toward covering

critical resource factor

The resource that limits operating capacity by its availability.

fixed costs and providing profit in relation to the "critical resource factor," in this case, shelf space. The **critical resource factor** is the resource that limits operating capacity by its availability. For example, in a manufacturing company, if machine hours are the most critical resource, a company should concentrate on the product for which revenues exceed variable costs by the highest margin per machine hour. Other critical resources in manufacturing companies might include labor hours, floor space, or special raw materials. Because shelf space is the critical resource factor for our retail store example, from a financial point of view, management should stock those products for which revenues exceed variable costs by the highest margin per square foot of shelf space.

To illustrate, we assume that Bolten Retail Company stocks potato chips and cookies. Let's further assume that its capacity, at least in the short term, is limited by the availability of only 20 square feet of shelf space for these two products. The revenue and cost data for one package each of potato chips and cookies are:

	Potato Chips	Cookies
Selling price per bag	$3.10	$3.50
Variable costs per bag	2.48	3.15
Contribution margin per bag	$0.62	$0.35
Percentage contribution margin (contribution margin ÷ selling price)	20%	10%

On the basis of this limited information, it would appear that potato chips are more profitable than cookies. The sale of one bag of potato chips will contribute $0.62 toward fixed costs and profit, whereas the sale of one package of cookies will contribute only $0.35.

Before Bolten can decide whether or not to emphasize potato chips, however, management must consider the extent to which each product uses the critical resource, limited shelf space. If a bag of potato chips takes up twice as much space as a package of cookies (two bags of potato chips occupy one square foot of shelf space, while four packages of cookies can occupy the same one square foot of shelf space), the sale of cookies will make a greater total contribution to profits than the sale of potato chips, as shown by the following calculations:[1]

	Potato Chips	Cookies
Contribution margin per unit	$0.62	$0.35
Packages per square foot	× 2	× 4
Contribution margin per square foot of shelf space	$1.24	$1.40

Even though potato chips have a higher contribution margin per unit of product ($0.62 versus $0.35), cookies have a higher contribution margin per square foot of shelf space ($1.40 versus $1.24), which is the critical resource. The management of Bolten Retail Company should stock cookies rather than potato chips, assuming that the company's only critical resource is shelf space.

However, if the demand for cookies is limited and Bolten never has potato chips for sale, will customers start shopping at other stores? In that case, Bolten should stock as many cookies as it can sell and use the balance of the critical resource for stocking potato chips. To illustrate, we assume that the market demand for cookies is 1,800 packages per month or an average of 60 per day. Because it takes only 15 square feet of shelf space (60 packages ÷ 4 packages per square foot) to store one day's worth of cookies, 5 square feet of shelf space are available to stock potato chips. This means that 10 bags of potato chips can be stocked. Assuming all 10 bags are sold during each day, the combined sales of cookies and potato chips will contribute $27.20 to cover fixed costs and provide a profit, as shown below.

> **STOP & THINK**
>
> Why do you think that most grocery stores allocate more space to breakfast cereals than to most other products?

	Daily Contribution Margin
Packages sold:	
Potato chips (10 bags × $0.62 per bag)	$ 6.20
Cookies (60 packages × $0.35 per package)	21.00
Total	$27.20

This analysis shows that from a financial perspective, the best use of the 20 square feet of shelf space is to use 15 square feet for cookies and 5 square feet for potato chips. Because demand for cookies is limited, only a $21 daily contribution margin can be earned by selling cookies. The other 5 feet of shelf space should be used to stock potato chips. Obviously, nonfinancial factors, such as customer satisfaction, would also have to be considered in making the final decision of how much of each product to stock.

---

[1] We are assuming that the company can sell all the potato chips and cookies it stocks. If it can't, or if one product sells faster than the other, rate of turnover must be considered.

CAUTION

It is essential to carefully and accurately identify the scarce resource and the quantity of the scarce resource consumed by each product. For example, in the store shelf space decision, if you don't carefully calculate the amount of space needed for cookies and potato chips and instead look only at the contribution margin per unit, an incorrect decision will be made. It is only when you consider the contribution margin per square foot of shelf space that the correct decision is made.

The foregoing analysis dealt with only two constraints: store shelf space and product demand. If a firm is further limited by other factors (such as the ability to buy certain amounts of particular products), management generally has to use the quantitative techniques of linear programming or simulation to help decide how many of each product to produce and/or sell. You can learn about this technique in advanced accounting or business management courses. Regardless of the number of constraints, though, the essence of the decision is to achieve the best short-term utilization of available resources.

REMEMBER THIS...

In deciding how to make the best use of critical resource factors, management should choose the item that provides the greatest contribution margin per unit of the most critical resource.

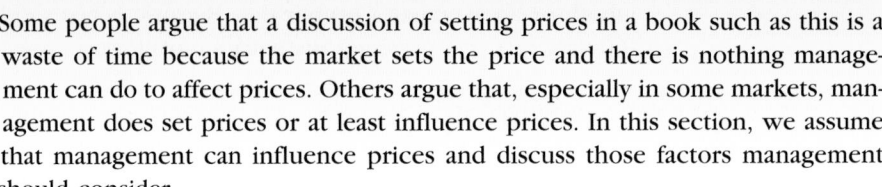

Setting Selling Prices

Use cost information in setting normal selling prices.

⑦ Some people argue that a discussion of setting prices in a book such as this is a waste of time because the market sets the price and there is nothing management can do to affect prices. Others argue that, especially in some markets, management does set prices or at least influence prices. In this section, we assume that management can influence prices and discuss those factors management should consider.

Pricing a product is partly a matter of guesswork because managers rarely know with any precision how price affects demand (e.g., how many more units could be sold if the price were to be lowered by a certain amount). In addition, other factors, such as advertising and packaging, affect the sale of a product.

The pricing process is further complicated by the fact that there are several broad categories of pricing decisions and the same cost information is not appropriate for all of them. Earlier, we considered the pricing of special orders. In this section, we cover the pricing of normal products. Other pricing categories, including the pricing of new products, are covered in advanced accounting and marketing texts.

CAUTION

In a purely competitive market (such as for commodities), sellers are price takers, and their costs are irrelevant in setting prices. In a market for differentiated products (such as for branded goods or for tailor-made items), no one "market" price exists, so production costs are an important input into the pricing decision process.

Normal Pricing of Products

In deciding whether to accept special orders, we stated that the price must be high enough to cover variable and incremental fixed costs. The price normally charged for a product or service, however, must be high enough to cover all costs (including production, selling, and administrative costs) and still provide a reasonable return on the owners' investments. Therefore, all costs (variable, as well as a fair share of fixed costs) are relevant to the pricing decision. In some cases, however, the final price may be set somewhat above or below the price suggested by total cost plus a reasonable return. This occurs when pricing decisions are based primarily on supply and demand, competition, and other market factors. For example, textbook prices are strictly competitive. Whether it costs $250,000 or $500,000 to produce a textbook, the price of the book has to be close to that of the nearest competitors.

In supplying cost data to aid management in normal pricing decisions, accountants may use a functional approach, summarizing costs by function (manufacturing, selling, or administrative), or a contribution approach, classifying costs by behavior (fixed or variable). To illustrate the two approaches, we assume that Kent Electronics (from the calculator example earlier in the chapter) is pricing a desk calculator. The relevant costs for each approach are as follows:

Functional Cost Approach

Direct materials	$ 6
Direct labor	8
Manufacturing overhead (200% × direct labor cost)	16
Total manufacturing cost	$30
Markup to cover selling and administrative expenses and provide a reasonable return on investment (0.40 × selling price)	20
Estimated normal selling price	$50

Contribution Approach

Direct materials	$ 6
Direct labor	8
Variable manufacturing overhead	7
Variable selling and administrative overhead expenses	4
Total variable costs	$25
Markup to cover fixed costs and provide a reasonable return on investment (0.50 × selling price)	25
Estimated normal selling price	$50

The markups calculated here are based on the selling price because marketing people generally use this approach. How do we calculate the markup as a percentage of the selling price before that price is known? If the markup is to be 40% of the selling price, as in our first example, the total manufacturing cost must be 60% of the selling price. So we simply divide the manufacturing cost by 60% to get the selling price ($30 ÷ 0.60 = $50). Then, the selling price minus the manufacturing cost is the markup ($50 – $30 = $20).

If a functional cost approach is used, the markup must be large enough to cover all selling and administrative costs and provide a reasonable return on investment. If a contribution approach is used, the markup must be large enough to cover all fixed costs and generate a reasonable return on investment.

REMEMBER THIS...

- For normal pricing of products, management should consider all costs, not just differential costs.
- With the functional cost approach, "costs" are defined as product costs, and the markup must cover period costs plus a reasonable return on investment.
- With the contribution approach, "costs" are defined as variable costs, and the markup must cover fixed costs plus a reasonable return on investment.

REVIEW OF LEARNING OBJECTIVES

(1) **Understand the concepts of sunk costs and differential costs and revenues, and be able to identify those costs and revenues that are relevant to making product and process decisions.**

- Differential costs are the future costs that change as a result of a decision. Only differential costs and revenues are relevant to decisions.
- Sunk costs are never relevant because they are past costs or future costs that cannot be changed.
- Qualitative factors must be considered.

(2) **Decide whether to accept or reject a special order.** When excess capacity exists, take a special order IF:

Special price > Variable costs + Direct fixed costs.

(3) **Determine whether a company should make a product itself or whether it should outsource the production to a supplier.** MAKE a product IF:

Cost of purchasing > Variable costs + Direct fixed costs +
Opportunity cost of alternative uses of the facilities.

(4) **Identify when a company should drop a product line or exit or enter a market.** KEEP a product line IF:

Revenue > Variable costs + Direct fixed costs +
Opportunity cost of alternative uses of the resources.

(5) **Determine whether to sell a joint product as it is or to process it further before selling it.** Process further IF:

Incremental revenue from the extra processing > Incremental processing costs incurred
after the split-off point.

(6) **Select the best use of a scarce resource.** Choose the item that provides the greatest contribution margin per unit of the most critical resource. The formula to use is:

Contribution margin per product ÷ Required units of scarce resource per product.

(7) **Use cost information in setting normal selling prices.**

- For normal pricing of products, management should consider all costs, not just differential costs.
- With the functional cost approach, "costs" are defined as product costs, and the markup must cover period costs plus a reasonable return on investment.
- With the contribution approach, "costs" are defined as variable costs, and the markup must cover fixed costs plus a reasonable return on investment.

KEY TERMS & CONCEPTS

common costs, 1089	differential costs, 1077	joint product costs, 1093	special order, 1081
critical resource factor, 1094	joint manufacturing process, 1092	opportunity cost, 1077	sunk costs, 1077
		outsourcing, 1084	

REVIEW PROBLEM

Whether to Make or Buy a Part

Schill Manufacturing Company makes lawn mowers. It has been buying a component from a regular supplier for $11.50 per unit. Because Schill recently has been operating at less than full capacity, the president is considering whether to make the part rather than purchase it. The estimated total cost of making the part under the company's costing system is $14.40, computed as follows:

Direct materials	$ 3.20
Direct labor	5.60
Manufacturing overhead (100% of direct labor cost)	5.60
Estimated total cost to make	$14.40

Variable manufacturing overhead costs are estimated to be 40% of direct labor cost. Fixed manufacturing costs that are not differential are 60% of direct labor cost.

Required:

Decide whether Schill should make or buy the component.

Solution

Differential-Cost Analysis		
	Cost to Make	**Cost to Buy**
Purchase price		$11.50
Direct materials	$ 3.20	
Direct labor	5.60	
Variable manufacturing overhead (40% of direct labor cost)*	2.24	
Differential cost to make the part	$11.04	
Differential cost to buy the part		$11.50
Cost savings by making the part	$ 0.46	

*Calculation: $5.60 × 0.40 = $2.24 variable manufacturing overhead.

Unless qualitative factors override the cost estimate, Schill should make the part rather than purchase it. The decision will be the same whether the calculation is based on differential costs only or on total costs.

DISCUSSION QUESTIONS

1. Many accounting systems are designed to collect financial information for the purpose of preparing financial statements. What problem does this create for an accountant who is asked to compile relevant data for use by managers to make product and process decisions? Explain.

2. What is a differential cost? Give an example of how differential costs are used by managers making product and process decisions.

3. Distinguish between variable costs and differential costs. Why is the distinction important?

4. Can a fixed cost be relevant to a decision? Explain.

5. What is a sunk cost? Why are sunk costs irrelevant in product and process decision making?

6. In deciding whether to replace an old asset with a new one, which of the following are differential revenues and costs?
   a. Cost of the new equipment
   b. Resale value of the old equipment
   c. Resale value of the new equipment
   d. Book value of the old equipment
   e. Operating costs of the new equipment

7. Why must business decisions be based on qualitative as well as quantitative information? Explain.

8. Explain what costs are generally relevant to make-or-buy decisions.

9. Explain why opportunity costs are not included in the accounting records.

10. What is the significance of idle capacity in determining the price of a special order?

11. If total manufacturing costs, including fixed manufacturing overhead, are larger than the price offered by a purchaser for a special order, the order should not be accepted because the profits of the company will be adversely affected. Do you agree? Explain. (Ignore qualitative factors.)

12. In deciding whether to exit or enter a market, what factors should be considered?

13. When should a segment (product, product line, division, etc.) be dropped? When should a segment be added?

14. Why is the contribution margin per unit of a critical resource more important than the contribution margin per unit of product in deciding which products to produce and sell?

15. What determines whether a product should be sold at the point of separation from a joint process or after further processing? (Assume that a decision is to be based solely on quantitative information.)

PRACTICE EXERCISES

PE 21-1   **Differential Costs, Sunk Costs, and Opportunity Costs**

LO1   Which one of the following statements is *false*?

a. A sunk cost is one that has already been incurred.

b. Differential costs can be eliminated in whole or in part by choosing one alternative over another.

c. Opportunity cost is the amount of profit given up by choosing one alternative over another.

d. A differential cost is one that cannot be avoided.

PE 21-2   **Sunk Costs**

LO1   Which one of the following would be considered a sunk cost?

a. Variable cost of materials to build a new product

b. Additional insurance for a new product line

c. The total amount paid to purchase investment securities last year; the securities have recently declined in value by 50%

d. Expected annual maintenance costs for new equipment

PE 21-3   **Differential Costs and Decision Making**

LO1   St. Mary Mills, Inc. (SMM) uses high-quality looms to manufacture its textile products. SMM has decided to replace one of its looms and has researched the following cost data on replacement looms. Using the following cost data, decide which alternative the company should pursue with respect to buying and operating a new piece of equipment. Use the differential-cost approach.

	Severn Manufacturing	Old Mill Supplies
Cost of new equipment	$61,300	$55,000
Lifetime service and maintenance contract	1,200	4,800
Resale value of old equipment	500	500
Expected fixed operating costs	400	120
Original cost of old equipment	20,000	20,000

PE 21-4

LO2

Special Order Pricing

The company is deciding whether to accept a special order. The company's costs for the most recent year were as follows:

Total variable costs	$2,800,000
Total fixed costs	1,300,000

The company produced 100,000 units in the most recent year. What is the minimum price per unit at which the company should accept the special order (ignoring any qualitative factors)?

PE 21-5

LO2

Special Orders–The Seller's Decision

At the end of a very mild winter, the company has enough raw materials to produce 1,000 coats, and the materials can be used only for coats. The material is very sensitive and will not be usable if it is not used immediately. The company does not expect to be able to receive the full sales price of $120 per coat, and the company needs production storage space to make room for the raw materials for its summer clothes inventory production. The company has received a special order from one of its customers for 1,000 coats at $70 per coat. The cost of making one coat (assuming a production run of 1,000 coats) is as follows:

Direct materials	$25 per coat
Direct labor	$40 per coat
Manufacturing overhead	$20 per coat

For the manufacturing overhead, $15 per coat relates to fixed overhead, primarily wages paid to special technicians who repair the equipment used to make the coats. These technicians are hired from an outside company and will not be hired if the coats are not made. Should the company accept the special order?

PE 21-6

LO3

Making or Buying Manufactured Parts

The company currently makes a part used in the production of its best-selling product. The company has the option to buy this same part from a supplier for $55 per part. The company uses 800 of these parts each period and has the following cost data for producing these 800 parts:

	Cost per Unit
Direct labor	$20
Direct materials	12
Variable manufacturing overhead	13
Fixed manufacturing overhead, direct*	7
Fixed manufacturing overhead, indirect*	10

*Based on 800 units per period. If the parts are purchased from the supplier, the direct fixed manufacturing overhead costs can be avoided.

Should the company buy the 800 parts per period from the supplier or continue to make them?

PE 21-7

LO4

Exiting a Market

Using the following information, decide whether the company should close any of its stores:

	Store 1	Store 2	Store 3
Sales revenue	$1,000,000	$1,200,000	$800,000
Variable costs	550,000	610,000	450,000
Direct fixed costs	200,000	310,000	305,000
Indirect fixed costs	70,000	70,000	70,000

PE 21-8   **Entering a Market**

LO4   Refer to the data in PE 21-7. The company's main customer is considering whether to merge with the company (and its three stores). If the merger takes place, the efficiencies associated with combining the stores with their main customer will cause variable costs at each of the three stores to decline by 25%. However, the merger will increase overall fixed costs by $300,000. Should the merger take place?

PE 21-9   **Additional Processing**

LO5   Panaca Pork Products produces and sells ham, bacon, and sausage. For years, Panaca has sold only one version of its three products. However, Panaca is now considering selling "premium" versions of each of its products. The following information is available:

	Number of Pounds Produced	Selling Price per Pound for Regular Product	Additional Processing Costs	Selling Price per Pound for Premium Product
Ham	1,000,000	$1.00	$120,000	$1.20
Bacon	400,000	0.90	90,000	1.10
Sausage	600,000	1.10	200,000	1.40

Before any additional processing costs, the total production cost for the 2,000,000 combined pounds of ham, bacon, and sausage is $1,400,000. Which, if any, of the three products (ham, bacon, and sausage) should Panaca sell as a premium product?

PE 21-10   **Contribution Margin Percentage**

LO6   Using the following information, compute the contribution margin percentage for each product.

	Product A	Product B
Selling price	$394	$140
Variable costs	256	77

PE 21-11   **Critical Resource Factor**

LO6   Refer to the data in PE 21-10. Product A requires three units of the company's critical resource, while Product B requires only two units. Compute the contribution margin per unit of critical resource to determine which product the company should emphasize in its marketing campaign.

PE 21-12   **Setting Selling Prices: Contribution Approach**

LO7   The company prices its products using a 40% markup on total variable cost to cover fixed costs and to provide a reasonable return on investment. Using the following data and the contribution approach to pricing products, estimate the normal selling price. *Note*: The markup will end up being 40% of the selling price.

	Cost per Unit
Direct materials	$10
Direct labor	17
Variable manufacturing overhead	13
Variable selling and administrative expenses	8

Fixed manufacturing overhead totals $80,000 per year. Fixed selling and administrative expenses are $55,000 per year. The average number of units sold per year is 5,000.

PE 21-13

LO7

Setting Selling Prices: Functional Cost Approach

Refer to PE 21-12. Assume that the company prices its products using a 30% markup on total manufacturing cost to cover selling and administrative expenses and to provide a reasonable return on investment. Using the following data and the functional cost approach to pricing products, estimate the normal selling price. *Note:* The markup will end up being 30% of the selling price.

EXERCISES

E 21-14

LO1

Relevant Costs

Gilliland Company provides maid services for local hotels. Last year the firm acquired a cleaning machine for $50,000. The firm expected to use the machine for five years. However, this year a new, more efficient machine has been introduced on the market. The accountant for Gilliland has determined that the annual total operating costs for the old machine are $120,000. The annual operating costs for the new machine would be $100,000, and the purchase price is $65,000. The president of Gilliland feels the company should not buy the new machine. He points out that the operating costs of $100,000 and the purchase price of $65,000 for the new machine, plus the original cost of the old machine of $50,000, are greater than the operating costs of the old machine.

1. Do you agree with the president?
2. What type of cost is the $50,000 purchase price of the old machine?

E 21-15

LO1, LO3

Qualitative Factors

Sturdy Chair Company manufactures wooden chairs. In producing the chairs, a great deal of scrap wood is created. The company currently uses the wood as fuel in a factory furnace. However, it has the opportunity to send the scrap wood to a subcontractor, who would turn it into pressed board to be used to produce small end tables as a new product of Sturdy Chair.

Identify any qualitative factors that Sturdy Chair Company might want to consider in deciding how to use the scrap wood.

E 21-16

LO2

Special Order Pricing

You are the controller for Tippets Watch Company, a manufacturer of high-quality watches. The company has excess watches, which it has not been able to market through its own distribution outlets. To utilize the excess capacity, the president is negotiating with a large department store chain to sell Tippets watches. He has asked you to estimate the minimum selling price below which Tippets should not accept an order from the retail chain. Cost information per watch is:

Direct materials	$38
Direct labor	24
Manufacturing overhead:	
Variable	14
Fixed	10
Selling and administrative expenses:	
Variable	5
Fixed	14

The fixed costs are the same whether or not the order is accepted.

1. What is the minimum selling price the company should accept based solely on cost information (not considering qualitative factors)?
2. Assume that the president agrees to sell 12,000 watches at a price of $89 per watch. What would be the expected increase in profit?

E 21-17

LO3

Make-or-Buy Decisions

Nelson Car Audio needs 500 amplifiers to complete this month's car stereo shipment. If Nelson Car Audio buys rather than makes the amplifiers, some of the facilities still cannot be used in another manufacturing activity. Twenty-five percent of the fixed manufacturing overhead costs are indirect and will still be incurred regardless of which decision is made. The per-unit costs of making and buying the amplifiers are:

Cost to make the amplifier:	
Direct materials	$ 25
Direct labor	50
Variable manufacturing overhead	35
Fixed manufacturing overhead	40
	$150
Cost to buy the amplifier from another company	$144

Identify the differential costs of making the amplifier as a basis for deciding whether to make or buy it.

E 21-18

LO3

Make-or-Buy Decisions

Miller Manufacturing builds and markets personal computers for home and small business use. The company has been approached by an outside supplier offering to provide LCD monitors to the company for $96 each. The company's marketing director negotiated the deal personally and is thrilled about how much cheaper it will be to purchase the monitors from outside. Producing the following cost data, the manager proudly proclaims, "Look, a $22.40 per-unit savings!" Miller Manufacturing currently sells 30,000 LCD monitors along with its personal computer sales.

	Per Unit	30,000 Units per Year
Direct materials	$ 44.80	$1,344,000
Direct labor	16.00	480,000
Variable manufacturing overhead	4.80	144,000
Fixed manufacturing overhead, direct	9.60	288,000
Fixed manufacturing overhead, indirect	43.20	1,296,000
Total cost	$118.40	$3,552,000

1. Assuming zero opportunity costs, should the company accept the outside offer?
2. If the monitors are purchased from outside, Miller can produce an alternative product that will contribute $600,000 per year toward covering indirect fixed overhead. Will this affect your decision in part (1)?

E 21-19

LO3

Make-or-Buy Decisions

Tricia Company has been manufacturing 9,000 units of part Y for its products. The unit cost for the part is as follows:

Direct materials	$ 9
Direct labor	24
Variable manufacturing overhead	12
Fixed manufacturing overhead	18
Total	$63

A supplier has offered to sell 9,000 units of part Y to Tricia for $54 each. If the part is purchased, Tricia can use its facilities to manufacture another product, which would generate a contribution margin of $12,000. Seventy-five percent of the fixed manufacturing overhead costs are indirect and will still be incurred even if the part is purchased.

Compute the net differential cost in deciding whether to make or buy the part.

E 21-20

LO3

Purchasing Services from Outside

Dr. Anderson, a local dentist, is considering reducing his office staff and outsourcing the management of his accounts receivable. Currently, he has an office manager and two part-time workers on his staff. One part-time employee spends almost 100% of her time sending out billing notices and following up on collections. Even then, Dr. Anderson is able to collect on only about 80% of the receivables. A collection agency wants Dr. Anderson's business. It will handle all billing and collection details for a monthly fee of $1,500. The agency believes it can deliver a 90% collection of receivables. Another firm, We Collect, Inc., has approached Anderson with a proposal that would shift all accounts receivable risk to We Collect, Inc. Anderson would receive 85% of all receivables automatically. Additional information follows:

Anderson's average yearly accounts receivable	$400,000
Anderson's average annual bad debt expense	80,000
Part-time accounts receivable employee salary	12,000

Which of the following alternatives should Anderson pursue concerning his accounts receivable?

1. Maintain status quo (part-time employee handling accounts receivable).
2. Outsource to collection agency.
3. Outsource to We Collect, Inc.

E 21-21

LO5

Joint Costs and Further Processing

Pure Paint Company has been known for years for its two excellent interior wall paints: Nice & Smooth and Rich & Thick. The company has discovered that by processing Rich & Thick further it could produce a slightly different paint.

Nice & Smooth and Rich & Thick are produced jointly at a cost of $160,000, which is allocated equally between them. If Rich & Thick were processed further, its selling price would increase by $2.25 per unit, and the additional cost per unit would be $1.80.

1. On the basis of the information given (and disregarding qualitative factors), should the company process Rich & Thick further? Do you have enough information to make a recommendation? Explain.
2. **Interpretive Question:** Is the joint cost of $160,000 relevant to this discussion? Why or why not?

E 21-22

LO5

Sell Now or Process Further

Colorado Steak Company (CSC) uses a joint process to manufacture three types of beef: roasts, steaks, and ground beef. Each product can be sold at the point of separation, or it can be processed further. All additional processing costs are directly traceable to each product that is processed further. Joint production costs for the year are $140,000 and are allocated to all three products on the basis of their sales values at the point of separation. The pertinent data accumulated by the accounting department for these products are:

Product	Units	Sales Value at Separation	Allocation of Joint Costs	Sales Value and Additional Costs of Processing Further	
				Sales Value	Additional Costs
Steak	18,000	$150,000	$70,000	$190,000	$24,000
Roast	20,000	120,000	56,000	150,000	40,000
Ground	10,000	30,000	14,000	60,000	25,000

1. Which products should Colorado Steak Company process further (after separation) in order to maximize its profits? Show computations.
2. Explain why you did or did not use the allocated joint costs in deciding which of the products to process further.

E 21-23
LO4

Discontinuing a Product Line

Swanton Company currently sells three products: desk calendars, pen sets, and paper-clip holders. The company is thinking of discontinuing the production and sale of paper-clip holders. However, because many customers buy the products as a set, Swanton estimates that the sales of the other two products will decrease by 20% if the paper-clip holders are discontinued.

Current data on each of the three products are provided below.

	Desk Calendars	Pen Sets	Paper-Clip Holders	Total
Units	40,000	20,000	14,000	
Sales revenue	$280,000	$240,000	$42,000	$562,000
Variable costs	160,000	160,000	45,000	365,000
Direct fixed costs	40,000	20,000	5,000	65,000
Indirect fixed costs	30,000	40,000	10,000	80,000

1. What is the segment margin of the paper-clip holders?
2. **Interpretive Question:** Would you recommend dropping the paper-clip holder product line? Why or why not?

E 21-24
LO4

Adding a New Product

Cuda, Inc., is thinking about adding a new product line. Marketing surveys indicate that sales of the new product would be 100,000 units. Each unit sells for $8. Direct variable costs would be $5.60 per unit, direct fixed costs would be $60,000, and $45,000 represents the company's indirect fixed costs. The company does not expect the new product to affect the sales of its other products.

Should Cuda, Inc., add the new product? Why or why not?

E 21-25
LO6

Contribution Margin per Unit of a Critical Resource

Haws Electronics produces two products, CD players and clock radios. Both products are extremely popular, and the company can sell as many of either product as it can produce. Haws Electronics can produce only a limited number of products, however, because only 12,000 direct labor hours are available due to the isolated location of the community. It takes four hours of direct labor to produce a CD player and three hours to produce a clock radio. The selling price of a CD player is $68, and the variable costs are $40. The selling price of a clock radio is $52, with variable costs of $28.

Which product should Haws Electronics produce if its direct labor hours are limited?

E 21-26
LO6

Critical Resource Constraints

B&B Manufacturing (BBM) makes two types of lawnmower engines which it supplies to lawnmower manufacturers: a turbo and a self-propelling engine. The company has agreed to a limited supply of skilled labor with the local machinist union of 9,000 labor hours. Due to supply constraints, BBM has been able to obtain only a limited number of engine bolts, a necessary part in the production process. Anticipated sales have exceeded capacity for both engines.

Information on each product is as follows:

	Turbo	Self-Propelling
Contribution margin per unit	$4	$5
Units produced per hour	3	2
Units produced per 100 bolts	60	80

Total labor hours available: 9,000 hours
Total bolts available: 30,000 bolts

1. Identify the critical resource constraint under which BBM must operate.
2. Which product should be produced?

E 21-27 **Pricing Regular Products**

LO7   Medical Care, Inc., is considering what price to charge for Sparkle, a toothpaste that is sold in its leased store at a hospital. The accountant has been asked to prepare an estimated normal selling price based on the costs that Medical Care incurs in making the product in a factory it operates. Costs of producing one tube of Sparkle are 20 cents for direct materials, 10 cents for direct labor, 20 cents for variable manufacturing overhead, and 10 cents for variable selling and administrative costs. Total direct fixed costs are $10,000. The company estimates that a markup of 40% of the selling price is necessary to cover the fixed costs and provide a reasonable return on investment.

1. Calculate the estimated normal selling price.
2. Would you recommend that the company obtain any other information before establishing a sales price?

PROBLEMS

P 21-28 **Special Order Pricing**

LO2   Midwest Company manufactures portable radios. Shop Smart, a large retail merchandiser, wants to buy 200,000 radios from Midwest Company for $12 each. The radio would carry Shop Smart's name and would be sold in its stores.

Midwest Company normally sells 420,000 radios per year at $16 each; its production capacity is 540,000 units per year. Cost information for the radios is as follows:

Production costs:	
Variable production costs	$7
Fixed manufacturing overhead ($2,100,000 ÷ 420,000 units)	5
Selling and administrative expenses:	
Variable	1
Fixed ($420,000 ÷ 420,000 units)	1

The $1 variable selling and administrative expenses would not be applicable to the radios ordered by Shop Smart because that is a single large order. Shop Smart has indicated that the company is not interested in signing a contract for less than 200,000 radios. Total fixed costs will not change regardless of whether the Shop Smart order is accepted.

Required:

1. Identify any opportunity costs that Midwest Company should consider when making the decision.
2. Determine whether Midwest Company should accept Shop Smart's offer.
3. **Interpretive Question:** What qualitative factors might be relevant to this decision?

P 21-29 **Make-or-Buy Decisions**

LO3   Logan Company manufactures several toy products. One is a large plastic truck, which requires a plastic truck body, two metal axles, and four rubber wheels. Logan currently manufactures and assembles all the parts.

Another toy company has offered to sell the parts to Logan at $1.95 per truck if 60,000 or more parts are purchased each year, and at $2.15 per truck if less than 60,000 parts are purchased. Logan is considering this offer. The space used in producing the parts could be used for a new toy, which is scheduled to begin production next year. If Logan continues to produce the parts for the plastic truck, the company will have to lease space from another company in an adjacent building to produce the new toy. The rent would be $16,100 per year.

(continued)

Other information related to the truck is:

	Produce Parts	Assemble Truck	Total
Direct materials	$1.30	$0.20	$1.50
Direct labor	0.30	0.20	0.50
Variable manufacturing overhead	0.25	0.15	0.40
Fixed manufacturing overhead	0.20	0.40	0.60
Total manufacturing costs	$2.05	$0.95	$3.00

The marketing department has estimated that sales for the plastic truck will be approximately 46,000 units per year for the next three years. The fixed manufacturing overhead is indirect and will still be incurred regardless of which decision is made.

Required:

1. Describe Logan Company's two alternatives for this decision.
2. What costs are relevant to the decision?
3. Which alternative should Logan Company select?
4. What would be the better decision had Logan not planned to produce the new toy?
5. **Interpretive Question:** What are some of the qualitative factors that Logan Company might consider in making the decision?

P 21-30

LO3

Choosing between Two Machines

Bruce's Bakery is thinking of making its own Danishes. Two machines, A and B, are being considered for purchase. The company now purchases the Danishes from an outside supplier for 20 cents each. The cost information for producing the Danishes would be:

	Machine A	Machine B
Variable costs per Danish	$0.16	$0.14
Annual fixed costs	$3,500	$5,000
Initial cost of machine	$10,000	$24,000
Salvage value at end of five years	$0	$8,000
Estimated life of machine	5 years	5 years

Required:

1. At a sales volume of 275,000 Danishes per year, which of these alternatives is best— buying the Danishes, using machine A, or using machine B? (Ignore the time value of money, and assume straight-line depreciation.)
2. At what level of production would you be indifferent between machine A and machine B? Which machine is preferable if production exceeds this volume?

P 21-31

LO3

Purchasing Services from Outside

Northeast Reinsurance Company is growing rapidly. As it has grown, it has added legal staff to provide for its legal services. One of the principals of the company is an attorney who has provided oversight over the growing legal department. However, she is now too busy to continue this "legal counsel" role. She suggests that the senior company attorney become an officer of the company and be given the title "legal counsel and secretary." Another of the principals is good friends with an attorney at a prestigious regional law firm. That law firm has offered to provide Northeast with legal services for an annual retainer of $500,000 plus an average billing rate of $100 per hour for all work done over 5,000 hours per year. It is expected that legal work, whether done inside or outside the company, will require about 6,000 hours this coming year and will probably increase by 10% a year thereafter. The current company legal staff may be able to handle the work load for two years before it

(continued)

will have to hire another attorney (at an expected salary and benefit package of $100,000). Other variable costs are expected to increase by 5% a year.

Additional information follows:

	Current Costs of Internal Legal Department
Salaries and benefits of legal staff	$350,000
Travel costs	80,000
Required continuing education costs	10,000
Legal support costs (library, computers, software, supplies, etc.)	100,000
Other variable costs	25,000
Allocated office overhead (depreciation, utilities, etc.)	40,000
Total costs of legal department	$605,000

Required:

1. What are the relevant costs for Northeast to consider in making this decision?
2. From a financial standpoint, should Northeast continue to use its own legal department for legal services or outsource this function to the regional law firm?
3. What other factors might Northeast consider in making this decision?

P 21-32
LO3

Unifying Concepts: Make-or-Buy Decisions (Differential Costs and Opportunity Costs)

Snow Corporation manufactures commercial freezers for use in restaurant kitchens. The company is planning to produce a new freezer suitable for large hotel kitchens. These smaller freezers require a component that Snow Corporation can either make or buy from a subcontractor. The subcontractor will sell the part for $29. The costs for making 18,000 units of the part are as follows:

Direct materials	$12 per unit
Direct labor	$9 per unit
Variable manufacturing overhead	$6 per unit
Fixed manufacturing overhead	$60,000*

*The $60,000 fixed manufacturing overhead includes $24,000 of indirect fixed costs allocated to the part and $36,000 for a production manager.

If the part is produced, Snow Corporation will use an idle machine it already owns. If the part is bought, the company plans to rent the machine and the factory space to another company for $8,000 and $14,000 a year, respectively.

Snow expects that, if the part is produced, the company will be able to schedule production so that no warehouse space will be needed. However, if the part is bought, Snow will need to use warehouse space, for which it will have to pay $2,000 a year in rent.

Required:

1. Identify any opportunity costs relevant to the decision to make or buy the component.
2. Determine the differential costs of making the product.
3. Determine the differential costs of buying the product.
4. **Interpretive Question:** Would you recommend that Snow make or buy the component? Why?

P 21-33
LO5

Processing Past the Point of Separation

Style Company manufactures three items, S1, S2, and S3, which are used in the production of fabrics. Each item can be sold at the point that all three are separated from the joint production process, or they can be processed further. Presently, S1 and S2 are processed past the point of separation. The joint cost of producing the three items to the point of

(continued)

separation is $450,000. The costs past the point of separation are variable and can be traced to each product. The $450,000 joint costs are allocated to each product equally.

The following information is available:

	Number of Units Produced	Selling Price per Unit at Point of Separation	Additional Processing Costs	Selling Price per Unit After Processing
S1	100,000	$10	$120,000	$12
S2	40,000	9	90,000	11
S3	60,000	11	?	13

Required:

1. Should S1 and S2 be processed after the separation point?
2. What maximum additional processing costs could be incurred to process S3 further and still leave a profit?

P 21-34   **Dropping a Product Line**

LO4   Bryce Baseballs manufactures baseballs, baseball bats, and baseball gloves. The company is thinking of dropping baseball gloves as a product line. The following report was prepared by the accounting department:

	Baseballs	Baseball Bats	Baseball Gloves	Total
Sales revenues	$ 240,000	$105,000	$ 25,000	$ 370,000
Variable costs	(185,000)	(70,000)	(12,000)	(267,000)
Contribution margin	$ 55,000	$ 35,000	$ 13,000	$ 103,000
Direct fixed costs	(20,000)	(10,000)	(13,500)	(43,500)
Segment margin	$ 35,000	$ 25,000	$ (500)	$ 59,500
Indirect fixed costs	(17,500)	(10,000)	(2,500)	(30,000)
Net income	$ 17,500	$ 15,000	$ (3,000)	$ 29,500

Required:

1. Should the baseball glove line be dropped? Why or why not?
2. **Interpretive Question:** What qualitative factors should be considered in deciding whether to drop the baseball glove line?

P 21-35   **Adding and Dropping Product Lines**

LO4   Park Manufacturing Company has been producing three products: Frisbees, Volleyballs, and Croquet. Now that the plant has been shifted to an assembly-line operation, a fourth product, Bocce, has been added. Each product has its own assembly-line operation, producing 25,000 units. Total indirect fixed costs of $200,000 are divided proportionately, based on the space allocated to each assembly line. Other pertinent information is given below.

	Frisbee	Volleyball	Croquet	Bocce
Selling price per unit	$8.00	$12.00	$24.00	$14.00
Variable cost per unit	$5.00	$9.15	$21.75	$12.75
Number of square feet	1,600	1,400	1,100	900

Required:

1. Prepare a schedule that shows net income for each product line.
2. Would total company income increase if the bocce balls were dropped? Why or why not?
3. **Interpretive Question:** If you could double the production of either the Frisbees, the Volleyballs, of the Croquet sets in place of having bocce balls, which would you choose? Why?

P 21-36

LO4

Shutting Down or Continuing Operations

End Trail Campground is open year-round. However, 80% of its revenues are generated from May through October. Because only 20% of the revenues are generated from November to April, the campground is considering closing during those months. The yearly revenues and cost information expected by End Trail for next year if the campground does not close are:

Camping fees	$1,800,000
Variable costs	990,000
Fixed costs ($40,000 per month)	480,000

The cost to close the campground at the end of October would be $20,000, and the cost to reopen in May would be $50,000. If the campground is closed, the total fixed costs are only $25,000 per month, rather than the $40,000 per month when the campground is open.

Required:

Determine whether End Trail Campground should close from November to April or remain open for the entire year.

P 21-37

LO6

Determining Production with a Critical Resource Limitation

Clarity Corporation produces three sizes of television sets: 10-inch screen, 19-inch screen, and 24-inch screen. The revenues and costs per unit for each size are as follows:

	Screen Size		
	10-inch	**19-inch**	**24-inch**
Selling price	$195	$325	$450
Variable costs:			
Direct materials	$ 55	$100	$126
Direct labor	80	120	180
Variable manufacturing overhead	40	60	90
Total variable costs	$175	$280	$396
Contribution margin	$ 20	$ 45	$ 54
Units ordered for next week	200	150	75

The company has a constraint on the amount of skilled labor available to produce television sets. Direct labor employees are paid $8 per hour. The total amount of labor time available for next week's production is 2,700 hours.

Required:

Given the units ordered for next week, which size or sizes of television sets should be produced and sold to maximize the company's profit?

P 21-38

LO6

Determining Production with a Critical Resource Limitation

A company is examining two of its products, X-121 and Y-707. The following information is being reviewed:

	X-121	**Y-707**
Unit selling price	$28.50	$21.00
Materials required per unit	$3.00	$1.50
Direct labor required per unit	$2.50	$1.25
Variable manufacturing overhead per unit	$0.50	$1.00
Production time per unit (in hours)	1.5	1

Required:

1. Which item should the company manufacture if there is no constraint on hours of production?
2. If full production capacity is 1,500 hours, and if the company can sell all the units it makes, which item should it manufacture? Why?

P 21-39

LO6

Contribution Margin per Unit of a Critical Resource

Dresser, Inc., manufactures three super-sports-hero dolls: Super Dunk, Pete Tulip, and Zonk. Production, however, is limited by the skilled labor necessary to produce these unique dolls. Data on each of the dolls are as follows:

	Super Dunk	Pete Tulip	Zonk
Contribution margin per doll	$9	$6	$8
Dolls produced per hour	30	43	40
Expected total market volume (units)	20,000	9,000	100,000
Total skilled labor hours available: 3,000 hours.			

Required:

Assuming that there are no relevant qualitative factors, how many dolls of each type should Dresser produce?

P 21-40

LO6

Unifying Concepts: Production and Advertising

Cole Company manufactures only two products—a battery charger and a testing machine for automobile engines. An average of 30,000 chargers and 50,000 testers are sold each year. This year, the company can afford only $60,000 for advertising the products, which is just enough to advertise one product effectively. The marketing manager expects that the sales of chargers will increase by 20% if they are advertised and that the sales of testers will increase by 10% if they are advertised.

The following information about the two products has been provided by the accountant:

	Charger	Tester
Selling price per unit	$70	$90
Variable cost per unit	$30	$40
Fixed cost per unit	$30	$40
Production time per unit (in hours)	2	4

Required:

1. If Cole had an unlimited number of labor hours, would you recommend that it advertise either of its products? If yes, which one and why?
2. Assume that Cole has a capacity of 260,000 labor hours. Should Cole still advertise? If so, which product should it advertise?

P 21-41

LO7

Normal Selling Price

Chojna Lighting Supply manufactures desktop and ceiling-mounted light fixtures. The company is seeking to come up with a reasonable price for its desktop executive model. Production costs for each unit follow:

Direct materials	$7 per unit
Direct labor	1.5 hours per unit
Direct labor rate	$4 per hour
Variable manufacturing overhead	$3 per labor hour
Variable selling and administrative costs	$2 per unit
Fixed overhead (direct)	$3 per unit
Markup of selling price to cover indirect overhead and expected profit	40%

Required:

Calculate the estimated normal selling price.

ANALYTICAL ASSIGNMENTS

AA 21-42
DISCUSSION

Buying from Inside or Outside the Company

E & B Company has two divisions, processing and finishing. The Finishing Division has been purchasing certain products from the Processing Division at a price of $80 per unit. (A unit consists of 100 yards of material.) The Processing Division has announced that, starting next month, it will raise its price to $100 per unit. As the manager of the Finishing Division, you object to this price and have indicated that you are planning to purchase these units of material from outside suppliers at a price of $85 per unit. You have asked the accounting department to furnish cost data to help you understand why the Processing Division's price has to be raised to $100 per unit. Following is the information supplied about the Processing Division's operations:

Units produced for Finishing Division	2,000
Variable production costs per unit	$60
Indirect fixed costs allocated to the Processing Division	$50,000
Normal profit per unit in Processing Division	$15

If the Finishing Division buys from outside suppliers, the facilities used by the Processing Division to manufacture these units for the Finishing Division will remain idle.
Answer the following questions:

1. If the Processing Division is successful in imposing the $100 price and the Finishing Division elects to buy from outside suppliers, what impact does this action have on the overall profit of E & B Company?
2. Explain why the variable production costs, the fixed costs, and the normal profit are, or are not, each relevant to this decision. (You are not being asked to discuss whether the $100 price is an appropriate price or whether the division managers should be allowed to maintain an autonomous posture in this decision.)
3. What additional factors should E & B Company's top management consider in resolving this matter?

AA 21-43
DISCUSSION

Sunk Costs

Sam Love owns and manages a small but growing service business. In fact, this year has been so good that Sam is moving his office to a larger, more centrally located site. In an effort to save on moving costs, Sam employs his brother Dan (who owns a large truck) to haul his office furniture and equipment. Unfortunately, Dan doesn't properly secure the rear door of the truck, and one of Sam's two copy machines winds up in a million pieces in the middle of the highway. As the two brothers survey the damage, Sam's office manager approaches and says, "Well, look on the bright side, the machine was half depreciated."
    Should Sam take comfort from this statement? Explain your answer.

AA 21-44
JUDGMENT CALL

You Decide: Which is more important to a company's overall success and profitability: quantitative or qualitative factors?

Often a company is judged based on the strength of financial indicators, such as sales revenue, net income, or earnings per share. However, many of these measures fail to incorporate intangible items, such as delivery time, quality control, and customer service. In a management accounting field setting, which factors are most important?

AA 21-45
REAL COMPANY
ANALYSIS

Microsoft

Find the most recent Form 10-K for **Microsoft**. Read through the report to determine how many segments of business exist within Microsoft. What approach does Microsoft appear to use in identifying operating segments within the company at large?

AA 21-46

Main Line Pictures, Inc., versus Kim Basinger

Hollywood produces a lot of entertainment, including accounting entertainment! In early 1993, the Superior Court of the State of California (Los Angeles County) heard a litigation suit filed by **Main Line Pictures, Inc.**, against the actress Kim Basinger for breach of contract. At issue was Basinger's decision to withdraw from a film project after making a verbal commitment to appear in it. The film, released in September 1993, was *Boxing Helena*. Didn't see it? That was the point of Main Line's lawsuit: the studio claimed a lot of people didn't see *Boxing Helena* because the actress who replaced Basinger (Sherilyn Fenn) did not have nearly the same box office appeal.

Main Line claimed damages due to an incremental difference in revenues and costs, which led to actual profits being less than expected, all due to not having Basinger in the film. An expert economist and an expert in film finance were called to testify regarding the appropriate size of the incremental revenue and cost differences. Hence, the case essentially became an accounting argument.

Main Line's lawyers argued that their client lost between $5.1 million and $9.7 million as a result of Basinger's withdrawal. The $5.1 million loss calculation is shown below (all amounts are in millions).

Minimum Damages, Plaintiff			
	With Basinger	**Without Basinger**	**Difference**
Foreign presales	$ 7.60	$ 2.70	$ 4.90
Domestic presales	3.00		3.00
Total revenue	$10.60	$ 2.70	$ 7.90
Production costs	(7.60)	(4.80)	(2.80)
Profit (loss)	$ 3.00	$(2.10)	$ 5.10

To understand the numbers above, you need to know a couple of things about revenues and costs in the movie business and this film in particular.

- It is extremely difficult to predict what a film will actually earn when released. There are *plenty* of examples of big budget films that did poorly at the box office, as well as inexpensive, independent films that have done very well. Hence, presale revenue (guaranteed minimum payments by a film distributor to the film producer) is the only sure revenue the producer can bank on when budgeting costs of making the film. If the film does well, then the distributor and producer share in the profits.
- After Basinger dropped out of the film, one of Main Line's partners loaned $1.7 million to the project, to be repaid out of domestic revenues.
- Often the producer will contract to share profits from presales, as well as incremental profits, with key actors. Basinger was to be paid a guaranteed $1 million to star in the film. In addition, she, her proposed co-star Ed Harris, and writer/director Jennifer Lynch were to be paid a total of 20.5% of the producer's net profits. On the other hand, Sherilyn Fenn and her co-star, Julian Sands, each received only a $100,000 guaranteed salary.
- After Basinger dropped from the film project, the producer made some changes to scale back production costs by $1.9 million.
- Often a movie project has many investing partners. Main Line had a partnership with Philippe Caland, who was, essentially, to receive 50% of net profits (after participation payments to the actors and writer), up to a maximum of $2 million.
- After withdrawing from *Boxing Helena*, Basinger received $3 million from a separate producer to star in *Final Analysis*.

Do you agree with the numbers presented above by the plaintiff? Consider all the information provided above and adjust the incremental profit analysis if needed. Be sure to defend your decision to use or not use each piece of information provided.

Source: Adapted from T. L. Barton, W. G. Shenkir, and B. C. Marinas, "Main Line vs. Basinger: A Case in Relevant Costs and Incremental Analysis," *Issues in Accounting Education*, Spring 1996, pp. 163–174.

AA 21-47

INTERNATIONAL

Ameripill Company

Located in Bartow, Alabama, the Pharmaceutical Division of **Ameripill Company** ranks among the top 15 drug companies in the world. The European Unit of the Pharmaceutical Division is divided into three markets: United Kingdom (U.K.), Germany, and France. Actual and budgeted operating reports for two recent years are presented below for these three markets.

	United Kingdom		Germany		France	
	Year 2 Budget	Year 1 Actual	Year 2 Budget	Year 1 Actual	Year 2 Budget	Year 1 Actual
Sales	$49,960	$48,080	$156,840	$137,440	$108,720	$102,560
Cost of sales	(21,982)	(21,155)	(65,872)	(57,995)	(53,414)	(50,254)
Direct expenses	(14,658)	(14,512)	(50,286)	(46,603)	(31,529)	(29,742)
Other income/expenses	(1,499)	(1,155)	(300)	(210)	(946)	(1,026)
Responsibility earnings	$11,821	$11,258	$ 40,382	$ 32,632	$ 22,831	$ 21,538
Interest income/expense*	(358)	(241)	(1,312)	(939)	(1,033)	(1,047)
Exchange gain/loss**	(142)	(338)	(150)	(210)	(272)	(286)
Division charges***	(1,629)	(1,640)	(4,700)	(4,123)	(3,262)	(3,077)
Earnings before taxes	$ 9,692	$ 9,039	$ 34,220	$ 27,360	$ 18,264	$ 17,128
Segment assets	$84,500	$88,860	$ 73,760	$ 72,900	$ 74,220	$ 73,460
Earnings before taxes	19.4%	18.8%	21.8%	19.9%	16.8%	16.7%
Return on assets	11.5%	10.2%	46.4%	37.5%	24.6%	23.3%

*Based on locally incurred debt.
**Based on the average Year 1 exchange rate with the United States.
***Fixed charge negotiated annually between the Bartow Division and the market subsidiary.

1. Analyze these reports carefully. Assuming that Ameripill requires a minimum ROA of 12%, should the company consider dropping the U.K. market?
2. Ameripill currently has a problem with one of the drugs sold in France. In the French market, Saincoeur is a highly successful treatment for heart-attack victims. (It is also sold under other names in all of Ameripill's markets.) Because of regulatory pressure in France, Saincoeur is being sold at a much lower price in France than in Germany or the United Kingdom. Despite the price ceiling, Saincoeur is a profitable product (barely) in France. However, word of the lower price is creating a lot of pressure in the neighboring markets to reduce the prices to a level similar to that of the French market. Saincoeur is a very profitable product in both Germany and the United Kingdom. How do these facts affect your previous decision regarding the U.K. market in part (1)?

Source: Adapted from S. F. Haka, B. A. Lamberton, and H. M. Sollenberger, "International Subsidiary Performance Evaluation: The Case of the Ameripill Company," *Issues in Accounting Education*, Spring 1994, pp. 168–190.

AA 21-48

ETHICS

Play World, Inc.

Roger Smith, the controller of Play World, Inc., a toy company, has just completed an analysis of a make-or-buy decision with respect to a particular part for one of the new toys the company is planning to manufacture. The result of the analysis clearly shows that the company should buy the part from one of the three available suppliers (based on written price quotations received from those suppliers within the past few weeks). Based on this analysis, Smith and the division manager, Kate Pfirman, agreed to proceed with placing an order. They issued instructions to the purchasing department indicating that the order should be placed for a price not higher than $3.40 per part. A few days later, Smith received a phone call from the purchasing department indicating that all three suppliers had raised their price to $4.00 per unit. It was a normal business practice to raise prices after written quotations had been issued.

It was immediately clear to Smith that it would be disadvantageous to his company to buy the part at the higher price. He discussed the new information with Pfirman, and they

(continued)

agreed to proceed with manufacturing plans to make the part internally. Smith thought it was rather strange that all three suppliers had raised their price to the same amount, but felt there was nothing he could do about it.

A few days later, Smith's secretary, Lynn Berry, asked if she could have a private conversation with him. Berry was obviously upset, so Smith asked her to come into his office and shut the door. Berry told him she was good friends with the secretary for the president of one of the suppliers from which Play World had planned to buy the part for the new toy. Berry's friend had casually mentioned that her boss had been on the phone with the other suppliers and they had agreed to raise the price for certain parts they were manufacturing to specified dollar amounts. Berry said she was reluctant to tell Smith because she didn't want her friend to get in trouble for revealing confidential information outside her company. For Smith, this information was the missing piece that explained why the price for the part had been raised to $4.00 by all three companies. Smith thanked Berry for the information and told her not to worry; he would keep the information to himself but would give some thought to what he would eventually do with what she had told him.

1. Who are the parties that are affected by this bid-rigging scheme?
2. What should Smith do with the information he received from Berry (keep in mind his responsibilities to the accounting profession, to his company, and to Berry)?

AA 21-49

WRITING

Airline Ticket Prices

If you have ever shopped for airline tickets, you are aware of the tremendous diversity in ticket prices for the same flight, even for those who sit in the same section (first-class, coach, etc.). Much of the difference is based on two factors: (1) when you bought your ticket and (2) whether you plan to stay over a Saturday night.

Write a one- to two-page paper describing why airline companies have so many different ticket prices. Also, why do you think it is important to the airline that clients fly back from their business trips on Sunday instead of Saturday?

Capital Investment Decisions

(1) **Understand the importance of capital budgeting and the concepts underlying strategic and capital investment decisions.** *Making decisions regarding the purchase of long-term assets or the start of a business project that will last more than one year is called capital budgeting. In these decisions, it is important to recognize that a dollar received right now is of greater value than a dollar to be received in the future; this is called the time value of money.*

(2) **Describe and use two nondiscounted capital budgeting techniques: the payback method and the unadjusted rate of return method.** *The payback method involves computing how many years of cash inflow it will take to pay for the original cost of the project; the faster the payback period, the more attractive the project. The unadjusted rate of return is a computation of the accounting return on assets (ROA) generated by a project; the higher the return, the better the project.*

(3) **Describe and use two discounted capital budgeting techniques: the net present value method and the internal rate of return method.** *A project's net present value is the value of the project over and above a benchmark return on the original investment; a company should only undertake projects with a positive net present value. The internal rate of return of a project is the actual return generated by the project, after considering the amount and timing of all cash flows.*

(4) **Understand the need for evaluating qualitative factors in strategic and capital investment decisions.** *In some long-term investment decisions, especially those for which the financial numbers don't indicate a clear choice, qualitative factors such as company image and community welfare become extremely important considerations.*

EXPANDED *material*

(5) **Use sensitivity analysis to assess the potential effects of uncertainty in capital budgeting.** *All decisions about the future involve estimates and forecasts. Prudent capital budgeting involves calculating the impact of these uncertainties.*

(6) **Explain how to use capital budgeting techniques in ranking capital investment projects.** *Usually a company doesn't have the management time or financing capacity to implement all of its attractive ideas, so an important part of capital budgeting is ranking acceptable projects in order to identify the best one.*

(7) **Explain how income taxes affect capital budgeting decisions.** *The relevant cash flows to use in making a capital budgeting decision are the after-tax cash flows. Higher income tax rates reduce cash flows from operations. However, the tax savings generated by deductions for depreciation are an important cash inflow to include in a capital budgeting analysis.*

FedEx is the largest air-freight company in the world. Frederick W. Smith, CEO and founder of FedEx, came up with his initial overnight-delivery idea as he was writing a term paper in 1965 as a Yale undergraduate. Smith's Yale professor was unimpressed with the idea and gave the paper a "C" grade. After serving two tours of duty in Vietnam as a Marine, Smith returned to the United States and began assembling the pieces to implement his idea. In 1971, Smith was optimistic about obtaining the contract to ship canceled checks around the country; he named his company "Federal Express" because the contract would have been with the Federal Reserve System. That contract never came to be, and Smith focused his attention on shipping small, time-sensitive packages through his hub-and-spoke air system centered in Memphis,

Tennessee. The inaugural night of service was March 12, 1973, but only six packages arrived at the 10,000-per-hour package handling system in Memphis. After further marketing in an expanded set of cities, a second start was attempted on April 17, 1973. That night, Federal Express handled 186 packages, and daily volume has climbed steadily ever since. In 2005, FedEx Express delivered over 3 million packages per day. In order to handle this many shipments, FedEx has become one of the largest users of airplanes and trucks in the world. As a result, managing these capital assets is a critical management activity at this company.

Sources: Robert A. Sigafoos, *Absolutely Positively Overnight!: The Unofficial History of Federal Express* (Memphis: St. Lukes Press, 1988).

How do FedEx and other companies decide which types of equipment to buy and what other capital investments to make? In this chapter, we examine that part of planning called capital budgeting, the systematic planning for long-term investments in operating assets (primarily property, plant, equipment, intangible assets, and natural resources). Capital budgeting techniques are also important in planning for a company's investments in people and information. For example, the most important decisions a university makes are not about where or when to build buildings but instead are about whom to hire for the university's faculty.

capital budgeting

Systematic planning for long-term investments in operating assets.

Capital budgeting differs from the types of planning already discussed in that it is more permanent and less retractable. A decision to increase inventory levels, for example, can be reversed within a relatively short time by cutting back on future purchases or by lowering prices to increase sales. Even a nonroutine decision to purchase, rather than make or deliver internally, a component or service can generally be changed without too much disruption to operations. On the other hand, a capital investment decision to purchase a fleet of freight aircraft at tens of millions of dollars each requires a long-term commitment of resources, a commitment that will probably be difficult and very expensive to change at a later date. Because of its long-term consequences, capital budgeting is an important part of a company's strategic plan.

Because capital budgeting involves long-range planning, the time value of money must be considered. But before we begin to explain how capital budgeting provides management with information for evaluating long-term investments in operating assets, we must introduce some basic concepts.

FYI

FedEx, along with most airlines, leases many of the airplanes it uses. Technically, these leases, which are often for long periods of time and are not cancelable, are not equivalent to the purchase of the airplanes. However, the same capital budgeting analysis used to evaluate a purchase is used to evaluate a long-term lease.

Conceptual Basis of Capital Budgeting

Understand the importance of capital budgeting and the concepts underlying strategic and capital investment decisions.

(1) The primary objective of a business is to generate a profit for its owners. Profitable businesses can be based on a low-cost strategy (such as **Wal-Mart**), a customer service strategy (such as **FedEx**), a product-branding strategy (such as **Coca-Cola**), and a variety of other business strategies. No matter what a company's underlying strategy, it must make long-term investment decisions in buildings, equipment, information technology, personnel, and so forth. Capital budgeting is the process of determining whether the future sales, cost savings, quality improvements, and other future benefits stemming from these strategic investment decisions are sufficient to justify the significant up-front costs associated with those decisions. In short, capital budgeting involves a comparison of the magnitude of up-front costs to the magnitude of estimated future multi-year benefits.

capital

The total amount of money or other resources owned or used to acquire future income or benefits.

The term **capital** may be defined broadly as any form of material wealth. As used in business, it is more specifically defined as the total amount of money or other resources owned or used by an individual or a company to acquire future income or benefits.

Thus, capital is something to be invested with the expectation that it will be recovered along with a profit, and capital budgeting is the planning for that investment. From a quantitative viewpoint, the success of an investment depends on the amount of net future cash inflows (or future cash savings) in relation to the cost (current cash outlays) of the investment. Ignoring the time value of money for the moment, if a company invests $10,000 and receives only $10,000 in the future, there has been only a return of the investment but no profit; in other words, there has been no return on the investment. However, if $15,000 is received in the future, there is not only a return of the original investment but also an additional return on the investment, or profit, of $5,000. Other things being equal, investors obviously wish to receive the greatest future benefits for the least investment cost.

Importance of Capital Investment Decisions in Planning

Three aspects of capital investment decisions are critical to long-run profitability:

1. *Large initial outlay.* Decisions to invest in assets such as land, buildings, and equipment usually require large outlays of capital. Firms making poor decisions involving these large assets will struggle to survive.
2. *Potential long-term impact on earnings.* Long-term investments, by definition, extend over several years. Thus, poor capital budgeting, resulting in bad investment decisions, is likely to have an adverse effect on earnings over a long period.
3. *Difficult to reverse course.* Long-term investments in land, buildings, and specialized equipment are much less liquid than other investments. Investments in stocks and bonds, for example, can usually be terminated by sale through regularly established markets at almost any time. It is much more difficult to dispose of capital assets.

Uses of Capital Budgeting: Screening and Ranking

Clearly, all long-term investment decisions are important. The larger the investment, however, the more critical is the need to budget for that expenditure. And the longer the time period, the more difficult it is to assess future outcomes and to plan accordingly. Following are some typical business decisions that can be better understood with capital budgeting techniques.

1. A machine breaks down. Should the manager have the machine repaired or replaced?
2. Should a pharmaceutical company hire a renowned research scientist and commit to supporting this scientist and her staff for the next 10 years?

3. Should a company add to its manufacturing facility or build a new, larger factory?
4. Should a professional sports team sign a long-term guaranteed contract for $252 million with a key player?
5. Should Company A purchase Company B and, if so, on what terms?

Situations such as these require careful consideration of all factors, qualitative as well as quantitative, and it is just as important for nonprofit organizations to make sound strategic and capital investment decisions as for-profit organizations. Thus, the concepts and techniques discussed in this chapter are applicable to all types of organizations—companies, governmental agencies, school districts, hospitals, municipalities, and so forth.

Capital budgeting analysis can help by answering two basic questions. First, does the investment make sense? That is, does it meet a minimum standard of financial acceptability? This is the **screening** function of capital budgeting. Second, is an investment the best among available acceptable alternatives? We determine this by ranking the alternatives. Before we discuss the screening and **ranking** of investment alternatives, we will briefly review the time value of money concept.

> **screening**
>
> Determining whether a capital investment meets a minimum standard of financial acceptability.

> **ranking**
>
> The ordering of acceptable investment alternatives from most to least desirable.

> **interest**
>
> The payment (cost) for the use of money.

The Time Value of Money

Like other commodities, money has value because it is a scarce resource. Therefore, a payment is generally required for its use. This payment is called **interest**. Because the time value of money is widely recognized, few people would consider hiding money under a mattress or otherwise keeping large amounts of idle cash; they realize that there is a significant opportunity cost in doing so. Money left idle will not earn interest from a bank, nor will it earn the potentially higher returns that can be obtained from investments in corporate stocks and bonds or real estate, for example.

Because money has value over time, the timing of expected cash flows is important in investment decisions. This is the essence of capital budgeting—comparing the cost of an investment with the expected future net cash inflows to decide whether, given the risks and available alternatives, the project should be undertaken. An investment made today will not generate cash inflows until the future, either periodically over a number of years or in a lump sum several years hence. Thus, for the comparison of cash flows to be accurate, all amounts should be stated at their value at one point in time, generally the present; this means that all future cash flows should be stated in terms of their present values. This mathematical process of adjusting future cash flows to their present values is called discounting.

The choice of the correct interest rate, or discount rate, to use in doing time value of money computations is extremely important. In fact, this is one of the topics emphasized in the field of finance. Generally speaking, managers use relatively high discount rates when evaluating projects or investments that involve a high degree of risk; an expectation of a high rate of return is necessary to entice a rational manager into undertaking a very risky project. In addition, a manager must consider what it will cost to obtain the funds to finance the project. We will return later to the problem of selecting a discount rate for making capital investment decisions.

In the remainder of this chapter and in the end-of-chapter exercises and problems, we will assume that you understand the concepts of present value and the underlying notion of the time value of money. If you do not, or if you want to refresh your memory, you might want to review the appendix to this chapter.

CAUTION

If you are using a business calculator, you might note that a more precise calculation of the present value of $100,000 to be received one year from now, if the interest rate is 10%, is $90,909.09. The $90,910 amount results from using present value tables. In this chapter, calculations using both present value tables and business calculators will be illustrated.

Discounting Cash Flows

Because of the time value of money, a difference in the timing of cash flows can make one investment more attractive than another, even if both involve the same total amount of money. To illustrate, we assume that project A will produce $100,000 at the end of one year and that project B will return $50,000 at the end of each year for two years. Both projects will generate a total return of $100,000. However, by using present value computations (reviewed in the chapter appendix) and assuming a discount (interest) rate of 10% per year, you will see that the discounted cash flows from project A are $90,910 and from project B are $86,775. In other words, if the appropriate discount rate is 10%, receiving $90,910 right now is the same as receiving $100,000 one year from now. Similarly, receiving $86,775 right now is the same as receiving $50,000 at the end of each year for the next two years. The difference in the present values of these two projects with the same total cash flows arises because with project A, the cash is received sooner. Cash received sooner is worth more because it can be put to productive use—invested, used to pay off loans, and so forth. If all other factors—that is, any qualitative considerations—are the same, an investor would be $4,135 (in today's dollars) better off by investing in project A.

Project A

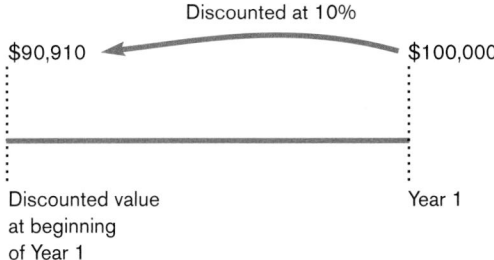

Project B

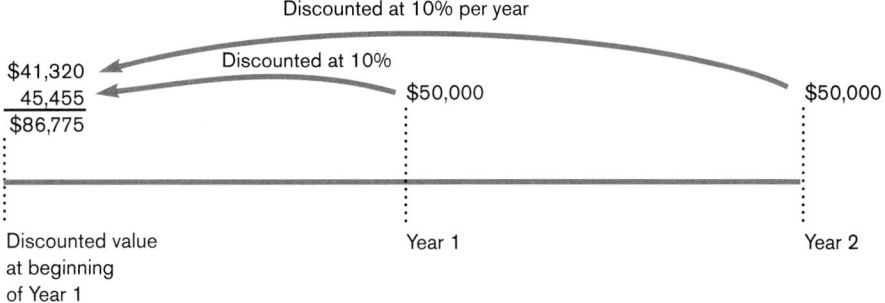

As the analysis above shows, discounted cash flows reflect the time value of money and should be considered in capital budgeting. For short-term investments, this approach does not significantly affect the results. Ignoring the time value of money can be misleading, however, when evaluating long-term projects.

The determination of net income in accordance with GAAP is based, as you know, on accrual concepts that recognize income when it is earned, not when cash is actually received. Thus, accounting net income doesn't necessarily coincide with cash flows. In capital budgeting, the focus is on cash flows because the computations are based on the returns that can be earned on alternative investments. To be able to do these computations, you need a solid understanding of how to measure cash inflows and outflows. In the following paragraphs, we provide some definitions and examples.

cash outflows

The initial cost and other expected outlays associated with an investment.

Cash Outflows Cash outflows include the initial cost of an investment plus any other expected future cash outlays associated with the investment. For example, suppose that a company purchases a drill press for $8,000 cash less a trade-in allowance of $500 for its old press. With maintenance expenses of $400 at the end of each year for the 5-year life of the press, and assuming a 12% discount rate, the present value of the cash outflows for the investment is computed as follows:

	Time Period	Cash Outflows	Present Value Factor	Present Value of Cash Outflows
Initial cash outlay	Today	$7,500	1.0000	$7,500
Future cash outlays	Years 1–5	400	3.6048*	1,442
Total present value of cash outflows				$8,942

*From Table II, 5 years at 12%.

CAUTION

In the examples used in this chapter, we provide the amounts of the future cash flows that are discounted. With real capital budgeting decisions, however, it is often very difficult to determine what the amounts of future cash inflows and outflows will be. With capital budgeting, we are dealing with future outcomes that are often difficult to project. It is this uncertainty about the future that makes capital budgeting so complex in the real world.

The $7,500 is invested immediately, so it is already stated at its present value. The $400 series of equal payments (an annuity) is to be extended over five years, so it must be discounted to its present value equivalent.

Maintenance expense is only one category of future cash outflows. Another is manufacturing overhead costs—such as heat, electricity, and rent—that may be incurred as a consequence of an investment. In addition, income taxes are expenses that must be considered in almost all capital budgeting decisions made by businesses. For simplicity, income taxes are ignored in the first part of this chapter; the impact of income taxes on capital budgeting decisions is explained in the expanded material section of the chapter. In brief, all current or expected cash outlays (expressed in terms of present values) should be considered as cash outflows in evaluating investments.

Note that some expenses, although deducted from revenues in arriving at accounting net income, do not involve actual cash disbursements and so should not be considered outflows in capital budgeting. It would obviously be wrong, for example, to include depreciation expense as an outflow, since no cash flow is directly involved.

cash inflows

Any current or expected revenues or savings directly associated with an investment.

Cash Inflows   Cash inflows include all current and expected future revenues or savings directly associated with an investment. For example, rent receipts, installment payments, and other revenues represent cash inflows. Returning to our earlier example, we now assume that the drill press is expected to generate annual revenues of $2,500 for five years, after which it can be sold as scrap for $750. The present value of the cash inflows for the investment is computed as follows:

	Time Period	Cash Inflows	Present Value Factor	Present Value of Cash Inflows
Future cash revenues	Years 1–5	$2,500	3.6048*	$9,012
Cash salvage value	Years 5	750	0.5674**	426
Total present value of cash inflows				$9,438

*From Table II, 5 years at 12%.
**From Table I, 5 years at 12%.

These revenues may be shown "net"—that is, reduced by any direct expenses, such as those for maintenance or materials and supplies. Thus, the net annual cash inflows from the drill press would be $2,100 per year ($2,500 − $400 maintenance expense).

Less obvious cash inflows are cash savings that occur when an investment reduces future costs. In brief, the present value of all cash that is likely to be received or saved as a result of an investment should be included as cash inflows.

> ### REMEMBER THIS...
>
> - Capital budgeting involves a comparison of the current and expected cash outflows and inflows in order to decide whether, given the risks and available alternatives, an investment should be made.
> - To make comparisons more meaningful, all future cash flows should be discounted to the present to reflect the time value of money.

Nondiscounted Capital Budgeting Techniques

Describe and use two nondiscounted capital budgeting techniques: the payback method and the unadjusted rate of return method.

(2) The four most commonly used capital budgeting techniques are:

1. the payback method,
2. the unadjusted rate of return method,
3. the net present value method, and
4. the internal rate of return method.

We will discuss the first two methods in this section and the latter two in the next section.

We have chosen the sequence of our discussion to parallel the pattern of most companies as they grow larger and become more sophisticated in the way that they make investment decisions. That is, companies generally first use the payback method or the unadjusted rate of return method because these techniques are relatively simple. Both of these techniques have a serious weakness, however, in that they ignore the time value of money. As a result, most companies eventually turn to either the net present value method or the internal rate of return method, both of which are more theoretically correct approaches to capital budgeting. The last two techniques are referred to as **discounted cash flow methods** because they use a discount rate in comparing the cash flows of investments.

discounted cash flow methods

Capital budgeting techniques that take into account the time value of money by comparing discounted cash flows.

Payback Method

payback method

A capital budgeting technique that determines the amount of time it takes the net cash inflows of an investment to repay the investment cost.

The **payback method** is widely used in business because it is simple to apply and it provides a preliminary screening of investment opportunities. It can also be used as a crude measure of a project's risk. Basically, this method is used to determine the length of time it will take the net cash inflows of an investment to equal the initial cash outlay. The payback period is a particularly important consideration for companies in a tight cash position. Assuming that the payback period is to be computed in years (any time period can be applied) and that equal cash flows are generated for each period, the simple formula for a project's payback period is:

$$\frac{\text{Investment cost}}{\text{Annual net cash inflows}} = \text{Payback period}$$

To illustrate the payback method, we will consider Kristi Felt's decision to purchase a personal computer, printer, and software for typing and printing essays and term papers for other students. A reasonably good PC, printer, and appropriate software will cost Kristi a total of $1,500. She can borrow the $1,500 from her parents, who require no interest but need to be repaid at the end of 18 months. Kristi expects to make $100 per month after paying for supplies and other related expenses. The payback period (in months) may be computed as follows:

$$\frac{\$1,500}{\$100} = 15 \text{ months}$$

Because Kristi would generate sufficient cash to recover the investment in 15 months, she could repay her parents within the agreed period of time (assuming she spends none of the money).

This is one of the strengths of the payback method: It can be used to determine whether an investment fits within an acceptable period for the use of funds. For example, a company's cash position may lead it to establish a rule of thumb that no investment with a payback period exceeding three years will be accepted. In such a situation, a manager may be obliged to select an investment alternative with a slightly lower rate of return but a shorter payback period.

The length of an acceptable payback period differs depending on the nature of the project. For example, a payback period of four years is very attractive if the investment is in a building that is expected to have a life of 30 years or more. However, if the investment is in a computer system upgrade that has a probable economic life of less than two years, then a four-year payback period is much too long.

The payback method has several weaknesses, however. One is that it measures the time needed to recover the initial outlay but does not consider the investment's overall profitability. Most investments are made in order to earn an acceptable return, not just to recover their costs. In our example, Kristi is not solely interested in recovering the $1,500 in the shortest time possible. Her purpose in buying the equipment is to earn some extra money. Assuming that the equipment will last for more than 15 months, Kristi not only will recover her initial investment, but will also generate subsequent earnings (at least $100 per month). Although the payback method may provide some clues about the advisability or risk of investments, it does not directly measure profitability.

To clarify this last point and show why the payback method must be used with care, consider a manager's decision to purchase one of two machines. Machine A costs $5,500 and is expected to generate $1,000 of net cash inflows annually. Machine B costs $3,500 and will produce $800 of net cash inflows annually. The payback period for machine A is 5.5 years ($5,500 ÷ $1,000); for machine B, the payback period is 4.4 years ($3,500 ÷ $800). Other things being equal, the payback method would indicate that the manager should purchase machine B because it would result in a shorter payback period. That is, its original cost would be recovered in a shorter time. However, if machine B were expected to last less than 4.4 years, such an investment would be unwise. The machine would not last long enough to recover its original cost, let alone generate any earnings.

Now suppose that both machines were estimated to have a 7-year life. Which machine would be the better investment? What if the estimated lifetimes of both machines were more than 10 years? Clearly, Machine B is less risky in that it will recover the initial investment sooner, but this doesn't mean that Machine B is more profitable. To compare these two investments properly, we would have to use one of the discounted cash flow methods (to be discussed later) in conjunction with the payback period.

 FYI

Companies that use the payback method generally require shorter payback periods for projects with less certain cash inflows or with less certain useful lives. For example, a shorter payback period would be required in evaluating an investment in an experimental computerized inventory system than for an investment in a new inventory storage facility.

This example highlights the other major weakness of the payback method: It does not take into account the time value of money. The payback method can give you a quick idea of the attractiveness of a project, but a serious analysis requires the use of the discounted cash flow methods discussed later in this chapter.

Unadjusted Rate of Return Method

unadjusted rate of return method

A capital budgeting technique in which a rate of return is calculated by dividing the increase in the average annual net income a project will generate by the initial investment cost.

Another commonly used capital budgeting technique is the **unadjusted rate of return method**. Also referred to as the simple rate of return method or the accounting rate of return method, the unadjusted rate of return is computed as follows:

$$\frac{\text{Increase in future average net income}}{\text{Initial investment cost}} = \text{Unadjusted rate of return}$$

To illustrate the unadjusted rate of return method, consider the following situation. Seal Right Company manufactures cans for fruits, vegetables, and other farm produce. Management wants to add a new, larger can size to the product line in order to take advantage of a potential demand for food storage items in the western states. This new can is expected to increase the company's annual revenues by an average of $51,500 a year for 10 years. The additional machinery needed to manufacture the can will cost $215,000. Assuming that there are no other expenses, the new can will increase annual net income by $30,000 each year; this $30,000 is computed as the difference between the $51,500 increase in revenues and the $21,500 ($215,000 ÷ 10 years) increase in annual depreciation. The unadjusted rate of return (or accounting return on assets) on the investment is $30,000 ÷ $215,000 = 14% (rounded).

While the payback and unadjusted rate of return methods do not consider the time value of money, they are widely used in practice because they involve simple computations and are so easy to use. In fact, smaller, unsophisticated companies are less likely than larger companies to use the more complex discounted methods.

Unlike the payback method, the unadjusted rate of return method attempts (although it is a "quick and dirty" attempt) to measure the profitability of an investment. A company compares the unadjusted rate of return with a preselected rate that it considers acceptable. Management invests only in projects with accounting rates of return that are equal to or greater than the established standard rate. This standard rate is often called

hurdle rate

The minimum rate of return that an investment must provide in order to be acceptable.

the **hurdle rate**, or the rate that must be cleared for a project to be acceptable. Thus, if Seal Right's hurdle rate is less than or equal to 14%, the project would be acceptable.

You need to understand that the unadjusted rate of return method has two important weaknesses. First, like the payback method, it does not consider the time value of money. The computation uses average future net income rather than expected future earnings discounted to the present. Second, in contrast to the payback method, the unadjusted rate of return uses GAAP-based income rather than cash flows. In effect, the unadjusted rate of return method is very similar to the traditional ROI (return on investment) calculation that has been in use in business for a long time. By omitting the time value of money and emphasizing income measures instead of cash measures, the unadjusted rate of return method can produce misleading results and incorrect long-term investment decisions. Hence, the unadjusted rate of return method must be used with extreme care.

The word "unadjusted" in the title of this technique refers to the fact that the calculations are not adjusted for the time value of money. You should also remember that this technique is based on *income* measures rather than *cash flow* measures.

Discounted Capital Budgeting Techniques

Describe and use two discounted capital budgeting techniques: the net present value method and the internal rate of return method.

③ Two widely used capital budgeting techniques recognize the time value of money—the net present value method and the internal rate of return method. Both methods apply discounted cash flow principles in determining the acceptability of an investment. The net present value method uses a standard discount rate (i.e., the hurdle rate) to restate all cash flows in terms of present values and then make comparisons. The internal rate of return method calculates the investment's "true" discounted rate of return and compares it with the firm's hurdle rate. Thus, an appropriate discount rate is extremely important in capital budgeting. Before explaining each of the two methods, we first discuss how to select an appropriate discount rate.

Selecting a Discount Rate

cost of capital

The average cost of a firm's debt and equity capital; equals the rate of return that a company must earn in order to satisfy the demands of its owners and creditors.

An excellent starting point for computing the correct discount rate is a company's cost of capital. The **cost of capital** is basically an average cost of a firm's debt (primarily bank loans and bonds) and its equity (primarily common and preferred stock and retained earnings). These costs are measured in terms of effective interest rates on bank loans and bonds and the rate of return expected to be earned by the company's stockholders. In essence, then, the cost of capital is the rate a company must earn in order to satisfy its owners and creditors.

The computation of the cost of capital is complex and beyond the scope of this book. However, the following example should help you understand the concept. Assume that 30% of a company's total capital is debt, 20% is equity from the issuance of stock, and 50% is equity from retained earnings. Upon analysis, the company has determined that the cost of its debt capital is 10%, and the cost of its equity capital is 22% from stock and 16% from retained earnings. (*Note:* The cost of equity capital from the issuance of new shares is considered to be higher because of the commissions, registration fees, and so forth, associated with the issuance of new shares.) The firm's cost of capital would be determined as follows:

Type	Cost of Capital	×	Weight	=	Average Cost of Capital
Debt (bonds)	10%	×	30%	=	3.0%
Equity (stocks)	22	×	20	=	4.4
Equity (retained earnings)	16	×	50	=	8.0
Total cost of capital			100%		15.4%

STOP & THINK

Assume you were trying to decide whether to purchase or lease an automobile and you wanted to use the net present value method to determine which alternative to choose. What factors would you consider in determining the rate at which to discount the future cash outflows (i.e., what factors would determine your personal cost of capital)?

The weighting procedure may seem fairly simple. As you will learn in more advanced courses, however, it is not always easy to calculate the costs of the different types of capital. This is because the necessary information is often not readily available or absolutely verifiable. For example, debt costs must be adjusted to an after-tax basis, and equity costs include some subjective elements, such as the opportunity cost of retained earnings. Although you now have a general understanding of the cost of capital, you will need further study in finance courses in order to be able to confidently use this concept.

As mentioned above, the cost of capital is a starting point in identifying an appropriate discount rate. The riskiness of a project should also be considered in choosing the appropriate discount rate. For example, the cost of capital computed earlier is 15.4%. If the company were considering a very risky project, a higher discount rate would be used because high-risk projects must yield higher-than-average returns in order to compensate for the increased probability of low or negative returns. The techniques of correctly computing risk-adjusted discount rates are beyond the scope of this text; however, remember that the selection of the right discount rate is critical in the execution of a useful capital budgeting analysis.

net present value method

A capital budgeting technique that uses discounted cash flows to compare the present values of an investment's expected cash inflows and outflows.

Net Present Value Method

The **net present value method** compares all expected cash inflows associated with an investment with the current and future cash outflows. All cash flows are discounted to their present values, giving recognition to the time value of money. For this reason, the net present value method is superior to both the payback method and the unadjusted rate of return method.

In general, the net present value method involves the following five steps:

1. *Estimate* the amount and timing of all cash flows associated with the investment.
2. *Evaluate* the riskiness of the cash flows in order to determine the appropriate discount rate to use in the present value calculations.
3. *Compute* the present values of all the expected cash inflows and outflows of the investment. (Note that most present value calculations assume end-of-year inflows and outflows.)
4. *Subtract* the total present value of the cash outflows from the total present value of the cash inflows. The difference is the investment's net present value.
5. *Decide* whether to undertake the investment. If the net present value of the investment is positive, or at least zero, the project is acceptable from a financial standpoint.

Steps 1 and 2, the estimation of the amount and timing of the cash flows and the selection of an appropriate discount rate, are the most difficult steps in evaluating a long-term investment. These steps are where business judgment, experience, and careful analysis of details separate managers that make good long-term investment decisions from those that make bad long-term investment decisions. Implementation of steps 1 and 2 is a topic for more advanced accounting and finance courses as well as being the object of much on-the-job training for young managers. For the illustrations in this chapter, the cash flows and the discount rate will be given so that we can focus on the calculations and decision process in steps 3, 4, and 5.

The following case illustrates the net present value method. The fleet manager of MBK Company is thinking of replacing an old truck before it begins to need major repairs. Because the company has limited funds and cannot spend more than $18,000, the manager is considering a small, fuel-efficient pickup truck that is presently selling for that amount. The truck would save the company $5,625 a year in gas and other expenses. The truck's estimated useful life is four years, and the expected salvage value is $1,800. The company uses a 10% discount rate. What is this investment's net present value? Should the truck be purchased?

Because the cash flows and the discount rate are given, we are assuming that steps 1 and 2 have already been completed. Step 3 of the net present value method is to use the predetermined discount rate to state all cash flows at their present values (rounded to the nearest dollar in this example).

Cash inflows:

Annual cash savings	×	Discount factor	=	Present value
$5,625	×	3.1699*	=	$17,831
Salvage value	×	Discount factor	=	Present value
$1,800	×	0.6830**	=	$1,229

Cash outflows:

Initial cost	×	Discount factor	=	Present value
$18,000	×	1.0000	=	$18,000

*From Table II, 4 years at 10%.
**From Table I, 4 years at 10%.

net present value

The difference between the present values of an investment's expected cash inflows and outflows.

Step 4 is to compute the **net present value**; that is, the difference between the present values of cash inflows and outflows.

Present value of inflows:

Cash savings	$17,831
Salvage value	1,229
Total	$19,060

Less present value of outflows:

Cost of truck	18,000
Net present value*	$ 1,060

*It is significantly easier to calculate the net present value using a calculator. We demonstrate the keystrokes for a Hewlett-Packard calculator below when we compute the internal rate of return. If you choose to use a calculator to compute the net present value on replacing the truck, the answer is $1,059.92.

FYI

Another way to think of the $1,060 net present value is that on the day the company decides to buy the truck, the market value of the company immediately increases by $1,060. This increase stems from the fact that the company has embarked on a course that involves exchanging cash flows with a present value of $18,000 for cash flows with a present value of $19,060. When viewed this way, it is obvious that a company should want to engage in as many positive net present value projects as possible.

The analysis in step 4 shows that investing in the truck would produce a positive net present value. In other words, after adjusting for the time value of money, purchasing the truck is like paying $18,000 in exchange for a stream of cash flows that is worth $19,060. Clearly, this is something that you would want to do. Thus, from a quantitative standpoint, it seems that the truck should be purchased. Exhibit 1 illustrates the process just described.

A common misinterpretation of the $1,060 net present value is that the acquisition of the truck will generate a net profit of just $1,060. Actually, because a 10% discount rate was used in evaluating the truck, the $1,060 net present value means that the investment in the truck will yield a net value gain of $1,060 OVER AND ABOVE the 10% hurdle rate. Similarly, a computed net present value of $0 does not mean that an investment just barely breaks even; instead, a $0 net present value means that the investment yields a return exactly equal to the discount rate used in evaluating the investment.

Managers must sometimes make least-cost decisions to fulfill certain imposed requirements at the lowest possible cost. For example, government regulations may require a company to purchase pollution-control equipment.

Before the company decides whether to purchase the truck, however, management must consider other factors. For example, a policy of support for U.S. car manufacturers or a lack of certain safety features on the truck might dictate a particular course of action. Qualitative factors are discussed in greater detail later in the chapter.

Least-Cost Decisions The net present value method generally assumes that an investment must be justified by cash savings or increased revenues. Sometimes, however, funds must be used to purchase assets regardless of whether they can be justified financially. Such situations arise, for example, when (1) government regulations require a firm to purchase safety or pollution-control equipment, (2) personnel contracts stipulate the establishment of retirement funds, or (3) a company is required to invest in cafeteria or recreational facilities, either to comply with a labor union contract or because management is persuaded that morale considerations warrant it.

Such situations may seem to be beyond help from capital budgeting. However, the net present value method may assist managers in making a **least-cost decision**—a decision that satisfies certain requirements at the lowest possible cost to the firm. The two major differences between least-cost decisions and all other capital budgeting decisions are:

least-cost decision

A decision to undertake the project with the smallest negative net present value.

1. Least-cost decisions are limited to alternatives that fulfill certain imposed requirements.
2. None of the alternatives may produce a positive net present value.

To illustrate, we will assume that New England Steel Company has been told by the Environmental Protection Agency to install a pollution-control device. One alternative

EXHIBIT 1	**Computing Net Present Value**					
		Present Time	**Year 1**	**Year 2**	**Year 3**	**Year 4**
Cost		$18,000				
Savings			$5,625	$5,625	$5,625	$5,625
Salvage value						1,800

	Time Period	**Cash Flows**	**Present Value Factor**	**Present Value of Cash Flows**
Present value of cash inflows:				
Savings	Years 1–4	$ 5,625	3.1699*	$17,831
Salvage value	Year 4	1,800	0.6830**	1,229
				$19,060
Present value of cash outflows:				
Cost	Today	(18,000)	1.0000	18,000
Net present value				$ 1,060

*From Table II, 4 years at 10%.
**From Table I, 4 years at 10%.

STOP & THINK

Over your lifetime, you will make many personal, long-term investments such as buying automobiles and buying a home. Are the capital budgeting techniques we have discussed in this chapter relevant to these personal decisions? Since you probably won't be earning a return on your automobile and home investments, what type of capital budgeting decisions are these?

would cost $1,000,000 immediately but would not add to operating costs. It would last for 10 years. A second alternative is a device that costs $200,000 immediately but would add $125,000 to annual operating costs. Like the first device, it would last 10 years. The firm uses a 12% discount rate. Which device should be purchased?

The first alternative involves no future cash inflows or outflows. Its outlay cost in net present value terms is its initial cash outlay of $1,000,000. The second alternative has an initial cost of $200,000 plus future cash outflows of $125,000 per year for the next 10 years. Therefore, its outlay cost in net present value terms would be:

Annual cash outflows	×	Discount factor	=	Present value
$125,000	×	5.6502*	=	$706,275
Initial cost				200,000
Net present value**				$906,275

*From Table II, 10 years at 12%.
**Using a calculator, the net present value of the outlay costs is $906,277.88.

FYI

This pollution-control example is somewhat misleading. Many companies have found that the effort to control emissions or reduce waste actually improves overall efficiency, turning environmental initiatives into positive net present value business projects.

Source: Martha Hamilton, "Generating Profit from the Waste Up," *The Washington Post,* April 12, 1995, p. F01.

If the company had a choice between installing and not installing, neither alternative would be acceptable because both net present values are negative. However, one of the alternatives must be accepted. Because a cost of $906,275 is less than a cost of $1,000,000, the second alternative should be chosen to minimize costs.

Internal Rate of Return Method

internal rate of return method

A capital budgeting technique that uses discounted cash flows to find the "true" discount rate of an investment; this true rate produces a net present value of zero.

internal rate of return

The "true" discount rate that will produce a net present value of zero when applied to the future cash flows of a capital investment.

The **internal rate of return method**, also known as the time-adjusted rate of return method or the discounted rate of return method, is similar to the net present value approach in that it emphasizes the profitability of investments and takes into account the time value of money. As a discounted cash flow method, it is superior to either the payback method or the unadjusted rate of return method. Some managers consider the internal rate of return method more difficult than the net present value method because the computations can be challenging. Some managers, however, prefer to analyze investment alternatives in terms of comparative rates of return rather than net present values.

The **internal rate of return** is defined as the "true" discount rate that an investment yields. For example, assume that your parents have $100,000 that they are considering investing in one of two ways—in a mutual fund containing the stocks of large U.S. companies or in your college education. They learn that the mutual fund investment will yield an average return of 12%. They estimate the increased value of your lifetime annual earnings stemming from your college education and calculate that, after adjusting for the time value of money, the investment in your college education will yield an average return of, say, 20% per year. The 20% number is the internal rate of return generated by an investment in your education; because this return is higher than the return your parents can

> ! **CAUTION**
>
> Of course, as mentioned earlier, there may be QUALITATIVE considerations that would cause your parents to invest in your education even if the MONETARY return were expected to be lower than what they could earn in the stock market.

earn on a mutual fund, they would naturally invest the $100,000 in your future.

Mathematically, the internal rate of return is the discount rate that yields a net present value of zero when applied to the cash flows of an investment—both inflows and outflows.

When using present value tables, the internal rate of return method involves three steps.

1. Calculate the present value factor by dividing the investment cost by the annual net cash inflows.
2. Using applicable present value tables and the life of the investment, find the present value factor closest to the number derived in step 1.
3. Using interpolation, if necessary, find the exact internal rate of return represented by the present value factor in step 1.

To help you understand this concept, we will again refer to MBK Company's plan to purchase a new truck. For the purpose of this explanation, however, we will ignore the truck's salvage value; later, we will show how to incorporate salvage value into the calculation. The calculations for the MBK example are as follows:

1. Calculate the present value factor with the following formula:

$$\frac{\text{Investment cost}}{\text{Annual net cash inflows}} = \text{Present value factor}$$

$$\frac{\$18,000}{\$5,625} = 3.2000$$

(Note that this is also the formula for calculating the payback period.)

2. In Present Value Table II, find the applicable row for the life of the investment. By moving across the table, you can find the present value factor closest to the number derived in step 1. In our example, the investment's life is known to be 4 years, so find row 4 and move across the row until you come to the factor 3.2397. This is the factor for 9%. The next factor, 3.1699, represents 10%. Since the factor is between these two numbers, the truck purchase yields between a 9% and 10% return.

interpolation

A method of determining the internal rate of return when the factor for that rate lies between the factors given in the present value table.

3. If necessary, use **interpolation** to find the exact internal rate of return. Interpolation is most easily visualized by setting up a table as follows:

	Rate of Return (Discount Rate)	Present Value Factors	
		High and True Factors	High and Low Factors
High factor*	9%	3.2397	3.2397
True factor		3.2000	
Low factor	10		3.1699
Differences	1%	0.0397	0.0698

*Note that the high factor is associated with the low rate and that the low factor is associated with the high rate.

The number 0.0397 is the difference between the high factor and the true factor determined in step 1. The number 0.0698 is the difference between the high factor and the low factor. One percent is the difference between the discount rates for the high and the low factors. To find the approximate rate of return in this example, you would make the following calculation:

$$\text{Internal rate of return} = 0.09 + \left(0.01 \times \frac{0.0397}{0.0698}\right) = 0.0957 \text{ or } 9.6\% \text{ (rounded)}$$

CAUTION

For you mathematicians, it is necessary to note that this interpolation process only approximates the internal rate of return. This is because the formulas generating the present value factors are nonlinear.

What we are doing is adding the proportion 0.0397 ÷ 0.0698 of the 1% difference to the low rate to get the true rate. The result, 9.6%, means that if the annual savings of $5,625 were discounted at 9.6%, the net present value of the investment would be zero. (Note that there may be slight differences due to rounding.)

The purpose of interpolation is to determine the "true" rate of interest indicated by the present value factor. Although the factor's true rate of interest is fairly easy to roughly estimate, interpolation produces a more precise estimate.

Computation of internal rates of return is one area in which knowledge of how to use a standard business calculator really pays off. For example, the internal rate of return in the MBK example could be computed using the following keystrokes with a Hewlett-Packard business calculator:

Hewlett-Packard Keystrokes:

1. −18,000: Press **PV** (you must enter the cash outflow as a NEGATIVE number)
2. 5,625: Press **PMT** (this is the annual cash inflow)
3. 4: Press **N** (number of years)
4. Press **I/YR** for the answer = 9.5642274%*

*If you get an interest rate of 114.77% (or a rate significantly different from the correct rate of 9.56%), you probably need to set your calculator to recognize one payment per year. Enter 1 and press the **P/YR** key.

FYI

A calculator actually computes the internal rate of return using a repeated interpolation process; most business calculators take a couple of seconds to come up with the final answer.

Using the Internal Rate of Return

To determine the value of an investment, management must compare the project's internal rate of return with the company's usual discount rate, often called the hurdle rate, or the rate that must be cleared for a project to be acceptable. If the internal rate is higher than or equal to the company's hurdle rate, the project is acceptable. If the internal rate is lower than the hurdle rate, the project is usually rejected. As with any of the capital budgeting techniques, even if the investment is acceptable from an internal rate of return standpoint, qualitative factors must still be considered before a final decision can be made.

The Problem of Uneven Cash Flows

In the truck example, annual cash flows were the same because salvage value was ignored. However, when salvage value is considered, the investment will have uneven cash flows. When this occurs, an annuity table cannot be used. Each cash flow has to be discounted back at an assumed discount rate until the net present value of all the cash flows discounted at this rate approximates zero. The rate that results after a trial-and-error process is the internal rate of return. A simplified example of this method is shown on page 1136. Although this can be a tedious procedure, it is facilitated by using a business calculator. For example, computing the internal rate of return of the MBK truck purchase, including consideration of the $1,800 salvage value cash inflow at the end of four years, would be done as follows using a Hewlett-Packard business calculator:

Hewlett-Packard Keystrokes:

1. −18,000: Press **PV** (again, remember to enter the cash outflow as a NEGATIVE number)
2. 5,625: Press **PMT**
3. 4: Press **N** (number of years)
4. 1,800: Press **FV** (this is a single inflow amount occurring at the end of the period of time indicated in step 3)
5. Press **I/YR** for the answer = 12.5774719%

Note that the internal rate of return is higher (12.6% vs. 9.6%) when the additional cash inflow from the salvage value is considered.

In addition to using present value tables and business calculators, net present values and internal rates of return can also be calculated using Excel spreadsheet functions. These calculations are illustrated in the appendix to this chapter.

Comparative Example of Capital Budgeting Techniques

To solidify your understanding of the capital budgeting techniques introduced thus far in this chapter, we present the example of Will's Pit Stop, a small service station that sells gasoline on a self-service basis as its only source of revenue. Because one wall of the enclosed station area is vacant, the manager has decided to install one or two food vending machines. A sales representative has suggested that a freezer for ice cream and other dairy items would do well. The freezer would cost $42,045. It has an estimated useful life of 10 years, with an expected salvage value of $4,000. The sales representative is confident that the freezer will generate revenues of $15,000 a year on goods that cost $7,600. The freezer will need $8,000 of servicing during its fifth year of operation. The increase in Will's average yearly net income if the freezer is purchased is estimated to be $3,500. Note that the difference between annual net cash inflows of $7,400 ($15,000 − $7,600) and the estimated average net income of $3,500 is due to noncash expenses, such as depreciation, and other accruals which are deducted on the income statement.

The manager of the station has come to you for advice, indicating that the firm's hurdle rate is 12%—Will's estimated cost of capital. Compute the payback period, the unadjusted rate of return, the net present value, and the internal rate of return of the project. Then give your recommendations. Note that companies generally do not analyze an investment with all these techniques. They are all used here for illustrative purposes.

1. *Payback period:*

$$\frac{\$50,045 \text{ (investment cost)}^*}{\$7,400 \text{ (annual net cash inflows)}} = 6.76 \text{ years}$$

*$42,045 initial investment + $8,000 servicing cost after 5 years.

Note that the salvage value is not considered here because it is received in the tenth year.

2. *Unadjusted rate of return:*

$$\frac{\$3,500 \text{ (increase in future average annual net income)}}{\$42,045 \text{ (initial investment cost)}} = 8.3\%$$

3. *Net present value:*

	Time Period	Cash Flows	Present Value Factor	Present Value of Cash Flows
Present value of cash inflows:				
Net revenues ($15,000 − $7,600)	Years 1–10	$ 7,400	5.6502*	$41,811
Salvage value	Year 10	4,000	0.3220**	1,288
Total cash inflows				$43,099
Present value of cash outflows:				
Initial cost	Today	$42,045	1.0000	$42,045
Servicing cost	Year 5	8,000	0.5674***	4,539
Total cash outflows				$46,584
Net present value				$ (3,485)

   *From Table II, 10 years at 12%.
  **From Table I, 10 years at 12%.
 ***From Table I, 5 years at 12%.

4. *Internal rate of return:*

   Since the cash flows are uneven due to the servicing cost and the salvage value, a trial-and-error process is required in computing the internal rate of return. From the net present value method, we can see that the 12% rate is too high. A 10% rate is selected for trial, and the net present value at that rate is calculated.

	Time Period	Cash Flows	Present Value Factor	Present Value of Cash Flows
Present value of cash inflows:				
Net revenues ($15,000 − $7,600)	Years 1–10	$ 7,400	6.1446*	$45,470
Salvage value	Year 10	4,000	0.3855**	1,542
Total cash inflows				$47,012
Present value of cash outflows:				
Initial cost	Today	$42,045	1.0000	$42,045
Servicing cost	Year 5	8,000	0.6209***	4,967
Total cash outflows				$47,012
Net present value				$ 0

   *From Table II, 10 years at 10%.
  **From Table I, 10 years at 10%.
 ***From Table I, 5 years at 10%.

   At 10%, the net present value is zero. Therefore, 10% is the internal rate of return.

   On the basis of the financial analysis, you should recommend rejection. The payback period is well within the life of the investment; however, it is not short enough to warrant any special consideration. The unadjusted rate of return is only 8.3%, and the internal rate of return of 10% is well under Will's hurdle rate, which means that the project's net present value is negative. Therefore, on the basis of the quantitative results, the manager should look for an opportunity that is more attractive financially. However, if the 10% rate is close enough to the 12% hurdle rate, perhaps qualitative factors, such as the probability that the additional customers attracted by the freezer items will also buy gas, might make the project acceptable.

> **REMEMBER THIS...**
>
> - Net present value (NPV) = Discounted value of cash inflows less discounted value of cash outflows
>   - If NPV $\geq$ 0, accept the project
> - Internal rate of return (IRR) = The "true" rate of return for an investment after considering the time value of money. Computationally, the IRR is the discount rate that results in an NPV exactly equal to zero.
>   - If IRR $\geq$ Hurdle rate, accept the project

Qualitative Factors in Strategic and Capital Investment Decisions

Understand the need for evaluating qualitative factors in strategic and capital investment decisions.

(4) In explaining the fundamental concepts of capital budgeting, we have focused on the financial (quantitative) aspects of analyzing investment alternatives. However, a discussion of capital budgeting is incomplete without mentioning factors that cannot be reduced to numbers. Sometimes qualitative factors can override quantitative analysis in strategic and capital investment decisions. Here, we consider three types of qualitative factors: (1) an investment's effect on the quality of products and services offered, (2) an investment's effect on the time with which products and services can be produced and delivered to customers, and (3) other qualitative factors. Thus far in the chapter, we have made the determination of whether a capital investment decision is a good one solely on the basis of its financial return, computed using one of four methods. If the financial return was positive, our conclusion was to invest; if the financial return was negative, we recommended that the project not be undertaken. However, organizations must carefully manage and balance decisions across three important aspects of decision making: cost, quality, and time.

Quality and time considerations can sometimes dictate that a capital investment should be made even if the financial returns don't justify the expenditure. For example, if buying a new machine will help the company produce higher quality products or deliver those products to its customers faster, the machine may be a good investment. Companies know that their competitors are doing everything possible to speed up delivery and increase quality. Thus, even if a company has a cost of capital of 12%, and an investment will return only 8%, if buying a machine will allow the company to deliver products or services faster than competitors, the purchase may be a good one. Likewise, if buying a machine will mean fewer defects, higher quality, and more satisfied customers, the purchase may be a good one. Companies must always be continuously improving in order to keep up with or surpass their competition. Unfortunately, capital investments often are long-term decisions that make continuous improvement difficult. Thus, even if a company has not completely recovered its investment in a capital project, recognizing that competitors have better or more efficient equipment may motivate a company to abandon an investment (a machine that works fine, for example) and make a costlier new investment that will allow the company to remain competitive. The impact of quality and time on capital budgeting decisions must not be underestimated. In fact, because of the need to continuously improve, companies generally prefer shorter capital investment opportunities so that they are more flexible, such as leasing or renting equipment and other operating assets where possible.

In addition to quality and time, there are a number of other qualitative factors that must be considered when making capital budgeting decisions. Consider, for example, consumer safety. In one lawsuit, a major U.S. automobile manufacturer was cited for producing cars that were not as safe as they should have been. The company was essentially accused of comparing the present value of the legal and other costs that might result from the unsafe condition of the cars with the cash savings from manufacturing the cars more cheaply, and of choosing the less expensive route. The question was then posed: What is the value of a life? This situation provides a dramatic illustration of the need to include qualitative factors in capital investment decisions.

Other qualitative factors include such matters as (1) government regulations, (2) pollution control and environmental protection, (3) worker safety, (4) company image and prestige, (5) preferences of owners and management, and (6) the general welfare of the community in which the company operates. Many more examples could be mentioned, but the point is that numbers alone do not control the investment decisions of a good manager. Quality, time, and other qualitative, as well as quantitative, factors should all be considered in reaching long-term investment decisions.

REMEMBER THIS...

Some of the qualitative factors that should be considered in making capital budgeting decisions are as follows:

- Impact on the timeliness of product or service delivery
- Impact on the quality of the product or service
- Legal exposure
- Government regulations
- Environmental impact
- Worker safety
- Company image
- Community welfare

EXPANDED *material*

In the previous sections of the chapter, we have explained the importance of capital budgeting and the concepts underlying strategic and capital investment decisions, including the time value of money. We have also described and illustrated the four most commonly used capital budgeting techniques. Finally, we have discussed briefly the need for evaluating qualitative factors in any investment decision. In the expanded material, we explain how to use sensitivity analysis in dealing with uncertainty in capital budgeting decisions and the concept of "capital rationing," which is the process of ranking capital investment projects. We also discuss the impact of income taxes on capital budgeting decisions.

Use sensitivity analysis to assess the potential effects of uncertainty in capital budgeting.

Dealing with Uncertainty in Strategic and Capital Investment Decisions

⑤ Throughout this chapter, we have applied capital budgeting techniques as though the future were certain. That is, we have assumed perfect knowledge of expected cash flows, the useful lives of assets, salvage values, and so forth. Actually, the future is almost always uncertain, and the applicable numbers are estimates. By using "**sensitivity analysis**," we can evaluate, at least to some extent, the degree to which an error in a particular estimate is likely to invalidate the decision reached. Essentially, sensitivity analysis is a method of examining the effect of changes in an estimate on the results of the calculations. We use sensitivity analysis to determine whether the conclusions still seem reasonable under modified circumstances.

sensitivity analysis

A method of assessing the reasonableness of a decision that was based upon estimates; involves calculating how far reality can differ from an estimate without invalidating the decision.

To illustrate this approach, we will consider the following situation. An asset can be purchased for $100,000; it is expected to provide $20,000 of annual net cash inflows. It has a 10-year life and an expected salvage value of $10,000. The hurdle rate is 8%. We can use either of the discounted cash flow techniques to assess this investment opportunity. For illustrative purposes, we use both.

Net present value method:

Discounted expected cash inflows ($20,000 × 6.7101*)	$134,202
Discounted disposal value ($10,000 × 0.4632**)	4,632
Net cash inflows	$138,834
Net cash outflows	100,000
Net present value***	$ 38,834

*From Table II, 10 years at 8%.
**From Table I, 10 years at 8%.
***Using a calculator, the net present value of the asset investment is $38,833.56.

Internal rate of return method:

$$\frac{\text{Investment cost } (\$100{,}000 - \$4{,}632)}{\text{Annual net cash inflows}} = \frac{\$95{,}368}{\$20{,}000} = 4.7684 \text{ Present value factor}$$

For 10 years, the internal rate of return is close to 16%.*

*Using a calculator, the internal rate of return of the asset investment is 15.72%. The method using the present value factor is a little bit off because the subtraction of the $4,632 is computed using the hurdle rate of 8% which, as demonstrated by the preliminary internal rate of return calculation, is too low in this context. If you do one more iteration of the present value factor calculation, this time using 16% to compute the present value of the $10,000, you get an IRR answer quite close to the 15.72% computed using a calculator.

The net present value is greater than zero, and the internal rate of return is considerably more than the minimum acceptable rate of 8%. Therefore, from a quantitative standpoint, we should accept this investment opportunity. But what about the uncertainties? What if $20,000 is not received each year? What if the asset does not last 10 years? What if the disposal value is less than $10,000? Sensitivity analysis enables us to evaluate the potential effect of each of these uncertainties.

If Expected Cash Flows Are Uncertain

To assess the amount of error we can tolerate in expected cash flows, we need to determine the break-even amount of net cash flow—that is, the annual cash flow that would earn the minimum rate of 8%. We accomplish this by determining the discounted net cost of the investment and dividing that amount by the present value factor for the minimum acceptable interest rate (8%) for 10 years.

Computations:

Initial cost	$100,000
Discounted disposal value	4,632
Net cost of investment	$ 95,368

$95,368 \div 6.7101$ (present value factor of 8%) = $14,213 cash flow return in order to break even.

We could then assess how likely it is that this project will generate annual cash flows of at least $14,213. Any amount above that, of course, would be acceptable with an 8% hurdle rate.

If Useful Life Is Uncertain

To assess the amount of error we can tolerate in the estimate that the asset will have a useful life of 10 years, we take the discounted net cost of the investment and divide it by the expected cash flows. This produces a present value factor of 4.7684. Looking under 8% interest in Table II, we find that this factor falls between 6 and 7 years. Thus, assuming that the $20,000 estimate of cash inflows is reliable, the asset does not have to last a full 10 years for the investment to be acceptable. In fact, only 7 years are necessary.

Computations:

$$\frac{\text{Net cost of investment}}{\text{Annual net cash inflows}} = \frac{\$95,368}{\$20,000} = 4.7684 \text{ at } 8\%$$

$$= \text{Between 6 and 7 years of useful life in order to break even}$$

If Disposal Value Is Uncertain

Usually, the disposal value is an insignificant factor in the investment decision. However, to see if it would make a difference in the acceptability of a project, we can assume it is zero. In our example, if the asset has a zero disposal value, the investment cost of $100,000 divided by $20,000 annual net cash inflows equals a 5.0 present value factor. For an assumed 10-year life, the return is between 15 and 16%, which is clearly acceptable according to our 8% hurdle rate.[1]

Computations:

$$\frac{\text{Initial investment cost}}{\text{Annual net cash inflows}} = \frac{\$100,000}{\$20,000} = 5.0 \text{ for 10 years}$$

$$= 15 \text{ to } 16\% \text{ return}$$

REMEMBER THIS...

To evaluate the potential effect of uncertainty about estimates of future amounts, use sensitivity analysis which involves addressing questions such as the following:

- What level of cash operating inflows will give the project an NPV of at least zero? What are the chances that this level of cash inflows will be achieved?
- What salvage value amount is large enough to give the project an NPV of at least zero? What are the chances that the salvage value will be at least this much?
- How long must the project last in order to have an NPV of at least zero? What are the chances that the project will last this long?

---

[1]In this example, we looked at the uncertainty of each variable separately. Using computer simulation, uncertainty in all variables could have been examined simultaneously.

Capital Rationing

Explain how to use capital budgeting techniques in ranking capital investment projects.

⑥ Thus far, we have dealt exclusively with the screening function of capital budgeting—that is, determining whether an investment meets a minimum standard of acceptability. In many cases, however, a company has not one but several investment opportunities, all of which offer returns in excess of the company's hurdle rate. Since a company's resources are limited, some projects should be given priority. The ranking function of capital budgeting enables management to select the most profitable investments first. Projects should not be ranked, however, until the screening process is completed.

Another factor to consider in ranking projects is whether particular projects are compatible, complementary, or mutually exclusive. We assume mutually exclusive projects in this section on ranking, that is, that each project is independent and adds neither an advantage nor a disadvantage to other projects. Certainly, there are situations where the acceptance of one project adds value, directly or indirectly, to another project and might therefore alter a ranking consideration. These factors, like the qualitative factors that we discussed earlier, may significantly influence the strategy involved in a capital investment decision.

capital rationing

Allocating limited resources among ranked acceptable investments.

The objective of ranking is to help a company use limited resources to the best advantage by investing only in the projects that offer the highest return. The process of allocating limited resources based on the ranking of projects is called **capital rationing**. Either the internal rate of return method or the net present value method may be used in ranking investments.

Ranking by the Internal Rate of Return Method

If the internal rate of return method is used, investments that pass the screening test are ranked in the order of their internal rate of return, from highest to lowest. This method is simple, requires no additional computations, and is widely used.

To illustrate the process, we will assume the following situation. Sundance Enterprises is considering six capital investment projects. Management requires a minimum return of 15% on its investments. The six projects are first screened, then ranked by their internal rates of return, as shown below.

Project	Expected Rate of Return	Screening Decision	Ranking Decision
A	10%	Reject	—
B	18	Accept	3
C	12	Reject	—
D	22	Accept	1
E	20	Accept	2
F	16	Accept	4

From a quantitative standpoint, Sundance should invest in all four of the projects that passed the screening test. If resources are limited, however, capital must be rationed. In this situation, the ranking process indicates that limited resources would be allocated to project D first, then to projects E, B, and F, respectively. This conclusion ignores the additional complications of the investments having different lives. It also does not consider differences in the size of the initial investment.

Ranking by the Net Present Value Method

If the net present value method is used for ranking investments, additional computations are necessary because the net present value of one investment usually cannot be directly compared with that of another. Only projects that require the same amount of investment are comparable. For example, you cannot directly compare an investment of $10,000 that produces a $2,000 net present value (project A) with a $20,000 investment that also results in a $2,000 net present value (project B), although project A intuitively seems more desirable because it generates the same amount of positive net present value with a smaller investment. To rank such projects, we need to compute a **profitability index**.

profitability index

The present value of net cash inflows divided by the cost of an investment.

$$\frac{\text{Present value of net cash flows}}{\text{Investment cost}} = \text{Profitability index}$$

Projects can then be ranked from highest to lowest in terms of their respective profitability indexes. The project with the highest profitability index should obviously be undertaken first; other projects will be undertaken according to the amount of resources available for investment.

To illustrate the ranking of projects using the net present value method, we will use the example in the preceding paragraph. The amount of the investment and its net present value are added to arrive at the present value of net cash inflows. Then, present value is divided by the investment cost to calculate a profitability index and respective ranking.

	Project A	Project B
Present value of net cash inflows	$12,000 (a)	$22,000 (a)
Investment cost	10,000 (b)	20,000 (b)
Net present value	$ 2,000	$ 2,000
Profitability index (a ÷ b)	1.20	1.10
Rank	1	2

Note that the profitability index must be 1.0 or greater for a project to be acceptable; this means that the net present value is at least zero.

Exhibit 2 summarizes the rules for making screening and ranking decisions using the net present value (with a profitability index) and the internal rate of return methods. Note that each technique leads management to the same screening decision. However, the methods may produce slightly different rankings. Remember that these rankings are estimates based on forecasted future cash flows. If the projects are so close in their quantitative characteristics that the two ranking methods produce slightly different rankings, it is probably the case that the final decision should focus on qualitative factors to identify the best project.

EXHIBIT 2   **Capital Budgeting Decision Rules**

Selected Capital Budgeting Techniques	Decision Rules	
	Screening	Ranking
Net present value method (NPV) using the profitability index (PI)	If PI > 1, invest If PI = 1, indifferent If PI < 1, don't invest	For two projects, a and b; If $PI_a > PI_b$, pick a, etc.
Internal rate of return (IRR)	If IRR > CC*, invest If IRR = CC, indifferent If IRR < CC, don't invest	For two projects, a and b; If $IRR_a > IRR_b$, pick a, etc.

*CC = cost of capital, or hurdle rate.

Explain how income taxes affect capital budgeting decisions.

Income Tax Considerations in Capital Budgeting Decisions

(7) To keep the concepts simple, when considering capital budgeting decisions thus far in the chapter, we ignored the effects of income taxes on capital budgeting decisions. Unfortunately, ignoring tax effects is not very realistic because capital budgeting decisions can be significantly affected by tax considerations. As an example of the income tax effects, the net cash inflows from the profits stemming from a project are reduced because those profits are taxed. On the other hand, any losses stemming from a project will generate tax deductions, leading to tax savings. And the depreciation of the cost of an investment also leads to cash savings. Such tax effects can be so significant that the net present value of the cash flows changes from positive to negative, or vice versa.

To illustrate these income tax effects, we will use the Will's Pit Stop example discussed earlier. Recall that the gas station owner was considering installing a freezer for ice cream and other dairy products. The cost of the freezer was $42,045. It was expected to have a salvage value of $4,000 at the end of its 10-year useful life and to generate revenues of $15,000 per year on goods that cost $7,600. Thus, the cash flow was expected to be $7,400 ($15,000 − $7,600). At the end of the fifth year, the freezer would need $8,000 of repairs and servicing. Based on this information, the management of Will's Pit Stop decided not to buy the freezer because, at a hurdle rate of 12%, the net present value was negative. Furthermore, the internal rate of return was only 10%.

In making this decision, management neglected to consider the income tax effects. Here, we will incorporate the tax effects of the investment, based on the following initial assumptions: (1) Will's Pit Stop is a corporation with an effective tax rate of 25%, and (2) the hurdle rate of 12% is an after-tax rate. Assumption (2) means that the calculation of the cost of capital reflects the after-tax cost of interest expense, which is a deduction in computing a corporation's tax liability.

To compute the present values of the cash inflows and outflows, we must first convert them to after-tax amounts. This conversion is accomplished as follows:

1. Income on the freezer before taxes was $7,400 ($15,000 revenues − $7,600 cost of goods sold). This $7,400 represents the before-tax net cash inflow from the freezer. At a 25% tax rate, the after-tax net cash inflow is $5,550 ($7,400 × 0.25 = $1,850; $7,400 − $1,850 = $5,550). In other words, the company keeps 75% (1.00 less the tax rate of 25%) of the before-tax net cash inflow from the freezer ($7,400 × 0.75 = $5,550).

2. We assume that, for income tax purposes, Will's Pit Stop uses straight-line depreciation over the 10-year life of the freezer. Also, in accordance with common practice

CAUTION

In this simple example, we have assumed that Will's Pit Stop uses straight-line depreciation. A real company is more likely to use the Modified Accelerated Cost Recovery System (MACRS) for income tax purposes. This tax depreciation system is based on the double-declining-balance depreciation method.

in computing depreciation for income tax purposes, we assume a zero salvage value. In the real world, without this zero salvage value assumption, the government would be in constant disputes with taxpayers over salvage value estimates. Given these assumptions, the amount of the annual depreciation deduction for income tax purposes is $4,204.50 [($42,045 − $0) ÷ 10 years]. Because this noncash depreciation amount is deducted from taxable income in the computation of the amount of income tax to be paid, Will's Pit Stop will save $1,051 ($4,204.50 × 0.25) each year in income tax payments. This amount is sometimes called the depreciation tax shield and is an important component of the cash inflows associated with any capital purchase.

3. By the end of 10 years, the entire cost of the freezer will have been depreciated. If the freezer is sold at the end of 10 years at its $4,000 estimated salvage value, there will be a $4,000 gain on the sale. This gain will be taxable as ordinary income at 25% (assuming no change in tax rates), so the after-tax cash inflow will be only $3,000 ($4,000 × 0.75).

4. The estimated repairs and servicing cost of $8,000 at the end of Year 5 is an expense deduction from the company's income for that year. Therefore, the net cost of this expense to the company is only $6,000 ($8,000 × 0.75).

These adjusted cash flows can now be used to compute the net present value of the cash inflows and outflows that would result if the freezer were purchased. The present values of these cash flows are presented in Exhibit 3 at three different discount rates: 8%, 10%, and 12%.

Three different rates are used to illustrate that the net present value decreases as the hurdle rate increases from 8 to 12%. In other words, as the rate of return increases, the present value of the cash inflow decreases in relation to the present value of the cash outflows. The point at which the present values of the inflows and outflows are equal reflects the expected internal rate of return. If the expected return is less than the company's hurdle rate, it is unlikely that the company will acquire the asset unless there are compensating qualitative factors.

Exhibit 3 shows that the tax effects on cash inflows and outflows, given a tax rate of 25%, reduce the internal rate of return on Will's Pit Stop's proposed freezer from a pretax 10% calculated earlier in the chapter to just under 8%. This occurs because taxes reduce the present value of the cash inflows more than they reduce the present value of the cash outflows. (Remember the initial cost is already at its present value.) If the tax rate were at the U.S. federal corporate rate of 35%, which is the rate that would be applicable to almost all large U.S. corporations, the internal rate of return would decrease even further. This is because the negative effect of the increased tax expense on gross margin is greater than the positive effect of the increased tax savings from the annual depreciation deduction and the deduction for repairs. In general, income taxes reduce the internal rate of return (as well as the net present value)—and the higher the tax rate, the greater the reduction.

For the company to justify purchasing the freezer in the face of a 12% hurdle rate, the company would have to increase its gross margin significantly (increase sales volume with the same freezer capacity). You should also keep in mind that when the net present value at a selected hurdle rate is at or near zero, important qualitative factors not incorporated into the calculations of net present value will be the primary determinants of whether the asset is acquired.

EXHIBIT 3 | Income Tax Effects of Capital Budgeting

Will's Pit Stop

Net Present Value of Cash Inflows and Outflows (25% Tax Rate)

Type of Cash Flow	Period	After-Tax Cash Flow	8% Present Value	8% Amount*	10% Present Value	10% Amount*	12% Present Value	12% Amount*
Inflows:								
Revenue less cost of goods sold								
(net of tax): ($15,000 − $7,600) × 0.75	Years 1–10	$ 5,550	6.7101	$37,241	6.1446	$34,103	5.6502	$31,359
Depreciation tax shield: $4,204.50 × 0.25	Years 1–10	1,051	6.7101	7,052	6.1446	6,458	5.6502	5,938
Salvage value ($4,000 × 0.75)	End of Year 10	3,000	0.4632	1,390	0.3855	1,157	0.3220	966
Total cash inflows				$45,683		$41,718		$38,263
Outflows:								
Initial freezer cost	Today	42,045	1.0000	$42,045	1.0000	$42,045	1.0000	$42,045
Repairs and servicing cost ($8,000 × 0.75)	End of Year 5	6,000	0.6806	4,084	0.6209	3,725	0.5674	3,404
Total cash outflows				$46,129		$45,770		$45,449
Excess cash inflow (outflow)				$ (446)		$ (4,052)		$ (7,186)

*After-tax cash flow × present value.

> **REMEMBER THIS...**
>
> - After-tax cash flow = Before-tax cash flow × (1 − Tax rate)
> - Depreciation tax shield = Depreciation deduction × Tax rate

Appendix: The Time Value of Money

Present Value and Future Value Concepts

The concepts of present value and future value are used to measure the effect of time on the value of money. To illustrate, if you are to receive $100 one year from today, is it worth $100 today? Obviously not, because if you had the $100 today you could either use it now or invest it and earn interest. If the $100 isn't to be received for one year, those options are not available. The present value of $1 is the value today of $1 to be received or paid in the future, given a specified interest rate. To determine the value today of money to be received or paid in the future, we must "discount" the future amount (reduce the amount to its present value) by an appropriate interest rate. For example, if money can earn 10% per year, $100 to be received one year from now is approximately equal to $90.91 received today.

Putting it another way, if $90.91 is invested today in an account that earns 10% interest for one year, the interest earned will be $9.09 ($90.91 × 10% × 1 year = $9.09). The sum of the $90.91 principal plus $9.09 interest would equal $100 at the end of one year. Thus, the present value of $100 to be received (or paid) in one year with 10% interest is $90.91. This present value relationship can be diagramed as follows:

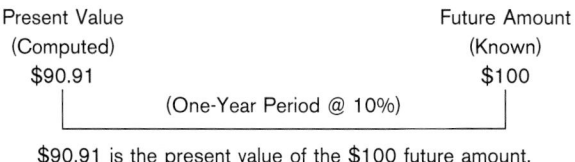

$90.91 is the present value of the $100 future amount.

The relationships in this diagram can be described in two ways. We have just looked at the relationship by recognizing that the $90.91 is the present value of $100 to be received one year from now when interest is 10%. In this example, the $100 to be received one year from now is known, and the present value of $90.91 must be computed. We are computing a present value amount from a known future value amount.

Another way to look at the relationship is on a future value basis. Future values apply when the amount today ($90.91) is known, and the future amount must be calculated. Future values are exactly the opposite of present values. Thinking in terms of future values, $100 is the future amount we can expect to receive in one year, given a present known amount of $90.91 when the interest rate is 10%. We can diagram this relationship as follows:

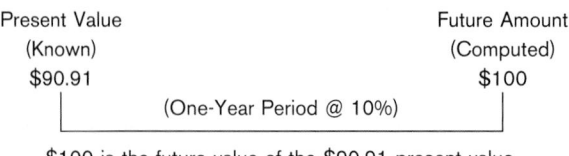

$100 is the future value of the $90.91 present value.

Present and future values can be calculated using formulas. However, if more than one period is involved, the calculations become rather complicated. Therefore, it is more convenient to use either a present value table or a calculator that gives the present value of $1 for various numbers of periods and interest rates (see Table I, page 1152) or a future value table that gives the future value of $1 for various numbers of periods and interest rates (see Table III, page 1154). We will illustrate the use of both a present value table and a future value table.

Present Value Table   To use a present value table, you simply locate the appropriate number of periods in the leftmost column and the interest rate in the row at the top of the table. The intersection of the row and column is the factor representing the present value of $1 for the number of periods and the relevant interest rate. To find the present value of an amount other than $1, multiply the factor in the table by that amount.

To illustrate the use of a present value table (Table I) to find the present value of a known future amount, assume that $10,000 is to be paid four years from today when the interest rate is 10%. What is the present value of the $10,000 payment?

Amount of payment	$10,000
Present value factor of $1 to be paid in 4 periods	
at 10% interest (from Table I)	×0.6830
Present value of payment	$ 6,830

This present value amount, $6,830, is the amount that could be paid today to satisfy the obligation that is due four years from now. As indicated, this procedure is sometimes referred to as "discounting." Thus, we say that $10,000 discounted for four years at 10% is $6,830. Stated another way, if $6,830 is invested today in an account that pays 10% interest, in four years the balance in that account would be $10,000.

The same present value computed in the previous example can be obtained using a business calculator. The necessary keystrokes are illustrated below. *Note*: The exact sequences of keystrokes illustrated are for a Hewlett-Packard business calculator; the keystrokes for other business calculators are similar if not exactly the same.

Hewlett-Packard Keystrokes for Present Value of a Single Payment:

1.   10,000: Press **FV** (this is the amount of the future payment)
2.   4: Press **N** (number of years)
3.   10: Press **I** (interest rate)
4.   Press **PV** for the answer = $6,830.13455 = $6,830 (rounded)

Future Value Table   To find the future value of an amount that is known today, you use a future value table. When using a future value table, you simply locate the appropriate number of periods in the leftmost column and the interest rate in the row at the top of the table. The intersection of the row and column is the factor representing the future value of $1 for the number of periods and the relevant interest rate. To find the future value of an amount other than $1, multiply the factor in the table by that amount.

To illustrate the use of a future value table (Table III), we will use the same information that was presented before, except that we will now assume that the present value of $6,830 is known, not the future amount of $10,000. Assume that we have a savings account with a current balance of $6,830 that earns interest of 10%. What will be the balance in that account in four years?

Present value in savings account	$ 6,830
Future value factor of $1 in 4 periods	
at 10% interest (from Table III)	×1.4641
Future value	$10,000*

*Rounded

Hewlett-Packard Keystrokes for Future Value of a Single Payment:

1. 6,830: Press **PV** (this is the amount of the current payment)
2. 4: Press **N** (number of years)
3. 10: Press **I** (interest rate)
4. Press **FV** for the answer = $9,999.80300 = $10,000 (rounded)

When computing future values, we often use the term *compounding* to mean the frequency with which interest is added to the principal. Thus, we say that interest of 10% has been compounded once a year (annually) to arrive at a future value at the end of four years of $10,000. If the interest is added more or less frequently than once a year, the future amount will be different.

The preceding example assumed an annual compounding period for interest. If the 10% interest had been compounded semiannually (twice a year) for four years, the calculation would have involved using a 5% (one-half of the 10%) rate for 8 periods (4 years × 2 periods per year) instead of 10% for 4 periods. To illustrate, what is the present value of $10,000 to be paid in four years if interest of 10% is compounded semiannually?

Amount of payment	$10,000
Present value factor of $1 to be paid in 8 periods	
at 5% interest (from Table I)	×0.6768
Present value of payment	$ 6,768

Thus, the present value of $10,000 to be paid in four years is $6,768 if interest is compounded semiannually. Likewise, if semiannual compounding is used to determine the future value of $6,768 in four years at 10% compounded semiannually, the result is as follows:

Present value in savings account	$ 6,768
Future value factor of $1 in 8 periods	
at 5% interest (from Table III)	×1.4775
Future value	$10,000*

*Rounded

Note that the present value ($6,768) is lower with semiannual compounding than with annual compounding ($6,830). The more frequently interest is compounded, the greater the total amount of interest deducted (in computing present values) or added (in computing future values).

Hewlett-Packard Keystrokes for Present Value of a Single Payment:

1. 10,000: Press **FV** (this is the amount of the future payment)
2. 8: Press **N** (number of semiannual periods)
3. 5: Press **I** (interest rate per semiannual period)
4. Press **PV** for the answer = $6,768.39362 = $6,768 (rounded)

Hewlett-Packard Keystrokes for Future Value of a Single Payment:

1. 6,768: Press **PV** (this is the amount of the current payment)
2. 8: Press **N** (number of semiannual periods)
3. 5: Press **I** (interest rate per semiannual period)
4. Press **FV** for the answer = $9,999.41844 = $10,000 (rounded up)

Since interest may also be compounded quarterly, monthly, daily, or for some other period, you should learn the relationship of interest to the compounding period. Semiannual interest means that you double the interest periods and halve the annual interest rate; with quarterly interest you quadruple the periods and take one-fourth of the annual interest rate. The formula for interest rate is:

$$\frac{\text{Yearly interest rate}}{\text{Compounding periods per year}} = \text{Interest rate per compounding period}$$

The number of interest periods is simply the number of periods per year times the number of years. That formula is:

$$\frac{\text{Compounding}}{\text{periods per year}} \times \frac{\text{Number}}{\text{of years}} = \frac{\text{Number of}}{\text{interest periods}}$$

The Present Value of an Annuity

In discussing present values and future values, we have assumed only a single present value or future value with one of the amounts known and the other to be computed. With liabilities, we generally know the future amount that must be paid and would like to compute the present value of that future payment.

Many long-term liabilities involve a series of payments rather than one lump-sum payment. For example, a company might purchase equipment under an installment agreement requiring payments of $5,000 each year for five years. Determining the value today (present value) of a series of equally spaced, equal amount payments (called annuities) is more complicated than determining the present value of a single future payment. If you were to try to calculate the present value of an annuity by hand, you would have to discount the first payment for one period, the second payment for two periods, and so on, and then add all the present values together. Because such calculations are time-consuming, a table is generally used (see Table II, page 1153). The factors in the table are the sums of the individual present values of all future payments. Based on the present value of an annuity of $1, the table provides factors for various interest rates and payments.

To illustrate the use of a present value of an annuity table (Table II), we will assume that $10,000 is to be paid at the end of each of the next 10 years. If the interest rate is 12% compounded annually, Table II shows a present value factor of 5.6502. This factor means that the present value of $1 paid each year for 10 years discounted at 12% is approximately $5.65. Applying this factor to payments of $10,000 results in the following:

Amount of the annual payment	$10,000
Present value factor of an annuity of $1 discounted for 10 payments at 12%	×5.6502
Present value	$56,502

This amount, $56,502, is the amount (present value) that could be paid today to satisfy the obligation if interest is 12%.

Hewlett-Packard Keystrokes for Present Value of an Annuity:

1. 10,000: Press **PMT** (this is the amount of the annual payments)
2. 10: Press **N** (number of payments)
3. 12: Press **I** (interest rate)
4. Press **PV** for the answer = $56,502.23028 = $56,502 (rounded)

Using Excel Spreadsheets for Time Value of Money Calculations

Because of the widespread use of laptop computers, many people now use functions available in Excel spreadsheets to do time value of money calculations. Three of those functions—PV, NPV, and IRR—are introduced in this section.

The following example will be used to illustrate the use of all three Excel functions. For simplicity, income taxes will be ignored.

Initial cost of machine	$10,000
Net annual cash inflows from the machine	$3,000
Salvage value at the end of the machine's useful life	$1,000
Useful life	5 years
Appropriate discount rate	12%

PV Excel Function

If you push the "Insert Function," or f_x button, in Excel, you can scan the menu of "Financial" functions and find the PV function. The function arguments for the PV function are as follows:

Rate   The discount rate, which is 12% in this example.

Nper   The number of periods, which is five years in this example.

Pmt   The regular annuity (or periodic, equal cash flow) amount. In this case, the annuity is $3,000.

Fv   The amount of any single cash flow to occur in the future. In this case, the salvage value is a single cash flow at the end of five years of $1,000.

Type   Indication of whether the cash flows occur at the beginning or the end of the periods. In the examples shown in this chapter, we have always assumed that cash flows occur at the end of the periods; this is indicated by leaving this field blank or by inserting a zero. If the cash flows occur at the beginning of the period, this is indicated by entering a one in this field. In this case, we will enter a zero to indicate that the cash flows occur at the end of the periods.

The completed set of Excel function arguments appears as follows:

Rate	.12
Nper	5
Pmt	3000
Fv	1000
Type	0

With these inputs, the value of the function is ($11,381.76). Note that Excel is designed such that the function returns a negative number. This can easily be remedied by placing a minus sign in front of the function. This calculation indicates that the net present value, or NPV, of this project is positive because the initial cost of the machine is just $10,000. Thus, the NPV is $1,381.76 ($11,381.76 − $10,000.00). This computation will be confirmed in an alternate way using the NPV Excel function.

NPV Excel Function

The annual cash flow information regarding the machine can be entered into a spreadsheet in the format shown on the next page. This format, rather than emphasizing the cash flows that come from each source (initial cost, annual cash inflows, or salvage value), instead emphasizes the net annual cash inflow or outflow from all sources. An advantage

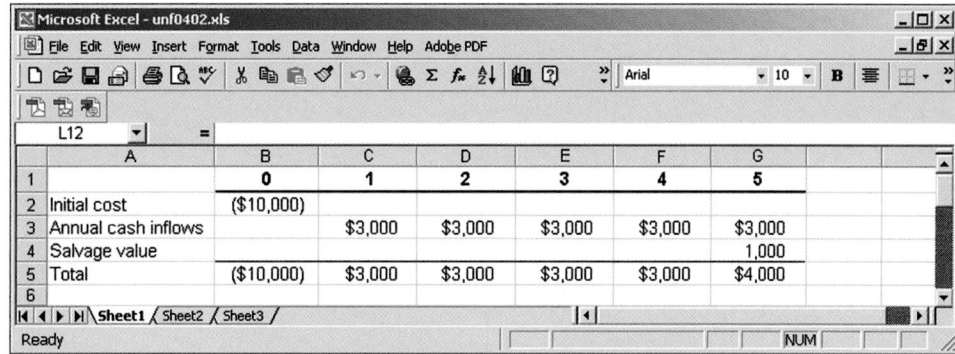

of presenting the cash flows in this fashion is that it allows for the use of the NPV function in Excel. If you push the "Insert Function," or f_x button, in Excel, you can scan the menu of "Financial" functions and find the NPV function. The function arguments for the NPV function are as follows:

Rate The discount rate, which is 12% in this example.

Value1 The range of spreadsheet cells containing the net annual cash flows. In this case, that range is C5:G5. This function requires that all cash flows occur at the end of the periods. Note that the initial outflow of $10,000 is not included in the C5:G5 range of cells because that outflow occurs at the beginning, not the end, of the first year.

The completed set of Excel function arguments appears as follows:

Rate .12
Value1 C5:G5

With these inputs, the value of the function is $11,381.76. Computation of the NPV of the project requires subtracting the initial cost of $10,000 from the present value of these net annual cash flows. Again, as computed previously, the NPV is $1,381.76.

IRR Excel Function

Another advantage of presenting the total net cash flows by year as shown in the preceding section is that it allows for the use of the IRR function in Excel. If you push the "Insert Function," or f_x button, in Excel, you can scan the menu of "Financial" functions and find the IRR function. The function arguments for the IRR function are as follows:

Values The range of spreadsheet cells containing the net annual cash flows. In this case, that range is B5:G5. In contrast to the NPV function, the IRR function requires that the first cash flow included in the function occur immediately.

Guess An initial estimate of the IRR. Because the IRR calculation involves an iterative interpolation process, the mathematical algorithm has to have a starting place. It is almost always safe to leave this field blank; if the field is blank, Excel uses 10% as the initial estimate.

The completed set of Excel function arguments appears as follows:

Values B5:G5
Guess .10

> **CAUTION**
>
> The NPV function assumes that the first cash flow included in the function occurs at the end of the first year. The IRR function assumes that the first cash flow occurs immediately.

With these inputs, the value of the IRR function is 17.23%. We expected an IRR greater than 12% because our previous computations demonstrated that the NPV (using a 12% discount rate) is greater than zero.

TABLE I

The Present Value of $1 Due in n Periods*

Period	1%	2%	3%	4%	5%	6%	7%	8%	9%	10%	12%	14%	15%	16%	18%	20%
1	.9901	.9804	.9709	.9615	.9524	.9434	.9346	.9259	.9174	.9091	.8929	.8772	.8696	.8621	.8475	.8333
2	.9803	.9612	.9426	.9246	.9070	.8900	.8734	.8573	.8417	.8264	.7972	.7695	.7561	.7432	.7182	.6944
3	.9706	.9423	.9151	.8890	.8638	.8396	.8163	.7938	.7722	.7513	.7118	.6750	.6575	.6407	.6086	.5787
4	.9610	.9238	.8885	.8548	.8227	.7921	.7629	.7350	.7084	.6830	.6355	.5921	.5718	.5523	.5158	.4823
5	.9515	.9057	.8626	.8219	.7835	.7473	.7130	.6806	.6499	.6209	.5674	.5194	.4972	.4761	.4371	.4019
6	.9420	.8880	.8375	.7903	.7462	.7050	.6663	.6302	.5963	.5645	.5066	.4556	.4323	.4104	.3704	.3349
7	.9327	.8706	.8131	.7599	.7107	.6651	.6227	.5835	.5470	.5132	.4523	.3996	.3759	.3538	.3139	.2791
8	.9235	.8535	.7894	.7307	.6768	.6274	.5820	.5403	.5019	.4665	.4039	.3506	.3269	.3050	.2660	.2326
9	.9143	.8368	.7664	.7026	.6446	.5919	.5439	.5002	.4604	.4241	.3606	.3075	.2843	.2630	.2255	.1938
10	.9053	.8203	.7441	.6756	.6139	.5584	.5083	.4632	.4224	.3855	.3220	.2697	.2472	.2267	.1911	.1615
11	.8963	.8043	.7224	.6496	.5847	.5268	.4751	.4289	.3875	.3503	.2875	.2366	.2149	.1954	.1619	.1346
12	.8874	.7885	.7014	.6246	.5568	.4970	.4440	.3971	.3555	.3186	.2567	.2076	.1869	.1685	.1372	.1122
13	.8787	.7730	.6810	.6006	.5303	.4688	.4150	.3677	.3262	.2897	.2292	.1821	.1625	.1452	.1163	.0935
14	.8700	.7579	.6611	.5775	.5051	.4423	.3878	.3405	.2992	.2633	.2046	.1597	.1413	.1252	.0985	.0779
15	.8613	.7430	.6419	.5553	.4810	.4173	.3624	.3152	.2745	.2394	.1827	.1401	.1229	.1079	.0835	.0649
16	.8528	.7284	.6232	.5339	.4581	.3936	.3387	.2919	.2519	.2176	.1631	.1229	.1069	.0930	.0708	.0541
17	.8444	.7142	.6050	.5134	.4363	.3714	.3166	.2703	.2311	.1978	.1456	.1078	.0929	.0802	.0600	.0451
18	.8360	.7002	.5874	.4936	.4155	.3503	.2959	.2502	.2120	.1799	.1300	.0946	.0808	.0691	.0508	.0376
19	.8277	.6864	.5703	.4746	.3957	.3305	.2765	.2317	.1945	.1635	.1161	.0829	.0703	.0596	.0431	.0313
20	.8195	.6730	.5537	.4564	.3769	.3118	.2584	.2145	.1784	.1486	.1037	.0728	.0611	.0514	.0365	.0261
25	.7798	.6095	.4776	.3751	.2953	.2330	.1842	.1460	.1160	.0923	.0588	.0378	.0304	.0245	.0160	.0105
30	.7419	.5521	.4120	.3083	.2314	.1741	.1314	.0994	.0754	.0573	.0334	.0196	.0151	.0116	.0070	.0042
40	.6717	.4529	.3066	.2083	.1420	.0972	.0668	.0460	.0318	.0221	.0107	.0053	.0037	.0026	.0013	.0007
50	.6080	.3715	.2281	.1407	.0872	.0543	.0339	.0213	.0134	.0085	.0035	.0014	.0009	.0006	.0003	.0001
60	.5504	.3048	.1697	.0951	.0535	.0303	.0173	.0099	.0057	.0033	.0011	.0004	.0002	.0001	†	†

*The formula used to derive the values in this table was $PV = F \dfrac{1}{(1 + i)^n}$ where PV = present value, F = future amount to be discounted, i = interest rate, and n = number of periods.

†The value of 0 to four decimal places.

TABLE II — The Present Value of an Annuity of $1 per Number of Payments*

Number of Payments	1%	2%	3%	4%	5%	6%	7%	8%	9%	10%	12%	14%	15%	16%	18%	20%
1	0.9901	0.9804	0.9709	0.9615	0.9524	0.9434	0.9346	0.9259	0.9174	0.9091	0.8929	0.8772	0.8596	0.8621	0.8475	0.8333
2	1.9704	1.9416	1.9135	1.8861	1.8594	1.8334	1.8080	1.7833	1.7591	1.7355	1.6901	1.6467	1.6257	1.6052	1.5656	1.5278
3	2.9410	2.8839	2.8286	2.7751	2.7232	2.6730	2.6243	2.5771	2.5313	2.4869	2.4018	2.3216	2.2832	2.2459	2.1743	2.1065
4	3.9820	3.8077	3.7171	3.6299	3.5460	3.4651	3.3872	3.3121	3.2397	3.1699	3.0373	2.9137	2.8550	2.7982	2.6901	2.5887
5	4.8884	4.7135	4.5797	4.4518	4.3295	4.2124	4.1002	3.9927	3.8897	3.7908	3.6048	3.4331	3.3522	3.2743	3.1272	2.9906
6	5.7985	5.6014	5.4172	5.2421	5.0757	4.9173	4.7665	4.6229	4.4859	4.3553	4.1114	3.8887	3.7845	3.6847	3.4976	3.3255
7	6.7282	6.4720	6.2303	6.0021	5.7864	5.5824	5.3893	5.2064	5.0330	4.8684	4.5638	4.2883	4.1604	4.0386	3.8115	3.6046
8	7.6517	7.3255	7.0197	6.7327	6.4632	6.2098	5.9713	5.7466	5.5348	5.3349	4.9676	4.6389	4.4873	4.3436	4.0776	3.8372
9	8.5660	8.1622	7.7861	7.4353	7.1078	6.8017	6.5152	6.2469	5.9952	5.7590	5.3282	4.9464	4.7716	4.6065	4.3030	4.0310
10	9.4713	8.9826	8.5302	8.1109	7.7217	7.3601	7.0236	6.7101	6.4177	6.1446	5.6502	5.2161	5.0188	4.8332	4.4941	4.1925
11	10.3676	9.7868	9.2526	8.7605	8.3064	7.8869	7.4987	7.1390	6.8052	6.4951	5.9377	5.4527	5.2337	5.0286	4.6560	4.3271
12	11.2551	10.5733	9.9540	9.3851	8.8633	8.3838	7.9427	7.5361	7.1607	6.8137	6.1944	5.6603	5.4206	5.1971	4.7932	4.4392
13	12.1337	11.3484	10.6350	9.9856	9.3936	8.8527	8.3577	7.9038	7.4869	7.1034	6.4235	5.8424	5.5831	5.3423	4.9095	4.5327
14	13.0037	12.1062	11.2961	10.5631	9.8986	9.2950	8.7455	8.2442	7.7862	7.3667	6.6282	6.0021	5.7245	5.4675	5.0081	4.6106
15	13.8651	12.8493	11.9379	11.1184	10.3797	9.7122	9.1079	8.5595	8.0607	7.6061	6.8109	6.1422	5.8474	5.5755	5.0916	4.6755
16	14.7179	13.5777	12.5611	11.6523	10.8378	10.1059	9.4466	8.8514	8.3126	7.8237	6.9740	6.2651	5.9542	5.6685	5.1624	4.7296
17	15.5623	14.2919	13.1661	12.1657	11.2741	10.4773	9.7632	9.1216	8.5436	8.0216	7.1196	6.3729	6.0472	5.7487	5.2223	4.7746
18	16.3983	14.9920	13.7535	12.6593	11.6896	10.8276	10.0591	9.3719	8.7556	8.2014	7.2497	6.4674	6.1280	5.8178	5.2732	4.8122
19	17.2260	15.6785	14.3238	13.1339	12.0853	11.1581	10.3356	9.6036	8.9501	8.3649	7.3658	6.5504	6.1982	5.8775	5.3162	4.8435
20	18.0456	16.3514	14.8775	13.5903	12.4622	11.4699	10.5940	9.8181	9.1285	8.5136	7.4694	6.6231	6.2593	5.9288	5.3527	4.8696
25	22.0232	19.5235	17.4131	15.6221	14.0939	12.7834	11.6536	10.6748	9.8226	9.0770	7.8431	6.8729	6.4641	6.0971	5.4669	4.9476
30	25.8077	22.3965	19.6004	17.2920	15.3725	13.7648	12.4090	11.2578	10.2737	9.4269	8.0552	7.0027	6.5660	6.1772	5.5168	4.9789
40	32.8347	27.3555	23.1148	19.7928	17.1591	15.0463	13.3317	11.9246	10.7574	9.7791	8.2438	7.1050	6.6418	6.2335	5.5482	4.9966
50	39.1961	31.4236	25.7298	21.4822	18.2559	15.7619	13.8007	12.2335	10.9617	9.9148	8.3045	7.1327	6.6605	6.2463	5.5641	4.9995
60	44.9550	34.7609	27.6756	22.6235	18.9293	16.1614	14.0392	12.3766	11.0480	9.9672	8.3240	7.1401	6.6651	6.2482	5.5553	4.9999

*The formula used to derive the values in this table was $PV = F\left(\dfrac{1 - \dfrac{1}{(1+i)^n}}{i}\right)$ where PV = present value, F = periodic payment to be discounted, i = interest rate, and n = number of payments.

TABLE III	Amount of $1 Due in *n* Periods																	
Period	1%	2%	3%	4%	5%	6%	7%	8%	9%	10%	12%	14%	15%	16%	18%	20%
1	1.0100	1.0200	1.0300	1.0400	1.0500	1.0600	1.0700	1.0800	1.0900	1.1000	1.1200	1.1400	1.1500	1.1600	1.1800	1.2000
2	1.0201	1.0404	1.0609	1.0816	1.1025	1.1236	1.1449	1.1664	1.1881	1.2100	1.2544	1.2996	1.3225	1.3456	1.3924	1.4400
3	1.0303	1.0612	1.0927	1.1249	1.1576	1.1910	1.2250	1.2597	1.2950	1.3310	1.4049	1.4815	1.5209	1.5609	1.6430	1.7280
4	1.0406	1.0824	1.1255	1.1699	1.2155	1.2625	1.3108	1.3605	1.4116	1.4641	1.5735	1.6890	1.7490	1.8106	1.9388	2.0736
5	1.0510	1.1041	1.1593	1.2167	1.2763	1.3382	1.4026	1.4693	1.5386	1.6105	1.7623	1.9254	2.0114	2.1003	2.2878	2.4883
6	1.0615	1.1262	1.1941	1.2653	1.3401	1.4185	1.5007	1.5869	1.6771	1.7716	1.9738	2.1950	2.3131	2.4364	2.6996	2.9860
7	1.0721	1.1487	1.2299	1.3159	1.4071	1.5036	1.6058	1.7138	1.8280	1.9487	2.2107	2.5023	2.6600	2.8262	3.1855	3.5832
8	1.0829	1.1717	1.2668	1.3686	1.4775	1.5938	1.7182	1.8509	1.9926	2.1436	2.4760	2.8526	3.0590	3.2784	3.7589	4.2998
9	1.0937	1.1951	1.3048	1.4233	1.5513	1.6895	1.8385	1.9990	2.1719	2.3579	2.7731	3.2519	3.5179	3.8030	4.4355	5.1598
10	1.1046	1.2190	1.3439	1.4802	1.6289	1.7908	1.9672	2.1589	2.3674	2.5937	3.1058	3.7072	4.0456	4.4114	5.2338	6.1917
11	1.1157	1.2434	1.3842	1.5395	1.7103	1.8983	2.1049	2.3316	2.5804	2.8531	3.4785	4.2262	4.6524	5.1173	6.1759	7.4031
12	1.1268	1.2682	1.4258	1.6010	1.7959	2.0122	2.2522	2.5182	2.8127	3.1384	3.8960	4.8179	5.3502	5.9360	7.2876	8.9161
13	1.1381	1.2936	1.4685	1.6651	1.8856	2.1329	2.4098	2.7196	3.0658	3.4523	4.3635	5.4924	6.1528	6.8858	8.5994	10.699
14	1.1495	1.3195	1.5126	1.7317	1.9799	2.2609	2.5785	2.9372	3.3417	3.7975	4.8871	6.2613	7.0757	7.9875	10.147	12.839
15	1.1610	1.3459	1.5580	1.8009	2.0789	2.3966	2.7590	3.1722	3.6425	4.1772	5.4736	7.1379	8.1371	9.2655	11.973	15.407
16	1.1726	1.3728	1.6047	1.8730	2.1829	2.5404	2.9522	3.4259	3.9703	4.5950	6.1304	8.1372	9.3576	10.748	14.129	18.488
17	1.1843	1.4002	1.6528	1.9479	2.2920	2.6928	3.1588	3.7000	4.3276	5.0545	6.8660	9.2765	10.761	12.467	16.672	22.186
18	1.1961	1.4282	1.7024	2.0258	2.4066	2.8543	3.3799	3.9960	4.7171	5.5599	7.6900	10.575	12.375	14.462	19.673	26.623
19	1.2081	1.4568	1.7535	2.1068	2.5270	3.0256	3.6165	4.3157	5.1417	6.1159	8.6128	12.055	14.231	16.776	23.214	31.948
20	1.2202	1.4859	1.8061	2.1911	2.6533	3.2071	3.8697	4.6610	5.6044	6.7275	9.6463	13.743	16.366	19.460	27.393	38.337
30	1.3478	1.8114	2.4273	3.2434	4.3219	5.7435	7.6123	10.062	13.267	17.449	29.959	50.950	66.211	85.849	143.37	237.37
40	1.4889	2.2080	3.2620	4.8010	7.0400	10.285	14.974	21.724	31.409	45.259	93.050	188.88	267.86	378.72	750.37	1469.7
50	1.6446	2.6916	4.3839	7.1067	11.467	18.420	29.457	46.901	74.357	117.39	289.00	700.23	1083.6	1670.7	3927.3	9100.4
60	1.8167	3.2810	5.8916	10.519	18.679	32.987	57.946	101.25	176.03	304.48	897.59	2595.9	4383.9	7370.1	20555.	56347.

TABLE IV — Amount of an Annuity of $1 per Number of Payments

Number of Payments	1%	2%	3%	4%	5%	6%	7%	8%	9%	10%	12%	14%	15%	16%	18%	20%
1	1.0000	1.0000	1.0000	1.0000	1.0000	1.0000	1.0000	1.0000	1.0000	1.0000	1.0000	1.0000	1.0000	1.0000	1.0000	1.0000
2	2.0100	2.0200	2.0300	2.0400	2.0500	2.0600	2.0700	2.0800	2.0900	2.1000	2.1200	2.1400	2.1500	2.1600	2.1800	2.2000
3	3.0301	3.0604	3.0909	3.1216	3.1525	3.1836	3.2149	3.2464	3.2781	3.3100	3.3744	3.4396	3.4725	3.5056	3.5724	3.6400
4	4.0604	4.1216	4.1836	4.2465	4.3101	4.3746	4.4399	4.5061	4.5731	4.6410	4.7793	4.9211	4.9934	5.0665	5.2154	5.3680
5	5.1010	5.2040	5.3091	5.4163	5.5256	5.6371	5.7507	5.8666	5.9847	6.1051	6.3528	6.6101	6.7424	6.8771	7.1542	7.4416
6	6.1520	6.3081	6.4684	6.6330	6.8019	6.9753	7.1533	7.3359	7.5233	7.7156	8.1152	8.5355	8.7537	8.9775	9.4420	9.9299
7	7.2135	7.4343	7.6625	7.8983	8.1420	8.3938	8.6540	8.9228	9.2004	9.4872	10.0890	10.7305	11.0668	11.4139	12.1415	12.9159
8	8.2857	8.5830	8.8923	9.2142	9.5491	9.8975	10.2598	10.6366	11.0285	11.4359	12.2997	13.2328	13.7268	14.2401	15.3270	16.4991
9	9.3685	9.7546	10.1591	10.5828	11.0266	11.4913	11.9780	12.4876	13.0210	13.5795	14.7757	16.0853	16.7858	17.5185	19.0859	20.7989
10	10.4622	10.9497	11.4639	12.0061	12.5779	13.1808	13.8164	14.4866	15.1929	15.9374	17.5487	19.3373	20.3037	21.3215	23.5213	25.9587
11	11.5668	12.1687	12.8078	13.4864	14.2068	14.9716	15.7836	16.6455	17.5603	18.5312	20.6546	23.0445	24.3493	25.7329	28.7551	32.1504
12	12.6825	13.4121	14.1920	15.0258	15.9171	16.8699	17.8885	18.9771	20.1407	21.3843	24.1331	27.2707	29.0017	30.8502	34.9311	39.5805
13	13.8093	14.6803	15.6178	16.6268	17.7130	18.8821	20.1406	21.4953	22.9534	24.5227	28.0291	32.0887	34.3519	36.7862	42.2187	48.4966
14	14.9474	15.9739	17.0863	18.2919	19.5986	21.0151	22.5505	24.2149	26.0192	27.9750	32.3926	37.5811	40.5047	43.6720	50.8180	59.1959
15	16.0969	17.2934	18.5989	20.0236	21.5786	23.2760	25.1290	27.1521	29.3609	31.7725	37.2797	43.8424	47.5804	51.6595	60.9653	72.0351
16	17.2579	18.6393	20.1569	21.8245	23.6575	25.6725	27.8881	30.3243	33.0034	35.9497	42.7535	50.9804	55.7178	60.9250	72.9390	87.4421
17	18.4304	20.0121	21.7616	23.6975	25.8404	28.2129	30.8402	33.7502	36.9737	40.5447	48.8837	59.1176	65.0751	71.6730	87.0680	105.9306
18	19.6147	21.4123	23.4144	25.6454	28.1324	30.9057	33.9990	37.4502	41.3013	45.5992	55.7497	68.3941	75.8364	84.1407	103.7403	128.1167
19	20.8190	22.8406	25.1169	27.6712	30.5390	33.7600	37.3790	41.4463	46.0185	51.1591	63.4397	78.9692	88.2118	98.6032	123.4135	154.7400
20	22.0190	24.2974	26.8704	29.7781	33.0660	36.7856	40.9955	45.7620	51.1601	57.2750	72.0524	91.0249	102.4436	115.3797	146.6280	186.6880
30	34.7849	40.5681	47.5754	56.0849	66.4388	79.0582	94.4608	113.2832	136.3075	164.4940	241.3327	356.7868	434.7451	530.3117	790.9480	1181.8816
40	48.8864	60.4020	75.4013	95.0255	120.7998	154.7620	199.6351	259.0565	337.8824	442.5926	767.0914	1342.0251	1779.0903	2360.7572	4163.2130	7343.8578
50	64.4632	84.5794	112.7969	152.6671	209.3480	290.3359	406.5289	573.7702	815.0836	1163.9085	2400.0182	4994.5213	7217.7163	10435.6488	21813.0937	45497.1908
60	81.6697	114.0515	163.0534	237.9907	353.5837	533.1282	813.5204	1253.2133	1944.7921	3034.8164	7471.6411	18535.1333	29219.9916	46057.5085	114189.6665	281732.5718

REVIEW OF LEARNING OBJECTIVES

(1) Understand the importance of capital budgeting and the concepts underlying strategic and capital investment decisions.

- Capital budgeting is the making of long-term decisions.
- Proper capital budgeting involves:
  - a comparison of the current and expected cash outflows and inflows associated with the decision and
  - discounting of those cash flows to the present to reflect the time value of money.

(2) Describe and use two nondiscounted capital budgeting techniques: the payback method and the unadjusted rate of return method.

- The payback and unadjusted rate of return methods are commonly used in business because they are simple to apply.
- The payback method measures the time required to recover the initial cost of an investment from future net cash inflows (investment cost divided by annual net cash inflows).
- The unadjusted rate of return method provides a measure of the accounting profitability of an investment (increases in future average annual net income divided by the cost of the investment).

(3) Describe and use two discounted capital budgeting techniques: the net present value method and the internal rate of return method.

- Net present value (NPV) = Discounted value of cash inflows less discounted value of cash outflows
  - If NPV $\geq$ 0, accept the project

- Internal rate of return (IRR) = The "true" rate of return for an investment after considering the time value of money. Computationally, the IRR is the discount rate that results in an NPV exactly equal to zero.
  - If IRR $\geq$ Hurdle rate, accept the project

(4) Understand the need for evaluating qualitative factors in strategic and capital investment decisions. Some of the qualitative factors that should be considered in making capital budgeting decisions are as follows:

- Impact on the timeliness of product or service delivery
- Impact on the quality of the product or service
- Legal exposure
- Government regulations
- Environmental impact
- Worker safety
- Company image
- Community welfare

EXPANDED

⑤ **Use sensitivity analysis to assess the potential effects of uncertainty in capital budgeting.** To evaluate the potential effect of uncertainty about estimates of future amounts, use sensitivity analysis which involves addressing questions such as the following:

- What level of cash operating inflows will give the project an NPV of at least zero?
- What salvage value amount is large enough to give the project an NPV of at least zero?
- How long must the project last in order to have an NPV of at least zero?

⑥ **Explain how to use capital budgeting techniques in ranking capital investment projects.**

- Screening determines whether projects are acceptable.
- Ranking enables management to select the most profitable investment first and thus use limited resources to the best advantage.
- Ranking may be accomplished by:
  - the internal rate of return or by
  - the net present value method using the profitability index.

⑦ **Explain how income taxes affect capital budgeting decisions.**

- After-tax cash flow = Before-tax cash flow × (1 − Tax rate)
- Depreciation tax shield = Depreciation deduction × Tax rate

KEY TERMS & CONCEPTS

capital, 1121
capital budgeting, 1120
cash inflows, 1124
cash outflows, 1123
cost of capital, 1128
discounted cash flow
   methods, 1125
hurdle rate, 1127

interest, 1122
internal rate of
   return, 1132
internal rate of return
   method, 1132
interpolation, 1133
least-cost decision, 1131
net present value, 1130

net present value
   method, 1129
payback
   method, 1125
ranking, 1122
screening, 1122
unadjusted rate of return
   method, 1127

EXPANDED

capital rationing, 1141
profitability index, 1142
sensitivity analysis, 1139

REVIEW PROBLEM

Capital Budgeting

High Flying Company has an opportunity to make an investment that will yield $1,000 net cash inflow per year for the next 10 years. The investment will cost $6,000 and will have no salvage value. After cost reductions and depreciation related to the new investment, the future average annual net income will increase $800.

Required:
Compute the following:

1. The payback period.
2. The unadjusted rate of return.
3. The net present value. (Use a 10% discount rate.)
4. The internal rate of return. (The hurdle rate is 10%.)

(continued)

Solution

1. The Payback Period

To compute the payback period, divide the investment cost by the annual net cash inflows.

$$\frac{\text{Investment cost}}{\text{Annual net cash inflows}} = \frac{\$6,000}{\$1,000} = 6 \text{ years}$$

2. The Unadjusted Rate of Return

To compute the unadjusted rate of return, divide the increase in future average annual net income by the initial investment cost.

$$\frac{\text{Increase in future average annual net income}}{\text{Initial investment cost}} = \frac{\$800}{\$6,000} = 13.3\%$$

3. The Net Present Value

To compute the net present value, first state in present value terms all expected cash outflows and inflows.

Present value of 10 annual payments of $1,000 discounted at 10%	$6,145
Present value of payment of $6,000 now	6,000
Net present value of project (present value of cash inflows minus present value of cash outflow)	$ 145

Since this investment's net present value is greater than zero, it is acceptable from a quantitative standpoint.

4. The Internal Rate of Return

To compute the internal rate of return, first compute the present value factor, as follows:

$$\frac{\text{Investment cost}}{\text{Annual net cash inflows}} = \frac{\$6,000}{\$1,000} = 6.0000$$

Next, use this present value factor to find the investment's internal rate of return in a present value table. Using Table II, find the row for 10 years, the life of the investment. Move across the row until you find the present value factor closest to 6.0000, which is 6.1446. This is the factor for 10%. Since 6.0000 is between 6.1446 and 5.6502, the investment's internal rate of return is between 10 and 12%. Next, use interpolation to find a more exact internal rate of return.

Rate of Return		**Present Value Factors**	
High factor	10%	6.1446	6.1446
True factor		6.0000	0.0000
Low factor	12		5.6502
Differences	2%	0.1446	0.4944

The number 0.1446 is the difference between the high factor and the true factor. The number 0.4944 is the difference between the high factor and the low factor. The difference between the high rate and the low rate is 2%. The proportion 0.1446 ÷ 0.4944 of this 2% difference must be added to the low rate to give the true internal rate of return.

$$\text{True internal rate of return} = 0.10 + \left(0.02 \times \frac{0.1446}{0.4944}\right) = 10.58\%$$

The internal rate of return could also be computed using the following keystrokes with a Hewlett-Packard business calculator:

(continued)

Hewlett-Packard Keystrokes:

1. −6,000: Press **PV** (you must enter the cash outflow as a NEGATIVE number)
2. 1,000: Press **PMT** (this is the annual cash inflow)
3. 10: Press **N** (number of years)
4. Press **I/YR** for the answer = 10.56%

Note that the answer obtained using table interpolation (10.58%) is very close to the actual internal rate of return of 10.56%.

Next, this internal rate of return is compared with the hurdle rate. Since it is greater, the investment is acceptable quantitatively. Note that this is the same decision reached by calculating the net present value.

DISCUSSION QUESTIONS

1. Define *capital budgeting*. Give two examples of long-term investment decisions that require capital budgeting.
2. Why do long-term capital investment decisions often have a significant effect on a company's profitability?
3. Why is the time value of money so important in capital budgeting decisions?
4. If the time value of money is so important, why isn't the timing of cash flows emphasized in the accounting cycle?
5. How is depreciation expense treated when the discounted cash flow methods are used? Why?
6. How are cost savings and increased revenues related in capital budgeting?
7. Identify four capital budgeting methods, and explain why some are considered better than others.
8. Why is the payback method inferior to the discounted cash flow methods? When is the payback method helpful?
9. What is the major weakness of the unadjusted rate of return method?
10. Does a net present value of zero indicate that a project should be rejected? Explain.

11. As the desired rate of return increases, does the net present value of a project increase? Explain.
12. Under what circumstances might a project with a negative net present value be accepted?
13. What discount rate yields a net present value of zero? How is it determined?
14. What is a company's hurdle rate? How is it used?
15. How do quality and time considerations affect capital budgeting decisions?
16. Identify several qualitative factors, other than quality and time considerations, that may affect strategic and capital investment decisions. Why are qualitative factors important?

EXPANDED *material*

17. How can we deal with uncertainties involved in capital budgeting?
18. Distinguish between the screening and ranking functions of capital budgeting.
19. Of what value is a profitability index in capital budgeting?
20. How do income taxes influence capital budgeting decisions?

PRACTICE EXERCISES

PE 22-1 **Capital Investment Decisions in Planning**
LO1 Which one of the following is *not* a reason why a company should carefully plan its capital investment decisions?
a. Capital investments usually require a large initial outlay of capital.
b. Capital investments are usually tied to management bonus plans.
c. Capital investment decisions affect earnings over a long period of time.
d. Capital investments are less liquid, so poor investment decisions are difficult to reverse.

PE 22-2

LO1

Screening, Ranking, and Discounting

Which one of the following statements is correct?

a. Screening is the process of finding the best among available acceptable alternatives.

b. Ranking is the process of determining whether an investment meets a minimum standard of financial acceptability.

c. For the comparison of cash flows to be accurate, all amounts should be stated at their value at the point in time when the cash flow occurs.

d. Cash received sooner is worth more than cash received later.

e. Generally speaking, managers use relatively low discount rates when evaluating investments that involve a high degree of risk.

PE 22-3

LO1

Discounting Cash Outflows

The company is deciding whether to invest in a certain capital investment. The investment requires an initial outlay of $55,000 and annual payments of $12,000 made at the end of the year for five years. The company's discount rate is 14%. What is the present value of cash outflows related to this investment?

PE 22-4

LO1

Discounting Cash Inflows

Refer to the data in PE 22-3. The company expects the new investment will generate revenues of $24,000 per year for the five years of the investment's life. At the end of the four years, the company expects the investment to have a salvage value of $20,000. What is the present value of cash inflows related to this investment? Should the company make this investment?

PE 22-5

LO2

Payback Method

The company paid $50,000 cash for a capital investment. The company expects the investment to generate net cash inflows of $8,400 per year. What is the payback period of this investment?

PE 22-6

LO2

Unadjusted Rate of Return Method

Refer to the data in PE 22-5. What is the unadjusted rate of return on the investment? *Note:* The investment is expected to have a useful life of 10 years, and the company uses straight-line depreciation with zero salvage value.

PE 22-7

LO1

Cost of Capital

Forty percent of a company's total capital is debt, 45% is from the issuance of stock, and 15% is equity from retained earnings. The company has determined that the cost of its debt capital is 8% and the cost of its equity capital is 20% from stock and 15% from retained earnings. Compute the company's average cost of capital.

PE 22-8

LO3

Net Present Value Method

Which one of the following investment opportunities would be rejected by a company that accepts all projects with net present values greater than zero?

a. Present value of inflows = $35,740; present value of outflows = $32,023.

b. Present value of inflows = $452,800; present value of outflows = $450,020.

c. Present value of inflows = $1,003,840; present value of outflows = $1,003,810.

d. Present value of inflows = $125,114; present value of outflows = $125,843.

e. Present value of inflows = $85,084; present value of outflows = $82,000.

PE 22-9

LO3

Least-Cost Decisions

The company is required to install a new piece of safety equipment. The company has two alternatives for the equipment. One alternative would cost $260,000 immediately but would not add to operating costs over the 5-year life of the equipment. The second alternative costs $75,000 immediately but would add $45,000 to annual operating costs for five years. The company uses an 8% discount rate. Which alternative should the company purchase?

PE 22-10 **Calculating Internal Rate of Return**

LO3 The company is considering an 8-year investment. The initial cost of the investment is $55,348. The investment will yield net cash inflows of $10,000 per year. What is the internal rate of return for this investment?

PE 22-11 **Internal Rate of Return Interpolation**

LO3 The company is considering whether to invest in a project with an initial cost of $538,000 that will provide annual net cash inflows of $82,500 for 10 years. Use interpolation to estimate the internal rate of return.

PE 22-12 **Uneven Cash Flows and Internal Rate of Return**

LO3 The company is considering whether to invest in a piece of equipment that requires an investment of $250,000 today. The project will provide net cash flows of $50,000 per year for eight years, and it will have a salvage value of $51,509 at the end of eight years. Calculate the internal rate of return. (*Hint:* The IRR is greater than 10%.)

PE 22-13 **Qualitative Factors in Strategic and Capital Investment Decisions**

LO4 Which one of the following is an important qualitative factor to consider when making strategic and capital investment decisions?
  a. Company image and prestige.
  b. Pollution control and environmental protection.
  c. Government regulation.
  d. Worker safety.
  e. All of the above are examples of important qualitative factors.

EXPANDED *material*

PE 22-14 **Uncertain Expected Cash Flows**

LO5 The company is considering an investment that costs $785,000 today and has a salvage value in 10 years of $137,714, but the company is not sure how much net annual cash inflow will be provided by the investment. The company has a discount rate of 7%. Compute the net amount of annual cash inflow required to break even.

PE 22-15 **Uncertain Useful Life**

LO5 The company is considering an investment that costs $500,000 today and will provide $90,000 each year in net cash inflow, but the company is not sure how long the investment will last. The company has a discount rate of 10%. Compute the number of years of useful life required for this investment to break even.

PE 22-16 **Ranking by the Internal Rate of Return Method**

LO6 The company is considering eight capital investment projects. The company has a minimum required internal rate of return of 13%. Screen and rank the eight capital investment projects using the internal rate of return.

Project		Expected Rate of Return
S	....	14%
T	....	24
U	....	20
V	....	10
W	....	17
X	....	9
Y	....	12
Z	....	18

PE 22-17   **Profitability Index**

LO6   The company is considering a project with a present value of net cash inflows of $1,340,000 and an initial investment cost of $973,000. What is the profitability index of this investment?

PE 22-18   **Ranking Using the Profitability Index**

LO6   Screen and rank the following projects using the profitability index.

	Project J	Project K	Project L	Project M
Present value of net cash inflows	$1,000,000	$500,000	$1,250,000	$250,000
Investment cost	950,000	430,000	1,280,000	205,000

PE 22-19   **Income Tax Considerations in Capital Budgeting Decisions**

LO7   The company has decided to invest in some equipment that costs $50,000 today and will generate cash inflows of $20,000 per year for the 5-year life of the equipment. At the end of the five years, the equipment will have no salvage value. The company will depreciate the equipment using straight-line depreciation. The company's tax rate is 30%, and its discount rate is 10%. Compute the net present value of this investment.

PE 22-20   **Income Tax Considerations in Capital Budgeting**

LO7   The company has decided to invest in new factory machinery that will decrease labor costs by $50,000 per year. The new machinery will cost the company $200,000 and has an expected salvage value of $20,000 after nine years. The corporate tax rate is 35%, and the company's discount rate is 12%. Compute the NPV of this investment. Should the company go ahead with the investment?

EXERCISES

Note: Unless otherwise indicated, the exercises and problems assume that all payments are made or received at the end of the year.

E 22-21   **Present Values**

LO1   Consider each part independently.
  1. Super-Fix Company would like to move its auto repair shop to a downtown location in order to attract more customers. What is the maximum Super-Fix should pay to purchase a building at the new location, assuming that the company needs to earn 12%? The new building will last 40 years. Super-Fix estimates that moving to the new location will result in a $10,000 increase in annual income.
  2. If Audrey Ostler buys a new small automobile that costs $14,000 and provides annual gasoline savings of $1,200, how long must she own the car before the savings justify its cost? Assume an 8% cost of capital.

E 22-22   **Time Value of Money**

LO1   Your late, rich uncle left you $250,000. The executor of the estate has asked if you would rather receive the full amount now or $30,000 a year for the next 40 years.
Which of these options would you take, assuming that your desired rate of return is:
  1. 10%?
  2. 12%?

E 22-23   **Payback Method**

LO2   The manager of Simple Company must choose between two investments. Project A costs $75,000 and promises cash savings of $15,000 a year over a useful life of 10 years. Project B costs $60,000, and the estimated cash savings are $13,000 per year over a useful life of 11 years. Using the payback method, determine which project the manager should choose.

E 22-24 **Unadjusted Rate of Return Method**

LO2 Um Good, Inc., a candy maker, is thinking of purchasing a new machine. A marketing firm has estimated that the new machine could increase revenues by $30,000 a year for the next five years. The expenses (including depreciation) directly relating to the machine total $100,000 ($20,000 × 5 years). The initial purchase cost would be $80,000. What is the unadjusted rate of return?

E 22-25 **Net Present Value Method**

LO3 The Carroll Broom Company is thinking of purchasing a new automatic straw-binding machine. The company president, Joan Carroll, has determined that such a machine would save the company $10,000 per year in labor costs. The machine would cost $46,500 and would have a useful life of 10 years and a scrap value of $500. The machine would require servicing after five years at a cost of $1,000. Carroll uses a discount rate of 16%. Compute the net present value. From a quantitative standpoint, should the machine be purchased?

E 22-26 **Least-Cost Decision**

LO3 The local fire department has determined the Sleep-Eazy Mattress Company is not in full compliance with local fire regulations. To comply, Sleep-Eazy has two alternatives: It may install an automatic sprinkler system, or it may hire a fire safety expert to make weekly fire safety checks. The automatic sprinkler system will cost $125,000, including installation charges, and will last for 10 years. It will have no salvage value. The entire system is virtually maintenance-free. The fire safety expert's fee is $18,000 per year. The cost of capital is 10%. Which alternative should Sleep-Eazy Mattress Company choose? Why?

E 22-27 **Internal Rate of Return**

LO3 Juan Gonzales, the president of Nogalis Corporation, is trying to decide whether he should buy a new machine that will improve production efficiency. The machine will increase cash inflows $5,000 a year for five years. It will cost $18,000, and there will be no salvage value. What is the internal rate of return?

E 22-28 **Cost of Capital**

LO1 Daphney Corporation has raised $200,000 in equity financing through the issuance of shares. Stockholders expect to earn an average of 20% per year on their equity investment in Daphney. In addition, the corporation has issued $100,000 of 10% bonds. The corporation has also accumulated $25,000 in earnings that have been retained in the company. Investors expect to earn about 16% on the earnings that are retained in the company. Using the weighting procedure discussed in the chapter, calculate Daphney Corporation's cost of capital. (Ignore taxes in calculating the cost of debt.)

E 22-29 **Net Present Value and Internal Rate of Return**

LO3 A real estate investment requires an initial outlay of $200,000 in cash. The investment will return a single sum cash payment of $438,490 after five years. The rate of return required on projects as risky as this one is 18%.

1. What is the net present value of this real estate investment?
2. What is the internal rate of return of this real estate investment?
3. Is this an attractive investment?

E 22-30 **Net Present Value and Internal Rate of Return**

LO3 A retired person has $700,000 in a retirement account. An insurance company is offering to give the retired person an annuity of $61,029 at the end of each year for the next 20 years in exchange for the $700,000. The retired person requires a rate of return of 8% on investments; this is the rate currently being earned in the retirement account.

1. What is the net present value of this exchange?
2. What is the internal rate of return implied in this exchange?
3. Should the retired person accept the exchange offered by the insurance company?

E 22-31   **Quality and Time Factors**

LO4   Tucker Yard Service Company is contemplating purchasing a new riding lawnmower for its business. One particular model has special features that enhance the cutting and the collecting of the mowed grass, but that mower is quite expensive. Another model is more basic and costs $1,000 less. The payback period on the more expensive model is estimated to be 3.5 years and on the less expensive model 2.5 years. The "bumper-to-bumper" warranties are two years and one year, respectively. From these limited data, what factors should Tucker consider in making this decision?

E 22-32   **Qualitative Considerations**

LO4   The Upscale Department Store has been plagued with shoplifting. The president, Hector Conrad, has suggested that the store hire a security force to "frisk" all customers as they leave the store. It is estimated that annual shoplifting losses are $100,000. Expenses associated with the security force are estimated to be $50,000 annually. Before Mr. Conrad makes his final decision, what other factors might he consider?

E 22-33   **Sensitivity Analysis**

LO5   You have accumulated $35,000 in a mutual fund account that pays 10% interest. You are offered the opportunity to buy 100 ounces of gold at $350 per ounce. The price of gold is expected to rise to $700 per ounce by the end of five years. You realize, however, that this is only an estimate.

   To what price would gold have to rise in order to earn a 10% return? (Note that the future value factor for $35,000 at 10% at the end of five years is 1.6105.)

E 22-34   **Screening Function**

LO6   Your company's cost of capital was determined to be 12%. Several investment alternatives are being considered, and the discounted cash flows have given the following results:

Net present value:
1. A new machine was analyzed, and a net present value of zero resulted.
2. A new product line was analyzed, and a negative net present value of $60 resulted.
3. An investment was being considered. The analysis yielded a net present value of $250.

Internal rate of return:
1. A plant expansion project promised a yield of 12%.
2. An investment in additional transport trucks would yield an internal rate of return of 10%.
3. The addition of another assembly line would add cash flows that would give an internal rate of return of 16%.

Determine which projects should be accepted as investment opportunities and which should be rejected.

E 22-35   **Ranking Projects**

LO6   Using net present value (NPV) analysis, a manager can select those projects that will maximize the present value of future cash flows. NPV analysis is a powerful tool; however, surveys of current practice indicate that the internal rate of return (IRR) method enjoys considerable popularity among decision makers. What would account for IRR's appeal? What are the drawbacks to using only the IRR method to rank projects?

E 22-36   **Profitability Index**

LO6   California Company is trying to determine the relative profitability of two alternative color, laser printers. Printer A requires an initial cash outlay of $4,000 and has a net present value

(continued)

of $250. Printer B requires an initial cash outlay of $3,000 and has a net present value of $175. Compute the profitability index of each printer. Which alternative is more profitable?

E 22-37 Income Tax Effects

LO7 Kade Corporation is considering purchasing a new piece of equipment. The equipment will cost $135,000 and is expected to have a useful life of five years. The gross cash flow savings is estimated to be $50,000 per year. The company will depreciate the cost of the asset for tax purposes using a 5-year useful life, zero salvage value, and the straight-line method. The company is in the 40% tax bracket (including federal, state, and local taxes).

1. Compute the after-tax cash flow savings on the asset.
2. Compute the after-tax internal rate of return that will equate the present value of the savings with the net outlay cost.

PROBLEMS

P 22-38 Net Present Value Method

LO3 A fast-food establishment is thinking of buying a new cooking grill and refrigeration unit. The costs of these new machines are $12,500 and $9,000, respectively. The installation costs of the new equipment will run about $800. It is estimated that 10% more customers can be served with the new equipment, which would mean an additional annual net cash flow of approximately $4,500. The salvage value of the old grill and refrigeration unit is estimated to be $1,000.

The firm's cost of capital is 12%. The equipment should last 10 years, at a minimum.

Required:
Using the net present value method, should the company purchase the new equipment? (Ignore income tax effects.)

P 22-39 Net Present Value Method–Uneven Cash Flows

LO3 Southside Junk Yard needs to buy a car smasher. The machine would add the following revenues to the business over the next three years:

Year 1 Cash savings = $30,000
Year 2 Cash savings plus additional scrap sales = $40,000
Year 3 Cash savings plus additional scrap sales = $55,000

The initial cost of the machine is $100,000. At the end of three years, its salvage value is estimated at $20,000. The firm has a cost of capital of 12%.

Required:
Using the net present value method, determine whether the company should purchase the machine. (Ignore income tax effects.)

P 22-40 Internal Rate of Return

LO3 You have been offered the opportunity to purchase a franchise of Sunshine Juice Stores. You will have to pay $258,635 for the initial investment in the store and its equipment, plus $30,000 per year for the lease payments and the franchise fee. The franchise contract obligates you for 10 years. Operating costs for each year will be $225,000, and the expected revenue is $298,000 a year. Your hurdle rate is 10%. Ignore income taxes.

Required:
1. Does this investment yield a satisfactory rate of return?
2. What qualitative factors might be considered?

P 22-41   **Internal Rate of Return and Hurdle Rate**

LO3   Nina Roberts has the opportunity to invest in a timber forest. She would have to invest $100,000. Revenues of $20,000 per year are projected for 20 years. However, these revenues will not begin coming in for five years because the timber must be seasoned before cutting and selling can begin. Ms. Roberts's hurdle rate is 10%. Ignore income taxes.

Required:

1. Calculate the internal rate of return, and determine whether or not Ms. Roberts should make the investment.
2. If Ms. Roberts has to borrow the $100,000 necessary for the investment from her bank at 12% interest, should she make the investment?
3. **Interpretive Question**: Why is it important for Ms. Roberts to determine her cost of capital before making this investment decision?

P 22-42   **Payback, Net Present Value, and Internal Rate of Return Methods**

LO2, LO3   Nucore Company is thinking of purchasing a new candy-wrapping machine at a cost of $370,000. The machine should save the company approximately $70,000 in operating costs per year over its estimated useful life of 10 years. The salvage value at the end of 10 years is expected to be $15,000. (Ignore income tax effects.)

Required:

1. What is the machine's payback period?
2. Compute the net present value of the machine if the cost of capital is 12%.
3. What is the expected internal rate of return for this machine?

P 22-43   **Internal Rate of Return**

LO3   The manager of Soft & Creamy Ice Cream is thinking of buying a new soft ice cream machine. The machine will cost $13,500 and will last 10 years. Soft ice cream sales are expected to generate $3,000 in income per year.

Required:

What is the internal rate of return on this project?

P 22-44   **Choosing among Alternatives**

LO3   Tom Thurlow wants to buy a boat but is short of cash. Two alternatives are available: Tom can accept $7,500 per year from his brother for partial ownership in the boat, or he can earn money by renting the boat to others. Rental income would be $10,000 per year. Under either alternative, the boat will last eight years. If Tom rents the boat out, he will have to pay $15,000 to overhaul the engine at the end of the fourth year.

Required:

Which alternative should Tom select, assuming that the cost of capital is 12% and that only quantitative considerations are involved?

P 22-45   **Lease-or-Buy Decision**

LO3   A small sales company is committed to supplying three sales representatives with new cars. The company has two alternatives. It can either buy the three cars and sell them after two years, or it can lease the cars for two years. The company uses a 16% discount rate. The information for each alternative is as follows:

Alternative 1: Buy

Cost	$36,000
Annual service costs	3,000
Anticipated repairs during the 1st year	700
Anticipated repairs during the 2nd year	1,500
Salvage value at the end of 2 years	10,000

Alternative 2: Lease
To lease the cars, the company would simply pay $20,000 a year for the two years.

(continued)

Required:

Assuming the lease is paid at the end of each year, determine the better alternative.

P 22-46   **Rent-or-Purchase Decision**

LO3

As one aspect of its business, New Lawn Company currently rents a ditch-digging machine for an average of $48 per job. A used machine is available for $995 but would cost $498 to repair. The machine, if purchased, would cost $800 a year to maintain and in two years would need a new chain costing $394. The used digger has a useful life of four years with no salvage value.

Required:

If the company averages 30 jobs a year and has a cost of capital of 10%, which alternative is more profitable?

P 22-47   **Sell-or-Rent Decision**

LO3

Clarence Gleason has inherited an apartment complex. He is now faced with the decision of whether to sell or to rent the property. A real estate adviser believes that Clarence should rent the property, because he could receive $65,000 per year for 10 years and then could sell the property for $500,000. A development company has offered Clarence $200,000 down and promises to pay $50,000 per year for the next 15 years. The land has a remaining mortgage of $130,000. If Clarence sells the complex, he will have to pay that sum now. If he rents the property, he will have to pay the mortgage of $130,000 over 10 annual payments. The mortgage rate is 12%. The cost of capital is 16%.

Required:

1. Calculate the net present value of each alternative.
2. **Interpretive Question:** Discuss the qualitative factors that might affect the decision to sell or rent.

P 22-48   **Unifying Concepts: Net Present Value and Internal Rate of Return Methods**

LO3

Julie Kowalis, an investment analyst, wants to know if her investments during the past four years have earned at least a 12% return. Four years ago, she had the following investments:

a. She purchased a small building for $50,000 and rented space in it. She received rental income of $8,000 for each of the four years and then sold the building this year for $55,000.

b. She purchased a small refreshment stand near the city park for $25,000. Annual income from the stand was $5,000 for each of the four years. She sold the stand for $20,000 this year.

c. She purchased an antique car for $5,000 four years ago. She sold it this year to a collector for $7,000.

Required:

1. Using the net present value method, determine whether or not each investment earned at least 12%.
2. Did the investments as a whole earn at least 12%? Explain.

P 22-49   **Sensitivity Analysis**

LO3, LO6

Falcon Manufacturing is a leading manufacturer of airframe components for small aircraft. Heidi Saxton, Falcon's operations manager, has submitted a request for a new piece of production equipment. Using the new machine, the company will be able to reduce expenses for both maintenance and labor. Data on the project are as follows:

(continued)

Initial investment	$80,000
Useful life	10 years
Salvage value of old machine	$1,500
Annual cash savings	$15,000
Salvage value of new machine	$10,000
Maintenance overhaul (Year 5)	$7,600
Cost of capital	12%

Assume all cash flows occur at the end of each year. (Ignore income tax effects.)

Required:

1. Using the above data, calculate the net present value of the investment. From a strictly quantitative standpoint, should the machine be purchased?
2. Suppose that Heidi receives another analysis that increases the cost of capital estimate to 14% and the new machine's salvage value to $17,000. Would the purchase still make sense?
3. Falcon's CEO, Kevin Davis, is responsible for approving all capital investment projects. Having spent his entire career dealing with one estimate after another, Kevin has asked you to consider two specific changes:
   a. Reduce annual cash inflows by 10%.
   b. Cut in half the estimated salvage value of new equipment.
   Using the original problem data, calculate the net present value using the CEO's two changes.

P 22-50

LO3, LO6

Net Present Value Used to Rank Alternatives

Taglioni's Pizza Company has to choose a new delivery car from among three alternatives. Assume that gasoline costs $3.00 per gallon and that the firm's cost of capital is 12%. The car will be driven 12,000 miles per year.

	Car 1	Car 2	Car 3
Cost	$26,000	$20,000	$23,000
Mileage per gallon	40	12	24
Useful life	5 years	5 years	5 years
Salvage value	$2,000	$500	$1,000

Required:

1. Which car should the company purchase?
2. How would your answer change if the price of gasoline decreased to $2 per gallon?

P 22-51

LO6

Screening and Ranking Alternatives

Sunshine Corporation is considering several long-term investments. Management wants to accept the two best projects, given the following data:

	Project				
	A	B	C	D	E
Present value of					
net cash inflows	$24,000	$44,000	$15,000	$30,000	$50,000
Investment cost	20,000	40,000	16,000	24,000	41,000

Required:

1. Determine the net present value and the profitability index for each project.
2. Which projects are acceptable using the profitability index as a screening tool?
3. What would be the ranking of the acceptable projects according to the profitability indexes?
4. **Interpretive Question:** What additional information would be needed to screen and rank the projects using the internal rate of return method? What are the decision rules using the IRR method for screening and ranking capital budgeting projects?

P 22-52

LO3, LO6

Unifying Concepts: Comparing the Internal Rate of Return and the Net Present Value Methods

Get Rich Corporation has to choose between two investment opportunities. Investment A requires an immediate cash outlay of $100,000 and provides after-tax income of $20,000 per year for 10 years. Investment B requires an immediate cash outlay of $1,000 and generates after-tax income of $350 per year for five years.

Required:

1. Using a cost of capital of 12%, calculate the net present value of each investment, and determine which one Get Rich should select.
2. Calculate the internal rate of return of each investment. On the basis of this method, which investment should Get Rich select?
3. **Interpretive Question:** How do you account for the difference in rankings? Under the circumstances, which method would you rely on for your decision?

P 22-53

LO2, LO3, LO4

Unifying Concepts: Payback and Internal Rate of Return

The management of Kitchen Shop is thinking of buying a new drill press to aid in adapting parts for different machines. The press is expected to save Kitchen Shop $8,000 per year in costs. However, Kitchen Shop has an old punch machine that isn't worth anything on the market and that will probably last indefinitely. The new press will last 12 years and will cost $41,595. (Ignore income tax effects.)

Required:

1. Compute the payback period of the new machine.
2. Compute the internal rate of return.
3. **Interpretive Question:** What uncertainties are involved in this decision? Discuss how they might be dealt with.

P 22-54

LO2, LO3, LO6

Unifying Concepts: Capital Rationing Using the Payback and Net Present Value Methods

Dino Corporation is trying to decide which of five investment opportunities it should undertake. The company's cost of capital is 16%. Owing to a cash shortage, the company has a policy that it will not undertake any investment unless it has a payback period of less than three years. The company is unwilling to undertake more than two investment projects. The following data apply to the alternatives:

Investment	Initial Cost	Expected Returns
A	$100,000	$30,000 per year for 5 years
B	50,000	25,000 per year for 6 years
C	30,000	8,000 per year for 10 years
D	20,000	7,000 per year for 6 years
E	10,000	3,500 per year for 3 years

Required:

1. Using the payback method, screen out any investment project that fails to meet the company's payback period requirement.
2. Using the net present value method, determine which of the remaining projects the company should undertake, keeping in mind the capital rationing constraint.
3. **Interpretive Question:** What advantages do you see in using the payback method together with other capital budgeting methods?

P 22-55

LO3, LO7

Income Tax Effects

Sylvania Manufacturing Company is considering the purchase of new equipment to perform operations currently being performed on less efficient equipment. The purchase price is $142,000 delivered and installed. A company engineer estimates that the new equipment

(continued)

will save $29,000 in labor and other direct costs annually. The new equipment will have an estimated life of 10 years and zero salvage value at the end of the 10 years. The equipment will be depreciated using a straight-line basis. The existing equipment has a book value of $4,000, a remaining economic life of five years, and can be disposed of now for $4,000. The company's average tax rate is 40% (including federal, state, and local taxes), and its after-tax cost of capital is 12%.

Required:
1. Should the new equipment be purchased?
2. What would the decision be if the cost of capital were 10%?
3. **Interpretive Question:** Assuming that the net present value of an investment in new equipment is so small that you are indifferent about whether to make the purchase or keep the old equipment, what other factors would you consider in making the decision?

ANALYTICAL ASSIGNMENTS

AA 22-56

DISCUSSION

Should We Purchase That New Copier?

Campus Print Shop is thinking of purchasing a new, modern copier that automatically collates pages. The machine would cost $22,000 cash. A service contract on the machine, considered a must because of its complexity, would be an additional $200 per month. The machine is expected to last eight years and have a resale value of $4,000. By purchasing the new machine, Campus would save $450 per month in labor costs and $100 per month in materials costs due to increased efficiency. Other operating costs are expected to remain the same. The old copier would be sold for its scrap value of $1,000. Campus requires a return of 14% on its capital investments.
1. As a consultant to Campus, compute:
   a. The payback period.
   b. The unadjusted rate of return.
   c. The net present value.
   d. The internal rate of return.
2. On the basis of these computations and any qualitative considerations, would you recommend that Campus purchase the new copier?

AA 22-57

DISCUSSION

Cost and Qualitative Factors in Capital Investment Decisions

Yoshika Landscaping is contemplating purchasing a new ditch-digging machine that promises savings of $5,600 per year for 10 years. The machine costs $21,970, and no salvage value is expected. The company's cost of capital is 12%. You have been asked to advise Yoshika relative to this capital investment decision. As part of your analysis, compute:
1. The payback period.
2. The unadjusted rate of return.
3. The net present value.
4. The internal rate of return.
What factors besides your quantitative analysis should be considered in making this decision?

AA 22-58

JUDGMENT CALL

You Decide: **Which measurement is more important when making a capital budgeting decision, net present value or improved customer satisfaction?**

Your company is considering purchasing a server to host the company Web site, which customers use to place their orders. When deciding on this new capital investment, you realize that the net present value of the purchase is negative, meaning the future cash flows associated with the server will not replace the initial investment. However, an important qualitative factor that should be considered with the purchase of a new server is the improved customer service and satisfaction that will be achieved as a result of the purchase. What should you do?

AA 22-59
JUDGMENT CALL

You Decide: **Should a project be accepted or rejected if the project has an internal rate of return that is less than the company's hurdle rate?**

You are the CFO for an automobile manufacturer. The board of directors is considering expanding the current product line to include sports utility vehicles. As you look at the new product line's internal rate of return, it is 12% and the company's overall discount rate is 15%. Should the new line be added to the company's existing lines? The board wants your input before they make a decision. What factors should you consider?

AA 22-60
REAL COMPANY
ANALYSIS

Microsoft

The section of **Microsoft**'s Form 10-K relating to management's discussion and analysis provides detail as to factors that might affect Microsoft's future and, as a result, the company's long-term decisions. Review the financial statements and the "Management Discussion and Analysis" section in Microsoft's most recent 10-K, and answer the following questions:

1. Microsoft has no long-term debt. Does that mean its cost of capital is zero? Explain.
2. Microsoft specifically states that the company "does not provide forecasts of future financial performance." If that is the case, how can it make any capital budgeting decisions?

AA 22-61
REAL COMPANY
ANALYSIS

The Boeing Company

As you probably know, **Boeing** builds airplanes. While most famous for the big 747, Boeing is continually developing newer models. Over the past several years, Boeing has been developing the 737 and 777 families of airplanes. In 1996, Boeing formed a joint venture with **General Electric** to develop planes that can fly over 6,000 miles without refueling.

1. What factors must Boeing consider when making the decision to produce a new family of airplanes like the 777? What would be the expected cash inflows, and what would be the expected cash outflows? Categorize the outflows into two types: one-time outflows and annual outflows.
2. The costs of developing a new family of airplanes are enormous. Why would Boeing agree to incur these costs when it is able to continue producing older model planes like the 747 and the 767? Frame this discussion in terms of a capital budgeting decision. That is, evaluate the opportunities in terms of cash inflows and cash outflows.

AA 22-62
INTERNATIONAL

DaimlerChrysler

DaimlerChrysler discloses the following information relating to its long-term debt in its 2002 annual report:

- 6.3% notes/bonds
- 2.6% commercial paper
- 5.3% liabilities to financial institutions

Ford Motor Company also provides information relating to its debt in the notes to its annual report. That information is given below.

- Secured indebtedness, 7.6%
- Unsecured senior indebtedness—notes and bank debt, 4.8%
- Unsecured subordinated indebtedness—notes, 9.4%

1. Assume that each company's debt is distributed equally across the various categories. Compute an average cost interest rate for each company.
2. If your answer from part (1) represented each firm's cost of capital, what would it tell you about the kinds of projects that DaimlerChrysler can undertake as compared to Ford?

AA 22-63
ETHICS

Wheeler, Nevada

The city council of Wheeler, Nevada, is faced with an important decision: whether or not to rezone a parcel of property and allow ChemStor, Inc., to purchase the land and build a chemical waste storage facility on the property. Several factors enter into the decision.

(continued)

a. The property is currently zoned for agricultural use and is surrounded by ranching operations in a rural community.

b. Several ranchers have joined together and offered to buy the property from the city over a 40-year period. In return for an agreed-upon interest rate of one point below prime, they will donate 20 acres of the land for a city park.

c. ChemStor has offered to pay cash for the land. Company management also points out that the facility will create about 25 new jobs for local residents and generate close to $100,000 a year in increased property taxes for the city.

d. ChemStor, a New Jersey-based company, learned of this property from its controller, who is a brother-in-law to one of the Wheeler City council members. ChemStor has offered a "finder's fee" for locating a waste storage site. The finder's fee would be split between the controller and the brother-in-law.

Identify the ethical and other issues involved in this capital investment decision.

AA 22-64
WRITING

Lease versus Buy

You are fresh out of college, have your first real job, and just received your first big paycheck. You decide you need some wheels. Off you go to the car dealer. You carefully review the various makes and models of cars, determine the price range you can afford, and select "YOUR FIRST CAR." You thought that was the hard part. Now you need to decide on financing. The salesperson says you can either borrow money to purchase the vehicle or you can lease the car.

What factors should you consider in making this capital budgeting decision? Identify those factors that should enter into the lease versus buy decision. Prepare a short memo discussing the pros and cons of leasing versus buying and identifying the cash inflows and outflows associated with each option.

Capital Budgeting and Relevant Costs for Decision Making

Franklin Bakery is considering buying a new doughnut-making machine. The cost of the machine is $10,000. The machine will last for 10 years and is expected to be worth $1,000 as scrap at that time. It is expected that the new machine will increase doughnut sales by 15,000 doughnuts per year. Each doughnut has a selling price of 50 cents.

The annual operating costs of the doughnut machine are projected to be as follows. *Note:* These cost projections are based on the forecasted sales level of 15,000 doughnuts per year.

Raw materials	$2,250
Direct labor	1,200
Variable production overhead	1,650
Variable selling costs	900
Direct fixed costs	3,000
Indirect fixed costs*	4,000

*The indirect fixed costs represent the routine allocation of general company overhead to projects. Actually, because of the efficiency and reliability of the machine, general fixed company overhead will go down by $3,700 as a result of the purchase of the new doughnut-making machine.

For simplicity, assume that all doughnut sales occur at the end of the year and that all costs are paid for in cash at the end of the year. Franklin Bakery has determined that the appropriate cost of capital to use in evaluating this doughnut machine is 16%.

Required:

1. With the numbers given, compute the net present value of the doughnut machine.
2. Assume that the appropriate cost of capital is 10% instead of 16%. Compute the net present value of the doughnut machine.
3. Assume again that the cost of capital is 16%. Now assume that the doughnut machine will increase production by 10,000 doughnuts per year instead of 15,000 doughnuts per year. This is within the relevant range. Compute the net present value of the doughnut machine.
4. Assume a cost of capital of 16% and an increase in production of 15,000 doughnuts per year. Now assume that the machine will cost $12,000 instead of $10,000 but that the machine will last 12 years instead of 10 years. The scrap value at the end of 12 years is still $1,000. Compute the net present value of the doughnut machine.

New Measures of
Performance 23

New Measures of Performance

After studying this chapter, you should be able to:

(1) Understand the concept of measuring Economic Value Added. *Economic Value Added (EVA®) measures the incremental income produced in excess of the economic cost of debt and equity invested in the company.*

(2) Describe the relationship between just-in-time (JIT) management systems and total quality management (TQM). *By reducing or removing inventory, organizations are disciplined to focus on significant improvements in quality and timeliness of processes. Management accounting can support this effort by tracking costs of quality in the organization.*

(3) Explain the fundamentals of building a Balanced Scorecard. *The Balanced Scorecard is a management model that organizes performance measures around four key objectives: financial, customer, internal process, and learning and growth performance.*

(4) Anticipate that both management accounting and financial accounting will continue to change and evolve. *Competition demands constant improvement, and the accounting discipline cannot avoid this reality. Hence, accounting continues to improve and expand the content, focus, and usefulness of the information provided to decision makers.*

Warren Buffett, nicknamed the "Oracle of Omaha," is perhaps America's most famous stock investor, businessman, and philanthropist. He has amassed an enormous fortune for himself and others from astute investments, particularly through his company **Berkshire Hathaway**. Buffett has run his investment company for over 40 years based on several core business principles. In an annual report to the shareholders, he stated one core principle as follows: "We feel noble intentions should be checked periodically against results. We test the wisdom of retaining earnings by assessing whether retention, over time, delivers shareholders at least $1 of market value for each $1 retained."[1] More simply put, Buffett believes strongly that the earnings and investments retained in Berkshire Hathaway belong to its shareholders, and that every dollar that he invests must deliver more value than what could be earned by the shareholder. Otherwise, he should return the dollar to its rightful owner. This is a very important principle of business— that a dollar invested must return some minimum earnings in order to deserve to stay invested.

Buffet's concept of establishing a benchmark of return on an investment was later captured in a new performance measure by **Stern Stewart & Co.**, a global consulting firm. In 1993 this measure was introduced broadly to the world in an important *Fortune Magazine* article[2] as Economic Value Added or EVA®. Over 300 companies now use EVA®; among the most

well-known: investment banks **Goldman Sachs** and **Credit Suisse**, **Best Buy**, **Coca-Cola**, **Dun & Bradstreet**, **Sprint**, **JC Penney**, **Quaker Oats**, **Toys "R" Us**, the **United States Postal Service**, and the health care company **Eli Lilly**. Many of these companies disclose their application of EVA® within their annual reports— allowing investors and creditors to evaluate the company based on its EVA® goals and criteria. This financial measure is seen as a highly useful calculation to measure the success of management to create financial value for the shareholders.

You remember that we introduced management accounting in Chapter 15 with DuPont's innovative performance measure in the early 1900s called ROI (return on investment). Management accounting will always be in a state of evolution. EVA® represents a number of emerging innovations in effective performance measurement. EVA® is not a perfect performance measure. It has its critics. Nevertheless, its development demonstrates a trend of continuous improvement in today's management accounting profession. In contrast to financial accounting, which is established by regulatory agencies to provide a common reporting platform, the evolution of management accounting represents a natural "survival of the fittest" as individuals and organizations work hard to identify new and unique measures that help professionals better plan, control, and evaluate unique organizations.

Yﾟou are now in the last chapter of this textbook. You've spent a lot of time studying many details concerning the process of creating and using accounting to add value to an organization. We've established that the management process involves planning, controlling, and evaluating business activities in order to compete well. We've also discussed managing these processes across three different types of firms: manufacturing, merchandising, and service. We understand that the accountant must customize a great variety of information sources to fit the specific strategic and operating needs of decision makers. The effort to "manage" this management accounting

process may cause you to feel a bit overwhelmed. Of all the information that is possible (and we've presented in this text only a subset of a growing list of possibilities), what information is best for a particular company? How do accountants and managers identify specific performance measures critical to surviving and thriving in the fast-paced, highly competitive, worldwide economy of the twenty-first century? More importantly, how does management accounting continue to improve performance measures in pace with innovations in products and processes and changes in markets and competition? There will always be a lot of discussion among managers and management accountants

---

[1] Warren Buffett, "To the Shareholders of Berkshire Hathaway Inc.," Berkshire Hathaway Annual Report, 1983.
[2] Shawn Tully, "The Real Key to Creating Wealth," *Fortune* (September 20, 1993), pp. 30–50.

on this very question. One approach to answering this question is the search for a single critical measure that captures all of the effects, both positive and negative, that go into managing a company. Many accountants and managers believe that the Economic Value Added measure effectively serves as a single *output* measure of performance. On the other hand, other professionals choose to focus on *input* performance measures using just-in-time (JIT) inventory systems and total quality management (TQM) measures. In midst of this debate, an alternative approach to performance measurement is gaining attention in many companies. The approach, called the "Balanced Scorecard," represents a set of critical input *and* output performance measures and no education on management accounting is really complete without some awareness of this approach.[3] Management accounting is in a constant state of evolution. In this final chapter, we explore some of the newer measures of performance arising in management accounting. We then conclude this textbook with a brief look at the future of accounting.

Adding Value to Investors' Money

Understand the concept of measuring Economic Value Added®.

① 1 Do you remember the **residual income** concept that we studied in Chapter 19? The formula is:

Operating profit − (Minimum required rate of return × Average total assets) = Residual income

This concept was first recognized by economists in the 1770s and is based on the premise that, in order for a firm to create wealth for its owners, it must earn more on its total invested capital than the cost of that capital.[4] To put it another way, part of the calculation of net income using financial accounting methods includes only the explicit costs of interest expense on debt. However, the residual income concept in management accounting includes all of the implicit costs of both debt and equity financing used by the organization.

residual income

The amount of operating income earned above a specified minimum rate of return on assets; used to evaluate investment centers.

Economic Value Added (EVA®)

A commercialized performance measurement system that emphasizes the incremental income an organization creates over and above the income required to cover the costs of capital invested by both debt and equity holders in the organization.

Economic Value Added (EVA®), as developed by **Stern Stewart & Co.**, is quite similar in many respects to the measurement for residual income. The formula is:

Net operating profit after tax − (Cost of capital × Invested capital) = EVA®

You can see obvious similarities as you compare the residual income formula with the formula for EVA®. However, it's important to understand the differences.

First, residual income is focused on operating profit before tax, while EVA® starts with net operating profit after tax (sometimes called NOPAT). The major difference is that EVA® includes the effect of taxes when calculating profit.

Second, residual income uses a minimum required rate of return (sometimes referred to as a hurdle rate) to measure the minimum level of income that should result from using the organization's assets. This hurdle rate is typically set by the executive managers and may be based on the cost of acquiring assets (or capital) for the organization. On the other hand, EVA® is absolutely focused on using the organization's specific cost of capital to establish the required return on funds invested in the organization. Sometimes called the **weighted average cost of capital** (or WACC), the cost of capital as used in EVA® is essentially the average return expected by both equity owners (or shareholders) and debt holders (see page 1180 for definition). In other words, WACC represents the investors' opportunity cost of taking

---

[3] The Balanced Scorecard Model was first presented in a series of articles in the *Harvard Business Review* by Robert S. Kaplan and David P. Norton: "The Balanced Scorecard-Measures That Drive Performance" (January-February 1992); "Putting the Balanced Scorecard to Work" (September-October 1993); "Using the Balanced Scorecard as a Strategic Management System" (January-February 1996). The most complete discussion on this theory is found in Kaplan and Norton's *The Balanced Scorecard: Translating Strategy into Action* (Boston, MA: Harvard Business School Press, 1996) and *The Strategy-Focused Organization: How Balanced Scorecard Companies Thrive in the New Business Environment* (Boston, MA: Harvard Business School Press, 2001).

[4] Gary Biddle, Robert Bowen, and James Wallace, "Evidence on EVA?®," *Journal of Applied Corporate Finance* (Summer 1999), pp. 69-79.

weighted average cost of capital (WACC)

The average cost of a firm's debt and equity capital, weighted by the relative amounts of each source of financing; equals the average rate of return that a company must earn on its invested capital in order to satisfy the demands of its owners and creditors.

on the risk of putting money into a company. In this textbook, we won't worry about the details of computing WACC as it can be a complicated measure that is best saved for an intermediate course in finance.

Finally, residual income combines the hurdle rate with average total assets to determine the minimum income required. Conversely, EVA® uses invested capital, which focuses on interest-bearing debt and all the equity invested in the organization. The critical difference is that EVA® excludes non-interest-bearing operating liabilities, such as accounts payable and wages payable, from the equation.[5] The reason for not including operating liabilities is because these obligations do not generate any explicit interest expense for the organization. These operating liabilities represent, effectively, a "free" source of assets for the organization to use to generate operating profits.

Applying the EVA® Concept

To help you better understand the EVA® concept and how its calculation differs from the residual income computation, let's explore together an example of a Triple-A baseball franchise that we'll call the Elkhart Eagles. Owning a Triple-A baseball team is a challenging business proposition. Not only is the franchise itself expensive, but successfully bringing a team to a new city typically involves building a new stadium or expanding an old one. Total costs can run more than $100 million, and a lot of debt financing must be raised in addition to the equity invested by the owners. In the case of our Elkhart Eagles, let's assume the investor group that owns the Elkhart Eagles franchise typically expects a 15% return on their investments. This rate of return effectively establishes for them a hurdle rate that is used to justify investment decisions. The total book value of the Eagles franchise assets is $120 million. A municipal bond was issued in the amount of $95 million to purchase the franchise and build the new Eagles stadium. In addition, the owners originally invested $13 million of their own money and have retained $4 million of past earnings in the franchise. Remember that Assets = Liabilities + Owners' Equity. Hence, the remainder of the team assets is funded through short-term operating liabilities ($120 million − $95 million − $13 million − $4 million = $8 million). The $8 million in short-term operating liabilities includes salaries and taxes payable, as well as other accounts payable to vendors, suppliers, etc. The average income tax rate for the franchise is 40% (this includes federal, state, and local taxes).

The operating profit on the Eagles franchise generally runs about $20 million per year (before tax). However, the Eagles hosted the All-Star game in 2007 which increased fan enthusiasm, driving up ticket sales throughout the season. At the end of that year, operating profit before tax was $22.5 million. The **return on investment (ROI)** for the year was nearly 19% ($22.5 million ÷ $120.0 million = 18.75%). The residual income for the year was $4.5 million computed as follows:

return on investment (ROI)

A measure of operating performance and efficiency in utilizing assets; computed in its simplest form by dividing operating profit by average total assets.

Operating profit − (Minimum required rate of return × Average total assets) = Residual income
$22.5 million − (15% × $120 million) = $4.5 million

However, the owners want to better understand the actual economic value being created by the franchise based on the actual cost of the debt and equity financing of the franchise. Hence, a finance consultant was employed who established the weighted average cost of capital for the Eagles franchise to be 12.5%. Because this rate is computed using the after-tax cost of debt, the owners felt that

---

[5] Therefore, invested capital assets in the EVA® equation can be computed as either:

Interest-bearing debt + Total equity

or can be computed as:

Total assets − Non-interest-bearing operating liabilities.

the EVA® calculation should appropriately be based on the net operating profit after tax (NOPAT). The EVA® performance measure was computed as follows:

Net operating profit after tax − (Cost of capital × Invested capital) = EVA®
[$22.5 million − ($22.5 million × 40%)] − [12.5% × ($120 million − $8 million)[6]] = EVA®
$13.5 million − $14 million = −$500,000

The owners learned that despite the improved operating profits in 2008, the franchise had actually used up $500,000 in economic value as a result of being unable to pay for the costs of capital invested by both debt and equity holders in the organization. In fact, they quickly determined that the Eagles franchise would need to generate approximately $23.3 million annually in pretax operating profits in order to pay for the costs of capital.[7] This fact provided some important insight to the owners about why it was that their profitable baseball franchise seemed to struggle financially to make ends meet. They resolved to make changes to the business operation in order to generate more revenue and investment value in light of the true economic costs of running their team. However, despite the important insight provided by the EVA® calculation, it didn't really help them understand *how* to better run their business. They would need to turn elsewhere for that understanding. Running a baseball team is actually a very complicated business process. It was clear to the team owners that no single performance measure was likely to support a very effective management effort.

REMEMBER THIS...

- A company is expected to earn at least enough income to pay for the economic cost of the debt capital and equity capital invested in the organization. This cost is essentially an expected rate of return on all the money invested in the company and is known as the weighted average cost of capital (or WACC).

- A relatively new measure has emerged to reflect the ability of a company to earn income above and beyond its cost of capital. This measure is called Economic Value Added (or EVA®). The formula is:

    Net operating profit after tax − (WACC × Invested capital) = EVA®

- A company's invested capital is equal to its interest-bearing debt and stockholders' equity.

Managing Time and Quality

Describe the relationship between just-in-time (JIT) management systems and total quality management (TQM).

(2) At the end of the previous section, we left the Eagles franchise managers with the realization that they needed to run their business better, but without the specific insight they need in order to know *how* to run the business better. In this section, we'll introduce some recent developments in measuring and managing performance in daily operations.

Remember in the introduction to Chapter 15 that management accounting has evolved as a result of competition. When one company or industry (or, in the new global economy, country) develops a better management accounting technique or measure, it then competes more strongly in the marketplace. Eventually, the success of the innovator puts pressure on other organizations to adopt the same

---

[6] Remember that Interest-bearing debt + Equity = Assets − Non-interest-bearing operating liabilities. In other words, $95 million + $13 million + $4 million = $120 million − $8 million.

[7] $14 million cost of capital ÷ (1 − 40%) = $23.33 million.

or a similar approach to their own management accounting systems. This was exactly the situation when U.S. companies began adjusting their management teams and management accounting systems to focus on quality and timeliness. In the 1980s, American manufacturers faced an assault from Japanese companies such as **Toyota** and **NEC**. These Japanese companies had mastered quality and inventory control, as well as speedier ways to get products to market. Western CEOs studied the competition, deconstructed what made it so good, adopted the better features of their rivals, and changed their management systems. Since then, this management focus on controlling the cost, quality, and timeliness of processes and organizations has had an impact on management accounting and has spread into U.S. merchandising and service industries, as well as into industries in other countries around the world.

JIT Inventory Systems

just-in-time (JIT)

A management philosophy that emphasizes removing all waste of effort, time, and inventory costs from the organization. One explicit result of JIT is the reduction or removal of needless inventory in a production system.

The effort of management to compete on measures of time and to make improvements involving time is captured in the concept of **just-in-time** (JIT) management processes. To understand JIT, you need to first understand how JIT is used to manage inventory, including raw materials inventory, work-in-process inventory, and finished goods inventory. Let's talk for a moment about inventory. What is the purpose of inventory in a manufacturing plant? This may seem obvious. Manufacturers and other organizations stockpile inventories in order to avoid shutdowns or slowdowns and to meet customer needs if suppliers are late or if production or delivery is slow. Occasionally (sometimes more than occasionally!), suppliers deliver raw materials that contain some defects, or the production process ruins some work-in-process, or a customer returns an unacceptable product. How do we deal with these unexpected surprises? The answer has been to "have a little extra on hand" so that bad parts or products can be replaced without having to interrupt the manufacturing process. Not surprisingly, production managers can get a little nervous when inventory levels get too low.

Because of concerns about risks due to scheduling and quality problems, companies establish policies to keep inventory levels at or above some minimal level. This minimum level of inventory is usually called a "safety stock." In fact, this safety stock of inventory can be thought of as a "just-in-case" buffer used to deal with problems and uncertainty in the organization. However, a number of years ago some pioneering accountants and business owners in Japan created a new competitive view of inventory management. They (like everyone else) realized that maintaining these inventories can be very expensive because of warehousing costs, interest costs incurred to finance inventory, and the opportunity cost of money tied up in stockpiled inventory. The real insight these Japanese business professionals had was that inventories are really only buffers that mask inefficient operations or product quality problems. Eliminate these timing and quality problems, and you no longer need the inventory buffers. By concentrating on improving product quality and timely deliveries, many Japanese companies became much more efficient and profitable when inventories were kept to a minimum or even eliminated. The emerging inventory systems that allow for the elimination of inventory stockpiles, inefficiency, and waste are referred to as just-in-time inventory systems. The competitive value of these new management systems eventually caught on and came to America.

JIT began as a management tool for manufacturing. So, when first learning about JIT, it's probably best to think of it in this context. In a manufacturing setting, JIT is a process by which only enough materials to satisfy immediate production are shipped to the job site. When JIT is functioning perfectly, companies take delivery from suppliers only as raw materials are needed for production and complete all inventory started during the day. In addition, inventory is completed only as it is ordered by customers and can be shipped immediately. As the name implies, materials are delivered "just in time" for production, and goods are manufactured "just in time" to meet customers' needs. As described earlier, JIT inventory systems started in Japan and have now been adopted successfully by a number of U.S. organizations. The results of JIT implementation are often dramatic. For example, at the time that JIT management systems began taking hold in the United States, one **AT&T** shop realized 54% improvement in quality yield, a 12-fold decrease in manufacturing time, an 88% reduction in scrap and rework, and a 95% increase in on-time deliveries.[8]

Measuring Time-Based Performance

Benefits such as those experienced by AT&T occur because companies that have adopted JIT have been able to avoid buildups of parts and materials and still ensure a smooth and orderly flow of goods to customers. JIT-based environments manage the flow of goods using a "pull" process. Essentially, this means that the final assembly stage for a product sends a signal known as a **kanban** to the preceding workstation indicating what parts and materials will be needed during the next few hours. The preceding workstation then sends similar signals all the way back through the manufacturing cycle, ensuring an orderly flow of products. Thus, the demand at the final assembly stage "pulls" the inventory through the production process only as it is needed. Using this system, nothing is produced unless customers demand it. At all stages, inventories are eliminated or reduced to the lowest possible level. Obviously, then, progress toward successful implementation of JIT is inventory related. Inventory reduction is not the primary purpose of JIT, but it is a consequence of JIT efforts to eliminate waste.

kanban

A Japanese word meaning "sign" or "card." In a JIT management system, *kanban* refers to a signaling system that pulls (rather than pushes) parts forward through the production system.

It is important to understand that JIT encourages accountants to emphasize providing time-based performance measures to management. Inventory pull systems using kanban signals are a critical element of a time-focused process. Critical success factors for many JIT manufacturing, service, and merchandising firms include improving timeliness of customer delivery and increasing the product or service provider's flexibility in handling customers' needs. Exhibit 1 provides a sample of appropriate performance measures that support these factors of success, which are particularly important in today's dynamic, customer-oriented environment.

JIT and Value-Added Activities

value-added activities

Necessary activities in a production or service process that customers identify as valuable and for which they are willing to pay.

non-value-added activities

Unnecessary activities in a production or service process that customers typically do not see or care about and for which they are unwilling to pay.

Another goal of the JIT management system is to add value to the product or service and to reduce or eliminate activities that do not add value. To be specific, **value-added activities** are essentially defined as those activities for which the customer is willing to pay. On the other hand, **non-value-added activities** are those for which the customer is not willing to pay. For example, clients in a law office are not interested in paying for the time spent running the payroll, organizing the file room, or computing billable hours. These are non-value-added activities. However, these clients should be willing to pay for court time and consultation time. These are clearly value-added activities that the law firm should emphasize. Under JIT, waste is considered to be anything other than the minimum amount of equipment, materials, parts, space, and workers' time that is essential to add desired value to a product. The result is careful management of time spent on value-added activities such as machining and assembly operations (for a manufacturer) and customer service and contact activities (for a service firm). More importantly, the JIT focus on eliminating waste emphasizes removing as much as possible the time spent on non-value-added activities such as setup work, materials handling, and inspection.

---

[8] F. B. Green, F. Amenkienan, and G. Johnson, "Performance Measures and JIT," *Management Accounting*, February 1991, pp. 50–54.

EXHIBIT 1   **Time-Based Performance Measures in a JIT Firm**

Customer Delivery Success Factor (On-time delivery to customers can be affected by suppliers, product design time, and the production process and distribution time.)		Provider Flexibility Success Factor (Manufacturing, service, and merchandising flexibility includes the ability to respond quickly to changes in customer demand and product design changes.)	
Measure	**Computation Method**	**Measure**	**Computation Method**
Customer on-time delivery	Number of on-time deliveries divided by total deliveries. Goal: higher	Lead time for new product introduction	Amount of time from idea to readiness for sale. Goal: lower
Supplier on-time delivery	Number of on-time deliveries divided by total deliveries. Goal: higher	Parts and product availability	Number of times a part or product is unavailable when requested. Goal: lower
Design cycle time	Amount of time from initial idea to readied plans. Goal: lower	Number of common parts	Number of parts in a product design common to other products. Goal: higher
Number of contract changes	Number of times a contract is changed. Goal: lower	Inventory level	Average level of inventory. Goal: lower
Schedule attainment	Number of unchanged schedules divided by total schedules. Goal: higher	Capacity utilization	Percentage of process capacity used in current operations. Goal: higher
Lead time	Amount of time from customer's initial request to final product or service delivery. Goal: lower	Downtime	Amount of time a manufacturing or service process was unavailable. Goal: lower
Setup time*	Amount of time required to set up a production run. Goal: lower	Setup time*	Amount of time required to set up a production run. Goal: lower
Throughput time*	Amount of time from beginning of production or service process until process conclusion. Goal: lower	Throughput time*	Amount of time from beginning of production or service process until process conclusion. Goal: lower

*Note that some performance measures are important to both customer delivery and flexibility success factors.

Source: Adapted from J. A. Hendricks, "Performance Measures for a JIT Manufacturer," *Management Accounting*, January 1994, pp. 26–30.

Total Quality Management

total quality management (TQM)

A management philosophy focused on increasing profitability by improving the quality of products and processes and increasing customer satisfaction, while promoting the well-being and growth of employees.

Toyota Motor Company began experimenting with JIT management systems in the 1950s. At about that same time an American management scientist named W. Edward Deming came to Japan and became a leading consultant in the quality revolution that began sweeping through that country in the 1960s. Deming's focus on controlling processes, improving systems, and empowering workers combined very well with the principles of a JIT system. Soon Deming established the concept of **total quality management (TQM)** which many Japanese industries implemented with great success. In honor of his work, Japan established the national Deming Prize to annually honor companies making significant improvements in the TQM process. During the 1980s, concerns about American competitiveness spurred many U.S. companies to take a new interest in quality. Several companies invited Deming, then in his eighties, back to the United States to challenge the "old way" of thinking about costs and quality. A hundred years earlier, Andrew Carnegie essentially built an empire in the steel industry with the following motto: "Watch the costs and the profits will take care of themselves." Deming revised this phrase to "Watch the *quality* and the profits will take care of themselves." The effect he and his colleagues have had on the way organizations work and compete is profound. Deming passed away in 1993 at the age of 93.

TQM is a management philosophy focused on increasing profitability by improving the quality of products and processes and increasing customer satisfaction while promoting the well-being and growth of the employees of the organization. Most managers, if asked, would say that their company seeks to improve quality, increase customer satisfaction, and take care of its employees. Implementing TQM, however, requires more than just endorsing the importance of quality in the company. An organization that has truly implemented TQM exhibits two defining characteristics. First, quality and continuous improvement are emphasized above all else within the organization. The premise here is one of priority. A company focused on TQM manages itself with the assumption that if product quality is high, customers will be satisfied and employees will be happy, and *then* profits can be expected. This contrasts with the assumption that the company cannot focus on quality until it is performing well financially. Second, TQM in the organization is the result of continuously planning, controlling, and evaluating improvement using specific measures. It is in this second assumption that management accounting systems can be built to interface well with TQM. By tracking costs and performance related to TQM activities, accounting can be used to support this critical trend in business management.

TQM and Management Accounting

statistical process control (SPC)

A statistical technique for identifying and measuring the quality status of a process by evaluating its output to determine if serious problems exist in the process.

Perhaps you've heard the term *statistical process control.* **Statistical process control (SPC)** is a technical tool that provides users with the ability to study, control, and improve processes of all types. Using statistical probability analysis, SPC provides management with the ability to know whether the errors in a production or service process are a signal that a serious problem exists in the process. Deming refined this early engineering tool and placed it squarely in the center of his TQM theory of management. Basically, Deming recognized that variation is a regular fact of life. No matter how carefully the fry cook at your local **McDonald's** prepares a set of hamburgers, each one will be slightly different from the others. This is a natural fact of variation. Frankly, it's probably not very important to you as a consumer that every McDonald's hamburger you purchase is *exactly* like every other hamburger made that day in that store. However, if you're in the business of manufacturing or purchasing baseballs to be used in major league games throughout the summer, you're probably quite interested in consistent product quality. If you're in the business of manufacturing or purchasing surgical scalpels, computer chips, or rocket boosters for the U.S. Space Shuttle Program, then consistent product quality may be even more important.

SPC is having a large effect on management accounting in many organizations today. An accountant usually doesn't need to perform statistical analysis and probability procedures in order to participate in the TQM effort. SPC work is typically the responsibility of engineers and statisticians. Nevertheless, using SPC to support TQM in a company involves a lot of cost management issues. It costs money to create low-variation, high-quality products and services. It costs money to inspect and measure processes in order to know when problems exist. On the other hand, Deming and others have taught us that it costs a great deal of money to allow high-variation, low-quality products and services to exist in our organizations. Tracking and managing these costs is an important part of the TQM effort and is often the responsibility of accountants.

Costs of Quality (COQ)

Let's use baseball manufacturing to help understand exactly how management accounting works with SPC to measure and report quality costs. You may be interested to learn that, although China produces 80% of the world's baseballs, every single baseball pitched in **Major League Baseball** is made in a Costa Rican factory owned by **Rawlings Sporting Goods Company**. A Rawlings baseball begins life as a "pill," a small sphere of cork and rubber enclosed in a rubber shell. The pill is tightly wound with three different layers of wool yarn, and then finished with a winding of cotton/polyester yarn. This "core" is then coated with a latex adhesive. Over this gooey hard lump must be sewn an extremely tight-fitting jacket of leather using exactly 216 raised stitches. Sewing on the cover is a major effort. No one has been able to successfully create a machine that can automatically stitch the cover on a professional baseball. Hence, Rawlings employs about 1,000 baseball sewing experts. In its factory, top sewing pros can sew four to six baseballs an hour, achieving perfect string tension by feel. A wooden press rolls the seams flat, and finished balls are stored in a dehumidifying room that shrinks the covers tight and protects the balls from tropical humidity that might make them bloat illegally. Baseballs are carefully inspected at the Rawlings plant before being packed for shipping. A baseball that turns out too skinny, too hefty, or otherwise off-spec is "blemmed." It's stamped "blem" for blemish and sold as a practice ball.[9]

To be used in the major leagues, a Rawlings baseball should weigh approximately 5.12 ounces and be 9.12 inches in circumference. As we pointed out, however, regardless of how hard the Rawlings Sporting Goods Company works to make sure its sewers are consistently producing baseballs of the perfect weight and size, variation occurs.[10] For the Rawlings plant, the important thing is to distinguish simple random variations in baseball weight and size that occasionally occur in a well-controlled production environment from systematic variations that occur more often when a poorly trained sewer is working or when low-quality leather is being used. Consider the following hypothetical example. Rawlings has determined upper and lower control limits for a baseball. Specifically, baseballs must weigh between 5 and 5.25 ounces and have a circumference between 9 and 9.25 inches. Exhibit 2 shows an SPC chart of measurements of daily baseball weights at Rawlings. As you can see, some of these measurements are outside the control limits, indicating that there are potentially serious quality problems in the factory. Although getting the production process back in control will require some management effort, the problem

F Y I

A Rawlings baseball doesn't last long in a major league game (average life is about six game minutes), but it has to be as perfect as possible. When a professional pitcher throws a ball toward home plate at nearly 100 miles per hour, the slightest blemish in stitching, size, or weight can be the difference between a strike and a home run, the difference between winning a pennant and having a disappointing season.

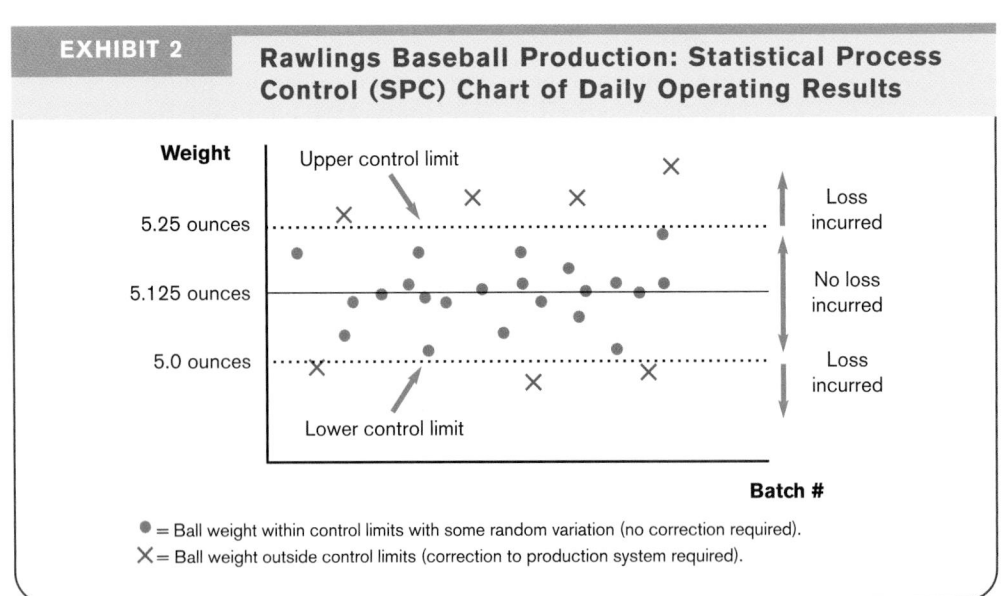

EXHIBIT 2   **Rawlings Baseball Production: Statistical Process Control (SPC) Chart of Daily Operating Results**

● = Ball weight within control limits with some random variation (no correction required).
X = Ball weight outside control limits (correction to production system required).

---

[9] Hannah Holmes, "The Skinny on Sewing Up Baseballs," at **http://www.discovery.com.**

[10] *Note:* This example uses fictitious production standards and results in the setting of an actual company. Data used to illustrate quality concepts in this text should not be construed as actual production standards and results for the Rawlings Sporting Goods Company.

costs of quality (COQ)

Costs spent to achieve high quality products and services, as well as costs spent when products fail to have high quality. The four types of costs of quality are prevention costs, appraisal costs, internal failure costs, and external failure costs.

prevention costs

Costs of quality that relate specifically to design, training, and other investments to ensure that processes are performed correctly the first time and that products and services meet customers' expectations.

appraisal costs

Costs of quality that relate specifically to the effort of inspecting, testing, and sampling activities performed in order to identify and remove low-quality products and services from the system.

internal failure costs

Costs of quality that relate specifically to the expenses that occur when low-quality products and services fail during production or before delivery to customers.

cannot go on unchecked. Blemmed baseballs cost Rawlings money because the balls cannot be sold at game prices. Worse, though, is the cost to Rawlings' reputation. If Major League Baseball switches to another supplier because of inconsistent quality at Rawlings, the long-term opportunity costs to Rawlings could be devastating.

Before Rawlings' production managers can begin working on a potential quality problem on the production floor, the management accountants need to answer a couple of important questions: "What is it costing Rawlings when it produces blemmed baseballs? What will it cost to get the production process back within control limits?" These questions are the initial step in identifying an important set of costs called "costs of quality." **Costs of quality (COQ)** are costs spent to achieve TQM, as well as costs spent when products and processes fail to have high quality. Once activities that relate to quality in the organization have been identified, the accountant must be able to track the costs of those activities in order to measure COQ. Joseph M. Juran, another American quality guru who, like Deming, was enormously influential in the Japanese quality movement, originally identified COQ as an important accounting concept. Eventually, Juran also returned from Japan to the United States with his COQ theories to guide notable companies such as **Texas Instruments, DuPont,** and **Xerox.** He understood that organizations need to balance costs of achieving quality against the costs of poor quality. Most importantly, he specifically defined four types of quality costs that form the COQ model: prevention costs, appraisal costs, internal failure costs, and external failure costs.

Prevention Costs **Prevention costs** are costs incurred to ensure that tasks are performed correctly the first time and that the product or service meets customer requirements. Examples of prevention costs include costs of process or product design, employee training, education of suppliers, preventive maintenance, and other quality improvement meetings and projects. In the case of Rawlings Sporting Goods, the quality of its baseballs is highly dependent on the quality of its raw materials and on the expertise of those who stitch on the leather covers. This company will likely spend a lot of money working with its suppliers and training its employees to build a quality product.

Appraisal Costs **Appraisal costs** are the amounts spent on inspection, testing, and sampling of raw materials, work in process, and finished goods and services. They include overhead expenses for quality inspectors, costs to adjust measuring and test equipment, and costs of associated supplies and materials. Rawlings performs extensive inspections to gather data similar to that shown in Exhibit 2. These inspections require individuals to spend time using special equipment to evaluate each ball for size, weight, color, stitching, etc. Both appraisal and prevention costs can be viewed as investments in the process of providing quality baseballs to Major League Baseball.

Internal Failure Costs Juran categorizes all the scrap and rework costs that are incurred to dispose of or fix defective products *before* they are shipped to the customer as **internal failure costs.** Costs of downtime or reduced yield due to production of defective parts or services are also included in this cost category. For example, if a Rawlings employee spends 10 minutes sewing a baseball, only to have the cover suddenly rip because of poor-quality leather, the company has lost money due to both

 F Y I

Rawlings baseballs are selected at random from each shipment to Major League Baseball and shot from an air cannon at a speed of 85 feet per second at a wall made of northern white ash (the wood used to make bats). Each tested ball must bounce back at between 0.514 and 0.578 of its original speed to be suitably lively for Major League Baseball.

the scrapped leather and the wages paid for 10 minutes of sewing a useless ball. In addition, all the materials and labor time spent previously winding, coating, and fitting the ball before the stitching work started are lost and become part of the internal failure costs. Clearly, Rawlings wants to be able to reduce scrap and sell more baseballs. Investments in prevention and appraisal work should reduce internal failure costs in the organization.

External Failure Costs   Internal failure costs are very expensive. Nevertheless, Rawlings would *much* rather experience an internal failure than an external failure (defined as failure after the product has been delivered to the customers). **External failure costs** are generally the highest costs of a poor-quality process. Some examples are the costs of processing complaints, customer returns, warranty claims, product recalls, field service, and product liability. The most serious type of external failure cost likely results from unhappy customers; because bad news travels fast, defects found by a customer can cause the firm to lose both market share and future profits. In fact, a **Ford Motor Company** survey indicates that a dissatisfied customer tells, on average, six other people. Sometimes the bad news can travel even faster. If a cover of a Rawlings baseball is pulled loose by a pitcher in the act of throwing a knuckleball during a game, the ball is immediately removed from the game. Obviously, more than six people instantly know about the product failure. Worse, though, is when significant product failure leads to news announcements and discussion in the media. In the last few years, you may recall some famous examples of publicized product failure involving software with bugs, unsafe tires on vehicles, medicine or medical procedures with unexpected side effects, and audit failures to capture fraudulent accounting practices.

Juran originally related all four of these COQ categories back to Deming's SPC model. He taught that if companies really understood the extent of failure costs, they would be willing to invest more in appraisal and prevention costs to keep more of their products performing within established control limits. Accountants should track these costs so that they can better manage the important relationship between costs of low-quality products and costs required to create high-quality products. This is an important relationship to manage. Obviously, high quality saves the company a lot of money as both internal and external product failures are reduced. On the other hand, high quality likely requires large investments in appraisal and prevention costs. Even though TQM requires that managers focus first on quality and then on profits, managers still need to understand how their commitment to TQM affects the company's bottom line (i.e., its profits). The dollar amounts involved in COQ are often quite large. Accountants add important competitive value to the organization when they are able to provide this important cost information. Hence, management accounting systems should identify appraisal and prevention activities, track the cost drivers of these activities, and establish performance measures that relate to reductions in failure costs and activities as a result of appraisal and prevention activities.

COQ Example

Let's return to our example involving the production of baseballs at Rawlings Sporting Goods Company. Rawlings has invested expensive time and equipment to inspect all baseballs represented on the graph in Exhibit 2. As you can see, there are a few baseballs whose individual weights are outside the control limits. Balls failing the test are marked "blems" and sold very cheaply as practice balls. Other balls are not even usable as practice balls and must be scrapped. (Remember that weight is not the only quality criterion at Rawlings. The company is inspecting and scrapping balls for size, stitching, and color problems as well.) In addition to the balls failing the SPC tests, as displayed in Exhibit 2, Rawlings may also occasionally deal with complaints from merchants, athletes, and other organizations involving balls that fail in "the field." Because of the company's high commitment to customer satisfaction, it incurs significant costs in handling these calls, providing replacement balls, and investigating the cause of the product failure back at the factory. To counter these problems, Rawlings is considering making a large investment in its inspection equipment and in better training for its factory workers. Additionally, it is considering a new supplier for some of its raw materials (there are significant costs involved in establishing the new supplier relationship). Rawlings has a difficult planning decision to make that will likely require an intelligent evaluation of the trade-offs across all its quality costs. Rawlings will invest in an increasing level of appraisal and prevention costs in order to increase the percentage of baseballs that conform to all control limits. As the quality of baseballs increases, failure costs decrease dramatically. However, achieving perfect quality requires higher and higher prevention and appraisal costs. Balancing the decreasing costs of product failure with the increasing costs of high quality requires combining *all* costs in order to compute total COQ. The idea is to find the quality level where total COQ is minimized. As an example, look at the fictitious cost numbers in the following table. As the percentage of baseballs that comply with all control limits (color, weight, diameter, etc.) increases, total appraisal and prevention costs increase. On the other hand, as the percentage of baseballs that comply with all control limits decreases, total failure costs increase. Rawlings needs to balance these costs by focusing on the appropriate level of quality in its production process. As you can see by inspecting the numbers presented, all quality costs are minimized in this example at 94% conformance where total COQ equals $2,237,155.

% of balls within all control limits	84%	86%	88%	90%	92%	94%	96%	98%	100%
Total appraisal & prevention costs	$ 100,037	$ 122,554	$ 156,347	$ 211,347	$ 311,850	$ 530,663	$1,164,270	$4,214,198	$44,172,984
Total internal & external failure costs	52,100,456	7,927,472	3,713,274	2,549,005	2,018,342	1,706,492	1,495,145	1,338,798	1,216,244
Total costs of quality (COQ)	$52,200,493	$8,050,026	$3,869,621	$2,760,352	$2,330,192	$2,237,155	$2,659,415	$5,552,996	$45,389,228

Locating COQ in the Accounting Records

It is important to see that tracking COQ within traditional accounting records can be challenging. Essentially, if the accountant desires to provide COQ data, most of these data are buried in the accounting records. As we discussed in previous chapters, many organizations traditionally categorize product costs as direct materials, direct labor, and overhead; and they categorize period costs as selling or general administrative. Quality costs used in the COQ model are typically spread throughout these traditional categories as shown below.

Prevention Costs		Appraisal Costs		Internal Failure Costs		External Failure Costs	
Cost Type	**Where Found**	**Cost Type**	**Where Found**	**Cost Type**	**Where Found**	**Cost Type**	**Where Found**
Process or product design	General administrative	Quality inspectors	Overhead	Scrap	Direct materials	Processing complaints & returns	Selling
Employee training	Overhead	Purchasing test equipment	Overhead (depreciation)	Rework	Direct labor	Product recalls	Selling or general administrative
Educating suppliers	General administrative	Adjusting test equipment	Overhead	Downtime	Direct labor and overhead or general administrative	Product liability	General administrative
Preventive maintenance	Overhead	Special supplies and materials	Overhead	Reduced yield	Direct materials and direct labor	Lost sales	Not found in the accounting system

Companies using a traditional cost accounting system may have some difficulty separating quality costs from other costs. However, companies using more modern management accounting systems should be able to identify activities related to many of these quality processes. Note that lost sales (one type of failure costs) are *not* found in the accounting system. Lost sales are an opportunity cost, and opportunity costs are typically not tracked within most accounting systems. Nevertheless, these are extremely important costs for the accountant to measure and provide to decision makers trying to plan, control, and evaluate the quality process in the organization. Lately, there has been some progress in the effort to track these important opportunity costs. This developing work in COQ accounting systems suggests that a more effective measurement of *all* of the opportunity costs of external failure events will encourage much higher standards of quality in goods and services than many companies currently practice. Estimating the opportunity costs of lost sales is a rather complex topic that is reserved for more advanced management accounting courses.

REMEMBER THIS...

- Just-in-time (JIT) is an inventory management system that focuses on removing all waste from a production or service process. JIT has a strong emphasis on costs and quality.

- JIT is also focused on timeliness and flexibility. Using a kanban signal, demand at the final assembly stage "pulls" the inventory through the production process only as it is needed. Using this system, nothing is produced until customers demand it.

- Total quality management (TQM) is an outgrowth of JIT systems. One of the main TQM tools is SPC (statistical process control). Companies use SPC to identify an acceptable range of variation in their products and services.

- Costs of quality (COQ) can be used to manage decision making based on SPC. There are four COQ categories:
  - Prevention costs (such as good product design and employee training).
  - Appraisal costs (such as inspection and testing).
  - Internal failure costs (such as scrap and employee downtime).
  - External failure costs (such as handling complaints, product recalls, and lost sales).

- The COQ information that accountants provide managers should illustrate how decreasing failure costs may be offset by increasing prevention and appraisal costs.

- Identifying quality costs can be a challenge because these costs are generally intermingled across all the product and period costs within many organizations' accounting systems.

- Perhaps the most important costs of quality are the opportunity costs of lost sales. These costs are typically not captured at all by traditional accounting systems.

Let's Take a Flight!

Explain the fundamentals of building a Balanced Scorecard.

(3) In the first section of this chapter, we used the example of a Triple-A baseball team to illustrate the mechanics and usefulness of the EVA® performance measure. With the insight from this measure on financial outcomes, the owners of the Elkhart Eagles are now faced with a need to better manage their ball club. The next section of this chapter then illustrated a number of performance measures that focus on managing the quality and timeliness of internal processes. The business of managing a baseball team is a unique and complicated business. In light of multiple input and output measures of performance, the owners wonder if there is an effective performance measurement model that will help them understand how to organize and relate together the right input measures to help them

achieve better financial performance in their unique organization. There is, and we'll illustrate it with a different example.

Imagine that a friend of yours is getting her airplane pilot's license and has invited you to sit in the passenger seat of the airplane during her next pilot's lesson. Your friend has not been taking flying lessons very long. However, as you listen to her enthusiastic description of past lessons as the two of you drive out to the airfield the next afternoon, you begin to really look forward to the experience. After parking the car and walking to the Cessna plane that waits on the tarmac, your friend introduces you to the flight instructor, and the three of you climb into the plane. Soon after you take your seat and buckle the seatbelt, your friend revs the engine and the small plane surges forward. The instructor is sitting next to your friend, providing advice and guidance as the plane taxis down the runway gathering speed for takeoff. Suddenly, as you peer over the shoulders of the instructor and your friend in front of you, you notice with some concern that the small plane's instrument panel is noticeably bare of the assortment of instruments, dials, gauges, and controls that are typically part of an airplane's cockpit. In fact, there appears to be only one gauge on the whole panel. Trying to make your question sound casual, you ask about the barren panel and the sole gauge. The instructor looks back over his shoulder to tell you that the gauge measures airspeed. The plane is nearing the end of the runway and is just about to lift off. After swallowing once or twice, you brave more questions about direction, altitude, fuel, temperature, and thrust. Aren't these items also important in flying a plane? Don't most planes have gauges to provide feedback to the pilot on details other than simply airspeed? The instructor agrees but indicates that your friend is currently concentrating on airspeed in her flying lessons. Once she excels at managing airspeed, perhaps the airspeed gauge will be switched for an altimeter, and she can then concentrate on managing altitude. The instructor tells you that he feels it's important to not make the pilot concentrate on too many things at the same time. You notice that your friend is concentrating very hard on the airspeed gauge as the plane noses up and lifts off from the ground. You swallow hard and tighten your seatbelt until it is very snug around your waist. For some reason, you're suddenly imagining about a hundred others places you'd rather be than sitting in this plane.

performance measures

A general term used to describe all measures designed to capture information about performance related to a particular activity or process.

Flying an airplane is a complicated process. To do it successfully requires that the pilot process a lot of information about various performance aspects of both the equipment and the environment. Managing a company such as a baseball franchise is certainly no less complicated. A lot has to happen in order for a company to perform well in its competitive environment as the demands of products, customers, and regulatory agencies change constantly. One of a management accountant's most important functions is to identify and implement **performance measures** that are focused on key strategic and operating plans established by management. These performance measures then become the primary means of controlling and evaluating business processes in the organization. What is the best performance measure for an accountant to provide for an organization? Frankly, there is no one best performance measure.

The Balanced Scorecard

Previous chapters in this textbook have typically focused on subsets of management accounting issues such as merchandising, cost measurement, or the evaluating process. However, in the remainder of this chapter we are not going to focus the discussion on any particular type of firm, strategic imperative, or management process. Instead, we present a *framework* that a management accountant can use to work with any of these issues. That framework is the Balanced Scorecard.

The **Balanced Scorecard** is a process to manage a set of performance measures that support directly the unique strategy an organization is trying to establish and follow (see page 1192 for definition). Exhibit 3 presents the framework of the Balanced Scorecard.

Balanced Scorecard

A management model designed to link together performance measures for financial, customer, internal process, and learning/growth perspectives that are unique to an organization's particular strategy.

The strategic performance measures that a company develops for itself are largely determined by how the organization answers the four basic questions listed in Exhibit 3. The answers to these questions then determine the management *objectives* for the organization, the *measures* that support those objectives, the immediate and long-term *targets* or goals for those measures, and what *initiatives* need to be put into place to begin working toward the targets. The entire Balanced Scorecard process is driven by the organization's overall vision or strategy.

At first glance, the Balanced Scorecard may not seem to be a very new idea. Shouldn't all performance measures support the organization's strategy? Hasn't management accounting always been focused on supporting the objectives of managers and executives to create a profitable company? Actually, although the purpose of management accounting is to establish performance measures that add value to the organization, too often these measures have been limited to periodic reports composed solely of financial measures. Advances in the technology and theory of computer systems today allow more information, more variety in information, and more timely information to be created and reported than ever before. The existence of better information capabilities provides an opportunity for accountants, working in conjunction with system technologists and organization executives, to significantly expand the definition of management accounting. As you study this chapter, you need to understand that the Balanced Scorecard is really a guiding theory of management, rather than an exact formula such as EVA®. It takes times to design and implement a customized scorecard for an organization. However, once created, each organization's own balanced scorecard is a direct view of its strategy, its plans, and its management processes. The idea that a balanced scorecard is extremely personal for each organization is captured in the following comment made by an executive as his division completed work on its first balanced scorecard:

> In the past, if you had lost my strategic planning document on an airplane and a competitor found it, I would have been angry, but I would have

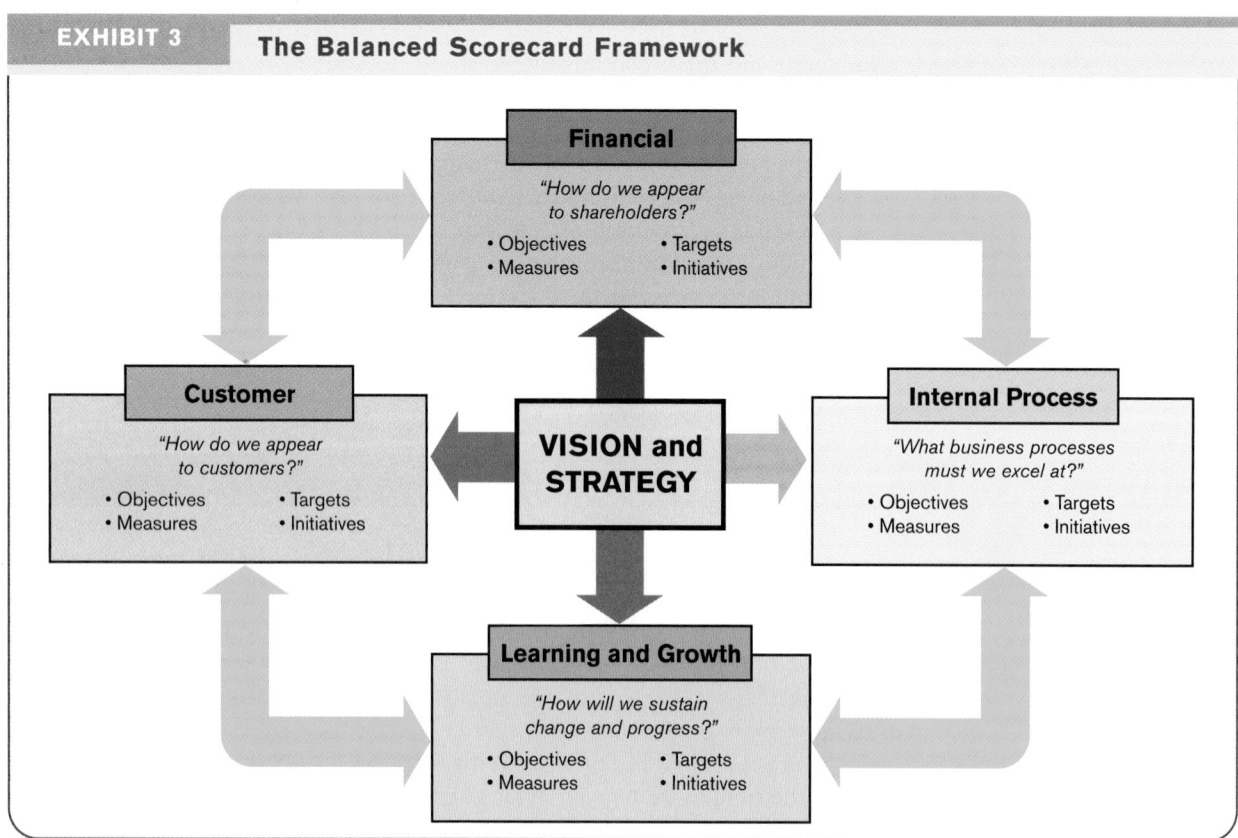

EXHIBIT 3   **The Balanced Scorecard Framework**

Financial
"How do we appear to shareholders?"
- Objectives
- Measures
- Targets
- Initiatives

Customer
"How do we appear to customers?"
- Objectives
- Measures
- Targets
- Initiatives

VISION and STRATEGY

Internal Process
"What business processes must we excel at?"
- Objectives
- Measures
- Targets
- Initiatives

Learning and Growth
"How will we sustain change and progress?"
- Objectives
- Measures
- Targets
- Initiatives

gotten over it. In reality, it wouldn't have been that big a loss. Or if I had left my monthly operating review somewhere and a competitor obtained a copy, I would have been upset, but, again, it wouldn't have been that big a deal. This balanced scorecard, however, communicates my strategy so well that a competitor seeing this would be able to block the strategy and cause it to become ineffective.[11]

Hence, there is no such thing as a *standard* balanced scorecard that any organization can use to operate successfully in its environment. Therefore, as we use example performance measures throughout the chapter to describe the Balanced Scorecard theory, you should remember that each organization must design its own performance measures that support its own particular strategy.

Adding Value with Performance Measures

Frankly, there are a number of problems associated with the performance evaluation methods currently used in many organizations. Current performance measurement systems in some organizations even encourage waste, inefficiency, and poor quality. For example, a measure that emphasizes purchase price may encourage the purchasing department to increase the purchase quantity to get a lower price but might ignore quality and speed of delivery. The results may be excess inventory, increased storage and other carrying costs, and failure to use suppliers with the best quality and service. If machine or labor utilization is the performance measure being emphasized, a supervisor may run a machine or employee team in excess of daily production requirements to maximize the performance measure. This may result in excess inventory or production that is not needed. Similarly, if the performance measure is focused solely on the number of units produced, poor-quality goods or inventory that is not desired by customers may be produced. A specific example from the former Soviet Union illustrates this point. Oil drillers, in competition with one another, received recognition and compensation based on the number of meters drilled. The award-winning team recognized by *Pravda* (Russia's leading newspaper) drilled meter upon meter but never struck oil. It seems that the first 100 meters of drilling do not require as much effort and expense as the second, third, fourth, and so on. The winning team drilled dry hole after dry hole. And the depth of these wells never exceeded 100 meters.

Every company ultimately must perform well financially in order to survive. Even not-for-profit organizations must be able to consistently pay their bills, including payrolls and loans, in order to survive over time. Other companies must consistently show profits, build equity, and provide a return to stockholders. The **DuPont Company** made a lot of money in the first half of the twentieth century by carefully tracking financial measures that contributed to consistent ROI performance. Remember, however, that successful management accounting methods are eventually copied by other organizations. Hence, strictly using ROI to manage an organization does not provide a competitive edge in today's economy. Organizations must continuously improve their management information processes in order to continue to compete. Traditional financial measures are being replaced in some organizations by new measures such as EVA®. And both traditional and cutting-edge financial measures are being vigorously supplemented in three new areas: customer service, internal process improvement, and learning and growth throughout the organization.

 FYI

In harmony with the idea of an instrument panel on an airplane, some companies prefer to refer to their strategic measurement systems as dashboards rather than scoreboards.

---

[11] R. S. Kaplan and D. P. Norton, *The Balanced Translating Strategy into Action* (Boston, MA: Harvard Business School Press, 1996), p. 148.

Customers

The first key to strong financial performance is customer satisfaction. Deming understood this concept well and used it to motivate the need for TQM in organizations. When companies understand what their customers value and what services and products they are willing to pay for, then these companies can design customer-focused performance measures that lead to growth in market share, increased revenues, and long-term profits.

There are two types of customer performance measures: leading measures and outcome measures. **Leading measures** focus on fulfilling customer expectations regarding cost, quality, and time factors. **Outcome measures** determine if the improvements in leading measures result in more satisfied, loyal customers. Therefore, it is important that there be a clear link between the company's efforts to provide low-cost, high-quality, timely products and services, and customer response to these efforts as demonstrated by increased market share and customer profitability (i.e., the company is able to earn sufficient profits by serving its customers). Exhibit 4 provides measures of customer-focused performance.

leading measures

Measures that, if successfully implemented, will support desired performance in other business activities. Note that some leading measures can also serve as outcome measures.

outcome measures

Measures of desired outcome performance in activities critical to an organization's strategic goals. Note that some outcome measures are also leading measures to support desired performance in other business activities.

Leading Measures of Customer Satisfaction   Understanding how and why customers care about cost, quality, and time measures of performance is absolutely essential in today's competitive markets. Naturally, most customers desire low-cost products and services. However, customer satisfaction is the result of the right combination of cost, quality, and time performance. As customers, we are willing to balance our demands for these three objectives. For example, when you mail a package across the nation, you are probably very comfortable making a trade-off decision. The **U.S. Postal Service**, like other package delivery companies, provides various delivery schedules (overnight, two days, three to five days), as well as some options regarding quality of service (contents insurance and registered delivery); each mailing option carries an appropriate price. When you select what mailing method to use, you've effectively communicated what *you* believe at that time to be the value-added services provided by the U.S. Postal Service—and you're willing to pay for those services.

Most companies have spent a great deal of effort understanding how their customers perceive value in terms of timeliness, quality, and price. For many companies, customers are more concerned with reliability than with the fastest delivery. **Toyota** demands deliveries from its suppliers to assembly plants within a one-hour time window. Early arrivals

EXHIBIT 4	**Performance Measures of Customer Satisfaction**

Leading Performance Measures

Cost	Quality	Time	
		Reliable Delivery	**Fastest Delivery**
• Purchase cost to customer	• Returns by customers	• Percentage of on-time deliveries	• Average response time for service call
• Delivery cost to customer	• Quality rankings by other agencies	• Number of production interruptions	• Time to complete contract
• Setup cost to customer	• Customer survey response		• Production cycle time
• Maintenance and repair cost to customer			

Outcome Performance Measures

Customer Retention	Customer Acquisition	Market Share
• Retention rates	• Acquisition rates	• Percent of total number of customers
• Number of defecting customers	• Number of new customers	• Percent of total dollars spent by customers
• Costs to retain customers	• Costs to recruit customers	• Percent of total units sold to customers

When you buy a car, the purchase price represents only part of the total cost of car ownership. You must also consider such costs as maintenance, repairs, and gas. In an effort to account for all costs incurred throughout the entire life of a product, some companies use life cycle costing.

of parts are as unacceptable as late deliveries. Hence, observers have sometimes witnessed delivery trucks driving around and around a Toyota assembly plant until it is time to deliver their goods. If you think about it, this is not really strange behavior. Have you ever scheduled a telephone repairperson to come to your home during the day? Your definition of "on time" is probably not sometime between 9:00 A.M. and 3:00 P.M., is it? Further, given a 1:00 P.M. appointment, you probably would not be particularly pleased at the repairperson's effort to "delight the customer" by arriving two hours early. Performance measures regarding reliability versus fastest delivery of goods or services depend on both the strategy of the company and the demands of its customers. Some examples of these types of measures are provided in Exhibit 4.

Customers compare timeliness and quality factors with price to evaluate the real value of a product or service. Many companies realize, however, that the purchase price of their product often does not represent the total cost to their customer. If you own a car, you may be painfully aware of this fact. The purchase price of your car is only part of its total cost. Maintenance, repairs, gas mileage, and insurance also combine with the original purchase price to determine the total cost of owning your car. Perhaps you wish you had spent a little more (or less) when purchasing your car in order to better balance the subsequent costs of owning your car. In an effort to account for costs that are an essential part of the total value of a product, some firms are turning to a concept known as life cycle costing. Essentially, **life cycle costing** is a method of costing that focuses on all costs that will be incurred throughout the entire life of a product. The life cycle approach to costing helps to ensure that no costs are omitted when evaluating performance and value. Hence, when evaluating customer satisfaction, an organization also needs to measure performance of its product or service in terms of *all* its costs for its customers. These cost measures are listed as leading performance measures in Exhibit 4.

Outcome Measures of Customer Satisfaction

An organization's focus on customers must be twofold. First, the company works to measure up to customer expectations regarding cost, quality, and time. Then the company must determine if its efforts are being rewarded with increased market share and customer profitability. **Market share** is the proportion of industry sales of a particular product or service that is controlled by a specific firm. Companies increase their market share in two ways: retaining current customers and acquiring new customers. Clearly, companies that cannot service their current customers better than competitors will be hard-pressed to maintain market share. Absolute customer satisfaction is key in this regard. Interestingly, when management accountants ignore expected future cash flows over a customer's life, they miss reporting the real cost (the opportunity cost) of losing customers. A relatively new management concept known as **customer relationship management (CRM)** emphasizes an increasingly clear fact that customer profitability over time really takes

life cycle costing

The process of measuring all costs involved in creating, producing, and using a product or service. Life cycle costing is not limited to costs incurred by the organization measuring these costs but also includes all costs incurred by the suppliers and the customers of the product or service.

market share

The percentage share one company receives of the total sales revenue in the economy for a particular product or service.

customer relationship management (CRM)

A corporate level strategy that focuses on creating and maintaining lasting relationships with its customers in order to establish long-term financial value for the organization.

off *if* the company can retain its customers' loyalty. This increased profitability over time is the result of increased purchases or higher account balances, reduced operating costs, and profits from referrals. Hence, customer retention rates are very important outcome measures that result from good performance of leading measures related to customers' overall costs, quality of product, and timeliness of delivery.

Once the company has established leading measures that result in high customer retention, it can turn its attention to acquiring new customers in order to grow its market share. Obviously, there is a strong relationship between loyal customers who speak enthusiastically about the company's product and the company's ability to win new customers. As a result, many companies identify customer loyalty as the best way to acquire new customers. In addition, companies also spend a great deal of effort and resources recruiting new customers. Hence, tracking performance in customer acquisition is a strategy of growth in market share. It is important to understand that there are many ways to successfully maintain and increase market share through customer retention and acquisition. However, retaining and recruiting customers *profitably* is important to strong financial performance. Hence, companies must track the costs spent recruiting new customers, as well as the costs spent retaining current customers. Using activity-based costing (ABC) to track the costs of activities necessary to recruit and retain customers can provide a company with the necessary information to identify desirable customers and to make important decisions to drop certain unprofitable customers. Management accountants who provide outcome measures of their companies' efforts to profitably grow market share can add competitive value to the management process. These customer outcome measures are listed in Exhibit 4.

Internal Processes

Effective management accounting that is built around the Balanced Scorecard can help organizations better understand how satisfying customers (using leading performance measures) relates to growth in customer profitability (using outcome measures). The next issue to be resolved is what processes within the organization must take place in order to satisfy the customer completely? Much of our work with management accounting in this textbook has focused on understanding how performance measures should support the manager's efforts to plan, control, and evaluate processes within the company. However, building performance measures that effectively support the goal of customer satisfaction requires that the management accountant first understand that there are three types of processes that must be in place in order to take care of the customer: innovation processes, operations processes, and service-after-sale processes. Examples of performance measures for management of internal processes are provided in Exhibit 5. Like the customer measures suggested in Exhibit 4, these internal process measures are categorized into cost, quality, and timeliness performance. Quality and timeliness measures are particularly related to the TQM concept.

Innovation Process Measures   We've talked very little in this textbook about planning, controlling, and evaluating the *innovation process*, which involves identifying new products and services, and then creating and bringing those products to market. The reason for this is that most of the management accounting effort has historically been focused

EXHIBIT 5	**Performance Measures of Internal Processes**		
	Innovation Processes	**Operations Processes**	**Service-after-Sale Processes**
Cost measures	• R&D costs per new product • Payback on R&D costs	• Unit-level costs • Batch-level costs • Product line costs	• Costs per service incidence • Costs of replacement parts
Quality measures	• Number of modifications required per design • Percentage of sales from new products	• Defects-per-million opportunities (six sigma) • Errors in customer service	• Customer requests handled on first call • Satisfaction survey responses
Time measures	• Lead time (from idea to working model) • Design cycle time	• Lead time (from order to delivery) • Production cycle time	• Lead time (from request to fulfillment) • Repair cycle time

on the operations process, which involves building goods or providing services that already exist. For example, accountants spend a great deal of effort developing budgets of operations, then measuring variances from standard costs of direct materials, direct labor, and manufacturing overhead. We focused on this particular management process in earlier chapters on budgets and control in cost, profit, and investment centers. However, the innovation process of identifying and creating new products is where much of a company's competitive edge is created. **Microsoft** spends a lot of money hiring some of the best minds in the software industry in order to ensure that it will continue to create new products that retain and recruit customers. As we move further into the new century, many businesses are spending more in their research, design, and development processes than they do to support their production and operating processes. Microsoft is a great example of this trend. If you look at its income statements for 2003 through 2006, you will see that this company often spends more money on research and development of new products than it spends providing current goods and services to its customers. These data are provided below.

	2003	**2004**	**2005**	**2006**
Cost of revenue	$6.06 billion	$6.72 billion	$6.03 billion	$7.65 billion
Research and development	$6.60 billion	$7.78 billion	$6.10 billion	$6.58 billion

Admittedly, many companies do not spend the kind of money on the innovation process that Microsoft does. Nevertheless, the resources invested in the innovation process for most companies are significant. It's important to the ultimate financial success of the organization that the critical effort to identify and develop new products and services is effectively managed. At some point, the money invested in the research and development (R&D) effort must provide financial returns. Hence, given the size of the investments made, it is important that organizations develop measures to evaluate the costs of their innovation processes. In addition, organizations should assess the effectiveness (e.g., the quality) of innovation work. Without proper controls, R&D work is at risk of simply taking too long. You're likely familiar with the old adage that "time is money." Clearly, any project that requires time extensions will cost more to complete. However, in the case of R&D, "time is opportunity!" The market is always moving. Organizations that take longer than their competitors to complete the research and development of new products or services may quickly find themselves seriously disadvantaged in the marketplace. Hence, organizations that manage well their innovation processes time will compete well in the marketplace. Performance measures that support the management of the innovation process will typically be custom built for each organization based on its strategic intent and on the particular nature of its R&D work. Exhibit 5 provides examples of cost, quality, and time-based measures for the innovation process.

Operations Process Measures   *Operations processes* involve all of the activities directly related to the sale of goods or services to customers, including receipt of customer orders, creation of products, and delivery of products. Accountants have traditionally focused on adding value to the operations processes by measuring cost, quality, and time performance. In the effort to support operations processes, many valuable accounting methods have been developed. As a result, several of the previous chapters have focused on helping you understand these methods. Though management accounting for operations processes has been in place for a long time, new methods continue to evolve in an effort to create information that has competitive value.

The concepts of activity-based costing (ABC) discussed in Chapter 17 represent some of the important cost measures created recently to fulfill competitive needs for organizations. An example of a quality measure for manufacturing processes that strongly impacts performance in the marketplace is **six sigma quality**. One of the famous measures of quality, six sigma quality is now becoming an important operations management tool for many types of merchandising and service firms. Sigma[12] is a statistical measure of variation in a product or process and is used to evaluate quality performance. Sigma measures also provide insight about probabilities. Specifically, when the incidence of a single error in the product or service process occurs at a distance of six sigma from the target value, then the probability that the process itself has quality problems is very low. To be precise (without getting into all the statistics involved), an operation process is said to have six sigma quality when defects in the process are occurring at the low rate of 3.4 defects per million opportunities—now that's a high-quality process! Other measures of cost, quality, and time that have competitive value continue to be developed and refined. Exhibit 5 provides some measures that exemplify the continuous improvements we now see in cost, quality, and time measures to support operations processes.

> **six sigma quality**
>
> A measure of quality based on statistical analysis. Products or services with six sigma quality have no more than 3.4 defects per million opportunities (e.g., parts or events).

Service-after-Sale Process Measures   *Service-after-sale processes* are of two types. One type of service-after-sale process involves the billing and collection of payments from customers. The other type involves the organization's commitment to warranty its product, including efforts to repair or replace products and provide post-sale support and guidance in the use of the product. If you've ever purchased a personal computer, you have likely had some experience with technical support to help you resolve a computer problem or simply to figure out how to better use your new computer. Depending on your experience with your computer merchant's technical support (or, for that matter, the post-sale support of any other product or service you've purchased), you probably have strong positive or negative feelings about the quality and timeliness of the support you received, and about the company itself! Do organizations create a competitive edge when they provide quality, timely post-sale support while controlling the costs of that support? You bet! Poor management of service-after-sale processes can result in many opportunity costs. Hence, management accountants also pay attention to management

F Y I

Lands' End is a garment mail-order merchant that exemplifies the growing trend of excellent service-after-sale to customers. Despite being a very large company (during peak seasons, close to 1,100 phone lines handle over 100,000 calls per day), it has established a strong reputation for customer service. The Lands' End guarantee has always been an unconditional one. It reads: "If you're not satisfied with any item, simply return it to us at any time for an exchange or refund of its purchase price." Land's End means every word of this guarantee, and has simplified it further with its trademark statement: GUARANTEED. PERIOD.®

---

[12] Sigma is the name of the Latin symbol σ and is used to represent a statistical measure more commonly known as "standard deviation."

of these processes using effective performance measures, some examples of which are provided in Exhibit 5.

Learning and Growth

Perhaps the most interesting example of continuous improvement in management accounting is found in the recent trend for accountants to help management teams better understand the process of building learning and growth within the organization. In order to survive and thrive in this competitive economy, an organization must continue to learn and grow. Or, to be more specific, the organization's employees, systems, and structure must learn, grow, and change in order to continuously build and improve internal processes and satisfy customers. Deming, for example, understood this need well and was an early advocate for organizations to focus on developing their people. Certainly, the demand of customers today is well described by the question, "What have you done for me lately?" Without learning and growth, internal processes stop improving, customers grow restless and defect, and financial performance stagnates. However, many might react rather strongly to the trend to create performance measures on learning and growth by challenging whether this kind of work is really management accounting at all! How does one measure learning and growth? Frankly, it's not a well-developed accounting discipline. However, because development in this area is rather slight, there is much opportunity for management accountants to create significant competitive value for their organizations by working to build good measures. Don't forget the lesson learned from Donaldson Brown and the DuPont ROI formula in the introduction to Chapter 15. Accountants who are able to provide information useful to plan, control, and evaluate critical business processes, regardless of the initial difficulty of the effort, will add the most value to their organization. By dividing this effort into leading measures and outcome measures (similar to the measures used to manage an organization's work with its customers), the Balanced Scorecard Model suggests some interesting possibilities for measuring performance in the learning and growth effort. Exhibit 6 illustrates some example measures that can be used for managing learning and growth performance.

Leading Measures of Learning and Growth   The ultimate result of building learning and growth in the organization is based on developing employee productivity. Employee productivity then leads to internal process improvements. Related to employee productivity is employee retention and employee satisfaction. These three issues form the desired outcome measures of learning and growth. Therefore, the organization should track performance in the productivity, retention rates, and satisfaction of its employees. However, managing improvements in these important outcome measures requires that management accountants identify the factors that result in high employee productivity, retention, and satisfaction. These factors form *leading* measures in learning and growth: employee capabilities, information system capabilities, and organizational structure capabilities.

Improvements in employee capabilities should lead to improvements in employee productivity. However, improving employee productivity does not necessarily mean that employees are satisfied with their work

CAUTION

Remember that management accounting is not a precisely defined discipline. Individual companies adapt good management accounting principles to fit specific information needs to plan, control, and evaluate their unique organizations. No where is this more true than with the Balanced Scorecard, particularly when it comes to measures of an organization's performance on learning and growth. Every organization will have a *very* specific view of what it means for that organization to learn and grow. Therefore, remember that Exhibit 6, as well as other exhibits in this chapter listing scorecard measures, provide measures that some companies might select from when developing an effective balanced scorecard. No two companies' scorecards are alike!

EXHIBIT 6	**Performance Measures of Learning and Growth**

Leading Performance Measures

	Employee Capabilities	Information Systems Capabilities	Organizational Structure Capabilities
Cost measures	• On-site training expense per employee • Off-site education expense per employee	• Total costs invested in computer systems within the organization • Systems R&D expense per total systems expense	• Costs invested in assessing and building new communication structures • Costs invested in activities to align goals within the company
Quality measures	• Number of new certifications or degrees • Percentage of employees participating in education activities	• System capability compared to competitor systems • Percentage of employees with access to personal computer	• Assessment of effective communication • Assessment of effective teamwork • Assessment of goal alignment
Time measures	• Average yearly training or education hours per employee • Time required to complete a training module	• Average life cycle time of personal computers (e.g., how often are machines upgraded?) • Time required to complete a system upgrade	• Amount of time spent in teamwork versus individual work • Average time to disseminate information or to receive employee feedback

Outcome Performance Measures

Employee Retention	Employee Satisfaction	Employee Productivity
• Employee turnover rate • Average employee years with company • Number of female managers • Average age of employees	• Survey of employee satisfaction • Percentage of employees having leadership opportunities • Management positions filled by inside versus outside recruits	• Output per employee • Billable hours per consultant • New ideas or patents per employee • Recognition of employees by customers

situation and are committed to staying with the company. If investments in employee capabilities are expected to result in higher satisfaction and retention rates among employees, then companies should also expect to see positive improvements in internal processes, customer care, and financial performance. Measures here can focus on the level of qualifications and certifications among employees, as well as investments made by the company in employee training and education.

In this information age, the strength of a company's information system structure is critical to employee productivity. To build an excellent organization, employees need relevant, accurate, and timely information on the results of their efforts to improve processes, satisfy customers, and strengthen financial performance within the organization. In addition to information systems, modern technology continues to provide significant opportunities for directly improving various business processes in all kinds of organizations. Performance measures on information systems and other types of technologies can focus on the quality of systems, accessibility to systems, and investments in systems.

Poorly run organizations can quickly damage employee satisfaction, as well as create confusion that limits employee productivity. Factors that define a well-run organization include effective communication; alignment of goals (i.e., everyone understands and is working toward the same goals); integration of team efforts across departments; and clearly defined planning, controlling, and evaluating processes. Measuring performance and capability in organizational structures is likely the most undefined and challenging "next step" for management accountants today. Nevertheless, this is important work. Organizations usually work very hard to create effective communication channels, to obtain buy-in from employees on company goals, to form an environment where people will work together, and to establish good management processes. Surveys of employees' perspectives are one good way to measure performance on the drive to create good organizational structure.

Outcome Measures of Learning and Growth   Examples of leading and outcome measures of learning and growth are provided in Exhibit 6. As accountants track these measures, it is critical that good performance in employee capabilities, information system capabilities, and organizational structure capabilities results in improvements in employee satisfaction, retention, and productivity. Obviously, then, management accountants can (and should) test the relationship between leading measures and outcome measures by evaluating satisfaction of employees using surveys; reporting on resignation trends within the company; and measuring employees' productivity in terms of volume, quality, and timeliness of output. When investments in employee education programs or improvements in information systems fail to improve employee outcome measures, then management accountants should provide useful information to better manage these critical processes. Otherwise, there is likely to be little improvement in internal processes, customer satisfaction, and (finally) financial performance. Are you getting the sense that linking together all performance measures within the organization may be a critical aspect of developing a balanced scorecard? If so, then you are on track with the final concept that we discuss in the next section.

Linking It All Together

So far in this chapter, and, for that matter, throughout this entire textbook, we have been discussing a *lot* of different performance measures! Do management accountants really need to track *all* these data in order to effectively support the management processes within their companies? Clearly, the answer is no. Too much information is often as harmful as too little. Managers and organizations can become overloaded with information. The key is to clearly identify the vision and strategy a company chooses to pursue, and then establish a set of performance measures that supports progress toward specific company goals. The Balanced Scorecard approach recognizes that management of a company requires information on financial, customer, internal process, and learning and growth activities. Further, performance measures of these activities are not limited to financial measures, but should include nonfinancial measures as well (e.g., quality and time-based measures). Perhaps the most important aspect of a Balanced Scorecard approach is that all measures must *link together* to eventually support the ultimate financial goals of a company.[13] Good performances on activities that do not directly or indirectly contribute to the ultimate goals the organization has established are obviously a waste of resources. Nevertheless, pointless investments in non-value-added activities probably occur in many organizations. Distinguishing non-value-added activities from value-added activities and identifying which performance measures successfully contribute to helping the company accomplish its strategic goals are the ideas behind linkages within a company's balanced scorecard.

To illustrate the importance of clearly linking performance measures in a balanced scorecard, look at Exhibit 7. It should be clear that the ability to achieve target financial goals such as a positive ROI or EVA® is closely linked to success on customer outcome measures (customer retention, customer acquisition, and market share). However, a company can increase its market share and still experience declining ROI because the type of customers it is serving, or the way it is serving its customers, does not lead to positive profits for the company. This is the concept of leading versus lagging indicators.

---

[13] The ultimate goals of an organization do not need to be financial profits in order to apply the Balanced Scorecard Model. For example, not-for-profit organizations (such as governments or charities) will likely emphasize service to constituents or clients as their ultimate strategic goals.

leading indicators

Measures that indicate the potential success of future business activities. Leading indicators are related to the concept "leading measures."

lagging indicators

Measures that indicate the success of past business activities. Lagging indicators are related to the concept "outcome measures."

Leading indicators are measures of performance that, if accomplished, should lead to a desired result. Measures of performance on the desired results are the **lagging indicators**. A company may desire positive ROI. However, the company does not really "manage" ROI directly; instead, it manages performance that *leads* to positive ROI. Hence, it is important that the company has clearly determined that there is a strong relationship between its leading and lagging indicators. In other words, a company may determine that high rates of customer acquisition should lead to improvements in its overall ROI. Nevertheless, if the company actually does acquire a lot of new customers but does not experience improved ROI performance, it likely needs to spend some time better identifying exactly what the real leading indicators are for improved profits in its industry.

As you can see in Exhibit 7, cause-and-effect relationships between leading and lagging indicators should exist throughout a company's balanced scorecard. Customer outcome measures are leading indicators for financial measures. If the company identifies the cost, quality, and time factors that customers care about, then improved performance in these activities will lead to good outcomes in customer retention, acquisition, and market share. Similarly, effective innovation, operations, and service-after-sale processes should lead to improved performance in customer leading measures. Continuous improvements in these internal processes are then linked to learning and growth outcome measures (i.e., employee retention, satisfaction, and productivity), which are linked to investments in leading measures of employee, information systems, and organizational structure capabilities. Exhibit 7 illustrates that most

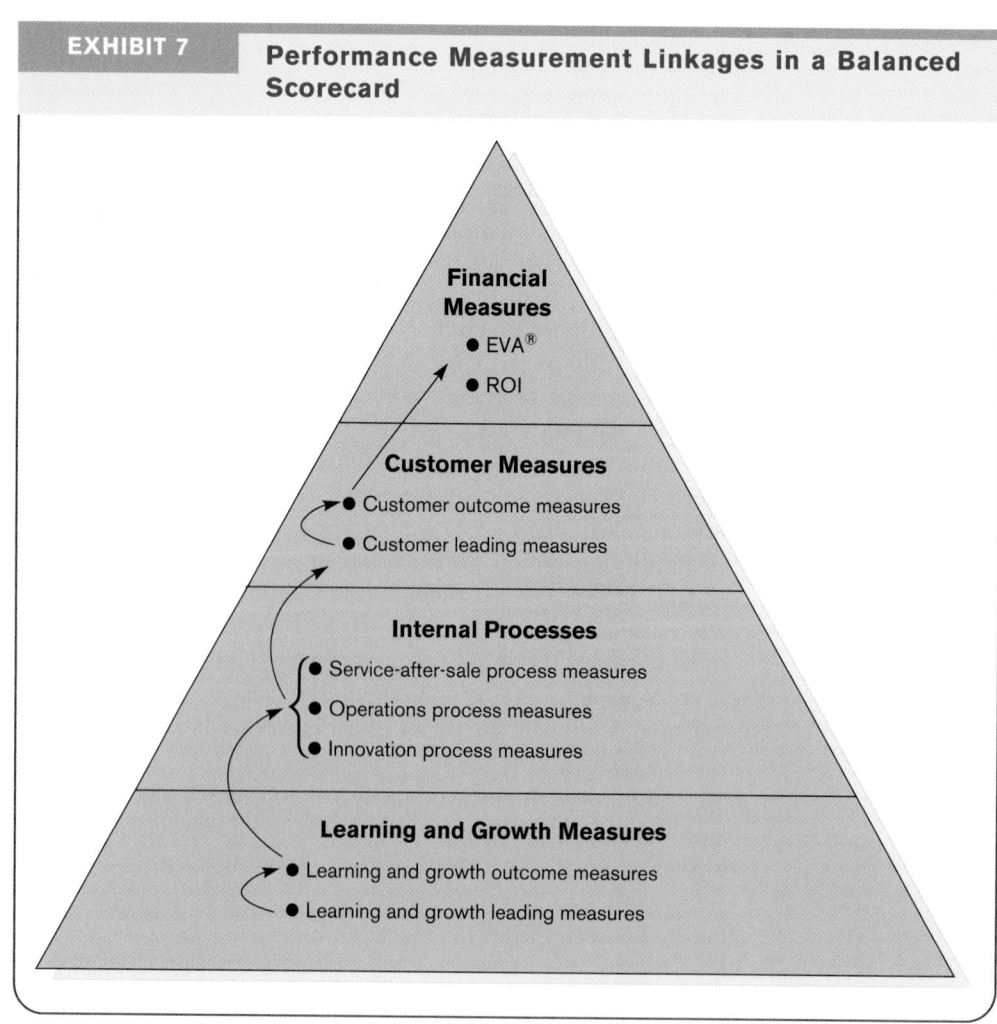

EXHIBIT 7   **Performance Measurement Linkages in a Balanced Scorecard**

performance measures serve as both leading and lagging indicators. When an accountant builds a performance measurement system based on this perspective, it should be clear that financial performance is no more important than performance related to internal processes or learning and growth effort. This is the concept of "balance" in a balanced scorecard. Further, traditional financial measures such as operating income or ROI are really "after the fact." The fact that a company is reporting either positive or negative profits is the result of *past* performance with customers, internal processes, and learning and growth efforts. Can an ROI measure be used to predict future performance? As illustrated in Exhibit 7, financial measures are the ultimate lagging indicators of a successful strategy. Managing an organization's strategy requires insight on leading performance measures. What we see from this reality is that the Balanced Scorecard is really a management system. Management accountants who want to add value to the organization must build and support effective management systems.

An Example Scorecard

Exhibit 8 shows a proposed balanced scorecard for our earlier example of a Triple-A baseball franchise (the Elkhart Eagles). Take a moment to examine this scorecard. Can you recognize the objectives this baseball organization has identified as important to its strategy? Can you identify linkages between its performance measures?

You might note that the financial goals and measures for the franchise are rather basic. The majority of companies in most industries are working to grow revenue and improve profitability. However, the Elkhart Eagles organization is demonstrating some innovation in measuring financial performance by its use of the EVA® metric. The customer goals are divided into leading and outcome measures. The franchise has linked comparative dollar value with alternative entertainment and fan satisfaction as important to its ability to increase its committed fan base (season ticket holders) and its ability to attract potential committed fans by selling single game tickets. Getting fans to commit early in the pre-season to attend games by purchasing season tickets seems to be important to growing revenue and profitability.

Innovation may be the most important way for a baseball franchise to compete with alternative forms of entertainment in the community. Accordingly, you can see that there are two measures supporting the process of keeping fans excited about returning to more games during the season. At the foundation of the Eagles' success must be its investments in its non-player employees. The nature of minor league baseball is that as soon as a player becomes particularly successful and can potentially start drawing fans to the ball park, he is called up to play on the major league team. Hence, the long-term success of the franchise has to be based on its "real employees." The Eagles franchise is committed to making substantial investments in training and is focused on building teamwork within the organization. The expectation is that these leading measures of learning and growth will link to improved employee retention and satisfaction, as well as support internal processes and customer service at the ball park.

 F Y I

No company would actually track as many measures as are being listed in Exhibits 4, 5, and 6. Like the baseball franchise example in Exhibit 8, most organizations will limit their balanced scorecard to between three and six measures in each of the four categories of financial, customer satisfaction, internal processes, and learning and growth.

As you consider the scorecard for the Elkhart Eagles, you may feel that some measures and linkages among measures may be missing. You are probably right! Nevertheless, in contrast to being solely focused on short-term financial performance, the managers and accountants in this franchise are on their way to creating a performance measurement system that truly incorporates the entire strategy of their organization. Studying this scorecard should make it clear to you that good performance measures can capture a unique strategy for a specific company.

EXHIBIT 8	Sample Balanced Scorecard for a Triple-A Baseball Franchise

Scorecard for the Elkhart Eagles

Strategic Objectives	Performance Measures
Financial Perspective	
• Growth	• Percent increase in average gate revenues per game
• Profitability	• Annual operating income
• Investment value	• EVA®
Customer Perspective	
Outcome objectives:	
• Market penetration	• Annual volume of individual game ticket sales
• Market retention	• Annual volume of season ticket sales
Leading objectives:	
• Relative entertainment cost	• Dollar comparison with local dinner and movie outing
• Customer satisfaction	• Spot surveys at games; annual season ticket holder surveys
Internal Processes Perspective	
Operations objectives:	
• Parking cycle time	• Average line length to park before game; average line length to exit after game
• Concessions process	• Average level of inventory; average time to fill a food or drink order
• Stadium management	• Cleanliness scores on seating area, restrooms, and exterior grounds; average time to post-game clean the stadium
Innovation objectives:	
• New products	• Annual increase in number of unique game day promotions
• New entertainment	• Annual increase in number of unique post-game performances
Learning and Growth Perspective	
Outcome objectives:	
• Employee retention	• Average non-player employee years with the franchise
• Employee satisfaction	• Annual non-player employee satisfaction survey
Leading objectives:	
• Employee capabilities	• Training costs invested per non-player employee; percent of employees participating annually in training
• Organizational structure capabilities	• Average weekly hours in teamwork settings; annual assessment of effective teamwork (by outside consultant)

There Is No "Quick Approach"

The Balanced Scorecard approach to performance measurement recognizes that every organization is unique. This is not the only tool available for organizations that desire to better manage strategy, information, and performance; but it is currently one of the most well-known. Hopefully, as you conclude your work with this textbook, it is clear that a manufacturing company will not manage itself the same as a merchandising or service company. Further, even companies competing within the same industry will each have different sets of goals, objectives, and strategies to attain a specific mission. The process of building a balanced scorecard takes time and effort. The management accountant must have a clear knowledge of both financial and management accounting concepts. Then the organization's specific strategy must be clearly and specifically defined in terms of cause-and-effect relationships (i.e., linkages) for its particular industry. What cost, quality, and time issues are important to compete successfully within a particular market? An organization cannot expect to be financially rewarded for world-class performance in response time to customer repair requests unless that type of response time is truly valued by its customers. Finally, measures must be developed, tested, and implemented into clear reporting systems that support effective planning, controlling, and evaluating procedures.

Management accountants can easily build elegant looking but irrelevant performance measurement systems. There are examples of this in far too many organizations. The best example of this bad situation is when accounting is determined to be a non-value-added activity in an organization, and managers simply ignore accounting data as they work on their own to build the company. One of the authors of this textbook is reminded of an experience of having dinner with a plant manager who had built his plant into one of the most successful divisions within the company. When asked how the plant controller's work figured into the division's successful implementation of cutting-edge management principles such as ABC or six sigma quality, the plant manager smiled grimly and indicated that the controller really had only two jobs in the organization. First, the controller was responsible for handling all requests from the external auditors. Second, the controller was simply to "stay out of his way!" He felt that the controller (the chief accountant in the organization) provided no information useful to him in his efforts to implement and execute strategy. Clearly, both the controller and the plant manager were missing important opportunities. The division was making significant investments in its accounting system without receiving any competitive benefits. The controller's reports were irrelevant to the core activities of the organization. How long would it be before one of the competitors in this division's market could effectively use management accounting to better implement its own strategy and seize the market?

Good management accounting requires that both managers and accountants work together to create information systems and performance measures that add value—that support the organization's unique strategy. This kind of work is not easy, nor is it done quickly. Management accountants must clearly understand the nature of critical business processes in the organization, as well as how managers and executives intend to strategically plan, control, and evaluate those processes. Linkages between activities must be tested. If performance in one activity does not lead to desired outcomes in customer service or financial performance, then relationships need to be reexamined. This is exciting work! The history of business in America has clearly demonstrated that successful organizations are willing to spend the necessary creative energy to really understand how the work they do adds value to the marketplace. The spirit of continuous improvement that is now prevalent throughout our economy requires that management accounting continue to identify and support opportunities to improve the cost, quality, and timeliness of the information it provides.

REMEMBER THIS...

- The Balanced Scorecard is an important management tool that integrates performance measures of financial, customer, internal process, and learning and growth activities within an organization. Both financial and nonfinancial measures are used in this new management model.

- A balanced scorecard, once created, is unique to each organization.

- It is critical that performance measures in a balanced scorecard are linked together in a series of leading and lagging indicators of performance. Therefore, learning and growth measures related to employees, information systems, and organizational structure must lead to improvements in the performance of internal process measures involving innovation, operations, and server-after-sale processes.

- Internal process measures should lead to improvements in customer measures that eventually result in improvements in customer retention and customer acquisition in the organization.

- The ultimate lagging measures in the organization are financial measures. All other measures in a balanced scorecard should lead to improvements in financial performance.

Accounting for Tomorrow

Anticipate that both management accounting and financial accounting will continue to change and evolve.

"There is a bulldozer of change coming. You can either be part of the bulldozer, or you can be part of the road." The Balanced Scorecard is one important example of continuous improvement that is characteristic of a competitive world economy that is always growing and changing. Managers and accountants in many organizations are creating new performance measurement systems that support dramatic improvements in products, processes, and people. These professionals understand that measures should focus on monitoring *all* critical activities in an organization in order to anticipate and prepare for future decisions, rather than simply report the financial effects of past decisions.

In this atmosphere of healthy competition and change, you can expect that new models and methods of management accounting will continue to be developed. Financial accounting is moving in this direction as well. Investors, creditors, and regulators are putting a lot of pressure on companies to make public more relevant and more timely information than is now contained in annual reports prepared using the financial accounting model first developed by Italian merchants in the 1300–1400s. The American Institute of Certified Public Accountants (AICPA) has commissioned a number of special committees to study demands for additional public data about companies and to propose new models of financial accounting. Robert Elliott, chairman of the AICPA in 2000/2001, is one of many leaders in industry who believe that accounting will continue to grow and mature as the global economy and technology grow. He describes the professional practice of a "new finance" that "encompasses hard-core management accounting topics such as cost management, discount rates, and capacity management; manufacturing issues including just-in-time production, distribution channel management, and competitive intelligence; and softer topics like benchmarking, performance measurement, and managing change." He says the new finance is "less about accounting and more about becoming strategic advisors and decision makers in our companies."[14]

Exhibit 9 illustrates one way to view the current direction of change that is necessary for accounting in today's marketplace. As you can see, the pressure on accounting to change is threefold. First, financial accounting is being pressured to provide *nonfinancial* data in public reports. Second, preparation of financial accounting reports has always focused on making reports objective, consistent, and reliable. However, users of financial accounting reports want these reports to emphasize more the *relevance* of information to important investing, lending, and regulatory decisions for individual companies. Finally, in an age when the Internet allows users to access and analyze huge amounts of data almost instantaneously, there is increased demand by decision makers trying to evaluate a company based on financial accounting to be able to access information *systems* throughout the year, rather than having to wait one to three months after the year-end for the company to release an annual report document; or, in the case of internal management accounting reports, having to wait days or weeks for cost, quality, and time analysis reports to be completed and delivered to management. It's difficult to predict how these demands will eventually affect the financial accounting reports provided by thousands of companies. However, it's not difficult to predict that changes are coming. This is a very exciting time to be preparing to enter the world of business. Regardless of whether you intend to actually work as an accountant, it is clear that accounting will dramatically impact the way you work. By understanding the concepts of financial and management accounting, as well as the great potential for continuous improvement in these areas, you will be better prepared to use accounting to personally add value to your organization.

---

[14] P. Fleming, "Steering a Course for the Future," *Journal of Accountancy* (November 1999), pp. 35–38.

EXHIBIT 9	The Future of Financial Accounting in Public Reports

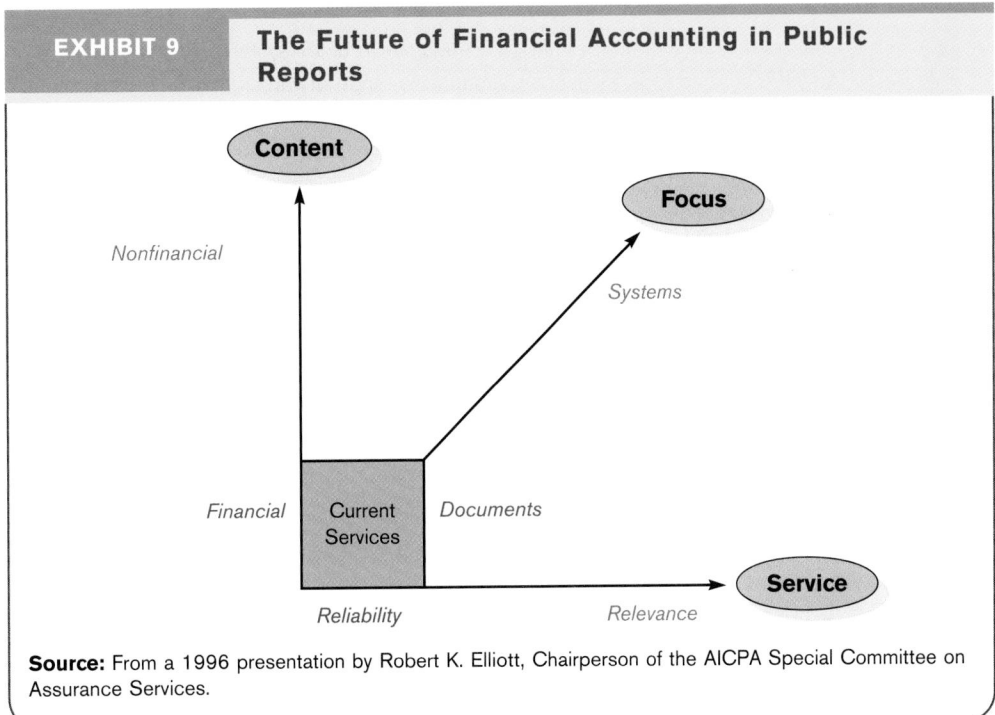

Source: From a 1996 presentation by Robert K. Elliott, Chairperson of the AICPA Special Committee on Assurance Services.

REMEMBER THIS...

- The accounting discipline, both financial and management accounting, has evolved over the years largely as result of the need to improve compliance and competitive usefulness. This evolution will continue in the future.
- The pressure on accounting to grow and change involves three essential areas:
  - the need to include nonfinancial measures in public accounting reports;
  - the need to better emphasize relevant, rather than just reliable, data; and
  - the need to allow continual access to data systems rather than periodic report documents.

REVIEW OF LEARNING OBJECTIVES

(1) Understand the concept of measuring Economic Value Added.

- Economic Value Added is an important new financial performance measure that is calculated as follows:

  Net operating profit after tax − (WACC × Invested capital assets) = EVA®

- The WACC in the formula is the weighted average cost of capital economic value. WACC represents a minimum rate of return that pays for the cost of long-term debt capital and stockholders' equity capital invested in the organization.

(2) Describe the relationship between just-in-time (JIT) management systems and total quality management (TQM).

- By reducing or removing inventory, just-in-time (JIT) management systems focus the organization on removing waste by emphasizing quality and time-based performance.

- Total quality management (TQM) is an outgrowth of JIT systems. Using statistical process control (SPC), companies identify an acceptable range of variation in their products and services.
- Costs of quality (COQ) is then used to manage decision making based on SPC. The four COQ categories are:
  - Prevention costs
  - Appraisal costs
  - Internal failure costs
  - External failure costs

(3) Explain the fundamentals of building a Balanced Scorecard.

- The Balanced Scorecard is a broad-scale model for identifying and relating together a number of unique performance measures that are viewed as critical to the strategy of a particular organization.
- Four specific perspectives are used to organize a balanced scorecard. Those perspectives and their linkages to each other are illustrated below.

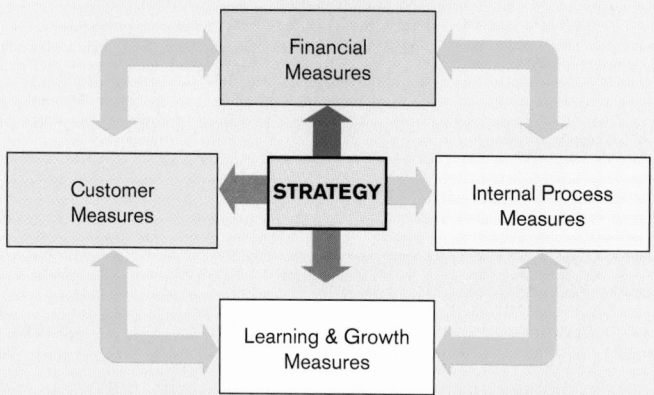

(4) Anticipate that both management accounting and financial accounting will continue to change and evolve.

- You should expect that today's competitive markets will continue to put pressure on both management and financial accounting to make some fundamental changes.
- One way to anticipate future changes in accounting is to watch current accounting services expand financial measures to include more nonfinancial measures that are based more on information systems than on paper documents and that emphasize increasing relevance to decision processes of many kinds of users.
- Accountants, as well as other business professionals, who can anticipate these needs will be best positioned to add value to their organizations throughout the future.

KEY TERMS & CONCEPTS

appraisal costs, 1187

Balanced
  Scorecard, 1192

costs of quality
  (COQ), 1187

customer relationship
  management
  (CRM), 1195

Economic Value Added
  (EVA®), 1179

external failure
  costs, 1188

internal failure
  costs, 1187

just-in-time (JIT), 1182

kanban, 1183

lagging indicators, 1202

leading indicators, 1202

leading measures, 1194

life cycle costing, 1195

market share, 1195

non-value-added
  activities, 1183

outcome measures, 1194

performance
  measures, 1191

prevention costs, 1187

residual income, 1179

return on investment
  (ROI), 1180

six sigma quality, 1198

statistical process
  control (SPC), 1185

total quality management
  (TQM), 1184

value-added
  activities, 1183

weighted average
  cost of capital
  (WACC), 1180

REVIEW PROBLEMS

Applying the EVA® Performance Measure to a Large Company

Rockwell International is a multinational company with the following financial results for 2009:

Rockwell International Income Statement (in millions)	
Revenue	$ 800
Cost of goods sold	(450)
Gross margin	$ 350
Operating expenses	(210)
Operating income*	$ 140

*Before interest and taxes

Balance Sheet (in millions)			
Current assets	$ 50	Current liabilities	$ 35
Noncurrent assets	375	Noncurrent liabilities	155
		Stockholders' equity	235
Total assets	$425	Total liabilities and equity	$425

The effective tax rate for Rockwell is 40%. The weighted average cost of capital (WACC) for the company is computed to be 10%.

Required:

Compute the Economic Value Added for Rockwell International.

Solution

The EVA® formula is as follows:

Net operating profit after tax − (WACC × Invested capital assets)
The net operating profit after tax is $140M × (1 − 40%) = $84M
The invested capital is $155M + $235M or $425M − $35M = $390M

Therefore, Rockwell's EVA® is as follows:

$84M − (10% × $390M) = $45M

Applying the Balanced Scorecard to a School District

Knowlton School District is currently developing a balanced scorecard to be used by all the schools in the district (K-12). At a meeting with all of the principals in the Knowlton School District, the following objectives were created for each of the five categories shown below. (Note that balanced scorecard categories can and should be adjusted to suit the specific needs of the organization.)

1. *Student Achievement*
   Objectives:
   - Student mastery of curriculum
   - Nationally competitive students
2. *Customer Satisfaction*
   Objectives:
   - Safe and enriching school environment
   - Parent satisfaction
   - Community involvement

(continued)

3. *Instructional and Administrative Processes*
   Objectives:
   - Effective instruction
   - Safe and efficient transportation
   - Well-maintained facilities
4. *Staff Learning and Growth*
   Objectives:
   - Competent staff
   - Staff satisfaction
5. *Financial Performance*
   Objective:
   - Sound fiscal management

Required:

For each of these objectives, provide one measure of performance that the school district could use.

Solution*

Many different measures could be used. Here are some possible measures.

	Goal Area	Objective	Measure
1.	Student Achievement	Student mastery of curriculum	• Proficiency tests in various subjects • Retention rates • Drop-out rates
		Nationally competitive students	• SAT scores • AP exam scores • Enrollments in college-credit courses
2.	Customer Satisfaction	Safe and enriching school environment	• Absenteeism and tardy rates • Participation in extracurricular activities • Perception of safety (student surveys)
		Parent satisfaction	• Scores on parent surveys • Number of parent complaints
		Community involvement	• Total volunteer hours • Dollars donated • Number of business partners
3.	Instructional and Administrative Processes	Effective instruction	• Percent of students in summer school • Percent of teachers certified in special programs • Percent of teachers using technology
		Safe and efficient transportation	• Accidents per million miles • On-time bus delivery
		Well-maintained facilities	• Accidents per student days • Scores on inspection reports • Level of backlogged maintenance reports
4.	Staff Learning and Growth	Competent staff	• Percentage of teachers with 7+ years of experience • Percentage of teachers with advanced degrees • Percentage of board-certified teachers
		Staff satisfaction	• Absenteeism rates • Percentage of teachers retiring early • Scores on teacher surveys
5.	Financial Performance	Sound fiscal management	• Sound fiscal management • Revenue variances of actual to budget • Expense variances of actual to budget • Fund balances

* This balanced scorecard is adapted from actual balanced scorecard for the Fulton County School System in Georgia in 2003. Current balanced scorecard reports are available at **http://www.fulton.k12.ga.us/**.

DISCUSSION QUESTIONS

1. What is invested capital, and how is it measured?
2. What is the total cost of capital for a company?
3. How can a company make a profit and yet not be profitable in the sense that it has negative value in the EVA® calculation?
4. What are three basic ways that a company can improve its EVA®?
5. How did the concept of just-in-time (JIT) change most companies' view that maintaining a minimum level of inventory was desirable? Use the measures of cost, quality, and time as you prepare your answer.
6. "The purpose of just-in-time (JIT) is to reduce inventory." Do you agree or disagree? Explain.
7. In what way do Edward Deming's ideas of total quality management (TQM) change Andrew Carnegie's slogan, "Watch the costs and the profits will take care of themselves"?
8. Briefly describe the four types of costs in costs of quality (COQ).
9. Why are external failure costs generally the highest of the costs of quality (COQ)?
10. Why is it unwise for a company to focus on only one performance measure while ignoring other performance measures?
11. Why do you think performance measures vary from company to company?
12. Why do you think there has been such a revolution in the way companies think about and measure their performance in recent years?
13. What is one way that traditional performance measurement systems, which have historically been tied to financial reporting, may be dysfunctional?
14. Describe the two classifications of customer performance measures.
15. What are the key ingredients of customer satisfaction?
16. Why doesn't the purchase price of a product equal the product's total cost to customers?
17. What are the two issues involved in managing a company's market share of its products?
18. What are the three types of processes that should be in place to effectively support customer satisfaction?
19. How can companies plan, control, and evaluate their innovation processes?
20. Is it possible for a company to spend more money on the innovation process than on providing goods and services to current customers?
21. What are the three leading measures of learning and growth in an organization?
22. What are some of the factors of effective organizational structures discussed in this chapter?
23. How do companies go about managing *directly* their return on investment (ROI)?
24. Pressure to provide better information to support the competitive needs of today's marketplace is resulting in fundamental changes in the accounting information that is being provided to managers, investors, and creditors. Identify the three primary areas of change.

PRACTICE EXERCISES

PE 23-1 **The Cost of Capital**

LO1   Which one of the following statements is *false*?
   a. The costs of capital for an organization include the interest costs expected by long-term debt holders and the return expected by the owners or stockholders.
   b. The cost of capital will generally include an implicit cost related to current obligations such as accounts payable and wages payable.
   c. The stockholders' equity in an organization, including retained earnings, represents assets that the company, at some point in the future, must pay to use.
   d. The cost of capital is measured as an average rate that reflects a combination of interest rates and expected rates of return in the organization.

PE 23-2 **Economic Value Added**

LO1   Which one of the following statements is *false*?
   a. Economic value added is a relatively new measure that is based on a traditional measure of residual income.
   b. Economic value added is an after-tax measure of value added by the organization to its owners.

(continued)

c. Economic value added requires a careful measure of the invested capital assets in order to determine the opportunity costs of those assets for those who provided the assets to the organization.

d. Economic value added is a measure very similar to net income and is essentially based on measuring the economic revenues of the organization.

PE 23-3   Calculating EVA®
LO1   Which one of the following is the correct formula for EVA®?

a. Net operating profit before tax – (Cost of capital × Invested capital)
b. Net operating profit after tax – (Cost of capital × Invested capital)
c. Net operating profit after tax – (Cost of capital × Total assets)
d. Net operating profit before tax – (Cost of capital × Total assets)

PE 23-4   Just-in-Time Inventory
LO2   Which one of the following statements is *false*?

a. Carrying large amounts of inventory can be very costly for a company.
b. JIT environments are usually "push" systems.
c. JIT inventory systems started in Japan.
d. JIT emphasizes reduction of non-value-added activities.
e. Under a JIT system, accountants are encouraged to provide time-based performance measures to management.

PE 23-5   Total Quality Management
LO2   Which one of the following statements is *false*?

a. Total quality management is simply a general endorsement of quality in a company.
b. W. Edward Deming was instrumental in the quality revolution in Japan during the 1950s.
c. Total quality management shifted some companies' focus from costs to quality.
d. Statistical process control can help management know whether a process has serious problems.

PE 23-6   Costs of Quality
LO2   Which one of the following is *not* a type of costs of quality?

a. Appraisal costs
b. Adaptive costs
c. Internal failure costs
d. Prevention costs
e. External failure costs

PE 23-7   The Balanced Scorecard
LO3   Which one of the following statements is *false*?

a. Companies that use the Balanced Scorecard do not need to focus on financial performance.
b. The Balanced Scorecard is not an exact formula that can be automatically implemented in any organization.
c. Companies using the Balanced Scorecard should implement performance measures that support the organization's goals.
d. Lower-level managers tend to pattern their efforts after the performance measures that upper-level management has implemented.

PE 23-8   Customer Satisfaction
LO3   Which one of the following statements is *false*?

a. Leading measures focus on fulfilling customer expectations.
b. Outcome measures focus on whether improvements in leading measures result in more satisfied customers.
c. A decreasing market share is a good indication of high customer satisfaction.
d. Companies that are not committed to quality products usually do not last long.

PE 23-9   **Internal Processes**

LO3   Which one of the following statements is *false*?

a. One type of service-after-sale process is the organization's commitment to warranty its product.

b. Research and development projects can require a very long payback period.

c. An operation process that has six sigma quality allows for only 3.4 defects per million opportunities.

d. One type of operations process is billing and collection of payments from customers.

PE 23-10   **Learning and Growth**

LO3   Which one of the following statements is *false*?

a. Developing employee productivity is an ultimate result of building learning and growth in an organization.

b. Poorly run organizations often have low employee morale.

c. Outcome performance measures, such as output per employee, can be used to estimate how well the leading performance measures, such as training hours per employee, add value to the organization.

d. Learning and growth measurement is a well-developed accounting discipline.

PE 23-11   **Linking It All Together**

LO3   Which one of the following statements is *false*?

a. All measures of a balanced scorecard should link together to eventually support the ultimate financial goals of a company.

b. A company should use every possible performance measure available.

c. Leading measures indicate the potential success of future business activities.

d. Too much information is often as harmful as too little information.

PE 23-12   **Performance Measurement Linkages**

LO3   Which one of the following represents the correct cause-and-effect sequence of leading and lagging measures in an organization?

a. Learning and Growth → Internal Processes → Customer → Financial

b. Financial → Learning and Growth → Internal Processes → Customer

c. Customer → Internal Processes → Learning and Growth → Financial

d. Internal Processes → Financial → Learning and Growth → Customer

PE 23-13   **Implementing a Balanced Scorecard**

LO3   Which one of the following statements is *true*?

a. The same balanced scorecard can be implemented at all organizations for maximum success.

b. Management accountants may build performance measurement systems that are irrelevant to the strategy of the organization.

c. A correctly implemented balanced scorecard usually fails to add value to the organization.

d. Two companies that have different performance measures will not be able to compete against each other.

PE 23-14   **Accounting for Tomorrow**

LO4   The accounting industry is currently facing pressure in each of the following areas *except*:

a. The need to better emphasize relevant, rather than just reliable, data.

b. The need to grow at a faster rate than the other industries to keep up with business demands.

c. The demand to allow continual access to data systems rather than periodic report documents.

d. The demand to include nonfinancial measures in public accounting reports.

EXERCISES

E 23-15
LO1

Measuring Invested Capital Assets

At the end of 2009, Hatch Industries had the following balance sheet:

Hatch Industries Balance Sheet For December 31, 2009			
Cash	$ 1,200	Accounts payable	$ 2,100
Inventory	5,500	Wages payable	3,700
Accounts receivable	3,200	Total current liabilities	$ 5,800
Total current assets	$ 9,900	Long-term liabilities	188,000
Equipment	78,000	Total liabilities	$193,800
Buildings	235,000	Common stock	220,000
Land	150,000	Retained earnings	59,100
Total assets	$472,900	Total liabilities and equity	$472,900

Hatch Industries would like to compute its EVA® for the year. Help the accountant at Hatch Industries prepare for that computation by determining invested assets from the balance sheet above.

E 23-16
LO1

Computing Economic Value Added

Firefly Travel Services has recently shifted its performance measurement system to include Economic Value Added (EVA®). The Firefly accountant gathered the following data for 2009:

Operating income	$ 275,000
Total assets	1,220,000
Current liabilities	18,000

The average tax rate on income for Firefly Travel Services is 32%. Assume that the WACC is 15.5%. Compute Firefly's EVA®.

E 23-17
LO1

Computing Economic Value Added

Jessica began a day care business three years ago and has worked hard to make it successful. She originally invested $4,000 of her own money and borrowed $5,000 from the bank to start her business. She has two employees and pays herself a management salary. She hopes to make a return on her $4,000 investment. With some help from her financial advisor, she determined that her expected rate of return on her investment combined with the rate of interest on her bank loan results in a weighted average cost of capital of 20%. The effective income tax rate on her business is 25%. She had $5,600 in operating income before interest and taxes this year. Her financial advisor helped her draw up the following balance sheet at the end of the year:

Jessi's Day Care Year-End Balance Sheet			
Cash	$ 1,000	Wages payable	$ 800
Supplies	350	Bank loan	5,000
Accounts receivable	850	Total liabilities	$ 5,800
Total current assets	$ 2,200	Capital contribution	4,000
Equipment	8,600	Retained earnings	1,000
Total assets	$10,800	Total liabilities and equity	$10,800

Compute the Economic Value Added (EVA®) for Jessi's Day Care.

E 23-18

LO2

Value-Added and Non-Value-Added Activities

Below is a list of activities performed by the Ibapah Bijou, a movie theater. Indicate whether each activity is a value-added activity (VA) or a non-value-added activity (NVA).

a. Redesigning the staff uniforms.

b. Cooking popcorn.

c. Counting the ticket stubs at night to make sure no one got in free.

d. Servicing the quadraphonic speaker system.

e. Paying for the rights to show the next movie starring Julia Roberts.

f. Paying a management fee for the employee pension fund.

g. Renting a storage facility to store the excess inventory of candy, uncooked popcorn, and soft drinks.

h. Paying the accounts payable.

i. Cleaning the white movie screens.

j. Scrubbing the theater floor to remove the sticky residue of spilled soft drinks.

E 23-19

LO2

Costs of Quality

Some of the costs in the list below are costs of quality. For each cost, indicate by the appropriate letter what type of cost it is: prevention cost (P), appraisal cost (A), internal failure cost (I), external failure cost (E), or not a cost of quality (N/A).

a. Cost of raw materials used in discarded, defective products

b. Salary of the president of the company

c. Cost to purchase product testing equipment

d. Lawsuit costs stemming from the sale of defective products

e. Cost to repair defective products before shipment

f. Employee quality training costs

g. Employee downtime caused by production halts to repair defective products

h. Cost of sampling raw materials to ensure quality

i. Customer warranty costs

j. Property taxes

k. Cost of lost reputation (i.e., lost sales)

l. Cost to help suppliers improve their product shipping procedures

m. Interest cost on short-term loans

n. Production process design costs

E 23-20

LO2

Costs of Quality

Sara's Stylish Suppers prepares food for wholesale to gourmet restaurants. Quality is very important to consumers of gourmet food. Following is a list of costs that Sara incurred during 2009:

Wages paid during downtime to fix machinery	$ 50,000
Cost of spoiled raw materials (cheese, meat, etc.)	85,000
Training cost for new food handlers	12,000
Wages paid to food samplers	15,000
Lawsuit settlements for severe food poisoning	134,000
Cost of refrigerator used to keep food fresh	75,000
Wages paid to quality inspectors	21,000
Wages paid to chefs who create new gourmet dishes	97,000
Wages paid for redoing poor quality food (found before delivery)	46,000

In addition, Sara's accountants estimated approximately $100,000 in lost sales due to restaurant managers who are unhappy with Sara's products and service.

Compute the total cost for each of the following categories:

1. Prevention costs

2. Appraisal costs

3. Internal failure costs

4. External failure costs

E 23-21   **Customer Satisfaction Performance Measures**

LO3   The following are possible performance measures of customer satisfaction:

1. Purchase cost to customer
2. Customer defection rate
3. Returns by customers
4. Number of new customers
5. Time to complete contract
6. Percent of total units sold
7. Customer survey response
8. Costs to recruit customers

Identify which of these measures are most likely to be considered leading measures and which are outcome performance measures. Also, if they are leading performance measures, identify whether they relate to cost, quality, or time. If they are outcome performance measures, identify whether they relate to customer retention, customer acquisition, or market share.

E 23-22   **Internal Processes Performance Measures**

LO3   The following are possible performance measures of internal processes:

1. Cost of replacement parts
2. Lead time (order to delivery)
3. Lead time (idea to working model)
4. Product returns per million
5. Payback on R&D costs
6. Percentage of sales from new products
7. Production defects per million
8. Repair cycle time
9. Cost of warranty repairs

Identify the type of performance measure (cost, quality, or time) and the related process (innovation, operations, or service-after-sale) for each of these measures.

E 23-23   **Performance Measures of Learning and Growth**

LO3   The following are performance measures of learning and growth:

1. Number of new certifications or degrees
2. Average life cycle time of personal computers
3. Assessment of effective communication
4. Employee turnover rate
5. Output per employee
6. Average yearly training or education hours per employee
7. Survey of employee satisfaction
8. Amount of time spent in teamwork versus individual work

Identify which of these learning and growth measures are leading performance measures and which are outcome performance measures. Also, if they are leading performance measures, identify whether they would be classified as cost, quality, or time measures and whether they relate to employee, information system, or organizational structure capabilities. If they are outcome performance measures, identify whether they relate to employee retention, employee satisfaction, or employee productivity.

E 23-24   **Balanced Scorecard Linkages**

LO3   The following are examples of performance measures in a balanced scorecard:

1. ROI
2. Percentage of employees having leadership opportunities
3. Repair cycle time
4. Quality rankings by other agencies
5. ROE
6. Design cycle time

(continued)

7. Six sigma

8. Systems R&D expense per total systems expense

Classify each of the above performance measures using the categories in Exhibit 7. For each measure, identify the type of lagging measure to which it links.

E 23-25

LO3

Classifying Balanced Scorecard Elements

Listed below are a number of scorecard measures for a manufacturing company.

a. Number of new customers

b. Percentage of customers who place multiple orders

c. Percentage of on-time deliveries

d. Number of worker accidents

e. Number of customer complaints about products

f. Number of employees who attend training seminars

g. Percentage of product defects

h. Percentage of back-ordered products

i. Customer satisfaction, as measured through periodic surveys

j. Unit product cost

k. Earnings per share

l. Gross margin on products

m. Employee turnover

n. Costs to retain customers

o. Amount of time spent in teamwork

Classify each performance measure according to the following:

1. *Perspective:* financial, customer, internal processes, or learning and growth

2. *Focus:* cost, quality, time, or overall financial (*Note:* Some measures may have more than one focus.)

3. *Relationship:* leading or outcome (*Note:* As the measure relates to other measures within its own perspective.)

E 23-26

LO3

Balanced Scorecard and Incentives

Recall from the chapter the discussion of the oil drillers from the former Soviet Union who won a production competition based on the number of meters drilled. Those drillers determined that the first 100 meters of drilling were the easiest, so they simply drilled dry wells that never exceeded 100 meters in depth. Naturally, management would be upset when the drillers' tactics were exposed. After all, management's objective was to drill wells and find oil.

1. Can you suggest to management an incentive system that would have prevented such behavior and would instead encourage the desired behavior?

2. Do you consider what the drillers did to be wrong or smart?

E 23-27

LO3

Thinking about the Balanced Scorecard

Albert Einstein once commented that "sometimes what can be counted doesn't count, and what can't be counted is what really counts." A business executive stated, "The first indication we don't know what we are doing is a preoccupation with numbers." How do you think these two statements relate to the Balanced Scorecard approach to performance measurement?

E 23-28

LO3

Applying the Balanced Scorecard to a Bank

You have just been hired as the CFO of Bridger Bank, a small community bank in your town. Management is currently in the process of creating a balanced scorecard management system. You have been given the following list of performance measures:

a. Return on equity

b. Sales calls to potential customers

c. Thank you calls or cards to existing customers

d. Lending income

e.   Number of new customers
f.   Referrals (a referral is when one employee suggests that a customer see another employee for more information about a bank product)
g.   Cross-sells (selling multiple products to one customer when the customer comes in for only one product)
h.   Employee training hours
i.   Nonlending income
j.   Employee turnover
k.   Customer satisfaction
l.   New products introduced
m.   Employee satisfaction
n.   Customer retention

1.   Classify these measures as learning and growth measures, internal processes, customer measures, and financial measures by grouping the measures in a column for each respective category.
2.   After classifying the measures in columns, draw arrows from the leading measures to the lagging measures. (*Hint:* Some measures may be both a leading and lagging measure, and some measures may be a leading or a lagging measure for more than one other measure.)

Note: This exercise is adapted from T. Albright, S. Davis, and A. Hibbets, "Tri-Cities Community Bank: A Balanced Scorecard Case," *Strategic Finance* (October 2001), pp. 54–59.

PROBLEMS

P 23-29
LO1

Applying the EVA® Performance Measure to a Start-Up Company

Two good friends, Mike Morley and John Baird, got together after graduating with MBA degrees in international business and decided to form an import business out of Thailand and Vietnam. Both had spent significant time in Southeast Asia during college working in the school's study abroad program. They recognized an opportunity to import sports clothing and shoes out of these two countries into the United States for sale to college students. They worked hard to identify good production facilities in Thailand and Vietnam that they felt employed workers fairly and safely. They felt that this was a critical selling point to college students who are typically sensitive to issues of worker exploitation. After securing distribution partners in 20 key universities across the United States, Mike and John felt ready to begin the business. They had secured a $250,000 loan to match the $250,000 investment made by a venture capitalist firm that targeted start-up business by recent MBA graduates. Having studied finance in their MBA program, Mike and John were able to effectively compute the weighted average cost of capital on their $500,000 fund to be 14.5%. They were also fortunate to be able to maintain $50,000 in inventory on account from their Thailand and Vietnam suppliers. Hence, Mike and John's first year of business was conducted with a total asset base of $550,000. At the end of the year, their net operating profit before interest and taxes was $88,000. John and Mike were pleased with the results of their first year of business, but they knew that the business needed to do better if it was to succeed.

Required:
1.   Compute the Economic Value Added for Mike and John's first year of operations (assume an effective income tax rate of 35%).
2.   Explain why the EVA® is different from operating profit for Mike and John's business.

P 23-30
LO1

Applying the EVA® Performance Measure to a Large Company

Sperry Space and Aeronautics is a research and development firm that contracts with the government to design specialized equipment for use in the NASA space shuttle program. Its income statements and year-end balance sheets for 2008 and 2009 are shown below. The board of directors for Sperry recently installed a new key performance measure for the company called Economic Value Added. Sperry's CEO worked with his management team to

(continued)

make the change in 2009. Based on the EVA® results, the CEO was concerned when he presented the financial report for 2009 at the first board meeting following the end of the year. As he began the presentation, he was just glad that Sperry was showing much better profit in 2009 than it had in 2008. His relief, however, was short-lived when the head of the finance committee on the board pointed out that EVA® loss in 2009 was actually more than the EVA® loss in 2008. When he asked the CEO for an explanation, the CEO was momentarily flustered. Why was it that operating income was improving, but EVA® was getting worse?

Sperry Space and Aeronautics

Financial Statements for 2009 and 2008

Income Statement (in thousands)	2009	2008
Revenue	$ 8,800	$ 8,600
Cost of sales	(4,100)	(3,900)
Gross margin	$ 4,700	$ 4,700
Operating expenses	(3,300)	(3,700)
Operating income before interest and tax	$ 1,400	$ 1,000

Balance Sheet (in thousands)

	2009	2008		2009	2008
Cash	$ 210	$ 100	Accounts payable	$ 20	$ 190
Supplies	120	70	Salaries payable	90	40
Accounts receivable	250	360	Total current liabilities	$ 110	$ 230
Total current assets	$ 580	$ 530	Bonds payable	5,000	5,000
Equipment	2,530	1,400	Total liabilities	$ 5,110	$ 5,230
Buildings	14,500	10,000	Common stock	15,000	10,000
Land	7,000	7,000	Retained earnings	4,500	3,700
Total assets	$24,610	$18,930	Total liabilities and equity	$24,610	$18,930

Required:
1. Compute the Economic Value Added for 2008 and 2009. Sperry's average tax rate is 45% and remained the same in both years. On the other hand, due to an increase in equity funding, the weighted average cost of capital increased from 10% in 2008 to 11% in 2009.
2. Explain why EVA® is getting worse in 2009 despite the fact that operating income is higher.

P 23-31

LO2

JIT Inventory

The president of Penman Corporation, John Burton, has asked you, the company's controller, to advise him on whether Penman should develop a just-in-time (JIT) inventory system. Your research concludes that there is a high cost associated with inventory storage facilities; that inventories use a large portion of the company's cash flow; and that because of the nature of the inventory, there is a significant amount of shrinkage. Research also shows that neither of Penman's two competitors uses a JIT inventory system. Most of Penman's employees are trained to do only one job and belong to a local union. The union is strong and, in the past, has opposed major production changes. The union believes major changes will result in the loss of union employees' jobs. Your research indicates that Penman's major production item (a fairly new product in the market) should continue to have strong sales growth.

Required:
1. Using the information provided, advise John Burton to either continue the present system or work to develop a JIT inventory system.

(continued)

2. Assume John decides to develop an inventory management system. He plans to evaluate the system after one year. List at least four possible performance measures John could use to evaluate the effectiveness of the system. Describe what information these measures would provide John.

P 23-32

LO2

Costs of Quality

DeeAnn Martinez is preparing to open her own CPA firm. DeeAnn is a smart businessperson and wants to maximize her profits. She has not yet decided whether to run a low-quality CPA firm (basically offering to sign the financial statements of anyone who will pay her fee), an average CPA firm, or a premium-quality CPA firm (competing head-to-head with large international accounting firms such as **Pricewaterhouse Coopers**).

DeeAnn has analyzed the costs of quality related to operating a CPA firm and has developed the following analysis:

- *Prevention costs:* The best way to ensure the quality of the audit is to increase the quality of the staff hired and to increase the time that the staff spends on each audit. DeeAnn realizes that hiring higher-quality staff will cost more.
- *Appraisal costs:* DeeAnn plans to inspect the work of the staff auditors by having audit managers review the work. The average salary rate for an audit manager (including all fringe benefits) is $50 per hour.
- *Internal failure costs:* Sometimes the audit team will do such a poor job that one of DeeAnn's audit partners will have to personally supervise the completion of the audit work. The average salary rate for an audit partner is $100 per hour.
- *External failure costs:* If investors or creditors rely on financial statements that later prove to be false, the audit firm that approved those financial statements will probably be sued. Of course, the frequency of being sued, and the cost of each lawsuit, will be higher if DeeAnn decides to provide low-quality audits.

DeeAnn has gathered the following numerical information about the costs of quality in relation to operating a CPA firm:

	Low Quality	Average Quality	Premium Quality
Prevention costs:			
Staff hours spent on audit	10 hours	30 hours	100 hours
Staff salary rate	$20/hour	$25/hour	$35/hour
Appraisal costs:			
Manager review of audit work	1 hour	5 hours	20 hours
Internal failure costs:			
Frequency of bad audits	1 in 3	1 in 10	1 in 50
Partner time to fix bad audit	10 hours	5 hours	3 hours
External failure costs:			
Frequency of lawsuits	1 in 5	1 in 40	1 in 100
Expected loss on each lawsuit	$200,000	$100,000	$100,000

Required:

1. Assume that the revenue from each audit is the same no matter what the quality of the audit. Therefore, in order to maximize her profits, DeeAnn must minimize the expected cost of each audit. Which type of audit firm—low quality, average quality, or premium quality—should DeeAnn operate in order to maximize her expected profit per audit? Show your calculations.

2. Comment on whether the assumption about revenue made in part (1) seems appropriate.

P 23-33

LO3

Applying the Balanced Scorecard to Manufacturing

Martin, Inc., manufactures pleasure and fishing boats. Management's goals and objectives for the company are:

(continued)

1. *Goal:* To be the industry leader in market share in North America.
   Objectives:

   - Maintain sufficient cash balances to assure liquidity and solvency
   - Expand sales within current markets
   - Introduce products into new markets

2. *Goal:* To provide excellent customer service.
   Objectives:
   - Provide boats that meet customer needs
   - Meet customer needs on a timely basis
   - Exceed customer quality standards
3. *Goal:* To be the industry leader in product innovations.
   Objectives:
   - Bring new boats and features to the market before competitors
   - Increase efficiency and productivity faster than competitors

Required:
For each of these objectives, provide one measure of performance the company could use.

P 23-34
LO3

Applying the Balanced Scorecard to a Small Business

You are an optometrist with your own practice. For the past 20 years, you have focused almost exclusively on profitability of your practice as your sole performance measure. In fact, you have been quite profitable. However, during the past two years, a number of new, low-cost, commercial optometric offices including **Lenscrafters**, **Wal-Mart**, **Shopko**, and even **Kmart** have opened in your practice area. As a result, your profitability has decreased to the point where you are barely breaking even. Because of your concern for your practice, you have asked a business consultant what you should do.

She has told you that your single-minded focus on profitability is no different than that of your new commercial competitors and has convinced you that these competitors will be more successful than you in making profits because they have lower cost structures than you do. She has suggested that you read her recently published book on the Balanced Scorecard measurement system and respond to the following questions:

Required:
1. Are your current success measures mostly financial, internal processes, learning and growth, or customer focused?
2. Has your focus been on cost, quality, or time measures, or on an appropriate balance of the three?
3. Thinking about your performance perspective (financial, customer, internal processes, and learning and growth), how could you distinguish yourself from the commercial optometrists and create value for your customers?
4. Are there ways you should change your focus regarding cost, quality, and time measures?

P 23-35
LO3

Applying the Balanced Scorecard to an Internet Company

ServiceComm, Inc. is a technology company that manufactures, installs, and services cellular towers for cellular phone companies. These towers provide greater connectivity for cellular users. They are a subcontractor for tower installation companies and provide service for most of the large cellular companies. Two years ago, ServiceComm had an initial public offering (IPO) where it raised $500 million in operating capital. With that money, it built a new factory and administrative building, and developed much of the infrastructure needed to serve as the regional leader in cellular infrastructure. The company gets most of its revenue from service contracts on the towers, and not the price of the tower installation itself. In its prospectus for the IPO, ServiceComm stated that its only critical performance measure of success was the number of cellular towers under service contract. It stated that if, in two years, it has 50,000 individual towers under service contract, then it would consider itself to

(continued)

be successful. Now, two years later, there are over 100,000 towers under contract within ServiceComm's system. Unfortunately, however, ServiceComm is still losing considerable amounts of money and is experiencing serious complaints about dropped calls and signal strength.

Required:

1. What do you think about ServiceComm's "number of towers under service contract" performance measure?
2. If, in fact, ServiceComm measures its success solely on the basis of the number of towers under service contract, what important performance measures is it ignoring?

P 23-36   **Applying the Balanced Scorecard to a University**

LO3   The dean of your business school has determined that there are four major drivers of success for her business school. Those success drivers are having outstanding (1) faculty, (2) students, (3) curricula, and (4) alumni and recruiter support.

Required:

Based on these drivers of success, develop a Balanced Scorecard management system that the dean could use to evaluate the operations of her school. Be specific and indicate the purpose of each measure. Make sure that you clearly include both leading and outcome measures in your balanced scorecard.

P 23-37   **Applying the Balanced Scorecard to a Church**

LO3   As an accountant and active member of a local church, you have been asked by your pastor to help him develop a Balanced Scorecard management system for the church. He is seriously interested in continuous improvement and believes that by identifying and monitoring the right performance measurements, the church will be more successful. In discussions with the pastor, you have determined that the scorecard should focus on the following four areas:

* Increase in learning and commitment of members
* Size of congregation and membership
* Respect in the community
* Amount of financial contributions

Required:

Develop a performance measurement system for these four areas that includes both leading and outcome measures that could be used by the pastor and his church to grow and measure the success of his ecumenical efforts.

ANALYTICAL ASSIGNMENTS

AA 23-38   **Understanding the Cost of Capital**

DISCUSSION   A friend of yours is currently the president of a large company. The two of you are having lunch one day when she asks your opinion on a decision she is trying to make about how to obtain funds for her company in order to cover several years of operating losses. She works with a good company and is confident that earnings are about to turn positive. As she talks about the decision, it is clear to you that she is leaning towards selling more stock in the company rather than issuing more debt. During the conversation, she states several times that new debt requires more interest expense, but that equity is largely "free money" in the sense the dividend payout rate is much lower than the company's interest rate. Further, the dividends paid out on the new equity will not affect earnings. You decide to explain to her the concept of Economic Value Added to help her better understand the full cost of adding more invested capital assets in the organization. During a pause in the conversation, she asks you, "So, do you agree with me that selling more stock in the company is clearly the way to resolve our operating loss problem?" How do you respond?

AA 23-39
DISCUSSION

Costs of Quality (Starving Sailor Restaurant)

You are the leader of a group of investors that is planning to open a nationwide chain of seafood restaurants that you will call "Starving Sailor Restaurant." You are preparing for a strategy meeting that will be held tomorrow. The investor group is considering two strategies for how the restaurant chain will be operated. One strategy, which you have titled "Classy," proposes to market the restaurant chain as the quality leader among seafood restaurants. The restaurants will be located in good neighborhoods, will offer choice seafood selections, and will have an excellent cleanup crew. Each restaurant will also have a trained manager on site during business hours to handle customer complaints in addition to a national troubleshooting team that will promptly fly to any location to investigate consistent patterns in customer complaints received via a toll-free complaint hotline.

You have titled the other strategy "Tight Budget." The restaurants will be located wherever cheap real estate can be found, will be staffed with the lowest-cost labor possible, and will focus on offering low-cost food. There will be no mechanism for receiving customer complaints, and the store manager will not be trained in customer satisfaction.

A significant portion of the investor group advocates the "Tight Budget" strategy, arguing that it offers the lowest operating costs and, therefore, the highest profit. You are worried that these investors may not have thought carefully about all the costs associated with this strategy. Using the costs of quality (COQ) categories, outline some of the major costs that will differ between these two restaurant strategies.

AA 23-40
DISCUSSION

Strategy for Developing a Balanced Scorecard

A company is interested in developing a Balanced Scorecard approach to evaluating and enhancing its performance. It is looking at two ways of accomplishing the task. The first is for top management to develop the scorecard and impose it on managers throughout the organization. The second is to involve managers, customers, and other stakeholders in a grassroots approach to determine what cost, quality, and time factors should be measured. Which of the two approaches would you recommend to the company?

AA 23-41
DISCUSSION

How Soon Can You Make Us a Balanced Scorecard?

You are currently the controller for a large manufacturing company. The president of the company calls you to his office and states the following: "I just went to a round-table discussion with presidents of other companies, and they told me that the most important development they had made in their companies was to implement balanced scorecards. I want you to drop whatever you are doing this week and develop a balanced scorecard for our company." You are vaguely aware of the Balanced Scorecard concept from your reading, but you aren't too sure what they are all about. As you begin to think about your upcoming task, you discover that your company does not have a strategic plan or mission statement. Is it realistic that the task given you by the president one that can be accomplished in a week (or even accomplished at all)? What is the effect of not having a strategic plan or mission statement to guide the development of a balanced scorecard for the company?

AA 23-42
DISCUSSION

Get Those Business School Ratings Up!

You are the dean of the business school at North Central University. You have recently gone through a strategic planning process involving representatives from all your stakeholder groups (students, staff, faculty, recruiters, alumni, administration, etc.). The result is a newly refined strategic plan, including a mission statement, underlying values, specific objectives and strategies, and assessment outcomes (performance measurements). One of your objectives is to increase the ranking of your business school by *Business News*, a magazine that annually ranks business programs in your region. Given your understanding of the Balanced Scorecard approach and the material covered in this textbook, answer the following questions:

1. Even though it takes longer, is it wise to involve various stakeholders in developing your strategic plan? Why or why not?
2. What are some likely strategies that might be implemented to increase your business school ranking? Explain.

AA 23-43
JUDGMENT CALL

You Decide: **Can a just-in-time inventory system help companies minimize inventory costs, or is JIT too expensive and cumbersome to implement?**

Lately, you have heard a lot of talk about just-in-time inventory systems and how they help companies, like **Wal-Mart**, keep track of inventory. You know that a JIT system can help track and keep inventory costs at a minimum, but is JIT really a viable option for all companies? For example, your neighbor works at a local automobile repair shop and he is always complaining about not having the right parts on hand, which causes him to get behind on his work. He can frequently be heard saying, "We always seem to run out of parts at the wrong time. Jan does a good job at trying to keep inventory in stock, but sometimes that job can get too big. Something else needs to be done or we are going to start losing customers!" How large does a company have to be and how much inventory must it have before JIT makes sense?

AA 23-44
JUDGMENT CALL

You Decide: **Does total quality management help a company revamp and improve its business operations, or is it too much of an administrative burden that takes away from the company's primary goals?**

Over the last 20 years, there have been many new developments in the area of total quality management. Companies strive to increase profitability by improving their products and processes. However, you are still a bit skeptical. At your current place of employment, your boss has heard about TQM and tries to meet at least every six weeks to talk about what is being done in implementing TQM and what could be improved. You don't see any benefits from the meetings. Nothing that is brought up in the meetings is ever implemented. It just seems to be an opportunity to meet with your friends and have a free lunch. Are you wasting your time?

AA 23-45
JUDGMENT CALL

You Decide: **By encouraging employees to work harder and to increase quality, are companies lowering overall costs, or are they increasing waste and inefficiency of materials?**

You have just been hired to work as a part-time accountant for a small, local flower shop. Jim, the manager, feels the costs of doing business (purchasing flowers, vases, etc.) are getting too high, and he has asked you to find a solution to this problem. The shop employs two full-time workers and one part-time worker. Jim's philosophy is if you use the highest quality, you will increase business through customer loyalty. However, you have found out that Jim has given the employees permission to use whatever means necessary to ensure the flower arrangements and bouquets are made of the highest quality, even if it means wasting a lot of materials to create the best flower products possible.

AA 23-46
JUDGMENT CALL

You Decide: **Should the Balanced Scorecard concept be a "one-size fits all," or is the Balanced Scorecard more effective when it is catered to and created with an individual company in mind?**

You have been introduced to the Balanced Scorecard idea through your classes in business school. At a recent family gathering, you began talking to your Uncle Richard about what you have learned. He has been president of a regional furniture store for the last 10 years and has tried to implement a balanced scorecard in his company, but with no success. Your uncle says, "I had a college buddy e-mail me his company's scorecard as an example. He works in the real estate industry and said that it has changed the way they do business. We tried to implement his scorecard in our business, but it just didn't make sense. It might work for some companies, but it sure doesn't work for mine!"

AA 23-47
REAL COMPANY
ANAYLSIS

Wal-Mart

Use the income statement and balance sheet for **Wal-Mart** (see Appendix A) to gather the necessary information to calculate Wal-Mart's Economic Value Added (EVA®) for 2006 and 2005. Wal-Mart's weighted average cost of capital (WACC) has been estimated to be anywhere between 8% and 13%.

1. Calculate 2006 and 2005 EVA® for Wal-Mart assuming a WACC of 8%.
2. Calculate 2006 and 2005 EVA® for Wal-Mart assuming a WACC of 13%.
3. How do the two WACC values affect the EVA® calculation?

AA 23-48
REAL COMPANY
ANALYSIS

Futura Industries

Remember the last time you walked through a grocery store? Did you notice all of the shelves holding the food? If you are like most people, you probably did not pay much attention to the shelves except to take the food off of them. The aluminum parts that make up the shelves in a grocery store (and other stores) are part of a product family known as aluminum extrusions. Many aluminum extrusions are manufactured by a company in Clearfield, Utah, called **Futura Industries**. While Futura's products are not very exciting, they are pretty important. Hence, the management process at Futura is as important as it is at any other type of company, and Futura Industries has a very interesting balanced scorecard. Futura Industries began in the 1930s producing a product called colfonite. During the late 1940s, it started producing aluminum extrusions. By 1979, the Seattle, Washington-based company had moved its entire company to Clearfield, Utah. Futura's current president, Sherrie Hayashi, has chosen to pursue her company's mission (Extraordinary Value through Extrusions) by careful alignment of the company's measures and tactics. She and the rest of the management staff at Futura have developed a balanced scorecard that has proven to be very successful in helping the company to grow.

> *Strategy of Futura:*
> Futura strives to insure financial growth and prosperity by developing customer intimacy, providing flawless new products, and identifying new opportunities in products and processes. In addition, it emphasizes speed and quality in operations, planning and delivery accuracy, and continual reduction of costs. Futura is also focused on working to improve its competencies, providing a safe, challenging, and enjoyable workforce, and hiring people who have its same values.

The following is an alphabetical list of Futura's balanced scorecard measures along with a definition of each measure:

Balanced Scorecard Measure	Definition
Accuracy of price quotes	Number of correct price quotes ÷ Total price quotes issued
Average job certification levels	Total sum of job certification levels ÷ Total employees
Birthday review	Score based on yearly review on date of employee's birthday
Cash return on total assets	Cash flow ÷ Total assets
Cost of plant scrap	Dollar value of scrapped material
Cost of rework	Dollar value of rework before sale
Customer complaints	Number of complaints ÷ Total number of customers
Customer satisfaction	Periodic customer surveys
Dollar value of products packaged per person	Total dollar value of product packed ÷ Number of employees working
Employees with one year or more turnover ratio	Number of employees employed for one year or more ÷ Total number of employees
Income growth	(Current year's income − Previous year's income) ÷ Previous year's income
Leadership survey	Yearly survey score of employees
Leadership turnover	Number of new employees in leadership positions ÷ Total number of employees in leadership positions
Margins on new products and standard products	Gross profit margin on new products and on standard products
On-time deliveries	Number of on-time deliveries ÷ Total deliveries
Percent of market in commercial retailing	Number of commercial retail customers ÷ Total number of customers
Percent of market in original equipment manufacturers (OEM)	Number of OEM customers ÷ Total number of OEM customers
Percent of sales from new products	Sales revenue from new products ÷ Total sales revenue
Pounds of products packaged per person	Number of pounds packed ÷ Number of employees working

(continued)

Balanced Scorecard Measure	Definition
Product returns	Number of items returned
Total company employee turnover	Number of new employees ÷ Total number of employees
Total finished goods turnover	Total cost of finished goods sold during year ÷ Average finished goods inventory
Total inventory turnover	Total cost of goods sold during the year ÷ Average inventory
Total production cost per direct labor hour	Total cost of production ÷ Total direct labor hours

Classify Futura's balanced scorecard measures into the four Balanced Scorecard categories: financial measures, customer measures, internal process measures, and learning and growth measures. Use Futura's strategy to help you determine how to classify each measure.

AA 23-49

INTERNATIONAL

Deming in Japan

As noted in this chapter, the ideas of W. Edward Deming received little attention in the United States in the late 1940s and early 1950s. Deming then moved to Japan where his ideas were accepted and implemented almost immediately. The result was that industries in Japan, such as automobile production, quickly developed a reputation for producing quality products. In the 1980s, the United States found itself trying to catch up to Japan in the race for quality products. Can you speculate as to why Deming's ideas were not readily accepted in the United States, yet were quickly adopted in Japan? To answer this question, you may need to recall your world history during the 1940s.

AA 23-50

ETHICS

"Family" Business

Martin Beemer is the purchasing manager for the police department in a large metropolitan city. The city has 13,000 police officers. The city currently purchases police uniforms from three different manufacturers, one of which is SunKing, International (a Korean company). Martin recently agreed (in private) with SunKing's vice president to give SunKing increased business if SunKing would hire his daughter as a "ghost" salesperson in the United States at a salary of $350,000 per year.

1. Do you believe the actions of Martin and SunKing are unethical? Fraudulent?
2. What internal process performance measures could the city have had in place in the purchasing department that could have revealed the kickback arrangement?

AA 23-51

WRITING

More Than Just the Numbers

You have found in your study of accounting that accountants generally focus on the numbers. Their job is to summarize financial results and provide information for decision makers. In this chapter, you have read about additional measures that are critical to a company's success: items like customer loyalty and satisfaction and employee productivity. Your assignment is to prepare a one- to two-page memo summarizing the following points:

1. Select an internal process measure, like research and development, and map out how the careful monitoring of that process will eventually show up in a financial measure like ROI.
2. Are accountants the best people to collect information on items such as customer satisfaction and customer loyalty? If not, who in a business would be best suited to collect this type of information?

Management's Discussion and Analysis of Results of Operations and Financial Condition
WAL-MART

Overview

Wal-Mart Stores, Inc. ("Wal-Mart" or the "Company") is a global retailer committed to improving the standard of living for our customers throughout the world. We earn the trust of our customers every day by providing a broad assortment of quality merchandise and services at every day low prices ("EDLP") while fostering a culture that rewards and embraces mutual respect, integrity and diversity. EDLP is our pricing philosophy under which we price items at a low price every day so that our customers trust that our prices will not change erratically under frequent promotional activity. Our focus for SAM'S CLUB is to provide exceptional value on brand-name merchandise at "members only" prices for both business and personal use. Internationally, we operate with similar philosophies. Our fiscal year ends on January 31.

We intend for this discussion to provide the reader with information that will assist in understanding our financial statements, the changes in certain key items in those financial statements from year to year, and the primary factors that accounted for those changes, as well as how certain accounting principles affect our financial statements. The discussion also provides information about the financial results of the various segments of our business to provide a better understanding of how those segments and their results affect the financial condition and results of operations of the Company as a whole. This discussion should be read in conjunction with our financial statements and accompanying notes as of January 31, 2006, and the year then ended.

Throughout this Management's Discussion and Analysis of Results of Operations and Financial Condition, we discuss segment operating income and comparative store sales. Segment operating income refers to income from continuing operations before net interest expense, income taxes and minority interest. Segment operating income does not include unallocated corporate overhead. Comparative store sales is a measure which indicates the performance of our existing stores by measuring the growth in sales for such stores for a particular period over the corresponding period in the prior year. For fiscal 2006 and prior years, we considered comparative store sales to be sales at stores that were open as of February 1st of the prior fiscal year and had not been expanded or relocated since that date. Stores that were expanded or relocated during that period are not included in the calculation. Comparative store sales is also referred to as "same-store" sales by others within the retail industry. The method of calculating comparative store sales varies across the retail industry. As a result, our calculation of comparative store sales is not necessarily comparable to similarly titled measures reported by other companies. Beginning in fiscal 2007, we changed our method of calculating comparative store sales. These changes are described in our Current Report on Form 8-K that we furnished to the SEC on February 2, 2006.

On May 23, 2003, we consummated the sale of McLane Company, Inc. ("McLane"), one of our wholly-owned subsidiaries, for $1.5 billion. As a result of this sale, we classified McLane as a discontinued operation in the financial statements for fiscal 2004. McLane's external sales prior to the divestiture were $4.3 billion in fiscal 2004. McLane continues to be a supplier to the Company.

Operations

Our operations are comprised of three business segments: Wal-Mart Stores, SAM'S CLUB and International.

Our Wal-Mart Stores segment is the largest segment of our business, accounting for approximately 67.2% of our fiscal 2006 net sales. This segment consists of three traditional retail formats, all of which are located in the United States, and Wal-Mart's online retail format, Walmart.com. Our traditional Wal-Mart Stores retail formats include:

- Supercenters, which average approximately 187,000 square feet in size and offer a wide assortment of general merchandise and a full-line supermarket;
- Discount stores, which average approximately 102,000 square feet in size and offer a wide assortment of general merchandise and a limited assortment of food products; and
- Neighborhood Markets, which average approximately 42,000 square feet in size and offer a full-line supermarket and a limited assortment of general merchandise.

Our SAM'S CLUB segment consists of membership warehouse clubs in the United States and the segment's online retail format, samsclub.com. SAM'S CLUB accounted for approximately 12.7% of our fiscal 2006 sales. Our SAM'S CLUBs in the United States average approximately 129,000 square feet in size.

As of January 31, 2006, our International operations were located in nine countries and Puerto Rico. Internationally, we generated approximately 20.1% of our fiscal 2006 sales. Outside the United States, we operate several different formats of retail stores and restaurants, including supercenters, discount stores and SAM'S CLUBs. Additionally, at January 31, 2006, we owned an unconsolidated 33.3% minority interest in Central American Retail Holding Company ("CARHCO"), a retailer operating in five Central American countries. In February 2006, we acquired a controlling interest in CARHCO.

The Retail Industry

We operate in the highly competitive retail industry in both the United States and abroad. We face strong sales competition from other discount, department, drug, variety and specialty stores and supermarkets, many of which are national chains. Additionally, we compete with a number of companies for prime retail site locations, as well as in attracting and retaining quality employees ("associates"). We, along with other retail companies, are influenced by a number of factors including, but not limited to: cost of goods, consumer debt levels, economic conditions, interest rates, customer preferences, employment, labor costs, inflation, currency exchange fluctuations, fuel prices, weather patterns and insurance costs. Our SAM'S CLUB segment faces strong sales competition from other wholesale club operators, as well as other retailers. Further information on risks to our Company can be located in Item 1A, Risk Factors, in our Annual Report on Form 10-K for the year ended January 31, 2006.

Management's Discussion and Analysis of Results of Operations and Financial Condition
WAL-MART

Key Items in Fiscal 2006

Significant financial items during fiscal 2006 include:

- Net sales increased 9.5% from fiscal 2005 to $312.4 billion in fiscal 2006, and net income increased 9.4% to $11.2 billion. Foreign currency exchange rates favorably impacted sales and operating income by $1.5 billion and $64 million, respectively, in fiscal 2006.
- Net cash provided by operating activities was $17.6 billion for fiscal 2006. During fiscal 2006, we repurchased $3.6 billion of our common stock under our share repurchase program and paid dividends of $2.5 billion. Additionally during fiscal 2006, we issued $7.7 billion in long-term debt, repaid $2.7 billion of long-term debt and funded a net decrease in commercial paper of $704 million.
- Total assets increased 15.0%, to $138.2 billion at January 31, 2006, when compared to January 31, 2005. During fiscal 2006, we made $14.6 billion of capital expenditures which was an increase of 13.0% over capital expenditures of $12.9 billion in fiscal 2005.
- When compared to fiscal 2005, our Wal-Mart Stores segment experienced an 8.2% increase in operating income and a 9.4% increase in net sales in fiscal 2006.
- SAM'S CLUB's continued focus on our business members helped drive an 8.2% increase in operating income on a 7.2% increase in net sales when comparing fiscal 2006 with fiscal 2005.
- Our International segment generated a net sales and operating income increase of 11.4% compared to fiscal 2005.

Company Performance Measures

Management uses a number of metrics to assess the Company's performance. The following are the more frequently used metrics:

- Comparative store sales is a measure which indicates the performance of our existing stores by measuring the growth in sales for such stores for a particular period over the corresponding period in the prior year. Our Wal-Mart Stores segment's comparative store sales were 3.0% for fiscal 2006 versus 2.9% for fiscal 2005. Our SAM'S CLUB segment's comparative club sales were 5.0% in fiscal 2006 versus 5.8% in fiscal 2005.
- Operating income growth greater than net sales growth has long been a measure of success for us. For fiscal 2006, our operating income increased by 8.4% when compared to fiscal 2005, while net sales increased by 9.5% over the same period. Our SAM'S CLUB segment met this target; however, the Wal-Mart Stores segment fell short of the target, while the International segment grew operating income at the same rate as net sales.
- Inventory growth at a rate less than that of net sales is a key measure of our efficiency. However, our increased purchases of imported merchandise and recent acquisition activity impact this measure. Total inventories at January 31, 2006, were up 8.2% over levels at January 31, 2005, and net sales were up 9.5% when comparing fiscal 2006 with fiscal 2005. Approximately 150 basis points of the fiscal 2006 increase in inventory was from increased levels of imported merchandise, which carries a longer lead time, and an additional 170 basis points was from the consolidation of The Seiyu, Ltd. and the purchase of Sonae Distribuição Brasil S.A.
- With an asset base as large as ours, we are focused on continuing to make certain our assets are productive. It is important for us to sustain our return on assets. Return on assets is defined as income from continuing operations before minority interest divided by average total assets. Return on assets for fiscal 2006, 2005 and 2004 was 8.9%, 9.3% and 9.2%, respectively. Return on assets in fiscal 2006 was impacted by acquisition activity in the fourth quarter.

Results of Operations

The Company and each of its operating segments had net sales (in millions), as follows:

Fiscal Year Ended January 31,	2006			2005			2004	
	Net sales	Percent of total	Percent increase	Net sales	Percent of total	Percent increase	Net sales	Percent of total
Wal-Mart Stores	$209,910	67.2%	9.4%	$191,826	67.3%	10.1%	$174,220	68.0%
SAM'S CLUB	39,798	12.7%	7.2%	37,119	13.0%	7.5%	34,537	13.5%
International	62,719	20.1%	11.4%	56,277	19.7%	18.3%	47,572	18.5%
Total net sales	$312,427	100.0%	9.5%	$285,222	100.0%	11.3%	$256,329	100.0%

Our total net sales increased by 9.5% and 11.3% in fiscal 2006 and 2005 when compared to the previous fiscal year. Those increases resulted from our expansion programs and comparative store sales increases in the United States. Comparative store sales increased 3.4% in fiscal 2006 and 3.3% in fiscal 2005. As we continue to add new stores in the United States, we do so with an understanding that additional stores may take sales away from existing units. We estimate that comparative store sales in fiscal 2006, 2005 and 2004 were negatively impacted by the opening of new stores by approximately 1% per year. We expect that this effect of opening new stores on comparable store sales will continue during fiscal 2007 at a similar rate.

During fiscal 2006 and 2005, foreign currency exchange rates had a $1.5 billion and $3.2 billion favorable impact, respectively, on the International segment's net sales, causing an increase in the International segment's net sales as a percentage of total net sales relative to the Wal-Mart Stores and SAM'S CLUB segments. Additionally, the decrease in the SAM'S CLUB segment's net sales as a percent of total Company sales in fiscal 2006 and 2005 when compared to the previous fiscal years resulted from the more rapid development of new stores in the International and Wal-Mart Stores segments than the SAM'S CLUB segment. We expect this trend to continue for the foreseeable future.

Our total gross profit as a percentage of net sales (our "gross margin") was 23.1%, 22.9% and 22.5% in fiscal 2006, 2005 and 2004, respectively. Our Wal-Mart Stores and International segment sales yield higher gross margins than our SAM'S CLUB segment. Accordingly, the greater increases in net sales for the Wal-Mart Stores and International segments in fiscal 2006 and 2005 had a favorable impact on the Company's total gross margin.

Operating, selling, general and administrative expenses ("operating expenses") as a percentage of net sales were 18.2%, 17.9% and 17.5% for fiscal 2006, 2005 and 2004, respectively. The increase in operating expenses as a percentage of total net sales was primarily due to a faster rate of growth in operating expenses in our Wal-Mart Stores and International segments, which have higher operating expenses as a percentage of segment net sales than our SAM'S CLUB segment. Operating expenses in fiscal 2006 were higher as a percentage of net sales because of increases in utilities, maintenance and repairs and advertising. Increases in these expenses in fiscal 2006 were partially offset by reduced payroll costs as a percentage of net sales. Operating expenses in fiscal 2005 were impacted by the Wal-Mart Stores and SAM'S CLUB segments' implementation of a new job classification and pay structure for hourly field associates in the United States. The job classification and pay structure, which was implemented in the second quarter of fiscal 2005, was designed to help maintain internal equity and external competitiveness.

Operating expenses in fiscal 2004 were impacted by the adoption of Emerging Issues Task Force Issue No. 02-16, "Accounting by a Reseller for Cash Consideration Received from a Vendor" ("EITF 02-16"). The adoption of EITF 02-16 resulted in an after-tax reduction in fiscal 2004 net income of approximately $140 million.

Interest, net, as a percentage of net sales increased from fiscal 2004 through fiscal 2006. The increase was due to higher borrowing levels and higher interest rates during the period from fiscal 2004 through fiscal 2006. The $186-million increase in interest, net, in fiscal 2006 consisted of a $221-million increase due to higher borrowing levels and $99 million due to higher interest rates, partially offset by a benefit from refund of IRS interest paid, reversal of interest on income tax accruals for prior years, and reduced levels of interest on fiscal 2006 income tax accruals. The $154-million increase in interest, net, in fiscal 2005 consisted of a $139-million increase due to higher borrowing levels, a $26-million decrease due to changing interest rates and a $41-million increase in interest on income tax accruals.

Our effective income tax rates for fiscal 2006, 2005 and 2004 were 33.4%, 34.7% and 36.1%, respectively. The fiscal 2006 rate was less than the fiscal 2005 rate due primarily to adjustments in deferred income taxes and resolutions of certain federal and state tax contingencies. The fiscal 2005 rate was less than the fiscal 2004 rate due to the October 2004 passage of the Working Families Tax-Relief Act of 2004, which retroactively extended the work opportunity tax credit for fiscal 2005. In addition, the fiscal 2004 effective tax rate was impacted by an increase in the deferred tax asset valuation allowance as a result of tax legislation in Germany. This legislation required us to reevaluate the recoverability of deferred tax assets in Germany, resulting in a $150 million increase in the fiscal 2004 provision for income taxes.

In fiscal 2006, we earned net income of $11.2 billion, a 9.4% increase over fiscal 2005. In fiscal 2005, we earned income from continuing operations of $10.3 billion, a 15.9% increase over fiscal 2004. Net income in fiscal 2005 increased 13.4% from fiscal 2004 largely as a result of the increase in income from continuing operations described above, net of the $193 million provided from the discontinued operations and sale of McLane in fiscal 2004.

Wal-Mart Stores Segment

Fiscal Year	Segment Net Sales Increase from Prior Fiscal Year	Segment Operating Income (in millions)	Segment Operating Income Increase from Prior Fiscal Year	Operating Income as a Percentage of Segment Sales
2006	**9.4%**	**$15,324**	**8.2%**	**7.3%**
2005	10.1%	14,163	9.7%	7.4%
2004	10.9%	12,916	9.1%	7.4%

The segment net sales increases in fiscal 2006 and fiscal 2005 from the prior fiscal years resulted from comparative store sales increases of 3.0% in fiscal 2006 and 2.9% in fiscal 2005, in addition to our expansion program. Market development strategies in fiscal 2006 continued to put pressures on comparative stores sales increases as new stores were opened within the trade area of established stores. We have developed several initiatives to help mitigate this pressure and to grow comparable store sales through becoming more relevant to the customer by creating a better store shopping experience, continual improvement in product assortment and an aggressive store upgrade program to be instituted over the next 18 months.

Management's Discussion and Analysis of Results of Operations and Financial Condition
WAL-MART

Our expansion programs consist of opening new units, converting discount stores to supercenters, relocations that result in more square footage, as well as expansions of existing stores. Segment expansion during fiscal 2006 included the opening of 24 discount stores, 15 Neighborhood Markets and 267 supercenters (including the conversion and/or relocation of 166 existing discount stores into supercenters). Two discount stores closed in fiscal 2006. During fiscal 2006, our total expansion program added approximately 39 million of store square footage, an 8.6% increase. Segment expansion during fiscal 2005 included the opening of 36 discount stores, 21 Neighborhood Markets and 242 supercenters (including the conversion and/or relocation of 159 existing discount stores into supercenters). Two discount stores closed in fiscal 2005. During fiscal 2005, our total expansion program added approximately 36 million of store square footage, an 8.6% increase.

Fiscal 2006 segment operating income was down 0.1% as a percentage of segment net sales. This decrease was driven by a 4 basis point decline in gross margin and an 8 basis point increase in operating expenses, partially offset by a slight increase in other income as a percentage of segment net sales. This gross margin decrease from

fiscal 2005 can be attributed to the continued increase in sales of our lower-margin food items as a percentage of total segment net sales, rising transportation costs, and the unfavorable impact of an adjustment to our product warranty liabilities in fiscal 2006. The segment's operating expenses as a percentage of segment net sales in fiscal 2006 were higher than fiscal 2005 primarily due to expense pressures from utilities and advertising costs.

While our fiscal 2005 segment operating income as a percentage of segment net sales was unchanged from fiscal 2004, segment gross margin and operating expenses as a percentage of segment net sales were each up 0.4% for the year. Our gross margin improvement in fiscal 2005 can be primarily attributed to our global sourcing effort and reductions in markdowns and shrinkage as a percentage of segment net sales for fiscal 2005 when compared to fiscal 2004. The segment's operating expenses in fiscal 2005 as a percentage of segment net sales were higher than fiscal 2004 primarily due to expense pressures from associate wages and accident costs. Wages primarily increased due to our new job classification and pay structure, which was implemented in the second quarter of fiscal 2005.

SAM'S CLUB Segment

Fiscal Year	Segment Net Sales Increase from Prior Fiscal Year	Segment Operating Income (in millions)	Segment Operating Income Increase from Prior Fiscal Year	Operating Income as a Percentage of Segment Sales
2006	**7.2%**	**$1,385**	**8.2%**	**3.5%**
2005	7.5%	1,280	13.7%	3.4%
2004	8.9%	1,126	10.1%	3.3%

Growth in net sales for the SAM'S CLUB segment in fiscal 2006 and fiscal 2005 resulted from comparative club sales increases of 5.0% in fiscal 2006 and 5.8% in fiscal 2005, along with our expansion program. Comparative club sales in fiscal 2006 increased at a slower rate than in fiscal 2005 primarily due to lower growth rates in certain fresh and hardline categories. The impact of fuel sales contributed 130 basis points and 121 basis points to fiscal 2006 and 2005 comparative club sales, respectively. We believe that a greater focus on providing a quality in-club experience for our members will improve overall sales, including sales in these categories. Segment expansion consisted of the opening of 17 new clubs in fiscal 2006 and 13 clubs in fiscal 2005. One club closed in fiscal 2006. Our total expansion program added approximately 3 million of additional club square footage, or 3.8%, in fiscal 2006 and approximately 3 million, or 3.7%, of additional club square footage in fiscal 2005.

Segment operating income as a percentage of segment net sales increased slightly in fiscal 2006 when compared to fiscal 2005. The increase was due to an improvement in operating expenses and other income as a percentage of segment net sales, partially offset by a slight decrease in gross margin as a percentage of segment net sales. Operating expenses as a percentage of segment net sales improved primarily due to lower wage and accident costs in fiscal 2006 when

compared to fiscal 2005, partially offset by the impact of increased utility costs. The increase in other income as a percentage of segment net sales was primarily the result of income recognized from higher membership sales in fiscal 2006. Gross margin as a percentage of net sales decreased due to strong sales in certain lower margin categories, including fuel and tobacco, during fiscal 2006.

Segment operating income as a percentage of segment net sales increased slightly in fiscal 2005 when compared to fiscal 2004 due to an improvement in gross margin, partially offset by an increase in operating expenses as a percentage of segment net sales and the impact of the adoption of EITF 02-16 in fiscal 2004. The improvement in gross margin was primarily a result of strong sales in higher margin categories. Operating expenses as a percentage of segment net sales increased due to higher wage costs resulting from our new job classification and pay structure, which was implemented in the second quarter of fiscal 2005. The adoption of EITF 02-16 resulted in a decrease to the segment's operating income in fiscal 2004 of $44 million.

International Segment

Fiscal Year	Segment Net Sales Increase from Prior Fiscal Year	Segment Operating Income (in millions)	Segment Operating Income Increase from Prior Fiscal Year	Operating Income as a Percentage of Segment Sales
2006	**11.4%**	**$3,330**	**11.4%**	**5.3%**
2005	18.3%	2,988	26.1%	5.3%
2004	16.6%	2,370	18.6%	5.0%

At January 31, 2006, our International segment was comprised of wholly-owned operations in Argentina, Brazil, Canada, Germany, South Korea, Puerto Rico and the United Kingdom, the operation of joint ventures in China and the operations of majority-owned subsidiaries in Japan and Mexico.

The fiscal 2006 increase in the International segment's net sales primarily resulted from improved operating execution, our international expansion program and the impact of changes in foreign currency exchange rates. In fiscal 2006, the International segment opened 698 units, net of relocations and closings, which added 52 million, or 39.2%, of additional unit square footage. This includes the acquisition of Sonae Distribuição Brasil S.A. ("Sonae") in Southern Brazil, which added 139 stores and 11 million square feet in December 2005, and the consolidation of The Seiyu, Ltd. in Japan, which added 398 stores and 29 million square feet in December 2005. Additionally, the impact of changes in foreign currency exchange rates favorably affected the translation of International segment sales into U.S. dollars by an aggregate of $1.5 billion in fiscal 2006.

The fiscal 2005 increase in the International segment's net sales primarily resulted from improved operating execution, our international expansion program and the impact of foreign currency exchange rate changes. In fiscal 2005, the International segment opened 232 units, net of relocations and closings, which added 18 million, or 15.6%, of additional unit square footage. This includes the acquisition of Bompreço S.A. Supermercados do Nordeste in Brazil, which added 118 stores and approximately 8 million square feet in February 2004. Additionally, the impact of changes in foreign currency exchange rates favorably affected the translation of International segment sales into U.S. dollars by an aggregate of $3.2 billion in fiscal 2005.

Fiscal 2006 sales at our United Kingdom subsidiary, ASDA, were 42.7% of the International segment net sales. Sales for ASDA included in our consolidated income statement during fiscal 2006, 2005, and 2004 were $26.8 billion, $26.0 billion, and $21.7 billion, respectively.

While fiscal 2006 International segment operating income as a percentage of segment net sales was unchanged from fiscal 2005, segment gross margin was up 0.5%. This improvement in segment gross margin was offset by an increase in operating expenses and a decrease in other income, both as a percentage of segment net sales. The International segment's improvement in gross margin is primarily due to a favorable shift in the mix of products sold toward general merchandise categories which carry a higher margin. The 0.3% increase in operating expenses was driven primarily by increased advertising, utility and insurance expenditures. Other income declined 0.2% in fiscal 2006 primarily due to a reduction

in current year rental income in Canada and a payroll tax recovery in Mexico in fiscal 2005. Fiscal 2006 operating income includes a favorable impact of $64 million from changes in foreign currency exchange rates.

The fiscal 2005 increase in segment operating income as a percentage of segment net sales compared with fiscal 2004 resulted primarily from a 0.3% improvement in gross margin. The improvement in gross margin was due to a favorable shift in the mix of products sold toward general merchandise categories. Fiscal 2005 operating income includes a favorable impact of $150 million from changes in foreign currency exchange rates.

Future financial results for our foreign operations could be affected by factors such as changes in foreign currency exchange rates, weak economic conditions, changes in tax law and government regulations in the foreign markets in which we operate.

Liquidity and Capital Resources

Overview

Cash flows provided by operating activities supply us with a significant source of liquidity. Our cash flows from operating activities were $17.6 billion in fiscal 2006 compared with $15.0 billion in fiscal 2005. The increase in cash flows provided by operating activities was primarily attributable to improved income from operations and improved inventory management resulting in accounts payable growing at a faster rate than inventory.

Our cash flows from operating activities of continuing operations were $15.0 billion in fiscal 2005, compared with $15.9 billion in fiscal 2004. This decrease was primarily attributable to differences in the timing of payroll, income and other taxes, supplier payments and the timing of the collection of receivables in fiscal 2005 compared with fiscal 2004.

In fiscal 2006, we paid dividends of $2.5 billion, made $14.6 billion in capital expenditures, paid $3.6 billion to repurchase shares of our common stock, received $7.7 billion from the issuance of long-term debt, repaid $2.7 billion of long-term debt and repaid $704 million of commercial paper (net of issuances).

Working Capital

Current liabilities exceeded current assets at January 31, 2006, by $5.0 billion, an increase of $622 million from January 31, 2005. Our ratio of current assets to current liabilities was 0.9 to 1 at January 31, 2006 and 2005. At January 31, 2006, we had total assets of $138.2 billion compared with total assets of $120.2 billion at January 31, 2005.

Management's Discussion and Analysis of Results of Operations and Financial Condition
WAL-MART

Company Share Repurchase Program

From time to time, we repurchase shares of our common stock under a $10.0 billion share repurchase program authorized by our Board of Directors in September 2004. During the first half of fiscal 2006, we repurchased $3.6 billion of shares under this repurchase program. No shares of our common stock were repurchased under this program in the third or fourth quarters of fiscal 2006. During fiscal 2005, we repurchased $4.5 billion of shares under the current and past authorizations. At January 31, 2006, approximately $6.1 billion of additional shares may be repurchased under the current authorization.

There is no expiration date for or other restriction limiting the period over which we can make our share repurchases under the program, which will expire only when and if we have repurchased $10.0 billion of our shares under the program. Under the program, repurchased shares are constructively retired and returned to unissued status. We consider several factors in determining when to make share repurchases, including among other things, our current cash needs, the ratio of our debt to our total capitalization, our cost of borrowings, and the market price of the stock.

Common Stock Dividends

We paid dividends totaling approximately $2.5 billion or $0.60 per share in fiscal 2006. The dividends paid in fiscal 2006 represent a 15.4% increase over fiscal 2005. The fiscal 2005 dividend of $0.52 per share represented a 44.4% increase over fiscal 2004. We have increased our dividend every year since the first dividend was declared in March 1974.

On March 2, 2006, the Company's Board of Directors approved an increase in annual dividends to $0.67 per share. The annual dividend will be paid in four quarterly installments on April 3, 2006, June 5, 2006, September 5, 2006, and January 2, 2007 to holders of record on March 17, May 19, August 18 and December 15, 2006, respectively.

Contractual Obligations and Other Commercial Commitments

The following table sets forth certain information concerning our obligations and commitments to make contractual future payments, such as debt and lease agreements, and contingent commitments:

		Payments due during fiscal years ending January 31,			
(In millions)	Total	2007	2008-2009	2010-2011	Thereafter
Recorded Contractual Obligations					
Long-term debt	$31,024	$ 4,595	$ 6,178	$ 7,516	$ 12,735
Commercial paper	3,754	3,754	–	–	–
Capital lease obligations	6,380	592	1,138	1,040	3,610
Unrecorded Contractual Obligations:					
Non-cancelable operating leases	9,683	797	1,461	1,220	6,205
Interest on long-term debt	14,823	1,419	2,374	1,848	9,182
Undrawn lines of credit	5,296	5,296	–	–	–
Trade letters of credit	2,593	2,593	–	–	–
Standby letters of credit	2,800	2,800	–	–	–
Purchase obligations	19,872	10,519	9,023	218	112
Total commercial commitments	$96,225	$32,365	$20,174·	$11,842	$31,844

Purchase obligations include all legally binding contracts such as firm commitments for inventory purchases, utility purchases, as well as commitments to make capital expenditures, software acquisition/license commitments and legally binding service contracts. Purchase orders for the purchase of inventory and other services are not included in the table above. Purchase orders represent authorizations to purchase rather than binding agreements. For the purposes of this table, contractual obligations for purchase of goods or services are defined as agreements that are enforceable and legally binding and that specify all significant terms, including: fixed or minimum quantities to be purchased; fixed, minimum or variable price provisions; and the approximate timing of the transaction. Our purchase orders are based on our current inventory needs and are fulfilled by our suppliers within short time periods. We also enter into contracts for outsourced services; however, the obligations under these contracts are not significant and the contracts generally contain clauses allowing for cancellation without significant penalty.

The expected timing for payment of the obligations discussed above is estimated based on current information. Timing of payments and actual amounts paid may be different depending on the timing of receipt of goods or services or changes to agreed-upon amounts for some obligations.

Off Balance Sheet Arrangements

In addition to the unrecorded contractual obligations discussed and presented above, the Company has made certain guarantees as discussed below for which the timing of payment, if any, is unknown.

In connection with certain debt financing, we could be liable for early termination payments if certain unlikely events were to occur. At January 31, 2006, the aggregate termination payment was $89 million. These two arrangements expire in fiscal 2011 and fiscal 2019.

In connection with the development of our grocery distribution network in the United States, we have agreements with third parties which would require us to purchase or assume the leases on certain unique equipment in the event the agreements are terminated. These agreements, which can be terminated by either party at will, cover up to a five-year period and obligate the Company to pay up to approximately $233 million upon termination of some or all of these agreements.

There are no recourse provisions which would enable us to recover from third parties any amounts paid under the above guarantees. No liability for these guarantees has been recorded in our financial statements.

The Company has entered into lease commitments for land and buildings for 60 future locations. These lease commitments with real estate developers provide for minimum rentals ranging from five to 35 years, which, if consummated based on current cost estimates, will approximate $95 million annually over the lease terms.

Capital Resources

During fiscal 2006, we issued $7.7 billion of long-term debt. The net proceeds from the issuance of such long-term debt were used to repay outstanding commercial paper indebtedness and for other general corporate purposes.

At January 31, 2006 and 2005, the ratio of our debt to our total capitalization was 42% and 39%, respectively. The fiscal 2006 consolidation of Seiyu and purchase of Sonae increased our debt to total capitalization at January 31, 2006, by 2.5 percentage points. Our objective is to maintain a debt to total capitalization ratio averaging approximately 40%.

Management believes that cash flows from operations and proceeds from the sale of commercial paper will be sufficient to finance any seasonal buildups in merchandise inventories and meet other cash requirements. If our operating cash flows are not sufficient to pay dividends and to fund our capital expenditures, we anticipate funding any shortfall in these expenditures with a combination of commercial paper and long-term debt. We plan to refinance existing long-term debt as it matures and may desire to obtain additional long-term financing for other corporate purposes. We anticipate no difficulty in obtaining long-term financing in view of our credit rating and favorable experiences in the debt market in the recent past. The following table details the ratings of the credit rating agencies that rated our outstanding indebtedness at January 31, 2006.

Rating agency	Commercial paper	Long-term debt
Standard and Poor's	A-1+	AA
Moody's Investors Service	P-1	Aa2
Fitch Ratings	F1+	AA
Dominion Bond Rating Service	R-1 (middle)	AA

In February 2006, we entered into a £150 million revolving credit facility in the United Kingdom. Interest on borrowings under the credit facility accrues at LIBOR plus 25 basis points.

Future Expansion

Capital expenditures for fiscal 2007 are expected to be approximately $17.5 billion, including additions of capital leases. These fiscal 2007 expenditures will include the construction of 20 to 30 new discount stores, 270 to 280 new supercenters (with relocations or expansions accounting for approximately 160 of those supercenters), 15 to 20 new Neighborhood Markets, 30 to 40 new SAM'S CLUBs (with relocations or expansions accounting for 20 of those SAM'S CLUBs) and 220 to 230 new units in our International segment (with relocations or expansions accounting for approximately 35 of those units). We plan to finance this expansion, and any acquisitions of other operations that we may make during fiscal 2007, primarily out of cash flows from operations.

Market Risk

In addition to the risks inherent in our operations, we are exposed to certain market risks, including changes in interest rates and changes in foreign currency exchange rates.

The analysis presented for each of our market risk sensitive instruments is based on a 10% change in interest or foreign currency exchange rates. These changes are hypothetical scenarios used to calibrate potential risk and do not represent our view of future market changes. As the hypothetical figures indicate, changes in fair value based on the assumed change in rates generally cannot be extrapolated because the relationship of the change in assumption to the change in fair value may not be linear. The effect of a variation in a particular assumption is calculated without changing any other assumption. In reality, changes in one factor may result in changes in another, which may magnify or counteract the sensitivities.

At January 31, 2006 and 2005, we had $31.0 billion and $23.8 billion, respectively, of long-term debt outstanding. Our weighted average effective interest rate on long-term debt, after considering the effect of interest rate swaps, was 4.79% and 4.08% at January 31, 2006 and 2005, respectively. A hypothetical 10% increase in interest rates in effect at January 31, 2006 and 2005, would have increased annual interest expense on borrowings outstanding at those dates by $48 million and $25 million, respectively.

At January 31, 2006 and 2005, we had $3.8 billion of outstanding commercial paper obligations. The rate, including fees, on these obligations at January 31, 2006 and 2005, was 3.9% and 2.9%, respectively. A hypothetical 10% increase in commercial paper rates in effect at January 31, 2006 and 2005, would have increased annual interest expense on the outstanding balances on those dates by $14 million and $11 million, respectively.

Management's Discussion and Analysis of Results of Operations and Financial Condition
WAL-MART

We enter into interest rate swaps to minimize the risks and costs associated with financing activities, as well as to maintain an appropriate mix of fixed- and floating-rate debt. Our preference is to maintain approximately 50% of our debt portfolio, including interest rate swaps, in floating-rate debt. The swap agreements are contracts to exchange fixed- or variable-rates for variable- or fixed-interest rate payments periodically over the life of the instruments. The aggregate fair value of these swaps was a gain of approximately $133 million and $472 million at January 31, 2006 and 2005, respectively. A hypothetical increase (or decrease) of 10% in interest rates from the level in effect at January 31, 2006, would result in a (loss) or gain in value of the swaps of ($103 million) or $104 million, respectively. A hypothetical increase (or decrease) of 10% in interest rates from the level in effect at January 31, 2005, would result in a (loss) or gain in value of the swaps of ($123 million) or $126 million, respectively.

We hold currency swaps to hedge the foreign currency exchange component of our net investments in the United Kingdom and Japan. In addition, we hold a cross-currency swap which hedges the foreign currency risk of debt denominated in currencies other than the local currency. The aggregate fair value of these swaps at January 31, 2006 and 2005, was a loss of $244 million and $169 million, respectively. A hypothetical 10% increase (or decrease) in the foreign currency exchange rates underlying these swaps from the market rate would result in a (loss) or gain in the value of the swaps of ($96 million) and $78 million at January 31, 2006, and ($90 million) and $71 million at January 31, 2005. A hypothetical 10% change in interest rates underlying these swaps from the market rates in effect at January 31, 2006 and 2005, would have an insignificant impact on the value of the swaps.

In addition to currency swaps, we have designated debt of approximately £2.0 billion as of January 31, 2006 and 2005, as a hedge of our net investment in the United Kingdom. At January 31, 2006, a hypothetical 10% increase (or decrease) in value of the U.S. dollar relative to the British pound would result in a gain (or loss) in the value of the debt of $359 million. At January 31, 2005, a hypothetical 10% increase (or decrease) in value of the U.S. dollar relative to the British pound would result in a gain (or loss) in the value of the debt of $380 million. In addition, we have designated debt of approximately ¥87.1 billion as of January 31, 2006 as a hedge of our net investment in Japan. At January 31, 2006, a hypothetical 10% increase (or decrease) in value of the U.S. dollar relative to the Japanese yen would result in a gain (or loss) in the value of the debt of $75 million.

Summary of Critical Accounting Policies
Management strives to report the financial results of the Company in a clear and understandable manner, although in some cases accounting and disclosure rules are complex and require us to use technical terminology. In preparing our consolidated financial statements, we follow accounting principles generally accepted in the United States. These principles require us to make certain estimates and apply judgments that affect our financial position and results of operations as reflected in our financial statements. These judgments and estimates are based on past events and expectations of future outcomes. Actual results may differ from our estimates.

Management continually reviews its accounting policies, how they are applied and how they are reported and disclosed in our financial statements. Following is a summary of our more significant accounting policies and how they are applied in preparation of the financial statements.

Inventories
We value our inventories at the lower of cost or market as determined primarily by the retail method of accounting, using the last-in, first-out ("LIFO") method for substantially all merchandise inventories in the United States, except SAM'S CLUB merchandise and merchandise in our distribution warehouses, which is based on the cost LIFO method. Inventories for international operations are primarily valued by the retail method of accounting and are stated using the first-in, first-out ("FIFO") method.

Under the retail method, inventory is stated at cost, which is determined by applying a cost-to-retail ratio to each merchandise grouping's retail value. The cost-to-retail ratio is based on the fiscal year purchase activity. The retail method requires management to make certain judgments and estimates that may significantly impact the ending inventory valuation at cost as well as the amount of gross margin recognized. Judgments made include the recording of markdowns used to sell through inventory and shrinkage. Markdowns designated for clearance activity are recorded at the time of the decision rather than at the point of sale, when management determines the salability of inventory has diminished. Factors considered in the determination of markdowns include current and anticipated demand, customer preferences and age of merchandise, as well as seasonal and fashion trends. Changes in weather patterns and customer preferences related to fashion trends could cause material changes in the amount and timing of markdowns from year to year.

When necessary, the Company records a LIFO provision each quarter for the estimated annual effect of inflation, and these estimates are adjusted to actual results determined at year-end. Our LIFO provision is calculated based on inventory levels, markup rates and internally generated retail price indices except for grocery items, for which we use a consumer price index. At January 31, 2006 and 2005, our inventories valued at LIFO approximated those inventories as if they were valued at FIFO.

The Company provides for estimated inventory losses ("shrinkage") between physical inventory counts on the basis of a percentage of sales. The provision is adjusted annually to reflect the historical trend of the actual physical inventory count results. Historically, shrinkage has not been volatile.

Impairment of Assets
We evaluate long-lived assets other than goodwill for indicators of impairment whenever events or changes in circumstances indicate their carrying values may not be recoverable. Management's judgments regarding the existence of impairment indicators are based on market conditions and our operational performance, such as operating income and cash flows. The variability of these factors depends on a number of conditions, including uncertainty about future events, and thus our accounting estimates may change from period

to period. These factors could cause management to conclude that impairment indicators exist and require that impairment tests be performed, which could result in management determining that the value of long-lived assets is impaired, resulting in a writedown of the long-lived assets.

Goodwill is not amortized, but is evaluated for impairment annually or whenever events or changes in circumstances indicate that the value of certain goodwill may be impaired. This evaluation requires management to make judgments relating to future cash flows, growth rates, and economic and market conditions. These evaluations are based on discounted cash flows that incorporate the impact of existing Company businesses. Historically, the Company has generated sufficient returns to recover the cost of goodwill and other intangible assets. Because of the nature of the factors used in these tests, if different conditions occur in future periods, future operating results could be materially impacted.

Income Taxes

The determination of our provision for income taxes requires significant judgment, the use of estimates, and the interpretation and application of complex tax laws. Significant judgment is required in assessing the timing and amounts of deductible and taxable items. We establish reserves when, despite our belief that our tax return positions are fully supportable, we believe that certain positions may be successfully challenged. When facts and circumstances change, we adjust these reserves through our provision for income taxes.

Self-Insurance

We use a combination of insurance, self-insured retention and self-insurance for a number of risks, including, without limitation, workers' compensation, general liability, vehicle liability and the Company's portion of employee-related health care benefits. Liabilities associated with the risks that we retain are estimated in part by considering historical claims experience, including frequency, severity, demographic factors, and other actuarial assumptions. In calculating our liability, we analyze our historical trends, including loss development, and apply appropriate loss development factors to the incurred costs associated with the claims made against our self-insured program. The estimated accruals for these liabilities could be significantly affected if future occurrences or loss development differ from these assumptions. For example, for workers' compensation and liability, a 1% increase or decrease to the assumptions for claims costs and loss development factors would increase or decrease our self-insurance accrual by $23 million and $62 million, respectively.

For a summary of our significant accounting policies, please see Note 1 to our consolidated financial statements that appear after this discussion.

Forward-Looking Statements

This Annual Report contains statements that Wal-Mart believes are "forward-looking statements" within the meaning of the Private Securities Litigation Reform Act of 1995. Those statements are intended to enjoy the protection of the safe harbor for forward-looking statements provided by that Act. These forward-looking statements include statements under the caption "Results of Operations" regarding the effect of the opening of new stores on existing stores' sales and the trend in the percentages that the net sales of certain of our business segments represent of our total net sales, under the caption "SAM'S CLUB Segment" regarding the improvement in net sales in the SAM'S CLUB Segment and under the caption "Liquidity and Capital Resources" in Management's Discussion and Analysis of Financial Condition and Results of Operations with respect to our capital expenditures, our ability to fund certain cash flow shortfalls by the sale of commercial paper and long-term debt securities, our ability to sell our long-term securities and our anticipated reasons for repurchasing shares of our common stock. These statements are identified by the use of the words "anticipate," "believe," "contemplate," "expect," "plan," and other, similar words or phrases. Similarly, descriptions of our objectives, strategies, plans, goals or targets are also forward-looking statements. These statements discuss, among other things, expected growth, future revenues, future cash flows, future capital expenditures, future performance and the anticipation and expectations of Wal-Mart and its management as to future occurrences and trends. These forward-looking statements are subject to certain factors, in the United States and internationally, that could affect our financial performance, business strategy, plans, goals and objectives. Those factors include the cost of goods, labor costs, the cost of fuel and electricity, the cost of healthcare benefits, insurance costs, catastrophic events, competitive pressures, inflation, accident-related costs, consumer buying patterns and debt levels, weather patterns, transport of goods from foreign suppliers, currency exchange fluctuations, trade restrictions, changes in tariff and freight rates, changes in tax and other laws and regulations that affect our business, the outcome of legal proceedings to which we are a party, unemployment levels, interest rate fluctuations, changes in employment legislation and other capital market, economic and geo-political conditions. Moreover, we typically earn a disproportionate part of our annual operating income in the fourth quarter as a result of the seasonal buying patterns. Those buying patterns are difficult to forecast with certainty. The foregoing list of factors that may affect our performance is not exclusive. Other factors and unanticipated events could adversely affect our business operations and financial performance. We discuss certain of these matters more fully, as well as certain risk factors that may affect our business operations, financial condition and results of operations, in other of our filings with the SEC, including our Annual Report on Form 10-K. We filed our Annual Report on Form 10-K for the year ended January 31, 2006, with the SEC on or about March 29, 2006. Actual results may materially differ from anticipated results described or implied in these forward-looking statements as a result of changes in facts, assumptions not being realized or other circumstances. You are urged to consider all of these risks, uncertainties and other factors carefully in evaluating the forward-looking statements. The forward-looking statements included in this Annual Report are made only as of the date of this report, and we undertake no obligation to update these forward-looking statements to reflect subsequent events or circumstances, except as may be required by applicable law.

Consolidated Statements of Income
WAL-MART

(Amounts in millions except per share data)

Fiscal Year Ended January 31,	2006	2005	2004
Revenues:			
Net sales	$312,427	$285,222	$256,329
Other income, net	3,227	2,910	2,352
	315,654	288,132	258,681
Costs and expenses:			
Cost of sales	240,391	219,793	198,747
Operating, selling, general and administrative expenses	56,733	51,248	44,909
Operating income	18,530	17,091	15,025
Interest:			
Debt	1,171	934	729
Capital leases	249	253	267
Interest income	(248)	(201)	(164)
Interest, net	1,172	986	832
Income from continuing operations before income taxes and minority interest	17,358	16,105	14,193
Provision for income taxes:			
Current	5,932	5,326	4,941
Deferred	(129)	263	177
	5,803	5,589	5,118
Income from continuing operations before minority interest	11,555	10,516	9,075
Minority interest	(324)	(249)	(214)
Income from continuing operations	11,231	10,267	8,861
Income from discontinued operation, net of tax	–	–	193
Net income	$ 11,231	$ 10,267	$ 9,054
Basic net income per common share:			
Income from continuing operations	$ 2.68	$ 2.41	$ 2.03
Income from discontinued operation	–	–	0.05
Basic net income per common share	$ 2.68	$ 2.41	$ 2.08
Diluted net income per common share:			
Income from continuing operations	$ 2.68	$ 2.41	$ 2.03
Income from discontinued operation	–	–	0.04
Diluted net income per common share	$ 2.68	$ 2.41	$ 2.07
Weighted-average number of common shares:			
Basic	4,183	4,259	4,363
Diluted	4,188	4,266	4,373
Dividends per common share	$ 0.60	$ 0.52	$ 0.36

See accompanying notes.

Consolidated Balance Sheets
WAL-MART

(Amounts in millions except per share data)

January 31,	2006	2005
Assets		
Current assets:		
Cash and cash equivalents	$ 6,414	$ 5,488
Receivables	2,662	1,715
Inventories	32,191	29,762
Prepaid expenses and other	2,557	1,889
Total current assets	43,824	38,854
Property and equipment, at cost:		
Land	16,643	14,472
Buildings and improvements	56,163	46,574
Fixtures and equipment	22,750	21,461
Transportation equipment	1,746	1,530
Property and equipment, at cost	97,302	84,037
Less accumulated depreciation	21,427	18,637
Property and equipment, net	75,875	65,400
Property under capital lease:		
Property under capital lease	5,578	4,556
Less accumulated amortization	2,163	1,838
Property under capital lease, net	3,415	2,718
Goodwill	12,188	10,803
Other assets and deferred charges	2,885	2,379
Total assets	$138,187	$120,154
Liabilities and shareholders' equity		
Current liabilities:		
Commercial paper	$ 3,754	$ 3,812
Accounts payable	25,373	21,987
Accrued liabilities	13,465	12,120
Accrued income taxes	1,340	1,281
Long-term debt due within one year	4,595	3,759
Obligations under capital leases due within one year	299	223
Total current liabilities	48,826	43,182
Long-term debt	26,429	20,087
Long-term obligations under capital leases	3,742	3,171
Deferred income taxes and other	4,552	2,978
Minority interest	1,467	1,340
Commitments and contingencies		
Shareholders' equity:		
Preferred stock ($0.10 par value; 100 shares authorized, none issued)	–	–
Common stock ($0.10 par value; 11,000 shares authorized, 4,165 and 4,234 issued and outstanding at January 31, 2006 and January 31, 2005, respectively)	417	423
Capital in excess of par value	2,596	2,425
Accumulated other comprehensive income	1,053	2,694
Retained earnings	49,105	43,854
Total shareholders' equity	53,171	49,396
Total liabilities and shareholders' equity	$138,187	$120,154

See accompanying notes.

Consolidated Statements of Shareholders' Equity
WAL-MART

(Amounts in millions except per share data)	Number of Shares	Common Stock	Capital in Excess of Par Value	Accumulated Other Comprehensive Income	Retained Earnings	Total
Balance – January 31, 2003	4,395	$ 440	$ 1,954	$ (509)	$ 37,576	$ 39,461
Comprehensive income:						
Net income from continuing operations					8,861	8,861
Net income from discontinued operation					193	193
Other comprehensive income:						
Foreign currency translation				1,685		1,685
Net unrealized depreciation of derivatives				(341)		(341)
Minimum pension liability				16		16
Total comprehensive income						10,414
Cash dividends ($0.36 per share)					(1,569)	(1,569)
Purchase of Company stock	(92)	(9)	(182)		(4,855)	(5,046)
Stock options exercised and other	8		363			363
Balance – January 31, 2004	4,311	431	2,135	851	40,206	43,623
Comprehensive income:						
Net income from continuing operations					10,267	10,267
Other comprehensive income:						
Foreign currency translation				2,130		2,130
Net unrealized depreciation of derivatives				(194)		(194)
Minimum pension liability				(93)		(93)
Total comprehensive income						12,110
Cash dividends ($0.52 per share)					(2,214)	(2,214)
Purchase of Company stock	(81)	(8)	(136)		(4,405)	(4,549)
Stock options exercised and other	4		426			426
Balance – January 31, 2005	4,234	423	2,425	2,694	43,854	49,396
Comprehensive income:						
Net income from continuing operations					11,231	11,231
Other comprehensive income:						
Foreign currency translation				(1,920)		(1,920)
Net unrealized depreciation of derivatives				228		228
Minimum pension liability				51		51
Total comprehensive income						9,590
Cash dividends ($0.60 per share)					(2,511)	(2,511)
Purchase of Company stock	(74)	(7)	(104)		(3,469)	(3,580)
Stock options exercised and other	5	1	275			276
Balance – January 31, 2006	4,165	$417	$2,596	$1,053	$49,105	$53,171

See accompanying notes.

Consolidated Statements of Cash Flows
WAL-MART

(Amounts in millions)

Fiscal Year Ended January 31,	2006	2005	2004
Cash flows from operating activities			
Income from continuing operations	$ 11,231	$ 10,267	$ 8,861
Adjustments to reconcile net income to net cash			
provided by operating activities:			
Depreciation and amortization	4,717	4,264	3,852
Deferred income taxes	(129)	263	177
Other operating activities	620	378	173
Changes in certain assets and liabilities, net of effects of acquisitions:			
Decrease (increase) in accounts receivable	(456)	(304)	373
Increase in inventories	(1,733)	(2,494)	(1,973)
Increase in accounts payable	2,390	1,694	2,587
Increase in accrued liabilities	993	976	1,896
Net cash provided by operating activities of continuing operations	17,633	15,044	15,946
Net cash provided by operating activities of discontinued operation	–	–	50
Net cash provided by operating activities	17,633	15,044	15,996
Cash flows from investing activities			
Payments for property and equipment	(14,563)	(12,893)	(10,308)
Investment in international operations, net of cash acquired	(601)	(315)	(38)
Proceeds from the disposal of fixed assets	1,049	953	481
Proceeds from the sale of McLane	–	–	1,500
Other investing activities	(68)	(96)	78
Net cash used in investing activities of continuing operations	(14,183)	(12,351)	(8,287)
Net cash used in investing activities of discontinued operation	–	–	(25)
Net cash used in investing activities	(14,183)	(12,351)	(8,312)
Cash flows from financing activities			
Increase (decrease) in commercial paper	(704)	544	688
Proceeds from issuance of long-term debt	7,691	5,832	4,099
Purchase of Company stock	(3,580)	(4,549)	(5,046)
Dividends paid	(2,511)	(2,214)	(1,569)
Payment of long-term debt	(2,724)	(2,131)	(3,541)
Payment of capital lease obligations	(245)	(204)	(305)
Other financing activities	(349)	113	111
Net cash used in financing activities	(2,422)	(2,609)	(5,563)
Effect of exchange rate changes on cash	(102)	205	320
Net increase in cash and cash equivalents	926	289	2,441
Cash and cash equivalents at beginning of year	5,488	5,199	2,758
Cash and cash equivalents at end of year	$ 6,414	$ 5,488	$ 5,199
Supplemental disclosure of cash flow information			
Income tax paid	$ 5,962	$ 5,593	$ 4,538
Interest paid	1,390	1,163	1,024
Capital lease obligations incurred	286	377	252

See accompanying notes.

Notes to Consolidated Financial Statements
WAL-MART

1 SUMMARY OF SIGNIFICANT ACCOUNTING POLICIES

Consolidation

The consolidated financial statements include the accounts of Wal-Mart Stores, Inc. and its subsidiaries ("Wal-Mart" or the "Company"). Significant intercompany transactions have been eliminated in consolidation. Investments in which the Company has a 20 percent to 50 percent voting interest and where the Company exercises significant influence over the investee are accounted for using the equity method.

The Company's operations in Argentina, Brazil, China, Germany, Japan, Mexico, South Korea and the United Kingdom are consolidated using a December 31 fiscal year-end, generally due to statutory reporting requirements. There were no significant intervening events which materially affected the financial statements. The Company's operations in Canada and Puerto Rico are consolidated using a January 31 fiscal year-end.

The Company consolidates the accounts of certain variable interest entities where it has been determined that Wal-Mart is the primary beneficiary of those entities' operations. The assets, liabilities and results of operations of these entities are not material to the Company.

Cash and Cash Equivalents

The Company considers investments with a maturity of three months or less when purchased to be cash equivalents. The majority of payments due from banks for third-party credit card, debit card and electronic benefit transactions ("EBT") process within 24-48 hours, except for transactions occurring on a Friday, which are generally processed the following Monday. All credit card, debit card and EBT transactions that process in less than seven days are classified as cash and cash equivalents. Amounts due from banks for these transactions classified as cash totaled $575 million and $549 million at January 31, 2006 and 2005, respectively.

Receivables

Accounts receivable consist primarily of receivables from insurance companies resulting from our pharmacy sales, receivables from suppliers for marketing or incentive programs, receivables from real estate transactions and receivables from property insurance claims. Additionally, amounts due from banks for customer credit card, debit card and EBT transactions that take in excess of seven days to process are classified as accounts receivable.

Inventories

The Company values inventories at the lower of cost or market as determined primarily by the retail method of accounting, using the last-in, first-out ("LIFO") method for substantially all merchandise inventories in the United States, except SAM'S CLUB merchandise and merchandise in our distribution warehouses, which is based on the cost LIFO method. Inventories of foreign operations are primarily valued by the retail method of accounting, using the first-in, first-out ("FIFO") method. At January 31, 2006 and 2005, our inventories valued at LIFO approximate those inventories as if they were valued at FIFO.

Financial Instruments

The Company uses derivative financial instruments for purposes other than trading to manage its exposure to interest and foreign exchange rates, as well as to maintain an appropriate mix of fixed and floating-rate debt. Contract terms of a hedge instrument closely mirror those of the hedged item, providing a high degree of risk reduction and correlation. Contracts that are effective at meeting the risk reduction and correlation criteria are recorded using hedge accounting. If a derivative instrument is a hedge, depending on the nature of the hedge, changes in the fair value of the instrument will either be offset against the change in fair value of the hedged assets, liabilities or firm commitments through earnings or recognized in other comprehensive income until the hedged item is recognized in earnings. The ineffective portion of an instrument's change in fair value will be immediately recognized in earnings. Instruments that do not meet the criteria for hedge accounting, or contracts for which the Company has not elected hedge accounting, are marked to fair value with unrealized gains or losses reported in earnings during the period of change.

Capitalized Interest

Interest costs capitalized on construction projects were $157 million, $120 million, and $144 million in fiscal 2006, 2005 and 2004, respectively.

Long-Lived Assets

Long-lived assets are stated at cost. Management reviews long-lived assets for indicators of impairment whenever events or changes in circumstances indicate that the carrying value may not be recoverable. The evaluation is performed at the lowest level of identifiable cash flows, which is typically at the individual store level. Cash flows expected to be generated by the related assets are estimated over the asset's useful life based on updated projections. If the evaluation indicates that the carrying amount of the asset may not be recoverable, any potential impairment is measured based on a projected discounted cash flow method using a discount rate that is considered to be commensurate with the risk inherent in the Company's current business model.

Goodwill and Other Acquired Intangible Assets

Goodwill is not amortized; rather it is evaluated for impairment annually or whenever events or changes in circumstances indicate that the value of certain goodwill may be impaired. Other acquired intangible assets are amortized on a straight-line basis over the periods that expected economic benefits will be provided. These evaluations are based on discounted cash flows and incorporate the impact of existing Company businesses. The analyses require significant management judgment to evaluate the capacity of an acquired business to perform within projections. Historically, the Company has generated sufficient returns to recover the cost of the goodwill and other intangible assets.

Goodwill is recorded on the balance sheet in the operating segments as follows (in millions):

January 31,	2006	2005
International	$11,883	$10,498
SAM'S CLUB	305	305
Total goodwill	$12,188	$10,803

The fiscal 2006 consolidation of The Seiyu, Ltd. and acquisition of Sonae Distribuição Brasil S.A. and the fiscal 2005 acquisition of Bompreço S.A. Supermercados do Nordeste resulted in increases to goodwill. In addition, changes in the International segment's goodwill result from foreign currency exchange rate fluctuations.

Leases

The Company estimates the expected term of a lease by assuming the exercise of renewal options where an economic penalty exists that would preclude the abandonment of the lease at the end of the initial non-cancelable term and the exercise of such renewal is at the sole discretion of the Company. This expected term is used in the determination of whether a store lease is a capital or operating lease and in the calculation of straight-line rent expense. Additionally, the useful life of leasehold improvements is limited by the expected lease term. If significant expenditures are made for leasehold improvements late in the expected term of a lease, judgment is applied to determine if the leasehold improvements have a useful life that extends beyond the original expected lease term or if the leasehold improvements have a useful life that is bound by the end of the original expected lease term.

Rent abatements and escalations are considered in the calculation of minimum lease payments in the Company's capital lease tests and in determining straight-line rent expense for operating leases.

Foreign Currency Translation

The assets and liabilities of all foreign subsidiaries are translated using exchange rates at the balance sheet date. The income statements of foreign subsidiaries are translated using average exchange rates. Related translation adjustments are recorded as a component of accumulated other comprehensive income.

Revenue Recognition

The Company recognizes sales revenue net of estimated sales returns at the time it sells merchandise to the customer, except for layaway transactions. The Company recognizes revenue from layaway transactions when the customer satisfies all payment obligations and takes possession of the merchandise. Customer purchases of Wal-Mart and SAM'S CLUB shopping cards are not recognized as revenue until the card is redeemed and the customer purchases merchandise by using the shopping card.

SAM'S CLUB Membership Fee Revenue Recognition

The Company recognizes SAM'S CLUB membership fee revenues both in the United States and internationally over the term of the membership, which is 12 months. The following table details unearned revenues, membership fees received from members and the amount of revenues recognized in earnings for each of the fiscal years 2006, 2005 and 2004 (in millions):

Fiscal Year Ended January 31,	2006	2005	2004
Deferred membership fee revenue, beginning of year	$ 458	$ 449	$ 437
Membership fees received	940	890	840
Membership fee revenue recognized	(908)	(881)	(828)
Deferred membership fee revenue, end of year	$ 490	$ 458	$ 449

SAM'S CLUB membership revenue is included in other income, net in the revenues section of the Consolidated Statements of Income.

The Company's deferred membership fee revenue is included in accrued liabilities in the Consolidated Balance Sheets. The Company's analysis of historical membership fee refunds indicates that such refunds have been nominal. Accordingly, no reserve existed for membership fee refunds at January 31, 2006 and 2005.

Cost of Sales

Cost of sales includes actual product cost, change in inventory, the cost of transportation to the Company's warehouses from suppliers, the cost of transportation from the Company's warehouses to the stores and clubs and the cost of warehousing for our SAM'S CLUB segment.

Payments from Suppliers

Wal-Mart receives money from suppliers for various programs, primarily volume incentives, warehouse allowances and reimbursements for specific programs such as markdowns, margin protection and advertising. Substantially all allowances are accounted for as a reduction of purchases and recognized in our Consolidated Statements of Income when the related inventory is sold.

Operating, Selling, General and Administrative Expenses

Operating, selling, general and administrative expenses include all operating costs of the Company that are not related to the transportation of products from the supplier to the warehouse or from the warehouse to the store. Additionally, the cost of warehousing and occupancy for our Wal-Mart Stores segment distribution facilities are included in operating, selling, general and administrative expenses. Because we do not include the cost of our Wal-Mart Stores segment distribution facilities in cost of sales, our gross profit and gross margin may not be comparable to those of other retailers that may include all costs related to their distribution facilities in costs of sales and in the calculation of gross profit and gross margin.

Notes to Consolidated Financial Statements
WAL-MART

Advertising Costs
Advertising costs are expensed as incurred and were $1.6 billion, $1.4 billion and $966 million in fiscal 2006, 2005 and 2004, respectively. Advertising costs consist primarily of print and television advertisements.

Pre-Opening Costs
The costs of start-up activities, including organization costs and new store openings, are expensed as incurred.

Share-Based Compensation
The Company recognizes expense for its share-based compensation based on the fair value of the awards that are granted. The fair value of stock options is estimated at the date of grant using the Black-Scholes-Merton option valuation model which was developed for use in estimating the fair value of exchange traded options that have no vesting restrictions and are fully transferable. Option valuation methods require the input of highly subjective assumptions, including the expected stock price volatility. Measured compensation cost is recognized ratably over the vesting period of the related share-based compensation award.

Share-based compensation awards that may be settled in cash are accounted for as liabilities and marked to market each period.

Insurance/Self-Insurance
The Company uses a combination of insurance, self-insured retention and self-insurance for a number of risks, including, without limitation, workers' compensation, general liability, vehicle liability and the Company-funded portion of employee-related health care benefits. Liabilities associated with these risks are estimated in part by considering historical claims experience, demographic factors, frequency and severity factors and other actuarial assumptions.

Depreciation and Amortization
Depreciation and amortization for financial statement purposes are provided on the straight-line method over the estimated useful lives of the various assets. Depreciation expense, including amortization of property under capital leases for fiscal years 2006, 2005 and 2004 was $4.7 billion, $4.3 billion and $3.9 billion, respectively. For income tax purposes, accelerated methods of depreciation are used with recognition of deferred income taxes for the resulting temporary differences. Leasehold improvements are depreciated over the shorter of the estimated useful life of the asset or the remaining lease term. Estimated useful lives for financial statement purposes are as follows:

Buildings and improvements	5 – 50 years
Fixtures and equipment	3 – 12 years
Transportation equipment	3 – 15 years

Income Taxes
Income taxes are accounted for under the asset and liability method. Deferred tax assets and liabilities are recognized for the estimated future tax consequences attributable to differences between the financial statement carrying amounts of existing assets and liabilities and their respective tax bases. Deferred tax assets and liabilities are measured using enacted tax rates in effect for the year in which those temporary differences are expected to be recovered or settled. The effect on deferred tax assets and liabilities of a change in tax rate is recognized in income in the period that includes the enactment date. Valuation allowances are established when necessary to reduce deferred tax assets to the amounts more likely than not to be realized.

In determining the quarterly provision for income taxes, the Company uses an annual effective tax rate based on expected annual income and statutory tax rates. The effective tax rate also reflects the Company's assessment of the ultimate outcome of tax audits. Significant discrete items are separately recognized in the income tax provision in the quarter in which they occur.

The determination of the Company's provision for income taxes requires significant judgment, the use of estimates, and the interpretation and application of complex tax laws. Significant judgment is required in assessing the timing and amounts of deductible and taxable items. Reserves are established when, despite management's belief that the Company's tax return positions are fully supportable, management believes that certain positions may be successfully challenged. When facts and circumstances change, these reserves are adjusted through the provision for income taxes.

Net Income Per Common Share
Basic net income per common share is based on the weighted-average outstanding common shares. Diluted net income per common share is based on the weighted-average outstanding shares adjusted for the dilutive effect of stock options and restricted stock grants. The dilutive effect of stock options and restricted stock was 5 million, 7 million and 10 million shares in fiscal 2006, 2005 and 2004, respectively. The Company had approximately 57 million, 59 million and 50 million option shares outstanding at January 31, 2006, 2005 and 2004, respectively, which were not included in the diluted net income per share calculation because their effect would be antidilutive as the underlying option price exceeded the average market price of the stock for the period.

Estimates and Assumptions
The preparation of consolidated financial statements in conformity with generally accepted accounting principles requires Management to make estimates and assumptions. These estimates and assumptions affect the reported amounts of assets and liabilities. They also affect the disclosure of contingent assets and liabilities at the date of the consolidated financial statements and the reported amounts of revenues and expenses during the reporting period. Actual results may differ from those estimates.

Reclassifications
Certain reclassifications have been made to prior periods to conform to current presentations.

2 COMMERCIAL PAPER AND LONG-TERM DEBT

Information on short-term borrowings and interest rates is as follows (dollars in millions):

Fiscal Year	**2006**	2005	2004
Maximum amount outstanding at any month-end	**$9,054**	$7,782	$4,957
Average daily short-term borrowings	**5,719**	4,823	1,498
Weighted-average interest rate	**3.4%**	1.6%	1.1%

At January 31, 2006 and 2005, short-term borrowings consisted of $3.8 billion of commercial paper. At January 31, 2006, the Company had committed lines of credit of $5.0 billion with 57 firms and banks, which were used to support commercial paper, and committed and informal lines of credit with various banks totaling an additional $693 million.

Long-term debt at January 31, consists of (in millions):

Interest Rate	Due by Fiscal Year	**2006**	2005
2.130 – 6.875%	Notes due 2010	**$ 4,527**	$ 4,500
5.250%	Notes due 2036	**4,279**	1,883
1.100 – 13.250%, LIBOR less 0.140%	Notes due 2007	**3,415**	3,164
2.875 – 8.380%, LIBOR less 0.1025%	Notes due 2008	**3,311**	1,500
0.1838 – 0.880%	Notes due 2011[1]	**3,308**	500
0.750 – 7.250%	Notes due 2014	**2,885**	2,883
3.000 – 3.375%	Notes due 2009	**2,800**	1,000
1.200 – 4.125%	Notes due 2012	**2,015**	2,000
5.750 – 7.550%	Notes due 2031	**1,890**	1,941
3.150 – 6.630%	Notes due 2016	**767**	–
2.950 – 5.006%	Notes due 2019[1]	**516**	500
5.300 – 6.750%	Notes due 2024	**266**	250
2.100 – 2.875%	Notes due 2015	**53**	–
2.000 – 2.500%	Notes due 2017	**41**	–
3.750 – 5.000%	Notes due 2018	**31**	–
5.170%	Notes due 2021	**25**	–
1.000 – 2.300%	Notes due 2013	**23**	–
4.150 – 5.875%, LIBOR less 0.0425%	Notes due 2006	**–**	2,597
	Other [2]	**872**	1,128
Total		**$31,024**	$23,846

(1) Includes put option on $500 million.
(2) Includes adjustments to debt hedged by derivatives.

The Company has two separate issuances of $500 million debt with embedded put options. For the first issuance, beginning June 2001, and each year thereafter, the holders of $500 million of the debt may require the Company to repurchase the debt at face value, in addition to accrued and unpaid interest. The holders of the other $500 million issuance may require the Company to repurchase the debt at par plus accrued interest at any time. Both of these issuances have been classified as a current liability in the Consolidated Balance Sheets.

Under the Company's most significant borrowing arrangements, the Company is not required to observe financial covenants. However, under certain lines of credit totaling $5.0 billion, which were undrawn as of January 31, 2006, the Company has agreed to observe certain covenants, the most restrictive of which relates to minimum net worth levels and amounts of additional secured debt and long-term leases. In addition, one of our subsidiaries has restrictive financial covenants on $2.0 billion of long-term debt that requires it to maintain certain equity, sales, and profit levels. The Company was in compliance with these covenants at January 31, 2006.

Long-term debt is unsecured except for $1.1 billion, which is collateralized by property with an aggregate carrying value of approximately $1.4 billion. Annual maturities of long-term debt during the next five years and thereafter are (in millions):

Fiscal Year Ended January 31,	Annual Maturity
2007	$ 4,595
2008	3,320
2009	2,858
2010	4,639
2011	2,877
Thereafter	12,735
Total	$31,024

The Company has entered into sale/leaseback transactions involving buildings while retaining title to the underlying land. These transactions were accounted for as financings and are included in long-term debt and the annual maturities schedule above. The resulting obligations are amortized over the lease terms. Future minimum lease payments during the next five years and thereafter are (in millions):

Fiscal Year Ended January 31,	Minimum Payments
2007	$ 9
2008	10
2009	10
2010	10
2011	10
Thereafter	211
Total	$260

Notes to Consolidated Financial Statements
WAL-MART

The Company had trade letters of credit outstanding totaling $2.6 billion at January 31, 2006 and 2005. At January 31, 2006 and 2005, the Company had standby letters of credit outstanding totaling $2.3 billion and $2.0 billion, respectively. These letters of credit were issued primarily for the purchase of inventory and insurance.

3 FINANCIAL INSTRUMENTS

The Company uses derivative financial instruments for hedging and non-trading purposes to manage its exposure to interest and foreign exchange rates. Use of derivative financial instruments in hedging programs subjects the Company to certain risks, such as market and credit risks. Market risk represents the possibility that the value of the derivative instrument will change. In a hedging relationship, the change in the value of the derivative is offset to a great extent by the change in the value of the underlying hedged item. Credit risk related to derivatives represents the possibility that the counterparty will not fulfill the terms of the contract. The notional, or contractual, amount of the Company's derivative financial instruments is used to measure interest to be paid or received and does not represent the Company's exposure due to credit risk. Credit risk is monitored through established approval procedures, including setting concentration limits by counterparty, reviewing credit ratings and requiring collateral (generally cash) when appropriate. The majority of the Company's transactions are with counterparties rated "AA-" or better by nationally recognized credit rating agencies.

Fair Value Instruments

The Company enters into interest rate swaps to minimize the risks and costs associated with its financing activities. Under the swap agreements, the Company pays variable-rate interest and receives fixed-rate interest payments periodically over the life of the instruments. The notional amounts are used to measure interest to be paid or received and do not represent the exposure due to credit loss. All of the Company's interest rate swaps that receive fixed interest rate payments and pay variable interest rate payments are designated as fair value hedges. As the specific terms and notional amounts of the derivative instruments exactly match those of the instruments being hedged, the derivative instruments were assumed to be perfect hedges and all changes in fair value of the hedges were recorded on the balance sheet with no net impact on the income statement.

Net Investment Instruments

At January 31, 2006, the Company is party to cross-currency interest rate swaps that hedge its net investments in the United Kingdom and Japan. The agreements are contracts to exchange fixed-rate payments in one currency for fixed-rate payments in another currency. The Company also has outstanding approximately £2.0 billion of debt that is designated as a hedge of the Company's net investment in the United Kingdom and ¥87.1 billion of debt that is designated as a hedge of the Company's net investment in Japan. All changes in the fair value of these instruments are recorded in other comprehensive income, offsetting the foreign currency translation adjustment that is also recorded in other comprehensive income.

Cash Flow Instruments

The Company is party to a cross-currency interest rate swap to hedge the foreign currency risk of certain foreign-denominated debt. The swap is designated as a cash flow hedge of foreign currency exchange risk. The agreement is a contract to exchange fixed-rate payments in one currency for fixed-rate payments in another currency. Changes in the foreign currency spot exchange rate result in reclassification of amounts from other accumulated comprehensive income to earnings to offset transaction gains or losses on foreign-denominated debt. The instrument matures in fiscal 2007.

The Company expects that the amount of gain or loss existing in other accumulated comprehensive income to be reclassified into earnings within the next 12 months will not be significant.

Fair Value of Financial Instruments

Instrument Fiscal Year Ended January 31, (in millions)	Notional Amount		Fair Value	
	2006	2005	**2006**	2005
Derivative financial instruments designated for hedging:				
Receive fixed-rate, pay floating rate interest rate swaps designated as fair value hedges	**$ 6,945**	$ 8,042	**$ 133**	$ 477
Receive fixed-rate, pay fixed-rate cross-currency interest rate swaps designated as net investment hedges (Cross-currency notional amount: GBP 795 at 1/31/2006 and 1/31/2005)	**1,250**	1,250	**(107)**	(14)
Receive fixed-rate, pay fixed-rate cross-currency interest rate swap designated as a cash flow hedge (Cross-currency notional amount: CAD 503 at 1/31/2006 and 1/31/2005)	**325**	325	**(120)**	(87)
Receive fixed-rate, pay fixed-rate cross-currency interest rate swap designated as a net investment hedge (Cross-currency notional amount: ¥52,056 at 1/31/2006 and 1/31/2005)	**432**	432	**(17)**	(68)
Receive floating rate, pay fixed-rate interest rate swap designated as a cash flow hedge	**–**	1,500	**–**	(5)
Total	**$ 8,952**	$11,549	**$ (111)**	$ 303
Non-derivative financial instruments:				
Long-term debt	**$31,024**	$23,846	**$31,580**	$25,016

Hedging instruments with an unrealized gain are recorded on the Consolidated Balance Sheets in other current assets or other assets and deferred charges, based on maturity date. Those instruments with an unrealized loss are recorded in accrued liabilities or deferred income taxes and other, based on maturity date.

Cash and cash equivalents: The carrying amount approximates fair value due to the short maturity of these instruments.

Long-term debt: Fair value is based on the Company's current incremental borrowing rate for similar types of borrowing arrangements.

Fair value instruments and net investment instruments: The fair values are estimated amounts the Company would receive or pay to terminate the agreements as of the reporting dates.

4 ACCUMULATED OTHER COMPREHENSIVE INCOME

Comprehensive income is net income plus certain other items that are recorded directly to shareholders' equity. Amounts included in accumulated other comprehensive income for the Company's derivative instruments and minimum pension liability are recorded net of the related income tax effects. The following table gives further detail regarding changes in the composition of accumulated other comprehensive income during fiscal 2006, 2005 and 2004 (in millions):

	Foreign Currency Translation	Derivative Instruments	Minimum Pension Liability	Total
Balance at January 31, 2003	$ (1,125)	$ 822	$ (206)	$ (509)
Foreign currency translation adjustment	1,685			1,685
Change in fair value of hedge instruments		(444)		(444)
Reclassification to earnings		103		103
Subsidiary minimum pension liability			16	16
Balance at January 31, 2004	560	481	(190)	851
Foreign currency translation adjustment	2,130			2,130
Change in fair value of hedge instruments		(235)		(235)
Reclassification to earnings		41		41
Subsidiary minimum pension liability			(93)	(93)
Balance at January 31, 2005	**$ 2,690**	**$ 287**	**$ (283)**	**$ 2,694**
Foreign currency translation adjustment	**(1,920)**			**(1,920)**
Change in fair value of hedge instruments		**157**		**157**
Reclassification to earnings		**71**		**71**
Subsidiary minimum pension liability			**51**	**51**
Balance at January 31, 2006	**$ 770**	**$515**	**$(232)**	**$ 1,053**

5 INCOME TAXES

The income tax provision consists of the following (in millions):

Fiscal Year Ended January 31,	**2006**	2005	2004
Current:			
Federal	**$4,646**	$4,116	$4,039
State and local	**449**	640	333
International	**837**	570	569
Total current tax provision	**5,932**	5,326	4,941
Deferred:			
Federal	**(62)**	311	31
State and local	**56**	(71)	2
International	**(123)**	23	144
Total deferred tax provision	**(129)**	263	177
Total provision for income taxes	**$5,803**	$5,589	$5,118

Income from continuing operations before income taxes and minority interest by jurisdiction is as follows (in millions):

Fiscal Year Ended January 31,	**2006**	2005	2004
United States	**$14,447**	$13,599	$12,075
Outside the United States	**$ 2,911**	2,506	2,118
Total income from continuing operations before income taxes and minority interest	**$17,358**	$16,105	$14,193

Notes to Consolidated Financial Statements
WAL-MART

Items that give rise to significant portions of the deferred tax accounts are as follows (in millions):

January 31,	2006	2005
Deferred tax liabilities		
Property and equipment	$2,355	$2,210
International, principally asset basis differences	1,141	1,054
Inventory	336	187
Other	265	230
Total deferred tax liabilities	$4,097	$3,681
Deferred tax assets		
International loss carryforwards and asset basis differences	$2,082	$1,460
Amounts accrued for financial reporting purposes not yet deductible for tax purposes	1,668	1,361
Stock-based compensation expense	248	258
Other	353	263
Total deferred tax assets	4,351	3,342
Valuation allowance	(1,054)	(526)
Total deferred tax assets, net of valuation allowance	$3,297	$2,816
Net deferred tax liabilities	$ 800	$ 865

The change in the Company's net deferred tax liability is impacted by foreign currency translation.

A reconciliation of the significant differences between the effective income tax rate and the federal statutory rate on pretax income is as follows:

Fiscal Year Ended January 31,	2006	2005	2004
Statutory tax rate	35.00%	35.00%	35.00%
State income taxes, net of federal income tax benefit	1.86%	2.30%	1.53%
Income taxes outside the United States	(1.75%)	(1.81%)	(0.20%)
Other	(1.68%)	(0.79%)	(0.27%)
Effective income tax rate	33.43%	34.70%	36.06%

Federal and state income taxes have not been provided on accumulated but undistributed earnings of foreign subsidiaries aggregating approximately $6.8 billion at January 31, 2006 and $5.3 billion at January 31, 2005, as such earnings have been permanently reinvested in the business. The determination of the amount of the unrecognized deferred tax liability related to the undistributed earnings is not practicable.

The Company had foreign net operating loss carryforwards of $4.7 billion at January 31, 2006. Of this amount, $1.3 billion related to the December 2005 consolidation of The Seiyu, Ltd. The recording of the related deferred tax asset of $525 million resulted in a corresponding increase in the valuation allowance. Any tax benefit ultimately realized from the Japan net operating loss carryforward will adjust goodwill. Net operating loss carryforwards of $1.4 billion expire in various years through 2011.

6 ACQUISITIONS AND DISPOSAL

Acquisitions

During December 2005, the Company purchased an additional interest in The Seiyu, Ltd. ("Seiyu"), for approximately $570 million, bringing the Company's total investment in Seiyu, including adjustments arising from the equity method of accounting, to $1.2 billion. Seiyu is a retailer in Japan, which operates 398 stores selling apparel, general merchandise, food and certain services. Following this additional purchase, the Company owns approximately 53.3% of Seiyu. Beginning on the date of the controlling interest purchase, the Company began consolidating Seiyu as a majority-owned subsidiary using a December 31 fiscal year-end. Seiyu's results of operations were not material to the Company. As a result of the consolidation of Seiyu, total assets and liabilities of $6.8 billion and $5.6 billion, respectively, were recorded in our financial statements. Goodwill recorded in the consolidation amounted to approximately $1.6 billion. The amount of assets and liabilities recorded in the consolidation of Seiyu are preliminary estimates made by management and will be finalized upon completion of the valuation of tangible and intangible assets and liabilities.

The minority interest in Seiyu is represented, in part, by shares of Seiyu's preferred stock which are convertible into shares of Seiyu common stock. If the minority holder of Seiyu's preferred stock proposes to sell or convert its shares of preferred stock, the Company has the right to purchase those shares at a predetermined price.

Through a warrant exercisable through December 2007, the Company can contribute approximately ¥154.6 billion, or $1.3 billion at a January 31, 2006, exchange rate of 117.75 yen per dollar, for approximately 538 million additional common shares of Seiyu stock. If the warrant is exercised, we would own approximately 71% of the stock of Seiyu by the end of December 2007. These calculations assume no conversion of Seiyu's preferred stock into common shares and no other issuances of Seiyu common shares.

In December 2005, the Company completed the purchase of Sonae Distribuição Brasil S.A. ("Sonae"), a retail operation in Southern Brazil consisting of 139 hypermarkets, supermarkets and warehouse units. The purchase price was approximately $720 million. Assets recorded in the acquisition of Sonae were $1.3 billion and liabilities assumed were $566 million. As a result of the Sonae acquisition, we recorded goodwill of $305 million and other identifiable intangible assets of $89 million. Sonae's results of operations, which were not material to the Company, are included in our consolidated financial statements following the date of acquisition using a December 31 fiscal year-end. The amount of assets and liabilities recorded in the purchase of Sonae are preliminary estimates made by management and will be finalized upon completion of the valuation of tangible and intangible assets and liabilities.

In September 2005, the Company acquired a 33.3% interest in Central American Retail Holding Company ("CARHCO"), a retailer with more than 360 supermarkets and other stores in Costa Rica, El Salvador, Guatemala, Honduras and Nicaragua. The purchase price was approximately $318 million, including transaction costs. In fiscal 2006, the Company accounted for its investment in CARHCO under the equity method. Concurrent with the purchase of the investment in CARHCO, the Company entered into an agreement to purchase an additional 17.7% of CARHCO in the first quarter of fiscal 2007 and an option agreement that will allow the Company to purchase up to an additional 24% beginning in September 2010. To the extent that the Company does not exercise its option to purchase the additional 24% of CARHCO, the minority shareholders will have certain put rights that could require the Company to purchase the additional 24% after September 2012. In February 2006, the Company purchased the additional 17.7% of CARHCO for a purchase price of approximately $212 million.

In February 2004, the Company completed its purchase of Bompreço S.A. Supermercados do Nordeste ("Bompreço"), a supermarket chain in northern Brazil with 118 hypermarkets, supermarkets and mini-markets. The purchase price was approximately $315 million, net of cash acquired. The results of operations for Bompreço, which were not material to the Company, have been included in the Company's consolidated financial statements since the date of acquisition.

Disposal

On May 23, 2003, the Company completed the sale of McLane Company, Inc. ("McLane"). The Company received $1.5 billion in cash for the sale. The accompanying consolidated financial statements and notes reflect the gain on the sale and the operations of McLane as a discontinued operation.

Following is summarized financial information for McLane (in millions):

Fiscal Year Ended January 31,	2004
Net sales	$4,328
Income from discontinued operation	$ 67
Income tax expense	25
Net operating income from discontinued operation	42
Gain on sale of McLane, net of $147 income tax expense	151
Income from discontinued operation, net of tax	$ 193

The effective tax rate on the gain from the sale of McLane was 49% as a result of the non-deductibility of $99 million of goodwill recorded in the original McLane acquisition.

7 SHARE-BASED COMPENSATION PLANS

As of January 31, 2006, the Company has awarded share-based compensation to executives and other associates of the Company through various share-based compensation plans. The compensation cost recognized for all plans was $244 million, $204 million, and $183 million for fiscal 2006, 2005, and 2004, respectively. The total income tax benefit recognized for all share-based compensation plans was $82 million, $71 million, and $66 million for fiscal 2006, 2005, and 2004, respectively.

On February 1, 2003, the Company adopted the expense recognition provisions of Statement of Financial Accounting Standards No. 123 ("SFAS 123"), restating results for prior periods. In December 2004, the Financial Accounting Standards Board issued a revision of SFAS 123 ("SFAS 123(R)"). The Company adopted the provisions of SFAS 123(R) upon its release. The adoption of SFAS 123(R) did not have a material impact on our results of operations, financial position or cash flows. All share-based compensation is accounted for in accordance with the fair-value based method of SFAS 123(R).

The Company's Stock Incentive Plan of 2005 (the "Plan"), which is shareholder-approved, permits the grant of stock options, restricted (non-vested) stock and performance share compensation awards to its associates for up to 210 million shares of common stock. The Company believes that such awards better align the interests of its associates with those of its shareholders.

Under the Plan and prior plans, stock option awards have been granted with an exercise price equal to the market price of the Company's stock at the date of grant. Generally, outstanding options granted before fiscal 2001 vest over seven years. Options granted after fiscal 2001 generally vest over five years. Shares issued upon the exercise of options are newly issued. Options granted generally have a contractual term of 10 years. The fair value of each stock option award is estimated on the date of grant using the Black-Scholes-Merton option valuation model that uses various assumptions for inputs, which are noted in the following table. Generally, the Company uses historical volatilities and risk free interest rates that correlate with the expected term of the option. To determine the expected life of the option, the Company bases its estimates on historical grants with similar vesting periods. The following tables represents a weighted-average of the assumptions used by the company to estimate the fair values of the Company's stock options at the grant dates:

Fiscal Year Ended January 31,	**2006**	2005	2004
Dividend yield	**1.9%**	1.1%	0.9%
Volatility	**24.9%**	26.2%	32.3%
Risk-free interest rate	**4.2%**	3.5%	2.8%
Expected life in years	**6.1**	5.3	4.5

Notes to Consolidated Financial Statements
WAL-MART

A summary of the stock option award activity for fiscal 2006 is presented below:

Options	Shares	Weighted-Average Exercise Price	Weighted-Average Remaining Life in Years	Aggregate Intrinsic Value
Outstanding at January 31, 2005	68,115,000	$ 46.79		
Granted	4,281,000	50.74		
Exercised	(4,208,000)	23.26		
Forfeited or expired	(8,645,000)	51.92		
Outstanding at January 31, 2006	59,543,000	$48.02	6.5	$163,326,000
Exercisable at January 31, 2006	32,904,000	$45.20	5.3	$162,240,000

The weighted-average grant-date fair value of options granted during the fiscal years ended January 31, 2006, 2005 and 2004, was $12.29, $11.92 and $14.89, respectively. The total intrinsic value of options exercised during the years ended January 31, 2006, 2005 and 2004, was $108.3 million, $221.6 million and $231.0 million, respectively.

Under the Plan, the Company grants various types of awards of restricted (non-vested) stock to certain associates. These grants include awards for shares that vest based on the passage of time, performance criteria, or both. Vesting periods vary. The restricted stock awards may be settled in stock, or deferred as stock or cash, based upon the associate's election. Consequently, these awards are classified as liabilities in the accompanying balance sheets unless the associate has elected for the award to be settled or deferred in stock. The fair value of the restricted stock liabilities is remeasured each reporting period. The total liability for restricted stock awards at January 31, 2006, was $61.1 million.

A summary of the Company's restricted (non-vested) stock award activity for fiscal 2006 is presented below:

Non-Vested Stock Awards	Shares	Weighted-Average Grant-Date Fair Value
Restricted Stock Awards at January 31, 2005	3,423,000	$ 46.63
Granted	2,955,000	$ 44.81
Vested	(383,000)	$ 44.78
Forfeited	(551,000)	$ 45.02
Restricted Stock Awards at January 31, 2006	5,444,000	$46.08

As of January 31, 2006, there was $157.9 million of total unrecognized compensation cost related to restricted stock granted under the Plan, which is expected to be recognized over a weighted-average period of 5.9 years. The total fair value of shares vested during the fiscal years ended January 31, 2006, 2005, and 2004, was $19.9 million, $33.9 million and $8.0 million, respectively.

During fiscal 2005, the Company began issuing performance share awards under the Plan, the vesting of which is tied to the achievement of performance criteria. These awards accrue to the associate based on the extent to which revenue growth and return on investment goals are attained or exceeded over a one- to three-year period. Based on the extent to which the targets are achieved, vested shares may range from 0% to 150% of the original award amount. Because the performance shares may be settled in stock or cash, the performance shares are accounted for as liabilities in the accompanying balance sheets. Outstanding performance shares, the related liability and unrecognized compensation cost as of January 31, 2006 and 2005, were not significant.

The Company's United Kingdom subsidiary, ASDA, also offers two other stock option plans to its associates. The first plan, The ASDA Colleague Share Ownership Plan 1999 ("CSOP"), grants options to certain associates. Options granted under the CSOP Plan generally expire six years from the date of grant, with half

vesting on the third anniversary of the grant and the other half on the sixth anniversary of the date of grant. Shares in the money at the vesting date are exercised while shares out of the money at the vesting date expire. The second plan, The ASDA Sharesave Plan 2000 ("Sharesave"), grants options to certain associates at 80% of market value on the date of grant. Sharesave options become exercisable after either a three-year or five-year period and generally lapse six months after becoming exercisable. Outstanding options under these plans as well as the related aggregate intrinsic value as of January 31, 2006, were not significant.

8 LITIGATION

The Company is involved in a number of legal proceedings. In accordance with Statement of Financial Accounting Standards No. 5, "Accounting for Contingencies," the Company has made accruals with respect to these matters, where appropriate, which are reflected in the Company's consolidated financial statements. The Company may enter into discussions regarding settlement of these matters, and may enter into settlement agreements, if it believes settlement is in the best interests of the Company's shareholders. The matters, or groups of related matters, discussed below, if decided adversely to or settled by the Company, individually or in the aggregate, may result in liability material to the Company's financial condition or results of operations.

The Company is a defendant in numerous cases containing class-action allegations in which the plaintiffs have brought claims under the Fair Labor Standards Act ("FLSA"), corresponding state statutes, or other laws. The plaintiffs in these lawsuits are current and former hourly associates who allege, among other things, that the Company forced them to work "off the clock," or failed to provide work breaks, or otherwise claim they were not paid for work performed. The complaints generally seek unspecified monetary damages, injunctive relief, or both. Class certification has yet to be addressed in a majority of the cases. Class certification has been denied or overturned in cases pending in Arizona, Arkansas, Florida, Georgia, Indiana, Louisiana, Maryland, Michigan, Nevada, New Jersey, North Carolina, Ohio, Texas, West Virginia and Wisconsin. Some or all of the requested classes have been certified in cases pending in California, Colorado, Massachusetts, Minnesota, Missouri, New Mexico, Oregon, Pennsylvania and Washington. Conditional certifications for notice purposes under the FLSA have been allowed in cases in Georgia, Michigan and Texas. The Company cannot estimate the possible loss or range of loss which may arise from these lawsuits.

The Company is a defendant in *Savaglio v. Wal-Mart Stores, Inc.*, a class-action lawsuit in which the plaintiffs allege that they were not provided meal and rest breaks in accordance with California law, and seek monetary damages and injunctive relief. A jury trial on the plaintiffs' claims for monetary damages concluded on December 22, 2005. The jury returned a verdict of $57,216,673 in statutory penalties and $115 million in punitive damages. The Company believes that it has substantial defenses to the claims at issue, and intends to challenge the verdict in post-trial motions and, if necessary, on appeal. Meanwhile, the plaintiffs' claims for injunctive relief have been tentatively set for trial in June 2006.

A putative class action is pending in California challenging the methodology of payments made under various Associate incentive bonus plans, and a second putative class action in California asserts that the Company has omitted to include bonus payments in calculating associates' regular rate of pay for purposes of determining overtime. As to the first case (*Cruz v. Wal-Mart Stores, Inc.*), the Company cannot estimate the possible loss or range of loss which may arise. The parties have entered into an agreement to settle the second case (*Fries v. Wal-Mart Stores, Inc.*), which must be approved by the court in order to become effective. If approved by the court, the settlement will include all class members who do not opt out of the settlement class. The amount to be paid by Wal-Mart under the settlement will not have a material impact on the Company's financial condition or results of operations.

The Company is currently a defendant in five putative class actions brought on behalf of assistant store managers who challenge their exempt status under state and federal laws, which are pending in California, Michigan, New Mexico and Tennessee. Conditional certification for notice purposes under the FLSA has been granted in one of these cases (*Comer v. Wal-Mart Stores, Inc.*). Otherwise, no determination has been made as to class certification in any of these cases. The Company cannot estimate the possible loss or range of loss which may arise from these lawsuits.

The Company is a defendant in *Dukes v. Wal-Mart Stores, Inc.*, a class-action lawsuit commenced in June 2001 and pending in the United States District Court for the Northern District of California. The case was brought on behalf of all past and present female employees in all of the Company's retail stores and warehouse clubs in the United States. The complaint alleges that the Company has engaged in a pattern and practice of discriminating against women in promotions, pay, training and job assignments. The complaint seeks, among other things, injunctive relief, front pay, back pay, punitive damages, and attorneys' fees. Following a hearing on class certification on September 24, 2003, on June 21, 2004, the District Court issued an order granting in part and denying in part the plaintiffs' motion for class certification. The class, which was certified by the District Court for purposes of liability, injunctive and declaratory relief, punitive damages, and lost pay, subject to certain exceptions, includes all women employed at any Wal-Mart domestic retail store at any time since December 26, 1998, who have been or may be subjected to the pay and management track promotions policies and practices challenged by the plaintiffs. The class as certified currently includes approximately 1.6 million present and former female associates.

The Company believes that the District Court's ruling is incorrect. The United States Court of Appeals for the Ninth Circuit has granted the Company's petition for discretionary review of the ruling. The Court of Appeals heard oral argument from counsel in the case on August 8, 2005. There is no indication at this time as to when a decision will be rendered. If the Company is not successful in its appeal of class certification, or an appellate court issues a ruling that allows for the certification of a class or classes with a different size or scope, and if there is a subsequent adverse verdict on the merits from which there is no successful appeal, or in the event of a negotiated settlement of the litigation, the resulting liability could be material to the Company. The plaintiffs also seek punitive damages which, if awarded, could result in the payment of additional amounts material to the Company. However, because of the uncertainty of the outcome of the appeal from the District Court's certification decision, because of the uncertainty of the balance of the proceedings contemplated by the District Court, and because the Company's liability, if any, arising from the litigation, including the size of any damages award if plaintiffs are successful in the litigation or any negotiated settlement, could vary widely, the Company cannot reasonably estimate the possible loss or range of loss which may arise from the litigation.

The Company is a defendant in *Mauldin v. Wal-Mart Stores, Inc.*, a class-action lawsuit that was filed on October 16, 2001, in the United States District Court for the Northern District of Georgia, Atlanta Division. The class was certified on August 23, 2002. On September 30, 2003, the court denied the Company's motion to reconsider that ruling. The class is composed of female Wal-Mart associates who were participants in the Associates Health and Welfare Plan at any time from March 8, 2001, to the present and who were using prescription contraceptives. The class seeks amendment of the Plan to include coverage for prescription contraceptives, back pay for all members in the form of reimbursement of the cost of prescription contraceptives, pre-judgment interest, and attorneys'

Notes to Consolidated Financial Statements
WAL-MART

fees. The complaint alleges that the Company's Health Plan violates Title VII's prohibition against gender discrimination in that the Health Plan's Reproductive Systems provision does not provide coverage for prescription contraceptives. The Company cannot estimate the possible loss or range of loss which may arise from this litigation.

The Company is a defendant in a lawsuit that was filed on August 24, 2001, in the United States District Court for the Eastern District of Kentucky. *EEOC (Janice Smith) v. Wal-Mart Stores, Inc.* is an action brought by the EEOC on behalf of Janice Smith and all other females who made application or transfer requests at the London, Kentucky, distribution center from 1995 to the present, and who were not hired or transferred into the warehouse positions for which they applied. The class seeks back pay for those females not selected for hire or transfer during the relevant time period. The class also seeks injunctive and prospective affirmative relief. The complaint alleges that the Company based hiring decisions on gender in violation of Title VII of the 1964 Civil Rights Act as amended. The EEOC can maintain this action as a class without certification. The Company cannot estimate the possible loss or range of loss which may arise from this litigation.

On November 8, 2005, the Company received a grand jury subpoena from the United States Attorney's Office for the Central District of California, seeking documents and information relating to the Company's receipt, transportation, handling, identification, recycling, treatment, storage and disposal of certain merchandise that constitutes hazardous materials or hazardous waste. The Company has been informed by the U.S. Attorney's Office for the Central District of California that it is a target of a criminal investigation into potential violations of the Resource Conservation and Recovery Act ("RCRA"), the Clean Water Act, and the Hazardous Materials Transportation Statute. This U.S. Attorney's Office contends, among other things, that the use of Company trucks to transport certain returned merchandise from the Company's stores to its return centers is prohibited by RCRA because those materials may be considered hazardous waste. The government alleges that, to comply with RCRA, the Company must ship from the store certain materials as "hazardous waste" directly to a certified disposal facility using a certified hazardous waste carrier. The Company contends that the practice of transporting returned merchandise to its return centers for subsequent disposition, including disposal by certified facilities, is compliant with applicable laws and regulations.

Additionally, the U.S. Attorney's Office in the Northern District of California has initiated its own investigation regarding the Company's handling of hazardous materials and hazardous waste and the Company has received administrative document requests from the California Department of Toxic Substances Control requesting documents and information with respect to two of the Company's distribution facilities. Further, the Company also received a subpoena from the Los Angeles County District Attorney's Office for documents and administrative interrogatories requesting information, among other things, regarding the Company's handling of materials and hazardous waste. California state and local government authorities and the State of Nevada have also initiated investigations into these matters. The Company is cooperating fully with the respective authorities.

The Company cannot estimate the possible loss or range of loss which may arise from this matter.

9 COMMITMENTS

The Company and certain of its subsidiaries have long-term leases for stores and equipment. Rentals (including, for certain leases, amounts applicable to taxes, insurance, maintenance, other operating expenses and contingent rentals) under operating leases and other short-term rental arrangements were $1.3 billion, $1.2 billion and $1.1 billion in 2006, 2005 and 2004, respectively. Aggregate minimum annual rentals at January 31, 2006, under non-cancelable leases are as follows (in millions):

Fiscal Year	Operating Leases	Capital Leases
2007	$ 797	$ 592
2008	751	588
2009	710	550
2010	634	526
2011	586	514
Thereafter	6,205	3,610
Total minimum rentals	$9,683	6,380
Less estimated executory costs		39
Net minimum lease payments		6,341
Less imputed interest at rates ranging from 3.0% to 29.0%		2,300
Present value of minimum lease payments		$4,041

The Company has entered into sale/leaseback transactions involving buildings and the underlying land that were accounted for as capital and operating leases. Included in the annual maturities schedule above are $429 million of capital leases and $140 million of operating leases.

Certain of the Company's leases provide for the payment of contingent rentals based on a percentage of sales. Such contingent rentals amounted to $27 million, $32 million and $38 million in 2006, 2005 and 2004, respectively. Substantially all of the Company's store leases have renewal options, some of which may trigger an escalation in rentals.

In connection with certain debt financing, we could be liable for early termination payments if certain unlikely events were to occur. At January 31, 2006, the aggregate termination payment was $89 million. These two arrangements expire in fiscal 2011 and fiscal 2019.

In connection with the development of our grocery distribution network in the United States, we have agreements with third parties which would require us to purchase or assume the leases on certain unique equipment in the event the agreements are terminated. These agreements, which can be terminated by either party at will, cover up to a five-year period and obligate the Company to pay up to approximately $233 million upon termination of some or all of these agreements.

There are no recourse provisions which would enable us to recover from third parties any amounts paid under the above guarantees. No liability for these guarantees has been recorded in our financial statements.

The Company has entered into lease commitments for land and buildings for 60 future locations. These lease commitments with real estate developers provide for minimum rentals ranging from 5 to 35 years, which if consummated based on current cost estimates, will approximate $95 million annually over the lease terms.

10 RETIREMENT-RELATED BENEFITS

In the United States, the Company maintains a Profit Sharing and 401(k) Retirement Savings Plan under which most full-time and many part-time associates become participants following one year of employment. The Profit Sharing component of the plan is entirely funded by the Company, with an additional contribution made by the Company to the associates' 401(k) component of the plan. In addition to the Company contributions to the 401(k) Retirement Savings component of the plan, associates may elect to contribute a percentage of their earnings. During fiscal 2006, participants could contribute up to 25% of their pretax earnings, but not more than statutory limits.

Associates may choose from among 13 different investment options for the 401(k) Retirement Savings component of the plan. For associates who did not make an election, their 401(k) balance in the plan is placed in a balanced fund. Associates are immediately vested in their 401(k) funds and may change their investment options at any time. Additionally, fully vested associates have the same 13 investment options for the Profit Sharing component of the plan. Associates are fully vested in the Profit Sharing component of the plan after seven years of service.

Annual contributions made by the Company to the United States and Puerto Rico Profit Sharing and 401(k) Retirement Savings Plans are made at the sole discretion of the Company, and were $827 million, $756 million and $662 million for fiscal 2006, 2005 and 2004, respectively.

Employees in foreign countries who are not U.S. citizens are covered by various post-employment benefit arrangements. These plans are administered based upon the legislative and tax requirements in the country in which they are established. Annual contributions to foreign retirement savings and profit sharing plans are made at the discretion of the Company, and were $244 million, $199 million and $123 million in fiscal 2006, 2005 and 2004, respectively.

The Company's subsidiaries in the United Kingdom and Japan have defined benefit pension plans. The plan in the United Kingdom was underfunded by $332 million and $419 million at January 31, 2006 and 2005, respectively. The plan in Japan was underfunded by $228 million at January 31, 2006.

11 SEGMENTS

At January 31, 2006, the Company and its subsidiaries were principally engaged in the operation of retail stores located in all 50 states, Argentina, Brazil, Canada, Germany, South Korea, Puerto Rico and the United Kingdom, through joint ventures in China, and through majority-owned subsidiaries in Japan and Mexico. The Company identifies segments based on management responsibility within the United States and in total for international units.

The Wal-Mart Stores segment includes the Company's supercenters, discount stores and Neighborhood Markets in the United States, as well as Walmart.com. The SAM'S CLUB segment includes the warehouse membership clubs in the United States as well as samsclub.com. At January 31, 2006, the International segment consisted of the Company's operations in Argentina, Brazil, China, Germany, Mexico, South Korea, Japan and the United Kingdom, which are consolidated using a December 31 fiscal year-end, generally due to statutory reporting requirements. There were no significant intervening events which materially affected the financial statements. The Company's operations in Canada and Puerto Rico are consolidated using a January 31 fiscal year-end. The amounts under the caption "Other" in the following table include unallocated corporate overhead. The Company's portion of the results of our unconsolidated minority interest in Seiyu prior to December 20, 2005, and our unconsolidated minority interest in CARHCO are also included under the caption "Other."

Notes to Consolidated Financial Statements
WAL-MART

The Company measures the profit of its segments as "segment operating income," which is defined as income from continuing operations before net interest expense, income taxes and minority interest. Information on segments and the reconciliation to income from continuing operations before income taxes and minority interest are as follows (in millions):

Fiscal Year Ended January 31, 2006	Wal-Mart Stores	SAM'S CLUB	International	Other	Consolidated
Revenues from external customers	$209,910	$39,798	$62,719	$ –	$312,427
Intercompany real estate charge (income)	3,454	547	–	(4,001)	–
Depreciation and amortization	1,922	296	1,043	1,456	4,717
Operating income (loss)	15,324	1,385	3,330	(1,509)	18,530
Interest expense, net					(1,172)
Income from continuing operations before income taxes and minority interest					$ 17,358
Total assets of continuing operations	$ 32,809	$ 5,686	$51,581	$48,111	$138,187

Fiscal Year Ended January 31, 2005	Wal-Mart Stores	SAM'S CLUB	International	Other	Consolidated
Revenues from external customers	$ 191,826	$ 37,119	$ 56,277	$ –	$ 285,222
Intercompany real estate charge (income)	2,754	513	–	(3,267)	–
Depreciation and amortization	1,561	274	919	1,510	4,264
Operating income (loss)	14,163	1,280	2,988	(1,340)	17,091
Interest expense, net					(986)
Income from continuing operations before income taxes and minority interest					$ 16,105
Total assets of continuing operations	$ 29,489	$ 5,685	$ 40,981	$ 43,999	$ 120,154

Fiscal Year Ended January 31, 2004	Wal-Mart Stores	SAM'S CLUB	International	Other	Consolidated
Revenues from external customers	$ 174,220	$ 34,537	$ 47,572	$ –	$ 256,329
Intercompany real estate charge (income)	2,468	484	–	(2,952)	–
Depreciation and amortization	1,482	249	810	1,311	3,852
Operating income (loss)	12,916	1,126	2,370	(1,387)	15,025
Interest expense, net					(832)
Income from continuing operations before income taxes and minority interest					$ 14,193
Total assets of continuing operations	$ 27,028	$ 4,751	$ 35,230	$ 38,396	$ 105,405

Certain information for fiscal years 2005 and 2004 has been reclassified to conform to current-year presentation.

In the United States, long-lived assets, net, excluding goodwill and other assets and deferred charges were $55.5 billion and $48.4 billion as of January 31, 2006 and 2005, respectively. In the United States, additions to long-lived assets were $11.8 billion, $9.8 billion and $8.1 billion in fiscal 2006, 2005 and 2004, respectively. Outside of the United States, long-lived assets, net, excluding goodwill and other assets and deferred charges were $23.8 billion and $19.7 billion in fiscal 2006 and 2005, respectively. Outside of the United States, additions to long-lived assets were $2.8 billion, $3.1 billion and $2.2 billion in fiscal 2006, 2005 and 2004, respectively. The International segment includes all real estate outside the United States. The operations of the Company's ASDA subsidiary are significant in comparison to the total operations of the International segment. ASDA sales during fiscal 2006, 2005 and 2004 were $26.8 billion, $26.0 billion and $21.7 billion, respectively. At January 31, 2006 and 2005, ASDA long-lived assets, consisting primarily of property and equipment, net, and goodwill, net, totaled $17.7 billion and $18.9 billion, respectively. The decline in ASDA's long-lived assets from January 31, 2005 to January 31, 2006 was largely due to foreign currency translation.

12 QUARTERLY FINANCIAL DATA (UNAUDITED)

(Amounts in millions except per share information)	April 30,	July 31,	October 31,	January 31,
		Quarters ended		
Fiscal 2006				
Net sales	**$70,908**	**$76,811**	**$75,436**	**$89,273**
Cost of sales	**54,571**	**58,787**	**57,988**	**69,045**
Gross profit	**$16,337**	**$18,024**	**$17,448**	**$20,228**
Net income	**$ 2,461**	**$ 2,805**	**$ 2,374**	**$ 3,589**
Basic and diluted net income per common share	**$ 0.58**	**$ 0.67**	**$ 0.57**	**$ 0.86**
Fiscal 2005				
Net sales	$64,763	$69,722	$68,520	$82,216
Cost of sales	49,969	53,533	52,567	63,723
Gross profit	$14,794	$16,189	$15,953	$18,493
Net income	$ 2,166	$ 2,651	$ 2,286	$ 3,164
Basic and diluted net income per common share	$ 0.50	$ 0.62	$ 0.54	$ 0.75

The sum of quarterly financial data will not agree to annual amounts due to rounding.

13 SUBSEQUENT EVENTS

On March 2, 2006, the Company's Board of Directors approved an increase in the Company's annual dividend to $0.67 per share. The annual dividend will be paid in four quarterly installments on April 3, 2006, June 5, 2006, September 5, 2006, and January 2, 2007 to holders of record on March 17, May 19, August 18 and December 15, 2006, respectively.

In February 2006, we entered into a £150 million revolving credit facility in the United Kingdom. Interest on borrowings under the credit facility accrues at LIBOR plus 25 basis points.

Report of Independent Registered Public Accounting Firm
WAL-MART

The Board of Directors and Shareholders,
Wal-Mart Stores, Inc.

We have audited the accompanying consolidated balance sheets of Wal-Mart Stores, Inc. as of January 31, 2006 and 2005, and the related consolidated statements of income, shareholders' equity and cash flows for each of the three years in the period ended January 31, 2006. These financial statements are the responsibility of the Company's management. Our responsibility is to express an opinion on these financial statements based on our audits.

We conducted our audits in accordance with the standards of the Public Company Accounting Oversight Board (United States). Those standards require that we plan and perform the audit to obtain reasonable assurance about whether the financial statements are free of material misstatement. An audit includes examining, on a test basis, evidence supporting the amounts and disclosures in the financial statements. An audit also includes assessing the accounting principles used and significant estimates made by management, as well as evaluating the overall financial statement presentation. We believe that our audits provide a reasonable basis for our opinion.

In our opinion, the financial statements referred to above present fairly, in all material respects, the consolidated financial position of Wal-Mart Stores, Inc. at January 31, 2006 and 2005, and the consolidated results of its operations and its cash flows for each of the three years in the period ended January 31, 2006, in conformity with U.S. generally accepted accounting principles.

We also have audited, in accordance with the standards of the Public Company Accounting Oversight Board (United States), the effectiveness of Wal-Mart Stores, Inc.'s internal control over financial reporting as of January 31, 2006, based on criteria established in *Internal Control – Integrated Framework* issued by the Committee of Sponsoring Organizations of the Treadway Commission and our report dated March 27, 2006 expressed an unqualified opinion thereon.

Ernst & Young LLP

Rogers, Arkansas
March 27, 2006

Report of Independent Registered Public Accounting Firm on Internal Control Over Financial Reporting
WAL-MART

The Board of Directors and Shareholders,
Wal-Mart Stores, Inc.

We have audited management's assessment, included in the accompanying Management's Report to Our Shareholders under the caption "Report on Internal Control Over Financial Reporting," that Wal-Mart Stores, Inc. maintained effective internal control over financial reporting as of January 31, 2006, based on criteria established in *Internal Control – Integrated Framework* issued by the Committee of Sponsoring Organizations of the Treadway Commission (the COSO criteria). Wal-Mart Stores, Inc.'s management is responsible for maintaining effective internal control over financial reporting and for its assessment of the effectiveness of internal control over financial reporting. Our responsibility is to express an opinion on management's assessment and an opinion on the effectiveness of the company's internal control over financial reporting based on our audit.

We conducted our audit in accordance with the standards of the Public Company Accounting Oversight Board (United States). Those standards require that we plan and perform the audit to obtain reasonable assurance about whether effective internal control over financial reporting was maintained in all material respects. Our audit included obtaining an understanding of internal control over financial reporting, evaluating management's assessment, testing and evaluating the design and operating effectiveness of internal control, and performing such other procedures as we considered necessary in the circumstances. We believe that our audit provides a reasonable basis for our opinion.

A company's internal control over financial reporting is a process designed to provide reasonable assurance regarding the reliability of financial reporting and the preparation of financial statements for external purposes in accordance with generally accepted accounting principles. A company's internal control over financial reporting includes those policies and procedures that (1) pertain to the maintenance of records that, in reasonable detail, accurately and fairly reflect the transactions and dispositions of the assets of the company; (2) provide reasonable assurance that transactions are recorded as necessary to permit preparation of financial statements in accordance with generally accepted accounting principles, and that receipts and expenditures of the company are being made only in accordance with authorizations of management and directors of the company; and (3) provide reasonable assurance regarding prevention or timely detection of unauthorized acquisition, use, or disposition of the company's assets that could have a material effect on the financial statements.

Because of its inherent limitations, internal control over financial reporting may not prevent or detect misstatements. Also, projections of any evaluation of effectiveness to future periods are subject to the risk that controls may become inadequate because of changes in conditions, or that the degree of compliance with the policies or procedures may deteriorate.

As indicated in the accompanying Management's Report to Our Shareholders, management's assessment of and conclusion on the effectiveness of internal control over financial reporting did not include the internal controls of The Seiyu, Ltd., and Sonae Distribuição Brasil S.A., both of which were acquired in fiscal 2006 and are included in the fiscal 2006 consolidated financial statements of Wal-Mart Stores, Inc. These entities represented, in the aggregate, 5.8% and 0.1% of total assets and total net sales, respectively, of the Company as of, and for the year ended, January 31, 2006. These acquisitions are more fully discussed in Note 6 to the consolidated financial statements for fiscal 2006. Our audit of internal control over financial reporting of Wal-Mart Stores, Inc. also did not include an evaluation of the internal control over financial reporting for these fiscal 2006 acquisitions.

In our opinion, management's assessment that Wal-Mart Stores, Inc. maintained effective internal control over financial reporting as of January 31, 2006, is fairly stated, in all material respects, based on the COSO criteria. Also, in our opinion, Wal-Mart Stores, Inc., maintained, in all material respects, effective internal control over financial reporting as of January 31, 2006, based on the COSO criteria.

We also have audited, in accordance with the standards of the Public Company Accounting Oversight Board (United States), the consolidated balance sheets of Wal-Mart Stores, Inc. as of January 31, 2006 and 2005, and the related consolidated statements of income, shareholders' equity and cash flows for each of the three years in the period ended January 31, 2006 and our report dated March 27, 2006 expressed an unqualified opinion thereon.

.

Ernst + Young LLP

Rogers, Arkansas
March 27, 2006

Management's Report to Our Shareholders
WAL-MART

Management of Wal-Mart Stores, Inc. ("Wal-Mart" or the "Company") is responsible for the preparation, integrity and objectivity of Wal-Mart's consolidated financial statements and other financial information contained in this Annual Report to Shareholders. Those consolidated financial statements were prepared in conformity with accounting principles generally accepted in the United States. In preparing those consolidated financial statements, management was required to make certain estimates and judgments, which are based upon currently available information and management's view of current conditions and circumstances.

The Audit Committee of the Board of Directors, which consists solely of independent directors, oversees our process of reporting financial information and the audit of our consolidated financial statements. The Audit Committee stays informed of the financial condition of Wal-Mart and regularly reviews management's financial policies and procedures, the independence of our independent auditors, our internal control and the objectivity of our financial reporting. Both the independent auditors and the internal auditors have free access to the Audit Committee and meet with the Audit Committee periodically, both with and without management present.

We have retained Ernst & Young LLP, an independent registered public accounting firm, to audit our consolidated financial statements found in this annual report. We have made available to Ernst & Young LLP all of our financial records and related data in connection with their audit of our consolidated financial statements.

We have filed with the Securities and Exchange Commission ("SEC") the required certifications related to our consolidated financial statements as of and for the year ended January 31, 2006. These certifications are attached as exhibits to our Annual Report on Form 10-K for the year ended January 31, 2006. Additionally, we have also provided to the New York Stock Exchange the required annual certification of our Chief Executive Officer regarding our compliance with the New York Stock Exchange's corporate governance listing standards.

Report on Internal Control Over Financial Reporting.
Management has responsibility for establishing and maintaining adequate internal control over financial reporting. Internal control over financial reporting is a process designed to provide reasonable assurance regarding the reliability of financial reporting and the preparation of financial statements for external reporting purposes in accordance with accounting principles generally accepted in the United States. Because of its inherent limitations, internal control over financial reporting may not prevent or detect misstatements. Management has assessed the effectiveness of the Company's internal control over financial reporting as of January 31, 2006. In making its assessment, management has utilized the criteria set forth by the Committee of Sponsoring Organizations ("COSO") of the Treadway Commission in *Internal Control – Integrated Framework*. Management concluded that based on its assessment, Wal-Mart's internal control over financial reporting was effective as of January 31, 2006. Management's assessment of the effectiveness of the Company's internal control over financial reporting as of January 31, 2006, has been audited by Ernst & Young LLP, an independent registered public accounting firm, as stated in their report which appears in this Annual Report to Shareholders.

Management's assessment of the effectiveness of the Company's internal control over financial reporting excluded The Seiyu, Ltd. and Sonae Distribuição Brasil S.A., both of which were acquired in fiscal 2006. These entities represented, in the aggregate, 5.8% and

0.1% of consolidated total assets and consolidated net sales, respectively, of the Company as of and for the year ended January 31, 2006. These acquisitions are more fully discussed in Note 6 to our consolidated financial statements for fiscal 2006. Under guidelines established by the SEC, companies are allowed to exclude acquisitions from their first assessment of internal control over financial reporting following the date of the acquisition.

Evaluation of Disclosure Controls and Procedures.
We maintain disclosure controls and procedures designed to provide reasonable assurance that information required to be timely disclosed is accumulated and communicated to management in a timely fashion. Management has assessed the effectiveness of these disclosure controls and procedures as of January 31, 2006, and determined they were effective as of that date to provide reasonable assurance that information required to be disclosed by us in the reports we file or submit under the Securities Exchange Act of 1934, as amended, was accumulated and communicated to management, as appropriate, to allow timely decisions regarding required disclosure and were effective to provide reasonable assurance that such information is recorded, processed, summarized and reported within the time periods specified by the SEC's rules and forms.

Report on Ethical Standards.
Our Company was founded on the belief that open communications and the highest standards of ethics are necessary to be successful. Our long-standing "Open Door" communication policy helps management be aware of and address issues in a timely and effective manner. Through the open door policy all associates are encouraged to inform management at the appropriate level when they are concerned about any matter pertaining to Wal-Mart.

Wal-Mart has adopted a Statement of Ethics to guide our associates in the continued observance of high ethical standards such as honesty, integrity and compliance with the law in the conduct of Wal-Mart's business. Familiarity and compliance with the Statement of Ethics is required of all associates who are part of management. The Company also maintains a separate Code of Ethics for our senior financial officers. Wal-Mart also has in place a Related-Party Transaction Policy. This policy applies to Wal-Mart's senior officers and directors and requires material related-party transactions to be reviewed by the Audit Committee. The senior officers and directors are required to report material related-party transactions to Wal-Mart. We maintain an ethics office which oversees and administers an ethics hotline. The ethics hotline provides a channel for associates to make confidential and anonymous complaints regarding potential violations of our statements of ethics, including violations related to financial or accounting matters.

H. Lee Scott
President and Chief Executive Officer

Thomas M. Schoewe
Executive Vice President and Chief Financial Officer

Fiscal 2006 End-of-Year Store Count
WAL-MART

State	Discount Stores	Supercenters	SAM'S CLUBs	Neighborhood Markets
Alabama	13	76	11	2
Alaska	7	0	3	0
Arizona	15	42	13	9
Arkansas	20	60	5	6
California	146	13	35	0
Colorado	13	44	15	0
Connecticut	28	4	3	0
Delaware	4	4	1	0
Florida	48	128	39	9
Georgia	15	101	21	0
Hawaii	8	0	2	0
Idaho	3	14	1	0
Illinois	79	51	28	0
Indiana	27	61	16	4
Iowa	18	37	7	0
Kansas	18	35	6	3
Kentucky	22	59	7	2
Louisiana	23	60	13	1
Maine	10	12	3	0
Maryland	33	8	12	0
Massachusetts	41	3	4	0
Michigan	37	40	25	0
Minnesota	31	21	13	0
Mississippi	12	53	6	1
Missouri	40	77	15	0
Montana	4	7	1	0
Nebraska	3	23	3	0
Nevada	8	15	5	6
New Hampshire	19	7	4	0
New Jersey	40	1	9	0
New Mexico	3	26	6	1
New York	48	35	18	0
North Carolina	34	78	19	0
North Dakota	7	1	2	0
Ohio	52	72	27	0
Oklahoma	29	53	8	15
Oregon	17	12	0	0
Pennsylvania	46	70	23	0
Rhode Island	7	1	1	0
South Carolina	14	49	9	0
South Dakota	1	10	2	0
Tennessee	16	81	16	6
Texas	62	253	70	30
Utah	2	26	7	5
Vermont	4	0	0	0
Virginia	20	61	13	0
Washington	21	19	3	0
W. Virginia	6	26	4	0
Wisconsin	34	43	11	0
Wyoming	1	8	2	0
U.S. Totals	**1,209**	**1,980**	**567**	**100**

International/Worldwide

Country	Discount Stores	Supercenters	SAM'S CLUBs	Neighborhood Markets
Argentina	0	11	0	0
Brazil	255*	23	15	2*
Canada	272	0	6	0
China	0	51	3	2
Germany	0	88	0	0
Japan	2‡	96‡	0	300‡
South Korea	0	16	0	0
Mexico	599†	105	70	0
Puerto Rico	9	5	9	31**
United Kingdom	294§	21	0	0
International Totals	**1,431**	**416**	**103**	**335**
Grand Totals	**2,640**	**2,396**	**670**	**435**

* Brazil includes 2 Todo Dias, 116 Bompreço and 139 Sonae.

‡ Japan includes 2 GM only, 96 general merchandise, apparel and food stores and 300 supermarkets. Japan excludes 45 Wakana units, which are take-out restaurants generally less than 1,000 square feet in size.

† Mexico includes 187 Bodegas, 16 Mi Bodegas, 1 Mi Bodega Express, 1 Mercamas, 53 Suburbias, 55 Superamas, 286 Vips and does not include Vips franchises.

** Puerto Rico includes 31 Amigos.

§ United Kingdom includes 236 ASDA stores, 10 George stores, 5 ASDA Living and 43 ASDA small stores.

APPENDIX B: Glossary

A

account An accounting record in which the results of transactions are accumulated; shows increases, decreases, and a balance.

accounting A system for providing quantitative, financial information about economic entities that is useful for making sound economic decisions. Accounting is often called the "language of business" because it provides the means of recording and communicating business activities and the results of those activities.

accounting cycle The procedure for analyzing, recording, summarizing, and reporting the transactions of a business.

accounting equation An algebraic equation that expresses the relationship between assets (resources), liabilities (obligations), and owner's equity (net assets, or the residual interest in a business after all liabilities have been met): Assets = Liabilities + Owners' Equity.

accounting model The basic accounting assumptions, concepts, principles, and procedures that determine the manner of recording, measuring, and reporting a company's transactions.

accounting system The procedures and processes used by a business to analyze transactions, handle routine bookkeeping tasks, and structure information so it can be used to evaluate the performance and health of the business.

accounts receivable A current asset representing money due for services performed or merchandise sold on credit.

accounts receivable turnover A measure used to indicate how fast a company collects its receivables; computed by dividing sales by average accounts receivable.

accrual-basis accounting A system of accounting in which revenues and expenses are recorded as they are earned and incurred, not necessarily when cash is received or paid.

accumulated other comprehensive income Certain market-related gains and losses that are not included in the computation of net income; for example, foreign currency translation adjustments and unrealized gains or losses on investments.

activity-based costing (ABC) A method of attributing overhead costs to products based on measurable factors that relate to activities that create overhead costs.

adjusting entries Entries required at the end of each accounting period to recognize, on an accrual basis, revenues and expenses for the period and to report proper amounts for asset, liability, and owners' equity accounts.

aging accounts receivable The process of categorizing each account receivable by the number of days it has been outstanding.

allowance for bad debts A contra account, deducted from Accounts Receivable, that shows the estimated losses from uncollectible accounts.

allowance method The recording of estimated losses due to uncollectible accounts as expenses during the period in which the sales occurred.

American Institute of Certified Public Accountants (AICPA) The national organization of CPAs in the United States.

amortization The process of cost allocation that assigns the original cost of an intangible asset to the periods benefited.

annual report A document that summarizes the results of operations and financial status of a company for the past year and outlines plans for the future.

annuity A series of equal amounts to be received or paid at the end of equal time intervals.

appraisal costs Costs of quality that relate specifically to the effort of inspecting, testing, and sampling activities performed in order to identify and remove low-quality products and services from the system.

arm's-length transactions Business dealings between independent and rational parties who are looking out for their own interests.

articulation The interrelationships among the financial statements.

asset turnover A measure of company efficiency, computed by dividing sales by total assets.

asset turnover ratio An overall measure of how effectively assets are used during a period; computed by dividing revenue by average total assets.

assets Economic resources that are owned or controlled by a company.

assets-to-equity ratio A measure of the number of dollars of assets a company is able to acquire using each dollar of equity; calculated by dividing assets by equity.

audit committee Members of a company's board of directors who are responsible for dealing with the external and internal auditors.

audit report A report issued by an independent CPA that expresses an opinion about whether the financial statements fairly present a company's financial position, operating results, and cash flows in accordance with generally accepted accounting principles.

available-for-sale securities Debt and equity securities not classified as trading, held-to-maturity, or equity method securities.

average collection period A measure of the average number of days it takes to collect a credit sale; computed by dividing 365 days by the accounts receivable turnover.

average cost An inventory cost flow assumption whereby cost of goods sold and the cost of ending inventory are determined by using an average cost of all merchandise available for sale during the period.

B

bad debt An uncollectible account receivable.

bad debt expense An account that represents the portion of the current period's credit sales that are estimated to be uncollectible.

balance sheet (statement of financial position) The financial statement that reports a company's assets, liabilities, and owners' equity at a particular date.

Balanced Scorecard A management model designed to link together performance measurers for financial, customer, internal process, and learning/growth perspectives that are unique to an organization's particular strategy.

bank reconciliation The process of systematically comparing the cash balance as reported by the bank with the cash balance on the company's books and explaining any differences.

basic earnings per share An earnings per share figure that divides net income by the number of shares of stock outstanding.

basket purchase The purchase of two or more assets acquired together at a single price.

batch-level activities Activities that take place in order to support a batch or production run, regardless of the size of the batch.

board of directors Individuals elected by the stockholders to govern a corporation.

bond A contract between a borrower and a lender in which the borrower promises to pay a specified rate of interest for each period the bond is outstanding and repay the principal at the maturity date.

bond carrying value The face value of bonds minus the unamortized discount or plus the unamortized premium.

bond discount The difference between the face value and the sales price when bonds are sold below their face value.

bond indenture A contract between a bond issuer and a bond purchaser that specifies the terms of a bond.

bond maturity date The date at which a bond principal or face amount becomes payable.

bond premium The difference between the face value and the sales price when bonds are sold above their face value.

bonus Additional compensation, beyond the regular compensation, that is paid to employees if certain objectives are achieved.

book value The value of a company as measured by the amount of owners' equity; that is, assets less liabilities.

bookkeeping The preservation of a systematic, quantitative record of an activity.

break-even point The amount of sales at which total costs of the number of units sold equal total revenues; the point at which there is no profit or loss.

budget A quantitative expression of a plan of action that shows how a firm or an organization will acquire and use resources over some specified period of time.

budget committee A management group responsible for establishing budgeting policy and for coordinating the preparation of budgets.

budgetary slack The process of inflating a department's budget request for resource inputs (e.g., materials, labor, time, etc.) or deflating the department's budget commitment to output (products, services, sales, etc.) so that the department manager can more easily achieve the budget.

budgeted product cost sheet A schedule of all of the product costs (i.e., the costs of direct materials, direct labor, and manufacturing overhead) used to create a single product.

budgeted service cost sheet A schedule of all of the service costs (i.e., the costs of supplies, wages and salaries, and overhead) used to provide a single service event.

business An organization operated with the objective of making a profit from the sale of goods or services.

business documents Records of transactions used as the basis for recording accounting entries; include invoices, check stubs, receipts, and similar business papers.

C

calendar year An entity's reporting year, covering 12 months and ending on December 31.

callable bonds Bonds for which the issuer reserves the right to pay the obligation before its maturity date.

capital The total amount of money or other resources owned or used to acquire future income or benefits.

capital budgeting Systematic planning for long-term investments in operating assets.

capital lease A leasing transaction that is recorded as a purchase by the lessee.

capital rationing Allocating limited resources among ranked acceptable investments.

capital stock The portion of a stockholders' equity that represents investment by owners in exchange for shares of stock. Also referred to as paid-in capital.

capitalized interest Interest that is recorded as part of the cost of a self-constructed asset.

cash Coins, currency, money orders, checks, and funds on deposit with financial institutions; the most liquid of assets.

cash budget A schedule of expected cash receipts and disbursements during the budget period.

cash dividend A cash distribution of earnings to stockholders.

cash equivalents Short-term, highly liquid investments that can easily be converted into cash.

cash flow adequacy ratio Cash from operations divided by expenditures for fixed asset additions and acquisitions of new businesses.

cash flow-to-net income ratio A ratio that reflects the extent to which accrual accounting assumptions and adjustments have been included in computing net income.

cash inflows Any current or expected revenues or savings directly associated with an investment.

cash outflows The initial cost and other expected outlays associated with an investment.

cash-basis accounting A system of accounting in which transactions are recorded and revenues and expenses are recognized only when cash is received or paid.

ceiling The maximum market amount at which inventory can be carried on the books; equal to net realizable value.

centralized company An organization in which top management makes most of the major decisions for the entire company rather than delegating decisions to managers at lower levels.

certified public accountant (CPA) A special designation given to an accountant who has passed a national uniform examination and has met other certifying requirements.

chart of accounts A systematic listing of all accounts used by a company.

classified balance sheet A balance sheet in which assets and liabilities are subdivided into current and long-term categories.

closing entries Entries that reduce all nominal, or temporary, accounts to a zero balance at the end of each accounting period, transferring their preclosing balances to a permanent balance sheet account.

common costs Overhead costs such as executive salaries or property taxes that cannot be attributed to and are not the responsibility of, specific products, departments, or business segments.

common stock The most frequently issued class of stock; usually, it provides a voting right but is secondary to preferred stock in dividend and liquidation rights.

common-size financial statements Financial statements achieved by dividing all financial statement numbers by total sales for the year.

comparative financial statements Financial statements in which data for two or more years are shown together.

compound journal entry A journal entry that involves more than one debit or more than one credit or both.

compounding period The period of time for which interest is computed.

comprehensive income A measure of the overall change in a company's wealth during a period; consists of net income plus changes in wealth resulting from changes in investment values and exchange rates.

conglomerates A company comprised of a number of divisions with those divisions often operating in different industries.

consignment An arrangement whereby merchandise owned by one party, the consignor, is sold by another party, the consignee, usually on a commission basis.

consolidated financial statements Statements that report the combined operating results, financial position, and cash flows of two or more legally separate but affiliated companies as if they were one economic entity.

contingency Circumstances involving potential losses or gains that will not be resolved until some future event occurs.

contra account An account that is offset or deducted from another account.

contributed capital The portion of owners' equity contributed by investors (the owners) in exchange for shares of stock.

contribution margin The difference between total sales and variable costs; the portion of sales revenue available to cover fixed costs and provide a profit.

contribution margin ratio The percentage of net sales revenue left after variable costs are deducted; the contribution margin divided by net sales revenue.

control activities (procedures) Policies and procedures used by management to meet their objectives.

control environment The actions, policies, and procedures that reflect the overall attitudes of top management about control and its importance to the entity.

controlling Implementing management plans and identifying how plans compare with actual performance.

conversion costs The costs of converting raw materials to finished products; include direct labor and manufacturing overhead costs.

convertible bonds Bonds that can be traded for, or converted to, other securities after a specified period of time.

convertible preferred stock Preferred stock that can be converted to common stock at a specified conversion rate.

corporation A legal entity chartered by a state; ownership is represented by transferable shares of stock.

cost behavior The way a cost is affected by changes in activity levels.

cost center An organizational unit in which a manager has control over and is held accountable for cost performance.

cost driver Numerical measure used to reflect the amount of a specific cost that is associated with a particular activity.

cost of capital The average cost of a firm's debt and equity capital; equals the rate of return that a company must earn in order to satisfy the demands of its owners and creditors.

cost of goods available for sale The cost of all merchandise available for sale during the period; equal to the sum of beginning inventory and net purchases.

Cost of Goods Manufactured schedule A schedule supporting the income statement that summarizes the total cost of goods manufactured and transferred out of the work-in-process inventory account during a period. These costs include direct materials, direct labor, and applied manufacturing overhead.

cost of goods sold The costs incurred to purchase or manufacture the merchandise sold during a period.

cost pool Total cost identified as being generated by a specific overhead cost activity.

cost principle The idea that transactions are recorded at their historical costs or exchange prices at the transaction date.

costs of quality (COQ) Costs spent to achieve high quality products and services, as well as costs spent when products fail to have high quality. The four types of costs of quality are prevention costs, appraisal costs, internal failure costs, and external failure costs.

cost-volume-profit (C-V-P) analysis Techniques for determining how changes in revenues, costs, and level of activity affect the profitability of an organization.

coupon bonds Unregistered bonds for which owners receive periodic interest payments by clipping a coupon from the bond and sending it to the issuer as evidence of ownership.

credit An entry on the right side of a T-account.

critical resource factor The resource that limits operating capacity by its availability.

cumulative-dividend preference The right of preferred stockholders to receive current dividends plus all dividends in arrears before common stockholders receive any dividends.

current assets Cash and other assets that can be easily converted to cash within a year.

current liabilities Liabilities expected to be satisfied within a year or the current operating cycle, whichever is longer.

current ratio A measure of the liquidity of a business; equal to current assets divided by current liabilities.

current-dividend preference The right of preferred stockholders to receive current dividends before common stockholders receive dividends.

customer relationship management (CRM) A corporate level strategy that focuses on creating and maintaining lasting relationships with its customers in order to establish long-term financial value for the organization.

D

date of record The date selected by a corporation's board of directors on which the stockholders of record are identified as those who will receive dividends.

debentures (unsecured bonds) Bonds for which no collateral has been pledged.

debit An entry on the left side of a T-account.

debt ratio A measure of leverage, computed by dividing total liabilities by total assets.

debt securities Financial instruments issued by a company that carry with them a promise of interest payments and the repayment of principal.

debt-to-equity ratio The number of dollars of borrowed funds for every dollar invested by owners; computed as total liabilities divided by total stockholders' equity.

decentralized company An organization in which managers at all levels have the authority to make decisions concerning the operations for which they are responsible.

declaration date The date on which a corporation's board of directors formally decides to pay a dividend to stockholders.

declining-balance depreciation method An accelerated depreciation method in which an asset's book value is multiplied by a constant depreciation rate (such as double the straight-line percentage, in the case of double-declining-balance).

defined benefit plan A pension plan under which the employer defines the amount that retiring employees will receive and contributes enough to the pension fund to pay that amount.

defined contribution plan A pension plan under which the employer contributes a defined amount to the pension fund; after retirement, the employees receive the amount contributed plus whatever it has earned.

depletion The process of cost allocation that assigns the original cost of a natural resource to the periods benefited.

depreciation The process of cost allocation that assigns the original cost of plant and equipment to the periods benefited.

detective controls Internal control activities that are designed to detect the occurrence of errors and fraud.

differential costs Future costs that change as a result of a decision; also called incremental or relevant costs.

diluted earnings per share An earnings per share figure that considers the effect on net income and shares outstanding of events that will likely occur in the future, such as the exercising of favorable stock options.

direct costs Costs that are specifically traceable to a unit of business or segment being analyzed.

direct labor Wages that are paid to those who physically work on direct materials to transform them into a finished product and are traceable to specific products.

direct labor budget A schedule of direct labor requirements for the budget period.

direct materials Materials that become part of the product and are traceable to it.

direct materials budget A schedule of direct materials to be used during the budget period and direct materials to be purchased during that period.

direct method A method of reporting net cash flows from operations that shows the major classes of cash receipts and payments for a period of time.

direct write-off method The recording of actual losses from uncollectible accounts as expenses during the period in which accounts receivable are determined to be uncollectible.

discounted cash flow methods Capital budgeting techniques that take into account the time value of money by comparing discounted cash flows.

disposable income Income left after withholdings and fixed expenses have been subtracted from gross salary; the amount left to cover variable expenditures.

dividend payment date The date on which a corporation pays dividends to its stockholders.

dividend payout ratio A measure of the percentage of earnings paid out in dividends; computed by dividing cash dividends by net income.

dividends Distributions to the owners (stockholders) of a corporation.

dividends in arrears Missed dividends for past years that preferred stockholders have a right to receive under the cumulative-dividend preference if and when dividends are declared.

double-entry accounting A system of recording transactions in a way that maintains the equality of the accounting equation.

DuPont framework A systematic approach for breaking down return on equity into three ratios: return on sales, asset turnover, and assets-to-equity ratio.

E

earnings (loss) per share (EPS) The amount of net income (earnings) related to each share of stock; computed by dividing net income by the number of shares of stock outstanding during the period.

Economic Value Added (EVA®) A commercialized performance measurement system that emphasizes the incremental income an organization creates over and above the income required to cover the costs of capital invested by both debt and equity holders in the organization.

effective-interest amortization A method of systematically writing off a bond premium or discount that takes into consideration the time value of money and results in an equal interest rate being used for amortization for each period.

employee stock options Rights given to employees to purchase shares of stock of a company at a predetermined price.

entity An organizational unit (a person, partnership, or corporation) for which accounting records are kept and about which accounting reports are prepared.

environmental liabilities Obligations incurred because of damage done to the environment.

equity method A method used to account for an investment in the stock of another company when significant influence can be imposed (presumed to exist when 20 to 50% of the outstanding voting stock is owned).

equity securities (stock) Shares of ownership in a corporation that can change significantly in value and that provide for a return to investors in the form of dividends.

equivalent units of production A method used in a process costing system to measure the production output during a period. Equivalent units of production essentially measures the "work done" by the center or department in terms of units of output.

estimated manufacturing overhead Budgeted manufacturing overhead costs that are used to establish the predetermined overhead rate.

evaluating Analyzing results, rewarding performance, and identifying problems.

exception reports Reports that highlight variances from, or exceptions to, the budget.

expenses Costs incurred in the normal course of business to generate revenues.

external auditors Independent CPAs who are retained by organizations to perform audits of financial statements.

external failure costs Costs of quality that relate specifically to the costs that occur when low-quality products and services fail after delivery to customers. These are often the most significant costs of quality to an organization.

extraordinary items Nonoperating gains and losses that are unusual in nature, infrequent in occurrence, and material in amount.

F

facility support activities Activities necessary to have a facility in place in order to participate in the development and production of products or services. However, these activities are not related to any particular line of products or services.

FIFO (first in, first out) An inventory cost flow assumption whereby the first goods purchased are assumed to be the first goods sold so that the ending inventory consists of the most recently purchased goods.

financial accounting The area of accounting concerned with reporting financial information to interested external parties.

Financial Accounting Standards Board (FASB) The private organization responsible for establishing the standards for financial accounting and reporting in the United States.

financial ratios Relationships between financial statement amounts.

financial statement analysis The examination of both the relationships among financial statement numbers and the trends in those numbers over time.

financial statements Reports such as the balance sheet, income statement, and statement of cash flows, which summarize the financial status and results of operations of a business entity.

financing activities Activities whereby cash is obtained from or repaid to owners and creditors.

finished goods Manufactured products ready for sale.

finished goods inventory Inventory that has completed the production process and is ready for sale to customers.

fiscal year An entity's reporting year, covering a 12-month accounting period.

fixed asset turnover The number of dollars in sales generated by each dollar of fixed assets; computed as sales divided by property, plant, and equipment.

fixed costs Costs that remain constant in total, regardless of activity level, at least over a certain range of activity.

fixed manufacturing overhead budget variance The difference between the standard (or budgeted) fixed manufacturing overhead established at the beginning of the reporting period and the actual fixed manufacturing overhead incurred.

flexible budget A quantified plan that projects revenues and costs for varying levels of activity.

floor The minimum market amount at which inventory can be carried on the books; equal to net realizable value minus a normal profit.

FOB (free-on-board) destination A business term meaning that the seller of merchandise bears the shipping costs and maintains ownership until the merchandise is delivered to the buyer.

FOB (free-on-board) shipping point A business term meaning that the buyer of merchandise bears the shipping costs and acquires ownership at the point of shipment.

Foreign Corrupt Practices Act (FCPA) Legislation requiring any company that has publicly-traded stock to have an adequate system of internal accounting controls.

foreign currency transaction A sale in which the price is denominated in a currency other than the currency of the seller's home country.

franchise An entity that has been licensed to sell the product of a manufacturer or to offer a particular service in a given area.

G

GAAP oval A diagram that represents the flexibility a manager has, within GAAP, to report one earnings number from among many possibilities based on different methods and assumptions.

gains (losses) Money made or lost on activities outside the normal operation of a company.

generally accepted accounting principles (GAAP) Authoritative guidelines that define accounting practice at a particular time.

generally accepted auditing standards (GAAS) Auditing standards developed by the PCAOB for public companies and AICPA for private companies.

goal congruence The selection of goals for responsibility centers that are consistent, or congruent, with those of the company as a whole.

going concern assumption The idea that an accounting entity will have a continuing existence for the foreseeable future.

goodwill An intangible asset that exists when a business is valued at more than the fair market value of its net assets, usually due to strategic location, reputation, good customer relations, or similar factors; equal to the excess of the purchase price over the fair market value of the net assets purchased.

gross margin method A procedure for estimating the amount of ending inventory; the historical relationship of cost of goods sold to sales revenue is used in computing ending inventory.

gross profit (gross margin) The excess of net sales revenue over the cost of goods sold.

gross sales Total recorded sales before deducting any sales discounts or sales returns and allowances.

H

held-to-maturity security A debt security purchased by an investor with the intent of holding the security until it matures.

high-low method A method of segregating the fixed and variable components of a mixed cost by analyzing the costs at the highest and the lowest activity levels within a relevant range.

historical cost The dollar amount originally exchanged in an arms'-length transaction; an amount assumed to reflect the fair market value of an item at the transaction date.

hurdle rate The minimum rate of return that an investment must provide in order to be acceptable.

I

impairment A decline in the value of a long-term operating asset.

income smoothing The practice of carefully timing the recognition of revenues and expenses to even out the amount of reported earnings from one year to the next.

income statement (statement of earnings) The financial statement that repots the amount of net income earned by a company during a period.

independent checks Procedures for continual internal verification of other controls.

indirect costs Costs normally incurred for the benefit of several segments within the organization; sometimes called common costs or joint costs.

indirect labor Labor that is necessary to a manufacturing or service business but is not directly related to the actual production of the manufactured or service product.

indirect materials Materials that are necessary to a manufacturing or service business but are not directly included in or are not a significant part of the actual product.

indirect method A method of reporting net cash flows from operations that involves converting accrual-basis net income to a cash basis.

intangible assets Long-lived assets without physical substance that are used in business, such as licenses, patents, franchises, and goodwill.

interest The payment (cost) for the use of money.

internal auditors An independent group of experts (in controls, accounting, and operations) who monitor operating results and financial records, evaluate internal controls, assist with increasing the efficiency and effectiveness of operations, and detect fraud.

internal control structure Safeguards in the form of policies and procedures established to provide management with reasonable assurance that the objectives of an entity will be achieved.

internal earnings targets Financial goals established within a company.

internal failure costs Costs of quality that relate specifically to the expenses that occur when low-quality products and services fail during production or before delivery to customers.

internal rate of return The "true" discount rate that will produce a net present value of zero when applied to the future cash flows of a capital investment.

internal rate of return method A capital budgeting technique that uses discounted cash flows to find the "true" discount rate of an investment; this true rate produces a net present value of zero.

Internal Revenue Service (IRS) A government agency that prescribes the rules and regulations that govern the collection of tax revenues in the United States.

International Accounting Standards Board (IASB) The committee formed in 1973 to develop worldwide accounting standards.

interpolation A method of determining the internal rate of return when the factor for that rate lies between the factors given in the present value table.

inventory Goods held for resale.

inventory shrinkage The amount of inventory that is lost, stolen, or spoiled during a period; determined by comparing perpetual inventory records to the physical count of inventory.

inventory turnover A measure of the efficiency with which inventory is managed; computed by dividing cost of goods sold by average inventory for a period.

investing activities Activities associated with buying and selling long-term assets.

investment center An organizational unit in which a manager has control over and is held accountable for cost, revenue, and asset performance.

J

job order costing A method of product costing whereby each job, product, or batch of products is costed separately.

joint manufacturing process When one material input is used to produce more than one product.

joint product costs The costs that a firm incurs before the point at which the different products are separated for further processing or immediate sale.

journal An accounting record in which transactions are first entered; provides a chronological record of all business activities.

journal entry A recording of a transaction where debits equal credits; usually includes a date and an explanation of the transaction.

journalizing Recording transactions in a journal.

junk bonds Bonds issued by companies in weak financial condition with large amounts of debt already outstanding; these bonds yield high rates of return because of high risk.

just-in-time (JIT) A management philosophy that emphasizes removing all waste of effort, time, and inventory costs from the organization. One explicit result of JIT is the reduction or removal of needless inventory in a production system.

K

kanban A Japanese word meaning "sign" or "card". In a JIT management system, *kanban* refers to a signaling system that pulls (rather than pushes) parts forward through the production system.

L

labor efficiency variance The extent to which the actual labor used varies from the standard quantity; computed by multiplying the difference between the actual quantity of labor used and the standard quantity of labor allowed by the standard rate.

labor rate variance The extent to which the standard labor rate varies from the actual rate for the quantity of labor used; computed by multiplying the difference between the standard rate and the actual rate by the quantity of labor used.

lagging indicators Measures that indicate the success of past business activities. Lagging indicators are related to the concept "outcome measures."

leading indicators Measures that indicate the potential success of future business activities. Leading indicators are related to the concept "leading measures."

leading measures Measures that, if successfully implemented, will support desired performance in other business activities. Note that some leading measures can also serve as outcome measures.

lease A contract that specifies the terms under which the owner of an asset (the lessor) agrees to transfer the right to use the asset to another party (the lessee).

least-cost decision A decision to undertake the project with the smallest negative net present value.

ledger A book of accounts in which data from transactions recorded in journals are posted and thereby summarized.

lessee The party that is granted the right to use property under the terms of a lease.

lessor The owner of property that is leased (rented) to another party.

leverage Borrowing that allows a company to purchase more assets than its stockholders are able to pay for through their own investment.

liabilities Obligations to pay cash, transfer other assets, or provide services to someone else.

life cycle costing The process of measuring all costs involved in creating, producing, and using a product or service. Life cycle costing is not limited to costs incurred by the organization measuring these costs but also includes all costs incurred by the suppliers and the customers of the product or service.

LIFO (last in, first out) An inventory cost flow assumption whereby the last goods purchased are assumed to be the first goods sold so that the ending inventory consists of the first goods purchased.

limited liability The legal protection given stockholders whereby they are responsible for the debts and obligations of a corporation only to the extent of their capital contributions.

line of credit An arrangement whereby a bank agrees to loan an amount of money (up to a certain limit) on demand for short periods of time, usually less than a year.

liquidity The ability of a company to pay its debts in the short run.

long-term assets Assets that a company needs in order to operate its business over an extended period of time.

long-term liabilities Liabilities that are not expected to be satisfied within a year.

long-term operating assets Assets expected to be held and used over the course of several years to facilitate operating activities.

lower-of-cost-or-market (LCM) rule A basis for valuing inventory at the lower of original cost or current market value.

M

management accounting The area of accounting concerned with providing internal financial reports to assist management in making decisions.

management by exception The strategy of focusing attention on significant deviations from standard costs or expectations.

manufacturing organizations Organizations that focus on using labor and/or machinery to convert raw materials into marketable products.

manufacturing overhead The indirect manufacturing costs associated with producing inventory.

manufacturing overhead budget A schedule of production costs other than those for direct labor and direct materials.

manufacturing overhead rate The rate at which manufacturing overhead costs are assigned to products; equals estimated manufacturing overhead costs for the period divided by the number of units of the activity base being used.

Market Adjustment—Trading Securities An account used to track the difference between the historical cost and the market value of a company's portfolio of trading securities.

market rate (effective rate or yield rate) of interest The actual interest rate earned or paid on a bond investment.

market share The percentage share one company receives of the total sales revenue in the economy for a particular product or service.

market value The value of a company as measured by the number of shares of stock outstanding multiplied by the current market price of the stock; the current value of a business.

master budget A network of many separate schedules and budgets that together constitute the overall operating and financing plan for the coming period.

matching principle The concept that all costs and expenses incurred in generating revenues must be recognized in the same reporting period as the related revenues.

materials price variance The extent to which the standard price varies from the actual price for the quantity of materials purchased or used; computed by multiplying the difference between the standard and actual prices by the quantity purchased or used.

materials quantity variance The extent to which the actual quantity of materials varies from the standard quantity; computed by multiplying the difference between the standard quantity of materials allowed and actual quantity of materials used by the standard price.

merchandising organizations Organizations that focus on buying products from manufacturers, then distributing those products to customers.

minority interest The amount of equity investment made by outside shareholders to consolidated subsidiaries that are not 100% owned by the parent.

mixed costs Costs that contain both variable and fixed cost components.

monetary measurement The idea that money, as the common medium of exchange, is the accounting unit of measurement, and that only economic activities measurable in monetary terms are included in the accounting model.

mortgage amortization schedule A schedule that shows the breakdown between interest and principal for each payment over the life of a mortgage.

mortgage payable A written promise to pay a stated amount of money at one or more specified future dates; a mortgage is secured by the pledging of certain assets, usually real estate, as collateral.

N

natural resources Assets that are physically consumed or waste away, such as oil, minerals, gravel, and timber.

net assets The owners' equity of a business; equal to total assets minus total liabilities.

net income (net loss) An overall measure of the performance of a company; equal to revenues minus expenses for the period.

net present value The difference between the present values of an investment's expected cash inflows and outflows.

net present value method A capital budgeting technique that uses discounted cash flows to compare the present values of an investment's expected cash inflows and outflows.

net purchases The net cost of inventory purchased during a period, after adding the cost of freight in and subtracting returns and discounts.

net realizable value The selling price of an item less reasonable selling costs.

net realizable value of accounts receivable The net amount that would be received if all receivables considered collectible were collected; equal to total accounts receivable less the allowance for bad debts.

net sales Gross sales less sales discounts and sales returns and allowances.

nominal accounts Accounts that are closed to a zero balance at the end of each accounting period; temporary accounts generally appearing on the income statement.

noncash items Items included in the determination of net income on an accrual basis that do not affect cash; for example, depreciation and amortization.

noncash transactions Investing and financing activities that do not affect cash; if significant, they are disclosed below the statement of cash flows or in the notes to the financial statements.

nonprofit organization An entity without a profit objective, oriented toward providing services efficiently and effectively.

non-value-added activities Unnecessary activities in a production or service process that customers typically do not see or care about and for which they are unwilling to pay.

notes to the financial statements Explanatory information considered an integral part of the financial statements.

NSF (not sufficient funds) check A check that is not honored by a bank because of insufficient cash in the check writer's account.

number of days' purchases in accounts payable A measure of how well operating cash flow is being managed; computed by dividing total inventory purchases by average accounts payable and then dividing 365 days by the result.

number of days' sales in inventory An alternative measure of how well inventory is being managed; computed by dividing 365 days by the inventory turnover ratio.

O

operating activities Activities that are part of the day-to-day business of a company.

operating capital Funds available for use in financing the day-to-day activities of a business.

operating lease A simple rental agreement.

operating leverage The extent to which fixed costs replace variable costs as part of a company's cost structure; the higher the proportion of fixed costs to variable costs, the faster income increases or decreases with changes in sales volume.

operational budgeting Managerial planning decisions regarding current operations and those of the immediate future (typically one year or less) that are characterized by regularity and frequency.

opportunity costs The benefits lost or forfeited as a result of selecting one alternative course of action over another.

organizational structure Lines of authority and responsibility.

other revenues and expenses Items incurred or earned from activities that are outside of, or peripheral to, the normal operations of a firm.

outcome measures Measures of desired outcome performance in activities critical to an organization's strategic goals. Note that some outcome measures are also leading measures to support desired performance in other business activities.

outsourcing An arrangement in which one company provides services for another company which has historically performed those services for itself.

out-of-pocket costs Costs that require an outlay of cash or other resources.

overapplied manufacturing overhead The excess of applied manufacturing overhead (based on a predetermined application rate) over the actual manufacturing overhead costs for a period.

owners' equity The ownership interest in the net assets of an entity; equals total assets minus total liabilities.

P

par value A nominal value assigned to and printed on the face of each share of a corporation's stock.

participative budgeting A bottom-up approach to budgeting that involves the full cooperation and participation of managers at all levels of the organization.

partnership An association of two or more individuals or organizations to carry on economic activity.

patent An exclusive right granted for 20 years by the federal government to manufacture and sell an invention.

payback method A capital budgeting technique that determines the amount of time it takes the net cash inflows of an investment to repay the investment cost.

pension An agreement between an employer and employees that provides for benefits upon retirement.

performance measures A general term used to describe all measures designed to capture information about performance related to a particular activity or process.

period costs Costs not directly related to a product, service, or asset. These costs are charged as expenses to the income statement in the period in which they are incurred.

periodic inventory system A system of accounting for inventory in which cost of goods sold is determined and inventory is adjusted at the end of the accounting period, not when merchandise is purchased or sold.

perpetual inventory system A system of accounting for inventory in which detailed records of the number of units and the cost of each purchase and sales transaction are prepared throughout the accounting period.

per-unit contribution margin The excess of the sales price of one unit over its variable costs.

physical safeguards Physical precautions used to protect assets and records, such as locks on doors, fireproof vaults, password verification, and security guards.

planning Outlining the activities that need to be performed for an organization to achieve its objectives.

post-closing trial balance A listing of all real account balances after the closing process has been completed; provides a means of testing whether total debits equal total credits for all real accounts prior to beginning a new accounting cycle.

postemployment benefits Benefits paid to employees who have been laid off or terminated.

posting The process of transforming amounts from the journal to the ledger.

predetermined overhead rate A rate at which estimated manufacturing overhead costs are assigned to products throughout the year; equals total estimated manufacturing overhead costs divided by a suitable allocation base, such as number of units produced, direct labor hours, direct materials used, or direct labor costs.

preferred stock A class of stock that usually provides dividend and liquidation preferences over common stock.

prepaid expenses Payments made in advance for items normally charged to expense.

present value of $1 The value today of $1 to be received or paid at some future date, given a specified interest rate.

present value of an annuity The value today of a series of equally spaced, equal-amount payments to be made or received in the future given a specified interest rate.

preventative controls Internal control activities that are designed to prevent the occurrence of errors and fraud.

prevention costs Costs of quality that relate specifically to design, training, and other investments to ensure that processes are performed correctly the first time and that products and services meet customers' expectations.

price-earnings ratio A measure of growth potential, earnings stability, and management capabilities; computed by dividing market value of a company by net income.

primary financial statements The balance sheet, income statement, and statement of cash flows, used by external groups to assess a company's economic standing.

principal (face value or maturity value) The amount that will be paid on a bond at the maturity date.

process costing A method of product costing whereby costs are accumulated by process or work centers and averaged over all products manufactured in a center or department during a particular production period. There are two methods of process costing: The FIFO method and the weighted-average method.

product costs Costs associated with products or services offered.

product line activities Activities that take place in order to support a product line, regardless of the number of batches or individual units actually produced.

production budget A schedule of production requirements for the budget period.

production cost report A document that compiles all the costs of a manufacturing center for a particular production period. The information on this report is used to control and evaluate production costs, as well as transfer costs and units of output from one manufacturing center to another.

production prioritizing Management's continual evaluation of the profitability of the various product lines and divisions within an organization so that products or divisions that are performing below expectations can be analyzed to identify problems and potential solutions.

profit center An organizational unit in which a manager has control over and is held accountable for both cost and revenue performance.

profit graph A graph that shows how profits vary with changes in volume.

profit margin (operating performance) ratio An overall measure of the profitability of operations during a period; computed by dividing operating profit by revenue.

profitability index The present value of net cash inflows divided by the cost of an investment.

property, plant, and equipment Tangible, long-lived assets acquired for use in business operations; include land, buildings, machinery, equipment, and furniture.

proprietorship A business owned by one person.

prospectus A report provided to potential investors that represents a company's financial statements and explains its business plan, sources of financing, and significant risks.

Public Company Accounting Oversight Board (PCAOB) Board of five full-time members established by the Sarbanes-Oxley Act to oversee the accounting and auditing profession.

purchases budget A schedule of projected purchases over the budget period.

R

ranking The ordering of acceptable investment alternatives from most to least desirable.

raw materials Materials purchased for use in manufacturing products.

raw materials inventory The inventory of raw materials that have not yet begun the production process.

real accounts Accounts that are not closed to a zero balance at the end of each accounting period; permanent accounts appearing on the balance sheet.

realized gains and losses Gains and losses resulting from the sale of securities in an arm's-length transaction.

receivables Claims for money, goods, or services.

registered bonds Bonds for which the names and addresses of the bondholders are kept on file by the issuing company.

regression line On a scattergraph, the straight line that most closely expresses the relationship between the variables.

relevant range The range of operating level, or volume of activity, over which the relationship between total costs (variable plus fixed) and activity level is approximately linear.

residual income The amount of operating profit earned above a specified minimum rate of return on assets; used to evaluate investment centers.

responsibility accounting A system of evaluating performance; managers are held accountable for the costs, revenues, assets, or other elements over which they have control.

responsibility center An organizational unit in which a manager has control over and is held accountable for performance.

retailers Second-tier merchants who typically purchase products from wholesalers to distribute to end-user customers. Many large retailers, however, often bypass wholesalers to purchase products directly from the original manufacturers.

retained earnings The amount of accumulated earnings of the business that have not been distributed to owners.

return on equity A measure of the amount of profit earned per dollar of investment, computed by dividing net income by equity.

return on investment (ROI) A measure of operating performance and efficiency in utilizing assets; computed in its simplest form by dividing operating profit by average total assets.

return on sales A measure of the amount of profit earned per dollar of sales, computed by dividing net income by sales.

return on sales revenue A measure of operating performance; computed by dividing net income by total sales revenue. Similar to profit margin.

revenue Increase in a company's resources from the sale of goods or services.

revenue budget A service entity's budget that identifies how much revenue (and often cash) will be generated during a period.

revenue recognition The process of recording revenue in the accounting records; occurs after (1) the work has been substantially completed and (2) cash collection is reasonably assured.

revenue recognition principle The idea that revenues should be recorded when (1) the earnings process has been substantially completed and (2) cash has either been collected or collectibility is reasonably assured.

S

sales budget A schedule of projected sales over the budget period.

sales discount A reduction in the selling price that is allowed if payment is received within a specified period.

sales mix The relative proportion of total sales dollars (or total units sold) that is represented by each of a company's products.

sales price variance The difference between the expected or standard price and the actual price multiplied by the actual quantity sold; measures that part of the variance between expected and actual sales revenue that is due to differences between expected and actual prices of goods.

sales returns and allowances A contra-revenue account in which the return of, or allowance for reduction in the price of, merchandise previously sold is recorded.

sales tax payable Money collected from customers for sales taxes that must be remitted to local governments and other taxing authorities.

sales volume variance The difference between the expected quantity and the actual quantity sold multiplied by the expected or standard price; measures that part of the variance between expected and actual sales revenue that is due to the difference between expected and actual volume of goods sold.

salvage value The amount expected to be received when an asset is sold at the end of its useful life.

Sarbanes-Oxley Act A law passed by Congress in 2002 that gives the SEC significant oversight responsibility and control over companies issuing financial statements and their external auditors.

scattergraph (visual-fit) method A method of segregating the fixed and variable components of a mixed cost by plotting on a graph total costs at several activity levels and drawing a regression line through the points.

screening Determining whether a capital investment meets a minimum standard of financial acceptability.

secured bonds Bonds for which assets have been pledged in order to guarantee repayment.

Securities and Exchange Commission (SEC) The government body responsible for regulating the financial reporting practices of most publicly-owned corporations in connection with the buying and selling of stocks and bonds.

segments Parts of an organization requiring separate reports for evaluation by management.

segment margins The difference between segment revenue and direct segment costs; a measure of the segment's contribution to cover indirect fixed costs and provide profits. In effect, segment margins are the operating profit created by the segment.

segment-margin ratios The segment margin divided by the segment's net sales revenue; a measure of the efficiency of the segment's operating performance and, therefore, of its profitability.

segment margin statement A profit and loss statement that identifies costs directly chargeable to a segment and further divides them into variable and fixed cost behavior patterns.

segregation of duties A strategy to provide an internal check on performance through separation of authorization of transactions from custody of related assets, separation of operational responsibilities from record-keeping responsibilities, and separation of custody of assets from accounting personnel.

selling and administrative expense budget A schedule of all nonproduction spending expected to occur during the budget period.

sensitivity analysis A method of assessing the reasonableness of a decision that was based upon estimates; involves calculating how far reality can differ from an estimate without invalidating the decision.

separate entity concept The idea that the activities of an entity are to be separated from those of the individual owners.

serial bonds Bonds that mature in a series of installments at specified future dates.

service organizations Organizations that focus on delivery of marketable services, such as legal advice or education, to individuals or other organizations.

service overhead budget The budget, prepared by service entities, that identifies projected costs associated with providing the service.

six sigma quality A measure of quality based on statistical analysis. Products or services with six sigma quality have no more than 3.4 defects per million opportunities (e.g., parts or events).

Social Security (FICA) taxes Federal Insurance Contributions Act taxes imposed on the employee and the employer; used mainly to provide retirement benefits.

special order An order that may be priced below the normal selling price in order to utilize excess capacity and thereby contribute to company profits.

specific identification A method of valuing inventory and determining cost of goods sold whereby the actual costs of specific inventory items are assigned to them.

standard cost system A cost-accumulation system in which standard costs are used as product costs instead of actual costs. The standard costs are then adjusted to actual costs when financial reports are created. This adjustment creates variances that are reported to management.

stated rate of interest The rate of interest printed on the bond.

statement of cash flows The financial statement that reports the amount of cash collected and paid out by a company during a period of time.

statement of comprehensive income A statement outlining the changes in accumulated comprehensive income that arose during the period.

statement of retained earnings A report that shows the changes in retained earnings during a period of time.

statement of stockholders' equity A financial statement that reports all changes in stockholders' equity.

static budget A quantified plan that projects revenues and costs for only one level of activity.

statistical process control (SPC) A statistical technique for identifying and measuring the quality status of a process by evaluating its output to determine if serious problems exist in the process.

stepped costs Costs that change in total in a stair-step fashion (in large amounts) with changes in volume of activity.

stockholders (shareholders) The owners of a corporation.

stockholders' equity The owners' equity section of a corporate balance sheet.

straight-line amortization A method of systematically writing off a bond discount or premium in equal amounts each period until maturity.

straight-line depreciation method The depreciation method in which the cost of an asset is allocated equally over the periods of an asset's estimated useful life.

strategic planning Broad, long-range planning usually conducted by top management.

sum-of-the years' digits (SYD) depreciation method The accelerated depreciation method in which a constant balance (cost minus salvage value) is multiplied by a declining depreciation rate.

sunk costs Costs, such as depreciation, that are past costs and do not change as a result of a future decision.

supplies budget The budget, prepared by service entities, that identifies projected supplies expenses over the budget period.

T

T-account A simplified depiction of an account in the form of a letter T.

target income A profit level desired by management.

term bonds Bonds that mature in one single sum at a specified future date.

time value of money The concept that a dollar received now is worth more than a dollar received in the future.

time-period concept The idea that the life of a business is divided into distinct and relatively short time periods so that accounting information can be timely.

times interest earned A measure of a borrower's ability to make required interest payments; computed as income before interest and taxes divided by annual interest expense.

total quality management (TQM) A management philosophy focused on increasing profitability by improving the quality of products and processes and increasing customer satisfaction, while promoting the well-being and growth of employees.

trading securities Debt and equity securities purchased with the intent of selling them should the need for cash arise or to realize short-term gains.

transactions Exchange of goods or services between entities (whether individuals, businesses, or other organizations), as well as other events having an economic impact on a business.

treasury stock Issued stock that has subsequently been reacquired by the corporation.

trial balance A listing of all account balances; provides a means of testing whether total debits equal total credits for all accounts.

U

unadjusted rate of return method A capital budgeting technique in which a rate of return is calculated by dividing the increase in the average annual net income a project will generate by the initial investment cost.

underapplied manufacturing overhead The excess of actual manufacturing overhead costs over the applied overhead costs for a period (based on a predetermined application rate).

unearned revenues Cash amounts received before they have been earned.

unit-level activities Activities that take place each time a unit of product is produced.

units-of-production method The depreciation method in which the cost of an asset is allocated to each period on the basis of the productive output or use of the asset during the period.

unrealized gains and losses Gains and losses resulting from changes in the value of securities that are still being held.

unrecorded liabilities Expenses incurred during a period that have not been recorded by the end of that period.

unrecorded receivables Revenues earned during a period that have not been recorded by the end of that period.

V

value-added activities Necessary activities in a production or service process that customers identify as valuable and for which they are willing to pay.

variable cost rate The change in cost divided by the change in activity; the slope of the regression line.

variable costs Costs that change in total in direct proportion to changes in activity level.

variable manufacturing overhead efficiency variance The difference between the standard variable manufacturing overhead allowed for the standard activity level and the standard variable manufacturing overhead predicated based on the actual activity level. This difference is then multiplied by the standard variable overhead cost rate. This variance effectively measures the efficiency of the underlying activity used to assign variable manufacturing overhead costs.

variable manufacturing overhead spending variance The difference between the variable overhead manufacturing costs as predicated by the actual activity cost driver and the variable manufacturing overhead costs actually incurred.

variance Any deviation from standard.

venture capital firm A company that provides needed cash to companies in return for an ownership interest.

volume variance The difference between the expected (or budgeted) production output established at the beginning of the reporting period and the actual production output. This difference is then converted into a dollar number by multiplying it by the standard fixed manufacturing overhead costs per unit.

W

wages and salaries budget The budget, prepared by service entities, that identifies projected labor costs involved directly in providing the service over the budget period.

weighted average cost of capital (WACC) The average cost of a firm's debt and equity capital, weighted by the relative amounts of each source of financing; equals the average rate of return that a company must earn on its invested capital in order to satisfy the demands of its owners and creditors.

wholesalers Top-tier merchants who typically deal directly with the original manufacturers to distribute products to retailers.

work in process Partially completed units in production.

work sheet A tool used by accountants to facilitate the preparation of financial statements.

work-in-process inventory Inventory that is partly completed in the production process, but not yet ready for sale to customers.

Z

zero-coupon bonds Bonds issued with no promise of interest payments; only a single payment will be made.

APPENDIX C: Check Figures*

Chapter 1
Not Applicable

Chapter 2
Exercises

2-20	(8) BS/A
2-22	(Z) Expenses in 2009 = $330
2-24	Total assets = $560,000
2-26	(4) EPS = $2.45
2-28	(1) Net income = $510,000
2-30	6/30/09 Retained earnings = $83,900
2-32	(1) Net cash provided by operating activities = $78,000
2-34	N/A
2-36	N/A

Problems

2-38	(2) Total long-term assets = $576,000
2-40	(2) Retained earnings $33,000
2-42	EPS = $34.14
2-44	Net income = $34,515
2-46	(2) 5/31/09 Retained earnings $216,910
2-48	(2) Net income for 2009 = $25,000
2-50	Cash at beginning of year $676,000

Chapter 3
Exercises

3-24	N/A
3-26	(2) OE—R
3-28	(3) Net income for 2009 = $17,500
3-30	(4) Debit to Accounts Payable = $15,000
3-32	(1) Debit to Compensation Expense = $105,000
3-34	N/A
3-36	7/23 Paid rent of $2,000
3-38	Retained Earnings = $40,300

Problems

3-40	(1) (c) Debit to Utilities Expense = $720
3-42	9/9 Debit to Insurance Expense = $1,500
3-44	3/4/09 Credit to Accounts Receivable = $2,500
3-46	5/15/09 Debit to Notes Payable = $2,500
3-48	(2) Total Debits = $134,000

Chapter 4
Exercises

4-24	(1) (b) Accrual-basis Net income = $39,533
4-26	(3) Unrecorded liability
4-28	(2) Adjusting entry—Debit to Subscription Expense = $131
4-30	(2) (b) Debit to Salaries Expense = $90,000
4-32	(2) Debit to Interest Expense = $5,625
4-34	(4) No adjusting entry
4-36	(1) Supplies on Hand = $2,000
4-38	(12) N
4-40	Credit to Retained Earnings = $107,100
4-42	Debit to Sales Revenue = $906,000
4-44	(2) Retained Earnings = $41,200

Problems

4-46	(d) Credit to Rent Revenue = $33,900
4-48	(1) Wages Expense for 2009 = $30,000
4-50	N/A
4-52	(1) Credit to Retained Earnings = $76,580
4-54	(1) Total assets = $820,000
4-56	(2) Ending Cash balance = $33,000

Chapter 5
Exercises

5-2	Total assets = $7,801,300

Chapter 6
Exercises

6-26	N/A
6-28	N/A
6-30	6/30 Debit to Sales Discounts = $800
6-32	(1) Bad debt expense = $5,200
6-34	(2) Ending Accounts Receivable = $1,340,000

---

* Note: Check figures are provided for even-numbered exercises and problems, where applicable.

6-36 (3) 12/31/09 Net accounts receivable = $149,010

6-38 2009 Debit to Bad Debt Expense = $66,000

6-40 (1) Boulder, Inc. Average Collection Period for Year 3 = 118 days

6-42 N/A

6-44 January 2010 Debit to Estimated Liability for Service = $760

6-46 (2) Debit to Miscellaneous Expenses = $50

6-48 (1) 3.2 billion Vietnamese dong

Problems

6-50 N/A

6-52 (b) Debit to Sales Returns and Allowances = $4,000

6-54 (1) Debit to Bad Debt Expense = $209,800

6-56 (3) (a) Debit to Allowance for Bad Debts = $3,500

6-58 (2) Credit to Accounts Receivable = $89

6-60 (3) 12/31/09 Net accounts receivable = $362,260

6-62 (1) Deposits in transit = $6,000

6-64 (2) Credit to Exchange Gain = $700

Chapter 7
Exercises

7-30 (4) Net purchases = $53,500

7-32 Ending inventory = $31,371

7-34 (5) Beginning inventory = $17,100

7-36 Debit to Inventory Shrinkage = $28,000

7-38 Cost of goods sold = $511,760

7-40 (1) Cost of goods sold = $7,050

7-42 Net purchases = $4,800

7-44 Burbank number of days' sales in inventory = 35.1 days

7-46 (1) (a) Gross margin = $60,000

7-48 (2) Debit to Purchases = $300

7-50 (1) Ending inventory = $120,000

7-52 Ending inventory = $500,000

Problems

7-54 (1) (d) Debit to Accounts Payable = $19,520

7-56 (10) Gross margin = $675

7-58 (2) Ending inventory LIFO = $45,885

7-60 (1) Net Purchases = $79,600

7-62 (1) 2009 Correct gross margin = $31,400

7-64 (1) (a) Gross margin FIFO = $9,336

Chapter 8
Exercises

8-22 (2) Credit to FICA Taxes Payable, Employer = $9,716

8-24 Total compensation expense = $660,000

8-26 Net pension asset = $340,000

8-28 (b) Pension expense = $13,000

8-30 (2) Income tax expense = $262,500

8-32 N/A

8-34 Gross margin = $8,500

Problems

8-36 (2) Debit to Salaries Payable = $8,289.70

8-38 (1) Compensation expense for 2009 = $666,667

8-40 (3) 2008 Pension obligation = $846,807

8-42 Operating income = $284,500

Chapter 9
Exercises

9-26 N/A

9-28 (1) Total cost = $50,000

9-30 (1) (b) Debit to Interest Expense = $78

9-32 Debit to Land = $112,500

9-34 (1) Depreciation expense = $2,000 per year

9-36 (2) Debit to Loss on Impairment = $200

9-38 (2) Debit to Loss on Sale of Truck = $2,000

9-40 (1) Debit to Amortization Expense, Patent = $6,800

9-42 (3) Market value of the net assets = $1,430,000

9-44 (1) Debit to Drilling Equipment = $185,000

9-46 (2) 2009 Book value = $522,006

9-48 (1) 2009 Depreciation expense = $10,048

9-50 2009 Depreciation expense = $14,667

Problems

9-52 N/A

9-54 (3) 12/31/09 Debit to Interest Expense = $23,954

9-56 (2) Alternative b = $42,150 per year

9-58   (2) Debit to Equipment = $50,400
9-60   (1) Credit to Cash = $114,000
9-62   (3) Debit to Depletion Expense = $210,000
9-64   Debit to Goodwill = $20,000
9-66   (1) Fixed asset turnover = 3.08
9-68   (3) Depreciation = $50,400
9-70   (2) 2009 Depreciation Expense = $7,520
9-72   (3) (c) Uranium Book Value = $24,000

Chapter 10
Exercises

10-24   (4) $10,997
10-26   (1) Payment = $75,481
10-28   12/31/09 Credit to Cash = $1,250
10-30   (2) Total Interest Paid = $17,072
10-32   (2) Debit to Rent (or Lease) Expense = $4,141
10-34   Total issuance price = $68,124
10-36   (3) 3/1/10 Debit to Bond Interest Expense = $4,200
10-38   (1) Debt ratio = 55.6%
10-40   (1) (b) Debit to Premium on Bonds = $100
10-42   (4) Bonds Payable Carrying Value = $51,772

Problems

10-44   (2) (a) $27,372
10-46   (2) Payment = $444.89
10-48   (2) 12/31/08 Debit to Interest Expense = $750
10-50   (1) (c) Debit to Lease Liability = $3,782
10-52   June 30 Issuance price of bonds = $1,010,720
10-54   (2) Debit to Bond Interest Expense = $22,500
10-56   Total liabilities = $1,025,300
10-58   (2) Debt ratio = 77.8%
10-60   (1) Debit to Cash = $99,000
10-62   (1) Issuance price of bonds = $138,961
10-64   (1) Credit to Premium on bonds = $22,939
10-66   (1) (d) Debit to Bond Interest Expense = $4,400
10-68   Case 2 Approximate effective interest rate = 12.7%

Chapter 11
Exercises

11-18   (2) Retained earnings = $130,150
11-20   (c) Credit to Dividends Payable = $76,720
11-22   (e) Credit to Dividends Payable = $79,800
11-24   (3) $1.69 per share
11-26   (2) Total dividends paid = $172,485
11-28   (2) $8.43 per share
11-30   Comprehensive income = $22,100

Problems

11-32   (3) (b) $861,000
11-34   (b) Credit to Treasury Stock = $44,800
11-36   (2) Total stockholders' equity = $269,600
11-38   (2) 2009 Preferred Stock Dividends = $206,000
11-40   Case B Dividend payout ratio = 0.143
11-42   (1) (b) $89,000
11-44   (2) Total stockholders' equity = $786,250
11-46   (1) (e) Debit to Retained Earnings = $30,200
11-48   N/A

Chapter 12
Exercises

12-20   12/31 Credit to Unrealized Gain on Trading Securities—Income = $1,560
12-22   12/31/09 Debit to Unrealized Increase/Decrease in Value of Available-for-Sale Securities—Equity = $27,500
12-24   Debit to Investment in Trading Securities = $20,500
12-26   Debit to Market Adjustment—Available-for-Sale Securities = $100
12-28   Credit to Cash = $35,620
12-30   (2) Total present value = $113,592
12-32   (1) 12/31 Debit to Bond Interest Receivable = $1,500
12-34   Total amount of Amortization = $3,285
12-36   (2) Credit to Dividend Revenue = $3,000
12-38   (1) Minority interest = $375

Problems

12-40   (c) Credit to Dividend Revenue = $200
12-42   (1) $2,500 unrealized loss

12-44   (1) 12/31 Credit to Bond Interest Revenue = $4,300

12-46   (3) Loss on sale of securities = $680

12-48   (1) 7/1 Debit to Cash = $1,650

12-50   (3) Debit to Realized Loss on Sale of Trading Securities = $3,000

12-52   (2) $3,000

12-54   (2) 12/31/09 Debit to Bond Interest Receivable = $418.90

12-56   (2) 3/20 Debit to Investment in Equity Method Securities = $2,560,000

12-58   (2) Corporation B Credit to Dividend Revenue = $12,500

12-60   N/A

Chapter 13
Exercises

13-18   N/A

13-20   (1) (d) Credit to Dividend Revenue = $6,300

13-22   Net increase in cash = $48,750

13-24   N/A

13-26   Net cash flows provided by operating activities = $74,400

13-28   Net cash flows provided by operating activities = $161,600

13-30   Net cash flows provided by operating activities = $90,800

13-32   Net cash flows used in investing activities = ($197,000)

13-34   Cash receipts from Customers = $415,500

13-36   N/A

Problems

13-38   (2) Net increase in cash = $74,300

13-40   (1) Net cash flows provided by operating activities = $13,000

13-42   (1) Net cash flows from operations = $24,540

13-44   Net income = $122,100

13-46   (1) Cash from operating activities = $707

13-48   (1) Cash paid for taxes = $13,700

Chapter 14
Exercises

14-34   (f) Total liabilities = $125,500

14-36   (1) 2009 Income tax expense as percentage of sales = 5.9%

14-38   (1) 2009 Total assets as percentage of sales = 23.6%

14-40   (1) Cost of goods sold = $161,000

14-42   (2) 2009 Return on sales = 5.0%

14-44   (1) Faulty's ROE = 8.7%

14-46   Profit Margin = 57.9%

14-48   (1) Retail jewelry stores' Return on Assets = 7.6%

14-54   (1) 2009 Cash flow-to-net income ratio = 0.75

Problems

14-56   (1) Current ratio = 1.79

14-58   (1) 2009 Operating income as percentage of sales = 7%

14-60   (1) 2009 Total operating expenses as a percentage of sales = 26.7%

14-62   (2) 2009 Asset turnover = 2.50

14-64   (1) (b) 2009 Debt ratio = 38.6%

14-66   N/A

14-68   N/A

Chapter 15
Exercises

15-16   N/A

15-18   N/A

15-20   Total manufacturing overhead = $73,000

15-22   N/A

15-24   N/A

15-26   (1) 151,899 tickets (rounded up)

15-28   (1) Variable cost = $11.80 per bat

15-30   (1) Segment profit for RX-5 = $18,840

15-32   (1) Segment profit = $4,350,000

Chapter 16
Exercises

16-24   N/A

16-26   (2) Total cost for Job #203 = $27,400

16-28   Predetermined overhead rate = $4.25 per direct labor hour

16-30   (1) (b) Predetermined overhead rate = $1.00 per hour

16-32   (2) Overapplied manufacturing overhead = $930

16-34   (2) Total manufacturing overhead in Job #315X = $4,734

16-36   (2) Cost of goods manufactured = $456,000

16-38   N/A

16-40   (2) Overapplied overhead = $21,800

16-42   Monday work done = 4.8 equivalent units

16-44 (1) Conversion Costs Equivalent units of production = 2,840

Problems

16-46 N/A
16-48 (1) Predetermined overhead rate = $4 per direct labor hour
16-50 (2) Total manufacturing overhead applied to Job #29 = $20,434
16-52 (1) (c) Cost per chair = $190.10
16-54 Total manufacturing costs = $614,833
16-56 (1) (b) Cost of goods manufactured = $700,000
16-58 N/A
16-60 N/A
16-62 Total costs transferred out = $186,354
16-64 (3) Total costs transferred out = $48,776.32

Chapter 17
Exercises

17-16 N/A
17-18 (1) Product B Gross margin = $(70,000)
17-20 (1) Standard Product Gross margin = $180,000
17-22 (1) Product Z Gross margin = $50,000

Problems

17-24 N/A
17-26 (1) (b) Standard total annual setups = 220
17-28 (1) Agricultural Products Gross margin = $150,000
17-30 (5) (a) Gross margin for 50 hp = $2,518
17-32 (3) Product 1 Gross margin percent = 24.2%
17-34 (3) Total manufacturing costs for Building Pipe = $227,040
17-36 (4) Operating profit = $300,000

Chapter 18
Exercises

18-18 Annual net deficit = $(117)
18-20 (2) May collections from customers = $60,830
18-22 Quarter 2 15″ Units to be produced = 2,625
18-24 (2) Payments to suppliers = $318,380
18-26 March Total direct labor cost = $37,480
18-28 Aluminum Bat Total unit cost = $73.13

18-30 (1) Budgeted wage expense = $180,000
18-32 Projected cash balance July 31, 2009 = $469,000
18-34 (1) Cash receipts from financing = $42,900
18-36 Net income = $46,800
18-38 (1) Net income = $107,400

Problems

18-40 (2) 23 months (rounded)
18-42 (2) Third Quarter Collections = $172,500
18-44 Total direct materials purchases = $4,028
18-46 (1) Chocolate Almond Bars Total unit cost = $16.50
18-48 (4) Total MOH costs = $5,577
18-50 (1) Total Revenues = $1,655,300
18-52 Expected annual income (loss) for 10 enrollees = $(13,500)
18-54 January Excess cash = $159,000
18-56 (3) Net cash provided by operating activities = $2,162,080
18-58 Net cash provided by operating activities = $89,000

Chapter 19
Exercises

19-22 (1) Illinois Variance = $100,000 U
19-24 (1) Materials price variance = $1,100 U
19-26 Materials price variance = $28,800 U
19-28 (2) Materials Quantity Variance = $275 U
19-30 (1) Labor efficiency variance = $1,600 U
19-32 (d) Standard labor cost per hour = $4.20
19-34 (1) Scranton Segment margin = $10,500
19-36 (2) Shampoo Sales price variance = $4,800 F
19-38 (f) ROI = 25%
19-40 (1) Residual income of New Investment = $1,000
19-42 (2) Volume variance = $90,000 U

Problems

19-44 (2) Europe Variance = $50,000 F
19-46 (1) Materials price variance = $18,000 F
19-48 (1) Actual costs of materials = $76,720
19-50 (2) Materials quantity variance = $320 U
19-52 Grocery Department Total margin = $40,000

19-54   (2) Tortillas Sales price variance = $760 F
19-56   (2) Calculator Segment margin = $4,000
19-58   (2) Joliet Asset turnover = 2.67
19-60   (4) Los Angeles ROI = 14.0%
19-62   (2) Residual income of the Proposed Investment = $1,500
19-64   (2) Variable overhead spending variance = $5,800 U
19-66   (1) First Quarter Fixed overhead budget variance = $4,000 F

Chapter 20
Exercises

20-26   (1) $2,000 per boat
20-28   (2) Variable cost rate = $1.875 per unit
20-30   (1) Total variable costs = $57,375 at 850,000 copies
20-32   (1) Profit = $238
20-34   (2) Contribution margin = $660,000
20-36   (1) (b) 40,000 units
20-38   (3) Approximate answers (based on graph) fixed costs $15,000; variable costs $12,000; and profits $3,000
20-40   N/A
20-42   (2) Profit = $267,000
20-44   (1) Break-even point in sales dollars = $437,500
20-46   (2) Kassandra Company Profit = $2,500

Problems

20-48   (1) Variable cost = $4 per unit
20-50   (1) Profit = $36,900
20-52   (3) Number of units sold = 7,560 units
20-54   (1) Contribution margin ratio = 20%
20-56   (1) (e) Total variable costs per unit = $12.50
20-58   (2) Break-even sales = $237,996
20-60   (1) Profit = $310,000
20-62   (1) Fixed cost element = $2,401 (rounded up)
20-64   (1) Spencer break-even point in sales dollars = $400,000

Chapter 21
Exercises

21-14   (1) Total relevant costs of the New Machine = $465,000
21-16   (1) Total variable costs = $81
21-18   (1) Cost Difference between making or buying = $624,000
21-20   Net expected benefit of Alternative 2 = $342,000
21-22   (1) Loss if Roast is processed further = $(10,000)
21-24   Product line contribution = $180,000
21-26   (2) Maximum production of Turbo Engine = 18,000 units

Problems

21-28   (1) Opportunity cost = $640,000
21-30   (1) Total 5-year cost to make Danishes with Machine B = $233,500
21-32   (2) Differential costs to make the part = $544,000
21-34   (1) Net income without Baseball Gloves = $29,500
21-36   Lost contribution if shut down = $162,000
21-38   (1) X-121 Contribution margin = $22.50
21-40   (2) Net contribution from advertising Charger = $30,000

Chapter 22
Exercises

22-22   (1) Present value = $293,372 (rounded)
22-24   Unadjusted rate of return = 22.5%
22-26   Net present value of cost of fire safety expert = $110,603 (rounded)
22-28   Total Average Cost of Capital = 16.8%
22-30   (1) Present value of future cash inflow (20 years) = $599,189 (rounded)
22-32   N/A
22-34   N/A
22-36   Printer A's Profitability index = 1.0625

Problems

22-38   Net present value = $4,126 (rounded)
22-40   (1) Internal rate of return = 10.51% (rounded)
22-42   (2) Net present value = $30,344
22-44   Present value of Alternative 1: Shared Ownership = $37,257 (rounded)
22-46   Present value to rent = $4,565 (rounded)
22-48   (1) Investment B Net present value = $2,897
22-50   (2) Net present value of Car 1 = $(27,028)
22-52   (1) Investment A Net present value = $13,004
22-54   (1) Investment C Payback period = 3.75 years

Chapter 23

Exercises

23-16   EVA = $690

23-18   (b) VA

23-20   (3) Internal failure costs = $181,000

23-22   N/A

23-24   N/A

23-26   N/A

23-28   N/A

Problems

23-30   (1) 2008: Invested capital = $18,700,000

23-32   (1) Low Quality Total expected audit cost = $40,583

23-34   N/A

23-36   N/A

A

B